MW00715214

MODERN FINANCIAL MANAGING

CONTINUITY AND CHANGE

PRELIMINARY EDITION

FRANK M. WERNER
Fordham University
Associate Professor of Finance

JAMES A.F. STONER
Fordham University
Professor of Management Systems

HarperCollins*CollegePublishers*

Acquisitions Editor: Kirsten D. Sandberg
Editor-in-Chief: Michael Roche
Developmental Editor: Edward L. Yarnell
Coordination, Text, and Cover Design: York Production Services
Electronic Production Manager: Christine Pearson
Electronic Page Makeup: York Graphic Services, Inc.
Printer and Binder: R.R. Donnelley & Sons Company
Cover Printer: The Lehigh Press, Inc.

About the cover illustration: Artist Roy Weimann has captured continuity and change in financial managing in his cover design. The shifting pyramid represents the modern business organization in today's dramatically changing business environment, removing layers of management to get closer to its customers and its operations. The dollar bill in the background represents finance, both as a critical part of the business environment and as an important component of every company's management system. Seen together, the dollar bill and pyramid symbolize the continuity and change inherent in the job of every financial manager: to apply and adapt the teachings of finance to the needs of an ever (and ever faster) changing world. Our special thanks go to Roy and to Clare Jett and Associates for making the cover illustration possible.

For permission to use copyrighted material, grateful acknowledgement is made to the copyright holders on p. C-1 which are hereby made part of this copyright page.

Modern Financial Managing—Continuity and Change, Preliminary Edition

Copyright © 1995 by HarperCollins College Publishers

All rights reserved. Printed in the United States of America. No part of this book may be used or reproduced in any manner whatsoever without written permission, except in the case of brief quotations embodied in critical articles and reviews. For information address HarperCollins College Publishers, 10 East 53rd Street, New York, NY 10022.

Library of Congress Cataloging-in-Publication Data
Werner, Frank M., 1944–
Modern Financial Managing—Continuity and Change/Frank M. Werner, James A.F. Stoner.—1st prelim. ed.
p. cm.
Includes index.
ISBN 0-673-99268-3 (hc.)
1. Finance. 2. Corporations—Finance. I. Stoner, James Arthur Finch, 1935– . II. Title.
HG173.W447 1995
658. 15—dc20 94-24899
CIP

94 95 96 97 9 8 7 6 5 4 3 2 1

To Marie, Allison, and Eric, who teach me over and over again how teamwork leads to quality.

FMW

To Barbara, Alexandra, and Carrie, who have waited an awfully long time for that vacation.

JAFS

BRIEF CONTENTS

DETAILED CONTENTS

TO THE INSTRUCTOR

Thank you and congratulations for adopting this book. We and the many leading finance professionals throughout North America who encouraged us to write it and who reviewed our work think you have made an important decision for your students and for global competitiveness. Change is never easy, as we ourselves found out when we began asking the questions that led to this textbook.

Modern Financial Managing—Continuity and Change is a new kind of finance text. Although all financial management texts cover finance, we know of no other "financial management" textbook that has anything to do with management. We're excited about the book (we *should* be, given that we devoted a good part of the last four years to its writing) since we believe this is the way we will all be seeing finance in the coming years. We hope we've communicated our excitement to you and your students

We have chosen the book's title with care, and each word has meaning for us:

- *Modern*—The book describes finance as it is practiced today in world-class companies.
- *Financial*—The book's core focus is on the finance function within a business organization.
- *Managing*—The book recognizes that financial analysis and decision making must be closely integrated with a company's management systems to be effective. We use the "ing" form of the verb *to manage* to communicate our belief that the activities of financial professionals within a business are not static and reactive but are proactive and constantly evolving.
- *Continuity*—The book is firmly connected to the rich history of finance theory and practice which continues to provide important guidance to business activities.
- *Change*—The book identifies that we are in a period of rapid change in the business environment. These are particularly exciting times for finance and finance professionals as new finance theories and techniques emerge—such as sophisticated applications of option theory, derivative securites, agency theory, and behavioral finance—and as the business environment rapidly evolves in response to the forces of globalization, quality, and diversity. Along with the rest of every business organization, finance is changing in order to survive.

"Teacher burnout."

1. Our Goals for the Book

In writing *Modern Financial Managing—Continuity and Change*, we set seven goals for ourselves:

To present finance in a clear and consistent manner The book is designed—through its choice of language, illustrations, and design—to be easy to read and use. The approach for analysis and problem-solving is straightforward and is applied consistently. The book is approachable and user-friendly, thanks to features such as its realistic cases and problem scenarios, cartoons, hypertext cross-references, and dual glossary.

To organize the book based on the way financial managers make decisions Analytical topics are organized by the methodology underlying analysis and decisions—incremental, process, and optimization—rather than the traditional balance sheet approach or theory-driven approach. This makes related topics easier to teach and easier for students to understand.

To make the book consistent with the direction of business education The book includes extensive material in response to four concerns of contemporary business education: (1) globalization, (2) ethics, (3) cross-disciplinary activities, and (4) small business. International content is integrated throughout the book. Ethics appears naturally in the context of the worldwide quality-management revolution. Cross-disciplinary activity, a requirement in modern business practice, is explicitly addressed wherever financial decision making is discussed. The special needs and limitations of small business appear throughout the book, making it applicable to organizations of all sizes.

To capture the implications of the quality revolution for financial practice The book uses the experiences of quality-leading companies to report the progress finance organizations are making in identifying and serving finance's customers and in improving finance's processes. A consistent theme throughout the book is bridging the gap between traditional and new management practices, a current fact of life for finance professionals we refer to as "living in both worlds."

To equal or surpass the best features of other textbooks We benchmarked over 50 features of both finance and nonfinance texts, looking for the best example(s) of each, and set out to do as well or better on every one.

To provide instructors flexibility in using the book The book contains full coverage for an introductory course of either one or two semesters. It can be used in a traditional financial management course, or in a survey of finance course since its broad coverage introduces many areas of finance, not just large corporation financial management. Wherever possible, we have put more-advanced subjects, more-detailed explanations, and derivations in appendixes to provide greater flexibility in assigning materials. Cross-reference footnotes connect material that appears in multiple chapters, helping instructors and students alike to tie pieces of the finance subject together.

To keep the size (and price) of the book reasonable Even with all its new coverage, the book has only 23 chapters.

2. Advantages for Students, Instructors, and Society

We think there are important advantages to a finance book that is consistent with the best management practice.

For students The approach of *Modern Financial Managing* makes students more attractive to employers, not only by teaching them the core competencies of finance but also by showing them how to use those skills effectively within a modern, world-class organization.

For instructors *Modern Financial Managing* permits instructors to teach best practice—financial managing as it is done in companies recognized as business leaders. It supports teaching, as students find the book intuitively clear and easy to read and understand. By integrating international and ethical issues throughout the book, it builds those subjects naturally into students' analyses and removes the need to treat them as separate topics.

For society *Modern Financial Managing* joins the increasing supply of educational materials attempting to change the way business schools prepare their students. Business is changing so fast today that schools often have understandable difficulty keeping up. The observation of Walt Kelly's lovable cartoon possum, Pogo, that "We have met the enemy, and it is us!" has been applied with some wisdom to business education. *Modern Financial Managing—Continuity and Change* is our contribution to moving business schools from being "part of the problem" to a "part of the solution" to the failures of many U.S. companies to compete successfully in global markets.

3. Who Should Use the Book

Because of its tone and approach, we believe *Modern Financial Managing* will be appreciated by instructors, students, and employers alike. It has been successfully class-tested at the undergraduate, M.B.A., and executive M.B.A. levels and has been reviewed during its development both by professors and by senior financial executives from some of North America's leading companies. We think the book is especially appropriate for nontechnical students, since it minimizes the use of derivations and formulas, and for students who are employed full- or part-time and who will immediately see the validity of the book's approach and its relevance to their work.

4. Pedagogical Aids

We have included many pedagogical aids to make your job of teaching easier and your students' job of learning more rewarding and more fun. Among the features to look for and take advantage of are:

Tightly integrated chapter structure Each chapter begins with a set of learning objectives entitled "Key Points You Should Learn from This Chapter." These points correspond precisely to the A-heads, or major sections of the chapter. At the end of each chapter is a "Summary of Key Points" that repeats and reviews the learning objectives.

Chapter opening and closing vignettes Each opening vignette describes a scenario faced by a finance professional and is designed to involve your students in the material by putting them "on the job." Each closing vignette shows how the concepts of the chapter can be used to address the opening issue. Since the closing vignettes do not give a single definitive answer (there rarely is one), the opening story can be used as a case for class discussion, homework, or examinations.

Presentation of current finance practices of world-class companies (and some not quite so accomplished) Three types of boxes are scattered throughout the book. "Finance in Practice" boxes describe recent activities of companies and business leaders as well as modern applications of finance theory. "Serving Finance's Customers" boxes illustrate how a finance organization can add value by meeting the needs of its internal and external customers. "Improving Finance's Processes" boxes describe examples of adding value to a corporation by doing finance's job more efficiently and effectively.

Frequent, clearly labeled, fully worked-out examples Students learn from examples, and we have tried to err on the side of too many rather than too few. Where the examples are closely linked to finance theory, we often have presented the example first, followed by the theory, rather than the other way around, so that the theoretical concepts may be related immediately to a shared and understood example. Examples are in a standard format: a problem scenario paragraph followed by a "Question," "Solution steps," and "Answer." Often the "Answer" contains further commentary to enhance students' understanding of the example.

Appeal to intuition rather than to formula While some students are very comfortable with mathematical presentations, all too many are not and never learn finance because of their "math anxiety." This is a shame because the majority of finance can be a very intuitive subject. We have avoided formulas wherever possible or placed them in appendixes where they are available for those who find them helpful. We have standardized the notation in the algebra that is included: in all cases, capital letters stand for a money amount (e.g., PV for present value) while lower case letters stand for a rate (e.g., t for the marginal tax rate).

Use of the financial calculator for time-value analyses We have purposely minimized the use of time-value tables with this text. Although some instructors find the tables useful for illustrating the basic time-value relationships, financial calculators are a universal tool in business today. It is the rare finance professional who does not use one; it is the rarer finance professional who still uses time-value tables. Also, it is often cheaper for a student to purchase a calculator than to buy the textbook itself. All problems involving time value are fully worked out, showing the correct keystrokes. At the end of the book you will find a calculator appendix "Using Your Financial Calculator" illustrating the location of each time-value key on the most widely used financial calculators. By illustrating how each time-value example may be solved with a financial calculator, the book provides students with extensive hands-on experience. Another advantage of moving from tables to the calculator is that our examples can be much more realistic and not confined to a narrow set of interest rates or time periods.

Use of visual aids Chart, tables, and maps are used throughout the book to support learning. Each discussion of financial market instruments features a copy of the relevant quote(s) from a recent edition of *The Wall Street Journal* as seen "Through the Looking Glass" in which we magnify a section of the newspaper to study the numbers in more detail.

Complete glossary, both in the margin, and at the end of the book The marginal glossary defines terms as they are encountered in the text, so students have the definitions when they need them. The end-of-text glossary is a reference students can go back to when they review and study. Also, the end-of-text glossary serves as a second index since each definition contains the number of the page on which the parallel marginal definition appears.

Questions that follow each chapter We have tried to make the chapter-ending questions both thought-provoking and useful for reviewing the chapter concepts. They may be used for homework, class discussion, or examinations.

Extensive set of homework problems The problems that follow each chapter are presented in the same order as the chapter material and are clearly labeled to identify the topic(s) they refer to. Problems come in pairs: problems 1 and 2 cover the same material; so do problems 3 and 4, problems 5 and 6, etc. You can assign one problem of each pair for homework and keep the other in reserve for classroom work, examinations, or for the student who asks for additional examples. The problems range from the simple to the complex—the first problems are narrowly targeted at specific concepts and relationships, while the later problems tend to be broader and integrate the chapter materials. Most problems have multiple parts in which the value of one variable is systematically changed. Students may do all the parts at one sitting or may save one or two parts for later review. When all parts of a problem have been completed, they illustrate the sensitivity of the result to the variable that was changed, providing another learning opportunity.

End-of-chapter cases These cases provide additional opportunities to explore the chapter concepts and may also be used for assignments and examinations.

End-of-book summary of mathematical relationships and summary of financial ratios These handy summaries can be used as study aids by students. They are also useful as reference materials for examinations if you permit students to bring in a list of formulas.

5. Supplements

We are creating a full set of supplements to accompany the book. For this preliminary edition there is:

- **An instructors manual** containing several suggested syllabi for both a one semester and full-year course; teaching notes for each chapter and case; and solutions to all questions and problems.
- **A test bank** with short-answer questions and problems available both in hard copy and on diskette for Macintosh and PC-compatible computers.

Additional supplements are planned for the four-color "first edition," due next year:

- **Transparency masters** of each figure and table in the text and of other materials to supplement classroom presentations.
- **A study guide** containing an outline of each chapter, worked out sample problems, and self tests.
- **A diskette** containing computerized versions of various end-of-chapter problems which may be used with many popular spreadsheet programs.
- ***Finance Tutor*** featuring a computerized tutorial program that students may use to review concepts and work a virtually unlimited number of additional problems at their own pace.

For both instructors and students there are three books summarizing our recent research findings:

- *Managing Finance for Quality—Bottom-Line Results from Top-Level Commitment,* published by ASQC Quality Press and the Financial Executives Research Foundation in 1994. Written for executives and practitioners, this book reports how the quality management revolution is changing financial management practice. The book includes case studies of five quality-leading companies—Corning Incorporated, Federal Express, Motorola, Solectron, and Southern Pacific. FERF, the research arm of the Financial Executives Institute, was the generous sponsor of this research.

- *Finance in the Quality Revolution—Adding Value by Integrating Financial and Total Quality Management,* published by the Financial Executives Research Foundation in 1993. This shorter version of *Managing Finance for Quality* contains an executive summary, the five case studies, and a chapter on "Lessons Learned." It was published for and distributed to the 11,000 senior financial executives and academics who are members of the Financial Executives Institute.
- *Remaking Corporate Finance—The New Corporate Finance Emerging in Quality-Leading Companies,* published by McGraw-Hill Primis in 1992. A monograph describing transformations in finance work as seen through the observations of senior executives from leading corporations, venture capitalists, consulting organizations, and universities.

6. Moving Forward Together

We have worked very hard to make this preliminary edition of *Modern Financial Managing—Continuity and Change,* an exciting and superior textbook. However, we believe that everything is subject to continuous improvement, and we know that you all have wonderful ideas that could enhance the book and its supplements. We would love to hear from you. Tell us how we can (further) assist your teaching in any way; help us make the book better. Feel free to contact us any time at:

Fordham University
Graduate School of
Business Administration
113 West 60th Street
New York, NY 10023

or

Finance Editor
HarperCollins
College Publishers
10 E. 53rd Street
New York, NY 10022

Frank: (212) 636-6213
Jim: (212) 636-6178

You are our customers, and delighting you and exceeding your expectations is and will always be our primary goal.

Acknowledgments

Writing a textbook takes the efforts of many people over many years. We extend our hearty thanks to all of them. Although we will never be able to thank each person adequately, we wish to identify those who played a particularly important role in the book's development.

The beginnings of this textbook were the teaching materials Frank Werner developed for use in his corporate finance classes at Fordham University and in the *Management Training Program—Finance* at Manufacturers Hanover Trust Company, now part of Chemical Banking Corporation. Thanks go to Corporate Professional Development staff at Manufacturers Hanover—especially Mort Glantz, Carol Johnson, Tom Kennedy, Tom McCaskill, Charlie Stipp, and Barbara Taylor—who helped Frank to identify the best content and sequencing of the materials, and to Dale Broderick, who, more than any other teacher, taught Frank how to write for the classroom.

In 1989, Frank and Jim began their work on the interrelationships between financial managing, globalization, and quality management by conducting the first of a series of graduate seminars with that theme. The seminars led to our stimulating and fruitful relationship with the Financial Executives Institute's research arm, the Financial Executives Research Foundation (FERF). FERF's research grants, and the strong support of Roland Laing and Bill Sinnett of FERF, gave us exceptional opportunities to work closely with many CFOs and other financial executives of companies that are leaders in changing financial management practice. These financial executives are showing how finance can add increasing value to their companies by recognizing and taking advantage of the opportunities arising from the integration of globalization, quality management, and financial practice. Many of the examples in this book are drawn from their successes in maintaining continuity while initializing change.

At Fordham, Frank and Jim have had the good fortune to work with excellent colleagues in an environment where good teaching is encouraged and supported. Our faculty colleagues, particularly Victor Marek Borun, John Finnerty, Marek Hessel, Marta Mooney, Walter O'Connor, Robert Wharton, and Milan Zeleny continue to provide much of that environment. Our deans past and present of the Fordham Schools of Business—Susan Atherton, Arlene Eager, Lauren Mounty, Ernest Scalberg, William Small, Sharon Smith, and Arthur Taylor—have consistently supported us emotionally and financially.

As we began to create the book, we class-tested each chapter extensively in the introductory courses at both the College and Graduate School of Business Administration. Hundreds of students provided written feedback as they read each chapter. While it is impossible to single out each by name, they are responsible for many of the book's examples and innovations. Particular thanks go to Fordham professors Christopher Blake, Sris Chatterjee, Iftekhar Hasan, and Rohinton Karanjia who used draft sections of the book in their classes and provided valuable feedback.

An early draft of the book was used by David Brunn, retired partner of Arthur Andersen, and Larry Grow, vice president and director of corporate financial plan-

ning at Motorola, in their pioneering course in quality corporate finance at the Lake Forest Graduate School of Management (LFGSM). Thanks are also due to Raymond Britt, president and Nancy Kin, associate dean of LFGSM for their foresight in creating interdisciplinary courses in their curriculum and who, in the best quality management sense, served as an excellent support system.

We received superb assistance from the staff and our student assistants at Fordham. Rosanne Conte, Frank's assistant in his role as associate dean of the Graduate School of Business, coordinated production of early versions of the manuscript. Our student assistants—Jean-Louis Boulmer, Eleonora Oropeza, Maribeth Holland, John Diego, Matthew Cannold, Terence Hales, Jennifer Carrobis, and Jeffrey Adams—also took responsibility for research and production work freeing us up to learn and write. Jennifer Carrobis took on the task of obtaining permissions to reprint all previously published materials; we thank her especially for our ability to use all those wonderful cartoons. Bobby Wen repeatedly played key roles in the early seminars and courses we conducted.

Perhaps our greatest intellectual debt is to the finance and quality professionals throughout the United States who taught us quality management and how it must be an integral part of the job of financial managing. In particular, we wish to single out:

Fred Allerdyce, CFO, American Standard
David Baldwin, former CFO, Florida Power and Light
Len Bardsley, former Manager, Continuous Improvement, Du Pont
Richard Buetow, VP and Director of Quality, Motorola
Chauncey Burton, Senior Quality Administrator, Finance, Federal Express
Jim Chambers, Assistant Treasurer, Corning Incorporated
Winston Chen, former Chairman, Solectron
W. Edwards Deming, consultant
Joe Doherty, Assistant VP—Finance, Southern Pacific
Keith Elliott, CFO, Hercules Corporation
Bill Fitton, Senior Manager, Corporate Financial Audit, Motorola
Justin Fox, Director—Quality, Southern Pacific
Blan Godfrey, Chairman and CEO, The Juran Institute
Larry Grow, VP and Director of Corporate Financial Planning, Motorola
Sandy Helton, VP and Treasurer, Corning Incorporated
David Hickie, former Executive VP and Vice-CFO, Motorola
Alan Hunter, CFO, Stanley Works
Ken Johnson, VP, Corporate Controller, and Director of Internal Audit, Motorola
Joseph M. Juran, Chairman Emeritus, The Juran Institute
Ralph Karthein, Controller, IBM Canada
Bob Lambrix, former CFO, Baxter International
Bill Latzko, President, Latzko Associates
Ken Leach, VP Administration, Globe Metallurgical
Karen May, VP, Corporate Audit, Baxter International
Paul Makosz, General Auditor, Gulf Canada Resources
Ko Nishimura, President and CEO, Solectron
Gabriel Pall, Vice President, The Juran Institute
James F. Riley, Vice President, The Juran Institute

Pete Sale, Team Member—Finance Reengineering, Baxter International
Paul Schnitz, Director, Corporate Operations Review Group, Raychem
Bob Siminoni, Director of Strategic Planning, Treasury, Westinghouse
Ben Stein, VP and General Auditor, American Standard
Kent Sterett, Executive VP, Quality, Southern Pacific
Kent Stemper, Director, Corporate Audit, Baxter International
Bob Talbot, VP, Management Services, IBM Credit Corporation
Susan Wang, CFO, Solectron
Len Wood, Corporate Operations Review Group, Raychem
Larry Yarberry, CFO Southern Pacific

In December 1992 we were introduced to Kirsten Sandberg, finance acquisition editor at HarperCollins College Publishers. Kirsten was quick to see the potential of our approach and immediately understood our desire to produce the book using quality management techniques. In a large sense, this book would not exist if it were not for her unfailing energy, good humor, and consistent faith in us and the project. With the support of her management, she put together a superb team of professionals at Harper and York Production Services who coached us and guided the book to its current form—Ed Yarnell and Joan Cannon, developmental editors; Lee Anne Fisher, district sales manager; Mike Roche, Editor-in-Chief; Christine Pearson, electronic production manager; Kate Steinbacher, senior marketing manager; Michael Weinstein, Vice President and Director of EDP; Kathi Kuntz, editorial assistant; Laura Skinger and Susan Bogle, and Kevin Bradley of York Production Services, production editors.

Ed Yarnell worked closely, patiently, and creatively with us in the final crunch, and arranged for our work to be read by the following academic and professional reviewers who responded to the manuscript in its various stages of completion and who gave us many good ideas for improvement:

Peter Bacon, Wright State University
Omar M. Benkato, Ball State University
T. K. Bhattacharya, Cameron University
James Booth, Arizona State University
Kuang C. Chen, California State University-Fresno
Michael C. Ehrhardt, University of Tennessee
Janet Hamilton, Portland State University
David W. Hickie, Motorola Corporation
Sherry L. Jarrell, Indiana University
H. Thomas Johnson, Portland State University
John M. Joseph, Jr., Thomas College
John Kensinger, University of North Texas
Russell L. Kent, Georgia State University
Nancy E. Kin, Lake Forest Graduate School of Management
Rose Knotts, University of North Texas
John H. Lea, Arizona State University
Bryan Malcolm, University of Wisconsin-Stout
Steven Mann, University of South Carolina
Kyle Mattson, Rochester Institute of Technology
Thomas H. McInish, Memphis State University

Vivian Nazar, Ferris State University
Chec K. Ng, Jackson State University
M. Megan Partch, University of Oregon
Shafiqur Rahman, Portland State University
Robert G. Schwebach, University of Wyoming
Hugh D. Sherman, York College of Pennsylvania
William B. Sloan, North Carolina State University
Steven H. Smith, Digital Equipment Corporation
Raymond E. Spudek, Incarnate Word College
David Y. Suk, Rider University
Kenneth R. Tillery, Middle Tennessee State
Philip M. Van Auken, Baylor University
Charles H. Wellens, Fitchburg State University
Len Wood, Raychem Corporation
Thomas V. Wright, St. Louis University
Robert M. Zahrowski, Portland State University

Finally, we both feel a debt of love and gratitude to our families—Marie, Allison, and Eric; and Barbara, Alexandra, and Carolyn—who accepted our many late nights at the office and frequent trips to visit finance and quality professionals with very few complaints and many warm welcomes upon our return. For both of us they formed our ultimate support system.

FMW
JAFS

TO THE STUDENT

Welcome to *Modern Financial Managing—Continuity and Change*. We have tried to make the book easy to read and learn from and a lot of fun as well. Unlike many introductory finance books, this one talks about two facets of finance: analytical finance, the theory that guides financial analysis and decision making (which is in all finance texts), and operational finance, the way finance is practiced in world-class companies (which is in no other finance text we know of). You are fortunate to have a professor who is forward-looking and in touch with the enormous changes taking place in business practice.

As you begin to study finance you are embarking on an exciting adventure, and we hope this book will be a good companion and guide. To help your learning further, we offer these suggestions:

Skim the entire book in advance Take an hour or so to look over the table of contents and to skim the glossary and index. Then read the "part openers," the short sections that begin each of the eight parts of the book, and read the section "Key Points You Should Learn from This Chapter" at the beginning of each chapter. By taking the time to do this at the beginning of the term, you will get a good overview of the subject and will be able to set each topic in the appropriate context when you get to it.

Read the section entitled "To the Instructor" It is always useful to know as much as possible of what is on your professor's mind. In our comments to your instructor, we have written about what is new and special about this book. We have described some of the major features of the book—most of which were designed to make your work as a student easier.

Put yourself in the chapter opening vignettes Each chapter opens with a scenario you might find yourself in (or may already have been in) at some point in your business career. Before you read the chapter, think of how you might try to deal with the situation our characters are facing. As you read the chapter, relate the concepts to the vignette, and see how much more you could add. When you reach the end of the chapter, and read the closing vignette, match up your observations with those of the protagonist. While there is rarely a single "right answer," finance provides helpful ways of approaching each problem. You will be delighted as you observe your thinking and analytical processes sharpen throughout the course.

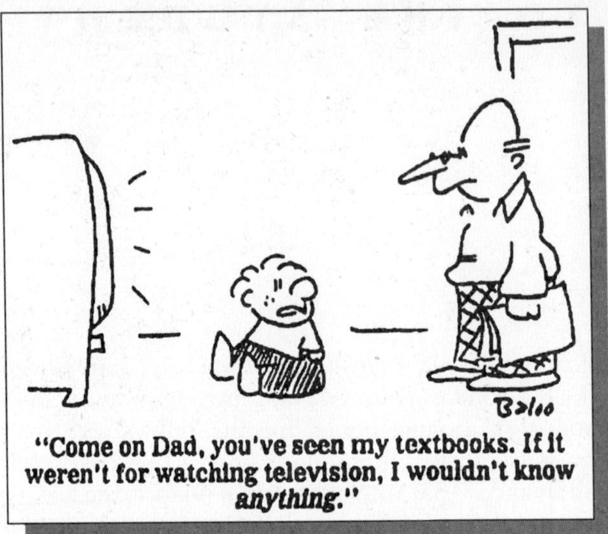

"Come on Dad, you've seen my textbooks. If it weren't for watching television, I wouldn't know *anything*."

Work each example problem you encounter while you are reading a chapter Take out your financial calculator and go through the problem step by step. Doing each problem will reinforce your reading and help you to become proficient at using the financial calculator which has become a universal tool of financial professionals. You will learn more, and the new knowledge will stay with you longer.

Relate the examples about company practices to your experiences If you have worked for a while, you have probably been involved in or seen similar examples of financial practice. However, even if you have little or no work experience, you have been a customer of business for years. In many ways, all the examples talk about universal phenomena: serving customers, increasing quality, improving work, discovering when benefits exceed costs, finding the best way to do something. In what ways are these examples different or the same as those you have experienced? What could you have done differently if you had this knowledge back then? What about these examples makes them illustrations of "world-class" performance?

Use the footnotes labeled "Cross-reference" as a hypertext device Whenever a reference is made to something that appears in another chapter, there is a footnote identifying that other location. Jump back and forth as needed to pick up and review supporting concepts.

Look carefully at the total results of each homework problem Where a problem has multiple parts, you may find yourself doing the same analysis several times. Feel free to do only one or two parts at first and come back to the rest later to reinforce your learning. However, when you have completed all parts of a repeating problem, look at the range of results. Observe how the results changed in response to the one variable that changed, an important insight beyond what is asked in the problem.

Take advantage of the end-of-book "Summary of Mathematical Relationships" and "Summary of Financial Ratios" These handy pages include every formula in the book and serve as useful references when doing homework problems or preparing for examinations.

Use the end-of-book "Glossary" as a second index When you wish to review a concept, you can look up the definition of a related term in the glossary. At the end of the definition you will find the number of the chapter and page on which the term was first defined. Turn to that page, and you are at the beginning of the section to review.

As we teach financial managing to our students at Fordham, we ask each student to write a weekly memo to us telling us how well we did each week as teachers and authors. Was the class clear and useful? Did this week's chapter read well or make no sense? What didn't you understand, and which parts of the chapter worked well for you? What could we do to make the book better? Hundreds of our students, at both the undergraduate and M.B.A. levels, have written those memos. They have taught us a huge amount, and helped us to improve the book significantly, even before this "preliminary" edition was published. We invite all of you to join our Fordham students as we continue to improve the book. Please address any comments, criticisms, and suggestions to either of us at:

Fordham University	or	Finance Editor
Graduate School of		HarperCollins
Business Administration		College Publishers
113 West 60th Street		10 East 53rd Street
New York, NY 10023		New York, NY 10022

We promise to read your letters and consider them seriously for the next edition. You are the ultimate customers of our work, and as we have learned from our studies of world-class companies, delighting you and exceeding your expectations must always be our primary goal.

Most important, as you study finance, HAVE FUN!! We know that there will be times during the course where many of you will be convinced that finance is anything else *but* fun, but this doesn't have to be so. We believe that one of the most important goals for every worker—whether a student, professor, finance professional, or anyone else—is to find what the renowned management thinker W. Edwards Deming called "joy in work." If you put in the effort to read carefully, to do the assigned problems, to go over the sticky points, to review your work, and to discuss the material with your friends who are also taking the course, you will be rewarded handsomely with useful and important learning that will last a lifetime. And as it has for your professor and us, finance will become a true labor of love.

ABOUT THE AUTHORS

Frank M. Werner is Associate Professor of Finance at the Schools of Business Administration and Associate Dean of The Graduate School of Business Administration of Fordham University. He received his Ph.D. in Finance from Columbia University in 1978. He also received an M.Phil. in Finance from Columbia in 1975 and an M.B.A. from Harvard in 1968. His undergraduate degree, also from Harvard, was in Engineering and Applied Physics in 1966. Dr. Werner is the author of a variety of journal articles, a computer-based simulation of corporate finance decision making, and numerous monographs and cases for instructional use. He is a member of the American Accounting Association, the American Economics Association, the American Finance Association, the American Society for Quality Control, the Financial Executives Institute, the Financial Management Association, and the Institute of Management Sciences. In addition to his responsibilities at Fordham, Dr. Werner advises companies in the areas of corporate finance and quality management. He has given seminars on various quality and finance topics, in both English and Spanish, throughout the United States as well as in Europe, Asia, South America, and the Caribbean.

James A.F. Stoner is Professor of Management Systems at the Schools of Business Administration of Fordham University. He received his Ph.D. from the MIT School of Industrial Management (now the Sloan School) in 1967. He also earned an S.M. in Management from MIT in 1961 and a B.S. in Engineering Science from Antioch College in 1959. Dr. Stoner is author and co-author of a number of books and journal articles. These include *Management*, sixth edition, Prentice Hall; *Introduction to Business*, Scott Foresman; and *World-class Managing—Two Pages at a Time*, Fordham University. He is a member of the Academy of Management; American Finance Association; Financial Executives Institute; Financial Management Association; American Society for Quality Control; and the Organizational Behavior Teaching Society, of which he is a former board member. In addition to his responsibilities at Fordham, Dr. Stoner advises several major companies on the movement toward quality management and teaches in executive seminars on quality and management. He has taught in executive programs in North and South America, Europe, Africa, and Asia. In 1992, Fordham University established the James A.F. Stoner Chair in Quality Leadership.

Drs. Werner and Stoner are the authors of three books studying changes in finance in companies that are leaders in quality management. *Remaking Corporate Finance—The New Corporate Finance Emerging in High-Quality Companies* (McGraw-Hill Primis, 1992), examines changes in the corporate finance function and the job of the Chief Financial Officer. *Finance in the Quality Revolution—Adding Value by*

Integrating Financial and Total Quality Management, (Financial Executives Research Foundation, 1993) and *Managing Finance for Quality—Bottom-Line Results from Top-Level Commitment* (ASQC Quality Press and the Financial Executives Research Foundation, 1994) report on new finance practices at five quality-leading companies. They are currently studying how progress in quality management is changing the internal audit process, the results to be published in book form at the beginning of 1995.

MODERN FINANCIAL MANAGING

CONTINUITY AND CHANGE

PART I

INTRODUCTION

In Part I we explore the role of financial managing in helping an organization achieve its goals. We look at the environment in which financial managers operate and review the various data sets used in financial analysis and decision making.

Chapter 1 is an introduction to finance and the task we call *financial managing.* We define finance, relate it to economics, and look at two ways to organize the subject. We then set finance in historical context by tracing its development over the last century. Today, finance is undergoing important changes in response to twin revolutions in global competition and management systems. We identify these changes and discuss how modern financial managing is a vital support system within a world-class organization helping it exceed the expectations of its stakeholders. We end the chapter with a look ahead at the rest of the book.

Chapter 2 explores the purpose of the firm. The chapter traces the modern finance goal—maximization of shareholder wealth—from its roots in the Industrial Revolution to its implementation today, paying special attention to the "agency problem" that arose as large organizations came to be led by professional managers rather than by their owners. We report how the agency problem has been addressed and how new management systems promise to reduce the problem further while providing new solu-

tions. We also look at how companies that have moved toward the new management systems are following a "sequenced goal approach" in which they focus on customer satisfaction and process improvement in order to maximize the wealth of their shareholders. Appendix 2A describes the three forms of organization used by U.S. companies. Appendix 2B examines incentives for managers designed to reduce agency costs.

Chapter 3 describes how all firms are in transition, somewhere en route from the ways of managing that have worked for many decades to something new. We describe and contrast the two systems and identify some of the limitations of the old system that precipitated the change. We also report on research into the ways in which financial managers are adapting to the new management system and how the practice of finance is changing. The chapter concludes with some observations about working in a changing world and implications for financial practitioners.

Chapter 4 identifies the information used in financial analysis and decision making. Five data sets are covered: (1) data about the people who are critical for a company's financial success, such as customers and employees; (2) data about the efficiency of the firm's processes; (3) managerial accounting data used for internal economic analyses; (4) financial accounting data reported publicly and used by financial analysts outside the company; and (5) data used to calculate the tax-related costs of company activities. The chapter identifies how the use of all data derives from theory and suggests some difficulties in making accurate use of data. Five appendixes follow Chapter 4, covering: (4A) break-even analysis, (4B) the U.S. personal income tax system, (4C) the U.S. corporate income tax system, (4D) analysis of financial accounting data, and (4E) the interrelationship of financial ratios.

CHAPTER 1

AN OVERVIEW OF FINANCIAL MANAGING

Liz Horne and Mike Cantrell shut the door to the conference room and sat down around the circular table. Liz spoke first, "This should be an interesting assignment. I really think the boss is right. The company could do a much better job of providing education for members of the finance organization."

Liz and Mike are on the staff of the chief financial officer (CFO) of their company. Earlier today, the CFO asked them to study the knowledge and skills within the finance department and to recommend what kind of education the company should provide to its finance employees.

Mike walked over to a flip-chart in the corner of the room and started making notes. He spoke as he wrote. "We could start by interviewing our colleagues. After all, they're the ones who know the most about what education they don't have."

"I'm not so sure," Liz replied. "How can they know what they don't know? Maybe we should talk to some experts in finance, like the professors at the university. They can tell us what our people should know. Then we can go around the department and see how everybody measures up."

"Do we want to ask only finance professors?" Mike countered. "When I was in school, I remember my teachers emphasizing how the various parts of any organization are interconnected. It seems to me that we have to look at the big picture and see how the finance department fits into the entire company. Why don't we try to list the various functions that the finance organization plays in the company and see where that takes us?"

Two hours later, the walls of the conference room were covered with Liz and Mike's notes. Liz sat back and looked around the room. "One thing is clear," she commented. "Finance certainly is a large and fascinating field. Our company's education program will have to cover a lot of ground."

Liz and Mike have a challenging task in front of them. As their brainstorming revealed, well-educated finance professionals are comfortable with two bodies of knowledge. First, they must understand finance theory, a particularly useful way to view how the worlds of money and business work. Over the years, students of finance have developed many useful techniques for the analysis and solution of business problems. Second, finance professionals must understand how finance relates to the rest of the organization and the external environment. The finance function serves as a support system—obtaining money resources and providing technical expertise. A seemingly brilliant solution to a financial problem that is not compatible with the way the rest of the organization or the external world functions is not really useful at all!

financial managing—the art of integrating financial theory and practice with the rest of an organization's management systems to support the delivery of low-cost, high-quality goods and services to customers and to maximize the value of the organization to its stockholders and other stakeholders

A successful business operates efficiently and effectively and maintains cooperative and productive relationships with people and other organizations. It delivers value to its customers—competitively priced, high-quality products and services that not only satisfy those customers but make them want to return to purchase more. An effective finance organization supports the company's relationships and operations. It helps the business deliver value to its customers and, as a result, deliver increased value to employees, suppliers, neighbors, and ultimately to investors. We call this task **financial managing.** In this book we discuss what financial managing is and how skillful financial managing can add value to any business organization.

Key Points You Should Learn from This Chapter

After reading this chapter you should be able to:

- Identify what the subject of finance deals with and how it differs from traditional economics, and divide finance into its component parts along two dimensions.
- Recount how the finance discipline evolved.
- Recognize why increased global competition and the global quality revolution are leading to changes in financial managing.
- Understand where the finance function fits within a business organization and why it is important for finance to be integrated with the rest of the business.
- Have a sense of what to expect in the remainder of this book.

Introductory Concepts—What Is Finance?

finance—the study and practice of how money is raised and used by organizations

Finance is a broad subject. In simplest terms, it covers anything to do with the use and management of money. Since money is a required ingredient in the recipe for all businesses, finance plays an important role in any business organization. Since businesses that run out of money cease to exist, skillful financial managing can easily be the difference between a successful and an unsuccessful company.

Of course, money is also a topic within the subject of economics, the discipline that has made the greatest contribution to financial theory and practice. The supply of and demand for money are very important issues in understanding how economies function. One group of economic theorists, the "monetarists," represented most notably by Nobel Prize winner Milton Friedman, argues that the money supply-demand relationship is practically the sole determinant of how well an economy performs. This book will touch on the **macroeconomic** implications of money where appropriate, but this is not our focus.

macroeconomics—the study of the functioning of economies taken as a whole

microeconomics—the study of individual units within an economy, specifically consumers and producing firms

Neither will we dwell on the micro side of economics, even though finance is an outgrowth of **microeconomics.** The branch of microeconomics commonly known as "the theory of the firm" has long dealt with the economics of a business organization but from a very narrow point of view. The organization is typically assumed to produce a product, as opposed to a service. It is studied in terms of the physical transformation of inputs into outputs: what is the optimal mix of land, labor, and capital to produce the firm's products at the lowest cost? What is the optimal mix of products to generate the highest revenue? It is also studied in terms of market structure: how should the firm price its product, and how much should the firm produce if it is a perfect competitor? an oligopolist? a monopolistic competitor? a monopolist?

The characteristics that distinguish finance from traditional economics are a focus on the business firm and the individual (hence finance is not quite macroeconomics) and a focus on financial flows rather than production transformations (hence it is not quite microeconomics either). Finance looks at how money enters the firm, is used within the firm, and exits the firm. It studies who gives the firm money and why, how best to raise and employ money, and how the firm distributes money. It seeks to discover the best ways to use money to maximize the firm's worth. Figure 1.1 diagrams the flow of money into and out from a typical firm and identifies the firm's **stakeholders,** all those affected by the actions of the business.

stakeholders—persons and organizations affected by the actions of a business firm

Like many broad subjects, it is helpful to divide finance into component parts for ease of understanding. Two useful divisions are: (1) by academic studies and career paths and (2) by areas of concern to financial managers.

1. Organizing Finance by Academic Studies and Career Paths

One useful way to categorize the subject of finance is by the academic studies and career paths you might follow should you choose to take additional finance

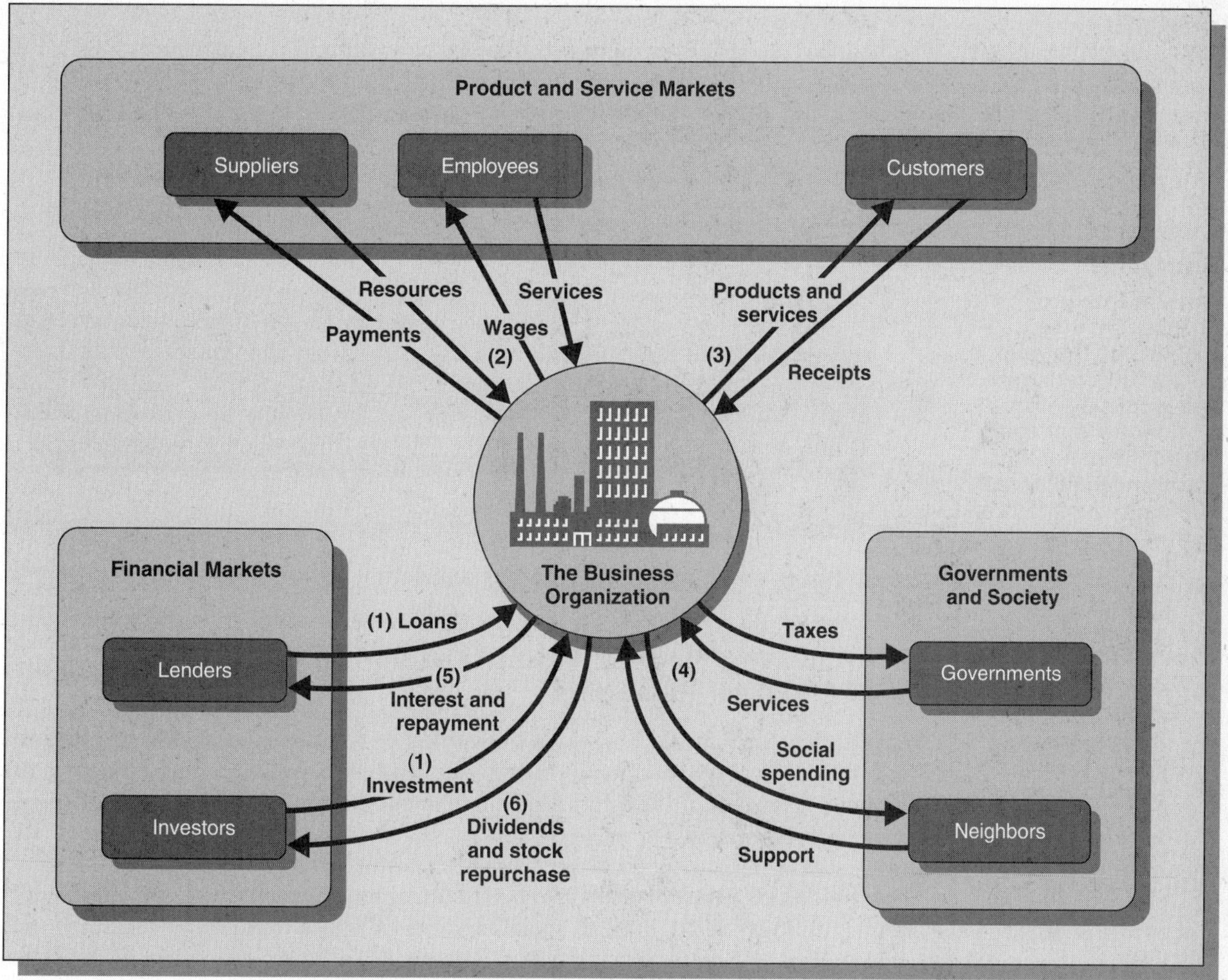

FIGURE 1.1
Money flows of a business. The firm (1) raises money, (2) purchases inputs and (3) sells outputs, (4) shares its profits with governments and society, (5) pays its debts, and (6) provides returns to its investors.

courses or work in a finance job. Most universities organize their finance curriculum into three broad tracks which correspond to the way many finance professionals organize job opportunities: (1) financial managing within an organization that produces and sells products and/or services, (2) analysis and management of investments, and (3) work within financial markets and institutions. Figure 1.2 shows these three paths and identifies some of the common course titles and job activities on each. Figure 1.2 also identifies an important insight: although this book concentrates primarily on the financial managing path, the key finance concepts you will encounter in the book underlie and are fully applicable to all three paths.

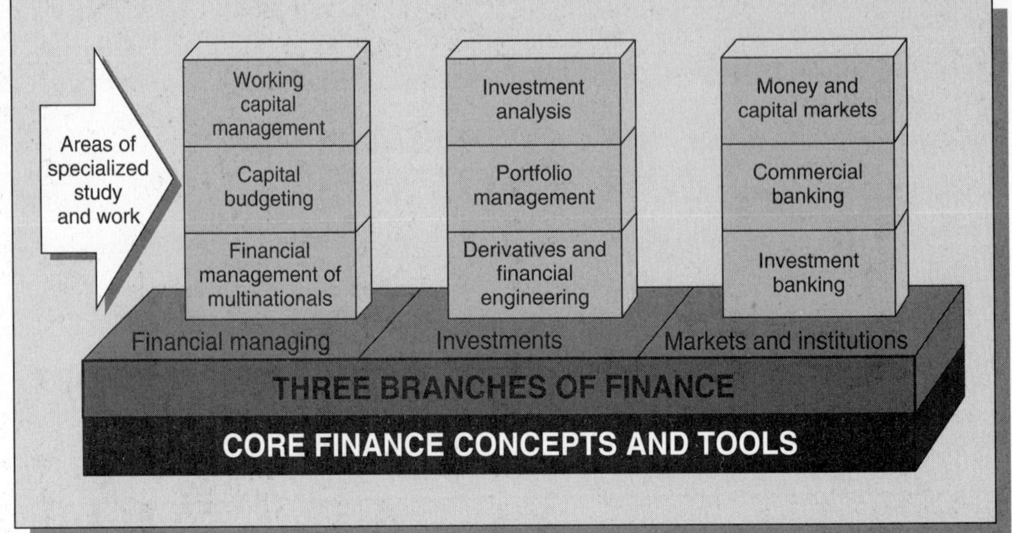

FIGURE 1.2
Three branches of finance. The core concepts of this book support further study and employment in (1) financial managing, (2) investment analysis and management, and (3) financial markets and institutions.

2. Organizing Finance Around the Concerns of Financial Managers

financial environment—the business and social forces which impact the financial operations of an organization

financial instrument—a document giving the holder a claim to present or future cash flows

security—a financial instrument such as a bond or share of stock

stock—a type of financial instrument that gives the holder ownership of a portion of a corporation

bond—a type of financial instrument that is a long-term loan, giving the holder the right to receive interest payments and repayment of the loan principal

investment banker—an individual or organization that specializes in helping firms issue new securities and in trading existing securities

Another useful way to categorize the subject of finance is to divide it into three broad areas as seen by someone managing finance within an organization: (1) the financial environment, (2) financial instruments, and (3) management of the finances of the business firm.

The financial environment The **financial environment** includes all the economic, political, legal, ethical, social, and other issues that define the surroundings within which financial people operate. It includes the financial markets, where lenders and investors provide money to business firms, and the product and service markets, where firms purchase resources and sell their products and services. It also includes the tax environment, within which income is shared with various governmental agencies.

Financial instruments **Financial instruments** are legal agreements giving investors ownership of the results of a business's operations. They include notes, such as bank loan agreements, and **securities,** such as **stocks** and **bonds.** Finance professionals active in the creation of financial instruments include **investment bankers,** who help the business firm to structure and issue securities; **commercial bankers,** who make loans to the firm; and professional investors and fund managers, who trade in the firm's securities to earn money for their clients. Financial managers study financial instruments to understand how and why (or why not) they can add value for these stakeholders and the firm.

Financial managing The **financial manager** is responsible for the money which enters, is used by, and leaves an organization. Accordingly, financial managers must understand in detail the firm's flow of money and must ensure that

commercial banker—an individual or organization that specializes in taking deposits from investors and in making loans to individuals and organizations

financial manager—a person responsible for analyzing and improving the money flows of an organization

money is consistently used in the best ways possible to further the company's objectives.

Of these three areas of financial managing activity, this book deals primarily with managing the finances of the business firm. It also includes information about the financial environment and financial instruments, because good financial managers base financial management decisions upon a solid understanding of all parts of the finance discipline. This book is also about managing financial processes and operations. Good financial managers understand and use not only the tools and techniques of finance but also the tools and techniques of management. One without the other is incomplete.

chief financial officer (CFO)—the senior finance professional responsible for all of a company's financial activities

If you choose to enter the finance area of a business, your first job typically will call for the use of technical finance skills; little management knowledge will be required. As you grow in responsibility within the firm, however, the nature of your job will change. While you will still need to be well versed in financial theory and practice, you will be managing tasks and people and dealing more frequently with senior managers. At this level, an understanding of management will be of significant help in your work. Eventually, you might reach the post of **chief financial officer (CFO)** or perhaps president of your company. Success at this level requires a thorough understanding of management.

The Development of the Finance Discipline

Finance as a discipline did not exist prior to the beginning of the twentieth century. Small businesses were the norm. Because they were small, they needed few financial resources and were believed to be efficient and self-regulating. The few large businesses were, for the most part, financed by a wealthy owner and a few equally wealthy banker friends. Although the concept of financial accounting had been around for centuries, there was no set of standards to make financial statements available or meaningful. The financial markets were the province of a few insiders. Little information about the firm was publicly available, and few outside the business and its associates were interested in the firm's finances.

Finance as we know it today evolved over the course of the twentieth century, as summarized in Figure 1.3. The first tentative analyses of the firm from a financial point of view were largely descriptive and followed the trends of the day. Between 1900 and 1910 the focus was on the building of the great trusts: merger, consolidation, and economies of scale. From 1910–1920, the focus shifted to include divestiture in response to early antitrust legislation. Also during this period, the Federal Reserve system was created and the banking system was studied intently. The boom of the 1920s encouraged firms to raise funds for expansion and redirected the descriptive focus of finance toward securities and the stock market. By 1930, the boom was over and finance followed soberly, turning its attention to describing reduction in scale and bankruptcy.

It was not until the mid-1930s that finance began to grow into its own as a discipline. John Burr Williams's development of the theory of time value marked a

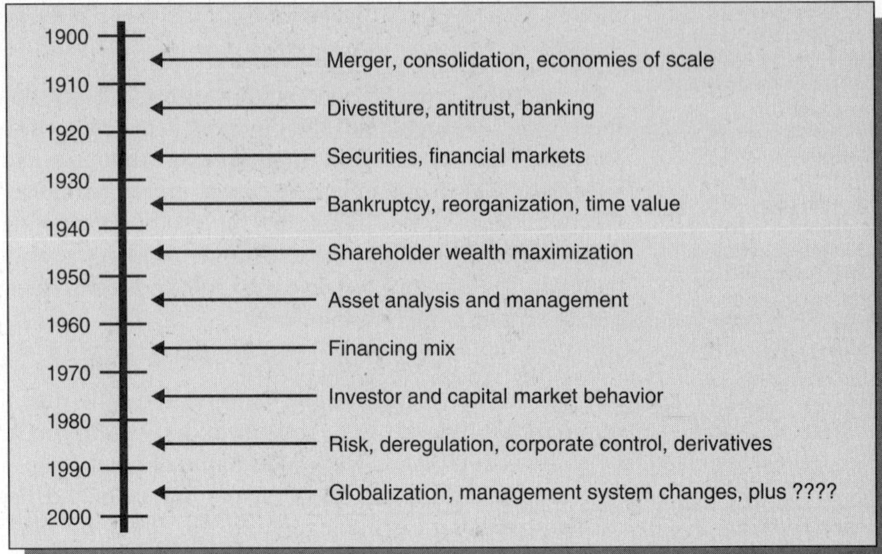

FIGURE 1.3
A timetable of financial thought. The finance discipline continues to evolve in response to changes in the business environment.

turning point in the history of finance.[1] Finance was no longer solely descriptive. For the first time, there was a theory that could instruct financial managers in what they *should* do to add value to the firm. After that, with a bit of a pause during World War II, finance spurted ahead in leaps and bounds. A goal of maximizing shareholder wealth was formulated (more about this in Chapter 2), and techniques and theories were developed to achieve this goal. Mathematics and statistics were married to finance, and the power of computers was harnessed to permit complex modeling.

During the 1950s the focus of these efforts centered on the analysis and management of assets, as time value theory was applied to the flows of money from asset purchases. By 1960, theories of liability/equity mix had begun to emerge, and the methods by which the firm raises money—for many years a subject only of description—got a thorough analytical treatment. The 1970s saw the development of theories of the behavior of investors and of capital markets. During these three decades, theories of risk were developed, permitting financial managers to quantify risk for the first time and relate it to return. As a result, the actions of firms were linked with the behavior of investors and capital markets, and financial managers could begin to quantify how shareholders might react to corporate financial decisions.

The early 1980s represented a period of major development within the field of finance in response to the economic legacy of the 1970s. The "oil shock" as the OPEC cartel sharply raised petroleum prices, the "currency shock" as world currencies floated free of gold and the dollar, and the "inflation shock" as prices rose at double-digit rates, all created a financial environment much more volatile than

[1] **Reference:** John Burr Williams published his insights in *The Theory of Investment Value* (Cambridge, Mass.: Harvard Univ. Press, 1938).

experienced at any time in recent history. Financial models were revised to incorporate these greater levels of variation. New financial instruments were developed to assist financial managers in coping with the increased risk.

The decade of the 1980s was also a period of wrenching change for many companies. In the early 1980s, a number of U.S. industries—the financial industry included—were partially or totally deregulated in response to competition from countries with less regulation and to the political success of "free-market" advocates. (Airlines, railroads, banks, and telecommunication companies are examples of industries that experienced significant deregulation.) Although finance theory provided much advice on managing in an increasingly deregulated world, not all newly deregulated industries made the transition easily, and the savings and loan crisis cost the country hundreds of billions of dollars. By the mid 1980s the "market for corporate control" was flourishing: U.S. business was engulfed in a wave of mergers and takeovers as "financial raiders" sought to acquire poorly performing companies and sell off the worst-performing units. *Junk bonds, greenmail,* and *leveraged buyout* became household words.

In the 1980s and early 1990s, we also witnessed events that are forcing us to rethink the basic premises of how organizations are managed and how the finance function contributes to that process. Existing management systems, consistent with traditional financial theory, were considered the best means for achieving a vibrant, innovative, and competitive business sector; yet we experienced competitive difficulties in industry after industry. We expected our businesses to lead the nation to global economic success, yet the United States—until recently the world's principal creditor nation—became the world's principal debtor nation and faces large and continuing balance-of-trade deficits year after year. Per capita income in the United States was stagnant, and income disparities widened—the rich became richer and the poor became poorer. These observations and many more like them have raised increasing concerns about the effectiveness of the total economic system and the role played by financial management. Today, managers are paying much more attention to management thinkers who have long been proposing new methods for running organizations. And finance thinkers are beginning to reformulate theories of finance to be consistent with these new approaches to management. This is an exciting time to be studying finance.

Two Major Forces for Change in Financial Managing

Two dramatic and closely related "revolutions" in the business environment are causing many financial managers to change important aspects of the way they think about their work and do their jobs. One is the breaking down of international barriers, which is significantly raising the level of global competitiveness. The other is a new way of managing that has produced remarkable successes and is challenging many widely held beliefs.[2]

[2] **Cross-reference:** In Chapter 3 we discuss seven types of change affecting financial managing. The two discussed in this chapter are so important that we have given them special attention—in this chapter, in Chapter 3, and throughout the book.

1. Global Business Competitiveness

Until the last twenty years or so, most business firms operated primarily in their domestic markets. Even those that had international operations focused primarily on their home markets. Where this was not the result of chauvinism (as in "buy American," for example), it was the result of tariff, distance, or other barriers. This has all changed.

The past two decades have been marked by the breakdown of international barriers. Today, business competition is truly global. Computer and telecommunications systems have linked the world, making it easier for companies to move their operations to the lowest-cost location. Tariffs are being reduced, and free trade is becoming the norm. The United States, Canada, and Mexico (signers of the North American Free Trade Agreement, or NAFTA); the European Community; and the Mercosur group of South American countries are three examples of blocs of nations which are removing most barriers to trade among themselves. It is difficult to be insulated and protected today. There are more competitors, and often the competition comes from a country with higher productivity, a better-educated work force, a stronger currency, more support from its government, or some other competitive advantage.

The result of this increased competitiveness is that the business firm must be much better than it has ever had to be if it is to survive and prosper. By 1990, the evidence was all around us, as three quotations from a single *Fortune* magazine article from that year indicate:

> During the 1980's American producers lost huge chunks of the market to foreign suppliers of computer chips and machine tools—high tech sectors crucial to industrial strength in the 21st century. In 1983, Japan's Ministry of Trade and Industry (MITI) analyzed U.S. and Japanese prowess in 40 key sectors of commercial technology, from assembly robots to skyscrapers. It found Japan lagging in nearly half. In an update of that study five years later, MITI concluded that the U.S. has held its lead in only one area (database software).[3]

Financial managers are finding that they have an important role to play in helping the firm compete globally. Consider the case of Alcoa Aluminum, whose worldwide success is due in large part to its ability to see finance in the context of its long-range competitive objectives:

> Alcoa developed its thriving export business only after getting whacked with what (Group Vice President Ronald R.) Hoffman calls a "cold towel in the face" by the Japanese. In 1980 the company was finishing a record year of earnings when the first Japanese competition arrived on American shores. The Japanese were selling (aluminum) sheet for 8% to 10% less than Alcoa and other American manufacturers. "But what our customers really applauded was the quality," says Hoffman. Rolling their sheet on equipment similar to Alcoa's, the Japanese were getting a cleaner surface finish, fewer imperfections, and a greater tolerance for high-speed canmaking processes.

[3] **Reference:** "Lifting American Competitiveness," *Fortune,* April 23, 1990, pp. 56–58.

> At first, says Hoffman, Alcoa refused to recognize the competitive threat. "We denied reality. We convinced ourselves that the Japanese were handpicking (only the best) coils of aluminum sheet to break into the U.S. market. But it didn't take a New York minute for us to figure out that we were going to get nailed over the next few years if we didn't follow up (and beat the quality of the Japanese product)."
>
> Alcoa committed $800 million to upgrade and stuck to its modernization plan even though earnings fell over the next few years and excess capacity flooded world markets. "We laid a lot of money out when not a lot of money was coming in," says Hoffman. "Now we have a profitable, noncyclical business in a market that has taken off."[4]

Or listen to Lee Iacocca, former chairman of Chrysler Corporation, who points out that the international competitive position of the American automobile industry was held back for years because of a narrow finance-based focus on production costs:

> When the U.S. consulting firm A.T. Kearney surveyed companies planning new facilities, more than half said pursuing lower costs was their chief goal. American business has to learn that costs of any kind are only half of the competitive equation: the customer wants value for money. . . . consumers fork over about $2,000 more for Japanese cars than for comparable American models because they think they are getting a better machine.[5]

In today's competitive environment, financial managers have to deal with many variables which can change from country to country. Instead of dealing in one currency, financial managers must operate in several. They must monitor the relative values of these currencies and protect the firm from adverse changes. Instead of dealing with one group of people with (perhaps) a common cultural heritage, financial managers must satisfy stakeholders with different value systems and attitudes about business and work. Instead of one tax system, they must integrate the effects of several. Instead of one legal system, financial managers must operate so as to be acceptable to many.

The political environment varies from country to country as well, and in some nations from week to week. Many countries welcome privately owned businesses and support their operations while others do not. In some nations resources may be freely purchased and sold, and profits may be freely remitted to the firm's home country; other nations place limits on these flows and require the business to negotiate with the government for these privileges. At the extreme, assets may be expropriated in some countries of the world. The effort now underway to transform the economies of eastern European nations and the republics of the former Soviet Union from central, state control to market driven is the most dramatic recent example of how quickly and completely the political environment can change.

---

[4] **Reference:** "Rewriting the Export Rules," *Fortune,* April 23, 1990, p. 92.

[5] **Reference and observation:** "Lessons From U.S. Business Blunders," in *Fortune,* April 23, 1990, p. 129. Because consumers were willing to pay more for Japanese-made cars, the Japanese automobile manufacturers could have higher costs than their American competitors and still be more profitable. Since the use of quality management techniques also enabled them to produce at lower costs than their American competitors, they had a twofold financial advantage!

2. The Global Quality Revolution

Closely related to increased global competitiveness is the emergence of a new way of managing that has revolutionized the way many successful companies around the world operate. Its hallmarks are a commitment to satisfying customers and outstanding success in doing so. On the customer side, the commitment is to exceed customer expectations on an ongoing basis by continuously improving the company's products and services and the processes that make and support them. On the success side, the accomplishment is the achievement of "revolutionary rates of quality improvement": very rapid development of new products, new features for existing products, and new services. The quality improvements include dramatic reductions in defects—not reductions of 5% or 10% in a few years but reductions of 99% in two years followed by another 99% so that defects are one ten-thousandth of what they were four years earlier. This way of managing aims for and achieves speed and perfection: rapid response to customers, competitors, technologies, and markets, and near-zero variation in everything the firm does. Its use by Japanese firms over the past 40 years transformed that nation's economy. From a devastated loser of World War II with a reputation for exporting cheap, low-quality products, Japan became one of the world's strongest economies and most formidable competitors.

Although keeping the customer happy and improving quality seem like obvious things to do, it is only recently that many American companies have discovered the power of new management approaches in achieving these goals. Company-wide use of these management practices in the United States dates from the late 1970s, when a few companies—primarily those losing markets to the Japanese—began serious study of the reasons for their competitors' success. By the mid-1980s, these management practices had begun to spread throughout the United States and to evolve into a truly new way of managing in some companies. As this way of managing was adopted, individual companies put their own unique label on what they were doing and fine-tuned the basics of these practices to their unique histories and competitive situations.

In the mid-1980s, a group of corporate leaders and quality experts began to convince the U.S. government of the importance of promoting revolutionary rates of quality improvement in all American companies. Impressed by the apparent success of the Deming Prize, a Japanese quality award named after an American, they advocated a similar type of public recognition for American companies. The award was to be a visible, public recognition of the power of this way of managing in achieving high levels of customer satisfaction, competitive success, and corporate survival. In 1988, the U.S. government awarded the first Malcolm Baldrige National Quality Awards, elevating the pursuit of quality by American business to a national priority.

> Much of the time, that level of quality produces healthy financial rewards. The first small company to win a Baldrige award, in 1988, was Cleveland's Globe Metallurgical, Inc. Its chief executive, Arden C. Sims, estimates that Globe's investments in quality have produced a 40–1 return. From 1986 to 1988, Globe cut operating expenses by a hefty $11.3 million, and its quality efforts continue to pare operating costs by about $4 million a year. Recently, Sims told the *Har-*

> *vard Business Review* that annual savings from quality efforts for his $115 million company should increase to about $13 million by 1995.[6]

In Europe, Asia, and Latin America similar changes in management practices were also occurring and similar awards were also being developed, such as the European Award for Quality and Mexico's National Quality Award.

These quality management practices are starting to have a profound impact on the conduct of finance in companies that adopt them. One of the most visible impacts is a greatly increased recognition of the importance of viewing an organization as a system. As companies adopt quality-focused management practices and adapt them to their own circumstances, they quickly discover that one core concept involves viewing the organization as a system tied together by processes that cross conventional functional boundaries. Every traditional department—including finance—must be involved in the company's quality-focused efforts for the company to obtain the full benefits of this powerful way of managing. The finance functions of many companies are learning that they can add considerable value to their firms by being full partners and participants in their company's quality management efforts.

Continuity and Change in Finance's Work

Even though the revolutions in global competitiveness and quality management are causing significant changes in many aspects of business, they are merely the latest in a long history of forces that have caused business practice to evolve. As we emphasize in Chapter 3 and throughout the book, finance work has always been a combination of the old and the new. Identifying and holding on to those things that still work well while discarding or improving those that no longer do is and will continue to be an important part of everyone's job.

This mixture of old and new, of continuity and change, is particularly visible when we look at finance's place in the organizational structure. For many years, in most organizations, the roles of financial managers have been set in the context of the pyramidal organization. Finance professionals have worked in a finance department, similar and parallel to other departments housing marketing, production, human resources, and other business specialists. However, this structure's inability to respond quickly and efficiently to today's competitive environment is causing many companies to rethink the way they are organized. And as organizational structure is changing, so too are organizational roles, including those of financial managers.

[6] **Reference:** "Quality: Small and Midsize Companies Seize the Challenge—Not a Moment Too Soon," *Business Week,* Nov. 30, 1992, p. 72.

1. Well-Established Financial Roles and Work

Traditionally, the finance function has been an independent organization within the firm, as shown in Figure 1.4, an organization chart of a typical business. The chief financial officer (CFO)—often carrying the title vice president of finance—normally reports to the president and is responsible for all money transactions within the firm and between the firm and outside parties. Below the CFO are the treasurer, controller, and often a third person who might be called director of financial analysis.

treasurer—the finance professional responsible for funding a company and for its day-to-day money flows

The **treasurer** manages relationships with commercial and investment banks and oversees the firm's investments in securities, such as its pension funds and investments of temporary excess cash. Treasury professionals manage the day-to-day cash balance and raise various forms of debt and equity financing. The treasurer also normally manages the credit department, which oversees the extension of credit to customers, the collection of accounts receivable, and the payment of accounts payable.

FIGURE 1.4

A traditional business organization. The organization is shaped like a pyramid with the "boss" on top and is separated into departments, each with responsibility for a different business function.

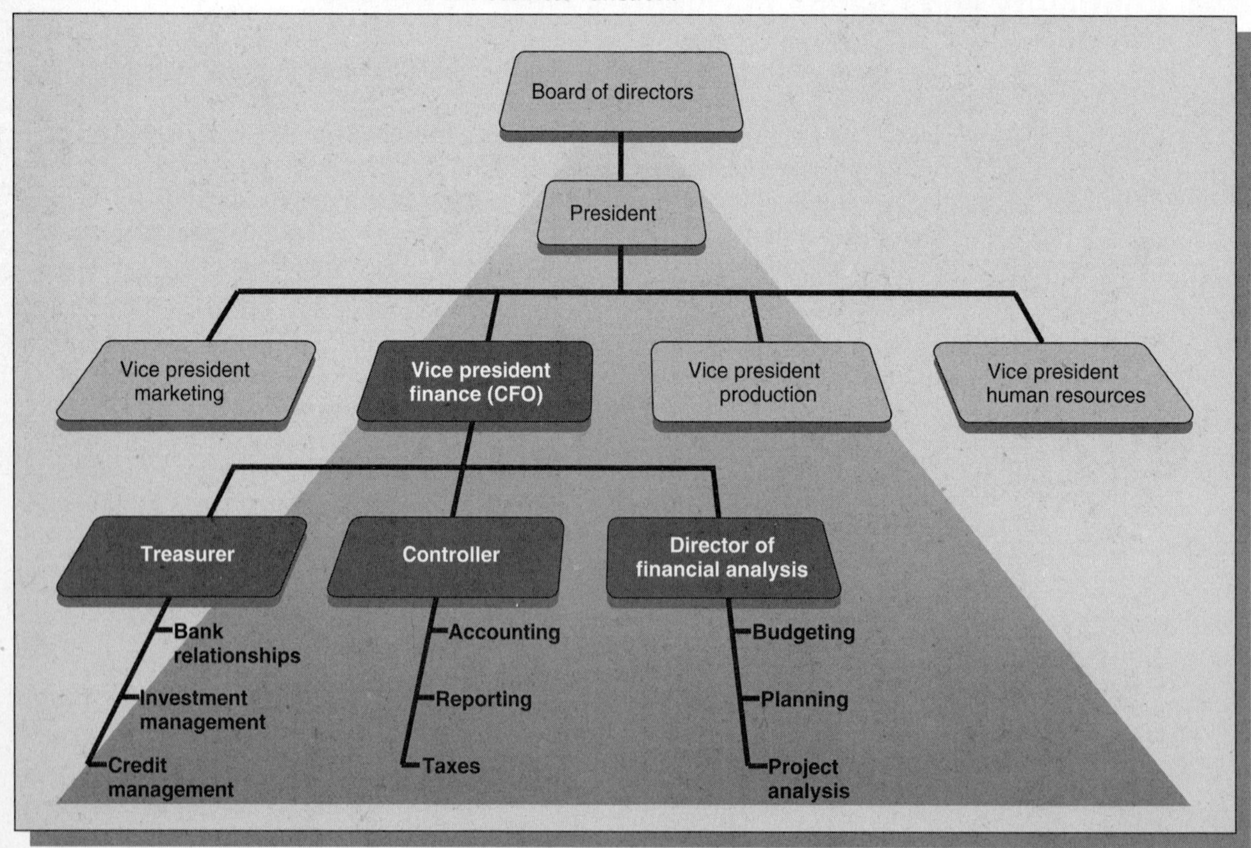

controller—the finance/accounting professional responsible for a company's financial record-keeping and reporting

The **controller** is usually the firm's chief accountant and manages its financial data. These activities include public reporting according to the rules of the Securities and Exchange Commission (SEC) and the Financial Accounting Standards Board (FASB), internal financial reporting for analysis and decision making, and preparation of the company's tax return.

director of financial analysis—the finance professional responsible for a company's financial analysis and planning

The **director of financial analysis** oversees the firm's financial planning activities including detailed budgeting and the technical analysis of the various investment projects the firm might initiate. In many firms, the financial analysis role is performed by the controller's office.

2. Problems with the Traditional Structure

The growing international competition faced by American companies and the need to improve quality and customer responsiveness have called attention to a series of problems arising in part from the traditional pyramidal structure of work and roles. Two of these problems are: (1) barriers to collaborative work between departments and functions within the organization and (2) a tendency to lose focus on customers. These problems frequently show up as slowness in responding to customer needs and competitive challenges.

Functional barriers Companies organized along functional lines are often sluggish in reacting to customers and change. The pyramid is designed for vertical communication, but most work flows across functions rather than up and down. This problem has always existed in pyramidal organizations; what is new is that increased global competitiveness has led many managers to believe this sluggishness may now be life-threatening to the organizations in which they occur.

The problem is primarily due to over-emphasis by each function or department on its own work and its own importance. The metaphor used by managers to describe this problem is the silo in which agricultural products are stored: a tall vertical cylinder with firm walls keeping the valuable contents from spilling out and unwanted rain, dirt, or insects from getting in. In business the issue is that managers in one "functional silo" fail to collaborate effectively with those in another.

Losing customer focus The second problem arises in part from the power and status differences in pyramidal organizations. With the officers of the business firm located at the top of the hierarchy, the understandable presumption of employees, as well as of the officers, is that the officers are much more important than employees. Employees often pay more attention to senior managers than to the firm's customers. And, since the "important" officers are far removed from customers, the "voice of the customer" is often barely audible when important decisions are made.

3. The Customer-Focused Organization

A new and quite different picture of the organization is illustrated in Figure 1.5, an organization chart drawn by the Nordstrom Corporation. The customer, the person who purchases the firm's goods and services, is on top being served by

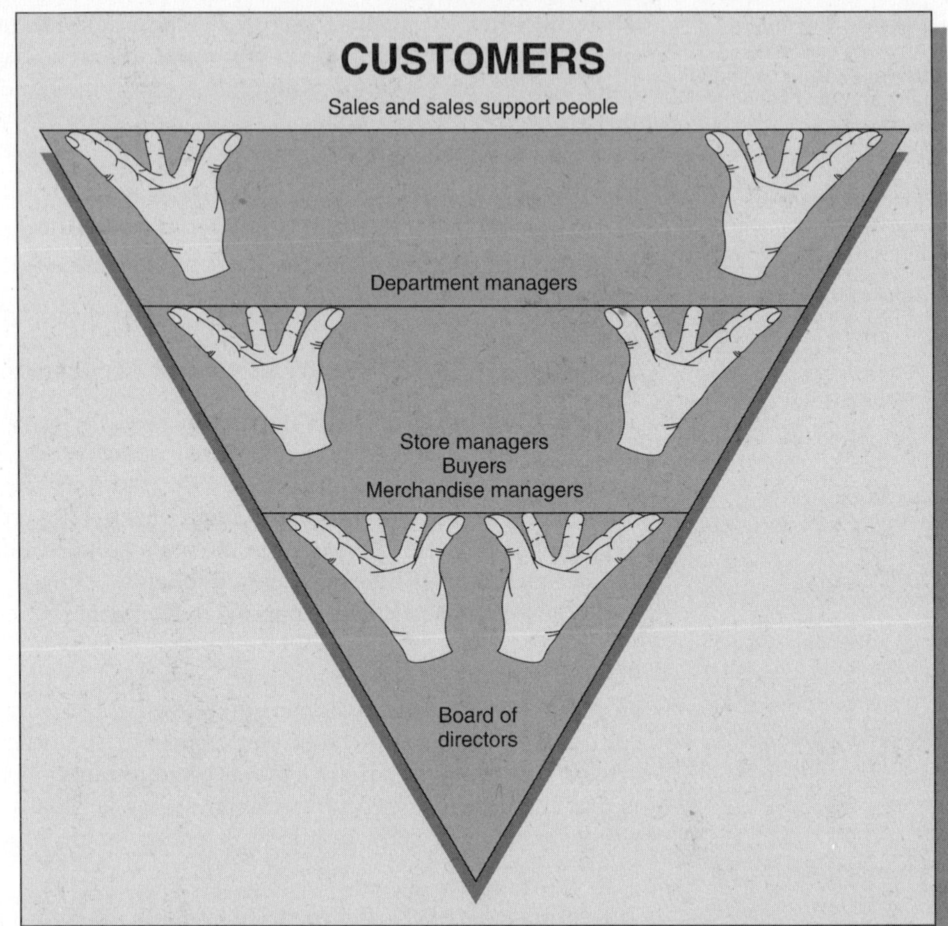

FIGURE 1.5
Nordstrom's inverted organizational pyramid. In this modern way of picturing organizational form, the customer is on top and a much flatter organization serves as a support system to help everyone exceed customer expectations.

the members of the organization. The modern quality-focused management system goes even further than Figure 1.5 suggests, identifying the customer as the most important person "in" any business firm. Effective organizations are learning to think and speak of customers as being part of the organization rather than outsiders, to talk of the production process starting and ending with the customer, and of managers supporting the workers and removing the barriers that prevent them from doing excellent work. One way in which this change of mind-set is communicated to organizational members is by drawing the organization chart in this very different way to emphasize the importance of customers and of organizational members who serve customers directly.

Figure 1.5 is similar to ones drawn for many years by companies like Bergen Brunswig, Dana Corporation, and Scandinavian Airline Systems (SAS). Notice that the higher the level of management, the lower the position in this organization structure. In this respect, the inverted pyramid is exactly the reverse of the traditional structure. The chart emphasizes the role of all managers in supporting those who serve the customer. Rather than directing and controlling subordinates, managers work to create an environment in which employees can do their jobs well. They improve processes, permitting excellent performance to become the norm. They eliminate barriers between the functions and departments rather than creating and protecting their "turf."

As finance professionals adapt to this new structure, some of the work of finance is changing and some is remaining the same. For example, the preparation of budgets and the evaluation of capital investment projects are becoming collaborative, team-based activities, yet the techniques used to evaluate the worth of future cash flows continue to be used just as they have been for decades. New financial managing activities are arising from the need to support the modern management practices being adopted throughout the organization—for example, the defining, collecting, and communicating of nonfinancial measures like customer satisfaction, defects in operations, and the length of time required to accomplish key organizational activities. Other practices, such as finance acting in a policing or inspecting role, are being eliminated as they are discovered to add no value to (and often reduce the value of) the business.

4. The Importance of Recognizing Finance's Supporting Role

The clear importance of finance's work might lead to the conclusions that finance is more important than other business functions and the finance discipline is the most important of all business disciplines. Since (1) the goal of the firm has been assumed to be the maximization of stockholder wealth, and since (2) many decisions leading to that goal occur within the financial arena, and since (3) the achievement of that goal is gauged by financial measures, it may seem only natural that all other business functions should be viewed as serving finance. Some teachers and financial managers have yielded to this temptation. They feel accounting's main function is to produce the data needed for financial decision making; accounting is criticized when its measures are not consistent with evaluating shareholder wealth. Marketing has to know when the costs of production and distribution exceed the benefits of serving the customer. Human resource management has to know when the cost of labor makes benefiting employees impossible.

"NOW THEY'RE TALKING! THIS SEMESTER, THE LIST OF COURSES MENTIONS HOW MUCH EACH COULD ADD TO YOUR INCOME AFTER GRADUATION."

In some respects these advocates of finance are correct. Proper financial managing is critically important to the success of the business firm. Indeed, there are numerous examples of how a company that pays little or no attention to financial managing fares poorly. Cost control, good investment decisions, wise financing choices, and all the other financial managing analyses and decisions considered in this book remain key requirements for business success. And financial mistakes will often show up much faster and with greater impact than mistakes in other organizational functions.

However, the revolutions in global competitiveness and quality management are teaching us that, in a much more important sense, finance is not uniquely important. Without the other components of the organization doing their work well, there is no work for finance to do at all. Failure anywhere else can also doom the organization. In this most important of all senses, all business functions are equally important. A well-run business is an integrated whole serving many clienteles. No one discipline dominates because the contributions of every part are necessary for success. For the value of the business to grow, all stakeholders must be served along several dimensions. A major challenge of the 1990s is to add many more financial managers to the ranks of those who combine a deep understanding of the value and importance of finance with a recognition of its role in supporting the contributions of other organizational functions.

The Organization of the Book

This book is organized into eight parts.

In Part I, we explore the purpose of the firm and the role of finance and of finance people in achieving that purpose. We identify the dimensions on which stakeholders measure the firm's performance and begin the discussion of how the firm might meet and exceed their expectations. We explore how rapid change, due to the globalization of business, the emergence of quality management, and other factors, is modifying every day the way we view the finance function. We review the various sets of data—from customers, processes, the environment, and tax and accounting records—that are used in financial decision making.

Since finance deals with money, Part II covers the basics of that resource. We study the time value of money: how the value of money depends critically upon when it is received or paid. We also examine the price of money, both as a function of time (interest rates) and of type (exchange rates).

Part III explores the concepts of risk and return, the framework used throughout financial theory to evaluate the value added by financial decisions. We define risk as seen by the firm's investors, identify what causes it, illustrate how to measure it, and identify how it plays an important role in determining investors' requirements. Next we examine how investors use this information to value financial instruments—bonds, stocks, and options. We conclude by showing how the requirements of investors can be integrated into an overall cost of capital funds for the firm.

Parts IV through VI discuss the common decisions facing financial managers. They are grouped according to the analytical technique used to study data and reach conclusions. In Part IV we examine how to make incremental decisions as we study capital budgeting and setting permanent working capital balances.

Part V looks at process decisions. We uncover various processes within the finance function and identify the tools available to analyze and improve them. We also explore how financial managers can contribute to improving processes involving multiple areas of the business.

Part VI is devoted to optimization decisions—decisions for which theory prescribes a "best" solution. These decisions include the degree of leverage, the mix of financing, the hedging of risk exposure, and the amount of the firm's dividend.

In Part VII, we examine the various sources of financing available to the firm. We begin by looking at techniques for identifying a company's financial needs. Next we profile the financial markets in which money is exchanged and the financial institutions that operate within those markets. The remainder of this part of the book looks at the various financial instruments—stocks, bonds, loans, etc.—used by financial managers to raise funds in the financial markets. Because debt securities come in many more varieties than equity instruments, we devote correspondingly more time to them. We also look at contingent equity claims, warrants and convertible securities, which increase the firm's financing flexibility.

Part VIII provides opportunities both to look back and to look ahead. We review what we know and what we do not know about the finance discipline. We comment on the benefits (and dangers) of finance as a way of thinking about business. And we invite each reader to join us and our academic and business colleagues in the ongoing inquiry into financial managing.

Three days after Liz Horne and Mike Cantrell put their initial ideas for a financial training program on flip-chart pages, they returned to the same conference room with their PCs to hammer out a short report to the CFO.

"Wow," said Liz, "you can learn a lot—and get pretty confused—in three days when you ask a question that a lot of smart people are interested in, can't you?"

"Yep," Mike replied. "The treasurer points out how different the finance course he took three decades ago was from the current business school syllabus we showed him. And then, in the same breath, he points out a bunch of concepts in that same syllabus that he learned 30 years ago and still uses today. It looks as if there's lots of change and lots of stability at the same time."

"Okay," said Liz, "here's my memory of what we agreed late yesterday: (1) there are some key concepts and tools to be learned; (2) finance has specialized skills and a unique role in the company. In that sense finance people are different—and at the same time, finance people are members of the whole organization; in that sense they are the same as everyone else. And (3) some of what finance does today will change and some will not . . . and nobody knows for sure which part is which.

"Let's summarize what the program might look like. We start with an introduction to finance and some of the changes occuring. Then we cover time value of money and money rates, and risk and return. From there we go to financial decision making. We finish up with a survey of financial markets and institutions. How does it sound?"

"It sounds like a new kind of textbook! Let's see what the CFO says," Mike responded, laughing.

Summary of Key Points

- **Identify what the subject of finance deals with and how it differs from traditional economics, and divide finance into its component parts along two dimensions.** Finance is about money: how a firm gets it, uses it, and distributes it. Finance draws heavily from economic thinking but is distinct from the economic discipline. Unlike macroeconomics, which looks at economies taken as a whole, finance studies individuals and business firms. Unlike microeconomics, which looks at physical transformations within a business, finance studies money flows. Finance may be divided into three areas of academic study and career paths: financial managing, investment analysis and management, and financial markets and institutions. The concerns of financial managers may also be divided into three areas: the financial environment, financial instruments, and financial managing. In addition, financial managers must know how to manage well to be successful.
- **Recount how the finance discipline evolved.** Finance evolved over the twentieth century from a descriptive subject to an analytic discipline. Theory, mathematics, statistics, and computing power have been joined to create a rich body of knowledge which can guide the financial manager in making good decisions. Of late, theorists have been recasting financial concepts in a broader framework in response to concerns about the performance of U.S. business and the economy.
- **Recognize why increased global competition and the global quality revolution are leading to changes in financial management.** As barriers to world trade have shrunk in recent years, the financial manager has found it necessary to think in global terms. Issues of competitiveness, multiple currencies, and multiple social and political environments have broadened the financial manager's job and have put pressure on the business firm to perform at ever higher levels. In addition, revolutionary rates of quality improvement in many industries have called attention to new, modern management practices far more effective than traditional ones. These modern practices are being adopted by companies around the world. These changes in the total management system of companies are leading to changes in the ways financial managers view and perform their own work.
- **Understand where the finance function fits within a business organization and why it is important for finance to be integrated with the rest of the business.** The need for rapid response in the global environment and the customer focus of modern management practices are encouraging financial managers to rethink the role of finance within the organization and to discover new ways to contribute to the company's success. At the same time, many well-established finance practices continue to be valid. In some companies finance functions are increasing their effectiveness by reintegrating themselves into the rest of the company rather than maintaining the departmental barriers that have separated them from other organizational units.
- **Have a sense of what to expect in the remainder of this book.** The book is divided into eight parts covering: (1) an introduction to financial managing, (2) the basics of money, (3) risk and return, (4) making incremental decisions, (5) making process decisions, (6) making optimization decisions, (7) sources of financing, and (8) looking ahead to exciting questions in financial managing.

Questions

1. How is the discipline of finance (a) similar to and (b) different from the discipline of economics?
2. Give an example of how each piece of the financial environment listed below affects the business firm:
   a. the economy
   b. the political scene
   c. the law
   d. ethical standards
   e. social norms
3. What does a financial manager do for a living?
4. What is a stakeholder? For each stakeholder listed below, identify its relationship to the business firm:
   a. customers
   b. employees
   c. suppliers
   d. governments
   e. neighbors
   f. lenders
   g. investors
5. What has happened over the past decade to change the competitive position of all business firms worldwide?
6. Why are some observers of the business scene drawing "upside-down" organization charts?
7. Why do you think finance is the most popular area of concentration at graduate schools of business?

CASE

JILL McDUFF

Jill McDuff stopped taking notes for a moment and looked around the room. One hour ago the eight other faces were those of strangers, but already it seemed to her as if she had known each of them much longer. Each face was different; yet in its own way, each was familiar. She glanced again at the name cards on the desk in front of each one. There was Shoji from Tokyo, Kim from Seoul, and Anisha from Bombay. Marek from Poland, Hamisi from Tanzania, Fernando from Spain, and João from Brazil. Each spoke with a different accent, yet each had a degree in finance. They were totally different, yet they were all the same.

Jill was from Glasgow, Scotland, where she was employed by a company that manufactured and distributed a range of products in its local market. Like her counterparts around the table, she had been invited to the headquarters of the Trinetics Corporation, a rapidly growing electronics firm in California's Silicon Valley, south of San Francisco Bay. Trinetics's business with multinational companies was increasing, and it was interested in establishing international sales and production relationships to serve its customers' overseas facilities more effectively. Each company invited to the meeting was highly respected in its country and was one that Trinetics thought would be an attractive partner. Since Jill's company was eager to attract more business from U.S. manufacturers, she had jumped at the chance to attend.

The eighth face belonged to Arthur Martin, Marty as he liked to be called, the person chairing the meeting. Marty was the chief financial officer (CFO) of Trinetics and was leading the company's project to expand its overseas business. He was presently in the midst of a formal presentation about Trinetics's product line: how Trinetics's products were of the highest quality, in high demand, and sure to represent a profitable line of business for each of the companies represented in the room.

When Marty finished his presentation and the group broke for coffee, Jill found herself in animated discussion with several of the others. She found the conversation fascinating and enjoyed learning more about this very diverse group. It struck her that this meeting was a microcosm of the changes many companies were facing in response to the globalization of business. As she returned to her chair, she jotted down three questions that she wanted to come back to later in the day. The questions on Jill's pad were:

1. What opportunities and barriers will Trinetics Corporation and my company face as they learn to do business together?
2. What old and new skills will Marty and the rest of us need in our new relationships?
3. What can I do, as a finance professional, to make sure the relationship between the companies operates as smoothly and profitably as possible?

CHAPTER 2
THE PURPOSE OF THE FIRM

Anne Spencer looked down at the notepad on her desk. An hour had passed since she had started to jot down her ideas, but her notes were still not coming together.

Anne was working for the firm's president, who had asked her to propose a mission statement for her company. The president had explained that the first part of the mission statement was to be a clear declaration of the firm's goal.

As a first step, Anne talked to senior managers in the company's various areas. The problem was that each manager gave her a different answer. The company's chief financial officer told her that the goal of the firm must be to maximize the firm's stock price; if the stock price were not kept up, shareholders—the owners of the firm—would not be fairly rewarded, the company could not raise capital funds at reasonable costs, and it could even be vulnerable to a takeover by corporate raiders. The vice president of marketing talked about satisfying customers to maintain and increase market share—if the firm did not satisfy its customers, it would soon go out of business. The head of production emphasized quality and productivity—unless the firm produced the highest quality products and services at low costs, it would lose business to its competitors. The human resources chief pointed out that the success of the firm depended on the performance of its people—training, developing, and rewarding employees had to be the firm's primary concerns.

Anne thought back to all the comments. If the firm had to have one goal, then clearly all of the above could not be the answer. But it seemed to her that every manager she talked to had a valid point. Perhaps the firm *should* pursue all of these agendas. But if so, just what was *the* goal of the firm?

Anne's problem is very real in many companies today. Each business function is acutely aware of the importance of its activities and is tempted to identify its own primary concern as *the goal* of the firm, the single most important objective for the company to pursue. Each argues that if its own goal is not made paramount, the firm will fare poorly.

For many years, the finance discipline has behaved in the same way, advancing its goal for the firm—maximizing the firm's stock price—as the single, most important one. This perspective has been widely accepted, and many corporations have adopted stock-price maximization as their single, most important goal. In today's changing business environment, however, managers and business thinkers have begun to question this approach and rethink the goal(s) of the firm. Many successful firms seem to be following a two-stage, or sequenced, goal approach: a *final* goal, associated with financial results, and a set of *operating* goals, for day-to-day managerial guidance. The traditional financial goal is appealing in its simplicity, yet it is difficult to explain the actions of many firms by assuming that they follow this goal in their daily operations. And when firms do follow the traditional financial goal on a day-to-day basis, they often produce results that are not in the best interests of their shareholders or their other stakeholders.

Anne is correct in believing that success in every area of the business is necessary for the firm to prosper. A firm without satisfied, productive employees is one that cannot produce high-quality products and services at low cost. Without such products and/or services, the firm cannot keep its customers and expand its market share. And without the ability to increase sales and lower costs, the company has no hope of increasing the value of its common stock. The successful firm in today's global marketplace is capable of integrating these goals and, by doing so, simultaneously meeting the needs of all its stakeholders.

Key Points You Should Learn from This Chapter

After reading this chapter you should be able to:

- Explain why it is important for a business to have goals.
- Explain why profit maximization was the original goal recommended for the firm by the early microeconomists.
- Explain why shareholder wealth maximization replaced profit maximization as the firm's financial goal.
- Identify the problems in maximizing shareholder wealth addressed by agency theory.
- Describe traditional approaches to minimizing agency costs and their pitfalls.
- Identify longstanding concerns about the undesirable side effects of shareholder wealth maximization being the goal of business firms.
- Explain how emerging new management methods and other approaches may reduce some of the concerns about agency conflicts and shareholder wealth maximization as a goal.

Introductory Concepts—The Importance of Goals

Before we can consider *what* the financial manager should do, we must first ask *why*. All decisions, financial or otherwise, can be judged only if they are measured against some **goal** or goals. A good decision is one that helps the company achieve its goals; a bad decision is one that moves the firm further away from its goals.

goal—the objective of (a business's) actions

1. The Need for Goals

The need for goals applies to all forms of endeavor, not just actions of a business firm. Consider personal decisions, for example. Why are you studying finance? There are many possible reasons. Is it to get a job? to get a better job? to make more money? to satisfy a demanding boss or parent? to meet an academic requirement? to broaden yourself as a person? to contribute to the well-being of society? to have fun? If you are studying finance for the right reasons, your efforts will prove rewarding. If you are studying finance for the wrong reasons, this could well be a frustrating and empty experience.

Or consider the decision to accept a new job. Is the new job right for you? The best way to approach the decision is first to be honest with yourself: what are your goals here? money? status? autonomy? personal growth? ability to contribute? intellectual challenge? If you clearly define your goals and ask how the new job measures up against those goals, you are far more likely to make a good decision than if you choose blindly.

Edgar finds his purpose.

Prior to the 1930s, before the finance discipline had developed any significant theory, the goal of finance was the microeconomic rule of maximizing profits. Since then, however, profits have been replaced by shareholder wealth as the number to maximize. Today, shareholder wealth maximization is itself being challenged by a much broader definition of the firm's goals.

2. The Role of Business in Society

Business plays a vital role in our society. It is the primary means by which the necessities of life—food, clothing and shelter—are manufactured and made available to the public. It provides jobs, which define much of our lives and give us much of our sense of self-worth. But business does much more. It provides pharmaceuticals and medical care. It provides banking, insurance, and pensions. It provides education at all levels. It engages in research and development activities, which bring us new products and services enhancing our lives. By freeing us from economic want, business allows us to pursue leisure activities. All societies require a healthy business sector, and a healthy business sector is required for a healthy society.

capitalist economic system—an economy marked by private ownership of businesses and the resources necessary for producing goods and services

Yet, in a **capitalist economic system** such as ours, society and business are quite distinct from each other. And while business firms can indeed benefit society, they are usually owned and operated by people for other reasons entirely. The entrepreneur who devotes time, energy, and money to creating and nurturing a business rarely makes benefit to society the primary goal of the firm. Rather, individuals create business firms for personal reasons, usually to make money. Since the Industrial Revolution, when the earliest businesses were formed, economists and philosophers have been examining whether, given the personal motivations of those who form and manage businesses, the actions of privately owned firms really do lead to a high degree of social welfare.[1]

The Microeconomic Goal: Profit Maximization

It was Adam Smith who first put forward the idea that individual business firms, each acting for its own benefit could, in the aggregate, benefit society. Over 200 years ago he wrote:

> (The businessman) by directing . . . industry in such a manner as its produce may be of greatest value . . . intends only his own gain, and he is in this, as in many other cases, led by an invisible hand to promote an end which was not

[1] **Observation:** This question, of the consistency between personal and societal goals, is particularly relevant in a capitalist economy, in which the means of production (businesses) are privately owned and separate from society as a whole. An alternate approach is that of Karl Marx, who, concerned about just this potential conflict of interest, proposed an economic system in which society owned all businesses. In this socialist economy, Marx argued, business and society would join together, and government would insure that business success equalled societal success. However, as recent events in socialist economies throughout the world (most notably in Eastern Europe and the former Soviet Union) have demonstrated, the side effects of socialism—centralization of political power, misallocation of resources due to the lack of market pricing signals, alienation of people—have repeatedly prevented the system from achieving either a well-functioning economy or a high degree of social welfare.

economic profits—the money returns to the investors in a firm

profit maximization—the act of managing a firm so as to increase its economic profits to the maximum possible level

competitive market—a market in which no participant has enough economic power to influence prices

efficient allocation of resources—directing the resources of an economy (money, labor, machinery, land, etc.) to those businesses where they can produce goods and services of the greatest value

accounting profits—the bottom number on an income statement using rules of measurement determined by accounting authorities

> a part of his intention. . . . pursuing his own interest he frequently promotes that of society more effectually than when he really intends to promote it.[2]

This most famous of passages offered the managers of the Industrial Revolution a simple primary goal. The object was for each firm to maximize **economic profits;** in practical terms this translated to efficiency of production. Since it was observed that firms that became more efficient survived and prospered, **profit maximization** attracted many adherents. As elaborated by subsequent economists, in highly **competitive markets,** with well-informed participants and prices accurately reflecting values, profit maximization by all businesses leads to the **efficient allocation of resources** and produces the greatest amount of those goods and services demanded by society at the lowest cost given the resources available.

Of course, when the early economists described the role of profits, they had no way of anticipating the complexity of modern business practice and the multiplicity of ways present-day accountants record and interpret financial numbers. In today's world, profits are not determined solely by economic activity; they are also defined by the accounting system. One firm can have many possible numbers for its **accounting profits,** depending on the choices made by its managers and accountants. It is increasingly difficult to measure profits and to know whether they are being maximized.

There are other difficulties as well with profit maximization as a goal—difficulties also not foreseen by Adam Smith and his followers. For one thing, profits do not come at once but over time, as firms invest their resources in long-term investment projects. As a result, investments with the same total profits might not have the same value.

Example

Different Timing for Two Profit Streams

Investments A and B both have a three-year life and total profits of $6,000. However, Investment B returns its profits earlier than Investment A.

	Profits from	
Year	**Investment A**	**Investment B**
1	$ 1,000	$ 3,000
2	2,000	2,000
3	3,000	1,000
Total	$ 6,000	$ 6,000

Question: Which investment will be preferred by the company's owners?

Answer: Although both investments have the same $6,000 *total* profits, there is considerable difference as to *when* the profits come. Based on this difference, the firm's owners would probably prefer Investment B, which earns the greater amount sooner. However, if the two investments have impacts beyond year 3, the answer could be different. For example, if Investment B's

[2] **Reference:** Adam Smith, *The Wealth of Nations*, 1776, bk. 1, chap. 2.

declining performance is the result of customer dissatisfaction and Investment A's performance resulted from a gain in market share that will continue in years 4, 5, and beyond, the firm's owners would probably prefer Investment A.

risk—the possibility that the result of some activity will not be exactly as (and particularly, will be worse than) forecast

Another difficulty is that of **risk,** the lack of certainty in the profits from an investment. Profits do not consider risk, but investors do.

Example

Different Risk Levels

Investments C and D both have a one-year life. However, each investment's profitability depends on the state of the economy.

	Profits from	
Event	**Investment C**	**Investment D**
Good economy	$ 50,000	$ 90,000
Poor economy	50,000	10,000
Average profits	50,000	50,000
Variability of profits	0	80,000

Question: Which investment will be preferred by the company's owners?

Answer: Although both investments have average (expected) profits of $50,000 (assuming good and bad economies are equally likely), there is considerable difference as to the *certainty* with which the profits will be received. The profits from Investment C will be $50,000 regardless of the state of the economy; however, Investment D could earn $90,000 or $10,000. The firm's owners would probably prefer Investment C which exposes them to much less risk than Investment D.

There is still one more problem with profits. In Adam Smith's day, the manager of a business was normally its owner and thus directly received its profits. Profits equaled return to the investor. Over time, however, as firms required additional equity capital to finance growth, shares of stock were sold to outside investors. Today, in most large companies, outside shareholders make up the majority of owners; the companies typically are run by **professional managers,** who own relatively little of the firm. In these firms the owners receive dividends and stock-price appreciation, which are rarely equal to the firm's profits. Profits no longer equal return to the investor.

professional managers—individuals employed by a firm to direct its activities because of their expertise. They are distinguished from owner-managers, individuals who find themselves managing a firm because they own it

Profits, then, do not convey enough information in a complex world. They are hard to measure, and they ignore the timing and riskiness of benefits. In addition, profits are something which happen within the firm, yet the firm's owners are often outside shareholders who do not receive the firm's profits as they are earned. For these reasons, finance turned away from maximizing *profits* as the goal of the firm and toward maximizing the *wealth* of the firm's owners.

The Traditional Finance Goal: Maximization of Shareholder Wealth

shareholder wealth—the total value of an investment in the common stock of a company, measured by the price at which the stock could be sold

For many years it has been accepted in finance that the proper goal of every business is to maximize the wealth of its owners. For a corporation, owned by shareholders, this is referred to as **shareholder wealth.** In this perspective, shareholders provide the investment needed to start and expand the firm, and most companies exist because of shareholders' desire to increase the value of their investment. Shareholders hire management, whose primary responsibility is to increase the wealth of their employers.

Shareholders obtain wealth from the firm in two ways: (1) dividends and other direct cash payments, and (2) appreciation in stock price. In general these two methods of adding to shareholder wealth do not conflict; that is, actions that lead to the ability to pay a high dividend stream are the same actions that increase the firm's stock price. It is therefore customary to equate the maximization of shareholder wealth with the maximization of stock price.

efficient capital market—a financial market in which security prices fully contain the meaning of all known information

By looking at stock price we avoid the problems of profit maximization. A well-functioning or **efficient capital market** should look beyond accounting choices and evaluate the timing and risk of promised benefits to determine their true worth.[3] Even though the price of a share of stock may be affected on a day-to-day basis by many factors having no relation to the performance of the firm, in the long-run the stock market will recognize all the components of value and reward stockholders whose managers act to increase their wealth.

In addition to rewarding shareholders justly for the use of their funds and for the risks they bear, it has further been accepted that the goal of maximizing shareholder wealth leads to two additional contributions to the economic welfare of society:

- *The effective allocation of new investment funds.* Companies often need infusions of additional money from outside investors to finance their operations. The firms most deserving of these funds are those that use the money best in satisfying the desires of their customers for goods and services. But firms that do an excellent job of satisfying their customers should be highly profitable and should have a high stock price. Therefore, firms that act to maximize their share price will be the ones that deserve to attract new investment capital. This is particularly important to financial managers, since a key part of their job is to raise money. Companies must always be positioned to obtain funds as needed.
- *The evaluation of investment risks.* As they consider giving their money to a business firm, investors evaluate the risks they would face. What is the likelihood that the firm will do well? be average? do poorly? fail? Investors in general are averse to taking risks and will do so only if properly compen-

[3] **Elaboration:** In financial terms, an efficient capital market is one in which security prices are always "correct" in that they reflect investors' best judgment about the future. All available information has been properly evaluated, and new information is rapidly analyzed and incorporated into security prices. Studies of the efficiency of the stock market (in particular of the New York Stock Exchange) have suggested a very high level of efficiency.

sated. They will demand a higher return from a risky investment than from one with less risk and will reduce the price they are willing to pay for the firm's stock if they see the company taking excessive risks. Management will be able to maximize the value of the firm's stock only if it can provide returns commensurate with the risks it takes.

signaling—the process of conveying economic information

Notice how investors provide a powerful signal to a company's management through the price they are willing to pay for the firm's stock. This **signaling** aspect of the stock market, providing feedback about risk and return levels, is considered one of its most important properties.

Figure 2.1 presents the logic of share-price maximization as the traditional financial goal of the firm. The ultimate objective is to achieve the greatest level of economic efficiency. An important requirement for economic efficiency is a vibrant, well-functioning business sector. This can only be achieved by private enterprise—entrepreneurial businesses willing to compete and take risks. If successful, many of these businesses will become large enough to require professional management, and ownership and management will become separated. Managers will be asked

FIGURE 2.1

The logic of share-price maximization. Private enterprise, professionally managed to maximize share price, should lead to the highest degree of economic efficiency.

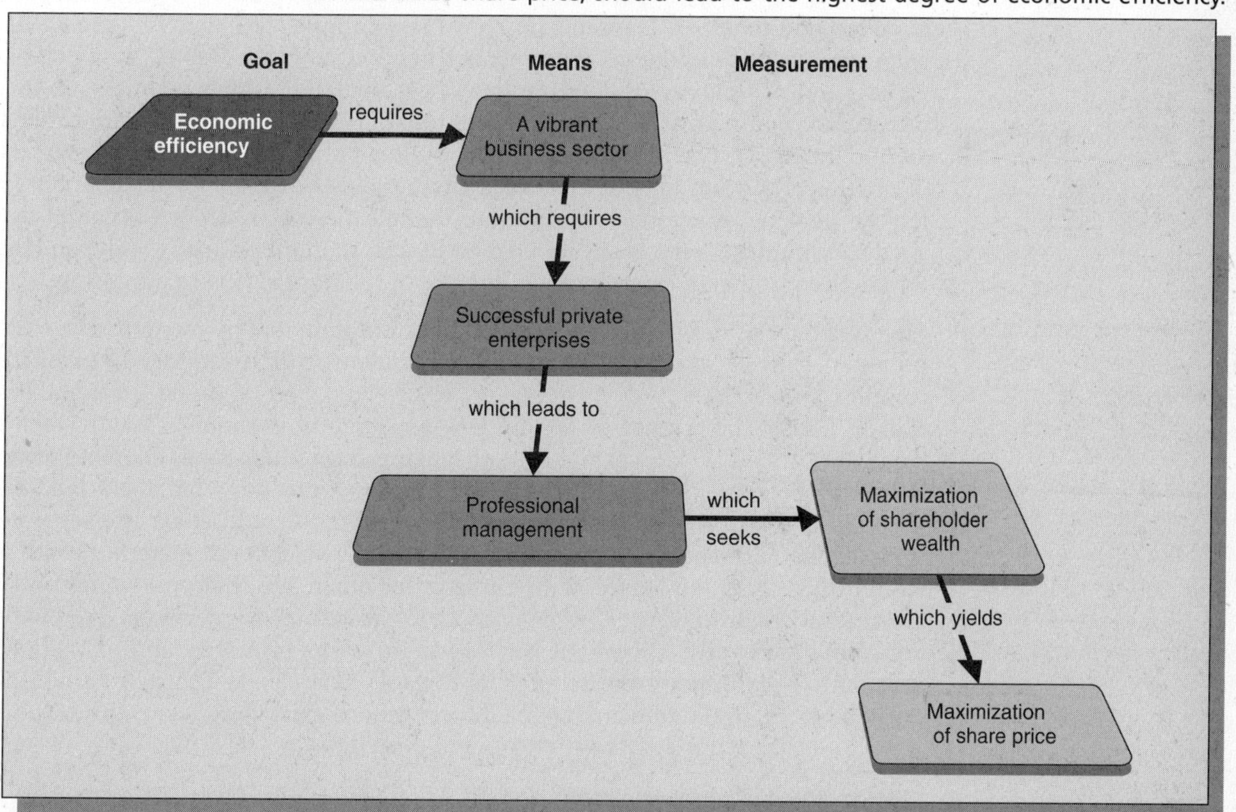

to act in the best interest of the owners, who will measure them by looking at how well they have added to the owners' wealth. Increased wealth will come through increased share price. In summary, then, we ask managers to work in the best interests of society, and we measure their success by how well they increase the firm's share price.

Agency Theory

Recently, finance academics and practitioners have devoted attention to describing and removing one particular barrier to effective shareholder wealth maximization: the differences in motives between a corporations' stockholders and its professional managers. These insights are summarized under the title, *agency theory*.

1. Background to Agency Theory

In agrarian societies prior to the Industrial Revolution, business dealings were quite simple. Most transactions were exchanges between farmers, shopkeepers, craftsmen, etc. Transactions were carried out face to face between parties who often knew each other personally. There was little need to be concerned about whether other parties to a transaction would fulfill their obligations.

With the arrival of the Industrial Revolution, much of this changed. To produce new and often complex products, a variety of labor and material resources had to be brought together. Transactions grew more complicated, many involving relationships between persons who did not know each other. Today, the number, variety, and complexity of goods and services demanded by consumers are immense. It is commonplace for a business to be operating in dozens of locations around the world, producing hundreds of different products, requiring thousands of raw materials and tens of thousands of employees. It is no longer possible to rely on personal relationships to ensure that all these transactions occur as desired. It would be very costly to engage in and monitor so many independent transactions; rather, a more formal structure of relationships is required.

The world of business in advanced economies is dominated by corporations. Corporations exist because they provide the formal structure necessary to organize complex transactions and, in doing so, reduce the cost of doing business. As Ronald Coase, the winner of the 1991 Nobel Prize in economics, has written[4], firms are formed whenever the cost of making individual transactions exceeds the additional costs of operating within a business. Consider what you would do if you had to arrange for the education of a child. You could enter into separate transactions with each teacher, with suppliers of instructional materials, with a landlord for classroom space, with a caterer for lunch, etc.; but you would probably find it easier to contract with a school to provide all the services. Even with all its internal overhead costs, it is cheaper—in terms of money and effort (and headaches!)—to employ the school. As a result, schools exist to deliver educational services. In the same manner, all corporations exist to deliver products and

---

[4] **Reference and observation:** Ronald Coase, "The Theory of the Firm," *Economica* 4(1937), pp. 386–405. Note how long it can take for excellent research to be honored—Coase published in 1937 but was not honored by the Nobel committee until 1991!

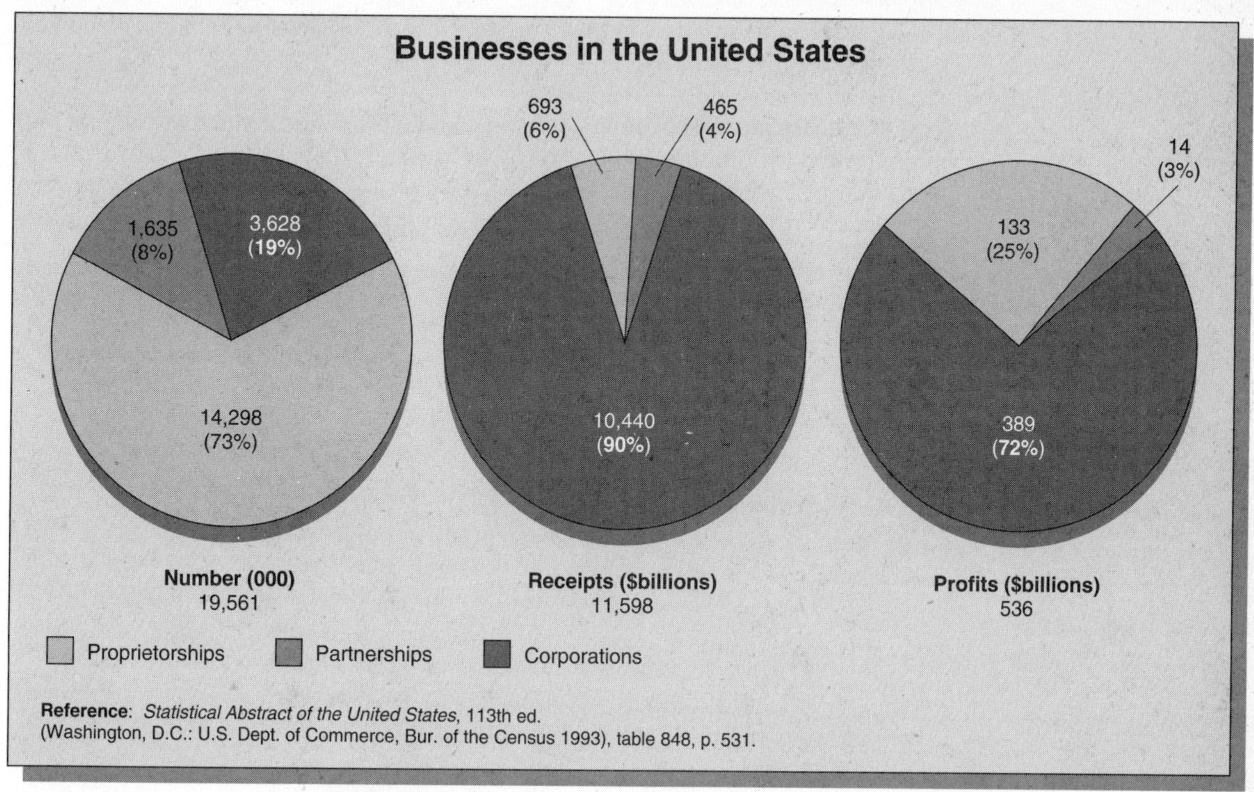

FIGURE 2.2
Recent statistics about U.S. businesses. Although only 19% of businesses are organized as corporations, they account for 90% of receipts (sales) and 72% of profits.

services cheaply and efficiently. As Figure 2.2 reveals, although corporations make up only 19% of business organizations in the United States, corporations tend to be large relative to proprietorships and partnerships and account for 90% of the receipts and 72% of the profits of all firms.[5]

2. The Agency Problem

principal—a person who employs another to act in his/her behalf

agent—a person who acts on behalf of and by the authority of another

agency problem—the possibility that an agent will not act in the best interests of his/her principal

As useful as corporations are, their existence does introduce a new problem into the maximization of owners' wealth. Recall that shareholders employ professional managers to run the business. Borrowing from legal terminology, we can identify shareholders as a corporation's **principals** and the firm's professional managers as the shareholders' **agents.** It is quite possible that the goals of the agents, who make the day-to-day decisions about the direction and activities of the firm, might differ from the goals of the principals. If so, the manager-agents might not act in the best interests of the shareholder-principals to maximize owners' wealth. This is the **agency problem.**

[5] **Cross-reference:** See Appendix 2A to learn more about the characteristics of proprietorships, partnerships, and corporations.

The agency problem arises from a variety of sources. The six problems discussed below are frequently cited.

The time horizon problem Because managers spend a relatively short time in any one position, they have a tendency to slight the long term, favoring decisions that pay off during their tenure on the job over those with longer-term payoff, for which they might receive no recognition. They are motivated to ignore

FINANCE IN PRACTICE

Is Executive Compensation Reasonable?

> No matter how you count it, the sum is staggering. It adds up to more than a half-million dollars a day, every day, for an entire year. Or $78,001 per hour. Enough to see 31.2 million first-run movies or buy 6.5 million tickets to Disneyland's Magic Kingdom.
>
> Hold your breath. Look over the number carefully. It's not a misprint: $203,010,590. That's what Michael D. Eisner, chairman of Walt Disney Co., made last year. It's more than any other chief executive of a public corporation has made in a single year—or probably in an entire career in the history of American business.

To put Michael Eisner's 1998 pay in further perspective:

> Eisner's pay, which puts him atop *Business Week's* 1993 survey of executive compensation, is nearly equal to the GNP of Granada.

Eisner's compensation came primarily from exercising options for 5.4 million shares of Disney stock he had been granted over the years since becoming CEO in 1984.

> There are some slight misgivings on Disney's board, though. In retrospect, Raymond L. Watson, head of Disney's compensation committee, believes the company's original deal with Eisner was flawed, because all his stock options were priced at market value when at least some could have been priced at a premium. "None of us in our wildest dreams ever imagined we'd be looking at a $200 million payday," says Watson. "But then again, we never thought we'd be talking about a market cap of $22 billion either." [Disney's market capitalization, or total stock market value, was over $22 billion in early 1994, up from $2.2 billion in 1984 when Eisner became Disney's CEO.]

Further concerns arise from the realization that Disney's success was the result of the efforts of all its employees.

> Eisner, however, didn't bring about Disney's comeback singlehandedly. It took the help of thousands of employees, from the people who keep Disney's theme parks clean to the artists in its animation studios. Yet Eisner and a few members of his senior management team have reaped most of the rewards.

And some students of executive pay, including former compensation consultant and author Graef Crystal, point out the weak link between executive pay and corporate performance:

> Although Crystal hasn't yet studied last year's pay, he says that only 2% of the variation in CEO pay packages in 1992 could be explained by the differences in company performance at the 180 largest corporations.

Reference: "That Eye-Popping Executive Pay," the annual survey of executive pay by *Business Week,* April 25, 1994, pp. 52–58.

good opportunities that do not produce measurable returns in the short term and to accept poor opportunities that do well in the short term but ultimately reduce owners' wealth. This is especially true if some portion of managers' compensation is based on the current year's profits. The manager-agents look good and receive their raises and promotions, but at the expense of the shareholder-principals.

The compensation problem Managers typically have considerable influence over their salaries independent of the "fair" value of their compensation. It is not uncommon to hear of executives who vote themselves large bonuses or other forms of compensation that have no connection to their firm's performance. The manager-agents are well paid, but at the expense of the shareholder-principals.[6]

perquisite ("perq")—compensation in a form other than money

The perquisite problem Managers often add to their earnings by increasing the nonmonetary forms of their compensation. They arrange for luxurious offices, company cars, and company-paid vacations. They carry company-paid credit cards which permit them to eat well and regularly attend plays, the opera, or the symphony. The manager-agents increase their overall compensation, but at the expense of the shareholder-principals.

The information problem Managers are insiders, privy to detailed knowledge about all facets of the firm's operations. Shareholders, on the other hand, are dependent on managers for their knowledge of the firm. As a result, managers can limit the information received by shareholders. This **information asymmetry** allows managers to make decisions without having to be fully accountable to the firm's owners. The manager-agents can get away with making decisions that favor their own interests at the expense of the shareholder-principals.

information asymmetry—the condition in which a firm's manager-agents know more about the firm than its shareholder-principals

The risk-preference problem Managers' attitudes toward risk may differ from shareholders' attitudes. Managers are often unwilling to take on risky opportunities that have a good chance of benefiting the firm's owners. If the opportunity succeeds, the managers will get little of the benefit; but if the opportunity fails, they may lose their jobs. Or the reverse might be true: a manager might take excessive risks not in the shareholders' best interests in the hope of obtaining a large bonus. The manager-agents make decisions that protect or enrich themselves at the expense of the shareholder-principals.

The retained earnings problem Managers may choose to maintain an excessively high level of cash in the business to provide a cushion against a poor economic environment. In this way they avoid being blamed for any cash shortages that might otherwise develop. They retain a higher degree of the firm's earnings than necessary and pay a lower dividend. The manager-agents protect themselves against poor times, but at the expense of the shareholder-principals.

agency cost—the reduction in a principal's wealth when an agent does not act in the principal's best interests

In each of these cases, the agency problem arises because the managers' best interests are not consistently the same as the owners' best interests. The company's owners suffer an **agency cost,** a reduction in their wealth. By contrast, the agency problem does not exist in a proprietorship, for in that case the manager <u>is</u> the owner—increased management compensation is simply a change in the form of

[6] **Reference:** This issue is discussed in detail in Graef S. Crystal's book *In Search of Excess* (New York, W.W. Norton, 1991).

the owner's wealth. Questionable management decisions may turn out to be mistakes, but they are not mistakes motivated by an agent's opportunity to take advantage of a principal.

3. Viewing Relationships as Contracts

contract—an agreement between parties specifying each party's role in the relationship

Recently a comprehensive theory of agency has been developed in finance.[7] Each relationship within the firm and between the firm and outsiders is seen as a **contract,** an agreement covering each party's rights and responsibilities. Some contracts are explicit, such as those between the firm and its suppliers, which are in written form and specify each facet of the relationship. Other contracts are implicit, not in written form but understood through verbal agreement and common business behavior, such as the amount of work per day a nonhourly employee owes the firm. Contracts often include terms that specify penalties for nonperformance, for example, lending agreements that stipulate that the lender can claim some of the firm's assets should the firm default on its promise to pay. Agency theory sees the firm as a **nexus of contracts,** a series of many such agreements between every party within and outside the business.

nexus of contracts—an interconnection of many contracts

One advantage of viewing the firm as a nexus of contracts is that it encourages us to focus on the relationships between the various parties within a business. The concept of a contract provides a framework for delineating each relationship, for discovering whether the parties to that relationship are working together in the best interests of the firm, and for examining what the parties are doing to align their goals.

Minimizing Agency Costs—Well-Established Approaches

The shareholder-principals of a corporation will want to minimize agency costs, since each dollar of agency cost saved is one more dollar available to them. In response, two broad methods of controlling agency costs have become well established: incentives (the carrot) and threats (the stick). We identify below three classes of incentives[8] and three threats as well as some limitations of these methods.

1. Incentives

The most common incentives are those that attempt to connect managers' compensation directly to increases in shareholder wealth. There are three variations on the theme.

Salary and bonus plans These approaches base the agent-managers' compensation on objectives that are negotiated at the beginning of the year. Salary

[7] **Reference:** The seminal work in agency theory is: Michael C. Jensen, and W. H. Meckling, "Theory of the Firm: Managerial Behavior, Agency Costs and Ownership Structure," *Journal of Financial Economics* 3(1976), pp. 305–360.

[8] **To delve further:** Appendix 2B describes the incentive approaches in more detail along with the agency problem each addresses and the conditions required for their success.

plans tie managers' salaries to their achievements. Bonus plans pay managers a base salary plus a bonus based on the company's financial performance.

Stock-related incentives These approaches reward managers with company stock to sharpen their focus on shareholder wealth. In the typical plan, a manager cannot cash out until some time has passed to maintain the manager's involvement for the longer term.

Dividend units This approach gives managers a bonus based on future dividends, tying compensation to the cash benefits shareholders receive.

2. Threats

A variety of oversight and control techniques exist at various levels in most corporations to prevent manager-agents from acting other than in the shareholders' best interests. These include the following mechanisms.

The firm's internal planning and control systems Planning makes public what is expected of everyone within the corporation, creating a benchmark against which to measure results. Knowing that their actions are subject to scrutiny by their senior management, managers are more careful about doing what is expected of them.

Corporate governance A corporation's board of directors exists to monitor and control the company's management. Knowing that their actions are subject to the scrutiny of the board of directors—which has direct responsibility for protecting shareholder interests—managers are more careful about developing and executing plans that will maximize shareholders' wealth.

The market for corporate control A corporation not acting in the best interests of its shareholders will experience a decline in stock price as investors perceive the firm to have less value. This makes it an inviting target for outsiders or frustrated managers who can buy enough shares to win control of the company, throw out board members and managers unresponsive to shareholder interests, and install new directors and managers more willing to act for the shareholders.

3. Problems with the Traditional Methods of Minimizing Agency Costs

The problems of using these well-established methods of reducing agency costs have long been recognized. Three broad problem areas stand out.

Dependence on financial measures Traditional incentive-oriented methods of dealing with agency costs often use profits or stock price as their measure of performance. Managers are encouraged to improve financial metrics over the time horizon most advantageous to them, which may not be in the best interests of shareholders.

Conflictual premise Traditional threat-oriented methods of dealing with agency costs emphasize the conflicts described by agency theory. In doing so they ignore areas of shared interests between principals and agents and discourage the development of win/win approaches to solving the agency problem.

Reliance on the vertical organizational structure Traditional approaches to dealing with the agency problem focus on contracts made between senior managers and their subordinates, following the vertical structure of the firm. However, the work of the organization and the relationships crucial for a firm's success are more likely to be horizontal, crossing departmental and functional lines. Building rewards on vertical relationships may discourage collaboration in horizontal relationships.

Concerns About Shareholder Wealth Maximization

The agency problem presents an important barrier to achieving the goal of shareholder wealth maximization and the economic benefits it can provide. However there is a larger issue. Earlier in this chapter we pointed out the separation between business and society characteristic of capitalist economies. Important concerns persist in most societies about whether an economy of corporations, each maximizing the wealth of its shareholders, produces undesirable side effects. We summarize these concerns under two questions: (1) Does accepting this goal yield a desirable mix of outcomes for society? (2) Does accepting it lead to desirable actions within corporations?

1. Outcomes for Society

Even when pursuit of shareholder wealth maximization yields the full advantages of economic efficiency its advocates claim for it, it may still not lead to the best mix of outcomes for society. A well-performing economy is only one facet—although a very important one—of a country's social welfare. Other aspects of social welfare must be successfully addressed for a nation to survive and prosper. In particular, is shareholder wealth maximization always consistent with society's notions of economic and social justice? Major concerns about this issue have persisted for years. In many countries it is the defining issue that separates social groups and political parties.[9]

Three topics regularly discussed as part of this debate are: (1) income inequality, (2) the failure of corporations to take socially responsible actions, and (3) poorly directed business activities.

Income inequality In most societies there is a widely held belief that there is a tradeoff between economic efficiency and equality of incomes. If the tradeoff does exist, companies acting to maximize shareholder wealth may be hurting society at the same time as they contribute to it. And even if these beliefs are not accurate, the debate could persist indefinitely because the relationship is so hard to test empirically.

---

[9] **Elaboration:** In the United States, for example, this division is the primary distinction between many of the positions of the Republican and Democratic parties. Although it is dangerous to summarize any one of a political party's positions in a few words, for the most part, the Republicans see the benefits from a well-functioning economy as a paramount goal and the precursor to most social possibilities, while the Democrats believe that more far-reaching social goals must be pursued in parallel to economic goals, even if that results in somewhat less economic efficiency.

Failure to take socially responsible actions Companies pursuing shareholder wealth maximization may perceive little or no incentive to use their resources to provide for the social welfare either of their employees or of nonemployees. For example, until mandated by legislation, many companies spent very little on workplace safety, employee health care, or employee pensions. And even though, when viewed in hindsight, the benefits companies derived from being more socially responsive might well have been greater than the costs in many cases (thus actually increasing the companies' success in pursuing shareholder wealth), this does not mitigate the social losses arising from the companies' earlier lack of social responsibility.

Poorly directed business activities The pursuit of shareholder wealth maximization leads to a mixture of products and services that is not always consistent with the needs or desires of the overall population. Rather it reflects the demands of those in the top portion of the income distribution. To some observers, it seems inconsistent with social welfare that there are over 50 brands of sugared cereals on the supermarket shelves at the same time that many people cannot find adequate shelter or health care. In a similar manner, profit maximization by itself does not discourage producing and marketing products and services harmful to society.[10] In fact, the more profitable an activity, the more it is encouraged by a goal that looks only at the benefits accruing to shareholders and ignores the costs borne by society.

2. Actions Within the Firm

At least four concerns exist about the internal operations of companies using shareholder wealth maximization as their goal. These concerns can be expressed in terms of four questions many managers have had trouble answering to their own satisfaction: (1) Is the shareholder wealth maximization goal a useful measuring stick? (2) Does it create the right image for the company? (3) Does it inspire employee commitment? (4) Does it encourage ethical behavior?

A useful measuring stick? To be useful in guiding day-to-day action, shareholder wealth maximization needs to provide clear and valid guidance to managers. Some financial managers are convinced it does exactly that. However, other finance professionals see limitations to share price maximization as a useful managerial guideline. Perhaps the greatest concern is about the temptation to take actions that increase short-run share price at the expense of long-run share price. Many financial managers believe it is possible to fool the market—at least in the very short run—to look good this week or month at the expense of things not going as well at some time in the future. They are very uncomfortable with measurement systems that encourage them to sacrifice the future strength of their company for current appearances of high performance.

[10] **Observation:** Illicit drugs, tobacco, and handguns are examples of highly profitable products that cause significant damage to many people.

Creating the right image? One major disadvantage of shareholder wealth maximization being the goal of a company is the message it sends to those outside the firm. The consistency between maximizing shareholder wealth and serving customers with excellence, treating suppliers with integrity as partners, and contributing to society has not been easy to communicate. The public is aware of so many examples of companies which in their single-minded search for profits have not achieved desirable social outcomes, that any company touting such a goal faces the task of explaining how its pursuit of only a high share price will lead to behavior different from that of other companies with apparently the same goal.

Inspiring commitment? Many managers are also concerned about the image this goal would project within their company. Think back to the most recent time you made a personal sacrifice in contributing to a company you were working for—when you inconvenienced yourself to go well beyond the minimum required of you and when you knew there was almost no likelihood you would be rewarded or even recognized for your extra effort. Did you put the company's interest ahead of your own in the hope that you would add 0.00000001 dollars to the value of each share in your company? We suspect not.[11]

Much more likely, you did what you did for a very different reason. Perhaps you did not want to let down an internal or external customer or a member of your work group. Maybe you cared about how the company would look if you did not put forth the extra effort, or perhaps the reason was simply that the personal pain of doing less than your best was greater than the sacrifice required to do what you knew was right. The trouble with telling people that the entire purpose of their work is to enrich someone else is that it sends the wrong message—that we are being used for a purpose that sounds less than noble to most of us and seems to demean our commitment and our sacrifices.

Encouraging ethics? Many managers believe that high corporate ethics are not just morally correct but also good business. However, the call for maximizing share price may not always carry with it an equally loud insistence on maintaining high ethical standards while doing so. Where the only goal is share price, ethics has sometimes taken a back seat to making more money.

Emerging New Approaches That Begin Re-Integrating Societal and Shareholder Interests

We have seen that the separation of managers from owners and the separation of firms from society raise concerns about the different interests served by the modern corporation. Shareholders' concerns over agency conflicts with managers certainly have merit, as do society's concerns about relying on shareholder wealth maximization to provide the best mix of benefits for the community. Both issues present problems that are real and may never be solved fully. However, the seri-

[11] **An invitation:** If that *was the reason,* please write or call us and tell us about it (our addresses and phone numbers are in the "To the Instructor" and "To the Student" sections at the beginning of the book). We are delighted to learn when our predictions are inaccurate. However, we don't anticipate getting many calls.

ousness of these concerns and frustrations in dealing with them, both within and outside corporations, continue to encourage new solutions. Three emerging approaches may offer new alternatives for reducing such concerns. They are: (1) a broader definition of the agency conflict, (2) efforts to align goals throughout the organization, and (3) a recognition of the value of a sequence of goals.

1. A Broader Definition of the Agency Conflict

The actions that managers take to enrich and benefit themselves at the expense of shareholders rarely harm simply their principals. Those actions very frequently damage the entire company and all its stakeholders. Whether the actions are self-promoted excessive compensation, self-protecting decisions that trade company opportunities for nonthreatening managerial tenure, or short time horizons that damage future company viability, all stakeholders are losers. Framing the agency problem exclusively in terms of losses borne by shareholders is a limited way to define the issue. Because many shareholders have only a transient involvement in the company and a very narrow interest at that, placing exclusive attention on possible losses borne by them runs the risk of obscuring and trivializing this much larger issue. Shareholders and all other stakeholders have a vital interest in the effective performance of manager-agents. Broadening the definition of the agency issue may be one step in gaining full support for finding more effective means of solving it.

2. Aligning Goals Throughout the Organization

The requirements of global competitiveness and the modern quality-focused management systems discussed in Chapters 1 and 3 stress the pursuit of harmony and alignment of interests of all parties within a company and between the firm and its environment. Unless all parts of a business work together, it is impossible to produce low-cost products and services of competitive quality. And without competitive products and services, the firm cannot survive, much less maximize shareholder wealth.

In Chapter 3 we will take a closer look at modern quality-focused management systems and how their evolution is affecting the corporate finance function. These modern management approaches offer new solutions to integrating the interests of shareholders and society as a whole and also to minimizing agency costs.

Using process-focused goals Modern quality-focused management approaches seek to concentrate every employee and manager's attention on the connection between the needs of customers and the internal productive processes that meet those needs. Efforts are directed toward improving the way the firm designs, produces, markets, delivers, finances, etc. its products and services. By doing so the firm lowers its costs while creating more value for its customers, often permitting it to charge premium prices. The result is increased profitability and share price, but this comes from a focus on processes not on financial numbers.

Building on people's integrity The framing of the agency conflict focuses on the dark side of our nature, our selfishness and lack of integrity, and ignores our good side, our trustworthiness and selflessness. Implicitly it says that organizations must be designed to protect themselves from those of us who cannot be trusted. In doing so, it invites all of us to respond in kind—to earn that distrust.

A major aspect of modern management approaches is the pursuit of organizational designs based on the "98% of us who can be trusted to work collaboratively with others in pursuit of valued organizational goals" rather than on the "2% who cannot be trusted to do so." One approach involves asking all organizational members to identify their customers and suppliers, inside or outside the firm, and to create **customer–supplier alignments.** These alignments permit both parties to gain a fuller understanding of the other's needs, permitting suppliers to meet and exceed their customers' expectations.

customer-supplier alignment—a close working relationship between two parties, one of whom supplies the other, to ensure that the needs of each are being met

Another approach is to support individuals and work units in designing, installing, and operating their own control methods—to operate under a system of self-control. Early experiences with such systems have been very encouraging, even at a stage when our knowledge and skills for developing them are quite modest.

Focusing on cross-functional relationships Modern quality-focused management approaches recognize that the formal organization chart is often an impediment to cooperation. As a result they place great emphasis on breaking down those barriers. Recall Figure 1.5, the inverted organizational pyramid, which represents some of the changes occurring in modern organizations. Organizations thinking of themselves in such a way work hard to forge the cross-functional relationships necessary to make their processes work smoothly and accurately.

3. A Sequence of Goals

To maximize stock price, management must integrate its goals into a sequence that builds from one goal to the next. Federal Express Corporation captures this concept in its motto "People, Service, Profits," which identifies the order in which value is created. Federal Express managers think first about their employees (the people in the motto): how to empower them and provide the resources they need to excel at their jobs, to act boldly on their own initiatives when unforeseen customer needs arise, and to improve every part of the company. Success with employees is the critical prerequisite for high-quality service. And sustained profitability is only possible after people and service have been taken care of. This is not to say that profits are a lower priority than people or service—rather, to achieve profits it is first necessary to have well-treated employees and well-served customers.

The Johnson & Johnson Company has described the sequenced goal approach as well as any company. The statement they call "Our Credo," is reprinted as Figure 2.3.

For the purpose of this book, we take this sequenced approach as the way to define the goal of the firm, which Anne Spencer was seeking at the beginning of this chapter. The sequenced goal approach translates in practice to continually striving to exceed the expectations of *all* stakeholders. In doing so firms will:

On a Day-to-Day Basis

1. Treat customers like royalty, providing the best possible products and services at attractive prices at all times.

Our Credo

We believe our first responsibility is to the doctors, nurses and patients,
to mothers and fathers and all others who use our products and services.
In meeting their needs everything we do must be of high quality.
We must constantly strive to reduce our costs
in order to maintain reasonable prices.
Customers' orders must be serviced promptly and accurately.
Our suppliers and distributors must have an opportunity
to make a fair profit.

We are responsible to our employees,
the men and women who work with us throughout the world.
Everyone must be considered as an individual.
We must respect their dignity and recognize their merit.
They must have a sense of security in their jobs.
Compensation must be fair and adequate,
and working conditions clean, orderly and safe.
We must be mindful of ways to help our employees fulfill
their family responsibilities.
Employees must feel free to make suggestions and complaints.
There must be equal opportunity for employment, development
and advancement for those qualified.
We must provide competent management,
and their actions must be just and ethical.

We are responsible to the communities in which we live and work
and to the world community as well.
We must be good citizens – support good works and charities
and bear our fair share of taxes.
We must encourage civic improvements and better health and education.
We must maintain in good order
the property we are privileged to use,
protecting the environment and natural resources.

Our final responsibility is to our stockholders.
Business must make a sound profit.
We must experiment with new ideas.
Research must be carried on, innovative programs developed
and mistakes paid for.
New equipment must be purchased, new facilities provided
and new products launched.
Reserves must be created to provide for adverse times.
When we operate according to these principles,
the stockholders should realize a fair return.

Johnson & Johnson

FIGURE 2.3
The Johnson & Johnson Company credo. Notice their use of the sequenced goal approach: first customers, then employees, then communities, and finally stockholders.

2. Treat employees fairly, paying a fair wage and providing employee benefits, excellent working conditions, and opportunities for personal and professional growth.
3. Treat suppliers and creditors with respect and courtesy, negotiating firmly yet also seeking win/win agreements and scrupulously honoring contracts.
4. Treat neighbors as it would wish to be treated by them in return.
5. Constantly strive to reduce costs, increase quality, and add to market share in all aspects of the business.

On a Long-term Basis

6. Treat shareholders to the high returns that will come from properly implementing the day-to-day actions.

The sequenced goal approach provides a practical method of achieving the traditional finance goal of shareholder wealth maximization by putting customers and other stakeholders first. Yet there is an irony here: as recounted in this chapter, firms that directly pursue high stock price may, in that pursuit, do many things that eventually drive their stock prices to progressively lower levels. In the sequenced goal approach, share price maximization still plays a role. But it is restored to its rightful original place—as the result of doing other things well and not as the first place for management to direct its attention. Only by first satisfying the firm's other stakeholders can management produce a successful and valuable firm.

Seemingly the reverse of the traditional goal, this far-from-new approach begins with customers and employees and ends with shareholders. By beginning with share price, management often can get derailed before reaching its other stakeholders. By beginning with customers and employees, the firm rarely gets derailed on the way to high stock price. In February 1989, the Coca-Cola Company published the following under the heading, "Our Goal":

> Our goal for the 1990s sounds deceptively simple. It is to expand our global business system, reaching increasing numbers of consumers who will enjoy our brands and products more and more often.
>
> With Coca-Cola as the centerpiece, ours is a worldwide system of superior brands and services through which we, our franchisees and other business partners deliver satisfaction and value to customers and consumers. By doing so, we enhance brand equity on a global basis. As a result, we increase shareholder wealth over time.[12]

Anne Spencer took out a clean piece of paper and began to write again. Her thinking about the goals of the firm was coming together and she found herself writing as fast as she could. She now understood that the various goals she had been given by her firm's senior managers were not at all incompatible as she once thought. The issue was really one of time horizon—how to sequence the goals.

[12] **Reference:** "Coca-Cola, A Business System Toward 2000: Our Mission in the 1990s," The Coca-Cola Company, Feb. 1989.

In the long run, her company had to become the most efficient economic organization possible to survive in the highly competitive global marketplace. This was consistent with share price maximization, the traditional goal of finance. In the short run, however, managing by share price could be dangerous and not lead to long-run value.

Day to day, the firm had to focus on its employees, its customers, and the quality of its products, services, and processes. Satisfied employees were required to produce high-quality output that would exceed the expectations of customers. And the revenue from those customers combined with low costs from high-quality processes would yield the earnings needed to drive up shareholder wealth.

Summary of Key Points

- **Explain why it is important for a business to have goals.** Goals are necessary to judge the value of any action. Since business has such an enormous effect on most aspects of society, it is important that the goal(s) of business be chosen wisely to provide maximum benefit.
- **Explain why profit maximization was the original goal recommended for the firm by the early microeconomists.** Early economists demonstrated that profit maximization leads to an efficient use of resources and a high degree of economic efficiency under conditions of perfect competition.
- **Explain why shareholder wealth maximization replaced profit maximization as the firm's financial goal.** As the world grew more complex in the post-World War II era, the difficulty of measuring profits, as well as the new dimensions of the timing and risk of benefits, convinced economists that a more comprehensive goal than profit maximization was needed. They concluded that an economy composed of firms acting to maximize their stock prices would achieve the classical benefits of economic efficiency. In addition it would provide for the effective allocation of investable funds and the proper evaluation of business-related risks.
- **Identify the problems in maximizing shareholder wealth addressed by agency theory.** Business firms exist because they provide goods and services at a lower cost than a series of separate transactions. However, in a corporation with professional management, the interests of the manager-agents are often not the same as those of the shareholder-principals. This "agency problem" leads to agency costs, reducing the value of the company to its owners. Agency costs arise from a variety of sources including differences in time-horizon and risk-aversion, management's control of its own compensation, information asymmetry, and attitudes toward retaining earnings. Agency theory frames the firm as a nexus of contracts, a series of implicit and explicit agreements among all parties affected by the firm which define relationships and are designed to limit potential conflicts of interest.
- **Describe traditional approaches to minimizing agency costs and their pitfalls.** Well-established methods of minimizing agency costs include the "carrots" of various incentive compensation schemes and the "sticks" of management control systems, corporate governance, and the market for corporate control. Accumulating evidence suggests that there are problems with these techniques. In particular, the use of financial measures for day-to-day managerial guidance, the emphasis on preventing conflict rather than building cooperation, and the focus on relationships delineated by the formal organization chart often prevent companies from achieving high shareholder wealth.
- **Identify longstanding concerns about the undesirable side-effects of shareholder wealth maximization being the goal of business firms.** Even strong advocates of shareholder wealth maximization have long recognized important social trade-offs inherent in this goal. Although an economy of firms acting to maximize shareholder wealth can achieve significant economic benefits, the accompanying social costs such as income inequalities, failure to take socially responsible actions, and poorly directed business activities are unattractive to most of us. Concerns about what may

happen when shareholder wealth is used to guide a company include difficulties in applying the concept in practice, problems communicating to society the advantages of this goal, the goal's weakness as a theme for inspiring commitment, and the goal's potential for encouraging selfish and unethical behavior.

- **Explain how emerging new management methods and other approaches may reduce some of the concerns about agency conflicts and shareholder wealth maximization as a goal.** A broader definition of the agency conflict may lead to wider concern about the issue and new approaches to reducing it. Aligning goals throughout the organization and a sequenced goal approach both emphasize the consistency of interests among parties. They provide more effective ways to manage, and they suggest that maximizing shareholder wealth can only be accomplished on a sustained basis by serving the needs of customers, employees, and other stakeholders on a day-to-day basis. If a sequence of goals is the way shareholder wealth maximization is pursued, many of the concerns about undesirable societal consequences of shareholder wealth maximization are reduced or removed.

Questions

1. If you were to start a business, what would you set as its goal? Suppose your business grew to employ 50 people. Would this change your answer? What if you had 1,000 employees?
2. What are the problems with the economic rule of maximizing profits? In what ways does the use of shareholder wealth as the firm's goal solve these problems?
3. Why is an efficient capital market necessary for the goal of maximizing shareholder wealth to be effective?
4. Give an example of an agency cost. If you were a shareholder of a company, how might you attempt to minimize it?
5. Identify an instance from your experience or readings in which a firm, aiming to maximize shareholder wealth, has caused damage to society.
6. What is the sequenced goal approach? Why is it important for managers to sequence their goals?
7. In what ways do the quotes from Johnson & Johnson and Coca-Cola relate to the primary theme of this chapter?

CASE

JOHN MOREHOUSE

"Exceed customer expectations." John Morehouse repeated the words to himself as he absentmindedly tapped a pencil on the desk in his hotel room. He figured that he must have heard that phrase 100 times today, yet the concept bothered him. John was attending a week-long seminar entitled "Managing for Total Quality." He had just finished dinner and was resting for a few minutes before joining a study group to prepare for tomorrow's session.

John was the CFO of his company. He had an MBA from a well-known school of business, where his finance professors had emphasized that the goal of the firm was to maximize its stock price. Indeed he had spent most of the past few years working hard to do just that. He considered himself successful, as well, because not once during the past decade had his company become the target of a takeover attempt, hostile or otherwise.

For comfort, John opened the finance textbook he had brought with him and turned to Chapter 1. He found the paragraph he was looking for:

> The goal of the firm is to maximize the wealth of its owners. These are the holders of the company's common stock. While shareholder wealth can come from either dividends or stock price appreciation, in practice maximizing wealth is the same as maximizing the price of the firm's common stock. Actions that increase the firm's stock price add value to the firm and should be taken; those that decrease stock price take away value and should be avoided.

To John, this clearly meant that his customers were the shareholders of the firm. It was their expectations that he had to meet and exceed. Wasn't a primary job of the finance department to ensure that other parts of the firm, less aware of the shareholder, acted in the shareholders' best interests? But the discussion earlier that day had talked about a different concept of customer: the purchaser of the company's goods and services. John took a sheet of paper and made a list of all the jobs done by his staff: raise capital funds, manage bank relationships, prepare budgets, evaluate investment projects, produce financial reports, etc. He found it difficult to see how the work of his department had anything to do with this customer. "Marketing deals with customers, of course, but certainly not finance," he thought, shaking his head. Yet he remained unsure.

As John left the room to join his study-group partners, he came back to that phrase, "Exceed customer expectations." Maybe the seminar leader was right in asking the group to rethink the concept of the customer. But if the common stockholders were not his customers, then who were? And just what could the finance department do to exceed their expectations?

APPENDIX 2A

FORMS OF BUSINESS ORGANIZATION

In the United States, businesses are organized into three legal forms: proprietorships, partnerships, and corporations. Each form is appropriate for a certain size and complexity of business. Each provides its owners certain benefits in practice

'SURE IT'S A PARTNERSHIP, ELWOOD, BUT IT'S A LIMITED PARTNERSHIP, AND YOU'RE THE ONE WHO'S LIMITED.'

and under the law. And, as we will see in Appendixes B and C to Chapter 4, corporations are taxed differently from proprietorships and partnerships.

Proprietorships Proprietorships are businesses owned by one person or one family. New businesses and small "mom and pop" stores are typically proprietorships. They are easy to start—there are no legal formalities other than perhaps a license—and they permit prompt and responsive decision making since authority is centered in the owner/operator. But proprietorships typically suffer from a lack of resources. Managerial talent is limited by the abilities of the owner. Financing is limited to the owner's finances plus what can be borrowed. Liability, on the other hand, is not limited to the firm's assets; the owner is personally responsible for the firm's debts and its products and services. As we will see, proprietors add the income from their business to any other personal income and pay taxes under the personal tax system.

general partnership—a partnership in which all partners share equally in decision-making authority and liability

limited partnership—a partnership in which some partners receive limited liability in return for limited authority

Partnerships Partnerships are businesses owned by some number of unrelated individuals. The partners sign an agreement that specifies each partner's responsibilities and rewards from the business. In **general partnerships,** all partners are equal and share in authority and liability; most operating partnerships such as accounting and law firms are organized in this way. Alternatively, the partnership may be a **limited partnership,** the form typically used by those organized for investment purposes. In this form, one or more "general partners," typically the organizers of the partnership, have the decision-making authority and assume full personal liability while the remainder are "limited partners," with limited authority but also a liability limited to the amount of their own investment. The Uniform Partnership Act and Uniform Limited Partnership Act, adopted in all 50 states, regulate partnership contracts and provide solutions when the partners have omitted something from their agreement. If any partner leaves the business, the partnership formally dissolves and a new partnership agreement must be drawn up. The presence of several partners provides a greater depth of managerial skills and access to more sources of financing as compared to a proprietorship. Like a proprietorship, however, partners add their business income to their personal tax returns.

Corporations Corporations are legal entities with rights and privileges separate from those of their owners. They live on regardless of who owns them. There is no "Uniform Corporation Act"; rather, each state has its own corporation law, and corporations often choose to incorporate in states with the most lenient laws, such as Delaware and Pennsylvania. In return for their investment, the corporation's owners receive shares of stock which may be sold to others, thus permitting ownership of the corporation to change freely and easily. Large corporations can free themselves from most of the limitations of proprietorships and partnerships. Since the managers need not be the owners, corporations can employ professional management. Financing opportunities are excellent: by selling small amounts of stock to many nonmanager owners, the corporation can raise significant amounts of equity, which then permits large-scale borrowing. In addition, the corporation's liabilities are not the responsibility of its owners—there is a legal separation of corporate and owner debts. As we will see, corporate profits are subject to a different tax than proprietorships and partnerships.

APPENDIX 2B

MANAGERIAL INCENTIVES FOR MINIMIZING AGENCY COSTS

Six incentives that attempt to connect managers' compensation directly to increases in shareholder wealth are described below, along with the agency problem they address and the conditions required for their success.

Salary and bonus plans The first two—salary and bonus plans—base the agent-managers' compensation on objectives that are negotiated at the beginning of the year.

Salary plans tie managers' salaries to their achievements. Managers are given, or negotiate with their supervisors, a set of goals for the upcoming year. Their salaries in that year and raises for the following year become a function of how fully they meet those objectives.

Bonus plans pay managers a base salary plus a bonus. The bonus may be calculated in many ways but is often a function of the firm's earnings. Bonus payments may be uniform across the company, based on the firm's overall earnings, or may be subdivided, with the managers of each unit of a company receiving a bonus based on their unit's earnings.

Large salary increases and bonuses can provide very strong incentive for current-year performance. They may also provide some encouragement to lay the groundwork for future high performance in coming years if managers plan or hope to remain with the company in the future.

For these approaches to reduce the agency problem, the compensation plans must develop performance objectives that increase shareholder wealth on a sustained basis—they must address the horizon problem effectively. They are often criticized for not doing so and sometimes even accused of worsening it. Uncertainty about their future with the company or a preference for greater rewards now than in the future can encourage managers to make decisions that yield immediate benefits on their performance dimensions but damage the company's future ability to perform well. Such decisions are likely to decrease shareholder wealth fairly quickly although not necessarily instantaneously.

Stock-related incentives The next three approaches seek to address the time horizon problem directly by rewarding managers for improvements in the company's stock price in the longer term. Each one provides stock in the company or a substitute for that stock, under conditions that encourage managers to seek high value for that stock in the future.

restricted stock—stock that cannot be sold prior to some trigger event taking place

Restricted stock plans augment managers' compensation with shares of the company's stock which they may not sell until some amount of time has passed and/or some financial goal has been met.

stock option—the right to buy shares of a company's common stock at a specified price within a specified time frame

stock appreciation rights—the right to be paid the difference between a company's stock price and some specified price

Stock option plans incorporate **stock options** into managers' compensation. A stock option gives its holder the right to buy shares of the company's stock at a predetermined price within a specified time period. If the company's stock price rises above the predetermined level, managers can buy shares from the company at that price. They may then hold the shares in hopes of continued appreciation or sell them right away at the higher market price for an immediate profit. A variation on the theme is **stock appreciation rights,** which behave exactly like stock options except that managers can receive the value inherent in the rights directly from the company without actually having to buy and then sell the company's stock.

performance units and shares—deferred compensation which may be converted to cash only if a company achieves its performance goals

Performance unit and share plans add another type of special agreement to managers' compensation. Managers receive **performance units,** typically worth a set dollar amount, or **performance shares,** whose value is equal to the day-by-day market price of the company's common stock. After a specified number of years has elapsed, managers are allowed to cash in their performance units or sell their performance shares back to the company. The number of units or shares that may be converted to cash is normally a function of the firm's financial performance over that time period.

For each of these three approaches to reduce agency costs, the time periods selected and performance goals chosen must encourage managers to make decisions that increase shareholder wealth.

dividend unit—the right to receive the dividends paid on a specific number of shares of stock as if the stock itself were owned

Dividend units A sixth technique—**dividend units**—creates a special agreement with managers that ties their future compensation to the future stream of dividends paid by the company. In doing so, this approach addresses both the time horizon and the retained earnings problem. Managers benefit when shareholders directly receive a cash payment. For this technique to reduce agency costs, the payment of cash dividends must be consistent with increased shareholder wealth.

Other incentives attempt to link managers' perceptions of the likelihood of their future success at the company with achieving stated corporate goals. The promotion of a successful manager is commonly broadcast throughout the company to encourage others to act in the same way. Competition between managers for a promotion is often created and made public in the hope of spurring each aspirant, and others as well, to a higher level of performance.

CHAPTER 3

CONTINUITY AND CHANGE IN FINANCIAL MANAGING

Alexandra McLean was pleased with the progress. All morning, her company's finance department had been wrestling with the competitive and environmental changes affecting their work. Now a consensus was forming about a topic to be explored in greater detail in the coming year.

Alex was CFO of an industrial products manufacturer located in the Pacific Northwest. With her colleagues, she was attending the finance department's annual four-day retreat to review last year's activities and set priorities for the next 12 months. The group's task was to list factors affecting the company and the finance organization, develop action plans for tasks to be done in the near future, and select a single major topic to be worked on during the coming year. After the retreat, a task force was to be selected from volunteers to study the topic, report back to the department, and see to it that appropriate actions were taken. They were using a process they had invented and which they playfully renamed every year; this year, the process was called: "SEE ALL" for "Sensing Environmental Events—Acting Like Lightning."

Five years ago, when she was the company's treasurer, Alex had convinced the group to build the annual project into their work. What pleased her the most was the realization that substantial changes in policies and procedures had emerged from each retreat. The first and fourth year's topics had been internationalization, the second was diversity, the third was ethics, and last year's topic was information technologies. The repeat for internationalization was stimulated by a conviction that some important additional opportunities for improvement had emerged, and by new opportunities that had arisen when the company expanded overseas two years ago. As Alex looked around the room, she was proud of her colleagues' work and eager to volunteer for this year's task force.

A team like Alexandra McLean's would have a rich set of topics to choose from each year. Many forces shape the practice of finance. As indicated by Chapter 1's description of the evolution of financial thought, theory and practice in finance change continuously. In this chapter we look at some current forces for change and their implications for financial managing. In doing so we will follow a series of steps similar to those used by Alex's task force.

Before you read further, we encourage you to make a list of five or ten forces that might have an important influence on how any company is run in the next few years. After each one, list two or three implications of that force that might influence what financial managers do. Then, refer back to it as you read the remainder of the chapter and discuss it with your instructor and peers. This will add to your pleasure and interest in reading the chapter and also to your learning.[1]

In this chapter we consider seven major forces for change and their broad implications. Not surprisingly, each of these topics will be ones you will see keep re-emerging throughout the book. After a broad review of these forces and some of their implications, we will do what Alex's task force is planning to do: select a single topic we think is relevant and give it more detailed consideration. The topic we have chosen is the global quality revolution and how it is changing the practice of financial managing, a topic that captures some elements of the other topics discussed more briefly in this chapter. In Chapter 23, the last chapter of the book, we will return to these forces for change and add some final observations and speculations.

Key Points You Should Learn from This Chapter

After reading this chapter you should be able to:

- Identify major forces for change currently affecting financial managing.
- Explain how those forces are influencing financial managing.
- Explain what is meant by the phrase *global quality revolution*.
- Explain why a global quality revolution might have important influences on financial managing.
- Identify some of the well-established aspects of financial practice that seem relatively unchanged and others that are changing in response to the quality revolution and the other current forces for change.

---

[1] **By the way:** There are no *right* or *wrong* answers to this exercise (or at least we won't know what they are until we look back some years from now).

Introductory Concepts—Forces for Change

We are living in a time of dramatic and accelerating change. Every day some new technology, social development, political movement, or other event appears and alters not only the content of the news but also the way we live and work. Only ten years ago individuals who predicted such things as the lifting of the iron curtain, the extent of the AIDS epidemic, the North American Free Trade Agreement, and many recent developments in information technologies were considered to be engaging in wild speculation. Today, events such as these are shaping our environment, and we must learn to respond to them as individuals and as members of business organizations if we are to survive, much less prosper.

1. The Consequences of Change

Change and the need to respond to it have always been characteristics of our environment. What is striking about change today, however, is its rapid pace and its dramatic consequences for many companies and industries.

- The U.S. banking industry hardly changed during the first three quarters of the century as it enjoyed considerable legal and competitive stability. Local personal relationships, unchanging products and services, and "bankers' hours" were the norm. Today, the industry has been deregulated, is rapidly consolidating and competing globally, and is struggling to use new technologies effectively.
- The U.S. automobile industry "owned" the domestic market until the 1970s. General Motors was the country's largest company and virtually defined the industry's products and practices. Today, foreign-owned manufacturers have captured a large portion of the market, and GM is struggling to catch up with its domestic and foreign rivals.
- The U.S. computer industry was dominated since its inception in the late 1940s by IBM, whose increasingly powerful mainframes and marketing sophistication were so effective that the U.S. government spent the entire decade of the 1970s attempting to break up the company's "monopoly." But where legal challenges failed, the changing environment succeeded. Today the microprocessor and software rule the industry; the most influential players are Intel and Microsoft; and IBM is struggling to adapt.

The rapid pace of change is making effective response more necessary at the same time that it is making it more difficult. In general, business organizations have not been very good at dealing with change. It is fascinating to study the lists of the 500 largest U.S. corporations published each year by *Fortune* and *Forbes* magazines. Far more interesting than which companies are on the lists is to discover which have dropped off. We might expect considerable stability from year to year; these are, after all, some of the biggest, wealthiest, most powerful organizations on the planet. The startling fact, however, is that some 40% of the companies on the list at the beginning of each decade are no longer on the list at decade's end. They have not kept up with change. They have lost out to their competitors, or they have merged with or been acquired by another company.

2. Major Forces for Change

The first step in dealing with change is understanding what is causing it to occur. Seven major forces for change in today's environment are: (1) increased international cooperation, communication, and competition; (2) revolutionary rates of improvement in the quality of goods and services; (3) increased diversity in organizations' work forces, customers, and suppliers; (4) rapid changes in technologies related to information production, analysis, and dissemination; (5) changes in ethical standards and expectations; (6) changes in the ways organizations are managed; and (7) changes in governmental policies and actions. Acting alone, and interacting among themselves, these forces are dramatically modifying business practice.[2]

Increased international cooperation, communication, and competition As late as the 1970s, most business was domestic, with companies primarily serving their national markets. Although the European Community was conceived in the late 1950s to reduce barriers to trade, it was still years away from having any real economic meaning. In the last 20 years, however, the economies of most of the world's nations have become significantly intertwined. The success of Japanese companies in penetrating foreign markets—notably in automobiles, banking, and electronics; the emergence of free trade areas throughout the world;[3] and the information and telecommunications technologies which supported these developments have created the "global village." Today, any company's partners and competitors can just as easily be half a world away as around the corner.

Revolutionary rates of improvement in the quality of goods and services New technologies of error detection, analysis, and prevention have permitted many companies to produce low-cost products at levels of quality unheard of only a decade ago. Whereas automobile warranties once rarely extended past one year, on some automobiles they now cover 100,000 miles of driving. We routinely expect electronic equipment to work for years without failure—so much so, that the retail electronics repair business is now nearly defunct. Today, in an increasing number of industries, it is impossible to compete without proficiency in these quality technologies.

Increased diversity in organizations' work forces, customers, and suppliers Changes in social norms and inexpensive worldwide transportation and communications have increased the probability that a company's next encounter will be with a person or organization from a different cultural background. We are in the midst of a major transformation as a society in our attitudes toward people different from ourselves. Rather than talking about how to "deal with"

---

[2] **Cross-reference:** Aspects of the first two of these forces—increased international cooperation, communication, and competition; and revolutionary rates of improvement in the quality of goods and services—were discussed in Chapter 1, pages 11–15.

[3] **Observation:** Although the European Community took 35 years to go from concept to today's relationships, the nations that have formed free trading areas more recently, including the signatories of NAFTA and Mercosur, expect to cut that time at least in half, another example of the increasing pace of change.

FINANCE IN PRACTICE

No More Television Sets from Motorola

In the mid-1970s, Motorola Corporation's television business was under considerable competitive pressure from Japanese manufacturers. Japanese-made TV sets were of much higher quality than Motorola's products and were capturing an increasing portion of the market. Motorola discovered that while 3 of every 200 sets they produced had defects and had to be fixed at the end of the assembly line, the Japanese were experiencing less than 1 defect per 1,000 sets. Japanese TVs were cheaper to make and failed less often. Motorola, which subsequently became a quality leader in the 1980s and 1990s, could not find an effective strategy for competing with such high levels of quality in the 1970s and sold its television business to Matsushita.

different people, companies are learning to embrace diversity and make it a positive and constructive force. Today, understanding different backgrounds and cultures is becoming a requisite of doing business.

Rapid changes in available information technologies In only 20 years, computers have moved from large, centralized, frigidly air-conditioned, tightly controlled rooms to everyone's work station, desk, and lap. Electronic networks and cellular communications connect company members to each other, to their customers and suppliers, and to databases holding vast amounts of information. E-mail is becoming as common as voice mail. Today, individual employees have immense and growing analytical power at their fingertips.

Changes in ethical standards and expectations Social norms are changing, and so is business conduct. Members of all racial, ethnic, and social groups increasingly expect nondiscriminatory behavior in the workplace. We are struggling to balance the requirement of any democracy for open discourse with our concerns for treating everyone fairly and equally, a conflict that often surfaces in discussions of "political correctness." Businesswomen have made the problems

FINANCE IN PRACTICE

A "Mini-United Nations"

A walk through the halls of just about any high-tech company in the Silicon Valley, south of San Francisco, is much like passing through the United Nations in New York or Geneva: it seems as if each office is staffed by a person from another part of the world. Dozens of languages are spoken and many cultures represented. The best of these companies recognize this diversity as a remarkable resource, especially when dealing with suppliers and customers that are similarly staffed or located in the countries their people once called home. Foreign-born employees who once might have been relegated to low-level jobs (even though they might have been well educated in their native lands) are now adding much greater value to their organizations, for example as members of sales and purchasing teams and as leaders of training sessions.

FINANCE IN PRACTICE

Reducing Costs Through Technology

A number of years ago, it was noted that if changes in the airline industry had been as swift as those in the computer industry, international travel would be very different. It would be possible to fly from Chicago to Tokyo in 12 minutes, at a cost of $2.50, in an airliner holding 6,000 passengers but the size of a cigarette pack. That was a few years ago—the example would be even more dramatic today: faster, cheaper, more powerful, smaller.

of sexual harassment and the "glass ceiling" more visible. We are looking more carefully at business leaders, due in part to the notoriety of recent fraudulent business activities, such as the insider trading scandals and savings and loan crisis of the 1980s and the BCCI scandal of the early 1990s. In the public arena, there has been a notable trend in many countries to hold politicians to ever higher moral standards. Today's rules of behavior are markedly different from those of even a few years ago.

Changes in the ways organizations are managed Over the past decade in the United States, management methods underwent the greatest change since scientific management and the assembly line revolutionized production early in the twentieth century. Many companies discovered they could operate more effectively by moving decision making "lower" in the organization, eliminating layers of management, and breaking down the "functional silos" that separated specialist units of the organization. Today, many companies are rethinking almost every facet of the way they operate.

Changes in governmental policies and actions In the United States, the 1980s was a decade of deregulation of industry. With technologies changing, governments concluded that natural monopolies were dissolving so that previously regulated companies would now respond to the discipline of the markets. Outside the United States, many countries began the shift toward market economies. Other countries—France, the United Kingdom, Chile, and Argentina, for example—moved to transfer state-owned companies to private owners. At the same time, many governments became much more active in working with domestic industries to increase their global competitive positions. Today, the interaction of business and government continues to evolve.

Implications of These Forces for Financial Managing

As the pace of change has accelerated, so has the need for all organizations to respond or risk being overcome by events. Yet not everything is changing. Some time-tested theories, methods, and behaviors will continue to work as well as ever; others will become less successful. Rapid change increases the need to identify and hold on to what works while simultaneously adapting to the ever new environment. It is this imperative that provided the title of this chapter, and the subtitle of the book, "Continuity and Change."

There are many implications for finance professionals in each of the seven change forces we have identified. For the most part, we discuss these implications throughout the book wherever we cover a topic that is changing. However, one implication transcends all finance activities: the imperative for intensified education and training. We use the word *education* to refer to the acquisition of broad knowledge related to a topic. *Training* refers to learning that can be focused on specific skills. In this view, we educate for living and train for earning a living—and both are necessary and valuable.

The need for increased education and training arises from every one of the seven change forces.

1. Globalization

The increased international involvement of businesses requires finance professionals to acquire many new skills. Some are for general business use, like mastering foreign languages, negotiating international business transactions, communicating with individuals from other cultures, and planning and operating within foreign economic systems. Others are more uniquely financial, such as transferring funds in various currencies across borders, arranging financing in foreign capital markets, and dealing with foreign exchange regulations.

2. Quality

The money most companies invest in quality management is overwhelmingly invested in training—not in machinery, not in new plants, and not on obtaining consultant advice. Failure to understand this fact can be costly.

3. Diversity

Coping with diversity demands education to understand and appreciate those different from ourselves and training to develop the skills required to work with others with different styles and ways of expressing themselves. As members of

FINANCE IN PRACTICE

Increasing Costs Through Technology at General Motors

General Motors' failure to make progress in dealing with its quality and cost problems in the early 1980s arose primarily from misunderstanding the importance of training. To lower costs and improve quality, GM invested heavily in automation, robotics, and new physical plant. Rather than improving its poorly functioning production and administrative processes, GM automated them. But automating a mess yielded only a bigger mess. If GM's finance officers had been able to steer the company away from the course it took, they could have saved the company billions of dollars in misinvested funds and even greater losses of revenues as market share declined.

finance departments are called upon to work with a wide variety of people from within and outside the organization, often on critical tasks with tight deadlines, the skills of establishing quick rapport with new acquaintances from very different backgrounds are skills that may be required at almost any time.

4. Information Technologies

The demands of finance work frequently require finance professionals to be among the early adopters of new information technologies. The accelerating pace of change has been particulary visible in information technologies, with new hardware and software doubling computing power every two years. Extensive and ongoing training is required just to keep up.

5. Ethics

A major source of unethical behavior is the failure to recognize an ethical issue when it arises—a failure that can be addressed through education. The issue is particularly relevant to finance since money is a major temptation to unethical behavior.

6. Management

The better trained finance members are, the more quickly and easily they can adapt as companies restructure and adopt new organizational practices. For example, one problem faced by companies that significantly alter the ways they are managed is the misalignment of well-established reward systems with new strategic imperatives and new ways of working together. Finance is the major player realigning these systems in most companies.

7. Government

As governments rethink and change their policies, including their relationships with business, finance organizations will have to estimate the financial implications of governmental actions passed into law or presented as proposals for the future. Learning the intricacies of new laws and regulations and new applications of old laws and regulations will itself be a full-time job.

FINANCE IN PRACTICE

Realigning Reward Systems at AT&T

When AT&T entered a competitive environment after a century of shelter as a monopoly, it faced the need for massive changes in its reward system. AT&T had a fully developed, successful reward system for managers and workers, which focused on careful adherence to well-polished procedures and rules. Now the company had to reward just the opposite behavior—especially aggressive marketing skills. It is taking years for the changes to be made, and during the transition the reward system will keep punishing the newly desired behaviors and rewarding old behaviors that no longer are useful.

A Global Quality Revolution

The phrase *global quality revolution* refers to a major change in the productive capabilities of businesses and other organizations. Starting in the early 1950s, a few manufacturers began finding ways to improve the quality of their products to previously unheard-of levels and to sustain what became called "revolutionary rates of quality improvement." Those early product-quality improvements led to changes in the relative competitiveness of entire nations, to changes in the ways organizations are managed, and in some cases to dramatic rates of improvement in services, like the ability to receive a package overnight anywhere in the country when Federal Express pioneered quality approaches in an American service industry 20 years ago.

1. Changes in Global Quality and Competitiveness

Although societies have always been interested in having high-quality goods and services available for consumption, the ability of individuals and organizations to produce such goods has, until the second half of this century, been very restricted. The means used to reduce errors and defects normally added considerably to the costs of production and frequently delayed completion of the goods. People became accustomed to paying more and waiting longer for more reliable, more defect-free items. In spite of conscientious efforts by managers and workers, the rate at which quality improvements were achieved was quite slow. At times an older product might even be less error-prone than a new one. For example, in the automobile industry, many buyers were convinced that it was quite risky to buy new models the first year they were sold—it was better to wait a year until the manufacturers had a chance to work the bugs out.

The situation is, of course, dramatically different today. Although most products are still not perfect, an increasing number are very close. Many manufacturers have been able to reduce the defects in their products by multiple orders of magnitude—going from measuring defects in electronic components, for example, in terms of percentages to measuring them in parts per million or even parts per billion. These revolutionary rates of quality improvement have, in turn, led to enormous changes in world economic and trade patterns, in standards of living, and in the growth or demise of companies and national industries. In terms of nations, the big economic beneficiary was Japan, which pioneered the translation of many quality concepts into effective production processes.

2. Quality-Driven Changes in Companies

Early quality improvements were achieved by changing quite dramatically the ways in which products were produced, not by simply working harder on the same old tasks. Initially, these changes occurred mostly in manufacturing operations. However, as quality management processes evolved over time, they have led to greater and greater changes in how companies are organized and managed. Among the most important are changes occurring in the areas of: (1) customer focus, (2) planning, (3) process management and improvement, (4) valid data, (5) new tools and methods, (6) employee empowerment, and (7) teamwork.

Area of Change	How Quality-Leading Companies Are Managed
Customer focus	Place a very high priority on satisfying customers, developing effective means for determining and anticipating what customers value, and communicating that information (*the voice of the customer*) throughout the organization.
Planning	Plan for revolutionary rates of quality improvement, integrating quality-improvement objectives and the steps to achieve them into the organization's business, financial, and strategic plans.
Process management and improvement	Manage and improve, continuously and dramatically, the horizontal, cross-departmental processes through which the actual work of the organization flows.
Valid data	Collect and use valid data in analysis and decision making and train members throughout the organization in the skills to collect and use such data.
New tools and methods	Train members throughout the organization to use a variety of tools and methods for improving process, product, and service quality.
Employee empowerment	Provide effective means for employees at all levels to take initiative in satisfying customers and in improving organizational processes.
Teamwork	Develop skills throughout the organization for members to work effectively and regularly on teams on a wide variety of important organizational tasks and develop ways to reward teams for success on those tasks.

FIGURE 3.1
Seven aspects of how quality-leading companies are managed. New management methods are emerging in each of these areas.

Figure 3.1 describes how quality-leading companies usually are managed in each of these areas.

3. Improvements in Service Quality

Major quality improvements occurred first in the production functions of manufacturing companies and were followed by similar improvements in the nonmanufacturing (service) functions of those manufacturing companies and in some service industries. However, in general, quality improvements in service activities have been smaller in magnitude than in manufacturing. They have also spread across service industries more slowly than in manufacturing. The fact that many services do not readily lend themselves to export contributes to the slower rate of quality improvement in services than in manufacturing. For example, for many years the British postal system has routinely delivered letters mailed in the morning to any address in London by the early afternoon. Yet, the American postal service has remained largely immune to a quality infection from the British. Although the U.S. postal system is improving somewhat and has undertaken some systematic quality initiatives, newspapers still carry occasional stories of letters taking longer to be delivered within the same city than the pony express required to deliver a letter from Kansas City to San Francisco a hundred years ago.

Although the rate of quality improvement in services is generally slower than in manufacturing, a wide spectrum of service industries including hospitals, government agencies, accounting firms, consulting companies, and even a few law

firms have adopted quality improvement techniques similar in many respects to those used by manufacturers and service businesses. Examples of dramatic improvements in service quality are occurring in increasing numbers.

Three Major Areas of Influence on Financial Managing

For almost any company, reaching a high level of performance on the dimensions shown in Figure 3.1 requires major changes in training programs, reward systems, recognition processes, skills of managers and workers—even changes in the ways people relate to each other within an organization. These changes can be so pervasive that many executives and authors refer to them as changes in the very *culture* of organizations.

Such changes throughout a company will most certainly be reflected in many ways in the work of finance. Three of the more important effects of the quality revolution on financial managing are: (1) its impact on business health and survival; (2) its impact on the expectations for the performance of finance departments; and, (3) its impact on ways finance's internal and external customers and suppliers do their work.

1. Quality, Maximizing Shareholder Wealth, and Business Survival

The global quality revolution has a very special implication for financial managers who must determine whether quality-based competitive changes pose a significant threat to or opportunity for their companies. Whether the firm's goal is stated in terms of maximizing shareholder wealth or in some other terms, it is hard to imagine a company achieving its goals by decaying into bankruptcy, the victim of competitors that can deliver goods and/or services of significantly higher quality. To fulfill their traditional responsibilities, chief financial officers must determine if the techniques of managing for quality are necessary for their company's survival. If they are necessary, those CFOs need to be active quality champions in their companies. Some, such as Alan Graf, senior VP and CFO of Federal Express, already are.

> I don't see how you can compete in the long run without embracing these (quality approaches). They are proven; there is no question about it anymore. It is a given fact. You had better get on board on these things or you are going to get left behind, and you are not going to be able to catch up.[4]

2. Expectations for Finance's Performance

Finance departments are discovering that when their company or some of their customers or suppliers are actively pursuing dramatic quality improvements, expectations for their own performance rise. The success of other parts of the company and of customers and suppliers brings with it pressure for finance to perform at equally high levels. If products are manufactured without error, why can't invoices be prepared properly the first time, every time? If a package can be delivered "absolutely, positively," across the country overnight, why can't finance deliver cash to the company's operating units in precisely the correct currency and amount, wherever and whenever it is required?

Pressures to achieve excellence come from inside the boundaries of the finance department as well as from outside. Members of finance expect their own department to perform at least as well as other organizational units. Heightened expectations are not restricted to performance outcomes. They also occur with respect to the means used to achieve the improvements in results. To the extent that finance professionals like the changes in management styles that support quality elsewhere in the company, they will expect to see them in their own department. And because of finance's exposure to and involvement in so many organizational activities, finance members and their customers and suppliers may expect the finance department to play a leadership role in anticipating and responding to change.

3. Requirements for Consistent Work Methods

In addition to changes in expectations about finance's performance, requirements for working with other units of the company and with its outside stakeholders are also changing. When others are using new types of data and analyzing it in new ways, finance needs to be able to do the same. When others are treating fi-

[4] **Reference:** James A.F. Stoner and Frank M. Werner, *Managing Finance for Quality—Bottom-line Results from Top-level Commitment* (Milwaukee: ASQC Quality Press, and Morristown, N.J.: Financial Executives Research Foundation), p. 141.

nance as a valued customer, finance is expected to respond in a similar manner. In organizations where working effectively in teams becomes a way of life, finance people who fail to master the same skills lose the power to contribute to the work of others and reduce the clarity and impact of finance's voice in company decisions.

Continuity and Change

In identifying how the pursuit of revolutionary rates of quality improvement is influencing financial managing, we are continually looking for both continuity and change. What is done the same and what is done differently? There are at least four places we might look for continuity and change: (1) in finance's well-established concepts and tools, (2) in the content of finance work, (3) in the functioning of finance's processes, and (4) in the ways in which finance goes about doing its work. In this section, we begin with the first two of these four topics: concepts and tools, and content of work. These are areas where the *lack* of change seems most striking—areas of continuity. Then we look at the other two issues: finance's processes and ways finance does its work—areas where change seems more striking than continuity.

1. Continuity

Areas of continuity include (1) core finance concepts and tools and (2) basic financial managing tasks.

Core finance concepts and tools Although new perspectives will always flow regularly into financial practice, the basic concepts and tools of finance do not seem to be changing dramatically as a result of the global quality revolution. Nor do they seem to be changing greatly in response to the six other forces for change discussed earlier in the chapter. Such things as the importance of cash flows and the time value of money, capital market efficiency, and the limited effects of financing choice on value continue as stable underpinnings for finance theory and practice. The importance of understanding interest rates and exchange rates is undiminished. Financial modeling remains focused on the monetary effects of alternative courses of action.

Basic financial managing tasks At present, finance's five basic work activities also continue to be necessary, whether or not a company or its industry is in pursuit of revolutionary rates of quality improvement. Finance people continue devoting their efforts to understanding finance's environment, making incremental decisions, making optimizing decisions, balancing risk and return, and managing finance's processes. Although these work activities are most notable for their continuity, the last one—managing finance's processes—has undergone enough change also to be worthy of inclusion in the following section on change in financial managing.

2. Change

The most notable current changes in financial managing involve (1) finance's own productive processes and (2) the ways finance goes about doing its work.

Improving finance's processes One of the most exciting areas of financial work today involves the improvement of financial processes. The excitement comes from the demonstrable impact such improvements have on corporate competitive strength and from the capacity to do finance's work in ways far superior to those of the past. It also comes from the intellectual challenges and satisfying collaborative working relationships that normally accompany such improvement activities.

Awareness that finance has its own processes has come almost as slowly to finance as it has to marketing, sales, human resources, and the corporate legal function. These corporate functions do not produce millions of physical products whose defects can be pointed to by customers and counted and displayed on graphs. As a result, the existence of "productive" processes in each of these support functions has been far less obvious than in manufacturing.

The lack of attention, until recently, to improving financial processes also arose in part from lack of belief that major improvements were possible and from lack of knowledge about how to make such improvements. However, these changes are so important for finance's contributions to organizations and so interesting to read about that we report examples of them throughout the book in boxes labeled "Improving Finance's Processes." We also devote two chapters, 13 and 14, to recognizing and improving financial processes. If current trends continue, the likelihood is very high that nearly everyone working in a financial activity within the next few years will be involved in improving some financial process or will work in financial processes improved by others. Process improvement is becoming a core part of finance's work.

Changing how finance does its work A second area of significant change in financial managing involves the ways finance does its work. These changes are reflected in how finance is coming to see its role in the organization and in the way finance people do their work each day. Figure 3.2 summarizes some of these changes in terms of ten ways finance people are moving toward an increasingly customer-oriented approach. The changes in Figure 3.2 are similar to a financial managing approach Patrick J. Keating and Stephen F. Jablonsky have called a "competitive-team orientation."

Keating and Jablonsky contrast the competitive-team orientation with two other financial managing approaches more consistent with the left side of Figure 3.2. They describe the competitive-team orientation as follows:

> Firms with this type of financial orientation are ones where financial work is focused on the market, those that integrate financial work into the business organization, and those that use the matrix style of management. Companies with this orientation stress commitment to using financial analysis to enhance the firm's core competitiveness and strategic competitiveness through customer service, financial leadership, value-added involvement with the management team, and a sophisticated knowledge of the business.[5]

[5] **Reference:** Patrick J. Keating, and Stephen F. Jablonsky, *Changing Roles of Financial Management—Getting Close to the Business* (Morristown, N.J.: Financial Executives Research Foundation, 1990), p. 6.

	More Emphasis on	Less Emphasis on
Perceptions, Relationships, and Roles		
Identification of finance's customer	All stakeholders—internal and external	Top management
Focus of finance's work	Processes as manageable drivers of quality, efficiency, and profitability; all costs and benefits—financial and non-financial; how results are achieved	Money and financial results; the accounting system
Attitude toward the management system	Assuming employees are okay and poor results come from weaknesses in the system	Assuming the system is okay and poor results come from employee weaknesses
Relationship to others	Being a problem-solving partner, integrated with the rest of the organization; the benefits from serving others; being proactive	Being an insular, independent overseer; potential conflicts of interest from serving others; being reactive
Roles of finance people	Being a partner, team member, teacher, and coach	Being an inspector, judge, and police officer
Ways of Working		
Measurement horizon	The long-term, regardless of whether the benefits and costs are immediately visible	Decisions that can be quickly evaluated by the financial markets
Handling of variation	Differentiating among causes of variation	Treating all variation as a problem
Methods of problem solving	Integrating systems and process perspectives into economic theory; seeking dramatic improvements; looking for quality and cycle time benefits	Economic theory taken by itself; seeking marginal improvements; decomposing problems for analysis; looking only for measurable financial benefits
Place in the organization	Distributing finance work and skills around the organization; finance as a conveyor of resources and information; encouraging self-control of resouce acquisition and utilization	Finance as a centralized data filter, controlling resource acquisition and utilization
The Purpose of the Firm		
Purpose	Delighting customers, improving products, services, and processes; serving all stakeholders well	Seeing shareholder wealth maximization as the only purpose

Reference: Adapted from James A. F. Stoner and Frank M. Werner, *Remaking Corporate Finance—The New Corporate Finance Emerging in High-quality Companies* (New York: McGraw-Hill Primis, 1992), p. 29; and *Managing Finance for Quality—Bottom-Line Results from Top-Level Commitment* (Milwaukee: ASQC Quality Press and Morristown, NJ: Financial Executives Research Foundation, 1994). p. 41.

FIGURE 3.2

Financial management changes observed in leading quality companies. Changes are visible in perceptions, relationships, and roles; ways of working; and the purpose of the firm.

3. Looking Ahead

In the coming chapters, you will find a number of reports on very specific ways in which some companies are bringing innovations into financial managing. Many but not all of those companies are leaders in integrating their financial managing practices with their customer-driven quality management systems. One useful set of questions to keep in mind as you read the book addresses the theme of continuity and change quite directly. The questions, used for many years by David B. Gleicher, a management consultant and executive, are summarized in three words: *continue, start,* and *stop*.

Continue

- What financial management practices continue to be performed as they have been in the past?
- What financial management practices continue to be performed but are performed in different ways?

Start

- What new financial management practices are starting to be performed?

Stop

- What old financial management practices are no longer being performed?

It is much too early in this book to go into the details of the answers to these questions since you are just starting to learn about finance. However, you may enjoy forming your own guesses about the answers as you progress through your course. We will return to these questions in the book's final chapter (Chapter 23) as we summarize some of the things you have learned.

A year had passed since Alexandra McLean attended her group's last annual retreat. As she drove toward this year's retreat, she played two thoughts around in her mind: a new name for the process the group called SEE—ALL last year, and the success of the last year's task force.

Her current candidate for this year's name for the process, SEE & ACT (Sense Environmental Events and Act Creatively Today), was too close to last year's name. "Anyway," she thought, "the group always chooses a better name than the one I suggest."

Alex was very pleased with the results of the task force, which had identified many of the impacts of the quality revolution for her company's finance function. Although the finance organization was already doing some things in a high-quality manner, dozens of opportunities for further systematic improvement were uncovered. Once again the changes that were implemented were at least as valuable as past ones, and more people had volunteered than ever before. So many people had volunteered, in fact, that Alex had withdrawn her name from the pool just before selections were made. She had explained truthfully that the topic was probably the one she was most interested in of all six so far, but she felt her withdrawal would give someone else a chance to make a visible contribution. And she trusted the process. The team would not need her to do an excellent job. She was delighted that the results proved she was correct in that assessment. And yet, it would have been so much more fun to be part of the team reporting on the project rather than part of the audience applauding their accomplishments.

Summary of Key Points

- **Identify major forces for change currently affecting financial managing.** Major forces for change include increased international cooperation, communication, and competition; revolutionary rates of improvement in the quality of goods and services; increased diversity in organizations' work forces, customers, and suppliers; rapid changes in technologies related to information production, analysis, and dissemination; changes in ethical standards and expectations; changes in the ways organizations are managed; and changes in governmental policies and actions.
- **Explain how those forces are influencing financial managing.** The forces have many implications for finance members. One of the most important is the need for additional training and education. Changes in finance's environment call for the development of many new skills—sometimes before other members of the organization need them.
- **Explain what is meant by the phrase *global quality revolution.*** The phrase *global quality revolution* is used most frequently to refer to revolutionary rates of improvement in the quality of products and services produced by firms in many different countries. These changes include dramatic improvements in response time and customer satisfaction and equally dramatic decreases in costs. A second, less common, interpretation focuses on changes occurring in the ways organizations that produce those goods and services go about doing their work—how they are now managed and interact with other parties.
- **Explain why a global quality revolution might have important influences on financial managing.** Such a revolution could influence the chances of survival of the finance department's company, its suppliers, and its customers. It could change the expectations held for finance's performance, and it could change the ways in which work is done by finance's internal and external customers. Because of finance's involvement in so many organizational activities and its wide exposure to many parts of the organization, finance members and their customers and suppliers may expect finance to play a leadership role in anticipating and responding to change that goes well beyond finance's traditional roles.
- **Identify some of the well-established aspects of financial practice that seem relatively unchanged and others that are changing in response to the quality revolution and the other current forces for change.** New perspectives will always flow regularly into financial practice, and new technologies like computers and ever more powerful software will continue to influence the work of finance. However, the basic concepts and conceptual tools of finance do not seem to be changing dramatically as a result of these current forces, nor are the basic types of financial work changing greatly. Such things as the tools of valuation, capital market efficiency, and the importance of having money sooner rather than later continue as stable underpinnings for financial theory and practice. The importance of understanding finance's environment, making incremental and optimizing decisions, balancing risk and return, and managing finance's processes continue to be the work of financial people. On the other hand, the possibility of improving dramatically the performance of finance's processes and the responsibility for making such improvements are new to most finance departments. Some departments are also changing appreciably their relationships and roles and the ways they work with their internal and external suppliers. Some are even speaking differently about the goal of maximizing shareholder wealth.

Questions

1. Why is the title of this chapter, and the subtitle of the book, "Continuity and Change"?
2. Identify seven forces for change in today's environment. Give an example of how each has affected business in general or a specific company.
3. Identify an industry affected significantly by recent environmental changes. List some of the ways the industry has been altered.
4. How are each of the seven forces for change transforming the way world-class companies view the education and training of their personnel?
5. What is the "global quality revolution"? Identify seven changes in companies currently taking place that are driven by this revolution.
6. Why has the rate of quality improvement in service industries and functions lagged behind the rate of quality improvement in manufacturing?
7. Identify three ways the quality revolution is influencing the practice of financial managing.
8. Which financial managing tools and activities appear *not* to be changing as a result of the global quality revolution?
9. Which financial managing tools and activities *do* appear to be changing as a result of the global quality revolution?
10. What is meant by the phrase "Continue, start, stop"? How does this concept relate to the study of financial managing?
11. Identify the following phrases. What is their connection to the global quality revolution?
    a. "Absolutely, positively."
    b. "Quality is Job 1."
    c. "It's amazing what we can do together."
    d. "A passion for perfection."
    e. "It just feels right."
    f. "Quality means the world to us."

CASE

CRISTINA LIBERATI

Cristina Liberati took a sip of her iced tea and frowned. "The world seems to be changing around me in ways that I don't know how to deal with," she said. "The skills that have always worked so well for me seem no longer to be what I need. I need some advice about what to do next."

Crissy was assistant controller of the largest division of a global, multiproduct company. She had joined the firm ten years ago after graduating from a highly respected business school. Crissy had chosen that school because of its strength in technical finance and had taken every high-level finance course at the school. An exceptional math student in high school, she had always been more comfortable with numbers than with interpersonal issues. Thinking back to her MBA days, she remembered how she couldn't wait for her management courses to end so she could return to the more technical subjects.

To help her sort through the issues, Crissy had invited a close friend who worked in finance for another company to join her for lunch. Now that they had ordered and the small talk was finished, it was time to turn to her concerns. "When I graduated from B-school, everything made so much sense. I was hired to do financial analysis with the department analyzing the company's expansion plans. My work went well, and I received regular promotions. As best I can tell, I am one of the youngest employees ever to make assistant controller. But lately, my assignments seem to have less and less to do with my strengths. Now that I'm managing a portion of the department, I have to deal with all those issues involving organizational behavior and human resources which I avoided in school. And to make matters worse, the CEO has announced that the company is going to adopt some form of total quality management which means more of the 'touchy-feely stuff.' I'm beginning to feel like a fish out of water."

"I think it may be time to consider some further education," Crissy's friend suggested. My company has been into quality management for several years now, and there are some topics I've recently been exposed to that could be very useful to you. But, I'm sure that a lot of your skills are still very valid. In fact, in some ways, quality management plays right to your strengths: it's very data-oriented and uses a wide variety of analytical tools to improve the business.

"I hope you're right," Crissy replied. "I guess what I'm most interested in is this: which of my skills are still useful? Which are outdated? And if I do look for more education and training, what different skills should I be learning now in order to continue contributing to my company and to grow personally and professionally?

CHAPTER 4
DATA FOR FINANCIAL DECISION MAKING

Stephen Lewis was worried. His company was profitable, yet there never seemed to be enough cash to meet all the firm's obligations. He had managed to pay all the firm's bills in the past, but just today he had received a telephone call from his banker threatening not to renew the company's line of credit unless the company improved its financial condition. He had assured the banker he would get to work to solve the problem immediately, but where to start?

And now, just when he needed to lock himself in the office, Stephen had a doctor's appointment to go to. He had made the appointment two months ago. Given his time pressure at work he wished he could cancel it, but Ann, his wife, would not hear of it. "Damn," he thought as he entered the doctor's office, "It's only a general physical examination. Why do I have to waste time on this now?"

Stephen's doctor carefully measured and recorded data on his physical condition. Then he compared Stephen's measurements to past data from his records and to standards for individuals of Stephen's age, height, and weight as published by the medical profession. He found that Stephen was essentially in good condition but could afford to lose 20 pounds. He told Stephen, "Take off the weight, and you'll feel a whole lot better. Your heart won't have to work as hard, you'll have much more energy, and you'll be able to get a lot more done. You'd be surprised how one improvement like that has so many ripple effects throughout your system."

On the way back to his office, Stephen thought about what his doctor had said. He wondered if the process by which the doctor had reached his diagnosis and prescription was in any way applicable to his problem at work.

Like a doctor who takes responsibility for the physical health of a patient, the financial manager is responsible for the financial health of a business. A healthy business, just as a healthy person, lives longer and is capable of pursuing many more interesting and rewarding activities. It has less stress and can more easily handle shocks to its system. It invests fewer resources to produce a profitable result, raising the return to all stakeholders.

In this chapter we look at the data required to make good financial decisions. Some of the data will help us understand the needs of the people with whom the company works: employees, customers, and suppliers. Other data will tell us how well financial processes are functioning and point toward opportunities for improvement. We look at data provided by the accounting system: the managerial accounting data used internally and the financial accounting data reported to the public. Still another data set deals with the company's relationship to governmental tax authorities. We also look at data about the firm created by outsiders, as they evaluate its performance. We close the chapter with a look at how some of the data can be used to compare the firm to other organizations.

Key Points You Should Learn from This Chapter

After reading this chapter you should be able to:

- Identify the meaning of *financial analysis* and the data used for financial decision making.
- Understand the importance of collecting information about customer and employee satisfaction.
- Appreciate the necessity of measuring the performance of financial processes.
- Prepare a cash flow table and recognize different types of costs.
- Realize that financial accounting data are a useful but imperfect source of information.
- Determine average and marginal tax rates.
- Understand why it is important to compare numbers when doing financial analysis.

Introductory Concepts—The Need for Good Data

financial analysis—the use of financial and other data to understand the financial health of an organization

Financial analysis is the task of using financial and other data to reach judgments about the financial health of an organization.[1] It is done within a company by financial managers as they work to keep the business healthy. It is also done outside the company by its stakeholders—investors, creditors, customers, suppliers, governments, unions—as they decide what actions they want to take in their interactions with the firm. In this chapter we look at the information used by financial managers, both financial data contained in the firm's accounting records and public financial statements, and nonfinancial data such as indicators of customer satisfaction and process quality.

The medical analogy is quite appropriate since, in performing financial analysis, we do virtually the same things as a doctor who analyzes and cares for a medical patient. First, we collect and organize data about the firm to describe its present condition in useful financial terms. Second, we use this information to diagnose the firm's strengths and weaknesses. This diagnosis identifies issues that require our immediate attention. Third, we use our knowledge of the firm, plus other data about similar firms and about the environment, to predict where financial problems are likely to arise in the future. Finally, we prescribe financial medicine if required to nurture the company back to full financial health, recommend a changed financial routine if required to improve its health, or simply advise the firm to continue doing what is working well to insure that a healthy firm stays that way.

While we identify data collection as the first step in financial analysis, there is actually a *prior* step: before we collect data, we must have theory. Without a theory we cannot know what information is relevant to study and hence to collect. Stephen Lewis's doctor used his knowledge of medical theory to select information that he knew would provide insight into Stephen's health.

The primary information set used by financial executives today is based on the traditional economic-financial theory of the firm, in which the fundamental objective of a business is to maximize owners' wealth. Thus financial managers collect measures of cash flow, profitability, liquidity, leverage, and resource use, because finance theory has discovered relationships between these numbers and value for the owners. *Health* is defined in financial terms. In many ways this traditional financial analysis has been quite successful in identifying problems and pointing toward better financial condition.

However, as we will see in a number of places in this book, many firms are in the midst of supplementing financial data with nonfinancial data. Financial managers are often major players in identifying meaningful nonfinancial data to collect, in collecting it, and in reporting it to the rest of the organization. In particular, companies that place a particularly high priority on customer satisfaction and continuous improvement of production and service processes are active in develop-

[1] **Observation:** While we look at a business organization in this chapter, the same concepts, with relatively minor modifications, can be used to analyze other types of organizations, both public and private.

ing new measures of the business to assess these components of its health. To improve customer satisfaction they collect data about customer dissatisfaction; to improve processes they measure them in ways that disclose their limitations. Today many companies are using customer and process data along with traditional financial measures to give a fuller picture of the firm.

People Data

Since satisfied people play an important role in the financial health of a business, it is important to collect and analyze data about their needs and about how pleased they are with the firm. Satisfied employees are the most important asset of many companies. They delight the customers they serve and contribute to process improvements leading to higher-quality products and services and to cost reduction. Satisfied customers raise the firm's revenues by buying its products and services again and again and by recommending the firm to others. Often they are willing to pay a premium price for what they perceive as superior quality.

As discussed in Chapters 2 and 3,[2] finance has customers both inside and outside the firm. Everyone who gets financial output—for example, the external customer who receives a bill, the supplier who receives a payment, the employee who receives a paycheck, the lender who receives an interest payment—is a customer of the finance function. It is important for financial managers to understand the needs of each of these customers and to measure how well they are being fulfilled. Many companies talk of customer/supplier alliances, close relationships between each customer and supplier, to emphasize the importance of working actively to improve these relationships by seeing them in cooperative terms. (At the same time, finance is a customer of other parts of the company, such as purchasing, which supplies data on material costs. It is equally important for finance people, acting as the customer, to form customer/supplier alliances with its suppliers to ensure that finance gets the inputs it needs on time, without error, and in the most useful form.)

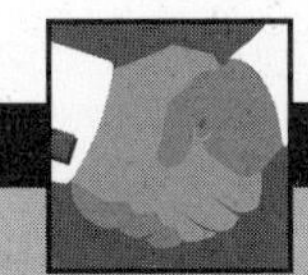

SERVING FINANCE'S CUSTOMERS

Collecting Customer Data at Solectron

The Solectron Corporation, a fast-growing contract manufacturer of electronic products located in California's Silicon Valley, asks each of its customers to fill out a "report card" every week. The form asks about Solectron's performance on five dimensions: product quality, on-time delivery, communication, service responsiveness, and overall company performance. Customers score the company on a letter-grade scale with a matching point score for each letter: A (100 points), A– (90), B (80), B– (75), C (0), and D (–100). Solectron's experience is that dissatisfied customers translate directly into lost revenues. Accordingly, the only acceptable score is a straight A; even an A– is well below the current corporate goal of 97%.

[2] **Cross-reference:** Pages 41–44 and 63.

Most data about customer satisfaction come from direct contact or from systematic surveys. Surveys may be taken of external customers and also of customers internal to the firm.

Many firms also survey employees to discover their concerns so these concerns may be promptly addressed. Some firms include questions about leadership, asking employees to rate their direct supervisor and the company's management in general. To ensure that management takes this information seriously, a company may incorporate it into its compensation policy. At Federal Express, for example, senior management can earn a full year-end bonus only if their leadership score on the employee survey has increased over the previous year's score.

Process Data

Every activity of finance professionals is part of a process, whether it be raising money, performing financial analysis, or producing internal reports. In a well-functioning company, these processes are understood, under control, and repeatable. They are also being studied to locate additional opportunities for improvement—either to continue reducing errors, waste, and rework or to shorten the time it takes to complete them.

Three ways that companies measure the performance of their processes are by calculating: (1) the absolute number of failures, (2) the relative number of failures—the number of failures as a fraction of the number of opportunities to fail, and (3) process cycle time.

1. Absolute Number of Failures

Individual processes can be measured by counting the number of times they fail to deliver the desired output. Simple tally sheets and graphs are often used to record the number of failures. A summary number, which captures the objective and indicates the functioning of the process, is identified and tracked. At Corning, Incorporated, these numbers are called "Key Results Indicators (KRIs)." For example, Corning's treasury is responsible for delivering cash throughout the company where and when needed. One of its goals is to have no missed deliveries, and it counts and plots—as one of its KRIs—the number of times per month

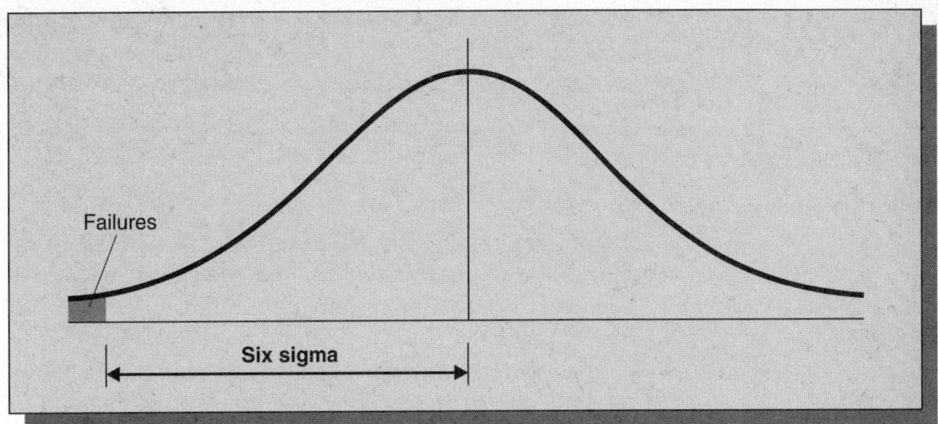

FIGURE 4.1
Six sigma. The area beyond six standard deviations from the mean is 3.4 millionths of the total area under the curve.

it fails to deliver, thereby failing to meet the needs of its internal customers. The graph of this KRI is prominently posted on the wall outside the corporate treasurer's office along with similar graphs of the treasury group's other KRIs.

2. Relative Number of Failures

six sigma—a statistical measure of process accuracy, only 3.4 errors per million opportunities

Where processes have many steps, or repeat many times, statistical techniques often are employed to measure process accuracy. One popular system, based on the number of failures per opportunity to fail, is known as **six sigma,** after the goal for process accuracy set by its creators. Developed at Motorola, Inc., six sigma is based on the normal (bell curve) probability distribution and represents the tiny area under one tail of the distribution further than six standard deviations from the mean, as illustrated in Figure 4.1.[3] Motorola's studies have shown that, without the application of systematic quality management, the norm for many human processes is to perform with approximately four sigma accuracy. This translates to 6,210 errors per million opportunities, a success rate of 99.38%. While this rate might seem quite high, customers of some processes normally demand significantly higher levels of performance. For example, the following has been compiled for an accuracy rate of 99.9%.[4] At 99.9% accuracy:

- Each day twelve babies will be given to the wrong parents by hospitals.
- Each day 107 incorrect medical procedures will be performed.
- Each year 20,000 incorrect drug prescriptions will be written.
- Each minute 1,314 phone calls will be misplaced by telecommunications services.
- Each hour 18,322 pieces of mail will be mishandled.
- Each hour 22,000 checks will be deducted from the wrong account.
- Each year 268,500 defective tires will be shipped.

[3] **Elaboration:** The six sigma calculation is actually a bit more involved since it allows for a shift of 1.5 standard deviations in the mean of the distribution.

[4] **Reference:** Natalie Gabel, "Is 99.9% Good Enough?," a supplement to *Training,* March 1991, Lakewood Publications. pp. 40–41.

When a process is operating at six sigma accuracy, however, there are only 3.4 defects per million opportunities, a 99.9997% success rate. At that level of precision, someone typing 20 pages of single-spaced text every working day would hit the wrong key roughly once a week.[5]

3. Cycle Time

cycle time—the time from the beginning to the end of any process or process step

If a process can be completed quickly, unnecessary costs are avoided, there is less chance for errors to creep in, and customers receive the output of the process in a more timely fashion. Many companies have begun to measure **cycle time**—the time it takes to complete each process, either in absolute hours or in person-hours—and to set goals for cycle time reduction. For example, after achieving six sigma accuracy in many of its processes by the end of 1992, Motorola set a new corporate goal of ten-times cycle time reduction in every process over the next five years. A process that now takes ten hours should take only one hour to complete five years hence. Cycle time reduction comes from process redesign to eliminate complexity and waste. Unnecessary steps are eliminated and the steps that remain are simplified. In doing so, errors are also reduced.

Managerial Accounting Data

Managerial accounting information consists of data collected by the firm's accounting system used in internal planning, analysis, and decision making. While generally coming from the same database as the information used to produce the company's public financial statements, it is not constrained by the pronouncements of the Financial Accounting Standards Board (FASB) or the Securities and Exchange Commission (SEC), the organizations that establish the rules for public reporting. Rather, the information can take any form management finds useful in its work.

Three particular aspects of managerial accounting data are useful to keep in mind as you study finance: (1) the difference between cash flows and accrual accounting data, (2) different types of costs, and (3) alternate methods of cost allocation. All three imply that the numbers available in the accounting system must be looked at carefully to see if they are appropriate for any specific analysis.

1. Cash Flows vs. Accrual Accounting Data

cash flow—money received or paid by an organization

Most financial analysis and decision making is based on cash flows. A **cash flow,** the receiving or paying of cash, is a real, tangible event and is clearly identifiable. Cash has clear and immediate value. A firm that has cash can use it to acquire resources or invest it to earn interest. A firm that must make a cash payment loses the opportunity to put that money to another use. If it is short of cash, the firm

[5] **Observation and cross-reference:** From this example it should be clear that systematic quality management is necessary for processes to reach six sigma accuracy. We look further at financial processes, their measurement and improvement in Chapters 13 and 14.

must raise the money, for example by borrowing it and incurring interest charges.

accrual accounting—a system of recording accounting numbers when economic events have been achieved

By contrast, the data appearing in accounting records often are not based on cash. Most companies use the **accrual accounting** system, in which revenues and expenses enter the accounting records when products or services are sold (for example, the accounts "sales revenue," or "cost of goods sold"), or as time passes (the account "interest expense" is an example). The amount of sales revenue will not equal the amount of cash brought in if there are accounts receivable. Similarly, the firm's expenses will differ from cash paid out if there are any payables. Throughout this book we will be careful to extract cash flow data from accounting records for use in financial analysis and decision making.

Whenever we need to summarize cash flows, we will use a format known as a "cash flow table." This is a spreadsheet in which each row represents an event producing a cash flow and each column stands for a point in time. Columns are identified with the date and/or a time-point number beginning with 0 to represent "now." The amount of each cash flow is inserted at the appropriate intersection. For clarity, it is common to use the accountant's convention of parentheses to indicate negative numbers since negative signs can easily be overlooked. After all numbers have been entered into the table, we total the amounts in each column to produce the net cash flow at each point in time.

Example

Cash Flow Table

A company is trying to organize the following cash flows:

- Buy a machine for $25,000 in 1995.
- Increase cash inflows by $15,000 in 1996, 1997, and 1998.
- Pay additional taxes of $8,000 in 1997.
- Sell the machine for $10,000 in 1998.

Question: Prepare a cash flow table to summarize this information.

Solution:

Event	Year 0 1995	Year 1 1996	Year 2 1997	Year 3 1998
Buy machine	(25,000)			
Additional cash inflows		15,000	15,000	15,000
Additional taxes			(8,000)	
Sell machine				10,000
Net cash flows	(25,000)	15,000	7,000	25,000

2. Types of Costs

Because the word *cost* is used in so many ways, it is important to distinguish among several types of costs which are particularly useful for the financial manager to understand.

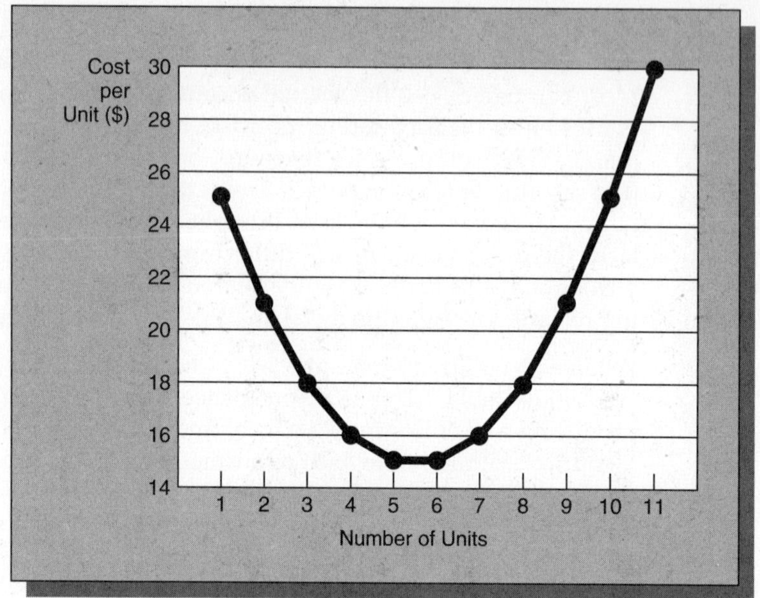

FIGURE 4.2
A U-shaped cost curve. Per-unit costs are normally high at first, then decline, and finally increase again.

total cost—the sum of the costs of making each unit

average cost—total cost divided by the number of units made

marginal cost—the cost of making one additional unit

Total, average, and marginal costs When a company manufactures many units of a product or provides many instances of its service, it is unlikely that every unit costs the same amount to create. It is normal for the first units of anything to be expensive to produce due to start-up costs and the unfamiliarity of employees with how to make them. As more is produced, efficiencies and learning set in, and costs decline. Eventually, resources become strained, and costs tend to rise again. Economists capture this pattern with the concept of the "U–shaped cost curve" illustrated in Figure 4.2. Note that each unit has a different cost, making it difficult to specify the cost of any one unit of product. The concepts of total, average, and marginal cost provide ways to describe this operating environment. As the words suggest, **total cost** is the sum of all costs, **average cost** is the cost per unit, and **marginal cost** is the cost of producing the next unit of output.

Example

Total, Average, and Marginal Cost

A company estimates the following costs to produce the first 11 units of its product:

Unit:	1	2	3	4	5	6	7	8	9	10	11
Cost:	$25	$21	$18	$16	$15	$15	$16	$18	$21	$25	$30

Question: What are the total and average costs to produce the first 10 units?

Solution steps:

Total cost = 25 + 21 + 18 + 16 + 15 + 15 + 16 + 18 + 21 + 25
= $190

Average cost = $190 / 10 = $19

Question: What is the marginal cost to produce the eleventh unit?

Answer: $30. The marginal cost is simply the cost of producing that unit.

Total and average cost numbers are particularly useful for analyzing long-term, optimization decisions. Marginal numbers, on the other hand, are used in analyzing short-run, incremental decisions.[6]

incremental cost—the additional cost from taking a particular action

Incremental cost The marginal cost concept is commonly extended to other actions beyond producing more of the firm's products or services. Whenever the company considers taking any action that will change its costs, the amount of the change is the **incremental cost.** Equally, we must consider any incremental revenues that will come from the change.

Example

Incremental Cost (and Revenue)

A company is considering the purchase of a new machine which is expected to increase revenues by $10,000 and increase costs by $6,000 per year. Because these numbers capture the changes from purchasing the new machine, they are incremental and must enter the analysis.

sunk cost—money previously spent

Sunk cost A **sunk cost** is money that was spent in the past. Since the cost has already taken place, it is unrecoverable—the fact that the money was spent is history and can never be changed. Sunk costs are always ignored in financial decision making.

Example

Sunk Cost

A company purchased a machine three years ago for $100,000. Today it is evaluating whether to sell it. Because the $100,000 was spent in the past, it is a sunk cost and should play no role in the analysis of whether to sell the machine.

opportunity cost—a benefit forgone by the making of a financial decision

Opportunity cost Often, a financial decision prevents a firm from obtaining some other benefit. Whenever this happens, the lost benefit, or **opportunity cost,** must be taken into account in analyzing the decision.

Example

Opportunity Cost

A company owns a building which is currently leased to another firm for $1,000 per month. It is considering whether to expand one of its product lines which would require the use of the building, resulting in the termination of the lease. The analysis of the expansion must take into account the opportunity cost of $1,000 per month, the income which would be lost if the building were taken off lease.

variable cost—a cost that changes with changes in sales

fixed cost—a cost that remains constant when sales changes

Variable and fixed costs Costs that vary as sales (and hence production volume) changes are called **variable costs.** By contrast, costs that remain fixed as sales changes are called **fixed costs.** For any analysis in which sales and production volume are expected to change, it is important to identify which costs are variable and which are fixed, since only the variable costs will be affected.[7]

---

[6] **Cross-reference:** We study optimization decisions, such as the best mix of financing, in Chapters 15–17. Incremental decisions, such as acquiring plant and equipment, are examined in Chapters 11 and 12.

[7] **Cross-reference:** One particular use of variable and fixed costs is break-even analysis, described in Appendix 4A.

Example

Variable and Fixed Costs

A company is evaluating the costs of increasing production of one of its products. Raw materials and direct production labor costs are variable, since they will increase as production levels increase, and must be included in the analysis. On the other hand, the costs of operating the company's administrative offices are fixed with respect to sales and production levels and will not enter the decision.

3. Cost Allocation

Often a financial manager needs to determine the cost of producing one unit of the firm's product. While this might seem simple in concept, it can be very difficult in practice.

direct cost—a cost directly traceable to the manufacture of a product or delivery of a service

indirect (overhead) cost—a cost not directly traceable to a product or service

cost driver—an activity that results in costs being incurred in operations

activity-based costing—a cost allocation method based on cost driver activities

Direct and indirect (overhead) costs Some costs can be easily connected to each product or service a firm produces. These are known as **direct costs.** For example, a firm that assembles machinery can keep track of the cost of each piece of raw material that goes into every unit it produces. (In reality, this may be cumbersome if there are many items of raw material, and the firm might estimate per-unit raw material costs using an average of some kind.) Other costs cannot easily be traced to individual products—the president's salary, for example. These are **indirect** (or **overhead**) **costs,** and they must be allocated to each unit produced if it is desired to include them in the cost of production.

Of particular concern to financial analysts are the indirect variable costs, those that would change if sales and production levels change. Because these costs are indirect, it is often difficult to project how they would change. One method is to connect these costs to each product by identifying an activity, known as a **cost driver,** which leads to incurring the cost. For example, some companies use total labor hours as the cost driver for the personnel department, since the department's workload is determined in large part by the number of employees, hence hours worked. Each product is then studied to determine how much of each cost driver activity is required per unit of product. With this information, it is possible to estimate how much of each indirect variable cost should be "attached" to each unit of product. The process of connecting costs to products through cost driver activities is known as **activity-based costing.**

Example

Activity-Based Costing

A company's personnel department spends $500 per year to support each employee. Production employees work a 40-hour week for 50 weeks per year and produce 100 units of product per hour on average.

Question: Using activity-based costing, determine the personnel department cost to be allocated to each unit of product if "labor-hours" is the cost driver.

Solution steps:

1. Calculate the total number of units of the cost driver, labor hours:
   Annual labor hours: 40 hrs/week × 50 weeks = 2,000 hours

2. Calculate the amount to allocate per labor hour:
   Total cost to be allocated: \$500
   Amount allocated per labor hour: \$500/2,000 = \$0.25
3. Allocate costs further to the individual unit:
   Production rate: 100 units per hour
   Amount allocated per unit: \$0.25/100 = \$0.0025

Answer: The company should allocate \$0.0025 to each unit produced.

Financial Accounting Data

Financial accounting data are information collected by the firm's accounting system which are used to produce the financial statements presented to the public: the income statement, balance sheet, and statement of cash flows. While generally coming from the same database as the information used for managerial accounting data, they are constrained by the pronouncements of the Financial Accounting Standards Board and the Securities and Exchange Commission, the organizations that establish the rules for public reporting.

Financial analysts need good information about the condition of the business to make a correct diagnosis. In testing the validity of financial accounting data, financial managers have an advantage over outside analysts since they can talk directly to the people who produced the data and often can see the raw records or details of calculations. Outside analysts generally have little access to this supporting information and may have to rely on the reputation of those who generated the data. U.S. securities law requires the financial statements of publicly held companies to be audited by a certified public accountant. Analysts looking at the financial statements of privately held companies, especially stakeholders with an interest in the firm, normally insist that they be audited as well. When looking at smaller firms, analysts often attempt to interview the firms' accountants directly.

The most serious potential problem with financial statements is that the data might be wrong to begin with. The firm might have made errors in collecting the data, or might not have correctly applied the rules of accounting in the preparation of its financial statements. In extreme cases, the financial data might be fraudulently constructed.

However, even in the majority of cases, when financial statements are prepared with perfectly correct data and conform precisely to financial accounting rules, there is still plenty of reason for analysts to be careful when using the information. Although public financial statements are required to conform to Generally Accepted Accounting Principles (GAAP),[8] GAAP rules are not always designed with the financial analyst in mind. In fact some of the rules make it quite difficult to reach meaningful conclusions from the financial statements. Three of the more important issues of concern to financial analysts are: (1) the use of dissimilar valuation methods, (2) the ability to use alternative numbers, and (3) the omission of important information.

---

[8] **Recommendation:** We encourage you to refer to your textbook in financial accounting if you need to refresh your knowledge of accounting principles.

1. Two Different Valuation Methods Mixed Together

A first concern is that two different and somewhat incompatible methods are used to value the firm's assets and liabilities. Monetary items, those that can be measured directly in money terms (cash, marketable securities, receivables, payables), are recorded at their cash value. However, nonmonetary items, those whose worth depends on future economic events (inventories, plant and equipment, receipts-in-advance) are valued at "historical cost"—for assets, the amount originally paid for them less depreciation; for liabilities, the amount received.

To accountants this makes sense. The alternative to historical cost is to estimate the money benefits the company will obtain from its nonmonetary assets and the costs of satisfying its nonmonetary liabilities, and any estimates of future benefits and costs clearly would be subjective and easy to misstate. To an analyst, however, historical cost can be just as arbitrary, since the depreciation formulas used may not relate at all to market conditions.

The use of two valuation methods complicates the comparison of asset and liability values. Two firms with the same numbers might be worth very different amounts.

Example

Different Valuation Methods

The Monetary Company and the Nonmonetary Company both report $10 million of assets on their 1994 balance sheets. Monetary Company's assets are primarily investments in Treasury bills and are carried at market value. Nonmonetary Company's assets are primarily land and buildings purchased ten years ago.

Question: Are the assets of both firms worth the same amount?

Answer: Most probably no! It is likely that Monetary Company's assets are worth close to the $10 million reported since they are carried at market value and probably could be sold for that amount. The value of Nonmonetary Company's assets, however, cannot be determined from the balance sheet. If their real estate is run down and in a poor location, it might be worth considerably less than $10 million. On the other hand, if it is well maintained and well located, its value could be far above the $10 million reported according to GAAP rules.

2. Alternative Numbers for the Same Event

A second problem with GAAP is the flexibility allowed accountants in the way an event may be described. This is considered necessary as it is believed that one rigid means of handling each accounting area might not fit all economic circumstances. Unfortunately, when management has a choice of accounting methods, it does not always choose the one that best describes the economics in question. Rather, managers often choose to put their best face forward—highest income, lowest costs, highest asset values—or to minimize taxes—lowest income, highest costs, lowest asset values. The unfortunate financial analyst, in search of the "truth," must often settle for something else.

Alternative accounting treatments show up throughout the financial statements. Some of the more common examples[9] are:

- Revenue alternatives—differences in the point in a company's economic process (production, sale, delivery, collection) when revenue is recognized (appears) on the income statement.
- Expense alternatives—differences in methods of measuring the use of nonmonetary assets such as inventory (alternatives include LIFO, FIFO, and average cost) and capital equipment (depreciation may be calculated using the straight-line method or one of several accelerated methods).
- Asset alternatives—differences in the treatment of inventory and capital equipment, as above, plus differences in how leases are recorded (as capital or operating leases) and in how acquisitions are handled (using the purchase or pooling-of-interests method).
- Liability alternatives—differences arising from the choice to include certain obligations or to treat them as "off-balance sheet" financing (such as contingent claims and nonconsolidated subsidiaries).

The variety of accounting treatments for a given event often makes it difficult to compare numbers. Two firms, identical except for accounting, might look very different to an analyst not aware of the accounting differences.

Example

Alternate Accounting Treatments

Two companies are identical in every respect except that First Company uses the first-in, first-out (FIFO) method to value its inventories while Last Company uses the last-in, first-out method (LIFO). The sum of beginning-of-year inventory value plus purchases of inventory this year is $800 for both companies; this amount will be allocated between ending inventory and cost of goods sold. However, prices have risen over the years. First Company, applying the lower, earlier prices to the product it sold this year, reported cost of goods sold of $500. Its inventory balance of $300 reflects the most recent price level. Last Company, on the other hand, reported cost of goods sold of $700 based on the higher, more recent prices, and applied earlier prices to value its inventory at $100. Both firms report $1,000 of assets other than inventory.

	First Company	Last Company
Inventory value	$ 300	$ 100
Other assets	1,000	1,000
Total assets	1,300	1,100
Cost of goods sold	500	700

[9] **Observation:** You will recognize some or all of these differences depending on how much accounting you have studied.

Question: Do the two companies look the same to financial analysts?

Answer: No! First Company appears to be more *profitable* since it reports that it produces at a lower cost (cost of goods sold of $500 versus $700) and owns more valuable assets ($1,300 versus $1,100) than Last Company. On the other hand, Last Company seems to be more *efficient*, reporting that it generates the same sales with less need for inventory ($100 versus $300) and total assets ($1,100 versus $1,300). In fact, of course, there is no real difference between the companies. The "difference" is only within the accounting records.

3. Important Information Omitted

With its focus on money transactions between the firm and outside parties, GAAP ignores data that might be of critical interest to some financial analysts. Some examples: Financial accounting does not measure the quality of a company's products and processes, increasingly important determinants of future success. Financial accounting places no value on human resources, yet in an increasingly knowledge-based world, the attitudes and skills of its employees may be among a company's most valuable assets. Financial accounting does not report on backlog of orders, a critical variable for firms with a long production cycle. Financial accounting does not value intangible assets that were not purchased—a company that has developed valuable patents, copyrights, or brand names finds little of that value reflected in its financial data.

Nevertheless, with all its problems, the financial information produced by a company is normally an excellent source of information for describing its financial health. While good analysts are appropriately skeptical and constantly searching for additional data to strengthen their conclusions, most analyses still begin with a thorough going over of the firm's financial statements.

Tax Data

An important stakeholder of every company is government. Governments provide essential services to business firms which enable them to function. These services range from the vital, such as encouraging and preserving a free market economic system or providing police to protect the safety of people and property, to the mundane, such as arranging for garbage collection. It is in the interest of every business that government functions well and that the interaction of business and government be mutually supportive.

In return for the services they provide, governments impose taxes on those they serve. Government services cost money, yet governments often lack the ability to charge directly for their use. Business, like other beneficiaries of government, is expected to pay its fair share.

There are various ways in which a government may elect to tax. Taxes may be imposed on profits, on costs, on value added, on sales, on asset values, or on any other measurement deemed fair and effective. Under the United States federal tax system (and most state and local tax systems as well), the tax most relevant to individuals and businesses is the income tax, a tax based on profits. In this sense, government is the partner of every individual and every business, since it takes a share of everyone's income.

tax evasion—not paying taxes which are owed to a government

tax avoidance—reducing a tax obligation within the framework of the law

If you and several friends were to form a business, you would probably go to some lengths to be sure you were sharing your profits fairly. You would no doubt consider it wrong to give extra income to some of your friends at the expense of the others. While it is indeed wrong to cheat the government out of taxes you legitimately owe, it is not wrong to pay the minimum amount of taxes that is consistent with the law. This is the difference between **tax evasion** and **tax avoidance**. Tax evasion is illegal. It cheats other taxpayers who must pay additional taxes to maintain the level of government services. By contrast, tax avoidance is quite legal and proper. There are many tax professionals who specialize in advising firms how to restructure their activities so less income will be subject to tax and in locating the tax calculation that results in minimum payments. As Justice Learned Hand pointed out:

> Any one may so arrange his affairs that his taxes shall be as low as possible; he is not bound to choose that pattern which will best pay the Treasury; there is not even a patriotic duty to increase one's taxes.[10]

A consistent theme throughout this book is that financial value comes from cash flows. A company that can produce high cash flows for its stakeholders is a valuable firm. Since taxes typically represent a large cash flow that goes to one stakeholder at the expense of the others, it is important for financial managers to understand the basics of the income tax system. In particular:

- Virtually every financial decision changes the amount of taxes the firm or its stakeholders will pay. It is thus impossible to evaluate a decision in financial terms without including the impact of taxes.
- If there are more ways than one to accomplish a goal, and if they differ in their tax impact, the value of the tax differential must enter the decision-making process for the comparison to be complete.[11]
- The government as a stakeholder requires only what is specified by the law, and a business fully satisfies its tax obligation by paying that amount. A firm that overpays its taxes is taking value away from the firm's other stakeholders. By not paying unnecessary taxes, the firm avoids lowering the value of the firm to its other stakeholders.

While we might wish for the certainty of a stable and predictable tax system, in practice tax rules are frequently revised. Taxes are the primary means by which governments fund themselves, and the financial needs of governments constantly change. Taxes are a powerful force to motivate economic decisions, and legisla-

[10] **Reference:** Learned Hand, in *Helvering v. Gregory,* 69 F. 2d 809, 810 (1934).

[11] **Elaboration:** The government recognizes this and often uses the tax code to motivate firms to act in ways judged beneficial to the public welfare. Two examples: A business that locates in an area deemed to be in need of economic revitalization can receive a reduction in its taxes. A business that employs minorities or the underprivileged can also receive a tax reduction. In both cases, it is the hope of the government that these tax savings will offset any other costs involved and make the socially responsible decision the economically more valuable decision as well.

tors regularly introduce new tax rules to change behavior.[12] Even the existing law has changes built in as rates and brackets adjust with the rate of inflation and as various provisions are phased in or out over several years. While the rules and rates used in this chapter are correct at the time of publication and while they are used in the book's examples and problems, they are certain to change. If you have to work with taxes in practice, we advise you to get up-to-date information from the tax authorities, from published tax guides, or from financial advisors.

average tax rate—the single number which, if multiplied by taxable income, produces the total amount of tax

It is important to distinguish between average and marginal tax rates. An **average tax rate** is found by dividing total taxes by total income. It is the one rate which if applied to total income would result in the figure for total taxes.

Example

Average Tax Rate

Tom's income is $30,000 and he must pay $6,000 in income taxes.

Question: What is Tom's average tax rate?

Solution: $6,000/$30,000 = 20%

Answer: Tom's average tax rate is 20%. (Regardless of what formula was actually used to calculate Tom's tax of $6,000, the same result would have been obtained if a single rate of 20% were used.)

marginal tax rate—the tax rate applicable to an incremental dollar of income

By contrast, a **marginal tax rate** is the tax rate that will be applied to the next dollar of income earned.

Example

Marginal Tax Rate

If Tom earns $1.00 more (raising his income to $30,001), he will pay $0.25 in additional taxes (raising his tax bill to $6,000.25).

Question: What is Tom's marginal tax rate?

Solution: $0.25/$1.00 = 25%

Answer: Tom's marginal tax rate is 25%. (Note that Tom's average tax rate has risen. It is now $6,000.25/$30,001 = 20.0001667%.)

flat rate tax system—a tax system with a single rate independent of income level

The simplest income tax system is a **flat rate** system, in which there is only one tax rate regardless of the level of income. In a flat rate system, there is no difference between average and marginal tax rates since there is only one rate.

Example

Flat Rate Tax System

Suppose that taxes are calculated as 20% of income. Megan's income is $60,000. Her tax obligation is therefore:

[12] **Elaboration:** An example is the "investment tax credit," a tax reduction for purchasing plant and equipment. A 7% credit (the business reduced its taxes by 7% of the cost of the property) was first introduced into the law in 1962 to encourage business expansion. In 1975, the credit was increased to 10%. It was removed from the tax code in 1986 as part of the major tax reform of that year, which significantly lowered tax rates in return for doing away with many deductions and credits. As this is written, some legislators are calling for restoring the investment tax credit in some form.

$$20\% \times \$60{,}000 = \underline{\underline{\$12{,}000}}$$

Megan's average tax rate is:

$$\$12{,}000/60{,}000 = \underline{\underline{20\%}}$$

Megan's marginal tax rate is also 20% since she would pay 20% tax on an additional $1.00 of income.

progressive tax system—a tax system in which the tax rate rises with income level

The U.S. income tax system is **progressive,** with the tax rate rising as income goes up. This is an attempt to be just by imposing greater taxes on those more able to pay. Under this system, income is divided into "brackets" with a different rate used to tax each bracket. In a progressive system, there can be a difference between average and marginal tax rates since there is more than one rate.

Example

Progressive Tax System

Now suppose that taxes are calculated by the following formula:

10% of the first $25,000 of income, plus
20% of the second $25,000 of income, plus
30% of all income over $50,000.

Megan's income is $60,000. Her tax obligation is:

10%	×	$25,000	=	$2,500
+ 20%	×	25,000	=	5,000
+ 30%	×	10,000	=	3,000
		$60,000		$10,500

Megan's average tax rate is:

$$\$10{,}500/60{,}000 = \underline{\underline{17.50\%}}$$

Megan's marginal tax rate, however, is 30% since she would pay 30% tax on an additional $1 of income.

Because of the progressive nature of U.S. tax rates and the complexity of determining taxable income, it can be quite time-consuming to calculate the correct amount of tax that results from a given transaction. To avoid unnecessary (but unfortunately very real) complications in the illustrations and problems of this book, we have chosen to treat all businesses as corporations subject to a flat tax rate of 34% or 35%, rates in the U.S. tax code that apply to many corporations.[13]

The Need to Compare Numbers

A common error in working with data is to use a number out of context. It does a doctor little good to know a person's weight, for example 150 pounds, and nothing else about the person. A weight of 150 pounds could be too low, too high, or quite good, but to determine this the doctor must have some other information

[13] **To delve further:** More detail about how income taxes are calculated in the United States is provided in Appendix 4B, "The U.S. Personal Income Tax System," and Appendix 4C, "The U.S. Corporate Income Tax System."

about the person (for example, height). In the same way, we must always make comparisons to make sense out of financial data. It is impossible to make a judgment about a business using one number alone.

Example

Attempting a Judgment with Only One Number

A company has a cash balance of $1 million.

Question: Is this cash balance sufficient? too high? too low?

Answer: There is no way to know without at least one other piece of data to compare to the $1 million so we can set the cash balance in context. One alternative is to compare the cash balance to the firm's size. Is it a small proprietorship?—if so, $1 million is likely much too large a cash balance. Is the company a giant corporation?—if so, $1 million is likely much too small. Another alternative is to look at the level and predictability of cash inflows and outflows. How much does the firm need to cover its day-to-day needs? Each comparison provides some insight; without comparison, the cash number is interesting perhaps, but not very informative.

There is a series of natural relationships between the financial numbers of any company, just as there are inherent relationships between a person's height and weight, or arm length and leg length, etc. A doctor uses an understanding of these relationships to spot those that seem to be abnormal. In a similar manner, as you learn more about which numbers to compare, you will develop the background and skill to locate many financial abnormalities within a business. The most common forms of financial comparison are common size financial statements, in which the numbers are recast to be percentages of a total, and financial ratios, in which one number is divided by another to put it into context.[14]

Three types of comparisons are generally used to test the meaning of financial and other data: (1) benchmark comparisons, (2) time-series comparisons, and (3) cross-section comparisons.

1. Benchmark Comparisons

benchmark comparison—comparison to a norm which is valid across many companies and/or industries

Whenever we compare a number to some standard value we are making a **benchmark comparison.** A benchmark is a norm that is valid across many companies and industries. For example, the number 2.0 has been a benchmark for the current ratio for many years. Financial analysts seek benchmark comparisons when they believe there is a universal relationship governing the numbers in question. However, because of the differences between companies and industries, there have been few useful financial benchmarks with which many analysts have felt comfortable.

[14] **To delve further:** More detail about common size financial statements and financial ratios is provided in Appendix 4D, "Analysis of Financial Accounting Data," and Appendix 4E, "The Interrelationship of Ratios." Also, at the end of the book is a "Summary of Financial Ratios" to be used as a quick reference.

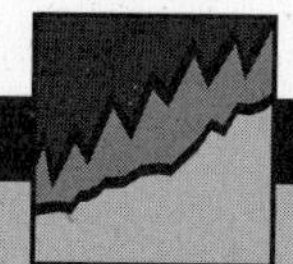

IMPROVING FINANCE'S PROCESSES

Financial Benchmarking at Southern Pacific

The Southern Pacific Transportation Company uses railroad industry data published by the United States Interstate Commerce Commission (ICC) in a very creative way. Each year, the ICC publishes its R1 report, a summary of financial and operating data from major U.S. railroads. Included in the report are detailed expense numbers for each company, that permit Southern Pacific to compare itself to its competitors. Southern Pacific uses the numbers to locate and prioritize opportunities for improvement and to support the company's shared belief that improvement is possible. Over the next decade, Southern Pacific is aiming to match or beat the best competitor in each cost category, which would make it the lowest-cost major western railroad in the United States.

competitive benchmarking—using the best example available, regardless of source, as the firm's target

Recently a new kind of benchmarking technique has been used by many companies to improve the quality of their products and services. In **competitive benchmarking,** we look for the *best* example of what we are trying to accomplish and set our goal to match or (preferably) exceed that standard. To illustrate, the manager of a real estate management company responsible for cleaning office buildings must set a standard for the level of cleanliness to strive for. Traditional benchmarking would have the manager compare the company's cleaning operation to those of similar real estate companies. Competitive benchmarking, on the other hand, would have the manager search for the best cleaning operation in any industry—perhaps in a hospital or in the "clean room" of a highly dirt-sensitive manufacturing facility. Some companies are now beginning to use competitive benchmarking to set financial standards and refusing to let traditional comparisons be their guide.

2. Time-Series Comparisons

time-series comparison—a tracking of some number across time to see if it is changing, and if so, the direction and amount of change

Whenever we can calculate measures for more than one year, we can study their trends across time. This is a **time-series comparison.** We can see which measures are deteriorating and which are improving. Often a time-series comparison gives us warning of a developing problem so we can take action before the problem becomes serious.

3. Cross-Section Comparisons

cross-section comparison—comparison of some number to equivalent data from other companies or from the industry over a common period of time

Whenever we have the same measure over a common period of time from more than one company we can make a **cross-section comparison.** We use a common time period to hold the environment constant. Then we can conclude that differences between measures must reflect differences between the firms and not just different points in the business cycle. We must also take care to be sure that other differences between the firms—size, product mix, markets, manufacturing technology, accounting policy, etc.—are not so great as to make comparisons meaningless. In part to overcome this problem, it is common to compare a company's

industry-average ratio—a ratio calculated by averaging the ratios of firms within an industry

ratios to **industry-average ratios.** This generally improves the analysis as it forces the comparison to reflect the overall economics of the industry in question.

It is important to note, however, that industry ratios are rarely good guides for financial managers. In some industries, even the "best" firms might be doing poorly, or business practice might not be up to date. And even if the industry is well managed, comparing a firm to the industry averages simply tests to see if the firm is average. Good financial managers do not use averages as their guide, for this leads to an average (mediocre) firm. This is another reason why the use of competitive benchmarking is becoming more and more widespread. By comparing themselves to the best, regardless of industry, businesses can break away from traditional thinking and identify possibilities for improvement.

Analysts normally calculate a company's ratios directly from its financial statements. To make a comparison with other companies and with industry groups, however, additional data are needed. Several information services collect financial data and report common ratios of companies and industries. Among the most popular sources are Standard & Poor's, Moody's Investor Services, Robert Morris Associates, and Dun & Bradstreet.

Stephen Lewis sat down at his desk, pulled out a pad of paper, and started to summarize his thoughts. On the way back from the doctor's office, he had contemplated the doctor's advice, and the connection between his personal health and the company's health was becoming clearer.

Diagnosing a company's problems was very similar to diagnosing a person's health problems. To understand his business and locate its problems it was necessary to have accurate data about the attitudes of key stakeholders, the functioning of key processes, the cash flows and costs of running the business, the overall financial performance of the firm, and the company's tax obligations. Stephen wrote down each item on a separate sheet of paper and listed underneath the information his company was currently collecting and using. It was clear there were significant gaps.

Just then the phone rang. It was the firm's banker calling back to ask whether Stephen had made any progress toward resolving the bank's cash flow concerns. "I sure have," Stephen replied with a smile. "It will be a couple of days before I can tell you how we'll lose the weight, but now I know where to look to find those extra 20 pounds!"

Summary of Key Points

- **Identify the meaning of *financial analysis* and the data used for financial decision making.** Financial analysis is the use of financial and other data to study the financial health of an organization. It is of interest to all stakeholders since they all benefit if the firm remains vibrant and healthy. It is of particular use to management as it can help uncover problems that deserve management's attention within the firm's finances. It makes use of data that conform both to the traditional economic-financial theory of the firm and to recent insights into the contributions of people and processes to financial health.
- **Understand the importance of collecting information about customer and employee satisfaction.** A first source of data is surveying customers and employees to discover their level of satisfaction. Customer satisfaction is an important determinant of a company's revenues. Employees' satisfaction affects their ability and willingness to use resources wisely and to improve the firm's processes to serve customers, improve quality, and reduce costs.
- **Appreciate the necessity of measuring the performance of financial processes.** Companies and their finance functions collect information on processes to locate opportunities for improvement. Through the use of charts and summary numbers such as the number of failures, six sigma performance, and cycle time, they can identify processes that are functioning poorly and can be improved.
- **Prepare a cash flow table and recognize different types of costs.** A cash flow table is a spreadsheet organizing cash flows by what causes them and when they take place. The managerial accounting system is used to obtain the data for internal decision making. It is important to isolate cash flows and to understand types of costs to insure that the correct data are used for each type of analysis.
- **Realize that financial accounting data are a useful but imperfect source of information.** An important source of data is the firm's financial statements. However, GAAP rules permit choices in the preparation of accounting numbers. Analysts must understand how the statements were prepared and must be careful in comparing financial data among firms. Particular concerns include the use of both monetary and historical cost valuation, LIFO vs. FIFO inventory treatment, differing depreciation formulas, etc. Analysts must also be alert to spot incorrect data.
- **Determine average and marginal tax rates.** A large part of a firm's income is paid to governments in the form of taxes. By understanding marginal and average tax rates and the workings of the tax code, financial managers can avoid overpayment and minimize the amount taken away from other stakeholders.
- **Understand why it is important to compare numbers when doing financial analysis.** Financial analysis typically involves comparisons since one number out of context is usually meaningless. We force comparisons of financial data by looking at numbers in the context of common size financial statements and ratios. We also compare numbers to benchmarks, across time, and to other comparable companies.

Questions

1. Why is it critical to have theory prior to collecting data about a company?
2. In what ways do the attitudes of customers and employees affect the financial worth of a business?
3. Identify a financial process. What information would you like to have in order to learn if it is functioning properly?
4. What is the meaning of "six sigma"? How does it differ from the normal success rate of human activity?
5. Distinguish between cash flows and accrual accounting data. When would you use each?
6. Give an example of each of the following costs:
   a. Total cost
   b. Average cost
   c. Marginal cost
   d. Incremental cost
   e. Sunk cost
   f. Opportunity cost
   g. Variable cost
   h. Fixed cost
   i. Direct cost
   j. Indirect cost
7. What is a cost driver? How is it used in cost allocation?
8. Why is it often difficult to compare the financial statements of similar companies?
9. What is the difference between tax evasion and tax avoidance? Give an example of each.

10. Distinguish between an average tax rate and a marginal tax rate. When would you use each number?
11. You have just learned that a company has 10,000 employees and have been asked to determine if this is good or bad. What would you like to learn to make that judgment?
12. Why is competitive benchmarking superseding traditional benchmarking?

Problems

1. **(Cash flow table)** A company is investigating an activity that would generate the following incremental cash flows over the next five years:

Purchase machinery immediately	$100,000
Increase revenues in years 1–2	30,000 per year
Increase revenues in years 3–5	50,000 per year
Reduce costs in years 1–5	20,000 per year
Pay additional taxes in years 2–4	10,000 per year

Prepare a cash flow table to summarize this information.

2. **(Cash flow table)** A company is investigating an activity that would generate the following incremental cash flows over the next four years:

Purchase an office building immediately	$250,000
Increase revenues in years 1–4	85,000 per year
Reduce costs in years 1–4	30,000 per year
Pay additional taxes in years 2–4	20,000 per year
Sell building in year 4	400,000
Pay tax when building is sold	50,000

Prepare a cash flow table to summarize this information.

3. **(Total, average, and marginal costs)** A company estimates the following costs to produce the first five units of its only product:

Unit 1	$100
Unit 2	90
Unit 3	83
Unit 4	79
Unit 5	76

a. What is the total cost to produce the five units?
b. What is the average cost per unit for the first five units?
c. What is the marginal cost to produce the second unit?
d. What is the marginal cost to produce the fifth unit?

4. **(Total, average, and marginal costs)** A company estimates the following costs to produce the first seven units of its only product:

Unit 1	$60
Unit 2	51
Unit 3	44
Unit 4	39
Unit 5	36
Unit 6	35
Unit 7	35

a. What is the total cost to produce the seven units?
b. What is the average cost per unit for the first seven units?
c. What is the marginal cost to produce the sixth unit?
d. What is the marginal cost to produce the seventh unit?

5. **(Activity-based accounting)** A company's finance department spends $10,000 each year producing the company's payroll. The company has 5,000 employees, each of whom receives a weekly paycheck (assume 52 weeks per year). Calculate the cost of the finance department to be allocated to each paycheck.
6. **(Activity-based accounting)** A company's purchasing department spends $500 each year buying a particular bolt used in the assembly of one of its products. The company buys 100,000 of these bolts annually, and each unit of product requires ten bolts. Calculate the cost of the purchasing department to be allocated to each product.

APPENDIX 4A

BREAK-EVEN ANALYSIS

break-even point—the level of sales at which revenues equal operating costs so that operating profit (EBIT) equals zero

contribution margin—the net amount brought into the firm by the production and sale of one unit of its product

contribution percentage—the net amount brought into the firm by the production and sale of one dollar of its product

A firm's **break-even point** is the level of sales at which operating profit (earnings before interest and taxes, or EBIT) exactly equals zero. With a lower level of sales the firm loses money, as it does not bring in enough to cover its costs. At levels of sales above the break-even point the firm is profitable, since the higher level of inflows now more than fully covers its costs.

Every time a firm produces and sells one unit of its product, it brings in a certain amount of money. This amount, the excess of sales price over the unit's variable cost, is called the firm's **contribution margin.**[1] An alternative measure of the same thing is **contribution percentage,** the amount of money brought in per dollar of sales.

These concepts are often captured by some simple algebra:

Let: P = Price at which each unit is sold
Q = Quantity of units produced and sold
S = Sales revenue in dollars = PQ
V = Variable production cost per unit
v = variable cost percentage (the fraction of each sales dollar which goes to variable costs)
F = Fixed cost level

Then: *Contribution margin* = $P - V$
Contribution percentage = $(1 - v)$

Examples

Contribution Margin and Contribution Percentage

A firm produces and sells only one product. The variable cost to make each unit is \$3.00. Units of product are sold for \$5.00 each.

Question: What is the firm's contribution margin?

Solution steps: Producing and selling one unit brings in \$5.00 and costs \$3.00. The difference is \$2.00.

(By formula: P − V = \$5.00 − \$3.00 = \$2.00)

[1] **Observation:** Of course, if the firm sells its product for less than the variable cost, its contribution margin is negative, and it will never be profitable!

Answer: The firm's contribution margin is $2.00.

Question: What is the firm's contribution percentage?

Solution steps: Since $5.00 of sales requires the firm to spend $3.00 on variable costs, each dollar of sales is accompanied by

$$\$3.00/\$5.00 = .60$$

or 60 cents of variable costs. This leaves 40 cents per dollar, or 40% as contribution.

$$\text{(By formula: } v = \$3.00/\$5.00 = .60$$
$$1 - v = 1 - .60 = .40 = 40\%)$$

Answer: The firm's contribution percentage is 40%.

It is common to measure a company's break-even point in units produced and sold (Q_{be}) and also in dollars of sales (S_{be}). Continuing with the algebra, at the break-even point, EBIT equals zero. Using unit quantities:

$$\text{EBIT} = \text{Revenue} - \text{Variable costs} - \text{Fixed costs} = 0$$
$$PQ_{be} - VQ_{be} - F = 0$$
$$Q_{be}(P - V) - F = 0$$
$$Q_{be}(P - V) = F$$
$$Q_{be} = \frac{F}{P - V}$$

Therefore, measured in units, a company's break-even quantity, Q_{be}, equals its fixed cost divided by its contribution margin.

Redoing the algebra using dollar quantities:

$$\text{EBIT} = \text{Revenue} - \text{Variable costs} - \text{Fixed costs} = 0$$
$$S_{be} - vS_{be} - F = 0$$
$$S_{be}(1 - v) - F = 0$$
$$S_{be}(1 - v) = F$$
$$S_{be} = \frac{F}{1 - v}$$

Therefore, measured in dollars, a company's break-even sales, S_{be}, equals its fixed cost divided by its contribution percentage.

Examples

The Break-Even Point

A firm produces and sells only one product. It costs the company $3.00 to make each unit, which is then sold for $5.00. In addition, the firm must pay $100,000 per year in fixed costs.

Question: What is the firm's break-even point in units?

Solution steps: Each unit produced and sold brings in a contribution margin of \$2.00. With \$100,000 of fixed costs to cover, the firm will have to sell 50,000 units, each netting \$2.00 to exactly cover the fixed costs and leave zero EBIT.

or, applying the break-even relationship:

$$Q_{be} = F/(P - V) = \$100{,}000/(\$5 - \$3)$$
$$= \$100{,}000/\$2 = 50{,}000 \text{ units}$$

Answer: The firm's break-even point is 50,000 units.

Question: What is the firm's break-even point in dollars?

Solution steps: Sixty cents of each dollar of sales goes toward variable costs, leaving a contribution percentage of 40%. With \$100,000 of fixed costs to cover, the firm will have to reach sales of \$250,000 so that the 40% is sufficient to exactly cover the fixed costs and leave zero EBIT.

Applying the break-even relationship:

$$S_{be} = F/(1 - v) = \$100{,}000/(1 - .60)$$
$$= \$100{,}000/.40 = \$250{,}000$$

Answer: The firm's break-even point is \$250,000 of sales.

Figure 4A.1 illustrates the break-even model graphically. Revenues begin at zero and rise directly with sales. Expenses begin at F, the firm's fixed costs and rise with sales as variable costs are added in. As long as sales price (P, the slope of the revenue line) exceeds variable cost (V, the slope of the expense line), revenues will eventually overtake costs. The level of sales at which that happens is the firm's break-even point.

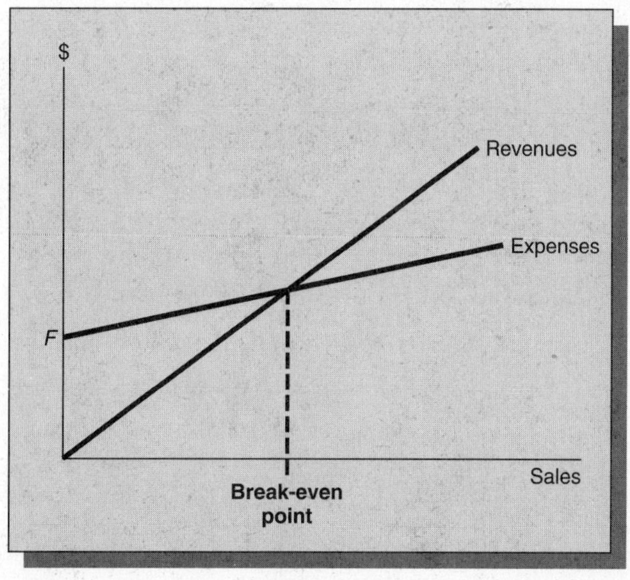

FIGURE 4A.1
The break-even model. A company breaks even when its revenues equal its expenses.

Because the break-even model connects the firm's sales volume to its expenses and profits, it is sometimes referred to as the "cost-volume-profit" model.

The break-even model is commonly used to get a sense of whether a new product would be financially viable.

Examples

Testing a New Product Using the Break-Even Model

A company is analyzing a proposal to produce and sell a new product. The product would cost $25.00 in variable costs to produce. Fixed costs to support the product are estimated to be $300,000 per year.

Question: If the firm plans to price the product at $40.00 each, how many units of the new product must be sold per year to break even?

Solution steps: Applying the break-even relationship:

$$Q_{be} = F/(P - V) = \$300{,}000/(\$40.00 - \$25.00)$$
$$= \$300{,}000/\$15.00 = 20{,}000 \text{ units}$$

Answer: The firm will break even if it can sell 20,000 units per year.

Question: If the firm's marketing analysts forecast the firm will only be able to sell 16,000 units per year, what price must be set in order to break even?

Solution steps: Applying the break-even relationship:

$$Q_{be} = F/(P - V)$$
$$16{,}000 = \$300{,}000/(P - \$25.00)$$
$$P - \$25 = \$300{,}000/16{,}000 = \$18.75$$
$$P = \$18.75 + \$25.00 = \$43.75$$

Answer: The firm will break even if it can price its product at $43.75.

The break-even model is also used to test the sensitivity of the firm's profits to changes in price or costs.

Examples

Testing Sensitivity Using the Break-Even Model

A company is worried about price competition in the market for its only product. Currently, the firm sells its product for $12, and pays $8 in variable costs to produce it. Fixed costs are $60,000 per year.

Question: What is the break-even quantity now?

Solution steps: Applying the break-even relationship:

$$Q_{be} = F/(P - V) = \$60{,}000/(\$12 - \$8)$$
$$= \$60{,}000/\$4 = 15{,}000 \text{ units}$$

Answer: The firm's break-even point is now 15,000 units.

Question: If the company is forced to lower its price to $11.00 per unit, what will happen to the break-even point?

Solution steps: Applying the break-even relationship:

$$Q_{be} = F/(P - V) = \$60{,}000/(\$11 - \$8)$$
$$= \$60{,}000/\$3 = 20{,}000 \text{ units}$$

Answer: At a price of \$11.00, the firm will have to produce and sell 20,000 units to break even.

Question: By how much must annual fixed costs be reduced to prevent the price decrease from raising the firm's break-even point?

Solution steps: Applying the break-even relationship:

$$Q_{be} = F/(P - V)$$
$$15{,}000 = F/(\$11 - \$8) = F/\$3$$
$$F = 15{,}000 \times \$3 = \$45{,}000$$

Answer: If the firm can reduce its fixed costs to \$45,000 per year, it can keep its break-even point at 15,000 units.

While the break-even model can provide useful insights into cost-volume-profit relationships, it does suffer from some important limitations:

- The model does not look across time periods but only compares numbers within a given period, for example a year. However, each year is rarely like any other. At best, break-even analysis can examine the immediate year, or a representative year.
- The model is a short-run tool only, as no costs are fixed in the long run.
- The model assumes that costs can be clearly classified into fixed and variable, something that is not always easily done.
- One-time cash flows, such as resource acquisition costs or salvage values, do not easily fit the model.
- The model is designed for linear cost and revenue functions, yet most firms do not face a constant variable cost percentage nor a constant sales price regardless of volume. Variable costs tend to follow the classic U shape: costs are high at low volumes, decrease as higher volume leads to efficiencies, and then shoot up again as even higher volume strains the firm's facilities. Unit prices tend to be low at low sales levels if discounted pricing is used to attract the first customers, tend to increase as volume reaches a "normal" level, and then tend to fall off again at high sales levels as markets become saturated and new demand must be stimulated.

Problems

1. **(Contribution margin and contribution percentage)** A company sells its one product for \$30 per unit. What are the firm's contribution margin and contribution percentage if the variable cost to produce the product is:

a. $18?
b. $23?
c. $27?
d. $32?

2. **(Contribution margin and contribution percentage)** A company produces its one product for a variable cost of $75 per unit. What are the firm's contribution margin and contribution percentage if it can sell the product for:

    a. $75?
    b. $85?
    c. $100?
    d. $150?

3. **(Break-even point)** A company produces its one product for a variable cost of $40 per unit. Fixed costs are $500,000 per year. What is the firm's break-even sales in units and dollars if it sells the product for:

    a. $35?
    b. $50?
    c. $65?
    d. $80?

4. **(Break-even point)** A company sells its one product for $150 per unit. Fixed costs are $1 million per year. What is the firm's break-even sales in units and dollars if its unit variable cost is:

    a. $115?
    b. $130?
    c. $145?
    d. $160?

5. **(Break-even point)** A company's fixed costs are $750,000 per year. What is the firm's break-even sales in dollars if it produces its one product at a variable cost percentage of:

    a. 30%?
    b. 40%?
    c. 50%?
    d. 60%?

6. **(Break-even point)** A company produces its one product at a variable cost percentage of 75%. What is the firm's break-even sales in dollars if annual fixed costs are:

    a. $ 300,000?
    b. $ 500,000?
    c. $ 1,000,000?
    d. $ 2,500,000?

7. **(Testing a new product)** A company is working on a new product that will cost $80 in variable costs to produce. Annual fixed costs associated with the product are estimated to be $500,000. How many units per year will the firm have to sell to break even if it prices its product at:

    a. $ 85?
    b. $ 100?
    c. $ 125?
    d. $ 140?

8. **(Testing a new product)** A company is working on a new product with estimated variable cost of $35 and annual fixed costs of $400,000. At what price must the firm sell the product to just break even if its marketing people estimate annual sales of:

    a. 10,000 units?
    b. 15,000 units?
    c. 25,000 units?
    d. 40,000 units?

9. **(Testing sensitivity)** A company sells its one product for $50.00 per unit. Annual fixed costs are $1 million and variable cost is $37.50 per unit. Calculate the firm's break-even point (each case is separate):

    a. Now
    b. If sales price can be increased to $60.00
    c. If variable costs increase to $40.00
    d. If fixed costs decrease to $950,000

10. **(Testing sensitivity)** A company sells its one product for $200 per unit. Annual fixed costs are $2 million and variable cost is $175 per unit. Calculate the firm's break-even point (each case is separate):

    a. Now
    b. If sales price is cut to $190
    c. If variable costs decrease to $170
    d. If fixed costs increase to $2,250,000

APPENDIX 4B

THE U.S. PERSONAL INCOME TAX SYSTEM

We look at income taxes levied on individuals for two reasons. First, individuals lend money to, and invest in, business firms. In return they hope to receive income in the form of interest, dividends, and capital gains. Since this income is taxed, they do not keep all that is paid to them. The way in which their income is taxed determines investors' ultimate after-tax returns and affects their decisions to invest in the first place.

Second, as we saw in Chapter 2, the majority of business firms in the United States are legally organized as proprietorships or partnerships. Income from proprietorships and partnerships is reported by the owners and partners on their personal income tax returns, and taxes are calculated at personal tax rates. Thus, it is the personal tax system and not the corporate tax system that applies to most businesses.

1. Gross Income

gross income—a tax term referring to total income

ordinary income—a tax term referring to income from providing goods and services

capital gains income—a tax term referring to income from asset sales

Gross income is the total income of an individual prior to subtracting certain adjustments, deductions, and exemptions permitted under the law. It is the sum of (1) **ordinary income,** the income earned from providing services and products to employers or customers, and (2) **capital gains income,** the profit or loss from selling an asset for a different price than its current value on the individual's tax records. Ordinary income and capital gains income must be separately identified as there is a ceiling to the tax rate for capital gains.[1]

Income must be further subdivided into three categories: (1) earned income, (2) investment income, and (3) passive income. Within each category, net profit or loss is calculated. The income from all categories that show a profit is then added together and becomes "gross income." Thus a loss from one type of income may not be used to offset income of another category and reduce taxes.[2] Instead, losses

[1] **Elaboration:** Prior to the 1986 tax act, capital gains on assets held for more than six months were taxed at only 40% of the rate applicable to ordinary income. When Congress lowered tax rates in 1986, it was feared that 40% of a much lower tax rate would be too low, and the special treatment of these "long-term capital gains" was eliminated. Presidential candidate George Bush made the establishment of a 15% rate on long-term capital gains a campaign pledge in 1988; as a compromise, Congress in 1990 established 28% as the maximum tax rate on capital gains.

[2] **Elaboration:** There are exceptions to this rule for those with limited incomes.

earned income—a tax term referring to income from personal services

investment income—a tax term referring to income from investment in financial assets

passive income—a tax term referring to income from business activities in which the individual plays little part

tax shelter—an investment whose purpose is to generate losses to reduce taxable income, hence taxes

get a different treatment depending on which income category they come from. **Earned income**[3] consists of wages, tips, and profits from a proprietorship or partnership in which the individual is an active participant. **Investment income** is earnings from investment activities including interest, dividends, and capital gains. **Passive income** is earnings from limited partnerships or other business activities in which the individual plays a negligible role. (Passive activities include most businesses set up as **tax shelters** designed solely to generate **paper losses.** By preventing these losses from offsetting other income, the three-part split of income makes most tax shelters worthless.)

Interest received from investing in state and local government bonds is generally exempt from U.S. taxes.[4] These **municipal bonds** can therefore carry a lower interest rate than comparable U.S. government or corporate bonds which are taxed by the federal government.

Examples

Municipal Bonds

Jeff, who lives in Concord, New Hampshire, is in the 28% federal tax bracket. He is choosing between a General Motors bond yielding 6.75% and a State of New Hampshire bond yielding 5.00%.

Question: Which bond provides the higher after-tax yield?

Solution steps:

1. Interest from the GM bond will be taxed at 28% leaving:

$$6.75\% - 28\% \ (6.75\%)$$
$$= 6.75\% - 1.89\% = \underline{\underline{4.86\%}}$$

after taxes.

2. The New Hampshire (municipal) bond pays $\underline{\underline{5.00\%}}$, and none of that will be taken away by taxes.

Answer: Jeff should choose the $\underline{\underline{\text{municipal bond}}}$.

Question: How high would the yield on the GM bond have to be before Jeff would prefer it to the municipal?

Solution steps: Jeff pays 28% in taxes, and keeps the other 72% of the interest on the GM bond. The after-tax yields would be the same if:

---

[3] **Observation:** The name is a bit misleading since there are those who would argue that all an individual's income is earned, not just the part that comes from personal work activities.

[4] **Elaboration:** Reciprocally, interest on U.S. government bonds is generally exempt from state and local income taxes. While this relationship had a legal beginning as a result of interpretations of the U.S. Constitution, its practical effect is to permit states and municipalities to borrow at a lower-than-market rate of interest to finance public projects. Also, most states and cities do not tax interest from bonds issued within that state. Thus, for example, to a resident of New York City, a municipal bond issued within New York State is "triple tax free" since no income tax has to be paid to the federal, state, or city governments.

$$
\begin{aligned}
\text{After-tax yield on GM bond} &= \text{After-tax yield on NH bond}\\
\text{GM Yield} - 28\%\ (\text{GM Yield}) &= 5.00\%\\
(100\% - 28\%)\ \text{GM Yield} &= 5.00\%\\
72\% \bullet \text{GM Yield} &= 5.00\%\\
\text{GM Yield} &= 5.00\%/.72 = \underline{\underline{6.94\%}}
\end{aligned}
$$

Answer: Jeff should choose the GM bond if its yield were above 6.94%.

paper loss—a loss according to tax calculations not accompanied by a similar loss of cash or market value

municipal bond—a bond issued by any government or government agency other than the federal government

adjusted gross income—a tax term referring to gross income less permitted subtractions

2. Adjusted Gross Income

From gross income, individuals are permitted to subtract contributions to retirement plans, alimony paid, and, if they are self-employed, the cost of health insurance policies. This means that health insurance and retirement plan contributions are not subject to tax, encouraging people to provide for their safety and old age. The subtraction of alimony is allowed since it is included as income on the tax return of the person receiving it. These adjustments reduce the income number on which tax will be calculated. The resulting subtotal is called **adjusted gross income.**

3. Deductions and Exemptions

Next, individuals are permitted to subtract their unreimbursed medical expenses (above 7.5% of adjusted gross income); taxes paid to state and local governments; interest paid on home mortgages (up to a limit); charitable contributions; allowable moving expenses; some job expenses not paid by employers (above 2% of adjusted gross income); and the amount of any significant unreimbursed losses

"Now, let's turn to page *two* of the 1040 form. . . ."

itemized deductions—a tax term referring to a detailed listing of expenses permitted as subtractions from income

standard deduction—a tax term referring to a statutory number that may be used instead of itemizing deductions

exemptions—a tax term referring to family size which determines a subtraction from income

taxable income—a tax term referring to the amount of income subject to tax

due to theft, fire, or some other casualty. Individuals may subtract all of their deductions, but if these **itemized deductions** are below a certain threshold, they may subtract a **standard deduction** instead. For 1994, the standard deduction is $3,800 for a single taxpayer and $6,350 for a married couple filing a joint return. In addition, individuals determine their number of **exemptions,** one for each family member. Each exemption means a further subtraction from income; in 1994 the number is $2,450 per exemption (the amount declines at high levels of adjusted gross income). The resulting total becomes **taxable income.**

4. Personal Tax Rates

Taxable income is used to determine the tax an individual owes. For the year 1994, the rates and brackets for the personal income tax are:

Single Individuals

15% of the first $22,750 of taxable income
+ 28% of taxable income from $22,750 to $55,100
+ 31% of taxable income from $55,100 to $115,000
+ 36% of taxable income from $115,000 to $250,000
+ 39.6% of taxable income over $250,000

Married Couples Filing a Joint Return

15% of the first $38,000 of taxable income
+ 28% of taxable income from $38,000 to $91,850
+ 31% of taxable income from $91,850 to $140,000
+ 36% of taxable income from $140,000 to $250,000
+ 39.6% of taxable income over $250,000

Under current law, the brackets change every year with inflation so that a taxpayer whose income rises solely due to inflation will not be pushed into a higher tax bracket. Prior to the adoption of this provision in 1986, individuals could easily become the victims of "bracket creep," in which their taxes rose faster than their income. This lowered real disposable income, depressing spending and the level of economic activity. Critics also pointed out that the government now had a motivation to actually encourage inflation since the resulting bracket creep provided government with an "inflation dividend" of higher tax revenues without any need to enact an unpopular tax increase.

Example

Calculating Personal Tax: Single Individual

Whitney, who is unmarried, calculates her 1994 taxable income to be $58,000.

Question: What will her tax obligation be?

Solution steps:

15% × $22,750	=	$ 3,412.50
+ 28% × ($55,100 − $22,750)	=	9,058.00
+ 31% × ($58,000 − $55,100)	=	899.00
		$13,369.50

Answer: Whitney will pay $13,369.50 in U.S. income taxes on her 1994 income.

Example

Calculating Personal Tax: Married Couple Filing Jointly

Betty and her husband, John, calculate their joint 1994 taxable income to be $95,000.

Question: What will their tax obligation be?

Solution steps:

15% × $ 38,000	=	$ 5,700.00
+ 28% × ($91,850 – $38,000)	=	15,078.00
+ 31% × ($95,000 – $91,850)	=	976.50
		$21,754.50

Answer: Betty and John will pay $21,754.50 in U.S. income taxes on their 1994 income.

5. Payment of Taxes

Even though individuals can wait until April 15 of the following year to file their tax return, they must pay their taxes as they earn money throughout the year, estimating how much they will owe by year-end. Wage earners do this by having taxes withheld from their regular paychecks. Self-employed individuals must make "estimated payments" four times during the year. If the full amount of tax has not been paid by year-end, the additional amount due is paid with the tax return.[5] If too much has been paid, a refund is due.[6]

Problems

1. **(Average and marginal tax rates)** Audrey Barton has taxable income of $75,000. She is unmarried.
   a. What is Audrey's average tax rate?
   b. What is Audrey's marginal tax rate?
2. **(Average and marginal tax rates)** Cheryl and David Enders have a joint taxable income of $110,000.
   a. What is their average tax rate?
   b. What is their marginal tax rate?
3. **(Municipal bonds)** Fred Graham, who is unmarried and lives in Dallas, Texas, forecasts his 1994 taxable income to be $40,000. He has saved $1000 and is thinking about buying either a General Motors Corporation bond yielding 7.00% or a State of Texas municipal bond yielding 5.50%.
   a. What is Fred's marginal tax rate?
   b. Which bond is better for Fred?
   c. At what tax bracket would Fred be indifferent to the two bonds?
   d. How much would the GM bond have to yield for Fred to be indifferent between it and the 5.50% Texas bond?

---

[5] **Elaboration:** A penalty is assessed if the underpayment at any point during the year is greater than 10% of the amount of tax owed as of that date.

[6] **Observation:** Even though many people look forward to receiving a tax refund, overpaying is a poor strategy. When you study the time value of money in Chapter 5, you will learn that there is a cost to paying an obligation earlier than its due date. By overpaying taxes, the individual loses value since it is the government that earns interest on the amount of the overpayment rather than the individual!

4. **(Municipal bonds)** Hilda Ibsen, who is unmarried and lives in Tacoma, Washington, forecasts her 1994 taxable income to be $90,000. She has saved $1,000 and is thinking about buying either a Boeing Corporation bond yielding 7.50% or a State of Washington municipal bond yielding 5.75%.
   a. What is Hilda's marginal tax rate?
   b. Which bond is better for Hilda?
   c. At what tax bracket would Hilda be indifferent to the two bonds?
   d. How much would the state of Washington bond have to yield for Hilda to be indifferent between it and the 7.50% Boeing bond?
5. **(Personal tax liability)** Jim King works selling life insurance in Los Angeles. In 1994 his salary was $65,000. Jim also received $1,000 of dividends from Texaco stock, $2,000 of interest from a city of Los Angeles bond, and $3,000 of interest from a corporate bond. His itemized deductions totalled $2,000. Jim is single and has only himself as an exemption.
   a. Determine Jim's U.S. federal taxable income.
   b. What is Jim's tax liability to the federal government for 1994?
6. **(Personal tax liability)** In 1994 Lee Nolan earned $45,000 from her job and her husband, Mike, earned $40,000 operating his own business. Mike contributed $4,500 of his income to his retirement plan. The Nolans also received $3,000 in interest and capital gains of $7,000 from investing in corporate bonds but sustained a $2,000 capital loss when Lee's brother-in law's hot stock tip proved to be not so hot. Because of high medical expenses, their itemized deductions totalled $15,000. Lee and Mike have two children.
   a. Determine the Nolan's U.S. federal taxable income.
   b. What is their tax liability to the federal government for 1994?

APPENDIX 4C

THE U.S. CORPORATE INCOME TAX SYSTEM

The calculation of corporate taxable income begins with the financial accounting income statement, since corporate taxable income derives from accounting income. To a large extent, taxable income is the same as before-tax accounting income. However, there are various differences between accounting and tax income, especially with respect to what to include as revenues and expenses and how to calculate those items that depend on formulas and estimation.

[1] **Elaboration:** Provided the shares are subject to market price risk and are held for more than 45 days. The result is that intercompany dividends are taxed at an effective maximum rate of 35% × 30% = 10.5%.

3-year class:	Some special tools, hogs, old horses
5-year class:	Automobiles, light trucks, tractors, computers and other office equipment, equipment used for research and development
7-year class:	Manufacturing machinery, office furniture and fixtures, refrigerators, dishwashers
10-year class:	Agricultural structures, fruit and nut trees and vines, ships
15-year class:	Wastewater treatment facilities, telephone switching facilities
20-year class:	Miscellaneous long-lived property
27.5-year class:	Residential rental real estate, such as apartment buildings
31.5-year class:	Nonresidential real estate, such as factories and office buildings

FIGURE 4C.1
The eight ACRS classes with examples of assets that fall into each class. These lifetimes must be used for depreciation calculations on business tax returns.

1. Revenues Receiving Special Treatment

The tax code excludes 70% of dividend income received by a corporation from taxable income[1]; corporations need only include the other 30%. This provision exists to avoid penalizing subsidiary-to-parent cash transfers made via the dividend process. If a subsidiary pays a dividend to its parent corporation, the dividend is, in effect, simply an internal cash transfer between two parts of a larger economic entity, and internal cash transfers are not subject to tax.

2. Expenses Receiving Special Treatment

accelerated cost recovery system—the depreciation method required for tax calculations in the United States

Under Section 179 of the tax code, up to $17,500 per year spent on depreciable assets may be expensed immediately and need not go through the depreciation process. This is intended to be a benefit to small businesses.

Whereas financial accounting uses the straight-line, declining balance, and sum-of-the-years digits methods for depreciation, the tax code specifies a depreciation method known as the (modified)[2] **accelerated cost recovery system** (ACRS, pronounced *"acres"* as if we were discussing a parcel of land.) Under ACRS, depreciation is calculated as a given percentage of the cost of the asset for each year of its depreciable life. All the tax preparer has to do is look up the appropriate percentage in tables prepared by the tax authorities.

Assets must be grouped into one of eight classes, where each class represents a specified depreciation life. Some examples are given in Figure 4C.1.

ACRS percentages are based on a variation of the "declining balance switching to straight-line method" of depreciation. A zero salvage value is used in the calculation. It is assumed the asset is purchased at the midpoint of the year regardless of the actual date of acquisition; this is the "half-year convention" and results in the otherwise strange-looking percentages for the first and last years. For the first four classes (3-, 5-, 7-, and 10-year lives) a 200% (double) declining balance

[2] **Elaboration:** ACRS was created in 1981 by the first tax-reform law passed during the Reagan administration. To encourage business to invest in plant and equipment, ACRS significantly shortened depreciation lives, increasing the present value of tax benefits from depreciation. ACRS was subsequently "modified" in 1986, when depreciation lives were lengthened again as part of the tax reform of that year.

Year	Three-year	Five-year	Seven-year	Ten-year
1	33.33%	20.00%	14.29%	10.00%
2	44.45	32.00	24.49	18.00
3	14.81	19.20	17.49	14.40
4	7.41	11.52	12.49	11.52
5		11.52	8.93	9.22
6		5.76	8.92	7.38
7			8.93	6.55
8			4.46	6.55
9				6.55
10				6.55
11				3.28
	100.00%	100.00%	100.00%	100.00%

FIGURE 4C.2
ACRS depreciation rates for assets in the three-, five-, seven-, and ten-year classes. The rates are based on the "double declining balance switching to straight line" method.

calculation is used—the resulting rates are shown in Figure 4C.2. A 150% declining balance calculation is used for 15-year and 20-year property.

Real estate (except land, which may not be depreciated for tax purposes, just as in financial accounting) is depreciated using the straight-line method. In the first year, the depreciation allowed depends on the month in which the asset is acquired. Any first year depreciation not allowed in the first year of ownership becomes the depreciation taken in the last (twenty-eighth or thirty-second) year of ownership.

Example

ACRS Depreciation

A corporation has just purchased a small delivery truck for $25,000.

Question: How much depreciation will the firm be allowed to expense on its tax return each year?

Solution steps:

1. Determine the appropriate ACRS life. Light trucks fall into the 5-year category.
2. Calculate each year's depreciation by multiplying the cost of the asset by the 5-year ACRS percentages:

Year	ACRS Percentage × Cost	=	Depreciation
1	20.00% × $25,000	=	$ 5,000
2	32.00 × 25,000	=	8,000
3	19.20 × 25,000	=	4,800
4	11.52 × 25,000	=	2,880
5	11.52 × 25,000	=	2,880
6	5.76 × 25,000	=	1,440
	100.00%		$25,000

3. The Differential Treatment of Interest vs. Dividends Paid

When a company pays interest to its creditors, the interest is fully deductible on its tax return as a normal business expense. Dividends to stockholders, however, are considered to be paid from after-tax income and are not a legitimate tax deduction. This difference is a very important characteristic of the tax law because it introduces a bias into the financing choices of business firms. Since interest is tax-deductible, paying interest lowers taxable income and thus lowers taxes. The net effect is to reduce the cost of borrowing—it is as if the government subsidizes business debt. (Borrow and the government will reduce your taxes!) No such subsidy is available for equity since dividend payments do not reduce taxes in any way.[3]

double taxation—the taxing of income twice: first as business income and then as income of the owner of the business

From the investor's point of view, the inability of a company to deduct dividends on its tax return leads to the **double taxation** of income paid as dividends. This income is first taxed as it is earned by the firm and then taxed again when it is paid to the investor.

Examples

Double Taxation

A corporation earns $10 million before taxes. It is in the 34% corporate income tax bracket and it elects to pay all earnings after taxes as dividends to its stockholders who are in the 28% personal income tax bracket.

Question: How much will the stockholders receive after both corporate and personal income taxes?

Solution steps:

1. The corporation will pay:

$$34\% \times \$10{,}000{,}000 = \$3{,}400{,}000$$

in taxes leaving earnings after tax of:

$$\$10{,}000{,}000 - \$3{,}400{,}000 = \$6{,}600{,}000$$

to be paid in dividends.

2. Shareholders will receive the $6,600,000 and pay:

$$28\% \times \$6{,}600{,}000 = \$1{,}848{,}000$$

in taxes leaving:

$$\$6{,}600{,}000 - \$1{,}848{,}000 = \$4{,}752{,}000$$

Answer: Shareholders will keep $4,752,000 after taxes.

Question: What effective rate of taxation does this imply?

[3] **Cross-reference:** We will explore this effect more fully when we consider the cost of raising capital funds in Chapter 10 and the optimal mix of debt vs. equity financing in Chapter 15.

Solution steps: Shareholders received $4,752,000 of the $10,000,000 earned by the firm. The difference of:

$$\$10,000,000 - \$4,752,000 = \$5,248,000$$

was taken by taxes on income. This implies an effective tax rate of:

$$\$5,248,000/\$10,000,000 = 52.48\%$$

Answer: Double taxation effectively subjects the firm and its shareholders to a 52.48% tax rate.

Some business firms retain most of their earnings, or do not pay dividends at all. Indeed, many firms have legitimate business needs that require substantial funding, including that from retained earnings. However, the tax authorities can assess a substantial penalty against a firm if they believe the firm is retaining earnings for the purpose of avoiding double taxation. This is known as the **improper accumulation** of retained earnings. Small firms are protected from this provision since the first $250,000 of earnings retained each year may not be considered improperly accumulated.

improper accumulation—a tax term referring to the "excessive" retention of earnings, hence not paying dividends, to avoid double taxation

4. Consolidated Tax Returns

A business with subsidiaries may combine the tax returns of the parent and any subsidiary which is at least 80% owned. Such combined returns are called **consolidated tax returns.** There are two major benefits of consolidated tax returns. First, any intercompany business which might otherwise be taxed, such as sales or dividends, disappears in the consolidation process. Second, the losses of one subsidiary can offset the earnings of another further lowering taxable income.

consolidated tax return—a tax return combining the income of a parent company and one or more of its subsidiaries

5. Corporate Tax Rates

If taxable income is positive, the corporation pays taxes at the following rates:[4]

15% of the first $50,000 of taxable income

+ 25% of the next $25,000 of taxable income

+ 34% of the next $25,000 of taxable income

+ 39% of the next $35,000 of taxable income

+ 34% of the next $9,665,000 of taxable income

+ 35% of the next $5,000,000 of taxable income

+ 38% of the next $3,333,333 of taxable income

+ 35% of taxable income above $18,333,333.

---

[4] **Elaboration:** The purpose of the progressive rate system is to tax small and marginally profitable corporations at lower rates than those which are highly profitable. However, the authors of the tax code reasoned that it was unfair to allow highly profitable firms to pay only 15% or 25% instead of 34% on their first dollars of income. The 39% rate was installed to undo the effect of the 15% and 25% rates for corporations with high incomes. Specifically, the benefit of paying 15% and 25% rather than 34% in the first brackets, which equals: *(footnote continued on the next page)*

Example

Calculating Corporate Tax

A corporation determines its taxable income to be $25 million.

Question: What will its U.S. income tax obligation be?

Solution steps:

15% × $	50,000 =	$ 7,500
+ 25% ×	25,000 =	6,250
+ 34% ×	25,000 =	8,500
+ 39% ×	235,000 =	91,650
+ 34% ×	9,665,000 =	3,286,100
+ 35% ×	5,000,000 =	1,750,000
+ 38% ×	3,333,333 =	1,266,667
+ 35% ×	6,666,667 =	2,333,333
	$25,000,000	$8,750,000

Short cut: Since the corporation's taxable income is greater than $18,333,333, the net effect of the detailed rate schedule is the same as a flat 35% rate:

35% × $25,000,000 = $8,750,000

Answer: The corporation will pay $8,750,000 in federal income taxes.

6. Loss Carryback and Carryforward

loss carryback—a tax term referring to the offsetting of income in prior years with a current loss to obtain a refund of taxes paid

loss carryforward—a tax term referring to the offsetting of current income with a loss in a prior year to reduce the firm's tax obligation

The **loss carryback** and **loss carryforward** provisions allow a firm to average out profits and losses over several years. If taxable income is negative, the corporation may "carry the loss back" to the past three years. This means that any taxes paid within the past three years on a comparable amount of income will be refunded to the corporation. If this year's loss exceeds the total of the past three years' income, the remaining loss may be "carried forward" for up to the next 15 years. While the corporation receives no immediate benefit from a carryforward, such losses can be used to offset income and reduce taxes in subsequent years.

7. "S Corporations"

Since the tax on corporate income is greater than the tax on a comparable amount of personal income, small businesses are often organized as proprietorships or partnerships to keep taxes down. On the other hand, the corporate form provides

---

(34% − 15%) × $50,000 = $ 9,500
(34% − 25%) × $25,000 = 2,250
$11,750

is precisely offset by the additional tax due to the 39% rate:

(39% − 34%) × ($235,000) = 5% × $235,000 = $11,750

Therefore, a company with taxable income in the range of $335,000 to $10 million, will pay the same tax as if it were simply subjected to a flat rate of 34%.
In exactly the same way, the 38% bracket is designed to offset the benefit of paying 34% instead of 35% on the first $10 million of income. A company with taxable income of $18,333,333 or greater will pay the same tax as if it were subjected to a flat rate of 35%.

subchapter S corporation— a corporation which has elected to be taxed as a partnership

a limitation of liability not available to proprietors or partners. A special section of the tax law, known as **Subchapter S,** permits small corporations to be taxed as partnerships thus getting both advantages.

Subchapter S status is particularly desirable in the first years of the life of a business. At this time, products and relationships are often untested and limited liability is particularly valuable. This is also a time when low revenues and high start-up costs can easily result in losses. If the business is taxed as a partnership, owners who are actively involved can use the losses to offset any other income they have. This produces an immediate reduction in their taxes. On the other hand, if the business were taxed as a corporation, it could not get any immediate tax relief since it would have no past income against which to carry the losses back. It could only carry the losses forward until some (unknown) year in the future when profits begin to appear.

Subchapter S status is also attractive to professionals such as doctors who could not maintain their practice without limited personal liability.

Problems

1. **(ACRS depreciation)** Queens Corporation has just purchased new equipment for its research and development laboratory costing $3 million. The equipment has a six-year economic life. Queens is in the 35% tax bracket.
   a. Into which ACRS class does this asset fall?
   b. Calculate the ACRS depreciation to be reported in each year of the equipment's economic life.
   c. By how much is Queens's tax liability reduced due to this depreciation in each year of the equipment's economic life?
   d. Assume that Queens depreciates the equipment differently on its public financial statements, using the straight-line method to zero salvage value over the equipment's economic life. By how much does taxable income differ from reported income in each of the next six years due to this difference?
2. **(ACRS depreciation)** Reeves Corporation has just purchased minicomputers for its staff at a cost of $750,000. Because of the speed of technological change in the computer industry, Reeves forecasts that the computers only have a three-year economic life. Reeves is in the 35% tax bracket.
   a. Into which ACRS class does this asset fall?
   b. Calculate the ACRS depreciation to be reported in each year of the computers' economic life.
   c. By how much is Reeves's tax liability reduced due to this depreciation in each year of the computers' economic life?
   d. Assume that Reeves depreciates the computers differently on its public financial statements, using the straight-line method to zero salvage value over the computers' economic life. By how much does taxable income differ from reported income in each of the next three years due to this difference?
3. **(Double taxation)** Southfield Corporation earned $2.00 per share before taxes of 35% in 1994. It then paid out all its earnings after tax as dividends. Tom Underhill, who owns 100 shares of Southfield Corporation, is in the 15% personal income tax bracket.
   a. Calculate Southfield's after-tax earnings per share (EPS).
   b. How much did Tom receive in dividends from Southfield Corporation in 1994?
   c. How much did Tom keep after paying taxes on his dividends?
   d. What was the effective tax rate on the income of Southfield Corporation, including both corporate and personal taxes?
4. **(Double taxation)** Victor Corporation earned $4.00 per share before taxes of 34% in 1994. It then paid out all its earnings after tax as dividends. Wanda Xavier, who owns 300 shares of Victor Corporation, is in the 31% personal income tax bracket.
   a. Calculate Victor's after-tax earnings per share (EPS).
   b. How much did Wanda receive in dividends from Victor Corporation in 1994?
   c. How much did Wanda keep after paying taxes on her dividends?
   d. What was the effective tax rate on the income of Victor Corporation, including both corporate and personal taxes?

5. **(Corporate tax liability)** Youngblood Corporation had earnings before interest and taxes (EBIT) of $15 million in 1994. It paid interest of $5 million to its creditors and $3 million in dividends to its stockholders.
   a. Determine Youngblood's U.S. federal taxable income.
   b. Calculate Youngblood's tax liability to the federal government for 1994.
   c. What is Youngblood's average tax rate?
   d. What is Youngblood's marginal tax rate?

6. **(Corporate tax liability)** Zebra Corporation had earnings before interest and taxes (EBIT) of $200,000 in 1994. It paid interest of $50,000 to its creditors and $75,000 in dividends to its stockholders.
   a. Determine Zebra's U.S. federal taxable income.
   b. Calculate Zebra's tax liability to the federal government for 1994.
   c. What is Zebra's average tax rate?
   d. What is Zebra's marginal tax rate?

7. **(Corporate tax liability)** Applejack Corporation had earnings from operations of $25 million in 1994. In addition, it received $1 million in interest and $5 million in dividends from investments. It paid interest of $7 million to its creditors and $4 million in dividends to its stockholders.
   a. Determine Applejack's U.S. federal taxable income.
   b. Calculate Applejack's tax liability to the federal government for 1994.

8. **(Corporate tax liability)** Buttermilk Corporation had earnings from operations of $150,000 in 1994. In addition, it received $20,000 in interest and $5,000 in dividends from investments. It paid interest of $40,000 to its creditors and $10,000 in dividends to its stockholders.
   a. Determine Buttermilk's U.S. federal taxable income.
   b. Calculate Buttermilk's tax liability to the federal government for 1994.
   c. What is Buttermilk's average tax rate?
   d. What is Buttermilk's marginal tax rate?

APPENDIX 4D

ANALYSIS OF FINANCIAL ACCOUNTING DATA

Financial accounting data[1] are typically analyzed by constructing comparisons between numbers. Two standard types of comparisons are common size financial statements and financial ratios. We illustrate the calculation and use of both in this appendix with the example of the Sunshine Company, a medium-sized manufacturing firm. Below are the Sunshine Company's financial statements for the last three years:

The Sunshine Company

Income Statements ($000 omitted)
For the Years Ending December 31

	1992	1993	1994
Sales	$22,746	$25,013	$26,897
Less: cost of goods sold	11,628	12,551	13,128
Gross profit	11,118	12,462	13,769
Less: operating expenses	8,021	9,114	10,044
Less: depreciation	843	861	1,154
Operating profit (EBIT[2])	2,254	2,487	2,571
Less: interest expense	994	902	813
Earnings before taxes (EBT)	1,260	1,585	1,758
Less: tax expense	428	539	598
Earnings after taxes (EAT)	$ 832	$ 1,046	$ 1,160
Less: dividends	500	625	625
Addition to retained earnings	$ 332	$ 421	$ 535
Earnings per share	$ 0.67	$ 0.84	$ 0.93

Notes:

1. All sales are on credit terms.
2. Purchases in 1992 = $3,887, 1993 = $4,246, in 1994 = $4,859.
3. Lease payments included in operating expenses in 1992 = $604, 1993 = $681, in 1994 = $747.
4. Federal tax rate = 34%.
5. Shares outstanding in 1992 = 1,250,000, in 1993 = 1,250,000, in 1994 = 1,250,000.
6. Stock price on December 31, 1992 = $7.88, on December 31, 1993 = $9.50, on December 31, 1994 = $11.75.

[1] **Tip:** This appendix draws heavily upon basic concepts in financial accounting. If you find yourself having any difficulty, it might be a good idea to review the first chapters of an introductory financial accounting textbook.

[2] **Abbreviation:** "EBIT" stands for "Earnings Before Interest and Taxes," and is the finance equivalent of the accountant's "operating profit."

The Sunshine Company

Balance Sheets ($000 omitted)
As of December 31

	1992	1993	1994
ASSETS:			
Cash	$ 2,026	$ 2,435	$ 2,239
Marketable securities	219	258	307
Accounts receivable	2,165	2,352	2,460
Inventories	2,251	2,336	2,367
Prepaids	464	481	504
Total current assets	7,125	7,862	7,877
Property, plant and equipment	8,937	9,250	10,034
Land	439	439	439
Total fixed assets	9,376	9,689	10,473
Total assets	$16,501	$17,551	$18,350
LIABILITIES:			
Accounts payable	$ 573	$ 638	$ 1,083
Wages payable	97	118	135
Taxes payable	64	79	90
Notes payable to banks	2,263	3,291	3,582
Current portion of long-term debt	500	500	500
Total current liabilities	3,497	4,626	5,390
Long-term liabilities	7,500	7,000	6,500
Total liabilities	10,997	11,626	11,890
EQUITY:			
Common stock ($1 par value)	1,250	1,250	1,250
Paid-in-capital	2,750	2,750	2,750
Retained earnings	1,504	1,925	2,460
Total equity	5,504	5,925	6,460
Total liabilities and equity	$16,501	$17,551	$18,350

The Sunshine Company

Statements of Cash Flows ($000 omitted)
For the Years Ending December 31

	1992	1993	1994
CASH FLOWS FROM OPERATIONS:			
Received from customers	$22,592	$24,826	$26,789
Paid to suppliers and employees	(19,652)	(21,681)	(22,764)
Interest paid	(994)	(902)	(813)
Income taxes paid	(414)	(524)	(587)
Net cash provided by operating activities	1,532	1,719	2,625

(Continued on pg. 114)

	1992	1993	1994
CASH FLOWS FROM INVESTMENTS:			
Payment for purchases of property, plant, and equipment	(1,075)	(1,174)	(1,938)
Net cash used for investing activities	(1,075)	(1,174)	(1,938)
CASH FLOWS FROM FINANCING:			
Proceeds from short-term borrowing	437	1.028	291
Repayment of long-term debt	(500)	(500)	(500)
Dividends paid	(500)	(625)	(625)
Net cash used for financing activities	(463)	(97)	(834)
NET INCREASE (DECREASE) IN CASH:	(6)	448	(147)
Cash and equivalents, beginning of year	2,251	2,245	2,693
Cash and equivalents, end of year	$ 2,245	$ 2,693	$ 2,546
RECONCILIATION OF NET INCOME TO CASH PROVIDED BY OPERATIONS:			
Net income	$ 832	$ 1,046	$ 1,160
Add Back: Depreciation	843	861	1,154
Subtract: Increase in			
Accounts receivable	(154)	(187)	(108)
Inventories	(81)	(85)	(31)
Prepaids	(14)	(17)	(23)
Add: Increase in			
Accounts payable	74	65	445
Wages payable	18	21	17
Taxes payable	14	15	11
Net cash provided by operations	$ 1,532	1,719	$2,625

As you read through this appendix, look for the financial strengths and weaknesses of the Sunshine Company. You will find that Sunshine has good control of its operating costs and its collections of accounts receivable but seems to have excess inventory. The company uses more debt financing than is typical in its industry, and this has led to high interest payments and low net profit margins. Although Sunshine appears to be reducing its debt, it has increased the length of time it takes to pay its bills, perhaps substituting one problem for another.

Common Size Financial Statements

common size financial statement—a financial statement in which the numbers are presented as percentages of the statement's total number, rather than in absolute money terms

Recall our comments earlier that single numbers taken out of context are not very useful. One quick and powerful way to provide a context to income statement and balance sheet numbers is to recast them in "common size" form. We do this by dividing each number by the statement's total number—sales for the income statement and total assets for the balance sheet. The resulting **common size financial statements** show each number in percentage, rather than in absolute terms. By recasting the statements in percentage terms, we immediately introduce a comparison for every number on the statements.

Using the example of the Sunshine Company:

The Sunshine Company

Common Size Income Statements
For the Years Ending December 31

	1992	1993	1994
Sales	100.00%	100.00%	100.00%
Less: cost of goods sold	51.12	50.18	48.81
Gross profit	48.88	49.82	51.19
Less: operating expenses	35.26	36.44	37.34
Less: depreciation	3.71	3.44	4.29
Operating profit (EBIT)	9.91	9.94	9.56
Less: interest expense	4.37	3.61	3.02
Earnings before taxes (EBT)	5.54	6.33	6.54
Less: tax expense	1.88	2.15	2.23
Earnings after taxes (EAT)	3.66	4.18	4.31
Less: dividends	2.20	2.50	2.32
Addition to retained earnings	1.46	1.68	1.99

The Sunshine Company

Common Size Balance Sheets
As of December 31

	1992	1993	1994
ASSETS:			
Cash	12.28%	13.88%	12.20%
Marketable securities	1.33	1.47	1.67
Accounts receivable	13.12	13.40	13.41
Inventories	13.64	13.31	12.90
Prepaids	2.81	2.74	2.75
Total current assets	43.18	44.80	42.93
Property, plant and equipment	54.16	52.70	54.68
Land	2.66	2.50	2.39
Total fixed assets	56.82	55.20	57.07
Total assets	100.00%	100.00%	100.00%
LIABILITIES:			
Accounts payable	3.47	3.64%	5.90%
Wages payable	0.59	0.67	0.74
Taxes payable	0.39	0.45	0.49
Notes payable to banks	13.71	18.75	19.52
Current portion of long-term debt	3.03	2.85	2.72
Total current liabilities	21.19	26.36	29.37
Long-term liabilities	45.45	39.88	35.43
Total liabilities	66.64	66.24	64.80
EQUITY:			
Common stock ($1 par value)	7.58	7.12	6.81
Paid-in-capital	16.67	15.67	14.99
Retained earnings	9.11	10.97	13.41
Total equity	33.36	33.76	35.20
Total liabilities and equity	100.00%	100.00%	100.00%

Now we can begin to understand the Sunshine Company's financial statements. From the percentage income statement we can determine the relationship of each cost to the amount of sales revenue. From the percentage balance sheet we can observe the mix of assets and financing employed.

Financial Ratios

A financial ratio, like any other mathematical ratio, is a fraction: a numerator over a denominator. It guarantees a comparison since at least two numbers are needed to construct it.

It is common to organize ratios into groups for presentation purposes. While there are several ways to do this, we favor a scheme that emphasizes the role of ratios in financial analysis. Thus each group below contains ratios that pertain to a specific question an analyst might have about the business. Although there are other ratios we could describe, those that follow are the most basic and most commonly used.

1. Ratios That Measure Profitability

An important measure of the health of a business is its ability to produce profits. Each ratio in this group measures the firm's profit level in some way. In measuring profits, they measure both revenues and costs. They differ in which income statement item is chosen to represent the firm's profit and in which measure profit is compared to. Often, ratios of this type are referred to as "measuring a rate of return."

Profitability compared to sales When we calculated the common size income statement for the Sunshine Company, we obtained each number as a percentage of total sales. Several of those percentages are the firm's profitability ratios:

Gross profit margin = gross profit/sales

Gross profit is sales less cost of goods sold. Cost of goods sold summarizes the costs of producing the firm's products. Sales is the sum of cost of goods sold and the firm's profit margin. As a result, this ratio measures the firm's pricing policy relative to its production costs. In a multiproduct firm, where each product has its own gross margin, changes in this ratio may be the result of a changing product mix.

For Sunshine:	1992: $11,118,000/$22,746,000 = 48.9%
	1993: $12,462,000/$25,013,000 = 49.8%
	1994: $13,769,000/$26,897,000 = 51.2%
Industry average[3]:	50.3%

[3] **Elaboration and cross-reference:** As discussed on pages 90–92, each ratio often tends toward a particular value in a given industry, reflecting that industry's production processes, trade practices, competitive picture, etc. As we present each ratio and illustrate its use with the example of the Sunshine Company, we will also present an industry average ratio for comparison. However, recall that average practice in any industry might not be an indicator of excellent performance. As a result, many firms today are comparing themselves to the best performer anywhere, regardless of industry.

Sunshine's gross profit margin is typical of the industry and has been improving slightly over the past three years. This suggests that Sunshine's cost of production and markup policy are similar to others in its industry.

Operating profit margin = EBIT/sales

Earnings before interest and taxes (EBIT) summarizes sales revenue less all operating expenses. Not included are financing costs and taxes. This ratio measures the firm's economic earnings, the earnings from delivering its products and services to customers. It is useful for comparing the economic performance of firms.

For Sunshine:	1992:	$2,254,000/$22,746,000 = 9.9%
	1993:	$2,487,000/$25,013,000 = 9.9%
	1994:	$2,571,000/$26,897,000 = 9.6%
Industry average:	8.9%	

Sunshine's operating profit margin is above the industry average, although it declined in 1994. This tells us that Sunshine's operating costs are below average for the industry.

Pre-tax profit margin = earnings before taxes/sales

This ratio measures the firm's profit after satisfying its creditors but before taxes and shareholders.

For Sunshine:	1992:	$1,260,000/$22,746,000 = 5.5%
	1993:	$1,585,000/$25,013,000 = 6.3%
	1994:	$1,758,000/$26,897,000 = 6.5%
Industry average:	7.2%	

Sunshine's pre-tax profit margin is below the industry average, although it has been rising over the past three years. This reflects the high (but declining) interest payments Sunshine has had to make over this period.

Net profit margin = earnings after taxes/sales

This ratio measures the profitability seen by shareholders as it takes all expenses into account.

For Sunshine:	1992:	$ 832,000/$22,746,000 = 3.7%
	1993:	$1,046,000/$25,013,000 = 4.2%
	1994:	$1,160,000/$26,897,000 = 4.3%
Industry average:	4.8%	

Like its pre-tax profit margin, Sunshine's after-tax profit margin is below the industry average, although improving.

Sunshine presented its data in the GAAP format, in which it grouped its expenses according to those related to the product (cost of goods sold) and those related to the passage of time (expenses such as rent or interest). On pages 81 and 82 we saw that a different expense classification, dividing costs according to those that are variable and those that are fixed, often makes good analytical sense. When using this alternate scheme for cost classification, we can calculate:

Contribution margin = contribution/sales

Recall that contribution is the subtotal of sales less variable costs. This ratio gives us the increase to the firm's profits from an additional dollar of sales. We study contribution margin more fully in the context of making incremental decisions in Part IV of this book and in Chapter 15 where we look at operating leverage.

Profitability compared to assets We are often interested in the firm's ability to generate sales from its investment in assets. Two ratios that look at this are:

Basic earning power = EBIT/average total assets

This ratio shows the firm's economic earnings in relation to its investment in assets.

For Sunshine: Average total assets:
1993: = ($16,501,000 + $17,551,000)/2 = $17,026,000
1994: = ($17,551,000 + $18,350,000)/2 = $17,950,500
1993: $2,487,000/$17,026,000 = 14.6%
1994: $2,571,000/$17,950,500 = 14.3%
Industry average: 12.3%

Sunshine's basic earning power is strong, two percentage points above the industry average. This reflects either a higher relative EBIT or the ability to use less (or less costly) assets.

Return on assets (ROA) = earnings after taxes/average total assets

This ratio shows the firm's total earnings in relation to its investment in assets.

For Sunshine: 1993: $1,046,000/$17,026,000 = 6.1%
1994: $1,160,000/$17,950,500 = 6.5%
Industry average: 6.4%

Sunshine's ROA is the same[4] as the industry. By comparing this ratio to basic earning power, we can see once again the effect of Sunshine's high interest payments: although Sunshine's EBIT (hence basic earning power) is strong, its net profit margin (and thus ROA) is not.

[4] **Observation:** Literally, Sunshine's ROA is *not* the same as the industry average, but the difference is too slight to be meaningful. Every ratio will vary somewhat due to the combined small effects of many factors, much like the way a person's body temperature is typically not constant but varies around 98.6°F. Doctors are trained to expect this natural variation and not react to it. In the same way the financial manager must also avoid the temptation to react to natural variation, for to do so would be to tamper with the firm based on a signal that does not indicate that something is wrong.

Note the use of *average* total assets in these ratios. Earnings come from the income statement and measure activity throughout the entire year. Total assets is a balance sheet figure which represents only one point in time, the balance sheet date. A fair comparison requires us to match profitability throughout the year with the (average) balance of assets also throughout the year. Whenever we compare an income statement or cash flow statement figure with the balance sheet, we will always try to use an average for the balance sheet number. A simple way to obtain the average, as we have done here, is to use the beginning-of-year and end-of-year figures: add them and divide by 2. The beginning-of-year figure, of course, is the prior year's balance sheet number. If you need more accuracy, you may average quarterly or even monthly numbers. However, sometimes only the end-of-year balance sheet is available or the analyst feels that the balance sheet data has not changed significantly during the year. In these cases it is common to simply use the end-of-year balance sheet numbers without taking an average.

Profitability compared to equity Still another way we can examine profitability is to compare it to the level of the shareholders' investment to learn if the company is providing shareholders a sufficient rate of return on their invested money.

Return on equity (ROE) = earnings after taxes/average total equity

When used with return on assets, this ratio shows how the firm uses leverage to raise its return on assets to a higher return for its shareholders.

For Sunshine: Average total equity:
1993: = ($5,504,000 + $5,925,000)/2 = $5,714,500
1994: = ($5,925,000 + $6,460,000)/2 = $6,192,500
1993: $1,046,000/$5,714,500 = 18.3%
1994: $1,160,000/$6,192,500 = 18.7%
Industry average: 15.2%

Sunshine uses more debt than the rest of the industry, hence it is able to "leverage up" its industry-average return on assets to produce a higher-than-industry-average ROE.

2. Ratios That Measure Effective Use of Working Capital

working capital—a firm's current assets minus its current liabilities

The term **working capital** refers to a firm's current assets and current liabilities.[5] Besides involving a large amount of money, these accounts require a great deal of day-to-day attention; current assets arrive daily and current liabilities must be paid when due. The first two of these ratios measure the firm's overall working capital position. The others measure how well the firm is managing one component of its working capital.

[5] **Elaboration and cross-reference:** Mathematically, *working capital* is normally used to mean current assets minus current liabilities. In day-to-day usage, however, the term is often used to refer to all current accounts taken together, regardless of any particular mathematical combination. See Chapters 12 and 16 for further elaboration.

liquidity—the ability to have access to cash quickly and in full amount

Measures of overall liquidity **Liquidity** refers to a company's ability to have cash as needed. If a firm has enough cash, it is liquid by definition. If its resources are not in the form of cash it is not liquid and it could have problems paying its current liabilities. The broadest measure of liquidity is the current ratio:

Current ratio = current assets/current liabilities

Current assets (such as cash and accounts receivable) are assets that are now cash or will turn into cash within the accounting period, typically the next year. Current liabilities (mostly payables) are obligations that must be paid within the accounting period. The current ratio, therefore, measures a firm's ability to generate cash to meet its upcoming obligations. A good current ratio is at least equal to 1.0, since, at that level, current assets equal current liabilities and are (barely) enough to cover the firm's current debts. If cash flows are variable, with inflows and outflows not coming at the same time, the average value of the current ratio should be above 1.0 so the firm can meet its obligations when cash inflows drop off.

A current ratio that is too high can be almost as bad as a very low current ratio. A very high current ratio could indicate an excess of current assets, a wasteful use of resources. It could also indicate inadequate use of current liabilities. A traditional rule-of-thumb used by many analysts is that a current ratio near 2.0 indicates that the current accounts are somewhat in balance.

For Sunshine:	1992:	$7,125,000/$3,497,000 = 2.04
	1993:	$7,862,000/$4,626,000 = 1.70
	1994:	$7,877,000/$5,390,000 = 1.46
Industry average:	1.96	

Sunshine's current ratio is below the industry average and worsening. We must look at the details of Sunshine's current accounts to find the problem(s). The ratios that follow will help our investigation.

The current ratio assumes that all current assets will indeed produce cash equal to the amount reported on the balance sheet. It also assumes that all current liabilities appear on the balance sheet at the amount actually due. However, while this is generally true for monetary assets and liabilities, it typically is not true for nonmonetary items. For example, if a company had a significant amount of inventory (a nonmonetary current asset carried at cost), cash receipts from selling the inventory should exceed the inventory's value by the firm's profit margin. If the firm had receipts in advance on its books (a nonmonetary current liability carried at the amount received) the cash payment required to satisfy that liability should be less than the book amount, again by the firm's profit margin. An analyst would have to recalculate the current ratio, replacing current assets with "cash likely to flow from current assets" and replacing current liabilities with "cash likely to be required to discharge current liabilities" to properly assess liquidity.

seasonal—a firm or market whose activity varies in a pattern throughout the year

Some companies are **seasonal,** their level of business changing throughout the year. In these firms there is a normal build-up of working capital, especially inventories and accounts receivable, as the busy season approaches, followed by a

"Now, depending on how we read these accounting figures, we have either an excess profit or an excess deficit."

reduction of working capital after the seasonal peak as inventories are sold and receivables are collected. The current ratio of a seasonal firm will fluctuate with the seasons as well, and the good analyst will calculate it at various points during the seasonal cycle to test the firm's liquidity throughout the year.

A stricter test of liquidity is the quick ratio:

Quick ratio = quick assets/current liabilities

For Sunshine: Quick assets = cash + securities + receivables:

1992: = \$2,026,000 + \$219,000 + \$2,165,000 = \$4,410,000
1993: = \$2,435,000 + \$258,000 + \$2,352,000 = \$5,045,000
1994: = \$2,239,000 + \$307,000 + \$2,460,000 = \$5,006,000

1992: \$4,410,000/\$3,497,000 = 1.26
1993: \$5,045,000/\$4,626,000 = 1.09
1994: \$5,006,000/\$5,390,000 = 0.93

Industry average: 1.02

Sunshine's quick ratio is slightly below the industry average as well as slightly below 1.00. Like its current ratio, Sunshine's quick ratio has been worsening.

Quick assets are those current assets that can be converted quickly to cash. Typically included as quick assets are cash (it's already cash), marketable securities (it only requires a phone call to the firm's securities broker to produce cash), and accounts receivable (which usually can be sold to a financial institution for cash). Typically omitted from quick assets is inventory that could be out of date or out of fashion. Inventory could also be work in process which might never be completed and would be of no use to anyone else. Also typically omitted are prepaid expenses, unless the money could be retrieved in an emergency. This ratio is a much narrower measure of liquidity than the current ratio. Analysts who forecast a crisis[6] in which the company has to raise cash immediately use this ratio to test the firm's ability to cover its obligations under that scenario.

Measures of the effective use of accounts receivable Companies extend credit to their customers to facilitate their customers' purchases and, hence, to increase sales. A well-managed receivables balance is then collected in a reasonable time so the money can be reused (turned over) to produce more products for additional customers. These ratios measure the speed with which the firm collects its accounts receivable. They are especially important for a company in which credit is an important competitive tool.

Accounts receivable turnover = credit sales/average accounts receivable

For Sunshine: Average accounts receivable:
1993: = ($2,165,000 + $2,352,000)/2 = $2,258,500
1994: = ($2,352,000 + $2,460,000)/2 = $2,406,000
1993: $25,013,000[7]/$2,258,500 = 11.1 times
1994: $26,897,000/$2,406,000 = 11.2 times

Industry average: 10.3 times

Collection period = (average accounts receivable/credit sales) × 360

For Sunshine: 1993: ($2,258,500/$25,013,000) × 360 = 33 days
1994: ($2,406,000/$26,897,000) × 360 = 32 days

Industry average: 35 days

Accounts receivable turnover is the number of times the firm sells and then collects each year. This equals the number of times each year the firm reuses the

[6] **Elaboration:** Because this ratio is particularly applicable in times of difficulty when the firm is being pushed to its financial limits, it is also called the *acid-test* ratio.

[7] **Cross-reference:** Note 1 to Sunshine's income statements on page 114 tells us that *all* their sales were on credit terms, hence credit sales equals total sales in this instance.

money invested in accounts receivable. Collection period expresses the same concept in days. It measures the time it takes (number of days after sale) to collect the typical receivable.

> Sunshine's accounts receivable turn over faster than the industry average leading to a shorter collection period. We can tentatively conclude that Sunshine manages its accounts receivable better than the average firm in its industry. Receivables are not causing the low degree of liquidity.

Since firms normally instruct their customers how long they may take before payment is due, a company's collection period may be compared to its invoice terms to test whether its customers are, on average, complying with its billing instructions.

Example

Testing the Collection Period

Sunshine's payment terms are "net 30" meaning that payment is due 30 days from the date of sale.

Question: Are Sunshine's customers paying their obligations on time?

Answer: Yes, they are. On average, Sunshine receives payment 32 days after sale. This is only 2 days more than the 30 days requested. It appears that Sunshine's customers are indeed paying as requested. The extra 2 days can easily be explained as time the "check is in the mail." (Note that the 32-day number is an *average* of the payment practices of all customers; it might hide the fact that some customers pay early while others pay very late.)

Credit sales is used in these ratios because only credit sales produce accounts receivable. When credit sales is not known, it is common to use total sales although this will overstate the turnover ratio and understate the collection period should there be any significant amount of cash sales.

Note the use of 360 to measure the number of days in the year. While some analysts insist on the precision of 365 or even 366 every fourth year, ambiguities within the accounting numbers are typically great enough so that 360 works very well. Using 360 days for the length of the year is also quite convenient, since it is easily divisible into halves, quarters, twelfths (it makes each month exactly 30 days), etc.

Measures of the effective use of inventories Traditionally, firms have invested in inventories for several reasons. Raw material and finished goods inventories were used to separate the production process from purchasing and sales in the belief that this would permit each to operate in the most efficient manner. Work-in-process inventories were used to "smooth" production. Finished goods and merchandise inventories were kept to provide immediate delivery and a choice of products to customers. The belief was that the costs associated with inventory were worth paying since they lowered production costs and increased sales.

just-in-time inventory system—a system in which inventory is received and produced only as needed keeping the balance of inventory-on-hand as close as possible to zero

Recently, a new inventory management system known as **just-in-time** has been adopted by many companies. Under this system, the ideal inventory balance is zero! Raw material is scheduled to arrive as it enters production; finished goods are produced as demanded by the customer. Work-in-process is kept to an absolute minimum. Just-in-time comes from the experiences of these companies that the benefits of holding inventories seem not to be worthwhile. Production can be smoothed in less costly ways than by holding inventory; in fact inventory is often found not to smooth production but to simply hide inefficiencies—production time too long, scrap and rework levels too high. Today there is a drive by companies in a wide variety of industries to use their inventories more effectively, and inventory balances are trending down.[8]

A well managed inventory balance, therefore, ties up as little (ideally none) of the firm's funds as possible. It permits the money invested to be turned over quickly to purchase the next round of inventory. These ratios measure the speed with which the firm moves its inventory. They are especially important for a firm in which inventory is perishable and must be turned over quickly to avoid spoilage or other damage.

Inventory turnover = cost of goods sold/average inventory

For Sunshine:	Average inventory:
	1993: = ($2,251,000 + $2,336,000)/2 = $2,293,500
	1994: = ($2,336,000 + $2,367,000)/2 = $2,351,500
	1993: $12,551,000/$2,293,500 = 5.5 times
	1994: $13,128,000/$2,351,500 = 5.6 times
Industry average:	7.3 times

Inventory days = (average inventory/cost of goods sold) × 360

For Sunshine:	1993: ($2,293,500/$12,551,000) × 360 = 66 days
	1994: ($2,351,500/$13,128,000) × 360 = 64 days
Industry average:	49 days

Inventory turnover is the number of times each year the firm reuses the money invested in inventories. Inventory days expresses the same concept in days. It measures the length of time the average item remains in inventory.

Sunshine holds on to inventory longer than the industry average and, as a result, turns over its inventory less frequently each year. It is likely that Sunshine has excess inventory; if inventory were reduced, its financial position would improve.

[8] **Cross-reference:** Just-in-time inventory appears again in Chapter 12 (pages 447-449) and Appendix 12B (pages 459-461) in the context of setting the permanent inventory balance.

Some analysts compute inventory ratios using sales in place of cost of goods sold, in part because of the practice of Dun & Bradstreet (D&B), a company that produces ratio and other credit-related information. D&B uses sales in these ratios as it cannot always get good data for cost of goods sold. However, this practice can lead to erroneous conclusions because it distorts the inventory ratios. Since sales contains profits as well as the cost of inventories, the inventory ratios now change with changing profit margins. A firm with a high gross profit margin would show a much higher inventory turnover than a firm which moves its inventory just as often but has a low gross profit margin. To measure inventory use accurately, the inventory balance should be compared to cost of goods sold.

Example

Distorting the Inventory Ratios

For 1994 Sunshine Company had an average inventory balance of $2,351,500 and cost of goods sold of $13,128,000. Its sales of $26,897,000 reflects a policy of pricing its products at approximately twice their cost to manufacture.

Question: What is the impact of using sales rather than cost of goods sold in the inventory ratios?

Solution steps:

Inventory turnover = $26,897,000/$2,351,500 = 11.4 times

and:

Inventory days = ($2,351,500/$26,897,000) × 360 = 31 days

Answer: The use of sales seriously distorts the ratios. As we calculated for 1994 using cost of goods sold, Sunshine turned over its inventory 5.6 times and the average item remained in inventory 64 days. An analyst who used sales instead of cost of goods sold would conclude Sunshine uses its inventory far more efficiently than it really does.

The inventory ratios are also affected by the accounting method—LIFO, FIFO or average cost—the firm uses. Analysts must be especially careful when comparing firms to be sure they use the same inventory method, as an earlier example in this chapter pointed out.

Measures of the effective use of accounts payable A well-managed firm pays its bills when due. Yet trade credit can be an important source of funds, especially for the smaller firm. These ratios measure the firm's ability, and perhaps willingness, to pay its obligations to suppliers.

Accounts payable turnover = purchases/average accounts payable

For Sunshine: Average accounts payable:
1993: = ($573,000 + $ 638,000)/2 = $605,500
1994: = ($638,000 + $1,083,000)/2 = $860,500
1993: $4,246,000[9]/$605,500 = 7.0 times
1994: $4,859,000/$860,500 = 5.6 times
Industry average: 9.7 times

[9] **Cross-reference:** Purchases are given in Note 2 to Sunshine's income statements on page 114.

Payables period = (average accounts payable/purchases) × 360

For Sunshine:	1993: ($605,500/$4,246,000) × 360 = 51 days
	1994: ($860,500/$4,859,000) × 360 = 64 days
Industry average:	37 days

Accounts payable turnover measures the number of times each year a company pays its accounts payable. More useful is the payables period ratio, which tells us how long it takes the firm to pay its bills. When compared with the terms of sale offered to the firm, we can determine whether the company is responsible and able to pay its obligations when due.

Sunshine takes longer to pay its trade creditors than the average of its peers. Consequently it has a higher balance of accounts payable. These numbers worsened considerably in 1994. It is likely that Sunshine is using accounts payable to finance its excess inventory and as a substitute for additional bank borrowing.

It is interesting to observe that some companies are discovering that by paying suppliers in advance when placing an order rather than waiting for an account payable to develop they reduce their paperwork costs and often receive goods and services of sufficiently higher quality to justify this apparent violation of time value of money.[10]

cash conversion cycle—the length of time from the outflow of cash to purchase inventory until the inflow of cash from the collection of accounts receivable

The cash conversion cycle The ratios that describe accounts receivable, inventories, and accounts payable in days can be combined to measure the firm's total commitment to working capital in support of its operations. This produces the **cash conversion cycle,** the time it takes to recover the funds invested in inventory and accounts receivable.

The cash conversion cycle is diagrammed in Figure 4D.1. Working capital activity begins when inventory is ordered, yet it is typical not to pay for inventory immediately (payables period). After some time has passed (inventory days), the firm sells its product. Still later (collection period), the customer pays and the firm retreives its cash (plus profits). Cash flows out when accounts payable are paid and does not flow back in until the corresponding account receivable is collected.

Algebraically:

Cash conversion cycle = inventory days + collection period − payables period

For Sunshine:	1993: 66 + 33 − 51 = 48 days
	1994: 64 + 32 − 64 = 32 days

[10] **Cross-reference:** We will study time value of money in Chapter 5 (look for Money Rule 2, "pay money later," on page 152), and we will examine trade credit in some detail, including this phenomenon, when we study short-term debt in Chapter 20.

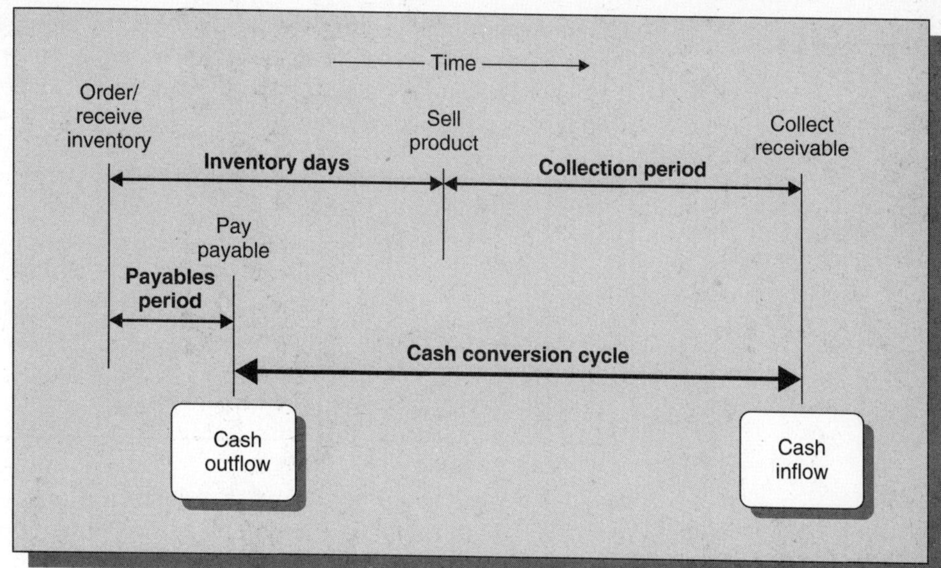

FIGURE 4D.1
The cash conversion cycle. The firm's cash is tied up in current assets from the time it pays its accounts payable to its suppliers until it collects its accounts receivable from its customers.

Industry average: 49 + 35 − 37 = 47 days

Sunshine's cash conversion cycle shortened dramatically in 1994, but this was due to the significant increase in its payables period. The shorter cash conversion cycle, therefore, does not reflect a more efficient turnover of working capital. Rather, it results from the decision to take longer to pay accounts payable. A healthier technique for reducing the cash conversion cycle would be to reduce the inventory balance, thus lowering inventory days.

While the length of the cash conversion cycle varies from industry to industry (the inventory days ratio is influenced by the nature of the production and selling process, and trade credit is often a function of industry practice), the shorter the cash conversion cycle the better. A short cash conversion cycle means that money invested in current assets comes back to the firm and can be reused quickly. A company can rapidly redirect its funds in response to changes in its environment. It also has a low reliance on outside funding to finance its investment in working capital.

3. Ratios That Measure the Use of Fixed and Total Assets

While the turnover concept is particularly applicable to current assets and liabilities since they flow into and out of the firm several times per year, it is also applied to a company's fixed assets, and to its total assets.

A measure of the productivity of fixed assets

Fixed asset turnover = sales/average fixed assets

This ratio captures the effectiveness of fixed assets in generating sales. It is meaningful for firms in which fixed assets are an important resource. Correspondingly, it has little meaning for firms whose sales do not depend on fixed assets, for example, many service companies.

For Sunshine: Average fixed assets:
1993: = ($9,376,000 + $ 9,689,000)/2 = $ 9,532,500
1994: = ($9,689,000 + $10,473,000)/2 = $10,081,000
1993: $25,013,000/$ 9,532,000 = 2.6 times
1994: $26,897,000/$10,081,000 = 2.7 times
Industry average: 2.5 times
Sunshine is very close to the industry average.

Recall that fixed assets are recorded at historical cost. A firm with old assets that have been depreciated to a low book value would show a higher turnover than a competitor with newer, less depreciated assets. Yet the second firm is probably in a better position, especially if its assets reflect more modern technologies.

A measure of the productivity of total assets

Total asset turnover = sales/average total assets

This ratio summarizes the relationship of all the firm's assets to its sales. It is effectively a weighted average of the accounts receivable turnover, inventory turnover, and fixed asset turnover ratios.

For Sunshine: Average total assets:
1993: = ($16,501,000 + 17,551,000)/2 = $17,026,000
1994: = ($17,551,000 + 18,350,000)/2 = $17,950,500
1993: $25,013,000/$17,026,000 = 1.5 times
1994: $26,897,000/$17,950,500 = 1.5 times
Industry average: 1.3 times
Sunshine's total asset turnover is slightly better than the industry average. This combines its very good accounts receivable turnover, its slightly above-average fixed asset turnover, and its poor inventory turnover.

4. Ratios That Measure the Choice and Management of Funding

How a firm chooses to finance itself is an important indicator of its risk as well as its ability to generate returns for its stakeholders. Each of these ratios looks at one part of the firm's financing choice.

Measures of the financing mix These ratios examine the mixture of debt and equity funds on the balance sheet. Creditors worry about too much debt since their interest and principal payments might be threatened. Shareholders, on the

financial leverage—the use of debt to magnify the returns to equity investors

other hand, enjoy the magnification of their earnings, or **financial leverage,**[11] which the judicious use of debt can provide. These ratios provide broad statements about the firm's financing mix.

The debt ratio = total liabilities/total assets

This ratio measures the fraction of the firm's assets financed with debt. Correspondingly, the remainder must be financed with equity.

For Sunshine:	1992: $10,997,000/$16,501,000 = .67 or 67%
	1993: $11,626,000/$17,551,000 = .66 or 66%
	1994: $11,890,000/$18,350,000 = .65 or 65%
Industry average:	52%

Sunshine relies excessively on debt financing. While it appears to have reduced its debt level slightly over the past two years, this might be the result of natural variation and not be meaningful.

The funded debt ratio = funded debt/total assets

Funded debt is debt on which interest must be paid. It does not include the various payables which carry no interest charge. This ratio gives a first, if general, picture of a company's interest obligations.

For Sunshine:	Funded debt = Notes payable to banks + long-term debt
	1992: $2,263,000 + ($500,000 + $7,500,000) = $10,263,000
	1993: $3,291,000 + ($500,000 + $7,000,000) = $10,791,000
	1994: $3,582,000 + ($500,000 + $6,500,000) = $10,582,000
	1992: $10,263,000/$16,501,000 = .62 or 62%
	1993: $10,791,000/$17,551,000 = .61 or 61%
	1994: $10,582,000/$18,350,000 = .58 or 58%
Industry average:	43%

The majority of Sunshine's debt requires interest payments. Sunshine has been reducing this ratio over the past two years. Note that since this ratio has declined faster than the debt ratio, Sunshine is not simply eliminating its debt; rather it is substituting accounts payable, which does not carry an interest obligation, for some of its funded debt.

The debt/equity ratio = total debt/total equity

This is a popular variation on the debt ratio, indicating the amount of debt relative to equity financing.

For Sunshine:	1992: $10,997,000/$5,504,000 = 2.0 times
	1993: $11,626,000/$5,925,000 = 2.0 times
	1994: $11,890,000/$6,460,000 = 1.8 times
Industry average:	1.1 times

A comparison of Sunshine to the industry reinforces our conclusion that Sunshine uses too much debt.

[11] **Cross-reference:** We will study financial leverage and the best mix of debt and equity financing in Chapter 15.

The assets/equity ratio = total assets/total equity

This is another variation on the debt ratio, highlighting the amount of assets supported by each dollar of equity financing.

For Sunshine:	1992:	$16,501,000/$5,504,000 = 3.0 times
	1993:	$17,551,000/$5,925,000 = 3.0 times
	1994:	$18,350,000/$6,460,000 = 2.8 times
Industry average:	2.1 times	

As of the end of 1994, Sunshine had $2.80 of assets for every $1.00 of equity financing. The remaining financing came from debt.

Measures of the ability to service debt The above ratios tell us the amount of debt a company has incurred. We need additional tests to determine whether the firm can make the payments its debt requires. The following ratios compare a firm's earnings to the amount it must pay to service its debt.

Times interest earned = EBIT/interest

This ratio compares operating earnings to interest. If its value exceeds 1.0, then earnings are sufficient to pay the year's interest obligation. Analysts look for a value in excess of 1.0, since earnings may well fluctuate in the future; 1.0 should be the absolute worst case for this ratio under any foreseeable economic scenario.

For Sunshine:	1992:	$2,254,000/$994,000 = 2.3 times
	1993:	$2,487,000/$902,000 = 2.8 times
	1994:	$2,571,000/$813,000 = 3.2 times
Industry average:	4.0 times	

Sunshine's higher-than-industry-average operating profit margin is offset by its high interest payments. Over the past two years, however, Sunshine has lowered its interest payments relative to operating income and therefore improved its times interest earned ratio, which is rising toward the industry average.

Sometimes a company obtains the use of a resource by making payments that are not called interest but, like interest, are contractual obligations. In this case, the times interest earned ratio must be modified or it will ignore some of the firm's required payments and will paint too positive a picture. A prime example is leased assets.[12] To assess the capability of a firm with a significant amount of leased assets to service its debt, lease payments should be removed from the expenses included in EBIT and should instead be added to interest. This reclassifies lease payments as a financing charge. A comparable adjustment should be made for any other debt-service payment not already called interest, regardless of its title.

Like all expenses on Sunshine's income statement, lease expense reduces profits, therefore EBIT has been reduced by this amount. To "remove" lease expenses from EBIT, we have to add the number back in. This will reverse its having been subtracted in the first place.

---

[12] **Cross-reference:** In Chapter 21 and Appendices 21A and 21B we will see how and why some firms choose to lease assets rather than to borrow money and buy the assets directly with the borrowed funds.

Example

Adjusting for Lease Payments When Calculating the Times Interest Earned Ratio

Sunshine Company leases a portion of the assets it uses in its business.

Question: How do Sunshine's lease payments affect its times interest earned ratio?

Solution steps:

1. Remove (add back) lease payments[13] from EBIT:
   1992: $2,254,000 + $604,000 = $2,858,000
   1993: $2,487,000 + $681,000 = $3,168,000
   1994: $2,571,000 + $747,000 = $3,318,000
2. Add lease payments to interest expense instead:
   1992: $994,000 + $604,000 = $1,598,000
   1993: $902,000 + $681,000 = $1,583,000
   1994: $813,000 + $747,000 = $1,560,000
3. Recompute times interest earned:
   1992: $2,858,000/$1,598,000 = 1.8 times
   1993: $3,168,000/$1,583,000 = 2.0 times
   1994: $3,318,000/$1,560,000 = 2.1 times

Industry average: 3.0 times

Answer: Like its peers, Sunshine uses leases in place of some debt financing. This is reflected in the lower adjusted times interest earned ratios for both Sunshine and the industry. Although improving, Sunshine's interest coverage is worse than the industry, both prior to and after the adjustment for lease payments.

Of course, interest is paid with cash, not with earnings. If EBIT is significantly different from the cash flow generated by operations, it is wise to recalculate the times interest earned ratio using operating cash flow in place of EBIT in the numerator.

Cash-flow-based times interest earned = cash from operations/interest

For Sunshine: 1992: $1,532,000/$994,000 = 1.5 times
1993: $1,719,000/$902,000 = 1.9 times
1994: $2,625,000/$813,000 = 3.2 times

Industry average: 4.7 times

Sunshine's cash flow from operations was much less than its EBIT in 1992 and 1993; for those years, cash-flow-based times interest earned was a better measure of the company's ability to meet interest obligations. For 1994, however, Sunshine's operating cash flow was similar to its EBIT, and the two times interest earned measures were the same. Note that the industry average ratio based on

[13] **Cross-reference:** Lease payments are given in Note 3 to Sunshine's income statements on page 114.

cash flow is higher than the ratio based on EBIT. To be comparable to its peers, Sunshine must raise its cash flow from operations to be above its EBIT.

Times interest earned ignores the repayment of principal. In effect it assumes that principal will not be repaid from earnings but will be "rolled over" by extending the maturity of the existing debt or by taking a new borrowing to repay the loan falling due. If earnings must be sufficient to pay both interest and principal, it is better to use:

$$\textbf{Fixed charge coverage} = \frac{\text{EBIT}}{\text{interest} + \text{principal}\left(\dfrac{1}{1-t}\right)}$$

Note the term $\frac{1}{(1-t)}$ multiplying the principal amount in the denominator (where t is the firm's marginal income tax rate). This

adjustment is required because it takes more than $1 of EBIT to repay $1 of debt principal. Debt principal is repaid with after-tax dollars. To repay $1 of principal, the firm must earn enough so that after taxes, there is $1 remaining. By contrast, interest is paid on a pre-tax basis, and $1 of EBIT will fully cover $1 of interest.

Example

Adjusting for Taxes in the Fixed Charge Coverage Ratio

Sunshine was required to repay $500,000 of debt principal (the current portion of its long-term debt) in each year, 1992, 1993, and 1994. It is in the 34% federal income tax bracket.

Question: How much did Sunshine have to earn to repay this amount?

Solution steps: $\left(\frac{1}{1-t}\right) = \left(\frac{1}{1-.34}\right) = \frac{1}{.66} = 1.5151515$

Sunshine must have $1.5151515 of EBIT to repay each $1.00 of principal since the government will first take $0.5151515 in taxes:

EBIT	$1.5151515
Less: Interest	0.0000000
EBT	1.5151515
Less: Tax (34%)	.5151515
EAT	$1.0000000

Answer: To repay $500,000 of principal, Sunshine must have EBIT of:

$500,000 (1.5151515) = $757,576

This ratio compares operating earnings to both interest and principal obligations. A value of 1.0 means earnings are just sufficient to cover both.

For Sunshine: 1992: $\frac{\$2{,}254{,}000}{\$994{,}000 + \$500{,}000\left(\dfrac{1}{1-.34}\right)}$

= $2,254,000/(994,000 + $757,576)
= $2,254,000/$1,751,576 = 1.3 times

$$1993: \quad \frac{\$2{,}487{,}000}{\$902{,}000 + \$500{,}000\left(\dfrac{1}{1-.34}\right)}$$

$$= \$2{,}487{,}000/(902{,}000 + \$757{,}576)$$
$$= \$2{,}487{,}000/\$1{,}659{,}576 = \underline{\underline{1.5 \text{ times}}}$$

$$1994: \quad \frac{\$2{,}571{,}000}{\$813{,}000 + \$500{,}000\left(\dfrac{1}{1-.34}\right)}$$

$$= \$2{,}571{,}000/(\$813{,}000 + \$757{,}576)$$
$$= \$2{,}571{,}000/\$1{,}570{,}576 = \underline{\underline{1.6 \text{ times}}}$$

Industry average: 2.4 times

Again, Sunshine lags the industry here.

Measures of payments against equity Some investors buy the shares of a company in order to receive regular dividends. Others prefer that the firm not pay dividends but rather retain and reinvest the firm's earnings. As we will see in Chapter 17, there is a variety of reasons why a particular dividend payout is appropriate for a given firm. These ratios measure the choice made by management.

Dividend payout ratio = dividends/earnings after taxes

For Sunshine:
- 1992: $500,000/$832,000 = .60 or 60%
- 1993: $625,000/$1,046,000 = .60 or 60%
- 1994: $625,000/$1,160,000 = .54 or 54%

Industry average: 46%

Retention ratio = earnings retained/earnings after taxes

For Sunshine:
- 1992: $332,000/$832,000 = .40 or 40%
- 1993: $421,000/$1,046,000 = .40 or 40%
- 1994: $535,000/$1,160,000 = .46 or 46%

Industry average: 54%

Sunshine pays out more of its earnings and retains less than the industry. This reduces the equity it can accumulate and adds to its reliance on debt.

Since earnings after taxes must be either paid out as dividends or retained, the sum of these two ratios must be 1.0.

5. Ratios That Measure the Market's Reaction to the Firm

The stock price of a firm is based on its current health plus forecasts of how well it will do in the future. These two ratios compare a firm's stock price to accounting measures of its current health. They gauge investors' reaction to the firm's condition and earnings and their optimism about the firm's future performance.

Price/earnings ratio = stock price/earnings per share

This ratio compares the firm's stock price to its most recent earnings. Firms with solid earnings, good future prospects, or relatively low risk will sell for a higher price earnings ratio than firms with weak earnings, poor prospects, or high risk.

For Sunshine:	1992: \$ 7.88/\$0.67 = 11.8 times
	1993: \$ 9.50/\$0.84 = 11.3 times
	1994: \$11.75/\$0.93 = 12.6 times
Industry average:	13.2 times

Sunshine's earnings are valued as worth a bit less than the average firm in its industry.

Market/book ratio = stock price/book value per share

Book value per share is total equity divided by the number of shares of common stock outstanding. This ratio compares stock price, the value of a company's equity in the market, to the firm's accountants' value for the same equity. Since accounting values are designed to err on the conservative side ("lower of cost or market"), this ratio is generally above 1.0 for a well-regarded firm.

For Sunshine:	Book value per share = total equity/shares outstanding
	1992: \$5,504,000/1,250,000 = \$4.40
	1993: \$5,925,000/1,250,000 = \$4.74
	1994: \$6,460,000/1,250,000 = \$5.17
	1992: \$ 7.88/\$4.40 = 1.8 times
	1993: \$ 9.50/\$4.74 = 2.0 times
	1994: \$11.75/\$5.17 = 2.3 times
Industry average:	2.3 times

Sunshine's market/book ratio has improved over the past two years until it is now equal to that of the average firm in its industry.

Another ratio compares the market value of the firm to the cost of reproducing the firm's assets at today's prices:

Tobin's q ratio = (market value of debt + equity)/replacement cost of assets

This ratio, named after James Tobin, the economist who proposed it[14], is an attempt to improve the market/book ratio to account for inflation. One reason a firm might have a high market/book ratio is if the firm purchased its assets some time ago at prices that are low by today's standards. This would result in the firm having a relatively low book value. Tobin's q substitutes replacement cost, hence today's prices, for book value. Also, since assets are claimed by all debt and equity holders, Tobin substituted the market value of all the firm's obligations for the market value of just the firm's stock in the numerator. If all a company can offer its investors is a minimum acceptable return on its assets, q should be equal to 1—that is, investors could get the same return from buying either the firm's assets or its stock. Well-managed firms typically have a q greater than 1, indicating

---

[14] **Reference:** James Tobin, "A General Equilibrium Approach to Monetary Theory," *Journal of Money, Credit, and Banking* 1 (Feb. 1969):15–29.

that the firm is more valuable than simply the sum of the value of its assets. This might be due to the quality of its processes, products, and services; to the abilities of its management; to a superior marketing capability; or to intangible assets such as brand names, trademarks, or copyrights. Tobin's q is often used as a guide to identify suitable candidates for acquisition: when a company's q is less than 1, it is cheaper to buy the company than to invest directly in comparable assets.

Example

Tobin's q Ratio

Sunshine Company is thinking of manufacturing beach chairs. It can either acquire a small beach chair company or directly buy the manufacturing equipment, distribution channels, etc. Its analysts have calculated Tobin's q ratio for the beach chair company to be .85.

Question: Is it cheaper to buy the company or buy the assets?

Solution steps:

Tobin's q ratio = (market value of debt + equity)/replacement cost of assets
= .85

Rearranging:

market value of debt + equity = .85 × replacement cost of assets

Answer: It is cheaper (only 85% as costly) to acquire the other company than to buy equivalent assets.

Analyzing the Cash Flow Statement

The cash flow statement is particularly interesting to financial analysts since cash plays such an important role in a company's functioning. This accounting statement shows where cash came from and how it was spent. Cash flows are separated into three sections: cash flows from operating activities, cash flows from investing activities, and cash flows from financing activities.

- Operating cash flows are those from the income-generating activities of the business—collections from customers, payments to suppliers and employees, and payments of interest and taxes. Interest and dividends received are also included in this category for purposes of consistency since they enter the calculation of net income.
- Investing cash flows include payments for the purchase of plant assets, receipts from selling plant assets, and the principal amounts of loans made by the business.
- Financing cash flows include the proceeds from borrowing and from selling stock, payments made to repay debt, and payments to owners for dividends and to repurchase shares.

The sum of cash flows from operations, cash flows from investments, and cash flows from financing gives the net change to the balance of the company's cash plus cash equivalents (such as marketable securities). This appears on the statement as the line "net increase (decrease) in cash," and is then reconciled to the difference between the beginning and ending balances of cash plus equivalents

Cash flow from operations is normally shown in the "direct" form, listing each major category of inflow and outflow. However, there is a second way to show cash flow from operations known as "indirect" form. It is called indirect because it begins with net income and then adjusts the income figure to remove any number that is the result of accounting accruals and does not represent cash flow. This table is often presented at the bottom of the cash flow statement under a title such as "reconciliation of net income to cash provided by operations."

Example

Understanding Cash Provided by Operations

Consider the "reconciliation of net income to cash provided by operations" section of the Sunshine Company's cash flow statement for 1994. It begins with net income of $1,160. This number is partially a cash number and partially an accrual number. To obtain the portion which is cash flow, we must remove all accrual effects:

Net income	$1,160
Add back: Depreciation	1,154
Subtract: Increase in	
Accounts receivable	(108)
Inventories	(31)
Prepaids	(23)
Add: Increase in:	
Accounts payable	445
Wages payable	17
Taxes payable	11
Net cash provided by operations	$2,625

By far, the most important item to remove from net income is depreciation. Depreciation reflects an accounting procedure, the reduction of the value of plant and equipment as time goes by. No cash is spent when an asset is depreciated, rather the depreciation reflects cash spent in some prior year. Since depreciation is a subtraction (expense) on the income statement, we remove it from net income by adding it back. A common error is to see depreciation added to net income and to conclude that net income and depreciation are separate sources of cash. We often hear sophisticated people who should know better refer to depreciation as a source of cash because of this presentation style. In fact, *depreciation can never be a source of cash.* A company can depreciate assets on its books as much as it wants and it will not have one cent more of money![15]

The other adjustments to Sunshine's net income reflect further differences between income and cash flow. Since accounts receivable increased, not all of Sunshine's sales was collected as cash. The increase to inventories means Sunshine spent more cash to acquire products than reflected in cost of goods sold. Similarly, the increase to prepaids indicates the company spent more money for these services than reflected in operating expenses. The increases to accounts,

[15] **Elaboration and cross-reference:** Of course, depreciation does produce a tax benefit, and in this sense it indirectly leads to the firm having more cash. As we saw in Appendix 4C, pages 106–108, depreciation calculated using the ACRS method is permitted as a deduction on the firm's tax return. On the cash flow statement, the tax benefit from depreciation is included in net income and is one of the numbers we do not wish to remove since it does represent cash flow.

wages, and taxes payable tell us that the corresponding expenses include money not yet paid, and the firm has more cash than the expense numbers would otherwise imply.

We look at the cash flow statement in three ways, (1) for internal consistency within each year, (2) for trends across time periods, and (3) as it compares to industry and competitive bencahmarks.

1. Internal Time-Period Consistency

There should be a match between the maturities of a firm's sources and uses of cash. Short-term sources are appropriate for short term uses. Long-term sources should fund long-term uses. Dividends should be funded by earnings and not by borrowing or through the sale of assets. A mismatch indicates poor financial managing and suggests that the firm will have problems resolving its obligations in the future.

At first look, Sunshine's 1994 cash flow statement looks good, with the $2,625,000 of operating cash flow more than sufficient to cover the $625,000 of dividends. But further examination shows a mismatch: Sunshine is using a short-term source (bank debt) to finance some long-term uses—in particular, all of the investment and financing uses are long term. The $625,000 of dividends and the $500,000 of long-term debt repayment represent money which will not come back to the firm. The $1,938,000 spent on new plant will take many years to return as the plant gradually produces product. In total, Sunshine spent $3,063,000 ($625,000 + $500,000 + $1,938,000) on long-term uses. However, only the $2,625,000 (and perhaps the $147,000 of cash reduction if Sunshine had excess cash) represents a long-term source of cash, a source that does not have to be repaid in the near term. Sunshine used $291,000 of short-term bank debt to help pay its long-term obligations. This raises the question: where will Sunshine get the cash to repay the bank debt when it falls due in the next few months?

2. Time-Series Analysis

It is useful to trace a firm's sources and uses of cash over a period of time to learn more about how a company raises and spends cash. In addition, it is not always possible to have internal time-period consistency in every year.

Over the three years 1992–1994, Sunshine raised its cash from operations and through borrowing from its bank. Cash was used for dividends; for debt retirement; and to increase property, plant, and equipment. Sunshine used bank debt to finance long-term uses throughout the period. On the other hand, Sunshine has shown a healthy increase in its source from operations over the three years. If the need for additional plant does not grow faster than its source of cash from operations, Sunshine may be on the verge of reducing its reliance on bank debt.

3. Cross-Section Analysis

It is useful to compare a firm's ability to bring in cash with its peers and with its industry in general to learn if the firm is more or less reliant on any particular source of funding. We can also compare a company's uses of cash with other firms and with the industry to test management's decisions about allocating its cash resources.

Questions

1. Why is it possible to talk of a "rule-of-thumb" number, such as 2.0, for the current ratio, but not have a comparable rule-of-thumb number for the times interest earned ratio?
2. If the value of one of a firm's ratios is cut in half, can we be sure that the firm's condition has improved?
3. Which ratios would be of most interest to:
   a. Managers?
   b. Customers?
   c. Shareholders?
   d. Creditors?
   e. Employees?
   f. Governments?
   g. Neighbors?
4. Why do industries that have low total asset turnover ratios tend to have high net profit margins and vice versa?
5. What would be the effect of inflation on ratios? How would an analyst take inflation into account in interpreting ratios?
6. Why are common size financial statements used for financial analysis instead of the actual statements themselves?
7. Why might an analyst pay more attention to average balance values in looking at a seasonal or growing firm than when studying a firm that remains constant throughout the year?
8. Is the fixed asset turnover ratio more relevant in the analysis of McDonald's Corporation or General Motors Corporation? Why?

Problems

1. **(Profitability)** A firm had the following income statement for last year:

Sales	$37,611
Less: Cost of goods sold	20,889
Gross profit	16,722
Less: Operating expenses	11,483
Less: Depreciation	1,575
Operating profit (EBIT)	3,664
Less: Interest expense	1,400
Earnings before taxes (EBT)	2,264
Less: Tax expense	792
Earnings after taxes (EAT)	$1,472

   Calculate the firm's:
   a. Gross profit margin ratio
   b. Operating profit margin ratio
   c. Pre-tax profit margin ratio
   d. Net profit margin ratio

2. **(Profitability)** A financial analyst calculated the following ratios from a firm's most recent income statement:

   Gross profit margin = 60%

   Operating profit margin = 27%

   Pre-tax profit margin = 14%

   The firm had sales of $500,000 and paid federal income taxes at a 35% rate.
   a. Reproduce the firm's income statement.
   b. Calculate the firm's net profit margin ratio.

3. **(Rates of return)** The firm of Problem 1 finances itself with equal amounts of liabilities and owners' equity. Calculate the firm's basic earning power, return on assets, and return on equity if its average total assets last year were equal to:
   a. $5,000
   b. $15,000
   c. $25,000
   d. $35,000

4. **(Rates of return)** A financial analyst calculated the following ratios from a firm's most recent financial statements:

   Operating profit margin = 22%

   Net profit margin = 6.5%

   Return on assets = 9%

   Return on equity = 14%

   The firm had sales of $2,500,000. Calculate the firm's:
   a. Earnings before interest and taxes (EBIT)
   b. Earnings after taxes (EAT)
   c. Average total assets
   d. Average total equity

5. **(Liquidity)** A firm has current assets at year-end consisting of:

Cash	$12,000
Marketable securities	5,000
Accounts receivable	22,000
Inventory (work-in-process)	8,000
Total current assets	$47,000

Calculate the firm's year-end current ratio and quick ratio if its current liabilities equal:

a. $10,000
b. $25,000
c. $40,000
d. $60,000

6. **(Liquidity)** A firm has a year-end current ratio of 1.85 and a quick ratio of 1.18. Total current assets equal $125,000. Calculate the firm's balance of:

a. Total current liabilities
b. Quick assets
c. Inventory

7. **(Seasonality)** A firm has the following partial quarterly balance sheets:

	Quarter 1	Quarter 2
Cash	$ 3,000	$ 1,000
Marketable securities	3,000	500
Accounts receivable	6,000	2,000
Inventory (work-in-process)	4,000	10,000
Total current assets	$16,000	$13,500
Total current liabilities	$10,000	$15,000

	Quarter 3	Quarter 4
Cash	$ 1,500	$ 2,000
Marketable securities	500	5,000
Accounts receivable	11,500	4,000
Inventory (work-in-process)	6,000	2,000
Total current assets	$19,500	$13,000
Total current liabilities	$12,000	$ 6,000

a. For each quarter, calculate the firm's current ratio and quick ratio.
b. In which quarter are the firm's ratios the strongest? why?
c. In which quarter are the firm's ratios the weakest? why?
d. Where is the firm's asset risk exposure in quarters 2 and 3?

8. **(Seasonality)** At the end of the first quarter, a firm has $50,000 of inventory. In the second quarter, all of the inventory is sold for $70,000 on 90-day credit terms. In the third quarter, the full $70,000 is collected as cash. The firm has no other inventory and has other current assets equal to $15,000. Total current liabilities remain constant at $40,000 throughout the period. Calculate the firm's current ratio and quick ratio:

a. At the end of the first quarter
b. At the end of the second quarter
c. At the end of the third quarter
d. How much of the change to the ratios is due to the firm's seasonality and how much is due to the recording of the $20,000 profit?

9. **(Accounts receivable)** A firm has annual sales of $5 million, of which 20% is for cash and the remainder is credit sales. What is the firm's accounts receivable turnover and average collection period if its average balance of accounts receivable is:

a. $250,000?
b. $500,000?
c. $750,000?
d. $1,000,000?

10. **(Accounts receivable)** A firm has annual sales of $9,000,000 and an average balance of accounts receivable of $500,000. What is the firm's accounts receivable turnover and average collection period if the percentage of its sales that is made on credit is:

a. 50%?
b. 75%?
c. 90%?
d. 100%?

11. **(Inventory)** A firm reported cost of goods sold of $100,000 last year. Determine the firm's inventory turnover and inventory days ratios if the firm maintained an average balance in inventory of:

a. $100,000
b. $50,000
c. $10,000
d. $1,000

12. **(Inventory)** A firm reported cost of goods sold of $2,500,000 last year. Determine the firm's average inventory balance if its:

a. Inventory turnover is 5 times
b. Inventory remains on hand for an average of 60 days
c. Inventory turnover is 15 times
d. Inventory remains on hand for an average of 5 days

13. **(Accounts payable)** A firm purchased $60,000 of merchandise inventory last year. Determine the firm's accounts payable turnover and payables period ratios if the firm maintained an average balance in the account "accounts payable—merchandise inventory" of:

a. $3,000
b. $6,000
c. $10,000
d. $20,000

14. **(Accounts payable)** A firm purchased $400,000 of merchandise inventory last year. Determine the average balance in the firm's account "accounts payable—merchandise inventory" if:
    a. Accounts payable turnover is 10 times
    b. It takes an average of 45 days to pay accounts payable
    c. Accounts payable turnover is 20 times
    d. It takes an average of 10 days to pay accounts payable
15. **(Cash conversion cycle)** Last year a firm had an inventory days ratio equal to 15 days and a payables period ratio equal to 30 days. Calculate the firm's cash conversion cycle if its collection period was:
    a. zero (all sales on a cash basis)
    b. 18 days
    c. 30 days
    d. 60 days
16. **(Cash conversion cycle)** Last year a firm had an inventory turnover ratio of 8 times and an accounts payable turnover ratio of 12 times. Calculate the firm's cash conversion cycle if its accounts receivable turnover was:
    a. 3 times
    b. 8 times
    c. 12 times
    d. 30 times
17. **(Fixed and total assets)** A firm had an average balance of total assets equal to $100,000 last year of which 40%, on average, were current assets. Calculate its fixed asset turnover ratio and total asset turnover ratio if the firm's sales was:
    a. $100,000
    b. $250,000
    c. $500,000
    d. $1,000,000
18. **(Fixed and total assets)** Last year a firm had a fixed asset turnover ratio of 6.5 times and a total asset turnover ratio of 4.2 times. Calculate the average balance of total assets, fixed assets, and current assets if sales was:
    a. $1,000,000
    b. $2,000,000
    c. $5,000,000
    d. $25,000,000
19. **(Financing mix)** A firm's year-end balance sheet reported total liabilities of $250,000 of which noninterest-bearing liabilities (accounts payable, wages payable, etc.) made up $75,000. Calculate the firm's debt ratio, funded-debt ratio, and debt/equity ratio if the firm's total assets equal:
    a. $1,000,000
    b. $750,000
    c. $450,000
    d. $300,000
20. **(Financing mix)** A financial analyst calculated the following ratios from a firm's year-end balance sheet

    Debt ratio = 45%

    Funded debt ratio = 35%

    The firm's year-end total assets were $900,000. Calculate the firm's year-end:
    a. Total liabilities
    b. Interest-bearing liabilities
    c. Noninterest-bearing liabilities
    d. Debt/equity ratio
21. **(Debt service)** A firm reported EBIT of $85,000 last year, which included lease payments of $20,000. The firm paid interest of $25,000 and repaid $15,000 of debt principal. Cash flow from operations was $100,000. The firm is in the 35% federal income tax bracket. Calculate the following ratios for this firm:
    a. Times interest earned
    b. Lease-adjusted times interest earned
    c. Cash-flow-based times interest earned
       (1) Without adjusting for leases
       (2) Including an adjustment for leases
    d. Fixed charge coverage
       (1) Without adjusting for leases
       (2) Including an adjustment for leases
22. **(Debt service)** A financial analyst calculated the following ratios from a firm's year-end financial statements:

    Times interest earned = 6 times

    Lease-adjusted times interest earned = 4.5 times

    Cash-flow-based times interest earned = 5 times

    Fixed charge coverage (excluding leases) = 3 times

    The firm had an EBIT of $500,000 and is in the 35% federal income tax bracket. For the current year, determine the firm's:
    a. Interest expense
    b. Lease payments
    c. Cash flow from operations
    d. Principal repayments
23. **(Dividends)** Last year a firm earned $65,000 after taxes. Calculate its dividend payout ratio and retention ratio if its dividend payment was:
    a. nothing
    b. $10,000
    c. $30,000
    d. $50,000

24. **(Dividends)** A firm is considering the cash-flow implications of its dividend policy. Last year's earnings were $140,000. Calculate the amount of its dividend and the amount of earnings retained, if it sets its dividend payout ratio at:
    a. zero
    b. 30%
    c. 65%
    d. 100%

25. **(Market value)** For the last several years, a firm has had 1 million shares of outstanding common stock. Last year the firm earned $3,500,000 after taxes and reported total assets of $2,000,000 and total liabilities of $1,200,000. Calculate the firm's price/earnings ratio and market/book ratio if its common stock is currently selling for a per-share price of:
    a. $10.00
    b. $25.00
    c. $40.00
    d. $75.00

26. **(Market value)** For the last several years, a firm has had 100,000 shares of outstanding common stock. Last year the firm earned $300,000 after taxes. Calculate the firm's stock price if its price/earnings ratio is currently:
    a. 5 times
    b. 12 times
    c. 20 times
    d. 35 times

APPENDIX 4E

THE INTERRELATIONSHIP OF RATIOS

Many commonly used ratios are calculated using sales (profitability ratios comparing profits to sales, accounts receivable ratios, fixed asset turnover, total asset turnover) or using total assets (profitability ratios comparing profits to assets, total asset turnover, debt ratios). As a result, a change in sales or a change in total assets affects the value of quite a few ratios at the same time. Years ago, analysts at the du Pont chemical company recognized that ratios were interrelated, and they devised a way to connect several of the more important ratios to focus attention on the underlying causes of a firm's performance.

1. The Basic du Pont Relationship

The basic du Pont relationship explains a firm's return on assets as the product of its net profit margin and total asset turnover ratios:

$$\textit{Return on assets} = \textit{net profit margin} \times \textit{total asset turnover}$$

This must be true from the way these three ratios are defined. Recall:

$$\begin{aligned} \text{Return on assets} &= \text{earnings after taxes/average total assets} \\ \text{Net profit margin} &= \text{earnings after taxes/sales} \\ \text{Total asset turnover} &= \text{sales/average total assets} \end{aligned}$$

Therefore, substituting the definitions for the ratios, we see that the equality holds:

$$\text{Return on assets} = \text{net profit margin} \times \text{total asset turnover}$$

$$\frac{\text{earnings after taxes}}{\text{average total assets}} = \frac{\text{earnings after taxes}}{\text{sales}} \times \frac{\text{sales}}{\text{average total assets}}$$

$$= \frac{\text{earnings after taxes}}{\text{average total assets}} \quad ✓✓$$

For Sunshine:[1]	1990:	Return on assets = 6.1%
		Net profit margin = 4.2%
		Total asset turnover = 1.5 times
		and: 6.1% = 4.2% × 1.5[2]
	1991:	Return on assets = 6.5%
		Net profit margin = 4.3%
		Total asset turnover = 1.5 times
		and: 6.5% = 4.3% × 1.5

2. The Extended du Pont Relationship

The extended du Pont relationship translates return on assets to return on shareholder's equity. It shows that a firm's return on equity is the product of its return on assets and its financial leverage expressed as the ratio of assets to equity:

$$\textit{Return on equity} = \textit{return on assets} \times \left(\frac{\textit{assets}}{\textit{equity}}\right)$$

Again, this relationship comes directly from the definitions of the ratios. Recall:

$$\text{Return on equity} = \text{earnings after taxes}/\text{average total equity}$$
$$\text{Return on assets} = \text{earnings after taxes}/\text{average total assets}$$

And substituting:

$$\text{Return on equity} = \text{return on assets} \times \frac{\text{assets}}{\text{equity}}$$

$$\frac{\text{earnings after taxes}}{\text{average total equity}} = \frac{\text{earnings after taxes}}{\text{average total assets}} \times \frac{\text{average total assets}}{\text{average total equity}}$$

$$= \frac{\text{earnings after taxes}}{\text{average total equity}} \quad ✓✓$$

For Sunshine:	Average total assets:	
	1990:	= ($16,501,000 + 17,551,000)/2 = $17,026,000
	1991:	= ($17,551,000 + 18,350,000)/2 = $17,950,500

[1] **Cross-reference:** The Sunshine Company is the ongoing example of Appendix 4D, "Analysis of Financial Accounting Data." We continue to use that company's financial reports in this appendix. The Sunshine Company's financial statements appear on pages 114–116.

[2] **Observation:** There is a bit of round-off error here.

Average total equity:
1990: = ($5,504,000 + $5,925,000)/2 = $5,714,500
1991: = ($5,925,000 + $6,460,000)/2 = $6,192,500
1990: Return on equity = 18.3%
Return on assets = 6.1%
Assets/equity = $17,026,000/$5,714,500 = 3.0 times
and: 18.3% = 6.1% × 3.0
1991: Return on equity = 18.7%
Return on assets = 6.5%
Assets/equity = $17,950,500/$6,192,500 = 2.9 times
and: 18.7% = 6.5% × 2.9

The extended du Pont relationship may also be written using all three ratios. Start with the extended relationship:

$$\text{Return on equity} = \text{return on assets} \times (\text{assets/equity})$$

Remember that the basic du Pont relationship is:

$$\text{Return on assets} = \text{net profit margin} \times \text{total asset turnover}$$

and, substituting:

$$\textit{Return on equity} = \textit{net profit margin} \times \textit{total asset turnover} \times \frac{\textit{assets}}{\textit{equity}}$$

3. Taking the Extended du Pont Relationship a Bit Further

The focus of the extended du Pont relationship is on return to shareholders.[3] Since shareholders' return comes primarily through stock price, we can expand the du Pont relationship forward to show how return on equity translates to share price. We can also identify how management of balance sheet and income statement accounts feeds into the du Pont ratios. Figure 4E.1 summarizes the du Pont relationship (identified by the darker boxes) and shows how it can be stretched in both directions. In each case, the two ratios next to each other are multiplied together to produce the ratio above.

Return on equity is multiplied by book value per share to produce earnings per share. This adjusts the overall return on equity to return per individual share of common stock.

$$\begin{aligned}\text{Earnings per share} &= \text{return on equity} \times \text{book value per share}\\ &= \frac{\text{earnings after taxes}}{\text{average total equity}} \times \frac{\text{average total equity}}{\text{number of shares}}\\ &= \frac{\text{earnings after taxes}}{\text{number of shares}} \quad \checkmark\checkmark\end{aligned}$$

[3] **Elaboration:** The analysts at du Pont who created this system were assigned the job of evaluating companies that du Pont might buy as part of its expansion after World War I. Since du Pont would be a stockholder of any company they acquired, return on equity was naturally one of their primary concerns.

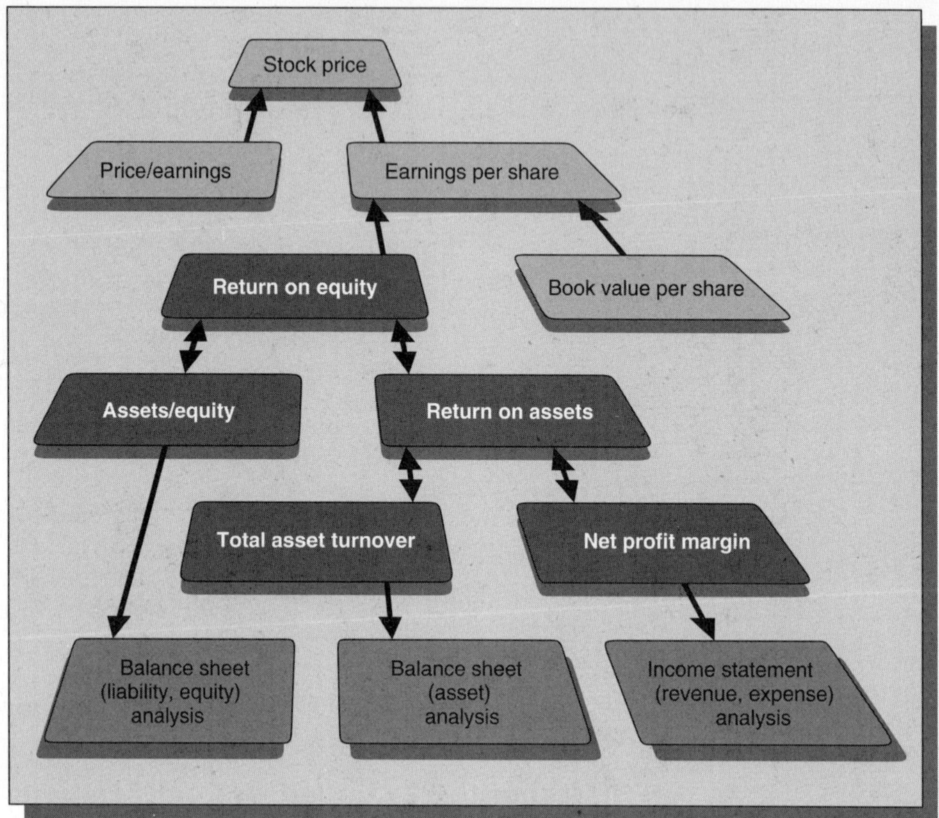

FIGURE 4E.1
Extending the du Pont relationship. The du Pont relationship, identified by the darker boxes, can be extended backward to the financial statements and forward to stock price.

Earnings per share is then further multiplied by the price/earnings ratio to give the firm's stock price.

$$\textit{Stock price} = \textit{earnings per share} \times \frac{\textit{price}}{\textit{earnings}}$$

4. Using the Extended du Pont Relationship

We can use the extended du Pont relationship in financial analysis and diagnosis. The relationship tells us that return on equity (ROE) comes from three sources:

- Net profit margin (NPM)—the firm's ability to produce profit from its sales.
- Total asset turnover (TAT)—the firm's ability to generate sales from its investment in assets.
- Assets/equity (A/E)—the firm's ability to use debt to fix the return going to creditors, hence direct proportionally more of its profits to its shareholders.

We can also use the extended du Pont relationship to learn about economic structure. Two firms with the same return on equity might arrive at that result by completely different paths.

Example

Using the Extended du Pont Relationship to Understand a Company's Financial Performance

A company has consistently underperformed its industry, producing a 12% return on equity as compared to the industry average of 19.6%.

Question: What is the reason for the company's poor ROE?

Solution steps: We know that:

$$ROE = NPM \times TAT \times A/E$$

so we focus on these ratios. Upon researching their values we find:

	Company	Industry
Net profit margin	2%	2%
Total asset turnover	2.0	3.5
Assets/equity	3.0	2.8

The company's NPM equals that of the industry, which suggests that its costs and pricing are in line with its peers. The company's TAT, however, is quite a bit lower than the industry average. This indicates a problem with asset utilization—perhaps the company has assets it does not need. In addition, the company's financial leverage is a bit higher than the industry average. Without this boost to ROE, the company's performance would have been even worse. (If there are unneeded assets that could be sold, the company could reduce its debt level and bring its financial leverage back in line with the industry.)

Answer: The problem appears to be with the company's assets.[4]

Example

Using the Extended du Pont Relationship as a Diagnostic Aid

A company's return on equity is down by 10%. Its net profit margin is down by 7% while total asset turnover is unchanged.

Question: Is the decrease in ROE due solely to lower profits?

Solution steps: We know that:

$$ROE = NPM \times TAT \times A/E$$

A 7% decline in NPM, all else unchanged, would decrease ROE by 7% as well. Therefore, either TAT or the firm's financial leverage (A/E) must also have decreased. But we know that TAT is unchanged. We conclude that A/E must be down.

Answer: The decrease in ROE is not due solely to the reduced NPM. Financial leverage accounts for some of the lowered ROE.

[4] **Elaboration:** Upon further analysis, we might find a good reason for the company's TAT to be so relatively low. Perhaps the company makes specialty or custom products that take a long time to produce or that require specialized machinery. But if this turns out to be the case, we would next focus on the NPM ratio, since a company with specialized products might not face a high degree of competition and might be able to produce higher-than-industry-average NPM to offset its low TAT. This reminds us that ratios are *general* indicators of health and always require further analysis prior to reaching a conclusion.

Example

Using the Extended du Pont Relationship as a Guide to Differences in Economic Structure

A retailer and a manufacturer both have a 20% return on equity.

Question: How does each firm achieve its 20% ROE?

Solution steps: When we research the firms we discover:

	NPM ×	TAT ×	A/E =	ROE
Retailer	0.5% ×	16 ×	2.5 =	20%
Manufacturer	5.0% ×	2 ×	2.0 =	20%

Answer: The retailer relies on a high total asset turnover, especially from the rapid movement of inventory. Because it is in a very competitive business, it cannot produce a high net profit margin. The manufacturer, on the other hand, obtains its return primarily from its net profit margin; with its need for a high level of fixed assets, it cannot produce a high total asset turnover. The retailer also uses a bit more financial leverage than the manufacturer.

Problems

1. **(Basic du Pont relationship)** A company has a net profit margin of 4%. Calculate its return on assets if it turns over its assets:
   a. Two times/year
   b. Three times/year
   c. Four times/year
   d. Five times/year
2. **(Basic du Pont relationship)** A company has a total asset turnover of six times/year. Calculate its return on assets if its net profit margin is:
   a. 2%
   b. 3%
   c. 4%
   d. 5%
3. **(Extended du Pont relationship)** A company's return on assets is 10%. Calculate its return on equity if its assets/equity ratio is:
   a. 1
   b. 2
   c. 3
   d. 4
4. **(Extended du Pont relationship)** A company's assets/equity ratio is 2. Calculate its return on equity if its return on assets is:
   a. 3%
   b. 6%
   c. 9%
   d. 12%
5. **(Understanding financial performance)** A company with a 6% net profit margin turns over its assets three times per year and has an assets/equity ratio of 2.5. Comparable figures for the industry are 5%, 4.2, and 3.0.
   a. Calculate the company's return on equity.
   b. Calculate the industry-average return on equity.
   c. Is the company outperforming or underperforming the industry?
   d. What is the reason for your result in part c?
6. **(Understanding financial performance)** A company with a 1.5% net profit margin turns over its assets ten times per year and has an assets/equity ratio of 2. Comparable figures for the industry are 2%, 8, and 1.5.
   a. Calculate the company's return on equity.
   b. Calculate the industry-average return on equity.
   c. Is the company outperforming or underperforming the industry?
   d. What is the reason for your result in part c?
7. **(Diagnosis)** A company's return on equity has risen in the past year by 20%; however, its net profit margin has remained unchanged over this period. What is the reason for the increased rate of return if its:
   a. Total asset turnover is also unchanged?
   b. Total asset turnover is up by 10%?
   c. Total asset turnover is up by 20%?
   d. Total asset turnover is up by 30%?
8. **(Diagnosis)** A company's return on equity has declined in the past year by 10%; however, its financial structure has remained unchanged over this period. What is the reason for the decreased rate of return if its:
   a. Total asset turnover is also unchanged?
   b. Total asset turnover is up by 10%?
   c. Total asset turnover is down by 10%?
   d. Total asset turnover is down by 20%?

PART II THE BASICS OF MONEY

In Part II we look at money, the central focus of financial managing.

Chapter 5 introduces time value of money, the fundamental concept that the value of money depends on both its amount and when it is received or paid. We develop the basic time value relationship and then systematically extend it to describe more complex patterns of cash flows and time periods less than one year. Appendix 5A further extends the time value concept to continuous compounding. Appendix 5B illustrates how to use the cash flow list feature of an advanced financial calculator. Appendix 5C presents the derivations of several time value formulas.

Chapter 6 looks at interest rates, the price of money. We first connect interest rates to time value and review the economic models that explain the level of interest rates. We then introduce a model of the components of interest rates that helps us organize their structure—why interest rates differ by maturity, risk, and taxability. Appendix 6A presents the derivation of the relationship relating expectations of future interest rates to the rates we observe today.

Chapter 7 explores exchange rates, the price of one currency relative to another. After describing various exchange rate systems, we look at spot and forward rates and how they are determined in the foreign exchange markets. We also examine the key relationships that determine relative currency values. Appendix 7A presents these relationships in a more formal, algebraic manner.

CHAPTER 5
THE TIME VALUE OF MONEY

Jay Herman boarded his morning train, settled in to a seat, and opened his attaché case. He took out the box containing his new financial calculator and the instruction manual that came with it. Jay smiled as he thought of how his wife had teased him about "one more high-tech toy," but even he was impressed by the number of buttons on the calculator and the size of the manual. This was one heck of a sophisticated "toy!"

Jay had recently joined the finance group of a medium-sized consumer products company. Because of his experience in manufacturing, his first assignment was to participate on a team studying improvements in an important production process. As preparation for that assignment, the company had provided him with the calculator.

Jay thought back to the group's last meeting, where group members had had a good discussion of process measurements, identified problems, and brainstormed solutions. The team had agreed that one solution looked particulary promising and should be studied further. Jay's role, as the finance person on the team, was to analyze the cash flow benefits and costs of implementing that solution and report back at the team's next meeting.

The cry of the conductor announcing the next station interrupted Jay's recollections. As he watched the throng on the platform squeezing toward the narrow train doors, Jay looked again at his new calculator. He remembered the awkwardness of the old time-value tables he had used in school, and realized how much he looked forward to learning how to use the calculator to help him make a positive contribution to the team's efforts.

As he gets more deeply into his analysis, Jay is going to find that the proposed process improvement will change his company's cash flows. There will be new costs and benefits while other costs and benefits will disappear. In addition to identifying the amounts of these changed cash flows, the team will have to estimate *when* they will occur so Jay can establish their "time value." Jay will indeed put his new financial calculator to very good use.

time value of money—the concept that the value of money depends on the date of its receipt or payment

Every organization is regularly receiving and paying money. Regardless of the size of the enterprise, time value underlies all financial decision making. A knowledge of the concepts of the **time value of money** is crucial for good financial managing.

Key Points You Should Learn from This Chapter

After reading this chapter you should be able to:

- Understand why the value of money depends on the time of its receipt or payment and, therefore, why money amounts can only be compared after they have been adjusted for time.
- Calculate the present value and future value of cash flows, the interest rate that describes any set of cash flows, and the length of time it takes to reach a financial goal.
- Analyze a set of uneven cash flows.
- Recognize when time value analysis can be simplified because the cash flows form a standard pattern.
- Identify the difference between a nominal rate, an effective rate, and the annual percentage rate (APR), and convert interest rates to equivalent rates for other periods of time.

Introductory Concepts—The Money Rules

If your rich uncle offered you a gift of either $100 or $150, which would you choose? Assuming there were no strings attached, most of us would choose the $150. We all know that it is better to have more money than less, other things being equal. The same concept works in the other direction as well. Suppose your uncle brought a car to your home and told you that you could own it by paying him either $3,000 or $4,000. What would you do? It is clearly better to pay only $3,000. In fact, if the car were really worth $4,000, buying it for $3,000 would add $1,000 to your wealth.[1] We summarize these ideas as Money Rule #1:

MONEY RULE #1: Value depends on the AMOUNT of money involved.
Choose to receive MORE.
Choose to pay LESS.

Suppose now that your uncle offered you a slightly different choice. You could have $100 today or the same $100 next year. Now which would you choose? Again, in the absence of "strings," most of us would choose to get the $100 today. Getting money sooner is better than getting it later. Turn the problem around. Which would you rather pay: $100 now or $100 a year from now? The better choice is to pay the $100 next year. These insights lead us to Money Rule #2:

MONEY RULE #2: Value depends on the TIMING of money flows.
Choose to receive money SOONER.
Choose to pay money LATER.

Of the several reasons why money depends on time, by far the most important is that money can be invested to earn positive interest rates. $100 received today can be invested to earn interest and to grow to be more than $100.[2]

Example

Earning Interest

If you deposited the $100 in a bank account that paid 6% interest, your $100 would grow to be $106 (the $100 deposit or "principal" plus 6% of the $100 or $6 interest). You would be $6 better off than if you simply got the $100 next year.

Virtually all business deals involve trades of money. We invest some money today with the expectation of receiving a greater amount in the future. We insist

[1] **Observation:** This is the basic idea underlying most financial transactions: buy something for less than it is worth to you. In particular, you could sell the car for its $4,000 value and turn the $1,000 gain into cash.

[2] **Elaboration:** Other reasons why time affects the value of money include the ability to take advantage of a special opportunity to purchase something, the loss of purchasing power due to inflation, and the risk associated with having to wait for a cash flow. However, if interest rates correctly contain compensation for postponing consumption, for inflation, and for risk, these concerns are all "priced" in today's rates and are included in the analysis of this chapter. We will explore the makeup of interest rates in more detail in the next chapter.

that we get back more than we invest in order to create a gain (that is, we follow the advice of Money Rule #1), but the very fact that we pay money now and receive money later creates an offsetting loss (we violate Money Rule #2). Every business deal, therefore, requires a comparison: we must determine if the gain from receiving more money than we invest outweighs the loss from investing today but not receiving the return on our investment until some later date. This is Money Rule #3:

> **MONEY RULE #3:** The value of a business deal involves a TRADEOFF between the amount of the money flows and the time of their receipt or payment

To make this test, we must first do a time value of money calculation since it is impossible to combine or compare cash flows and values that occur at different times. This is Money Rule #4:

> **MONEY RULE #4:** Money flows can only be compared after they have been adjusted for their time value

Sometimes the appropriate time value calculation is simple enough so that you can do it without any computational help.

Example

Calculating a Rate of Return: A Simple Case

You have the opportunity to invest $100 today in order to receive $125 in one year. What is the rate of return on this investment? The answer is 25%, and most people can easily do this calculation in their heads. If you were able to do this, your brain is functioning at least as well as a low-level financial calculator.

Most of the time, however, time value calculations are too complex for even the geniuses among us, and we must rely on a calculator, computer, or computer-generated table of numbers to give us the solution.[3]

Example

Calculating a Rate of Return: A More Difficult Case

You have the opportunity to invest $100 today in order to receive $40 one year later plus $60 one year after that, plus $50 after three years. What is the rate of return on this investment? Most people cannot do this calculation without some computational help. The answer is 22.40%, a result that required an advanced financial calculator to compute. Don't be too upset if you couldn't solve this problem in your head!

---

[3] **Elaboration:** This book is written with the assumption that students will have financial calculators available for their use. Financial calculators are far more efficient and capable than the limited time-value tables they replaced. In addition, they have become standard equipment in most modern businesses. They can be purchased for as little as $20, making them cheaper than many school supplies, including textbooks. (Time-value tables are included on pages 874–878 and instructions for their use are included in this book for those students and instructors who might wish to explore their use. In particular the solution to each time value example in this chapter is illustrated using both technologies.)

FINANCE IN PRACTICE

The U.S. Government Learns About Time Value of Money

After a three-year $500,000 study, the federal government says it's following a money-saving rule common to business: Collect receipts early and pay bills late.

The Office of Management and Budget says a series of efforts to accelerate the collection of federal revenues, channel more cash balances into interest-paying accounts and stop paying certain bills early is generating "savings" of $450 million a year.

Summing up the budget report, OMB Director James McIntyre said: "These actions allow the government, in the same manner as private firms, to make the most out of the time value of money it holds, collects and disburses, thereby reducing its debt requirements and resulting interest costs."

Federal interest costs will amount to $64.3 billion this year [1980].

Reference: "Get Receipts Sooner and Pay Bills Later Is New Federal Rule," The *Wall Street Journal,* Aug. 18, 1980, p. 3.

The concept of time value of money is perhaps the single most important concept in all of finance. It underlies the analysis of all investments and all forms of financing. In this chapter we will develop the basics of time value analysis. These techniques will then be applied over and over in many of the subsequent chapters.

The Fundamental Relationship

The amount of interest money can earn depends on the following three factors:

- Its amount (the principal)
- The interest rate it can earn (rate)
- How long it is invested (time)

simple interest—interest paid only on the initial principal and not on previously paid interest

You most likely saw this idea for the first time in elementary school, where you were taught the relationship for **simple interest:**

$$\text{Interest} = \text{Principal} \times \text{Rate} \times \text{Time}$$

This formula is true as long as the interest earned is removed (withdrawn) from the investment as it is paid. In business, however, it is much more usual for interest earnings not to be withdrawn from an investment. When interest earnings remain in an investment, they become part of the principal and earn interest in subsequent periods of time. This phenomenon, interest paid on previous interest, is called **compound interest.**

compound interest—interest paid on both the initial principal and previously paid interest

The fundamental time value of money relationship is the compound interest formula:

$$\textit{Future value} = \textit{present value}\ (1 + \textit{interest rate})^{\textit{number of time periods}}$$

You will see where this relationship comes from as we solve the first set of examples that follow.

The compound interest formula contains four variables. We will use the following notation to refer to them (we will add additional notation later as needed):

> **FV** = **Future Value:** a single cash flow or value at the end of a time frame.
>
> **PV** = **Present Value:** a single cash flow or value at the beginning of a time frame.[4]
>
> **n** = **number of time periods** between present and future value.
>
> **r** = **rate of interest** per time period. Also represented by the letter **i** when the financial calculator is to be used.

Using this notation, we can rewrite the compound interest formula as:

$$FV = PV(1 + r)^n$$

The potentially difficult part of this equation is the term $(1 + r)^n$. As a result, tables of values of $(1 + r)^n$ have been used for many years to simplify the calculation effort.[5] Figure 5.1 is an excerpt from Table 1, the table to use when calculating the future value of a present amount. Each row represents a value of **n,** each column a value of **r.** To use the table, follow one of two strategies, depending on which variable is the unknown:

1. If **FV** is the unknown, look up the value of $(1 + r)^n$ at the intersection of row **n** and column **r.** Then multiply that number by **PV** to obtain **FV.**
2. If **n** or **r** is the unknown, rearrange the future value equation to obtain the value of $(1 + r)^n$:

$$(1 + r)^n = FV/PV$$

Then (a) if you are solving for **n,** scan across the row for **n,** until you find the number closest to your value of $(1 + r)^n$ and look at the top of that column to find **r.**

FIGURE 5.1
Using a time value table. The tables can be used to obtain the value of $(1 + r)^n$ or to solve for **n** or **r.**

TABLE 1 Future Value Factors [FV of $1 after n periods at interest rate r = $(1 + r)^n$]

	1%	2%	3%	4%	(5%)	6%	7%
1	1.0100	1.0200	1.0300	1.0400	1.0500	1.0600	1.0700
2	1.0201	10404	1.0609	1.0816	1.1025	1.1236	1.1449
3	1.0303	1.0612	(1) 1.0927	(1.1249)	1.1576	1.1910	(2b) 1.2250
4	1.0406	1.0824	1.1255	1.1699	1.2155	1.2625	1.3108
5	1.0514	1.1041	(2a) 1.1593	1.2167	**1.2763**	1.3382	1.4026
6	1.0615	1.1262	1.1941	1.2653	1.3401	1.4185	1.5007
(7)	1.0721	1.1487	1.2299	1.3159	1.4071	**1.5036**	1.6058
8	1.0829	1.1717	1.2668	1.3686	1.4775	1.5938	1.7182

1. When you know **n** and **r** and are solving for **FV**
2a. When you know **FV** and **n** and are solving for **r**
2b. When you know **FV** and **r** and are solving for **n.**

[4] **Elaboration:** Since most business problems begin today (the present) and extend into the future, the terms *present value* and *future value* have become the standard usage for *beginning value* and *ending value.*

[5] **Cross-reference:** We have included such a table at the end of this book—it's identified as "Table 1—Future Value Factors"—as well as three additional tables for other time value problems.

(b) If you are solving for **r**, scan down the column for **r** until you find the number closest to your value of $(1 + r)^n$ and look at the left of that row to find **n.** (Note: it is also possible that the unknown is **PV,** but Table 2 is typically used for that problem.)

The problems may also be solved with a financial calculator by plugging in the data of the problem and letting the machine handle the arithmetic. The first three variables, **FV, PV,** and **n,** correspond precisely to the labels on the keys of your financial calculator. However, it is usual for calculators to use some variation of the letter "i" (such as **i, i%, %i,** or **I%YR**) rather than "r" to represent the interest rate.[6]

In solving time value problems we start with the values of three of the variables and then solve for the fourth. It does not matter which three we know and which is the unknown variable. In the examples that follow, we will illustrate all four possibilities, solving for: (1) future value, (2) present value, (3) the time period between two cash flows, and (4) the interest rate which joins two cash flows.

future value—a single cash flow or value at the end of a time frame

compounding—adding compound interest to a present value to produce a future value

1. Finding Future Value

Whenever we wish to determine the amount to which an investment will grow if our money earns interest for some period of time, we are looking for a **future value.** Solving for a future value is often referred to as **compounding** a present value.

Example

Compounding for One Year

Suppose you plan to deposit $1,000 into a bank account that pays 10% interest.

Question: How much will you have in your account after one year?

Solution steps:

1. Identify the data you have to work with. The $1,000 is a **present value,** a single beginning cash flow. You are also given the 10% **rate** and that the **number of time periods** (years) is one.
2. Identify what you are calculating. The answer will be a **future value,** a single value at the end of the one-year time frame.
3. Plug in the data and calculate the result. You can do this in several ways:
   a. By formula:

$$\begin{aligned} FV &= \text{Principal} + \text{interest} \\ &= PV + r \cdot PV \\ &= 1{,}000 + .10\ (1000) \\ &= 1{,}000 + 100 = \underline{\underline{1{,}100}} \end{aligned}$$

[6] **Elaboration:** In formulas, the rate of interest is always expressed in decimal form, thus 10% is represented as .10. In financial calculators, however, the rate of interest is always entered in percentage form. You would enter 10% into the calculator by keying in 10, not .10. Our choice of the letter **r** for formulas and **i** for calculators is intended to make this distinction. However, since time value tables are used with formulas, we will use **r** to denote the interest rate, even though most tables (ours included) show rates in percentage form.

Or, using the compound interest relationship:

$$\begin{aligned} FV &= PV\,(1 + r)^n \\ &= 1{,}000\,(1.10)^1 \\ &= 1{,}000\,(1.10) = \underline{\underline{1{,}100}} \end{aligned}$$

b. Using the time-value tables:

(1) Write the time value formula:

$$FV = PV(1 + r)^n$$

(2) Since **r** and **n** are known, look up the time value factor. Factors for the future value of a single present value are found in Table 1.

(3) Substitute into the formula and solve:

$$\begin{aligned} FV &= 1{,}000\,(1.1000) \\ &= \underline{\underline{1{,}100}} \end{aligned}$$

	8%	9%	10%	11%
1	~~1.0800~~	~~1.0900~~ ►	1.1000	1.1100
2	1.1664	1.1881	1.2100	1.2321
3	1.2597	1.2950	1.3310	1.3676
4	1.3605	1.4116	1.4041	1.5181
5	1.4693	1.5386	1.6105	1.6851
6	1.5869	1.6771	1.7716	1.8704
7	1.7138	1.8280	1.9487	2.0762
8	1.8509	1.9926	2.1436	2.3045
9	1.9990	2.1719	2.5379	2.5580
10	2.1589	2.3674	2.5937	2.8394
11	2.3316	2.5804	2.8531	2.1518
12	2.5182	2.8127	3.1384	3.4985
13	2.7196	3.0658	3.4523	3.8833
14	2.9372	3.3417	3.7975	4.3104

c. By financial calculator:

Key in 1,000, change the sign to negative,[7]
and press [PV]
Key in 10 and press [i]
Key in 1 and press [n]
Compute [FV] = 1,100

Answer: $1,100. You will still have your principal of $1,000 plus you will have earned interest equal to 10% of $1,000 or $100.

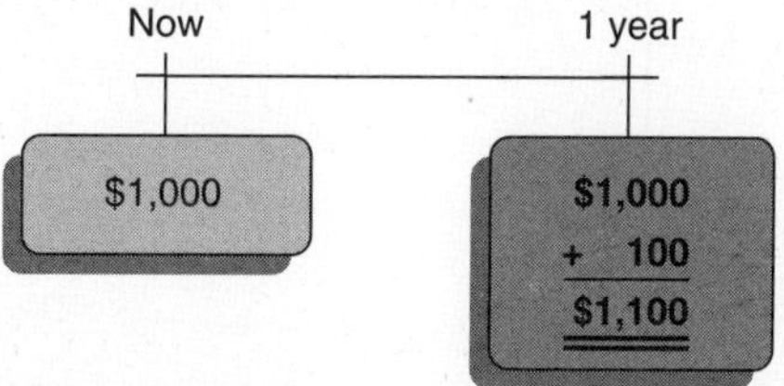

Example

Compounding for Two Years

Suppose you leave your $1,000 deposit in the bank for a second year.

Question: How much will you have in your account after two years if you can continue to earn 10% interest?

[7] **Elaboration:** A minus sign attached to a cash flow identifies it as an outflow while a positive cash flow is an inflow. In this problem we are telling the calculator we will *invest* 1,000 (hence the minus sign). The calculator responds with an answer of positive 1,100 indicating that in return for *giving* 1,000, we will *get* 1,100. Some older calculators will not accept the minus sign in front of the 1,000 present value. If so, simply enter the 1,000 as a positive number. Since the purpose of the negative sign is to distinguish cash outflows (−) from cash inflows (+), these older calculators will most likely not be able to handle complex patterns of cash flows.

Solution steps:

1. By formula (looking at the second year):

$$\begin{aligned} FV &= \text{Principal} + \text{interest} \\ &= PV + r \bullet PV \\ &= 1{,}100 + .10\ (1{,}100) \\ &= 1{,}100 + 110 = \underline{\underline{1{,}210}} \end{aligned}$$

Or, using the compound interest relationship (looking at both years together):

$$\begin{aligned} FV &= PV\ (1 + r)^n \\ &= 1{,}000\ (1.10)^2 \\ &= 1{,}000\ (1.21) = \underline{\underline{1{,}210}} \end{aligned}$$

2. Using the time-value tables:

a. Write the time value formula:

$$FV = PV(1 + r)^n$$

b. Since **r** and **n** are known, look up the time value factor. Factors for the future value of a single present value are found in Table 1.

c. Substitute into the formula and solve:

$$\begin{aligned} FV &= 1{,}000\ (1.2100) \\ &= \underline{\underline{1{,}210}} \end{aligned}$$

	8%	9%	10%	11%
1	1.0800	1.0900	1.1000	1.1100
2	1.1664	1.1881	1.2100	1.2321
3	1.2597	1.2950	1.3310	1.3676
4	1.3605	1.4116	1.4041	1.5181
5	1.4693	1.5386	1.6105	1.6851
6	1.5869	1.6771	1.7716	1.8704
7	1.7138	1.8280	1.9487	2.0762
8	1.8509	1.9926	2.1436	2.3045
9	1.9990	2.1719	2.5379	2.5580
10	2.1589	2.3674	2.5937	2.8394
11	2.3316	2.5804	2.8531	2.1518
12	2.5182	2.8127	3.1384	3.4985
13	2.7196	3.0658	3.4523	3.8833
14	2.9372	3.3417	3.7975	4.3104

3. By financial calculator:

Key in 1,000, change the sign to negative, and press [PV]
Key in 10 and press [i]
Key in 2 and press [n]
Compute [FV] = $\underline{\underline{1{,}210}}$

Answer: $\underline{\$1{,}210}$. By the end of the first year your account will have grown to $1,100. In the second year you will earn 10% interest on $1,100, or $110.

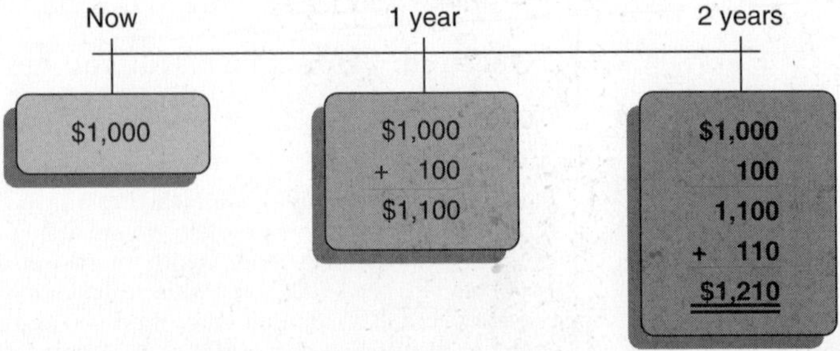

Example

Compounding for Three Years

Finally, suppose your $1,000 deposit remains in the bank and continues to earn 10% interest for a third year.

Question: How much will you have in your account after three years?

Solution steps:

1. By formula (looking at the third year):

$$\begin{aligned} FV &= \text{Principal} + \text{interest} \\ &= PV + r \bullet PV \\ &= 1{,}210 + .10\ (1210) \\ &= 1{,}210 + 121 = \underline{\underline{1{,}331}} \end{aligned}$$

Or, using the compound interest relationship (looking at the three years together):

$$\begin{aligned} FV &= PV\ (1 + r)^n \\ &= 1{,}000\ (1.10)^3 \\ &= 1{,}000\ (1.331) = \underline{\underline{1{,}331}} \end{aligned}$$

2. Using the time-value tables:
   a. Write the time value formula:

   $$FV = PV(1 + r)^n$$

   b. Since **r** and **n** are known, look up the time value factor. Factors for the future value of a single present value are found in Table 1.
   c. Substitute into the formula and solve:

   $$\begin{aligned} FV &= 1{,}000\ (1.3310) \\ &= \underline{\underline{1{,}331}} \end{aligned}$$

	8%	9%	10%	11%
1	1.0800	1.0900	1.1000	1.1100
2	1.1664	1.1881	1.2100	1.2321
3	~~1.2597~~	~~1.2950~~ →	**1.3310**	1.3676
4	1.3605	1.4116	1.4041	1.5181
5	1.4693	1.5386	1.6105	1.6851
6	1.5869	1.6771	1.7716	1.8704
7	1.7138	1.8280	1.9487	2.0762
8	1.8509	1.9926	2.1436	2.3045
9	1.9990	2.1719	2.5379	2.5580
10	2.1589	2.3674	2.5937	2.8394
11	2.3316	2.5804	2.8531	2.1518
12	2.5182	2.8127	3.1384	3.4985
13	2.7196	3.0658	3.4523	3.8833
14	2.9372	3.3417	3.7975	4.3104

3. By financial calculator:

Key in 1,000, change the sign to negative,
and press [PV]
Key in 10 and press [i]
Key in 3 and press [n]

Compute [FV] = $\underline{\underline{1{,}331}}$

Answer: $1,331. By the end of the second year your account will have grown to $1,210. In the third year you will earn 10% interest on $1,210, or $121.

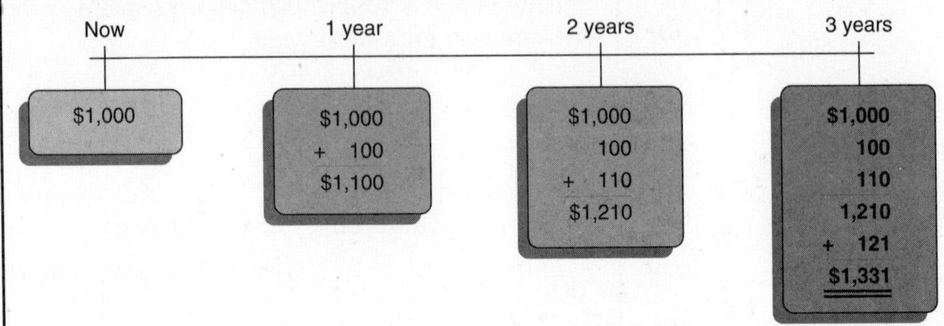

Do you see a pattern here? In each year, you get back the beginning principal and earn interest on that amount. Another way to say this is that each year's beginning principal is multiplied by (1 + r), where the "1" represents the return of principal and the "r" adds on the interest:

After 1 year: $FV = PV\ (1 + r)$

In the second year, the principal is $[PV(1 + r)]$, and

After 2 years: $FV = [PV(1 + r)] \bullet (1 + r) = PV\ (1 + r)^2$

In the third year, the principal is $[PV(1 + r)(1 + r)]$, and

After 3 years: $FV = [PV(1 + r)(1 + r)] \bullet (1 + r) = PV\ (1 + r)^3$

Continuing the pattern:

After n years: $\boldsymbol{FV = PV\ (1 + r)^n}$

and this is the compound interest relationship!

2. Finding Present Value

present value—a single cash flow or value at the beginning of a time frame

discounting—removing compound interest from a future value to produce a present value

Whenever we wish to determine how much we must invest today to produce a given future value, we are looking for a **present value.** An important use of this calculation is to establish a price for benefits we expect to receive in the future. Solving for a present value is often referred to as **discounting** a future cash flow.

The present value of a future amount is found by rearranging the compound interest formula to solve for **PV**:

$$PV = \frac{FV}{(1 + r)^n} = FV \frac{1}{(1 + r)^n}$$

Just like solving for future value, we can solve this equation in one of three ways: (1) directly, by plugging in values of **FV, r,** and **n;** (2) with the aid of a time value table, in this case "Table 2—Present Value Factors," to obtain a value for $1/(1 + r)^n$; or (3) with a financial calculator.

Example

Finding a Present Value (Discounting)

You can purchase an investment that will return $50,000 in five years, and you wish to earn an annual rate of return of 15%.

Question: How much should you pay for this investment?

Solution steps:[8]

1. Using TVM tables:

   a. Write the relevant time value formula:

   $$PV = FV/(1 + r)^n$$

   b. Since **r** and **n** are known, look up the time value factor. Factors for the present value of a single future value are found in Table 2.

   c. Substitute into the formula and solve:

   $$PV = 50{,}000\ (.4972)$$
   $$= 24{,}860$$

	13%	14%	15%	20%
1	0.8850	0.8772	0.8696	0.8333
2	0.7831	0.7695	0.7561	0.6944
3	0.6931	0.6750	0.6575	0.5787
4	0.6133	0.5921	0.5718	0.4823
5	~~0.5428~~	~~0.5194~~	**0.4972**	0.4019
6	0.4803	0.4556	0.4323	0.3349
7	0.4251	0.3996	0.3759	0.2791
8	0.3762	0.3506	0.3269	0.2326
9	0.3329	0.3075	0.2843	0.1938
10	0.2946	0.2697	0.2472	0.1615
11	0.2607	0.2366	0.2149	0.1346
12	0.2307	0.2076	0.1869	0.1122
13	0.2042	0.1821	0.1625	0.0935
14	0.1807	0.1597	0.1413	0.0779

2. Using the financial calculator:[9]

   CLEAR the time value part of your calculator[10]
   Key in 50,000 and press FV
   Key in 15 and press i
   Key in 5 and press n
   Compute PV = −24,858.84

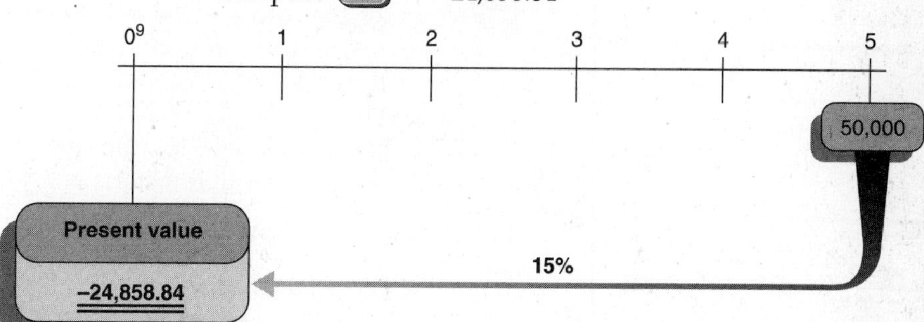

[8] **Observation:** Note the (small) difference between the calculator solution and the answer found with the table. The calculator result is the more precise one. There is round-off error when using time value tables since the time-value factors are rounded to four decimal places. For small dollar amounts this error is not meaningful.

[9] **Tip:** Don't forget to clear the part of your calculator that stores time value information before each calculation to prevent numbers left over from prior problems from accidently entering your current analysis. On most calculators, this is *not* done by pressing the **C** or **CLR** key (which simply clears the display), but rather by pressing a key or key sequence labelled **CLEAR TVM, CLEAR FIN, CLEAR DATA, CLEAR ALL,** or the like.

[10] **Observation:** We often will use a time line such as this one to diagram time value problems. Each number marks the end of a year, hence the label "1" means the end of the first year, etc. "0" (literally the end of the 0th year) stands for the *beginning* of the first year (or "now"), the point at which present values are normally located.

Answer: If you pay (notice that the present value calculates as a negative number—thus "pay") $24,858.84, you will earn exactly 15% per year over the five-year period.

3. Finding a Time Period

We may wish to determine how long it would take, given a rate of interest, for a present value to grow to a particular future amount.

Example

Finding a Time Period

You have $10,000 today and wish to see it grow to be $37,000. You can earn interest at an annual rate of 8%.

Question: How long will this take?

Solution steps:

1. Using TVM tables:

   a. Write the relevant time value formula:

   $$FV = PV\ (1 + r)^n$$

   b. Since **n** is the unknown, rearrange the equation to solve for the time value factor:

   $$(1 + r)^n = FV/PV$$
   $$= 37{,}000/10{,}000 = 3.7000$$

   c. Factors for the future value of a single present value are found in Table 1. Scan down the 8% column until you reach the number closest to 3.7000. Then look left to find the number of years for that factor:

   $$n = 17 \text{ years}$$

	6%	7%	8%	9%
11	1.8983	2.1049	2.3316	2.5804
12	2.0122	2.2522	2.5182	2.8127
13	2.1329	2.4098	2.7196	3.0658
14	2.2609	2.5785	2.9372	3.3417
15	2.3966	2.7590	3.1722	3.6425
16	2.5404	2.9522	3.4259	3.9703
17	2.8928	3.1588	**3.7000**	4.3276
18	2.8543	3.3799	3.9960	4.7171
19	3.0256	3.6165	4.3157	5.1417
20	3.2071	3.8697	4.6610	5.6044
21	3.3996	4.1406	5.0338	6.1088
22	3.6035	4.4304	5.4365	6.6586
23	3.8197	4.7405	5.8715	7.2579
24	4.0489	5.0724	6.3412	7.9111

2. Using the financial calculator:

   CLEAR the time value part of your calculator
   Key in −10,000 and press PV
   Key in 37,000 and press FV
   Key in 8 and press i
   Compute n = 17

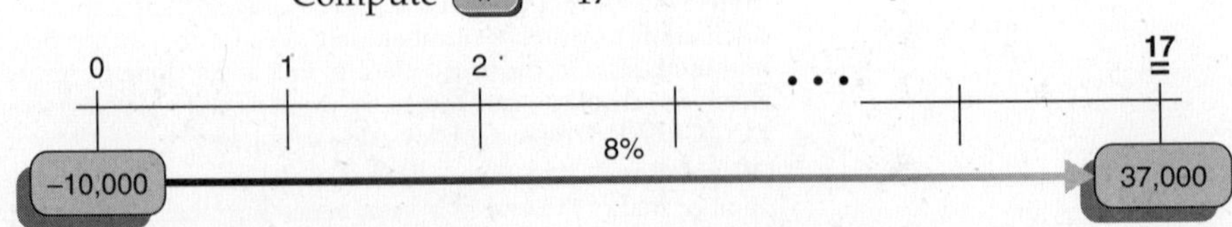

Answer: It will take 17 years.

4. Finding an Interest Rate

We often wish to learn what interest rate, compounded over a specified number of time periods, would make a present value grow to a given future amount.

Example

Finding an Interest Rate

You have \$10,000 today and wish to see it grow to be \$170,000 in 25 years.

Question: What interest rate will accomplish this?

Solution steps:

1. Using TVM tables:

   a. Write the relevant time value formula:

   $$FV = PV\ (1 + r)^n$$

   b. Since **r** is the unknown, rearrange the equation to solve for the time value factor:

   $$(1 + r)^n = FV/PV$$
   $$= 170{,}000/10{,}000 = 17.000$$

   c. Factors for the future value of a single present value are found in Table 1. Scan across the 25 year row until you reach the number closest to 17.000. Then look up to the top of that column to find the interest rate for that factor:

   $$i = 12\%$$

	11%	12%	13%	14%
18	6.5436	7.6880	9.0243	10.575
19	7.2633	8.6128	10.197	12.056
20	8.0623	9.6463	11.523	13.743
21	8.9492	10.804	13.021	15.668
22	9.9336	12.100	14.714	17.861
23	11.026	13.552	16.627	20.362
24	12.239	15.179	18.788	23.212
25	~~13.586~~ →	**17.000**	21.231	26.462
26	15.080	19.040	23.991	30.167
27	16.739	21.325	27.109	34.390
28	18.580	23.884	30.633	39.204
29	20.624	26.750	34.616	44.693
30	22.892	29.960	39.116	50.950
31	25.410	33.555	44.201	58.083

2. Using the financial calculator:

   CLEAR the time value part of your calculator
   Key in −10,000 and press PV
   Key in 170,000 and press FV
   Key in 25 and press n
   Compute i = 12.00%

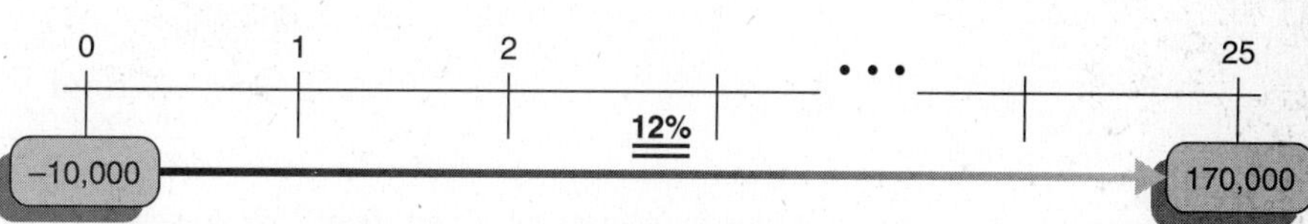

Answer: You will reach your goal if you can earn 12.00%.

Multiple Cash Flows—Uneven Flows

So far we have looked at calculations involving two cash flows only: one present value and one future value. While many problems are of that type, a good number require that we analyze more than two cash flows. When finding a present or future value (as opposed to finding an interest rate, which requires that all cash flows be considered together), one strategy is to analyze each cash flow individually and then combine the results.[11]

Example

Present Value of Uneven Cash Flows

The state lottery promises a grand prize of $1,000,000. The winner will be paid $100,000 per year for the first three years, $200,000 per year for the two years after that, and $300,000 in the sixth year. If 8% is the appropriate rate of interest, what is the lottery really worth today? (Note that even though the winner receives the advertised $1,000,000 in cash, the lottery must be worth less than that since the winner does not receive all of the money at once!)

Question interpreted: Find the present value of this package of cash flows.

Solution steps: Calculate each present value individually and then add them together:

1. Using TVM tables:
   a. Write the relevant time value formula:

$$PV = FV\ (1 + r)^n$$

   b. Since **r** and **n** are known, look up the time value factors for each number of years. Factors for the present value of a single future value are found in Table 2.

   c. Substitute each cash flow and time value factor into the formula in turn and solve:

	6%	7%	8%	9%
1	0.9434	0.9346	0.9259	0.9174
2	0.8900	0.8734	0.8573	0.8417
3	0.8396	0.8163	0.7938	0.7722
4	0.7921	0.7629	0.7350	0.7084
5	0.7473	0.7130	0.6806	0.6499
6	0.7050	0.6606	0.6302	0.5963
7	0.6651	0.6627	0.5835	0.5470
8	0.6274	0.5820	0.5403	0.5019
9	0.5919	0.5439	0.5002	0.4604
10	0.5584	0.5083	0.4632	0.4224
11	0.5268	0.4751	0.4289	0.3875
12	0.4970	0.4440	0.3971	0.3555
13	0.4688	0.4150	0.3677	0.3262
14	0.4423	0.3878	0.3405	0.2992

PV = 100,000 (.9259) = $ 92,590
PV = 100,000 (.8573) = 85,730
PV = 100,000 (.7938) = 79,380
PV = 200,000 (.7350) = 147,000
PV = 200,000 (.6806) = 136,120
PV = 300,000 (.6302) = 189,060
Total $729,880

[11] **Cross-reference and observation:** See Appendix 5B for a time-saving method of solving these problems using the cash flow list feature of the more sophisticated financial calculators. Since that method begins with inputting all the cash flows of the problem, it can also be used to solve for a rate of interest.

2. Using the financial calculator:

CLEAR the time value part of your calculator, then:

	Key in			
Year	As FV	As n	As i	Compute PV
1	100000	1	8	$ −92,592.59
2	100000	2	8	−85,733.88
3	100000	3	8	−79,383.22
4	200000	4	8	−147,005.97
5	200000	5	8	−136,116.64
6	300000	6	8	−189,050.89
			Total	$−729,883.19[12]

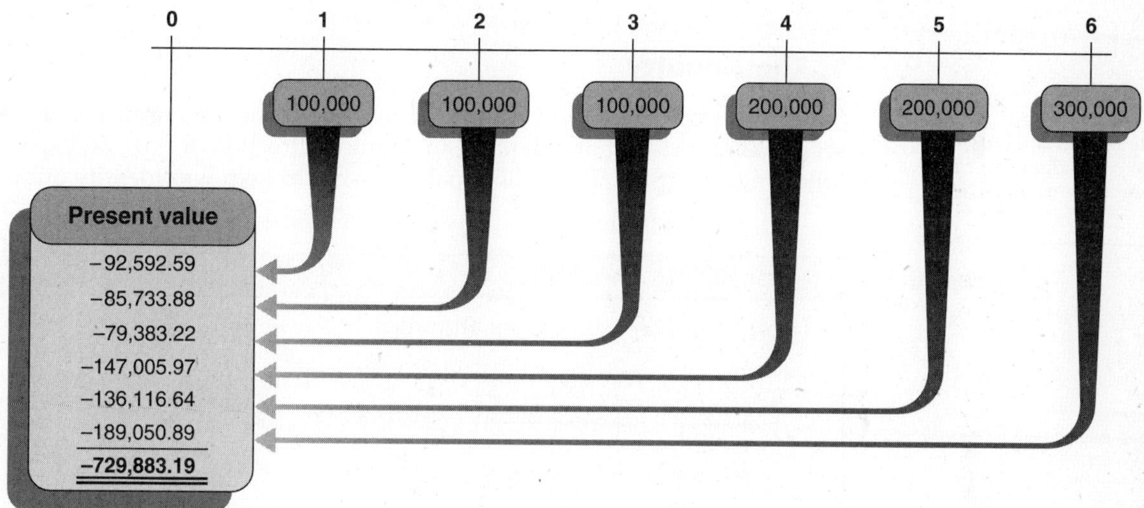

Answer: Winning this lottery is worth only $729,883.19 and not $1 million if 8% measures the value of time.

Multiple Cash Flows—Cash Flows That Form a Pattern

Sometimes the cash flows of a problem form a pattern for which a quick solution already exists. If we recognize these patterns when they occur, we can save ourselves much time (and increase the odds that we get the correct answer as well!).

---

[12] **Elaboration and observation:** The negative sign attached to the answer can be interpreted as follows: If a person *invested* (an outflow, hence negative) $729,883.19 today at 8% interest, the investment would grow exactly to provide the six cash flows of this problem. Thus $729,883.19 is the "correct price" to *pay* (−) for this investment in order to earn 8%. Of course, if you could buy these cash flows for the price of a lottery ticket, you would be way ahead!

Consider, for example, the problems facing John Platini, a lending officer at the Local National Bank. Yesterday, a customer wishing to purchase a house asked John to calculate how much she could borrow if she could repay $1,000 per month. Since the bank makes such home mortgage loans for a 30-year period (360 months), John had to calculate 360 present values and add them together. Today, another customer inquired about borrowing $20,000 and offered to repay the loan in ten annual installments. John was asked to calculate the amount of each payment, ten equal future values whose combined present value is $20,000. John is going to be doing a lot of calculations, many by trial-and-error, unless we can give him some help.

Fortunately the mathematics has been worked out for these and similar problems and is included in our financial calculator. We will look at three patterns of cash flows: (1) the annuity, (2) the growing cash stream, and (3) the perpetual annuity or "perpetuity."

1. The Annuity

annuity—a series of cash flows that are equal in amount, direction of flow, and time distance apart

Both problems facing John Platini involve annuities. An **annuity** is defined as a set of cash flows that are identical in amount, direction of flow, and spacing. The following examples of cash flow patterns should help you identify annuities:

Examples

Recognizing Annuities

These cash flow patterns *are* annuities:

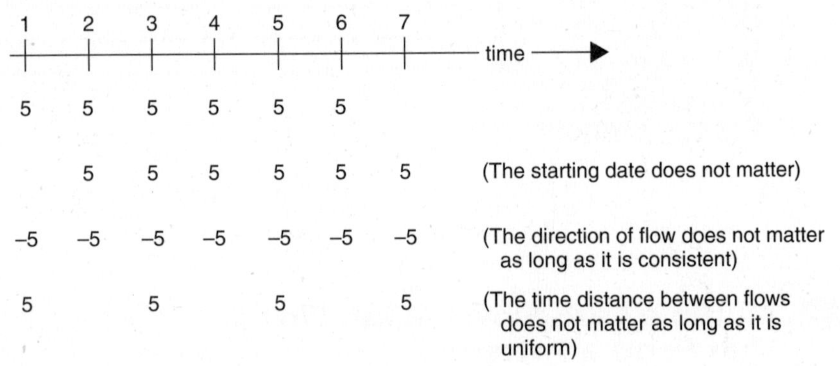

These cash flow patterns *are not* annuities:

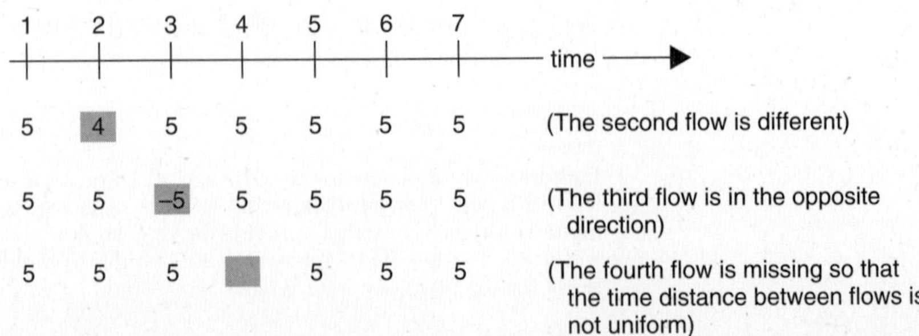

Annuity calculations Like the problems we have already examined, we can solve annuity problems using either time value tables or a financial calculator. The variable we use for each cash flow in an annuity is **PMT** which stands for the word **PayMenT.** You may have noticed there is a fifth time value key on your calculator labeled **PMT.** This is the key we use for an annuity.

payment—one of the cash flows in an annuity

There are two annuity formulas, one for the present value of an annuity and one for future value. As you might expect, these formulas are somewhat more complex than the formulas for the present and future values of a single cash flow. The future value of an annuity is given by:

$$FV = PMT\left(\frac{(1+r)^n - 1}{r}\right)$$

To simplify our notation, we will refer to the last term of this equation as the future value annuity factor (FVAF), and write:

$$FV = PMT \times FVAF$$

Table 3 contains future value annuity factors for representative values of **r** and **n.** The formula for the present value of an annuity is:

$$PV = PMT\left(\frac{1 - \frac{1}{(1+r)^n}}{r}\right)$$

We will also simplify the way we write this equation by identifying the last term as the present value annuity factor (PVAF):

$$PV = PMT \times PVAF$$

Table 4 contains present value annuity factors for representative values of **r** and **n.**

With time value tables or our financial calculator we can do five types of annuity calculations. We can compute (1) the present value of an annuity, (2) the amount of each annuity payment, (3) the future value of an annuity, (4) the length of an annuity, or (5) the interest rate in an annuity. With the help of John Platini, the banker, we will look at each calculation:

Example

Present Value of an Annuity

John's first problem involved finding the present value of an annuity, in this case the amount of a loan. His customer was willing to pay $1,000 per month for 360 months. Suppose John's bank charges 1% interest per month (or roughly 12% per year—we will look at this relationship later in this chapter) on this loan. How much can John lend?

Question: What is the present value of this annuity?

Solution steps:

1. Using TVM tables:
   a. Write the relevant time value formula:

PV = PMT × PVAF

b. Since **r** and **n** are known, look up the time value factor. Factors for the present value of an annuity are found in Table 4.

	1%	2%	3%	4%
34	28.703	24.499	21.132	18.411
35	29.409	27.355	21.487	18.665
40	32.835	37.355	23.115	19.793
50	39.196	31.424	25.730	21.482
60	44.955	34.761	27.676	22.623
70	50.169	37.499	29.123	23.395
80	54.888	39.745	30.201	23.915
360	97.218	49.960	33.333	25.000
999	99.995	50.000	33.333	25.000

c. Substitute into the formula and solve:

$$PV = 1{,}000\ (97.218)$$
$$= 97{,}218.00$$

2. Using the financial calculator:

CLEAR the time value part of your calculator

Key in 1,000 and press PMT

Key in 360 and press n [13]

Key in 1 and press i

Compute PV = −97,218.33

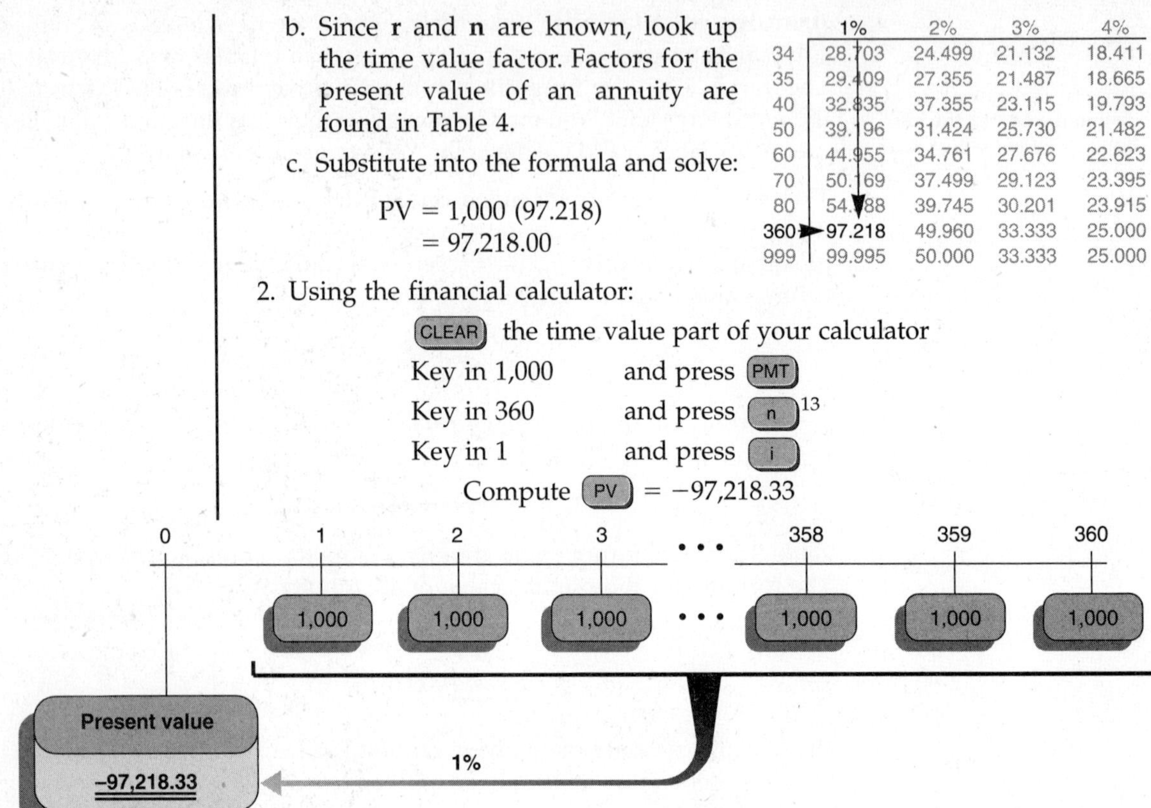

Answer: If the loan is for $97,218.33, John's customer's payments of $1,000 per month will repay the loan plus interest at the rate of 1% per month in 360 months or 30 years.

Example

Amount of an Annuity

John's second problem involved finding the amount of an annuity. His customer wished to borrow $20,000 to be repaid in ten equal annual installments. John's bank charges 14% annual interest on this loan.

Question: How much will each annuity payment be?

Solution steps:

1. Using TVM tables:

a. Write the relevant time value formula:

$$PV = PMT \times PVAF$$

b. Since **r** and **n** are known, look up the time value factor. Factors for the present value of an annuity are found in Table 4.

	12%	13%	14%	15%
3	2.4018	2.3612	2.3216	2.2832
4	3.0373	2.9745	2.9137	2.8550
5	3.6048	3.5172	3.4831	3.3522
6	4.1115	3.9975	3.8887	3.7845
7	4.5638	4.4226	4.2883	4.1604
8	4.9676	4.7988	4.6389	4.4873
9	5.3282	5.1317	4.9464	4.7716
10	5.6502	5.4262	5.2161	5.0188
11	5.9377	5.6869	5.4527	5.2337
12	6.1944	5.9176	5.6603	5.4206.

[13] **Looking ahead:** Note that the unit of time in this problem is months. More on this later in this chapter.

c. Substitute into the formula and solve:

$$20{,}000 = \text{PMT}\ (5.2161)$$

$$\text{PMT} = 20{,}000/5.2161 = 3{,}834.28$$

2. Using the financial calculator:

CLEAR the time value part of your calculator

Key in 20,000 and press PV

Key in 10 and press n

Key in 14 and press i

Compute PMT = −3,834.27

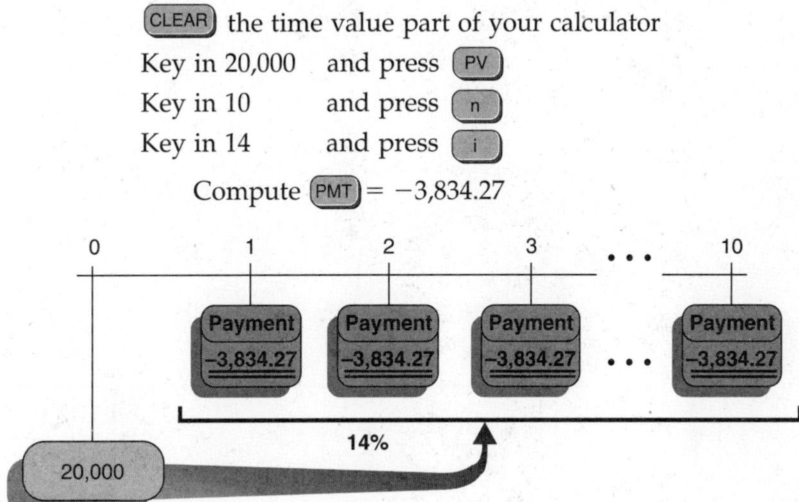

Answer: If the customer pays $3,834.27 in each of the next ten years, she will exactly repay the $20,000 loan plus interest at the annual rate of 14%.

Example

Future Value of an Annuity

John's bank offers Individual Retirement Accounts (IRAs)[14] to the public. A customer has just opened an IRA that pays 7% per year. He plans to deposit $2,000 per year for the next 25 years. How much will be in the account at the end of the 25 years?

Question: What is the future value of this annuity?

Solution steps:

1. Using TVM tables:

a. Write the relevant time value formula:

$$FV = PMT \times FVAF$$

b. Since **r** and **n** are known, look up the time value factor. Factors for the future value of an annuity are found in Table 3.

	5%	6%	7%	8%
18	28.132	30.906	33.999	37.450
19	30.539	33.760	37.379	41.446
20	33.066	36.786	40.995	45.762
21	35.719	39.993	44.865	50.423
22	38.505	43.392	49.006	55.457
23	41.430	46.996	53.436	60.893
24	44.502	50.816	58.177	66.765
25	47.727	54.865	63.249	73.106
26	51.113	59.156	68.676	79.954
27	54.669	63.706	74.484	87.351
28	58.403	68.528	80.698	95.339

[14] **Elaboration:** Individual Retirement Accounts were enacted into law by the U.S. Congress to encourage people to provide for their own retirement and to supplement the Social Security system. Eligible individuals can deposit up to $2,000 per year. IRAs get a very favorable tax treatment: the amount deposited each year can be deducted from income for tax purposes and neither it nor the interest earned becomes taxable until the money is withdrawn, presumably many years later.

c. Substitute into the formula and solve:

$$FV = 2{,}000\ (63.249)$$
$$= 126{,}498.00$$

2. Using the financial calculator:

CLEAR the time value part of your calculator
Key in −2,000 and press PMT
Key in 7 and press i
Key in 25 and press n
Compute FV = 126,498.08

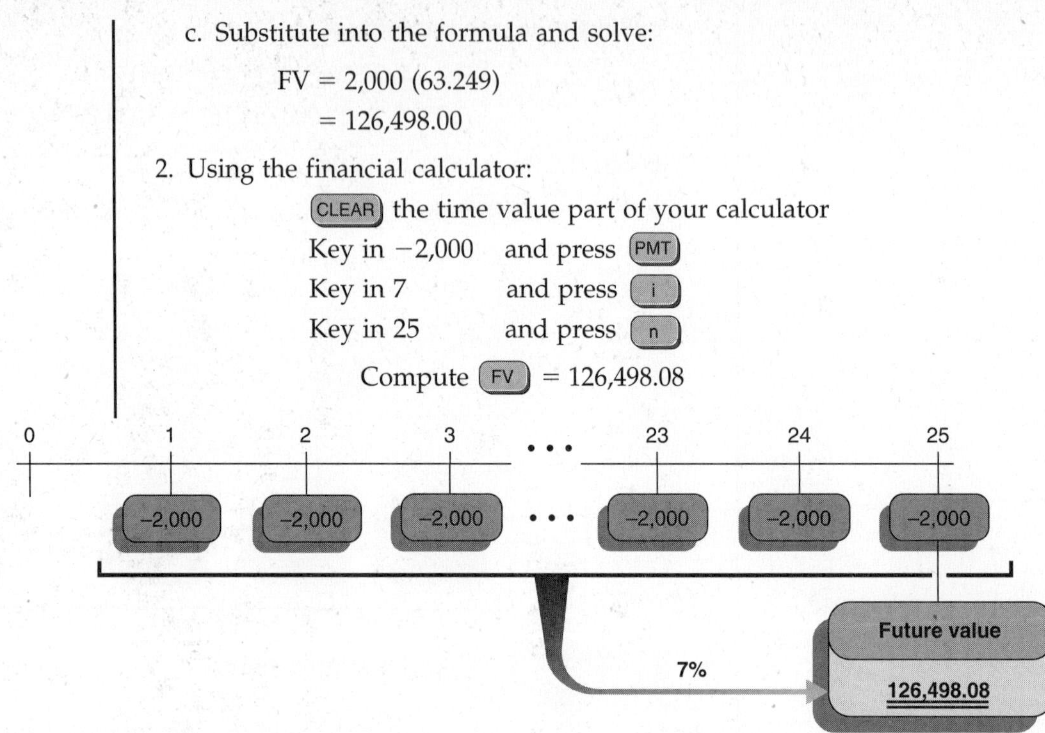

Answer: The customer's account will have a balance of $126,498.08 at the end of the 25 years.

Example

Length of an Annuity

A young couple has asked John for some advice. They have a goal of accumulating $337,500 to afford the cost of sending their one-year-old quadruplets to college. They can afford to invest $10,000 per year. John suggests a **certificate of deposit** (or **CD**) which pays 8% interest. How long will it take for their account to total $337,500?

certificate of deposit—a receipt for a bank deposit in which the depositor commits not to withdraw funds from the bank for a specified period of time in return for a better rate of interest

Question: What is the length of this annuity?

Solution steps:

1. Using TVM tables:

a. Write the relevant time value formula:

$$FV = PMT \times FVAF$$

b. Since **n** is the unknown, rearrange the equation to solve for the time value factor:

$$FVAF = FV/PMT$$
$$= 337{,}500/10{,}000 = 33.750$$

	6%	7%	8%	9%
10	13.181	13.816	14.487	15.193
11	14.972	15.784	16.645	17.560
12	16.870	17.888	18.977	20.141
13	18.882	20.141	21.495	22.953
14	21.015	22.550	24.215	26.019
15	23.276	25.129	27.152	29.361
16	25.673	27.888	30.324	33.003
17	[illegible].210	30.840	**33.750**	36.974
18	30.906	33.999	37.450	41.301
19	33.760	37.379	41.446	46.018
20	36.786	40.995	45.762	51.160

c. Factors for the future value of an annuity are found in Table 3. Scan down the 8% column until you reach the number closest to 33.750. Then look left to find the number of years for that factor:

n = 17 years

2. Using the financial calculator:

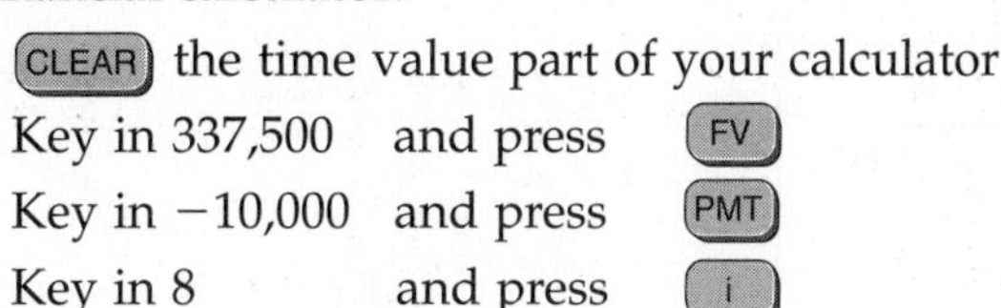

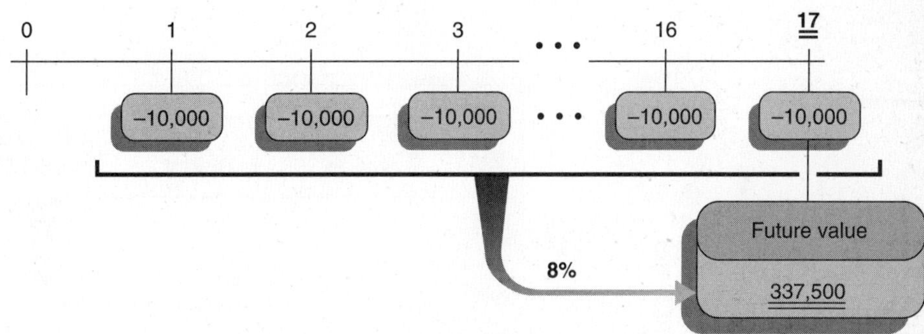

Answer: It will take the family 17 years to reach their goal, exactly the time they have available.

Example

Interest Rate in an Annuity

John's bank normally makes personal loans at a 14% annual interest rate. Recently, however, the bank made a special offer to its customers: customers could borrow $10,000 to be repaid with 5 equal annual payments of $2,850. What interest rate is the bank offering on this loan?

Question: What is the interest rate in this annuity?

Solution steps:

1. Using TVM tables:

a. Write the relevant time value formula:

$$PV = PMT \times PVAF$$

b. Since **r** is the unknown, rearrange the equation to solve for the time value factor:

$$PVAF = PV/PMT$$
$$= 10{,}000/2{,}850 = 3.5088$$

	11%	12%	13%	14%
1	0.9009	0.8929	0.8850	0.8772
2	1.7125	1.6901	1.6681	1.6467
3	2.4437	2.4018	2.3612	2.3216
4	3.1024	3.0373	2.9745	2.9137
5	3.6959	3.6048	3.5172	3.4331
6	4.2305	4.1114	3.9975	3.8887
7	4.7122	4.5638	4.4226	4.2883
8	5.1461	4.9676	4.7988	4.6389
9	5.5370	5.3282	5.1317	4.9464
10	5.8892	5.6502	5.4262	5.2161
11	6.2065	5.9377	5.6869	5.4527
12	6.4924	6.1944	5.9176	5.6603
13	6.7499	6.4235	6.1218	5.8424
14	6.9819	6.6282	6.3025	6.0021

c. Factors for the present value of an annuity are found in Table 4. Scan across the 5 year row until you reach the number closest to 3.5088. Then look up to the top of that column to find the interest rate for that factor:

$$i = 13\%$$

2. Using the financial calculator:

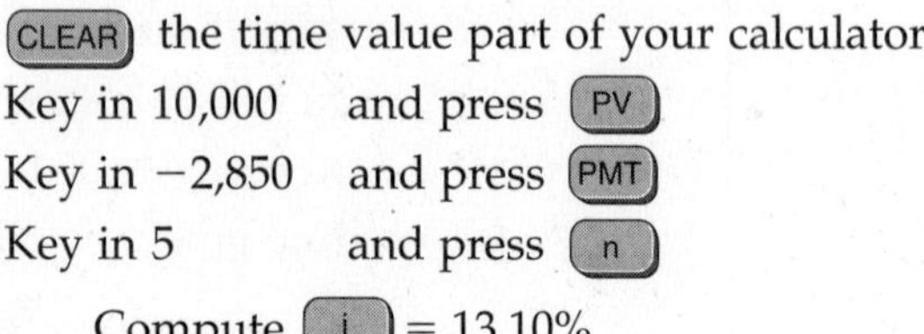

CLEAR the time value part of your calculator
Key in 10,000 and press PV
Key in −2,850 and press PMT
Key in 5 and press n
Compute i = 13.10%

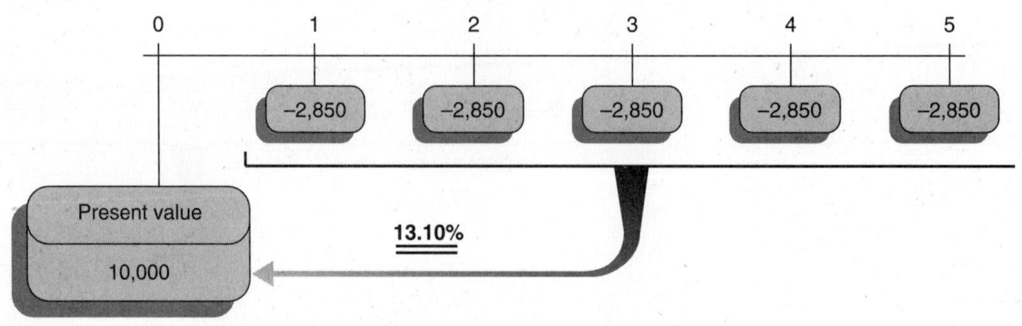

Answer: The loan carries an interest rate of 13.10%.

ordinary annuity (annuity in arrears, END annuity)—an annuity in which the cash flows occur at the end of each time period

Ordinary annuities vs. annuities due All of the above examples were illustrations of what are referred to as **ordinary annuities** (also **annuities in arrears** or **END annuities**). In these annuities, the cash flow in each period comes at the end of that period. For example, in a typical loan, the borrower waits until the end of each period (month, quarter, year, etc.) to make a payment.

Some financial deals involving annuities, however, require payments at the beginning of each period. If you rent an apartment or lease a car, for example, you are normally expected to make your payments on the first of each month. These annuities are called **annuities due** (also **annuities in advance** or **BEGIN annuities**).

annuity due (annuity in advance, BEGIN annuity)—an annuity in which the cash flows occur at the beginning of each time period

Since the timing of cash flows is critical to their worth, annuities due differ in present and future value from comparable ordinary annuities. Our time value tables were designed for ordinary annuities; we must modify the factors to use them for annuities due. The modifications are both simple and clever as Figure 5.2 illustrates; they can be done so quickly and easily that there is no need to construct separate tables for annuity due factors. To obtain a FVAF for an annuity due, look up the factor for one more period of time and subtract 1. To obtain a PVAF for an annuity due, look up the factor for one less period of time and add 1.

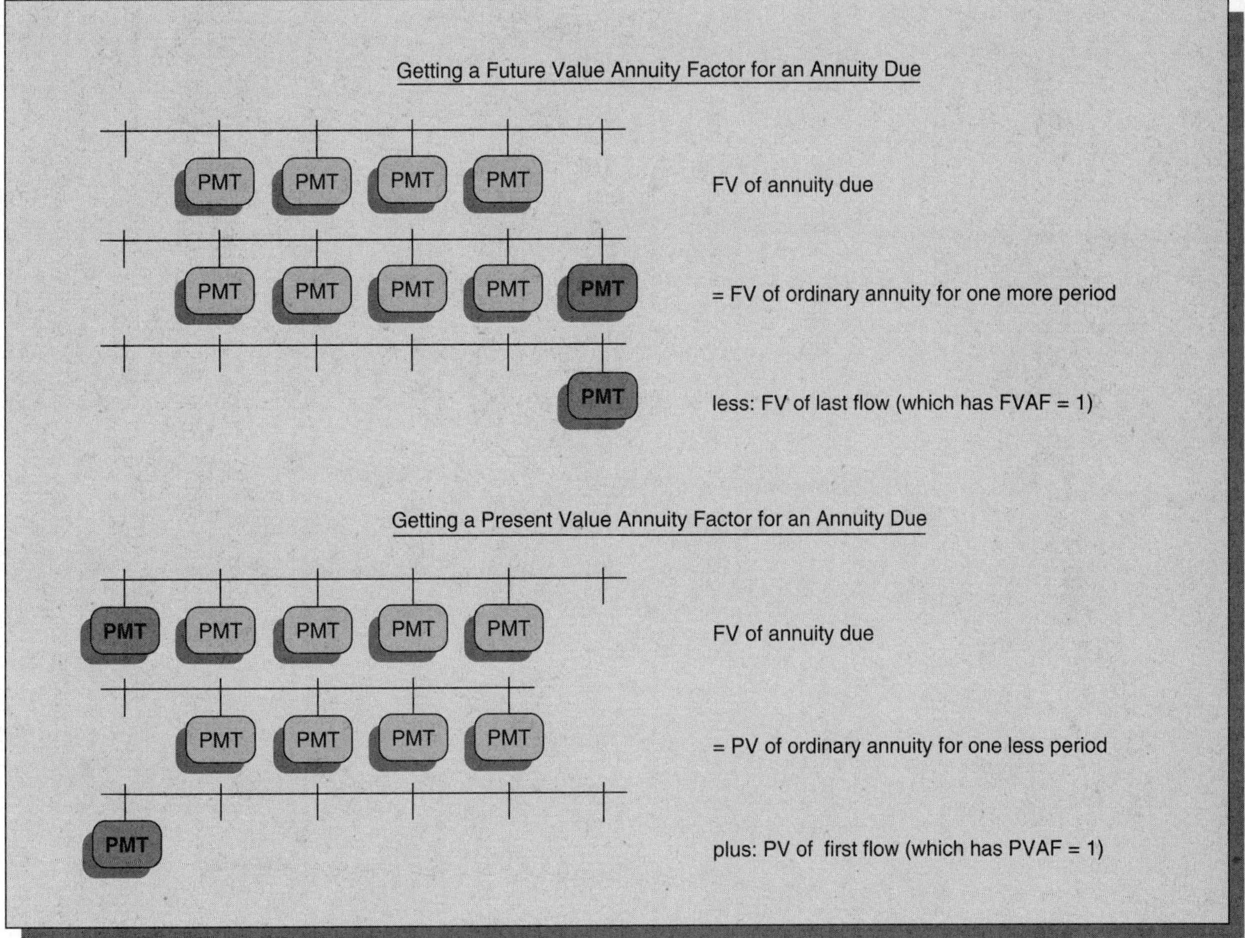

FIGURE 5.2
TVM factors for annuities due. These factors are obtained by making a simple adjustment to the factors for ordinary annuities.

The financial calculator deals with this by providing a way to switch from an **END** setting to a **BEGIN** setting.[15] In the above examples the annuities were all ordinary annuities, and your calculator had to be set to **END** for you to get the correct answer. Now we look at both alternatives.

Example

Ordinary Annuity

Consider Rita Thomas, who is putting away money to pay for her retirement. Rita's plan is to deposit $2,500 at the end of each year into a bank account which pays 7% annual interest. She expects to make deposits for 30 years.

Question: How much will Rita have at the end of the 30 years?

---

[15] **Tip:** Each financial calculator has its own method for switching between **END** and **BEGIN.** See your calculator manual or the calculator appendix at the back of this book for specifics.

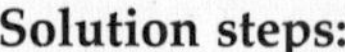

Solution steps:

1. Using TVM tables:
   a. Write the relevant time value formula:

   $$FV = PMT \times FVAF$$

   b. Since **r** and **n** are known, look up the time value factor. Factors for the future value of an annuity are found in Table 3.

   c. Substitute into the formula and solve:

   $$FV = 2{,}500\ (94.461)$$
   $$= 236{,}152.50$$

	5%	6%	7%	8%
23	41.430	46.996	53.436	60.893
24	44.502	50.816	58.177	66.765
25	47.727	54.865	63.249	73.106
26	51.113	59.156	68.676	79.954
27	54.669	63.706	74.484	87.351
28	58.403	68.528	80.698	95.339
29	62.323	73.640	87.347	103.97
30	66.439	79.058	**94.461**	113.28
31	70.761	84.802	102.07	123.35
32	75.299	90.890	110.22	134.21
33	80.064	97.343	118.93	145.95
34	85.067	104.18	128.26	158.63
35	90.320	111.43	138.24	172.32
40	120.80	154.76	199.64	259.06

2. Using the financial calculator:

   [CLEAR] the time value part of your calculator
   Be sure your calculator is set for [END]
   Key in −2,500 and press [PMT]
   Key in 7 and press [i]
   Key in 30 and press [n]
   Compute [FV] = 236,151.97

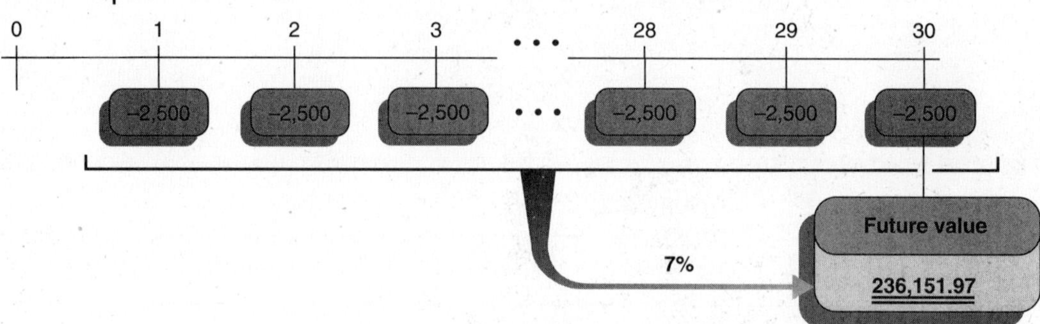

Answer: Rita will have $236,151.97 at the end of the 30th year.

Example **Annuity Due**

Recently, a friend suggested to Rita that she make her deposits at the beginning of each year, rather than at the end of each year. In this way, the friend pointed out, each deposit could earn one year's extra interest.

Question: If Rita follows her friend's advice, how much will she have at the end of the 30 years?

Solution steps:

1. Using TVM tables:

   a. Write the relevant time value formula:

   $$FV = PMT \times FVAF$$

   b. Since **r** and **n** are known, look up the time value factor. Factors for the future value of an annuity are found in Table 3. For a future value annuity due factor, obtain the factor for one more period of time and subtract 1:

	5%	6%	7%	8%
25	47.727	54.865	63.249	73.106
26	51.113	59.156	68.676	79.954
27	54.669	63.706	74.484	87.351
28	58.403	68.528	80.698	95.339
29	62.323	73.640	87.347	103.97
30	66.439	79.058	94.461	113.28
31	70.761	84.80	**102.07**	123.35
32	75.299	90.890	110.22	134.21
33	80.064	97.343	118.93	145.95
34	85.067	104.18	128.26	158.63
35	90.320	111.43	138.24	172.32
40	120.80	154.76	199.64	259.06
50	209.35	290.34	406.53	573.77
60	353.58	533.13	813.52	1253.2

   FVAF for 7%, 31 years = 102.07

   102.07 − 1 = 101.07

   c. Substitute into the formula and solve:

   $$FV = 2{,}500\ (101.07)$$
   $$= \underline{\underline{252{,}675.00}}$$

2. Using the financial calculator:

   CLEAR the time value part of your calculator
   Switch your calculator setting to BEG
   Key in −2,500 and press PMT
   Key in 7 and press i
   Key in 30 and press n
   Compute FV = 252,682.60

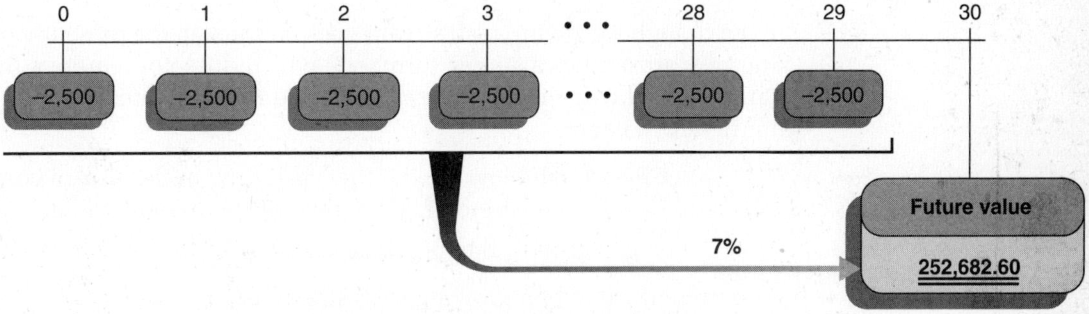

0 1 2 3 ... 28 29 30

−2,500 −2,500 −2,500 −2,500 ... −2,500 −2,500

7%

Future value
252,682.60

Answer: With beginning-of-year deposits, Rita will have $252,682.60 at the end of the 30th year.

Notice that if Rita makes her deposits at the beginning of every year, she accumulates $16,530.63 more than if she waited until the end of the year to make the deposits. The difference of $16,530.63 is exactly 7% of $236,151.97, reflecting one year's extra interest on all of her deposited money. Her friend was right!

2. The Growing Cash Stream

Van Hoffmann's close friend has given him a hot tip—buy the common stock of Techno-Industries, Inc., the new darling of Wall Street. Van understands that the stock's price is a present value, but he is having difficulty using time value techniques to calculate how much he should be willing to pay for each share. In particular, he is concerned that the annuity calculations he has just learned will not work here. For one thing, Van does not know how long the firm might remain in business—corporations like Techno-Industries are going concerns with no end-of-life in sight—yet annuities are defined in part by their finite length. For another, the cash flows Van expects to receive, the firm's dividend payments, are not likely to be constant year-in and year-out, yet annuity cash flows must be constant by definition.

growing cash stream—an infinitely long series of equally spaced cash flows in which each flow is greater than the previous one by a constant rate of growth

Van needs to learn about the **growing cash stream** relationship for present value. A growing cash stream is defined as an infinitely long series of equally spaced cash flows in which each is greater than the previous one by a constant rate of growth.

Example

Recognizing a Growing Cash Stream

The following set of cash flows fit the growing cash stream relationship. The rate of growth is 10%:

Cash flow 1: $10,000

Cash flow 2: $11,000 (10% more than $10,000)

Cash flow 3: $12,100 (10% more than $11,000)

Cash flow 4: $13,310 (10% more than $12,100)

etc., forever . . .

Even though a growing cash stream goes on forever, the present value of a growing cash stream has a simple form, one which does not require a financial calculator to solve. We already have the variable **r** for the interest rate, but we need a bit of new notation:

$\mathbf{CF_1}$ = **Cash Flow #1,** the first cash flow in the stream coming one period after the time of the present value.

g = **growth rate** of the cash flows.

The present value of a growing cash stream is:

$$PV = \frac{CF_1}{r - g}$$

Example

Growing Cash Stream

Now we can help Van with his stock investment. Suppose Van forecasts that Techno-Industries will pay a $2.00 per share dividend in one year, and that the dividend payment will grow at a rate of 6% for the foreseeable future. Van wants a 16% annual rate of return on this investment.

Question: How much is Techno-Industries common stock worth to Van?

Solution steps:

$$PV = \frac{CF_1}{r - g} = \frac{\$2.00}{.16 - .06} = \$20.00$$

Answer: The stock is worth $20.00 per share to Van. If he buys it at that price and his forecasts come true, he will earn his desired 16% rate of return.

Note two things about this relationship. First, since we are working with an equation and not the time value part of the financial calculator, both rates (r and g) were used in their decimal form (.16 rather than 16%; .06 rather than 6%). Second, the relationship only works when the value of r is greater than the value of g. Otherwise the formula is not valid and it gives incorrect results.

3. The Perpetuity

perpetuity—an annuity that continues forever; also, a growing cash stream with a zero rate of growth

A special case of the growing cash stream is the **perpetuity.** A perpetuity is a growing cash stream with a growth rate equal to zero. This makes every cash flow in the perpetuity the same amount. Another way of looking at a perpetuity is as an annuity that goes on forever. In fact, the word *perpetuity* is a special finance word made up from the words ***perpetual annuity.***

When g = 0, the growing cash stream present value relationship reduces to:

$$PV = \frac{PMT}{r}$$

(since every cash flow is the same, there is no need to distinguish the first one by the notation CF_1 here. PMT—payment—will do just fine. It is still required, however, that the first payment occur one period after the time of the present value.)

Example

Perpetuity

Van Hoffmann is also looking at the preferred stock of Techno-Industries which pays a $12.00 annual dividend per share, with the next dividend due in one year. Since Van considers Techno-Industries' preferred stock to be a bit less risky than the company's common stock, he only requires a 15% rate of return on this investment.

Question: How much is Techno-Industries' preferred stock worth to Van?

Solution steps:

$$PV = \frac{PMT}{r} = \frac{\$12.00}{.15} = \$80.00$$

Answer: The stock is worth $80.00 per share to Van. If he buys it at that price and his forecasts come true, he will earn his desired 15% rate of return.

Matching Rate and Period

In our previous examples, we did not pay too much attention to the length of a "period." With one exception (the mortgage loan example on pages 167–168) the length of one period equalled one year. Since it is common business practice to quote interest rates on an annual basis, beginning our studies with illustrations in which each period was one year made sense. But as the mortgage problem pointed out, we often need to analyze problems in which each period of time is something other than one year. There are many examples where this arises:

- Bonds typically pay interest every six months. An analysis of the value of a bond requires that we define the period of time as six months long.
- Common stock typically pays dividends every quarter, or three months. An analysis of the value of a share of stock requires that we define the period of time as three months long.
- Most consumer loans require monthly payments. An analysis of such a loan requires that we define the period of time as one month long.
- Most banks calculate interest on Visa and MasterCard balances on a daily basis. An analysis of one of these accounts requires that we define the period of time as one day long.

Fortunately, there is a simple way to deal with this. Time value calculations will always be valid if the interest rate and the time period match.

- To analyze the bond, make one period equal to six months. Then **n** becomes the number of six-month periods and **i** becomes the six-month (semi-annual) interest rate.
- To analyze the stock, make one period equal to three months. Then **n** becomes the number of three-month periods and **i** becomes the three-month (quarterly) interest rate.
- To analyze the consumer loan, make one period equal to one month. Then **n** becomes the number of months and **i** becomes the one-month (monthly) interest rate.
- To analyze the credit card account, make one period equal to one day. Then **n** becomes the number of days and **i** becomes the one-day (daily) interest rate.

The need to match the interest rate to the time period often requires that we convert the rate we are given (for example, an annual rate) to an equivalent rate for a different time period (for example, a monthly rate). The following terminology is used to identify the different types of interest rates we will encounter:

nominal interest rate—a quoted rate of interest

A **nominal interest rate** is a quoted rate. It is not used directly in time value calculations, but it serves as the basis for obtaining the interest rate which will be used.

Example

Nominal Interest Rate

The Local National Bank advertises that it pays "8%, compounded quarterly" on deposits that remain in the bank for one year. In this usage, 8% is a nominal rate.[16] The bank will not actually use the number 8% in its interest calculations.

effective interest rate—a true rate of interest which summarizes the total change in value over some period of time

An **effective interest rate** is a true interest rate which summarizes the total change in value over some period of time. This is the rate that is used in time value calculations.

Example

Effective Interest Rate

Local National Bank's advertising discloses that the nominal rate of 8% will be applied as "2% per quarter producing an annual yield of 8.24%". In the next part of this chapter we will learn that the effective rate offered by the bank is 2% per quarter (the "effective quarterly rate") or 8.24% for the full year (the "effective annual rate").

Nominal and effective rates can refer to any length period of time. As a result it is common to add a word to identify the period. For nominal interest rates:

If the period is . . .	the rate is called the . . .	and is abbreviated
One year	nominal annual rate	NAR
Six months	nominal semi-annual rate	NSR
Three months	nominal quarterly rate	NQR
One month	nominal monthly rate	NMR
One day	nominal daily rate	NDR
Unspecified	nominal periodic rate	NPR

For effective interest rates:

If the period is . . .	the rate is called the . . .	and is abbreviated
One year	effective annual rate	EAR
Six months	effective semi-annual rate	ESR
Three months	effective quarterly rate	EQR
One month	effective monthly rate	EMR
One day	effective daily rate	EDR
Unspecified	effective periodic rate	EPR

1. Converting from a Nominal to an Effective Rate

It is easy to convert a nominal interest rate to an equivalent effective interest rate: simply divide by the frequency of compounding. If:

p = compounding periods—the number of times compounding takes place.

[16] **Tip:** Whenever a rate is compounded more frequently than once per year, the rate can immediately be identified as nominal.

then:[17]

$$Effective\ rate = \frac{nominal\ rate}{p}$$

Examples

Converting from Nominal to Effective

John Platini knows that Local National Bank's competitors also advertise a nominal annual rate of 8% on one-year deposits but differ in the frequency of compounding they offer to their customers.

Question: What effective periodic rate is each bank offering?

Solution steps:

Bank	Quote	Effective Rate	
A	8% compounded semi-annually	ESR = 8%/2	= 4.0000%
LNB	8% compounded quarterly	EQR = 8%/4	= 2.0000%
B	8% compounded monthly	EMR = 8%/12	= 0.6667%
C	8% compounded daily	EDR = 8%/365	= 0.0219%

Answer: The effective rate is the 8% nominal rate divided by the compounding frequency.

Question: How much would a $15,000 deposit in each of the four banks (Bank A, Local National Bank (LNB), Bank B, and Bank C) grow to after 5 years?

Solution steps: Find the future value at the different rates offered by each of the four banks.[18]

1. Key in −15,000 and press PV
2. Carefully match rate and period:

Bank	Key in the Effective Rate as i	Key in the Number of Periods in 5 years n	Compute FV
A	4.0000% per half-year	5 × 2 = 10 half-years	22,203.66
LNB	2.0000% per quarter	5 × 4 = 20 quarters	22,289.21
B	0.6667% per month	5 × 12 = 60 months	22,348.13
C	0.0219% per day	5 × 365 = 1825 days	22,369.12

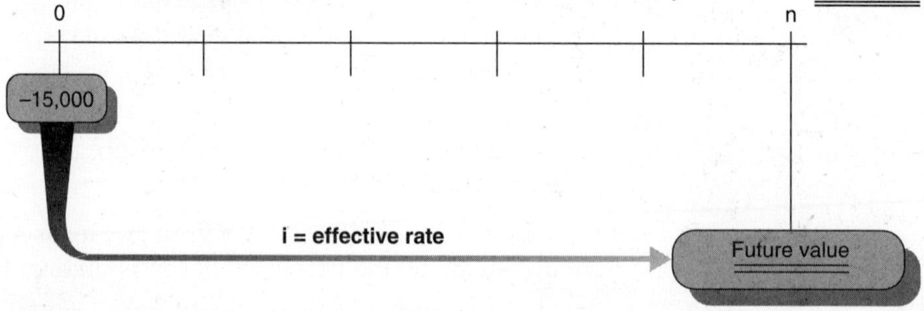

[17] **Observation and cross-reference:** For very high values of p this formula breaks down. In Appendix 5A we look at "continuous compounding," what happens to the effective rate as p becomes infinitely large.

[18] **Looking ahead:** From this point on, all solutions will be illustrated as they are done on the financial calculator.

Answer: The resulting balances are given in the table above. As you might expect, the more frequently compounding takes place, the greater future value a depositor will have.

If a problem contains an annuity, the value of **n** *must* be the number of annuity payments. This means that the length of one period of time *must* be the distance between payments, and the interest rate *must* be the effective rate for that period. If we have an interest rate for any other period of time, we must first convert it before completing the time value calculation.

Example

Matching the Interest Rate to the Time Period

John recently arranged an automobile loan for a customer who borrowed $15,000 at a nominal annual rate of 15% to be repaid over four years in (end-of-) monthly payments. How much is each payment?

Question: What is the amount of this annuity?

Solution steps:

1. There will be 48 payments, so **n** must equal 48 (months).
2. Since **n** is measured in months, **i** must be an effective *monthly* rate. The 15% rate is nominal, so:

$$\text{EMR} = 15\%/12 = 1.25\%$$

3. Using the financial calculator:

CLEAR the time value part of your calculator:
Switch your calculator setting to END
Key in 15000 and press PV
Key in 48 and press n
Key in 1.25 and press i
Compute PMT = −417.46

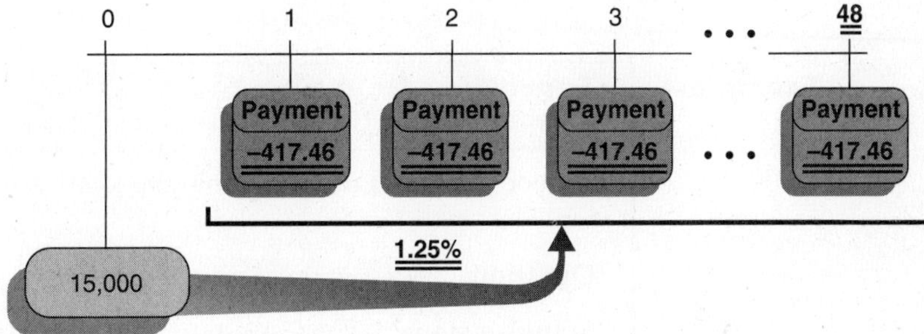

Answer: The monthly payment will be $417.46

2. Converting from an Effective to a Nominal Rate

The process of going from an effective interest rate to an equivalent nominal interest rate is exactly the reverse of going from nominal to effective: multiply (instead of divide) by the frequency of compounding:

$$Nominal\ rate = effective\ rate \times p$$

Examples

Converting from Effective to Nominal

Bank D pays interest at an effective semi-annual rate (ESR) of 6%.

Question: What is the equivalent nominal annual rate (NAR)?

Solution steps: There are two half-years in a year.

$$\text{NAR} = 6\% \times 2 = 12\%$$

Answer: The nominal annual rate is 12%.

Bank E uses an effective monthly rate (EMR) of 1.5% in calculating interest on its Visa and MasterCard accounts.

Question: What is the equivalent nominal annual rate (NAR)?

Solution steps: There are 12 months in a year.

$$\text{NAR} = 1.5\% \times 12 = 18\%$$

Answer: The nominal annual rate is 18%.

3. Converting from an Effective Rate to an Effective Rate for a Longer Period of Time

Often we need to find the summary effect of applying an effective rate over several compounding periods. This is simply another application of future value. In general (remember that EPR stands for "effective periodic rate," the general term for any period of time, and p is the number of compounding periods):[19]

$$EPR_{longer\ period} = (1 + EPR_{shorter\ period})^p - 1$$

Examples

Converting from Effective to Effective: Shorter to Longer Period

A deposit at the Local National Bank earns interest at the rate of "2% per quarter."

Question: What is the equivalent effective semi-annual rate (ESR)?

Solution steps: There are two quarters in a half-year, so p = 2.

[19] **Tip:** On most calculators, the exponent key is labeled y^x. On a few it is identified by ^.

$$ESR = (1 + EQR)^p - 1$$
$$= (1.02)^2 - 1 = 1.0404 - 1 = .0404 = 4.04\%$$

Answer: The effective semi-annual rate is 4.04%

Question: What is the equivalent effective annual rate (EAR)?

Solution steps: There are four quarters in a year, so p = 4.

$$EAR = (1 + EQR)^p - 1$$
$$= (1.02)^4 - 1 = 1.0824 - 1 = .0824 = 8.24\%$$

Answer: The effective annual rate is 8.24%

John Platini is thinking again about his three competitors, all of whom quoted an annual rate of 8% but differed in frequency of compounding.

Question: Compared to Local National Bank, what effective annual rates are John's competitors offering?

Bank	Compounds	Effective Periodic Rate	Effective Annual Rate	
A	semi-annually	ESR = 4.00%	$(1.04)^2 - 1$	= 8.16%
LNB	quarterly	EQR = 2.00%	$(1.02)^4 - 1$	= 8.24%
B	monthly	EMR = 0.6667%	$(1.006667)^{12} - 1$	= 8.30%
C	daily	EDR = 0.0219%	$(1.000219)^{365} - 1$	= 8.32%

Answer: The resulting rates are given in the table above. Observe that the more frequently compounding takes place, the greater the effective annual rate.

4. Converting from an Effective Rate to an Effective Rate for a Shorter Period of Time

Often we need to reverse the above process and find a rate which, when compounded, will produce a summary rate. We use the same relationship, but in reverse:[20]

$$EPR_{shorter\ period} = (1 + EPR_{longer\ period})^{1/p} - 1$$

Example

Converting from Effective to Effective: Longer to Shorter Period

Local National Bank permits customers to earn 8% interest on a particular deposit. However, bank policy does not permit any compounding within the year on this account. (Thus, 8% is not only the quoted or nominal annual rate (NAR), but also the effective annual rate (EAR) in this case.)

Question: What effective periodic interest rate would be earned by a depositor who invested for less than one year?

[20] **Tip:** Use the reciprocal key on your calculator, typically labeled 1/x, to change the exponent p to 1/p. For example, to calculate $(1.08)^{1/365}$: enter 1.08, press the exponent key, enter 365, press the reciprocal key, and then complete the calculation with the = key.

Deposit Period	1/p	Effective Periodic Rate[21]
1 day	1/365	EDR = $(1.08)^{1/365} - 1$ = 0.0211%
15 days	15/365	EHR = $(1.08)^{15/365} - 1$ = 0.3168%
1 month	1/12	EMR = $(1.08)^{1/12} - 1$ = 0.6434%
3 months	1/4	EQR = $(1.08)^{1/4} - 1$ = 1.9427%
6 months	1/2	ESR = $(1.08)^{1/2} - 1$ = 3.9230%
9 months	3/4	E9R = $(1.08)^{3/4} - 1$ = 5.9419%

Answer: The resulting rates are given in the table above. Each rate, when compounded for one year, produces an effective annual rate of 8%.

5. The Annual Percentage Rate (APR)

Because a given interest rate can be expressed in many ways (nominal, effective, annual, semi-annual, quarterly, etc.), it is easy for someone who is untrained in the concepts we are studying in this chapter to become confused. In 1968, the U.S. government passed legislation with the goal of preventing a financial institution from quoting one rate while actually using another. The law, popularly known as the "Truth in Lending Act," requires that a "true" interest rate, called the **annual percentage rate** (APR), be calculated and disclosed to most potential borrowers and lenders.

annual percentage rate—a standardized interest rate which must be disclosed to borrowers and lenders under U.S. law

Unfortunately, the law is not perfect. Some financial institutions quote the nominal annual rate for the APR while others quote the effective annual rate. Still others quote whichever rate is to their advantage.

Example

Keeping the APR Down

Monthly interest charged on a personal loan is calculated as 1% of the outstanding balance. Under the law, the APR could be quoted as either:

$$\text{The nominal annual rate (NAR)} = 1\% \times 12 = 12.00\%, \text{ or}$$
$$\text{The effective annual rate (EAR)} = (1.01)^{12} - 1 = 12.68\%$$

The more likely quote would be the NAR of 12.00% as it makes the interest rate the borrower is paying appear lower.

Example

Keeping the APR Up

Monthly interest paid on a time deposit is calculated as 0.65% of the outstanding balance. Under the law, the APR could be quoted as either:

$$\text{The nominal annual rate (NAR)} = 0.65\% \times 12 = 7.80\%, \text{ or}$$
$$\text{The effective annual rate (EAR)} = (1.0065)^{12} - 1 = 8.08\%$$

The more likely quote would be the EAR of 8.08% as it makes the interest rate the depositor is receiving appear higher.

---

[21] **Observation:** We use EHR for effective half-month rate, and E9R for effective 9-month rate in this example. These abbreviations are convenient but are not as widely used as the others such as EAR, ESR, etc.

Jay Herman put the calculator and instruction manual back into his attaché case. The train was pulling into the central station, and passengers were getting ready to make the final part of their journey to work. Jay had practiced a variety of the sample problems in the instruction manual, and by now the concepts and the location of the calculator keys were becoming familiar.

Analysis of financial values began with cash flows. To bring cash flows together, it was necessary to do time value calculations. This meant organizing the cash flows carefully by when they were expected to occur, choosing the time value model that fit the pattern of the cash flows, entering them into the calculator, and solving for the unknown quanity.

Jay stood up and eased into the aisle, flowing with the crowd toward the platform. As he left the station, he found himself smiling. If the rest of financial analysis was like this, it was certainly going to be a lot of fun!

Summary of Key Points

- **Understand why the value of money depends on the time of its receipt or payment and, therefore, why money amounts can only be compared after they have been adjusted for time.** The value of money depends on *two* things, its amount and the time of its receipt or payment. A larger sum of money is more valuable than a smaller sum. Receiving money sooner and paying it later is more valuable than later receipt or earlier payment, as additional interest may be earned. Since almost every business deal involves a payment today (present value) in order to get greater receipts in the future (future value), there is a natural tradeoff between the two characteristics of how much and when. To analyze a business deal, it is necessary to perform time value of money calculations.
- **Calculate the present value and future value of cash flows, the interest rate that describes any set of cash flows, and the length of time it takes to reach a financial goal.** The fundamental relationship of time value is the compound interest formula that relates a present value and a future value through a rate of interest that can be earned over a period of time. If we know three of the variables, we can solve for the fourth.
- **Analyze a set of uneven cash flows.** Uneven cash flows can be analyzed individually or can be entered into a high-level financial calculator or computer program to be analyzed together.
- **Recognize when time value analysis can be simplified because the cash flows form a standard pattern.** Many time value problems involve multiple cash flows. When the flows do not form a pattern, we must analyze them individually, a process made considerably easier by the cash flow list feature of a modern financial calculator. However, if cash flows are in the pattern of an annuity, a growing cash stream, or a perpetuity, we can use the relationships developed for these cash flow patterns to simplify our work considerably.
- **Identify the difference between a nominal rate, an effective rate, and the annual percentage rate (APR), and convert interest rates to equivalent rates for other periods of time.** Any quoted rate is a nominal rate. However, nominal rates often do not include the impact of compounding within the year. An effective rate is a "true" rate, containing the effect of within-year compounding. To prevent misleading quotations, the U.S. Government requires the use of the annual percentage rate. Although this rate significantly narrows the range of confusion, it does not eliminate confusion completely since several alternative calculations meet the legal requirement. For time value analysis to be correct, the definition of interest rate and time period must be consistent. Often this requires that we convert an interest rate to an equivalent rate for some other time period. Nominal rates can be converted to effective rates and vice-versa, and effective rates can be converted to equivalent effective rates for a different period of time.

Einstein discovers that time is actually money.

Questions

1. What is the relationship between a future value and a present value?
2. Some economists argue that people increase their savings when interest rates rise since they can earn more money. Suppose you were putting money away with the goal of raising $50,000 in five years. Would an increase in interest rates increase the amount of money you saved?
3. What is the relationship among an annuity, a perpetuity, and a growing cash stream?
4. If you had the choice of receiving interest compounded annually or monthly, which would you choose? Why?
5. A well-known advertisement by American Express urged travelers returning home to keep their travelers' checks rather than cash them in. The reason given was to have cash in an emergency, but could American Express have had any other reason for encouraging this behavior?
6. Why do airlines often insist that you pay for your ticket on the date you book your flight rather than the date you actually fly?

Problems

1. **(Basic future value)** If you invest $15,000 today at 9% annual interest, how much will you have in:
   a. 1 year?
   b. 2 years?
   c. 5 years?
   d. 10 years?

2. **(Basic future value)** How much will you have in 5 years if you invest $25,000 for a 5-year period at an annual interest rate of:
   a. 25%?
   b. 12%?
   c. 7%?
   d. 0%?

3. **(Basic present value)** You have been told you will receive $75,000 at some time in the future. In the meantime you can earn interest at an annual rate of 6%. How much is the $75,000 worth to you today if the time you must wait for its receipt is:
   a. 1 year?
   b. 2 years?
   c. 5 years?
   d. 10 years?

4. **(Basic present value)** You are due to receive $30,000 in 7 years. How much is it worth to you today if you can earn interest at an annual rate of:
   a. 25%?
   b. 12%?
   c. 7%?
   d. 0%?

5. **(Basic time period)** You have $10,000 today. How long will it take for you to double your money if you can earn interest at an annual rate of:
   a. 5%?
   b. 8%?
   c. 15%?
   d. 100%?

6. **(Basic time period)** If you can earn interest at an annual interest rate of 9%, how long will it take for $25,000 to grow to be:
   a. $30,000?
   b. $40,000?
   c. $75,000?
   d. $100,000?

7. **(Basic interest rate)** What annual interest rate does it take to make $45,000 grow to be $60,000 in:
   a. 3 years?
   b. 5 years?
   c. 10 years?
   d. 20 years?

8. **(Basic interest rate)** What annual interest rate, earned over 8 years, will make an initial $17,500 grow to be:
   a. $20,000?
   b. $25,000?
   c. $35,000?
   d. $50,000?

9. **(Present value of uneven cash flows)** Find the present value (as of today) of the following cash flow streams at an interest rate of 8%:

Year	Stream A	Stream B	Stream C
1	$1,000	$4,000	$5,000
2	2,000	2,000	4,000
3	3,000	3,000	3,000
4	4,000	1,000	2,000
5	5,000	5,000	1,000

10. **(Present value of uneven cash flows)** You wish to set aside a fund of money to provide for your elderly parents. You estimate you will need $25,000 at the end of each of the next 5 years and $15,000 at the end of each of the five years after that. What amount of money, deposited today, will provide these funds if you can earn at an annual interest rate of 6%?

11. **(Future value of an ordinary annuity)** If you save $5,000 at the end of each year for 15 years, how much will you have accumulated if you can earn at an annual interest rate of:
    a. 6%?
    b. 10%?
    c. 12%?
    d. 15%?

12. **(Future value of an ordinary annuity)** If you can earn at an annual interest rate of 8% per year, how much will you have accumulated if you save $3,000 at the end of each of the next:
    a. 5 years?
    b. 10 years?
    c. 15 years?
    d. 20 years?

13. **(Future value of an annuity due)** Redo Problem 11 assuming that you make your deposits at the beginning of each year.

14. **(Future value of an annuity due)** Redo Problem 12 assuming that you make your deposits at the beginning of each year.

15. **(Amount of an ordinary annuity)** How much must you pay at the end of each year to repay a $50,000, 14% annual interest rate loan if you must make:
    a. 10 payments?
    b. 15 payments?
    c. 20 payments?
    d. 30 payments?

16. **(Amount of an ordinary annuity)** How much must you deposit at the end of each of the next 10 years to accumulate $50,000 if you can earn interest at an annual interest rate of:

    a. 3%?
    b. 5%?
    c. 7%?
    d. 9%?

17. **(Amount of an annuity due)** Redo Problem 15 assuming that you make your payments at the beginning of each year.

18. **(Amount of an annuity due)** Redo Problem 16 assuming that you make your deposits at the beginning of each year.

19. **(Present value of an ordinary annuity)** You wish to create a bank account from which you can withdraw $10,000 per year at the end of each of the next 10 years. How much must you deposit today to provide these benefits if you can earn at a rate of:

    a. 5%?
    b. 12%?
    c. 16%?
    d. 20%?

20. **(Present value of an ordinary annuity)** You have asked your banker for a loan and stated that you are willing to repay the loan with annual end-of-year payments of $1,500. Your banker responded by informing you that the annual interest rate would be 12%. How much can you borrow if the loan is for a period of:

    a. 2 years?
    b. 5 years?
    c. 7 years?
    d. 10 years?

21. **(Present value of an annuity due)** Redo Problem 19 assuming that you make your withdrawals at the beginning of each year.

22. **(Present value of an annuity due)** Redo Problem 20 assuming that you make your loan payments at the beginning of each year.

23. **(Length of an ordinary annuity)** You have saved $250,000 and wish to retire today. For how many years can you draw $30,000, at the end of each year, if you can continue to earn interest at an annual rate of:

    a. 5%
    b. 8%
    c. 10%
    d. 11%

24. **(Length of an ordinary annuity)** You plan to make deposits into a retirement account and have set a goal of having $2 million in the account when you retire. You forecast you can earn interest at an annual rate of 6%. How many years will it take for you to reach your retirement goal if, at the end of each year, you deposit:

    a. $10,000?
    b. $20,000?
    c. $30,000?
    d. $40,000?

25. **(Length of an annuity due)** Redo Problem 23 assuming that you make your withdrawals at the beginning of each year.

26. **(Length of an annuity due)** Redo Problem 24 assuming that you make your deposits at the beginning of each year.

27. **(Interest rate in an ordinary annuity)** An insurance fund advertises that if you invest $50,000 today, you will receive a fixed amount at the end of each of the next 20 years. What interest rate are they giving you if the annual amount is:

    a. $ 3,500?
    b. $ 5,000?
    c. $ 7,500?
    d. $ 10,000?

28. **(Interest rate in an ordinary annuity)** You have decided to start saving for your children's education and want to accumulate $250,000. You can afford to deposit $15,000 into your education fund at the end of each year. What annual interest rate must you earn if you need to reach your savings target in:

    a. 6 years?
    b. 8 years?
    c. 10 years?
    d. 12 years?

29. **(Interest rate in an annuity due)** Redo Problem 27 assuming that the fund pays you at the beginning of each year.

30. **(Interest rate in an annuity due)** Redo Problem 28 assuming you make your deposits at the beginning of each year.

31. **(Growing cash stream)** You have the opportunity to buy the stock of a company which is expected to pay a $3.50 dividend in one year and grow thereafter at an annual rate of 4%. If you require a 16% rate of return on this investment, how much is the stock worth to you?

32. **(Growing cash stream)** The stock of a company that is expected to pay a $1.75 dividend in one year and

grow thereafter at an annual rate of 11% is currently selling for $35.00 per share. What rate of return does the market require on this security?

33. **(Perpetuity)** A certain preferred stock pays a $14.00 annual dividend. The next dividend is expected in one year. How much is the stock worth to you if you require a rate of return of:
    a. 10%?
    b. 14%?
    c. 17%?
    d. 20%?

34. **(Perpetuity)** You can buy a preferred stock that pays a $12.50 annual dividend, the next dividend due in one year. What rate of return does the stock offer if you can buy it for:
    a. $75.00?
    b. $90.00?
    c. $100.00?
    d. $120.00?

35. **(Converting interest rates)** Convert the following nominal annual rates to effective rates for the compounding period.
    a. 12%, compounded quarterly
    b. 9%, compounded semi-annually
    c. 11%, compounded monthly
    d. 16%, compounded daily

36. **(Converting interest rates)** Convert the following nominal annual rates to effective rates for the compounding period.
    a. 13% compounded daily
    b. 4% compounded weekly
    c. 10%, compounded quarterly
    d. 7%, compounded semi-annually

37. **(Converting interest rates)** Convert the following effective periodic interest rates to their nominal annual equivalent:
    a. 3% per quarter
    b. 1% per month
    c. 0.04% per day
    d. 0.35% per week

38. **(Converting interest rates)** Convert the following effective periodic interest rates to their nominal annual equivalent:
    a. 0.015% per day
    b. 0.8% per month
    c. 3% per quarter
    d. 6% per half year

39. **(Converting interest rates)** The four banks in town offer the following interest rates:

Bank	Rate offered
A	10%, compounded quarterly
B	10.50% with no compounding
C	0.80% per month
D	10.4%, compounded semi-annually

    a. Find the effective annual rate (EAR) offered by each bank.
    b. Which bank offers the highest rate?

40. **(Converting interest rates)** A bank officer is examining four rates to offer its customers on an automobile loan:

    9.60%, compounded semi-annually
    9.50%, compounded quarterly
    9.40%, compounded monthly
    9.30%, compounded daily

    a. Find the effective annual rate (EAR) that corresponds to each rate.
    b. If all other terms of the loan are identical,
       (1) Which rate earns the most for the bank?
       (2) As a customer, which rate do you prefer?

41. **(Converting interest rates)** Find the present value of an ordinary annuity of $500 per quarter for five years at an interest rate of:
    a. 8%, compounded annually
    b. 8%, compounded semi-annually
    c. 8%, compounded quarterly
    d. 8%, compounded monthly

42. **(Converting interest rates)** Find the future value of an ordinary annuity of $2,000 per quarter for ten years at an interest rate of:
    a. 6%, compounded annually
    b. 6%, compounded quarterly
    c. 6%, compounded monthly
    d. 6%, compounded daily

APPENDIX 5A

CONTINUOUS COMPOUNDING

In Chapter 5, John Platini, our banker friend, compared his bank to three others, all of which offered a nominal annual interest rate of 8%. He found that the effective annual rate increased as interest was compounded more frequently within a year. John's calculations are summarized below:

Bank	Compounds	Effective Rate	Effective Annual Rate	
A	semi-annually	ESR = 4.00%	$(1.04)^2 - 1$	= 8.16%
LNB	quarterly	EQR = 2.00%	$(1.02)^4 - 1$	= 8.24%
B	monthly	EMR = 0.6667%	$(1.006667)^{12} - 1$	= 8.30%
C	daily	EDR = 0.0219%	$(1.000219)^{365} - 1$	= 8.32%

We can take this concept to the extreme: what happens if compounding is so frequent that the compounding time period becomes infinitesimally small. This is the case known as continuous compounding.

The time value of money relationship has a special form for continuous compounding:

$$FV = PV \times e^{rt}$$

and the effective periodic rate is:

$$EPR = e^{rt} - 1$$

FV, PV and **r** have the same meaning as before. The new variables are:

t = time: this variable replaces **n.** It is measured in years.

e = a constant: this number is the base of the natural logarithms and has the value 2.718281828. . . .

Example

Continuous Compounding

John wants to see the effect of continuous compounding at the rate of 8%.

Question: If interest is paid for one year at the rate of "8%, compounded continuously," what is the effective annual rate of interest (EAR)?

Solution steps: For the effective *annual* rate, t = 1.

$$\begin{aligned} \text{EAR} &= e^{rt} - 1 \\ &= (2.718281828)^{(.08)(1)} - 1 = 1.083287 - 1 \\ &= .0833 = 8.33\% \end{aligned}$$

Answer: The effective annual rate is 8.33%. This is only slightly greater than the rate of 8.32% from daily compounding.

Problems

1. **(Continuous compounding)** Find the effective annual rate that is equivalent to:
   a. 6%, compounded continuously
   b. 9% compounded continuously
   c. 12%, compounded continuously
   d. 15%, compounded continuously

2. **(Continuous compounding)** If you invest $10,000 at the rate of 11%, compounded continuously, how much will you have accumulated after:
   a. 1 month?
   b. 6 months?
   c. 1 year?
   d. 5 years?

APPENDIX 5B

USING A CASH FLOW LIST ON A FINANCIAL CALCULATOR

Most modern financial calculators have a cash flow list feature which permits them to compute the present value of an uneven series of cash flows. In Chapter 5 we looked at the value of winning the state lottery. The problem was:

> The state lottery promises a grand prize of $1,000,000. The winner will be paid $100,000 per year for the first three years, $200,000 per year for the next two years, and $300,000 in the sixth year. If 8% is the appropriate rate of interest, what is the lottery really worth?

Earlier, the best we could do was to calculate the present value of each cash flow separately and add up the results:

	Key in			
Year	As FV	As n	As i	Compute PV
1	100,000	1	8	$-92,592.59
2	100,000	2	8	-85,733.88
3	100,000	3	8	-79,383.22
4	200,000	4	8	-147,005.97
5	200,000	5	8	-136,116.64
6	300,000	6	8	-189,050.89
			Total	$-729,883.19

With six cash flows this process was not too bad, but imagine if we had 50 cash flows!

A calculator that has a cash flow list feature permits us to enter each cash flow in chronological order, enter the 8% interest rate, and press one button for the answer. The procedure is as follows:[1]

1. Clear the calculator:

   Call up the cash flow menu (if required).

   CLEAR the cash-flow-list part of your calculator.

2. Enter the cash flows:

   0 as FLOW (there is no receipt or payment at time-point 0)

   100,000 as FLOW 1

   3 as TIMES the number of repeats for cash flow 1

   200,000 as FLOW 2

   2 as TIMES the number of repeats for cash flow 2

   300,000 as FLOW 3

3. Enter the interest rate:

   8 as i

4. Calculate the result:

   Press NPV for the answer = $729,883.20 (the one-penny difference is due to round-off error when each cash flow was analyzed individually).

net present value—the present value of all benefits from a proposed investment less the present value of all costs, using the weighted-average cost of capital as the discount rate

NPV stands for **net present value,** the sum of the present values of all of the cash flows in the problem.[2] The use of the word *net* reminds us that the outflows are considered negative flows. NPV therefore equals the sum of the present values of the cash inflows minus the sum of the present value of the cash outflows (much like "net income" is the sum of a firm's revenues minus the sum of the firm's expenses). On your calculator, NPV is the key to press whenever you are computing a present value using the cash flow list feature.

Another use for the cash flow list feature is to calculate an interest rate within an uneven stream of cash flows. This is possible if there are both cash outflows and cash inflows. The procedure is the same as above through Step 2. There is no need to enter an interest rate since you are asking the machine to calculate one. Recall this example:

> You have the opportunity to invest $100 today in order to receive $40 one year later, plus $60 one year after that, plus $50 after three years. What is the rate of return on this investment?

---

[1] **Tip:** Again, the exact steps differ slightly from one calculator to another. The steps shown here are typical. Check your calculator manual for the specifics of your machine. An appendix illustrating the steps on 6 popular financial calculators appears at the end of this book.

[2] **Cross-reference:** The cost of capital is the subject of Chapter 10. In Chapter 11, we will learn why net present value should be calculated using the "weighted-average cost of capital" if it is to be useful for investment decision-making.

We calculated the answer, 22.40%, using the cash flow list feature. Here's how it is done:

1. Clear your calculator:

   Call up the cash flow menu (if required).

   CLEAR the cash-flow-list part of your calculator.

2. Enter the cash flows:

   −100 as FLOW 0

   40 as FLOW 1

   60 as FLOW 2

   50 as FLOW 3

3. Calculate the result:

   Press IRR for the answer = 22.40%.

internal rate of return—the rate of return from an investment

IRR stands for **internal rate of return,** the rate of return that is earned when you invest money (negative cash flow) today in order to receive money (positive cash flow) later.[3] On your calculator, IRR is the key to press whenever you are computing an interest rate using the cash flow list feature.

Some calculators can also calculate net future value (NFV) and net uniform series (NUS) from a list of cash flows. Net future value is the compound value of the cash flows as of the date of the last flow in the list. Net uniform series is the amount of an ordinary annuity with the same length as the list of cash flows that has the same net present and net future values.

Problems

1. **(Cash flow list)** A certain investment promises to return the following cash flows to you at the times indicated:

Year	Cash flow
1	$ 6,000
2	8,000
3	10,000
4	10,000
5	10,000
6	12,000
7	12,000

   a. What is the net present value (NPV) of these cash flows at an interest rate of 6%?
   b. What is the net present value (NPV) of these cash flows at an interest rate of 10%?
   c. What is the net present value (NPV) of these cash flows at an interest rate of 14%?
   d. If the cost of the investment is $40,000, what is the investment's internal rate of return (IRR)?

2. **(Cash flow list)** A bank has proposed the following annual payments to repay a $100,000 loan:

Year	Cash flow
1	$30,000
2	30,000
3	30,000
4	20,000
5	20,000

   a. What is the net present value (NPV) of the loan repayment cash flows at an interest rate of 5%?
   b. What is the net present value (NPV) of the loan repayment cash flows at an interest rate of 8%?
   c. What is the net present value (NPV) of the loan repayment cash flows at an interest rate of 11%?
   d. What is the interest rate on this loan?

[3] **Cross-reference:** The use and limitations of internal rate of return are covered in Chapter 11 and Appendix 11B.

APPENDIX 5C

DERIVATION OF TIME VALUE FORMULAS

In this appendix we derive four time value formulas: (1) the present value of an ordinary annuity, (2) the future value of an ordinary annuity, (3) the present value of a perpetuity, and (4) the present value of a growing cash stream. The four derivations are remarkably similar in form, and all involve the same steps:

- Write out the relationship as an equation.
- Multiply both sides of the equation by the factor $(1 + r)$—for the growing cash stream, also divide both sides by $(1 + g)$—to create a second, similar equation.
- Subtract the first equation from the second equation. On the right-hand side, all terms but two will cancel out (disappear).
- Rearrange the remaining algebra to solve for the desired variable.

1. Present Value of an Ordinary Annuity

The relationship is:

$$PV = \sum_{i=1}^{n} \frac{PMT}{(1+r)^i}$$

$$= \frac{PMT}{(1+r)} + \frac{PMT}{(1+r)^2} + \frac{PMT}{(1+r)^3} + \ldots + \frac{PMT}{(1+r)^{n-1}} + \frac{PMT}{(1+r)^n}$$

Multiply both sides by $(1 + r)$. On the right side of the equation, this will decrease the power of each divisor by 1:

$$(1+r)\,PV = PMT + \frac{PMT}{(1+r)} + \frac{PMT}{(1+r)^2} + \frac{PMT}{(1+r)^3} + \ldots + \frac{PMT}{(1+r)^{n-1}}$$

Subtract the first equation from the second. Notice that, on the right side of the equation, all of the terms cancel each other out except the first term of the second equation (PMT) and the last term of the first equation $[PMT/(1 + r)^n]$:

$$(1+r)\,PV - PV = PMT - \frac{PMT}{(1+r)^n}$$

Now rearrange the algebra. Distribute the $(1 + r)$ on the left side of the equation and factor out PMT on the right side:

$$PV + rPV - PV = PMT\left(1 - \frac{1}{(1+r)^n}\right)$$

The PV and $-$PV on the left side of the equation cancel each other out leaving rPV:

$$rPV = PMT\left(1 - \frac{1}{(1 + r)^n}\right)$$

Finally divide both sides by r:

$$PV = PMT\left(\frac{1 - \frac{1}{(1 + r)^n}}{r}\right)$$

2. Future Value of an Ordinary Annuity

The relationship is:

$$FV = \sum_{i=0}^{n-1} PMT\ (1 + r)^i$$

$$= PMT + PMT\ (1 + r) + PMT\ (1 + r)^2 + PMT\ (1 + r)^3 + \ldots + PMT\ (1 + r)^{n-1}$$

Multiply both sides by (1 + r). On the right side of the equation, this will increase the power of each (1 + r) multiplier by 1:

$$(1 + r)\ FV = PMT\ (1 + r) + PMT\ (1 + r)^2 + PMT\ (1 + r)^3 + \ldots + PMT\ (1 + r)^{n-1} + PMT\ (1 + r)^n$$

Subtract the first equation from the second. Notice that, on the right side of the equation, all of the terms cancel each other out except the last term of the second equation [PMT$(1 + r)^n$] and the first term of the first equation (PMT):

$$(1 + r)FV - FV = PMT\ (1 + r)^n - PMT$$

Now rearrange the algebra. Distribute the (1 + r) on the left side of the equation and factor out PMT on the right side:

$$FV + rFV - FV = PMT\ [(1 + r)^n - 1]$$

The FV and $-$FV on the left side of the equation cancel each other out leaving rFV:

$$rFV = PMT\ [(1 + r)^n - 1]$$

Finally divide both sides by r:

$$FV = PMT\left(\frac{(1 + r)^n - 1}{r}\right)$$

3. Present Value of a Perpetuity

The relationship is:

$$PV = \sum_{i=1}^{\infty} \frac{PMT}{(1 + r)^i}$$

$$= \frac{PMT}{(1 + r)} + \frac{PMT}{(1 + r)^2} + \frac{PMT}{(1 + r)^3} + \ldots + \frac{PMT}{(1 + r)^{\infty-1}} + \frac{PMT}{(1 + r)^{\infty}}$$

Multiply both sides by (1 + r). On the right side of the equation, this will decrease the power of each divisor by 1:

$$(1 + r)\ PV = PMT + \frac{PMT}{(1 + r)} + \frac{PMT}{(1 + r)^2} + \frac{PMT}{(1 + r)^3} + \ldots + \frac{PMT}{(1 + r)^{\infty - 1}}$$

Subtract the first equation from the second. Notice that, on the right side of the equation, all of the terms cancel each other out except the first term of the second equation (PMT) and the last term of the first equation [$PMT/(1 + r)^{\infty}$]:

$$(1 + r)\ PV - PV = PMT - \frac{PMT}{(1 + r)^{\infty}}$$

Now rearrange the algebra. Distribute the (1 + r) on the left side of the equation. On the right side, the last term [$PMT/(1 + r)^{\infty}$] can be dropped out; it must equal zero since its denominator is infinitely large:

$$PV + rPV - PV = PMT$$

The PV and −PV on the left side of the equation cancel each other out leaving rPV:

$$rPV = PMT$$

Finally divide both sides by r:

$$PV = \frac{PMT}{r}$$

4. Present Value of a Growing Cash Stream

The relationship is:

$$PV = \sum_{i=1}^{\infty} \frac{CF_i}{(1 + r)^i}$$

$$= \frac{CF_1}{(1 + r)} + \frac{CF_2}{(1 + r)^2} + \frac{CF_3}{(1 + r)^3} + \ldots + \frac{CF_{\infty - 1}}{(1 + r)^{\infty - 1}} + \frac{CF_{\infty}}{(1 + r)^{\infty}}$$

In a growing cash stream, each cash flow differs from the prior flow by the factor (1 + g) where g is the growth rate. Therefore $CF_2 = CF_1(1 + g)$, $CF_3 = CF_2(1 + g) = CF_1(1 + g)^2$, etc., and the relationship can be rewritten:

$$PV = \frac{CF_1}{(1 + r)} + \frac{CF_1(1 + g)}{(1 + r)^2} + \frac{CF_1(1 + g)^2}{(1 + r)^3} + \ldots + \frac{CF_1(1 + g)^{\infty - 2}}{(1 + r)^{\infty - 1}} + \frac{CF_1(1 + g)^{\infty - 1}}{(1 + r)^{\infty}}$$

Multiply both sides by (1 + r) and divide by (1 + g). On the right side of the equation, this will decrease the power of each (1 + r) divisor and each (1 + g) multiplier by 1. Also, the first term on the right side will wind up with (1 + g) in the denominator:

$$\frac{(1+r)}{(1+g)}PV = \frac{CF_1}{(1+g)} + \frac{CF_1}{(1+r)} + \frac{CF_1(1+g)}{(1+r)^2} + \frac{CF_1(1+g)^2}{(1+r)^3} + \ldots + \frac{CF_1(1+g)^{\infty-2}}{(1+r)^{\infty-1}}$$

Subtract the first equation from the second. Notice that, on the right side of the equation, all of the terms cancel each other out except the first term of the second equation $[(CF_1/(1+g)]$ and the last term of the first equation $[CF_1(1+g)^{\infty-1}/(1+r)^{\infty}]$:

$$\frac{(1+r)}{(1+g)}PV - PV = \frac{CF_1}{(1+g)} - \frac{CF_1(1+g)^{\infty-1}}{(1+r)^{\infty}}$$

Now rearrange the algebra. Multiply each term by $(1+g)$:

$$(1+r)PV - (1+g)PV = CF_1 - \frac{CF_1(1+g)^{\infty}}{(1+r)^{\infty}}$$

Distribute the $(1+r)$ and $(1+g)$ on the left side of the equation. On the right side, *if* $r > g$ the last term $[CF_1(1+g)^{\infty}/(1+r)^{\infty}]$ can be dropped out; it will equal zero since its denominator will be infinitely larger than its numerator[1]:

$$PV + rPV - PV - gPV = CF_1$$

The PV and −PV on the left side of the equation cancel each other out leaving $rPV - gPV$:

$$rPV - gPV = CF_1$$

Now factor out PV on the left side:

$$PV(r-g) = CF_1$$

Finally divide both sides by $r - g$:

$$PV = \frac{CF_1}{r-g}$$

[1] **Observation:** This is why the growing cash stream formula is valid only when $r > g$. If $r < g$ the present value of a growing cash stream is infinite as seen by the last term which becomes infinitely large. If $r = g$, the above equation reduces to $0 = 0$ and becomes useless, although in this case the present value is infinite as well.

CHAPTER 6
INTEREST RATES

Sandra Maglen found herself nodding in agreement. The treasurer's point made perfect sense: her company had to do a better job of responding to conditions in the general economy. Sandra thought back to her economics classes in college and smiled as she remembered a favorite professor who was fond of pointing out how the macroeconomy affected the microeconomy. Perhaps she would write a letter to the professor to reestablish contact and to let him know that some of his teachings remained with her.

The treasurer went on, "The immediate issue is that the CFO received a call today from one of the major financial rating agencies saying that we've been put on a 'credit watch.' The boss fears that our ratings might slip. If that happens we would have to pay more to borrow. We can't be competitive if our costs rise like that. But the larger issue is that we shouldn't have gotten into this position in the first place. Let's see if we can come up with a strategy for avoiding these kinds of problems altogether."

Sandra and several others were asked to form a team to research and write a report identifying key relationships affecting the interest rates the firm paid on its debt. The team agreed to collect their thoughts and materials and get together later that afternoon. Back at her desk, Sandra took her old college economics books off the shelf and blew off the dust. She leafed through several pages and began to recall that interest-rates depend on a variety of factors. She jotted down some thoughts and made a note to collect some recent economic data prior to the meeting.

Interest rates are prices—the price to rent money. Of all the prices in an economy, interest rates are perhaps the most important, since money is such a universal commodity. They have a profound effect on the functioning of an economy and all of its components, and upon a wide range of business decisions. Except where determined by government regulation, they are set in competitive markets by the forces of supply and demand.

The problem on which Sandra has been asked to work is one that all firms face. In addition to understanding the general level of interest rates, it is important to understand the structure of rates—why all borrowers do not pay the same rate to raise money (and, correspondingly, why lenders receive different returns on their investments). With that knowledge, Sandra and her team can help the finance function provide financing at the lowest possible cost.

Key Points You Should Learn from This Chapter

After reading this chapter you should be able to:

- Demonstrate the inverse relationship between interest rates and present value.
- Describe how the supply of and demand for money interact to determine the base level of interest rates.
- Subdivide any interest rate into its components.
- Explain why interest rates differ by maturity of obligation.
- Understand how risks impact interest rates.
- Understand how taxes impact interest rates.

Introductory Concepts—Interest Rates and Present Value

Interest rates play several important roles within the economy. They balance the supply of, and demand for, money—thus permitting the market for money to clear. In doing so, they ration credit, providing it to those borrowers who can promise the highest rates of return and shutting out those with poor-yielding investments. In addition, governments, as major suppliers and demanders of money, use interest rates as a key component of economic policy, pushing rates lower to stimulate growth or raising them to slow inflation.

Interest rates are also critical for business decision making. As we saw in Chapter 5, every business decision involving money flows should be analyzed using time value of money calculations. But time value calculations require the use of an interest rate. As rates change, the value of business decisions changes as well. In particular, *interest rates and present values move in opposite directions.* As interest rates rise, the present value of future benefits declines, making investment alternatives less valuable. By contrast, as interest rates decline, present values rise and investment alternatives become correspondingly more valuable.

The Inverse Relationship Between Interest Rates and Present Value

You can purchase an investment that will return $100,000 in five years. How much should you pay if you require a rate of return of 10%? 12%? 14%? 16%?

Question: What is the present value at each interest rate?

Solution steps: (using the financial calculator):

CLEAR the time value part of your calculator

Key in 100,000 and press FV

Key in 5 and press n

Key in each rate in turn and press i

Compute PV

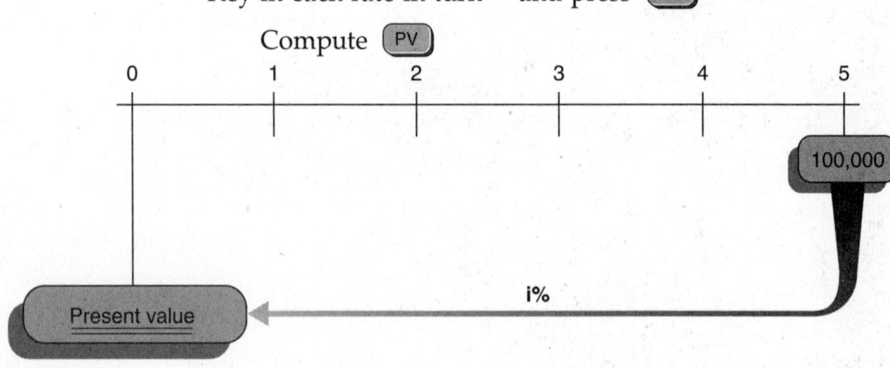

Answer:

Rate i	Present Value PV
10%	$ −62,092.13
12	−56,742.69
14	−51,936.87
16	−47,611.30

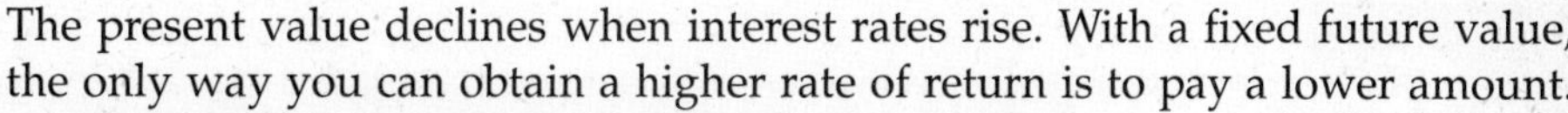

The present value declines when interest rates rise. With a fixed future value, the only way you can obtain a higher rate of return is to pay a lower amount.

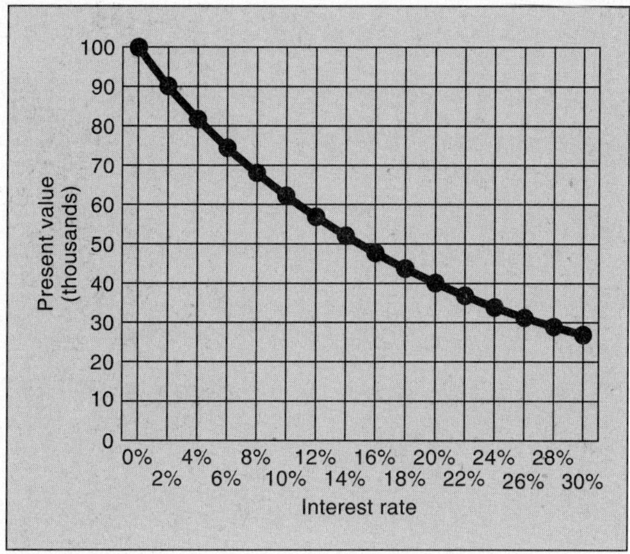

The graph shows the inverse relationship between interest rates and present values using the data of this example (Future value = \$100,000, five years). Notice as the interest rate rises, present value declines.

Financial managers study interest rates as they plan future business activity. They forecast the future level of rates to plan the level of their investment and financing actions. They forecast the speed with which rates might change to plan the timing of their investment and financing actions. Financial managers who anticipate and respond wisely to interest rates can add significant value to their organization.

The Base Level of Interest Rates

base level of interest rates—the level of interest rates common to all financial instruments in the economy

As we will see throughout this chapter, there are many interest rates. However, all interest rates are affected by certain underlying economic conditions. When those conditions change, all rates change together. We call the rate determined by common economic conditions the **base level of interest rates**. Economic theorists have used several models to explain the base level of interest rates. All are supply-demand models; they differ in which forces are assumed to be behind the supply of and demand for money. We look briefly at four: (1) classical theory, (2) liquidity preference theory, (3) loanable funds theory, and (4) rational expectations theory.

1. The Classical Theory of Interest Rates

classical theory of interest rates—a theory of interest rate determination focusing on household savings and business investment

An early explanation of the base level of interest rates was the **classical theory of interest rates** deriving from the work of the classical economists.[1] The classical the-

[1] **References:** The classical theory is particularly associated with Eugen von Bohm-Bawerk and Irving Fisher. Their original, classical works are Eugen von Bohm-Bawerk, *The Positive Theory of Capital* (New York: Macmillan, 1891); and Irving Fisher, *The Theory of Interest* (New York: Macmillan, 1936).

FINANCE IN PRACTICE

Reacting to Changes in Interest Rates

The decline in interest rates in the early 1980's encouraged financial managers to rethink their financing strategies. Some refinanced existing debt obligations.

> TriMas Corp. is starting 1992 off with a new, slimmer balance sheet. With interest rates at a 28-year low, the Ann Arbor (Mich.) maker of such gritty gear as trailer hitches got its bankers on the phone. And just like that, the deep-in-debt company refinanced $88 million of $128 million in debt from a 1988 spin-off. By cutting the rate it pays by two whole percentage points, and by retiring the remaining $40 million debt balance, TriMas eased its yearly interest payments by a welcome $5.4 million.

Others turned to the stock markets.

> After a four year drought, Wall Street underwriters are flush with equity deals. Issuers have been lured to market by a surprising new appetite for equities among investors, who are fleeing the rock-bottom rates paid on bank certificates and money funds.

The interest rate decline was particularly advantageous to small businesses.

> For smaller companies, the markets are making expansion possible again. Medical Care International Inc., the nation's largest operator of outpatient surgical centers, is using $115 million in debentures it issued to add as many as 10 centers this year to its current 80. Dallas-based Medical Care, which must pay up to 9.9% on other bonds, is shelling out just 6.75% for these. Says CEO Donald E. Steen: "I can't imagine a better market."

However, larger companies benefitted as well.

> For large, well-established companies, the new environment offers wonderful flexibility. A month ago, Walt Disney Co. was thinking about raising $220 million for its TV production unit via a new-fangled investment vehicle dubbed ZEBRA, for zero-based rate adjustment security. This paid a modest 4% but allowed investors to share Disney's profits, once hoped-for hits like its new "Dinosaurs" move into syndication. Suddenly, two days before Christmas, Disney cancelled the ZEBRA. Why? When it needs to, it can borrow from banks for less.

For many companies, the savings were substantial.

> Luckiest among debt-heavy companies are those with floating-rate debt—that is, with rates pegged to such benchmarks as the prime rate, which banks charge their most creditworthy customers, or the London interbank offered rate, used by banks dealing in U.S. currency held in Europe. RJR Nabisco Inc. pays just 0.62 points over LIBOR, now 4.4%. Result: an interest tab of only 5% on its $3.5 billion in bank loans. Compare that with the 12.3% RJR paid in 1989."

Reference: "A Stampede for Cheaper Money," *Business Week,* Jan. 20, 1992, pp. 26–27.

ory focused on household savings as the primary source of the supply of money and upon business investment as the primary demand. According to this theory, households—individuals and families—change their level of savings as interest rates change. This is because they view interest earnings as a *reward for deferring consumption*. Households save more when rates rise and save less as rates fall; this pat-

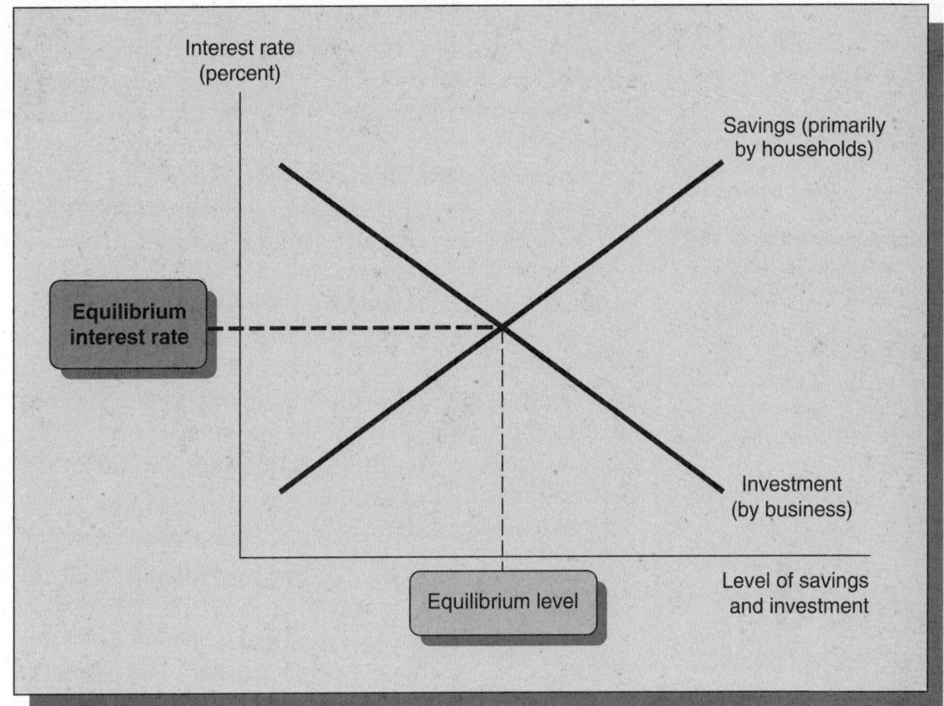

FIGURE 6.1
The base rate of interest in the classical theory. Money is supplied by household savings and demanded by businesses for investment in plant and equipment.

tern is reflected in the upward-sloping supply curve, labeled "Savings," in Figure 6.1. (It was recognized that businesses also save through purchases of securities and through retention of earnings and governments save if they run a budget surplus, but these sources were considered minor compared to household savings.) The demand for money came primarily from businesses that adjust their level of investment in capital equipment as interest rates change. They invest more when interest rates fall since low interest rates improve the present value of investment benefits and vice-versa.[2] The downward-sloping demand curve, labeled "Investment," captures this. The interest rate adjusts until supply equals demand, producing the equilibrium interest rate and the equilibrium level of savings and investment.

2. Liquidity Preference Theory

liquidity preference theory—a theory of interest rate determination focusing on individuals' reasons for holding cash and on the money supply as determined by the central bank

A second explanation of the base level of interest rates is the **liquidity preference theory** of John Maynard Keynes.[3] It emerged in the twentieth century in response to changes in the economic environment and to omissions of the classical theory. As the banking system grew in importance, it was observed that banks, through their money creation process, were important suppliers of money. In addition, time value of money theory was developed and the relationship between interest rates and security prices became understood.

[2] **Cross-reference:** We introduced the relationship of interest rates to present values in Chapter 5 and will look at how this affects the value of investment opportunities in Chapter 11.

[3] **Reference:** John Maynard Keynes, *The General Theory of Employment, Interest and Money* (New York: Harcourt Brace Jovanovich, 1936).

liquidity—the ability to have access to cash quickly and in full amount

Transactions motive—the desire to hold cash for day-to-day spending needs

precautionary motive—the desire to hold cash for unanticipated spending needs

speculative motive—the desire to hold cash for investment purposes in anticipation of rising interest rates

Keynes suggested that the primary reason individuals demanded money was their desire for **liquidity**. He separated the demand for money into three motives: **the transactions motive**—money held to make daily purchases; **the precautionary motive**—money held as a reserve, since transaction needs cannot be estimated precisely; and the **speculative motive**—money held to take advantage of good future investment opportunities. According to Keynes, the transactions and precautionary demands do not depend on interest rates but rather on income, price levels, and business activity. However, the speculative demand is related to interest rates. When interest rates are low, investors will hold speculative cash; they will not want to invest when rates are low and, given time value of money relationships, security prices are high. As interest rates rise, security prices will fall and investors will hold less speculative cash as they invest in the lower-priced securities. At very high interest rates, investors will hold little speculative cash. High interest rates are thus the *reward demanded by investors to surrender their liquidity*. In Figure 6.2 the demand curve begins at the sum of the transactions and precautionary demands. Beyond that amount (to the right on the graph) the demand for money increases (moves further rightward) as interest rates fall, due to the speculative demand.

In the Keynesian model, the supply of money is the amount available from the central bank. Keynes assumed that, in setting the level of the money supply, central banks were motivated by broad political and social forces and not by interest rates. He thus made the money supply constant with respect to interest rates in his model. As a result, we draw the money supply curve as a vertical line in Figure 6.2.

FIGURE 6.2
The base rate of interest in liquidity preference theory. Money is supplied by the central bank and demanded by individuals and businesses for transactions, precaution, and speculation.

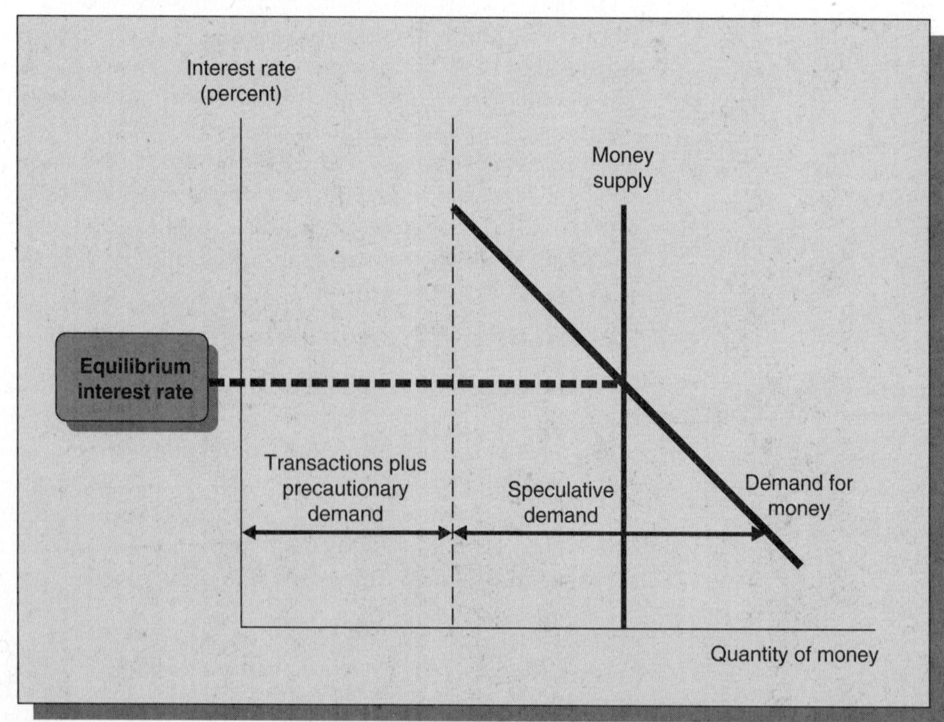

3. Loanable Funds Theory

Both the classical and liquidity preference theories have major limitations. The classical theory is generally considered a long-run theory. It is not very good at explaining short-run rate movements since it is based on savings habits and investment productivity, factors that are believed to be slow in changing. By contrast, liquidity preference is seen as a short-run theory, unable to explain long-run interest rate trends, because it ignores (implicitly holds as constant) important macroeconomic variables such as income, investment, and price levels. In the 1960s and 1970s, a third theory, the **loanable funds theory**, was developed to provide a more general and comprehensive explanation of the base level of interest rates.

loanable funds theory—a theory of interest rate determination focusing on money available for borrowing and lending

loanable funds—money, in whatever form, available for borrowing and lending

econometric model—a computer-based model of all or some part of the macroeconomy, in which the relationships between variables are represented by a set of simultaneous equations

Loanable funds theory identifies a new concept, **loanable funds**— money, in whatever form, that can be borrowed or lent by any participant in the economy. The supply of loanable funds comes from domestic savings and the reduction of cash balances by households, businesses, and governments (via budget surpluses); money creation by commercial banks; and lending by foreigners to domestic borrowers. The demand for loanable funds is the sum of all the demands for borrowing: domestically from consumers, businesses, and the government, and also from foreign individuals and organizations. Each component of supply and demand can be studied individually and related to its causal factors, which may change in relative importance over time. The model is diagrammed in Figure 6.3. A particular attraction of this model is that it fits well inside larger **econometric models** of the macroeconomy and therefore connects to other important economic variables.

FIGURE 6.3
The base rate of interest in loanable funds theory. Money is supplied and demanded by many different individuals and organizations, each of which can be studied individually.

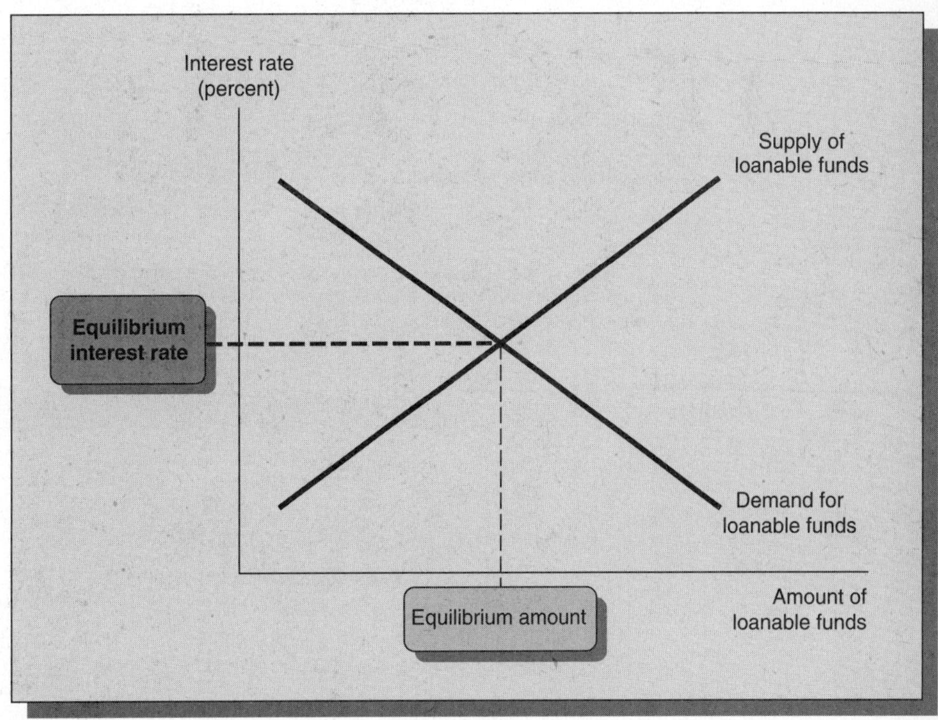

4. Rational Expectations Theory

rational expectations theory—a theory of interest rate determination focusing on the way in which individuals predict and process information

In recent years, concepts of market efficiency have been applied to interest rates. The **rational expectations theory** argues that the market for money displays the same efficiency often ascribed to the market for securities. Investors are rational in that they promptly and accurately assess the meaning of any newly received information which bears upon interest rates. Interest rates therefore reflect all publicly known information, are always at equilibrium levels, and change promptly as new information arrives.

Rational expectations theory is the most general of all the explanations of the base level of interest rates. No underlying relationships are specified. No data are identified as particularly important. The theory simply states that if a piece of information is meaningful to financial market participants, they will promptly incorporate it into their analyses and it will just as quickly be reflected in interest rates.

The Components of Interest Rates

A particularly useful way to study interest rates is the model of the economist Irving Fisher.[4] In Fisher's model, any interest rate may be subdivided into three components: a pure rate of interest, a premium for inflation, and a premium for risk. As with other interest rate calculations, the proper formulation of this model requires multiplication by terms of the form (1 + r) to ensure that the three effects "compound" upon each other:[5]

$$\begin{aligned} \textit{Nominal rate} &= (1 + \textit{pure rate})\,(1 + \textit{inflation premium})\,(1 + \textit{risk premium}) - 1 \\ &= (1 + r_p)\,(1 + r_i)\,(1 + r_r) - 1 \end{aligned}$$

[4] **Reference:** Irving Fisher, "Appreciation and Interest," *Publication of the American Economics Association,* Aug. 1896.

[5] **Elaboration:** Expanding the equation gives:

$$\begin{aligned} \text{Nominal rate} &= (1 + r_p)\,(1 + r_i)\,(1 + r_r) - 1 \\ &= r_p + r_i + r_r + r_p r_i + r_p r_r + r_i r_r + r_p r_i r_r \end{aligned}$$

Because the last four (cross-product) terms are small relative to the first three terms, they are often omitted (with some loss of accuracy), and the model is written in its additive form:

$$\begin{aligned} \text{Nominal rate} &= r_p + r_i + r_r \\ &= \text{pure rate} + \text{inflation premium} + \text{risk premium} \end{aligned}$$

Example

The Fisher Model—Multiplicative vs. Additive Forms

If:

the pure rate of interest (r_p) = .03
the inflation premium (r_i) = .05
the risk premium (r_r) = .06

then the full (multiplicative) Fisher model gives:

$$\begin{aligned} \text{Nominal rate} &= (1 + r_p)\,(1 + r_i)\,(1 + r_r) - 1 \\ &= (1.03)\,(1.05)\,(1.06) - 1 = .1464 = \underline{\underline{14.64\%}} \end{aligned}$$

while the additive form of the model gives:

$$\text{Nominal rate} = r_p + r_i + r_r = 3\% + 5\% + 6\% = \underline{\underline{14.00\%}}$$

Even though the difference between the two calculations can be significant, the additive form of the model is very commonly used due to its simplicity.

nominal rate of interest—a quoted rate; in this context, the rate of interest including the premiums for inflation and risk

The **nominal rate of interest** is the all-inclusive interest rate that is quoted with respect to any financial instrument. This is the same usage as in the time value of money, where the quoted rate is also called the *nominal rate*. In Fisher's model, the nominal rate is constructed from three components: a pure rate, a premium for inflation, and a premium for risk.

1. Components of the Fisher Model

pure rate of interest—the interest rate prior to inclusion of the premiums for inflation and risk

The **pure rate of interest** (r_p) is the starting point of Fisher's model. This is the rate of interest that would exist if there were no anticipated inflation or forecasted risk. Since it is rare for those conditions to exist, it is unusual to observe the pure rate of interest in practice. Nevertheless, the concept is useful as it permits us to separate out and focus on expectations of inflation and risk, two primary determinants of any particular interest rate.

inflation premium—the component of interest rates demanded by investors as compensation for anticipated inflation

purchasing power—the value of money measured by the goods and services it can purchase

The **inflation premium** (r_i) is the addition to interest rates demanded by investors as compensation for anticipated inflation. If investors anticipate no inflation over the life of an investment, the premium for inflation equals zero. However, if investors forecast a non-zero inflation rate, the inflation premium becomes non-zero as well. Investors must receive enough added return to protect the **purchasing power** of their money.

Example

Increasing Interest Rates to Protect Purchasing Power

Sandra Maglen has $1,000 and wishes to invest it to increase her purchasing power by 8% during the next year. She anticipates inflation to raise prices by 5% over that period.

Question: What rate of interest must she earn to achieve her goal?

Solution steps: Sandra needs to end the year with:

$$\$1{,}000\ (1.05) = \$1{,}050$$

simply to stay even with price increases. To make her purchasing power grow by 8% as well, she must earn an additional 8%:

$$\$1{,}050\ (1.08) = \$1{,}134$$

This is a 13.40% increase in her starting $1,000.

Alternatively:

$$\begin{aligned}\text{Required rate} &= (1 + \text{rate prior to inflation})\ (1 + \text{inflation premium}) - 1\\ &= (1.08)\ (1.05) - 1 = .1340 = 13.40\%\end{aligned}$$

Answer: With 5% inflation, Sandra must earn 13.40% to achieve her 8% growth in purchasing power.

risk premium—the component of interest rates demanded by investors as compensation for risk

The **risk premium** (r_r) is the addition to interest rates demanded by investors as compensation for assuming the risk of an investment. If the investment is risk-free, the premium for risk equals zero. As the perceived risk of an investment rises, so too does the required risk premium.[6]

[6] **Cross-reference:** We will study risk premiums and how they can be measured in Chapter 8.

THE KING WILL NOW OUTLINE HIS 153-POINT PROGRAM TO COMBAT INFLATION!
I CAN REMEMBER WHEN HE HAD A TEN-POINT PROGRAM
SAME ONE

real rate of interest—the rate of interest excluding the premium for inflation

Real rate The rate of interest prior to considering inflation is called the **real rate of interest**. The real rate measures the increase to an investor's purchasing power. Disregarding the inflation premium, the Fisher model reduces to:

$$\textit{Real rate} = (1 + \textit{pure rate})\ (1 + \textit{risk premium}) - 1$$
$$= (1 + r_p)\ (1 + r_r) - 1$$

Example

The Real Rate of Interest

Continuing the example (from footnote 5, page 206): Investors are assessing the common stock of the Xerox company to determine what rate of return they should demand. They have concluded:

1. the pure rate of interest (r_p) = .03,
2. they will require an inflation premium (r_i) = .05, and
3. the uncertainties of the Xerox Company's future indicate a risk premium (r_r) = .06

We calculated (in footnote 5) that investors would require a nominal rate of interest of 14.64%. However, their real rate of interest is only:

$$\text{real rate} = (1 + r_p)\ (1 + r_r) - 1$$
$$= (1.03)\ (1.06) - 1 = .0918 = \underline{\underline{9.18\%}}$$

Although the investors will receive a 14.64% rate of return, their purchasing power will increase by only 9.18%.

risk-free rate of interest—the rate of interest excluding the premium for risk; it is the rate available on a risk-free investment

Risk-free rate The rate of interest prior to considering risk is called the **risk-free rate of interest**. The yields on short-term securities issued by a strong and solvent government, and backed by the power of that government to tax, are generally considered to be examples of the risk-free rate.[7] Disregarding the risk premium, the Fisher model reduces to:

$$\textit{Risk-free rate} = (1 + \textit{pure rate})\ (1 + \textit{inflation premium}) - 1$$
$$= (1 + r_p)\ (1 + r_i) - 1$$

[7] **Elaboration:** Examples are U.S. government Treasury bills and U.K. government gilts.

Example

The Risk-free Rate of Interest

Continuing the example (from footnote 5, page 206):

If: the pure rate of interest (r_p) = .03, and
the inflation premium (r_i) = .05

then the risk-free rate of interest is:

$$\text{Risk-free interest rate} = (1 + r_p)(1 + r_i) - 1$$
$$= (1.03)(1.05) - 1 = .0815 = \underline{\underline{8.15\%}}$$

2. Interest Rates in Different Countries

Interest rates differ among countries (or more accurately, among currencies). Using the Fisher model, we can pinpoint the reasons for these differences.

First, there could be differences in the pure rate of interest among countries. These could stem from a variety of sources. Savings habits might differ because

FINANCE IN PRACTICE

Different Interest Rates Around the World

In its edition of May 27, 1994, the *Financial Times* reported the following interest rates for "benchmark government bonds," ten-year maturity bonds issued by governments around the world that are widely seen as indicators of the level of interest rates in their country of origin:

Country	Maturity Date	Yield
Australia	August 2003	9.11%
Belgium	April 2004	7.72
Canada	June 2004	8.51
Denmark	December 2004	7.70
France	April 2004	7.07
Germany	May 2004	6.87
Italy	January 2004	9.48
Japan	June 2003	3.73
Netherlands	January 2004	6.97
Spain	October 2003	9.65
United Kingdom	November 2004	8.26
United States	May 2004	7.11

Reference: *Financial Times,* May 27, 1994, p. 22.

of cultural or economic reasons.[8] Attitudes toward borrowing might not be the same. Differences in banking systems might lead to differences in cash-on-hand requirements or differences in money creation. The access by foreigners to domestic funds might differ. Any of these factors could make the supply of or demand for loanable funds differ among countries and lead to different interest rates.

Second, the anticipated rates of inflation might differ among countries. Investors will require higher rates of interest to protect their purchasing power in countries with greater anticipated inflation rates.

Third, risk levels might differ among comparable investments in different countries or currencies. This might be due to cultural or political issues, to the relative strengths of the governments and economies in question, or to other legal and social matters.

Example

Differences in Interest Rates Between Countries

Sandra wishes to understand the rate of return investors will demand from the stock of a U.S. company and the stock of a comparable Japanese company. From the data for the economies of the U.S. and Japan and for selected U.S. and Japanese companies she has concluded:

In the United States:

$$\text{the pure rate of interest } (r_p) = .03$$
$$\text{the inflation premium } (r_i) = .05$$
$$\text{the risk premium } (r_r) = .06$$

$$\text{Required rate of return} = (1 + r_p)\,(1 + r_i) - (1 + r_r)\,1$$
$$= (1.03)\,(1.05)\,(1.06) - 1 = .1464 = \underline{\underline{14.64\%}}$$

In Japan:

$$\text{the pure rate of interest } (r_p) = .02$$
$$\text{the inflation premium } (r_i) = .03$$
$$\text{the risk premium } (r_r) = .05$$

$$\text{Required rate of return} = (1 + r_p)\,(1 + r_i)\,(1 + r_r) - 1$$
$$= (1.02)\,(1.03)\,(1.05) - 1 = .1031 = \underline{\underline{10.31\%}}$$

Sandra has discovered that Japanese companies will have an advantage over their American counterparts in raising funds. The Japanese companies can raise money more cheaply since their investors will accept a lower rate of return.

[8] **Observation:** For example, it has been observed that the savings rate in Japan is significantly higher than that in the United States. This increases the supply of loanable funds in Japan vis-à-vis the U.S. and contributes to a lower pure rate of interest.

The Term Structure of Interest Rates

maturity—the time remaining until the expiration of a security

yield—the rate of return available from a security

Investors and financial managers have long been interested in the relationship between a security's **maturity** and its **yield**. In part, this is because they constantly face the choice of selling and/or buying alternative financial instruments with a wide range of maturities. At one end of the maturity spectrum are loans with a maturity of "overnight" or even one or two hours. At the other end are shares of stock whose lifetime is undefined, representing ownership in a going concern. In between are thousands of securities with every maturity imaginable.

term structure of interest rates—the relationship between a security's yield and maturity

The relationship between yield and maturity, all other factors held constant, is known as the **term structure of interest rates**.

To observe the term structure, it is necessary to have many securities that differ in maturity but not in any other way. The best selection of securities that fits this specification in the United States is U.S. Treasury issues—bills, bonds and notes. All are backed by the "full faith and taxing power" of the U.S. federal government, so there is no apparent risk differential.

Figure 6.4 is an excerpt from *The Wall Street Journal*'s daily quotations of U.S. Treasury issues as of mid-1994.[9] The Treasury borrows money to fund day-to-day government operations and the national debt by issuing "Bonds, Notes & Bills." While there are a few other differences among them, the primary distinction is their maturity: bills are issued with maturity of 1 year or less, notes for maturities of 1 to about 10 years, and bonds for maturities up to 30 years. It is popular in the investment community to call the Treasury bond with the longest maturity the "long bond."

yield curve—a graph of the term structure, most commonly of U.S. Treasury securities

Yields of the Treasury securities from Figure 6.4 are graphed in Figure 6.5, a graph popularly known as a **yield curve**. While it is possible to draw a yield curve using other securities, the term is most often applied to Treasury issues. In the more than 100 years that yield curves have been observed, their shape has either been upward sloping (up to the right) as in Figure 6.5, or downward sloping (down to the right) or primarily flat, as in Figure 6.6. Of these, the upward-sloping yield curve has been the most common by far, so much so that an upward-sloping yield curve is commonly called a **normal yield curve** and a downward-sloping curve an **inverted yield curve**.

normal yield curve—an upward-sloping yield curve in which long-term rates exceed short-term rates

inverted yield curve—a downward-sloping yield curve in which short-term rates exceed long-term rates

Over the years, four theories have been developed to explain the shape of the yield curve. These are: (1) the expectations hypothesis, (2) the liquidity preference hypothesis, (3) the segmentation or hedging hypothesis, and (4) the preferred habitat hypothesis. All four have some logical and empirical support.

1. The Expectations Hypothesis

expectations hypothesis—a theory of the term structure focusing on investors' forecasts of future interest rates

According to the **expectations hypothesis**, the long-term rates we see today are (geometric) averages of today's short-term rates and the short-term rates investors expect in the future. This is because investors determine a holding period for their

[9] **References:** *The Wall Street Journal*, May 6, 1994, p. C-22

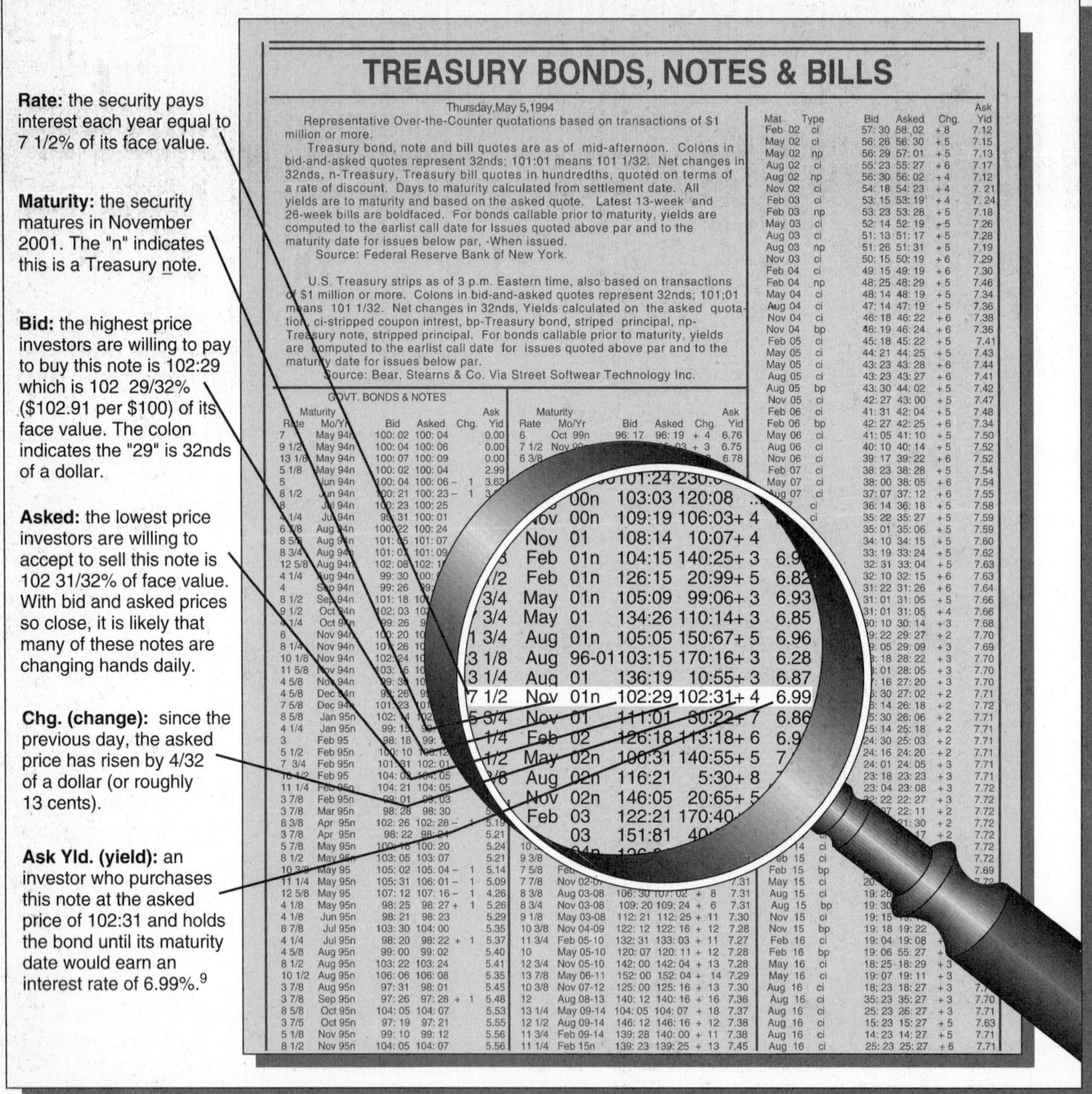

Rate: the security pays interest each year equal to 7 1/2% of its face value.
Maturity: the security matures in November 2001. The "n" indicates this is a Treasury note.
Bid: the highest price investors are willing to pay to buy this note is 102:29 which is 102 29/32% ($102.91 per $100) of its face value. The colon indicates the "29" is 32nds of a dollar.
Asked: the lowest price investors are willing to accept to sell this note is 102 31/32% of face value. With bid and asked prices so close, it is likely that many of these notes are changing hands daily.
Chg. (change): since the previous day, the asked price has risen by 4/32 of a dollar (or roughly 13 cents).
Ask Yld. (yield): an investor who purchases this note at the asked price of 102:31 and holds the bond until its maturity date would earn an interest rate of 6.99%.[9]

TREASURY BONDS, NOTES & BILLS

Thursday,May 5,1994

Representative Over-the-Counter quotations based on transactions of $1 million or more.

Treasury bond, note and bill quotes are as of mid-afternoon. Colons in bid-and-asked quotes represent 32nds; 101:01 means 101 1/32. Net changes in 32nds, n-Treasury, Treasury bill quotes in hundredths, quoted on terms of a rate of discount. Days to maturity calculated from settlement date. All yields are to maturity and based on the asked quote. Latest 13-week and 26-week bills are boldfaced. For bonds callable prior to maturity, yields are computed to the earlist call date for Issues quoted above par and to the maturity date for issues below par, -When issued.

Source: Federal Reserve Bank of New York.

U.S. Treasury strips as of 3 p.m. Eastern time, also based on transactions of $1 million or more. Colons in bid-and-asked quotes represent 32nds; 101;01 means 101 1/32. Net changes in 32nds, Yields calculated on the asked quotation, ci-stripped coupon intrest, bp-Treasury bond, striped principal, np-Treasury note, stripped principal. For bonds callable prior to maturity, yields are computed to the earlist call date for issues quoted above par and to the maturity date for issues below par.

Source: Bear, Stearns & Co. Via Street Softwear Technology Inc.

GOVT. BONDS & NOTES

Maturity Rate	Mo/Yr	Bid	Asked	Chg.	Ask Yld
7	May 94n	100:02	100:04		0.00
9 1/2	May 94n	100:04	100:06		0.00
13 1/8	May 94n	100:07	100:09		0.00
5 1/8	May 94n	100:02	100:04		2.99
5	Jun 94n	100:04	100:06	− 1	3.62
8 1/2	Jun 94n	100:21	100:23	− 1	[illegible]
8	Jul 94n	100:23	100:25		[illegible]
4 1/4	Jul 94n	99:31	100:01		[illegible]
6 7/8	Aug 94n	100:22	100:24		[illegible]
8 5/8	Aug 94n	101:05	101:07		[illegible]
8 3/4	Aug 94n	101:07	101:09		[illegible]
12 5/8	Aug 94n	102:08	[illegible]		[illegible]
4 1/4	Aug 94n	99:30	[illegible]		[illegible]
4	Sep 94n	99:26	[illegible]		[illegible]
8 1/2	Sep 94n	101:18	[illegible]		[illegible]
9 1/2	Oct 94n	102:03	[illegible]		[illegible]
4 1/4	Oct 94n	99:26	[illegible]		[illegible]
6	Nov 94n	100:20	[illegible]		[illegible]
8 1/4	Nov 94n	101:26	[illegible]		[illegible]
10 1/8	Nov 94n	102:24	[illegible]		[illegible]
11 5/8	Nov 94n	[illegible]	[illegible]		[illegible]
4 5/8	Nov 94n	99:30	[illegible]		[illegible]
4 5/8	Dec 94n	99:26	[illegible]		[illegible]
7 5/8	Dec 94n	101:23	[illegible]		[illegible]
8 5/8	Jan 95n	102:14	[illegible]		[illegible]
4 1/4	Jan 95n	99:15	[illegible]		[illegible]
3	Feb 95	98:18	[illegible]		[illegible]
5 1/2	Feb 95n	100:10	100:12		[illegible]
7 3/4	Feb 95n	101:31	102:01		[illegible]
10 1/2	Feb 95	104:03	104:05		[illegible]
11 1/4	Feb 95n	104:21	104:05		[illegible]
3 7/8	Feb 95n	99:01	99:03		[illegible]
3 7/8	Mar 95n	98:28	98:30		[illegible]
8 3/8	Apr 95n	102:26	102:28	− 1	5.19
3 7/8	Apr 95n	98:22	98:24		5.21
5 7/8	May 95n	100:18	100:20		5.24
8 1/2	May 95n	103:05	103:07		5.21
10 3/8	May 95	105:02	105:04	− 1	5.14
11 1/4	May 95n	105:31	106:01	− 1	5.09
12 5/8	May 95	107:12	107:16	− 1	4.26
4 1/8	May 95n	98:25	98:27	+ 1	5.26
4 1/8	Jun 95n	98:21	98:23		5.29
8 7/8	Jul 95n	103:30	104:00		5.35
4 1/4	Jul 95n	98:20	98:22	+ 1	5.37
4 5/8	Aug 95n	99:00	99:02		5.40
8 1/2	Aug 95n	103:22	103:24		5.41
10 1/2	Aug 95n	106:06	106:08		5.35
3 7/8	Aug 95n	97:31	98:01		5.45
3 7/8	Sep 95n	97:26	97:28	+ 1	5.48
8 5/8	Oct 95n	104:05	104:07		5.53
3 7/5	Oct 95n	97:19	97:21		5.55
5 1/8	Nov 95n	99:10	99:12		5.56
8 1/2	Nov 95n	104:05	104:07		5.56

Maturity Rate	Mo/Yr	Bid	Asked	Chg.	Ask Yld
6	Oct 99n	96:17	96:19	+ 4	6.76
7 1/2	Nov 99[illegible]	[illegible]	[illegible]	+ 3	6.75
6 3/8	[illegible]	[illegible]	[illegible]	[illegible]	6.78
[illegible]	[illegible]	101:24	230:[illegible]	[illegible]	[illegible]
[illegible]	00n	103:03	120:08	..	[illegible]
[illegible]	Nov 00n	109:19	106:03	+ 4	[illegible]
[illegible]	Nov 01	108:14	10:07	+ 4	[illegible]
[illegible]	Feb 01n	104:15	140:25	+ 3	6.9[illegible]
[illegible]	Feb 01n	126:15	20:99	+ 5	6.82
[illegible] 3/4	May 01n	105:09	99:06	+ 3	6.93
[illegible] 3/4	May 01	134:26	110:14	+ 3	6.85
[illegible] 3/4	Aug 01n	105:05	150:67	+ 5	6.96
[illegible] 1/8	Aug 96-01	103:15	170:16	+ 3	6.28
[illegible] 1/4	Aug 01	136:19	10:55	+ 3	6.87
7 1/2	Nov 01n	102:29	102:31	+ 4	6.99
5 3/4	Nov 01	111:01	30:22	+ 7	6.86
[illegible]	Feb 02	126:18	113:18	+ 6	6.9[illegible]
[illegible]	May 02n	100:31	140:55	+ 5	[illegible]
[illegible]	Aug 02n	116:21	5:30	+ 8	[illegible]
[illegible]	Nov 02n	146:05	20:65	+ 5	[illegible]
[illegible]	Feb 03	122:21	170:40	[illegible]	[illegible]
[illegible]	03	151:81	40:[illegible]	[illegible]	[illegible]
10 [illegible]	[illegible] 04n	[illegible]	[illegible]	[illegible]	[illegible]
9 3/8	[illegible]	[illegible]	[illegible]	[illegible]	[illegible]
7 5/8	Feb [illegible]	[illegible]	[illegible]	[illegible]	[illegible]
7 7/8	Nov 02-07	[illegible]	[illegible]	[illegible]	7.31
8 3/8	Aug 03-08	106:30	107:02	+ 8	7.31
8 3/4	Nov 03-08	109:20	109:24	+ 6	7.31
9 1/8	May 03-08	112:21	112:25	+ 11	7.30
10 3/8	Nov 04-09	122:12	122:16	+ 12	7.28
11 3/4	Feb 05-10	132:31	133:03	+ 11	7.27
10	May 05-10	120:07	120:11	+ 12	7.28
12 3/4	Nov 05-10	142:00	142:04	+ 13	7.28
13 7/8	May 06-11	152:00	152:04	+ 14	7.29
10 3/8	Nov 07-12	125:00	125:16	+ 13	7.30
12	Aug 08-13	140:12	140:16	+ 16	7.36
13 1/4	May 09-14	104:05	104:07	+ 18	7.37
12 1/2	Aug 09-14	146:12	146:16	+ 12	7.38
11 3/4	Feb 09-14	139:28	140:00	+ 11	7.38
11 1/4	Feb 15n	139:23	139:25	+ 13	7.45

Mat	Type	Bid	Asked	Chg.	Ask Yld
Feb 02	ci	57:30	58:02	+ 8	7.12
May 02	ci	56:26	56:30	+ 5	7.15
May 02	np	56:29	57:01	+ 5	7.13
Aug 02	ci	55:23	55:27	+ 6	7.17
Aug 02	np	56:30	56:02	+ 4	7.12
Nov 02	ci	54:18	54:23	+ 4	7.21
Feb 03	ci	53:15	53:19	+ 4	7.24
Feb 03	np	53:23	53:28	+ 5	7.18
May 03	ci	52:14	52:19	+ 5	7.26
Aug 03	ci	51:13	51:17	+ 5	7.28
Aug 03	np	51:26	51:31	+ 5	7.19
Nov 03	ci	50:15	50:19	+ 6	7.29
Feb 04	ci	49:15	49:19	+ 6	7.30
Feb 04	np	48:25	48:29	+ 5	7.46
May 04	ci	48:14	48:19	+ 5	7.34
Aug 04	ci	47:14	47:19	+ 5	7.36
Nov 04	ci	46:18	46:22	+ 6	7.38
Nov 04	bp	46:19	46:24	+ 6	7.36
Feb 05	ci	45:18	45:22	+ 5	7.41
May 05	ci	44:21	44:25	+ 5	7.43
May 05	ci	43:23	43:28	+ 6	7.44
Aug 05	ci	43:23	43:27	+ 6	7.41
Aug 05	bp	43:30	44:02	+ 5	7.42
Nov 05	ci	42:27	43:00	+ 5	7.47
Feb 06	ci	41:31	42:04	+ 5	7.48
Feb 06	bp	42:27	42:25	+ 6	7.34
May 06	ci	41:05	41:10	+ 5	7.50
Aug 06	ci	40:10	40:14	+ 5	7.52
Nov 06	ci	39:17	39:22	+ 6	7.52
Feb 07	ci	38:23	38:28	+ 5	7.54
May 07	ci	38:00	38:05	+ 6	7.54
Aug 07	ci	37:07	37:12	+ 6	7.55
[illegible]	ci	36:14	36:18	+ 5	7.58
[illegible]	ci	35:22	35:27	+ 5	7.59
[illegible]	[illegible]	35:01	35:06	+ 5	7.59
[illegible]	[illegible]	34:10	34:15	+ 5	7.60
[illegible]	[illegible]	33:19	33:24	+ 5	7.62
[illegible]	[illegible]	32:31	33:04	+ 5	7.63
[illegible]	[illegible]	32:10	32:15	+ 6	7.63
[illegible]	[illegible]	31:22	31:26	+ 6	7.64
[illegible]	[illegible]	31:01	31:05	+ 5	7.66
[illegible]	[illegible]	31:01	31:05	+ 4	7.66
[illegible]	[illegible]	30:10	30:14	+ 3	7.68
[illegible]	[illegible]	[illegible]:22	29:27	+ 2	7.70
[illegible]	[illegible]	[illegible]:05	29:09	+ 3	7.69
[illegible]	[illegible]	[illegible]:18	28:22	+ 3	7.70
[illegible]	[illegible]	[illegible]:01	28:05	+ 3	7.70
[illegible]	[illegible]	[illegible]:16	27:20	+ 3	7.70
[illegible]	[illegible]	[illegible]:30	27:02	+ 2	7.71
[illegible]	[illegible]	[illegible]:14	26:18	+ 2	7.72
[illegible]	[illegible]	[illegible]:30	26:06	+ 2	7.71
[illegible]	[illegible]	25:14	25:18	+ 2	7.71
[illegible]	[illegible]	24:30	25:03	+ 2	7.71
[illegible]	[illegible]	24:16	24:20	+ 2	7.71
[illegible]	[illegible]	24:01	24:05	+ 3	7.71
[illegible]	[illegible]	23:18	23:23	+ 3	7.71
[illegible]	[illegible]	23:04	23:08	+ 3	7.72
[illegible]	[illegible]	[illegible]:22	22:27	+ 3	7.72
[illegible]	[illegible]	[illegible]	22:11	+ 2	7.72
[illegible]	[illegible]	[illegible]	21:30	+ 2	7.72
[illegible]	[illegible]	[illegible]	[illegible]17	+ 2	7.72
[illegible] 14	ci	[illegible]	[illegible]	[illegible]	7.72
Feb 15	ci	[illegible]	[illegible]	[illegible]	7.72
Feb 15	bp	[illegible]	[illegible]	[illegible]	7.69
May 15	ci	20:[illegible]	[illegible]	[illegible]	[illegible]
Aug 15	ci	19:26	[illegible]	[illegible]	[illegible]
Aug 15	bp	19:30	[illegible]	[illegible]	[illegible]
Nov 15	ci	19:15	[illegible]	[illegible]	[illegible]
Nov 15	bp	19:18	19:22	[illegible]	[illegible]
Feb 16	ci	19:04	19:08	+ [illegible]	[illegible]
Feb 16	bp	19:06	55:27	+ [illegible]	[illegible]
May 16	ci	18:25	18:29	+ 3	[illegible]
May 16	ci	19:07	19:11	+ 3	[illegible]
Aug 16	ci	18;23	18:27	+ 3	7.7[illegible]
Aug 16	ci	35:23	35:27	+ 3	7.70
Aug 16	ci	25:23	25:27	+ 3	7.71
Aug 16	ci	15:23	15:27	+ 5	7.63
Aug 16	ci	14:23	14:27	+ 5	7.71
Aug 16	ci	25:23	25:27	+ 6	7.71

FIGURE 6.4

Through the Looking Glass: Prices and yields of U.S. Treasury securities. Each day *The Wall Street Journal* reports information for every security the Treasury has issued.

[10] **Observation and cross-reference:** This example illustrates the inverse relationship between interest rates (the bond's yield) and present values (the bond's price) discussed on pp. 200–201. For this bond, the yield has declined from 7 1/2% to 6.99% and the price has responded by climbing from 100% to 102 31/32% of face value. We will examine the relationship of bond prices and yields more closely in Chapter 9 and study other characteristics of bonds in Chapter 21.

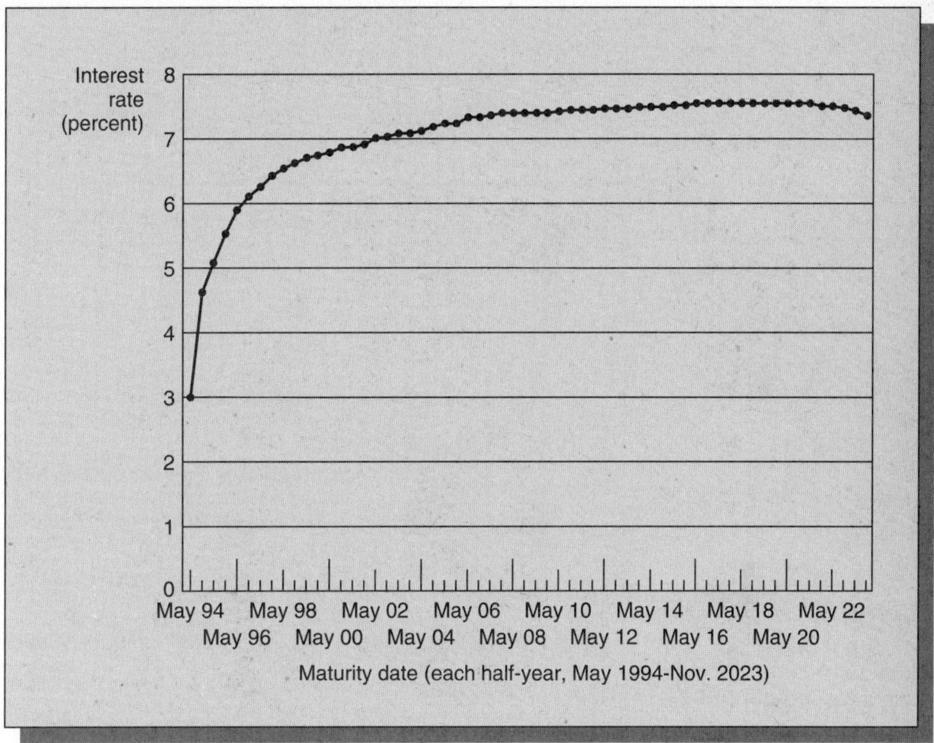

FIGURE 6.5
Yields of U.S. Treasury securities, May 5, 1994. On that date the yield curve was normal, or upward-sloping.

investment activities and do not care whether they own only one security for their desired holding period or a succession of shorter-term securities. They will choose the better alternative and, interacting in the financial markets, will produce an equilibrium condition in which the overall return for any holding period is precisely the same, as pictured in Figure 6.7.

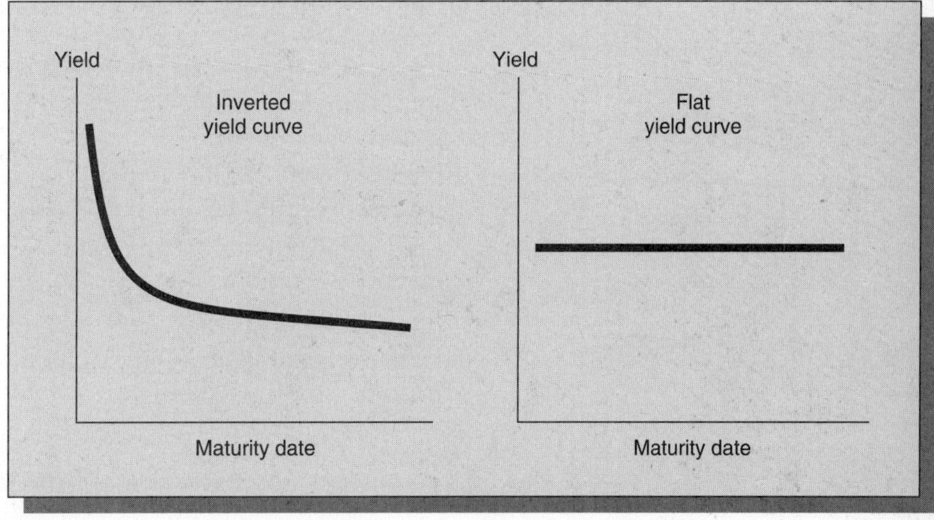

FIGURE 6.6
Less common yield curves. In addition to sloping upward (normal), the yield curve can slope downward (inverted) or be flat.

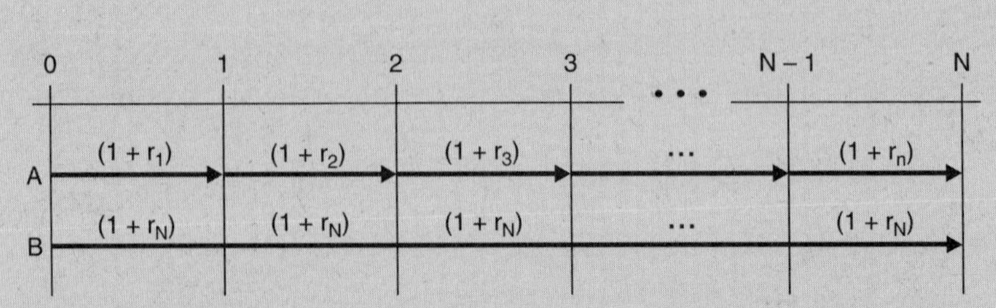

An investor who desires to invest for N years could choose to:

Alternative A: Hold a succession of one-year maturity securities. The first will yield an interest rate of r_1 so that each dollar invested at time-point 0 would grow to be $(1 + r_1)$ at time-point 1. The second will yield r_2, increasing the investor's value by $(1 + r_2)$ in the second year, etc.,

or

Alternative B: Hold one security with an N-year life yielding r_N each year so that $1 invested at time-point 0 would grow by $(1 + r_N)$ each year, or by $(1 + r_N)^N$ after N years.

When the financial markets are in equilibrium, the two alternatives will yield the same overall return.

FIGURE 6.7
The logic of the expectations hypothesis. At market equilibrium, the total return will be the same from holding any succession of securities over any N-year period.

The equilibrium relationship of the expectations hypothesis can be summarized as follows for any number of years, N:

$$(1 + r_N)^N = (1 + r_1)\,(1 + r_2)\,(1 + r_3)\ldots(1 + r_n)$$

where: r_N = the interest rate <u>available today</u> on a security with an N-year maturity (for example, if N = ten years, then r_N is the interest rate quoted today on a ten-year security),[11]

r_1 = the interest rate <u>available today</u> on, a one-year maturity security (held in year 1)

r_2 = the interest rate investors <u>forecast</u> for a one-year maturity security held in year 2,

r_3 = the interest rate investors <u>forecast</u> for a one-year maturity security held in year 3,

. . .

r_n = the interest rate investors <u>forecast</u> for a one-year maturity security held in year n.

[11] **Tip:** Since r_N is the rate of return each year for N years, the value of this security grows by the factor $(1 + r_N)^N$. Don't forget to include the exponent N when you write this term of the equation.

The term to the left of the equal sign is the total compound return earned by investors who purchase a bond with a maturity of N years (for example, if N = 5, this is the effective annual rate on a five-year Treasury bond). On the right of the equal sign is the total compound return investors would earn by purchasing a series of one-year bonds instead, one per year for N years (for example, five one-year maturity Treasury notes, one after the other). At equilibrium, the equation is in balance, and investors are indifferent to either investment strategy.

Examples

How the Expectations Hypothesis Explains Long-term Yields

The yield available on a one-year maturity U.S. Treasury bond is 6.5%. The consensus of investors' expectations is that one year from now a one-year maturity Treasury bond will yield 7.5%, and two years from now a one-year maturity Treasury bond will yield 8%.

Question: What is the equilibrium rate on a two-year Treasury bond?

Solution steps: An investor who buys the one-year bond today, and then reinvests in the one-year bond available a year from now, would earn:

$$(1 + r_{2\ years})^2 = (1 + r_{first\ year})\ (1 + r_{second\ year})$$
$$(1 + r_{2\ years})^2 = (1.065)\ (1.075)$$
$$(1 + r_{2\ years})^2 = 1.144875$$
$$(1 + r_{2\ years}) = (1.144875)^{1/2} = 1.069988$$
$$r_{2\ years} = .069988 = 7.00\%$$

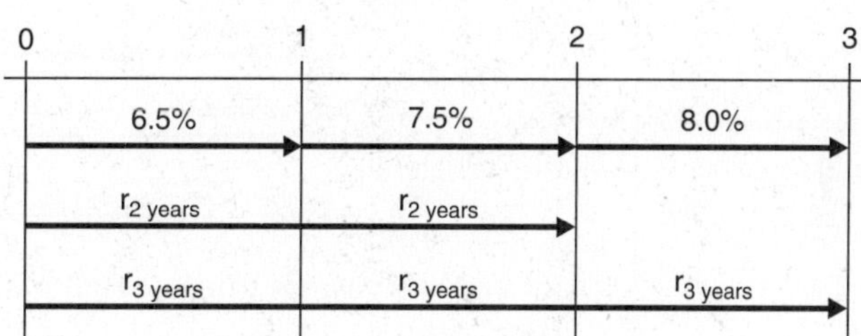

Answer: The two-year Treasury bond will yield 7.00%

Question: What is the equilibrium rate on a three-year Treasury bond?

Solution steps: An investor who buys the one-year bond today, and reinvests in another one-year bond a year from now and in a third one-year bond a year after that, would earn:

$$(1 + r_{3\text{-}years})^3 = (1 + r_{first\ year})\ (1 + r_{second\ year})\ (1 + r_{third\ year})$$
$$(1 + r_{3\text{-}years})^3 = (1.065)\ (1.075)\ (1.08)$$
$$(1 + r_{3\text{-}years})^3 = 1.236465$$
$$(1 + r_{3\text{-}years}) = (1.236465)^{1/3} = 1.073315$$
$$r_{3\text{-}years} = .073315 = 7.33\%$$

Answer: The three-year Treasury bond will yield 7.33%

The analysis can be done in the opposite direction to discover the forecasts of future interest rates embedded in the yield curve.

Examples

Reading the Yield Curve

The following yields are available on U.S. Treasury bonds of one, two and three year maturity:

One-year maturity: 7.25%
Two-year maturity: 8.05%
Three-year maturity: 8.40%

Question: What interest rate are investors forecasting for a one-year maturity U.S. Treasury bond one year from now?

Solution steps: An investor who buys the two-year bond today will earn 8.05% each year and:

$$(1 + r_{\text{2 years}})^2 = (1 + r_{\text{first year}})\,(1 + r_{\text{second year}})$$
$$(1.0805)^2 = (1.0725)\,(1 + r_{\text{second year}})$$
$$1.167480 = (1.0725)\,(1 + r_{\text{second year}})$$
$$(1 + r_{\text{second year}}) = 1.167480 \,/\, 1.0725 = 1.088560$$
$$r_{\text{second year}} = .088560 = 8.86\%$$

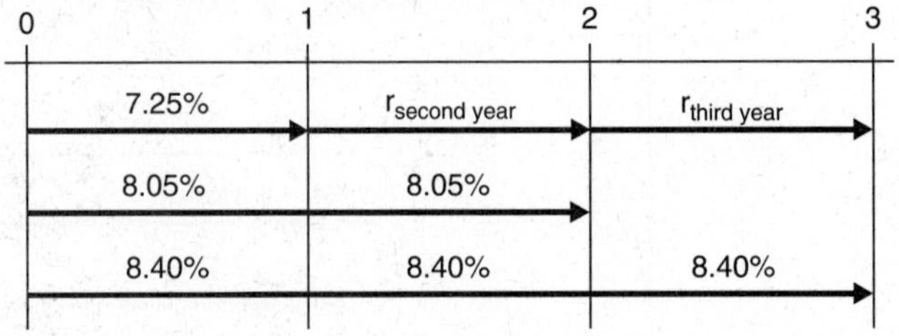

0 1 2 3

7.25% $r_{\text{second year}}$ $r_{\text{third year}}$

8.05% 8.05%

8.40% 8.40% 8.40%

Answer: Investors forecast that a one-year Treasury bond will yield 8.86% in one year.

Question: What interest rate are investors forecasting for a one-year maturity U.S. Treasury bond two years from now?

Solution steps: An investor who buys the three-year bond today will earn 8.40% each year, and:

$$(1 + r_{\text{3 years}})^3 = (1 + r_{\text{2 years}})^2\,(1 + r_{\text{third year}})$$
$$(1.0840)^3 = (1.0805)^2\,(1 + r_{\text{third year}})$$
$$1.273761 = (1.167480)\,(1 + r_{\text{third year}})$$
$$(1 + r_{\text{third year}}) = 1.273761 \,/\, 1.167480 = 1.091035$$
$$r_{\text{third year}} = .091035 = 9.10\%$$

Answer: Investors forecast that a one-year Treasury bond will yield 9.10% in two years.

According to the expectations hypothesis, an upward-sloping yield curve indicates that investors expect interest rates to rise, while a downward-sloping curve is a forecast of falling rates. The flat yield curve is typically seen as a transition state between a normal and an inverted curve, and vice-versa.

The shape of the yield curve changes with the business cycle, and economists have used the expectations hypothesis to explain these changes. At the bottom of the cycle, the supply of resources exceeds demand. Investors' concerns about price increases are small, and the yield curve is slightly upward-sloping. As the economy expands, however, some resources become scarce, their price is bid up, and investors begin to expect further price increases. Incorporating this anticipated inflation into their yield requirements, investors produce an upward-sloping yield curve. When the economy crests and begins to contract, investors reverse their forecasts. Now they predict a drop in demand for resources and with it, an easing of inflationary pressures. Investors incorporate their forecast of declining inflation into their yield requirements—and the yield curve becomes inverted and remains downward-sloping until the next expansionary phase of the business cycle begins.

2. The Liquidity Preference Hypothesis

liquidity preference hypothesis—a theory of the term structure focusing on investors' loss of liquidity as maturities lengthen

default risk—the risk that a borrower will delay or not make scheduled payments, or otherwise violate a loan agreement

Interest-rate risk—the risk that interest rates will rise, reducing the value of securities

A second theory of the term structure is the **liquidity preference hypothesis**. This theory points out that most Treasury securities are really not risk-free since they are price-sensitive to interest rates. Investors in Treasuries do avoid **default risk**. However, if the securities have a maturity longer than a few days, investors cannot escape **interest-rate risk**, the risk that interest rates will rise, reducing the bond's price. Should this happen, investors would lose some liquidity. Since long-term securities are more price-sensitive than short-term securities, long-maturity bonds are more risky than short-maturity bonds. Investors, preferring liquidity, will demand higher yields on the longer-term instruments. As a result, this theory claims it is impossible to construct a yield curve with securities that are identical in risk.

According to the liquidity preference hypothesis, all yield curves have a greater upward tilt (or lesser downward tilt) than they would otherwise have, since longer maturities demand a higher yield.

3. The Segmentation or Hedging Hypothesis

segmentation or hedging hypothesis—a theory of the term structure focusing on investors' desire for specific maturity instruments to hedge their liabilities

hedge—to balance liabilities with assets of equal amount and maturity

Both the expectations and liquidity preference hypotheses assume that investors are indifferent to the maturities of the bonds they hold: an investor who wishes a holding period of eight years, for example, has many, equally attractive, ways to reach that goal. The third explanation of the term structure, the **segmentation or hedging hypothesis**, discards that assumption. Investors are assumed to select the maturities of their investments to **hedge**, or match the maturities of, specific liabilities. For example, the manager of a pension fund might select maturities based on when money will be needed to pay retirement benefits. As a result, all maturities are not substitutes for one another since investors have preferences for specific maturities. In this view, each maturity is a separate market, that is, the market for bonds is "segmented" by maturity. Each maturity market has its own supply and demand and hence its own equilibrium interest rate. The yield curve is simply a presentation of many separate interest rate determinations on one graph.

According to the segmentation or hedging hypothesis, yield curves can have any shape.

4. The Preferred Habitat Hypothesis

preferred habitat hypothesis—a theory of the term structure that incorporates elements of the other three theories

Attempts to synthesize theories of the term structure have led to a fourth theory. The **preferred habitat hypothesis** begins in the same way as the segmentation/hedging argument. Investors choose preferred maturities based on their desire to hedge liabilities. However, they do not stick slavishly to those maturities. Rather they take advantage of particularly good investment opportunities at the neighboring maturities. Thus, while the various maturities are somewhat segmented, the separation between maturity markets is weak and investors easily cross over to other maturities within a range that is their preferred habitat.

Example

Moving Around Within a Preferred Habitat

One of Sandra Maglen's responsibilities is to manage a portfolio of investments for the firm's pension fund. Recently she was assigned the task of investing retirement contributions with actuarially determined benefits to be paid out in 15 years. As a result, her preference is to invest in 15-year securities to insulate the investment from interest-rate risk (in 15 years she will receive the face value of the bonds, and she will not be affected by price changes along the way). Today, 15-year U.S. Treasury bonds are yielding 8.85%. However, 14-year Treasuries are yielding 9.15%. Sandra does the following calculation:

If she invests in the 15-year maturity bonds, each dollar will grow to:

$$\begin{aligned} FV &= PV\,(1 + r)^n = PV\,(1 + r_{15\text{ years}})^{15} \\ &= \$1.00\,(1.0885)^{15} = \$3.57 \end{aligned}$$

after fifteen years.

On the other hand, if she invests in the 14-year maturity bonds, each dollar will grow to:

$$\begin{aligned} FV &= PV\,(1 + r)^n = PV\,(1 + r_{14\text{ years}})^{14} \\ &= \$1.00\,(1.0915)^{14} = \$3.41 \end{aligned}$$

after 14 years. In the fifteenth year, she will only need to earn:

$$\begin{aligned} FV = PV\,(1 + r)^n &= PV\,(1 + r_{\text{fifteenth year}})^1 \\ \$3.57 &= \$3.41\,(1 + r_{\text{fifteenth year}}) \\ (1 + r_{\text{fifteenth year}}) &= \$3.57 \,/\, \$3.41 = 1.0469 \\ r_{\text{fifteenth year}} &= .0469 = 4.69\% \end{aligned}$$

to do as well over the 15-year period as if she had selected the 15-year maturity bonds.

Sandra is convinced she will be able to earn more than 4.69% in the fifteenth year, so she selects the 14-year maturity bonds.

The Risk Structure of Interest Rates

An important component of interest rates is the premium for risk. Investors generally are risk averse, requiring higher returns to take on greater risk. Thus any element of a security which adds risk raises the interest rate on that instrument. Among the common risk-adding elements are:

- Default risk—the possibility that a borrower will be unable to live up to the loan agreement. Sometimes default is not critical to value, as when a borrower fails to deliver a document called for under the agreement. Usually, however, default is serious and involves late or missing payments, reducing the time value of the payment stream.

FINANCE IN PRACTICE

Increasing Default Risk Pushes General Motors to Take Drastic Action

In December 1991, General Motors Corporation announced one of the most drastic corporate retrenchments in American business history. While GM's problems had been building for over a decade, the final blow was the threat of Standard & Poor's (S & P), a company that evaluates default risk, to lower the "ratings" of GM's securities.

> In 1991, GM lost, on average, $1,500 on every one of the more than 3.5 million cars and trucks it made in North America. It ended the year with barely more than 35% of a U.S. market that bought fewer than 13 million new cars and light trucks; in 1979 the market exceeded 14 million and GM commanded 46% of it. . . .
>
> By 1995, GM will close six assembly plants and 15 other factories, reducing its capacity by one-fifth so that it can operate profitably with a 35% market share. In the process it will cut 74,000 blue- and white-collar jobs, trimming its work force to half the size it was in 1985. . . .
>
> A series of horrific events in the fall of 1991 forced [GM Chairman Robert] Stempel to move. One top GM official allowed that even the direst of pessimists could not have foreseen the company's predicament. Despite a sunburst of new models and heavy buyer incentives, GM was selling 600,000 fewer cars and trucks than in 1990. . . . After losing $2 billion in 1990, GM now faced a companywide deficit of $3 billion in 1991. Seeing GM running short of cash, and with economic recovery nowhere in sight, Standard & Poor's announced in November that it was putting GM on a "credit watch." For a company that once routinely luxuriated in Triple–A ratings, the prospect of a downgrading was not only an embarrassment but a financial menace. Borrowing costs for GMAC, which is GM's finance arm, could increase by $200 million or more annually.
>
> The company's deteriorating fiscal condition got the attention of GM's board of directors. At their regular December 9 meeting, in Washington, D.C., the directors pushed Stempel to move faster to cut costs by closing plants and getting rid of white-collar workers.

Reference: "Can GM Remodel Itself?," *Fortune,* Jan. 13, 1992, pp. 26–34.

- Interest-rate risk—the possibility that interest rates will rise, reducing the value of securities. Investors who needed their cash back prior to a security's maturity date would have to sell it in the market and take a loss. Interest rate risk is particularly severe in long-maturity securities and motivates investors to prefer shorter-maturity instruments.

reinvestment risk—the risk that interest rates will fall, limiting reinvestment opportunities

- **Reinvestment risk**—the possibility that interest rates will be low at the time an investment matures leaving investors with poor reinvestment opportunities. This motivates investors to prefer longer-maturity instruments so they can "lock in" a rate of return. Note that interest-rate risk and reinvestment risk have opposite effects.

marketability risk—the risk that a security will be difficult, hence costly, to sell

- **Marketability risk**—the projected difficulty of selling a security. An investor might have to take a loss to sell a security with poor marketability.

call risk—the risk that a lender will retire a security prior to maturity, taking a good earning opportunity away from an investor

- **Call risk**—the possibility that the issuer might take the security away. Many securities have a call feature as part of their structure, giving the issuer the option to terminate the borrowing agreement prior to maturity. While investors are compensated for giving up the security, the compensation normally is insufficient to prevent a loss in value. Companies are motivated to call their debt when interest rates have fallen and they can refinance at a lower rate of interest. Investors can therefore lose a relatively high-earning security at just the time when interest rates have fallen and reinvestment opportunities are poor.

We will look at these risks in more detail as we study bonds and other forms of debt financing in Chapters 9, 20, and 21.

The Tax Structure of Interest Rates

As we saw in Appendix 4B, not all securities are taxed in the same way. In particular, while income from federal government securities (such as U.S. Treasury bonds) is subject to federal taxes, it is not taxed by state and municipal authorities. Conversely, income from bonds issued by state and local governments (municipal bonds or "munis") is not taxed by the federal system and typically not taxed by the issuing state or locality. (See Figure 6.8)

Investors are ultimately interested in their final, or after-tax, returns and would prefer not to lose a portion of their interest earnings to taxes. They are attracted

FIGURE 6.8
Who taxes what? While government bonds escape some taxes, income from corporate bonds is taxed by all levels of government.

Issuer	Taxed by			
	Federal	Issuing state	Other states	Locality
U.S. government	X			
State or local government			X	
Corporation	X	X	X	X

Example

Calculating After-Tax Yields

Sandra Maglen lives in Maryland. She pays federal income taxes at a marginal rate of 28% and state taxes at a marginal rate of 7%. As she examines various investment alternatives, she discovers the following:

If she purchases a bond yielding 8% issued by a corporation, her income would be taxed by both state and federal authorities at a total rate of 28% + 7% = 35%. After taxes she would keep:

$$8\% - 35\%\,(8\%) = 8\%\,(1 - .35)$$
$$= 8\%\,(.65) = \underline{\underline{5.20\%}}$$

If she purchases a U.S. Treasury bond yielding 8%, her income would be taxed only by the federal authorities at a rate of 28%. After taxes she would keep:

$$8\% - 28\%\,(8\%) = 8\%\,(1 - .28)$$
$$= 8\%\,(.72) = \underline{\underline{5.76\%}}$$

If she purchases a bond yielding 8% issued by the state of Virginia (or any other state or local bond not issued in Maryland), her income would be taxed only by the State of Maryland at a rate of 7%. After taxes she would keep:

$$8\% - 7\%\,(8\%) = 8\%\,(1 - .07)$$
$$= 8\%\,(.93) = \underline{\underline{7.44\%}}$$

However, If she purchases a state of Maryland bond yielding 8%, her income would not be taxed at all. She would keep the full 8%.

to investments that are taxed at low rates and thus increase the demand for tax-advantaged securities relative to those without tax preferences. In response, the prices of tax-advantaged securities rise and their pre-tax yields fall, while the reduced demand for fully taxed securities lowers their prices and raises their pre-tax yields.[12] The pressure on prices continues until the average investor (that is, the investor in the average tax bracket) finds no remaining yield benefit from tax-advantaged securities. At market equilibrium, therefore, pre-tax yields have adjusted so that after-tax yields for the average investor-taxpayer on all securities of comparable risk and maturity are the same.

Example

Pre-Tax Yields that Produce Equivalent After-Tax Yields

Suppose that, on average, investors are in the 28% marginal federal income tax bracket and the 6% marginal state tax bracket. Bond F and Bond S are identical except that Bond F was issued by the federal government while Bond S was issued by a state government.

[12] **Reminder and cross-reference:** Recall that we began this chapter by pointing out that interest rates and present values move in opposite directions. On pp. 200–201 we illustrated how changing interest rates alter present values by examining the worth of a potential investment evaluated at alternative rates. In this example, the direction of the effect is the opposite (changing prices alter interest rates) but the relationship is precisely the same.

Question: What is the equilibrium relationship between the pre-tax yields of these two bonds?

Solution steps:

1. Calculate the after-tax yield from each bond:

$$\begin{aligned} \text{After-tax yield on bond F} &= \text{Pre-tax yield}_F - 28\%\ (\text{Pre-tax yield}_F) \\ &= \text{Pre-tax yield}_F\ (1 - .28) \\ &= \text{Pre-tax yield}_F\ (.72) \\ \text{After-tax yield on bond S} &= \text{Pre-tax yield}_S - 6\%\ (\text{Pre-tax yield}_S) \\ &= \text{Pre-tax yield}_S\ (1 - .06) \\ &= \text{Pre-tax yield}_S\ (.94) \end{aligned}$$

2. At equilibrium the after-tax yields will be equal. Equate them and solve for the ratio of the pre-tax yields:

$$\begin{aligned} \text{After-tax yield}_F &= \text{After-tax yield}_S \\ \text{Pre-tax yield}_F\ (.72) &= \text{Pre-tax yield}_S\ (.94) \\ \text{Pre-tax yield}_F &= (.94\ /\ .72)\ \text{Pre-tax yield}_S \\ \text{Pre-tax yield}_F &= (1.31)\ \text{Pre-tax yield}_S \end{aligned}$$

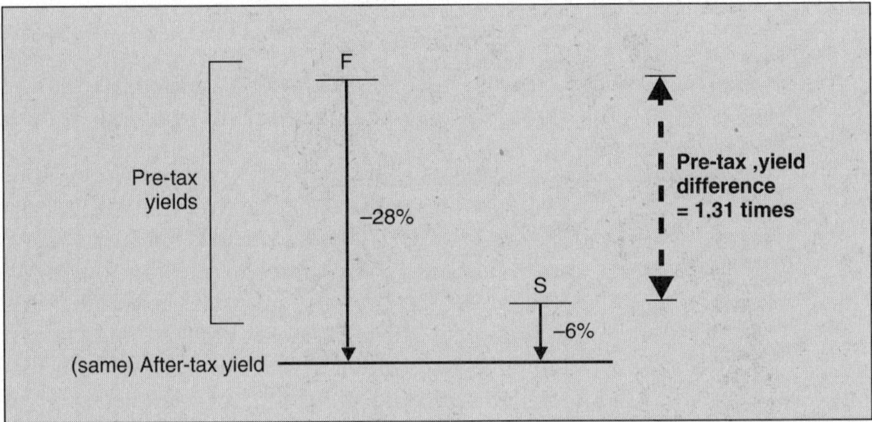

Answer: At equilibrium, the federal bond will yield 1.31 times the yield of the state bond so that, on average, investors will be indifferent between them after their personal income taxes are considered.

Sandra Maglen walked into the conference room and took a seat. Since the meeting that morning she had reread the section in one of her textbooks dealing with the level and structure of interest rates. Shortly, the room filled up and the team began discussing the firm's rising cost of borrowing. Sandra waited for a lull in the conversation before she spoke.

"The Fisher model identifies that interest rates consist of three components: pure, inflation, and risk. The pure rate of interest and investors' forecasts of inflation depend on the overall economy and have nothing to do with our company. That leaves risk. If the analysts at the rating agencies are concerned about our securities, they must be seeing an increased level of risk."

The discussion quickly turned to what information the analysts might be looking at and to what company activities, if any, might be causing the increased risk perception. The team decided to work closely with the rating agencies to identify to management the most significant risk factors.

As the meeting came to a close, Sandra thought again about her former professor. She made herself a promise to write a letter that afternoon to share her experiences and to renew a relationship.

Summary of Key Points

- **Demonstrate the inverse relationship between interest rates and present value.** As an important component of present value calculations, interest rates help determine the financial worth of all decisions. Since higher interest rates increase the difference between present and future values, the worth of a forecasted future benefit declines as interest rates rise, and vice-versa.
- **Describe how the supply of and demand for money interact to determine the base level of interest rates.** Over the years, several theories have been advanced to explain the general level of interest rates. Classical theory emphasizes household saving and business investment. Liquidity preference theory looks at the supply of money from the central bank and the reasons (motives) why individuals hold money. Loanable funds theory attempts to be more inclusive by incorporating several sources of supply and demand for money resources. Overlaying these theories is the concept of rational expectations, hypothesizing that interest rates, like stock prices, are always at an equilibrium determined by publicly available information.
- **Subdivide any interest rate into its components.** The Fisher model decomposes interest rates into a pure rate, inflation premium, and risk premium. By examining each component, we can obtain insight into various rates and understand why rates differ among investments and countries. In particular, we can identify the risk-free rate of interest and the real rate of interest and relate them to the nominal rates we observe.
- **Explain why interest rates differ by maturity of obligation.** The term structure of interest rates is the relationship of rates to the maturity of securities. Three theories, each of which seems to be somewhat true, are offered to explain it. Expectations theory argues that the term structure reflects expectations of future interest rates, primarily due to forecasts of inflation. Liquidity preference theory points out that investors' liquidity decreases with maturity, making longer-term securities inherently more risky and requiring higher rates of return. The hedging/segmentation theory argues that each maturity is a separate market and should be considered independent of the others. A synthesis of these theories, the preferred habitat theory, argues that interest rates contain all three effects.
- **Understand how risks impact interest rates.** Differences in yields often come from risk differences, since investors demand higher returns to take risks. Default risk is the probability of nonpayment. Interest-rate risk is the possibility of decline in value should interest rates rise. Reinvestment risk is the danger of being unable to continue to earn high rates should rates fall. Marketability risk is the likelihood that it will be costly to sell a security. Call risk is the chance that a security will be redeemed by its issuer prior to maturity.
- **Understand how taxes impact interest rates.** Differences in yields also come from tax differences. Although corporate bonds are taxed by all levels of government, the federal government does not tax municipal securities, and vice-versa. Investors ultimately receive returns after their personal taxes and take their personal tax rates into account when pricing securities.

Questions

1. Why do securities prices rise when interest rates fall, and vice-versa?
2. What happens to a company's ability to raise funds when interest rates rise? when interest rates fall?
3. Identify the key determinants of supply and demand that affect the base level of interest rates in the:

   a. Classical theory of interest rates
   b. Liquidity preference theory of interest rates
   c. Loanable funds theory of interest rates
4. Do you think investors are rational in their assessment of interest rates? What evidence can you think of to support your conclusion?
5. Identify the terms of the Fisher equation. What factors cause each term to take on its value?
6. Identify the following concepts:

   a. Nominal rate of interest
   b. Pure rate of interest
   c. Real rate of interest
   d. Risk-free rate of interest
7. Can you think of any examples in which you or some company has changed its behavior in response to inflation?
8. Why do American economists typically base the term structure of interest rates on U.S. Treasury securities?
9. Explain the term structure of interest rates using each of the four theories of term structure.
10. Interest-rate risk and reinvestment risk are often considered opposite sides of a coin. Why might this be so?
11. Assume the average investor is in the 28% marginal federal income tax bracket. If you were in the 15% tax bracket, would you prefer to invest in U.S. or state bonds? What if you were in the 31% tax bracket?
12. How could investors who own homes in more than one state use the concepts of this chapter to select which home should be their legal residence?

Problems

1. **(Fisher model)** The pure rate of interest is 3%, and investors demand an inflation premium of 4%. What interest rate should they demand if they require a risk premium of:

   a. 0%?
   b. 2%?
   c. 5%?
   d. 8%?
2. **(Fisher model)** The pure rate of interest is 3.5%, and investors require a 4% risk premium of a certain investment. What interest rate should they demand if they require an inflation premium of:

   a. 3%?
   b. 6%?
   c. 9%?
   d. 15%?
3. **(Using the Fisher model)** The rate of interest available on a certain security is 14%. If the pure rate of interest is 3.25%, what risk premium do investors demand if they require an inflation premium of:

   a. 2%?
   b. 4%?
   c. 6%?
   d. 8%?
4. **(Using the Fisher model)** The rate of interest available on a certain security is 17%. If the pure rate of interest is 3.75%, what inflation premium do investors require if they require a risk premium of:

   a. 0%?
   b. 3%?
   c. 8%?
   d. 11%?
5. **(Components of the interest rate)** The pure rate of interest is 3%, and investors require an inflation premium of 6% and a risk premium of 4% to invest in a certain security. What is the:

   a. Nominal rate of interest on the security?
   b. Real rate of interest on the security?
   c. Risk-free rate of interest on securities of this maturity?
6. **(Components of the interest rate)** The pure rate of interest is 3.5%, and investors require an inflation premium of 3% and a risk premium of 6% to invest in a certain security. What is the:

   a. Nominal rate of interest on the security?
   b. Real rate of interest on the security?
   c. Risk-free rate of interest on securities of this maturity?
7. **(International interest rates)** The interest rate on a ten-year U.S. Treasury bond is 7%, and the rate on a ten-year U.K. gilt (the British equivalent of a treasury bond) is 12%. If the pure rate of interest is 3.75% in each country, what is the difference in anticipated ten-year inflation rates between the U.S. and the U.K.?
8. **(International interest rates)** The expected return on a share of Exxon stock in the U.S. is 17% while the rate of return expected on a share of Royal Dutch Shell stock in the Netherlands is 15%. If the pure rate

of return is 3% in each country and the required risk premium is 8% for each company's stock, find the anticipated long-term inflation rate in each country.

9. **(Term structure)** One-year maturity treasury bonds currently yield 7.25%, and investors expect the following rates of return on one-year investments in the future:

One year from now:	8.25%
Two years from now:	8.75%
Three years from now:	9.15%
Four years from now:	9.35%

Calculate the two-year, three-year, four-year, and five-year equilibrium risk-free interest rates, as of today. Sketch this term structure.

10. **(Term structure)** One-year maturity treasury bonds currently yield 9.75%, and investors expect the following rates of return on one-year investments in the future:

One year from now:	8.50%
Two years from now:	7.90%
Three years from now:	7.60%
Four years from now:	7.40%

Calculate the two-year, three-year, four-year, and five-year equilibrium risk-free interest rates, as of today. Sketch this term structure.

11. **(Reading the term structure)** Today's *Wall Street Journal* quotes the following U.S. Treasury bond rates:

One-year maturity:	5.80%
Two-year maturity:	6.75%
Three-year maturity:	7.45%
Four-year maturity:	7.75%
Five-year maturity:	7.95%

a. Assuming that the expectations hypothesis is perfectly correct (unbiased), what one-year risk-free interest rates are investors forecasting for the four years following this year?

b. If the liquidity preference hypotheses is also correct, how does this change your answers to part (a)?

12. **(Reading the term structure)** Today's *Wall Street Journal* quotes the following U.S. Treasury bond rates:

One-year maturity:	13.20%
Two-year maturity:	11.85%
Three-year maturity:	10.75%
Four-year maturity:	10.15%
Five-year maturity:	9.85%

a. Assuming that the expectations hypothesis is perfectly correct (unbiased), what one-year risk-free interest rates are investors forecasting for the four years following this year?

b. If the liquidity preference hypotheses is also correct, how does this change your answers to part (a)?

13. **(After-tax equivalent yields)** On average, investors are in the 28% marginal federal income tax bracket. What pre-tax yield on a U.S. Treasury bond would produce the same after-tax yield as a municipal bond issued by a state with the average investing taxpayer in the:

a. 2% marginal income tax bracket?
b. 5% marginal income tax bracket?
c. 7% marginal income tax bracket?
d. 10% marginal income tax bracket?

14. **(After-tax equivalent yields)** On average, investors in a certain state are in the 4% marginal state income tax bracket. What pre-tax yield on a U.S. Treasury bond would produce the same after-tax yield as a municipal bond issued by that state if the average investing taxpayer is in the:

a. 0% marginal federal income tax bracket?
b. 15% marginal federal income tax bracket?
c. 28% marginal federal income tax bracket?
d. 31% marginal federal income tax bracket?

APPENDIX 6A

DERIVATION OF THE EXPECTATIONS HYPOTHESIS RELATIONSHIP

This is an application of future value. Recall the basic time value equation from Chapter 5:

$$FV = PV\ (1 + r)^n.$$

After n years, investors who elect to invest in the N-year security will have:

$$FV = PV\ (1 + r_N)^N.$$

Those who choose the succession of one-year securities instead will wind up with:

$$FV = PV\ (1 + r_1)\ (1 + r_2)\ (1 + r_3) \ldots (1 + r_n).$$

Investors will select the alternative that provides the higher future value. But this will change the demand for each kind of security, which will change their prices and yields, until, at equilibrium, the two future values are equal:

$$PV\ (1 + r_N)^N = PV\ (1 + r_1)\ (1 + r_2)\ (1 + r_3) \ldots (1 + r_n).$$

or, cancelling out the PV:

$$(1 + r_N)^N = (1 + r_1)\ (1 + r_2)\ (1 + r_3) \ldots (1 + r_n).$$

CHAPTER 7

EXCHANGE RATES

As the jet touched down, Ray Levitt let out a sigh. One-half of the sigh represented relief at the safe landing, for although he often flew on business trips, Ray was always a bit apprehensive about an airplane's ability to return to earth. The other half was Ray's reaction to returning to the United States. He had enjoyed this trip and was sad to see it come to an end.

Ray worked for the treasury group of a company that manufactured in six countries overseas and had sales offices in several others as well. As a result, the company dealt in many currencies in addition to the U.S. dollar. Among the treasury group's responsibilities was management of the company's foreign exchange exposure. However, treasury was having difficulty responding to the foreign exchange needs of each business unit. A preliminary study had suggested that at least part of the problem was the quality of information coming to the treasury group from the foreign units.

While abroad, Ray had met with finance professionals from each business unit he visited. His purpose was to collect information about how each unit measured its foreign exchange exposure and communicated it to the central treasury organization. Unless what was happening now was fully understood, Ray thought, there was no hope of improving it.

Back at his office, Ray called a meeting of everyone involved in the foreign exchange exposure problem. He reported on his trip and invited the group to form a team to study the process further and improve it.

Exchange rates are prices—the price of one currency in terms of another. Like interest rates, exchange rates change with economic and political conditions. And just as interest rates affect the value of all cash flows, the value of trade and investment that crosses borders depends crucially on the level of exchange rates.

As Ray Levitt knows, an effective financial manager must be aware of exchange rate relationships and the positive and negative effects that variations in exchange rates can have on the firm. Every dollar lost to currency movements is one less dollar available to meet stakeholder needs. Good financial managing requires an understanding of the forces that move exchange rates so they may be predicted and their effects anticipated. The financial success of a business is commonly measured in its domestic currency, a value often significantly influenced by exchange rates. In addition, it is important to understand and have access to the various risk-management products designed to insulate the firm from changing foreign exchange rates.[1]

Key Points You Should Learn from This Chapter

After reading this chapter you should be able to:

- Describe fixed and floating exchange rate systems and their variations.
- Express exchange rates as direct, reciprocal, and cross rates, and illustrate how geographic and triangular arbitrage maintain exchange rate relationships.
- Define the meaning of spot and forward rates.
- Demonstrate how the relationship between spot and forward rates is determined by five parity relationships and enforced by covered interest arbitrage.
- Identify how changes in exchange rates affect businesses dealing in multiple currencies.

[1] **Cross-reference:** In Chapter 17 we will look briefly at techniques for hedging foreign exchange exposure.

Introductory Concepts—Exchange Rate Systems

(foreign) exchange rate—the value of one currency in terms of another

foreign exchange risk—the possibility of variation in exchange rates which makes uncertain the value of assets, liabilities, cash flows, and income denominated in a foreign currency

There are more than 150 currencies in the world. Unfortunately, the **rate of exchange** among them is not stable. This creates problems for any business that operates across borders; while $100 might buy £65 today, the same $100 might only buy £62 tomorrow—or it might buy £67 tomorrow. As a result of this **foreign exchange risk,** the value of all business denominated in foreign currencies takes on an added degree of uncertainty.

Early foreign exchange was based on a "gold standard," with gold and other precious metals serving as the common international currency. To trade internationally one needed access to gold; therefore local markets in gold effectively determined exchange rates. While the price of gold varied somewhat from place to place, it did not vary dramatically but remained within a "band" reflecting the cost of transporting it.[2] This system worked as long as the volume of international trade was small and not in excess of the available supply of gold. It continued until the mid-1940s.

Toward the end of World War II, the (about to be) victorious western nations gathered in Bretton Woods, New Hampshire, to grapple with forecasts of a dramatically increased postwar volume of international transactions and the need to restore financial stability to a highly destabilized world. Out of that meeting came a new system for international currency relationships.[3] Dubbed the "Bretton Woods system," the plan called for the U.S. dollar to supplement the supply of gold as the standard for foreign exchange. As a result, world trade would not be limited by the availability of gold and international trade would be freed from physical money. The United States would stand ready to buy or sell gold at the fixed price of $35 per ounce, and each country would price its currency in terms of dollars. Anyone receiving dollars could exchange them for gold; in fact the dollar was "as good as gold!"

fixed exchange rate system—a system in which exchange rates are kept constant by government policy

The Bretton Woods system was a **fixed exchange rate system** since each participating currency had a fixed relationship to every other currency through the dollar. This achieved the sought-after stability among currencies, and international investment and trade grew dramatically after the war. Governments were encouraged to pursue fiscal and monetary policies consistent with a stable currency. Businesses could forecast that exchange rates would remain constant and that there would be no foreign exchange risk. Assets were insulated from devaluation and liabilities from increasing. Income and cash flow were not dependent on the variability of exchange rates.

Although the Bretton Woods system was appealing in many ways, it had its flaws. While it called for stable currency relationships, it could not repeal the underlying

[2] **Elaboration:** As long as the price of gold was not too far out of line in any one location, it did not pay for traders to take advantage of the price discrepancy, since the cost of transportation outweighed the profit from the price differential.

[3] **Elaboration:** The Bretton Woods conference also created an infrastructure to support the new international financial system including the World Bank, to provide resources to developing countries, and the International Monetary Fund, to serve as a central bank to governments in need of additional reserve currency.

economic forces that lead currencies to grow or decline in value. Fundamentally, exchange rates reflect the supply of and demand for each currency in comparison to the others. We examined factors which affect the supply of and demand for money in Chapter 6. When we turn our attention to exchange rates, the most important factors are transactions between domestic entities and foreigners. These flows are summarized periodically in the national accounting data of each country as the country's **balance of payments.** For fixed exchange rates to remain stable, each country's balance of payments must be in balance, and this is rarely the case.

balance of payments—the net difference between money inflows and outflows for a country during a period of time

A country's balance of payments reflects the desire of foreigners to acquire its currency for investment and to pay for the country's exports, balanced by the desire of domestic individuals to spend their currency on foreign investment and imports. If inflows and outflows are not in balance, there will be a surplus or deficit in the balance of payments. For example, if Argentina consistently imports more than it exports, it will have a deficit in its balance of payments. The foreign currency earnings from its exports will not fully pay for its imports, and the Argentine central bank will have to spend its holdings of reserve currencies (such as U.S. dollars) to pay for the remainder.[4] Foreigners will accumulate increasing amounts of Argentine pesos, but there will be little they can buy with them. The value of the peso will decline relative to other currencies.

At first, the Bretton Woods system was able to deal with these economic imbalances. The United States ran a strong balance-of-payments surplus and returned foreign currency to various countries through business investment and government aid programs. It was the weaker countries of the world that occasionally had to adjust the value of their currencies against the dollar, and, with so much economic power residing in the United States, the other countries had little choice but to go along with the system. By the mid-1960s, however, conditions had changed. Other countries, now economically stronger, became less willing to devalue their currencies. When they found they had no choice but to adjust exchange rates, the changes typically were large and late. The United States began to have sizable and continuing deficits in its balance of payments,[5] and its holdings of gold fell to levels deemed too low to back the domestic currency, much less the currencies of the western world. In 1971 the United States announced that it would no longer convert dollars to gold on request, and the Bretton Woods system was dead. By March 1973, most of the western nations permitted their currencies to adjust freely in the marketplace.

floating exchange rate system—a system in which exchange rates are allowed to change freely with market conditions

managed (dirty) float—a system in which government influences a floating exchange rate system through central bank intervention in the currency markets

pegged float—a system in which a currency is fixed against another which itself is free to float against other currencies

Today we have a mixture of various exchange rate systems in the world. In theory, most countries follow a **floating exchange rate system,** in which their currencies adjust in value on a continuous basis in the public foreign exchange markets. However, almost all countries attempt to influence the value of their currencies on occasion by having their central bank enter the markets to buy or sell in large quantities (the so-called **managed** or **dirty float**), thus changing the balance between supply and demand. Other countries tie or **peg** the value of their

[4] **Elaboration:** The country could also print more of its own money or borrow to cover its obligations (and would have to if its reserve currency balances were insufficient to cover the deficit) but these actions would eventually lead to the same result.

[5] **Observation:** This was due in part to the resurgence of other economies leading to a decline in U.S. exports and a dramatic increase in imports and in part to the added outflows necessary to fight the war in Vietnam.

joint float—a system in which several currencies are fixed against each other but float as a unit against other currencies

money to another currency, either because the other currency is quite stable or because it plays an important economic role in their own currency's value. A particularly interesting case is the **joint float** of the European Monetary System in which the participating countries maintain fixed exchange rates among themselves but allow their currencies as a group to float against the rest of the world.

Understanding Market Quotations

Figure 7.1 is a sample of exchange rate quotations taken from *The Wall Street Journal*.[6] The table lists countries with which the U.S. conducts significant trade. After each country name, the name of its currency appears in parentheses. The numbers across the table are the exchange rates, the price of that currency against the U.S. dollar. For some currencies, 30-, 90-, and 180-day forward rates are given as well. We will refer to Figure 7.1 throughout this chapter as we explore these concepts and illustrate the relationships among various exchange rates.

1. Direct Rates

direct exchange rate—the number of units of domestic currency required to purchase one unit of a foreign currency

The first two columns of Figure 7.1 are **direct rates** (also called "American" rates) for the two most recent trading days, the number of U.S. dollars required to purchase one unit of each foreign currency.

Example

Direct Exchange Rates

In the first column of Figure 7.1 locate the entry for Britain. As of the date of these quotations, it takes $1.4990 to purchase one British pound. Further down the same column is the entry for Japan. As of the date of these quotations, it takes $.009723 to purchase one Japanese yen.

2. Reciprocal Rates

reciprocal exchange rate—the number of units of a foreign currency required to purchase one unit of domestic currency

The two right-hand columns of Figure 7.1 are **reciprocal rates** (also called "European" rates) for the two most recent trading days, the number of units of each foreign currency required to purchase one U.S. dollar.

Example

Reciprocal Exchange Rates

In the third column of Figure 7.1 locate the entry for Britain. As of the date of these quotations, it takes £.6671 to purchase one U.S. dollar. Further down the same column is the entry for Japan. As of the date of these quotations, it takes ¥102.85 to purchase one U.S. dollar.

Reciprocal rates get their name because they are indeed the reciprocals of their corresponding direct rates.

---

[6] *The Wall Street Journal*, May 6, 1994, p. C15.

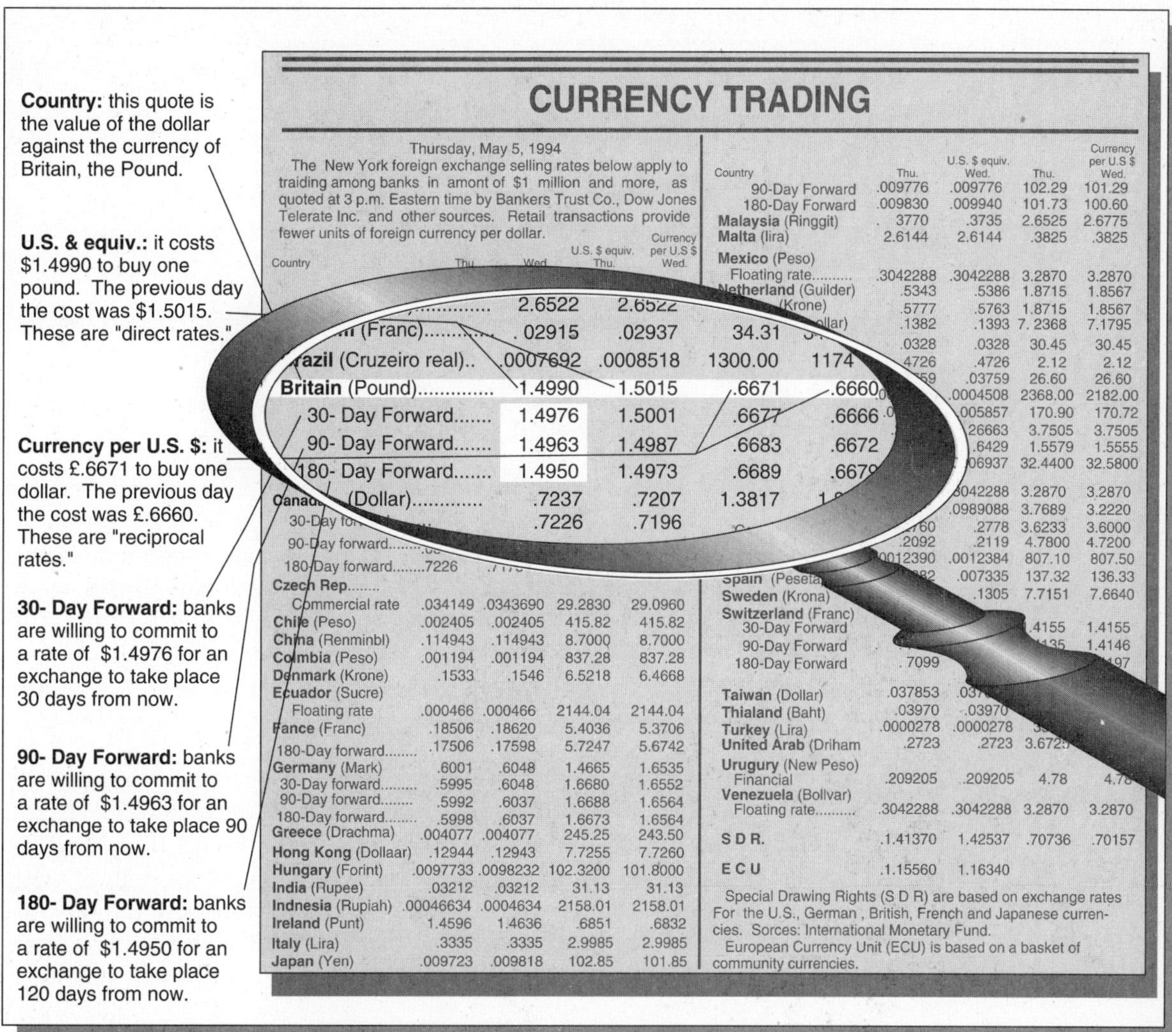

Country: this quote is the value of the dollar against the currency of Britain, the Pound.
U.S. & equiv.: it costs $1.4990 to buy one pound. The previous day the cost was $1.5015. These are "direct rates."
Currency per U.S. $: it costs £.6671 to buy one dollar. The previous day the cost was £.6660. These are "reciprocal rates."
30- Day Forward: banks are willing to commit to a rate of $1.4976 for an exchange to take place 30 days from now.
90- Day Forward: banks are willing to commit to a rate of $1.4963 for an exchange to take place 90 days from now.
180- Day Forward: banks are willing to commit to a rate of $1.4950 for an exchange to take place 120 days from now.

CURRENCY TRADING

Thursday, May 5, 1994

The New York foreign exchange selling rates below apply to traiding among banks in amont of $1 million and more, as quoted at 3 p.m. Eastern time by Bankers Trust Co., Dow Jones Telerate Inc. and other sources. Retail transactions provide fewer units of foreign currency per dollar.

Country	U.S. $ equiv. Thu.	U.S. $ equiv. Wed.	Currency per U.S $ Thu.	Currency per U.S $ Wed.
....	2.6522	2.6522		
(Franc).............	.02915	.02937	34.31	
Brazil (Cruzeiro real)..	.0007692	.0008518	1300.00	1174
Britain (Pound).............	1.4990	1.5015	.6671	.6660
30- Day Forward.......	1.4976	1.5001	.6677	.6666
90- Day Forward.......	1.4963	1.4987	.6683	.6672
180- Day Forward.......	1.4950	1.4973	.6689	.667
Canada (Dollar).............	.7237	.7207	1.3817	
30-Day forward	.7226	.7196		
90-Day forward........				
180-Day forward........	.7226			
Czech Rep........				
Commercial rate	.034149	.0343690	29.2830	29.0960
Chile (Peso)	.002405	.002405	415.82	415.82
China (Renminbl)	.114943	.114943	8.7000	8.7000
Colmbia (Peso)	.001194	.001194	837.28	837.28
Denmark (Krone)	.1533	.1546	6.5218	6.4668
Ecuador (Sucre)				
Floating rate	.000466	.000466	2144.04	2144.04
Fance (Franc)	.18506	.18620	5.4036	5.3706
180-Day forward........	.17506	.17598	5.7247	5.6742
Germany (Mark)	.6001	.6048	1.4665	1.6535
30-Day forward.........	.5995	.6048	1.6680	1.6552
90-Day forward........	.5992	.6037	1.6688	1.6564
180-Day forward........	.5998	.6037	1.6673	1.6564
Greece (Drachma)	.004077	.004077	245.25	243.50
Hong Kong (Dollaar)	.12944	.12943	7.7255	7.7260
Hungary (Forint)	.0097733	.0098232	102.3200	101.8000
India (Rupee)	.03212	.03212	31.13	31.13
Indnesia (Rupiah)	.00046634	.0004634	2158.01	2158.01
Ireland (Punt)	1.4596	1.4636	.6851	.6832
Italy (Lira)	.3335	.3335	2.9985	2.9985
Japan (Yen)	.009723	.009818	102.85	101.85
90-Day Forward	.009776	.009776	102.29	101.29
180-Day Forward	.009830	.009940	101.73	100.60
Malaysia (Ringgit)	. 3770	.3735	2.6525	2.6775
Malta (lira)	2.6144	2.6144	.3825	.3825
Mexico (Peso)				
Floating rate..........	.3042288	.3042288	3.2870	3.2870
Netherland (Guilder)	.5343	.5386	1.8715	1.8567
(Krone)	.5777	.5763	1.8715	1.8567
llar)	.1382	.1393	7. 2368	7.1795
	.0328	.0328	30.45	30.45
	.4726	.4726	2.12	2.12
		.03759	26.60	26.60
		.0004508	2368.00	2182.00
		.005857	170.90	170.72
		.26663	3.7505	3.7505
		.6429	1.5579	1.5555
		.06937	32.4400	32.5800
		.3042288	3.2870	3.2870
		.0989088	3.7689	3.2220
		.2778	3.6233	3.6000
	.2092	.2119	4.7800	4.7200
	.0012390	.0012384	807.10	807.50
Spain (Peseta)		.007335	137.32	136.33
Sweden (Krona)		.1305	7.7151	7.6640
Switzerland (Franc)				
30-Day Forward			1.4155	1.4155
90-Day Forward				1.4146
180-Day Forward	. 7099			
Taiwan (Dollar)	.037853			
Thialand (Baht)	.03970	.03970		
Turkey (Lira)	.0000278	.0000278		
United Arab (Driham	.2723	.2723	3.6725	
Urugury (New Peso)				
Financial	.209205	.209205	4.78	4.78
Venezuela (Bollvar)				
Floating rate..........	.3042288	.3042288	3.2870	3.2870
S D R.	.1.41370	1.42537	.70736	.70157
E C U	.1.15560	1.16340		

Special Drawing Rights (S D R) are based on exchange rates For the U.S., German , British, French and Japanese currencies. Sorces: International Monetary Fund.

European Currency Unit (ECU) is based on a basket of community currencies.

FIGURE 7.1

Through the Looking Glass: Exchange rate quotations. Each number is the price of a foreign currency versus the U.S. dollar.

Example

Relating Direct and Reciprocal Exchange Rates

The direct rate in the U.S. for the British pound is $1.4990 per pound. Taking the reciprocal of $1.4990 gives:

$$1/(\$1.4990 \text{ per pound}) = £.6671 \text{ per dollar}$$

which is the reciprocal rate. The direct rate in the U.S. for the Japanese yen is $.009723 per yen. Taking the reciprocal of $.009723 gives:

$$1/(\$.009723 \text{ per yen}) = ¥102.85 \text{ per dollar}$$

which is the reciprocal rate.

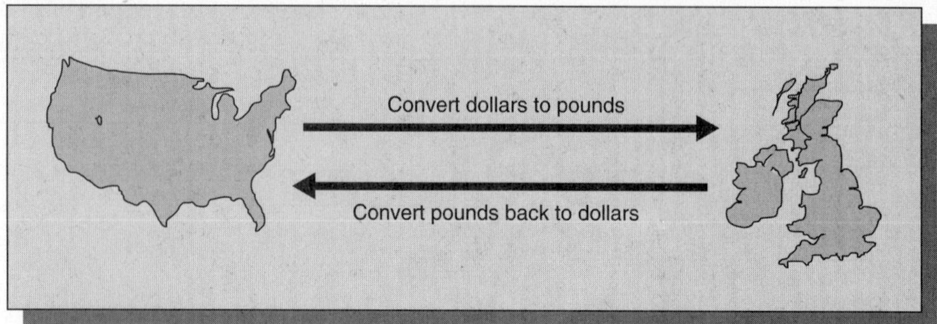

FIGURE 7.2
Geographic arbitrage. Two simultaneous foreign exchange transactions will yield an arbitrage profit when a currency quote is not at equilibrium.

Even though direct and reciprocal rates are substitutes for one another, it is common to use the number greater than one, rather than the fractional number, when quoting exchange rates. (There are some exceptions to this rule based on tradition.) Often the quotation does not specify whether the quote is the direct or reciprocal rate; it is up to the reader/listener to fill in the remainder of the relationship.

Example

Choosing the Rate to Quote

The exchange rate between the dollar and the pound could be quoted as "1.4990" or as ".6671." It would be more common to quote it as "1.4990" with the listener filling in "dollars per pound." The exchange rate between the dollar and the yen could be quoted as ".009723" or as "102.85." It would be more common to quote it as "102.85" with the listener filling in "yen per dollar."

3. Geographic Arbitrage

geographic arbitrage—the simultaneous buying and selling of two currencies to take advantage of a discrepancy in their reciprocal relationship

Reciprocal rates should always be the mathematical reciprocals of their corresponding direct rates, and vice-versa. For example, if you were to exchange dollars for pounds, then immediately exchange the pounds back for dollars, you should end up with exactly the same amount of dollars you began with.[7] If not, it would be possible to use the technique of **geographic arbitrage** to profit from the difference. You could purchase one currency at the lower exchange rate and simultaneously sell it at the higher exchange rate.[8] This would continue until the banks realized they were losing money and returned the exchange rates to their reciprocal equilibrium.[9] Geographic arbitrage is shown schematically in Figure 7.2.

[7] **Observation:** In practice, you would have to pay fees to each of the banks, so you would wind up with fewer dollars than you started with.

[8] **Observation:** This is a classic application of the old financial rule: "buy low, sell high!"

[9] **Observation:** In practice, a bank will often temporarily quote an off-equilibrium exchange rate on purpose to accumulate or dispose of a particular currency for a client or for its own account.

Examples

Geographic Arbitrage

The direct exchange rate between the dollar and the pound is \$1.4990 (and the reciprocal rate is £.6671). However, a bank quotes an "off-equilibrium" reciprocal rate of £.6500.

Question: Starting with dollars, how can you make an arbitrage profit from this discrepancy?

Solution steps:

1. Identify how to take advantage of the off-equilibrium rate: Since £.6500 per dollar is *less* than the equilibrium rate of £.6671, it is a cheap price and you want to *buy* dollars at that rate. You will buy pounds at the equilibrium rate.
2. Make the two exchanges:
   a. For each \$1, buy pounds at the equilibrium rate of £.6671 per dollar and get £.6671.
   b. Take your £.6671 to the bank offering £.6500 and convert back to (buy) dollars, getting £.6671/£.6500 = \$1.026.

Answer: You will make an arbitrage profit of \$0.026 per dollar.

Suppose the bank quotes an "off-equilibrium" reciprocal rate of £.6800 instead.

Question: Starting with dollars, how can an arbitrageur profit from this discrepancy?

Solution steps:

1. Identify how to take advantage of the off-equilibrium rate: Since £.6800 per dollar is *greater than* the equilibrium rate of £.6671, it is an expensive price and you do not want to buy dollars at that rate. You want to *sell* dollars (buy pounds) at £.6800 per dollar and buy your dollars back at the equilibrium rate.
2. Make the two exchanges:
   a. For each \$1, buy pounds at the bank offering £.6800 per dollar and get £.6800.
   b. Take your £.6800 to a bank offering the equilibrium rate of £.6671 and convert back to (buy) dollars, getting £.6800/£.6671 = \$1.019.

Answer: You will make an arbitrage profit of \$0.019 per dollar.

4. Cross Rates

Figure 7.1 gives us the price of currencies in terms of the U.S. dollar, but not the relationship of the non-dollar currencies to each other. However, it is easy to calculate these other exchange rates. Any two foreign currencies may be related to each other if we have the relationship, direct or reciprocal, between each of them and a third currency. The process is either to multiply or to divide the two rates we have to eliminate the third currency. When an exchange rate is calculated in this way, we identify it as a **cross rate.**

cross rate—the price of one foreign currency in terms of another, calculated via their relationships to a third currency

Examples

Calculating Cross Rates

The dollar-pound exchange rate is \$1.4990 per pound. The yen-dollar exchange rate is ¥102.85 per dollar.

Question: What is the yen-pound cross rate?

Solution steps: Since the common currency (dollars) is in the numerator of the first rate (dollars/pound) and in the denominator of the second rate (yen/dollar), multiply to cancel out the dollars:

$$1.4990 \frac{\text{dollars}}{\text{pound}} \times 102.85 \frac{\text{yen}}{\text{dollar}} = 154.17 \frac{\text{yen}}{\text{pound}}$$

Answer: The cross rate is ¥154.17 per pound.

The yen-dollar exchange rate is ¥102.85 per dollar. From the entry under Germany in Figure 7.1, the mark-dollar exchange rate is DM1.6665 per dollar.

Question: What is the yen-mark cross rate?

Solution steps: Since the common currency (dollars) is in the denominator of both rates (yen/dollar and marks/dollar), divide to cancel out the dollars:

$$\frac{102.85 \frac{\text{yen}}{\text{dollar}}}{1.6665 \frac{\text{marks}}{\text{dollar}}} = 102.85 \frac{\text{yen}}{\text{dollar}} \times \frac{1}{1.6665} \frac{\text{dollars}}{\text{mark}} = 61.716 \frac{\text{yen}}{\text{mark}}$$

Answer: The cross rate is ¥61.716 per mark.

The dollar-pound exchange rate is \$1.4990 per pound. From the entry under Ireland in Figure 7.1, the dollar-punt exchange rate is \$1.4596 per punt (also called the Irish pound with symbol: IR£).

Question: What is the punt-pound cross rate?

Solution steps: Since the common currency (dollars) is in the numerator of both rates (dollars/pound and dollars/punt), divide to cancel out the dollars:

$$1.4990 \frac{\text{dollars}}{\text{pounds}} \div 1.4596 \frac{\text{dollars}}{\text{punt}} = 1.0270 \frac{\text{punt}}{\text{pound}}$$

Answer: The cross rate is IR£1.0270 per pound.

5. Triangular Arbitrage

triangular arbitrage—the simultaneous buying and selling of three currencies to take advantage of a discrepancy in a cross rate

Cross rates, like reciprocal rates, must always remain in equilibrium. Should a bank quote an exchange rate that is not the mathematical cross rate between all other pairs of exchange rates, investors will use the technique of **triangular arbitrage** to profit from the off-quote. As with geographic arbitrage, the method is si-

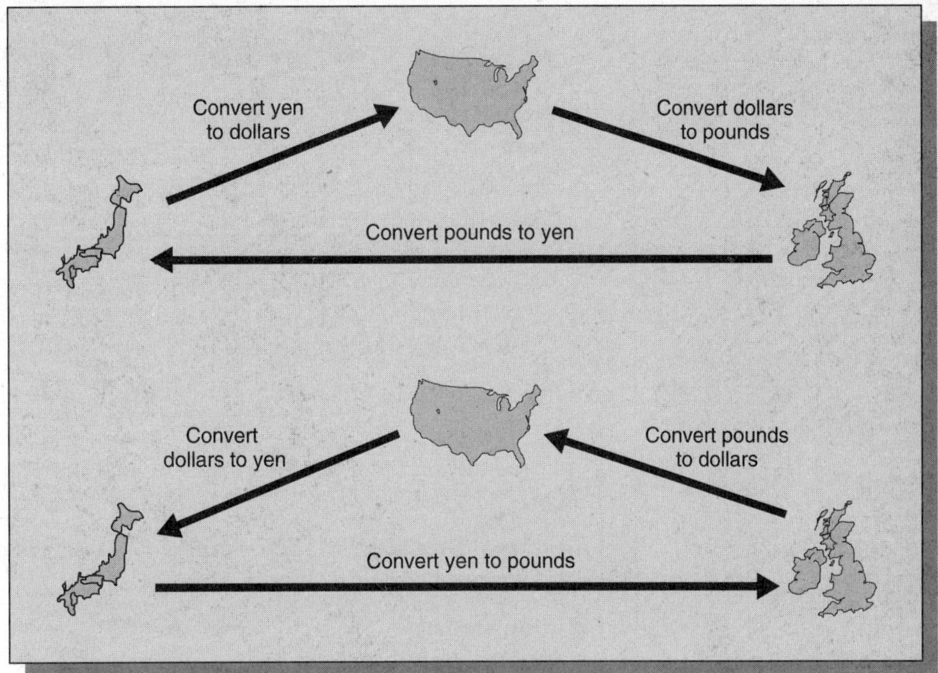

FIGURE 7.3
Triangular arbitrage. Three simultaneous foreign exchange transactions will yield an arbitrage profit when cross rates are not at equilibrium.

multaneously to purchase at the lower exchange rate and sell at the higher exchange rate and continue until the rates return to their cross-rate equilibrium.

Figure 7.3 shows the two possible paths for triangular arbitrage among the dollar, pound, and yen. In the top diagram, dollars are exchanged for pounds, then the pounds are exchanged for yen, and finally the yen are exchanged for dollars. In the bottom diagram, dollars are exchanged for yen, then the yen are exchanged for pounds, and finally the pounds are exchanged for dollars. Which path to take depends on the direction of "error" in the cross rate, as the examples illustrate.

Most foreign exchange arbitrage, both geographical and triangular (as well as the covered interest arbitrage we will encounter later in this chapter), is done in the trading rooms of major commercial banks. These banks actively buy and sell currencies for their customers and themselves. As a result, they know this market well and can make arbitrage transactions at little incremental cost. Further, they *must* watch exchange rates closely, for they can become the losers if arbitrage is done by others.

Examples

Triangular Arbitrage

Since the exchange rate between the dollar and the pound is \$1.4990 and the exchange rate between the yen and the dollar is ¥102.85, the correct cross rate is ¥154.17 per pound. However, a bank quotes an off-equilibrium yen-pound rate of ¥157.00 per pound.

Question: Starting with dollars, how can you make an arbitrage profit from this discrepancy?

Solution steps:

1. Identify how to take advantage of the off-equilibrium rate. Since ¥157.00 per pound is *greater than* the equilibrium rate of ¥154.17, it is an expensive price and you do not want to buy pounds at that rate. You want to *sell* pounds (buy yen) at that rate. Your path will be *dollars–pounds–yen–dollars*.
2. Make the three exchanges:
   a. For each \$1.00, buy pounds at \$1.4990 and get \$1.00/\$1.4990 = £.6671.
   b. Take your £.6671 to the bank offering the high cross rate and buy yen getting £.6671 × ¥157.00 = ¥104.735.
   c. Buy dollars with your ¥104.735 getting ¥104.735/¥102.45 = \$1.0223.

Answer: You will make an arbitrage profit of \$0.0223 per dollar.

Suppose another bank quotes an off-equilibrium yen-pound rate of ¥152.00 per pound.

Question: Starting with dollars, how can you make an arbitrage profit from this discrepancy?

Solution steps:

1. Identify how to take advantage of the off-equilibrium rate. Since ¥152.00 per pound is *less than* the equilibrium rate of ¥154.17, it is a cheap price and you want to buy pounds at that rate. Your path will be: *dollars–yen–pounds–dollars*.
2. Make the three exchanges:
   a. For each \$1.00, buy yen at ¥102.85 and get ¥102.85.
   b. Take your ¥102.85 to the bank offering the low cross rate and buy pounds getting ¥102.85/¥152.00 = £.6766.
   c. Buy dollars with your £.6766 getting £.6766 × \$1.4990 = \$1.0142.

Answer: You will make an arbitrage profit of \$0.0142 per dollar.

Spot and Forward Rates

spot (exchange) rate—an exchange rate available for the immediate trade of currencies

forward exchange contract—a contract binding the parties to a future trade of currencies on a specified date and at a specified exchange rate, the forward rate

Exchange rates for transactions today are called **spot rates.** Each rate we have looked at so far was a spot rate—\$1.4990 per pound, ¥102.85 per dollar, DM1.6665 per dollar, \$1.4596 per punt. To use these rates we would have to be ready to exchange our money for the other currency right away.[10] But it is also possible to sign a foreign exchange agreement providing for the actual exchange of currency to take place some time in the future. Such agreements are called **forward exchange contracts** and the rates quoted today are **forward rates.**

[10] **Elaboration:** Common banking practice is to allow two days, the "settlement period," from the time of agreement until the currency must be delivered to the bank.

forward (exchange) rate—an exchange rate for a contract to be entered into today (forward contract) but with the trade of currencies to take place on a specified future date

There is an active market for forward contracts in the major currencies. Referring back to Figure 7.1, we can find 30-day, 90-day, and 180-day forward rates for the U.S. dollar vs. the British pound, Canadian dollar, French franc, German mark, Japanese yen and Swiss franc. Since many export-import transactions specify delivery and payment in 30 or 90 or 180 days, quotes are published for these periods. However, contracts are available for interim periods as well. It is difficult to obtain forward contracts for periods much longer than 180 days as banks are normally unwilling to guarantee an exchange rate very far in advance.

Example

Forward Exchange Rates

In the first column of Figure 7.1, locate the entry for Britain. It currently takes \$1.4990 to purchase one British pound at spot. Immediately below are the forward rate quotes: \$1.4976 for a 30-day forward contract, \$1.4963 for a 90-day forward contract, and \$1.4950 for a 180-day forward contract.

Look at the third column of Figure 7.1. It now takes £.6671 to purchase one U.S. dollar at spot. Immediately below are the forward rate quotes: £.6677 for a 30-day forward contract, £.6683 for a 90-day forward contract, and £.6689 for a 180-day forward contract.

Notice that the dollar-pound forward rates are not equal to the spot rate. In this example the dollar-pound forward rates decline systematically as the contract period lengthens, while the pound-dollar forward rates increase with time. Later in this chapter we will examine the forces which determine the pattern of forward rates. For now two observations are useful. First, the spot and forward rates taken together form somewhat of a mini-term structure, the relationship of the exchange rate to the maturity of the forward contract. Second, it is common to describe the relationship between the forward and spot rates using the concepts of forward discount and forward premium.

forward discount—the condition when forward rates are less than the spot rate, also the amount of the difference

forward premium—the condition when forward rates are greater than the spot rate, also the amount of the difference

To say that one currency trades at a **forward discount** relative to another is to say that a forward contract is cheaper to purchase than a spot contract. Conversely, when a currency trades at a **forward premium** relative to another currency, a forward contract is more expensive to purchase than a spot contract. In the above example, the pound is trading at a forward discount to the dollar since the dollar-pound forward rates are less than the spot rate. It is cheaper to purchase forward pounds with dollars than to purchase pounds at spot. Yet at the same time, the dollar is trading at a forward premium to the pound since the pound-dollar forward rates are greater than the spot rate. It is more expensive to purchase forward dollars with pounds than to purchase dollars at spot.

Forward rates have the same reciprocal rate characteristic as spot rates. Therefore, in comparing two currencies, it will always be true that if currency A is trading at a forward discount to currency B, then currency B will trade at a forward premium to currency A. As one forward rate rises the reciprocal forward rate must decline, and vice-versa.

Forward discounts and premiums are generally quoted in the foreign exchange markets in percentage terms on a nominal annual basis using the formula:

$$\textit{Forward discount or premium} = \frac{\textit{forward} - \textit{spot}}{\textit{spot}} \times \frac{12}{\textit{months forward}}$$

In this relationship, the first term is the rate of discount (if negative) or premium (if positive) for the contract period. The second term annualizes the rate using the nominal (multiplicative) calculation.

Examples

Calculating Forward Discounts and Premiums

From Figure 7.1, the dollar-pound spot rate is \$1.4990 and the 30-day (one month) forward rate is \$1.4976.

Question: What is the percentage forward discount?

Solution steps:

$$\text{Forward discount} = \frac{\$1.4976 - \$1.4990}{\$1.4990} \times \frac{12}{1}$$

$$= -0.000934 \times 12 = -.0112 = -1.12\%$$

Answer: The pound is trading at a 30-day forward discount (note the minus sign in the result) to the dollar of 1.12%.

From Figure 7.1, the 180-day (six-month) forward rate is \$1.4950.

Question: What is the percentage forward discount?

Solution steps:

$$\text{Forward discount} = \frac{\$1.4950 - \$1.4990}{\$1.4990} \times \frac{12}{6}$$

$$= -0.002668 \times 2 = -.0053 = -0.53\%$$

Answer: The pound is trading at a 180-day forward discount (note the minus sign in the result) to the dollar of 0.53%.

From Figure 7.1, the pound-dollar spot rate is £.6671 and the 30-day (one month) forward rate is £.6677.

Question: What is the percentage forward premium?

Solution steps:

$$\text{Forward premium} = \frac{£0.6677 - £0.6671}{£0.6671} \times \frac{12}{1}$$

$$= 0.000899 \times 12 = .0108 = 1.08\%$$

Answer: The dollar is trading at a 30-day forward premium (note that the result is positive) to the pound of 1.08%.

From Figure 7.1, the 180-day (six month) forward rate is £.6689.

Question: What is the percentage forward premium?

Solution steps:

$$\text{Forward premium} = \frac{£0.6689 - £0.6671}{£0.6671} \times \frac{12}{6}$$

$$= 0.002698 \times 2 = .0054 = 0.54\%$$

Answer: The dollar is trading at a 180-day forward premium (note that the result is positive) to the pound of 0.54%.

The second and fourth columns of Figure 7.1 provide the prior day's direct and reciprocal rate quotations for each currency. It is common to measure the daily variation in an exchange rate on a percentage basis:

$$\textit{Daily percentage change} = \frac{\textit{today's rate} - \textit{yesterday's rate}}{\textit{yesterday's rate}}$$

Example

Calculating Daily Percentage Changes to Exchange Rates

From Figure 7.1, Thursday's dollar-pound spot rate was \$1.4990. Wednesday the rate was \$1.5015.

Question: What was the percentage change from Wednesday to Thursday?

Solution steps:

$$\text{Daily percentage change} = \frac{\$1.4990 - \$1.5015}{\$1.5015} = -0.0017 = -0.17\%$$

Answer: The pound decreased (note the result is a negative percentage) in value by 0.17% as compared to the dollar.

Equilibrium Relationships Among Spot and Forward Rates

Geographic arbitrage and triangular arbitrage are the forces that insure that reciprocal rates and cross rates always maintain their equilibrium relationships. Similar forces define and maintain equilibrium relationships between spot rates, changes to those spot rates, and between spot and forward rates. The primary underlying variable is inflation, and each rate is connected to inflation and anticipated changes in inflation in some way.

Figure 7.4 presents these relationships in a schematic diagram, showing how the spot and forward rates between two countries, for example the U.S. and Mexico, are formed. The spot rate is primarily a function of the difference in price levels in the two countries according to the mechanism of absolute purchasing power parity. Forward rates result from the difference between forecasts of inflation in the two countries but are formed by a more complex process. The Fisher effect translates differential inflation forecasts into different interest rates in the two countries. The inflation forecast difference and interest rate difference between the countries then lead to a forecast of how the spot rate will change over time according to relative purchasing power parity and the international Fisher effect.

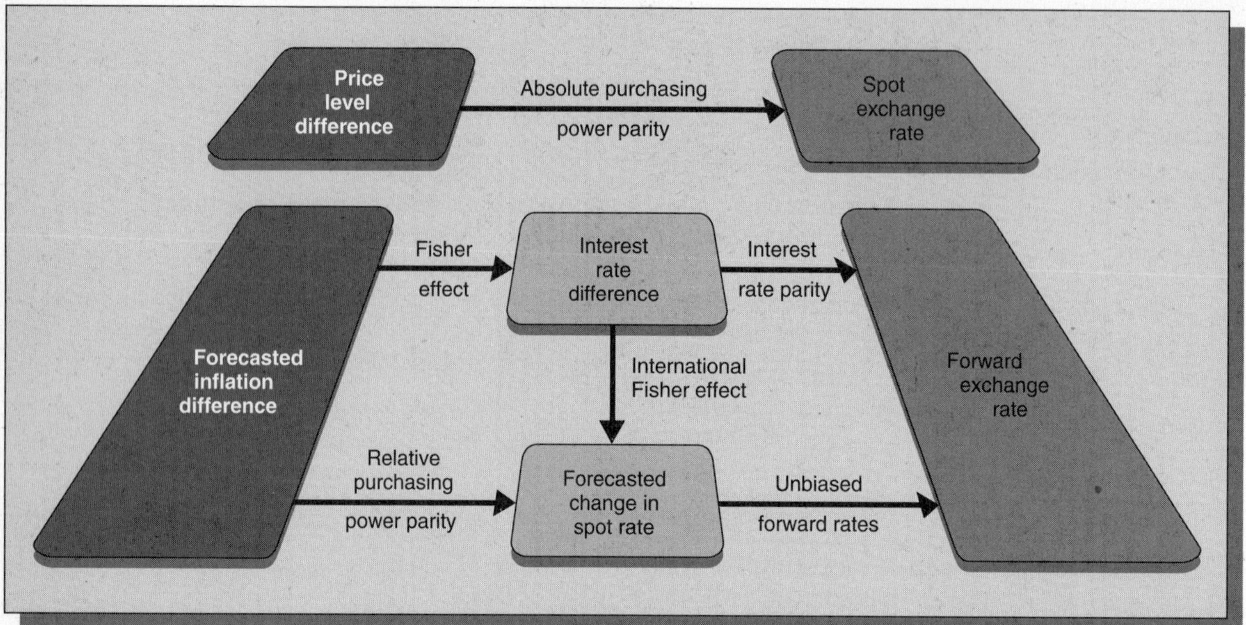

FIGURE 7.4
Forces that establish spot and forward rates. Spot rates depend on price-level differences while forward rates stem from differences in forecasted inflation.

Finally the interest rate difference produces the forward exchange rate via interest rate parity, a result that is reinforced by financial market participants using the forecasts of the spot rate to calculate unbiased forward rates.

Each of these effects is described and illustrated below. They are summarized in Figure 7.5. In addition, algebraic forms of the Fisher effect, the international Fisher effect, absolute and relative purchasing power parity, and interest rate parity are presented in Appendix 7A.

1. The Fisher Effect

Fisher effect—a relationship that holds that, at equilibrium, real rates are the same in all currencies

As we saw in Chapter 6, the Fisher equation identifies that the nominal rate of interest is made up of the real rate of interest and the anticipated inflation rate. Investors are interested in real returns, the increase to their purchasing power. To estimate real returns, they forecast inflation rates in various countries and remove inflation from interest rates. The **Fisher effect** holds that, at equilibrium, *real returns are the same in all currencies.* If they were not, investors would move their money to the country with the higher real returns to improve their investment performance. The resulting high demand for investments in that country would raise their price and lower their real returns, and hence nominal interest rates, until equilibrium were reached. This is shown in Figure 7.4 by the arrow linking forecasts of inflation differences with interest rates differences between countries.

Fisher effect	Real rates are the same in all currencies.
Purchasing power parity	Absolute: The spot rate between two currencies equals the ratio of price levels between the countries.
	Relative: The change in spot rate between two currencies is equal to the ratio of the changes in the relative price levels between the countries.
International Fisher effect	The difference in interest rates between two countries is an unbiased predictor of the future spot rate.
Forward rates as unbiased predictors	Forward rates equal investor's predictions of future spot rates.
Interest rate parity	Interest rate differentials between two countries are offset by the difference in spot and future rates.

FIGURE 7.5
The five parity conditions. These relationships determine spot and forward rates among currencies.

Example

Fisher Effect Equilibrium

Investments of a given risk level offer a 17% return in the United States and a 25.83% return in Mexico. However, the expected inflation rate is 6% in the United States and 14% in Mexico. Using the Fisher equation:

$$\text{Nominal rate} = (1 + \text{real rate})(1 + \text{inflation premium}) - 1$$

$$= (1 + r_r)(1 + r_i) - 1$$

solving for the real rate :

$$\text{Real rate} = \frac{(1 + \text{nominal rate})}{(1 + r_i)} - 1$$

In the U.S.:

$$\text{Real rate} = \frac{1.17}{1.06} - 1 = \underline{\underline{10.377\%}}$$

In Mexico:

$$\text{Real rate} = \frac{1.2583}{1.14} - 1 = \underline{\underline{10.377\%}}$$

The real rates of return are the same.

2. Purchasing Power Parity

absolute purchasing power parity—a relationship that holds that, at equilibrium, the spot exchange rate between two currencies is equal to the ratio of the price levels between the countries

Parity of purchasing power exists when goods and services cost the same regardless of the currency in which they are purchased. The **absolute** form of **purchasing power parity** holds that, at equilibrium, unless changed by government intervention, *the spot exchange rate between two currencies is equal to the ratio of the price levels between the countries.* This is because individuals and businesses have the ability to do their purchasing and selling in either country. If purchasing power parity did not hold, the price of goods and services would be cheaper in one currency and purchasers would wish to acquire that currency. By doing so, they would bid up that currency's price. At the same time, there would be lowered demand for the more expensive currency and it would fall in value. At equilibrium, buyers and sellers would be indifferent to which currency they used. The left-hand side of Figure 7.4, in which price level differences are connected to spot rate differences, identifies this effect.

Example

Absolute Purchasing Power Parity Equilibrium

In the United Kingdom it costs £66.71 to buy a basket of goods that costs $100.00 in the United States. The spot dollar-pound exchange rate is $1.4990. A U.S. resident could spend $100.00 in the United States, or could exchange the dollars for $100.00/$1.4990 = £66.71 and buy the same goods in the United Kingdom. Absolute purchasing power parity exists.

relative purchasing power parity—a relationship that holds that, at equilibrium, the change in the spot exchange rate between two currencies is equal to the ratio of the changes in relative price levels between the countries

A dynamic formulation of purchasing power parity, the relative form, holds that *the change in the spot exchange rate between two currencies is equal to the ratio of the changes in relative price levels between the countries.* Since price levels reflect inflation, **relative purchasing power parity** relates spot rates to inflation rates. If inflation rates are identical in two countries, prices will remain in proportion and

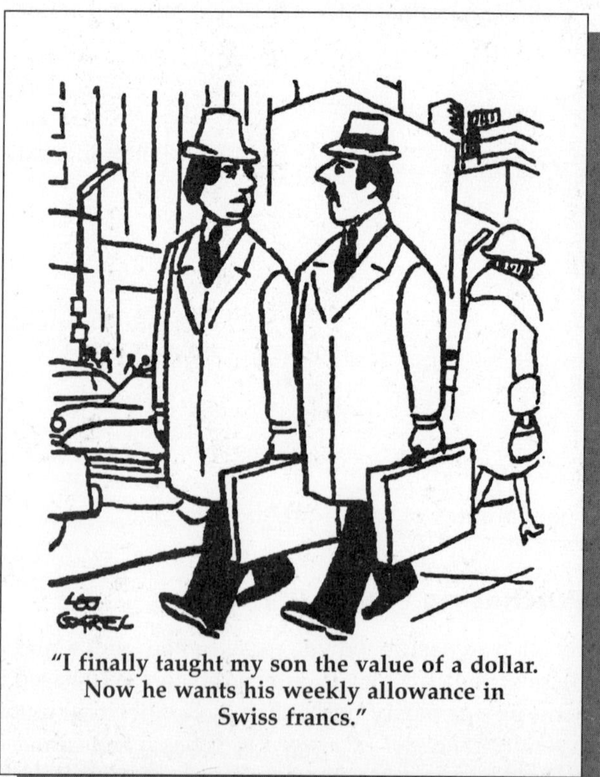

"I finally taught my son the value of a dollar. Now he wants his weekly allowance in Swiss francs."

the spot rate for the two currencies will not change. However, if inflation rates are different between two countries, prices will rise faster in the country with the higher rate of inflation, and that nation's currency will depreciate relative to the other's in proportion to the inflation rate differential. This is shown on Figure 7.4 by the arrow connecting forecasts of inflation differences with forecasts of changes in the spot rate between currencies.

Example

Relative Purchasing Power Parity Equilibrium

In the coming year, prices in Mexico are expected to increase by 14% while prices in the United States are expected to increase by 6%. Today the peso-dollar exchange rate is M$3.2870 per dollar. Relative purchasing power parity forecasts that the peso-dollar exchange rate will increase to:

$$\left(\frac{1.14}{1.06}\right) \times \text{M\$3.2870} = 1.07547 \times \text{M\$3.2870}$$
$$= \underline{\underline{\text{M\$3.5351 per dollar}}}$$

3. The International Fisher Effect

international Fisher effect—a relationship that holds that, at equilibrium, the difference in interest rates between two countries is an unbiased predictor of the future spot rate

Combining the Fisher effect and purchasing power parity gives the **international Fisher effect.** If interest rates between two countries differ primarily because of inflation rates (the Fisher effect), and if the difference in inflation rates causes proportional changes in spot rates (relative purchasing power parity), then it follows that the difference in interest rates between two countries leads to proportional changes in spot rates. In its pure form, the international Fisher effect holds that *the difference in interest rates between two countries is an unbiased predictor of the future spot rate.* ('*Unbiased*' implies that if one were to forecast future spot rates using differences in interest rates, the forecasts would be neither consistently high nor consistently low but would center on the actual number.) This relationship appears in Figure 7.4 as the arrow connecting interest rate differences with the forecast change in the spot rate.

Example

International Fisher Effect Equilibrium

The interest rate on a typical investment in Mexico is 25.83% and in the United States, 17%. The ratio of the two future value factors:

$$\frac{1.2583}{1.17} = 1.07547$$

predicts a 7.547% change in the peso-dollar exchange rate:

$$\text{M\$3.2870} \times 1.07547 = \underline{\underline{\text{M\$3.5351}}}$$

4. Forward Rates as Unbiased Predictors of Future Spot Rates

The international Fisher effect tells us that interest rate differentials predict future spot rates. Investors, armed with this insight could profit if forward rates differed from those predictions. They could lock in a forward transaction now and then convert the currency back at a more favorable rate. At equilibrium, *forward rates must equal investors' predictions of future spot rates.* In Figure 7.4, the arrow connecting the forecast of changes in the spot rate and forward exchange rates captures this notion.

Example

Forward Rates as Predictors of Future Spot Rates

The one-year forward peso-dollar rate is M$3.5351 per dollar. This is a forecast of what the spot rate will be in one-year's time.

5. Interest Rate Parity

interest rate parity—a relationship that holds that, at equilibrium, interest rate differentials between two countries are offset by the differences between spot and forward rates.

Following up the Fisher effect, if investors could obtain higher real returns in one particular country, they would move money into that country's currency to take advantage of this earning opportunity. The demand for that currency would be high and its spot price would rise. But at the same time, investors would want to arrange for the transfer of their investment proceeds back to their home country; they would buy forward contracts to lock in their gain. **Interest rate parity** holds that, at equilibrium, *interest rate differentials between two countries are offset by the difference between spot and forward rates.* Any gain from a higher interest rate is exactly lost to a devaluing exchange rate. In Figure 7.4, interest rate parity is indicated by the arrow connecting interest rate differences and forward exchange rates.

Example

Interest Rate Parity Equilibrium

Equal risk investments earn 17% in the United States and 25.83% in Mexico. The spot peso-dollar exchange rate is M$3.2870, and the one-year forward rate is M$3.5351.

An investor with $100 can invest in the United States at 17% and anticipate that the $100 will grow to be $117 in one year.

Alternatively the investor can attempt to take advantage of the higher rate of return in Mexico by:

1. Buying Mexican pesos at spot and receive $100 × 3.2870 = M$328.70.
2. Investing in Mexico at 25.83% for an anticipated value of M$3.2870 × 1.2583 = M$413.60 in one year.
3. Converting pesos back to dollars at year-end. To avoid the risk of what the spot rate will be one year from now, the investor might purchase a forward contract to guarantee the rate of exchange. If so, the pesos will convert back to M$413.60/3.5351 = $117

There is no advantage to investing in one country over the other!

The interest rate parity relationship is often written using the following formula:

$$\textit{Forward rate}_{\left(\frac{\textit{currency A}}{\textit{currency B}}\right)} = \textit{spot rate}_{\left(\frac{\textit{currency A}}{\textit{currency B}}\right)} \times \frac{1 + r_A}{1 + r_B}$$

This equation says that the forward exchange rate between two currencies (units of currency A per unit of currency B) equals the spot rate multiplied by a ratio composed of the interest rates for each currency. If r_A and r_B are monthly rates, the formula gives the equilibrium 1-month forward rate, if r_A and r_B are quarterly rates, the formula gives the equilibrium 3-month forward rate, and so on.

Example

Interest Rate Parity Formula

Country A is Mexico and Country B is the United States. The one-year nominal interest rate in Mexico is 25.83%, the one-year nominal interest rate in the United States is 17%, and the spot peso–dollar exchange rate (A/B = peso/dollar) is M$3.2870.

Question: What forward rate is consistent with the interest rate parity?

Solution steps:

$$\text{Forward rate} = \text{M\$3.2870} \times \frac{1.2583}{1.17} = \text{M\$3.5351}$$

Answer: The equilibrium forward rate is 3.5351 pesos per dollar.

covered interest arbitrage—simultaneous borrowing and lending in two currencies, coupled with spot and forward exchange contracts to take advantage of a discrepancy in the interest rate parity relationship

The mechanism which enforces interest rate parity is known as **covered interest arbitrage.** In this process, investors enter into four simultaneous contracts: a loan, a certificate of deposit, a spot currency exchange, and a forward exchange contract. If interest rate parity does not hold, the investor realizes an immediate arbitrage profit.

Example

Covered Interest Arbitrage: Foreign Borrowing

Equal risk investments earn 17% in the United States and 25.83% in Mexico. The spot peso-dollar exchange rate is M$3.2870, but a bank quotes a one-year forward rate of M$3.6000, not the equilibrium rate of M$3.5351. Since the quoted forward rate promises more pesos than the equilibrium rate, structure the arbitrage to *buy forward pesos.*

Enter into four simultaneous transactions:

1. Borrow any amount, for example M$328.70, in Mexico at the prevailing rate of 25.83%. In one year you will owe M$328.70 × 1.2583 = M$413.60.
2. Convert the pesos at spot to dollars receiving M$328.70/3.2870 = US$100.00.
3. Invest the US$100.00 in the United States at the prevailing rate of 17%. In one year you will have US$117.00.
4. At the forward rate of M$3.6000, you will need to convert US$114.89 (= M$413.60/3.6000) to fully pay off your Mexican debt. Sign a forward contract guaranteeing your ability to convert this amount.

The remaining US$2.11 ($117.00 – $114.89) is your arbitrage profit!

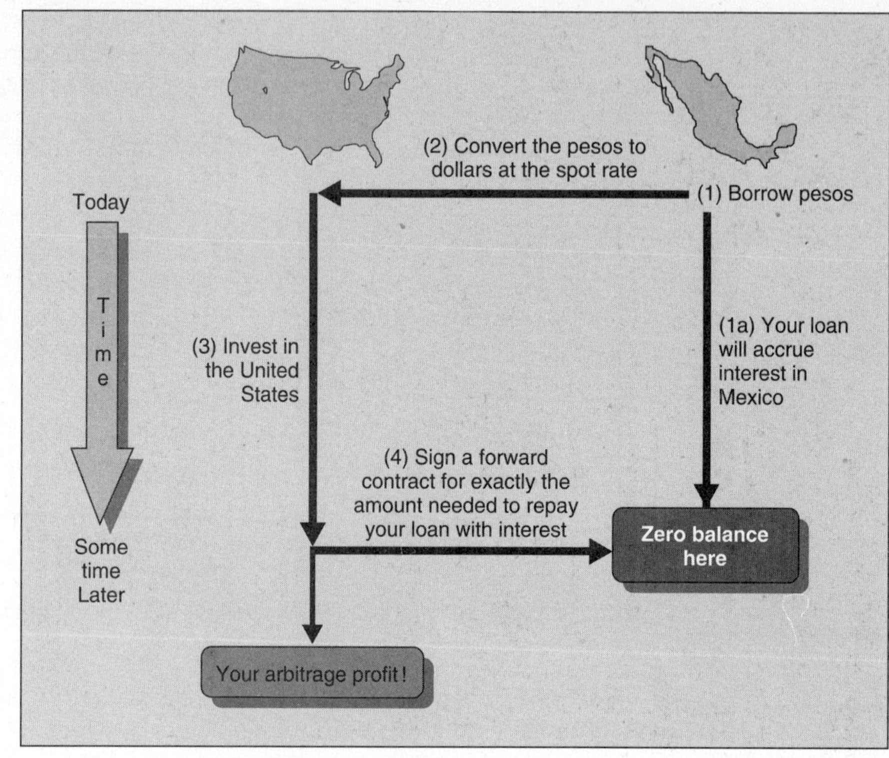

Example

Covered Interest Arbitrage: Domestic Borrowing

Now suppose a bank quotes a one-year forward rate of M$3.4000 instead of the equilibrium rate of M$3.5351. Since this forward rate is below equilibrium (i.e. fewer pesos per dollar), structure the arbitrage to *buy forward dollars* (sell forward pesos).

Enter into four simultaneous transactions:

1. Borrow any amount, say US$100.00, in the United States at the prevailing rate of 17%. In one year you will owe US$117.00.
2. Convert the dollars at spot to pesos receiving US$100.00 × 3.2870 = M$328.70.
3. Invest the M$328.70 in Mexico at the prevailing rate of 25.83%. In one year you will have M$413.60.
4. Sign a forward contract guaranteeing your ability to convert your M$413.60 to dollars at the forward rate of M$3.4000. This will give you US$121.65 (= M$413.60/3.4000). Use US$117.00 to fully pay off your U.S. debt.

The remaining US$4.65 is your arbitrage profit!

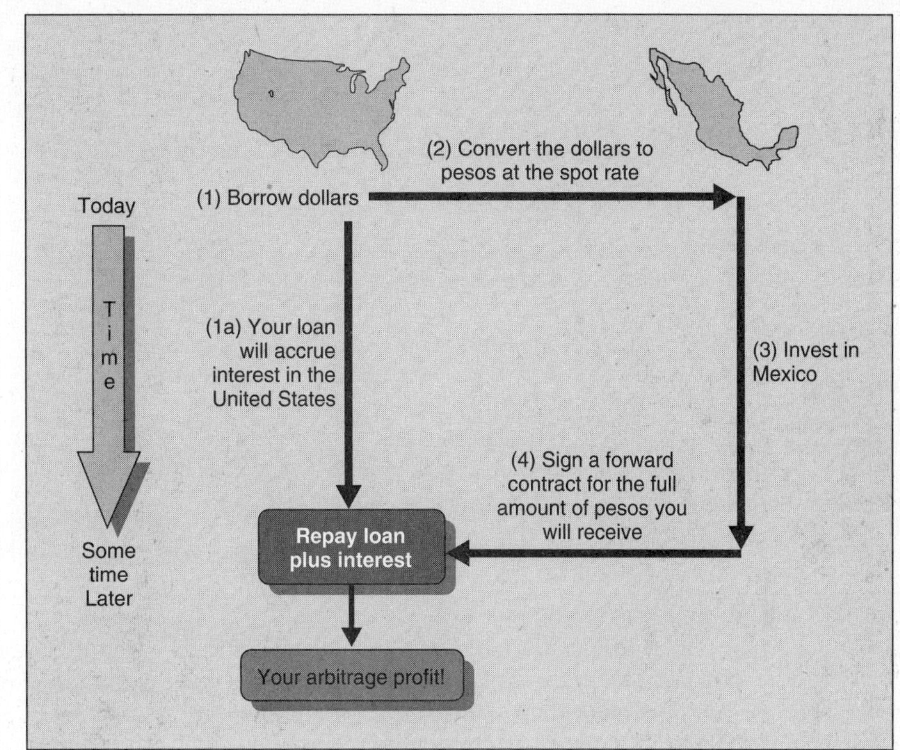

Since typically there are different interest rates for borrowing and lending, and for buying and selling foreign exchange (so financial institutions can make a profit), covered interest arbitrage works only up to a point, and interest rate parity does not hold precisely. Nevertheless, along with the other four equilibrium exchange rate relationships, it provides a powerful description of spot and forward rates.

Business Exposure to Exchange Rates

Foreign exchange risk affects businesses in three ways: transaction exposure, translation exposure, and economic exposure.

transaction exposure—exposure to foreign exchange losses on day-to-day transactions due to adverse exchange rate movements

Businesses that engage in foreign trade face **transaction exposure.** Such companies regularly enter into contracts for the purchase of materials and for the sale of their products and services. Often there is a time lag between the analysis and pricing of a contract and the date of receipt or payment of the foreign exchange. If the relevant exchange rate moves against the firm during that time, the firm will suffer a loss. In Chapter 17 we look at methods for protecting the firm from transaction exposure.

translation exposure—exposure to reduction of accounting income and values due to adverse exchange rate movements

Translation exposure affects the accounting statements of the multinational firm. The various accounts of the firm must be consolidated to produce annual financial statements; amounts measured in foreign currencies must be translated to the firm's home currency for this purpose. FASB Statement No. 52, Foreign Currency

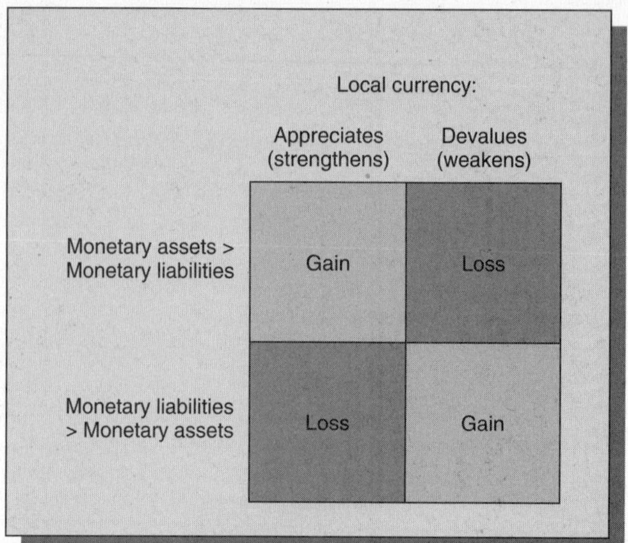

FIGURE 7.6
Economic exposure. A company's risk from changing exchange rates depends on the balance of its monetary assets and liabilities.

Translation, requires that all balance sheet amounts denominated in a foreign currency be translated to home currency at the exchange rate prevailing on the statement date. This makes the home-currency values of foreign accounts subject to change with exchange rates. In addition, the changes to equity due to asset and liability revaluation must pass through the income statement as profit or loss. Other income statement items must be translated at the weighted-average exchange rate for the accounting period. A significant shift in exchange rates could eliminate a large part, or perhaps all, of a firm's reported profits. And while accounting profits are not cash flows and do not directly represent financial value, they typically give stakeholders important information as to the health and possible future direction of the firm. Accounting losses due to exchange rate movements could well accompany or precede real financial losses.

economic exposure—exposure to a reduction in monetary asset values, an increase in monetary liabilities, or a reduction in cash flow due to adverse exchange rate movements

Firms are also subject to **economic exposure,** a term typically used to describe the risk of loss in the money value of assets, liabilities, and cash flows. A firm's assets and liabilities may be classified as monetary or nonmonetary.[11] If a monetary asset or liability is denominated in foreign currency, such as local accounts receivable and payable, then it is exposed to foreign exchange risk. As measured in a company's home currency, foreign-denominated monetary assets lose value when the foreign currency devalues (weakens), while foreign-denominated monetary liabilities become more costly if the foreign currency appreciates (strengthens). Nonmonetary assets and liabilities on the other hand, for example plant or some liabilities of service, are not denominated in money terms and are somewhat insulated from exchange-rate movements. Figure 7.6 shows that the effect on a firm of a shift in the exchange rate depends on the relationship of its monetary assets and liabilities. A firm anticipating a devaluation of the local currency would be wise to have many monetary liabilities and few monetary assets while

[11] **Elaboration and tip:** A monetary asset (such as cash) is defined by its money value, while a nonmonetary asset (for example, plant and equipment) is not. See your accounting textbook for a further review if you find it useful.

a firm expecting the local currency to appreciate should follow the reverse strategy, insuring that its monetary assets exceed monetary liabilities.

All of a firm's future cash flows denominated in a foreign currency are likewise subject to loss of value. This means that every estimate of future flows, for whatever purpose, must be examined for the risk of foreign exchange loss. We will look at this issue in more depth when we study financial decision making later in the book.

Ray Levitt emerged from the elevator and walked to an area where several members of the treasury group had their desks. He arrived just in time to join an animated discussion of the differences in assumptions about foreign exchange exposure that several of the company's foreign units seemed to be making.

A week had passed since Ray had returned from his trip, and much had already been accomplished. There had been no shortage of volunteers to form the process improvement team Ray had proposed, and one staffer, particularly skilled at computer technology, had already set up the company's electronic mail system so the foreign-based professionals could participate fully. Members of the team were currently engaged in flow-charting the way information was gathered and transmitted to the central treasury group.

As the discussion continued, Ray thought back to his meetings abroad. The company's foreign exchange exposure consisted of three parts: transaction, translation, and economic. To deal with each, the company had to be able to forecast possible exchange-rate variations and model their impact on the company's cash flows, income, and balance sheet values. Ray smiled inwardly as he looked at the faces of his colleagues; if their enthusiasm was any indication, it was clear the treasury organization was moving quickly toward a fuller understanding of the entire foreign exchange process.

Summary of Key Points

- **Describe fixed and floating exchange rate systems and their variations.** The world has passed through several exchange-rate eras. Prior to World War II, an informal gold standard prevailed. This was expanded and formalized at Bretton Woods, and for over 25 years, exchange rates were fixed. But underlying economic forces ultimately made the Bretton Woods system unworkable, and it was scrapped in the early 1970s. Today most exchange rates are free to float with economic conditions, but governments often intervene in the currency markets. The joint float of the European Monetary System is an attempt to regain some of the stability of fixed rates in a floating-rate environment.
- **Express exchange rates as direct, reciprocal, and cross rates, and illustrate how geographic and triangular arbitrage maintain exchange rate relationships.** Exchange rates may be direct—dollars per unit of foreign currency; reciprocal—foreign currency per dollar; or cross—two currencies related via a third. These rates form a pattern at all times. Should rates deviate from the pattern, they will quickly be brought back into equilibrium by financial market traders engaging in geographic and triangular arbitrage.
- **Define the meaning of spot and forward rates.** Spot rates are exchange rates for the immediate trade of currencies. Forward rates are for contracts to be signed today for the future trade of currencies. In general, forward rates are not equal to spot rates but

FINANCE IN PRACTICE

Protecting Against Exchange Rate Fluctuations

Just because exchange rates are . . . volatile, it doesn't mean your profits have to be. The world's most important currencies often have exchange rates as unpredictable as a volcano. This can play havoc with your profits if you're an importer. Or with your returns if you're an investor.

So at Barclays we've introduced . . . a certificate which you can buy over the counter at any of our branches. Each certificate is negotiable and entitles you to buy or sell the currency equivalent of £5,000 at a specified exchange rate within a certain period.

Say, for example, you believe that in three months time you will need £30,000 worth of dollars to pay for a consignment of goods. To make sure the exchange rate you'll get in three months time is the same as you've used today, you simply buy six [certificates] entitling you to exchange them for the £30,000 worth of dollars at a preselectable rate. Until you actually use the certificates (if you use them at all) all you have to pay out is a small premium. You can even sell . . . these certificates [to others] or offer them back to the bank before their expiry date, if you find you don't need them.

Our [certificates] are available against the US$ or DM. And have proved a highly effective and flexible insurance policy for many smaller importers and exporters or investors.

Reference: Excerpted from an advertisement by Barclays Bank, appearing in "The Euromoney Annual Foreign Exchange Review," *Euromoney*, May 1987.

exhibit a forward discount (lower than spot) or premium (greater than spot).

- **Demonstrate how the relationship between spot and forward rates is determined by five parity relationships and enforced by covered interest arbitrage.** Five economic relationships, the Fisher effect, purchasing power parity, the international Fisher effect, forward rates as unbiased predictors, and interest rate parity interconnect spot rates and forward rates with inflation and interest rates. Together, they provide a theoretical basis for rate relationships and a set of equilibrium conditions to which all rates must adhere.
- **Identify how changes in exchange rates affect businesses dealing in multiple currencies.** Any firm that deals in more than its domestic currency faces foreign exchange risk through transaction exposure, translation exposure, and economic exposure. As rates vary they change the value of the firm's assets, liabilities, and equity, as well as its income and cash-flow stream. It is important to be able to predict these exposures to take the appropriate steps to minimize their impact.

Questions

1. What was the Bretton Woods system? What were its strong points? Why did it ultimately break down?
2. Distinguish between a fixed exchange rate system and a floating exchange rate system.
3. What is meant by the terms:
   a. Managed float?
   b. Pegged float?
   c. Joint float?
4. What is the relationship between direct and reciprocal exchange rates?
5. Do you have to fly between the United States and the United Kingdom to engage in geographic arbitrage between the dollar and the pound? Why or why not?
6. Why must cross rates always be near or at equilibrium?
7. What is a forward rate? Why might a business person be interested in it?
8. What pattern of forward rates characterizes a currency trading at

a. A forward discount?
b. A forward premium?

9. Identify the following concepts:
   a. The Fisher effect
   b. The international Fisher effect
   c. Absolute purchasing power parity
   d. Relative purchasing power parity
   e. Interest rate parity
10. Why might a bank's currency traders announce an exchange rate not equal to the equilibrium value, even if they are fully aware that the bank will lose money to arbitrageurs?
11. Identify:
    a. Transaction exposure
    b. Translation exposure
    c. Economic exposure

    What events might trigger each of these business risks?

Problems

1. **(Reciprocal rates)** Find the reciprocal rate between the U.S. dollar and the Swiss franc if the direct rate is:
   a. $0.7500
   b. $0.7850
   c. $0.8025
   d. $0.8385
2. **(Reciprocal rates)** Find the direct rate between the U.S. dollar and the Spanish peseta if the reciprocal rate is:
   a. Pt88.75
   b. Pt90.25
   c. Pt94.30
   d. Pt96.60
3. **(Geographic arbitrage)** Indicate how you would use geographic arbitrage to take advantage of the following reciprocal rate relationships:
   a. Direct rate is 4.8750, reciprocal rate is quoted as .2225.
   b. Direct rate is 7.3841, reciprocal rate is quoted as .1275.
   c. Direct rate is 1.6000, reciprocal rate is quoted as .6250.
   d. Direct rate is 428.32, reciprocal rate is quoted as .002510.
4. **(Geographic arbitrage)** Indicate how you would use geographic arbitrage to take advantage of the following reciprocal rate relationships:
   a. Direct rate is 5.2020, reciprocal rate is quoted as .1885.
   b. Direct rate is 2.0164, reciprocal rate is quoted as .5068.
   c. Direct rate is 6.2500, reciprocal rate is quoted as .1600.
   d. Direct rate is 1254.87, reciprocal rate is quoted as .0007789.
5. **(Cross rates)** Find the cross rates between the Japanese yen, now trading at ¥132.20 per U.S. dollar and:
   a. The Bahrain dinar, now trading at $2.6525 per dinar.
   b. The Canadian dollar, now at C$1.1602 per U.S. dollar.
   c. The French franc, now at FF5.0500 per U.S. dollar.
   d. The Peruvian new sol, now at $1.9904 per new sol.
6. **(Cross rates)** Find the cross rate between the German mark, now trading at DM1.4850 per U.S. dollar and:
   a. The Belgian franc, now trading at BF30.62 per U.S. dollar.
   b. The British pound, now trading at $1.9570 per pound.
   c. The Irish punt, now trading at $1.7930 per punt.
   d. The Italian lira, now at L1,117.00 per U.S. dollar.
7. **(Triangular arbitrage)** The dollar-Swiss franc spot rate is $0.7962. Indicate how you would use triangular arbitrage to take advantage of the following cross rate relationships:
   a. The dollar-(Portuguese) escudo spot rate is $0.007522, and the cross rate is SF0.009550 per escudo.
   b. The (Finnish) markka-dollar spot rate is FM3.5955, and the cross rate is SF0.3445 per markka.
   c. The dollar-(Indian) rupee spot rate is $0.05435, and the cross rate is SF0.06826 per rupee.
   d. The (Netherlands) guilder-dollar spot rate is *f*1.6750, and the cross rate is SF0.7642 per guilder.
8. **(Triangular arbitrage)** The dollar-French franc spot rate is $0.19802. Indicate how you would use triangular arbitrage to take advantage of the following cross rate relationships:
   a. The dollar-(Colombian) peso spot rate is $0.001780, and the cross rate is FF0.01010 per peso.
   b. The (Austrian) schilling-dollar spot rate is As10.46, and the cross rate is FF0.4828 per schilling.
   c. The dollar-(Danish) krone spot rate is $0.1748, and the cross rate is FF0.8675 per krone.
   d. The (Japanese) yen-dollar spot rate is ¥132.20, and the cross rate is FF0.04020 per yen.

9. **(Forward discount or premium)** Calculate the forward premium for the dollar priced in Swiss francs if the spot rate is SF1.2560 per dollar and the forward rates are:

   a. 30-day forward rate: SF1.2576.
   b. 60-day forward rate: SF1.2592.
   c. 90-day forward rate: SF1.2603.
   d. 180-day forward rate: SF1.2643.

10. **(Forward discount or premium)** Calculate the forward discount for the Canadian dollar priced in U.S. dollars if the spot rate is $0.8619 per Canadian dollar and the forward rates are:

    a. 30-day forward rate: $0.8590.
    b. 60-day forward rate: $0.8557.
    c. 90-day forward rate: $0.8542.
    d. 180-day forward rate: $0.8484.

11. **(Daily rate changes)** Calculate the daily percentage changes for the following exchange rates:

    a. Spot Argentinean pesos, which were P1.01 per U.S. dollar yesterday and are P1.02 per U.S. dollar today.
    b. Spot Netherlands guilders, which were *f*1.6710 per U.S. dollar yesterday and are *f*1.6750 per U.S. dollar today.
    c. 180-day forward Japanese yen, which were ¥132.67 per U.S. dollar yesterday and are ¥132.80 per U.S. dollar today.
    d. Spot Spanish pesetas, which were Pt93.15 per U.S. dollar yesterday and are Pt93.45 per U.S. dollar today.

12. **(Daily rate changes)** Calculate the daily percentage changes for the following exchange rates:

    a. Spot Australian dollars, which were A$1.2739 per U.S. dollar yesterday and are A$1.2857 per U.S. dollar today.
    b. 90-day forward Canadian dollars, which were C$1.1680 per U.S. dollar yesterday and are C$1.1707 per U.S. dollar today.
    c. Spot Danish krone, which were Kr5.7070 per U.S. dollar yesterday and are Kr5.7214 per U.S. dollar today.
    d. Spot Singapore dollars, which were S$1.7310 per U.S. dollar yesterday and are S$1.7255 per U.S. dollar today.

13. **(Fisher effect)** The one-year risk-free rate of interest is 7% in the United States and 9% in Canada. If the Fisher effect holds exactly, what is the one-year inflation premium required by Canadian investors if the one-year inflation premium in the United States is:

    a. 0%?
    b. 2%?
    c. 3%?
    d. 6%?

14. **(Fisher effect)** The one-year inflation premium required by U.K. investors is 8% and by U.S. investors is 5%. If the Fisher effect holds exactly, what is the one-year risk-free rate of interest in the United Kingdom if the one-year risk-free rate of interest in the United States is:

    a. 7%?
    b. 8%?
    c. 10%?
    d. 12%?

15. **(Absolute purchasing power parity)** For absolute purchasing power parity to be true, what must the spot dollar-mark exchange rate be if the cost in Germany of a basket of goods and services that costs $100 in the United States is:

    a. DM140?
    b. DM145?
    c. DM150?
    d. DM155?

16. **(Absolute purchasing power parity)** For absolute purchasing power parity to be true, what must the spot yen-dollar exchange rate be if the cost in the United States of a basket of goods and services that costs ¥10,000 in Japan costs:

    a. $70?
    b. $75?
    c. $80?
    d. $85?

17. **(Relative purchasing power parity)** In the coming year, prices in Peru are expected to increase by 75%. Today the spot dollar-new sol exchange rate is $1.9904. What is the forecast of the spot exchange rate one year from now according to relative purchasing power parity if the forecast of inflation for the next year in the United States is:

    a. 3%?
    b. 5%?
    c. 10%?
    d. 25%?

18. **(Relative purchasing power parity)** In the coming year, prices in Spain are expected to increase by 12% while prices in the United States are expected to increase by 6%. What is the forecast of the spot peseta-dollar exchange rate one year from now according to relative purchasing power parity if the spot peseta-dollar exchange rate is now:

a. Pt85?
b. Pt90?
c. Pt105?
d. Pt120?

19. **(International Fisher effect)** The one-year rate of return on a typical investment in Belgium is 18% and in the United States 15%. What one-year future spot rate is predicted by the international Fisher effect if the spot franc-dollar exchange rate is:

a. BF25?
b. BF28?
c. BF32?
d. BF35?

20. **(International Fisher effect)** The one-year risk-free rate of return in Germany is 5% and in the United States 7%. What one-year future spot rate is predicted by the international Fisher effect if the spot dollar-mark exchange rate is:

a. $0.60?
b. $0.65?
c. $0.70?
d. $0.75?

21. **(Interest rate parity)** It is possible to borrow and lend for one year in the United States at 12% and in Canada at 15%. What is equilibrium one-year forward rate according to interest rate parity if the spot rate is:

a. US$0.80?
b. US$0.90?
c. US$1.00?
d. US$1.10?

22. **(Interest rate parity)** It is possible to borrow and lend for three months in the United States at a nominal annual rate of 12% and in Ireland at a nominal annual rate of 16%. What is equilibrium three-month forward rate according to interest rate parity if the spot rate is:

a. $1.60?
b. $1.75?
c. $1.90?
d. $2.05?

23. **(Covered interest arbitrage)** It is possible to borrow and lend for one year in the United States at 10% and in England at 18%. The spot dollar-pound exchange rate is $1.9570. Indicate how you would use covered interest arbitrage to take advantage of the following one-year forward dollar-pound rates:

a. $1.9026
b. $1.8567
c. $1.8243
d. $1.7953

24. **(Covered interest arbitrage)** It is possible to borrow and lend for six months in the United States at a nominal annual rate of 14% and in Japan at nominal annual rate of 8%. The spot yen-dollar exchange rate is ¥132.20. Indicate how you would use covered interest arbitrage to take advantage of the following six-month forward yen-dollar rates:

a. ¥125.84
b. ¥128.49
c. ¥131.07
d. ¥134.55

APPENDIX 7A

EQUILIBRIUM EXCHANGE RATE RELATIONSHIPS

The foreign exchange rate equilibrium relationships are often expressed in algebraic form. To do so we need some simple notation.

Let:

$s(0)$ = spot exchange rate now (at time 0)

$s(1)$ = spot exchange rate one period from now

$f(0)$ = forward exchange rate now (at time 0) for the period

$P(0)$ = price level now (at time 0)

$P(1)$ = price level forecast for one period from now

r_n = nominal rate of interest for the period

r_r = real rate of interest for the period

r_i = inflation premium for the period

As we will compare exchange rates and interest rates between two countries, we will add additional subscripts as follows:

For interest rates:

A = rate in Country A (so, for example, r_{nA} represents the nominal rate of interest in country A)

B = rate in Country B

For exchange rates:

A/B = units of Country A's currency required to buy one unit of Country B's currency (so, for example, if Country A is the US and Country B the UK, $s(0)_{A/B}$ becomes $s(0)_{US/UK}$ and represents the US-UK spot exchange rate expressed as dollars per pound).

Also, recall the Fisher equation from Chapter 6:

$$\text{Nominal rate} = (1 + \text{real rate})\ (1 + \text{inflation premium}) - 1$$

$$r_n = (1 + r_r)(1 + r_i) - 1$$

which can be rearranged to solve for the real rate of interest:

$$(1 + r_n) = (1 + r_r)(1 + r_i)$$

$$(1 + r_r) = (1 + r_n) / (1 + r_i)$$

$$r_r = [(1 + r_n) / (1 + r_i)] - 1$$

1. The Fisher Effect

The Fisher effect holds that *real rates of return are the same in all currencies:* Using the Fisher equation for our two countries, Country A and Country B:

In Country A: $r_{rA} = [(1 + r_{nA}) / (1 + r_{iA})] - 1$

In Country B: $r_{rB} = [(1 + r_{nB}) / (1 + r_{iB})] - 1$

And, if the real rates are equal:

$$r_{rA} = r_{rB}$$

$$[(1 + r_{nA}) / (1 + r_{iA})] - 1 = [(1 + r_{nB}) / (1 + r_{iB})] - 1$$

$$(1 + r_{nA}) / (1 + r_{iA}) = (1 + r_{nB}) / (1 + r_{iB})$$

This equation can be further rearranged in any of a variety of ways; for example it is also commonly written:

$$(1 + r_{nA}) / (1 + r_{nB})] = (1 + r_{iA}) / (1 + r_{iB})$$

2. Absolute Purchasing Power Parity

Absolute purchasing power parity holds that *the spot exchange rate between two currencies is equal to the ratio of the price levels between the countries.* Therefore, at time 0:

$$s(0)_{A/B} = P(0)_A/P(0)_B$$

3. Relative Purchasing Power Parity

Relative purchasing power parity holds that for any time period *the change in the spot exchange rate between two currencies is equal to the ratio of the changes in the relative price levels between the countries.* Therefore:

Change in spot exchange rate between countries A and B:

$$s(1)_{A/B}/s(0)_{A/B}$$

Change in price level in Country A: $P(1)_A/P(0)_A$

Change in price level in Country B: $P(1)_B/P(0)_B$

And:

$$s(1)_{A/B}/s(0)_{A/B} = [P(1)_A/P(0)_A] / [P(1)_B/P(0)_B]$$

Also, since the inflation premium in today's interest rates is equal to the forecast of the change in price level, in each country

$$(1 + r_i) = P(1) \ / \ P(0)$$

so that the relative purchasing power parity equation may also be written:

$$s(1)_{A/B}/s(0)_{A/B} = (1 + r_{iA}) \ / \ (1 + r_{iB})$$

4. The International Fisher Effect

The international Fisher effect holds that *the difference in interest rates between two countries is an unbiased predictor of the future spot rate.* This can be derived as follows:

The relationship for relative purchasing power parity is:

$$s(1)_{A/B}/s(0)_{A/B} = (1 + r_{iA}) \ / \ (1 + r_{iB})$$

From the Fisher effect, the right-hand side of the above equation is also equal to the ratio of the nominal rates, so:

$$s(1)_{A/B}/s(0)_{A/B} = (1 + r_{nA}) \ / \ (1 + r_{nB})$$

and multiplying through by $s(0)_{A/B}$ gives:

$$s(1)_{A/B} = [(1 + r_{nA}) \ / \ (1 + r_{nB})] \times s(0)_{A/B}$$

5. Interest Rate Parity

Interest rate parity holds that *the interest rate differentials between two countries are offset by the difference between spot and forward rates.* Consider the returns to residents of Country A who have one unit of currency to invest and who must select between investing in Country A or Country B:

If they invest in Country A at nominal interest rate r_{nA}, the unit of currency A will grow to an end-of-period value of:

$$(1 + r_{nA})$$

If they invest in Country B, they will:

1. Exchange the unit of currency A for currency B and get

   $$1 \ / \ s(0)_{A/B}$$

   units of currency B.
2. Invest this amount in Country B at nominal interest rate of r_{nB} and have

   $$[1 \ / \ s(0)_{A/B}] \ (1 + r_{nB})$$

   at the end of the period.
3. Purchase a forward exchange rate contract to lock in a rate of $f(0)_{A/B}$ for converting back at the end of the period. This will produce an end-of-period value of

   $$[1 \ / \ s(0)_{A/B}] \ (1 + r_{nB}) \ [f(0)_{A/B}]$$

According to interest rate parity, the two end-of-period values must be equal. Therefore:

$$(1 + r_{nA}) = [1 / s(0)_{A/B}] (1 + r_{nB}) [f(0)_{A/B}]$$

and rearranging, we get an expression for the forward rate: the spot rate multiplied by the ratio of one plus the nominal interest rate in each country.

$$f(0)_{A/B} = s(0)_{A/B} \times [(1 + r_{nA}) / (1 + r_{nB})]$$

PART III RISK AND RETURN

In Part III we study the interrelationship of risk and return, the framework used in finance theory for evaluating financial managing decisions.

Chapter 8 elaborates on risk. We define risk, describe reactions to it, establish the relationship of risk to financial value, and identify the three primary sources of risk. We then develop two models that relate risk to the rate of return required by investors: a total risk model for a stand-alone investment and a portfolio risk model, the capital asset pricing model (CAPM), for an asset held as part of a diversified portfolio.

Chapter 9 is devoted to valuation, how time value and risk can help us determine the worth of various financial instruments. We identify the value of a security as a present value that is independent of investors' holding periods. We distinguish between value and price. Then we study the valuation of bonds, preferred stock, and common stock. Appendix 9A introduces the Black-Scholes model for valuing a call option.

Chapter 10 examines the cost of capital, the rate of return a company must earn to satisfy its investors. We present the process of calculating a cost of capital: determining investors' required rates of return, calculating the cost of a capital source, integrating the cost of each capital source to produce an overall cost of capital, and producing a cost of capital schedule. We then illustrate each step as it applies to a company financed by bonds, preferred stock, and common stock. We also look at the role a cost of capital plays in management decision making. Appendix 10A extends the cost of capital framework to short-term debt.

CHAPTER 8
RISK

Cathy Stewart stared at the open door to her office and reflected on what had just happened. Not more than one minute ago, Mike Shield, one of her best employees, had stormed out of her office in an extremely distraught state of mind. It was clear that Mike would not be very productive today, and Cathy wondered how this incident would affect Mike's willingness to contribute to the organization in the future.

Cathy was the CFO of a small company that provided service to customers seven days a week. Last week, Cathy's boss had circulated a memo "informing" certain employees that they would have to report to work on alternate Saturdays. As the father of a small child, Mike felt he could not afford to work on Saturday. More important, he was enraged at what he considered a cavalier attitude toward employees' personal lives by the company's management.

Cathy thought back to last week, to a meeting with the company's investment bankers in which the topic was the market profile of the company's stock. At issue was the high amount of risk investors felt they were taking and how that risk level raised the rate of return the investors demanded. Cathy understood that if investors required a higher level of return, it would be more difficult to raise money and the price of the company's stock would be depressed.

Cathy remembered something Mike had said when he objected to working on Saturday: "Why are they making it so risky to be employed here?" As she mulled over how to respond to Mike's concerns, Cathy wondered whether the risk Mike was feeling was in any way connected to the risks the investment bankers were concerned about.

Cathy is dealing with one of the most fundamental issues in finance, how to understand risk and the effects of risk on a company's operations and value. Over the years, finance theorists have developed a comprehensive theory of risk as it affects the shareholder—how to define it, measure it, and estimate its impact on stock price. Today we are beginning to understand that each stakeholder of the firm faces risks and that all of these risks must be successfully addressed if the firm is to succeed and prosper.

In this chapter we define *risk* and identify why it is important. We then identify different types of risk and learn what events cause them. We also draw upon basic concepts in probability and statistics to measure risk and to reach important conclusions about the relationship of risk to the financial value of the firm.

Key Points You Should Learn from This Chapter

After reading this chapter you should be able to:

- Define *risk* and know why it is important to the financial manager.
- State the relationship between risk and financial value.
- Describe the three primary sources of risk faced by a firm.
- Measure the risk of a single security held by itself and relate this level of risk to investors' required rate of return.
- Measure the risk of a security held in a diversified portfolio and relate this level of risk to investors' required rate of return.

Introductory Concepts—What Is Risk and Why Does It Matter?

Risk is the chance that something will come out worse than planned. If we cross the street, our plan is to get to the other side safely. The risk in crossing the street is the chance that we might be injured in the process. The same concept is true in finance. For example, if we invest in the common stock of a company, we anticipate a fair rate of return on our investment. The risk is that we may earn less than anticipated.

Different streets have different levels of risk. The likelihood of injury in crossing a back country road is much less than that of crossing a busy urban freeway. Similarly, in finance, different investments have different levels of risk. A deposit in a federally insured bank account that pays a fixed, stated rate of interest has much less risk than an investment in a new biotech startup company.

The extreme risk outcome is a total failure to get anything in return for the time and money invested. For a customer, this could be paying for something that does not work or otherwise meet the customer's needs. For a supplier, this could mean investing in a relationship that is abruptly terminated. For an employee, total failure means losing one's job. For a creditor, failure means not being repaid. And for an investor, total failure is the bankruptcy of the company so that the investment becomes worthless.

risk seeker—an individual willing to pay to assume additional risk

Social scientists have identified three possible attitudes toward risk. Some people find risk something that increases value. Such people are called **risk seekers,** and they look for opportunities to add risk to their activities. In fact, risk seekers are willing to pay more for something if it contains an element of risk. Gambling in Las Vegas, bungee jumping, and taking mind-altering drugs are examples of activities that are pursued by risk seekers. In each case, the individuals (or their money) are safer if they avoid the activity. In each case, they pay for the opportunity to be in the risky situation. In each case, the thrill from the risk itself is an important part of the reward from the activity.

risk averter—an individual willing to pay to avoid risk

Other people dislike risk and find that it reduces value. These people are called **risk averters.** Risk averters look for opportunities to subtract risk from their ac-

Calvin and Hobbes by Bill Watterson

tivities. They stay away from risky situations and buy insurance when risk cannot be avoided. In financial markets, they insist on an increased rate of return on their invested money as compensation for the risks they take.

risk neutral—indifferent to risk

Of course, it is possible that some people are indifferent to risk. For them risk is irrelevant, and they will make decisions without taking risk into consideration. We call these people **risk neutral.**

When it comes to money, most people hold a combination of all three attitudes. For small amounts of money, they act as risk seekers and are willing to take small risks. For example, many people enjoy buying a lottery ticket, even though with the state taking its percentage off the top, they stand to win less on average than they pay for the ticket. The risk of losing is high, but the amount of money at risk is very low. In this case the added excitement from the possibility of winning—however tiny—more than compensates for the small added cost.

For slightly larger amounts of money, people tend to become risk neutral. They might, for example, purchase tickets to a play without ever thinking that the risk of not enjoying the production should lower the ticket price.

However, as the amount of money at risk increases further and becomes a significant fraction of a person's total wealth, almost all people become risk averters. For example, there are few of us who will gamble everything we own on a lottery ticket or move a long distance to take a job with an organization we know nothing about. Now the potential for significant loss dominates our thinking and outweighs any thrill from the risk.

At the level of a business, large amounts of money are at risk. As a result, it is reasonable that the key stakeholders of a business—customers, suppliers, employees, creditors, and investors—act as risk averters, a conclusion borne out by research into human and financial market behavior. If each stakeholder of the firm is a risk averter, then each will demand some form of compensation to assume risk. And in each case, the demand for that compensation will drain value from the firm and leave it worse off.

- For customers the risk of poor product or service quality reduces the price they are willing to pay. Over time it also reduces the amount they are willing to purchase, which further lowers the firm's revenues.
- For suppliers the risk of an unstable relationship increases the prices they charge the firm. They build in protection against the possibility that their investment in tooling up might not be fully recouped. They are less willing to work with an unpredictable customer or invest additional time and money, which further increases the firm's costs.
- For employees the risk of job changes and termination increases the wage the company must pay to attract and hold its staff. And as Cathy Stewart found out at the beginning of this chapter, employees who feel at risk tend to reduce their willingness to contribute to the firm in general.
- For creditors the risk of default increases the interest rate they must earn on loans to the company. They further protect themselves by writing restrictive loan agreements that limit the firm's degrees of operating and financial freedom.

Each of these risks—as seen by customers, suppliers, employees, and creditors—reduces the firm's profitability and adds uncertainty to its cash flow stream. For the firm's investors, the risk of lower and less-predictable income raises the rate of return they demand from the firm, increasing the firm's "cost of capital"[1] and reducing its stock price.

Risk and Financial Value

In Chapter 6 we introduced the Fisher interest rate equation:[2]

$$\textit{Nominal rate} = (1 + \textit{pure rate})\ (1 + \textit{inflation premium})\ (1 + \textit{risk premium}) - 1$$
$$= (1 + r_p)\ (1 + r_i)\ (1 + r_r) - 1$$

which, since the risk-free rate is the combination of the pure rate and the inflation premium, could also be written in the following form:

$$\textit{Nominal rate} = (1 + \textit{risk-free rate})\ (1 + \textit{risk premium}) - 1$$
$$= (1 + r_f)\ (1 + r_r) - 1$$

The Fisher equation illustrates the impact of risk on the rates of return investors require. If an investment is perceived as being risky, investors will ask not only for the risk-free rate, the interest rate appropriate for a risk-free investment, but also for a risk premium.

Example

How Risk Increases Nominal Rates

Investors are currently demanding a rate of return of 5% on a U.S. Treasury bill considered risk-free.

Question: What rate of return will investors require from an investment in Gorman Industries (GI) stock if the appropriate risk premium is 7%?

Solution steps: Using the Fisher equation:

$$\text{Nominal rate} = (1 + \text{risk-free rate})\ (1 + \text{risk premium}) - 1$$
$$= (1 + r_f)\ (1 + r_r) - 1$$
$$= (1.05)\ (1.07) - 1$$
$$= .1235 = 12.35\%$$

Answer: Investors will require a rate of return of 12.35%.

The level of risk estimated by investors will determine the value of the risk premium (r_r) and hence the required rate of return.

---

[1] **Cross-reference:** Cost of capital is the subject of Chapter 10.

[2] **Cross-reference:** The Fisher model is discussed on pp. 206–210.

Example

How a Higher Risk Premium Leads to a Higher Required Rate of Return

Investors are still demanding a rate of return of 5% on a U.S. Treasury bill considered risk-free. However, because of recent setbacks, investors now see Gorman Industries stock as a riskier investment.

Question: What rate of return will investors require from an investment in GI stock if the appropriate risk premium has risen to 8%?

Solution steps: Using the Fisher equation:

$$\begin{aligned}\text{Nominal rate} &= (1 + \text{risk-free rate})\ (1 + \text{risk premium}) - 1\\ &= (1 + r_f)\ (1 + r_r) - 1\\ &= (1.05)\ (1.08) - 1\\ &= .1340 = 13.40\%\end{aligned}$$

Answer: Now investors will require a rate of return of 13.40%.

As financial value is the present value of the benefits investors expect to receive, financial value declines as interest rates go up.

Examples

How Financial Values Decline With Higher Interest Rates

Investors estimate that Gorman Industries will produce a perpetuity of benefits of $5.00 per year for each common share.

Question: What was the value of GI stock when investors demanded a risk premium of 7%.

Solution steps: With a 7% risk premium, investors required a 12.35% rate of return. Using the perpetuity model:

$$\begin{aligned}\text{Value} &= \text{PV of perpetuity} = \text{PMT} \ / \ r\\ &= \$5.00 \ / \ .1235 = \$40.49 \text{ per share}\end{aligned}$$

Answer: GI stock was worth $40.49 per share.

Question: What happened to the value of GI stock when investors raised their required risk premium to 8%.

Solution steps: With a 8% risk premium, investors now require a 13.40% rate of return. Using the perpetuity model:

$$\begin{aligned}\text{Value} &= \text{PV of perpetuity} = \text{PMT} \ / \ r\\ &= \$5.00 \ / \ .1340 = \$37.31 \text{ per share}\end{aligned}$$

Answer: The increase in perceived risk lowered GI's stock price from $40.49 to $37.31, a decline of $3.18, or 7.85%.

In summary, then, when investors perceive a high level of risk, they will require a high rate of return and the firm's financial value will be reduced. Other things equal, the value of a firm can be increased by reducing the risks to which investors are exposed.

Sources of Risk

Figure 8.1 identifies the forces which create risk in a firm's financial results. As the figure reveals, each firm faces three primary sources of risk.

environmental risk—unexpected changes outside the firm that impact its operations

The first source of risk is **environmental risk,** which comes from events outside the firm. This includes changes in the business and economic climate, actions of competitors, technological advances, revaluation of currency prices, political limitations such as restrictions on transferring currency or other resources from one country to another, etc. While the firm typically cannot influence these forces, it can prepare for them so that if they occur, plans are in place to minimize their negative impact. In addition, good strategic planning often finds ways to position the firm to take advantage of these events.

process risk—unnecessary variability caused by systems within the firm that are out of control

The second source of risk is **process risk,** which comes from unnecessary variability within the firm itself. This includes problems due to out-of-control production operations as well as complications caused by dissatisfied customers, employees, and suppliers. If the firm's internal processes are functioning well, the only variability is the small amount of natural variation found in all processes. By contrast, poorly functioning processes vary greatly in their output and tend to magnify any problems due to changes in the environment.

business risk—the total variability of a firm's operating results

Taken together, the combination of environmental risk and process risk is known as **business risk** in that it describes the variability of the operating results of the business. In financial terms, business risk is variability in the firm's operating profit stream.

financial risk—the increased variability in a firm's financial results caused by its financing mix

The third source of risk, known as **financial risk,** comes from the financing mix the firm chooses. A firm that finances with debt adds the magnification of leverage to its profit and cash flow. For the creditors, financial risk is the risk of default on the debt. For stockholders, leverage magnifies any variability in the firm's operating profit and cash flow, a topic we will explore more fully in Chapter 15.

FIGURE 8.1

Sequence of risks. Variability from the environment is magnified by the firm's process variability, which is further magnified by the firm's financing mix.

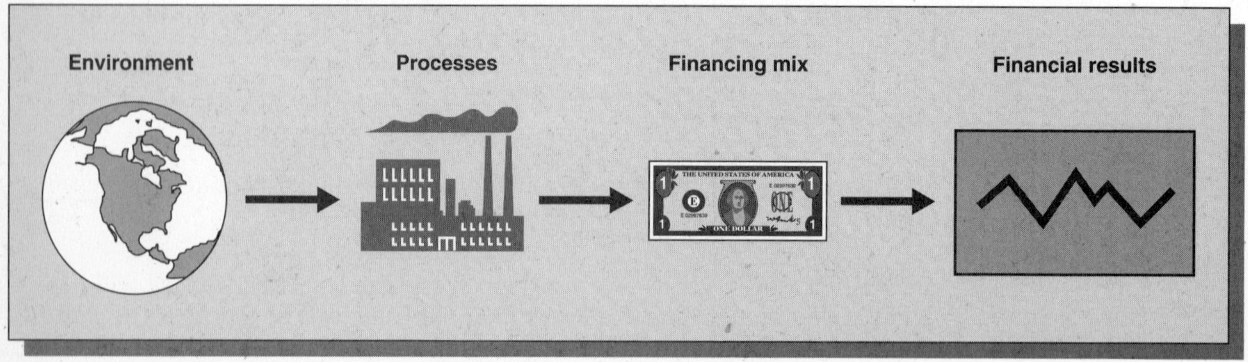

FINANCE IN PRACTICE

Excessive Financial Risk at Pan Am

The airline industry is characterized by high debt levels. Large amounts of money are required to purchase and maintain an up-to-date fleet, and the planes serve as excellent collateral for borrowing. However, the industry also has a high degree of environmentally caused business risk since the demand for both business and leisure air travel is very sensitive to the economy. In Pan American's case, the combination of high financial risk piled upon high business risk proved fatal. Each time the economy turned down, Pan Am's cash flow dried up. Throughout the 1970s and 1980s, Pan Am raised cash to stay aloft by selling its assets—the Intercontinental Hotel chain, its headquarters building in New York City; its Pacific routes, the Boston–New York–Washington shuttle, and its Latin American routes. Finally, there was nothing left to sell, and the once proud carrier that "opened the world" crash landed, a victim of excessive financial risk.

These three risk factors cascade, one upon the other. Risks from the environment are magnified by risks due to faulty processes, and that result is then further magnified by the leverage built into the financing mix. The stability of the firm's financial results reflects the combination of these three risk sources.

Measuring Risk—The Total Risk Model

Since risk creates variability in a firm's financial results, it is common to use elementary statistical concepts to measure risk. In this section we look at the risk of a single asset taken by itself. In the next section, we acknowledge that most assets are not held alone but rather as part of a portfolio of assets, and we look at risk in that context.

1. Probability Distributions

To say that something is uncertain is to say that we cannot predict its outcome precisely. However, if we can identify possible outcomes and identify the probability of each outcome occurring, we can apply some elementary concepts in probability and statistics to the problem.

probability distribution—a listing of all possible results of some activity showing the chance of each result taking place

A **probability distribution** is a listing of possible outcomes along with the chance that each will occur. For example, if we flip a fair coin, there is a 50% chance of getting heads and a 50% chance of getting tails. The probability distribution for this event is therefore:

Outcome	Probability
Heads	50% = .50
Tails	50% = .50
	100% = 1.00

The probabilities of all outcomes taken together must add up to 100% (or 1.00) if we are including every possible outcome.

A probability distribution for the returns from an investment looks much the same. Each outcome, usually shown as a rate of return, is listed along with its probability. Often there is a third column describing the underlying economic conditions which lead to each outcome. Consider, for example, an investment in common stock. In general, the better the economy, the more likely the company is to prosper, leading to increased dividends and a higher stock price, hence to high rates of return. Conversely, the worse the economy, the less likely the company is to prosper, leading to reduced dividends and a lower stock price, therefore to low rates of return.

Suppose you are considering an investment in the stock of one of two companies, AMR Corporation (American Airlines) and Con Edison (the New York City–area utility). AMR's performance is very dependent on economic conditions which influence the volume of business and leisure travel. By contrast, Con Edison's business is relatively stable as demand for gas and electricity depends on population trends and the weather and is somewhat independent of the business cycle.

Example

Probability Distributions for Two Investments

Investors have simplified their forecasts of the economy to five possibilities—boom, good times, average times, bad times, and recession—and have constructed the following probability distributions for returns from investing in AMR and Con Edison:

State of the Economy	Probability of This State of the Economy	Rate of Return from	
		AMR Corp.	Con Edison
Boom	10% = .10	75%	30%
Good times	20 = .20	40	20
Average times	40 = .40	20	12
Bad times	20 = .20	−10	5
Recession	10 = .10	−40	−10
	100% = 1.00		

From the example we see that investors estimate a 10% chance of a boom, in which case Con Edison should do well (a 30% rate of return) and AMR should do very well (returning 75%). Investors also estimate a 10% chance of a recession, in which case both companies are expected to do poorly, although AMR (a 40% loss) is expected to fare worse than Con Edison (down 10%). Because AMR is so much more dependent on the economy than Con Edison, its performance is estimated to vary much more widely, both in a boom and in a recession.

2. Expected Value

expected value—the weighted average of the forecasted rates of return from an investment

Looking a bit further at the numbers in the above example, it appears that AMR, on average, is expected to provide a higher rate of return than Con Edison. It is useful to have one number that captures the average anticipated level of returns; a common measure used for this is the **expected value** of the probability distribution.

The expected value of a probability distribution is calculated by taking each forecasted outcome, multiplying it by the probability of its occurrence, and summing the results.[3]

Example

Expected Values of Two Investments

Working with the probability distributions for returns from investing in AMR and Con Edison:

		AMR Corp.		Con Edison	
State of the Economy	**Probability (1)**	**Return (2)**	**Product (1) × (2)**	**Return (3)**	**Product (1) × (3)**
Boom	.10	75%	7.5%	30%	3.0%
Good times	.20	40	8.0	20	4.0
Average times	.40	20	8.0	12	4.8
Bad times	.20	−10	−2.0	5	1.0
Recession	.10	−40	−4.0	−10	−1.0
	1.00		17.5%		11.8%

The expected rate of return from an investment in AMR stock is 17.5% and from Con Edison stock is 11.8%

3. Graphing Probability Distributions

It is common to illustrate probability distributions by graphing them. Figure 8.2 shows the graphs of the probability distributions for AMR Corp. and Con Edison.

While it is convenient to estimate probability distributions as if there were only a few states of the economy that could take place, in reality there are many possible states of the economy—a continuum of possibilities. Figure 8.3 extends the probability distributions of AMR Corp. and Con Edison to be continuous distributions by filling in probabilities for the remaining possible rates of return. This produces smooth curves. As is true of all probability distributions, the sum of all the probabilities must equal 1.00, hence the total area under each curve equals 1.00. With an infinite number of possible rates of return, this means that the probability of any one particular rate of return occurring is infinitesimally small.

4. Variance and Standard Deviation

From Figure 8.3, we can see that the probability distribution for Con Edison is quite a bit narrower than the distribution for AMR Corp. This means there is less of a chance that Con Edison's rate of return will deviate far from its expected value than will that of AMR. In particular, there is a smaller chance that Con Edison's rate of return will be significantly below its expected value—precisely the concept of risk discussed earlier in the chapter.

[3] **Cross-reference:** Formulas for expected value and the other statistical calculations discussed in this chapter are given in the Summary of Mathematical Formulas at the end of the book.

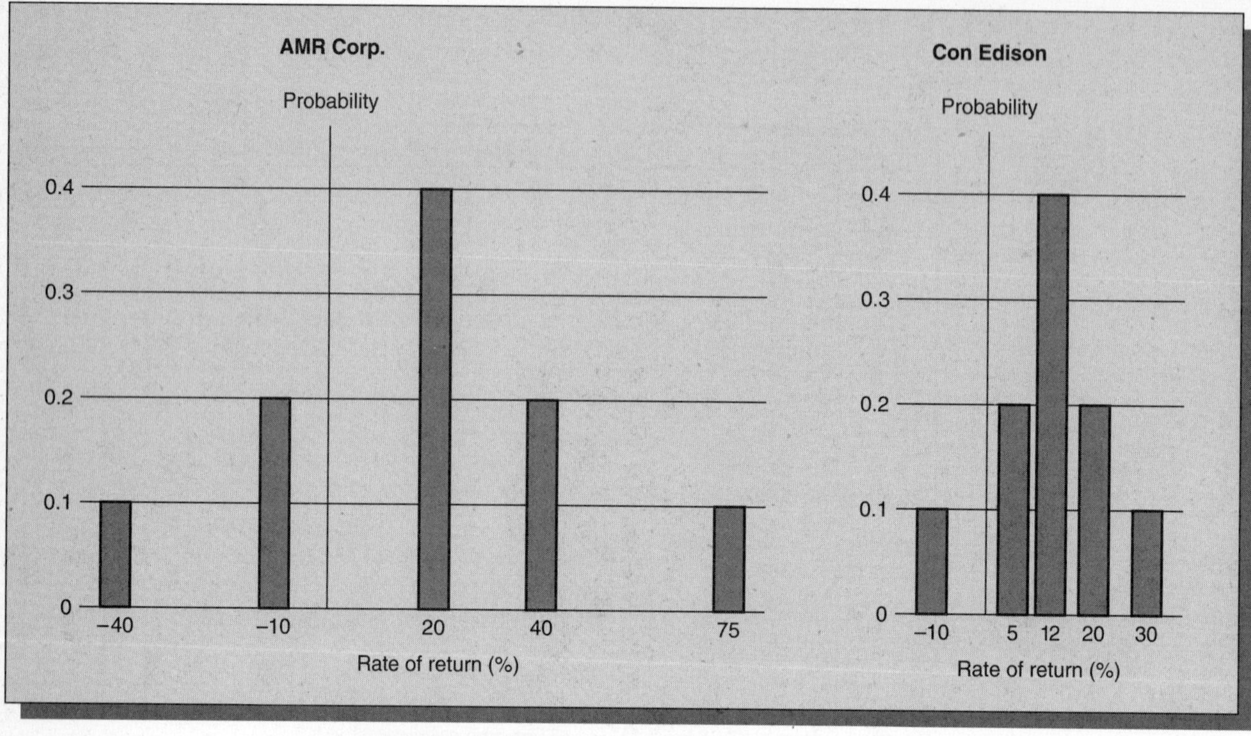

FIGURE 8.2
Probability distributions for AMR Corp. and Con Edison. The returns from AMR are expected to vary over a much wider range than the returns from Con Edison.

FIGURE 8.3
Continuous probability distributions for AMR Corp. and Con Edison. In reality there are many possible rates of return from each security.

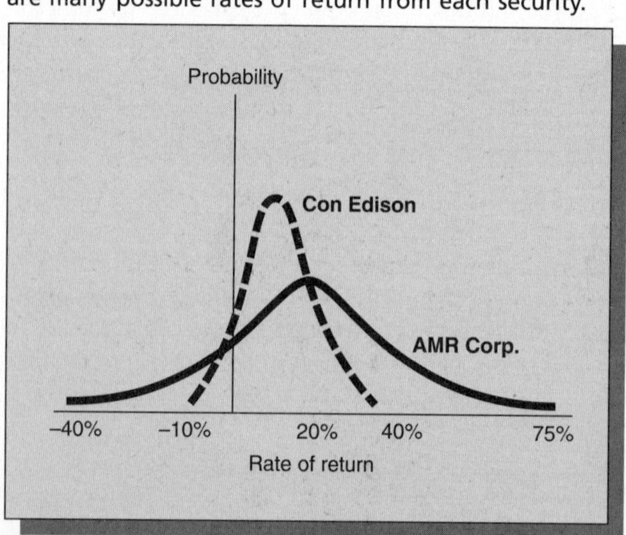

variance—a measure of the variability of rates of return

standard deviation—the square root of the variance

It is common to use the concepts of variance and standard deviation to measure the width of a probability distribution, and as a result, variance and standard deviation are used in finance to measure the risk of financial returns. The **variance** (written as σ^2) of a probability distribution is a measure of how far each possible outcome deviates from the distribution's expected value. It is calculated by: (1) obtaining the deviation of each outcome by subtracting the expected value, (2) squaring the deviations to eliminate any difference between positive and negative deviations, and (3) calculating a weighted average of the results using the probabilities as weights in the same way as we calculated the expected value. The **standard deviation** (σ) is the square root of the variance and has the virtue that its unit of measure is rate of return (whereas variance is measured as "rate of return squared," an awkward concept).

Example

Variance and Standard Deviation of Two Investments

Working with the probability distributions for returns from investing in AMR and Con Edison:

1. AMR Corp. (expected return = 17.5%)

State of the Economy	Probability (1)	Return (2)	Deviation (3) = (2) − 17.5	Deviation^2 (4) = (3)^2	Product (1) × (4)
Boom	.10	75%	57.5%	3306.25	330.625
Good times	.20	40	22.5	506.25	101.250
Average times	.40	20	2.5	6.25	2.500
Bad times	.20	−10	−27.5	756.25	151.250
Recession	.10	−40	−57.5	3306.25	330.625
	1.00				916.250

and $\sqrt{916.250} = 30.27\%$

The variance of AMR's expected returns is 916.250 and the standard deviation is 30.27%.

2. Con Edison (expected return = 11.8%)

State of the Economy	Probability (1)	Return (2)	Deviation (3) = (2) − 11.8	Deviation^2 (4) = (3)^2	Product (1) × (4)
Boom	.10	30%	18.2%	331.24	33.124
Good times	.20	20	8.2	67.24	13.448
Average times	.40	12	.2	.04	.016
Bad times	.20	5	−6.8	46.24	9.248
Recession	.10	−10	−21.8	475.24	47.524
	1.00				103.360

and $\sqrt{103.360} = 10.17\%$

The variance of Con Edison's expected returns is 103.360 and the standard deviation is 10.17%.

The calculations confirm our visual observations that Con Edison stock has less risk than AMR stock since Con Edison has a much lower variance and standard deviation.

If the distribution of returns for a security is estimated to be normal (bell-shaped), then roughly 68% of the probability lies within plus-or-minus one standard deviation from the expected value, about 95% lies within plus-or-minus two standard deviations, and well over 99% lies between plus-or-minus three standard deviations.

Example

Interpreting the Standard Deviation of Returns

Con Edison's expected return is 11.8% and its standard deviation is 10.17%. This tells us that investors are forecasting that the probability is 68% that the rate of return on Con Edison stock will fall between:

$$11.8\% - 10.17\% = 1.63\%$$

and

$$11.8\% + 10.17\% = 21.97\%$$

68% of probability
1σ 1σ
1.63 11.8 21.97

By contrast, AMR's expected return is 17.5% and its standard deviation is 30.27%. This tells us that investors are forecasting that the probability is 68% that the rate of return on AMR stock will fall between:

$$17.5\% - 30.27\% = -12.77\%$$

and

$$17.5\% + 30.27\% = 47.77\%$$

Again, these numbers point out how much riskier AMR stock is compared to Con Edison stock.

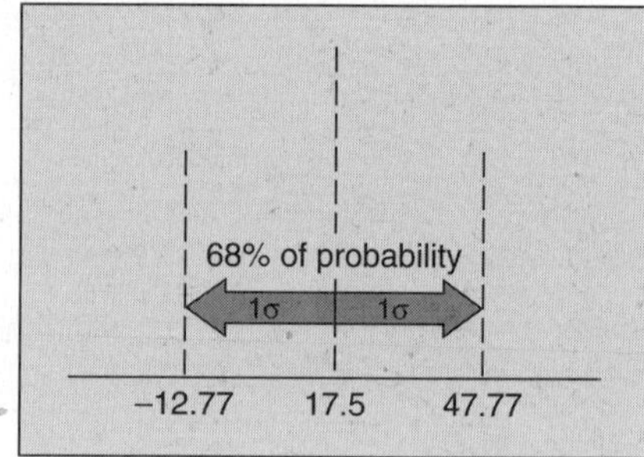

5. Coefficient of Variation

coefficient of variation—standard deviation divided by expected value

Sometimes we are comparing two investments whose expected returns are significantly different. In this case, it is useful to calculate the **coefficient of variation** of each investment to put its standard deviation into context. By dividing standard deviation by expected value, the coefficient of variation gives the risk per unit of return.

Example

The Coefficient of Variation

Investors have estimated an expected return of 50% and a standard deviation of 18% for Biosystems, Ltd., a young, high-tech company. They have also estimated an expected return of 12% and a standard deviation of 8% for Old-Line Metals, Inc., a mature foundry. At first glance, Biosystems has the greater risk since its standard deviation is more than twice that of Old-Line. However, additional insight is provided by calculating the coefficients of variation:

For Biosystems: 18% / 50% = 0.36

For Old-Line: 8% / 12% = 0.67

Relative to its expected value, Biosystems has the lower risk. In addition, there is little probability of sustaining a loss on an investment in Biosystems, while there is a much higher chance of loss for Old-Line stock.

The coefficient of variation is less useful in comparing AMR and Con Edison, whose expected returns are not so dramatically different.

Con Edison's expected return is 11.8% and its standard deviation is 10.17%. Its coefficient of variation is therefore:

10.17% / 11.8% = 0.86

AMR's expected return is 17.5% and its standard deviation is 30.27%. Its coefficient of variation is therefore:

30.27% / 17.5% = 1.73

These numbers only continue to point out that AMR stock is riskier than Con Edison stock.

6. The Capital Market Line (CML)

capital market line (CML)—a graph of investors' required rate of return as a function of an asset's total risk

It is common to summarize the risk-return relationship for a single asset using the **capital market line (CML).** The CML, illustrated in Figure 8.4, shows the relationship between the expected return and total risk from investing in a single

FIGURE 8.4

The capital market line (CML). For an individual asset, investors' required rate of return increases with total risk (σ).

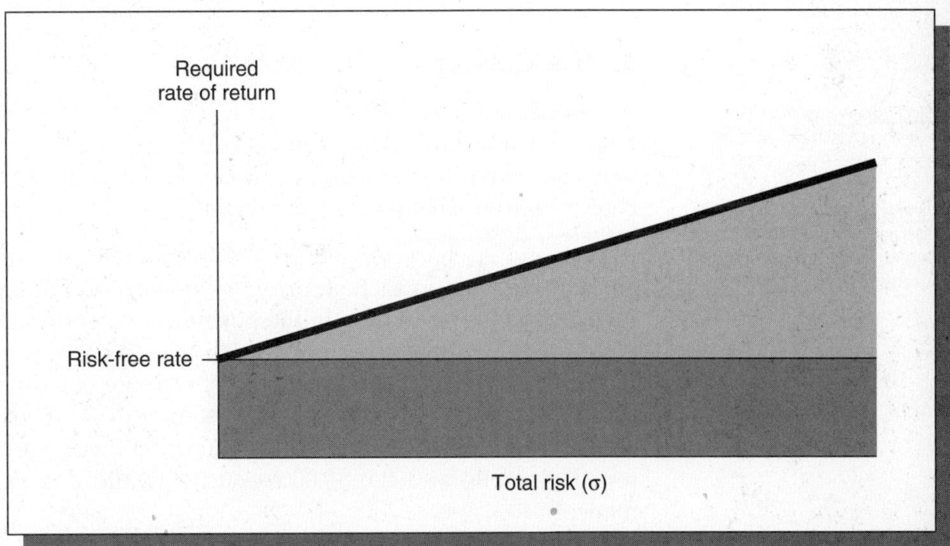

asset. At the left of the graph are assets with no risk, which return the risk-free rate. Further to the right on the graph lie the risky assets. The graph's upward slope reflects investors' risk aversion as they insist on higher rates of return to compensate for taking on riskier investments.

The equation of the CML is that of a straight line:

$$\textit{Required rate of return} = r_f + (\textit{slope}) \times \sigma$$
$$= r_f + (\textit{price of total risk}) \times \sigma$$

price of total risk—the additional return demanded by investors to take on one unit of total risk

where the slope is the **price of total risk,** the added return required per unit of standard deviation. Note that the CML is consistent with the additive version of the Fisher model:

$$\text{Nominal rate} = r_f + r_r$$
$$= r_f + (\text{price of total risk}) \times \sigma$$

For a single asset, r_r, the risk premium, equals the price of total risk multiplied by σ, the total risk of the investment.

Measuring Risk—The Portfolio Risk Model

So far we have treated each investment as if it were the only one owned by an investor. However, most investors do not put all their eggs in one basket. Rather, they spread their money across several investments. Intuitively, this makes sense. An investor who holds only one security is particularly vulnerable to any setback in that one investment. An investor who holds several securities, on the other hand, has spread the risk; low returns from one security will often be offset by higher returns from the others, and a poor performance by one security is far less of a concern. In this section, we look at the risk and return of a portfolio of investments.

1. The Concept of a Portfolio

portfolio—a group of investments held at the same time

diversify—to spread your money across several investments, i.e., to purchase a portfolio

A **portfolio** of investments is simply a group of investments held together. If you have $5,000 to invest, and you choose to buy $1,000 worth of each of five securities, you own a five-security portfolio. When you purchase a portfolio, you have chosen to **diversify** your investments.

A portfolio is characterized by the investments included in it and also by the amount invested in each security. As we will see, the securities in which more is invested play a larger role in the portfolio's performance than those with little invested. In the above example you elected to invest an equal amount in each of the five securities, and they will all contribute equally to the portfolio's risk and return. By contrast, had you chosen to invest $3,000 of your $5,000 in one of the securities and $500 in each of the four others, you would be holding a quite different portfolio and the $3,000 security would dominate the portfolio's performance.

2. Portfolio Returns

The rate of return from a portfolio is simply the weighted average of the returns from each security in the portfolio where the weights reflect how much money is invested in each security.

Example

Rate of Return from a Portfolio

Cathy Stewart owns a portfolio consisting of $3,000 worth of AMR stock and $7,000 worth of Con Edison stock.

Question: What is the expected rate of return from Cathy's portfolio?

Solution steps: Calculate the weighted average rate of return given that 30% of her money is invested in AMR and the other 70% in Con Edison.

Security	Expected Return	Percent of Portfolio	Product
AMR	17.5%	30%	5.25%
Con Edison	11.8	70	8.26
			13.51%

Answer: The portfolio has an expected return of 13.51%. Since Cathy has more than half (70%) of her money in Con Edison, the portfolio's expected return is closer to that investment's 11.8% expected return than it is to AMR's expected return of 17.5%.

Since the expected return from a portfolio is an average, it will always lie somewhere in the middle of the expected returns from each security that makes up the portfolio (13.51% lies between 11.8% and 17.5%). It is impossible to produce higher expected returns by investing in a portfolio!

3. Portfolio Risk

The real benefit from a portfolio lies in its risk-reducing ability, because, unlike the expected return, the risk of a portfolio is not simply the weighted average of the risks of its components. Rather, the standard deviation of a portfolio is almost always lower than the weighted average of the standard deviations of the component securities. To illustrate, suppose Cathy Stewart is thinking of "investing" $1,000 in the flip of a coin.[4] If heads comes up she earns 40% and gets back $1,400 (her initial $1000 plus $400). If tails comes up she loses 20% or $200 and only retrieves $800 as shown in the table. This is certainly a risky "investment" (with expected return of 10% or $100 and standard deviation of 30% or $300). There is a 50% chance Cathy will lose money.

[4] **Observation:** A foolish thing to do, perhaps, but the beginning of a very good illustration of the portfolio risk reduction effect.

Outcome	Probability	Payoff
Heads	.50	−40%($1,000) = $400
Tails	.50	−20%($1,000) = −$200

Suppose, instead, Cathy elects to diversify and invest $500 in each of two coin flips instead. The possible outcomes from this "two-investment portfolio" are:

Outcome		Probability	Payoff		
Coin 1	Coin 2		From Coin 1	From Coin 2	Total
Heads	Heads	.25	40%($500) = $200	40%($500) = $200	$400
Heads	Tails	.50	40%($500) = $200	−20%($500) = −$100	$100
Tails	Heads		−20%($500) = −$100	40%($500) = $200	
Tails	Tails	.25	−20%($500) = −$100	−20%($500) = −$100	−$200

This portfolio has the same 10% (or $100) expected rate of return as the single-flip "investment," but the standard deviation is lower: 21.213% (or $212.13).[5] There is now a 50% chance that Cathy will earn the expected $100 return, and only a 25% chance she will lose money. She has reduced her risk without giving up any expected return!

correlation coefficient—a measure of the relationship between the returns from two investments

The amount of risk reduction that comes from combining investments into a portfolio depends on the relationship among the investments. In the coin flip example, the two investments (coin flips) were independent of each other—the result of the first flip had no bearing on the outcome of the second. In statistical terms, there was zero correlation between the flips. The statistical measure known as the **correlation coefficient** (written as r) captures this idea. r can range from + 1 (perfect correlation: the two investments go up together and down together in perfect synchronization), through zero (no relationship: the two investments are completely independent of one another, like the coin flips), to − 1 (perfect negative correlation: when one investment goes up the other always goes down, and vice versa). If r = 1, the portfolio is no different than each of its components and risk is not reduced. However, it is rare to find perfectly correlated investments. Most pairs of investments have a correlation less than + 1 and can be combined to reduce risk. And the lower the correlation between the investments in a portfolio, the more they tend to move in opposite directions, and the greater the risk reduction.

Example

Risk of a Portfolio with Correlation Coefficient of + 1

Five years ago, Mike Shield invested in a portfolio of two stocks that were perfectly positively correlated (r = + 1). He invested an equal amount of money in each. The returns from this investment were:

[5] **Observation:** We have not illustrated the calculation of the expected return or standard deviation of Cathy's investments. Interested students are invited to check our numbers using the formats on pp. 271 and 273.

Year	Stock A	Stock B	Mike's Portfolio
1990	30%	30%	30%
1991	10	10	10
1992	−20	−20	−20
1993	50	50	50
1994	10	10	10
Average return	16%	16%	16%
Standard deviation	23.3%	23.3%	23.3%

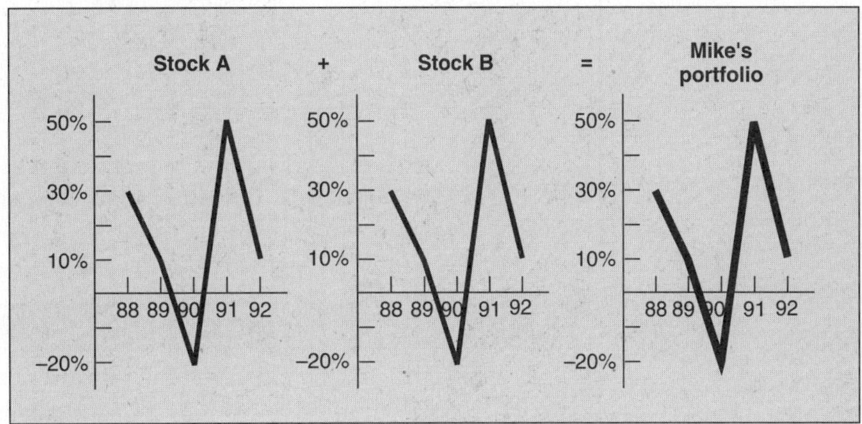

Since the two stocks moved precisely with one another, Mike's portfolio performed no differently than each of the individual stocks, and the portfolio had the same standard deviation as each stock. Diversification did not reduce risk.

Example

Risk of a Portfolio with Correlation Coefficient Between −1 and +1

Five years ago, Mike Shield invested in a second portfolio of two stocks that were somewhat positively correlated (r = +0.757). He invested an equal amount of money in each. The returns from this investment were:

Year	Stock A	Stock C	Mike's Portfolio
1990	30%	19%	24.5%
1991	10	38	24.0
1992	−20	−28	−24.0
1993	50	33	41.5
1994	10	18	14.0
Average return	16%	16%	16.0%
Standard deviation	23.3%	23.3%	21.9%

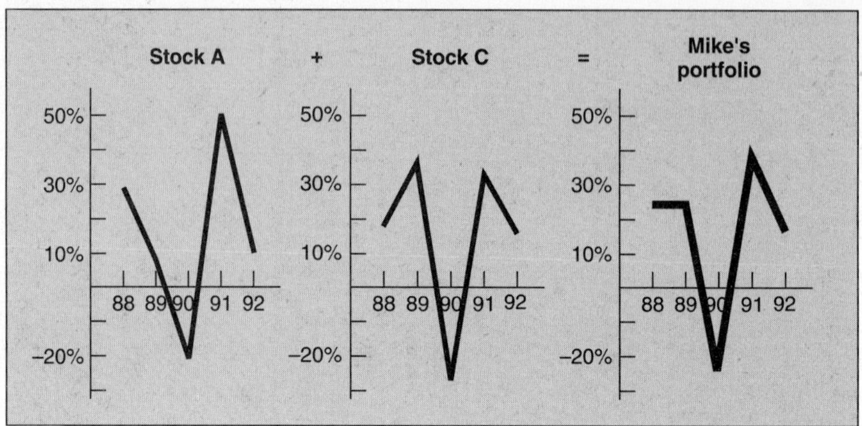

Since the two stocks did not move precisely with one another, Mike's portfolio had a lower standard deviation than each stock. Diversification reduced risk.

Example

Risk of a Portfolio with Correlation Coefficient of −1

Five years ago, Mike Shield invested in a third portfolio of two stocks that were perfectly negatively correlated (r = −1). He invested an equal amount of money in each. The returns from this investment were:

Year	Stock A	Stock D	Mike's Portfolio
1990	30%	2%	16%
1991	10	22	16
1992	−20	52	16
1993	50	−18	16
1994	10	22	16
Average return	16%	16%	16%
Standard deviation	23.3%	23.3%	0%

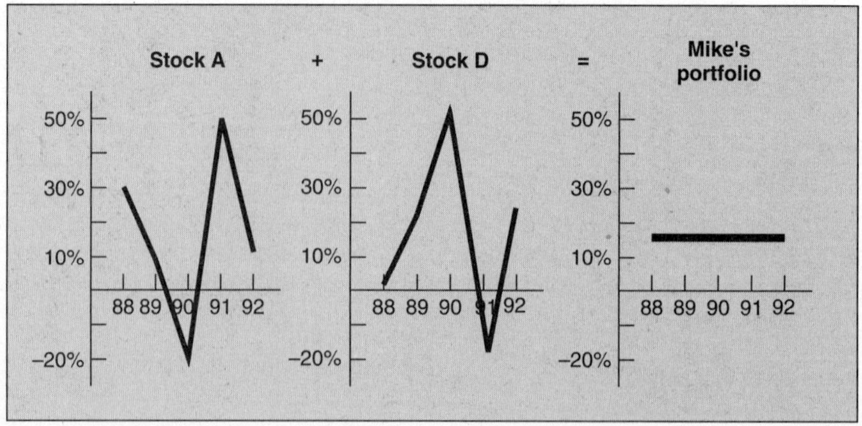

> Since the two stocks moved precisely opposite to one another, the upswings in one stock were cancelled out by the downswings from the other, and Mike's portfolio provided a constant rate of return. Diversification completely eliminated risk.

Both U.S. federal and state law recognize the risk reducing benefits from a portfolio and require financial institutions to hold a diverse portfolio of investments. Insurance companies, for example, must spread their investments among many securities, and banks can lend no more than a small portion of their assets to any one borrower. The many available **mutual funds** make it possible for every investor, even one with a small amount of money to invest, to own a share of a broadly diversified portfolio.

mutual fund—a pool of money from many investors which is invested in a portfolio of securities

4. Systematic and Unsystematic Risk

Total risk may be decomposed into two components: systematic risk and unsystematic risk. This division is important because diversification affects each component differently. In this section we identify these two components of total risk and begin the discussion of how investors can use diversification to reduce them.

All investments are tied in some way to the overall economy. When employment rises, or inflation goes down, or the dollar falls against foreign currencies every investment is affected in some way. The variability caused by these environmental risk sources is known as **systematic risk** because it is due to the overall economic system.

systematic risk—the variability in an investment's rate of return caused by factors that impact all investments

Systematic risk is what causes investments to be correlated. If companies that export are helped by a weaker dollar, all exporters will do better as a group if the dollar declines in value. At the same time, importers will fare worse as the falling dollar increases the price of foreign goods. A portfolio of the stocks of exporters would have a high degree of correlation, as would a portfolio composed only of the stocks of importers. A portfolio of some importers and some exporters would have a much lower correlation. In the same manner, companies in a given industry have a high degree of correlation since they tend to be affected similarly by economic events. As a result, a portfolio of only steel manufacturers would not be very diversified.

Unsystematic risk is the variability that is not shared by other companies. Much of a company's unsystematic risk comes from the variability in its internal processes—variability specific to that firm. Other sources of unsystematic risk are product successes and failures, patent and other legal issues, and personnel problems such as management shakeups and strikes. Since, by definition, the unsystematic risk of one company is unrelated to the unsystematic risk of other companies, there is no correlation between changes in rates of return due to these factors. This means that in *any* portfolio of securities, unsystematic movements tend to cancel each other out and lower risk—in the same way as Cathy Stewart's two-coin-flip portfolio reduced her risk.

unsystematic risk—the variability in an investment's rate of return caused by factors that only impact that investment

Figure 8.5 shows what happens when portfolios of various size are constructed at random, a process known as **naive diversification.** Small portfolios (at the left

naive diversification—the construction of a portfolio at random

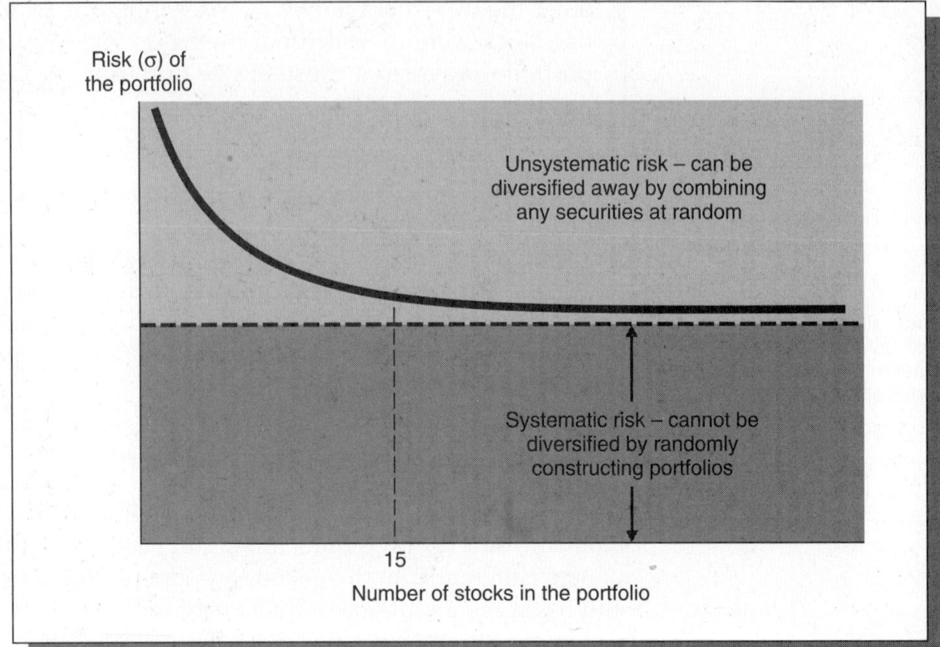

FIGURE 8.5
How unsystematic risk can be diversified away by naive diversification. Any portfolio of 15 or more securities has virtually no unsystematic risk.

side of the graph) have both systematic and unsystematic risk. In larger portfolios, unsystematic risk is diversified away as the unsystematic movements in each security's returns are offset by the unsystematic movements of the others. By the time the portfolio has grown to about 15 securities, most of the unsystematic risk has been eliminated. By contrast, systematic risk cannot be diversified away by naive diversification. This is because random combinations of securities will not necessarily have the low correlations required to reduce systematic risk. To reduce systematic risk through diversification, we must combine securities that have a low correlation with each other, not just combine securities at random.

In the same way that the returns from companies in a given industry tend to be more highly correlated than returns from companies chosen from a variety of industries, the securities of companies from one country are more highly correlated than an international selection of investments. This is because all companies in a country are affected by that country's economy while the economies of different countries are often not highly correlated. In the global economy, systematic risk comes only from those factors that have a consistent impact on more than one economy. Figure 8.6 points out that, compared to a portfolio composed only of domestic investments, an internationally diversified portfolio has less systematic risk, permitting much greater naive diversification.

5. Beta

characteristic line—the relationship of an investment's rate of return to the overall rate of return available in the market

It is useful to have a measure of systematic risk, the way each firm responds to changes in the overall economy. Figure 8.7 shows the **characteristic lines** of three investments, a plot of the rate of return from the investment versus the rate of re-

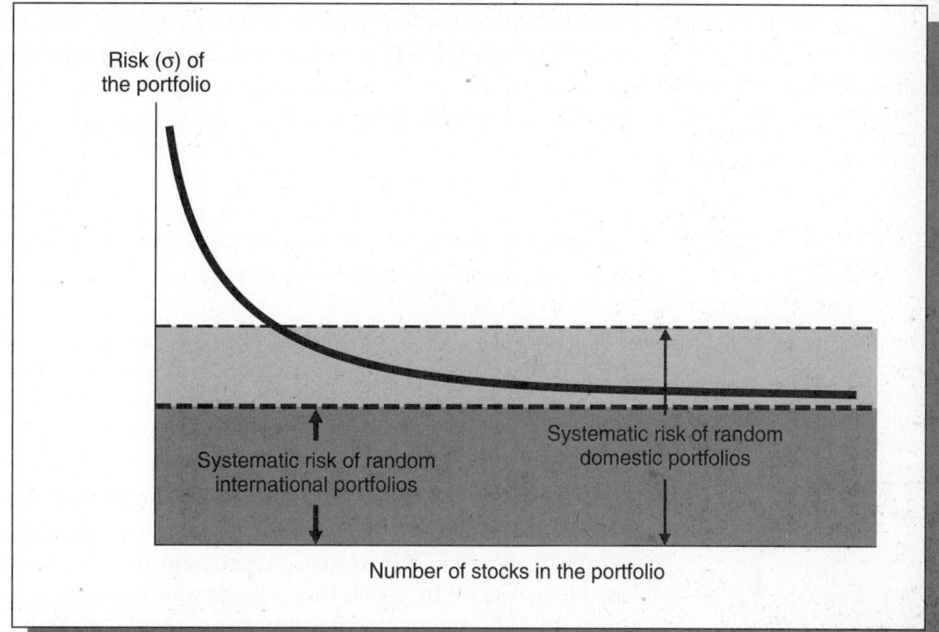

FIGURE 8.6
International naive diversification. Since economies are not perfectly correlated, diversifying internationally permits further risk reduction.

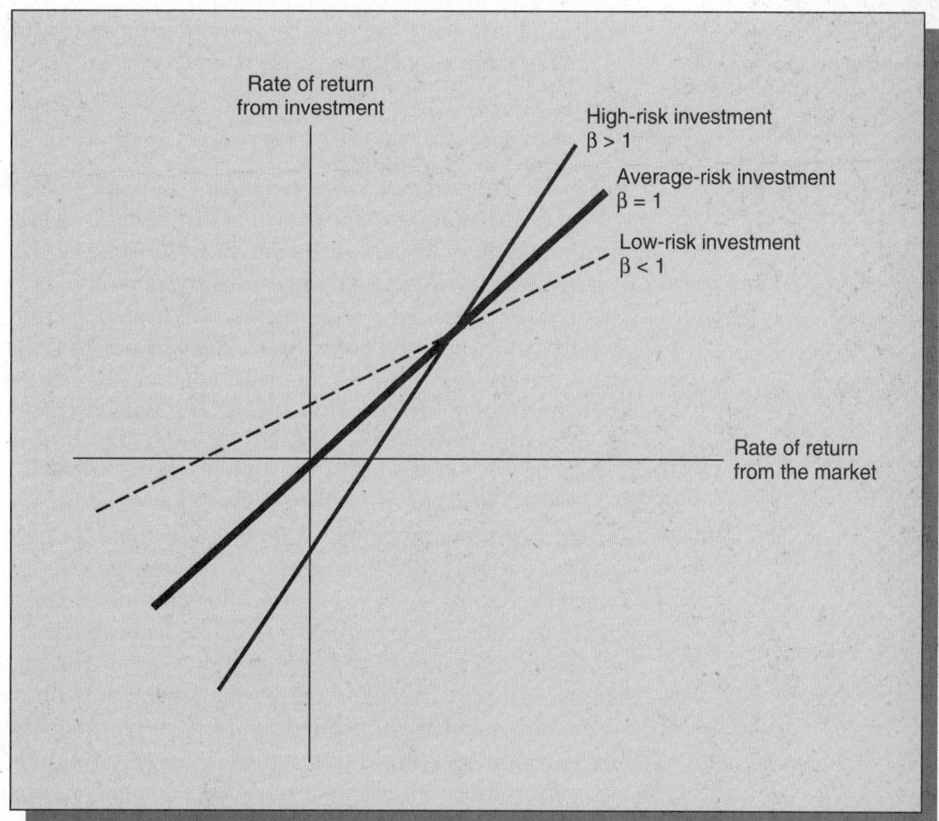

FIGURE 8.7
The characteristic lines of three securities. Beta, the slope of the line, measures how that security's returns respond to stock market movements.

turn available from investing in the economy as a whole. For convenience, the rate of return from the economy is typically measured by a major stock market index, such as the Standard & Poor's 500 stock index, and is called the **market return.** A low-risk investment has a characteristic line with a gradual slope, indicating that its rate of return is not too sensitive to changes in the economy. An average-risk investment has a characteristic line with a slope of 1 (a 45-degree line) and moves up and down at the same rate as the economy. A high-risk investment has a characteristic line with a steep slope, indicating that it is particularly sensitive to changes in the economy.

market return—the rate of return from the economy, commonly measured by a major stock market index

The slope of an investment's characteristic line is known as that investment's **beta.** Beta equals 1 for an average-risk investment, which means that the investment's rate of return closely follows the market. If the market moves up by 5%, an average-risk investment will also move up by 5%; if the market moves down by 5%, the investment will move down by 5%. A high-risk investment has a beta greater than 1: a 5% increase in the market will cause this investment to rise by more than 5%, while a 5% market decline will push this investment down by more than 5%. A low-risk investment has a beta less than 1, and a 5% change in the market will cause this investment to change by less than 5%. (Of course, no stock follows the market precisely—betas measure average responses to market movements over time.) Because it rises by a greater amount than the market when stock prices are rising, an investment with a beta above 1 is called an **aggressive security** and is sought after in an up market. By contrast, an investment with beta less than 1 moves by a smaller amount than the market and is known as a **defensive security** because it tends not to lose much of its value in a down market.

beta—the numerical relationship between the returns from an investment and the returns from the overall market

aggressive security—an investment with a beta greater than 1

defensive security—an investment with a beta less than 1

Industrial stocks in general tend to have values of beta that are distributed around the market average of 1. Securities of companies which are quite sensitive to condition of the economy, for example airlines like AMR, have high betas. Stocks of companies that are less influenced by the state of the economy, like Con Edison, have low betas. Figure 8.8 illustrates these points by listing the betas of the stocks that make up the Dow Jones industrial, transportation, and utility averages, three widely followed indexes of stock market performance constructed from groups of securities. All of the transportation stocks have a beta greater than 1, reflecting their high level of risk. The utilities, by contrast, have low betas which indicate their relative stability. In between are the betas of the industrial stocks which represent a broad cross-section of industries.

If a portfolio is sufficiently diversified so that all unsystematic risk has been eliminated, the only risk remaining is the systematic—the risk connected with the overall economy. As a result, for a well-diversified portfolio, its beta measures its risk. The beta of a portfolio, much like the expected return of a portfolio, can be calculated by taking the weighted average of the betas of its component investments. Adding another security changes the portfolio beta by the amount invested in the new security multiplied by the new security's beta. Therefore, beta captures the marginal risk of adding a security to a well-diversified portfolio. *In an environment in which investors diversify, beta becomes the appropriate measure of the risk of an investment.*

The Stocks that Make Up the Dow Jones Averages and Their Betas

30 Industrials		20 Transportations		15 Utilities	
Alcoa	1.20	Airborne Freight	1.50	American Electric Power	.65
American Express	1.50	Alaska Air	1.15	Centerior Energy	.55
Allied Signal	1.05	American President Lines	1.15	Commonwealth Edison	.65
AT&T	.95	AMR	1.35	Consolidated Edison	.75
Bethlehem Steel	1.35	Burlington Northern	1.15	Consolidated Natural Gas	.70
Boeing	1.05	Carolina Freightways	1.20	Detroit Edison	.70
Caterpillar	1.15	Conrail	1.30	Houston Industries	.60
Chevron	.75	Consolidated Freightways	1.15	Niagara Mohawk Power	.75
Coca Cola	1.15	CSX	1.20	North American Energy	.90
Walt Disney	1.25	Delta Airlines	1.15	Pacific Gas & Electric	.70
Du Pont	1.00	Federal Express	1.20	Panhandle Eastern	1.00
Exxon	.65	Norfolk Southern	1.10	Peoples Energy	.80
General Electric	1.15	Roadway Service	1.15	Philadelphia Electric	.70
General Motors	1.10	Ryder	NMF	Public Service Enterprises	.70
Goodyear	1.10	Santa Fe Pacific	1.25	SCE Corporation	.65
IBM	.90	Southwest Airlines	1.50		
International Paper	1.00	UAL	1.40		
Kodak	NMF	Union Pacific	1.05		
McDonalds	1.05	USAir Group	1.70		
Merck	1.10	XTRA	1.10		
JP Morgan	1.20				
Philip Morris	1.20				
Proctor & Gamble	1.10				
Sears	NMF				
Texaco	.65				
3M	1.45				
Union Carbide	NMF				
United Technologies	1.00				
Westinghouse	1.20				
Woolworth	1.25				

NMF = Nonmeaningful figure (insufficient or statistically insignificant data)

Reference: *The Value Line Investment Survey,* vol. 49, nos. 23–35, Feb 18–May 6, 1994.

FIGURE 8.8

Beta coefficients of the Dow Jones stocks. The Transportations are aggressive while the Utilities are defensive. The betas of the Industrials are distributed around the market average beta of 1.00.

7. The Security Market Line (SML)

security market line (SML)—a graph of investors' required rate of return as a function of an asset's portfolio (systematic) risk

It is common to summarize the risk-return relationship for a portfolio or for an asset held in a portfolio by using the **security market line (SML),** as shown in Figure 8.9. The SML illustrates the relationship between the expected return from investing in an asset and its portfolio risk. At the left of the graph are assets with no risk, which return the risk-free rate. Further to the right lie the risky assets. The graph's upward slope reflects investors' risk aversion as they insist on higher rates of return to compensate for taking on riskier investments.

Since the market average beta is 1.00, investments with betas equal to 1 reflect the risk of the market as a whole. These securities would be expected to provide a rate of return equal to that of the market in general, a rate known as the "rate of return on the market portfolio." This point is illustrated by the dotted lines on the graph.

The equation of the SML is that of a straight line:

$$\textit{Required rate of return} = r_f + (\textit{slope}) \times \beta$$
$$= r_f + (\textit{market price of risk}) \times \beta$$

market price of risk—the additional return demanded by investors to take on one unit of portfolio risk

where the slope is the price of portfolio risk, typically called the **market price of risk,** the added return required per unit of beta. In Figure 8.9, investors' required rate of return rises from the risk-free rate (r_f) to the required rate of return on the market portfolio (r_m) as beta goes from zero to one. Since the slope of a straight line is $\Delta y/\Delta x$, the market price of risk must be:

$$\frac{\Delta y}{\Delta x} = \frac{r_m - r_f}{1 - 0} = r_m - r_f$$

which is the difference between the rate of return currently required on an average risk stock or portfolio and today's risk-free rate. Including this detail, the SML can be written:

$$\textit{Required rate of return} = r_f + (r_m - r_f)\ \beta$$

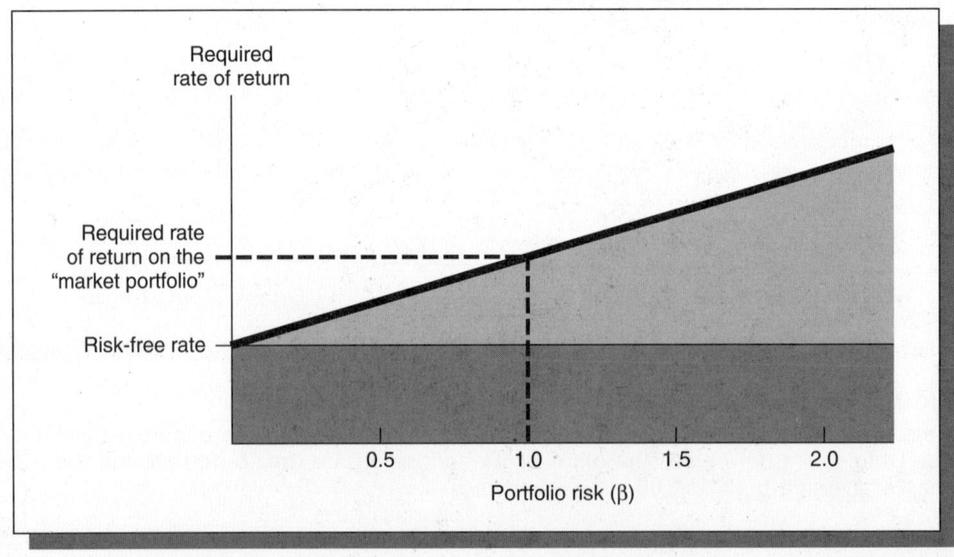

FIGURE 8.9
The security market line (SML). For an asset held as part of a portfolio, investors' required rate of return increases with portfolio risk (β).

Like the capital market line, this equation is also consistent with the additive version of the Fisher model:

$$\text{Nominal rate} = r_f + r_r$$
$$= r_f + (r_m - r_f)\ \beta$$

Here r_r, the risk premium, equals the market price of risk ($r_m - r_f$) multiplied by β, the portfolio risk of the investment.

Example

Using the Security Market Line to Obtain Required Rates of Return

AMR stock has a beta of 1.35, and Con Edison has a beta of .75. The risk-free rate is 5% and market price of risk is 8.5%.

Question: What is the required rate of return on a stock of average risk, on AMR stock, and on Con Edison stock?

Solution steps:

1. Average-risk stock—Recall that the average-risk stock has a beta of 1:

$$\text{Required rate} = r_f + (\text{market price of risk}) \times \beta$$
$$= 5\% + 8.5\% \times 1.00$$
$$= 5\% + 8.5\% = 13.5\%$$

2. AMR stock:

$$\text{Required rate} = r_f + (\text{market price of risk}) \times \beta$$
$$= 5\% + 8.5\% \times 1.35$$
$$= 5\% + 11.475\% = 16.475\%$$

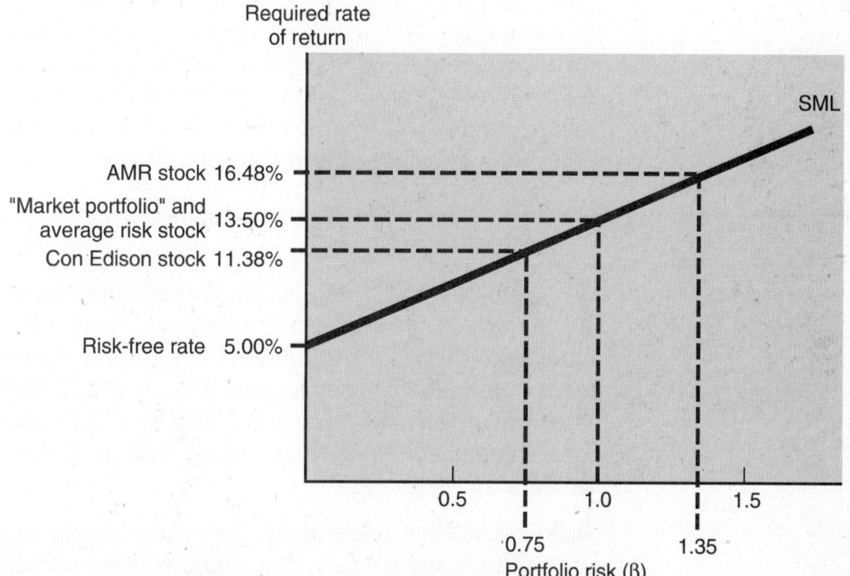

3. Con Edison stock:

$$\text{Required rate} = r_f + (\text{market price of risk}) \times \beta$$
$$= 5\% + 8.5\% \times 0.75$$
$$= 5\% + 6.375\% = 11.375\%$$

Answer: Investors will require a rate of return of 11.38% on the low-risk Con Edison stock, 13.50% on the average-risk stock, and 16.48% on the high-risk AMR stock.

Earlier we pointed out that an investor can eliminate unsystematic risk through naive diversification by simply constructing any portfolio of 15 or more investments. Since naive diversification is so easy and costless, the financial markets provide no added return to those who take on unsystematic risk. Eliminating systematic risk, on the other hand, is not costless but requires combining assets that do not respond in tandem to economic forces, the concept captured by beta. A low-beta investment, with its low correlation with the economy, tends to reduce the systematic risk of a portfolio, as opposed to a high-beta investment which can add risk. Accordingly, low-beta securities are highly desirable and sell at high prices and low rates of return. High-beta securities are risky, and investors insist on much higher rates of return as compensation.

As we shall explore more fully in the next chapter, investors use the required rate of return on an investment as an important input in setting an investment's market price. The security market line relationship, relating required rates of return to beta, thus also tells us something about the appropriate price for an asset that is likely to be held in a portfolio in the capital markets. As a result, finance theorists have given this model the name **capital asset pricing model (CAPM).**

capital asset pricing model (CAPM)—the finance model relating asset prices and rates of return to the asset's beta, its impact on the risk of a well-diversified portfolio

The security market line differs from the capital market line in that the CML relates return to total risk while the SML relates return to portfolio risk. The CML is the appropriate model to use when evaluating assets that will not be held in a portfolio, for example, when evaluating the worth of a small business fully owned by its founder who owns few other investments. The SML is the appropriate model to use when valuing a publicly traded security, one that most likely appears in many investment portfolios. This insight, that the correct measure of investment risk depends on the context in which investments are held, is one of the important discoveries of modern financial theory.

Cathy Stewart hung up the phone. She had just finished giving the good news to Mike Shield. Earlier that day she had convinced her company's president to withdraw the memo that had so enraged Mike and to empower a team of the affected employees to work on a better solution to the problem. Mike was clearly relieved, and Cathy also felt a lot better. As she reflected on Mike's complaint, she found herself a bit more comfortable with the issues the incident had triggered.

Risk comes from uncertainty, from not knowing what will happen. When people predict there will be risk, they increase their demands on the firm. The concept is the same whether the subject is rates of return provided to stockholders, product quality delivered to the customers, or the job environment as perceived by employees like Mike. An important role of managing is to reduce perceived risk levels to get the most from every contributor to the company's success.

For investors holding portfolios of securities, the relationship between Mike and the company was not very important. It was part of their unsystematic risk and was easy to diversify away. To Mike, on the other hand, his job was his only financial resource and not simply one component of a larger portfolio. Mike had no way to "diversify away" his on-the-job risk.

Cathy made a note to examine the systematic and unsystematic risk of her company's stock. She was certain that this would help her understand and then address the risk levels the company's stockholders were seeing. She sat back and smiled as she recognized how her understanding of finance had broad applicability throughout the company.

Summary of Key Points

- **Define *risk* and know why it is important to the financial manager.** Risk is the chance that an outcome might turn out to be worse than expected. It is important to financial managing because the firm's stakeholders are risk averters when it comes to investments of large amounts of time, energy, and money; they require additional compensation for assuming a greater amount of risk. As a result, high risk levels are costly—value can be added to the firm and all its stakeholders by keeping risk levels low.
- **State the relationship between risk and financial value.** The Fisher model of interest rates identifies risk premiums as an important component of rates. Financial values, the present values of expected future cash flows, are inversely related to interest rates. Accordingly, a firm that exposes its stakeholders to high risks must produce higher rates of return to adequately reward its stakeholders.
- **Describe the three primary sources of risk faced by a firm.** There are three sources of risk for the business firm. Environmental risk comes from changes external to the business—economic, technological, attitudinal, etc. Process risk results from unnecessary variability inside the firm. Combined, environmental risk and process risk are known as *business risk*. The third risk is financial risk, the added variability of the firm's profit and cash flow stream due to the firm's financing mix.
- **Measure the risk of a single security held by itself and relate this level of risk to investors' required rate of return.** Risk can be measured using basic statistical concepts. Forecasts of future events are translated into probability distributions. The expected value of the distribution measures the amount of return and, for a single investment, standard deviation measures the risk. The coefficient of variation is useful when comparing choices that differ significantly in expected return. The capital market line summarizes the return-risk relationship for a single asset.
- **Measure the risk of a security held in a diversified portfolio and relate this level of risk to investors' required rate of return.** Many investments are held as part of diversified portfolios. While the expected value of returns from a portfolio is an average of the expected values of the individual components, the standard deviation is not. Rather, it depends on the correlation between the returns from the portfolio's investments, and this enables portfolios to reduce investment risk. A high degree of positive correlation results in little risk reduction while a low or negative correlation permits much of the risk to be eliminated. At the extreme, investments with a perfect negative (–1) correlation can be combined to eliminate all of the risk. The capital asset pricing model shows that risk can be subdivided into the systematic and the unsystematic. Unsystematic risk, the variability of each investment that is not related to any other, can be eliminated with naive diversification (any combination of assets will suffice) and therefore carries no added rate of return. Systematic risk, the variability related to broad economic factors, affects all investments and is not so easily eliminated. To measure systematic risk, we calculate an investment's beta, the way in which its returns change with the economy. Since reducing systematic risk requires finding low-beta investments, beta is the relevant risk variable for investments held in diversified portfolios. The security market line provides the relationship of required rates of return to beta.

Questions

1. What is risk? Give an example of a risk faced by each of the following stakeholders:
   a. Customers
   b. Employees
   c. Suppliers
   d. Governments
   e. Neighbors
   f. Lenders
   g. Investors
2. If risk is the chance of loss, why is the standard deviation used as a risk measure when it measures variation both below and above the expected value?
3. Are you risk averse, risk neutral, or a risk seeker? Is your answer absolute or can you think of circumstances where you might have each of these attitudes?
4. Give an example of each of the following risks faced by the firm:
   a. Environmental risk
   b. Process risk
   c. Financial risk
5. When is the coefficient of variation a useful risk measurement concept?
6. What is a portfolio? Why do people diversify their investments? Why is it better to diversify across countries than only within one country?
7. Under what circumstance would the risk of a portfolio be the same as the riskiness of its component parts?
8. Why is it not too useful to diversify by buying the stocks of five companies in the same industry?
9. Why is naive diversification called *naive*? What does it do?
10. Comment on the accuracy of the following assertion: "It is easy to diversify away unsystematic risk, but it is impossible to eliminate systematic risk."
11. Even though the unsystematic risk within one company does not affect the risk of a holder of a large portfolio, it may still be relevant to that investor. Why?
12. What is the beta of a security? Connect it to the following concepts:
    a. Low-risk security
    b. Average-risk security
    c. High-risk security
    d. Aggressive security
    e. Defensive security
13. Why do transportation stocks have high betas while utilities have low betas?
14. Identify the:
    a. Capital market line
    b. Security market line

    Distinguish between them. When should each be used?
15. How would the security market line change if:
    a. Investors' forecast of inflation changed?
    b. Investors' level of risk aversion changed?
16. The AT&T company sponsors a well-known "Collegiate Investment Challenge," in which students simulate managing a $500,000 stock portfolio and compete to see who can produce the highest-value portfolio by the end of the game. What portfolio of stocks is likely to be the winning one?

Problems

1. **(Required rates of return)** U.S. Treasury bills currently return 4.5%. Determine the required rate on an investment with a risk premium of:
   a. 2%
   b. 4.5%
   c. 7%
   d. 9.5%
2. **(Required rates of return)** U.S. Treasury bills currently return 5%. Determine the risk premium investors are demanding if their required rate of return is:
   a. 5%
   b. 7.5%
   c. 10%
   d. 12.5%
3. **(Probability distributions of returns)** Investors have made the following forecast about the returns from investing in securities issued by two companies:

State of the economy	Probability of this state of the economy
Boom	15% = .15
Good times	25 = .25
Average times	35 = .35
Bad times	20 = .20
Recession	5 = .05
	100% = 1.00

State of the economy	Rate of Return from Company A	Company B
Boom	50%	25%
Good times	30	20
Average times	20	15
Bad times	−5	5
Recession	−25	0

a. Graph each probability distribution.
b. Calculate the expected return of each distribution.
c. Calculate the standard deviation of each distribution.
d. In terms of total risk, which security is riskier? How do you conclude this?

4. **(Probability distribution of returns)** Investors have made the following forecast about the returns from investing in securities issued by two companies:

State of the economy	Probability of this state of the economy
Boom	5% = .05
Good times	20 = .20
Average times	50 = .50
Bad times	15 = .15
Recession	10 = .10
	100% = 1.00

State of the economy	Rate of Return from Company C	Company D
Boom	25%	50%
Good times	20	30
Average times	15	20
Bad times	5	−5
Recession	0	−25

a. Graph each probability distribution.
b. Calculate the expected return of each distribution.
c. Calculate the standard deviation of each distribution.
d. In terms of total risk, which security is riskier? How do you conclude this?

5. **(Coefficient of variation)** Using the forecasts of Problem 3:

a. Calculate the coefficient of variation for each security.
b. Which security is riskier according to the standard deviation?
c. Which security is riskier according to the coefficient of variation?
d. Why do the two measures give the results they do?

6. **(Coefficient of variation)** Securities E and F have the following expected returns and standard deviations:

	E	F
Expected return	10%	65%
Standard deviation	8%	25%

a. Calculate the coefficient of variation for each security.
b. Which security is riskier according to the standard deviation?
c. Which security is riskier according to the coefficient of variation?
d. Why do the two measures give the results they do?

7. **(The capital market line)** The risk free rate of interest is 4% and the price of total risk is 0.5.

a. Write the equation of the capital market line.
b. What is the required rate of return on a security with a standard deviation of 5%?
c. What is the required rate of return on a security with a standard deviation of 10%?
d. What is the required rate of return on a security with a standard deviation of 15%?

8. **(The capital market line)** The capital market line is given by:

$$\text{Required rate} = .06 + 0.4\ \sigma$$

a. What is the risk-free rate of interest?
b. What is the value of the price of total risk?
c. What is the required rate of return on a security with a standard deviation of 12%?
d. What is the standard deviation of a security with a required rate of return of 14%

9. **(Rate of return on a portfolio)** A portfolio has been constructed from the following securities:

Security	Expected return	Amount invested
K	15%	\$5,000
L	9	3,000
M	20	2,000

a. What is the expected rate of return from this portfolio?
b. If Security L is sold, what will be the expected return of the remaining two-stock portfolio?
c. If the investor buys \$10,000 of Security N, with expected return of 12%, and adds it to the portfolio, what will be the expected return of the resulting four-stock portfolio?

d. If the investor sells $2,000 of Security K, what will be the expected return of the remaining three-stock portfolio?

10. **(Rate of return on a portfolio)** A portfolio has been constructed from the following securities:

Security	Expected return	Amount invested
P	5%	$40,000
Q	18	25,000
R	15	35,000

a. What is the expected rate of return from this portfolio?
b. If Security Q is sold, what will be the expected return of the remaining two-stock portfolio?
c. If the investor buys $50,000 of Security S, with expected return of 10%, and adds it to the portfolio, what will be the expected return of the resulting four-stock portfolio?
d. If the investor sells $20,000 of Security R, what will be the expected return of the remaining three-stock portfolio?

11. **(Risk of a portfolio)** Stocks T, U, and V have provided the following returns to investors over the past five years:

Year	Stock T	Stock U	Stock V
1990	15%	15%	5%
1991	−10	−10	30
1992	20	20	0
1993	35	35	−15
1994	5	5	15

a. What was the average annual rate of return on each stock?
b. What would have been the average rate of return on a portfolio composed of 50% of Stock T and 50% of Stock U?
c. What would have been the average rate of return on a portfolio composed of 50% of Stock T and 50% of Stock V?
d. Which securities are positively correlated? negatively correlated?

12. **(Risk of a portfolio)** You are thinking of investing half of your money into each of two stocks, both of which have a 50%–50% chance of earning 25% or earning only 5%.

a. What is the expected rate of return from each stock?
b. What is the standard deviation of returns from each stock?
c. What is the standard deviation of your planned portfolio?
d. Why have you lowered your risk by investing in the two securities instead of just one?

13. **(Beta)** ABC Transport has a beta of 1.3 while Central Gas and Power has a beta of .70

a. Which stock is aggressive?
b. Which stock is defensive?
c. If the market rose by 20%, what would happen to the value of each on average?
d. If the market fell by 10%, what would happen to the value of each on average?

14. **(Beta)** Classify the following stocks as aggressive, average, or defensive and identify if its beta is less than 1, equal to 1, or greater than 1:

a. Stock rises by 30% in response to a market rise of 20%.
b. Stock rises 10% in response to a market rise of 10%.
c. Stock falls 15% in response to a market decline of 20%.
d. Stock falls 10% in response to a market decline of 10%.

15. **(Beta of a portfolio)** ABC Transport has a beta of 1.3 while Central Gas and Power (CGP) has a beta of .70. What is the beta of a portfolio of these two securities if the amount of each is:

a. 20% ABC, 80% CGP?
b. 40% ABC, 60% CGP?
c. 60% ABC, 40% CGP?
d. 80% ABC, 20% CGP?

16. **(Beta of a portfolio)** A portfolio manager currently holds a diversified portfolio of 30 stocks. The amount invested in each stock is $10,000, and the portfolio beta is 1.05. What would happen to the portfolio beta under each of the following scenarios?

a. Another stock is added to the portfolio: amount $10,000, beta 1.05.
b. One of the stocks with beta 1.05 is sold.
c. Another stock is added to the portfolio: amount $10,000, beta 1.50.
d. One of the stocks with beta 0.75 is sold.

17. **(The security market line)** The risk-free rate of interest is 7%, and the risk premium for a stock with beta of 1 is 6%. XXX stock has a beta of 0.85, and YYY stock has a beta of 1.2.

a. What is the equation of the SML?
b. Draw the SML.
c. What is the required rate of return on XXX stock?
d. What is the required rate of return on YYY stock?

18. **(The security market line)** The pure rate of interest is 3%, investors demand a 5% inflation premium on long-term investments, and the risk premium for a stock with beta of 1 is 7%. ZZZ stock has a beta of 1.35.
    a. What is the required rate of return on ZZZ stock?
    b. Suppose investors increase their inflation premium to 6%. What is the new required rate of return on ZZZ stock?
    c. Now suppose investors increase their risk premium for a stock with beta of 1 to 8% (the inflation premium is still 5%). What is the new required rate of return on ZZZ stock?
    d. Now suppose investors decrease their estimate of ZZZ's beta to 1.25% (the inflation premium is still 5%, and the risk premium is still 7%). What is the new required rate of return on ZZZ stock?

CHAPTER 9
VALUATION

"I know it's difficult to forecast stock prices." Steve Payne listened carefully as the CFO of his firm continued. "But in order to raise money for the company at the cheapest cost, we have to have a pretty good sense of whether our stock price is relatively low or high. Otherwise, we'll never know the right time to sell new shares".

Steve was a recent business school graduate working in the company's finance group. Because of its rapid rate of growth in recent years, his company found itself making frequent trips to the financial markets to raise funds through bond and stock sales. Steve had been assigned to participate on a team modeling the value of the firm's securities. He looked around the room; every member of the team was present. Steve returned his attention to the CFO, who was still speaking.

"If we can sell shares when our stock price is at a relative high, we don't have to sell so many shares to raise our target amount of money. This means less dilution for existing shareholders." The CFO concluded his remarks with encouragement for the team.

As the CFO left the room, Steve joined the other members of his team to brainstorm an approach to the problem. He looked forward to getting to know the other team members. Most of all, he felt comfortable that he could apply what he had learned in his finance courses to this assignment.

The problem Steve's team is grappling with is one of the most fundamental in finance. Every company that raises funds from outside investors must make decisions about the timing of security issues. A financial manager who can consistently raise money when security prices are relatively high can save the business a lot of money.

The value of a company's securities is of considerable importance to financial managers for other reasons as well. Recall from our discussion of the goal of the firm in Chapter 2 that when a company successfully exceeds the expectations of its customers and other stakeholders, it will grow and prosper. This will increase the value of the firm, hence the value of its securities, rewarding existing investors. New investors will be attracted to the firm, further increasing the demand for its securities and putting additional upward pressure on their prices. And, since the long-term goal of the firm is to maximize the wealth of its shareholders through a high stock price, understanding the valuation of securities is an important part of understanding the financial results of publicly-owned companies.

Key Points You Should Learn from This Chapter

After reading this chapter you should be able to:

- Discuss why the value of a security is a present value and is independent of how long an investor plans to hold it.
- Describe the difference between value and price.
- Calculate the value and yield of traditional, zero-coupon, and perpetual bonds.
- Calculate the value and yield of preferred stock.
- Calculate the value and rate of return of common stock.
- Discuss the characteristics of options on common stock.

Introductory Concepts—What Is Value?

Valuation is the process of establishing the worth of a stream of cash flows. Any set of cash flows may be valued, regardless of their source. In this chapter we examine the cash flows leaving the firm to service its securities — stocks and bonds. In later chapters we will use the same concepts to value the cash flows from the firm's internal investments.

The ability to place a value on money flows is one of the most important jobs of financial managers. Most business decisions have a financial impact, and financial managers serve as a key resource to others in the firm, helping them to understand the money value of alternative courses of action. Financial managers are also responsible for the firm's relationship to investors; in this capacity they must understand how the decisions of the firm affect the value of the firm's bonds and stock.

required rate of return—the minimum acceptable rate of return on an investment which will appropriately compensate the investor for time and risk

The basic valuation model used in this chapter is the present value model: a security's value is the present value of the cash flows its holder expects to receive. The interest rate used to calculate the present values must be the rate the investor needs to earn to justify buying the series of cash flows. As we saw in Chapter 6, this rate must take into account the overall level of interest rates as well as the riskiness of the cash flows.[1] We call this rate, which differs for each investment, the **required rate of return.** Investors who pay the calculated value and receive the anticipated cash flows will indeed earn their required rate of return.

Example

Finding the Value of a Cash Flow

Steve Payne is considering the purchase of a note which promises one payment: $1,000 in exactly one year. He anticipates receiving the $1,000 on schedule, and requires a 15% return if he is to make this investment.

Question: What is the value of this note to Steve?

Solution steps: Calculate the present value of the cash flow Steve anticipates receiving:

CLEAR the time value part of your calculator

Key in 1,000 and press FV

Key in 1 and press n

Key in 15 and press i

Compute PV = −869.57

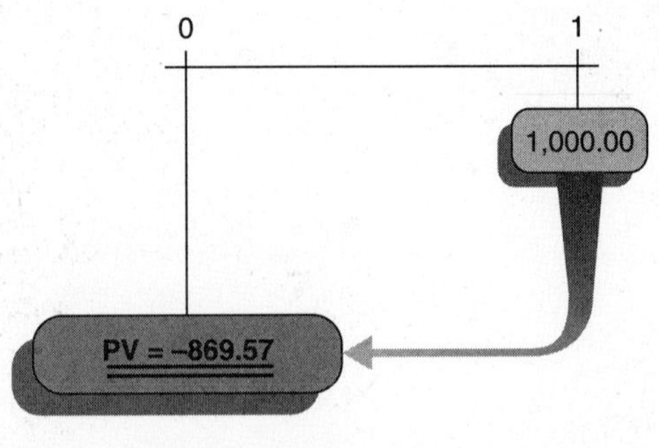

Answer: The note is worth $869.57 to Steve. If he pays this amount and receives the $1,000 in one year, he will earn his required rate of return of 15%.

[1] **Cross-reference:** For review, refer back to the Fisher model of interest rates on pages 206–210.

Check on answer:

CLEAR the time value part of your calculator

Key in −869.57 and press PV

Key in 1,000 and press FV

Key in 1 and press n

Compute i = 15%

An important concept which applies to all the financial instruments in this chapter is that the value of a security is independent of how long the investor actually plans to hold it. We will take advantage of this insight to simplify our modeling by calculating values as if each security is held until its maturity date (forever, in the case of a perpetual security). The reason is straightforward. To sell a security prior to its maturity date requires finding another investor. That investor, using the same valuation process, will be willing to pay an amount equal to the present value of the remaining cash flows, the same value the original investor would receive by not selling. Therefore, investors will forecast that they will receive the same cash benefits no matter how long they hold the security.

Examples

Value Does Not Depend on Holding Period

Steve is looking at another note, which pays $500.00 at the end of each of the next two years. He again anticipates that the issuer will pay on schedule and requires a 15% return on his money.

Question: What is the value of this note to Steve if he plans to hold it for the full two years?

Solution steps: Calculate the present value of the cash flows Steve anticipates receiving:

CLEAR the time value part of your calculator

Key in 500 and press PMT, set END

Key in 2 and press n

Key in 15 and press i

Compute PV = −812.85

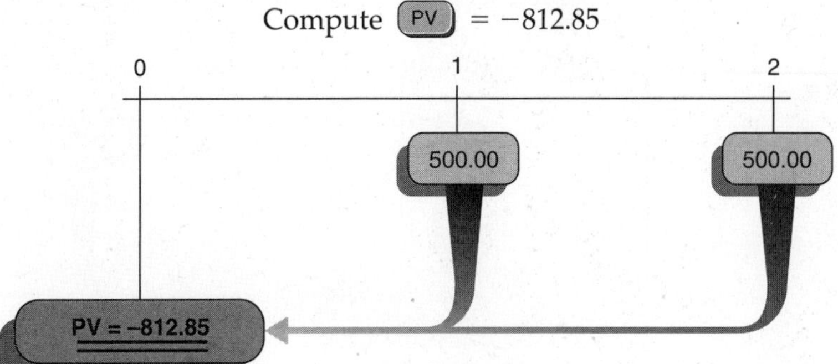

Answer: The note is worth $812.85 to Steve.

Question: What would the note be worth to Steve if he planned to sell it immediately after receiving the first $500 in one year.

Solution steps: Steve will receive the first $500 payment plus the market value of the note when he sells it in one year.

1. Find the market value of the note in one year. This will be the value of the note to investors at that time, the present value of the second $500 to be received in another year:

   CLEAR the time value part of your calculator
   Key in 500 and press FV
   Key in 1 and press n
   Key in 15 and press i
   Compute PV = −434.78

   Steve forecasts he will sell the note for $434.78 in one year.
2. Summarize the cash flows Steve anticipates: in one year he expects to receive the first $500 payment plus $434.78 from selling the note = $934.78.
3. Calculate the present value of Steve's anticipated cash flows:

   CLEAR the time value part of your calculator
   Key in 934.78 and press FV
   Key in 1 and press n
   Key in 15 and press i
   Compute PV = −812.85

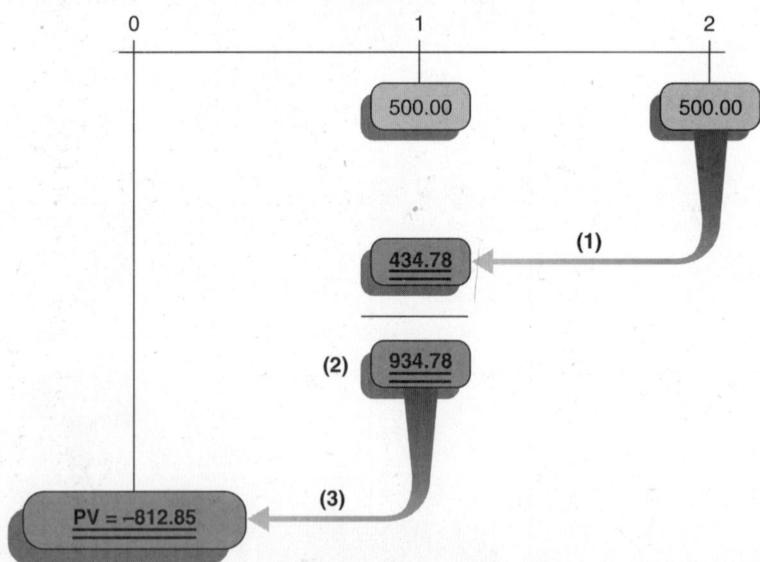

Answer: The note is worth $812.85 to Steve, *the same value he calculated assuming he held it until maturity!*

Value Vs. Price

There is an important distinction between value and price. In this chapter we discuss *value,* what something is worth. *Price* refers to what something sells for. We know from our everyday experience that not all things carry a price equal to their value. In fact, in many cases, price and value differ considerably. For example, air is free, yet it is invaluable to life. By contrast, precious gems are priced well above their value to most people.

For securities, the relationship of price to value depends upon the level of efficiency of the financial marketplace. If the market is efficient, so that a security's price reflects all information about that company, then price equals value. Academic studies of the security markets have generally found a high degree of efficiency.[2] However, not all markets have been extensively studied, and there are many investors who believe there are significant inefficiencies in some markets. They look for companies with prices substantially different from value to purchase securities when they are "undervalued" and sell them when they are "overvalued." These investors fall into two groups:[3]

1. Technical analysts—those who believe that mass psychology (fear, greed, exuberance, etc.) are significant factors in the setting of prices. They study investors' behavior and trends of security prices to detect investors' attitudes. Technical analysts predict price movements as continuations or reversals of these trends. They generally pay little attention to value but buy, sell, or hold based on their predictions of price movements.
2. Fundamental analysts—those who believe that security prices tend to oscillate around their values. At any particular time, however, a security's price could differ significantly from its value due to faulty or incomplete examination of economic and other information by security analysts. Fundamental analysts study company, industry, economic, and political data looking for clues to value that other analysts have missed. They avoid predicting price movements other than to assert that mispriced securities will eventually be priced correctly as other analysts discover the insights they have unearthed.

The more the future cash flows from an investment are uncertain, the more opportunity there is for price to diverge from value.[4] Investors have a much easier time forecasting the future cash flows from a bond—which specifies the cash flows it promises to pay—than from a share of common stock, where future cash flows depend upon the firm's future economic performance. As a result, price is generally close to value for notes and bonds. Technical and fundamental analysts pay most of their attention to stocks.

[2] **Cross-reference:** Security market efficiency is discussed on pp. 30–31 and pp. 709–711.

[3] **Cross-reference:** We discuss these two approaches to investing a bit further in Chapter 19, pp. 708–709.

[4] **Observation and cross-reference:** And as we saw in Chapter 8, there will be more risk and investors will require a higher rate of return.

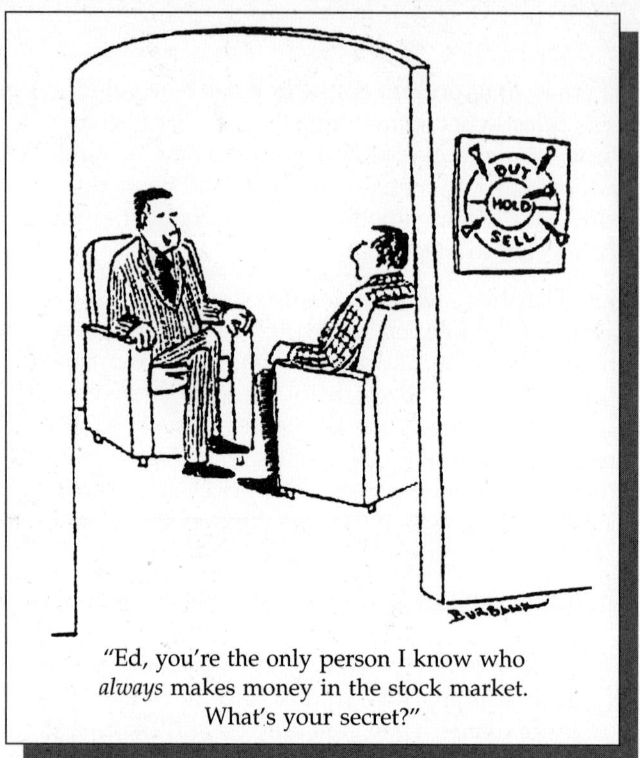

"Ed, you're the only person I know who *always* makes money in the stock market. What's your secret?"

Bond Valuation

The cash flows from a bond anticipated by investors are the regular (coupon) interest payments plus the payment of the face, or maturity, value promised in the bond indenture.

1. Traditional Bond

traditional bond—a bond that returns a fixed periodic interest payment plus a fixed principal value at maturity

coupon— the amount of cash interest paid annually by a bond

A **traditional bond** has both an interest **coupon** and a face value. Interest is normally paid at six-month intervals, so the appropriate version of investors' required rate of return is their effective semiannual rate (ESR). As we will examine further in Chapter 21, corporate bonds typically have a maturity value of \$1,000, and a bond's coupon rate multiplied by its face value defines the annual interest payment.

An investor who buys a traditional bond purchases two cash flow streams: the interest payments—which form an annuity, and the face value—a single future value at the bond's maturity date. In formula terms, the present value of a traditional bond is therefore:

$$\text{Price of bond} = \text{PV of interest annuity} + \text{PV of face value}$$

$$= \text{PMT}\left(\frac{1 - \dfrac{1}{(1 + r)^n}}{r}\right) + \text{FV}\left(\frac{1}{(1 + r)^n}\right)$$

$$= \text{PMT} \times \text{PVAF} + \text{FV} \times \text{PVF}$$

Just like all present value problems, we can find the price of a traditional bond in any of three ways.

- We can use the full mathematical formula, substituting in the bond's semiannual interest payment for **PMT,** the bond's face value for **FV,** the number of half-years to maturity for **n,** and investors' semiannual required rate of return for **r.**
- We can use time value tables, looking up present value factors for the interest annuity (**PVAF**) and for the face value (**PVF**) for our values of **n** and **r.**
- We can use our financial calculators, plugging in the values for **i, n, PMT,** and **FV,** and solving for **PV** in one calculation.

Although we encourage you to be aware of each of these three solution methods, we will continue to solve the example problems in this book using the financial calculator.

Example

Value of a Traditional Bond

Steve is considering the purchase of a traditional bond issued by Lydan Corporation, which has a $1,000 face value, a 12% coupon paid semi-annually, and which matures in 25 years. He anticipates that Lydan will make payments on schedule, and he requires a rate of return of 6% per half-year if he is to make this investment.

Question: What is the value of this bond to Steve?

Solution steps:

1. Identify the cash flows Steve anticipates receiving: With a 12% coupon, the bond pays 12% of $1,000 = $120 per year, or $60 each half-year for 50 half-years. He will also be paid the bond's face value when it matures 50 half-years from now.

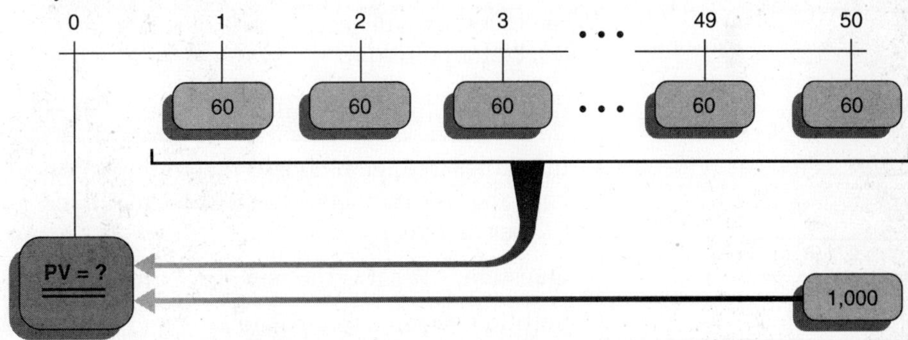

2. Calculate the present value of these cash flows:

CLEAR the time value part of your calculator
Key in 60 and press PMT, set END
Key in 1,000 and press FV
Key in 50 and press n
Key in 6 and press i
Compute PV = −1000

Answer: The bond is worth $1,000 to Steve, its face value.

par bond—a bond with a price equal to its face value

discount bond—a bond with a price less than its face value

premium bond—a bond with a price greater than its face value

Because this bond carries an interest coupon (12% annually, or 6% per half-year) exactly equal to Steve's required rate of return, it is worth precisely its face value to him. And if the consensus of investors is that 6% per half-year is the appropriate required rate of return, the bond will be a **par bond**, priced at its face value as well. However, if a bond pays a coupon different from investors' required rate of return, it will sell at either a **discount** from, or a **premium** to, its face value.

When investors require a rate of return greater than a bond's coupon, the bond will sell at a discount.

Example

Bond Selling at a Discount

Investors have revised their opinion of the Lydan Corporation bond (perhaps they perceive greater risk) and now require a rate of return of 7% per half-year.

Question: What is the new price of this bond?

Solution steps: Recalculate the bond's present value at a 7% rate:

CLEAR the time value part of your calculator

Key in 60	and press PMT, set END
Key in 1,000	and press FV
Key in 50	and press n
Key in **7**	and press i

Compute PV = −861.99

Answer: The bond is now selling for $861.99, a discount of ($1,000 − 861.99 =) $138.01 from its face value.

When investors will accept a rate of return lower than a bond's coupon, the bond will sell at a premium.

Example

Bond Selling at a Premium

Investors have again revised their opinion of the Lydan Corporation bond (perhaps the risk they perceive has declined) and now require a rate of return of 5% per half-year.

Question: What is the new price of this bond?

Solution steps: Recalculate the bond's present value at a 5% rate:

CLEAR the time value part of your calculator

Key in 60	and press PMT, set END
Key in 1,000	and press FV
Key in 50	and press n
Key in **5**	and press i

Compute PV = −1,182.56

Answer: The bond is now selling for $1,182.56, a premium of ($1,182.56 − 1,000.00 =) $182.56 above its face value.

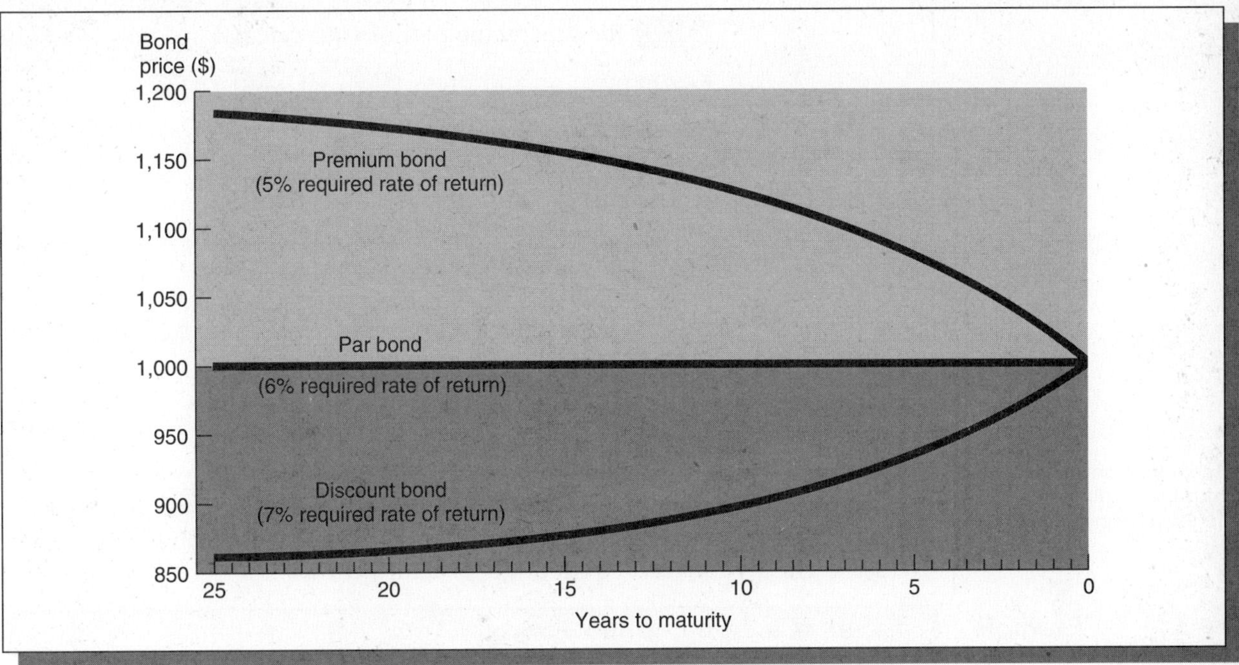

FIGURE 9.1
Price change of Lydan bonds over time (assuming investors' required rate of return remains constant). A bond's price converges on its face value as it approaches maturity.

Even if investors' required rate of return does not vary, the price of a discount or premium bond will change over time. With each passing year, investors are closer to receiving the bond's maturity value. As a result, a bond's present value is less affected by the discounting process (fewer periods of discounting) and it approaches its face value. Thus, the prices of all bonds converge on maturity value as the years go by. Figure 9.1 summarizes this pattern.

Example

Change in a Bond's Value as It Approaches Maturity

Investors still require a rate of return of 5% per half-year from the Lydan Corporation bond. Last year, with 50 half-years until maturity, they priced it at $1,182.56 (previous example). One year has now passed.

Question: What is the new price of this bond?

Solution steps: Recalculate the bond's present value now that it has only 48 half-years of life remaining:

CLEAR the time value part of your calculator

Key in 60 and press PMT, set END

Key in 1,000 and press FV

Key in 48 and press n

Key in 5 and press i

Compute PV = −1,180.77

Answer: The bond's price has declined to $1,180.77, a reduction of ($1,182.56 − 1,180.77) = $1.79.

2. Zero-Coupon Bond

zero-coupon bond—a bond which makes no cash interest payments

Zero-coupon bonds have no coupon, only a final maturity value. Since there are no cash interest payments, we do not have to use an interest rate that matches any particular payment period. Instead, we can value "zeros" directly by using investors' effective *annual* required rate of return (EAR).

Example

Value of a Zero-Coupon Bond

Steve is also considering the purchase of a $1,000 face value, zero-coupon bond that matures in 18 years. He requires an annual rate of return of 13% to make this investment.

Question: What is the value of this bond to Steve?

Solution steps:

1. Steve will receive only one cash flow from this bond: its face value when it matures 18 years from now.

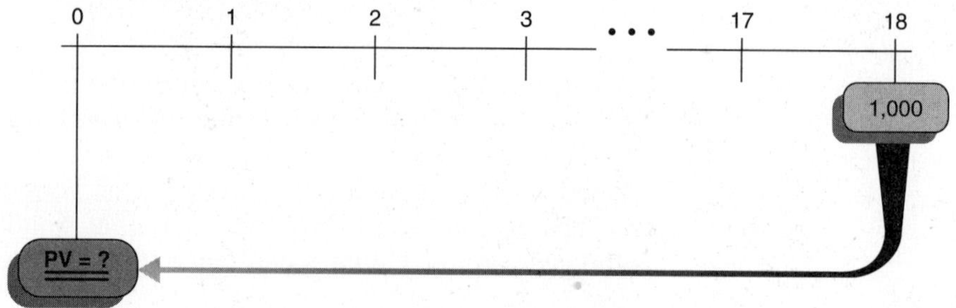

2. Calculate the present value of these cash flows:

CLEAR the time value part of your calculator

Key in 1,000 and press FV

Key in 18 and press n

Key in 13 and press i

Compute PV = −110.81

Answer: The bond is worth $110.81 to Steve, a deep discount from its face value.

deep discount bond—a bond with a price significantly less than its face value

When a bond sells at a price significantly below its face value, it is said to be selling at a **deep discount.** Zero-coupon bonds with more than a few years remaining until maturity must sell at a deep discount since the entire return has to come from the difference between their price and maturity value.

3. Perpetual Bond

perpetual bond—a bond with no maturity date

There are some bonds that have a perpetual lifetime with no maturity date. For such a **perpetual bond,** the appropriate present value model is the perpetuity model:[5]

$$\text{PV} = \frac{\text{PMT}}{\text{r}}$$

The payment is the interest coupon "C," and the interest rate is investors' required rate of return "r_b" where the subscript "b" stands for bonds. If interest is paid on a semi-annual basis, this is investors' required effective semi-annual rate (ESR). For a perpetual bond, therefore, the present value model is written:

$$Value = PV = \frac{C}{r_b}$$

Example

Value of a Perpetual Bond

The British government issued perpetual bonds in the year 1815 with a £1,000 face value and a 3% coupon paid semi-annually. Today the market demands a 7% annual yield on these bonds.

Question: What is the value of each bond?

Solution steps:

1. Determine the semi-annual interest coupon:

$$\text{Annual coupon} = 3\% \text{ of } £1{,}000 = £30$$

$$\text{Semi-annual coupon} = £30\ /\ 2 = £15$$

2. Determine the required effective semi-annual rate (ESR):[6]

$$(1.07)^{1/2} - 1 = 3.4408\%$$

3. Apply the model for the present value of a perpetuity:

$$\text{Value} = \text{PV} = \frac{\text{C}}{\text{r}_\text{b}}$$

$$= \frac{£15}{.034408} = £435.95$$

Answer: Each bond is worth £435.95 to an investor who wishes to earn 7%.

---

[5] **Cross-reference:** The perpetuity present value model was introduced in Chapter 5 on pg. 177.

[6] **Cross-reference:** Converting from an effective rate to an equivalent effective rate for a different time period is discussed in Chapter 5, pp. 182–184.

4. Nontraditional Bonds

A company will sometimes issue a bond with a nontraditional mix of interest coupons and face value to meet a specific need. The value of such a bond remains the present value of its cash flows. While perhaps slightly more difficult to calculate, the concept and meaning of the bond's value are unchanged.

5. Yield-to-Maturity

yield-to-maturity—the rate of return an investor would earn from a bond if it were purchased at today's price and held until its maturity date—provided it made all promised payments

So far, we have been calculating a bond's value given its promised cash flows and investors' required rate of return. However, we can reverse the calculation. Given the bond's promised cash flows and its price, we can calculate the rate of return an investor who paid today's price would earn. If we consider all the bond's promised cash flows—from today until its maturity date—the rate of return we calculate is called the bond's **yield-to-maturity** (YTM).

Example

Calculating Yield-to-Maturity

A bond issued by the Gary Corporation has a $1,000 maturity value, a 7% coupon paid semi-annually, and is due to mature in ten years. It is currently selling for a price of $885.[7]

Question: What is the yield-to-maturity of this bond?

Solution steps:

1. Identify the cash flows promised by this bond: With a 7% coupon, the bond will pay 7% of $1,000 = $70 per year or $35 each half-year for the next 20 half-years. It will also pay its $1,000 maturity value 20 half-years from now.
2. Calculate the interest rate embedded in these cash flows:

   CLEAR the time value part of your calculator

   Key in 35 and press PMT, set END

   Key in 1,000 and press FV

   Key in 20 and press n

   Key in −885 and press PV

   Compute i = 4.3745% per half-year
3. Annualize the interest rate:[8]

$$\text{YTM} = (1.043745)^2 - 1 = 8.94\%$$

Answer: The bond's yield to maturity is 8.94%.

[7] **Elaboration:** This price would be quoted in the financial press and by bond traders as 88 1/2, meaning 88.5% of maturity value.

[8] **Elaboration:** It is common practice to quote bond yields as *nominal* annual rates rather than effective annual rates, a number called the "bond equivalent yield." Thus, the financial press would report the yield on this bond as:

$$4.3745\% \times 2 = 8.75\%$$

Investors wishing to spend a bond's interest income—for example elderly persons using investment income to supplement social security and/or pensions—prefer a bond's yield to come in the form of regular cash interest payments. Other investors without the need for current cash flow from their bond investments—for example, younger persons with sufficient current income from their jobs—often prefer to postpone taking cash from a bond investment, especially since that also postpones taxes on that income. The yield-to-maturity from a bond can be subdivided into the **current yield,** the portion of the yield that comes from the interest coupon, and the **capital gains (or loss) yield**, the portion of the yield that comes from the growth (or decline) in the bond's value. The current yield for a period of time is calculated as the periodic interest coupon divided by the beginning-of-period market price:

current yield—the portion of a bond's yield coming from interest payments

capital gains yield—the portion of a security's yield coming from growth in value

$$\textit{Current yield} = \frac{\textit{periodic interest coupon}}{\textit{beginning-of-period market price}}$$

The capital gains yield over a period of time is the change in market price over the time period divided by the beginning-of-period price:

$$\textit{Capital gains yield} = \frac{\textit{change in market price}}{\textit{beginning-of-period market price}}$$

Example

Decomposing a Bond's Yield-to-Maturity

The Gary Corporation bond of the previous page has a market price of $885 and a yield-to-maturity of 4.3745% per half-year.

Question: What current yield and capital gains yield would an investor receive by holding the bond for the next six months? Assume investors' required rate of return does not change during this period.

Solution steps:

1. Calculate the bond's price after six months have passed (with 19 half-years of life remaining):

   CLEAR the time value part of your calculator

   Key in 35 and press PMT, set END

   Key in 1,000 and press FV

   Key in 19 and press n

   Key in 4.3745 and press i

   Compute PV = −888.7142

2. Calculate the two yields:

   Current yield = $35 / $885 = 3.9548%

   Capital gains yield = ($888.7142 − 885.00) / $885.00 = 0.4197%

Answer: The bond's semi-annual yield-to-maturity of 4.3745% comes in the form of a current yield of 3.9548% plus a capital gains yield of 0.4197%.

Check on answer:	Current yield	3.9548%	
	+ Capital gains yield	0.4197	
	= Yield-to-maturity	4.3745%	✓✓

A par bond, with price equal to maturity value, has no capital gains yield; all its yield comes from its interest coupon. If investors require a greater yield than a bond provides through its interest coupon, they price the bond at a discount. This increases the current yield and builds in a capital gains yield as well. On the other hand, if investors find the interest coupon provides more than their required rate of return, they bid up the bond's price in an attempt to purchase it, and the bond sells at a premium. This reduces the current yield and builds in a negative capital gains yield (capital loss), further lowering their rate of return.

6. Yield-to-First-Call

Some bonds have a call option attached to them giving the issuer the right to retire the bonds prior to their maturity date. Companies are motivated to call their bonds if they no longer need the money, if the bonds have unusually constraining covenants attached, or—most often—when interest rates have fallen and it is possible to refinance the debt at a cheaper interest rate.[9] If an investor believes that a bond might be called, it makes more sense to calculate the **yield-to-first-call** rather than the yield-to-maturity.

yield-to-first-call—the rate of return an investor would earn from a bond if it were purchased at today's price, made all promised payments, and were then called at the first possible opportunity

The typical call provision gives the firm the right to retire the bonds by paying investors face value plus a penalty payment, often equal to one-year's interest. Also, it usually specifies that the bond may not be called until some time has passed but may be called freely thereafter. The yield-to-call will therefore depend on when the call takes place. However, it is usual to calculate the yield-to-*first*-call, assuming that if it is in the company's interest to call the bond at all, it will do so at the first possible opportunity.

Calling a bond to refinance debt when interest rates have fallen takes value away from the firm's bondholders. They lose an investment paying a comparatively high rate of return and must accept a lower interest rate when they reinvest their money. Stockholders, on the other hand, benefit from the call. The firm lowers its interest payments and hence increases its earnings after taxes. To protect themselves, bondholders demand a greater rate of return on callable bonds than on equivalent bonds without a call feature, especially when they forecast interest rates to fall.

Example

Yield-to-First-Call

Gary Corporation can call its bond issue (from pp. 306 and 307) after five years by paying investors face value plus one-year's interest ($1,000 + $70 = $1,070).

Question: What is the bond's yield-to-first-call?

[9] **Cross-reference:** A call is an option—options and their value are discussed later in this chapter on pp. 318–321 and in Appendix 9A. The call feature on bonds is discussed in more detail in Appendix 21C, which also illustrates the analysis of whether it is profitable for a company to call a bond issue.

Solution steps:

1. Calculate the interest rate received by an investor who purchases the bond today and loses it in five years (ten half-years) to management's exercise of its call option:

   CLEAR the time value part of your calculator

   Key in −885 and press PV

   Key in 35 and press PMT, set END

   Key in 1,070 and press FV

   Key in 10 and press n

   Compute i = 5.5728% per half-year

2. Annualize the interest rate:

$$(1.055728)^2 - 1 = 11.46\%$$

Answer: This bond's yield-to-first-call is 11.46%.

7. Holding-Period Yield

Our previous examples have assumed that investors' required rates of return remain constant. If this were not true, the price of a bond could change significantly, and the lucky (or unlucky) investor who held the bond could receive a capital gains (or loss) yield quite different from the expected yield. The actual rate of return investors receive, incorporating all the cash flows they experience, is called their **holding-period yield.** This rate can only be determined after an investor sells the bond and all the investor's cash flows are known.

holding-period yield—the rate of return an investor actually earns from an investment

Example

Holding-Period Yield

Steve Payne bought the Gary Corporation bond for $885. He planned to hold it for several years anticipating a semi-annual yield-to-maturity of 4.3745% (an annual YTM of 8.94% as calculated on p. 306). However, interest rates fell during the next six months, and at the end of the half-year, investors only required a semi-annual yield-to-maturity of 3.75%. Steve sold the bond after holding it for six months.

Question: What was Steve's holding-period yield?

Solution steps:

1. Calculate the bond's price at the time Steve sold it:

   CLEAR the time value part of your calculator

   Key in 35 and press PMT, set END

   Key in 1,000 and press FV

   Key in 19 and press n

   Key in 3.75 and press i

   Compute PV = −966.46

2. Calculate the interest rate Steve received by analyzing the cash flows he experienced in the one period he held the bond:

CLEAR the time value part of your calculator

Key in −885 and press PV

Key in 35 and press PMT, set END

Key in 966.46 and press FV

Key in 1 and press n

Compute i = 13.1593% per half-year

3. Annualize the interest rate:

$$(1.131593)^2 - 1 = 28.05\%$$

Answer: Because interest rates fell, the bond's price rose quickly. Steve did not realize his anticipated 8.94% rate of return. Instead he did much better, earning a holding-period yield of 28.05%.

8. Bond Quotations

Figure 9.2 is an excerpt from *The Wall Street Journal*'s daily quotations of bonds traded on the New York Stock Exchange as of mid-1994.[10] The newspaper quotes each bond's coupon rate, year of maturity, current yield, and price, as well as the number of bonds traded that day and the change in the bond's price since the prior trading day.

Preferred Stock Valuation

The cash flows from preferred stock anticipated by investors are the dividends the stock promises to pay.

1. Fixed-Rate Preferred Stock

Fixed-rate preferred stock promises a fixed dividend, usually paid every quarter (three months). Also, it is normal that preferred stock has no set maturity but promises its dividend flow for as long as the firm is in existence. If we can view the business as a "going concern," the dividend flow may be projected as a perpetual annuity of benefits. Accordingly, the appropriate present value model is the perpetuity model.

The payment is the dividend, typically represented by "D_p", and the interest rate is the rate of return required from this stock by investors, represented by "r_p,"

[10] **Reference:** *The Wall Street Journal*, May 25, 1994, p. C–19.

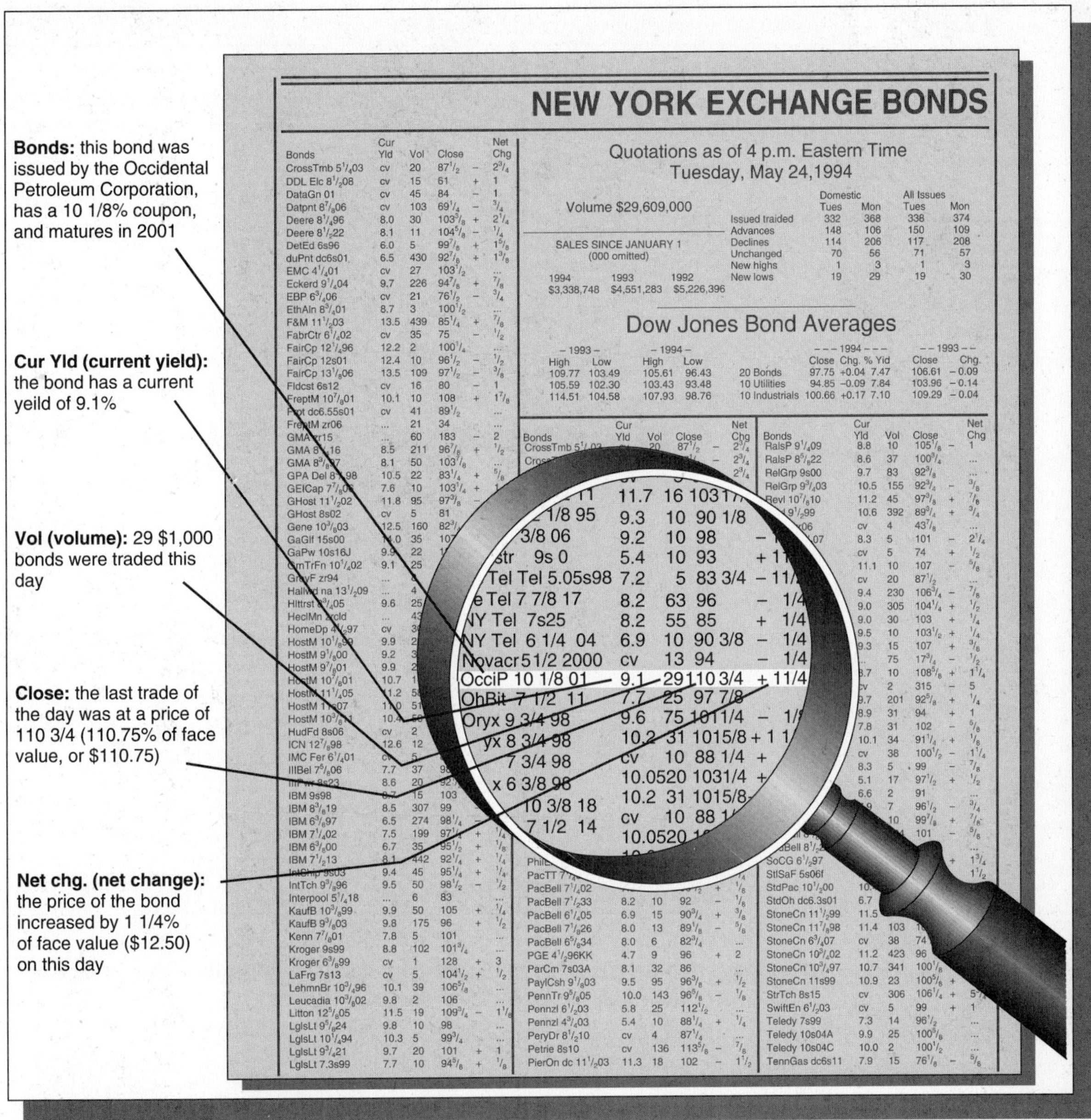

FIGURE 9.2
Through the Looking Glass: New York Stock Exchange bond quotations. Each day *The Wall Street Journal* reports price and yield information.

where the subscript "p" stands for *preferred*. If dividends are paid on a quarterly basis, this is investors' required effective quarterly rate (EQR). For preferred stock, therefore, the present value model is written:

$$Value = PV = \frac{D_p}{r_p}$$

Example

Value of Fixed-Rate Preferred Stock

Central Maine Power Co. preferred stock pays a quarterly dividend based on an annual dividend rate of \$7.88 per share. Today the market demands a 8.385% annual yield on this stock.

Question: What is the value of this stock?

Solution steps:

1. Determine the quarterly dividend:

$$\$7.88/4 = \$1.97$$

2. Determine the effective quarterly rate (EQR):

$$(1.08385)^{1/4} - 1 = 2.0334\%$$

3. Apply the model for the present value of a perpetuity:

$$\text{Value} = \text{PV} = \frac{D_P}{r_P}$$

$$= \frac{\$1.97}{.020334} = \$96.88$$

Answer: The stock is worth \$96.88 per share to investors and will sell for this amount.

The preferred stock valuation model can be solved for rate of return,[11] given the periodic dividend and the market price. Rearranging the algebra gives:

$$\textit{Yield} = r_p = \frac{D_p}{\textit{market price}}$$

Example

Yield of Fixed-Rate Preferred Stock

Chase Manhattan Corporation has an outstanding issue of preferred stock which pays a quarterly dividend based on an annual dividend rate of \$2.08 per share. Today the market price of this stock is \$26.50.

Question: What is the yield on this stock?

Solution steps:

1. Determine the quarterly dividend:

$$\$2.08/4 = \$0.52$$

---

[11] **Elaboration:** The financial press reports the rate of return on preferred stock as the annual dividend divided by its market price. For the Central Maine Power preferred this is:

$$\$7.88/\$96.88 = 8.13\%$$

Since this calculation ignores the quarterly nature of the dividend payments, it misses the benefit to the shareholder of not having to wait until the end of the year to receive all the year's dividends. 8.13% is the *nominal* annual rate of return but investors are really demanding an *effective* annual rate (EAR) of 8.385%.

2. Apply the model for the yield of preferred stock:

$$r_P = \frac{D_P}{\text{market price}}$$

$$= \frac{\$0.52}{\$26.50} = 1.9623\%$$

3. Annualize the yield:

   a. Effective yield = $(1.019623)^4 - 1 = 8.08\%$

   b. Nominal yield = $1.9623 \times 4 = 7.85\%$

Answer: The stock yields 8.08% (although it will be quoted in the financial press as yielding 7.85%).

2. Variable-Rate Preferred Stock

Variable-rate preferred stock provides corporate treasurers the opportunity to purchase a high-yielding, tax-advantaged, marketable security.[12] Variable-rate preferred stock adjusts its dividend with changes in interest rates to maintain a relatively constant value. As interest rates can change every day, the dividend is reset at least as frequently as once per week. As a result, the value of this stock never strays much away from its face value, typically $100 per share.

Common Stock Valuation

The cash flows from common stock are the dividends the stock promises to pay. Unlike preferred stock, however, dividends may vary considerably from quarter to quarter—there is no implication the dividend will remain constant or even be paid at all. In addition, the dividend stream may continue for a long time since the firm is a going concern. All this makes it very difficult to forecast the future dividends of any business and hence place a value on its common stock.

1. The Dividend-Growth Model

To simplify the common-stock valuation problem, it is usual to assume that future dividends will grow according to some pattern. By far the simplest and therefore easiest pattern to work with is constant growth. By assuming that a company's dividends will grow forever at a constant rate, we can use the growing cash stream present value model to value the firm's stock. When the growing cash

[12] **Elaboration and cross-reference:** The high yield is due to the greater risk of the preferred stock compared to other marketable securities—refer back to the Fisher model, Chapter 6, pp. 206–210. The tax advantage is the result of the law that makes 70% of dividends paid from one corporation to another tax free, as discussed in Appendix 4C, p. 106.

stream model is used for this purpose, it is typically referred to as the "dividend-growth model."[13] Recall that the growing cash stream model has the form:

$$\text{Present value} = \frac{CF_1}{r - g}$$

The first cash flow is the first dividend to be received one period from now, written as "D_1". The interest rate is investors' required rate of return, represented by "r_c", where the subscript "c" stands for common stock. "g" is the rate of growth of dividends anticipated by investors. For common stock, therefore, the present value model is written:

$$Value = PV = \frac{D_1}{r_c - g}$$

Normal practice is for corporations to pay dividends on a quarterly basis; in this case r_c is investors' required effective quarterly rate (EQR) and g their forecast of quarterly growth.

Example

Value of Common Stock—Constant Growth

Coca Cola common stock pays a quarterly dividend based on an annual dividend rate of $0.68 per share. Investors expect the company's dividend to grow at a rate of 12% as far into the future as they can forecast. Today the market demands a 14% annual rate of return from Coca Cola stock.

Question: What is the value of this stock?

Solution steps:

1. Determine the quarterly dividend:

$$\$0.68/4 = \$0.17$$

2. Determine the effective quarterly rate (EQR):

$$(1.14)^{1/4} - 1 = 3.3299\%$$

3. Determine the quarterly growth rate:

$$(1.12)^{1/4} - 1 = 2.8737\%$$

4. Apply the dividend-growth model:

$$\begin{aligned} \text{Value} = \text{PV} &= \frac{D_1}{(r_c - g)} \\ &= \frac{\$0.17}{.033299 - .028737} \\ &= \frac{\$0.17}{.004562} \\ &= \$37.26 \end{aligned}$$

Answer: The stock is worth $37.26 per share to investors and will sell for this amount.

[13] **Elaboration and cross-reference:** It is also widely known as the "Gordon model" or the "Gordon-Shapiro model" after the finance professors who suggested this application and wrote extensively about it. The model was introduced in Chapter 5 on pp. 176–177.

The dividend-growth model uses dividends—cash flow to investors—as the basis for value. But what about a company that does not pay a dividend? According to the model, the value of a nondividend-paying firm should be zero, yet many companies retain all their earnings and are not worthless. The reason is that the value of a company may not depend primarily on the amount of its dividend payment.[14] Rather, value stems from the ability to earn money. Dividends are the result of earnings. To value a company that pays little or no dividends, many investment analysts apply the dividend-growth model to the company's earnings numbers or to its cash flow from operations.

It would be unusual for any company to grow at a constant rate forever—economic, technological, and competitive conditions are far too variable. Therefore the dividend-growth model is only an approximation to the value of a share of stock. The best we can hope for is that the growth rate we forecast is an adequate summary of the *average* growth rate of the company. Nevertheless, the advantage of simplifying our calculations often outweighs the disadvantage of the approximate nature of our answer.

2. The Two-Stage Growth Version of the Dividend-Growth Model

One of the requirements of the dividend-growth model is that the growth rate must be less than investors' required rate of return; otherwise the model gives incorrect results (a negative value for a company growing at a rapid rate). To apply the model to a company for which a high growth rate is forecasted, we often use the two-stage version of the model. In this version, we divide our forecast of the company's future into two periods of time: a first time period during which we forecast high growth, followed by a second time period during which we forecast a lower, more normal growth rate. We calculate the present value of each cash flow individually during the first time period and apply the dividend-growth model only to the second time period, where the conditions of the model are met: constant growth at a rate less than the required rate of return.

Example

Value of Common Stock—Two-Stage Growth

Synthetic Genetics Corporation has grown at a 25% annual rate for the past several years. Investors anticipate this will continue for four years more, after which competition will intensify and the company's annual growth rate will decline to 10% and remain at that level for the foreseeable future. The company makes a single dividend payment annually; its last dividend, recently paid, was $2.50 per share. Investors require a 16% rate of return from Synthetic Genetics' common stock.

Question: What is the value of this stock?

[14] **Cross-reference:** We will explore the dividend decision of the firm in some depth in Chapter 17.

Solution steps:

1. Calculate the dividends individually for the next four years, the high-growth period:[15]

$$D_1 = \$2.50 \times 1.25 = \$3.13$$

$$D_2 = \$3.13 \times 1.25 = \$3.91$$

$$D_3 = \$3.91 \times 1.25 = \$4.89$$

$$D_4 = \$4.89 \times 1.25 = \$6.11$$

2. Calculate the next dividend, the first dividend of the normal growth period:

$$D_5 = \$6.11 \times 1.10 = \$6.72$$

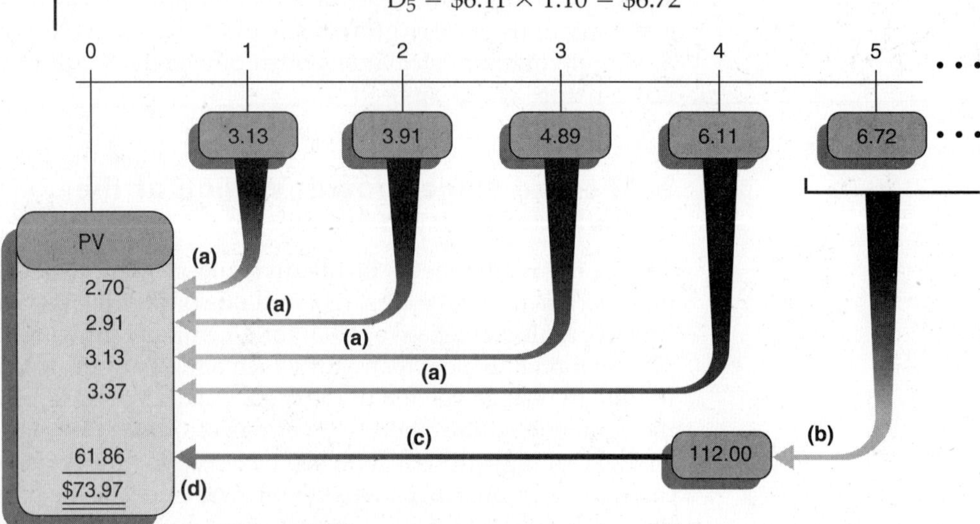

3. Calculate the present value of these cash flows:

   a. Calculate the present value of each of the first four dividends individually:

   CLEAR the time value part of your calculator

   Key in 3.13, 3.91, 4.89, 6.11 and press FV

   Key in 1, 2, 3, 4 and press n

   Key in 16 and press i

   Compute PV = −2.70, −2.91, −3.13, −3.37

   b. Calculate the value of all subsequent dividends using the dividend-growth model. This gives a value at time point 4 since the model assumes that the first cash flow is one period later in time:

---

[15] **Tip:** Multiplying each dividend by 1.25 increases it by 25%, and is the easy way to calculate the next dividend at a 25% growth rate. Note: this is the same calculation as the basic time value of money formula—a future value is a present value multiplied by (1 + r).

$$PV = \frac{D_1}{r_c - g} = \frac{\$6.72}{.16 - .10}$$

$$= \frac{\$6.72}{.06} = \$112.00$$

c. Discount the result of step (b) back to the present:

CLEAR the time value part of your calculator

Key in 112.00 and press FV

Key in 4 and press n

Key in 16 and press i

Compute PV = −61.86

d. Add up the present values to get the total value of this stock's future dividends.

Answer: The stock is worth $73.97 per share to investors and will sell for this amount.

3. The Rate of Return from Common Stock

The dividend-growth model may be rearranged to solve for r_c, the forecasted rate of return from holding common stock:

$$Rate\ of\ return = r_c = \frac{D_1}{stock\ price} + g$$

dividend yield—the portion of a stock's rate of return coming from dividend payments

While this model holds precisely only if we forecast constant growth, it shows that, just as with bonds, the return from an investment in common stock can be decomposed into two parts. The first term (D_1 / stock price) is the stock's expected **dividend yield**, the return coming in the form of regular cash payments and the equivalent of a bond's current yield. The second term (g) is the expected growth rate of the company's dividend stream and translates into the stock's capital gains yield.

Example

Rate of Return on Common Stock—Constant Growth

Reconsider the Coca Cola common stock example on p. 314. Assume investors anticipate a $0.17 quarterly dividend which is expected to grow thereafter at a quarterly rate of 2.8737%. The stock currently sells for $37.26 per share.

Question: Subdivide the stock's quarterly rate of return into the dividend yield and the capital gains yield.

Solution steps: Calculate the two yields:

Quarterly dividend yield = D_1 / price = $0.17 / $37.26 = 0.4562%
Quarterly capital gains yield = g = 2.8737%

Answer: The stock's quarterly rate of return of 3.3299% comes in the form of a dividend yield of 0.4562% plus a capital gains yield of 2.8737%.

Check on answer:

Quarterly dividend yield	0.4562%
+ Quarterly capital gains yield	2.8737
= Total quarterly rate of return	3.3299% ✓✓

4. Stock Quotations

Figure 9.3 is taken from *The Wall Street Journal*'s daily quotations of stocks traded on the New York Stock Exchange as of early 1994.[16] Preferred and common stocks of listed companies trade side by side.

Option Valuation

A contingent claim is one whose existence depends on some event happening. For example, suppose you have purchased collision insurance on your car. If you do not get into an accident, you have no claim on the insurance company—it owes you nothing. However, if you crumple a fender, you now have the right to a payment from the company. Your claim is contingent on an accident taking place.

option—the right to buy or sell an asset at an agreed-upon price during a specified time period

Contingent claims arise throughout business. In finance, perhaps the most common form of contingent claim is an **option**, the right to buy or sell something at an agreed-upon price during an agreed-upon period. Suppose, for example, you buy an option on a parcel of land. If you do not use your option, you have no claim on the land. If you exercise your option to buy, you do have a claim. In this case, your claim on the land is contingent on your use of the option.

1. Option Terminology

call—an option to buy

put—an option to sell

A **call** option is the right to buy something, for example a share of stock. The seller, or "writer," of a call option receives a payment in return for giving the buyer of the call the right to buy the stock. A **put** option is the right to sell something. Like the writer of a call, the writer of a put option receives a premium in return for giving this right to the put's buyer. Note that a call and a put are *not* opposite sides of the same contract, since only one party has the right to use the option.

It is useful to learn some other option terminology:

- An option's "exercise or strike price" is the agreed-upon purchase or sale price. In some option contracts, the exercise price remains constant over the life of the option. Other options specify that the exercise price will change if an identified event takes place, such as a stock dividend or split.
- The "expiration date" of an option is the date after which the option becomes worthless. An "American option" may be exercised at any time prior to its expiration while a "European option" is one that can only be exercised on its expiration date.

[16] **References:** *The Wall Street Journal*, Feb. 9, 1994, p. C-4.

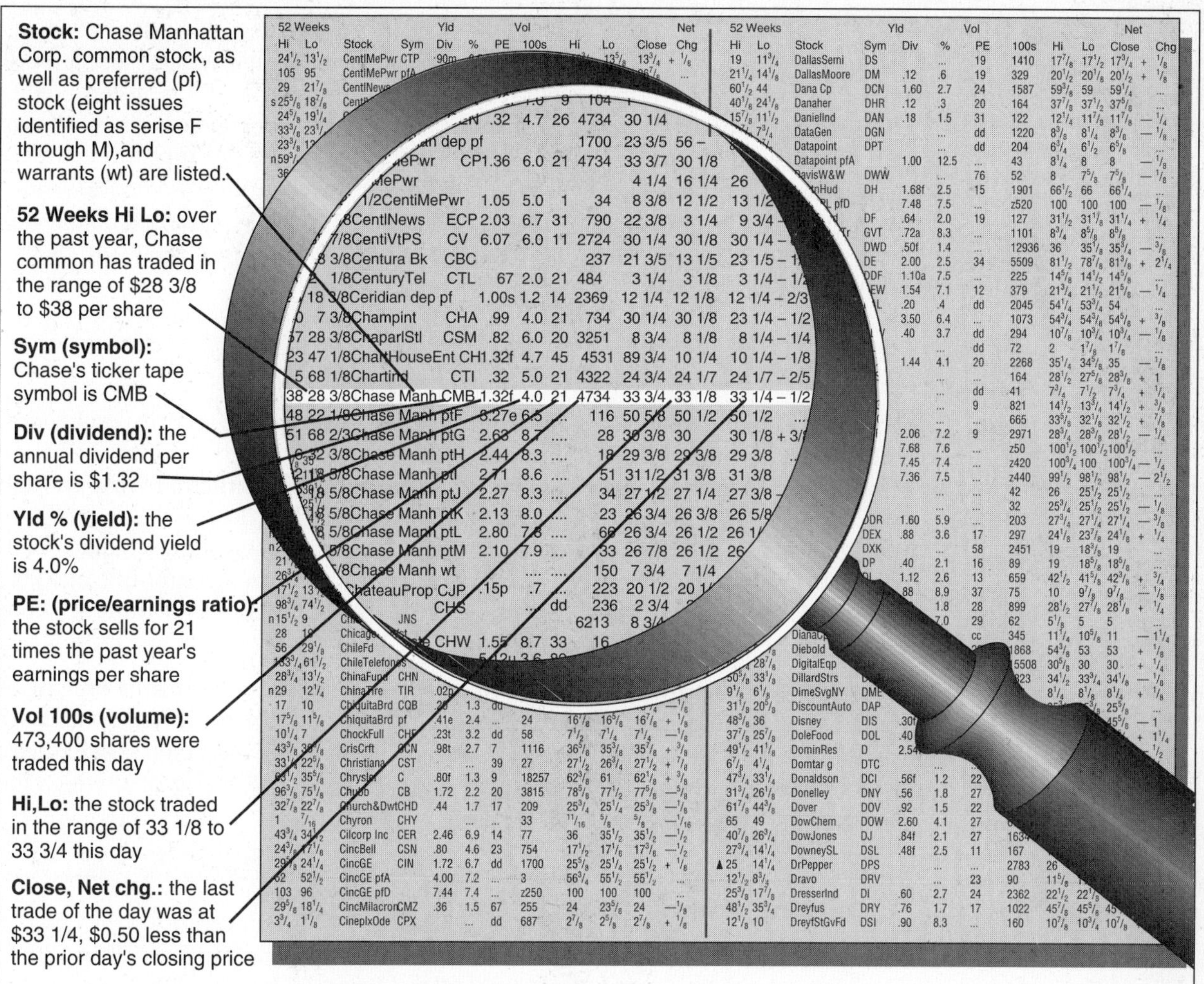

Stock: Chase Manhattan Corp. common stock, as well as preferred (pf) stock (eight issues identified as serise F through M),and warrants (wt) are listed.
52 Weeks Hi Lo: over the past year, Chase common has traded in the range of $28 3/8 to $38 per share
Sym (symbol): Chase's ticker tape symbol is CMB
Div (dividend): the annual dividend per share is $1.32
Yld % (yield): the stock's dividend yield is 4.0%
PE: (price/earnings ratio): the stock sells for 21 times the past year's earnings per share
Vol 100s (volume): 473,400 shares were traded this day
Hi,Lo: the stock traded in the range of 33 1/8 to 33 3/4 this day
Close, Net chg.: the last trade of the day was at $33 1/4, $0.50 less than the prior day's closing price

FIGURE 9.3

Through the Looking Glass: New York Stock Exchange stock quotations. Each day *The Wall Street Journal* reports summary price and trading information for the securities of listed companies.

- The option "premium" is the price paid by the buyer to the writer of the option for the purpose of obtaining the right inherent in the option.
- An option is "in the money" if it can be used today to buy or sell at a bargain price. It is "out of the money" if it is cheaper to buy or sell without using the option. For example, a call option to purchase IBM stock at a strike price of $50 is in the money if IBM is selling for more than $50 per share and is out of the money if the price of IBM stock is below $50.

2. The Value of an Option

The value of an option is a bit more complicated to calculate than the value of stocks and bonds, for two reasons. First, the future cash flow the option holder will receive depends upon the performance of the underlying stock. Second, it is difficult to quantify the risk of an option, hence determine the appropriate interest rate to use in the present value calculation. In the 1970s, however, professors Black and Scholes found a remarkably clever way to resolve these problems and write a formula for the value of a European call option. We present the Black–Scholes model in Appendix 9A.

3. Option Quotations

Options on common stock are traded on several of the major security exchanges. Prior to the opening of option trading by the Chicago Board Options Exchange (CBOE) in 1974, options had no standard form, and it was difficult to find enough buyers and sellers for any one option to make a market. To solve this problem, the CBOE limited the variety of option contracts traded on the exchange. Each contract covers 100 shares of stock, has a strike price which is a multiple of $5.00, and expires on the third Friday of the month. The success of this approach convinced the other exchanges to follow suit.

Figure 9.4 is taken from *The Wall Street Journal*'s daily quotations of exchange-traded options on common stock.[17] For each common stock on which options are traded, all allowable call and put contracts are listed, along with their strike prices, expiration dates, volume (number of contracts traded), and the price at which the last trade of the day took place.

3. Options Combined with Other Securities

Many securities have options attached or are hybrids of a pure security and one or more options. In general, the value of these financial instruments is simply the sum of the values of their parts. Some options add value for investors. For example, a convertible feature incorporated into a bond or preferred stock issue gives the investor the right to exchange the security for another, usually common stock. The value of a convertible bond or preferred share is the sum of the value of the underlying security if it did not contain the option *plus* the value of the conversion option.[18]

Other options reduce investors' value. We saw, for example, that it is common for bonds to contain a call option, giving management the right to retire the bonds prior to their maturity date. The value of a callable bond to an investor is its value if it did not contain the call feature *less* the value of the option.

---

[17] **Reference:** *The Wall Street Journal*, Feb. 9, 1994, p. C–12.

[18] **Cross-reference:** We discuss convertible securities more fully in Chapter 22, pp. 811–813.

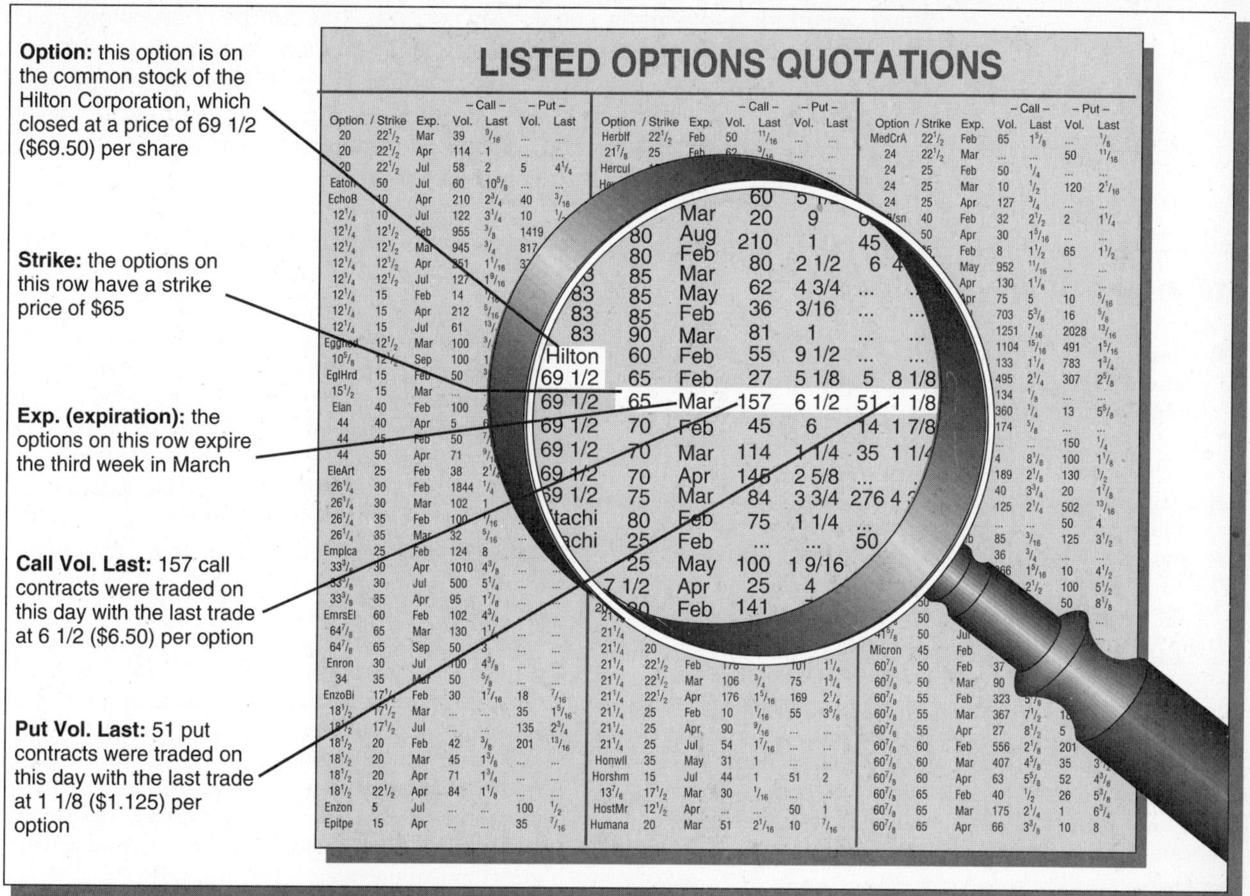

LISTED OPTIONS QUOTATIONS
Option: this option is on the common stock of the Hilton Corporation, which closed at a price of 69 1/2 ($69.50) per share
Strike: the options on this row have a strike price of $65
Exp. (expiration): the options on this row expire the third week in March
Call Vol. Last: 157 call contracts were traded on this day with the last trade at 6 1/2 ($6.50) per option
Put Vol. Last: 51 put contracts were traded on this day with the last trade at 1 1/8 ($1.125) per option

FIGURE 9.4

Through the Looking Glass: Option quotations. *The Wall Street Journal* summarizes trading on all U.S. exchanges.

Steve Payne looked up at the flip-charts taped to the wall. On one of them was written the dividend-growth model, in both its one-stage and two-stage forms. Steve's company had historically paid a regular dividend, so the team had begun its work with those classic stock valuation formulas.

The value of the company's stock could be modeled as the present value of the dividends anticipated by investors. This made sense and was consistent with the method of valuing any security. But that word *anticipated* had given the team a lot of trouble. Who were the relevant investors? What was their required rate of return? And how could the team learn what dividends they anticipated?

Steve waited for a chance to speak. "My sense is that our task here is not much different from many of the analyses I've seen in finance. At first, the tough part appears to be learning to use the various models. But pretty soon it becomes apparent that the real work is in getting good data to put into the models. Nevertheless, these present value relationships do an excellent job in pointing us in the direction we should be looking to find the information we need.

Summary of Key Points

- **Discuss why the value of a security is a present value and is independent of how long an investor plans to hold it.** Financial value comes from receiving cash, and any security can be seen as a stream of anticipated future cash flows. Time value of money analysis—in particular, present value—is the technique for finding today's value of a future cash flow stream. In this chapter we looked at the present value of the cash flows anticipated by investors in bonds and stocks. The value of any security can be found by calculating the present value of the security's cash flows assuming that the first investor holds it until maturity—or forever in the case of perpetual bonds and stock. This is because investors who expect to sell a security prior to its maturity date forecast a sale price equal to the present value of the remaining cash flows—an even trade—resulting in the same present value as if they hold on until maturity.
- **Describe the difference between value and price.** This chapter is primarily concerned with *value*, the worth of a security to any one investor. The *price* of a security will reflect the consensus forecast of future cash flows and the overall rate of return required by investors. In efficient markets, investors process information quickly and price tends to equal value. However, many observers of the investment scene believe that price and value diverge regularly and meaningfully.
- **Calculate the value and yield of traditional, zero-coupon, and perpetual bonds.** Bonds can be valued by calculating the present value of the cash flows investors expect, using their required rate of return as the discount rate. The appropriate present value model depends on the cash-flow structure of the bond. The calculation may be reversed to calculate a bond's yield-to-maturity, yield-to-first-call, or holding-period yield. Yield-to-maturity may be decomposed into current yield, the portion coming from cash distributions, and capital gains yield, the portion coming from growth in value.
- **Calculate the value and yield of preferred stock.** Like bonds, fixed-rate preferred stock can be valued by calculating the present value of the cash flows investors expect, using their required rate of return as the discount rate. The appropriate present value model is the perpetuity model since preferred stock promises a constant dividend with no maturity date. The calculation may also be reversed to calculate the stock's yield given its market price. Variable-rate preferred stock maintains a constant value since the dividend adjusts to market conditions.
- **Calculate the value and rate of return of common stock.** Common stock can also be valued by calculating the present value of the cash flows investors expect, using their required rate of return as the discount rate. The appropriate present value model is the growing cash stream model since common-stock dividends may be forecasted to grow with the firm. Reversing the calculation produces the stock's rate of return, which may be decomposed into dividend yield, the portion coming from cash distributions, and capital gains yield, the portion coming from growth in value.
- **Discuss the characteristics of options on common stock.** An option is a contingent claim, one whose value depends on the value of the underlying stock. A call is an option to buy while a put is an option to sell. Options are characterized by their exercise price, expiration date, and price or premium. An option is in the money if it can be used to obtain a bargain price and is out of the money if it cannot.

Questions

1. What determines investors' required rate of return from a bond or stock?
2. What is the relationship of the value of a security to the holding period of investors? Why is this so?
3. Distinguish between the value of a security and its price. Under what conditions would value equal price?
4. What is the philosophy of technical security analysts? What is the philosophy of fundamental security analysts?

5. Identify the following:
   a. Traditional bond
   b. Par bond
   c. Discount bond
   d. Premium bond
   e. Zero-coupon bond
   f. Perpetual bond
6. What happens to the value of a discount bond as it approaches its maturity date? What happens to the value of a premium bond as it approaches its maturity date?
7. If a zero-coupon bond never pays an interest coupon, how do investors earn anything?
8. Identify the following:
   a. Yield-to-maturity
   b. Current yield
   c. Capital gains yield
   d. Yield-to-first-call
   e. Holding-period yield
9. From a valuation point of view, what is the difference between a perpetual bond and fixed-rate preferred stock?
10. According to the dividend-growth model, a stock that pays no dividends is worthless! Discuss this statement.
11. Why is the two-stage version of the dividend-growth model often used instead of the basic (one-stage) version?
12. Why is an option a contingent claim?
13. Identify the following terms about an option on common stock:
    a. Call option
    b. Put option
    c. Exercise price
    d. Expiration date
    e. In the money
    f. Out of the money
14. Why is an "out of the money" option:
    a. Not worthless if time remains until its expiration?
    b. Worthless at its expiration date?
15. Most holders of "in the money" options do not use them to buy the underlying stock, even on the option's expiration date, but instead sell them to other investors. Why do you think this is so?

Problems

1. **(Traditional bond)** The Texaco Corporation has outstanding an issue of $1,000 face value, 8 1/2% semi-annual coupon bonds which mature in 15 years. Calculate the value of one bond to an investor who requires a nominal annual rate of return of:
   a. 7%
   b. 8.5%
   c. 10%
   d. 11.5%
2. **(Traditional bond)** The Chrysler Corporation has outstanding an issue of $1,000 face value, 10.95% semi-annual coupon bonds which mature in 26 years. Calculate the value of one bond to an investor who requires a nominal annual rate of return of:
   a. 10%
   b. 11%
   c. 15%
   d. 18%
3. **(Bond price over time)** USAir Corporation has outstanding an issue of $1,000 face value, 8 1/2% semi-annual coupon bonds which mature in 15 years. Today investors require an effective annual rate of return of 14%.
   a. Calculate the price of these bonds today.
   b. Calculate the price of these bonds 5 years from now if market interest rates do not change.
   c. Calculate the price of these bonds 5 years from now if investors' effective annual required rate of return declines to 11%.
   d. Calculate the price of these bonds 14 years from now assuming investors' effective annual required rate of return:
      (1) declines to 10%.
      (2) remains at 14%.
      (3) increases to 18%.
4. **(Bond price over time)** Occidental Petroleum Corporation has outstanding an issue of $1,000 face value, 11 3/4% semi-annual coupon bonds which mature in 20 years. Today investors require an effective annual rate of return of 10.5%.
   a. Calculate the price of these bonds today.
   b. Calculate the price of these bonds 7 years from now if market interest rates do not change.
   c. Calculate the price of these bonds 14 years from now if market interest rates do not change.
   d. Calculate the price of these bonds 20 years from now if market interest rates do not change.
5. **(Zero-coupon bond)** Allied Chemical Corporation has outstanding an issue of $1,000 face value zero coupon bonds which mature in ten years. Calculate the value of one bond to an investor who requires an effective annual rate of return of:
   a. 9%
   b. 11%
   c. 13%
   d. 15%

6. **(Zero-coupon bond)** Motorola Corporation has outstanding an issue of $1,000 face value zero coupon bonds which mature in 18 years. Calculate the value of one bond to an investor who requires an effective annual rate of return of:

   a. 8%
   b. 12%
   c. 15%
   d. 18%

7. **(Perpetual bond)** The UK government has issued £1,000 face value perpetual bonds carrying a 7% coupon paid semiannually. Calculate the value of one bond to an investor who requires a nominal annual rate of return of:

   a. 5.5%
   b. 7%
   c. 8.5%
   d. 10%

8. **(Perpetual bond)** The government of Switzerland has issued SF1,000 face value perpetual bonds carrying a 4% coupon paid semiannually. Calculate the value of one bond to an investor who requires a nominal annual rate of return of:

   a. 3%
   b. 4%
   c. 6%
   d. 8%

9. **(Yield-to-maturity)** Litton Industries has outstanding an issue of $1,000 face value, 12 5/8% semi-annual coupon bonds which mature in 14 years. Calculate the bond's yield-to-maturity if its current market price is:

   a. $ 875
   b. $ 950
   c. $1,000
   d. $1,080

10. **(Yield-to-maturity)** Citicorp has outstanding an issue of $1,000 face value, 8.45% semi-annual coupon bonds which mature in 16 years. Calculate the bond's yield-to-maturity if its current market price is:

    a. $ 800
    b. $1,000
    c. $1,150
    d. $1,300

11. **(Components of yield-to-maturity)** For each of the four cases in Problem 9, decompose the yield-to-maturity over the next six months on the Litton Industries bonds into the current yield and the capital gains yield, assuming investors' required rate of return does not change.

12. **(Components of yield-to-maturity)** For each of the four cases in Problem 10, decompose the yield-to-maturity over the next six months on the Citicorp bonds into the current yield and the capital gains yield, assuming investors' required rate of return does not change.

13. **(Yield-to-first-call)** Assume that the Litton Industries bonds of Problem 9 can be called after seven years by paying investors face value plus one-year's interest. For each of the four cases, calculate the yield-to-first-call.

14. **(Yield-to-first-call)** Assume that the Citicorp bonds of Problem 10 can be called after ten years by paying investors face value plus one-year's interest. For each of the four cases, calculate the yield-to-first-call.

15. **(Holding-period yield)** Assume you purchase one Litton Industries bond of Problem 9, hold it for five years, and then sell it for $975. For each of the four purchase prices given, calculate your holding-period yield.

16. **(Holding-period yield)** Assume you purchase one Citicorp bond of Problem 10, hold it for two years, and then sell it for $1,200. For each of the four purchase prices given, calculate your holding-period yield.

17. **(Preferred stock value)** General Motors preferred stock pays a quarterly dividend based on an annual dividend rate of $5 per share. Calculate the value of one share to an investor who requires an effective annual rate of return of:

    a. 6%
    b. 9%
    c. 12%
    d. 15%

18. **(Preferred stock value)** Ohio Edison preferred stock pays a quarterly dividend based on an annual dividend rate of $7.36 per share. Calculate the value of one share to an investor who requires an effective annual rate of return of:

    a. 5%
    b. 8%
    c. 11%
    d. 14%

19. **(Preferred stock yield)** Calculate the yield of the General Motors preferred stock of Problem 17 if its market price per share is:

    a. $ 30
    b. $ 65
    c. $ 85
    d. $100

20. **(Preferred stock yield)** Calculate the yield of the Ohio Edison preferred stock of Problem 18 if its market price per share is:

    a. \$ 60
    b. \$ 80
    c. \$100
    d. \$120

21. **(Common stock—constant growth)** The common stock of the Kellogg Company pays a quarterly dividend based on an annual dividend rate of \$2.12 per share. Calculate the value of one share to an investor who requires an effective annual rate of return of 14% and who forecasts that Kellogg's dividends will grow at a constant annual rate of:

    a. 0%
    b. 4%
    c. 7%
    d. 10%

22. **(Common stock—constant growth)** The common stock of the Seagrams Company pays a quarterly dividend based on an annual dividend rate of C\$2.12 (Canadian dollars) per share. Calculate the value of one share to an investor who requires an effective annual rate of return of 12% and who forecasts that Seagrams' dividends will grow at a constant annual rate of:

    a. –5%
    b. 0%
    c. 5%
    d. 15%

23. **(Common stock—two-stage growth)** The McDonald's Corporation recently paid an annual dividend of \$0.34 per share. Investors forecast the company's dividend will grow at a 23% annual rate for the next three years, after which the growth rate will settle down to 8% for the foreseeable future. Investors require a 15% effective annual rate of return on this stock.

    a. Calculate the dividends forecast by investors for the next four years.
    b. Calculate the present value of the first three dividends.
    c. Calculate the present value of the dividends during the normal growth period.
    d. Calculate the total value of McDonald's estimated future dividends.

24. **(Common stock—two-stage growth)** Merck Pharmaceuticals Company recently paid an annual dividend of \$2.24 per share. Investors forecast the company's dividend will grow at a 35% annual rate for the next five years, after which the growth rate will settle down to 11% for the foreseeable future. Investors require a 16% effective annual rate of return on this stock.

    a. Calculate the dividends forecast by investors for the next six years.
    b. Calculate the present value of the first five dividends.
    c. Calculate the present value of the dividends during the normal growth period.
    d. Calculate the total value of Merck's estimated future dividends.

25. **(Common stock—rate of return)** The stock of the Gillette Corporation recently paid a quarterly dividend based on an annual dividend rate of \$1.08 per share. Investors anticipate the company's dividend will grow at an annual rate of 10% for the foreseeable future. Calculate the stock's quarterly dividend yield and capital gains yield and the quarterly and annual total rate of return if one share of Gillette stock is currently selling for:

    a. \$45
    b. \$60
    c. \$75
    d. \$90

26. **(Common stock—rate of return)** The stock of the JCPenney Corporation recently paid a quarterly dividend based on an annual dividend rate of \$2.64 per share. The stock is currently selling for \$50 per share. Calculate the stock's quarterly dividend yield and capital gains yield and the quarterly and annual total rate of return if investors anticipate the company's dividends will grow for the foreseeable future at an annual rate of:

    a. –2%
    b. 0%
    c. 7%
    d. 12%

27. **(Bond prices and maturity)** AT&T Corporation has two \$1,000 face value bond issues outstanding with an 8 5/8% semi-annual coupon. One issue matures in 16 years and the other matures in 35 years.

    a. Calculate each bond's price if investors require a nominal annual rate of return of 8 5/8%.
    b. Calculate each bond's price if investors require a nominal annual rate of return of 5%.
    c. Calculate each bond's price if investors require a nominal annual rate of return of 12%.
    d. Comment on the pattern of price changes you observe.

28. **(Bond prices and maturity)** Compare the 9 5/8% semi-annual coupon bonds of Occidental Petroleum, which mature in 8 years, with those of Southwestern Bell, which mature in 29 years. Both have a $1,000 face value.

    a. Calculate each bond's price if investors require a nominal annual rate of return of 9 5/8%.
    b. Calculate each bond's price if investors require a nominal annual rate of return of 6%.
    c. Calculate each bond's price if investors require a nominal annual rate of return of 13%.
    d. Comment on the pattern of price changes you observe.

APPENDIX 9A

THE BLACK-SCHOLES OPTION PRICING MODEL

Professors Fischer Black and Myron Scholes have derived a model for calculating the price of a European call option, a right to buy which may be exercised only on its expiration date. In this appendix we present the logic of their derivation and the form of their model.

Black and Scholes observed that the value of a call option on a share of common stock is known with certainty on its expiration date. If the stock's price is less than the exercise price of the call, the option will be worthless (out of the money), since it is cheaper to purchase the stock in the market without using the call. On the other hand, if the stock's price exceeds the call's exercise price (the option is in the money), the option will be worth the difference between the stock price and exercise price, the savings from using the option to purchase the stock. Figure 9A.1 shows these possibilities for a call option with exercise price of $30 per share. To the left of $30, the call is worthless. To the right of $30, the call's value rises dollar for dollar with the price of the underlying stock.

riskless hedge—a combination of investments which have a certain outcome

Since the prices of a stock and its call option are precisely connected at the call's expiration date, Black and Scholes realized it is possible to construct a **riskless hedge,** a combination of shares of stock and option contracts that leads to a fixed, i.e., riskless, outcome regardless of fluctuations in share price. In efficient capital markets, a riskless investment position should return the risk-free rate of interest. The Black Scholes model is based on this insight: the price of a call option should be an amount that makes the return from a riskless portfolio of stocks and options equal to the risk-free rate.

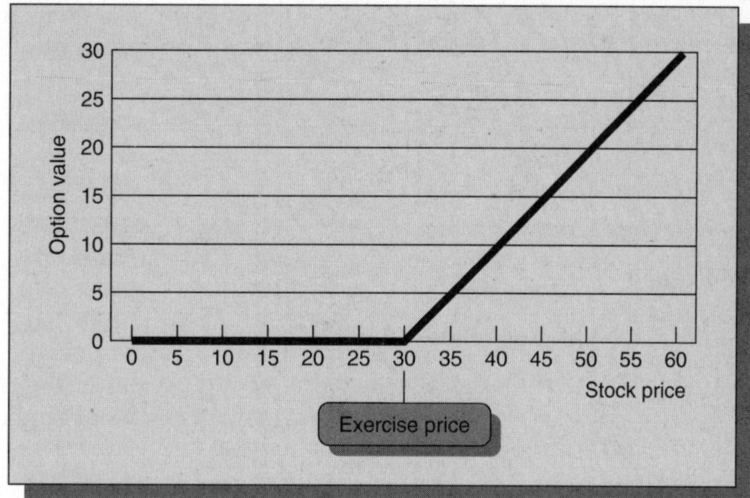

FIGURE 9A.1
The value of a call option at expiration. The call is either worthless or worth the difference between stock and exercise prices.

In practice, stock prices can vary considerably over any period of time, and the Black-Scholes model takes this into account. However, to simplify the presentation, the following examples assume that there are only two stock prices—or states—possible at the time the call option expires.[1]

Example

Constructing a Two-State Riskless Hedge

Xerox Corporation common stock is currently selling for $60 per share. A call option with one-month maturity is available with an exercise price of $63. In one month the stock could have one of two values: $65 or $55.

Question: What will the value of the option be in each state?

Solution steps:

1. If the stock goes to $65, the option will be worth $2, the discount available by purchasing the stock at the option's exercise price of $63.
2. If the stock goes to $55, the option will expire worthless since no investor would want to use it to purchase the stock for $63 when it is available in the market for $55.

Question: What is the hedge ratio, the number of options to combine with each share of stock to achieve the perfect hedge?

[1] **Elaboration:** Midway through the derivation of their model, Black and Scholes find they have reproduced the "heat-transfer equation of physics," a complex formula which requires the use of the integral calculus to solve. The two-state examples which follow are indeed much simpler!

Solution steps: The hedge ratio is the ratio of the range of values for the stock ($65 to $55) to the range of values for the option ($2 to $0):

$$\frac{65 - 55}{2 - 0} = \frac{10}{2}$$

$$= 5 \text{ options per share}$$

Question: Show that a hedge constructed by purchasing one share of Xerox stock and selling five call options is riskless.

Solution steps:

1. If the stock goes up to $65, the owner of the calls will use them. The investor (who sold the calls) will lose $2 per option for a net position of:

Own:	one share at $65	=	$ 65
Owe:	$2 on each of 5 calls	=	(10)
			$ 55

2. If the stock goes down to $55, the calls will be worthless and their owner will not use them. The investor's net position will be:

Own:	one share at $55	=	$ 55
Owe:	$0 against the calls	=	(0)
			$ 55

Conclusion: In either state the investment is worth $55. No variation is possible, hence there is no risk.

In the following example we use the Black-Scholes logic and some simple algebra to solve for an option's price by setting the present value of the certain benefit from a riskless hedge equal to the cost of purchasing that hedge.

Example

Valuing a Call Option Using a Two-State Riskless Hedge

Steve Payne is interested in purchasing a one-month call option with exercise price of $63 on Xerox stock. He forecasts that the stock, currently $60 per share, will be worth either $65 or $55 in one month, the two states of the previous example. The one-month risk-free rate is 0.4%

Question: What is the value of the option?

Solution steps:

1. Let X be the price of the call option. To find that value, Steve analyzes a riskless hedge. If he were to construct such a hedge, Steve would purchase one share of stock at $60 and sell five option contracts for $X each (receiving $5X in total) for a net outlay of:

$$\$60 - \$5X$$

2. In return, Steve would lock in a certain return of $55 in one month (as calculated in the previous example). At the risk-free rate of interest, this has present value of:

$$\frac{\$55}{1 + r_f} = \frac{\$55}{1.004} = \$54.78$$

3. Since the cost of the riskless hedge should be its fair present value, we can equate the above two expressions and solve for X:

$$\$60 - \$5X = \$54.78$$

$$\$5X = \$5.22$$

$$X = \$1.04$$

Answer: The value of the option is $1.04.

In the two-state examples above, the value of a call option is a function of its exercise price ($63, which is an input to the hedge ratio), the price of the stock today ($60), the risk-free rate of interest for the time until the option expires (0.4% for one month), and the anticipated future stock price in the two possible states ($55 and $65). In the more general case where many future stock prices are possible, it is necessary to use a more complex formulation for ending stock price. Black and Scholes modeled this by incorporating the variance of the stock's rate of return, one measure of the possible change in the stock's price, into their derivation. The resulting Black-Scholes equation is:

$$C = SN(d_1) - \frac{E}{e^{rt}}N(d_2)$$

where:

C = Call price

S = Stock price

E = Exercise price of the option

e = 2.71828 . . ., a constant, the base of the natural logarithms

r = the annual risk-free interest rate

t = the time until expiration in years

σ^2 = the **variance** of the rate of return of the stock

N(d) = the cumulative standard normal probability function: the probability that a normally distributed random variable with mean of zero and standard deviation of 1 will be less than d

The factors d_1 and d_2 are calculated by the following equations:

$$d_1 = \frac{ln\left(\frac{S}{E}\right) + \left(r + \frac{\sigma^2}{2}\right)t}{\sigma\sqrt{t}}$$

$$d_2 = \frac{ln\left(\frac{S}{E}\right) + \left(r - \frac{\sigma^2}{2}\right)t}{\sigma\sqrt{t}} = d_1 - \sigma\sqrt{t}$$

where *ln* represents the natural logarithm. $N(d_1)$ and $N(d_2)$ are then obtained from a table of the normal probability distribution found in the back of almost any statistics book.

Although the Black-Scholes model is intuitively appealing, it can be a bit overwhelming at first. It is easier to understand if digested a piece at a time.

- Recall that the value of an in-the-money call option at expiration is the difference between stock price and exercise price. The Black-Scholes model has exactly this form: the value of a call option is the difference between two numbers, the first based on the stock price and the second based on the exercise price.
- There is a potential time value mismatch in the data since the call option's price and the stock price are values today while the exercise price is a future value at the time of the option's expiration. The Black-Scholes model solves this problem by discounting the option's exercise price to the present by dividing by e^{rt}, the present value factor for interest rate r and time t when interest is compounded continuously.[2]
- $N(d_1)$ is the hedge ratio required to construct a riskless hedge stated in shares of stock per option. It balances the number of shares and options in the equation, adjusting the stock price to be consistent with the one option represented by the exercise price (E) in the second term.
- $N(d_2)$ does not have a simple interpretation by itself. Its role, however, when combined with $N(d_1)$, is to adjust the equation for the option's changing value as the time to expiration declines. Note that since the area under any probability distribution must equal 1.00 (or 100%), $N(d_1)$ and $N(d_2)$, each a portion of the total area, must both be less than 1.

Four of the five numbers required to use the Black-Scholes model—stock price (S), exercise price (E), the risk-free rate (r), and the time until the option expires (t)—are known precisely at any time. Only the variance of rates of return of the stock (σ^2) must be estimated. This is usually done from data about past stock price movements adjusted by any new insights and forecasts of the company's future stock price behavior.

Example

Black-Scholes Model

Steve Payne is interested in purchasing a one-month call option with exercise price of $63 on Xerox stock. The stock is currently selling at $60 per share, and the risk-free rate is 4.90%. Steve estimates the variance of the stock's rate of re-

[2] **Elaboration and cross-reference:** Black and Scholes used continuous compounding in their derivation to avoid having to specify a compounding period and to simplify their mathematics. In this book, continuous compounding was discussed briefly in Appendix 5A for just this purpose.

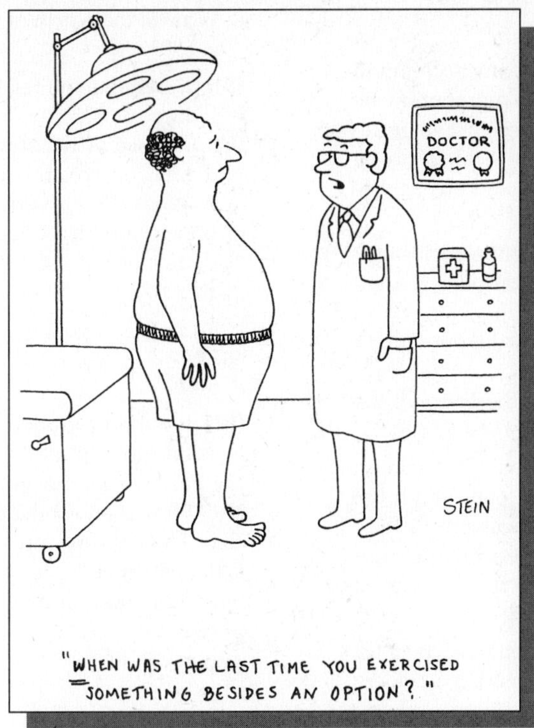
DOCTOR
STEIN
"WHEN WAS THE LAST TIME YOU EXERCISED SOMETHING BESIDES AN OPTION?"

turn to be 20%. Then, using a calculator with a natural logarithm function and table of the standard normal distribution, he calculates $N(d_1) = .390$ and $N(d_2) = .341$

Question: What is the value of the option according to the Black-Scholes model?

Solution steps:

1. Calculate the time to expiration in years:

$$1 \text{ month} = 1/12 \text{ year} = .0833 \text{ years}$$

2. Plug the variables into the Black Scholes model:

$$C = 60 \times .390 - \left(\frac{63}{(2.71828)^{.049 \times .0833}}\right) \times .341$$

$$C = 23.40 - 21.40 = \$2$$

Answer: The call option is worth $2.00

The Black-Scholes model was derived for a European option, one that cannot be exercised until its expiration date. American call options can be exercised prior to maturity and thus might have a different value. However, professor Robert Merton has shown that it never pays to exercise an American option prior to its maturity date. Accordingly, the value of an American call option must be equal to that of a European call option, and the model is valid for both.

Problems

1. **(Two-state riskless hedge)** A company's common stock is selling for $35 per share. In one month the stock price is expected to either increase to $40 or decrease to $30. Consider a call option on one share of the stock with a one-month maturity and an exercise price of $33.
   a. What will be the value of the option in each state?
   b. What hedge ratio is required to construct a riskless hedge?
   c. What is the worth of the option if the one-month riskless rate of interest is 0.5%?
   d. What will happen to the worth of the option if the one-month riskless rate of interest rises to 0.6%?
2. **(Two-state riskless hedge)** A company's common stock is selling for $90 per share. In one month the stock price is expected to either increase to $105 or decrease to $75. The one-month riskless rate of interest is 0.45%. Consider a call option on one share of the stock with a one-month maturity.
   a. What will be the value of the option in each state?
   b. What hedge ratio is required to construct a riskless hedge?
   c. What is the worth of the option if its exercise price is $93?
   d. What is the worth of the option if its exercise price is $98?
3. **(Black-Scholes model)** A company's common stock is selling for $35 per share. Based on an analysis of the variance of the stock's rate of return, the factor $N(d_1)$ has been estimated to be .673 and $N(d_2)$ to be .602. What is the worth of a call option on one share of the stock with a one-month maturity and an exercise price of $33 if the risk-free rate of interest is:
   a. 3%?
   b. 4%?
   c. 5%?
   d. 6%?
4. **(Black-Scholes model)** A company's common stock is selling for $90 per share. Based on an analysis of the variance of the stock's rate of return, the factor $N(d_1)$ has been estimated to be .438 and $N(d_2)$ to be .386. The risk-free rate of interest is now 4.5%. What is the worth of a call option on one share of the stock with a one-month maturity if its exercise price is:
   a. $80?
   b. $85?
   c. $90?
   d. $95?

CHAPTER 10
THE COST OF CAPITAL

Amy Graham refilled her coffee cup and returned to the conference table. The director of financial analysis for her company was pointing to a flip-chart in the corner of the room. "I've put the Irving Fisher interest rate model up on this chart. Remember that all interest rates are composed of pure, inflation, and risk factors. It is important that we understand each component of the rates of return demanded by our investors if we are to come up with a meaningful number."

As a new member of her company's financial analysis staff, Amy was part of the group responsible for bringing a finance perspective to the analysis of the firm's investment decisions. Today, the group was meeting to update the calculation of the firm's cost of capital.

The meeting had begun with a review of the current state of the financial markets presented by the chief economist of the firm's bank. This led to a discussion of the level and structure of interest rates and forecasts of where rates might be in 3, 6, and 12 months. Now the group was talking about ways to measure investors' perceptions of the riskiness of the firm's securities.

Amy raised her hand. "I'm still not sure how we should handle the fact that we raise money from a variety of sources—we've already talked about banks, long-term creditors, and stockholders, just for starters. I can't believe that all of them want the same rate of return from us. In fact. if the modeling we're doing is correct, they should want different rates of return. After all, they hold financial instruments that differ in maturity and risk. How do we put it all together?"

Amy's question points out a fundamental financial dilemma all companies face. A proposed use of funds adds value to a firm if it generates benefits in excess of the requirements of the company's stakeholders. Yet, every firm has multiple stakeholders, and they each have their own requirements. Which stakeholders' requirements should be used to test whether a proposed use of money is acceptable? Fortunately, finance theory provides a practical solution to Amy's concern, recommending that a firm first meet the needs of its noninvestor stakeholders and then test the remaining cash flows against the cost of capital, a single rate integrating the requirements of all financial investors.

The cost of a firm's capital, like the cost of the other resources it uses, is a significant determinant of its ability to be competitive. A company that can raise low-cost capital has an important edge over its competition. When its capital costs are low, a company can price aggressively and still be profitable. It can plow more funds into research and development and into other product and service improvements. And by generating high rates of return it can increase the benefits it provides to all of its stakeholders. Accordingly, a key part of the financial manager's responsibility is to minimize capital costs, a job that begins with a thorough understanding of where the firm's cost of capital comes from and how it is constructed.

Key Points You Should Learn from This Chapter

After reading this chapter you should be able to:

- Discuss the meaning of the cost of capital and how the establishment of a cost of capital affects management decision making.
- Describe the process of calculating a cost of capital.
- Determine an investor's required rate of return.
- Calculate the cost of a capital source.
- Integrate the cost of a firm's capital sources to produce its cost of capital.
- Graph a firm's cost of capital schedule.

Introductory Concepts—The Nature of the Cost of Capital

cost of capital—the minimum rate of return a firm must earn on new investments to satisfy its creditors and stockholders

The **cost of capital** is an interest rate—the minimum interest rate a firm must earn on its investments to add value for its stakeholders. It is closely related to investors' required rates of return, a concept we explored in the last chapter, but it goes beyond the requirements of investors to include other costs of raising money that investors do not see.

1. The Cost of Capital Is an Incremental Cost

In economic terms, the cost of capital is a firm's opportunity cost.[1] Every time a company invests money, it makes a choice. By accepting one investment, it forgoes the opportunity to invest elsewhere. One "alternate investment" is for the company to return the funds to its investors and let them put the money into some other earning opportunity. Investors will demand this if the firm cannot do better than they can elsewhere. Accordingly, the firm must earn a rate of return above this opportunity cost to satisfy its investors.

The cost of capital concept is incremental in nature. Every new investment opportunity requires management either to raise new money or to reinvest money already within the firm, money that otherwise could be returned to investors. Ei-

"They're not as young as they look . . . they have a 4½% mortgage!"

[1] **Cross-reference:** The concept of an opportunity cost was introduced in Chapter 4, p. 81.

ther way, by making an investment, the firm is asking investors to forgo some other investment opportunity that could earn at today's level of interest rates. *The cost of capital is thus always calculated using the rates of return investors would require today to provide new funds to the firm.*

2. The Effect of the Cost of Capital on the Organization

Establishing a cost of capital provides a powerful signal to members of an organization as to what is acceptable financial behavior. It states loudly and clearly that an investment idea that cannot better that benchmark will be rejected out of hand. Individuals hoping to get approval for their proposals will be motivated to spend time recasting their work into a form that can be tested against the cost of capital. Done properly, this can be a healthy discipline. Done poorly, it can lead to much destructive behavior.

If the cost of capital analysis is too tightly managed by the finance function, it can place too much authority in the hands of finance. This can lead finance to adopt a "judge and jury" role, making decisions about ideas on which it is often not well qualified to pass judgment. This also erects barriers between business departments and works against cooperative teamwork within the organization.

At the other extreme, if the cost of capital is not used under the guidance of those with financial expertise, it is in danger of being used incorrectly by those hoping to have their pet projects approved. Numbers will be twisted to look good and lose all their meaning in the process.

The cost of capital typically will differ among the various parts of the organization. Each unit of a company has its own spectrum of risks, different from the other parts of the business. Accordingly, each unit has its own beta and requires its own risk premium. Further, the different parts of a business often provide access to individualized funds, sources of money not available to other units of the organization. To the extent a business unit can obtain low-cost funds, it lowers its cost of capital vis-à-vis the rest of the organization. The wise financial manager works closely with the various parts of the business to foster an understanding about the cost of capital so it is not used or seen as a tool of arbitrary discrimination.

Properly used, the cost of capital becomes a shared understanding of the financial requirements of the business—a guide helping everyone within the organization grasp what is needed for successful financial performance.

The Process of Calculating a Cost of Capital

The calculation of a cost of capital proceeds through five steps:

1. *Identify the sources of capital the firm will use.* Only these sources enter the cost of capital calculation; the firm has no obligation to people or organizations that are not its stakeholders. We began our consideration of sources of financing in Appendix 4D when we saw that financial leverage ratios are

often used to test the wisdom of the firm's financing decisions. We will continue the analysis of financing choice in Chapter 15, where we examine the mix of debt and equity, and in Chapter 16, where we study the mix of debt maturities. In this chapter we will assume that the firm has already made these decisions.

2. *For each source of financing the firm plans to use, determine the required rate of return demanded by the supplier(s) of those funds.* The cost of capital begins here since its purpose is to test potential uses of funds to see if they produce the returns investors want. Where the investor is a professional, such as a banker or a private investor, we only need to ask. However, if we are raising funds from many investors in the public markets, it is impossible to learn investors' required rate of return by asking. First, it is difficult to phrase the question in a way that conveys precisely the correct meaning to each respondent. Second, it is unlikely that investors would give the desired answer; rather they might ask for a much higher rate of return in the hopes of motivating management to do better. Third, we would have to ask all potential investors. As a result, we use other means to estimate investors' required rate of return for publicly issued securities.

cost of a source of funds—the rate a firm must earn from the use of funds to provide the rate of return required by that investor

flotation costs—the total amount paid to third parties in order to raise funds

3. *Convert each required rate of return to the* ***cost of that source of funds.*** Since we plan to use the cost of capital to qualify the firm's potential investments, we need a number that captures all the benefits and obligations the firm will experience if it raises these funds. The cost of a source of capital is found by adjusting investors' required rate of return by the effects of flotation costs and income taxes. **Flotation costs,** the costs associated with issuing a security, add to the cost of capital by requiring a company to earn not only the investors' required rate of return, but also enough to cover these extra costs. By contrast, whenever the cash paid to investors is a legitimate deduction on a firm's tax return—interest payments, for example—the government effectively reduces the cost of that source of capital by reducing the firm's tax payments.
4. *Integrate the various capital costs into one overall cost of capital for the firm.* The typical company raises money from a variety of sources, each with its own cost. Yet we want to produce a single number that the firm can use to test the adequacy of the returns on investments it might undertake. We use the relative proportion of each financing source to produce a "weighted-average" cost of capital.
5. *Extrapolate the cost of capital into a cost of capital schedule, projecting how the cost of capital will change with the amount of financing the firm attempts to acquire.* In general, firms use the least-expensive sources of financing first, and, when these run out, turn to more-expensive sources of money. As a result, a company that needs to raise large amounts of funding will find its cost of capital rising.[2]

[2] **Alternate point of view:** We have shown this pattern in Figure 10.1 in the graph of the cost of capital schedule by drawing a line that starts off horizontal and then curves up as capital costs increase. However, there is some evidence that as large firms raise an increasing amount of money, the cost of capital declines before it increases due to economies of scale in raising funds.

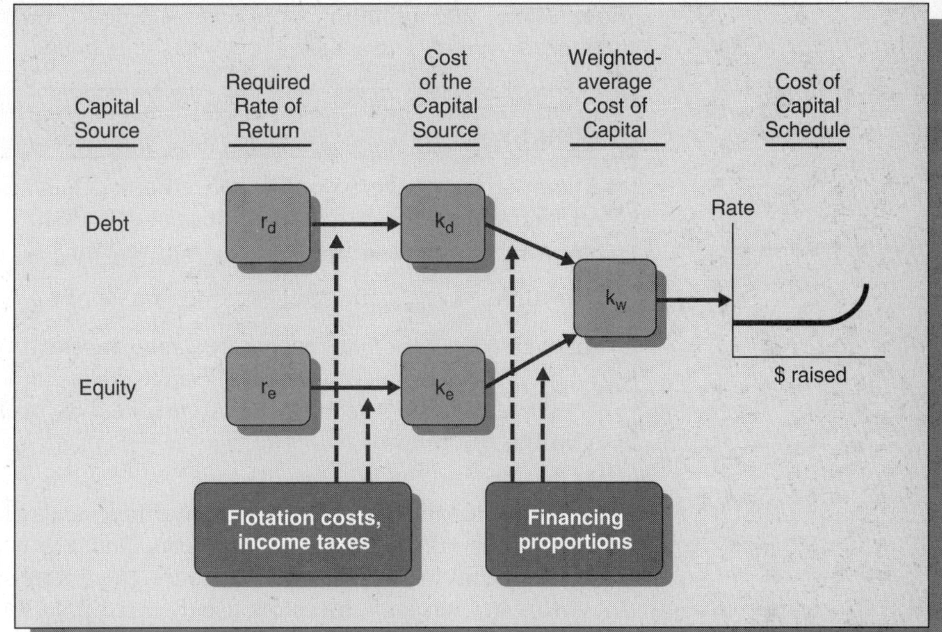

FIGURE 10.1 The process of calculating a cost of capital. Required rates of return first are converted into "costs" by incorporating flotation and income tax effects and then are combined by taking a weighted average.

Figure 10.1 summarizes this process. In Figure 10.1, we introduce the notation used to represent these concepts. "r" stands for investors' required rate of return, and "k" stands for the cost of that source of capital. The subscripts are "d" for debt, "e" for equity, and "w" for the weighted-average. As needed, we will introduce additional subscripts to denote more specific forms of debt and equity: "b" for bonds, "ps" for preferred stock, "cs" for common stock, and "re" for retained earnings; and in Appendix 10A: "wp" for wages payable, "ap" for accounts payable, "ria" for receipts-in-advance, and "bnp" for bank notes payable.

In the remainder of this chapter we will learn how to perform each of the five steps in turn.

Determining Required Rates of Return

Professional investors normally quote their required rate of return when asked. Sometimes the quotation is uncomplicated and gives the required rate of return directly.

Example

A Quotation That Directly Gives the Required Rate of Return

A loan officer at the First Finance Bank offers a $10 million ordinary interest loan for one year at a fixed annual rate of 12%. 12% is r_{bnp}, the bank's required rate of return.

More often, the quotation contains sufficient complexity to require further analysis.

Example

A Quotation That Does *Not* Directly Give the Required Rate of Return

A loan officer at the Second Finance Bank offers a $10 million ordinary interest loan for one year at a fixed annual rate of 10% plus a 2% origination fee and a 15% compensating balance requirement.[3]

Question: Is r_{bnp}, the bank's required rate of return, equal to 10%?

Answer: r_{bnp}, the bank's required rate of return on this loan, is not simply the 10% rate quoted by the bank since the fee and balance requirement complicate the loan's cash flows. We must solve for the interest rate embedded in this quotation.

If we are not dealing with a professional investor, we must use other means to calculate investors' required rate of return. One way is to infer their required rate from their behavior, in particular from the price they set on the firm's securities. As we saw in Chapter 9, investors use their required rate of return as the discount rate to set security prices. By doing the calculation in reverse we can use the price we observe to derive the required rate of return.

Example

Inferring the Required Rate of Return from Security Prices

Investors have set a price of $950 on the $1,000 face value bonds of the Miron Company. The bonds have an 11.80% semi-annual coupon and mature in seven years.

Question: What is r_b, the rate of return required by bond investors?

Solution steps:

1. Identify the cash flows promised by this bond. With an 11.80% coupon, the bond pays 11.80% of $1,000 = $118 per year, or $59 each half year for 14 half-years. It will also pay its maturity value 14 half-years from now.

	Year 0	Half-years 1–14	Half-year 14
Price/par	($950)		$1,000
Interest		$59	

2. Calculate the interest rate embedded in these cash flows:

   CLEAR the time value part of your calculator

   Key in −950 and press PV

   Key in 1,000 and press FV

[3] **Elaboration and cross-reference:** A loan origination fee is paid to the lender at the time the loan is taken. A compensating balance is a noninterest-bearing deposit that must be kept at the bank as long as the loan remains outstanding. We will look at these concepts, and how to determine the effective annual interest rate in this kind of loan, in Chapter 20.

Key in 59 and press PMT, set END

Key in 14 and press n

Compute i = 6.4531%

3. Annualize the interest rate:

$$YTM = r_b = (1.064531)^2 - 1 = 13.32\%$$

Answer: Investors' required rate of return from these bonds, r_b, is their yield to maturity of 13.32%.

The required rate of return on common stock traded in the capital markets may also be estimated as a combination of the risk-free rate of interest and an appropriate risk premium by using the capital asset pricing model presented in Chapter 8.

Example

Deriving the Required Rate of Return on Common Stock from the Capital Asset Pricing Model

The common stock of the Miron Company has a beta of 1.15. U.S. Treasury bonds currently yield 8.55%, and the market price of risk is estimated to be 8.3%.

Question: What is r_{cs}, the required rate of return of investors in this stock?

Solution steps: Apply the capital asset pricing model:

$$r_{cs} = r_f + (\text{market price of risk}) \times \beta$$

$$= 8.55\% + (8.3\%) \times 1.15$$

$$= 8.55\% + 9.55\% = 18.10\%$$

Answer: Investors require an 18.10% rate of return from Miron Company stock.

Calculating the Cost of a Capital Source

The cost of a source of financing, like investors' required rate of return, is an interest rate. And like the required rate of return, it is typically found by organizing the cash flows associated with the financing and solving for the embedded rate of interest. It differs from the required rate of return in that it is more inclusive. While the required rate of return calculation looks only at the cash flows between the investor and the firm, the cost-of-a-capital-source calculation adds in the other cash flows the firm experiences as a result of taking the financing. Thus, while the required rate of return describes the *cash flows experienced by the investor,* the cost of a capital source describes the *cash flows experienced by the firm.*

There are two cash flows that arise from taking on financing which are experienced by the firm but not by investors: flotation costs and corporate income taxes.

1. Flotation Costs

Flotation costs include all amounts paid to third parties to arrange the issue of securities: underwriting fees, selling fees, legal fees, printing costs, filing fees, etc. Some sources of financing—bank loans, for example—can be obtained without flotation costs. Others—for example, the public sale of bonds or stock—typically require investment banking and legal assistance. If flotation costs must be paid, the cost of that source of funds will be greater than investors' required rate of return.

Examples

How Flotation Costs Raise the Cost of a Capital Source

Miron Company's investment banker has advised the firm that it would be possible to sell at face value a new issue of $100.00 preferred stock with a $13.00 annual dividend paid quarterly and that they would charge 6% of face value to underwrite the issue.

Question: What is r_{ps}, the required rate of return of investors willing to purchase this new preferred stock issue?

Solution steps: Solve for the interest rate *investors* will experience if they buy this preferred stock. (Recall that preferred stock is a perpetuity.)

1. Obtain the cash flows:

$$\text{Quarterly dividend} = \$13.00/4 = \$3.25$$

2. Organize the investors' cash flows:

	Year 0	Quarters 1–∞
Buy stock at face value	($100.00)	
Dividend		$3.25
Net cash flows	($100.00)	$3.25

3. Solve for the interest rate using the model for the present value of a perpetuity:

$$\text{Quarterly rate} = \frac{D_{ps}}{\text{price}}$$

$$= \frac{\$3.25}{\$100.00} = 3.25\%$$

4. Annualize the rate:

$$r_{ps} = (1.0325)^4 - 1 = 13.65\%$$

Answer: Investors require a 13.65% rate of return to invest in Miron Company's proposed preferred stock issue.

Question: What is k_{ps}, the cost to Miron Company of this preferred stock?

Solution steps: Solve for the interest rate *the firm* will experience if it issues this preferred stock.

1. Organize the firm's cash flows *including flotation cost* (6% of the planned $100 face value = $6 per share):

	Year 0	Quarters 1–∞
Sell stock at face value	$100.00	
Dividend		($3.25)
Flotation cost	(6.00)	
Net cash flows	$ 94.00	($3.25)

2. Solve for the interest rate using the model for the present value of a perpetuity:

$$\text{Quarterly cost} = \frac{D_{ps}}{\text{net proceeds}}$$

$$= \frac{\$3.25}{\$94.00}$$

$$= 3.4574\%$$

3. Annualize the rate:

$$k_{ps} = (1.034574)^4 - 1 = 14.56\%$$

Answer: The cost, k_{ps}, to Miron Company of this new preferred stock capital is 14.56%. This is greater than investors' required rate of return of 13.65%. If Miron company issues the preferred stock, it will have to earn 14.56% from investing the proceeds both to pay the flotation cost and to return 13.65% to its investors.[4]

2. Corporate Income Taxes

The tax law of each country determines which expenses are deductible for tax purposes and which are not. In most countries, including the United States, deductible expenses include production, operating, and interest expenses but do not include principal amounts on loans or dividends, both of which are paid after taxes. A financing source that permits additional tax deductions lowers the firm's taxable income, reducing the taxes it must pay. The firm can use this "released" money for partial payment of its obligation to the investors—in effect the government provides a subsidy to the firm. As a result, a financing source that permits a company to increase its tax deductions will have a cost less than investors' required rate of return.

Examples

How the Corporate Income Tax Lowers the Cost of a Capital Source

Miron Company can privately place an issue of $1,000.00 face value, 30-year bonds. The bonds would carry a 10.70% interest coupon paid semi-annually and would be purchased by the investor at par. Since the issue would be privately placed, there would be no flotation cost. Miron is in the 35% marginal income tax bracket.

[4] **Elaboration:** Another way to look at the effect of flotation costs is to notice that, while each investor pays $100.00 for a share of the new preferred, Miron Company only receives $94.00. With less than the full amount to invest, each dollar has to earn at a higher rate of return to bring in the required quarterly $3.25.

Question: What is r_b, the required rate of return of the investor willing to purchase this new bond issue?

Solution steps: Solve for the interest rate *investors* will experience if they buy this bond issue.

1. Identify the cash flows promised by this bond. With a 10.70% coupon, the bond pays 10.70% of $1,000.00 = $107.00 per year or $53.50 each half-year for 60 half-years. It will also pay its maturity value 60 half-years from now. The price is par value or $1,000.00 per bond.

	Year 0	Half-years 1–60	Half-year 60
Principal	($1,000.00)		$1,000.00
Interest		$53.50	

2. Calculate the interest rate embedded in these cash flows:

CLEAR the time value part of your calculator

Key in −1,000 and press PV

Key in 1,000 and press FV

Key in 53.50 and press PMT, set END

Key in 60 and press n

Compute i = 5.35%

3. Annualize the interest rate:

$$YTM = r_b = (1.0535)^2 - 1 = 10.99\%$$

Answer: The investor requires a 10.99% rate of return to buy Miron Company's proposed bond issue.

Question: What is k_b, the cost to Miron Company of this bond financing?

Solution steps: Solve for the interest rate *the firm* will experience if it issues these bonds.

1. Calculate the tax savings from deducting interest payments:

$$\text{Tax savings} = 35\% \times \$53.50 = \$18.73.$$

2. Organize the firm's cash flows *including the tax savings:*

	Year 0	Half-years 1–60	Half-year 60
Principal	$1,000.00		($1,000.00)
Interest		($53.50)	
Tax savings		18.73	
Net cash flows	$1,000.00	($34.77)	($1,000.00)

3. Calculate the interest rate embedded in these cash flows:

CLEAR the time value part of your calculator

Key in 1,000 and press PV

Key in −34.77 and press PMT, set END

Key in −1,000 and press FV

Key in 60 and press n

Compute i = 3.477%

4. Annualize the interest rate:

$$k_b = (1.03477)^2 - 1 = 7.08\%$$

Answer: The cost, k_b, to Miron Company of this new bond capital is 7.08%. This is less than investors' required rate of return of 10.99%. If Miron company issues the bonds, it will only have to earn 7.08% from investing the proceeds to be able to return 10.99% to its investor. The remainder of the 10.99% return will come from the cash redirected from tax payments to the investor.[5]

Figure 10.2 identifies in summary form how long-term financing sources are affected by flotation costs and income taxes. In general, if a security is sold to the public the firm will incur flotation costs. Income taxes will be reduced for debt financing since interest payments (but not dividends) are tax-deductible. Notice that all four combinations are possible: a financing source can result in both flotation costs and tax reductions (publicly placed debt), flotation costs but no tax reductions (publicly placed preferred and common stock), tax reductions but no flotation costs (privately placed debt), or neither flotation costs nor tax reductions (retained earnings and privately placed preferred and common stock).

The Cost of Various Capital Sources

Every prospective entry on the right-hand side of a firm's balance sheet represents a possible source of financing. While they differ in many respects—different investors, different maturities, different degrees of flexibility, different claims, different risk exposures, etc.—each financial source used by the firm makes up one piece of its overall cost of capital. Financial managers must evaluate each of

[5] **Elaboration:** A simplified method to calculate the after-tax cost of financing when payments to the investor are tax-deductible is to multiply the (pre-tax) required rate of return by (1 − the tax rate). In this case, using the semi-annual numbers:

$$\text{Semi-annual } k_b = \text{semi-annual } r_b \times (1 - .35)$$

$$\text{Semi-annual } k_b = 5.35\% \times (.65) = 3.477\%$$

This method will work providing the tax law requires that deductions be taken at the time interest accrues against the financing obligation. Should the law specify any other timing for tax-deductions, this calculation will fail. In particular, if tax deductions can be taken prior to the dates when interest accrues, the firm will receive its tax subsidies earlier—which will make them more valuable—and its cost of capital will be further reduced. On the other hand, if tax deductions must be deferred beyond the dates on which interest accrues, they will be less valuable; the firm's cost of capital will not be as heavily subsidized and will not be reduced as much.

Financing source		Flotation cost	Reduced corporate income tax
Long-term debt (bonds)	Private placement		X
	Public issue	X	X
Preferred stock	Private placement		
	Public issue	X	
Common equity	Retained earnings		
	Private placement		
	Public issue	X	

FIGURE 10.2
Summary of additional cash flows. Public issues incur flotation costs while interest on debt reduces corporate income taxes.

these funding sources and determine first the required rate of return, and then the cost of each. Nevertheless, the primary funding sources for many companies are the long term sources: bonds, preferred stock and common stock. As a result, we consider these three sources in the remainder of this chapter.[6]

Since the calculation of the cost of a funding source is typically an extension of the calculation of the required rate of return (adding in the cash flows for flotation costs and corporate income taxes), we will illustrate these two steps in combination in the examples of this section. In each case we will follow a two-step process:

1. Calculate investors' required rate of return by studying the market price and the cash flows anticipated by investors in an existing security of comparable risk and maturity to the proposed new issue.
2. Calculate the cost of the funding source by laying out the cash flows the firm would experience if it were to issue new securities to give investors the required rate of return determined in step 1.

1. Bonds

Bonds have an explicit cost due to their interest obligation, however, the interest is tax-deductible which lowers the cost of bond financing. If sold to the general public, a new issue will most likely have flotation costs as well. The tax treatment of flotation costs depends on the tax law; in the U.S., flotation costs on debt instruments must be capitalized and amortized over the life of the issue.[7] Thus, there is a second small tax subsidy for debt with flotation costs.

Examples

The Cost of Bonds

Miron Company has $100,000.00 face value of outstanding bonds consisting of 100 $1,000.00 face value bonds with a 14.20% semi-annual coupon. The issue will mature in 20 years and is currently selling for 102.5 ($1,025.00 per bond).

[6] **Cross-reference:** The cost of short-term financing sources is discussed in Appendix 10A.

[7] **Accounting review:** This means flotation cost must be treated just like a machine subject to straight line depreciation. The company cannot deduct the flotation cost when the bond is issued but must spread it out evenly, deducting a small amount each (half-) year.

Miron's investment banker has advised that it would require a 4% underwriting fee to place a new 20-year issue of comparable risk. Miron is in the 35% marginal tax bracket.

Question: What is r_b, the required rate of return of Miron's bond investors today?

Solution steps: Use the outstanding bond to calculate investors' required rate of return by solving for the interest rate *the investors* will experience:

1. Identify the cash flows promised by this bond. With a 14.20% coupon, the bond pays 14.20% of $1,000 = $142 per year or $71 each half year for 40 half-years. It will also pay its maturity value 40 half-years from now.

	Year 0	Half-years 1–40	Half-year 40
Price/par	($ 1,025.00)		$1,000.00
Interest		$71.00	

2. Calculate the interest rate embedded in these cash flows:

CLEAR the time value part of your calculator

Key in −1,025 and press PV

Key in 71 and press PMT, set END

Key in 1,000 and press FV

Key in 40 and press n

Compute i = 6.9143%

3. Annualize the interest rate:

$$\text{YTM} = r_b = (1.069143)^2 - 1 = 14.31\%$$

Answer: Investors require a 14.31% rate of return, r_b, from Miron's existing bonds.

Question: What is k_b, the cost to Miron of a new issue of bond financing if the interest coupon on the new bonds is set so they will sell at par value?

Solution steps: Solve for the interest rate *the firm* will experience on the proposed new issue:

1. Since investors now require a semi-annual yield of 6.914%, a new issue would have to carry a coupon of 6.914% × $1,000.00 = $69.14 per half-year to sell at par.
2. Calculate flotation costs and tax savings:

Flotation cost = 4% × $1,000.00 = $40.00 per bond

Tax saving from deducting interest each half-year

= 35% × $69.14 = $24.20

Tax saving from deducting flotation cost:

Amount deducted each half-year

= $40.00/40 half-years = $1.00.

Tax saving each half-year = 35% × $1.00 = $0.35

3. *Include flotation costs and income taxes in the cash flows:*

	Year 0	Half-years 1–40	Half-year 40
Principal	$1,000.00		($1,000.00)
Interest		($69.14)	
Flotation	(40.00)		
Tax-interest		24.20	
Tax-flotation		.35	
	$ 960.00	($44.59)	($1,000.00)

4. Calculate the interest rate embedded in these cash flows:

CLEAR the time value part of your calculator

Key in 960 and press PV

Key in −44.59 and press PMT, set END

Key in −1,000 and press FV

Key in −40 and press n

Compute i = 4.6821%

5. Annualize the interest rate:

$$k_b = (1.046821)^2 - 1 = 9.58\%$$

Answer: The cost of this financing, k_b, is 9.58%. Miron must invest the money to earn at least 9.58%.

2. Preferred Stock

Because preferred stock pays a dividend and not interest, payments to investors are not tax deductible. In addition, under United States tax law flotation costs on a stock issue may not be deducted on the firm's tax return. As a result, in the U.S. preferred stock receives no tax subsidy at all.

Example

The Cost of Preferred Stock

Miron Company has $25,000.00 par value of outstanding preferred stock, consisting of 250 shares with $100.00 face value each currently selling for $87.50. The stock pays a quarterly dividend based on an annual dividend rate of $12.00 per share. Miron's investment banker has advised that it would require a 6% underwriting fee to place a new issue of comparable risk.

Question: What is r_{ps}, the required rate of return of Miron's preferred stock investors today?

Solution steps: Use the outstanding preferred stock to calculate investors' required rate of return by solving for the rate *the investors* will experience:

1. Determine the quarterly dividend:

$$\$12.00/4 = \$3.00$$

2. Organize the investors' cash flows:

	Year 0	Quarters 1–∞
Buy stock	($87.50)	
Dividend		$3.00

3. Apply the model for the present value of a perpetuity:

$$\text{Quarterly rate} = \frac{D_{ps}}{\text{price}}$$

$$= \frac{\$3.00}{\$87.50}$$

$$= 3.4286\%$$

4. Annualize the rate:

$$r_{ps} = (1.034286)^4 - 1 = 14.44\%$$

Answer: Investors require a 14.44% rate of return, r_{ps}, from Miron's existing preferred stock.

Question: What is k_{ps}, the cost to Miron of a new issue of preferred stock financing if the dividend on the new stock is set so it will sell at par value?

Solution steps: Solve for the rate *the firm* will experience on the proposed new issue:

1. As investors now require a 3.43% quarterly yield from Miron Company preferred stock, a new issue would have to carry a quarterly dividend of 3.43% × $100.00 = $3.43 to sell at par.
2. Calculate flotation costs:

$$6\% \times \$100.00 = \$6.00 \text{ per share}$$

3. *Include flotation costs in the cash flows:*

	Year 0	Quarters 1–∞
Sell stock	$100.00	
Dividend		($3.43)
Flotation	(6.00)	
	$ 94.00	($3.43)

4. Solve for the interest rate using the model for the present value of a perpetuity:

$$\text{Quarterly cost} = \frac{D_{ps}}{\text{net proceeds}}$$

$$= \frac{\$3.43}{\$94.00}$$

$$= 3.6489\%$$

5. Annualize the rate:

$$k_{ps} = (1.036489)^4 - 1 = 15.41\%$$

Answer: The cost, k_{ps}, to Miron Company of this new preferred stock capital is 15.41%. Miron must earn at least 15.41% on the money to justify its preferred stock financing.

3. Common Stock

A company that wishes to increase its common equity financing can do so in either of two ways. First, it can simply retain earnings. The earnings of a firm represent the residual increase in value not claimed by other stakeholders. By electing not to pay this as a dividend, management forces shareholders to increase the amount they have invested in the firm. Alternatively, management may choose to sell new shares of stock. These may be sold to existing shareholders or, more usually, to new investors.

Regardless of the source of new equity, the required rate of return is the same. Investors see no difference between the money they paid in and the money that management (re)invested for them. As a result, there is only one required rate of return for both retained earnings and for a new common stock issue. In addition, common stock financing, like preferred-stock financing, gets no tax subsidy, since neither its dividends nor flotation costs may be deducted on the firm's tax return.

However, there is a difference in the cost of these two common equity sources due to flotation costs. Notice that there are no flotation costs associated with retained earnings—a firm does not have to pay third parties to keep what it already has. By contrast, it is normal to use the services of an investment banker to sell a new stock issue. As a result, *the difference in flotation costs is the only distinction between the cost of retained earnings and the cost of a new common stock issue.*

Examples

The Cost of Common Equity

Miron Company has 10,000 shares of common stock outstanding currently selling for $25.00 per share. The stock recently paid a $0.56 per share quarterly dividend. Investors forecast that the firm will grow at a 2% quarterly rate for the foreseeable future. Miron expects to retain $20,000.00 in the coming year. Should it require additional equity financing, it will sell shares of stock to the public; its investment banker has advised that it would require an 8% underwriting fee to place any new issue.

Question: What is r_{cs}, the required rate of return of Miron's common stock investors today?

Solution steps: Use the outstanding common stock to calculate investors' required rate of return by solving for the rate *the investors* will experience:

1. Forecast the next dividend by incorporating the 2% growth rate:

$$D_1 = \$0.56\ (1.02) = \$0.5712$$

2. Apply the dividend-growth model:

$$\text{Quarterly rate} = \frac{D_1}{\text{price}} + g$$

$$= \frac{\$0.5712}{\$25.00} + .02$$

$$= .022848 + .02 = .042848 = 4.2848\%$$

3. Annualize the rate:

$$r_{cs} = (1.042848)^4 - 1 = 18.27\%$$

Answer: Investors require an 18.27% rate of return, r_{cs}, from Miron's existing common stock.

Question: What is k_{re}, the cost to Miron of retaining additional earnings?

Answer: $k_{re} = r_{cs} = 18.27\%$. With no flotation cost nor tax subsidy, *the cost of retained earnings always equals investors' required rate of return.*

Question: What is k_{cs}, the cost to Miron of a new issue of common stock?

Solution steps: Solve for the rate *the firm* will experience on the proposed new issue:

1. Calculate the net proceeds to Miron of a new stock issue.

$$\text{Flotation cost} = 8\% \times \$25.00 = \$2.00 \text{ per share.}$$

$$\text{Net proceeds} = \$25.00 - 2 = \$23.00 \text{ per share.}$$

2. Apply the dividend-growth model:

$$\text{Quarterly rate} = \frac{D_1}{\text{net proceeds}} + g$$

$$= \frac{\$0.5712}{\$23.00} + .02$$

$$= .024835 + .02 = .044835 = 4.4835\%$$

3. Annualize the rate:

$$r_{cs} = (1.044835)^4 - 1 = 19.18\%$$

Answer: The cost, k_{cs}, to Miron of a new stock issue is 19.18%. Miron must earn a return on these funds of at least this amount to satisfy its common stockholders.

The required rate of return and cost of common stock we calculated using the dividend-growth model are necessarily rough estimates. Unlike debt sources and preferred stock, which specify their future cash flows, common stock does not. While we see the market price investors set on common stock, we can only guess at the future cash flows they forecasted and used to calculate that price. If we guess correctly, our estimates of the required rate of return and cost of common stock will be good; if we guess incorrectly we could be far off the mark.

Because it is difficult to obtain a precise figure for the cost of common equity financing, two other approaches are commonly used to confirm the accuracy of our calculations, (1) the capital asset pricing model, and (2) the "bond-yield-plus" model.

Capital asset pricing model Earlier in this chapter we used the capital asset pricing model to estimate investors' required rate of return on Miron Company stock. The number we obtained there, 18.10% is sufficiently close to our number above, 18.27% to give us some comfort.

Bond-yield-plus model Another device for estimating the required rate of return on common stock is to calculate the required rate for a company's bonds and add a further risk premium. Common stock should be a riskier investment than bonds and should therefore yield a higher rate of return. From historical evidence, the appropriate incremental risk premium for many companies seems to be in the neighborhood of 4%. Applying this logic to the required rate of return we calculated for Miron Company's bonds:

$$r_{cs} = r_b + \text{about } 4\%$$
$$= 14.31\% + \text{about } 4\% = \underline{\underline{\text{about } 18.31\%}}$$

This technique produces a number that is similar to the other two, further increasing our comfort level. It is likely that the required rate of return on Miron's common stock is somewhere in the 18–19% range.

Calculating the Overall Cost of Capital

Miron raises capital from various sources. If the funds could be kept in separate bundles—so that the money raised from bondholders was never mixed with the money raised from bankers or with the money raised from stockholders, etc.—then Miron could use the cost of each funding source as the minimum rate of return it must earn using that money. For example, money with a 10% cost would be invested to earn more than 10%, while money with a 14% cost would have to earn more than 14%. However, the funds raised from various sources quickly get mixed together within a business; it is nearly impossible to look at any one dollar and identify its source. In addition, firms often undertake costly investment projects which require funding from more than one source. As a result, it is appropriate for Miron to calculate and use a single number for its cost of capital.

weighted-average cost of capital (WACOC)—a synonym for "cost of capital" emphasizing the method by which it is constructed

marginal cost of capital (MCC)—a synonym for "cost of capital" emphasizing its use as a measure of the marginal cost of capital funds

Miron's overall cost of capital resources will be a composite of the cost of each capital source. To calculate the single number we identify as Miron's cost of capital, we take a weighted average of the cost of each source of funding used by the firm. The resulting number is commonly known as the **weighted-average cost of capital (WACOC),** reflecting its method of construction. It is also known as the **marginal cost of capital (MCC)** to emphasize its use as a marginal cost; that is, it measures the cost to the firm of raising its next dollar of capital where that dollar is composed of funding from various sources.

target capital structure—the percentage mix of financing sources management plans to use in the future

The weights used in calculating the WACOC should be taken from the firm's **target capital structure,** management's plan for raising funding in the future. Recall that the WACOC is intended to be an incremental figure, the cost of raising the *next* dollar of financing. We took care in calculating the cost of each capital source to look at today's requirements of investors. We must take equal care to ensure that our calculation combines these funds in a mix that reflects management's most up-to-date plans.[8]

Example

Calculating the WACOC

Miron Company's management has announced a target capital structure consisting of 40% bond financing, 10% preferred stock financing, and 50% common equity financing.

Question: What is Miron's WACOC?

Solution steps: Construct a table of funding costs[9] and proportions (the target capital structure) and calculate the weighted average:

Funding Source	Cost	Proportion	Cost × Proportion
Bonds	9.58	40%	3.832
Preferred stock	15.41	10	1.541
Common equity	18.27	50	9.135
		100%	14.508%

Answer: Miron has a WACOC of 14.51%. If each of Miron's investments earn this amount or more, the proceeds will be sufficient to give all investors their required rate of return.

Producing the Marginal Cost of Capital Schedule

Notice that the cost figure used for common equity in Miron Company's WACOC calculation (above) was 18.27%, the cost of retained earnings. Miron faced a choice of using retained earnings or issuing new stock, costing 19.18%, to increase its equity financing. By selecting retained earnings first, Miron's financial manager chose the cheaper source of funding. It will always be to a firm's advantage, other things equal, to select the cheapest financing alternatives first. The firm should turn to more expensive capital only after the cheaper sources of financing are exhausted.

If a firm attempts to raise a large amount of capital at any one time, it will eventually exhaust its cheaper sources of financing. As it substitutes more expensive

[8] **Elaboration:** Sometimes an analyst outside the firm does not know management's target capital structure yet must still approximate the firm's cost of capital. In this case it is usual to assume that the firm is currently at its target capital structure and take the weights from the mix of funds on the firm's most recent balance sheet. When doing this, analysts typically use the market value of each balance sheet item rather than its book value in order to reflect current market conditions and to avoid the incompatibilities of the financial accounting system.

[9] **Cross-reference:** Miron's funding costs are carried forward from the previous examples in this chapter: bonds on pp. 346–348, preferred stock on pp. 348–350, and common equity on pp. 350–352.

cost of capital schedule—a graph showing how a firm's cost of capital will increase with the amount of capital it attempts to raise

break point—a point on the cost of capital schedule where the firm's cost of capital increases

capital for the cheaper funds, its cost of capital will rise. The summary picture of this process is the **cost of capital schedule,** a graph showing the firm's cost of capital as a function of the amount of new financing that it raises. Item by item, each component of the cost of capital will have to be replaced by a more expensive source; its cost will go up, and the weighted average will go up as well. Each time this happens, we have reached a **break point** in the cost of capital schedule.

To locate the break points in a firm's cost of capital schedule, we need two pieces of information: how much of the cheaper source of financing can be raised before it runs out, and what proportion of the total financing mix comes from that source. If management sticks to its target capital structure, the amount of financing newly raised from every source always equals its proportion of the total new financing. The following equation restates this point:

$$\text{Amount of money from each source} = \text{its proportion} \times \text{total new financing}$$

Rearranging gives the form we use to calculate the break points:

$$\textit{Total new financing} = \frac{\textit{amount of money from each source}}{\textit{its proportion}}$$

Example

Finding a Break Point in the Cost of Capital Schedule

Miron Company forecasts it will retain $2 million of new earnings in the coming year. Common equity is 50% of the target capital structure.

Question: How much total financing can Miron raise before it will have used up its new retained earnings and will have to turn to the more expensive new stock issue?

Solution steps:

$$\text{Total new financing} = \frac{\text{amount from this source}}{\text{its proportion}}$$

$$= \frac{\$2{,}000{,}000}{.50} = \$4{,}000{,}000$$

Answer: Miron can raise a total of $4 million of new financing (of which 50% will be the $2 million of new retained earnings and the other 50% will be a mix of the remaining financing sources) before it will exhaust its supply of retained earnings.

After the break point we recalculate the WACOC, substituting the higher-priced new stock issue for the cheaper retained earnings.

Example

Recalculating the WACOC After the Retained Earnings Break Point

If Miron Company raises more than $4 million of total new capital it will have to substitute newly issued stock with cost of 19.18% for retained earnings which cost 18.27%.

Question: What is Miron's WACOC after the break point?

Solution steps: Redo the table making the substitution on the "common equity" line:

Funding Source	Cost	Proportion	Cost × Proportion
Bonds	9.58	40%	3.832
Preferred stock	15.41	10	1.541
Common equity	**19.18**	50	**9.590**
		100%	14.963%

Answer: Miron WACOC goes up from 14.51% to 14.96%.

Figure 10.3 is the cost of capital schedule for the Miron Company as far as we have gone in this chapter. We have found two costs of capital separated by one break point. However, it is likely that there will be additional break points on the cost of capital schedule as Miron studies its other sources of financing to predict when they will run out and have to be replaced with more expensive sources.

Amy Graham listened intently to her peers as the meeting continued. After her earlier questioning, the group had begun an animated discussion of integrating the various components of the firm's cost of capital. By this point Amy felt she had a good grasp of how to construct that number.

The cost of capital was a combination of the rates of return required by all the company's financial investors. It was obtained by calculating a weighted average of the cost of each financial source, using the proportion of each source in

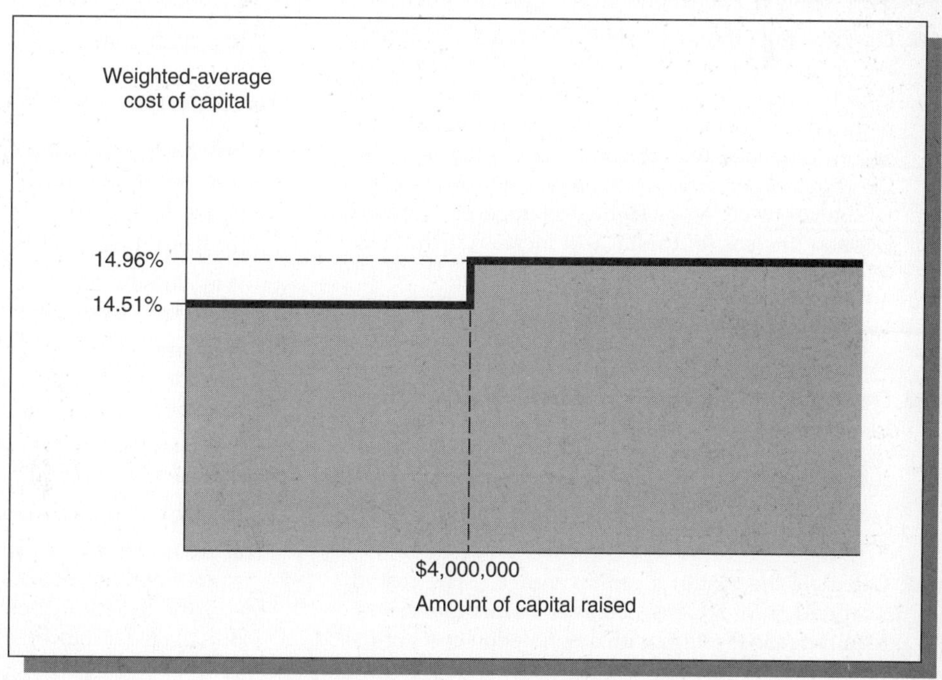

FIGURE 10.3
Cost of capital schedule for the Miron Company. The first $4 million of new funds will have a cost of capital of 14.51%; additional funds will cost 14.96%.

the firm's financing mix as the "weights." The costs were derived by adding flotation costs and income tax reductions (if any) to each investor group's required rate of return.

As the meeting wound to a close, Amy began to wonder some more about the needs of the nonfinancial stakeholders: the firm's employees and customers for example. Might it be possible to include their requirements into some kind of expanded cost of capital calculation, perhaps transforming it into a "cost of all resources" analysis? If so, what would such an analysis look like? And how might it be used? Amy smiled as she realized she was asking important questions about the future of finance theory.

Summary of Key Points

- **Discuss the meaning of the cost of capital and how the establishment of a cost of capital affects management decision making.** The cost of capital is the minimum rate of return a firm must earn on its new investments to meet the financial requirements of its investors. It is the firm's opportunity cost, capturing the requirement that the firm must earn more than investors' alternate opportunities. The cost of capital is an incremental concept measuring the cost of raising the next dollar of funds. As such it is always calculated with the most current information about investor needs and market conditions. Because the cost of capital can be an important determinant of what activities are supported within the firm, it must be used wisely in a collaborative team-oriented manner.
- **Describe the process of calculating a cost of capital.** We construct the cost of capital for a firm in five steps: (1) select financing sources, (2) determine investors' required rates of return, (3) incorporate flotation costs and income taxes into the analysis to fully describe the firm's experience, (4) combine the various capital sources by taking a weighted average, and (5) project how the cost of capital will increase if the firm attempts to raise large amounts of money. The final output of the process is the cost of capital schedule, a graph projecting the firm's cost of capital as a function of its fund-raising plans.
- **Determine an investor's required rate of return.** Required rates of return can be obtained from professional investors by asking. When investors are not able to give a meaningful quote, we infer required rates from market data. This is commonly done using cash-flow-based models and statistical risk models.
- **Calculate the cost of a capital source.** The cost of a capital source is calculated by combining investors' required rate of return with any flotation costs or income tax flows associated with the financing. A useful way to do this is to organize the cash flows the firm will experience due to the financing and then calculate the interest rate embedded within those flows.
- **Integrate the cost of a firm's capital sources to produce its cost of capital.** When the cost of each capital source has been determined, they are combined into a weighted-average cost of capital, using the firm's target capital structure as the weights.
- **Graph a firm's cost of capital schedule.** The cost of capital schedule shows how a firm's capital costs will rise as it raises more and more money. Each time a firm exhausts its supply of a capital source, it must turn to more expensive financing. This causes a break in the cost of capital schedule, and the firm's WACOC rises. There is one break for every increase in capital costs.

Questions

1. In what sense is the cost of capital an opportunity cost? An opportunity cost to whom?
2. Distinguish between an investor's required rate of return and the cost of that source of funding.
3. Why does flotation cost raise the cost of capital while the federal income tax lowers capital costs?
4. Why are estimates of the cost of capital more accurate for bond financing than for common stock financing?
5. Is it possible that there could be sources of financing that have a zero cost?
6. For what funding sources:
   a. are flotation costs applicable?
   b. are flotation costs never applicable?
   c. is the federal income tax subsidy applicable?
   d. is the federal income tax subsidy never applicable?

7. What is the difference between the cost of retained earnings and the cost of financing through the sale of common stock?
8. What weights should be used in calculating the weighted-average cost of capital?
9. What is meant by a *break point* in the cost of capital schedule? What causes a break point to happen?
10. Why do we often draw the cost of capital schedule as upward sloping? Under what circumstances might it be downward sloping?

Problems

1. **(Bonds)** A company has an outstanding issue of $1,000 face value bonds with a 9.5% semi-annual coupon and 20 years remaining until maturity. The bonds are currently selling at a price of 90 (90% of face value). An investment bank has advised that a new 20-year issue could be sold for a flotation cost of 5% of face value. The company is in the 35% tax bracket.
   a. Calculate investors' required rate of return today.
   b. What coupon would have to be placed on the new issue in order for it to sell at par?
   c. Calculate the flotation cost and tax savings from the proposed new issue.
   d. Calculate the cost of the new bond financing.
2. **(Bonds)** A company has an outstanding issue of $1,000 face value bonds with a 8.75% semi-annual coupon and 10 years remaining until maturity. The bonds are currently selling at a price of 82.50 (82.50% of face value). The company wishes to sell a new bond issue with a 30-year maturity. Their investment bank has advised that (1) the new 30-year issue could be sold for a flotation cost of 3% of face value, and (2) current yield curves indicate that 30-year maturity bonds yield a nominal 75 basis points (0.75%) more than 10-year maturity bonds on average. The company is in the 35% tax bracket.
   a. Calculate investors' required rate of return today.
   b. What coupon would have to be placed on the new issue in order for it to sell at par?
   c. Calculate the flotation cost and tax savings from the proposed new issue.
   d. Calculate the cost of the new bond financing.
3. **(Preferred stock)** A company has an outstanding issue of $100 face value fixed-rate preferred stock with a quarterly dividend based on an annual dividend rate of $10 per share. The stock is currently selling at $75 per share. An investment bank has advised that a new preferred-stock issue could be sold for a flotation cost of 8% of face value. The company is in the 35% tax bracket.
   a. Calculate investors' required rate of return today.
   b. What annual dividend rate would have to be placed on the new issue in order for it to sell at par?
   c. Calculate the flotation cost and tax savings from the proposed new issue.
   d. Calculate the cost of the new preferred-stock financing.
4. **(Preferred stock)** A company has an outstanding issue of $100 face value fixed-rate preferred stock with a quarterly dividend based on an annual dividend rate of $18 per share. The stock is currently selling at $110 per share. An investment bank has advised that a new preferred-stock issue could be sold for a flotation cost of 6% of face value. The company is in the 35% tax bracket.
   a. Calculate investors' required rate of return today.
   b. What annual dividend rate would have to be placed on the new issue in order for it to sell at par?
   c. Calculate the flotation cost and tax savings from the proposed new issue.
   d. Calculate the cost of the new preferred-stock financing.
5. **(Common equity—dividend-growth model)** Today, you looked at *The Wall Street Journal* and a stock prospectus to read about a company whose stock you follow. You discovered the following:

Closing stock price	$14.00 per share
Earnings announcement	$3.00 per share
Earnings five years ago	$2.00 per share
Dividend payout ratio	40.0% of earnings
Flotation cost for a new stock issue	7.5% of market price

   Based on the above data:
   a. Calculate the company's quarterly growth rate of earnings for the past five years.
   b. Calculate the anticipated dividend one quarter from now, assuming no change in growth rate.
   c. Calculate investors' required rate of return from the company's common stock.
   d. Calculate the company's cost of retained earnings and cost of a new stock issue.
6. **(Common equity—dividend-growth model)** A company's common stock is currently selling at $24.00 per share and pays a quarterly dividend based

on an annual dividend rate of $1.60 per share. Investors forecast that dividends will grow at an annual rate of 7% for the foreseeable future. An investment bank has advised that a new common stock issue could be sold for a flotation cost of 7% of face value.

a. Calculate the quarterly growth rate of dividends forecast for the company.
b. Calculate the anticipated dividend one quarter from now.
c. Calculate investors' required rate of return from the company's common stock.
d. Calculate the company's cost of retained earnings and cost of a new stock issue.

7. **(Common equity—capital asset pricing model)** Today, you looked at *The Wall Street Journal* and the *Value Line Survey* to read about a company whose stock you follow. You discovered the following:

Treasury bond yield	7.75%
Company's beta	1.3

Calculate investors' required rate of return from the company's common stock if the market price of risk is:

a. 6.5%
b. 7.2%
c. 8.3%
d. 9.5%

8. **(Common equity—capital asset pricing model)** Treasury bonds currently yield 8.5%, and the market price of risk has been estimated to be 8.3%. Calculate investors' required rate of return from a stock with beta coefficient of:

a. 0
b. .75
c. 1.0
d. 1.25

9. **(Common equity—bond-yield-plus-premium model)** A company's stock has produced a historical return of 4% above its long-term bond yield. What would this relationship predict for investors' required rate of return from the common stock if the bond yield were:

a. 9%?
b. 12%?
c. 15%?
d. 18%?

10. **(Common equity—bond-yield-plus-premium model)** A company's stock has produced a historical return of 5% above its long-term bond yield. What would this relationship predict for investors' required rate of return from the common stock if the bond yield were:

a. 8%?
b. 11%?
c. 13%?
d. 16%?

11. **(Weighted average cost of capital—weights)** A company has the following right-hand side of its balance sheet:

Bonds payable	$100,000
Preferred stock (250 shares)	25,000
Common stock (100,000 shares)	75,000
Total Liabilities + Equity	$200,000

Bonds payable are currently priced at 85 (85% of face value) in the market, preferred stock is selling at $110 per share, and common stock is selling at $5 per share. Management has announced that it wishes to move toward a capital structure composed of 40% debt and 60% equity. Of the equity, 15% is to be preferred stock with the remainder common stock. Calculate the weights to be used in the weighted-average cost of capital calculation if the weights are based on:

a. The company's book values
b. The company's market values
c. Management's target capital structure
d. Which of the above three alternatives is best? Why?

12. **(Weighted average cost of capital—weights)** A company has the following right-hand side of its balance sheet:

Bonds payable	$250,000
Preferred stock (1000 shares)	100,000
Common stock (200,000 shares)	400,000
Total Liabilities + Equity	$750,000

Bonds payable are currently priced at 115 (115% of face value) in the market, preferred stock is selling at $70 per share, and common stock is selling at $20 per share. Management has announced that it wishes to move toward a capital structure composed of 65% debt and 35% equity. Of the equity, 10% is to be preferred stock, with the remainder common stock. Calculate the weights to be used in the weighted average cost of capital calculation if the weights are based on:

a. The company's book values
b. The company's market values
c. Management's target capital structure
d. If management's target weights were not known, which of the other two weighting schemes would you use? Why?

13. **(Weighted-average cost of capital—calculation)** A company has the following capital costs and target capital structure:

	Cost	Proportion
Bonds payable	9.0%	35%
Preferred stock	15.5	20
Common stock	17.5	45
Total Liabilities + Equity		100%

Calculate the company's weighted-average cost of capital under each of the following scenarios:

a. It is calculated correctly.
b. The financial manager accidently omits the preferred stock from the calculation.
c. The financial manager accidently treats the preferred stock as if it were the same as common stock.
d. The financial manager accidently weighs each financing source equally.

14. **(Weighted-average cost of capital—calculation)** A company has the following capital costs and target capital structure:

	Cost	Proportion
Bonds payable	8.25%	50%
Preferred stock	11.0	10
Common stock	13.5	40
Total Liabilities + Equity		100%

Calculate the company's weighted-average cost of capital under each of the following scenarios:

a. It is calculated correctly.
b. The financial manager accidently omits the bonds payable from the calculation.
c. The financial manager accidently treats the preferred stock as if it were the same as bonds payable.
d. The financial manager accidently weighs each financing source equally.

15. **(Cost of capital schedule—one break point)** A company plans to raise new capital as follows:

	Cost	Proportion
Bonds payable	9.0%	35%
Preferred stock	15.5	15
Common equity (retained earnings)	17.5	50
Total Liabilities + Equity		100%

The firm forecasts it can retain $1 million of new earnings. If it requires additional common equity, it will have to raise it by selling a new issue of common stock at a cost of 18.5%.

a. Calculate the company's weighted-average cost of capital using new retained earnings as the equity source.
b. Locate the break point in the cost of capital schedule caused by running out of new retained earnings.
c. Calculate the company's weighted-average cost of capital after it substitutes the new stock issue for retained earnings.
d. Draw the cost of capital schedule.

16. **(Cost of capital schedule—one break point)** A company plans to raise new capital as follows:

	Cost	Proportion
Bonds payable	7.5%	30%
Preferred stock	10.0	10
Common equity (retained earnings)	11.5	60
Total Liabilities + Equity		100%

The firm forecasts it can retain $4 million of new earnings. If it requires additional common equity, it will have to raise it by selling a new issue of common stock at a cost of 13.0%.

a. Calculate the company's weighted-average cost of capital using new retained earnings as the equity source.
b. Locate the break point in the cost of capital schedule caused by running out of new retained earnings.
c. Calculate the company's weighted average cost of capital after it substitutes the new stock issue for retained earnings.
d. Draw the cost of capital schedule.

17. **(Cost of capital schedule—multiple break points)** The firm of Problem 15 also forecasts the following: (1) if it sells more than an additional $250,000 of bonds, the cost of bond financing will rise to 10.0%, and (2) if it sells more than an additional $400,000 of preferred stock, the cost of preferred-stock financing will rise to 16.5%.

a. Calculate the break point caused by running out of the cheaper bond financing.
b. Calculate the break point caused by running out of the cheaper preferred-stock financing.
c. Calculate the weighted-average cost of capital in each interval.
d. Redraw the cost of capital schedule.

18. **(Cost of capital schedule—multiple break points)** The firm of Problem 16 also forecasts the following: (1) if it sells more than an additional $6 million of bonds, the cost of bond financing will rise to 9.0%, and

(2) if it sells more than $5 million of common stock, the cost common stock financing will rise to 15.0%.

a. Calculate the break point caused by running out of the cheaper bond financing.
b. Calculate the break point caused by running out of the cheaper common stock financing.
c. Calculate the weighted-average cost of capital in each interval.
d. Redraw the cost of capital schedule.

APPENDIX 10A

THE COST OF SHORT-TERM FUNDING SOURCES

In Chapter 10, we calculated the cost of a firm's long-term financing sources—bonds, preferred stock, and common stock—and computed an overall cost of this long-term capital. For many companies these are the primary sources of financing. Other firms however, especially small firms which do not have much access to the long-term capital markets, raise a significant portion of their external financing from short-term sources, especially bank loans and trade payables.

In this appendix, we extend the traditional cost of capital analysis to encompass a company's short-term funding sources. We begin by looking at the cost of four common current liabilities: (1) institutional payables, the noncontractual liabilities that arise from standard payment practices, (2) trade payables, the firm's accounts payable balance, (3) receipts-in-advance, payments to the firm for future products and services, and (4) bank notes payable, loans taken from the firm's banks.[1] Then we show how the calculation of a firm's cost of capital can be expanded to include these short-term sources.

1. Institutional Payables

At the top of the list of a firm's current liabilities are its institutional payables: wages payable, interest payable, taxes payable, etc. For the most part these sources of financing are free since the firm pays no explicit interest or other comparable charge to have them.

---

[1] **Tip and cross-reference:** If you are not familiar with the characteristics and structure of current liabilities, you wish to refer back to your accounting textbook and also look ahead to Chapter 20, where we examine short-term debt in more detail.

Examples

The Cost of Wages Payable

Jilline Products Company has a weekly payroll of \$5,000. Employees are paid at various intervals, and receive their pay, on average, two weeks after they earn it. As a result, Jilline's wages payable account has an average balance of two weeks' wages or \$10,000.

Question: What is r_{wp}, the rate of return required by Jilline's employees who permit the firm to hold on to each dollar of their wages for two weeks?

Answer: Zero! Jilline's employees do not get any additional pay as a result of the two-week delay in payment.

Question: What is k_{wp}, the cost of the \$10,000 of wages payable financing used by Jilline?

Answer: Zero! Jilline pays nothing for the use of this money.[10]

2. Trade Payables

The accounts payable of a firm are typically free financing until the discount date but have an explicit cost if the firm extends its payables period beyond that time.

Examples

The Cost of Accounts Payable

Jilline Products Company has \$20,000 of accounts payable. The first \$5,000 have terms of 2/10,net 30; Jilline takes the discount on these accounts and pays its suppliers on day 10. The remaining \$15,000 have terms of 1/10,net 75; Jilline forgoes the discount on these accounts and pays the full amount on day 75. A small company, Jilline is in the 34% income tax bracket.

Question: What is r_{ap}, the required rate of return, on the first \$5,000 of accounts payable to Jilline's suppliers?

Answer: Zero! Jilline's suppliers do not get any additional payment in return for waiting ten days to be paid.

Question: What is k_{ap}, the cost of the first \$5,000 of accounts payable financing used by Jilline?

Answer: Zero! Jilline pays nothing for the use of this money.

Question: What is r_{ap}, the required rate of return on the other \$15,000 of accounts payable to Jilline's suppliers?

Solution steps: Solve for the interest rate *the suppliers* will experience:

1. Identify the cash flows. If Jilline paid on day 10, its suppliers would receive \$0.99 for each \$1.00 of Jilline's accounts payable. Since Jilline does not pay until day 75, however, its suppliers do not get \$0.99 on day 10, but instead receive the full \$1.00 65 days later.

[10] **Observation:** By using this \$10,000, Jilline avoids getting financing from another source—perhaps a bank loan which would carry an interest charge. This is indeed advantageous financing!

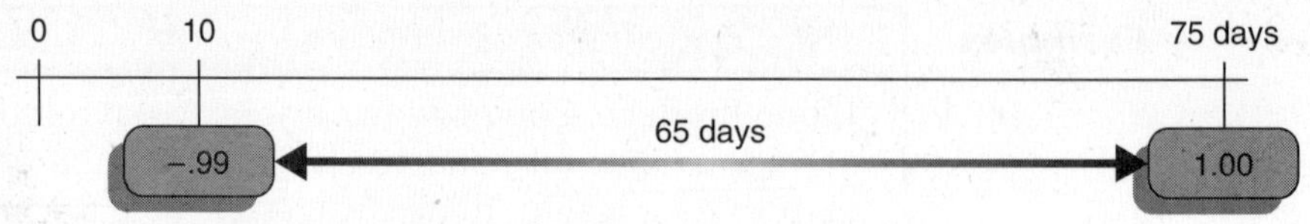

2. Calculate the interest rate embedded in these cash flows:

CLEAR the time value part of your calculator

Key in –.99 and press PV

Key in 1.00 and press FV

Key in 65/365 and press n (65/365th of a year)

Compute i = 5.81%

Answer: The required rate of return, r_{ap}, is 5.81%.

Question: What is k_{ap}, the cost of the other $15,000 of accounts payable financing used by Jilline?

Solution steps: Solve for the interest rate *the firm* will experience:

1. *Include flotation costs (none here) and income taxes in the cash flows.* Jilline keeps $0.99 on day 10 but pays $1.00 65 days later. The extra $0.01 eventually becomes a tax-deductible expense (in cost of goods sold or operating expense) and reduces the firm's taxes by $0.01 × 34% = $0.0034. Assuming this benefit comes on day 75, the firm's net outlay is reduced to $1.00 – 0.0034 = $.9966 on that date.

2. Calculate the interest rate embedded in these cash flows:

CLEAR the time value part of your calculator

Key in .99 and press PV

Key in –.9966 and press FV

Key in 65/365 and press n (65/365th of a year)

Compute i = 3.80%

Answer: The cost of this financing, k_{ap}, is 3.80%. Jilline only needs to earn 3.80% on this money to justify forgoing the discount of 1/10, net 75.

3. Receipts-in-Advance

Receipts-in-advance represent payments to the firm by customers in advance of receiving goods or services. It is zero-cost financing if the firm receives the same amount it would have received at a later date. However, if the firm gives a discount for early payment, there is a cost for this source of funding.

Examples

The Cost of Receipts-in-Advance

Jilline gives its customers a 4% discount if they pay when they place an order. Receipts-in-advance average $10,000, and orders are delivered two months later.

Question: What is r_{ria}, the rate of return required by (in this case offered to) Jilline's customers for early payment?

Solution steps: Solve for the interest rate *customers* will experience:

1. Identify the cash flows. For each $1.00 of product Jilline sells, its customers pay $.96 immediately instead of $1.00 in two months.

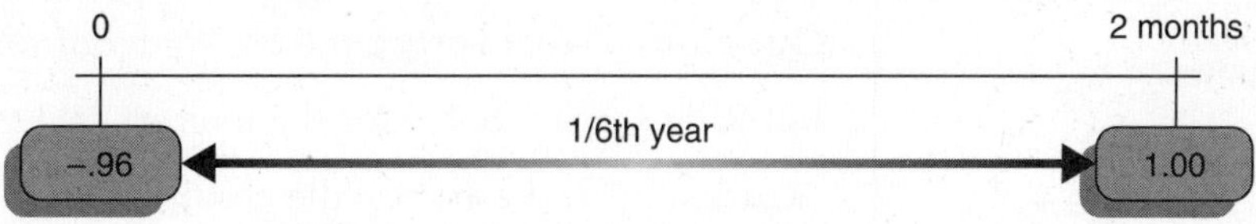

2. Calculate the interest rate embedded in these cash flows:

   CLEAR the time value part of your calculator

   Key in −.96 and press PV

   Key in 1.00 and press FV

   Key in 1/6 and press n (1/6th of a year)

   Compute i = 27.75%

Answer: Jilline is offering its customers a very attractive 27.75% rate of return for making early payment.

Question: What is k_{ria}, the cost of the receipts-in-advance financing used by Jilline?

Solution steps: Solve for the interest rate *the firm* will experience:

1. *Include flotation costs (none here) and income taxes in the cash flows.* Jilline gets $0.96 on day 0 but forgoes $1.00 two months later. The $0.04 discount lowers Jilline's income and reduces its taxes by $0.04 × 34% = $0.0136. Assuming this benefit comes when Jilline delivers its products, the firm's forgone revenue is reduced to $1.00 − 0.0136 = $.9864 on that date.
2. Calculate the interest rate embedded in these cash flows:

   CLEAR the time value part of your calculator

   Key in .96 and press PV

   Key in −.9864 and press FV

   Key in 1/6 and press n (1/6th of a year)

   Compute i = 17.68%

Answer: The cost of this financing, k_{ria}, is 17.68%. Jilline must earn 17.68% on this money to justify its discount policy.

4. Bank Notes Payable

Bank loans have an explicit cost due to the interest and other fees, etc., that are charged. There rarely are flotation costs, but the interest and fees are tax deductible.

Examples

The Cost of Bank Notes Payable

Jilline Company maintains an average balance of $40,000 of bank notes payable. This is an ordinary interest loan for one year at an annual rate which is currently 11% plus a 1% origination fee and a 12% compensating balance requirement.

Question: What is r_{bnp}, the bank's required rate of return?

Solution steps: Solve for the interest rate *the bank* will experience:

1. Identify and organize the cash flows:

Interest = 11% × $40,000 = $4,400

Origination fee = 1% × $40,000 = $400

Balance requirement = 12% × $40,000 = $4,800

	Year 0	Year 1
Loan principal	($40,000)	$ 40,000
Interest		4,400
Origination fee	400	
Compensating balance	4,800	(4,800)
Net cash flows	($34,800)	$39,600

2. Solve for the interest rate:

CLEAR the time value part of your calculator

Key in −34,800 and press PV

Key in 39,600 and press FV

Key in 1 and press n

Compute i = 13.79%

Answer: The bank's required rate of return, r_{bnp}, is 13.79%.

Question: What is k_{bnp}, the cost of the bank note financing used by Jilline?

Solution steps: Solve for the interest rate *the firm* will experience. There is no flotation cost but there will be a tax reduction:

1. Compute the tax savings:
   From deducting fee at time point 0: 34% × $400 = $136.
   From deducting interest at time point 1: 34% × $4,400 = $1,496.
2. *Include the tax savings with the other cash flows:*

	Year 0	Year 1
Cash flows before tax	$34,800	($39,600)
Tax benefits	136	1,496
Net cash flows	$34,936	($38,104)

3. Solve for the interest rate:

CLEAR the time value part of your calculator

Key in 34,936 and press PV

Key in −38,104 and press FV

Key in 1 and press n

Compute i = 9.07%

Answer: The cost of bank-note financing, k_{bnp}, is 9.07%. Jilline must invest this money to earn at least 9.07%.

Including Short-Term Funding Sources in the Cost of Capital Calculation

Every funding source must be included in the WACOC calculation, regardless of whether it is debt or equity, current or long-term, or has a zero or non-zero cost. In the example that follows, we calculate the Jilline Products Company's cost of capital assuming the company uses a combination of the long-term sources of funds we studied in Chapter 10 and the short-term sources we discussed in this appendix. The cost of each short-term financing source is the number calculated in the examples of this appendix; the cost of Jilline's long-term capital and Jilline's target capital structure are new information supplied for the problem.

Example

Including Short-Term Funding Sources in the WACOC Calculation

Jilline Products Company's management has announced the target capital structure (given in the column titled "Proportion") below:

Question: What is Jilline's WACOC?

Solution steps: Construct a table of funding costs and proportions and calculate the weighted average:

Funding Source	Cost	Proportion	Cost × Proportion
Wages payable	0.00%	4%	.0000%
Accounts payable	0.00	2	.0000
Accounts payable	3.80	6	.2280
Receipts-in-advance	17.68	3	.5304
Bank notes payable	9.07	10	.9070
Bonds	10.50	20	2.1000
Preferred stock	13.75	10	1.3750
Common equity	16.00	45	7.2000
		100%	12.3404%

Answer: Jilline's WACOC, including its short-term funding sources, is 12.34%.

Problems

1. **(Wages payable)** A company maintains an average balance of wages payable of $25,000, and employees receive no extra compensation due to the delay in payment. Calculate the cost of wages payable financing if, on average, the time between employees' earning their wages and being paid is:
   a. 5 days
   b. 7 days
   c. 10 days
   d. 14 days
2. **(Wages payable)** A company pays its employees, on average, ten days after they earn their wages. At the last salary negotiation with the firm's labor union, the company agreed to include an additional payment in each paycheck as compensation for the delay in payment. The firm is in the 34% tax bracket. Calculate the required rate of return and the cost of wages payable financing if the additional amount is:
   a. 0.1% of salary
   b. 0.25% of salary
   c. 0.5% of salary
   d. 1% of salary
3. **(Accounts payable)** A company has an average balance of accounts payable of $55,000. Terms offered to the company and its response are as follows:

Balance	Terms offered	Company's response
$ 8,000	1/10, net 60	Pays on day 60
15,000	1/10, net 45	Pays on day 45
20,000	2/10, net 45	Takes discount
12,000	2/10, net 30	Takes discount

   The company is in the 35% tax bracket. Calculate the required rate of return and the cost of accounts payable financing for:
   a. The first $8,000 of accounts payable
   b. The next $15,000 of accounts payable
   c. The next $20,000 of accounts payable
   d. The last $12,000 of accounts payable
4. **(Accounts payable)** A company has an average balance of accounts payable of $105,000. Terms offered to the company and its response are as follows:

Balance	Terms offered	Company's response
$10,000	1/15, net 75	Pays on day 75
30,000	2/10, net 90	Pays on day 90
25,000	1/15, net 45	Pays on day 45
40,000	3/10, net 30	Takes discount

   The company is in the 34% tax bracket. Calculate the required rate of return and the cost of accounts payable financing for:
   a. The first $10,000 of accounts payable
   b. The next $30,000 of accounts payable
   c. The next $25,000 of accounts payable
   d. The last $40,000 of accounts payable
5. **(Receipts-in-advance)** Tickets for New York Newts home games go on sale six months prior to the date of the game. A ticket costs $25 if purchased at the gate; however, advance tickets may be purchased up to the day prior to the game at a discount price of $20. The franchise pays taxes at a 35% rate. Calculate the required rate of return and the cost of receipts-in-advance financing if a sports fan purchases a discount ticket:
   a. Six months in advance
   b. Three months in advance
   c. One month in advance
   d. One day in advance
6. **(Receipts-in-advance)** *Modern Financial Managing Monthly*, the well-known magazine, costs $4 per copy if purchased on the newsstand. However, it is possible to purchase a one-year subscription. The publisher is in the 34% tax bracket. Calculate the required rate of return and the cost of receipts-in-advance financing if the one-year subscription price is:
   a. $30
   b. $36
   c. $42
   d. $48
7. **(Bank notes payable)** It is possible to obtain a $70,000 one-year ordinary-interest loan from the Skeptical National Bank at a fixed interest rate, plus a 1.5% origination fee and a 15% compensating balance. Calculate the bank's required rate of return and the cost of bank-notes-payable financing for a borrower in the 35% tax bracket if the interest rate quoted is:
   a. 8%
   b. 10%
   c. 12%
   d. 14%
8. **(Bank notes payable)** A company has been offered a $250,000 one-year ordinary-interest loan with a fixed interest rate of 14% and a compensating balance requirement. The company is in the 34% tax bracket. Calculate the bank's required rate of return and the cost of bank-notes-payable financing to the company if the compensating balance requirement is:
   a. 10%
   b. 15%
   c. 20%
   d. 25%

9. **(Weighted-average cost of capital—weights)** A company has the following right-hand side of its balance sheet:

Accounts payable	$ 15,000
Bank notes payable	30,000
Bonds payable	100,000
Preferred stock (250 shares)	25,000
Common stock (100,000 shares)	75,000
Total Liabilities + Equity	$ 245,000

Accounts and notes payable are carried at market value. Bonds payable are currently priced at 85 (85% of face value) in the market, preferred stock is selling at $110 per share, and common stock is selling at $5 per share. Management has announced that it wishes to move toward a capital structure composed of 40% debt and 60% equity. Of the debt, 70% is to be bonds payable, with the remainder split evenly between accounts and bank notes payable. Of the equity, 15% is to be preferred stock, with the remainder common stock. Calculate the weights to be used in the weighted-average cost of capital calculation if the weights are based on:

a. The company's book values
b. The company's market values
c. Management's target capital structure
d. Which of the above three alternatives is best? Why?

10. **(Weighted-average cost of capital—weights)** A company has the following right-hand side of its balance sheet:

Wages payable	$ 40,000
Accounts payable	65,000
Bonds payable	250,000
Preferred stock (1000 shares)	100,000
Common stock (200,000 shares)	400,000
Total Liabilities + Equity	$ 855,000

Wages and accounts payable are carried at market value. Bonds payable are currently priced at 115 (115% of face value) in the market, preferred stock is selling at $70 per share, and common stock is selling at $20 per share. Management has announced that it wishes to move toward a capital structure composed of 65% debt and 35% equity. Of the debt, 50% is to be bonds payable, 35% accounts payable, and 15% wages payable. Of the equity, 10% is to be preferred stock, with the remainder common stock. Calculate the weights to be used in the weighted-average cost of capital calculation if the weights are based on:

a. The company's book values
b. The company's market values
c. Management's target capital structure
d. If you did not know management's target weights, which of the other two weighting schemes would you use? Why?

11. **(Weighted-average cost of capital—calculation)** A company has the following capital costs and target capital structure:

	Cost	Proportion
Wages payable	0%	5%
Accounts payable	0	10
Bank notes payable	7.5	15
Bonds payable	9.0	25
Preferred stock	15.5	5
Common stock	17.5	40
Total Liabilities + Equity		100%

Calculate the company's weighted-average cost of capital under each of the following scenarios:

a. It is calculated correctly.
b. The financial manager accidently omits the zero-cost financing sources from the calculation.
c. The financial manager accidently weighs each financing source equally.
d. The financial manager accidently omits the current liabilities from the calculation.

12. **(Weighted-average cost of capital—calculation)** A company has the following capital costs and target capital structure:

	Cost	Proportion
Wages payable	0%	15%
Accounts payable	0	10
Bank notes payable	6.0	20
Common stock	13.5	55
Total Liabilities + Equity		100%

Calculate the company's weighted-average cost of capital under each of the following scenarios:

a. It is calculated correctly.
b. The financial manager accidently omits the zero-cost financing sources from the calculation.
c. The financial manager accidently weighs each financing source equally.
d. The financial manager accidently omits the current liabilities from the calculation.

PART IV MAKING INCREMENTAL DECISIONS

In Part IV we look at incremental decisions, decisions that focus on what is changing. Our goal is to determine whether a company would be better off if it said yes to a proposal to modify its resources or activities. In incremental analysis we look only at cash flows which change as a result of accepting the proposal under consideration. We also use the classic rule of microeconomics: Are the benefits from accepting the proposal greater than the costs?

Chapter 11 examines capital budgeting, the task of identifying investments in long-term assets that add value to the firm. We discuss its importance and identify the data used in capital budgeting by presenting eight data rules. We show how to organize and analyze the data. Appendix 11A illustrates the benefit of accelerated depreciation for tax purposes. Appendix 11B presents the mathematical limitations of the IRR technique. Appendix 11C discusses ranking investment projects. Appendix 11D reviews four other capital budgeting techniques.

Chapter 12 applies incremental analysis to permanent working capital, the base level of a firm's current resources. We show how the data for a permanent working capital decision can be organized and analyzed in the same way as capital budgeting. We then illustrate decisions involving the firm's balances of cash, accounts receivable, and inventories. Appendix 12A demonstrates that net annual benefit will always agree with net present value. Appendix 12B looks at the classic economic order quantity inventory model and just-in-time inventory management.

CHAPTER 11

CAPITAL BUDGETING

Rick Daniel stared at the computer screen and shook his head. The numbers did not seem to make sense. How could an investment with such obvious potential have such a low value?

Rick was an analyst in the corporate finance group of a large corporation. He had been assigned the task of evaluating the proposed purchase of a new kind of machinery which promised to reduce dramatically the cost of producing the company's highest-volume product. From his classes in finance, Rick knew that the proper method of analysis began with a complete summary of the incremental cash flows from accepting the project. But when he put the numbers into his spreadsheet program, the resulting calculations did not seem to be at all correct.

Puzzled, Rick printed out his spreadsheet and took the page to one of the group's senior analysts for advice. The analyst first looked at Rick's mathematics. Next, the analyst questioned Rick about his assumptions: where the numbers came from and how Rick had decided which numbers to include in the analysis. Rick took notes as he answered each question.

When he returned to his desk, Rick reviewed his notes. He had written a list of leads to follow up—leads that could improve his numbers and analysis. As he began to prioritize his follow-up actions, Rick thought back to his introductory finance course and realized that it was time to do a thorough review of the basics of capital budgeting.

A key part of the job of financial managing is to advise senior management of the value of potential uses of the firm's money. One important use is investment in long-term plant and equipment, the resources economists call a firm's "capital." As Rick Daniel is rediscovering, understanding whether a proposed capital expenditure is wise requires careful attention to researching and analyzing every consequence of the proposed change.

Finance as a discipline has been a pioneer in developing techniques for the analysis of long-term investment alternatives. Yet financial people have been widely blamed for many companies' lack of attention to long-term investment. While this may seem contradictory, there is much truth to both observations. Poor application of finance theory can easily lead to poor managerial judgments. In this chapter we will explore the methodology of evaluating investment projects as well as the pitfalls that can lead to myopic, short-term decision making.

Key Points You Should Learn from This Chapter

After reading this chapter you should be able to:

- Discuss the importance of capital budgeting to business success.
- Identify the data used in capital budgeting.
- Organize cash flow data for capital budgeting analysis.
- Use the techniques of net present value (NPV) and internal rate of return (IRR) to judge the worth of a capital project.
- Describe how quality-management techniques can improve the capital budgeting process.

Introductory Concepts—The Importance of Capital Budgeting

capital budgeting—the process of discovering, evaluating, and deciding whether to pursue investments in long-term assets

capital budget—a financial plan showing a firm's intended outlays for long-term assets

Capital budgeting is the widely used term for the process of evaluating potential investments in long-term assets. In Appendix 18E we will study the cash budget, the projection of the firm's day-to-day (or at least month-to-month) cash flow needs for the next year. Here we look at the **capital budget,** the parallel plan for spending money to acquire long-term resources.

Capital budgeting is important to any firm that makes significant use of plant and equipment, land, and other long-term assets. For one thing, long-term assets may make up 50% or more of the total assets of a company. Thus, capital budgeting may be the technique used to qualify the acquisition of a large amount of the firm's resources. Second, the decision to acquire—or not to acquire—capital resources has a major impact on the financing of the firm. Expenditures on assets require the company to make parallel and integrated decisions about where and in what form to raise funds. In addition, the effects of capital budgeting decisions stay with the firm for a long time. The wise acquisition of long-term assets can often be the difference between a business that is competitively strong, with opportunities for growth and market penetration, and a business that is weak and uncompetitive.

Even for the financial manager of a firm with little investment in capital assets, capital budgeting is an important technique to know and use well. As we will see

FINANCE IN PRACTICE

The Decline of American Manufacturing

Ask the chiefs of America's largest companies why American manufacturing has declined over the past decade, and they'll give you a long list of reasons. . . . They blame poorly educated employees, a lack of capital investment, and the focus on short-term thinking they say Wall Street demands. . . .

One explanation may be found on the bosses' résumés. Only 32% of the chief executives of industrial companies have spent most of their careers in manufacturing, while 27% have shimmied their way up through finance. . . .

Many of the chiefs think America fell out of love with manufacturing. Their favorite explanation, with a number of variations, is that Wall Street's to blame. . . . There was gold in the financial district and no dirty fingernails. . . . John Burns of Vista Chemical suspects that the zeitgeist is shifting. Reason: "There may be a feeling now that these people who understand the numbers don't understand the company."

Wall Street, say many of the CEOs, also forced manufacturing managers into poor decisions. Nearly a fifth of the chiefs criticized management's short-term focus, some of it forced, they say, by investors' quarterly earnings demands. Says [Arrow Electronics CEO Stephen] Kaufman: "The emphasis in American management is on making the quick buck, and that leads to avoiding long-term investments, either in product development or in manufacturing processes."

Reference: Terence P. Paré, "Why Some Do It the Wrong Way," *Fortune,* May 21, 1990, pp. 75–76.

in subsequent chapters, the techniques of capital budgeting are not only applicable to long-term asset decisions, they can be easily extended to deal with many choices affecting current assets as well. In addition, the logic we develop in this chapter is of considerable use in other, nontraditional, areas where finance-trained people are becoming more frequently involved. Often, when working with a team drawn from throughout the organization, the incremental thinking of this chapter is the finance person's greatest contribution.

Identification of Data

To make sound capital budgeting decisions, it is necessary to keep eight data rules in mind. The first seven identify the numbers to *include* in the analysis and the last specifies what to *exclude:* (1) Use cash flow numbers only. (2) Use incremental numbers only. (3) Include changes in every functional area of the business. (4) Include changes across the full life cycle of the product or service. (5) Include forecasted inflation in the cash flow estimates. (6) Consider the impact of the decision on quality and cycle time. (7) Consider the options implicit in the decision. (8) Do not contaminate the numbers of any one project with the firm's financing flows.

The rules are summarized in Figure 11.1. We will look at each rule in turn.

1. Use Cash Flow Numbers Only

Since financial value comes from cash flows, it is important to measure the impact of a decision in cash flow terms. In particular, we avoid accrual accounting revenue and expense numbers. The amount and timing of these figures are highly dependent on financial accounting rules which are made by people and change from time to time. There are alternative treatments for a single event within financial accounting; as a result, the same economic event can be described in several different ways. By concentrating on cash flows, we avoid the risk of distorting business decisions because of the selection among accounting alternatives.

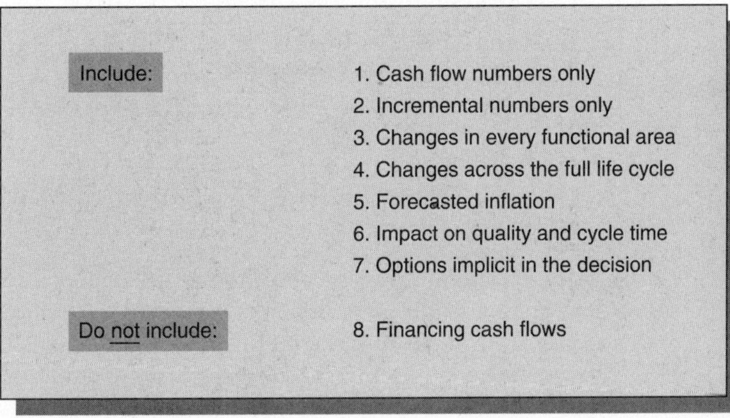

Include:
1. Cash flow numbers only
2. Incremental numbers only
3. Changes in every functional area
4. Changes across the full life cycle
5. Forecasted inflation
6. Impact on quality and cycle time
7. Options implicit in the decision
Do not include:
8. Financing cash flows

FIGURE 11.1
Eight data rules of capital budgeting. The rules provide a reminder of what to include and what not to include in capital budgeting analysis.

For financial accounting, the business might be required to recognize income at one point in time, even though the associated cash flows take place over a much longer period. Alternatively, the financial statements might spread revenues or expenses over several time periods even though the cash flow was received or paid in one lump sum. Perhaps the most common example is depreciation expense:

Example

Using Cash Flow and Not Depreciation Expense

Three companies are considering the purchase of the identical machine for $100,000. All three would depreciate it over five years to zero salvage value on their financial statements; but Company A would use straight-line depreciation, Company B would use sum-of-the-years-digits depreciation, and Company C would use double-declining-balance depreciation.

Question: What figure should each firm use in its capital budgeting analysis for the cost of the machine?

Answer: All three should use the same number: $100,000 at the date of purchase. This is the cash they must give up to acquire the machine. The differences between the three depreciation conventions are arbitrary and have nothing to do with the cost of the asset.

2. Use Incremental Numbers Only

As we discussed in the opening pages to this part of the book, incremental decisions are made by ignoring cash flows that do not change with the decision. One type of cash flow that cannot change with the decision, and therefore is a good example of a number that should not be included in capital budgeting analysis, is a sunk cost—a cash flow that took place in the past.

Example

Using Incremental Numbers and Not Sunk Costs

A firm has spent $10 million over the years to purchase plant and equipment. It is presently considering a proposal to spend $100,000 for another machine.

Question: Which figure should the firm use in its capital budgeting analysis for the cost of the machine?

Answer: $100,000. The decision to purchase the new machine involves this amount only. The $10 million is a sunk cost and cannot be changed by saying yes or no to the purchase of the new machine.

3. Include Changes in Every Functional Area of the Business

Capital budgeting projects can change cash flows throughout the business. While some changes will be obvious, others may be quite subtle and not immediately visible. Traditional cost accounting—grouping costs by functional area, cost center, profit center, etc.—is often inadequate to point out the financial interconnections throughout the organization. The analyst must adopt an activity-based approach, searching across all functional areas of the firm for cash flows that will change.[1] Not to do so would be to miss some of the incremental cash flows from accepting the proposal.

Example

Using Activity-Based and Not Local Numbers

A firm is considering a change to its product which would reduce production costs by \$0.50 per unit but add \$0.75 per unit to warranty service costs.

Question: Which figure should the firm use in its capital budgeting analysis for the per-unit cash flow change?

Answer: −\$0.25 per unit (\$0.50 − 0.75). While the impact on warranty service costs may not be immediately visible to those who attempt to lower production costs, its impact is real. It doesn't pay to save \$0.50 in the factory only to lose \$0.75 in the service department.

4. Include Changes Across the Full Life Cycle of the Product or Service

life-cycle numbers—numbers which cover the full life-span of some activity and which are not limited to any time period

Just as financial analysts must search across all functional areas of the firm, so too must they examine the entire life span of the activity for which a change is proposed. Traditional cost accounting often fails to provide sufficient information due to its focus on period-by-period reporting. The analyst must adopt a **life-cycle** approach considering all changes which might occur during the life span of the activity to be altered. Not to do so would be to miss some of the incremental cash flows from accepting the proposal.

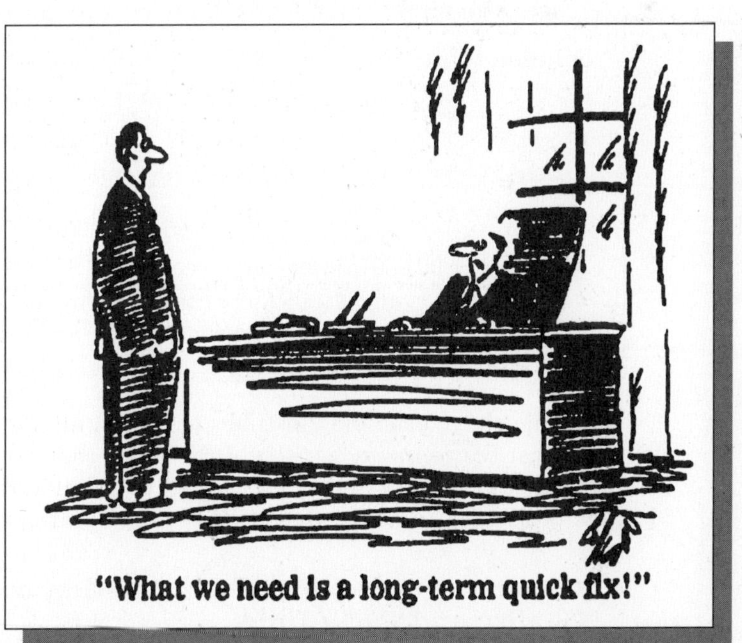
"What we need is a long-term quick fix!"

[1] **Cross-reference:** Activity-based costing is introduced in Chapter 4, pp. 82–83.

Example

Using Life-Cycle and Not Single-Period Numbers

A firm is considering a change that would reduce production costs by $2.00 per unit but result in production machinery wearing out faster: new machinery would have to be purchased in three years instead of five.

Question: Which figure should the firm use in its capital budgeting analysis for the cash flow change?

Answer: A figure that includes both the $2.00 and the cost to replace the machinery earlier. While the replacement of machinery is still in the future, the earlier replacement date translates into a more costly expenditure when time value of money is taken into account. The two effects must be balanced against one another.

5. Include Forecasted Inflation in the Cash Flow Estimates

Inflation can create a tangible change to cash flows. If left out, future cash flow estimates will tend to be understated.

Example

Using Nominal and Not Real Numbers

A firm is considering whether to market a new product. It expects to sell 500 units of the product in each of the next three years. It would price the product at $1,000 per unit in the coming year. Inflation is forecasted to be 8% per year for each succeeding year, and management believes it could increase its prices with the general level of prices over that period.

Question: Which figures should the firm use in its capital budgeting analysis for receipts from the sale of the new product?

Solution steps: Year 1: Receipts = 500 units × $1,000 = $500,000

Year 2: Price = $1,000 (1.08) = $1,080

Receipts = 500 units × $1,080 = $540,000

Year 3: Price = $1,080 (1.08) = $1,166

Receipts = 500 units × $1,166 = $583,000

Answer: $500,000 for the first year, then $540,000, then $583,000. The economic environment will allow the firm to increase its prices which will bring in additional cash flow. Ignoring inflation and using $500,000 for each year's receipts would not be accurate.

While the above example illustrates including inflation in revenue forecasts, it is likely that the company's costs for the new product will increase as well due to the same inflationary forces. The impact of inflation must be included in all cash flow projections, whether they are forecasts of inflows or outflows.

6. Consider the Impact of the Decision on Quality and Cycle Time

Capital budgeting proposals which affect the quality of a firm's products and services, or the cycle time of its production processes, will typically result in changes to cash flows well beyond what is immediately apparent. These quality and cycle time-related cash flows can easily be large and far outweigh the obvious cash flow changes. An estimate of them must be included in the analysis.

Example

Including Quality-Related Cash Flows

A firm is considering the installation of a new telephone system to improve its ability to respond to customer inquiries. While the team working on the project has not been able to identify significant cost savings, there is a shared feeling that increased customer satisfaction will lead to more repeat sales and to attracting new customers.

Question: Which figures should the firm use in its capital budgeting analysis for the new telephones?

Answer: The analysis must include an estimate of the quality-related benefits as well as the cost of the telephone system. Increased sales would produce new cash inflows which should not be ignored. Further, if the system were *not* installed, the firm might lose customers; a second incremental benefit of the new system is retaining the business of those customers who might otherwise go elsewhere. To estimate the value of new sales and existing customers retained, the analysts might interview members of the company's sales and marketing staff. They might also interview members of other companies that have installed similar telephone systems.

7. Consider the Options You Get if You Make the Decision

Capital budgeting proposals are often rejected because the future benefits from the investment are not easily quantifiable. This is especially true in research and development, where it is difficult to know what products or services will emerge from the R&D or what the marketplace will look like in the future. Yet if a firm

FINANCE IN PRACTICE

Using Options in Capital Budgeting at Merck

When [Merck & Company] considered the idea first for [an automated] drug packaging and distribution plant, the labor savings didn't justify the investment. Moreover, with no prior experience with robots, Merck also wasn't certain about the technical success.

"It was a tricky thing to convince management. But options valuation allowed engineers to articulate a whole range of outcomes and their benefits," says Judy Lewent, chief financial officer at Merck. The management agreed to take an "option" on automating the plant, and results from the pilot project since early this year [1990] have clarified the potential future benefits to the point that the company is now willing to expand automation to its diverse manufacturing operations.

Reference: Amal Kumar Naj, "In R&D, the Next Best Thing to a Gut Feeling," *The Wall Street Journal*, May 21, 1990, p. A–12.

rejects all such R&D efforts while its competitors push ahead, it could find itself at a severe disadvantage in the future.

One way to deal with this dilemma is to view accepting investments whose returns are speculative as the equivalent of purchasing a call option.[2] The firm spends some amount today (the option premium) to develop its knowledge, technology, expertise, etc., in return for the right (capability) to enter the market at some future date.

8. Do Not Contaminate the Numbers of Any One Project with the Firm's Financing Flows

The techniques for evaluating capital budgeting projects (discussed later in this chapter) test each potential investment against the firm's cost of capital. Since the role of the cost of capital is to bring the company's financing cash flows into the decision, we exclude financing flows from the description of the investment project itself. Otherwise we would be "double-counting," incorporating the financing flows twice.

Example

Omitting Financing Flows from the Description of the Investment Project

A firm is considering an investment project which would cost $100 today and return $115 in exactly one year. It will finance the project with capital costing 10% (it will cost $10, due in one year, to finance the $100 investment).

Question: Should the $10 financing cost be included in the project's cash flows?

Answer: No! The cost of capital does not enter the analysis at this stage. Do not deduct the $10 financing cost from the $115 to produce a $105 net return. Since the next step in evaluating the project will be to test its cash flows against the firm's 10% cost of capital, deducting the $10 would result in using the 10% number twice in the analysis.

Organizing the Data

In the remainder of this chapter we will use cash flow tables to organize the data for each capital budgeting problem. This is the same approach we used when we calculated the cost of each source of capital in Chapter 10. Recall that a cash flow table is a spreadsheet that summarizes cash flows by the date they are forecasted to occur, making it easy to do the required time value of money calculations.

The cash flows most often changed by capital budgeting decisions can be conveniently grouped into four categories: cash flows from (1) purchasing a new asset, (2) selling an existing asset, (3) changes in operations resulting from the asset purchase and/or sale, and (4) changes in the working capital required to support a

[2] **Cross-reference:** We discussed options in Chapter 9. The option valuation model presented in Appendix 9A can be used to place a value on estimates of uncertain future benefits.

Category	Cash flow	Treatment
Cash flows from purchasing an asset	Initial cost	Cash outflow when purchased
	Tax savings due to depreciation	Cash inflow (reduced outflow) each year depreciation may be taken
	Terminal value	Cash inflow when the asset is sold (adjusted by tax if a capital gain or loss is reported)
Cash flows from selling an existing asset	Sale price	Cash inflow when sold
	Tax on sale	Cash outflow if a gain on sale is reported; cash inflow (reduced outflow) if a loss on sale is reported
	Tax savings forgone due to no longer being able to depreciate the asset	Cash outflow (increased taxes) each year depreciation would have been taken if the asset were not sold
	Terminal value forgone from no longer having the asset to sell on its original termination date	Cash outflow (lost cash inflow)
Cash flows from operations	Changed receipts or payments from having the new asset and/or not having the old asset	Cash inflows and/or outflows over the lifetime of the new and/or old asset(s)
	Taxes paid or saved as changed receipts and payments enter the tax return as changes to income	Cash inflows and/or outflows over the lifetime of the new and/or old asset(s)
Cash flows from the investment in supporting working capital	The cost of acquiring additional working capital when a new asset is purchased	Cash outflow when the asset, and hence the supporting working capital, is purchased
	The cash from selling working capital no longer required when an asset is sold	Cash inflow when the asset, and hence the supporting working capital, is sold

FIGURE 11.2
The most common changes to cash flows in capital budgeting analyses. The cash flows have been grouped into four categories for convenience.

new asset or no longer required when an asset is sold. These categories are summarized in Figure 11.2.

Some of Figure 11.2 is self-explanatory—for example, the first line which identifies the cash outflow when a new asset is purchased. Other cash flow treatments require an understanding of basic accounting and tax rules—for example the calculation of the tax impact of changes to depreciation expense.[3] The last category—changes to supporting working capital—might require a bit more explanation. Often an investment in long-term assets triggers an accompanying change in related current assets (different inventory levels, changed receivable levels if sales is projected to change, etc.). These working capital changes involve cash flows and must be included in the capital budgeting analysis. However, there is no standard pat-

[3] **Cross-reference and recommendation:** Depreciation for corporate tax returns is done using the MACRS (modified accelerated cost recovery system) as described in Appendix 4C, pp. 107–108. The same rules apply to business assets owned by proprietorships and partnerships. See your accounting textbook if you desire further review of depreciation or of other accounting calculations such as the gain or loss when an asset is sold.

tern for these flows. Sometimes the additional working capital must be acquired along with the long-term asset—for example, an inventory of spare parts for a new machine. At other times, working capital is added in increments over the long-term asset's life—for example, additional accounts receivable as a new plant produces sales growth over time. On occasion, the new working capital becomes a permanent part of the company's resources; while in other cases, some or all of it can be sold or recaptured when the underlying long-term asset is no longer needed. Because there are so many possibilities, financial analysts study capital budgeting proposals carefully to estimate the amounts and timing of their working capital requirements. But this level of detail is beyond the scope of this book. Accordingly, we have adopted the simplification that the working capital requirements of capital budgeting proposals may be summarized, whenever they appear, with only two cash flows:

- A cash outflow to represent the purchase of supporting working capital when a long-term asset is acquired
- A cash inflow of equal amount, representing the recovery of the investment in supporting working capital when the long-term asset is sold and the working capital is no longer needed.

In cash flow table form, capital budgeting cash flows may be organized as shown in Figure 11.3:

Cash flows in all four categories are illustrated in the following examples:

Example

Organizing Cash Flow Data for Capital Budgeting

A real estate company is considering the purchase of a parcel of land for $1,000,000. Management forecasts it would hold the land for five years, during which time there would be no receipts or costs associated with the property. At the end of the five years, the land would be sold for a price forecasted to be $1,500,000. The firm is in the 35% income tax bracket.

Question: Organize the cash flows for this capital budgeting analysis.

FIGURE 11.3
Cash flow table (spreadsheet) for capital budgeting decisions. The table organizes the data into four categories of cash flows.

	Year 0	Years 1–n	Year n
Buy asset	(Cost)		
Tax—new depreciation		Reduced taxes	
Terminal value			Recovery
Sell asset	Sale price		
Tax—gain/loss on sale	Tax in/outflow		
Tax—lost depreciation		(Increased taxes)	
Lost terminal value			(Lost recovery)
Operating cash flows		Changed in/outflows	
Tax—changed income		Tax on above	
Working capital assets	(Investment)		Recovery
Net cash flows			

Solution steps:

1. The purchase and sale price for the land are given. We must calculate the tax the company will pay when it sells the land:

Gain on sale = \$1,500,000 − 1,000,000 = \$500,000

Tax on gain = 35% × \$500,000 = \$175,000

2. Construct a cash flow table:

	Year 0	Year 5
Buy the land	(\$1,000,000)	
Sell the land		\$1,500,000
Tax—gain on sale		(175,000)
Net cash flows	(\$1,000,000)	\$1,325,000

Answer: This project will require the firm to pay \$1,000,000 at its inception in return for a forecasted \$1,325,000 in five years.

Example

Organizing Cash Flow Data for Capital Budgeting

A company is considering a change to its production process to improve the quality of its product. The change would cost \$10,000 in released working time for the quality improvement team (during which they could not continue with their other productive work) plus a celebration event at the end of the project. Improving the process is expected to bring in new cash revenue of \$15,000 per year in each of the next four years. The firm is in the 35% income tax bracket.

Question: Organize the cash flows for this capital budgeting analysis.

Solution steps:

1. The wage cost and new revenue are given. We must calculate the tax changes due to these two new cash flows:

Tax benefit from deducting salary expense
= 35% × \$10,000 = \$3,500

Tax obligation on new revenue
= 35% × \$15,000 = \$5,250 / year

2. Construct a cash flow table:

	Year 0	Years 1–4
Pay the team members	(\$10,000)	
Tax—salaries	3,500	
New cash revenue		\$15,000
Tax—new revenue		(5,250)
Net cash flows	(\$ 6,500)	\$ 9,750

Answer: This project will require the firm to pay \$6,500 at its inception in return for a forecasted annuity of benefits of \$9,750 per year for four years.

Example

Organizing Cash Flow Data for Capital Budgeting

A manufacturing company is considering the purchase of a machine to reduce waste in its production process. The machine would cost $110,000, have a ten-year life, and be depreciated for tax purposes to a $10,000 salvage value using the straight-line[4] method. The company forecasts that the machine would save the firm $33,000 in each of the ten years of its life and that it could be sold for its $10,000 salvage value at the end of the ten years. The firm is in the 35% income tax bracket.

Question: Organize the cash flows for this capital budgeting analysis.

Solution steps:

1. The purchase and sale price for the machine are given as is the annual savings. We must calculate the tax benefits from depreciating the machine and the tax obligations from reporting higher income due to the annual operating savings:

$$\text{New depreciation} = (\$110{,}000 - 10{,}000)/10 = \$10{,}000/\text{year}$$

$$\text{Tax benefit} = 35\% \times \$10{,}000 = \$3{,}500/\text{year}$$

$$\text{Tax on operating savings} = 35\% \times \$33{,}000 = \$11{,}550/\text{year}$$

2. Construct a cash flow table:

	Year 0	Years 1–10	Year 10
Buy the machine	($110,000)		
Tax—new depreciation		$ 3,500	
Terminal value			$10,000
Operating cash flows		33,000	
Tax—changed income		(11,550)	
Net cash flows	($110,000)	$24,950	$10,000

Answer: This project will require the firm to pay $110,000 at its inception in return for a forecasted annuity of benefits of $24,950 per year for ten years plus a single cash benefit of $10,000 at the end of the tenth year.

[4] **Elaboration and cross-reference:** Although the U.S. tax code requires businesses to use the "modified accelerated cost recovery system (MACRS)" to depreciate assets on their tax returns, we use the straight-line method throughout this chapter to keep the illustrations simple and manageable. See Appendix 11A for further discussion of the worth of accelerated depreciation.

Example

Organizing Cash Flow Data for Capital Budgeting

A transportation company is considering the replacement of several trucks to reduce down-time, thus providing better on-time delivery service. The existing trucks were purchased three years ago for $75,000 and are being depreciated over their eight-year life to a $15,000 salvage value using the straight-line method. They could be sold today for $35,000. New trucks would cost $100,000, have a five-year life, and be depreciated for tax purposes to a $20,000 salvage value, also using the straight-line method. The company forecasts that the new trucks would reduce operating costs by $5,000 per year; in addition, increased customer satisfaction would add $20,000 per year to cash revenues. As long as the new trucks are around, the company must carry an increased inventory of spare parts costing $2,500. At the end of the five years, the new trucks would be sold for $25,000. The firm is in the 35% income tax bracket.

Question: Organize the cash flows for this capital budgeting analysis.

Solution steps:

1. The purchase and sale price for the new trucks are given, as are the sale price of the old trucks, the annual operating benefits, and the required increase to working capital assets. We must calculate the various tax effects:

New trucks:

New depreciation = ($100,000 − 20,000)/5 = $16,000/year

Tax benefit due to new depreciation = 35% × $16,000
= $5,600/year

Book value when sold = accounting salvage value = $20,000

Projected gain on sale = $25,000 − 20,000 = $5,000

Tax obligation due to gain on sale = 35% × $5,000 = $1,750

Old trucks:

Depreciation/year = ($75,000 − 15,000)/8 = $7,500

Tax obligation due to lost depreciation = 35% × $7,500
= $2,625/year

Current book value = $75,000 − (3 × $7,500) = $52,500

Loss on sale = $52,500 − 35,000 = $17,500

Tax benefit due to loss on sale = 35% × $17,500 = $6,125

Operating cash flows:

Tax obligation on cost saving = 35% × $5,000 = $1,750/year

Tax obligation on new revenues = 35% × $20,000 = $7,000/year

2. Construct a cash flow table:

	Year 0	Years 1–5	Year 5
Buy the new trucks	($100,000)		
Tax—new depreciation		$5,600	
Terminal value			$25,000
Tax—gain on sale			(1,750)
Sell the old trucks	35,000		
Tax—loss on sale	6,125		
Tax—lost depreciation		(2,625)	
Lost terminal value			(15,000)
Operating cash flows			
Cost savings		5,000	
Tax—cost savings		(1,750)	
New cash revenue		20,000	
Tax—new revenue		(7,000)	
Working capital assets	(2,500)		2,500
Net cash flows	($ 61,375)	$19,225	$ 10,750

Answer: This project will require the firm to pay a net $61,375 at its inception in return for a forecasted annuity of benefits of $19,225 per year for five years plus a single cash benefit of $10,750 at the end of the fifth year.

Reaching a Decision

The cash flow table for a capital budgeting proposal gives a summary of the project's projected cash flows organized by when they are expected to occur. In this form the data are perfectly arranged for evaluation using time value of money tools. The use of time value analysis is necessary since long-term asset investments, by their very nature, involve cash flow changes at a variety of points in time—from the project's inception into the future—and, as we originally saw in Chapter 5, it is impossible to compare cash flows unless they are adjusted for time.

There are two widely used methods of applying time value analysis to a table of cash flows: (1) net present value and (2) internal rate of return. Both reduce the cash flow data to a single number. Both test that number against the firm's weighted-average cost of capital to determine if the investment project returns an amount sufficient to give investors their required rate of return. If so, the company should accept the proposed investment as it will add value for the firm's stakeholders; if not, the proposed investment should be rejected since to accept it would reduce the firm's worth.[5]

[5] **Elaboration and observation:** Net present value (NPV) is the theoretically correct method, calculating the projected value added to the company from undertaking the proposed project. But internal rate of return (IRR) is a perfect substitute for NPV in many cases. Where this is so, many finance professionals prefer IRR since they find it easier to communicate and understand ("The proposed investment earns a 30% rate of return"). IRR, a rate of interest, is easily compared to other interest rates in the economy, especially the company's cost of capital. NPV on the other hand, a dollar amount, may seem like a more abstract concept ("The proposed investment would add $5,000 to the company's value measured in today's dollars"), and is more difficult to relate to the cost of financing the proposed capital budgeting project. See Appendix 11B for a discussion of those cases where IRR breaks down.

In what follows, we look further at these two methods and apply them to the four investments for which we developed cash flow tables on the previous pages.

1. Net Present Value (NPV)

net present value—the present value of all benefits from a proposed investment less the present value of all costs, using the weighted-average cost of capital as the discount rate

The **net present value** of a series of cash flows is the difference, or net, between the present value of all benefits and the present value of all costs. Alternatively, given the convention that cash inflows are written with a positive sign while cash outflows are treated as negative, net present value is simply the sum of the signed present values of all the cash flows. By combining the benefits and costs of a proposed project, NPV performs a (time-value-of-money adjusted) cost-benefit analysis.

The interest rate used to calculate net present value must be the cost of capital appropriate for the investment project. By using the cost of capital to discount future cash flows to their present value, NPV tests those flows to see if they represent a growth in value in excess of "the rate the firm must earn on new investments to return to investors their required rate of return."

When net present value is positive, benefits exceed costs and the proposal should be accepted. When net present value is negative, the reverse is true: costs are greater than benefits and the proposal should be rejected.

Examples

Calculating Net Present Value

In considering the land investment on pp. 380–381, the real estate company produced a cash flow table with the following summary numbers:

	Year 0	Year 5
Net cash flows	($1,000,000)	$1,325,000

The company's weighted-average cost of capital is 12%.

Question: Calculate the proposal's net present value.

Solution steps:

1. Since the outflow takes place at "year 0," its present value is its face value of $1,000,000.
2. Use the financial calculator to obtain the present value of the benefit:

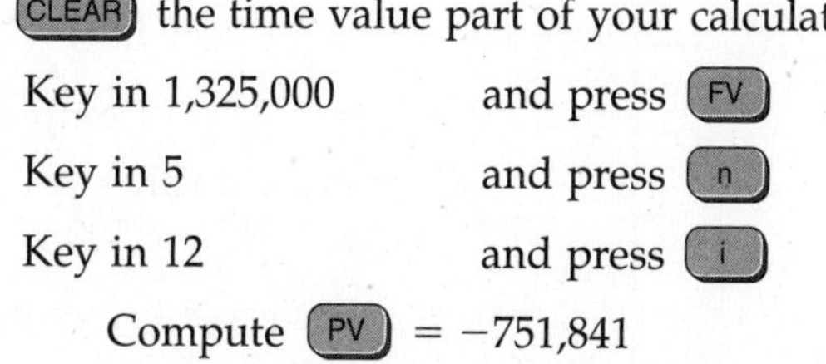

CLEAR the time value part of your calculator
Key in 1,325,000 and press FV
Key in 5 and press n
Key in 12 and press i
Compute PV = −751,841

(The negative sign indicates that $751,841 is the fair price to pay today for a benefit of $1,325,000 to be received in five years if the goal is to earn 12%. In this context, however, since we are evaluating a benefit, we ignore the negative sign and treat the $751,841 as a positive amount: the equivalent today to receiving $1,325,000 in five years.)

3. NPV = present value of benefits − present value of costs
= $751,841 − 1,000,000 = −$248,159

Answer: This project's net present value is −$248,159.

Question: Should the firm accept this proposal?

Answer: No! NPV is negative. To accept would be to give away $1,000,000 in return for future benefits worth only $751,841. The firm would lose $248,159 of value if it accepted the proposal.

Notice that net present value measures the change in value to the firm from accepting a proposal. This is always true and reinforces the decision rule that positive-NPV proposals are to be accepted while negative-NPV proposals should be rejected. In the previous example, the real estate firm's value would be reduced by $248,159 if the proposal were accepted.

Examples

Calculating Net Present Value

In considering the quality improvement investment on p. 381, a company produced a cash flow table with the following summary numbers:

	Year 0	Years 1–4
Net cash flows	($6,500)	$9,750

The company's weighted-average cost of capital is 9%.

Question: Calculate the proposal's net present value.

Solution steps:

1. Since the outflow takes place at year 0, its present value is its face value of $6,500.
2. Use the financial calculator to obtain the present value of the annuity of benefits:

   CLEAR the time value part of your calculator

   Key in 9,750 and press PMT, set END

   Key in 4 and press n

   Key in 9 and press i

   Compute PV = −31,587

3. NPV = present value of benefits − present value of costs
= $31,587 − 6,500 = $25,087

Answer: This project's net present value is $25,087.

Question: Should the firm accept this proposal?

Answer: Yes! NPV is positive. To accept would be to give away only $6,500 in return for benefits worth $31,587. The firm would add $25,087 to its value if it accepted the proposal.

By setting the calculator to **END,** we have adopted the usual convention: to assume that all cash inflows during a year come at the end of that year. This simplifies the NPV calculation. It is a conservative assumption as it tends to reduce the worth of investments by treating benefits during the year as coming later in time. Normally, the error introduced by this assumption is small; however, if NPV calculates very close to zero, it might be worthwhile to place the cash flows more precisely within the year and recalculate NPV.

Examples

Calculating Net Present Value

In considering the waste reduction investment on p. 382, a company produced a cash flow table with the following summary numbers:

	Year 0	Years 1–10	Year 10
Net cash flows	($ 110,000)	$ 24,950	$ 10,000

The company's weighted-average cost of capital is 10%.

Question: Calculate the proposal's net present value.

Solution steps:

1. Since the outflow takes place at year 0, its present value is its face value of $110,000.
2. Use the financial calculator to obtain the present value of the annuity of benefits:

   CLEAR the time value part of your calculator

   Key in 24,950 and press PMT, set END

   Key in 10,000 and press FV

   Key in 10 and press n

   Key in 10 and press i

   Compute PV = −157,162

3. NPV = present value of benefits − present value of costs
   = $157,162 − 110,000 = $47,162

Answer: This project's net present value is $47,162.

Question: Should the firm accept this proposal?

Answer: Yes! NPV is positive.

Examples

Calculating Net Present Value

In considering the replacement of trucks on pp. 383–384, a transportation company produced a cash flow table with the following summary numbers:

	Year 0	Years 1–5	Year 5
Net cash flows	($61,375)	$19,225	$10,750

The company's weighted-average cost of capital is 10%.

Question: Calculate the proposal's net present value.

Solution steps:

1. Since the outflow takes place at year 0, it's present value is its face value of $61,375.
2. Use the financial calculator to obtain the present value of the annuity of benefits:

CLEAR the time value part of your calculator

Key in 19,225 and press PMT, set END

Key in 10,750 and press FV

Key in 5 and press n

Key in 10 and press i

Compute PV = −79,553

3. NPV = present value of benefits − present value of costs
   = $79,553 − 61,375 = $18,178

Answer: This project's net present value is $18,178.

Question: Should the firm accept this proposal?

Answer: Yes! NPV is positive.

2. Internal Rate of Return (IRR)

internal rate of return—the discount rate that equates the present value of all benefits from a proposed investment to the present value of all costs

The **internal rate of return** of a capital budgeting proposal is the interest rate that makes the present value of the project's benefits exactly equal to the present value of the project's costs. Alternatively, it is the discount rate at which the project's net present value is equal to zero. Effectively, it is *the* interest rate returned by the investment project. Since it includes all benefits and costs in its computation, IRR, like NPV, performs a complete, time-value-of-money-adjusted, cost-benefit analysis.

It is not necessary to use the weighted-average cost of capital in the calculation of internal rates of return, since IRR is itself an interest rate. However, to use IRR as a decision tool, a proposed project's IRR must be compared to the cost of capital appropriate for that project. If the IRR exceeds the cost of capital, the investment project provides a rate of return in excess of that needed to compensate investors and the proposal should be accepted. Conversely, if the IRR is less than the cost of capital, the project does not earn a high enough rate of return and the proposal should be rejected.

Examples

Calculating Internal Rate of Return

In considering the land investment on pp. 380–381, the real estate company produced a cash flow table with the following summary numbers:

	Year 0	Year 5
Net cash flows	($1,000,000)	$1,325,000

The company's weighted-average cost of capital is 12%.

Question: Calculate the proposal's internal rate of return.

Solution steps: Use the financial calculator to solve for the interest rate which connects the cash flows:

CLEAR the time value part of your calculator

Key in −1,000,000 and press PV

Key in 1,325,000 and press FV

Key in 5 and press n

Compute i = 5.79%

Answer: This project's internal rate of return is 5.79%.

Question: Should the firm accept this proposal?

Answer: No! The project's IRR of 5.79% is less than the 12% cost of capital. The firm must earn 12% on its funds—this investment does not achieve that rate of return.

Examples

Calculating Internal Rate of Return

In considering the quality-improvement investment on p. 381, a company produced a cash flow table with the following summary numbers:

	Year 0	Years 1–4
Net cash flows	($6,500)	$9,750

The company's weighted-average cost of capital is 9%.

Question: Calculate the proposal's internal rate of return.

Solution steps: Use the financial calculator to solve for the interest rate that connects the cash flows:

CLEAR the time value part of your calculator

Key in −6,500 and press PV

Key in 9,750 and press PMT, set END

Key in 4 and press n

Compute i = 145.90%

Answer: This project's internal rate of return is 145.90%.

Question: Should the firm accept this proposal?

Answer: Yes! The project's IRR of 145.90% is greater than the 9% cost of capital. The firm must earn 9% on its funds—this investment achieves a rate of return far in excess of that standard.

Examples

Calculating Internal Rate of Return

In considering the waste reduction investment on p. 382, a company produced a cash flow table with the following summary numbers:

	Year 0	Years 1–10	Year 10
Net cash flows	($110,000)	$24,950	$10,000

The company's weighted-average cost of capital is 10%.

Question: Calculate the proposal's internal rate of return.

Solution steps: Use the financial calculator to solve for the interest rate that connects the cash flows:

CLEAR the time value part of your calculator

Key in −110,000 and press PV

Key in 24,950 and press PMT, set END

Key in 10,000 and press FV

Key in 10 and press n

Compute i = 19%

Answer: This project's internal rate of return is 19%.

Question: Should the firm accept this proposal?

Answer: Yes! The project's IRR of 19% exceeds the 10% cost of capital.

Examples

Calculating Internal Rate of Return

In considering the replacement of trucks on pp. 383–384, a transportation company produced a cash flow table with the following summary numbers:

	Year 0	Years 1–5	Year 5
Net cash flows	($61,375)	$19,225	$10,750

The company's weighted-average cost of capital is 10%.

Question: Calculate the proposal's internal rate of return.

Solution steps: Use the financial calculator to solve for the interest rate that connects the cash flows:

CLEAR the time value part of your calculator

Key in −61,375 and press PV

Key in 19,225 and press PMT, set END
Key in 10,750 and press FV
Key in 5 and press n
Compute i = 20.31%

Answer: This project's internal rate of return is 20.31%.

Question: Should the firm accept this proposal?

Answer: Yes! The project's IRR of 20.31% exceeds the 10% cost of capital.

3. Choosing the Appropriate Cost of Capital

Correct decisions using the NPV and IRR techniques require an accurate measure of the cost of capital. Financial managers need to keep two things in mind as they select the number to be used in any capital budgeting analysis: (1) a company's cost of capital changes as financial market conditions change and (2) the appropriate cost of capital for a proposed investment project is dependent on that project's risk.

Changing conditions A company's cost of capital changes regularly. As we saw in Chapter 10, the cost of capital is the rate of return a company must earn on a new use of funds to satisfy its creditors and investors. Its calculation begins

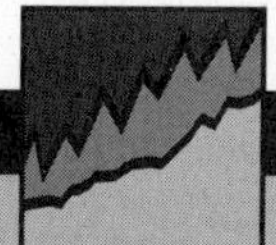

IMPROVING FINANCE'S PROCESSES

Evaluating Investments in Customer Service at Polaroid

The Customer Service group at Polaroid Corporation, the maker of cameras and film for instant photography, uses an innovative version of internal rate of return to evaluate investments in customer service. Prior to using the model, the group found it difficult to convince senior management that investments in service quality would provide an acceptable rate of return, generating sufficient new cash inflows to offset the costs of providing the additional service. Now the group constructs a cash flow model that explicitly identifies customer behaviors that, if changed, would increase cash inflows. Incremental outflows are the costs of the enhanced service. For each service initiative, values are calculated for the change(s) in behavior that would yield the company's minimum required IRR (its cost of capital). For example, the behavior change examined for a decision to provide pre-sale customer support was the percentage of leads that would subsequently become sales. The behavior change for a proposal to provide immediate replacement of defective cameras was the number of film packs the customer would purchase each month. Now when a proposed investment is presented to management, attention is immediately drawn to the most critical variables. Management can use forecasts of customer reactions to make the investment decisions. Customer groups can be segmented to provide the optimal service level to each. And unlike previous analyses, the new system is easy to understand and communicate to top management.

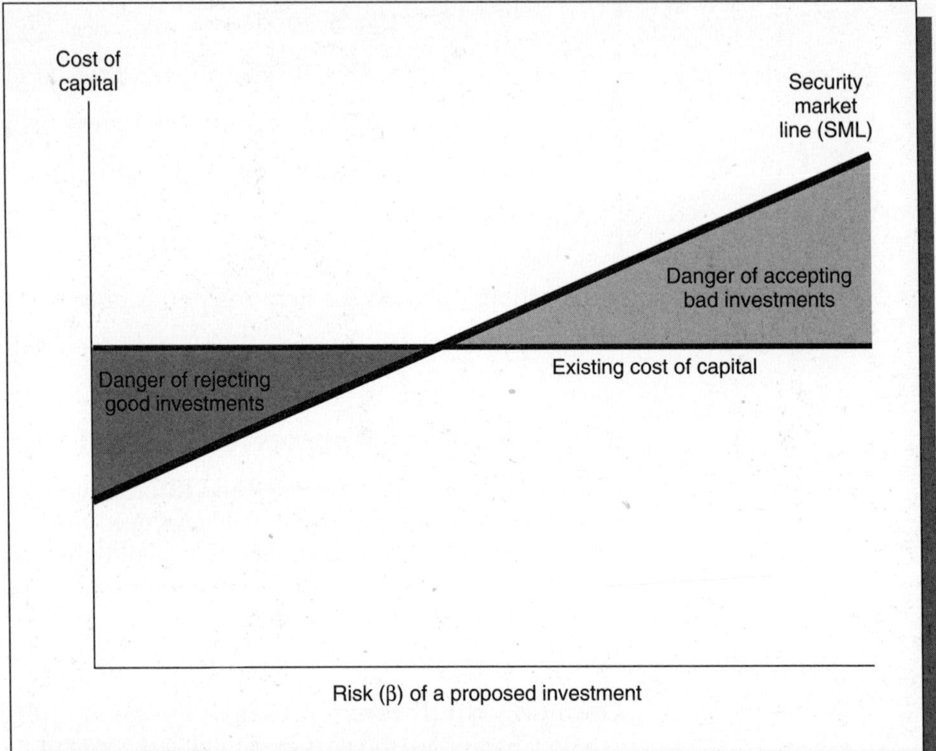

FIGURE 11.4
The appropriate cost of capital for a proposed investment project is a function of the project's beta. The existing cost of capital is valid only at the firm's current risk level.

with the rates of return required by the company's suppliers of funds, each of which incorporates the general level of interest rates and a premium for risk as delineated by the Fisher model we studied in Chapter 6. The cost of capital is then assembled by incorporating flotation costs, income tax effects, and the mix of financing used. As interest rates fluctuate, as risk perceptions shift, as flotation costs change, and as different tax rates affect the company, the cost of capital adjusts accordingly.

Risk appropriate A company's cost of capital can also differ for each capital budgeting project it considers since the risk premium its investors will demand depends on the risk of the project itself. The capital asset pricing model (CAPM) tells us that when an asset is held as part of a well-diversified portfolio, the relevant measure of its risk is its beta—the relationship of that asset's returns to the returns available from the economy as a whole. Each investment a company makes becomes one asset in the portfolio of assets held by the company and, through its securities, held by the company's investors.

The relationship between beta and the appropriate rate of return is captured by the security market line (SML),[6] which is drawn in Figure 11.4. Also on the graph

[6] **Cross-reference:** The capital asset pricing model is developed in Chapter 8, pp. 276–288. The security market line is introduced on pp. 286–288.

is the company's existing cost of capital, calculated without reference to the betas of proposed capital budgeting projects and hence shown as a horizontal line. Notice that the existing cost of capital is the correct rate to apply to a proposed capital budgeting investment only at one level of risk: the firm's current risk level where the two lines cross. To the left of that intersection, the proposed project is less risky than the firm; the existing cost of capital is too stringent a test and its use runs the risk of rejecting good projects. To the right of the intersection of the two lines, the proposed project is more risky than the firm; the existing cost of capital is too lenient a test and its use runs the risk of accepting poor projects.

Managing the Capital Budgeting Process

Although the majority of this chapter has been devoted to the cash-flow and time-value-of-money-based techniques of analyzing capital budgeting proposals, management of the capital budgeting process is also important. Once you have learned the analytical methods, it is relatively easy to organize cash flows and calculate net present values and internal rates of return. It is much more difficult to get good data to work with.

Many companies have begun to look at the *process* by which capital budgeting information is developed, qualified, communicated, and approved. Some are finding ways to standardize the flow of information and to ensure that the supporting assumptions and other related data necessary for accurate preparation and insightful interpretation are available as needed. One company that has reported the results of such an effort is Alcoa:

> In January 1989, a team at Alcoa undertook a project that will take many years to evaluate: the improvement of the company's capital expenditure decision process.
>
> By 1989, senior management had become increasingly concerned about their choice of capital investment projects. Key capital indicators like net income divided by total capital expenditures over a five-year period, and property, plant, and equipment divided by number of employees lagged behind the numbers of competitors against which the company was benchmarking itself. Capital expenditures as a percentage of sales also lagged relative to a set of benchmarked companies drawn from a variety of industries.
>
> To improve the process, Alcoa's top management empowered a sixteen-person cross functional/cross divisional high-level team, including seven vice presidents. The team reviewed past studies on capital effectiveness including post-completion analyses of major projects. Cause and effect relationships that contributed to the problem of "less-than-ideal" capital expenditure decisions were also explored.
>
> In particular, the team focused on problems concerning the requests for capital projects that are communicated to management via a formal Request for Authorization (RFA) package. These RFA packages justify proposed capital projects and must be approved at different management levels depending on the amount of each request. The consensus was that the RFA process was seriously flawed as it did not consistently:
>
> - Provide the right technical and business information to make the decision.
> - Reveal the underlying quality problem-solving process used to arrive at the decision to recommend a capital investment.

- Provide quantifiable documentation that allows project results to be verified.
- Provide appropriate accountability for project success.

By the end of 1989, the team had developed, pilot tested, and distributed new RFA guidelines to all Alcoa locations for use on new projects. One important change was development of a "Decision Analysis Summary (DAS)." The DAS provides strategic, market, and manufacturing process context for interpreting and deciding upon RFA schedules. It also reveals, in summarized form, some of the detailed analyses that underlie the RFAs and which were not previously provided to project reviewers.[7]

Another attempt to improve the capital budgeting process is Federal Express' technique known as the Business Case Approach:

> The Business Case Approach (BCA) is a process for analyzing projects that are likely to have an impact throughout the company. The approach emphasizes a broad company-wide focus rather than a narrow financial or departmental one and the building of a team bringing diverse perspectives, including the financial perspective, into the analysis at early stages.
>
> Most of the financial analysis takes place during repeated iterations as the project concept and design evolve rather than at the end when the project design has been completed. Along the way, financial models of the project and its implications are assembled, so that the repeated iterations may be analyzed as alternative approaches.
>
> The BCA process does not end when a completed proposal is presented to senior management nor when senior management makes its decision on the project. Instead, the modelling and documentation developed during the design process are retained. If the project is accepted, implementation alternatives can then be reconsidered at key decision points. For example, procedural steps can be modified based on test results or contracts can be restructured before execution as information on equipment reliability becomes available. If, on the other hand, the project is rejected, the BCA modelling provides a means to reconsider the original proposal or other ones as new technological and market information becomes available.[8]

Rick Daniel put down the advanced finance text and turned back to his spreadsheet. He had just finished rereading several chapters on capital budgeting. He was happy to discover that he had remembered most of it but was equally happy that he had located several ideas that could be applied to his current task. One chapter in particular, on how to search methodically for good data, had confirmed some of the senior analyst's suggestions.

---

[7] **References:** James A.F. Stoner, Frank M. Werner, and the Corporate Finance—IPM Study Group, *Remaking Corporate Finance—The New Corporate Finance Emerging in High-Quality Companies* (McGraw-Hill Primis, 1992), p. 49. The original report is: Manny Rosenfeld, "A Quality-based Capital Decision Process," *IMPRO-90 Conference Proceedings* (Wilton, Conn.: The Juran Institute, 1990), p. 7D-24–7D-36.

[8] **Reference:** James A.F. Stoner, and Frank M. Werner, *Finance in the Quality Revolution—Integrating Financial and Total Quality Management*. Morristown, N.J.: Financial Executives Research Foundation, 1993) pp. 54–56.

The cash flow numbers had been entered into the appropriate columns of the spreadsheet, reflecting estimates of when those cash flows would occur. The cost of capital was realistic. And the spreadsheet program was correctly calculating the project's net present value and internal rate of return. The problem seemed to be with the completeness of the data.

As he returned the text to his bookshelf, Rick thought back to his finance class on capital budgeting and remembered a statement his professor seemed to emphasize: "After a while, the NPV and IRR calculations become routine; getting good data is the difficult part of the job." Rick smiled wryly as he realized that his current problem was teaching him just how true that statement was.

Summary of Key Points

- **Discuss the importance of capital budgeting to business success.** Capital budgeting is the process of evaluating potential long-term investments. Due to their long-term nature, investments in these assets have a major impact on the firm's ability to compete and survive. The techniques of capital budgeting are applicable to other incremental decisions and form an important component of the financial manager's skills.
- **Identify the data used in capital budgeting.** There are eight rules which specify the data that should and should not enter into capital budgeting analysis: (1) use cash flow numbers only, (2) use incremental numbers only, (3) include changes in all functional areas, (4) include changes across the life cycle, (5) include forecasted inflation, (6) consider quality and cycle time impacts, (7) consider the options implicit in the decision, and (8) leave the financing flows out.
- **Organize cash flow data for capital budgeting analysis.** It is useful to organize the data of a capital budgeting decision into a cash flow table which summarizes cash flows by time of occurrence. This makes the data ready for analysis using time-value-of-money methods.
- **Use the techniques of net present value (NPV) and internal rate of return (IRR) to judge the worth of a capital project.** Two time-value calculations are applied to the cash flows of a capital budgeting proposal to reach a decision whether to invest. Net present value (NPV) compares the present value of the proposal's benefits to the present value of its costs to determine which is greater. The NPV number measures the value added to (or subtracted from) the firm by going ahead with the investment. When NPV is positive, benefits exceed costs and the project should be accepted. When NPV is negative, costs exceed benefits and the project should be rejected. A project's IRR is its rate of return. When a project's IRR exceeds the appropriate cost of capital, the project should be accepted as it returns more than the minimum amount required to satisfy investors. When a project's IRR is less than the cost of capital, the project should be rejected as the return is insufficient to meet investors' needs. The cost of capital used to evaluate each proposed project must reflect current market conditions and be adjusted to match the risk of the project.
- **Describe how quality-management techniques can improve the capital budgeting process.** Recently, quality-management techniques have been applied to the capital budgeting process to improve the quality of cash flow data and to ensure that the appropriate financial, market, and strategic information reaches decision makers as needed. In the Business Case Approach financial analysts work in partnership with other organization members to model investment decisions, permitting financial implications to be seen and addressed throughout a project's design and development.

Questions

1. Why does capital budgeting analysis pay attention only to cash flows?
2. What is a sunk cost? Why is it ignored in capital budgeting?
3. What would happen to a capital budgeting analysis if inflation were omitted from the cash flow estimates?
4. What is meant by the "option" inherent in a capital budgeting decision?
5. A financial analyst included the interest cost of the debt used to buy new machinery in the cash flows from a capital budgeting project. Is this correct or incorrect? Why?

6. What function does a cash flow table play in capital budgeting analysis?
7. What is the meaning of:

   a. Net present value?
   b. Internal rate of return?

   In what ways are they the same, and how do they differ?
8. Why is the net present value of a capital budgeting project equal to zero when its internal rate of return is used as the discount rate?
9. True or false (and why?): The NPV technique uses the firm's cost of capital in its calculation, but the IRR technique does not. Therefore, the cost of capital is relevant only if capital budgeting projects are evaluated using NPV.
10. What is the danger of applying one cost of capital to all proposed capital budgeting projects?

Problems

1. **(Identifying cash flows)** An analyst has prepared the following data as part of a proposal to acquire a new machine:

Cost to purchase machine	$40,000
Cost to install machine	1,000
Cost of new electric wiring	2,000
First-year depreciation of machine	4,000
Sales tax on purchasing machine	3,000
Economic salvage value of the machine	10,000
Accounting salvage value of the machine	8,000

   a. Which of the above figures should enter the capital budgeting analysis?
   b. What figure should enter the capital budgeting analysis as the investment at year zero?
   c. Which of the above figures should not enter the capital budgeting analysis?
   d. Will any of the items you list in part c have a later impact on the firm's cash flows? If so, what?

2. **(Identifying cash flows)** A company is considering switching from accelerated to straight-line depreciation on its GAAP financial statements to reduce its depreciation expense and boost income.

   a. What effect will this change have on the firm's reported income?
   b. What is the financial value of this decision?
   c. Suppose the company made the same switch on its tax returns. Now what is the financial value of this decision?
   d. Given your answers to parts a–c, why do many companies make this change in choice of depreciation method?

3. **(Identifying incremental cash flows)** An analyst has prepared the following data as part of a proposal for an addition to the firm's plant:

Cost to build addition	$ 500,000
Book value of existing plant	7,000,000
Cost for new machinery	200,000
Cost of new electric wiring	30,000
Amount spent on study to date	2,000
Increase to working capital to support machinery	60,000
Interest on loan taken to finance the addition	40,000

   a. Which of the above figures should enter the capital budgeting analysis? Why?
   b. Which of the above figures should not enter the capital budgeting analysis? Why?
   c. Suppose you found that $15,000 of working capital currently in use elsewhere within the company could perform double duty by supporting this facility as well. How would this change your answers to parts a and b?
   d. Suppose you found that the land under the plant would have been sold to a real estate developer for $1,500,000 if the addition were not built. How would this change your answers to parts a and b?

4. **(Identifying incremental cash flows)** Last week, your firm bought a fleet of trucks for $200,000 to begin a delivery service business. Today, someone came up with the idea to use the trucks to sell ice cream to suburban children door to door. Converting the trucks would cost $75,000. You have been asked to work on this capital budgeting project.

   a. What is the role of the $200,000 in your ice cream analysis?
   b. What is the role of the $75,000 in your ice cream analysis?
   c. What other information would you need to know about the trucks before making this decision?
   d. What other information not about the trucks would you need to know before making this decision?

5. **(Identifying nominal numbers)** A company is considering an investment that would cost $25,000 and return a net after-tax cash flow of $8,000 per year in each of the next five years.

a. Assume these figures include inflation forecasts. What numbers should enter the capital budgeting analysis?
b. Now assume the above figures do *not* include inflation, which is forecast to be 6% per year. What numbers should enter the capital budgeting analysis?
c. Why must the cash flows used in capital budgeting contain the impact of inflation?
d. What would be the bias if the impact of inflation were left out?

6. **(Identifying nominal numbers)** A company is considering an investment that would cost $70,000 and return a net after-tax cash flow of $10,000 per year in each of the next seven years.

a. Assume these figures include inflation forecasts. What numbers should enter the capital budgeting analysis?
b. Now assume the above figures do *not* include inflation, which is forecast to be 9% per year. What numbers should enter the capital budgeting analysis?
c. Why does inflation affect only one of the numbers above and not the other?
d. Does inflation appear anywhere else in the capital budgeting analysis? If so, where?

7. **(Organizing cash flows)** Judy Entrepreneur is considering the purchase of a machine for $100,000; the machine would be depreciated to a $20,000 salvage value over an eight-year period using the straight-line method. During its life, the machine would improve Judy's annual cash earnings by $25,000 per year. The firm expects to sell the machine for its $20,000 salvage value at the end of the eight years. The firm's federal tax rate on income is 35%. Calculate the incremental cash flows from:

a. The purchase of the machine
b. The depreciation of the machine
c. The operation of the machine
d. The sale of the machine

8. **(Organizing cash flows)** Joe Businessperson is considering the purchase of a machine for $650,000. The machine would be depreciated to a $50,000 salvage value over a nine-year period using the straight-line method and would bring in incremental cash income of $80,000 in each year. However, the firm expects to sell the machine for $60,000 at the end of the nine years. The firm's federal tax rate on income is 35%. Calculate the incremental cash flows from:

a. The purchase of the machine
b. The depreciation of the machine
c. The operation of the machine
d. The sale of the machine

9. **(NPV, IRR)** A company can invest $200,000 in a capital budgeting project that will generate the following forecasted cash flows:

Years	Cash flow
1–4	$75,000

The company has a 14% cost of capital.

a. Calculate the project's net present value.
b. Calculate the project's internal rate of return.
c. Should the firm accept or reject the project?
d. At what cost of capital would the firm be indifferent to accepting or rejecting this proposal?

10. **(NPV, IRR)** A company can invest $3 million in a capital budgeting project that will generate the following forecasted cash flows:

Years	Cash flow
1–16	$275,000

The company has an 8% cost of capital.

a. Calculate the project's net present value.
b. Calculate the project's internal rate of return.
c. Should the firm accept or reject the project?
d. At what cost of capital would the firm be indifferent to accepting or rejecting this proposal?

11. **(NPV, IRR)** A company can invest $200,000 in a capital budgeting project that will generate the following forecasted cash flows:

Year	Cash flow
1	$110,000
2	150,000
3	120,000
4	200,000

The company has a 10% cost of capital.

a. Calculate the project's net present value.
b. Calculate the project's internal rate of return.
c. Should the firm accept or reject the project?
d. What is the value added to the firm if it accepts this proposed investment?

12. **(NPV, IRR)** A company can invest $1,600,000 in a capital budgeting project that will generate the following forecasted cash flows:

Year	Cash flow
1	$500,000
2	720,000
3	300,000
4	600,000

The company has a 13% cost of capital.

a. Calculate the project's net present value.
b. Calculate the project's internal rate of return.
c. Should the firm accept or reject the project?
d. What is the value added to the firm if it accepts this proposed investment?

13. **(Organizing cash flows, NPV, IRR)** A company is evaluating the purchase of Machine A. The new machine would cost $120,000 and would be depreciated for tax purposes using the straight-line method over an estimated ten-year life to its expected salvage value of $20,000. The new machine would require an addition of $30,000 to working capital. In each year of Machine A's life, the company would reduce its pre-tax costs by $40,000. The company has a 12% cost of capital and is in the 35% marginal tax bracket.

a. Identify the incremental cash flows from investing in Machine A.
b. Calculate the investment's net present value (NPV).
c. Calculate the investment's internal rate of return (IRR).
d. Should the company purchase Machine A? Why or why not?

14. **(Organizing cash flows, NPV, IRR)** A company is evaluating the purchase of Machine X to improve product quality. The new machine would cost $1,000,000 and would be depreciated for tax purposes using the straight-line method over an estimated seven-year life to its expected salvage value of $125,000. The new machine would require an addition of $100,000 to working capital. In each year of Machine X's life, the company would increase its pre-tax receipts by $400,000. The company has an 11% cost of capital and is in the 35% marginal tax bracket.

a. Identify the incremental cash flows from investing in Machine X.
b. Calculate the investment's net present value (NPV).
c. Calculate the investment's internal rate of return (IRR).
d. Should the company purchase Machine X? Why or why not?

15. **(Organizing cash flows, NPV, IRR)** This problem follows Problem 13. It is now five years later. The company did buy Machine A, but just this week Machine B came on the market; Machine B could be purchased to replace Machine A. If acquired, Machine B would cost $80,000 and would be depreciated for tax purposes using the straight-line method over an estimated five-year life to its expected salvage value of $20,000. Machine B would also require $30,000 of working capital but would save an additional $20,000 per year in pre-tax operating costs. Machine A's salvage value remains $20,000, but it could be sold today for $40,000.

a. Identify the incremental cash flows from converting to Machine B.
b. Calculate this investment's net present value (NPV).
c. Calculate this investment's internal rate of return (IRR).
d. Should the company convert to Machine B? Why or why not?

16. **(Organizing cash flows, NPV, IRR)** This problem follows Problem 14. It is now four years later. The company did buy Machine X, but just today Machine Y came on the market; Machine Y could be purchased to replace Machine X. If acquired, Machine Y would cost $750,000 and would be depreciated for tax purposes using the straight-line method over an estimated three-year life to its expected salvage value of $150,000. Machine Y would require $160,000 of working capital but would add an additional $300,000 per year to pre-tax receipts. Machine X's salvage value remains $125,000, but it could be sold today for $100,000.

a. Identify the incremental cash flows from converting to Machine Y.
b. Calculate this investment's net present value (NPV).
c. Calculate this investment's internal rate of return (IRR).
d. Should the company convert to Machine Y? Why or why not?

17. **(Adjusting the cost of capital for risk)** A company with a 13% cost of capital is evaluating four independent potential capital budgeting proposals with the following forecasted internal rates of return (IRRs) and betas:

Proposal	IRR	Beta
A	12%	.85
B	10	1.00
C	16	1.10
D	14	1.25

The market price of risk is 8.5%, and the risk-free rate of interest is currently 4%.

a. Write the equation of the security market line (SML).
b. Calculate the required rate of return on each investment according to the SML.
c. Which projects would be accepted by using the existing cost of capital?
d. Which projects would be accepted by using a risk-adjusted cost of capital for each project based on the SML?

18. **(Adjusting the cost of capital for risk)** A company with a 14% cost of capital is evaluating four independent potential capital budgeting proposals with the following forecasted internal rates of return (IRRs) and betas:

Proposal	IRR	Beta
W	15%	1.40
X	19	1.15
Y	11	.90
Z	12	.65

The market price of risk is 8%, and the risk-free rate of interest is currently 5%.

a. Write the equation of the security market line (SML).
b. Calculate the required rate of return on each investment according to the SML.
c. Which projects would be accepted by using the existing cost of capital?
d. Which projects would be accepted by using a risk-adjusted cost of capital for each project based on the SML?

APPENDIX 11A

THE VALUE OF ACCELERATED DEPRECIATION

Money Rule No. 2 points out that, other things equal, it is advantageous to delay cash outflows. Compared to the straight-line method, accelerated depreciation does just that. By permitting a company to depreciate an asset earlier in its life, accelerated depreciation moves income to the later years of the asset's use. And as income comes later, so do the tax payments that attach to it. When the U.S. Congress approved accelerated depreciation for tax purposes in the early 1950s, and then introduced the even more-accelerated ACRS system in 1981, it was explicitly reducing the cost of thc tax payments associated with long-term asset purchases in the hope of stimulating corporate investment.

Example

The Value of Accelerated Depreciation

A company wishes to determine the value of electing ACRS depreciation instead of straight-line depreciation for its tax return.[1] It recently purchased an asset for $100,000 with a ten-year economic life and zero salvage value. The asset falls into the seven-year ACRS class. The company has a weighted-average cost of capital of 12% and is in the 35% tax bracket.

Question: What are the differences in depreciation, income, and taxes each year, and what is the present value of the tax differences between the two depreciation methods?

Solution steps:

1. Calculate yearly depreciation under each method, find the difference (which is also the difference in income), and multiply by the tax rate to calculate the tax difference:

Year	Straight-Line Depreciation	ACRS Rate	ACRS Depreciation	Depreciation Difference	Tax Difference
1	$ 10,000	14.29%	$ 14,290	$ 4,290	$1,501.50
2	10,000	24.49	24,490	14,490	5,071.50
3	10,000	17.49	17,490	7,490	2,621.50
4	10,000	12.49	12,490	2,490	871.50
5	10,000	8.93	8,930	(1,070)	(374.50)
6	10,000	8.92	8,920	(1,080)	(378.00)
7	10,000	8.93	8,930	(1,070)	(374.50)
8	10,000	4.46	4,460	(5,540)	(1,939.00)
9	10,000			(10,000)	(3,500.00)
10	10,000			(10,000)	(3,500.00)
	$100,000		$100,000	0	0.00

2. Discount the tax difference numbers to the present using the firm's 12% cost of capital. You can do this by discounting each number individually and summing the results or by using the cash flow list feature of a financial calculator as shown below.[2]

If needed:

call up the cash flow menu

CLEAR the cash-flow-list part of your calculator

Enter:

0 as FLOW 0

1,501.50 as FLOW 1

5,071.50 as FLOW 2

2,621.50 as FLOW 3

[1] **Observation:** Assuming it has this choice.

[2] **Cross-reference:** The use of the cash flow list feature of a financial calculator is discussed in Appendix 5B.

871.50 as FLOW 4

−374.50 as FLOW 5

−378 as FLOW 6

−374.50 as FLOW 7

−1,939 as FLOW 8

−3,500 as FLOW 9, 2 TIMES

12 as i

Compute NPV = $4,057.80

Answer: The ability to use ACRS depreciation is worth $4,057.80 more to this company than if it had to use the straight-line method. In effect, the government has increased its subsidy of the asset's purchase price by this amount.

APPENDIX 11B

MATHEMATICAL LIMITATIONS OF THE IRR TECHNIQUE

In the four capital budgeting problems illustrated in Chapter 11, net present value and internal rate of return gave the same result. Both rejected the real estate investment, and both accepted the other three. However, this is not always the case. While NPV works all the time, there are some mathematical limitations to the IRR method which make it difficult or impossible to use in some situations.

1. The Standard Project

standard project—an investment project in which all cash outflows precede all cash inflows

An investment project in which the summary cash flow numbers are characterized by the cash outflows coming first followed only by cash inflows is called a **standard project.** We denote a standard project by the symbol (− , +) where the signs correspond to the sequence of cash flows. For a standard project, IRR works precisely as described in the body of this chapter: there can be only one IRR; if IRR exceeds the cost of capital, the investment should be accepted; if IRR is less

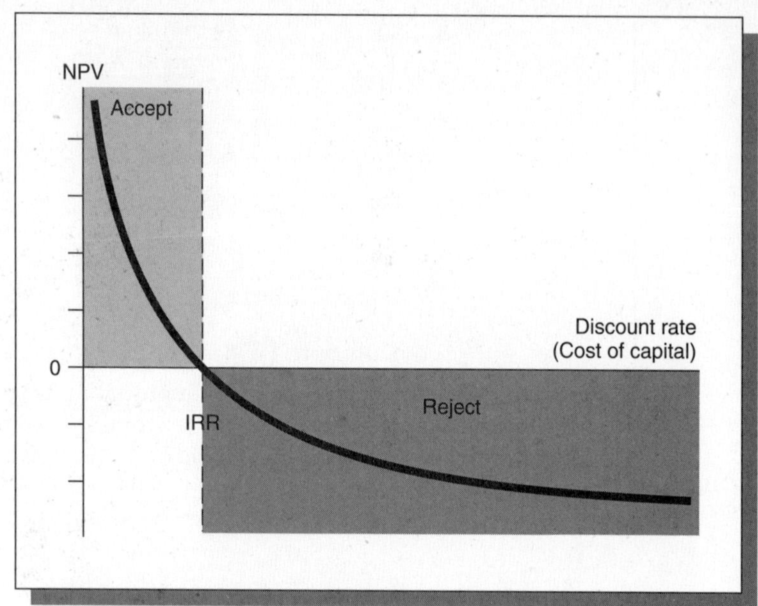

FIGURE 11B.1
NPV profile of a standard (− , +) project. For a standard project, NPV and IRR always agree.

than the cost of capital, the project should be rejected. *For a standard project, IRR is a perfect substitute for NPV—they may be used interchangeably.*

net present value profile—a graph of an investment project's net present value as a function of the discount rate

A popular way to illustrate this concept is with a graph known as a **net present value profile.** Figure 11B.1 is the NPV profile for a standard project. At low discount rates NPV is high, and vice versa. The discount rate that produces a zero NPV—the point where the graph intersects the horizontal axis—is the IRR. Notice that to the left of the IRR point, both the NPV and IRR methods signal to accept the investment: NPV is positive, and the IRR exceeds (is to the right of) the discount rate, i.e., the cost of capital. To the right of the IRR point, both methods signal reject: NPV is negative here, and the discount rate (cost of capital) is greater than the investment's IRR.

2. Other Cash Flow Patterns

There are three other common cash flow patterns: (1) opposite projects, (2) projects with no IRR, and (3) projects with multiple IRRs.

opposite project—an investment project in which all cash inflows precede all cash outflows

Opposite project An investment project in which the summary cash flow numbers are characterized by the cash *inflows* coming first followed only by cash *outflows* is an **opposite project.** We denote an opposite project by the symbol (+,−) where the signs again correspond to the sequence of cash flows. While an opposite project has only one IRR, that IRR must be interpreted in the opposite direction from that of a standard project: if IRR exceeds the cost of capital, the investment should be rejected; if IRR is less than the cost of capital, the project should be accepted. This is because an opposite project is the equivalent of raising money, obtaining an immediate inflow in return for later outflows. Whereas we wish to earn (standard projects) at high rates of return, it is best when raising money to do so at the lowest rates possible. An IRR below the cost of capital indicates the ability to obtain funds at a low, attractive rate and should be pursued. An IRR above the cost of capital signifies that the project is the equivalent of raising money at too high a cost and should be avoided. *For an opposite project, IRR remains a perfect substitute for NPV as long as it is interpreted correctly.*

Figure 11B.2 is the NPV profile for an opposite project. At low discount rates NPV is low, and vice versa. The discount rate that produces a zero NPV—the point where the graph intersects the horizontal axis—is still the IRR. Notice that to the left of the IRR point, both the NPV and IRR methods signal to reject the investment: NPV is negative, and the IRR exceeds (is to the right of) the discount rate, i.e., the cost of capital. To the right of the IRR point, both methods signal accept: NPV is positive here, and the discount rate (cost of capital) is greater than the investment's IRR.

No IRR An investment project in which the summary cash flow numbers are *only* inflows (+,+) or *only* outflows (−,−) *has no IRR.*

Figure 11B.3 is the NPV profile for a (+,+) project. For any discount rate NPV is positive, indicating that the project should be accepted no matter what the company's cost of capital. However, there is no need to calculate NPV to reach this conclusion—it may be reached merely by looking at the cash flows since in every period the net flows are positive.

Figure 11B.4 is the NPV profile for a (−,−) project. For any discount rate NPV is negative, indicating that the project should be rejected no matter what the company's cost of capital. Again, there is no need to calculate NPV to reach this conclusion—it may be reached merely by looking at the cash flows since in every period the net flows are negative.

FIGURE 11B.2
NPV profile of an opposite (+,−) project. When NPV is positive, IRR is always less than the firm's cost of capital.

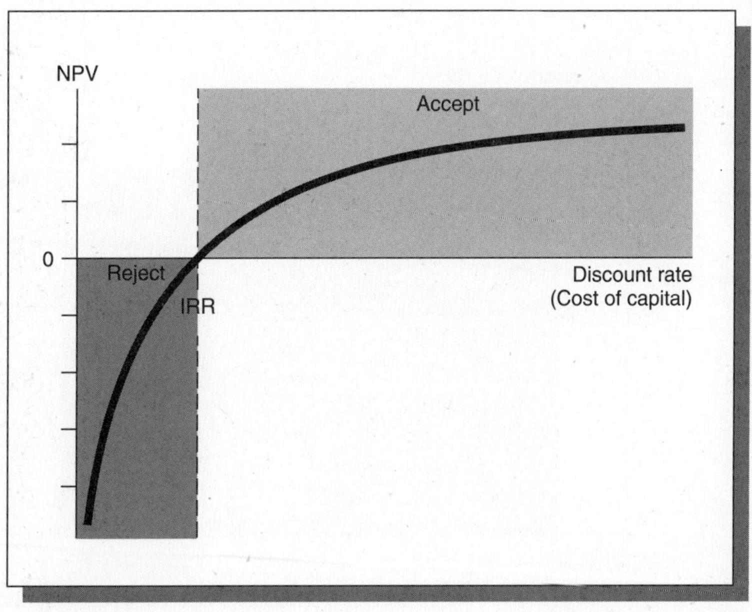

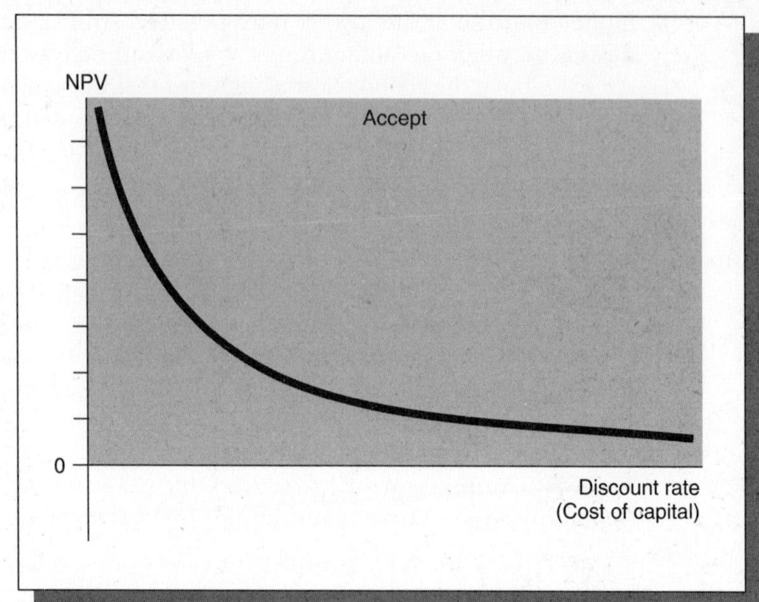

FIGURE 11B.3
NPV profile of an (+,+) project. NPV is positive for any cost of capital, and there is no IRR.

Multiple IRRs An investment project in which the summary cash flow numbers are characterized by alternating cash inflows and outflows can have more than one, or *multiple IRRs.* We denote these projects by (−,+,−. . .) or (+,−,+. . .) where the signs once again correspond to the sequence of cash flows. There can be as many IRRs as there are reversals in direction of cash flow. For example a (−,+,−) project could have two IRRs (minus-*to*-plus-*to*-minus) while a (−,+,−,+)

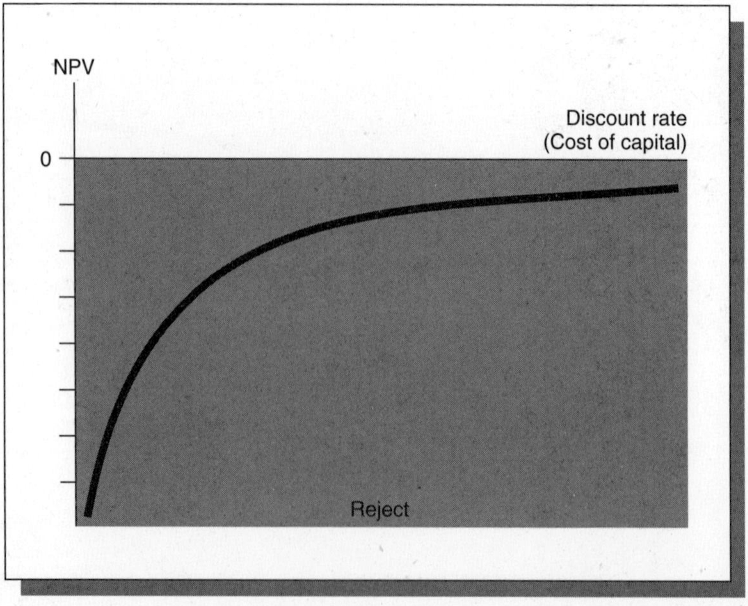

FIGURE 11B.4
NPV profile of a (−,−) project. NPV is negative for any cost of capital, and there is no IRR.

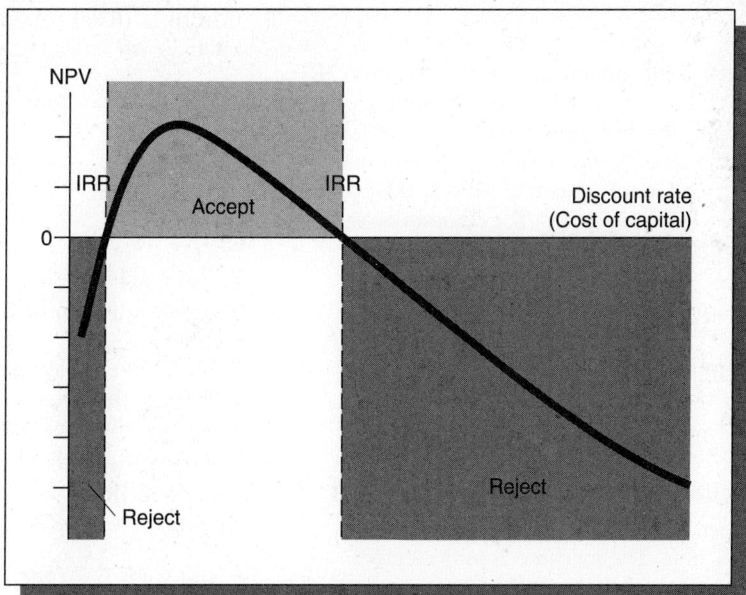

FIGURE 11B.5
NPV profile of a project (−,+,−) with multiple IRRs. IRR loses its economic meaning, but NPV remains valid.

project could have three (minus-*to*-plus-*to*-minus-*to*-plus), etc. Further, the IRRs need not be real numbers; they could be imaginary (containing the square root of –1) or complex (containing trigonometric components).

Figure 11B.5 is the NPV profile for a project with multiple IRRs. The graph cuts through the horizontal axis in two places, each of which is mathematically an IRR. However, although mathematically valid, it is very difficult to give an economic meaning to multiple IRRs. Which one is correct? Or are both correct (and what does that mean?) or neither? When there are multiple IRRs, it is best not to pay attention to them and use NPV instead.

3. Comparing IRR to a Yield Curve

Even when there is one clearly defined and usable IRR, IRR as a decision tool suffers from another problem. In all the illustrations of this chapter we assumed that each firm has one cost of capital which holds from period to period. However, the yield curve is rarely flat. It is likely that the firm's cost of capital is really a series of rates, one for each period into the future, which captures the shape of the yield curve.

This refinement poses no conceptual problem for the NPV method—we simply do our discounting period by period, changing the discount rate as we ride along the yield curve. However, IRR cannot handle multiple costs of capital. A project's IRR is a composite rate representing the overall earnings forecasted for an investment over some period of time. It must be compared to a single cost of capital. In the other direction, it is impossible to subdivide an IRR into separate rates for each period. And even if we could, it would be awkward to come to a definitive accept/reject decision on the basis of multiple comparisons between IRR components and cost of capital components.

Problems

1. **(Opposite project)** A company has the opportunity to sell an old machine. The machine is fully depreciated to a zero book value but could be sold for $5,000. If the company did not sell the machine, it would be able to use it for four more years and save $3,000 in pre-tax costs in each of those years. The company has a 10% cost of capital and is in the 35% marginal tax bracket.
   a. Calculate the net present value (NPV) of this decision.
   b. Calculate the internal rate of return (IRR) of this decision.
   c. Should the company sell the machine? Why or why not?
   d. Interpret the IRR you calculated.
2. **(Opposite project)** A company has the opportunity to sell an old machine. The machine is fully depreciated to a zero book value, but could be sold for $20,000. If the company did not sell the machine, it would be able to use it for two more years and save $11,000 in pre-tax costs in each of those years. The company has a 13% cost of capital and is in the 35% marginal tax bracket.
   a. Calculate the net present value (NPV) of this decision.
   b. Calculate the internal rate of return (IRR) of this decision.
   c. Should the company sell the machine? Why or why not?
   d. Interpret the IRR you calculated.
3. **(Multiple IRRs)** A company has projected the following cash flows for an investment project:

Year	Cash flow
0	−$8,000
1	27,000
2	−20,000

   a. Calculate this project's net present value (NPV) at a discount rate of 5%, 9.78%, 50%, 127.71%, and 200%.
   b. Sketch the project's NPV profile graph.
   c. What is this project's internal rate of return (IRR)?
   d. Should the project be accepted if the company's cost of capital is 14%? Why or why not?
4. **(Multiple IRRs)** A company has projected the following cash flows for an investment project:

Year	Cash flow
0	−$50,000
1	300,000
2	−275,000

   a. Calculate this project's net present value (NPV) at a discount rate of 5%, 12.92%, 100%, 387.08%, and 500%.
   b. Sketch the project's NPV profile graph.
   c. What is this project's internal rate of return (IRR)?
   d. Should the project be accepted if the company's cost of capital is 10%? Why or why not?

APPENDIX 11C

RANKING INVESTMENT PROJECTS

In Chapter 11 we examined the process of accepting or rejecting proposed investment projects. A project is acceptable if its net present value is positive, or alternatively for a standard project, if its internal rate of return exceeds the firm's cost of capital. All projects that meet the NPV and IRR tests should be taken as each adds to the value of the firm. However, this conclusion assumes that each project under consideration can be accepted independently of any other and that the firm faces no capital or other limitations. Should either of these assumptions be untrue, the firm will have to rank its choices.

independent investment projects—investment projects where acceptance of one does not have anything to do with the decision to accept or reject the other

Two investment projects are said to be **independent** of each other if each stands by itself, so that the firm may evaluate each one without regard to the other.

Example

Independent Investment Projects

A firm's research laboratory has come up with two new product ideas. Each has been given to a development team which is in the process of estimating the costs and benefits of taking the product to market. Depending on the results of the analyses, the firm will accept neither, one, or both of the proposals.

mutually exclusive investment projects—investment projects where acceptance of one precludes acceptance of the other, and vice-versa

Often, however, investment projects are not independent but instead are **mutually exclusive.** This is the case when they are alternatives to one another and the firm must choose between them. Now the projects must be ranked in order of value.

Example

Mutually Exclusive Investment Projects

A firm requires additional plant capacity and has developed two alternative expansion proposals. One involves building a facility in Ohio, while the other would locate the new plant in Kentucky. Financial analysis of the two alternative shows both to have a positive NPV and an IRR above the firm's cost of capital. The firm will only build one new plant.

A second reason why a firm might have to rank projects in order of value is if its resources are limited and it cannot afford to accept all investments that pass the IRR and NPV tests. Any one of several resources might be in short supply. The firm might be unable to raise sufficient funds to purchase all acceptable investments. Skilled employees might not be available soon enough. Accepting many new investment projects at once might excessively strain the ability of the firm's personnel to deliver quality products and services, prompting management to slow the firm's rate of expansion. Resource limitations are a particular concern of small firms which, unlike their large counterparts, have limited managerial depth and equally limited access to the capital and labor markets.[1]

Example

Resource Limitations

A firm's capital budgeting analysis identifies ten investment projects with positive NPVs and IRRs above the firm's cost of capital. To accept all ten the firm would have to raise $50 million, yet at present the firm's assets total only $10 million. The firm's investment banker advises that, at most, the firm will be able to raise $8 million in new funds this year.

Why NPV and IRR Often Disagree

Since both NPV and IRR are measures of an investment project's worth, it would seem that ranking projects involves simply selecting those with the highest NPV or highest IRR. Unfortunately, this does not work too well since the NPV measure often produces a ranking that differs from that produced by IRR.

Example

NPV and IRR Produce Different Rankings

Consider the three acceptable investment projects analyzed in this chapter:

Project	NPV	IRR
Quality improvement	$25,087	145.90%
Waste reduction	47,162	19.00
Truck replacement	18,178	20.31

The quality improvement project is ranked second by NPV but first by IRR. The waste reduction project is ranked first by NPV but third by IRR. And the truck replacement project is ranked third by NPV but second by IRR.

When NPV and IRR rank investment projects differently, it is due to one or both of two reasons: the projects differ in their lives or differ in their sizes.

1. Different Lives

The NPV of a project depends on how long that project lasts. Even if a project has a low IRR, given enough time it can accumulate a substantial NPV.

[1] **Elaboration:** Much of finance theory was developed assuming the firm was a large corporation with unlimited access to all resources. As a result, in the unlikely occurrence that a firm could not raise as much capital as needed to fund all acceptable investment projects, it was believed that the problem must be in the capital markets and not with the firm. This scenario, in which the capital markets limit the money available to any one firm, is called "capital rationing."

Examples

Comparing Investment Projects with Different Lives

A firm finds itself choosing between two investment projects, each of which costs $100,000. The first has a one-year life, returning $120,000 at the end of the year. The other has a five-year life, returning $200,000 at the end of the fifth year. The firm has a 10% cost of capital.

Question: Determine the NPV and IRR of the one-year project:

Solution steps:

1. NPV:

   a. Since the outflow takes place at year 0, its present value is its face value of $100,000.

   b. Use the financial calculator to obtain the present value of the benefit:

      CLEAR the time value part of your calculator
      Key in 120,000 and press FV
      Key in 1 and press n
      Key in 10 and press i
      Compute PV = −109,091

   c. NPV = present value of benefits − present value of costs
      = $109,091 − 100,000 = $9,091

2. IRR:

   Use the financial calculator to solve for the interest rate that connects the cash flows:

      CLEAR the time value part of your calculator
      Key in −100,000 and press PV
      Key in 120,000 and press FV
      Key in 1 and press n
      Compute i = 20.00%

Answer: The one-year project's NPV is $9,091 and its IRR is 20.00%.

Question: Determine the NPV and IRR of the five-year project:

Solution steps:

1. NPV:

   a. Since the outflow takes place at year 0, its present value is its face value of $100,000.

   b. Use the financial calculator to obtain the present value of the benefit:

CLEAR the time value part of your calculator

Key in 200,000 and press FV

Key in 5 and press n

Key in 10 and press i

Compute PV = −124,184

c. NPV = present value of benefits − present value of costs

= $124,184 − 100,000 = $24,184

2. IRR:

Use the financial calculator to solve for the interest rate that connects the cash flows:

CLEAR the time value part of your calculator

Key in −100,000 and press PV

Key in 200,000 and press FV

Key in 5 and press n

Compute i = 14.87%

Answer: The five-year project's NPV is $24,184 and its IRR is 14.87%.

Even though the five-year project earns at the lower IRR (14.87% vs. 20%), it builds up a greater NPV than the one-year project ($24,184 vs. $9,091) since it continues for five years.

2. Different Sizes

The NPV of a project also depends on how much money is invested. A large project may build up a high NPV even if it has a low IRR.

Examples

Comparing Investment Projects of Different Sizes

A firm finds itself choosing between two investment projects, each of which has a one-year life. The first costs $10,000 and returns $15,000 at the end of the year. The other costs $1,000,000 and returns $1,250,000 at the end of the year. The firm has a 10% cost of capital.

Question: Determine the NPV and IRR of the $10,000 project:

Solution steps:

1. NPV:

a. Since the outflow takes place at year 0, its present value is its face value of $10,000.

b. Use the financial calculator to obtain the present value of the benefit:

CLEAR the time value part of your calculator

Key in 15,000 and press FV

Key in 1 and press [n]

Key in 10 and press [i]

Compute [PV] = −13,636

c. NPV = present value of benefits − present value of costs

= $13,636 − 10,000 = $3,636

2. IRR:

Use the financial calculator to solve for the interest rate that connects the cash flows:

[CLEAR] the time value part of your calculator

Key in −10,000 and press [PV]

Key in 15,000 and press [FV]

Key in 1 and press [n]

Compute [i] = 50.00%

Answer: The $10,000 project's NPV is $3,636 and its IRR is 50.00%.

Question: Determine the NPV and IRR of the $1,000,000 project:

Solution Steps:

1. NPV:

a. Since the outflow takes place at year 0, its present value is its face value of $1,000,000.

b. Use the financial calculator to obtain the present value of the benefit:

[CLEAR] the time value part of your calculator

Key in 1,250,000 and press [FV]

Key in 1 and press [n]

Key in 10 and press [i]

Compute [PV] = −1,136,364

c. NPV = present value of benefits − present value of costs

= $1,136,364 − 1,000,000 = $136,364

2. IRR: Use the financial calculator to solve for the interest rate that connects the cash flows:

[CLEAR] the time value part of your calculator

Key in −1,000,000 and press [PV]

Key in 1,250,000 and press [FV]

Key in 1 and press [n]

Compute [i] = 25.00%

Answer: The $1,000,000 project's NPV is $136,364 and its IRR is 25.00%.

Even though the $1,000,000 project earns at the lower IRR (25% vs. 50%), it builds up a greater NPV than the $10,000 project ($136,364 vs. $3,636) since ten times as much money is involved.

Terminal Value Analysis

A useful technique for ranking investment projects which solves the problems of different size and life is known as terminal value analysis. Terminal value analysis "standardizes" investment projects by explicitly asking what will happen to a common amount of money (hence same size) over a common time frame (hence same life). The common amount is the cost of the most expensive alternative under consideration. The time horizon is the life of the longest alternative. If one of the projects ends or otherwise returns money to the firm prior to the terminal date, we assume that the money will be reinvested and we consider the increased value from reinvestment along with the value added by the original projects.

terminal value—the projected future value of a sum of money consisting of the value added by investing it in a project currently under consideration plus the additional value added by reinvesting the proceeds up to the end of a common time horizon

1. Terminal Value

For every project under consideration, we calculate a **terminal value,** the amount our investment is projected to grow to if we accept that project and then follow up by reinvesting all money returned to the firm until the terminal date. The project that starts the firm down the road to the greatest terminal value is the one to accept.

Examples

Comparing Investment Projects with Different Lives

Reconsider the choice between the one-year and five-year investment projects. The company's financial analysts project that if it accepts the one-year project, it will be able to reinvest the $120,000 returned at the end of the first year at a rate of 15% for the next four years.

Question: Determine the terminal value for both projects.

Solution steps: Since the more expensive project (in this case both of them) costs $100,000, and since the longer project has a five-year life, we trace $100,000 invested over five years.

1. Five-year project: This project keeps the $100,000 fully invested for the five years. Its terminal value is simply the $200,000 expected at the end of the five years.
2. One-year project: This project returns $120,000 at the end of the first year. If the money is reinvested at 15% for the remaining four years, the $120,000 will grow to:

CLEAR the time value part of your calculator

Key in −120,000 and press PV

Key in 4 and press n

Key in 15 and press [i]

Compute [FV] = 209,881

Answer: The one-year project's terminal value is $209,881 while the five-year project's is $200,000.

Question: Which project should the firm select?

Answer: Select the one-year project. By beginning with this project and then reinvesting the $120,000 of proceeds at 15%, the firm will end the next five years better off than if it chooses the five-year project.

2. Fully Invested Net Present Value and Internal Rate of Return

Terminal value analysis compares investment alternatives by tracing a common amount of money over a common lifetime, explicitly taking opportunities for reinvestment into account. The project that leads to the greatest terminal value is the better one to choose. Once we have calculated terminal values, we can also calculate two other measures to reinforce this comparison—a net present value and an internal rate of return.

fully invested NPV (NPV*)—the total net present value of a project and any subsequent reinvestment

fully invested IRR (IRR*)—the rate of return from the combination of a project and any subsequent reinvestment

We define **fully invested NPV** (sometimes written **NPV***) as the net present value of the combination of the initial project and any reinvestment that follows. Similarly, we define **fully invested IRR (IRR*)** as the internal rate of return of the combination. Both calculations use only three numbers as inputs: the initial outlay, the time horizon, and the terminal value. When using these measures to compare projects, the calculations use the same numbers for initial outlay and time horizon. Accordingly, the project with the greatest terminal value must also have the highest fully invested NPV and also the highest fully invested IRR. All three measures may be used interchangeably to select the better project.

Examples

Fully Invested NPV and IRR

In the previous example, we calculated terminal values for the one-year and five-year investment projects by establishing a common investment amount of $100,000 and a common time horizon of five years. The terminal value of the one-year project was $209,881, and the terminal value of the five-year project was $200,000. We concluded that the one-year project was preferable since it led to the greater terminal value.

Question: What is the fully invested net present value of each project?

Solution steps: Recall that the firm's cost of capital is 10%.

1. One-year project:

   a. Since the outflow takes place at year 0, its present value is its face value of $100,000.

   b. Use the financial calculator to obtain the present value of the terminal value:

CLEAR the time value part of your calculator

Key in 209,881 and press FV

Key in 5 and press n

Key in 10 and press i

Compute PV = −130,320

c. NPV* = PV of terminal value − PV of costs

= $130,320 − 100,000 = $30,320

2. Five-year project:

a. Since the outflow takes place at year 0, its present value is its face value of $100,000.

b. Use the financial calculator to obtain the present value of the terminal value:

CLEAR the time value part of your calculator

Key in 200,000 and press FV

Key in 5 and press n

Key in 10 and press i

Compute PV = −124,184

c. NPV* = PV of terminal value − PV of costs

= $124,184 − 100,000 = $24,184

Answer: The one-year project's NPV* is $30,320 while the five-year project's is $24,184. NPV* agrees with the terminal value numbers: the one-year project is better.

Question: What is the fully invested internal rate of return of each project?

Solution steps: Use the financial calculator to solve for the interest rate that connects the cash flows:

1. One-year project:

CLEAR the time value part of your calculator

Key in −100,000 and press PV

Key in 209,881 and press FV

Key in 5 and press n

Compute i = 15.98%

2. Five-year project:

CLEAR the time value part of your calculator

Key in −100,000 and press PV

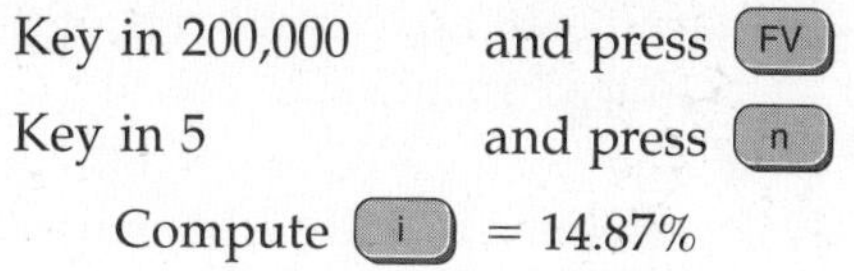

Answer: The one-year project's IRR* is 15.98% while the five-year project's is 14.97%. Just like NPV*, IRR* agrees with the terminal value numbers: the one-year project is better.

We can interpret the fully invested NPV and IRR numbers further. NPV* is the total present value provided by the initial project and any subsequent reinvestment. It is the sum of two numbers: the NPV of the project taken by itself and the added NPV coming from reinvestment. IRR* is the weighted-average rate of return provided by the initial project and subsequent reinvestment. Since it is an average, it must lie between the IRR of the project and the reinvestment rate (which is the IRR provided by reinvesting the funds).

Figure 11C.1 illustrates these points.

- The one-year project has an NPV of $9,091. When we add four years of reinvestment at 15% we find an NPV* of $30,320. Accordingly, reinvestment must provide the difference, an additional $21,229 of value.
- The IRR of the one-year project is 20%. If we reinvest at 15%, our money

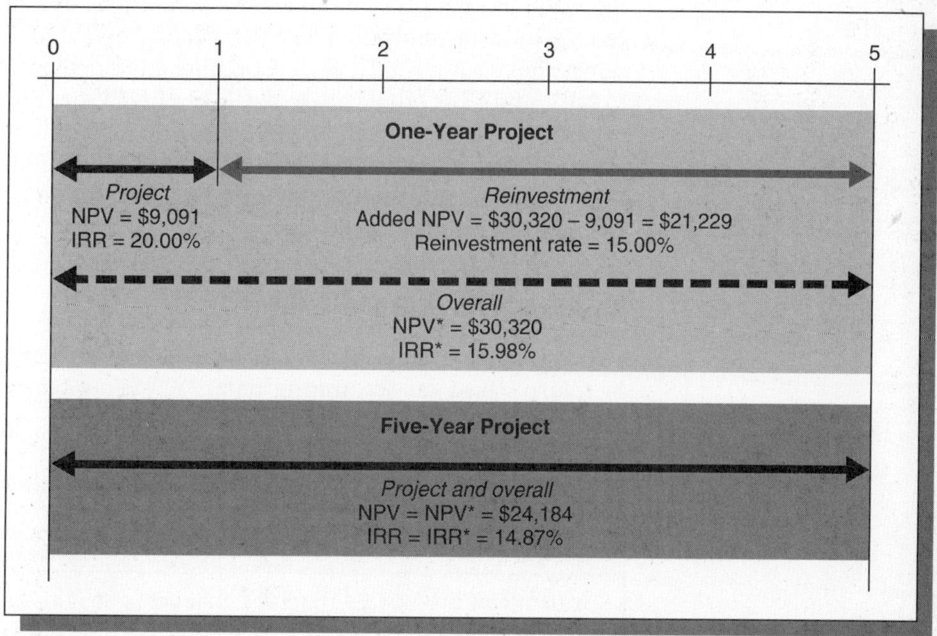

FIGURE 11C.1
Comparison of the two projects. NPV* is the sum of the NPVs from the project and reinvestment; IRR* is the (weighted) average rate of return.

will earn an average rate of $15.98%, the IRR*: one year at 20% followed by four years at 15%.

- The five-year project requires no reinvestment for this analysis. With no reinvestment to add additional value, the NPV* and IRR* of this project are identical to its NPV and IRR.

APPENDIX 11D

FLAWED DECISION TECHNIQUES—HISTORICAL FINANCIAL MODELS

As we saw in this chapter, the analysis of capital investments requires good data and proper analysis. Finance theory identifies incremental cash flows as the correct data and net present value (and sometimes internal rate of return) as the correct method of analysis. Over the years, however, finance theorists and practitioners have suggested a variety of other analytical methods. Some are alternatives to NPV and IRR, others are extensions of NPV or IRR to deal with the ranking of investment choices. Each is flawed: it works sometimes, but is also prone to give wrong answers. However, several are still used in conjunction with NPV and IRR because of the information they do contain. In this appendix, we look at four of the more popular alternatives.

1. Accounting Rate of Return

Accounting rate of return is just what its name suggests, the calculation of a rate of return based on accounting data. We encountered this idea in Appendix 4D, when we saw the "return on assets" and "return on equity" ratios. For an investment project, the accounting rate of return is a similar ratio: the average annual increase to income divided by the average value of the project's assets.

Example

Calculating Accounting Rate of Return

A firm can invest in a machine that costs $6,000. The machine has a three-year life and will be depreciated over that period to a zero salvage value using the straight-line method. The firm forecasts that in each of the three years, the machine will reduce operating costs by $3,250. It is in the 34% tax bracket.

Question: What is this proposal's accounting rate of return?

Solution steps:

1. Determine the depreciation schedule for the machine:

    Annual depreciation = ($6,000 − 0) / 3 = $2,000

    Value during: first year = $6,000

    second year = $6,000 − $2,000 = $4,000

    third year = $4,000 − $2,000 = $2,000

2. Obtain the average annual increase to income (in this case, the increase to income is the same in all three years):

ΔRevenue		$ 0
−ΔExpenses:		
ΔOperating costs	$−3,250	
ΔDepreciation	+2,000	−1,250
ΔEBIT		1,250
−ΔInterest		0
ΔEBT		1,250
−ΔTaxes (34%)		425
ΔEAT		$ 825

3. Obtain the average value of the project's assets:

    ($6,000 + 4,000 + 2,000) / 3 = $4,000

4. Calculate the accounting rate of return:

    $825 / $4,000 = 20.63%

Answer: This project's accounting rate of return is 20.63%.

As a capital budgeting measure, accounting rate of return suffers from several fatal flaws. First, it does not use cash flows. As we have seen, accrual accounting income figures and asset values depend on accounting conventions and do not always fully reflect the underlying economics. Income and investment change from year to year. At best, accounting rate of return can use average income and average investment, thereby glossing over differences from year to year. Further, accounting rate of return ignores the time value factor. As calculated by the accounting rate of return method, a dollar of income in one year is worth the same as a dollar of income in the next, yet we know that the value of money declines when we have to wait to receive it. In addition, it is difficult to compare accounting rate of return to the firm's cost of capital since they are calculated by entirely different means.[1]

[1] **Elaboration:** Accounting rate of return was popular before time value of money became widely understood. The concept of a time-value-based cost of capital was unknown at that time. As a result, accept/reject decisions were made by a rough sense of what rate of return was acceptable and what was too low and not by any formal comparison to a cost of capital.

2. Payback

The payback method was the technique in common use prior to the wide acceptance of NPV and IRR. It was the first method that focused on cash flows and the first to introduce time into the analysis.

payback period—the length of time until an investment project has returned its initial investment

To use payback, we calculate an investment project's **payback period,** how long it takes to recover the money invested.

Example

Calculating the Payback Period

In the waste-reduction investment we considered in Chapter 11 beginning on p. 383, we produced a cash-flow table with the following summary numbers:

	Year 0	Years 1–10	Year 10
Net cash flows	($ 110,000)	$ 24,950	$ 10,000

Question: Calculate the proposal's payback period.

Solution steps:

1. Subtract each year's cash flow from the initial outlay in turn:
   At year 0, the firm has $110,000 to recover.
   After year 1, the firm still has to recover $110,000 – $24,950 = $85,050.
   After year 2, the firm still has to recover $85,050 – $24,950 = $60,100.
   After year 3, the firm still has to recover $60,100 – $24,950 = $35,150.
   After year 4, the firm still has to recover $35,150 – $24,950 = $10,200.
2. Since $10,200 is less than the year 5 projected inflow of $24,950, the firm will recover the remaining $10,200 and be fully paid back in year 6. More precisely, the firm will receive the remaining $10,200 (10,200/24,950 =) 41% of the way through year 6.

Answer: This project's payback period is 4 years plus, or more precisely, 4.41 years.

When using the payback method, a project is accepted if it has a "short enough" payback period, and rejected if its payback period is "too long."

Payback suffers from three problems. First, while it does consider time, it does not include the interest rate concept which makes time value so powerful. Second, it ignores the timing of cash flows during the payback period as well as any cash flows after the payback period. Third, it is impossible to know what is an acceptable payback period and what time period is so long as to be unacceptable.

Example

Problems with Payback—Payback Ignores Time Value

Consider an investment of $1,000,000 which returns $1,000,001 in one month. The payback period is one month, a very short time, yet this investment has a very low rate of return (.0012%) and should be rejected.

Consider another investment of $1 which returns $1,000,000,000 in ten years.

The payback period is ten years, a period typically considered too long to be acceptable, yet this investment has a very high rate of return (694.33%) and should be accepted.

Example

Problems with Payback—Payback Ignores the Timing of Cash Flows During the Payback Period and Any Cash Flows After the Payback Period

Consider the following three investments that each cost $1,000 and return the following cash flows:

	Year 1	Year 2	Year 3	Year 4	Year 5
Investment A	0	0	0	1,000	
Investment B	999	0	0	1	
Investment C	0	0	0	1,000	1,000,000

Payback cannot distinguish them; all three have a payback period of four years.

Example

Problems with Payback—There Is No Good Criterion

Reconsider the waste-reduction investment, for which we calculated a payback period of 4.41 years. It is impossible to know whether this time period is acceptable or too long.

3. Profitability Index

profitability index—the net present value of benefits per dollar invested

Profitability index is a variation on net present value that was developed to compare projects when a choice must be made between them. An investment's **profitability index** is calculated as the NPV of benefits divided by the cost of the investment. As a result, the profitability index attempts to capture benefits per dollar invested.

For simple accept/reject decisions, the profitability index is compared to the number 1. If the present value of benefits exceeds the present value of costs, the numerator is greater than the denominator and the profitability index is greater than 1. Should the present value of benefits be less than the present value of costs, the numerator is less than the denominator and the profitability index is less than 1. Accordingly, a profitability index above 1 signals accept while a value below 1 is the reject signal.

For comparisons between projects, the alternative with the higher profitability index is considered the more valuable since it returns a greater present value per dollar invested.

Examples

Calculating Profitability Index

In the land investment we considered in Chapter 11 beginning on p. 380, we produced a cash flow table with the following summary numbers:

	Year 0	Year 5
Net cash flows	($1,000,000)	$1,325,000

The company has a weighted-average cost of capital of 12%.

Question: Calculate the proposal's profitability index.

Solution steps:

1. Use the financial calculator to obtain the present value of the benefit:

   CLEAR the time value part of your calculator

   Key in 1,325,000 and press FV

   Key in 5 and press n

   Key in 12 and press i

   Compute PV = −751,841

2. Divide the present value of benefits by the initial outlay:

   751,841/1,000,000 = .7518

Answer: This project's profitability index is .7518. For each dollar of investment, it produces slightly over 75 cents in present value of benefits.

Question: Should the firm accept this proposal?

Answer: No! The project's profitability index is less than 1. The present value of benefits is less than the (present value of) costs.

The profitability index method suffers from two primary flaws. First, unlike NPV, it cannot handle a (+, −, +) or (−, +, −) project[2] since it is based on the idea of a single outflow at the beginning of the project. Second, it can't adequately deal with projects of different size, often producing a ranking different from what NPV would indicate.

Example

Problems with Profitability Index

Consider the following two investments available to a company with a cost of capital of 10%:

	Year 0	Year 1
Investment A:	(100)	150
Investment B:	(1,000)	1,200

Question: Do the profitability indexes of the two investments agree with their NPVs?

Solution steps:

1. Investment A:

   a. Use the financial calculator to obtain the present value of the benefit:

[2] **Cross-reference:** See Appendix 11B for a discussion of investment projects with "nonstandard" cash flows.

CLEAR the time value part of your calculator

Key in 150 and press FV

Key in 1 and press n

Key in 10 and press i

Compute PV = −136.36

b. Profitability index = 136.36/100 = 1.36

c. NPV = 136.36 − 100 = 36.36

2. Investment B:

a. Use the financial calculator to obtain the present value of the benefit:

CLEAR the time value part of your calculator

Key in 1,200 and press FV

Key in 1 and press n

Key in 10 and press i

Compute PV = −1090.91

b. Profitability index = 1,090.91 / 1,000 = 1.09

c. NPV = 1,090.91 −1,000 = 90.91

Answer: Investment A's NPV is $36.36 and its profitability index is 1.36, while Investment B's NPV is $90.91 and its profitability index is 1.09. According to NPV, Investment B adds more value to the firm. However, profitability index ranks Investment A as better. Profitability index fails to be consistent with NPV!

4. Modified Internal Rate of Return (MIRR)

In Appendix 11C we saw how terminal value calculations can be used to bring reinvestment opportunities into the ranking of mutually exclusive capital budgeting projects. The technique involves establishing an investment horizon and calculating a terminal value—and if desired, a fully invested NPV (NPV*) and fully invested IRR (IRR*)—for each project. All three measures correctly rank the alternatives. Modified internal rate of return is an attempt to calculate a fully invested IRR for a single project over its own lifetime. Its goal is to obtain a more representative rate-of-return figure for the project and to improve on the ability of IRR to rank alternative projects.

Early attempts to deal with the conflict between NPV and IRR in ranking investment projects discussed the "reinvestment assumptions" made by each method. While, in fact, neither method makes any assumptions about reinvestment at all but looks only at the cash flows of the project itself, the following relationships were observed:

- When reinvestment takes place at the cost of capital, NPV* equals the project's NPV since reinvesting at the cost of capital neither adds nor subtracts any further value. In this case, ranking by NPV is valid.

- When reinvestment takes place at a rate equal to the project's IRR, IRR*—the average of the two rates—equals the project's IRR. In this case, ranking by IRR is valid.

These observations led to the popular but erroneous statements:

- "The NPV method assumes that reinvestment takes place at the company's cost of capital."
- "The IRR method assumes that reinvestment takes place at each project's unique IRR."

It seemed highly coincidental that the cash returned from an investment would be reinvested at a rate equal to, or even similar to, the project's IRR. Much more likely was that reinvestment would take place at a rate near the cost of capital, a more conservative view as well. Finance theorists concluded that since NPV's "reinvestment assumption" was the more realistic, NPV was the better measure for ranking projects.

modified internal rate of return (MIRR)—the fully invested IRR of a project assuming reinvestment at the cost of capital

Modified internal rate of return (MIRR) is a fully invested IRR calculation that assumes reinvestment takes place at the firm's cost of capital. Like IRR*, it is the average rate of return of an investment project plus all subsequent reinvestment until the date of the project's last cash flow.

Example

Modified Internal Rate of Return

In the quality improvement investment we considered in Chapter 11 beginning on p. 381, we produced a cash flow table with the following summary numbers:

	Year 0	Years 1–4
Net cash flows	($6,500)	$9,750

The company's weighted-average cost of capital is 9%. While the project has an IRR of 145.90%, it is highly unlikely that the cash flows returned in years 1 through 3 can be reinvested at that same rate.

Question: Calculate the proposal's modified IRR.

Solution steps:

1. Calculate the project's terminal value assuming reinvestment is at the 9% cost of capital.

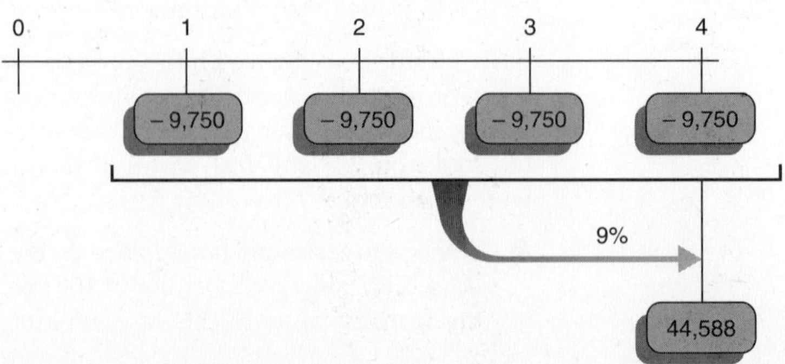

CLEAR the time value part of your calculator

Key in −9,750 and press PMT, set END

Key in 4 and press n

Key in 9 and press i

Compute FV = 44,588.01

2. Calculate the MIRR:

CLEAR the time value part of your calculator

Key in −6,500 and press PV

Key in 44,588 and press FV

Key in 4 and press n

Compute i = 61.84%

Answer: This project's MIRR is 61.84%. Although the project's IRR is 145.90%, reinvestment at 9% reduces the fully invested rate of return substantially.

Although MIRR takes reinvestment into account, the assumption that reinvestment will be at the cost of capital is not always a realistic one. Further, when used to compare projects, MIRR like IRR does not always produce rankings equivalent to those given by NPV. Terminal value analysis, incorporating the company's best forecasts of reinvestment opportunities, remains the best way to rank mutually exclusive projects.

CHAPTER 12
PERMANENT WORKING CAPITAL

Marie Kaye stared through the window that was the front wall of her office and shook her head slowly. Outside were row after row of desks. She glanced at her watch; it was 7:30 A.M. Monday morning. Soon the desks would be occupied by the clerks who processed the company's accounts receivable—at last count there were 43 clerks in the department.

Marie had recently been appointed controller of her company. Among her responsibilities were customer billing and collection of outstanding accounts, areas that had proved quite problematic. Customers routinely complained that invoices were difficult to understand, sometimes even incorrect, and responded by withholding payment. Marie had recently added 10 clerks to the department in an effort to correct the problems and reduce the company's collection period, which was well above the industry average, yet little progress had been made. Even with the additional staff, every clerk remained busy all day and many had to work overtime to clear their desks.

Last week Marie had attended a professional meeting, at which she talked to the controllers of several competitors and similar companies in other industries. She was surprised to learn that some companies she considered comparable to hers operated their billing and receivables function with fewer than 10 employees and had far fewer outstanding accounts. She made some notes about assembling a team to tackle the problem and vowed to go in first thing Monday morning to get an early start.

Marie looked at her watch again; it was 7:45. She was eager for the work day to begin so she could discuss the problem with her colleagues and put together the team.

Working capital management involves day-to-day dealings with the firm's stakeholders: customers, suppliers, employees, bankers, etc. In fact, many stakeholders' primary experience with the company is through its working capital activities. To manage these resources, financial managers must understand how their work affects stakeholders and, in turn, how stakeholder actions affect them. Marie is discovering that successful working capital management requires not only good application of finance theory, but also the use of quality-management information and tools to ensure that stakeholder needs are being met.

Working capital management provides an excellent opportunity for financial managers to add value to their organizations. In many companies, fully half of the investment in assets—and up to 90% of the effort of the finance organization—are in the current accounts. In this chapter we examine the nature of working capital, how the financial tools of incremental decision making can be applied to decisions about the level of permanent working capital, and how an awareness of quality-management issues can improve the worth of these decisions.

What You Should Learn from This Chapter

After reading this chapter you should be able to:

- Separate working capital into permanent and temporary components.
- Organize permanent working capital data into cash flow terms.
- Describe the components of a firm's cash balance and analyze decisions involving accelerating cash in transit.
- Analyze proposed changes to a firm's permanent accounts receivable balance.
- Analyze plans to change the level of permanent inventory and understand the importance of a just-in-time inventory system.

Introductory Concepts—Types of Working Capital

working capital—liquid resources available for the day-to-day operations of the firm

Working capital is the term commonly used to summarize the financial resources available for a firm's day-to-day operations. These must be liquid resources, available as cash (or convertible to cash) when required. Working capital includes cash and marketable securities—the most liquid of resources—and also the somewhat less liquid resources of accounts receivable, inventories, and prepaid expenses. Each is necessary for the firm to conduct its business, yet each is costly to maintain. One concern of financial managers is that their companies maintain adequate, but not excess, working capital.

A primary use of current resources is to pay debts as they fall due. The funds available for day-to-day operations may be considered the amount left over after resources have been allocated to pay current liabilities. As a result, working capital is normally represented as the difference between current assets and current liabilities:[1]

Working capital = current assets − current liabilities

1. Permanent Vs. Temporary Working Capital

Our examination of working capital in this chapter is organized by balance sheet account—cash, accounts receivable, inventory, etc.—since each account has its own characteristics. However, it is useful and important first to divide working capital in a different way: into "permanent" working capital and "temporary" working capital, a distinction that cuts across all the working capital accounts. We do this because permanent working capital decisions are analyzed differently from decisions to make temporary adjustments in working capital balances. In this chapter we look primarily at permanent working capital; temporary working capital is treated in Chapter 16.

In Figure 12.1, we graph a typical firm's balance sheet over time. The lines slope upward, representing a growing firm, but the picture would be equally valid if the company were unchanging or declining in size. On both sides of the equal sign, the bottom area represents the long-term: long-term assets on the left and long-term liabilities and equity on the right. Above the first dividing line are the current accounts—current assets and current liabilities—and each of these is subdivided into a permanent and a temporary component.

permanent working capital—the level of working capital required at all times

Permanent working capital is the base level of working capital, the amount required independent of daily, seasonal, or cyclical variations in business activity. It is made up of permanent current assets and permanent current liabilities. The firm needs its permanent working capital on a continuous basis. Even though a company's cash, accounts receivable, inventory, etc. turn over more frequently than once per year, and therefore are considered current assets by accounting, there will be some minimum *level* of each of these resources required at all times. It is

[1] **Elaboration:** An alternative usage is to let *working capital* equal only a firm's current assets and use the term *net working capital* to represent current assets minus current liabilities.

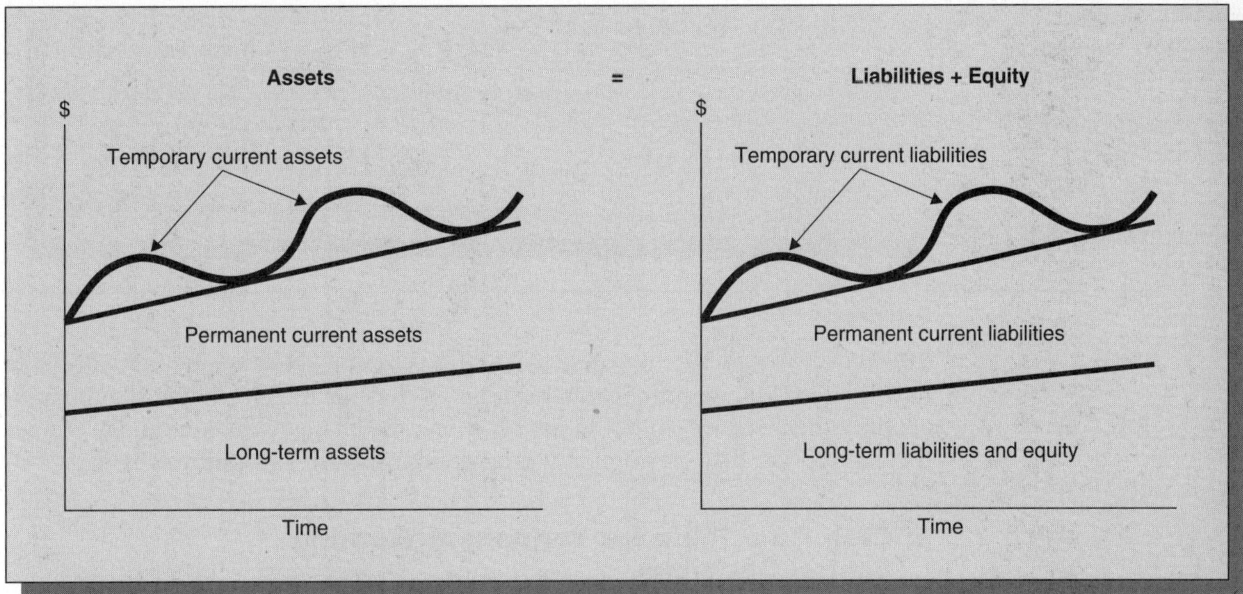

FIGURE 12.1
Levels of assets and claims across time for a growing firm. Current assets and liabilities can be divided into a permanent level plus temporary fluctuations.

impossible to operate without cash for liquidity. Extending trade credit, hence creating accounts receivable and payable, is normal practice in most industries. Some amount of inventory is a requirement for both merchandising and manufacturing. Therefore, *even though permanent working capital appears on the accounting books in the current accounts, which suggests that it is short-term in nature, it is really a long-term requirement.*

temporary working capital—increases to working capital due to fluctuations in business activity

Temporary working capital is the amount above the base level which is the result of variations in business activity. It is caused by three simultaneous processes. First, the business cycle increases and decreases the resource needs of all businesses over a multiyear time period. Second, most firms are seasonal, having an annual cycle of activities. Third, daily events impact resource needs since revenues and expenses, and cash inflows and outflows, rarely balance on a day-to-day basis. Receivables and collections follow the pattern of sales. Expenses and payments, on the other hand, are commonly tied to the day of the month. In contrast to permanent working capital, temporary working capital is short-term in nature.

Organizing and Analyzing Permanent Working Capital Data

Decisions about the level of permanent working capital are made in the same way as capital budgeting decisions—we identify incremental cash flows, organize them into a cash flow table, and apply time value of money analysis. There is only one

FIGURE 12.2
Cash flow table for permanent working capital decisions. The right-hand column is labeled "Years 1–∞" since these changes often have an indeterminate life.

	Year 0	Years 1–∞
Investment	(Cost) or recovery	
Operating cash flows		Changed in/(out)flows
Tax—changed income		Tax on above
Net cash flows		

difference between the two analyses, and it is minor: while plant and equipment have a finite life, working capital can be around for the entire life of an organization. Whenever we do not know how long the change will continue, we make the assumption that the company is a "going concern" with infinite life.

1. Cash Flow Table for Permanent Working Capital Decisions

Figure 12.2 is a generic cash flow table for permanent working capital. Notice that it is identical to the cash flow tables we used for capital budgeting[2] except that there is no column for "year n," the last year of the investment's life. Rather, the right-hand column is labeled "years 1–∞," representing all years from the first year of change to the end of the company's existence. As with the table for capital budgeting, this column would have to be separated into several columns if the cash flows from the proposed change differed from year to year. This simplified table is intended to illustrate the form of permanent working capital decisions; we will provide more detail as we examine each working capital item later in this chapter.

Because changes to permanent working capital are treated as having an indefinite life, the appropriate time value model to apply to the ongoing cash flows is the perpetuity (perpetual annuity) model.[3] Recall that for a perpetuity:

$$PV = \frac{PMT}{r}$$

and, rearranging the algebra, the interest rate embedded in a perpetuity, which for a permanent working capital decision is the internal rate of return, is:

$$r = \frac{PMT}{PV}$$

Examples

The Value of Permanent Working Capital Cash Flows

A proposed change to permanent working capital promises the following cash flows:

[2] **Cross-reference:** The cash flow table for capital budgeting decisions was introduced on p. 380.
[3] **Cross-reference:** The model for the present value of a perpetuity first appears on p. 177.

	Year 0	Years 1–∞
Investment	($50,000)	
Operating cash flow		$10,000
Tax (34%)		(3,400)
Net cash flows	($50,000)	$ 6,600

Question: What is the net present value of this decision if the firm's cost of capital is 10%?

Solution steps:

1. Since the outflow takes place at year 0, its present value is its face value of −$50,000.
2. Use the perpetuity model to calculate the present value of the ongoing cash flows:

$$PV = PMT/r = \$6,600/.10 = \$66,000$$

3. NPV = present value of benefits − present value of costs

$$= \$66,000 - 50,000 = \$16,000$$

Answer: The proposed investment has a net present value of $16,000.

Question: What is the internal rate of return of this decision?

Solution steps: Use the perpetuity model to calculate the rate of return in the cash flows, letting the year 0 outlay be the value of the variable PV:

$$r = PMT/PV = \$6,600/\$50,000 = 13.20\%$$

Answer: The proposed investment has an internal rate of return of 13.20%.

Question: Should this proposed investment be pursued?

Answer: Yes! Its NPV is greater than zero and its IRR exceeds the firm's cost of capital.

2. Net Annual Benefit

The assumption that the ongoing cash flow change will continue indefinitely at a constant level is troubling to many people—it is, after all, difficult to predict next year's cash flows much less flows many years into the future. As a result, some analysts prefer to use a third rearrangement of the perpetuity model:

$$PMT = r \times PV$$

net annual benefit (NAB)—the amount by which the annual benefit from an investment exceeds the amount required to cover the firm's cost of capital

and calculate **net annual benefit (NAB).** With this technique, we calculate the cash flow required each year to support the money invested and test this number against the actual benefit provided. If net annual benefit is positive, we accept the proposed project, and we reject the proposal if net annual benefit is negative.[4]

[4] **Elaboration:** In investments with an initial cash flow followed by a perpetuity, such as those in this chapter, net annual benefit will *always agree* with net present value. When one is positive, the other will also be positive, etc. Therefore, they are perfect substitutes for each other. See Appendix 12A for a demonstration of why this must be true.

Example

Net Annual Benefit

A proposed change to permanent working capital promises the following cash flows:

	Year 0	Years 1–∞
Net cash flows	($50,000)	$6,600

Question: What is the net annual benefit of this decision if the firm's cost of capital is 10%?

Solution steps:

1. Use the perpetuity model to calculate the annual benefit required given the amount of the initial investment:

$$PMT = r \times PV = .10 \times \$50,000 = \$5,000$$

2. NAB = actual annual benefit − required annual benefit

$$= \$6,600 - 5,000 = \$1,600$$

Answer: The net annual benefit is $1,600. Each year, this investment returns the $5,000 required to support the $50,000 capital investment *plus* an additional $1,600 which adds to the value of the firm.

Permanent Cash

The line "cash" on a firm's balance sheet refers to money held in any of several forms. These include coins and currency, demand (checking) deposits, and time (savings) deposits. Some companies also include marketable securities with their cash balance. Because there are so many varieties of "cash," this balance sheet line is often labelled "cash and cash equivalents."

Business organizations hold cash for several reasons. Perhaps the most obvious is to pay for the operating and capital resources required to run the business. Like individuals, firms hold cash for their transactions needs and also hold extra cash as a precaution in case their spending needs unexpectedly increase.[5] There are also other, less obvious reasons why firms hold cash. Large deposit balances often reduce the fees and other charges levied by banks for services such as processing of checks, credit checking, currency conversion, and letters of credit. A high cash balance raises a firm's current and quick ratios,[6] making it appear more solvent to potential creditors. Holding (or electing not to hold) cash in a particular location or currency can also minimize currency movements, thereby reducing costs and risks: the cost of excessive foreign exchange transactions, the cost of taxes on money transfers, the risk of limitations on cash movement, and the risk of expropriation due to adverse political events.

[5] **Cross-reference and elaboration:** The transactions, precautionary, and speculative motives for holding cash were introduced in Chapter 6: see pp. 203–204. Unlike individuals, businesses are not thought to hold a significant amount of cash for speculative purposes.

[6] **Cross-reference:** The current and quick ratios are discussed in Appendix 4D, pp. 122–124.

1. Cash Allocation

A company's treasury function allocates its cash (1) among the various possible types and (2) among different currencies.

Types of cash Coins and bills are kept for retail transactions and petty cash, although this amount is usually held to a minimum since it earns no interest and is exposed to theft. The appropriate local balance differs among each business location due to the nature and volume of business conducted. It also differs among countries due to differences in financial customs: the frequency of credit card use, the method by which workers are paid (cash or check), the convenience and cost of the local banking system, and the significance of the underground economy.

Additional cash is kept in the form of demand (checking) deposits, which commonly earn a low or zero rate of interest and are also held to a minimum level. Analytically, a firm's optimal checking balance is a complex function of several variables. Generally the balance increases with (1) volume of transactions including regular (payroll, purchases, taxes, dividends) and irregular (capital expenditures, debt retirement) flows and (2) variability of cash flows. It decreases with (1) efficiency of cash management and (2) access to financial markets. Sometimes a firm holds a larger deposit balance than its analysis recommends because of the requirements of a loan agreement.

Extra cash beyond the minimum required for currency and demand deposits is normally invested to earn interest in bank time deposits or marketable securities.

Different currencies Companies operating multinationally also must decide how much cash to maintain in each currency. The minimum requirement is to keep enough cash for local operating and investment needs. Beyond that amount, company treasurers must consider several additional issues. Cash is kept away from any country in which local political intervention could block the firm's ability to convert it and/or remove it. Cash is held in currencies that are expected to increase in value and not in those that are expected to depreciate. One loss of value comes from the fees incurred in exchanging currencies, so foreign exchange transactions are typically kept to a minimum. Cash is also often moved to currencies where investments earn the highest interest rates.[7]

When a company does business in several currencies, it commonly "nets out" all accounts receivable and accounts payable among its units. Thus, if Subsidiary A owes \$100 to Subsidiary B, and Subsidiary B owes \$120 to Subsidiary A, the two units will settle by B paying \$20 to A. This reduces currency movements and exchanges, keeping their cost down.

Finance professionals debate the benefits of managing cash from a centralized treasury department versus spreading out cash management responsibilities to a

---

[7] **Elaboration and cross-reference:** Recall "interest rate parity," the equilibrium condition that connects forward exchange rates to the difference in interest rates between countries pp. 246–247. The only way to benefit from moving cash into a high-interest-rate currency is to take the risk that the money can be exchanged back without loss of value. While an aggressive treasurer will move cash balances among countries to benefit from high interest rates and/or anticipated exchange rate movements, many treasurers choose not to expose their companies to these risks.

SERVING FINANCE'S CUSTOMERS

No Missed Cash Deliveries at Corning, Incorporated

The Treasury Division of Corning, Incorporated, the large multinational glass and ceramic products manufacturer, evaluates its performance in meeting its customers' requirements with a set of measurements the company calls Key Results Indicators (KRIs). For the Cash Management group, one KRI is the number of times Treasury fails to deliver the exact amount of cash needed by a company unit where and when required. Corning Treasury's goal is to have a KRI of zero—no missed cash deliveries.

firm's operating units. In general, centralized cash management lessens the likelihood that one unit is holding excess cash while another is short and must borrow. One central amount can serve as the precautionary balance for multiple locations. Borrowing costs are lowered as borrowing is done on a larger scale. Larger and more frequent transactions provide treasury personnel increased experience and expertise. On the other hand, decentralized cash management reduces the number of times cash is moved among units. This lowers the transaction costs associated with currency movements and exchange. It also permits the individual units to establish and maintain better relationships with local financial institutions.

2. Managing Cash in Transit

receivables float—the dollar amount of incoming checks that have been mailed but have not yet been collected

payables float—the dollar amount of outgoing checks that have been written but have not yet been covered by bank deposits

Every dollar (or pound, or franc, etc.) of operating cash flowing through a company follows a similar path, diagrammed in Figure 12.3. The process begins when a customer mails a check to the company, initiating a period of **receivables float** during which "the check is in the mail." Some days later, the company receives the check and deposits it in its bank. Now the money is "in the company's control," and can be withdrawn and invested to earn interest. Later, when the company must pay a supplier, it writes a check; although it usually does not deposit the amount back into its bank account until just before the check clears. The period between writing a check and the check clearing can be divided into a period of **payables float** and a period during which the cash is sitting in the bank waiting to be paid out.

FIGURE 12.3
Operating cash flow into and out from a company. Customers mail checks to the firm, and the money is then used to make payments to suppliers.

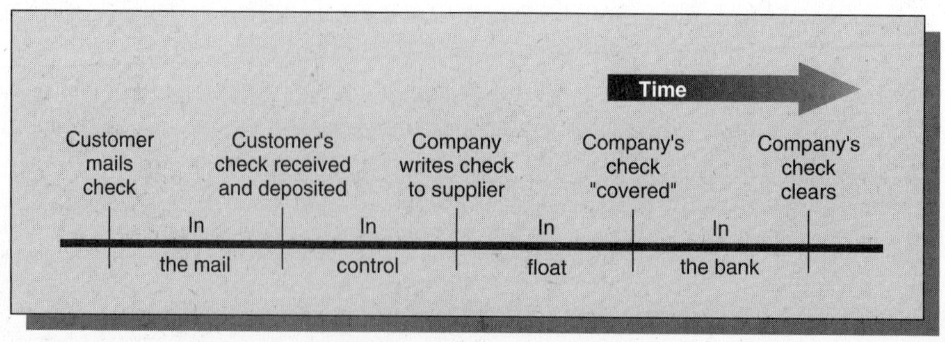

Receivables float cannot earn interest (although payables float normally does), nor is it usual for money sitting in a demand account waiting to be paid out to earn much interest. These amounts represent idle funds that cannot be used elsewhere, money that has an opportunity cost determined by the firm's cost of capital.

Example

The Cost of Idle Funds in Transit

It takes five days on average for customers' checks, averaging $50,000 per day, to reach a company. Once received, the money is invested to earn interest until required for payments to suppliers. Deposits, averaging $40,000 per day, are made to cover the company's checks one day before they clear. The company has a cost of capital of 12%.

Question: What is the annual cost of these idle funds?

Solution steps:

1. Multiply the number of idle days by the average daily cash flow to obtain the total sum of idle money:

$$\text{Idle money} = (5 \text{ days} \times \$50{,}000) + (1 \text{ day} \times \$40{,}000) = \$290{,}000$$

2. Multiply the total idle money by the cost of capital:

$$\$290{,}000 \times 12\% = \$34{,}800$$

Answer: The annual cost of idle funds is $34,800. $290,000 is tied up in transit and cannot be used elsewhere, requiring the firm to raise another $290,000 at an annual cost of $34,800.

lock box—a post office box to which customers mail their payments

concentration banking—the practice of instructing customers to mail payments to a local bank which then forwards the payment electronically

Because idle funds in transit are costly, financial managers attempt to reduce receivables float by accelerating collections and reduce idle "in-bank" funds by delaying disbursements. Accelerating collections translates to speeding up the mail. One way to do this is by instructing customers to mail payments to a **lock box,** a post office box used only for customer checks. A messenger from the company's commercial bank empties the lock box at regular intervals and takes the checks directly to the bank for deposit; the checks avoid the delay of being delivered to the company which then has to take them to the bank. Companies doing business in widely spread locations often also use **concentration banking,** in which customers mail their checks to a local lock box. There they are picked up by a local bank which then "concentrates" the funds by forwarding them electronically to the company's bank. With concentration banking, the time mail takes to travel long distances is avoided since all mail delivery is local.

A decrease in funds in transit is a permanent reduction to the firm's working capital needs and is analyzed using the perpetuity technique introduced earlier in this chapter. Interestingly, the change shows up on the accounting books not as a decrease to cash, but as a decrease in the accounts receivable balance since money owed the company is being collected more rapidly.

Example

Accelerating Collections

A company receives cash inflows of $1,000,000 per day from customers scattered across North America. For an annual fee of $300,000, its bank has proposed to implement a lock box/concentration banking system which would cut receivables float from an average of five days to two days. The company's cost of capital is 12% and it is in the 35% tax bracket.

Question: What is the value of the proposed system? Should it be implemented?

Solution steps:

1. Calculate the receivables float that can be eliminated:

Float now	= 5 days × $1,000,000 =	$5,000,000
Float with new system	= 2 days × $1,000,000 =	$2,000,000
Reduction in float		$3,000,000

2. Organize the cash flows: The company will pay $195,000 each year after taxes to free up $3,000,000.

	Year 0	Years 1–∞
Investment—float eliminated	$3,000,000	
Operating cash flow—fee		($300,000)
Tax (35%)		105,000
Net cash flows	$3,000,000	($195,000)

3. Calculate the value of the system using any of the three variations of the perpetuity model:

a. NPV:

PV of benefits = $3,000,000 since all benefits come at year 0

PV of costs = PMT/r = $195,000/.12 = $1,625,000

NPV = $3,000,000 − 1,625,000 = $1,375,000

b. IRR:[8]

IRR = r = PMT/PV = $195,000/$3,000,000 = 6.50%

c. NAB:[9]

Annual cost of float = r × PV = .12 × $3,000,000 = $360,000

Annual cost of the proposed system = $195,000

NAB = $360,000 − 195,000 = $165,000

[8] **Elaboration and cross-reference:** Notice that this is an "opposite project," in which a cash inflow is followed by cash outflows. In this case, the accept signal for the IRR measure is an IRR less than the cost of capital. Refer to Appendix 11B pp. 402–403 for further explanation.

[9] **Elaboration:** Since this is an opposite project, the words describing the costs and benefits reverse from the example given on p. 430. There is a cash inflow projected for year 0, representing the money currently invested; when we multiply this by the cost of capital, we get the annual cost of having this money tied up ("annual cost of the float"). The year 1–∞ flow represents the cost of freeing up the receivables float, hence the "annual cost of the proposed system." The net annual benefit reflects the exchange: in each year paying the cost of the proposed system to avoid the cost of float.

Answer: The proposal has an NPV of $1,375,000, an IRR of 6.50%, and an NAB of $165,000. Since NPV and NAB exceed zero (and IRR is less than the cost of capital for this "opposite project") the system should be implemented.

Today there is a movement to encourage customers to avoid the postal system altogether by making payments through direct electronic transfer between banks. At first glance it would seem that customers would balk at such a system since they benefit from keeping their money for the period of float. However, in addition to eliminating receivables float in its entirety, direct electronic transfer eliminates the majority of the costs of a mail-based system: invoicing, paper, postage, handling, reconciliation of accounts, and the cost of rework when an error occurs. In many cases, the savings to both parties exceeds the cost of the float and can be shared between the parties.

Delaying disbursements is normally done by waiting until the last permissible date to make a payment. For example, if a company is given payment terms of "net 30 days" in which it is expected to pay 30 days from the invoice date, it will wait the full 30 days before it writes and mails its check. However, as with receivables, there are costs to maintaining an accounts payable system geared to payment on the last day. Some companies are finding that these costs exceed their earnings from payables float, making it cost effective to pay suppliers as early as the date an order is placed.

Permanent Accounts Receivable

Accounts receivable represent money owed the firm by its customers. Many large retailers (Macy's, JCPenney, Sears, etc.), and companies that sell to other businesses tend to extend credit themselves. They obtain data about each customer's financial condition, determine whether the customer is creditworthy, establish the customer's credit line—the maximum amount of credit the company is willing to extend, send the customer regular invoices, and then monitor the customer's

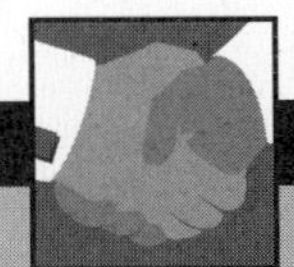

SERVING FINANCE'S CUSTOMERS

Paying Suppliers Upon Placing an Order at Motorola

In response to complaints from suppliers about slow payment of invoices, Motorola's finance department studied the company's accounts payable process. The analysis found that 1% of Motorola's expenditures accounted for fully 50% of its vendor-related paperwork. In response, Motorola scrapped its existing purchasing system and signed long-term commitments with suppliers of low-cost, high-volume goods, such as toilet paper and pencils. Vendors were told they had to perform at high quality levels to keep Motorola as a customer. In return, Motorola started paying those vendors by attaching a check to the purchase order and now pays by electronic transfer. Today, Motorola saves much more in reduced administrative costs than the value of the payables float.

performance in paying when due. Some large companies do the same but through a wholly owned finance subsidiary: examples are General Motors through General Motors Acceptance Corporation (GMAC), IBM through IBM Credit Corporation, and General Electric through GE Credit Corporation.

Discount stores and small retailers, on the other hand, tend to avoid accounts receivable. Rather they sign on with one or more of the national credit card organizations (Discover, Master Card, Optima, Visa). Customers can make purchases without cash, but it is the card company that extends the credit. The merchant is paid quickly by the card company, which then collects from the customer. Should the customer take longer than one month to pay, it is the card company that collects the interest.

Whether a company sells for cash or chooses to extend credit depends on the nature of the customer and the nature of the product. Many business customers will pay for their purchases only when presented with an invoice and then only with a check, both to avoid holding currency and to ensure an adequate paperwork trail. Selling to these firms requires extending credit. At the retail level, large and expensive products—automobiles, refrigerators, etc.—tend to be sold on credit. They are easy to identify, making good loan collateral. Also, many customers cannot afford them unless they can pay over an extended period of time.

Figure 12.4 is a cash flow table for permanent accounts receivable decisions. It is an expanded version of Figure 12.2, listing the investment and operating cash flows common to accounts receivable decisions. There are three potential changes to the amount the firm has invested in its accounts receivable process, four potential changes to annual operating cash flow, and a potential change to income taxes. Where the numbers may be calculated by a formula, the relationship is given in the cash flow columns.

FIGURE 12.4

Cash flow table for permanent accounts receivable decisions. The table organizes the data into three changes to the level of investment, four changes to operating cash flows, and the change to taxes.

	Year 0	Years 1–∞
Investment		
Accounts receivable	ΔAR × variable cost %	
Other working capital		
Changed collection period	(Sales/day × contribution %) × ΔCP	
Operating cash flows		
Contribution from sales		ΔSales × contribution %
Bad debts		ΔSales × % bad debts
Discounts		Discount % × affected sales
Administrative costs		
Tax—changed income		Tax on above
Net cash flows		

The potential changes in investment are:

- The change in the money invested in accounts receivable itself, calculated by taking the projected change in accounts receivable and multiplying it by a variable cost percentage to remove the profit portion.
- The change in other working capital, such as inventory and cash, which is not calculated by a standard formula.
- The changed value from receiving profits earlier or later, calculated as the daily profit flow (sales/day × contribution percentage) multiplied by the change, if any, in the collection period.

The potential changes in operating cash flows are:

- The change in profits, calculated as the change in sales multiplied by the firm's contribution percentage.
- The change in bad debt losses, calculated as the change in sales multiplied by the percent that become bad debts.
- The change in discounts granted, calculated as the discount percentage multiplied by the sales affected by the discount.
- The change in administrative costs, which is not calculated by a standard formula.

The change in taxes is the net change to operating cash flows multiplied by the firm's marginal tax rate.

A firm that extends credit to its customers must make three decisions that define its credit policy: (1) credit standards—who is an acceptable credit customer, (2) payment date—when is the customer expected to pay, and (3) price changes—what discounts may be taken for early payment and what finance charges will be added if payments are late. Each variable affects the level of the firm's permanent accounts receivable. We look at each in turn.

1. Credit Standards

To qualify acceptable credit customers, companies create scoring systems based on data about the customer's financial condition, stability, and past payment performance. Business customers are asked to provide financial statements and supporting data which are used for ratio and other financial analysis. Individuals are asked to fill out a form in which they report their income and their financial, employment, and family status. When available, information is obtained from credit reporting agencies, such as Dun & Bradstreet for businesses and TRW Credit for individuals. A common system is to divide credit applicants into three groups. Those with the highest scores receive credit immediately, those with the lowest scores are rejected for credit, and those in the middle are investigated further before a decision is made.

Extending credit to riskier customers increases sales, and hence profits, but adds to administrative costs and exposes the firm to additional bad debts. Contracting credit reduces these costs but also reduces sales and profits.

Example

Credit Standards

Marie Kaye's company currently extends credit to applicants scoring 150 or more points on its credit qualification scale. Marie is interested in the value of extending credit to applicants who score 145–149 points. She has prepared the following forecasts:

a. Sales to the new customers will total $20,000,000 per year

b. The new customers will pay in 90 days on average (assume a 360-day year for convenience)

c. Five percent of the new sales will become bad debts and will not be collected

d. No discounts will be offered to the new customers

e. Administering the additional accounts will cost $100,000 per year.

Marie's company has variable costs equal to 70% of sales, is in the 35% marginal income tax bracket, and has a 12% cost of capital.

Question: Should the company extend credit to these customers?

Solution steps:

1. Calculate the incremental cash flows:

   a. Incremental investment:

      (1) From the concept of the collection period ratio,[10] (90 days/360 days) = 1/4 of the new sales will be outstanding as receivables at any time:

      $$1/4 \times \$20{,}000{,}000 = \$5{,}000{,}000$$

      Of this, 70% represents the company's cost, the amount the company invested to create the receivables:

      $$70\% \times \$5{,}000{,}000 = \$3{,}500{,}000$$

      (2) There is no change anticipated to other working capital.

      (3) Existing customers are not changing their payment habits.

   b. Incremental operating cash flows:

      (1) Contribution margin = (1 − 70%) = 30%, so contribution from new sales:

      $$30\% \times \$20{,}000{,}000 = \$6{,}000{,}000$$

      (2) New bad debt losses:

      $$5\% \times \$20{,}000{,}000 = \$1{,}000{,}000$$

      (3) No discounts are being offered to these customers.

      (4) Incremental administrative costs are given as $100,000

[10] **Cross-reference:** Financial ratios are presented in Appendix 4D and summarized at the end of the book. The collection period ratio appears on pp. 124–125.

c. Income taxes will increase (an outflow) by:

35% ($6,000,000 – 1,000,000 – 100,000) = $1,715,000

2. Organize the cash flows into a cash flow table:

	Year 0	Years 1–∞
Investment		
Accounts receivable	($3,500,000)	
Operating cash flows		
Contribution from sales		$6,000,000
Bad debts		(1,000,000)
Administrative costs		(100,000)
Taxes on changed income		(1,715,000)
Net cash flows	($3,500,000)	$3,185,000

3. Calculate the value of the proposal using any of the three variations of the perpetuity model:

a. NPV:

PV of costs = $3,500,000 since all costs come at year 0

PV of benefits = PMT/r = $3,185,000/.12 = $26,541,667

NPV = $26,541,667 – 3,500,000 = $23,041,667

b. IRR:

IRR = r = PMT/PV = $3,185,000/$3,500,000 = 91.00%

c. NAB:

Required annual benefit = r × PV = .12 × $3,500,000 = $420,000

Actual annual benefit = $3,185,000

NAB = $3,185,000 – 420,000 = $2,765,000

Answer: The proposal has a NPV of $23,041,667, an IRR of 91.00%, and a NAB of $2,765,000. Since NPV and NAB exceed zero and IRR is greater than the cost of capital, credit should be extended to these new customers. In fact, the return is so attractive that Marie should consider analyzing the value of extending credit to potential customers scoring even lower on her company's credit qualification scale.

2. Payment Date

The invoice sent to a customer identifies when payment is due with terms such as net 30 (payment due in 30 days) or net 45 (payment due in 45 days). Permitting payment at a later date increases a company's investment in accounts receivable and slows its collection of profits but might encourage customers to increase their purchases. Shortening the time for payment, on the other hand, reduces the investment in receivables and accelerates profit collection but may reduce sales.

Example

Payment Date

Marie Kaye's company has a product line with sales of $7,800,000. She is curious about the impact of changing payment terms from net 60 to net 30 as customers are not paying their bills until the seventy-fifth day on average. Marie has prepared the following forecasts:

a. Customers will pay more quickly, reducing the collection period to 40 days (assume a 360-day year for convenience)

b. Her company will be able to reduce its idle cash balance by $25,000, freeing that money for other use

c. Some customers will take their business elsewhere and $600,000 of sales will be lost.

Marie's company has variable costs equal to 70% of sales, is in the 35% marginal income tax bracket, and has a 12% cost of capital.

Question: Should the payment date be changed?

Solution steps:

1. Calculate the incremental cash flows:
   a. Incremental investment:
      (1) From the collection period ratio, the accounts receivable balance is currently

      (75 days/360 days) × $7,800,000 = $1,625,000

      If the change is implemented, the accounts receivable balance will decline to

      (40 days/360 days) × $7,200,000 = $800,000

      a change of

      $1,625,000 − 800,000 = $825,000

      Of this, 70% represents the company's cost, the amount the company invested to create the receivables:

      70% × $825,000 = $577,500

      (2) Other working capital: idle cash will decline by $25,000

      (3) The customers who do not leave will speed up their payments. Daily profit flow from these customers is

      30% × ($7,200,000/360) = $6,000

      and if collected (75 − 40 =) 35 days earlier, adds value of:

      $6,000 × 35 days = $210,000

   b. Incremental operating cash flows:
      (1) Contribution lost from departing sales:

      30% × $600,000 = $180,000

(2) Bad debts are not forecast to change.

(3) No discounts are being offered to these customers.

(4) Administrative costs are not forecast to change.

c. Income taxes will decrease (an inflow) by:

$$35\% \times \$180{,}000 = \$63{,}000$$

2. Organize the cash flows into a cash flow table:

	Year 0	Years 1—∞
Investment		
Accounts receivable	$577,500	
Other working capital	25,000	
Changed collection period	210,000	
Operating cash flows		
Contribution from sales		($180,000)
Taxes on changed income		63,000
Net cash flows	$812,500	($117,000)

3. Calculate the value of the proposal using any of the three variations of the perpetuity model:

a. NPV:

PV of benefits = $812,500 since all at year 0

PV of costs = PMT/r = $117,000/.12 = $975,000

NPV = $812,500 − 975,000 = ($162,500)

b. IRR:

IRR = r = PMT/PV = $117,000/$812,500 = 14.40%

c. NAB:

Annual cost of the existing investment = r × PV
= .12 × $812,500 = $97,500

Annual cost of the proposed investment = $117,000

NAB = $97,500 − 117,000 = ($19,500)

Answer: The proposal has a NPV of ($162,500), an IRR of 14.40%, and an NAB of ($19,500). Since NPV and NAB are less than zero (and IRR is greater than the cost of capital for this "opposite project"), payment terms should not be shortened.

3. Price Changes

Discounts are often offered to business customers for early payment, such as in the terms 2/10, net 30, which gives the customer a choice: take a 2% discount (pay 98%) within ten days, or pay 100% by the thirtieth day. Granting discounts reduces a company's investment in accounts receivable and speeds up its collection of profits at the cost of the discount foregone. Eliminating existing discounts increases the investment in receivables and slows profit collection but does not give away profit dollars.

Example

Discounts

Marie Kaye's company has another product line with sales of $9,000,000 on terms of net 60. Customers pay on time, so the average collection period is 60 days. Marie is interested in the effect of offering a 2% discount by changing payment terms to 2/10, net 60. She has prepared the following forecasts:

a. Eighty percent of the customers will take the discount and pay on the tenth day (assume a 360 day year for convenience)

b. The other 20% of customers will continue to pay on the sixtieth day.

Marie's company has variable costs equal to 70% of sales, is in the 35% marginal income tax bracket, and has a 12% cost of capital.

Question: Should the company offer the discount?

Solution steps:

1. Calculate the incremental cash flows:
   a. Incremental investment:
      (1) From the collection period ratio, the accounts receivable balance is currently

      $$(60 \text{ days}/360 \text{ days}) \times \$9{,}000{,}000 = \$1{,}500{,}000$$

      If the change is implemented, the collection period will become

      $$(80\% \times 10 \text{ days}) + (20\% \times 60 \text{ days}) = 20 \text{ days}$$

      and the accounts receivable balance will decline to

      $$(20 \text{ days}/360 \text{ days}) \times \$9{,}000{,}000 = \$500{,}000$$

      a change of

      $$\$1{,}500{,}000 - 500{,}000 = \$1{,}000{,}000$$

      Of this, 70% represents the company's cost, the amount the company invested to create the receivables:

      $$70\% \times \$1{,}000{,}000 = \$700{,}000$$

      (2) There is no change anticipated to other working capital.

      (3) On average, customers will speed up their payments. Daily profit flow is

      $$30\% \times (\$9{,}000{,}000/360) = \$7{,}500$$

      and if collected (60 − 20 =) 40 days earlier, adds value of:

      $$\$7{,}500 \times 40 \text{ days} = \$300{,}000$$

   b. Incremental operating cash flows:

(1) Sales is not forecasted to change.

(2) Bad debts are not forecasted to change.

(3) Customers taking the discount purchase

$$80\% \times \$9{,}000{,}000 = \$7{,}200{,}000$$

If they take a 2% discount they will reduce their payments by

$$2\% \times \$7{,}200{,}000 = \$144{,}000$$

(4) Administrative costs are not forecasted to change.

c. Income taxes will decrease (an inflow) by:

$$35\% \times \$144{,}000 = \$50{,}400$$

2. Organize the cash flows into a cash flow table:

	Year 0	**Years 1–∞**
Investment		
Accounts receivable	$ 700,000	
Changed collection period	300,000	
Operating cash flows		
Discounts		($144,000)
Taxes on changed income		50,400
Net cash flows	$1,000,000	($ 93,600)

3. Calculate the value of the proposal using any of the three variations of the perpetuity model:

a. NPV:

PV of benefits = $1,000,000 since all come at year 0

PV of costs = PMT/r = $93,600/.12 = $780,000

NPV = $1,000,000 − 780,000 = $220,000

b. IRR:

IRR = r = PMT/PV = $93,600/$1,000,000 = 9.36%

c. NAB:

Annual cost of the existing investment = r × PV

= .12 × $1,000,000 = $120,000

Annual cost of the proposed investment = $93,600

NAB = $120,000 − 93,600 = $26,400

Answer: The proposal has a NPV of $220,000, an IRR of 9.36%, and a NAB of $26,400. Since NPV and NAB exceed zero (and IRR is less than the cost of capital for this "opposite project"), the discount should be offered.

A second form of price change occurs when interest is added to an overdue account balance. Since this is identical to transforming the receivables balance into a loan, it is treated in Chapter 20 which deals with short-term debt.

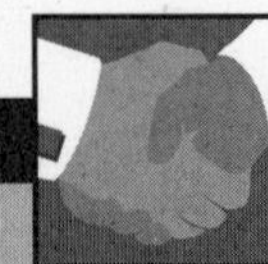

SERVING FINANCE'S CUSTOMERS

Reducing Billing "Contentions" at Southern Pacific

When a survey of customers identified billing accuracy as the finance process with which they were most dissatisfied—fully 13% of all bills were objected to as wrong, "contentions" in the jargon of the industry—the controller's office at Southern Pacific Transportation Company began a project to improve the process. Quality-improvement teams improved the data flow from marketing to billing, realigned the billing group to be more consistent with the marketing organization's structure, constructed a common pricing database, and studied how to simplify the railroad's pricing structure. Customers active in quality management joined with Southern Pacific in the effort. Today, contentions have been significantly reduced, and since the reduction in contested invoices represents millions of dollars of receivables per day, the company's cash flow has improved dramatically.

Permanent Inventory

In a manufacturing company, inventory comes in three forms: raw materials, work-in-process, and finished goods. A selling company carries merchandise inventory. Each type of inventory plays an important role in the production and/or sales process, yet there is a high cost to maintaining excessive inventories. A good permanent inventory policy balances the benefits and costs.

Raw materials inventory prevents the production process from becoming idle while waiting for material inputs to arrive. By uncoupling the purchasing and production processes, raw materials may allow each to become more efficient.[11] Work-in-process is a necessary by-product of a multiple-step production process; at any time, some work is partially completed and between steps. Finished goods serve to uncouple production and sales. The amount of finished goods inventory can range from near zero for a company that produces to order, to a somewhat larger amount for a company that wishes to respond promptly to customer orders but whose production process is not so flexible. Merchandise inventory is generally a major investment for a selling company whose sales depends on having a variety of products—brands, sizes, styles, etc.—in each sales location. Most firms carry inventories of consumables as well—spare parts for machinery and office equipment, office supplies, light bulbs, etc.—to avoid the slowdown or shutdown of work for want of an inexpensive or difficult-to-obtain resource.

Set against these benefits are the costs of holding inventories. Inventory must be financed, so every dollar of inventory incurs a cost of capital. There are costs to ordering raw materials and merchandise inventory: purchasing, transportation, receiving, testing, and accounting. Storing inventory requires physical space, han-

[11] **Observation and cross-reference:** Although decoupling the purchasing and production processes *may* allow each to become more efficient, the opposite is true in many companies. We discuss such situations on pp. 447–449.

shrinkage—the loss of inventory for any reason

dling, data management, and insurance. Inventory on hand is subject to **shrinkage** through physical damage, evaporation, chemical change, obsolescence, theft, etc.

1. Permanent Finished Goods and Merchandise Inventory

Figure 12.5 is a cash flow table for permanent finished goods and merchandise inventory decisions. Like Figure 12.4 for accounts receivable, it also is an expanded version of the generic Figure 12.2. There are two potential changes to the amount the firm has invested in its inventory process, three potential changes to annual operating cash flow, and a potential change to income taxes. Where the numbers may be calculated by formula, the relationship is given in the cash flow columns.

The potential changes in investment are:

- The change in the money invested in inventory itself, calculated as the projected change in the inventory account.
- The change in other working capital, such as accounts receivable and cash, which is not calculated by a standard formula.

The potential changes in operating cash flows are:

- The change in profits, calculated as the change in sales multiplied by the firm's contribution percentage.
- The change due to shrinkage, calculated as a percentage of inventory value.
- The change in administrative costs, which is not calculated by a standard formula.

The change in taxes is the net change to operating cash flows multiplied by the firm's marginal tax rate.

FIGURE 12.5
Cash flow table for permanent inventory decisions. The table organizes the data into two changes to the level of investment, three changes to operating cash flows, and the change to taxes.

	Year 0	Years 1–∞
Investment		
Inventory	ΔInventory	
Other working capital		
Operating cash flows		
Contribution from sales		ΔSales × contribution %
Shrinkage		% Inventory
Administrative costs		
Tax—changed income		Tax on above
Net cash flows		

Example

Permanent Inventory

Marie Kaye's company has a product line with sales of $10,000,000 and a finished goods inventory turnover of 12 times, much higher than the industry average. The president of Marie's company considers the high turnover proof of good inventory control. The sales manager, however, has pointed out that this policy leads to stockouts and lost sales and has recommended doubling inventory levels.

With the sales manager, Marie has prepared the following forecasts:

a. Sales will increase by $1,250,000.
b. Losses due to theft and damage will increase by 1% of the additional inventory.
c. Administrative costs for ordering and storing the additional inventory will increase by $50,000.
d. The balance of accounts receivable will increase by $100,000.

Marie's company has a gross margin of 25%, variable costs equal to 70% of sales, is in the 35% marginal income tax bracket, and has a 12% cost of capital.

Question: Should the finished goods inventory be doubled?

Solution steps:

1. Calculate the incremental cash flows:
   a. Incremental investment:
      (1) With a 25% gross margin, cost of goods sold is 75% of sales, or

$$75\% \times \$10{,}000{,}000 = \$7{,}500{,}000$$

and, since it turns over 12 times per year, finished goods inventory totals

$$\$7{,}500{,}000/12 = \$625{,}000$$

If inventory is doubled, the increase will be another $625,000

      (2) Other working capital: accounts receivable will increase by $100,000. With variable costs equal to 70% of sales, this will require an incremental investment of

$$70\% \times \$100{,}000 = \$70{,}000$$

   b. Incremental operating cash flows:
      (1) With variable costs equal to 70% of sales, contribution margin is 30%, so contribution from new sales is

$$30\% \times \$1{,}250{,}000 = \$375{,}000$$

      (2) Shrinkage on new inventory

$$1\% \times \$625{,}000 = \$6{,}250$$

      (3) Incremental administrative costs are given as $50,000
   c. Income taxes will increase (an outflow) by:

35% × ($375,000 − 6,250 − 50,000) = $111,563

2. Organize the cash flows into a cash flow table:

	Year 0	Years 1–∞
Investment		
Inventory	($625,000)	
Other working capital	(70,000)	
Operating cash flows		
Contribution from sales		$375,000
Shrinkage		(6,250)
Administrative costs		(50,000)
Taxes on changed income		(111,563)
Net cash flows	($695,000)	$207,187

3. Calculate the value of the proposal using any of the three variations of the perpetuity model:
   a. NPV:

PV of costs = $695,000 since all come at year 0

PV of benefits = PMT/r = $207,187/.12 = $1,726,558

NPV = $1,726,558 − 695,000 = $1,031,558

   b. IRR:

IRR = r = PMT/PV = $207,187/$695,000= 29.81%

   c. NAB:

Required annual benefit = r × PV = .12 × $695,000 = $83,400

Actual annual benefit = $207,187

NAB = $207,187 − 83,400 = $123,787

Answer: The proposal has an NPV of $1,031,558, an IRR of 29.81%, and an NAB of $123,787. Since NPV and NAB exceed zero, and IRR is greater than the cost of capital, doubling the finished goods inventory adds value to the firm. Further analysis will be required to determine if doubling inventory is the optimal solution.

2. Raw Materials and Work-in-Process Inventory

As we noted earlier, many companies use inventories to decouple purchasing, production, and sales, believing that each function can operate more efficiently if inventories are used to smooth the flow from one process to another. Recent improvements in managing production and in reintegrating purchasing, production, and sales have challenged this long-held belief. These new processes are often called **just-in-time manufacturing.**

just-in-time manufacturing—a system of integrating purchasing, production, and sales so each task is done only when required

In just-in-time manufacturing, raw materials, and work-in-process inventories are kept at the minimum levels required for smooth production operations. The ultimate goal is just-in-time delivery, in which inventory arrives as needed and not a moment before. Suppliers deliver raw materials hours or even minutes before they enter production. Work-in-process emerges from one production step just as it is required for the next. While a perfect just-in-time system is an ideal, the concept has led producing companies to discover inefficiencies in their production processes that were not previously visible.

Without a just-in-time system, it is easy for errors in production to be treated as special events rather than as signals to improve the process. Improperly manufactured products are pulled from production and the defects fixed by other workers. For many years the American automobile manufacturers operated this way, repairing cars after they left the assembly line. Defective cars continued to be manufactured, and it was widely understood that the quality of American-made automobiles lagged behind that of Japanese automobiles. The absence of a just-in-time system also accepts a buildup of work-in-process inventory at various points on the assembly line. The emphasis is often on keeping the line moving rather than studying how the production process might be redesigned to eliminate the problem that led to the accumulation of inventory.

A just-in-time system for raw materials requires a high degree of alignment with suppliers. Suppliers must be able to adjust their deliveries to the company's production needs. They must also produce to the same quality standards since there is no buffer of extra raw materials to substitute for a delivery of defective parts. To create this alignment, companies are changing their relationships with suppliers. For example, Globe Metallurgical, Inc., a manufacturer of precision castings and a 1988 recipient of the Malcolm Baldrige National Quality Award, routinely works with its suppliers to train them in high-quality production methods. Motorola, another 1988 Baldrige Award winner, announced that it would terminate business with any supplier that is not in a position to apply for the Baldrige Award by 1995.

Just-in-time has also led to a movement toward single suppliers. Once a supplier has been identified that can consistently deliver high-quality materials where and when required, the need for a second source may disappear. Many companies have concluded that it is better to direct 100% of the business to the single supplier to make the business more important for that supplier and to get that much more devotion to the relationship.

FINANCE IN PRACTICE

Just-in-Time at Apple Computer

Apple Computer, Inc. is a leader among American business in employing the just-in-time system for its raw materials inventory. At the plant in Fremont, California, where the Macintosh computer line is produced, suppliers are expected to deliver one-third of a day's production requirements three times per day. Each supplier is given three five-minute windows when the loading dock will be open for them and must meet these delivery targets to keep Apple's business. In return, Apple has embraced the single-supplier concept and promised to give as much business as possible to those suppliers that can meet Apple's quality and delivery targets.

"First of all, a hardy 'well done' to Tyler for a most remarkable improvement in our cash flow situation."

A widely used model of minimizing the cost of raw materials inventory is the "economic order quantity model" which is presented in Appendix 12B. Early implementations of this model ignored the inefficiencies in the production process caused by keeping more than the absolute minimum amount of raw materials and pointed toward keeping considerable quantities of raw materials on hand. When the model is solved with the costs of production inefficiencies included, the solution is very consistent with just-in-time.

Working Capital Liabilities

Current liabilities—accounts payable, accruals (wages payable, taxes payable, interest payable, etc.), short-term debt, and receipts in advance—make up the other half of the working capital equation. Because each of these accounts represents some form of short-term borrowing, they are treated together in Chapter 20, "Short-term Debt." In addition, the optimal level of working capital—the best combination of working capital assets and working capital liabilities—is discussed in Chapter 16, "Risk Management and Temporary Working Capital."

"Hey, how about a break for lunch," one member of the team asked, looking toward Marie Kaye. Marie glanced at her watch; it was almost 1:00 PM! After what had seemed like an eternity waiting for the day to begin, the morning had flown by. Marie had invited members of her staff to brainstorm the company's accounts receivable problems, and there was no shortage of volunteers. Everyone had made important contributions during the morning's discussion, and by now the walls of the conference room were covered with the team's notes.

Marie had begun the meeting with a review of the company's receivables policy: credit standards, payment date, and discount terms. She had put her staff's most recent cash flow analyses on the table, and after a general discussion of incremental analysis techniques, breakout groups had reviewed the assumptions and calculations. There was general agreement that the company's policy was reasonable, given the assumptions that had been made about customer behavior.

But it quickly became apparent that the group did not understand the behavior of their customers: why they were not paying as they had been forecasted to do. Part of the problem seemed to be with the format of the invoices since customers complained they were difficult to understand (even though they made perfect sense to everyone in the room), and the team made plans to form a joint controller/customer task force to work on the issue. Part of the problem was the errors in some invoices, and another task force was formed to trace the billing process to discover where and why errors arose.

As Marie left the room and walked toward the company's cafeteria, she felt a strong sense of accomplishment. She was having fun blending the traditional skills of financial analysis with the team-based work of quality management, and more than ever she was convinced of the need to combine the two to do her new job well.

Summary of Key Points

- **Separate working capital into permanent and temporary components.** Working capital represents a company's liquid resources available for daily use. Some is permanent, a base level required on an ongoing basis. The remainder is temporary, the changes around the base level due to the business cycle, seasonality, and the vagaries of day-to-day transactions.
- **Organize permanent working capital data into cash flow terms.** Permanent working capital decisions are analyzed using a cash flow table and the perpetuity time value of money model; there is no comparable standard form of analysis for temporary working capital decisions.
- **Describe the components of a firm's cash balance and analyze decisions involving accelerating cash in transit.** Cash includes coins and bills, demand deposits, and time deposits, and may be held in various currencies. Traditionally, companies have accelerated collections and delayed disbursements so cash in transit does not remain idle. Today, there is a trend toward immediate, often electronic, payment systems to reduce processing costs. Excess cash is moved to marketable securities to earn interest.
- **Analyze proposed changes to a firm's permanent accounts receivable balance.** A firm establishes its permanent accounts receivable balance through its decisions about credit standards, payment date, and price changes: discounts for early payment and interest added to overdue balances. Decisions are incremental, testing each proposed alternative and accepting changes that have a positive NPV or NAB or an acceptable IRR. Accounts receivable will change temporarily in response to specific customers' needs and circumstances.
- **Analyze plans to change the level of permanent inventory and understand the importance of a just-in-time inventory system.** Permanent inventory can provide benefits in manufacturing and sales but can also carry a high cost. As with accounts receivable, decisions about permanent inventory balances require incremental analysis. Raw materials and work-in-process are kept to the minimum amount consistent with production efficiency, using a just-in-time delivery system.

Questions

1. What are the two usages for the term *working capital*?
2. Distinguish between permanent working capital and temporary working capital. Why is the difference important to financial managers?
3. In what ways is the cash flow table used to organize the data for permanent working capital asset decisions similar to and different from the cash flow table used in capital budgeting?

4. What is a project's "net annual benefit"? Why is this measure used in evaluating permanent working capital asset decisions?
5. Are you comfortable with the assumption that permanent asset decisions are truly permanent—that is, their effects continue forever? Why or why not?
6. Discuss how a corporate treasurer allocates the firm's cash balance. What are the factors taken into account in making the allocation?
7. What is "float"? Why is it of concern to the financial manager? Discuss the advantages and/or disadvantages to receivables float and payables float.
8. How does a lock box-concentration banking system impact a firm's float?
9. When does a company move cash from its noninterest-bearing demand account to marketable securities?
10. What are the three components of a firm's credit policy? What does each entail?
11. What special considerations enter the credit granting decision when the customer is paying in a foreign currency?
12. What are the costs and benefits of maintaining inventories? What does this tell you about the movement toward just-in-time systems?
13. The Economic Order Quantity (EOQ) model, presented in Appendix 12B, is a widely accepted method of calculating the permanent inventory balance, yet we did not use it to analyze the inventory decision on pp. 446–447. Why?
14. In the example on pp. 446–447, we concluded that doubling the firm's inventory balance would add value to the company. Should Marie Kaye make this recommendation? What additional recommendations might she make based upon her analysis?

Problems

1. **(Calculating working capital)** A company's current asset balance is $500,000. Calculate its working capital and current ratio if its current liabilities equal:
   a. $200,000
   b. $350,000
   c. $500,000
   d. $650,000
2. **(Calculating working capital)** A company's working capital equals $2,000,000. Calculate its balance of current liabilities and its current ratio if the company's current assets equal:
   a. $6,000,000
   b. $5,000,000
   c. $4,000,000
   d. $3,000,000
3. **(Changes to working capital)** A company has current assets of $1,500,000 and current liabilities of $800,000. Calculate the change to the company's working capital and current ratio from the following transactions (treat each case separately):
   a. Collecting $100,000 of accounts receivable
   b. Paying $100,000 of accounts payable
   c. Purchasing $100,000 of plant and equipment for cash
   d. Selling $100,000 of common stock
4. **(Changes to working capital)** A company has current assets of $5,000,000 and current liabilities of $2,000,000. Calculate the change to the company's working capital and current ratio from the following transactions (treat each case separately):
   a. Purchasing $500,000 of inventory on credit (accounts payable)
   b. Recording $500,000 of depreciation
   c. Moving $500,000 from cash to marketable securities
   d. Recognizing $500,000 of receipts in advance as being earned
5. **(Perpetuity analysis)** A company with a 11% cost of capital is considering an investment that would cost it $300,000 today in return for a perpetuity of benefits of $45,000.
   a. Calculate the project's NPV
   b. Calculate the project's IRR
   c. Calculate the project's NAB
   d. Should the investment be accepted? (Interpret your results from parts a, b, and c.)
6. **(Perpetuity analysis)** A company with a 9% cost of capital is considering scaling back its operations. $1,750,000 would be released from investment in current assets, but the firm would forgo a perpetuity of benefits of $250,000.
   a. Calculate the project's NPV
   b. Calculate the project's IRR
   c. Calculate the project's NAB
   d. Should the investment be accepted? (Interpret your results from parts a, b, and c)
7. **(Funds in transit)** It takes three days on average for customers' checks, averaging $75,000 per day, to reach a company. Also, the company makes deposits averaging $60,000 to its bank account one day before its checks clear. The company has a 12% cost of capital.
   a. What is the amount of idle money
      (1) In the mail?
      (2) In the bank?

b. What is the total amount of idle money in transit?
c. What is the annual cost of the funds
(1) In the mail?
(2) In the bank?
d. What is the total annual cost of the idle funds?

8. **(Funds in transit)** It takes six days on average for customers' checks, averaging $200,000 per day, to reach a company. Also, the company makes deposits averaging $160,000 to its bank account one-half day before its checks clear. The company has a 10% cost of capital.
   a. What is the amount of idle money
      (1) In the mail?
      (2) In the bank?
   b. What is the total amount of idle money in transit?
   c. What is the annual cost of the funds
      (1) In the mail?
      (2) In the bank?
   d. What is the total annual cost of the idle funds?

9. **(Accelerating collections)** A company receives cash inflows of US$6 million per day from customers in North America. Checks take six days on average to arrive, but a large commercial bank has proposed to implement a lock box-concentration banking system for a $3 million annual fee which would cut the time a check is in receivables float to an average of three days. The company's marginal tax rate is 35%. What is the value of the proposed system to the company, and should it be implemented, if the company's cost of capital is:
   a. 8%?
   b. 10%?
   c. 12%?
   d. 15%?

10. **(Accelerating collections)** A company with a 12% cost of capital receives cash inflows from customers throughout the United States and Canada. Checks take 5 days on average to arrive, but a large commercial bank has proposed to implement a lock box-concentration banking system for a $250,000 annual fee which would cut the time a check is in receivables float to an average of 1 1/2 days. The company's marginal tax rate is 35%. What is the value of the proposed system to the company, and should it be implemented, if the company's daily cash inflows average:
    a. $150,000?
    b. $300,000?
    c. $450,000?
    d. $600,000?

11. **(Credit standards)** A company is considering extending credit to a group of customers who have not previously met the company's credit standards. The company forecasts that the new customers would purchase $80,000 per year, would pay in 75 days on average (assume a 360-day year), and would default on 8% of their purchases. It would cost $5,000 per year to administer the new accounts. The company's variable costs average 80% of sales, it is in the 35% marginal tax bracket, and it has a 9% cost of capital.
    a. Calculate the incremental cash flows from accepting this proposal.
    b. Organize your cash flows from part a into a cash flow table.
    c. Calculate the proposal's NPV, IRR, and NAB.
    d. Should credit be extended to the new customers?

12. **(Credit standards)** A company is considering withdrawing credit from a group of customers who are not paying on time. These customers purchase $200,000 per year, pay in 120 days on average (assume a 360-day year), and default on 15% of their purchases. The company would save $15,000 in administrative costs per year and could reduce its idle cash balance by $5,000 if it terminated these accounts. The company's variable costs average 60% of sales, it is in the 35% marginal tax bracket, and it has a 13% cost of capital.
    a. Calculate the incremental cash flows from accepting this proposal.
    b. Organize your cash flows from part a into a cash flow table.
    c. Calculate the proposal's NPV, IRR, and NAB.
    d. Should credit be withdrawn from these customers?

13. **(Payment date)** A company with annual sales of $5,000,000 is considering changing its payment terms from net 30 to net 45 to accommodate customers who are having difficulty in paying their bills. The company forecasts that customers would respond by: (1) paying on day 50 rather than on day 40 as at present (assume a 360-day year), (2) increasing their purchases by $100,000 per year, and (3) reducing their bad debts to 1.4% of sales from 1.5% of sales. The company also forecasts that its idle cash balance would increase by $50,000 but administrative costs would be reduced by $20,000. The company's variable costs average 75% of sales, it is in the 35% marginal tax bracket, and it has a 11% cost of capital.
    a. Calculate the incremental cash flows from accepting this proposal.
    b. Organize your cash flows from part a into a cash flow table.

c. Calculate the proposal's NPV, IRR, and NAB.
d. Should the company lengthen its payment terms?

14. **(Payment date)** A company with annual sales of $22,000,000 is considering changing its payment terms from net 40 to net 30 to encourage customers to pay more promptly. The company forecasts that customers would respond by paying on day 30 rather than on day 45 as at present (assume a 360-day year) but would decrease their purchases by $400,000 per year. The company also forecasts that its idle cash balance would decrease by $100,000 and administrative costs would be reduced by $50,000. The company's variable costs average 65% of sales, it is in the 35% marginal tax bracket, and it has a 12% cost of capital.
    a. Calculate the incremental cash flows from accepting this proposal.
    b. Organize your cash flows from part a into a cash flow table.
    c. Calculate the proposal's NPV, IRR, and NAB.
    d. Should the company shorten its payment terms?

15. **(Discounts)** A company with annual sales of $2,500,000 on terms of net 30 and a collection period of 40 days (assume a 360-day year) is considering offering its customers terms of 2/15, net 30. The company forecasts that 60% of the customers would take the discount and pay on day 15 while the remaining 40% would pay on day 35 on average. Customers are also expected to increase their purchases by $100,000, and the company forecasts that its idle cash balance would decrease by $60,000. The company's variable costs average 75% of sales, it is in the 35% marginal tax bracket, and it has a 10% cost of capital.
    a. Calculate the incremental cash flows from accepting this proposal.
    b. Organize your cash flows from part a into a cash flow table.
    c. Calculate the proposal's NPV, IRR, and NAB.
    d. Should the company offer the discount?

16. **(Discounts)** A company with annual sales of $900,000 on terms of 2/10, net 30 is considering eliminating the discount and simplifying its terms of sale to net 30. Only 25% of customers take the discount and pay on day 10 (assume a 360-day year), the rest pay on day 30 on average. The company forecasts that if the discount were eliminated, its collection period for all sales would become 30 days, its idle cash balance would increase by $1,000, and administrative costs would decrease by $3,000. The company's variable costs average 70% of sales, it is in the 35% marginal tax bracket, and it has a 10% cost of capital.
    a. Calculate the incremental cash flows from accepting this proposal.
    b. Organize your cash flows from part a into a cash flow table.
    c. Calculate the proposal's NPV, IRR, and NAB.
    d. Should the company eliminate the discount?

17. **(Permanent inventory)** A retail clothing store with sales of $6,000,000 is considering increasing its merchandise inventory by 50%. Currently the inventory days ratio is 20 days (assume a 360-day year). The company forecasts that this would increase sales by $500,000 but shrinkage would also increase from 2% of sales to 2.5% of sales. The annual cost of handling the new inventory is forecasted to be $30,000. In addition, the balance of accounts receivable is forecasted to increase by $50,000. The company has a gross margin of 60%, its variable costs average 55% of sales, it is in the 35% marginal tax bracket, and it has a 12% cost of capital.
    a. Calculate the incremental cash flows from accepting this proposal.
    b. Organize your cash flows from part a into a cash flow table.
    c. Calculate the proposal's NPV, IRR, and NAB.
    d. Should the company increase its inventory?

18. **(Permanent inventory)** A sporting goods store with sales of $2,250,000 is considering decreasing its merchandise inventory by 40%. Currently its inventory days ratio is 25 days (assume a 360-day year). The company forecasts that this would decrease sales by $60,000 but shrinkage would also decrease from 3% of sales to 2.5% of sales, the cost of handling inventory would decline by $7,500, and the balance of accounts receivable would decrease by $10,000. The company has a gross margin of 65%, its variable costs average 45% of sales, it is in the 35% marginal tax bracket, and it has a 13% cost of capital.
    a. Calculate the incremental cash flows from accepting this proposal.
    b. Organize your cash flows from part a into a cash flow table.
    c. Calculate the proposal's NPV, IRR, and NAB.
    d. Should the company decrease its inventory?

APPENDIX 12A

WHY NAB ALWAYS AGREES WITH NPV

In Chapter 12, we introduced a new time value measure, net annual benefit (NAB). NAB is preferred by some analysts for the type of problems we encountered in this chapter: problems with one cash flow at "year 0" followed by a perpetuity of cash flows in "year 1–∞." For this cash flow pattern NAB always agrees with net present value. When one is positive the other is also positive, and both signal to accept the decision. When one is negative the other is negative, both signaling to reject. And when one is zero the other is zero as well. In this appendix we demonstrate why this must be so.

Consider an investment project with the following net cash flows:

	Year 0	Years 1–∞
Net cash flows	$A	$B

where $A and $B are any amounts. Also, let the firm's cost of capital be represented by the variable r. Since $A comes at year 0 and $B is a perpetuity, the net present value of this project is:

$$\text{NPV} = \text{A} + \frac{\text{B}}{\text{r}}$$

and the project's net annual benefit is:

$$\text{NAB} = \text{r} \times \text{A} + \text{B}$$

Rearranging the equation for net present value gives:

$$\text{A} = \text{NPV} - \frac{\text{B}}{\text{r}}$$

and substituting this expression for A into the equation for NAB gives:

$$\begin{aligned}\text{NAB} &= \text{r} \times \left(\text{NPV} - \frac{\text{B}}{\text{r}}\right) + \text{B} \\ &= \text{r} \times \text{NPV} - \text{B} + \text{B}\end{aligned}$$

$$\boldsymbol{NAB = r \times NPV}$$

Therefore, for a decision with this pattern of cash flows, NAB is always equal to the net present value multiplied by the firm's cost of capital. Since costs of capital are positive numbers, NAB will always take on the same sign as NPV.

Effectively, NAB calculates the benefit from the first year of the project. If all subsequent years are identical to the first, a project that adds value in the first year of its life will add value in every subsequent year as well, and vice versa. In practice, however, each year's cash flows will not be identical. As time passes, we will learn more and refine our cash flow forecasts. NAB directs our focus to the upcoming year and encourages us to reanalyze the decision each time our forecasts improve.

APPENDIX 12B

THE ECONOMIC ORDER QUANTITY MODEL

For many years, one of the most widely used business decision tools has been the economic order quantity (EOQ) model for determining the optimal balance of raw materials or merchandise inventory. Although other optimization models are discussed in Part VI of this book, we include the EOQ model in this chapter because it is applied to permanent working capital decisions. We present the model in this appendix; it appears again in Appendix 16A as the Baumol model for setting the optimal target cash balance.

1. The Traditional Model

economic order quantity—the quantity of inventory to purchase with each order to minimize inventory costs

The **economic order quantity** is the dollar amount of inventory to purchase with each order to minimize total inventory costs. The model makes the following assumptions:

- There is only one type of inventory, and it arrives and is used on a uniform, predictable, continuous basis throughout the year with no seasonal increases or decreases in manufacturing or sales.
- Revenues are not dependent on the level of inventory, so that minimizing costs is the same as maximizing value.
- All costs of inventory can be grouped into two categories: ordering costs and carrying costs. **Ordering costs** include all costs necessary to purchase the inventory: the purchasing organization, shipping and handling, receiving, and accounting. **Carrying costs** include the costs of storing the inventory once it arrives: warehousing, handling, insurance, shrinkage, record keeping, and the cost of the invested capital.

ordering costs—the annual costs of acquiring inventory

carrying costs—the annual costs of storing inventory

Figure 12B.1 is a graph of ordering costs, carrying costs, and total inventory costs as a function of order quantity. Ordering costs are considered to be directly proportional to the number of times inventory is ordered and are represented by the downward-sloping line. If each order is for a small quantity, there will be many inventory orders and ordering costs will be very high. However, if each order is for a large amount, inventory will not have to be reordered frequently, and ordering costs will be low. By contrast, carrying costs are inversely related to the number of times an inventory order is placed and are shown as the upward-sloping straight line. Small, frequent orders mean low inventory balances and low carrying costs. Large, infrequent orders result in high inventory balances and high carrying costs.

The U-shaped line at the top of the graph represents total inventory costs, the sum of ordering costs and carrying costs. For low order sizes (frequent orders), total cost is high due to high ordering costs. As order size increases (less frequent orders), ordering costs come down rapidly and total costs decline. However, as order size continues to increase (infrequent but large orders), carrying costs begin to dominate ordering costs and total costs rise again. The EOQ is at the point where total cost is at a minimum. It is found by using the differential calculus: we write an equation for total cost, take the first derivative, and set the derivative equal to zero.

The model solves to:

$$EOQ = \sqrt{\frac{2SO}{C}}$$

FIGURE 12B.1
How the economic order quantity is determined. The EOQ is the order size that produces the minimum total cost for ordering and carrying inventory.

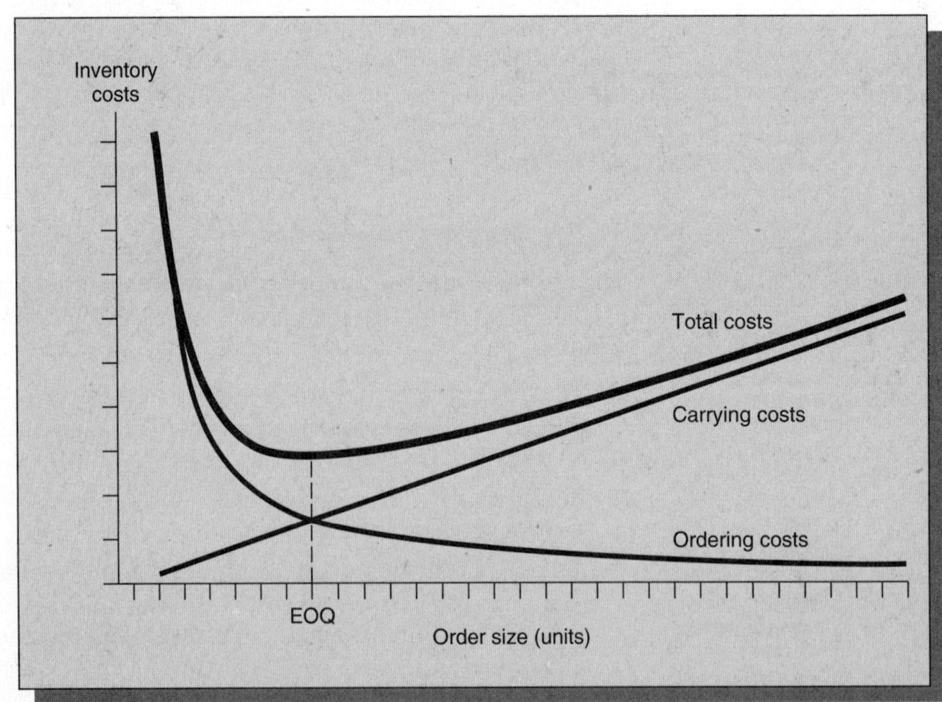

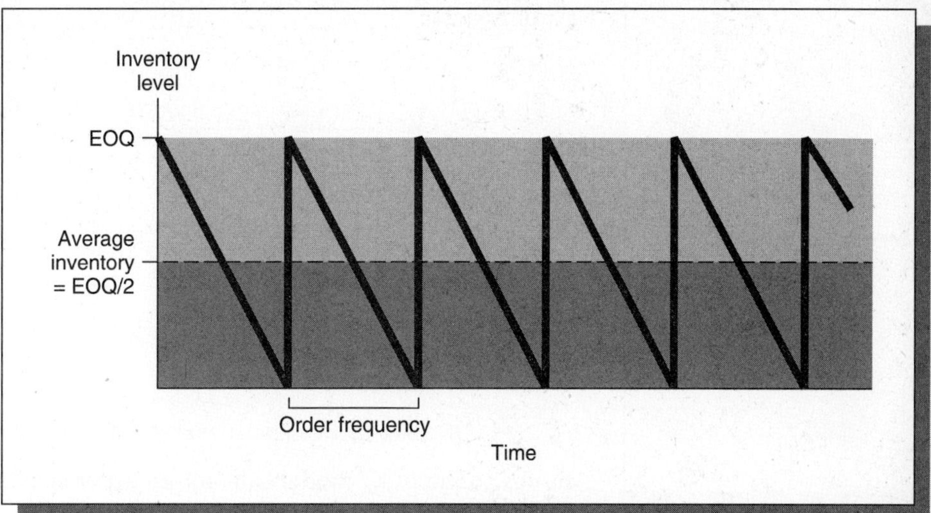

FIGURE 12B.2
A firm's inventory level from the EOQ model. Inventory is used uniformly until it runs out, at which point an arriving order increases inventory back to its high point, the EOQ.

where the variables are:

S = annual usage of the inventory item (the variable S comes from **S**ales of merchandise inventory)

O = **O**rdering cost per order

C = **C**arrying cost per unit per year

Figure 12B.2 illustrates the inventory pattern of an idealized company using the EOQ model. Inventory orders arrive at regular intervals, raising the inventory balance from zero to the EOQ. Inventory is then used/sold uniformly. The next order is timed to arrive at precisely the point at which inventory again goes to zero. The company's average inventory level will be the midpoint of the pattern, or simply one-half the EOQ. The model also concludes that the firm will place:

$$\textit{Orders per year} = \frac{S}{EOQ}$$

with frequency (assuming a 360-day year) of:

$$\textit{Order frequency} = \frac{360}{\textit{orders per year}}$$

Example

Economic Order Quantity

Marie Kaye wishes to apply the economic order quantity model to a particular raw material. Her company uses 112,500 units of the item each year. Marie has determined that each order costs $50 to place and her firm spends $5 per year to store each unit.

Question: If Marie uses the EOQ model for this inventory item, what will be the economic order quantity, the average inventory level, the number of orders per year, and the frequency of placing orders?

Solution steps:

1. EOQ

$$EOQ = \sqrt{\frac{2SO}{C}} = \sqrt{\frac{2 \times 112{,}500 \times 50}{5}} = \sqrt{2{,}250{,}000} = 1{,}500$$

2. Average inventory

$$EOQ/2 = 1{,}500/2 = 750$$

3. Number of orders per year

$$S/EOQ = 112{,}500/1{,}500 = 75$$

4. Order frequency

$$360/(\text{orders per year}) = 360/75 = \text{every 4.8 days}$$

Answer: The EOQ model calls for an order size of 1,500 units ordered every 4.8 days. The company will place 75 orders per year and maintain an average inventory of 750 units.

The square root in the EOQ formulation indicates there are economies of scale in inventory investment. For example, if sales or usage were to double, the EOQ would increase by only the square root of 2, or 1.414. Thus, inventory investment does not have to keep pace with production or sales in a growing firm.

Example

Economic Order Quantity: Increased Usage

Marie's company is planning to increase its rate of production. She has been asked to examine the implications of an increase in usage of raw material from 112,500 units to 162,500 units per year.

Question: At this higher level of usage, what does the EOQ model prescribe for the economic order quantity, the average inventory level, the number of orders per year, and the frequency of placing orders?

Solution steps:

1. EOQ

$$EOQ = \sqrt{\frac{2SO}{C}} = \sqrt{\frac{2 \times 162{,}500 \times 50}{5}} = \sqrt{3{,}240{,}000} = 1{,}800$$

2. Average inventory

$$EOQ/2 = 1{,}800/2 = 900$$

3. Number of orders per year

$$S/EOQ = 162{,}500/1{,}800 = 90$$

4. Order frequency

$$360/(\text{orders per year}) = 360/90 = \text{every 4 days}$$

Answer: The EOQ model calls for an order size of 1,800 units ordered every four days. The company will place 90 orders per year and maintain an average inventory of 900 units. Although usage is projected to increase by 44% (from 112,500 to 162,500) the EOQ only rises by 20% (1,500 to 1,800) illustrating economies of scale.

stock out—to run out of inventory

safety stock—extra inventory kept on hand to minimize the chance the firm will stock out

When the rate at which inventory is used or sold is not constant, or if it is difficult to guarantee on-time delivery of arriving inventory, it is possible to **stock out.** Firms have traditionally used **safety stocks,** a base level of extra inventory, to prevent stocking out and losing sales or disrupting production. Figure 12B.3 illustrates the use of safety stocks, both to cover speedy usage of inventory and delays in arrival of replacement stocks. In the first inventory cycle, usage increases and the firm must dip into its safety stock to meet demand. Inventory is below normal when the next order arrives, so the arriving stocks do not raise the inventory balance to the level of the EOQ. To avoid running low again, the subsequent order must be placed early. The fourth delivery of inventory arrives late, and once again the firm must use inventory from its safety stock.

2. Incorporating the Costs from Defective Production

Recently, companies have discovered a new category of costs associated with inventories: the costs of waste, inefficiency, and rework that arise when inventory obscures faulty production. This suggests that carrying costs are much higher than

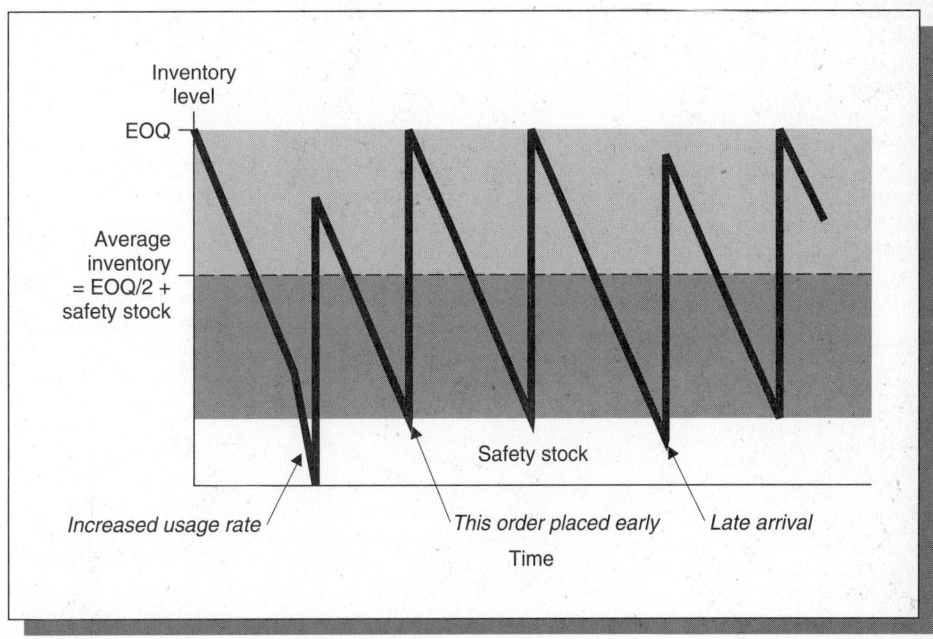

FIGURE 12B.3
EOQ inventory levels with safety stocks. Safety stocks have been the traditional method of protecting against production disruptions and lost sales due to stockouts.

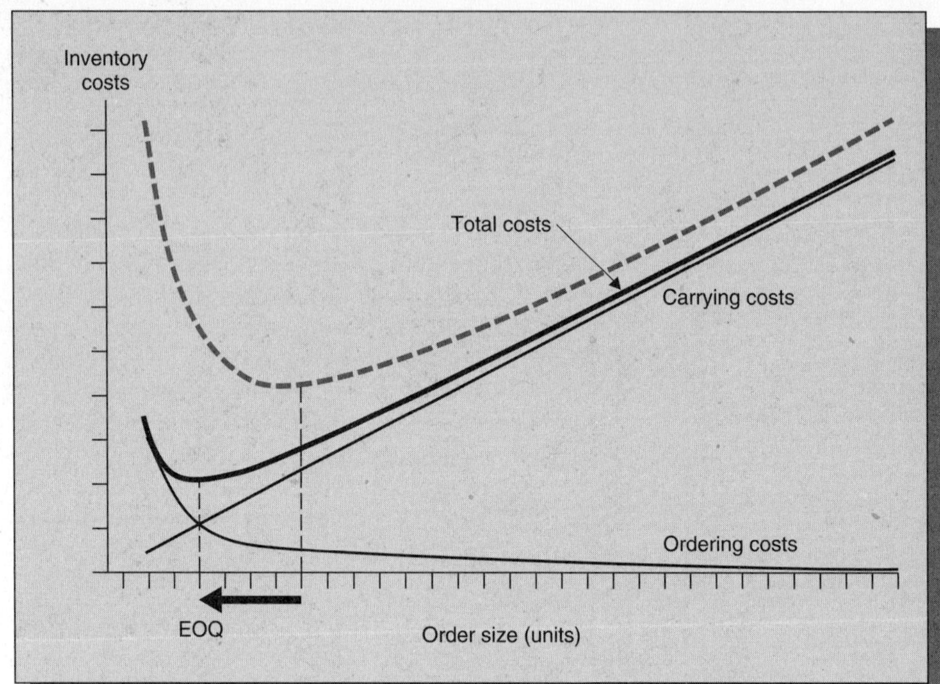

FIGURE 12B.4
The EOQ model including the costs of faulty production. The solution moves to the left, indicating that companies should hold less inventory.

FIGURE 12B.5
The EOQ model including the costs of faulty production and reduced ordering costs. The solution moves farther to the left and approaches zero—i.e., a just-in-time inventory system.

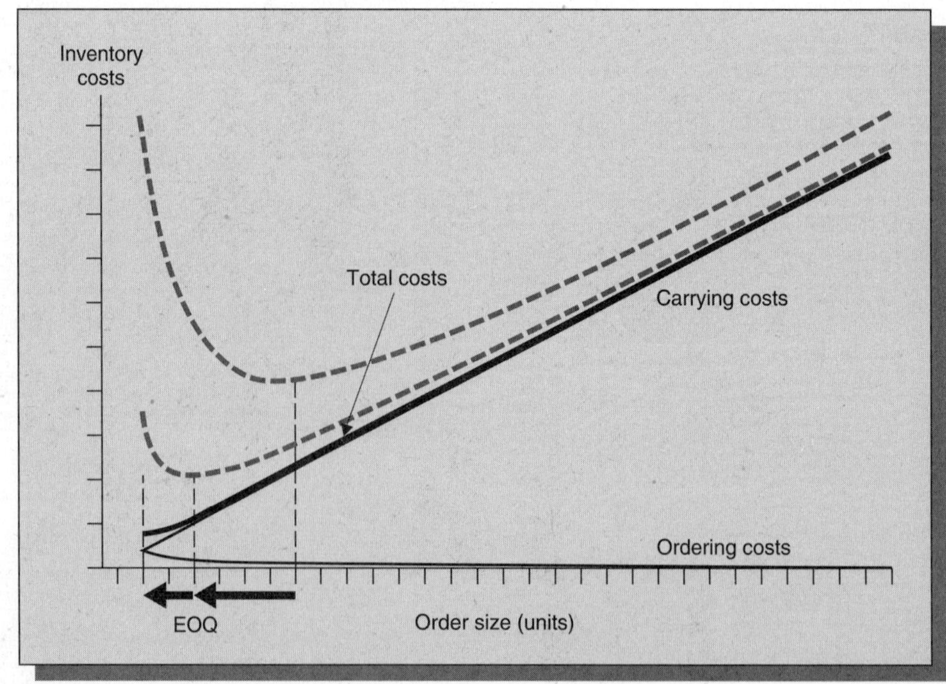

traditionally believed. In Figure 12B.4 we have reproduced the EOQ model but with increased carrying costs. Notice that the solution moves toward a lower inventory balance.

As companies increase their use of single, high-quality suppliers for each inventory item, ordering costs decrease. Evaluating and dealing with multiple suppliers is ended, receiving inspections are eliminated, returns and rework cease, and accounting and record keeping are simplified. In Figure 12B.5, we have again reproduced the EOQ model, this time with both increased carrying costs and lower ordering costs. Once again, the solution moves toward a lower inventory balance. In fact, as illustrated, the EOQ begins to approach zero, consistent with a just-in-time inventory policy.

Problems

1. **(Economic order quantity)** A manufacturing company uses 1,500,000 units of a particular raw material item each year. It costs $35 to place each order and $6 per year to store each unit. Using the EOQ model, calculate the:
   a. EOQ
   b. Average inventory balance
   c. Number of orders per year
   d. Order frequency
2. **(Economic order quantity)** A hardware wholesaler sells 400,000 of a particular bolt every year. It costs $55 to place each order with the manufacturer and $0.01 per year to store each bolt. Using the EOQ model, calculate the:
   a. EOQ
   b. Average inventory balance
   c. Number of orders per year
   d. Order frequency
3. **(EOQ—sensitivity)** A manufacturing company pays $75 to place an order and $3.50 per year to store each unit of raw material. Find the EOQ if usage is:
   a. 100,000 units per year
   b. 200,000 units per year
   c. 400,000 units per year
   d. 800,000 units per year
4. **(EOQ—sensitivity)** A merchandising company sells 250,000 of a certain product each year. Find the EOQ if:
   a. Ordering cost is $50 and annual carrying cost is $4
   b. Ordering cost is $50 and annual carrying cost is $8
   c. Ordering cost is $100 and annual carrying cost is $4
   d. Ordering cost is $100 and annual carrying cost is $8
5. **(EOQ—sensitivity)** A manufacturing company that is implementing quality management is discovering that its carrying costs for a particular item of raw material are higher than previously thought. Each year the company purchases 50,000 units at an ordering cost of $80. Find the EOQ if the firm's estimate of its carrying costs becomes:
   a. $3
   b. $6
   c. $9
   d. $12
6. **(EOQ—sensitivity)** A merchandising company that is implementing quality management is moving to a single-source supplier for a particular inventory item. Each year the company purchases 120,000 units which cost $5 each per year to carry. Find the EOQ if the firm's ordering costs decline to:
   a. $65
   b. $45
   c. $25
   d. $5

PART V MAKING PROCESS DECISIONS

In Part V we look at process decisions, decisions about how the finance organization does its work. We focus on business processes which affect financial managing and which financial managers can affect. The goal is to identify, analyze, and improve these processes. Improving financial and other organizational processes is becoming an increasingly important part of financial managing. And the tools and techniques of quality management that have been used so successfully in manufacturing, marketing, personnel, etc., are just as applicable in finance.

Chapter 13 explores understanding financial processes. We define a work process and distinguish the tasks of managing and improving financial processes from other financial managing activities. We identify financial processes focused on both internal and external customers, and introduce ways to depict the nature of these processes, describe how they transform inputs to outputs, and measure their performance.

Chapter 14 discusses how financial processes may be improved. We identify key factors that enable revolutionary rates of improvement in any process. We then describe three sets of quality management tools and apply them to financial processes. The chapter concludes with examples of how such approaches have been used by leading companies to make significant improvements in their financial processes. Appendix 14A presents the basic analytic tools and Appendix 14B summarizes a set of behavioral tools for process improvement.

CHAPTER 13
RECOGNIZING AND UNDERSTANDING FINANCIAL PROCESSES[1]

Bill Librasco was getting into the flow of his argument now. Looking at Jan Baxter and Hamid Allarani with a smile, he started what they all called a "patented Librasco lecture." "Look, I know we have to get more done with less in finance just as in the rest of the company. But quality management is not what we need. It may be a good idea to do that stuff elsewhere in the company, I really don't know, but we can't do it in finance.

"First, we don't produce widgets here. We produce decisions, and advice, and consultation . . . and we catch some errors and make sure other departments don't get sloppy. But the finance department is not a factory and finance people aren't like factory workers. Even if we could figure out a way to apply a few of the concepts and tools here, we couldn't get our people to use them. We are more skeptical, better educated, and more professional—not the type of folks who do that kind of stuff.

"And, we don't have the time. We have more important things to do than go to classes on how to 'empower' a team to move the water cooler to a place that makes everyone happier. For example, our boss took it in the ear last night about the increase in receivables. I have to be on the phone most of today to collect some of the overdue bills. Now *that's* worth a lot to the company! So,

---

[1] **Acknowledgment:** This chapter draws heavily on the work of members of the Juran Institute whose assistance is gratefully acknowledged.

let's not waste our time trying to get finance people to do something impossible that they don't want to do and that would be trivial even if they did it."

As Bill took a deep breath, Jan and Hamid laughed and applauded quietly. When Bill started laughing too, Jan turned to Hamid and said, "You win again. I thought he'd be a quick learner because he's so smart. But you were right; all through this conversation he's been using his brains to prove it can't be done, rather than trying to figure out how it can be done." Turning away, with a twinkle in her eye, she said to Hamid: "Let's go find someone to work with who isn't as smart as Bill and hasn't yet figured out why it can't be done."

They had taken only half of a step to leave before Bill said, "Okay, you two. You've hooked me again. What are the details of the project you want me to volunteer for *this* time! But make it brief, I really do have to collect some receivables to get the heat off *our* boss."

The project Bill will eventually volunteer for will be one that many other financial managers have been undertaking in the last few years: to figure out how to accomplish a great deal more useful work with fewer resources. Many will look at systematic quality management as one possible approach. They may do so because other parts of their companies are achieving successes using such approaches. Or they may do so because they recognize that finance has many processes, and one of the fundamental building blocks of quality management is process improvement. However, Bill and others will not be excited about the opportunity to improve finance's processes until they realize that finance has processes and that improving processes is an excellent way to do more with less.

For Bill and many others, the first step in improving finance's processes is to recognize that finance—like all the rest of the organization *does have processes.* This chapter looks at recognizing and understanding financial processes. We will follow Bill, Jan, and Hamid as they investigate how a focus on processes can help their company with its receivables problem. In the next chapter we will see how the team can improve the process in which the receivables problem is embedded.

Key Points You Should Learn from This Chapter

After reading this chapter you should be able to:

- Define a work process and distinguish the tasks of managing and improving financial processes from the other financial managing tasks.
- Describe and give examples of five groups of external-customer-focused financial processes and two groups of internal-customer-focused financial processes.
- Use three concepts to describe the nature of financial processes and five steps to describe how a financial process transforms inputs into outputs.
- Identify five concepts useful in measuring process performance and describe two other attributes of well-designed processes.

Introductory Concepts—Financial Processes

Bill Librasco is not alone in being slow to recognize that finance has processes of its own. However, when he thinks for a moment about the definition of a process, he may discover many financial processes around him: billing, cash management, making investment decisions, writing checks, closing the corporate books, and even collecting accounts receivable.

work process—a series of work activities intended to produce a specific result

We will define a **work process** as "a series of work activities intended to produce a specific result." A somewhat more rigorous definition is: "a series of definable, predictable, and repeatable work activities, consisting of people, equipment, procedures, and material, organized to produce a specific result."[2] We will use the words *process* and *work process* interchangeably. Each company has a number of major business processes, such as order fulfillment and working capital management, and many subprocesses that make up each major business process, such as the invoicing, shipping, and collections subprocesses of the order fulfillment process. When effectively designed and integrated these processes and their component subprocesses produce an effective **business system:** "a collection of integrated work processes that constitute an entire business organization."[3]

business system—the set of integrated and overlapping work processes that constitute an entire business organization

Figure 13.1[4] illustrates a business (or any other) process. The process is composed of a series of activities and subprocesses with inputs from a supplier and outputs to a customer. The dotted lines show two sets of feedback loops. The larger ones, on the left and right of the diagram, are labeled "customer requirements and satisfaction." They represent information about what customers actually want and how satisfied they are with the products and services provided by the process—how well the process meets or exceeds customer requirements. The second, smaller feedback loops in the diagram are labeled "results." These are the actual products or services provided by the process.

Figure 13.1 calls attention to two important outcomes of a process: the actual products and services produced and the satisfaction (or dissatisfaction) the products and services create when used by the customer. Recently, many financial managers have become less willing to assume that finance's processes are producing exactly the services and financial products their customers need and are much more willing to investigate how effective those products and services are in meeting the needs of finance's customers.[5]

---

[2] **Reference:** *American Express Quality Leadership Glossary.* (New York: American Express Company, Sept. 1992), p. 6.

[3] **Reference:** A rich discussion of the business and other organizational systems is given in Steven Cavaleri and Krzysztof Obloj, *Management Systems: A Global Prospective* (Belmont, Calif.: Wadsworth, 1993), p. 13.

[4] **Source:** Adapted, with adjustments, from *Business Process Quality Management* (Wilton, Conn.: The Juran Institute, 1993). Used with permission.

[5] **Elaboration:** The feedback loops in Figure 13.1 can be interpreted in terms used by some influential quality-management professionals. The customer requirements part of the customer requirements and satisfaction feedback loop is called "the voice of the customer." The feedback loop dealing with the results of the process is called "the voice of the process." The extent to which these two voices coincide determines customer satisfaction. See William W. Scherkenbach, *Deming's Road to Continual Improvement* (Knoxville, Tenn.: SPC Press, 1991).

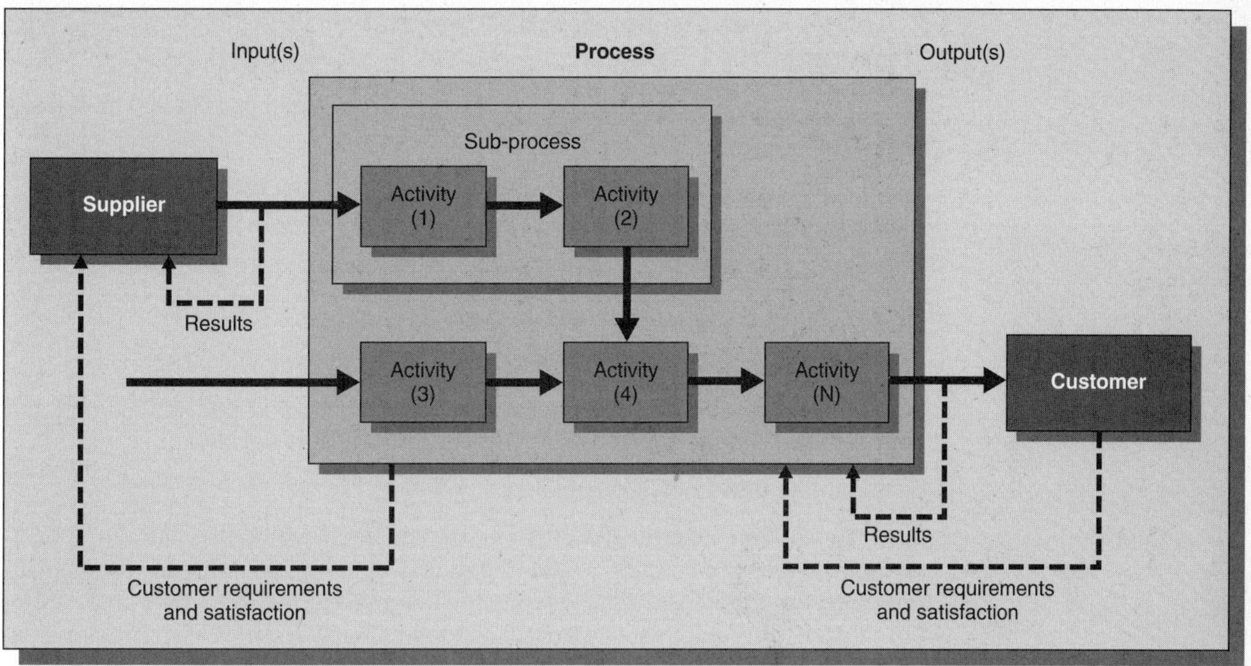

FIGURE 13.1
A business process. Process activities transform inputs from suppliers into outputs for customers.

1. Two Themes

One major theme of this chapter and the next is the similarity of financial processes and other organizational processes. Financial processes are similar to production processes, marketing processes, research and development processes, personnel processes—and even to legal processes. The similarity of these processes, once it is recognized, provides a useful vehicle for helping members of different departments and functions work together on shared process problems. It also makes a uniform language for describing and understanding processes possible and useful.

A second major theme is the usefulness of quality-management tools in improving financial processes. Finance's processes, purposes, and members are similar enough to those of the rest of the company to enable it to use the same quality-management approaches that work elsewhere in the organization. Of course, finance does have its own unique aspects; however, the similarities are large enough to enable finance to use approaches like the ones that work elsewhere. Therefore, process improvements achieved in other parts of the organization may provide useful models for finance, and much of what we say in this chapter and the next about recognizing, understanding, and improving financial processes will also be true for other organizational processes.

2. An Increasingly Important Financial Management Task

In Chapter 1, we discussed five major financial management tasks. Three tasks emphasize analysis and decision making:

1. Obtaining financing and selecting long-term investments
2. Managing day-to-day financial flows
3. Balancing the risks and returns faced by the firm and its stakeholders.

One task emphasizes study, analysis, and advice:

4. Serving as a resource about financial markets and sources of financing.

The fifth task also involves considerable study, analysis, and decision making, but it emphasizes two new dimensions—operations and improvement:

5. Operating and improving financial processes.

This fifth task can be understood by viewing the finance function as "a little business within a larger business." Like the overall organization, finance receives inputs from suppliers inside and outside the company, adds value by transforming those inputs, and delivers its work to customers. Recently, increased pressures on organizations to improve their competitiveness have led them to look much more carefully at how finance runs its own business and to look at ways for finance to increase its contributions while lowering its costs.

Although improving its own processes has always been an important part of finance's work and a key way to do more with less, it has frequently not been given high priority by finance and other organizational members. This low priority came about in part because many finance people, like Bill, were not aware of the processes around them, so they were not likely to think in terms of improving them. It also came about because few finance members had the tools to make significant, sustainable improvements in financial and other processes.

3. Two Supporting Tasks

Finance professionals are involved in two other tasks that support the five listed. These tasks—"distributing" the tools of finance and working on cross-functional teams—are so deeply embedded in finance's other tasks that they are not likely to be thought of as distinct activities. As a result they are easily overlooked. We mention them separately at this point because they are becoming increasingly visible and important as finance strives to increase its contributions to the total organization.

In pursuit of higher levels of achievement with fewer resources, finance members are spending more of their time developing ways of making financial management tools available to other organizational members and coaching and training them in the use of those techniques. Effectively, they are distributing the tools of finance throughout the organization, enabling other parts of the organization to do some of the work traditionally performed by finance. They are also working in teams composed of members from many parts of the organization (cross-func-

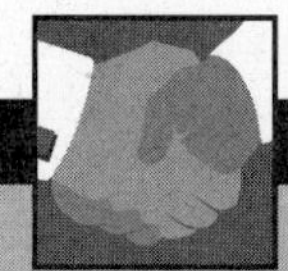

SERVING FINANCE'S CUSTOMERS

The Evolving Internal Audit Process at Gulf Canada Resources

The internal audit staff at Gulf Canada Resources, Ltd., a Canadian oil and gas producer with annual revenues of about $1 billion, has achieved considerable success with a process called "control self-assessment" which seeks to avoid win/lose gamesmanship. Rather than relying on the audit staff to find all the areas for improvement in the organizational units that are being audited, the staff now spends much of its time training members of the local units on methods for assessing their own control environment. Members of the unit being audited evaluate and seek areas for improvement in their own managerial, financial, and information systems. In the first three years that the new self-assessment process was in place, it uncovered far more control issues—opportunities for improvements in the control environment—than in the three preceding years, when traditional auditing methods had been used. The seriousness of the issues identified was also greater. The self-assessment process was catching more and bigger fish than the expert auditors had been able to do working in the traditional manner. Because the auditors are now being seen more as coaches and partners than as police officers, judges, and juries rolled into one, they are far more effective than before in protecting the company from losses and reducing the costs of operating the business.

Reference: P. G. Makosz and B. W. McCuaig, "Ripe for a Renaissance." *Internal Auditor* (Dec. 1990): 43–49.

tional teams) to improve the integration of financial processes and information systems with the organization's other work processes.[6]

One place where distributed finance and working on cross-functional teams are visibly improving financial processes is in internal audit, a specialized unit within the finance function. Usually performed by individuals with strong accounting backgrounds, internal auditing involves periodic evaluation of an organization's managerial, financial, and information systems to assure that they are designed and implemented effectively to achieve corporate objectives. A traditional challenge in the audit process has been to avoid a win-lose relationship between the auditors and the parts of the company being audited. It is easy for a relationship to develop in which the auditors are heroes only if they find something wrong and the auditees are heroes only when the auditors cannot find areas to criticize. The temptation can be strong to hide problems from the auditors, in hopes of fixing them before the next audit. All too frequently, such covered-up problems fester and worsen rather than being corrected. And even if they are corrected, it is

[6] **Reference:** For a very interesting discussion of changes in financial management roles see Patrick J. Keating and Stephen F. Jablonsky, *Changing Roles of Financial Management: Getting Close to the Business* (Morristown, N.J.: Financial Executives Research Foundation, 1990). These changing roles are also discussed in the context of quality management in James A.F. Stoner and Frank M. Werner, *Finance in the Quality Revolution* (Morristown, N.J.: Financial Executives Research Foundation, 1993, and *Managing Finance for Quality* (Milwaukee: Quality Press and Morristown, NJ: Financial Executives Research Foundation, 1994).

difficult to learn from them and share the learning around the organization since both their existence and cure must be kept secret. Distributing finance expertise throughout the organization and applying it in the context of cross-functional teams is allowing some companies to change the dynamics of the auditor/auditee relationship with dramatic results.

Recognizing Financial Processes

If Jan and Hamid decide to start Bill's "process education" by looking for places where finance has its own processes, they might well start where we started with this book. Figure 13.2, which also appeared as Figure 1.1, suggests a whole set of financial processes involving external customers and suppliers.

FIGURE 13.2
Money flows in a business. Each flow of money or financial data is part of a financial process.

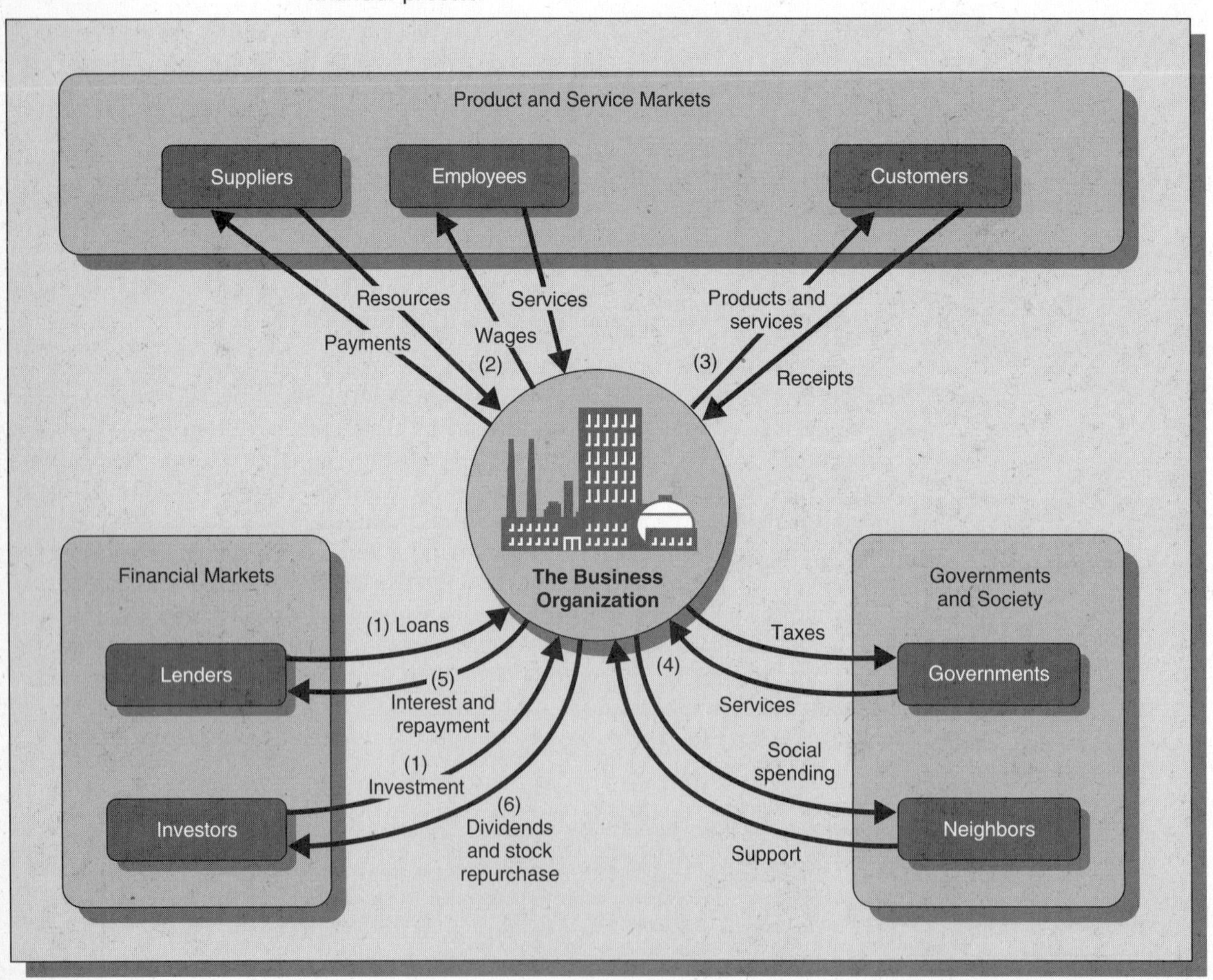

1. Processes with External Customers or Suppliers

Wherever money or financial data are exchanged between the organization and its outside stakeholders, a financial process exists. Financial processes directly visible to individuals and other entities outside the formal boundaries of the organization include processes for handling transactions with: (1) customers, (2) suppliers, (3) governments and local communities, (4) lenders, and (5) investors.

(Ultimate external) customers Financial processes with the organization's ultimate external customers include such activities as preparing, issuing, and collecting bills; extending credit; and providing cost estimates.

External suppliers Financial processes with the organization's external suppliers include verifying the accuracy of invoices and paying the bills, arranging for credit from suppliers or perhaps extending credit to them, and evaluating bids and cost estimates.

Governments and local communities Financial processes with governments include paying taxes, providing financial information, and reporting on compliance with regulations. Financial processes with local communities include contributing to educational, charitable, and social activities.

Lenders Financial processes with lenders include borrowing, servicing and repaying debt, arranging stand-by credit facilities, and obtaining trade financing.

Investors Financial processes with equity investors include paying dividends; issuing, transferring, and retiring equity shares; and reporting to shareholders and analysts on the organization's past and likely future competitive and financial performance.

2. Processes with Internal Customers or Suppliers

In addition to financial processes involving external customers and suppliers, finance is also involved in a great many processes whose customers and suppliers are members of the organization—internal customers and suppliers. Figure 13.3 lists some of those processes. The figure shows two major categories of financial processes serving internal customers and suppliers. The first are processes whose customers are the organization's employees. The second are processes whose customers and suppliers are units of the organization that need finance's contributions to conduct the organization's business.

Employee-focused processes Financial processes directed toward the organization's employees include the calculation and payment of normal compensation, commissions, overtime, and special incentive bonuses if those are used; withholding and payment of employee-related taxes, dues, insurance, health care costs and other contributions; investment in and management of pension funds; and payment of retirement benefits.

Customer/Supplier	Processes Dealing with:
	Customers are Employees
Employees	base compensation, bonuses, tax withholding, dues, insurance deductions, pension fund investments and management, retirement payments
	Customers are Other Organizational Units
International units	foreign exchange transactions for investments, sales and purchases across borders, dividend repatriation, investment project analysis, international capital allocations, operating budgets
Domestic divisions	investment project analysis, capital allocations, divisional performance evaluation criteria, divisional performance compensation arrangements and calculations
Marketing	sales plans and budgets, sales commission arrangements and calculations, pricing analysis
Production/operations	capital investment analysis, capital allocations, operating plans and budgets
Human resources	compensation plans and budgets; analyses of retirement, insurance, health care costs
Corporate secretary	dividend payments and policies, investor relations

FIGURE 13.3
Typical financial processes involving finance's internal customers and suppliers. A large portion of financial managing deals with activities internal to the company.

Processes supporting the day-to-day management of the organization Financial processes are also a part of almost all of the internal management processes used to conduct the organization's business. These activities include investment project evaluation, sales planning and budgeting, long-range and strategic planning, human resource budgeting, internal auditing, working with outside auditors, and setting and measuring objectives.

Understanding Financial Processes

Once a process becomes visible, there are a series of useful concepts for describing it, for understanding how it functions—including its "results"—and for improving it. In this section, we divide these concepts into two categories: (1) concepts for describing the nature of a process, and (2) concepts for describing what a process does. In the last major section of this chapter, we will discuss ways of measuring the performance of financial and other processes.

1. Describing the Nature of a Process

The concepts "process boundary," "adding value," and "supplier-processor-customer" roles are helpful in recognizing that a process exists and in seeing the nature of a specific process.

When Bill's team members start thinking of the "receivables problem" as occurring in a financial process, they will very quickly find themselves asking, "Where does the receivables process begin and where does it end?" They are asking about the boundaries of the process.

process boundary—the line separating a process from other business activities

The **boundary of a process** is the conceptual line drawn for a specific purpose that distinguishes what is part of the process from what is not part of it. The phrase, *for a specific purpose,* is very important in understanding the concept of process boundary. For most processes, the boundary can be drawn in many logical places. Should we consider the process of collecting a receivable to begin with picking up the phone to call the customer about an overdue account? Or should it begin with reviewing the entire pile of overdue accounts to decide which one to call? Or perhaps we should go back much, much further and start where the invoice is sent to the customer, or even before the sale is made. The answer is frequently not obvious, and *the purpose for which the process is being defined is the key to drawing the boundary.*

"Gee," said Hamid. "When we started to draw the process boundaries around collecting receivables, I thought the answer was clear. The process starts when the customer fails to pay on time. But now that does not seem at all like a good way to look at things. The more we try to draw a picture of the collectibles process, the further back I want to go."

adding value—making the output of a process worth more for its customers

Adding value is a phrase used to describe those activities performed within a process that make the resulting product or service of greater value to the process customer. If we define our receivables collection process to begin far enough back to include issuing the invoice, then one value-added step is easy to spot. Correctly calculating the cost of the products shipped and generating a simple, easy-to-read invoice add value for final customers by simplifying their work. Well-prepared invoices allow customers to make payment without having to obtain clarification about ambiguous invoice items or corrections of erroneous ones. They avoid delays required to resolve errors and clarify confusions.

customer-processor-supplier—the three simultaneous roles played by everyone involved in a process

If Bill's team members start drawing a picture of the receivables process, using Figure 13.1 as a guide, they will quickly see three roles played by the people involved. Each member of a process can be looked at as being simultaneously a **customer-processor-supplier.** For example, the person in Bill's receivables collection group who picks up the phone to call a customer is:

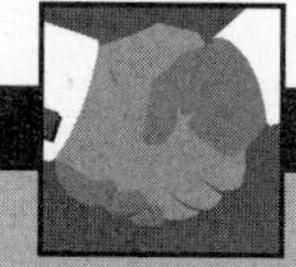

SERVING FINANCE'S CUSTOMERS

Adding Value to the Receivables Process at Hewlett-Packard

In 1988 the Hewlett-Packard Corporation discovered it had a serious problem with its accounts receivable. Many customers were not paying their bills promptly, and the balance of overdue accounts had skyrocketed. The first thought of HP's finance organization was to press customers to make their payments. Instead, a quality team worked with customers to understand how and why the receivables process had broken down. One of the team's findings was that HP's invoices were difficult to read and sometimes wrong. Today, HP sends its customers clear and accurate invoices that make it easy to pay.

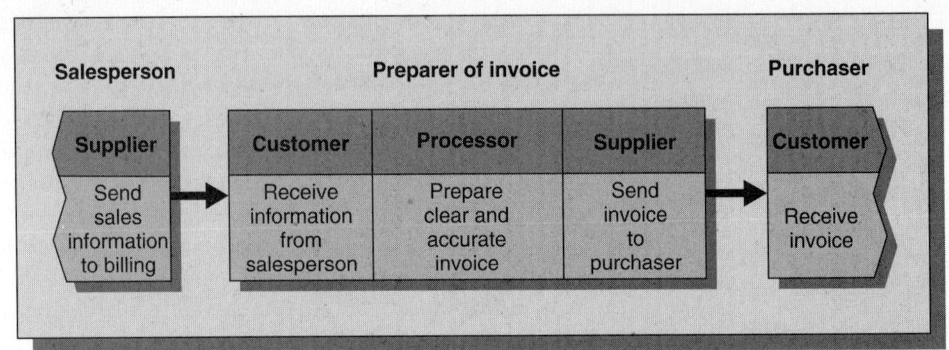

FIGURE 13.4
The three roles in a process. Each participant is simultaneously a customer, processor, and supplier.

1. A customer of the preceding subprocess or task.
2. A processor adding value by completing a task.
3. A supplier to a subsequent subprocess or task.[7]

Figure 13.4 illustrates the three roles for the person who issues invoices. We have already described who the customer of the invoicing process might be (the purchaser of the goods) and how value could be added (by preparing a clear and accurate invoice). The salesperson who provides information on the customer and details of the sale would be a supplier to the invoicing process.

There might be more than one supplier or customer, of course, and value might be added in a number of ways. For example, another supplier might be a stock clerk who verifies that the goods are on hand before the invoice is prepared; value might be added by dispatching the invoice by EDI (electronic data interchange), and other customers might include a shipping clerk who will dispatch the goods once a copy of the invoice is received by the shipping department.

Illustrating these concepts is easy if we set the boundaries of the process so broadly that we can select a clear example. However, if we choose narrow boundaries to focus on a small process (really a subprocess) we might have some problem identifying where value is added. For example, what about Bill when he calls customers about overdue invoices? Where is the value added? That is a good question, and we will return to it shortly.

2. Describing What a Process Does

Processes convert inputs into outputs. One approach to describing the important elements of how a process does so consists of five steps: (1) describing the product or service produced, (2) specifying the customer(s), (3) specifying the suppliers and their inputs, (4) describing each task within the process, the sequences of tasks, and who performs each one, and (5) describing the characteristics of satis-

[7] **Reference:** *Total Quality Management: A Practical Guide* (Wilton, Conn.: The Juran Institute, 1991) pp. 1-11–1-15.

factory inputs and outputs of the process. These steps are described below and illustrated for the process investigation stimulated by Bill Librasco's "receivables collection problem."

Describing the product or service If Bill's team focuses very narrowly on the activity of collecting the overdue receivables, the team might describe the products of the collection process as either "a deposited payment for the invoice" or a "written-off invoice." These two definitions of the products are shown in the *very* abbreviated diagram of the collection process in Figure 13.5. In some situations, that narrow a focus may be appropriate. However, a focus that takes a more encompassing view of the process—with process boundaries that include more activities—is frequently more useful.

If they take a broader view, the team might see the process as producing "payments for sales." In this perspective, the process includes issuing the original invoices, collecting most of them on time without incident, and dealing with some that are not paid in a timely manner. Overdue receivables would be viewed as some form of "defect" requiring **rework,** a frequently used term in studying and improving processes. The term *rework* suggests a useful way of looking at the question of how Bill is adding value when he calls customers about overdue invoices. Bill is doing rework because other things were not done right the first time by Bill's company or the customer's. The job may be necessary, but it is not adding value in the sense we defined earlier. If this task could be eliminated by improving the process, everyone—especially the customer—would be more satisfied.

rework—an activity performed to correct an error or omission in an earlier stage of a work process

As some companies have recognized that problems in executing financial transactions have cost them customers, revenues, and profits, improving financial processes has become a higher-priority part of finance's work. Reducing or eliminating rework and other nonvalue-adding activities in financial processes has become one of the more exciting challenges for members of finance.

FIGURE 13.5
The collection process. In this flow chart, the product of the process is defined as a collected or written-off receivable.

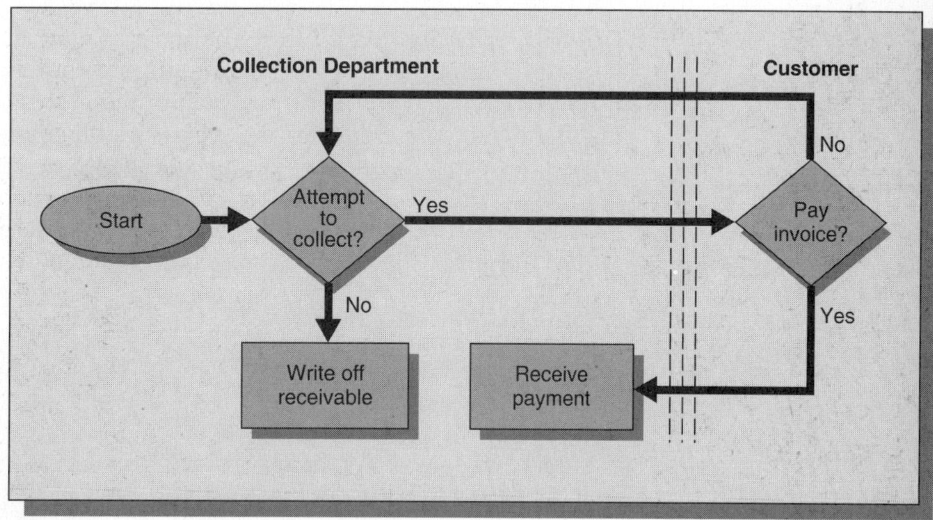

Specifying customer(s) Customers of the collection process could include many individuals and entities. In describing the process, Bill's team will certainly identify the actual buyer of the product or service who, hopefully, pays the invoice. The treasury function of Bill's company is also a customer when it deposits the check received in payment. Other customers could include a supplier in a new role. For example, the salesperson who made the sale may receive information on how smoothly or roughly the payment process went. The credit analyst who keeps records on payment performance and makes decisions on extending credit on future sales would be another customer.

> As they kept trying to describe the collection process, Jan started agreeing more and more with Hamid about the process boundaries: "I find that I keep wanting to add new internal customers to the process as we understand it better—treasury, sales, credit.
>
> "And I keep seeing how our external customers differ. Not all customers who have not paid are the same. There are many reasons for not paying, and some of them seem to be our fault."

Identifying suppliers and inputs By asking the question, "Who are the suppliers?" the team may start identifying others not yet shown in Figure 13.5. For example, the team might decide that the sales department should be shown as a process supplier—because accurate sales information is necessary for preparing accurate invoices. That thought might well lead to the decision that it is desirable to include the group that prepares the invoice explicitly in the diagram and also to include the treasury function, which receives and deposits payment for the invoice. Figure 13.6 expands the collection process a bit further to show these additional suppliers and customers of the process. If the team chooses to include these new actors in the process it is studying, it will be taking a step toward a more encompassing process definition—looking at a sales payment or an order fulfillment process rather than at an overdue invoice collection process.

Describing tasks As the team continues its work describing the process, it may keep discovering steps, actors, and products within the process that it had not anticipated. Each activity performed within the process must be described, including identifying who performs the activity and the order in which it is performed. Figure 13.7 expands one step of the collection process, the step identified in Figure 13.6 as "make collection effort," to illustrate how it might be described in a little more detail. Not surprisingly, the expansion of what looks like a single step in Figure 13.6 reveals a series of connections involving other actors in Figure 13.7.

> Over a two-month period, the team members succeeded in finding time to work on the project for quite a few hours while also accomplishing their normal work. Getting together at lunch, Bill tried to sum up their progress: "I think we have something here, but it's sure not as simple as we thought. We keep finding that the collection process is a lot more than

picking up a phone and calling someone. And people are not paying their invoices for a lot more reasons than shortage of cash. Weaknesses in the order fulfillment process throughout our company are significant contributors to the problem.

"I think looking only at the process of collections would be missing the boat. We need a bigger vision, a better understanding of process analysis, and more resources and time. Let's ask for them and do the job right. Agreed?"

Describing satisfactory inputs and outputs The team might identify three satisfactory products of the sales payment process. One would be a clearly written, accurate invoice showing the exact items shipped and the date of shipment with agreed terms of sale. The second would be a shipping confirmation—showing when the items were shipped—that arrives at the customer's purchasing office by EDI or by fax within 30 minutes of actual shipment. The third would be a check in the proper amount arriving at the corporate billing office within the time specified in the terms of sale. One satisfactory input might be an accurately

FIGURE 13.6
The collection process expanded. The sales and invoicing departments are suppliers, and treasury is another customer of the process.

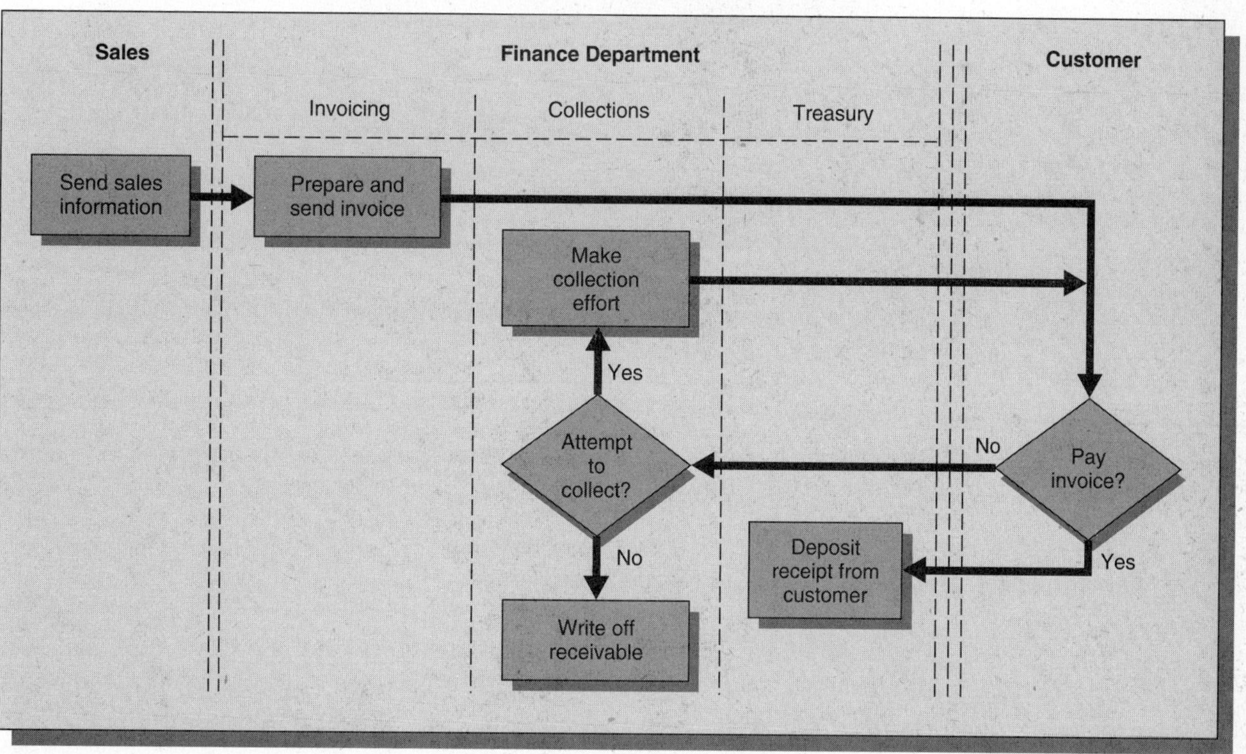

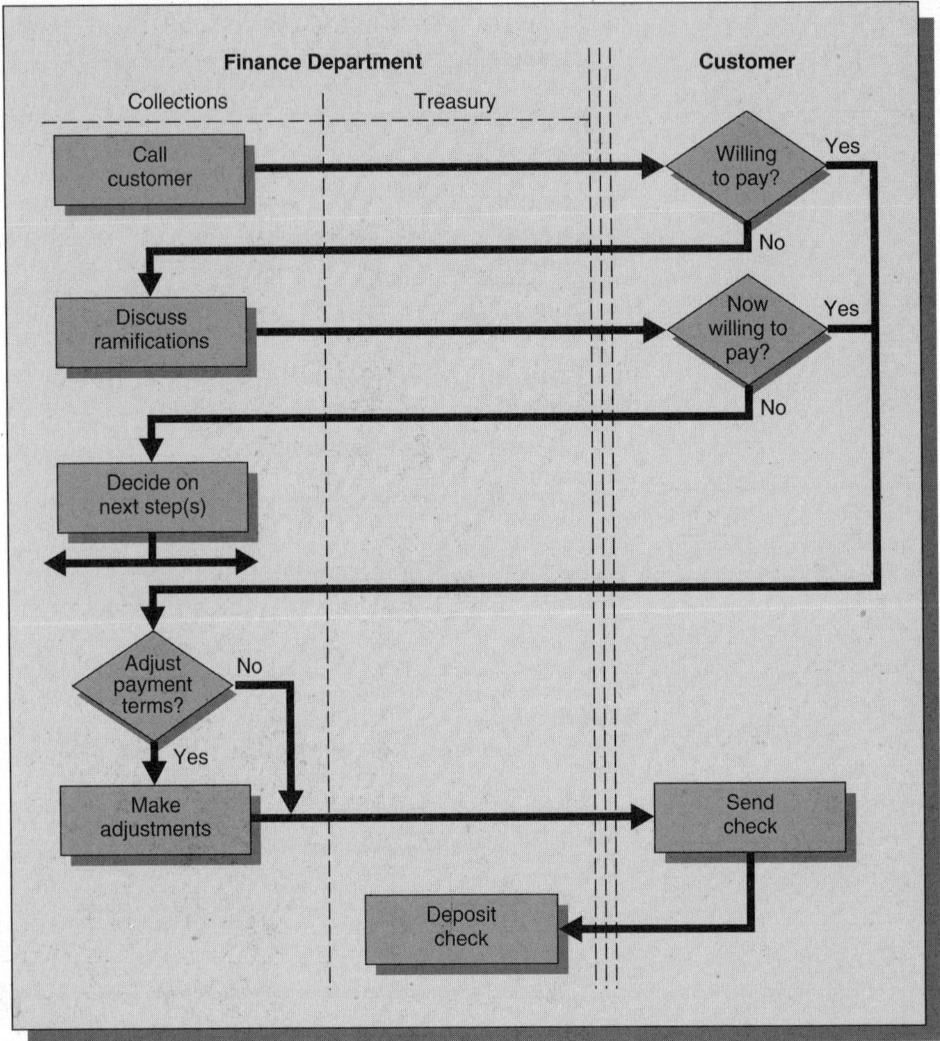

FIGURE 13.7
One step of the collection process further expanded. Each process task may consist of many subtasks.

completed statement of sales information prepared by the salesperson and forwarded to finance's invoicing department on the day of sale.

Measuring Financial Process Performance

In addition to developing a diagram of the sales payment process, Bill's team will also want to collect data on the performance of the process. We will look at a variety of process performance dimensions—five that are frequently measured (effectiveness, efficiency, cycle time, stability, and capability), and two more that are also important but by their nature difficult to measure (adaptability and robustness).

1. Effectiveness and Efficiency

Bill's team may find it useful to distinguish between performance measures that focus on the effectiveness of the process and those that deal with the efficiency of the process. This distinction has long been emphasized by the well-known management writer, teacher, and consultant, Peter Drucker. Drucker describes *effective* as "doing the right things," and *efficient* as "doing things right."

The first type of measure captures how well the process satisfies its customers—the people or organizations the process is intended to serve. The second type of measure looks at how well the process uses resources.

This distinction enables us to make a point dear to the heart of many managers: effectiveness is more important than efficiency. A popular quote from Peter Drucker is that "the greatest danger is getting better and better at doing that which should not be done at all." It is important to emphasize the pre-eminence of effectiveness because early attempts to improve processes sometimes focus too heavily on doing things better, losing sight of whether those things should be done in the first place. Improving processes just for the sake of improving them is not likely to be the best way to spend time and money.

2. Measures of Process Effectiveness

There are two dimensions of process effectiveness: the performance of the process in producing what it is supposed to produce and its performance in meeting and exceeding customer expectations—producing what the customer wants. The former type of measurement is frequently referred to as "conformance to specifications" and the latter as "conformance to requirements." Obviously, the latter measure is the more important one, but the former is also necessary and important.

Conformance to specifications The first set of measures determines whether the process is doing what it is intended to do. Are invoices paid by the twentieth day after receipt, were investment projects evaluated with the correct cost of capital, have the financial forecasts used the agreed-upon set of assumptions about economic growth rates and price inflation? These measures are collectible at the end of the process when the "final product or service" is available for inspection. Similar measures are also collectible "inside the process" at the end of each activity or subprocess.

Customer satisfaction—conformance to requirements Measures of customer satisfaction seek to determine how well a product or service meets or exceeds customer expectations. These measures are often based on customer surveys, which ask questions about reactions to the company's products and services. Many nonsurvey measures of customer satisfaction are also available, such as customer complaints, product or service rejections by customers, decline in repeat sales to established customers, and so on.

3. Measures of Process Efficiency

Measures of process efficiency assess the success of the process in meeting customer needs at low cost. Indicators of process efficiency include the total resources used in achieving a specific result, the amount of time in which useful work is actually done (value added time) divided by total time to complete the process, and many others. Most such measures are logical and traditional in the sense of dividing easily recognized outputs by easily recognized inputs and do not require explanation. One measure, "cost of poor quality," is an unusual one and does require discussion.

cost of poor quality—the sum of all unnecessary costs due to process and product quality being less than perfect

The **cost of poor quality** is a concept that has played a significant role in the history of quality management and one of particular interest to financial managers. Conceptually, the cost of poor quality is the total of all costs that are incurred because the product or service is less than perfect. These costs have three components: appraisal, internal failure, and external failure costs. Appraisal costs are the inspection costs incurred to determine if products and services conform to design specifications (if products were always perfect, they would not need to be inspected). Internal failure costs are the costs of correcting defects discovered before the products or services have reached the customer. Finally, external failure costs are the costs associated with defective products or services that are delivered to the customer.[8]

This last category, external failure costs, includes those that are normally borne by the producer, such as warranty costs, refunds, complaint adjustments, and costs of handling returns and replacements. However, external costs also include some the producer may never learn about, such as failures of the product or service that turn satisfied customers into ex-customers or failures that create problems for customers that they cannot trace to a particular cause. This latter category contains costs that quality expert W. Edwards Deming referred to as "the most important (types) of costs—those which are unknown and unknowable."

4. Cycle Time—A Particularly Powerful Measure

The concept of cycle time (the time from start to finish of an activity) was introduced in Chapter 4.[9] Cycle time is a particularly powerful measure because it is frequently tied closely to effectiveness, efficiency, or both.

The close tie between cycle time and effectiveness arises because quick response—short cycle time—is frequently a key component of customer satisfaction. A travel reimbursement paid within 12 hours is much more pleasing to an employee than one made three weeks later. Being served as soon as one walks into the bank is much more likely to be satisfying than waiting 20 minutes in line for a bank teller. One of the reasons companies engage contract manufacturers like Solectron Corporation to produce products for them is the contract manufacturers' ability to produce the items faster than the purchasing companies' own production facilities. The manufacturing departments of the purchasing companies support the

[8] **Elaboration:** The phrase *cost of poor quality* is replacing an earlier phrase, the *cost of quality*, that contained one additional item: prevention costs. Prevention costs are the costs of making sure defects never arise in the first place, for example, the costs incurred in the careful design of a product or process. Both terms continue to be used, but we find the *cost of poor quality* to be more useful and less open to misunderstanding.

[9] **Cross-reference:** See Chapter 4, p. 78.

use of contract manufacturers as a means of satisfying their own internal customers—sales and marketing—as well as the company's external customers. Getting products to the market faster and responding faster to new orders increase their revenues and profitability.

The close tie between cycle time and efficiency arises from the ways dramatic improvements in cycle time are now being achieved in many organizations. When improved cycle time starts with gaining a deep understanding of a process and the customer needs it serves, and is then achieved by redesigning the process to remove nonvalue-added steps and to simplify and error-proof those that remain, faster normally becomes better and cheaper. Processes redesigned in these ways have fewer opportunities for error and normally require fewer resources. Thus they provide the same or better quality at lower cost, achieving greater efficiency. In the next chapter we report how Motorola's finance function reduced the length of time required to consolidate its worldwide financial statements at the end of each month ("closing the books"). In doing so, it also reduced the number of errors in the process and reduced costs. Faster was better and cheaper. (Of course, if reduced cycle time is achieved by having more people work faster and harder in the identical process, the shorter cycle time is likely to be more expensive and more error-prone. It will be less efficient and may well be less effective if increased dissatisfaction from greater errors outweighs increased satisfaction from faster cycle time.)

5. Process Stability

process stability—the variation in the output of a process

Process stability refers to the extent to which a process exhibits low variation in its output—how free it is from the types of "sporadic spikes" shown in Figure 13.8. Bill's team can choose from among a great many possible measures of process performance and stability. The measure chosen in Figure 13.8 is the percentage of invoices not paid on time. (For Bill's company, "on time" might be defined as within 30 days from mailing of the invoice.) Other measures the team might have used are dollars of receivables outstanding and dollar value of invoices paid on time. (In Figure 13.8, the good direction is downward—overdue receivables are treated as defects. Showing improvement as a decline in defects is a common practice in presenting process data.)

natural variation—the random variation inherent in any process

The concept of variation is one of the cornerstones of the global quality revolution.[10] Even when processes are running smoothly and are said to be "in control" or stable, they continue to demonstrate **natural variation** in their outputs. For example, at any given time some purchasers will experience competitive problems, causing them to delay their payments and increasing the number of invoices becoming overdue. For no identifiable reason, a few more customers will have such problems in some months and in other months fewer customers will have those problems. The amounts of overdue accounts receivable will fluctuate accordingly without a predictable pattern.

---

[10] **References:** Good references on variation are: Myron Tribus, "The Germ Theory of Management," ms. undated; Brian L. Joiner and Marie A. Gaudard, "Variation, Management, and W. Edwards Deming." *Quality Progress* (1990) pp. 29–37, and William W. Scherkenbach, *Deming's Road to Continual Improvement* (Knoxville, Tenn.: SPC Press, 1991).

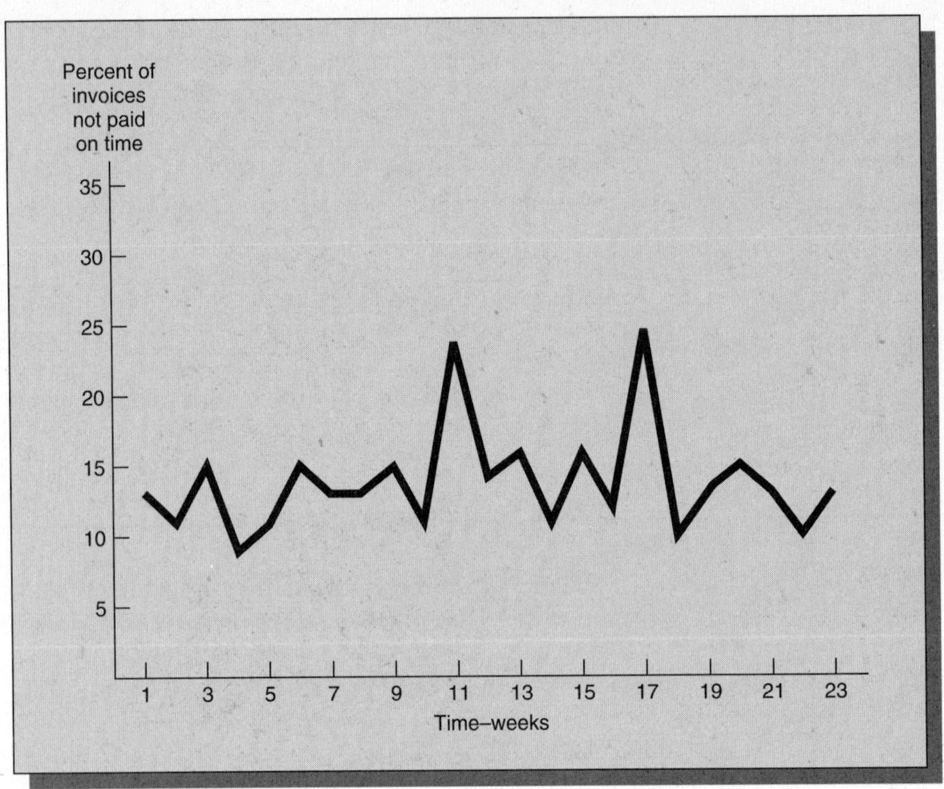

FIGURE 13.8
Process stability. The upward spikes indicate the process is unstable.

However, when a process is not running smoothly—when it is not stable—additional variation occurs from special events. For example, if invoices were incorrectly addressed and delayed in the mail, there would be a surge of overdue payments—even though customers paid promptly after receiving the late invoice. Serious problems in getting service on past sales could cause customers to withhold payments to "get the company's attention" and get the service problem handled. And, of course, a business recession might slow the rate at which customers pay. Each of these three events could cause a "spike" of increased overdue receivables. However, only the first two are within the direct control of the company, and only the first is a problem occurring within the receivables process.

common causes of variation—factors that cause natural variation in a stable process

special causes of variation—factors that cause excessive variation and make a process unstable

The natural variation in outputs of a stable process is said to come entirely from **common causes**—factors inherent in the process. A normal number of clerical errors in calculating invoice dollar amounts, which lead in turn to delays in payment, would be an example of a common cause. Special events, like a new, improperly trained invoicing clerk who calculates invoice values from an out-of-date price list would be an example of a **special cause.** The resulting errors could well lead to an increase in late payments.

At present most companies do not understand the distinction between common causes of variation and special causes. As a result, in most companies much more management time is devoted to "chasing spikes"—finding and correcting errors arising from special causes—rather than to reducing common cause variation—

i.e., improving the process. This relative allocation of effort is supported by the way each problem typically arises: the sporadic spikes of special causes show up as crises needing immediate management attention while the chronic waste from common causes is an everyday occurrence, often accepted as inevitable. Bill's situation at the beginning of the chapter is an example of just such a circumstance—Bill does not have time to study and improve the receivables process because he has to spend time on rework: calling customers to try to collect overdue invoices. When he puts out this fire, the management system is likely to call him to another fire . . . until this one breaks out once again.

6. Process Capability

process capability—how well a process functions under normal operating conditions

Process capability refers to the extent to which a process will yield the intended output under normal operating conditions. For example, Bill's company may be completely satisfied if 80% of its invoices are paid promptly and if the percentage of uncollected invoices is held to 2% a year. If the collection process is able to yield that performance it is said to be capable. Whether or not a process is capable depends not only on the performance of the process but also on the expectations of it. The process in Figure 13.8 is capable if the standard for it is on-time collection of 75% of invoices (25% or fewer are paid late). If the standard is 90% paid on time, the process is not capable.

A major impact of the global quality revolution on finance, as well as on all other parts of companies, is in the definition of process capability. Processes that used to be considered adequate or good or even excellent are now considered inadequate (no longer capable). A company fully satisfied with a book-closing process requiring ten days may consider the process wholly inadequate when it discovers other companies are closing their books in two days at lower costs with fewer errors.

7. Process Adaptability and Robustness

Two additional concepts are useful in understanding process performance: adaptability and robustness. These concepts are somewhat different from the preceding ones because they have more of a "what if" nature. Rather than reporting what is happening on a day-to-day basis, they indicate what might happen if something unusual occurs. However, they are important attributes which financial professionals will attempt to design into a new process or into one that is being improved.

process adaptability—the ease and speed with which a process can be modified

Process adaptability refers to how easily and quickly a process can be adjusted to changing conditions. For example, during tight economic times, an adaptable sales-invoicing-collection process might involve applying more stringent credit standards to potential new customers if financially weak new customers are more likely to default than in normal times. It might simultaneously involve extending more generous payment terms to reliable customers who are likely to survive the difficult times. Or it might respond with a different variation on the same theme: aggressively extending credit to a few targeted new customer prospects who may grow into key long-term customers after the recession passes. A process in which such steps can be taken promptly and smoothly would be adaptable.

process robustness—the ability of a process to meet performance objectives when inputs and operating conditions vary

Process robustness refers to how well a process will continue to meet its stated performance objectives when it is subjected to variations in quality of inputs or operating conditions. For example, a robust collection process might contain a clearly defined training subprocess that reduces the risk that an improperly trained invoicing clerk would make the types of errors noted earlier. It might also have a built-in automatic checking step that alerts the invoicing clerk that the prices being entered on the invoices are not consistent with a file containing the current prices. With such elements, the process might continue to yield high-quality outcomes even when some shocks to the system occur.

Both of these aspects of performance will become apparent at various times when a process is subjected to unusual shocks, but they will not be apparent in the normal day-to-day functioning of the process. They are, however, important factors to consider in understanding, designing, and improving any process.

8. Finance's Role in Measuring Process Performance

Finance members have two major involvements with process performance measures. First, in some companies they have started collecting data from their own internal and external customers on finance's performance in meeting their needs. Second, as the "custodian of the numbers" used in running the business, finance

SERVING FINANCE'S CUSTOMERS

Raising the Visibility of Process Measures at IBM Credit

At IBM Credit Corporation the finance organization plays a leadership role in reporting both traditional financial results and process measures. Each unit of the company is asked to identify two process-related measures, one relating to quality and the other to cycle time, to be included in finance's regular monthly reports. As custodians of the data, finance insures that the information is impartial, accurate, and timely. Today at IBM Credit, process measures are becoming as visible and as important as financial measures.

is beginning to play a vital role in collecting and reporting data from external and internal customers of others in the organization.

Jan Baxter and Hamid Allarani exchanged amused glances as Bill Librasco collapsed into his chair but kept talking with his usual passion. "I don't know what you two are smiling about. We have been trying for two weeks to get the CFO and her staff to listen to what we have to say about the accounts receivable problem, but I don't think we have moved them one step forward. They simply do not see that the problems come from the process. First they blame the manager and the department, then our customers, and then the sales force. Next they'll probably blame the banks because interest rates are too high, or competitors, or the government. They simply can't see that accounts receivable is a process like any other process. Even the back-of-the-envelope study we did gives good hints on how to improve the process dramatically. Why won't they let us form a team officially and really dig into the process? I'll bet dollars to donuts that the payback period from such a team would be less than six months, and if the IRR is less than 200%, I'll push a peanut with my nose from the CFO's office to the water cooler. Ah, come on now, what are you two laughing at? I'm serious."

Hamid looked at Bill and said: "Hey, don't be so pessimistic. We made good progress the last few months. The whole team learned a lot about the receivables situation, you have become a quality champion—or perhaps I should say a "quality fanatic"—and our boss did promise to go to that seminar on quality in finance. I think she has learned a lot more than you realize. That's not so bad for slipping this extra work into all our regular responsibilities. Look, we even learned that we only need four and a half hours of sleep at night! I declare the project a complete success."

Summary of Key Points

- **Define a work process and distinguish the tasks of managing and improving financial processes from the other financial managing tasks.** A work process is a series of work activities intended to produce a specific result. As organizations adopt modern customer-focused quality-management practices, their finance members spend more time working in teams to improve financial and other organizational processes. In addition, members of finance continue to work on the traditional and continuing financial management tasks: (1) obtaining financing and selecting long-term investments, (2) managing short-term financial flows, (3) balancing risk and returns in daily and longer-term decisions, and (4) serving as a company resource about financial markets and sources of financing.

- **Describe and give examples of five groups of external-customer-focused financial processes and two groups of internal-customer-focused financial processes.** Financial processes focused on individuals and other entities outside the formal boundaries of the organization include processes for handling transactions with (1) customers, (2) suppliers, (3) governmental entities, (4) creditors, and (5) shareholders. Financial transactions with external customers and suppliers include such activities as paying and collecting bills. Transactions with governmental entities include paying taxes. Creditor transactions include borrowing, servicing, and repaying debt. Shareholder transactions include arranging for payment of dividends. Financial processes focused on internal customers include (1) processes related to employees, such as the calculation and payment of normal compensation and bonuses, and (2) processes involving other management activities. Financial processes also are part of almost all of the internal management processes used to conduct the organization's business; one example is evaluating investment projects.

- **Use three concepts to describe the nature of financial processes and five steps to describe how a financial process transforms inputs into outputs.** The boundary of a process is the conceptual line drawn for a specific purpose that distinguishes what is part of the process from what is not part of it. *Adding value* is a phrase used to describe those activities performed within a process that make the resulting product or service of greater value to the ultimate and final consumer of the product or service. The three-part roles of customer-processor-supplier describe each participant in a process as being simultaneously a customer of the preceding subprocess or task, a processor adding value by completing a task, and a supplier to a subsequent subprocess or task. Describing a process involves (1) describing the product or service produced by the process, (2) specifying the customer(s) of the product or service, (3) identifying suppliers who provide inputs to the process and specifying what inputs they provide, (4) describing each of the activities performed within the process and identifying who performs those activities, and (5) describing the characteristics of satisfactory inputs to the process and satisfactory products or services produced by the process.

- **Identify five concepts useful in measuring process performance, and describe two other attributes of well-designed processes.** Process performance can be measured in terms of effectiveness, efficiency, cycle time, stability, and capability. The key measurement of effectiveness is customer satisfaction—how well a product or service meets or exceeds customer expectations. Efficiency measures the ability of a process to meet customer needs at low cost. Cycle time measures seek to report the length of time that elapses between the start of an activity and its completion. Measures of process stability indicate the extent to which a process exhibits low variation, arising only from random causes built into the process rather than from identifiable, sporadic shocks to the process. Process capability refers to the extent to which a process will yield the intended output under normal operating conditions. Two other attributes of well-designed processes are adaptability (the ability of a process to be adjusted easily and quickly to changing conditions) and robustness (the ability of a process to continue to meet its stated performance objectives when it is subjected to variations in quality of inputs or operating conditions).

Questions

1. Why are the collections activities of a company considered a process? What is the benefit of thinking of it in this way?
2. What is the relationship of a work process to a business system?
3. Name five finance processes with *external* customers or suppliers. For each, identify at least one supplier and one customer.
4. Name five finance processes with *internal* customers or suppliers. For each, identify at least one supplier and one customer.

5. What is a process boundary? Identify the process boundary of the payroll process. Explain the purpose of drawing the boundary as you did.
6. What are the three roles played by anyone as seen in process terms. Pick any finance activity within the payroll process and identify how these three roles take place.
7. What is rework? Can you think of a situation in which you experienced rework in a financial process? (Hint: Consider the bursar/financial aid office of your school.)
8. Many of the companies that have tried to use the cost of poor quality as a management tool have given up. Why do you think they have done so?
9. Why is cycle time one of the most important measures of quality performance?
10. "All processes have natural variation." Comment on this statement.
11. Distinguish between common causes and special causes of variation.
12. How could this chapter be improved to make it more valuable to you?

CASE

DONNA MELE

"I still can't see what quality has to do with Corporate Finance." Donna Mele looked up at her subordinates for a response, and seeing none, she went on. "I can understand why manufacturing is hot on it. After all, they're the ones who have to turn out products that don't fail five minutes after the customer takes them out of the box. But what in the world do we do that has anything to do with quality management? I just don't understand how we can use this quality approach in our work!"

Earlier that day, at the regular monthly meeting of the executive committee, the CEO had asked everyone to think about how to move the company toward a quality-management approach. As CFO, Donna, like the other department heads, had agreed to come up with some ideas about implementing quality techniques in her area. Donna remembered what the CEO had said:

> "The quality movement is no longer a matter of choice. Look at how the Japanese used quality to beat the pants off us in the consumer electronics industry and in automobiles. If we don't get on board as fast as we can, our competitors surely will and we will lose out to them. I'm convinced that we have to implement quality in everything we do from the top to the bottom of this organization and everywhere in between. That's why I am asking each of you to identify those areas of your operation that would benefit from a total quality approach and to report back at our next meeting."

Donna went on: "What the boss said made lots of sense, but what troubles me is that everything I've read about quality tells me it has to do with a production environment. Just-in-time inventory and multiproduct assembly lines are fine if you are making a product. But our 'product' in finance is information. We produce and analyze data. We evaluate the financial impact of decisions. We arrange for money, most of which is simply notations on some bank's records. I don't see anything that we do that is amenable to these quality techniques."

On the other hand, Donna was well aware of the inroads that the quality movement had made in American business. She had read *Thriving on Chaos* and several of the more recently published books on quality, and she had some sense of what distinguished systematic quality management from the older "quality control" approach. She knew, for example, that today's focus was on exceeding customers' expectations and on continuous improvement of processes, trying to build quality in at the beginning rather than identify and rework faulty output after the fact. As a result, she was reasonably comfortable—happy in fact—that the CEO had become a convert to quality management.

Donna looked up at her staff and gave a wry chuckle. "Let's get to work," she said. "How about a brainstorming session? Let's take five minutes or so and write down as many corporate finance activities as we can identify that might be improved by the application of systematic quality management techniques."

CHAPTER 14 IMPROVING FINANCIAL PROCESSES[1]

The day Jan Baxter, Hamid Allarani, and Bill Librasco's boss returned from the finance and quality-management seminar, Jan said to Hamid and Bill, "I don't know whether to celebrate or panic."

Their boss, the company's CFO, had really been turned on by the seminar. She "rewarded" the team with a new assignment, one to be added to their already large collection of individual responsibilities. The new task was wide open: "Get Finance started in quality management." No other guidance. No other directions. And no indication, as of yet, of what resources would be available.

"Ohhhhh boy," said Hamid to his friends, exhaling slowly, "Now we've really done it. Where do we start?"

There are a variety of ways Hamid's team could "get started in quality management." The team could start learning and using the statistical and process improvement tools that are widely used by companies that have achieved rapid improvements in quality. It could study selected financial processes in other organizations and attempt to adapt the more promising approaches to its own company. It could start an inquiry into finance's mission in the total organiza-

[1] **Acknowledgment:** This chapter draws heavily on the work of members of the Juran Institute whose assistance is gratefully acknowledged.

tion with the intent of developing a new mission statement. One way many quality experts recommend starting is by improving a highly visible process important to the organization—especially a process with a history of chronic problems that traditional approaches have not solved. The receivables problem from the previous chapter might be just such a project.

Financial managers are vitally interested in achieving high-quality processes in finance and in all other parts of the company because of their importance for company profitability and survival. We begin this chapter by reviewing three determinants of the rate at which quality improvements take place and then introduce key concepts of process improvement. Next, we review some of the tools used in managing and improving processes and present one team-based approach for doing so. Finally, we present three examples of improvements in financial processes.

Key Points You Should Learn from This Chapter

After reading this chapter you should be able to:

- Describe three key factors in achieving revolutionary rates of quality improvement in financial processes and the rest of the organization.
- Describe three key concepts for bringing about systematic quality improvement.
- Describe three sets of quality-management tools used to improve financial and other processes.
- Describe one systematic approach for improving financial and other processes.
- Describe three examples in which quality-management tools and approaches have been used to improve financial processes.

Introductory Concepts—Three Keys to Revolutionary Rates of Improvement

One hallmark of the global quality revolution is the repeated success of many organizations in achieving revolutionary rates of quality improvement—not just 5% or 10% reductions in costs or defects, and not merely shortening cycle time from 30 days to 28. Financial executives in companies with such achievements talk of successes such as a 50% reduction in costs, ten times improvement in quality in two years, doubling market share, and cutting cycle time from eight days to four hours. These dramatic improvements come from many sources. Three very important ones are (1) internal projects, (2) external borrowing, and (3) broad organizational changes. This chapter will focus primarily on the first source. But the other two are also important to keep in mind because finance can play important roles in bringing their potential benefits to the organization.

1. Internal Projects

Systematic, team-based quality-improvement projects are seen by many managers and quality experts as the single most important key to revolutionary rates of quality improvement. Dr. Joseph M. Juran, one of America's pre-eminent quality experts, has repeatedly asserted that "All improvement takes place project by project."[2] The extent to which team-based quality-improvement projects contribute to dramatic rates of improvement is a function of three factors: (1) number of teams, (2) project importance combined with team effectiveness, and (3) spread of team results.

Numbers The first factor is simply the number of teams in place. The greater the number of teams, the greater the opportunity to discover or invent improved processes. Literally hundreds of teams were working on quality-improvement projects at Florida Power and Light Company when it was on the road to becoming the first non-Japanese company to win Japan's Deming Prize for quality. Xerox Corporation's Business Products and Systems Division, a 1989 Baldrige Award winner, also had hundreds of such teams in place.

Importance and effectiveness The second factor has two components: the importance of each project undertaken and the effectiveness of the team in executing its work. Teams that select projects with the potential for big improvements in many places throughout the organization have the opportunity to make large contributions if they execute their work well. Teams that undertake projects with only small or moderate possibilities for improvement in a single or a few parts of the organization are not likely to have a major impact, even if their projects are big successes. And whether or not a team achieves its potential contribution from a given project is a function of how well and how quickly it executes the project.

---

[2]**Reference:** For example, "The Last Word: Lessons of a Lifetime in Managing for Quality." Seminar at Mahwah, N.J., Aug. 16, 1993.

Spread The third factor is the extent to which the learning and approaches from successful projects are spread throughout the organization. Insights from these projects can assist others in their improvement efforts. The achievements of a single team can be leveraged greatly if new knowledge is replicated quickly in other places.

2. External Borrowing

The second major source of revolutionary rates of quality improvement is adopting and adapting improvements from other organizations. Like internal projects, the amount of contribution from external borrowing depends on the number of ideas borrowed, their importance, and the extent to which they are replicated throughout the borrowing organization.

Many good ideas are borrowed by the same types of teams described above, but it is useful to list external borrowing as a separate source for at least two reasons. First, all companies that have made dramatic improvements in quality have also made significant progress in defeating one of the major barriers to organizational improvement—the "NIH syndrome." NIH stands for "not invented here," an all too common attitude that rejects the successes of other companies, or even other departments within the same company, because they were not developed by one's own organizational unit. Major new opportunities for improvement occur when organizations become aggressive in adopting others' useful ideas. Such companies, like the textile company Milliken Corporation, refer to adopting good ideas from others as "stealing shamelessly" and are proud of their ability to bury NIH as a company attitude.

A second reason for emphasizing this source of improvement is because of the growing importance, in finance and elsewhere, of a quality-improvement tool known as "competitive benchmarking," used for making such borrowing a systematic part of managing. Competitive benchmarking is discussed later in this chapter.

3. Broad Organizational Changes

Changes that align the individual elements of the organization with emerging modern management practices can also make major contributions to improved organizational performance. Such changes are also necessary to support and sustain the two sources of improvement just discussed. The transition from traditional management methods to modern customer-focused, quality-based management practices involves many changes throughout an organization. These changes include increased participation of employees in decision making, greater commitment to using valid data, breaking down barriers that weaken effective collaboration among organizational departments, and many others.[3]

[3] **Cross-reference:** We discussed some of the new management methods emerging in high-quality companies in Chapter 3 and summarized them in Figure 3.1 on p. 61.

The secret to the success of this type of contribution is to have a reasonably clear vision of what the emerging management system looks like so individuals and parts of the organization can be supported in moving toward that vision. Improvements in this realm are usually "opportunistic" in the good sense of opportunism—seeing an unpredictable opportunity to move the organization forward and acting in a timely way when that opportunity arises. Jan, Hamid, and Bill made just such a contribution when they talked their boss into attending the finance and quality-management seminar. The training from that seminar helped her to align her knowledge, values, and priorities with the organizational requirements for sustaining rapid improvement. Her open invitation "to get started in quality management" provides another such chance.

Systematic Process Improvement

As Bill, Hamid, and Jan's team continues its inquiry into process improvement, having a fuller understanding of process management and improvement methods will be useful. It is also likely that distinguishing between large- and small-scale improvements will be helpful.

1. A Model of Process Management and Improvement

Figure 14.1 presents a widely used model of process-management activities that is receiving increasing attention from financial managers. This diagram has been called the "Juran Breakthrough Cycle" and the "Juran Trilogy." It suggests how

FIGURE 14.1

The Juran Triology. Quality planning, quality control, and quality improvement combine to improve work processes.

Source: J. M. Juran, *Juran on Planning for Quality*. (New York, The Free Press, 1988), p. 12.

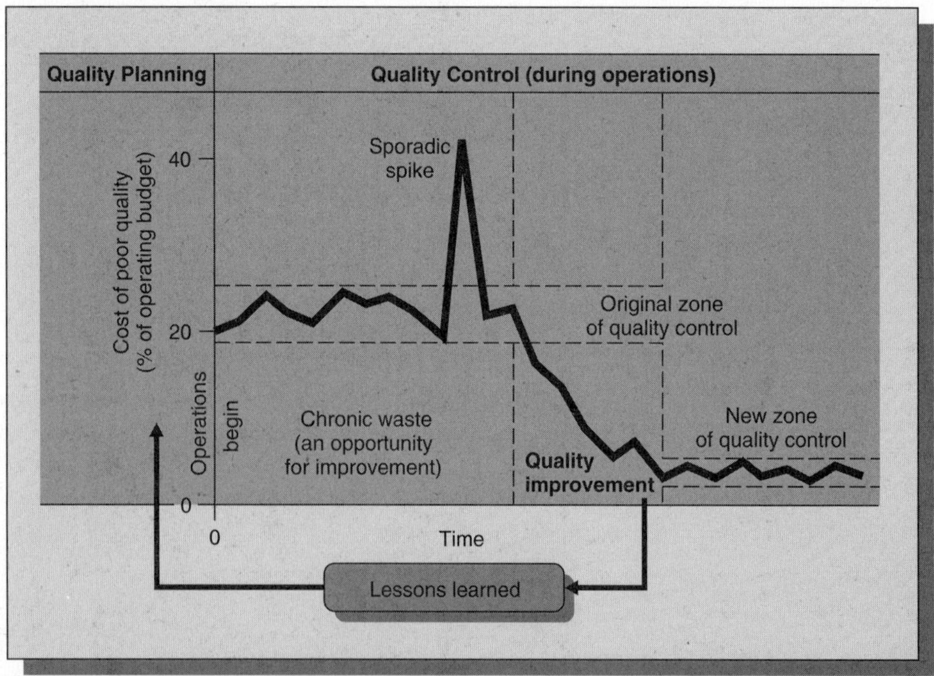

the quality-related costs of a process can be brought down over time. The cycle has three parts focused on process quality: quality planning, quality control, and quality improvement. The vertical dimension (y-axis) is the cost of poor quality, the cost to the company of known and unknown errors from weaknesses in the process. The horizontal dimension (x-axis) is time. The vertical axis could also be used to record the number of defects or errors in a process, such as the number of payroll checks incorrectly written or the amount of accounts receivable overdue more than 30 days. The figure is normally drawn so that downward movement over time indicates improvement.

Quality planning The first activity in achieving excellent financial processes is quality planning—creating processes that will be able to meet established goals under a wide range of operating conditions. Most financial (and other organizational) processes in use today were not originally designed with quality in mind. Rather, they simply grew over time, being modified as new demands were placed on them and with patchwork changes made when they seemed not to work very well. Such processes often present opportunities for dramatic improvements in customer satisfaction; reductions in cycle time, defect rates, and costs; and increased work enjoyment for the organizational members who work in them.

Quality control Juran describes the next stage—using Figure 14.1 as his illustration—in terms familiar to any of us who have struggled to function in a system that doesn't work very well:

> Following the planning, the process is turned over to the operating forces. Their responsibility is to run the process at optimal effectiveness. Due to deficiencies in the original planning, the process runs at a high level of chronic waste. That waste was planned into the process, in the sense that the planning process failed to plan it out. Because the waste is inherent in the process, the operating forces are unable to get rid of the chronic waste. If it does get worse (sporadic spike), a fire fighting team is brought in to determine the cause or causes of this abnormal variation. Once the cause(s) has been determined, and corrective action is taken, the process again falls into the zone defined by the "quality control" limits.[4]

In most companies, the large area of chronic waste has become accepted as normal, a cost of doing business. As long as sporadic spikes do not occur too often, the performance of the process is considered satisfactory. A major impact of the quality revolution has been the discovery that the large area of chronic waste in Figure 14.1 is not inevitable—that it can be removed, producing enormous positive impacts on market share, revenue, costs, and profitability.

Quality improvement The third stage of the breakthrough cycle is quality improvement. In this stage, systematic approaches of the types discussed in this chapter are used to achieve dramatic improvements in the process. The chronic waste that had become accepted by managers and nonmanagers alike as "the best we can do, given the way things are around here" is eliminated. The starting point is to begin seeing the chronic waste as no longer inevitable and acceptable.

---

[4] **Reference:** J. M. Juran, "The Quality Triology." *Quality Progress,* Aug. 1986, p. 20.

2. Small- and Large-Scale Improvements

Kaizen—small- and moderate-scale continuous improvement in all phases of an organization

Kaizen, or small-scale continuous improvement, is a term popularized in the United States by Masaaki Imai in his 1986 book of that title. Imai describes Kaizen as "continuing improvement in personal life, home life, social life, and working life. When applied to the workplace, Kaizen means continuing improvement involving everyone—managers and workers alike."[5] Although the definition given above is quite encompassing, the word Kaizen has come to be used to describe small- and moderate-scale improvements (the "singles" of baseball) rather than very large ones (the "home runs" and "grand slams").

In the same book, Imai uses the term *innovation* to refer to those homers and grand slams. He speaks of innovation as large-scale endeavors that seek to achieve dramatic improvements. We will use the term "large-scale improvement" to refer to this concept because the word innovation has many other meanings and its use in this very specialized way invites misunderstanding.

Imai is critical of the overreliance of Western managers on such large-scale improvement attempts and their slowness to embrace Kaizen. He observes correctly that many innovation projects are undertaken with a results-oriented (focusing on the "ends") approach which ignores the power of a process-oriented approach (focusing on the "means"). Although his criticisms are well founded, increasing numbers of American companies have adopted small-scale improvement processes in recent years and have also learned to undertake large-scale improvement projects in the same quality-process-based ways that small projects are undertaken. For these companies, Imai's criticism is no longer as valid as it once was.

However, it is useful to distinguish between the two major modes of improvement: many, many small and medium-sized improvement projects and a few major very large-scale improvement projects. Both have important roles to play in an organization's achievement of greater competitiveness. One value in the distinction is the insight it offers into post-World War II management practice in Japan and the United States. As quality management evolved in Japan, companies became progressively more proficient in Kaizen while remaining only moderately adept at large-scale improvement. Until very recently, the great majority of U.S. companies maintained a strong bias for large-scale improvement, paying little or no attention to the small-scale continuous improvements of Kaizen. In fact, for most of the postwar period, "continuous improvement" was not even part of the vocabulary of most U.S. business people.

We will use the term *project-by-project improvement* to refer to the organizationwide use of numerous teams working on continuous improvement projects. The projects will include the small and medium-sized Kaizen projects as well as large-scale improvement projects.

3. Organizational Transformation

Organizational transformation refers to the large and small changes in all components of an organization as it moves from one state to another. The changes de-

[5] **Reference:** Masaaki Imai, *KAIZEN: The Key to Japan's Competitive Success* (New York: McGraw-Hill, 1986), p. xx.

"Which tie says, 'Here's the man responsible for positive cash flow from an outmoded operation in a depressed industry'?"

scribed in Chapter 3 are only some of those that companies have undergone in their pursuit of revolutionary rates of quality improvement. They impact the values, management style, training systems, and virtually all aspects of an organization. They are often called a "change in organizational culture."

Many of the changes in modern financial management practices described in this book are part of this process of organizational transformation. As American and other companies adjust to a world of increasing competitiveness, all parts of the organization experience new pressures for change. The changes occurring in finance are also occurring in the other functional areas of the organization—accounting, marketing, human resources, legal, and so on.

Process Improvement Tools

Three sets of quality-management tools used by some innovative finance departments can be readily identified: quantitative-statistical-analytical tools; behavioral tools; and competitive benchmarking. These tools are widely used by managers and nonmanagers alike in companies pursuing revolutionary rates of quality improvement.

FIGURE 14.2
Ten core values and concepts of systematic quality improvement. All ten must be in place for a company to achieve Baldrige Award-level quality.

Source: 1994 Award Criteria—Malcolm Baldrige National Quality Award, pp. 2–4.

- Customer-driven quality
- Leadership
- Continuous improvement
- Employee participation and development
- Fast response
- Design quality and prevention
- Long-range outlook
- Management by fact
- Partnership development
- Corporate responsibility and citizenship

1. Quantitative-Statistical-Analytical Tools

Figure 14.2 presents the ten core values of systematic quality improvement identified in the application for the Malcolm Baldrige National Quality Award. One of these particularly close to the heart of most financial managers is "management by fact." Central to management by fact is a strong commitment to use data for analysis and decision making rather than to rely too heavily on opinion and judgment. And central to gathering and using data well are a set of quantitative-statistical-analytical tools some of which are listed in Figure 14.3. These seven are frequently called the "seven classical tools of statistical process control."[6]

For our work in financial managing at this stage, it is not necessary for most readers to learn how to use these tools or even to learn their names and nature if they are not already familiar with them. However, it is important to remember four things about the basic tools in Figure 14.3 and Appendix 14A. First, all are fairly simple to learn and use. The most difficult requires roughly eighth-grade arithmetic skills for full mastery. Second, in most organizations that have made great progress in quality improvement, virtually all organizational members are familiar with the tools and are able to use them. Third, these tools are used repeatedly to improve organizational processes, products, and services; to communicate about problems, opportunities, and improvements; and to accomplish myriad daily tasks. Using these tools becomes simply a part of everyday work to get the job done.

FIGURE 14.3
The seven classical tools of statistical process control. These tools form the basis for gathering and analyzing process data.

- Bar charts and histograms
- Pareto charts
- Scatter diagrams
- Run charts
- Control charts
- Cause-and-effect (also called *Ishikawa* or *fishbone*) diagrams
- Flow charts

[6] **Cross-reference:** The "seven classical tools" are discussed further in Appendix 14A.

FIGURE 14.4
Selected behavioral tools of quality management. These tools enable employee development and participation in quality improvement.

- Brainstorming
- Nominal group technique
- Task-force management processes
- Self-directed, self-managing, and self-leading work teams
- Active listening
- QIT (quality-improvement team) processes
- Process reengineering techniques (or business process quality-improvement techniques)

The fourth thing to remember may be the most important of all for individuals studying finance. Although these tools do not require sophisticated mathematical skills, some of them do use numbers intensively. Many Americans are quite uncomfortable with mathematics and are unsure of their ability to handle numerical tasks. Individuals interested in financial managing are much less likely to have such fears and to suffer from what John Allen Paulos called "innumeracy" in his best-selling book with that title. Because of their comfort with numbers, financial managers are well placed to play leading roles in adopting these tools and in teaching them to others. Therefore, it is quite important that students of finance get to know these tools and their potential for contributing to a company's financial health and success.

Appendix 14A also lists some additional analytical tools that are being adopted by many organizations. Some are fairly sophisticated analytical tools. Others are specialized planning and analysis tools. Unlike the basic tools in Figure 14.3, these are not likely to be understood and used by the great majority of organizational members in their daily work. However, they are being used more and more frequently by organizational members with the appropriate training.

2. Behavioral Tools

Examples of behavioral tools are listed in Figure 14.4.[7] These tools can be seen as key vehicles for realizing another of the ten values listed in the Baldrige application: employee participation and development.

Again, it is not necessary to master these tools as part of this course, but, like the basic quantitative tools, a few things about them are important to remember. First, these behavioral tools are learned by virtually all organizational members. Second, they are widely used in daily work in companies making rapid progress in quality improvement.

Points one and two are directly parallel to the first two points about the quantitative tools, but points three and four are not. Third, unlike the basic quantitative tools, many of these behavioral tools are not easy to use. And fourth, individuals interested in financial managing may not have any special advantages in learning to use them. All of these behavioral tools are conceptually fairly easy to understand, like the nominal group technique and effective task-force management

[7] **Cross reference:** The behavioral tools are discussed further in Appendix 14B.

processes. And all are within the intellectual and interpersonal capabilities of virtually every organizational member. But most require the development of considerable interpersonal skills for effective use and considerable personal behavioral discipline to continue their use over and over again. In the "heat" of day-to-day managing, it is easy to forget to use these behavioral tools. Ironically, successes with them in the past may create a temptation to take a shortcut or to forget to use them in the future. Yet in spite of these difficulties, many organizations and many financial managers have made major progress in adopting these tools.

3. Competitive Benchmarking

Competitive benchmarking is a term used in quality management to describe the activity of discovering and achieving outstanding products, services, and processes. It involves identifying a superb example of a process, service, or product; setting that example as a standard to be matched or exceeded; and then doing so. One version of the competitive benchmarking process—based upon the system used at Xerox, a leader in developing benchmarking in America—is illustrated in Figure 14.5, which identifies ten steps in the process composing four major categories: planning, analysis, integration, and action.

Competitive benchmarking has become a widely used tool in companies committed to quality management. Motorola's success in shortening the time required to close its corporate books each month is described later in this chapter. However, closing the books is only one of many financial processes Motorola has improved dramatically. As a result of these successes, many activities of Motorola's finance function have become the competitive benchmark for other companies. Financial managers from Motorola frequently share information on its processes with their counterparts at companies seeking to discover better ways to do business.

FIGURE 14.5
Competitive benchmarking at Xerox. There are ten steps to the process.

Source: Robert C. Camp, "A Bible for Benchmarking, by Xerox." *Financial Executive,* Jul./Aug. 1993, p. 26.

Planning

1. Identify what is to be benchmarked.
2. Identify comparative companies.
3. Determine data collection method and collect data.

Analysis

4. Determine current performance levels.
5. Project future performance levels.
6. Communicate benchmark findings and gain acceptance.

Integration

7. Establish functional goals.
8. Develop action plans.

Action

9. Implement specific actions and monitor progress.
10. Recalibrate benchmarks.

FINANCE IN PRACTICE

Benchmarking Financial Numbers at Southern Pacific

When the Southern Pacific Transportation Company began its companywide quality initiative, one early action was to identify major areas of improvement by using publicly available data. The Interstate Commerce Commission prepares and distributes "R1 Reports"—detailed operating and cost data on all major railroads based upon annual submissions by each railroad. Early in the company's quality efforts, the finance department began issuing annual reports that compared Southern Pacific's own R1 data with data from its major competitors. The reports included two calculations of the savings for each "line item" (cost category)—first, the savings if Southern Pacific matched the average performance of its competitors and second, the savings achievable if it matched the performance of its best competitor in each category. These comparisons are an important input to Southern Pacific's process for setting quality-improvement priorities.

Project-by-Project Process Improvement

Companies pursuing revolutionary rates of quality improvement use teams following a systematic step-by-step process. In pursuing their goal of delighting customers, some teams place more emphasis on reducing errors, some on eliminating unnecessary steps, and some on reducing the time required to complete activities, but each emphasis supports the other two.

For the smaller Kaizen-type projects, many companies have found it useful to record and display the progress of each team on a "quality storyboard." Figures 14.6 and 14.7 show one such multistep quality-improvement process and the storyboard that is used with it. The larger projects we called "large-scale improvements" are also attacked in team-based ways, but the process might be called a task-force project, "process reengineering," or "business process quality management."

If Bill, Hamid, and Jan had been able to define the receivables problem from the previous chapter as a fairly small, self-contained process, then a small-scale continuous improvement project—using a storyboard—would have been an appropriate approach. Since their project grew into a much larger piece of work, they very likely would have chosen to use the larger-scale process reengineering approach.

FIGURE 14.6
A quality storyboard process. The process has six steps.

1. Identify a project.
2. Establish the project.
3. Diagnose the cause.
4. Remedy the cause.
5. Hold the gains.
6. Replicate results and nominate new projects.

IDENTIFY PROJECT	ESTABLISH PROJECT		CURRENT STATUS		
	SELECT TEAM	VERIFY MISSION	RECENT MINUTES	CURRENT ACTIVITIES	CAN YOU HELP?
DIAGNOSE CAUSE					
ANALYZE SYMPTOMS	CONFIRM OR MODIFY MISSION	FORMULATE THEORIES	TEST THEORIES		IDENTIFY ROOT CAUSE(S)
REMEDY CAUSE					
EVALUATE ALTERNATIVES	DESIGN REMEDY	DESIGN CONTROLS	DESIGN FOR CULTURE	PROVE EFFECTIVENESS	IMPLEMENT

FIGURE 14.7
Quality storyboard. Progress on each step of a quality project is tracked and displayed.
Source: The Juran Institute. Used with permission.

The philosophy behind these team-based approaches is that: "Truly revolutionary improvement requires:

1. identifying . . . the most important opportunities,
2. assembling the right team to make the improvement,
3. realizing the maximum benefit from each quality improvement project, and
4. completing each project as quickly as the particular problem will permit."[8]

The quality storyboard process shown in Figure 14.6 has six steps, each of which has a series of substeps. There are many versions of this storyboard approach. Some, like the one in Figure 14.6, involve as few as 6 steps while others have as many as 12. Teams using the process give their members formal roles, such as team leader, facilitator, timekeeper, and scribe (recorder of the team's work). The progress of the team is usually recorded regularly on the storyboard, which is displayed in a prominent place.

The storyboard in Figure 14.7 records progress on the first four steps and allows space to include some additional information. We will discuss each step and illustrate it with a typical financial process.[9]

[8] **Reference:** *Quality Improvement Storyboard* (Wilton, Conn.: The Juran Institute) 1992, p. 1.

[9] **Reference:** The storyboard example and Figures 14.6 and 14.7 are based upon *Quality Improvement Storyboard* and *Quality Improvement Pocket Guide* (Wilton, Conn.: The Juran Institute, 1992 and 1993, respectively).

1. Identify a Project

Identifying high-priority opportunities for improvement involves nominating and evaluating possible projects, selecting one, and then asking whether the proposed project will represent a quality improvement once it is completed.

To illustrate, we will use a problem Jan, Hamid, and Bill's company tackled later: dealing with increasing complaints about late and incorrect paychecks. Calculating and issuing paychecks is one of the processes performed by their finance department. When this process started performing poorly, large amounts of employee energy and time were absorbed in unproductive activities as the errors were corrected. Bad feelings also resulted, captured in such phrases as, "You folks in finance are always telling us how to run our business yet you can't even write a check properly." Correcting this situation became a high-priority improvement project so "the company could put this distraction behind it and get on with its real work."

2. Establish the Project

Establishing the project involves preparing a mission statement for the project team, selecting the right team to accomplish the mission, and then verifying that both mission and team are appropriate and have the requirements for success.

The mission statement for improving the paycheck issuing process read, "to assure accurate and timely payment to every employee every time." Team members consisted of volunteers: two from the payroll office, one from human resources, a benefits administrator, one from an operating unit (in this case a factory), a computer programmer, and one from the sales organization (because sales commissions are a major part of compensation in that department).

3. Diagnose the Cause

The third step involves analyzing symptoms of the problem to be solved by the project, using the greater understanding of the project situation developed in the analysis to confirm or modify the original mission statement, formulating and testing theories, and then identifying the **root cause** of the problem.

root cause—the single cause most important in creating a problem

A variety of payroll process symptoms were identified. These included delays in issuing checks; incorrect calculations of overtime, commissions, and deduction of benefits. Checks were also repeatedly mailed to the wrong address for some employees. Possible causes included poorly designed forms for collecting data, delays in providing information on overtime earnings to the payroll department, ineffective processes for incorporating new data on employee benefits deductions into calculations of those deductions, and clerical errors in actually writing the paychecks. Data about each of these were collected. Analysis of the data indicated that more than 50% of recent errors appeared to come from illegible information provided by the factory on overtime hours worked, and the team identified this as the root cause of the problem.

4. Remedy the Cause

In the fourth step, the team evaluates alternatives for removing the root cause(s) and selects one to try out. The team develops that alternative in detail and evaluates it against the project mission. Means for measuring and evaluating the consequences of implementing the selected alternative are developed. Possible organizational cultural barriers and likely resistances to the planned changes are identified and plans made to overcome them. The alternative is pilot-tested, the results assessed, adjustments made, and then a plan for larger-scale implementation is developed and implemented if warranted.

Because of the seriousness of the immediate problem, the team developed a new form for reporting overtime even though they had other ideas about making major changes in the process. Actually, two supervisors in the factory and two payroll clerks designed the form over lunch while the rest of the team watched. Use of the new form immediately reduced errors in overtime calculations by 95% beginning the following month. Additional changes introduced soon afterward reduced other errors substantially.

5. Hold the Gains

To hold the gains achieved by the new process, quality controls are designed with an emphasis on building into the design a high level of self-control by the members operating the process. Steps are taken to reduce the possibility of error in using the remedy—to foolproof it. Systems are then set up to report results and the controls are documented.

The new overtime form was designed so that employees entered information by filling in prenumbered boxes instead of writing numbers in their own handwriting. The team then arranged for the writing of a computer program that could read the information into the main payroll program directly from the darkened boxes on the forms. Not only did this improve accuracy, it also eliminated the need for three payroll clerks to devote time to overtime entries. The clerks were reassigned to work adding greater value.

6. Replicate Results and Nominate New Projects

The final step in the improvement cycle extends the improvement to similar situations in other parts of the organization and contributes to restarting the improvement cycle by identifying possible new projects. Each attempt to replicate the improvement involves a severely abbreviated repeat of key elements of the previous five steps.

As part of the replication step, other problems are identified that have root causes the same as or similar to those remedied by the original project. For example, the team discovered a number of other processes in which poorly designed forms were creating significant numbers of data-entry errors. The appropriateness of applying the remedy to each new problem and situation is verified, necessary adjustments to the new situation are made, and particular attention is paid to overcoming resistance to change in the new situations. If the remedy is successful, appropriate alterations are made in designing and auditing the controls and in foolproofing the remedy.

The learning that has occurred during each improvement project is used to develop nominations for new projects. New-project nominations frequently come from one of three sources: (1) additional causes of the original problem (ones in addition to the root cause that was remedied by the project), (2) additional deficiencies in the process uncovered by the team in the course of its work, and (3) root causes from other projects that may emerge as a common theme in a series of problems.

Although the paycheck team dramatically reduced the number of errors in preparing paychecks, the biggest contribution of the team was starting in motion a series of other changes. Over the next two years the calculation of overtime was greatly simplified as were other personnel calculations. The company's time cards were replaced with a bar coded identification badge which was read automatically whenever workers started and ended the work day. A simple software program made overtime and other calculations, with error rates of less than three per year. Address change errors were reduced by sending employees a printout of the change and asking for verification. Check-mailing problems were removed by arranging direct deposit of pay for all employees.

Three Examples of Improvements in Financial Processes

Throughout this book we have presented many examples of ways finance has used quality approaches to serve its customers better and to improve its processes. For example, in Chapter 11 we described how Alcoa redesigned its capital budgeting process and how Federal Express developed a new approach to project development and decision making for complex technological investments. In this section we present three more examples of improvements in financial processes and we present them in somewhat greater detail than most of the other examples. The three are (1) closing the books at Motorola, (2) reengineering Ford's accounts payable process, and (3) "distributing" credit analysis to Solectron's salespeople.

1. Closing the Books at Motorola[10]

In the early 1980s, the finance function of Motorola, the large manufacturer of electronic and communications equipment, recognized the need to join the company's progress in improving quality at a revolutionary rate. The pilot application in finance was the process of closing the corporate books each month—consolidating the financial statements from all units of the company.

[10] **Reference:** James A.F. Stoner and Frank M. Werner, *Finance in the Quality Revolution* (Morristown, N. J.: Financial Executives Research Foundation, 1993), pp. 68–70.

As the project began, the monthly close averaged 9 working days. As a result, an updated forecast for the coming month was not available until 11 or 12 working days of that month had passed. The monthly operating committee meeting to review the prior month's activities and the current month's plan was typically held a week later. Management was getting information for last month with the next already two-thirds over. And many people in the Motorola financial function around the world worked very hard at the end of every month to provide this information.

To improve this business process, Motorola set the ambitious goal of reducing the closing time to 4 days by the first quarter of 1990 and 2 days by the end of 1992. As David Hickie, at that time senior vice president and assistant chief financial officer, pointed out,

> If you tell people to close the books in 7 days instead of 8, they will figure out how to do it very easily. They will work a little overtime over the weekend. If you say do it in 6 days, they will work on Sunday. But they would not change what they were doing. When we told them to do it in 4 days and that we would not let them use the weekend as a crutch, they had to look at a fundamental change in the process.

In examining the closing process, Motorola found that much of the cycle time was absorbed correcting erroneous journal entries, waiting for data from overseas units, and entering and correcting data in a headquarters computer. Efforts to improve these situations led to a decrease in monthly journal entry errors from roughly 8,000 to 2; direct forwarding of overseas data to the United States rather than through three intermediate locations that routinely approved the data after considerable delay; and bringing back in-house the data-entry activity that was performed by an outside contractor—a change that sped up data entry and reduced errors.

Commenting on the improved process, Ken Johnson, vice president and corporate controller, identifies the advantages of closing the books quickly.

> In addition to the cost savings, the early close frees up several hundred finance people for each day removed from the process. They can devote their attention to more important things than just preparing the numbers—like helping our people run the business.

By July 1992, Motorola's finance organization had reduced monthly closing time from 9 days to 2 days. In July 1991, Motorola was able to report that speeding up the monthly close from the sixth to fourth day had saved the company $20 million per year. Motorola expects a further $10 million annual savings now that it has reached a 2-day close.

2. Reengineering Ford's Accounts Payable Process[11]

Early in the 1980s, the Ford Motor Company investigated ways of improving its accounts payable process. At that time more than 500 people worked in the accounts payable department of Ford's North American operations. Plans to intro-

[11] **References:** Michael Hammer and James Champy, *Reengineering the Corporation* (New York, HarperCollins, 1992), pp. 39–44; Michael Hammer, "Reengineering Work: Don't Automate, Obliterate." *Harvard Business Review* July–Aug. 1990:104–112; *Business Process Quality Management*, 2nd edition, "Discussions and Team Exercises" (Wilton, Conn.: The Juran Institute, 1993), pp. 27–33.

duce automation and other changes were developed, promising a 20% reduction in the number of workers required to pay Ford's suppliers.

This improvement looked impressive to Ford until a team that visited Mazda's operations in Japan reported that Mazda required only five employees to pay its suppliers. Although the companies differed considerably in size, the difference in staffing was too great to be explained on that basis. Even after adjusting for the size differences of the two companies, Ford concluded that its accounts payable staff was at least five times larger than it should have been.

With a new goal of accomplishing the work with far more than a 20% reduction in staffing, an accounts payable improvement team studied the business process used to pay suppliers. The study indicated that members of the department spent most of their working time resolving discrepancies in data they received at the last step in the payment process.

As shown in Figure 14.8, the purchasing/payment process involved the matching of three documents. When purchasing departments ordered goods, they issued a purchase order to the supplier and sent a copy to accounts payable. When the supplier shipped the goods, it forwarded an invoice to accounts payable. When one of Ford's receiving docks received the goods, it forwarded a receiving document to accounts payable. When all three documents reached the accounts payable department, they were compared. If they matched, a check for the invoice was written and dispatched. If they did not match, an investigation was started to re-

FIGURE 14.8
Ford's old purchasing/payments process. Three documents had to match exactly before payment was made.

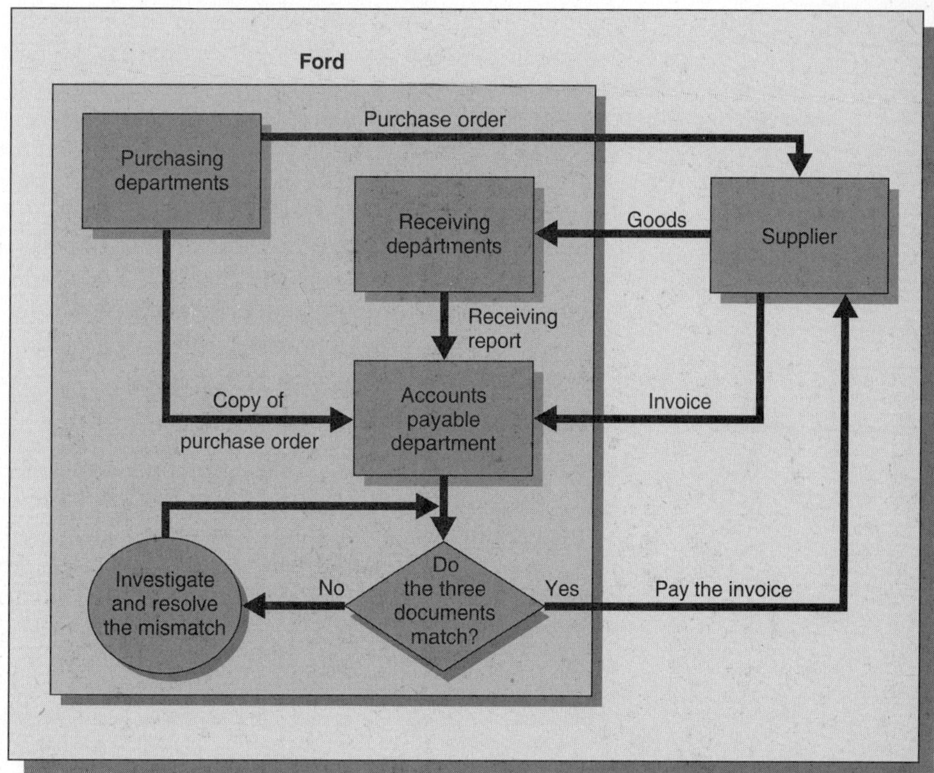

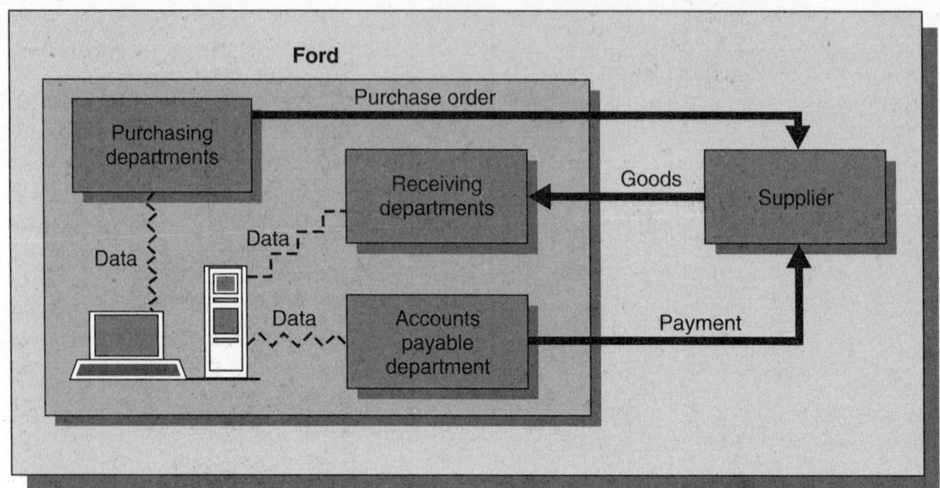

FIGURE 14.9
Ford's new purchasing/payments process. Most of the paperwork and document matching has been eliminated.

solve any discrepancies. With 14 data items on all three documents requiring matching, members of the department spent most of their time trying to resolve mismatches.

The business process was redesigned to eliminate the supplier's invoice and the receiving department's report and to reduce the number of items needing matching from 14 to 3: part number, quantity, and supplier code. In the new process, Figure 14.9, Ford sends a purchase order to the supplier but does not send a copy to accounts payable. Instead, it enters data on the order into a database accessible by all receiving docks. It also requests the supplier not to send an invoice to Ford. When goods arrive at a loading dock, the receiving clerk checks the database to see if the delivered goods match the order. If they match exactly, the shipment is accepted. If not, they are rejected and the carrier returns them to the supplier. When the receiving dock enters the arrival information into the database, the information is automatically transmitted to accounts payable, and the computer makes payment to the supplier at the appropriate time. The new process requires only about 150 workers and saves millions of dollars every year.

3. "Distributing" Credit Analysis to Solectron's Salespeople[12]

Solectron is a fast-growing contract manufacturer of electronic subassemblies, a rapidly changing, highly competitive business with very narrow profit margins. Contract manufacturers perform assembly and manufacturing operations for other companies. They compete not only with each other but also with the manufacturing operations of their own customers. Their success depends on their abil-

[12] **Reference:** James A.F. Stoner and Frank M. Werner, *Finance in the Quality Revolution* (Morristown, N.J.: Financial Executives Research Foundation, 1993), pp. 100–102.

ity to produce at lower costs, greater speed, higher quality, or some combination of these three.

Over the years Solectron has developed an effective team-based process for identifying promising customer prospects, evaluating them and making decisions on their suitability. However, recent attempts to improve a step that used to come relatively late in the prospect identification process has improved considerably finance's contribution to the entire process. That step involves the decision on the creditworthiness of the prospect and the amount of credit the prospect would be eligible to receive.

In Solectron's early days, there was no formal procedure for checking a customer's creditworthiness. The company was small and did not have appreciable financial resources to extend to customers. In addition, early customers tended to be well-established companies or were identified as prospects through personal contacts and were well known to management. By the mid-1980s, however, Solectron had grown to the point where extension of credit was becoming increasingly important and appropriate as it expanded its customer base.

In 1985 to 1986, finance developed an internal credit matrix, a fairly elaborate and traditional credit analysis process similar to commercial bank systems. Unfortunately, the system proved quite cumbersome. Since few members of the sales force had finance skills or desired to take time away from selling, credit analysis was done within the finance organization. Salespeople lost considerable time as they contended for the attention of the company's sole analyst, lobbied for credit approval, and were forced to wait for the credit decision. It was difficult to be responsive to prospects. A negative decision meant that the time invested with a potential customer was wasted, leaving the sales staff, and very likely the rejected prospect, angry and frustrated.

In early 1992, Myron Lee, financial manager with credit responsibility, introduced a simplified process. Finance divides potential customers into three groups: "A customers," those who are large and financially healthy and for whom no credit check is required; "B customers," the middle-sized prospects for which it is important to check credit; and "C customers," those that are financially weak and are not to be pursued unless a special strategic rationale exists. Salespeople are free to pursue A customers without further financial review. For B customers, the salesperson now fills out a credit scoring sheet developed by Myron and his colleagues. The form uses easily obtainable data and is simple to fill out. A potential customer's score translates directly into the credit line Solectron is willing to extend.

The new process has empowered the sales staff to make preliminary credit decisions and has eliminated the frustration of the prior system. Salespeople now know how finance will react before approaching a customer and no longer waste time selling to unacceptable credit risks. Because it is so easy to understand, the form itself teaches the sales staff how and why finance makes the credit decision. Finance staffers are now seen as a support system and are no longer the "bad guys" who interfere with sales. By distributing some of his skills to the sales force, Myron Lee eliminated much of his routine work and now devotes more time to supporting strategic marketing decisions.

Hamid, Jan, and Bill were only three of the dozen individuals who worked on the receivables cross-functional QIT (quality-improvement team) in the previous 11 months. They were also the lowest three in terms of the organization's formal hierarchy. Yet, their boss and all of the other team members recognized that in some sense it was uniquely "their project." And the achievements of the team and of the other organizational members who contributed to the project's success were, in a special way, an acknowledgement of their initiative in "getting started on quality in finance."

In that 11 months, the team had put remedies in place that cut overdue receivables by more than 80%. Changes included many "upstream" activities like more precise specification of sales contracts, less frequent partial shipments, and more timely completion of the service manuals that were part of many sales agreements. There were also changes in more traditional finance responsibilities, including easier to read invoices, more accurate invoice information, and the beginnings of electronic invoicing and payment arrangements with a few of the more sophisticated customers.

By far the most amusing discovery by the team was that 40% of the "overdue receivables" were not overdue at all—they were simply the result of customers deciding not to pay invoices for partial shipments: a legitimate decision even though the items left out of partial shipments were almost always minor items that did not inconvenience the customer and that carried very low price tags. However, awaiting payment was a wise financial decision for the customer—it provided free financing of the purchase, sometimes for as long as six months!

As the team met for the last time to celebrate its successes, Jan grinned at Bill and said, "Well, Quality Champion, now that you don't have to spend so much time on the telephone collecting overdue receivables, I wonder if you'd care to volunteer to find some ways to measure the revenue-increasing benefits of high quality?"

Bill just smiled.

Summary of Key Points

- **Describe three key factors in achieving revolutionary rates of quality improvement in financial processes and the rest of the organization.** Revolutionary rates of quality improvement arise from: (1) team-based projects, (2) borrowing from other organizations, and (3) other organizational changes. Team-based contribution is a function of four factors: the number of teams, the importance of the projects they undertake, the success of their projects, and the extent to which successful projects are replicated throughout the organization. Contribution from borrowing from other organizations depends on the number of ideas borrowed, their importance, and the extent to which they are replicated. Broad changes that align the organization with modern quality-management methods offer additional opportunities for improvement and are necessary for supporting and sustaining the first two sources of rapid improvement.
- **Describe three key concepts for bringing about systematic quality improvement.** (1) The Juran Breakthrough Cycle describes systematic quality improvement as quality planning, quality control, and quality improvement. This cycle can be applied to major business processes (macroprocesses) or portions of such processes (microprocess or subprocesses).

(2) *Kaizen* or *continuous improvement* refers to many small incremental changes made rapidly and continually. Quality improvement also comes from much larger-scale changes made in one or a few discrete steps. Both can lead to dramatic improvements, and both are used to improve financial processes. (3) *Organizational transformation* refers to the systematic change of so many aspects of an organization, including its financial systems, that the resulting organization differs significantly from its original state.

- **Describe three sets of quality-management tools used to improve financial and other processes.** Financial managers and other organizational members use: (1) a set of statistical, quantitative, and analytical tools (including Pareto charts, control charts, and cause and effect diagrams); (2) a set of behavioral techniques or tools (including brainstorming, nominal group technique, and business process reengineering); and (3) competitive benchmarking to improve financial and other organizational processes.
- **Describe one systematic approach for improving financial and other processes.** Almost all companies making dramatic improvements in quality use some form of team-based systematic quality-improvement process. Such processes consist of a series of 6 to 12 clearly defined sequential steps. Team members fulfill roles such as leader, facilitator, time-keeper, and scribe. Team progress is frequently charted and communicated through a quality storyboard. Typical steps include: (1) selecting a high-priority process to improve; (2) establishing the improvement to be achieved and building a team to make the improvement; (3) diagnosing the problem, collecting data, and identifying the root cause; (4) selecting and trying out a remedy; (5) building systems to support the improvement over time; and (6) extending the remedy to other parts of the organization and developing ideas for new projects (so the cycle can return to step 1).
- **Describe three examples in which quality-management tools and approaches have been used to improve financial processes.** (1) Motorola reengineered its process for closing its worldwide corporate books each month, reducing errors and rework, reducing the time required from nine days to two, and saving more than $30 million per year. (2) Ford Motor Company redesigned its accounts payable process, freeing-up more than 70% of the departmental members for more productive work, reducing errors, increasing supplier and employee satisfaction, and saving millions of dollars each year. (3) Solectron redesigned its credit approval process to enable sales representatives to determine whether a potential customer would eventually receive credit at the very beginning of the customer prospecting task rather than late in the process. By doing so, the company avoids wasting customer development efforts, speeds credit approval, and avoids disappointing the sales staff and rejected customers.

Questions

1. What does Dr. Joseph M. Juran mean when he says "All improvement takes place project by project"?
2. What three factors influence the impact of team-based quality-improvement projects on the rate of companywide improvement? Why is each of the three important?
3. Describe the three components of Juran's "Quality Trilogy."
4. Distinguish between small-scale (Kaizen) and large-scale quality improvements. What is the role of each in systematic quality management?
5. Describe a process from your own experience that performed poorly because quality was not planned in from the beginning.
5. Can you think of a situation in your own experience in which poor quality was intentionally planned into a process, product, or service?
6. What are the "seven classical tools of statistical process control"?
7. Identify seven behavioral used in quality management tools.
8. What is competitive benchmarking? Identify an example of an excellent process, product, or service you think might be good enough to benchmark.
9. Describe six steps in a typical quality storyboard process. Pick a finance process and describe how each of the steps could be applied to a process improvement project.
10. What do the three examples of improvements in finance processes (Motorola, Ford, and Solectron) have in common? How do they illustrate the concepts of this chapter?

CASE

CHIP DONNELLO

"I don't believe it!" Chip Donnello exclaimed as he tossed the memo down on his desk. The memo was from the company's assistant financial vice president and controller and read as follows:

> On September 22nd, a memo was sent to all personnel announcing a change to the method for distributing payroll checks for employees not enrolled in the direct payroll deposit program and advices[13] for all employees. The change in distribution method began with the October 29th payroll and has been used for three payroll distributions.
>
> There were two primary reasons for the change. The first was to address concerns related to late and undelivered payroll checks by the U.S. postal system. The second was to reduce payroll distribution costs for the company as a whole.
>
> We have discussed the change with several departmental administrators and found that there are significant concerns regarding confidentiality and privacy. Notwithstanding the fact that the payroll check and advice design, including the paper stock itself, was modified to further protect the confidential information contained in the sealed envelope, this concern is widespread. We understand that many offices are taking the payroll envelopes received from the payroll department and are enclosing them in an additional envelope and readdressing them prior to placing them in employees' office mail boxes. Some offices are mailing them, via U.S. mail, to the person's home.
>
> It is clear that departmental concerns and their resultant actions have not allowed the company to make payroll distribution more efficient and less costly. In fact, the practices being followed currently are extremely inefficient and very costly. Given these facts, it is only logical to revert to the payroll distribution system that was in place on October 29th.
>
> Therefore, effective December 10th, the payroll department will once again mail all payroll checks and advices to the recipient's home address as contained within the company's human resource system.

Chip looked again at the memo and reflected on the events they recounted. "I wonder how else the payroll department could have handled it?" he thought.

---

[13] **Elaboration:** An "advice" is a statement listing the employee's gross salary and all deductions for taxes, health benefits, retirement plans, etc. At Chip's company, it is sent to each employee on each pay date.

APPENDIX 14A

ANALYTICAL TOOLS OF PROCESS IMPROVEMENT

A series of quantitative, statistical, and analytical tools are widely used for improving processes, products, and services in organizations that are achieving revolutionary rates of quality improvement. Some of the tools have been used for so long and by so many people that they have received nicknames, such as "the classical tools of statistical process control (or 'of quality management')." In this appendix, we first describe a basic set of these tools and then mention some other tools that are not yet as widely known or used.

Because we are concerned with understanding and improving financial processes, our description will emphasize the application of these tools to processes although they are used for describing and analyzing a wide variety of things. Used alone or in combination, they provide data and visual pictures of the internal processes that underlie a company's products and services, whether those processes be the production of widgets on a shop floor, the movement of expense-account vouchers through a finance department, or the analysis of capital expenditure opportunities by a cross-functional team.

1. The "Classical Tools of Statistical Process Control"

Seven of these tools are the: (1) histogram, (2) Pareto chart, (3) run (trend) chart, (4) control chart, (5) scatter diagram, (6) flow chart, and (7) cause-and-effect chart. These "basic seven" are widely used, in part because of their simplicity. They require no sophisticated mathematics—indeed, nothing more than ordinary arithmetic. They may, of course, be used in combination with more complex analytical tools, but these seven are frequently the only analytical tools needed by a team working to improve a process.

Histograms Histograms are familiar to anyone who has ever had an introductory statistics course and are widely found in newspapers and business publications. As illustrated in Figure 14A.1, they use bars to show the frequency distribution of a process or other phenomenon. Essentially, they divide the data points falling along a curve into easily calculated groups (e.g., deciles) and thus display the characteristics of a variable and its variation.

Analysis of the overall shape of a histogram—for example, large or small variance, skewness to the right or left—gives clues to problems in the process, such as variation larger than expected or measurements averaging above or below normal.

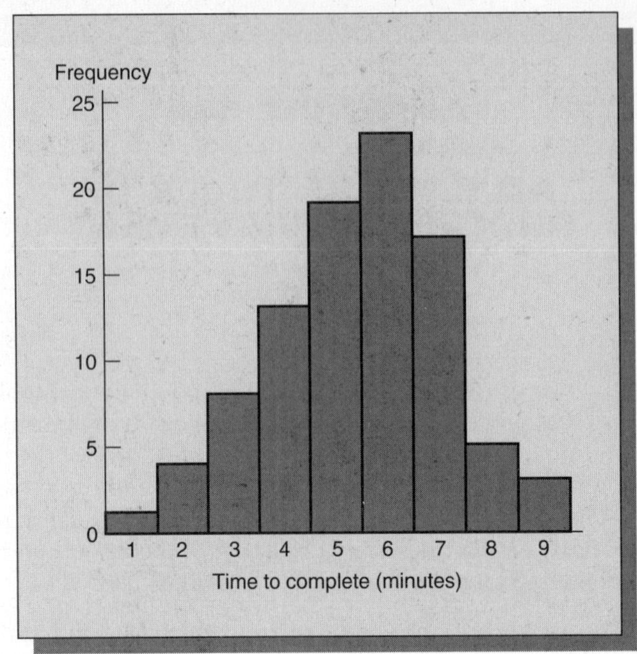

FIGURE 14A.1
Histogram. A histogram shows the frequency and distribution of some process or phenomenon.

Pareto charts A Pareto chart is a special kind of histogram, as shown in Figure 14A.2. It is a bar chart that organizes data to show the number of times something, such as a problem, occurs in a process. The most frequently occurring item is placed on the left of the chart, followed by the remaining items in declining order of frequency. This provides a visual picture of which items occur many times and which occur only occasionally. An additional line is often added to the chart,

FIGURE 14A.2
Pareto chart. A Pareto chart is a histogram ordered by frequency of occurrence, often showing a cumulative frequency line.

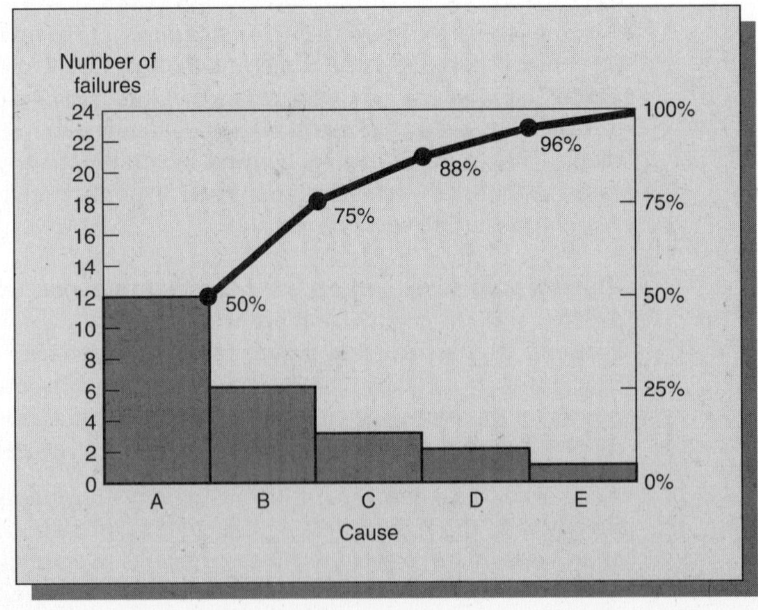

beginning at the top of the first (tallest) bar, showing the cumulative frequency for each item in the chart.

Pareto charts are useful in determining which problems to attack first to make the largest impact on results since they distinguish between the few problems that occur many times (the "vital few") and the many problems that each occur only a few times (the "trivial many").

Run (trend) charts Run, or trend, charts are also very familiar because of their wide use in popular and business publications. Figure 14A.3 is a typical run chart. Although normally shown as a line rather than a bar, these charts are much like histograms. They show the magnitudes of items over time—such as sales each month of the year or daily stock prices. In their simplest form they may be little more than checklists designed to tabulate the outcomes of the process being observed.

By providing a visual representation of the data, a run chart makes it easier to detect trends in the data points and changes in averages over the longer term than if the data were presented in a table. An "average" line, based on the data set being plotted, is often included in the chart. Patterns also may emerge which provide insight into natural process variation or seasonality in the data.

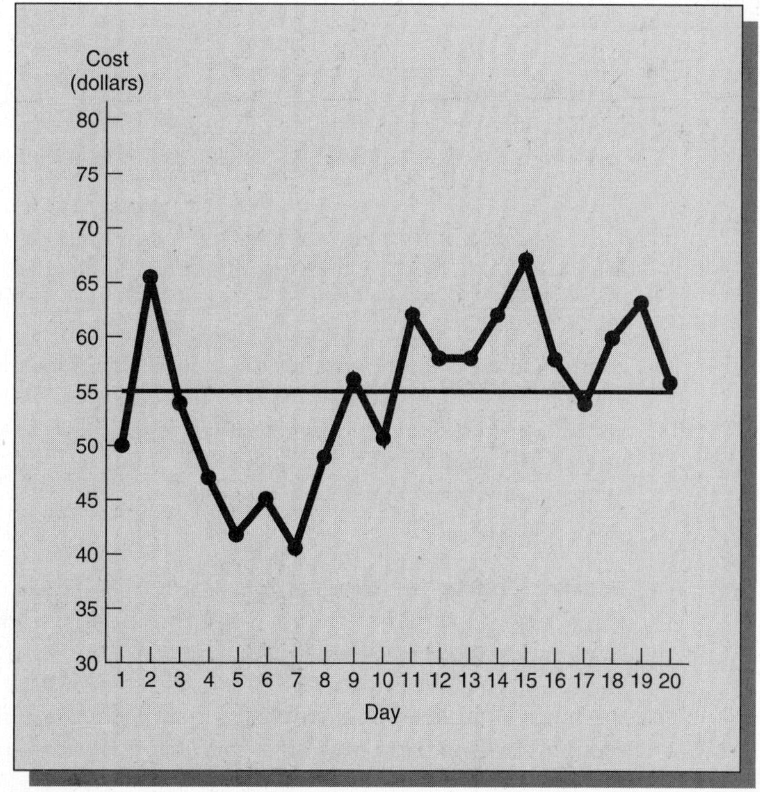

FIGURE 14A.3
Run (trend) chart. A run chart is a plot of the value of some variable over time, often with a line showing the average value.

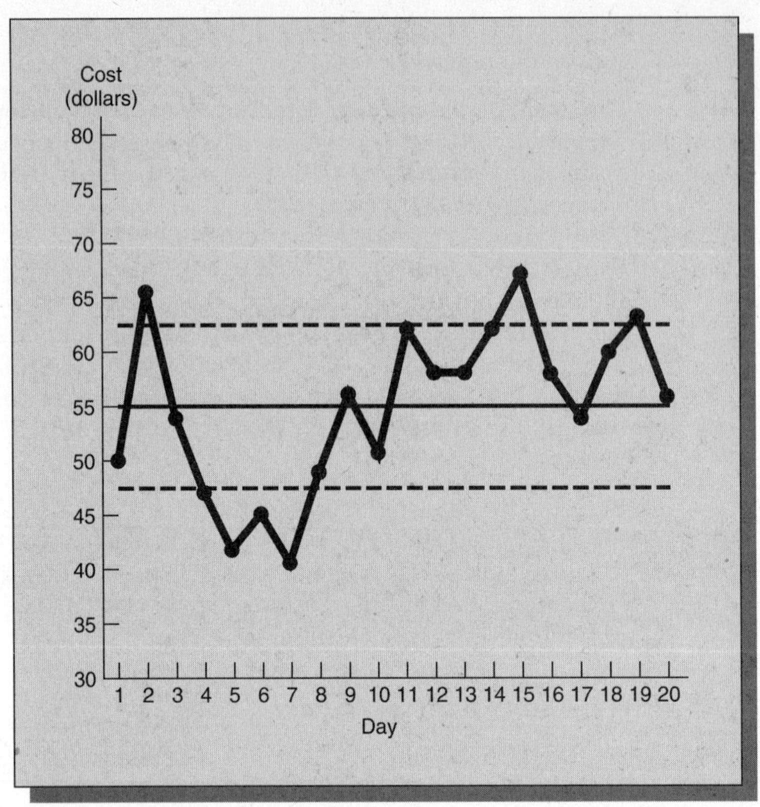

FIGURE 14A.4
Control chart. A control chart is a run chart with control limits added to identify "out-of-control" events.

Control charts Control charts are run charts incorporating additional information. They provide a visible indication of the range of variation occurring in a process and provide guidance for determining whether a process is demonstrating unusual behavior.

The additional information is shown as two lines called *control limits,* the dotted lines in Figure 14A.4. Control limits are calculated statistically using data from the process. The control limits are used to help interpret whether particular data points in the chart are normally occurring events or unusual ones. For example, control charts call attention to unusual occurrences, like the spike in Figure 14.1, allowing special cause variation to be separated from common cause (natural) variation. Guidelines for interpreting control charts drawn from statistics, such as how to interpret a number of successive points falling above or below the process average, enable conclusions to be drawn about possible changes in the process being studied.

Scatter charts (or diagrams) Scatter charts are used to study the relationships between variables. In process improvement efforts, they are used to develop hypotheses about cause-and-effect relationships that can lead to making process changes. The chart is drawn with one variable on the vertical axis and another on the horizontal axis. For example, in manufacturing, the variables might be "time required to assemble a unit" and "number of parts in the unit" (or perhaps "hours of training per assembly-line worker"). In finance it might be "time required to process an invoice" as a function of size of order or unit of currency.

As illustrated in Figure 14A.5, data points are plotted for the values of variable 1 at given values of variable 2. After sufficient points are plotted, the resulting "cloud" of points may exhibit a pattern. The degree of concentration of the points and their pattern indicate the strength and nature of the relationship, if any. For process improvement work, visual inspection of the pattern is frequently all that is required to take the next analytical step. However, when more rigorous analysis is appropriate, statistical analysis techniques, such as linear regression, are easily accessible on PCs for testing the strength of the relationships.

Flow charts Flow charts, such as the one shown in Figure 14A.6, are familiar to many of us because of their use in computer programming for organizing the sequence of steps in a program. They are graphic representations of each individual step or decision in a process. They show the interconnection of the steps—how one step follows from another. Writing down and formalizing these steps often leads to discoveries about how the process "really works" or to insights about improving a process by streamlining or redesigning it.

Cause-and-effect charts Cause-and-effect charts show possible causes of a problem or event in an organized way. They are also called "Ishikawa diagrams," in honor of the man who popularized their use, and "fishbone diagrams" because

FIGURE 14A.5
Scatter chart (or diagram). A scatter chart is a plot of one variable against another to make any relationship visual and easier to spot.

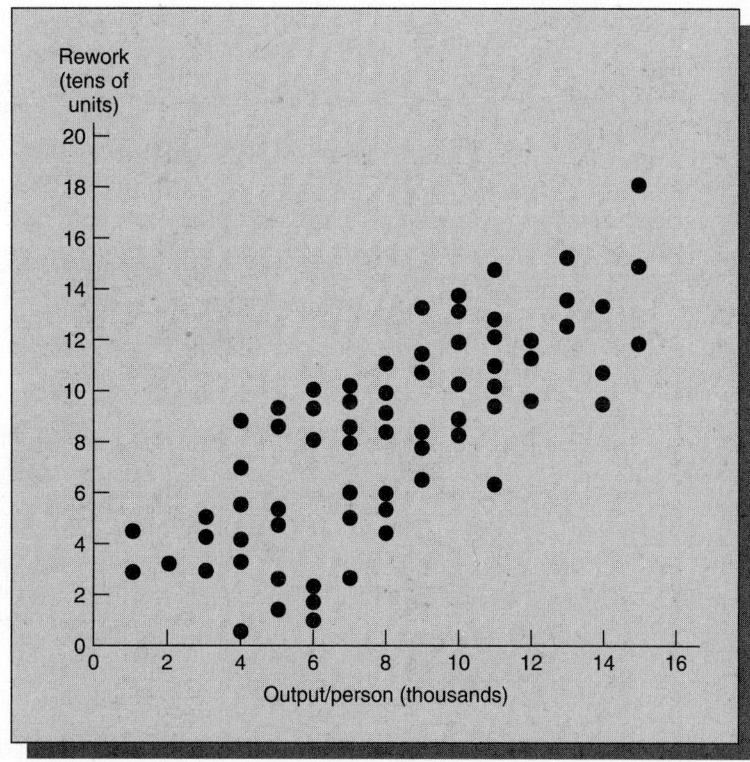

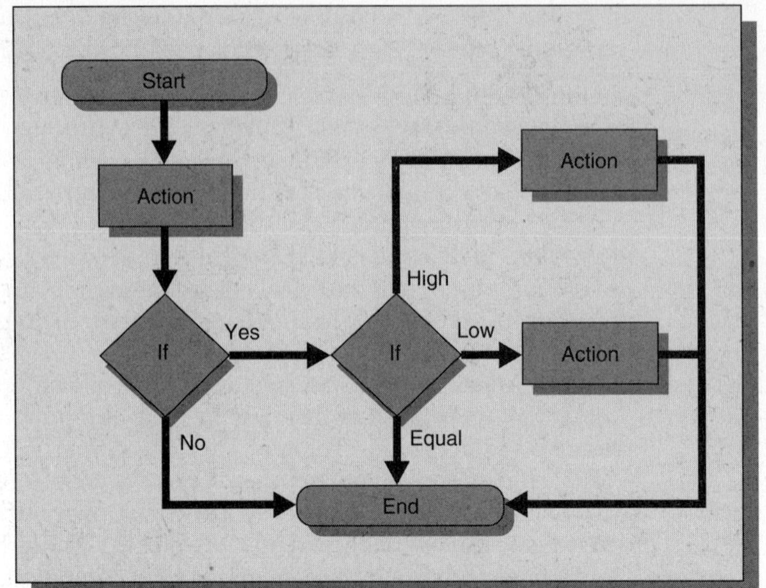

FIGURE 14A.6
Flow chart. A flow chart is a picture of the steps in a process showing their sequencing and interconnections.

of their shape. Broad categories of possible causes of problems in a process are labeled on branches sprouting from the center line. The four categories *plant, policies, procedures,* and *people* (sometimes *machines, material, methods,* and *manpower*) are frequently used as seen in Figure 14A.7. Smaller branches containing further refinements on the theme are then added to each of the larger ones summarized by the branch category. The final result looks like a fish skeleton, hence the name *fishbone.* Cause-and-effect diagrams can be seen as simple maps showing how a variety of factors contribute to high or low process performance. This perspective facilitates

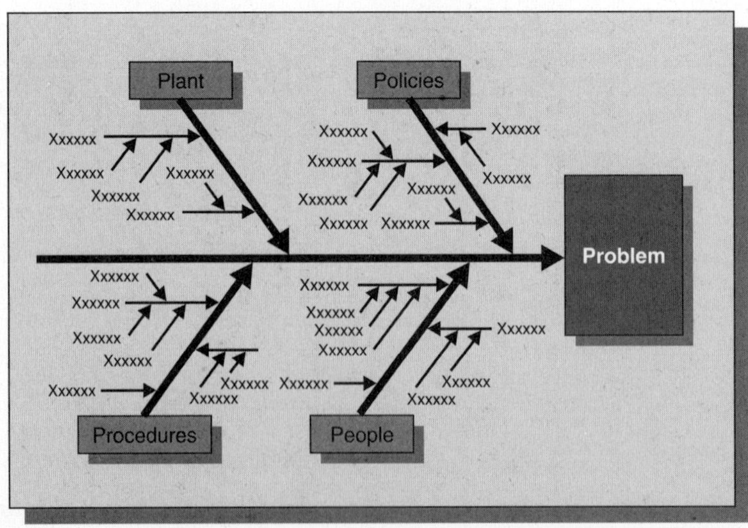

FIGURE 14A.7
Cause-and-effect chart. A cause-and-effect chart is a map showing how various factors contribute to an outcome.

the generation of hypotheses about which inputs may be most likely to cause the problem under investigation, thus suggesting promising targets for improvement.

2. Other Basic Analytical Tools

Check sheets Check sheets are forms used to collect data and sometimes are classified as one of the classical tools of quality management. They are worksheets where the number of occurrences of one or more selected variables are recorded.

Stratification Stratification is a technique that is often useful in analyzing data with different attributes, for example data collected from many different sources. The variety within the data may tend to obscure important patterns. Stratification sorts the data by obvious, unifying criteria, such as *type* of customer, *location* of accounting offices, *department* paying late, transactions by *time* of day, and so on. The other analytical tools are then used on the resulting data subgroups. Considerable insight into a problem may often be gained by sorting data this way before analyzing it further.

3. The "Seven New Tools" and More Sophisticated Statistical Tools

The tools listed above are used by virtually all organization members. Two other sets of analytical tools are used by fewer organization members but are still important.

One set is sometimes called the "seven new tools of management and planning." They have been popularized in the United States by the quality training and consulting organization GOAL/QPC and by Shigeru Mizuno.[1]

The seven new tools are:

- Affinity diagrams—used to organize large amounts of nonnumerical data into logical groupings.
- Interrelationship digraphs—used to determine and show the relationships among factors in complex, multifactor situations.
- Tree diagrams—used to determine and show the paths and tasks needed to accomplish goals and all related subgoals.
- Prioritization matrices—used to prioritize items, such as tasks, issues, and alternative courses of action by applying specified, weighted criteria.
- Matrix diagrams—used to show the relations between each item in two sets of items, such as ideas and issues.
- Process design program charts (PDPC)—used to show the events and contingencies that may occur when moving from a problem statement to possible solutions.

---

[1]**References:** Mizuno's book is *Management for Quality Improvement: The 7 New QC Tools,* (Cambridge Mass.: Productivity Press, 1988). The description of these tools is based upon Michael Brassard, *The Memory Jogger Plus+,* (Methuen, Mass.: GOAL/QPC, 1989).

- Activity network diagrams—used to plan and monitor progress on complex projects and to determine optimal sequences of tasks, minimal project completion time, and critical time paths for project completion. *Activity network diagram* is a new name for the type of well-established management tool long known to engineers and managers as PERT (program evaluation and review technique) and CPM (critical path method).

The other group is composed of a set of more advanced statistical tools such as "design of experiments" and "Taguchi methods." These statistical techniques are more sophisticated and are used mainly by engineers comfortable with statistics and by statisticians. One of their main uses is to determine which variables are most important in complex situations where the simpler tools are not sufficiently effective or efficient.

APPENDIX 14B

BEHAVIORAL TOOLS OF PROCESS IMPROVEMENT

A set of behavioral tools or techniques are as widely used for improving processes, products, and services as are the quantitative, statistical, and analytical tools presented in Appendix 14A. As in that appendix, our description emphasizes the use of these quality-management tools for improving processes, although they too are used for improving products and services.

Seven behavioral tools are listed in Figure 14.4 and presented in this appendix. The concept of behavioral tools for process improvement is much less well understood than the concept of analytical tools. As a result, there is not yet clear agreement about which behavioral tools of process improvement are the most important or even most frequently used—we do not yet have an agreed-upon set of "classical behavioral tools of process improvement." The seven behavioral tools presented here are, however, ones that are used in many organizations to improve processes and in other aspects of managing.

1. Brainstorming

Brainstorming is a technique developed by Alex S. Osborn in the late 1940s for generating creative advertising ideas. It has been adopted in quality management to generate large numbers of suggestions, such as possible causes of a problem. Used in its original form, brainstorming involves collecting as many ideas as possible with no concern for their apparent value and under strict rules forbidding criticism, evaluation, or discussion of the ideas as they are being presented. Members sit together, volunteer ideas spontaneously, and produce a list of everything mentioned. The open atmosphere encourages sharing nonconventional thoughts and often helps generate ideas well beyond those the members bring to the session.

2. Nominal Group Technique

Nominal group technique (often erroneously called brainstorming) is a structured method developed in the 1970s by Andre L. Delbecq, Andrew H. Van de Ven, and David H. Gustafson that incorporates a form of brainstorming but then goes much further. Ideas, such as possible causes of a problem, are collected, their meanings clarified, and the most promising ones identified ("prioritized"). In some versions of this technique, plans for taking action are developed as part of the same working session.

3. Task Force Management Processes

This term is used to refer to various techniques for managing a group of organizational members assigned to address a particular problem or opportunity. A wide variety of task forces exist, and members may be volunteers or appointed. Many organizations have developed detailed guidelines for selecting task-force members, clarifying and negotiating the details of a group's mission, determining how resources will be acquired, establishing how the group members will work on the project both during group meetings and between meetings, and specifying how the group's results will be used by the organization.

4. Self-Directed, Self-Managing, and Self-Leading Work Teams

These three terms are used to describe groups of organizational members that do the normal on-going work of an organization—work that would otherwise be performed in "command groups" by managers or supervisors and their subordinates. These groups have varying degrees of authority to determine what type of work they will do, how it will be done, and perhaps even how it will be evaluated. The groups may have authority to select and remove group members and to allocate rewards for performance. The group members often have no formal supervisor to whom they report in the traditional sense.

5. Active Listening

Active listening is a communication technique, and skill, that involves paying careful attention to another person and guards against the many behaviors that interfere with one person's ability to communicate with another. Methods for focusing attention on the other party and for verifying that one has heard accurately what the other party is saying play important roles in this technique. Another term referring to these techniques is *nondirective interviewing*.

6. QIT (Quality-Improvement Team) Processes

QIT processes are systematic ways of identifying areas for improvement and then making the improvements. They are normally taught in organized training programs and use a formal step-by-step process involving explicit team-member roles such as facilitator, leader, and time keeper. The storyboard process described in this chapter is a representative QIT process. QITs normally work on an organization's numerous smaller processes and subprocesses.

7. Process Reengineering and Business Process Quality-Management Techniques

These two terms refer to systematic, team-based ways of improving large-scale processes. Although similar to QIT techniques in many respects, they both differ from QIT techniques in terms of the size of the projects undertaken, some of the methods used, and the amount of resources and time devoted to their solution. They differ from each other mainly in terms of continuity. The term *process reengi-*

neering usually refers to a more ad hoc way of improving business (or other) processes—"one-shot" efforts directed at dramatic improvements of particularly important or trouble-plagued processes. *Business process quality management* usually refers to the continual and on-going improvement of major processes under the leadership of formally designated "process owners." Repeatedly achieving dramatic process improvements is one of the regular and major managerial responsibilities of the process owners. The scale of process improvement sought is just as large as in process reengineering, but the improvement efforts are conducted repeatedly over time under the same leader.

PART VI
MAKING OPTIMIZATION DECISIONS

In Part VI we look at optimization decisions, attempts to determine the "best" value of one or more financial variables. Our goal is to find numbers that produce the highest worth for the company and its stakeholders.

Chapter 15 discusses leverage and the optimal mix of debt vs. equity financing. We show how fixed costs magnify companies' earnings and changes to their earnings. We review why a company's financing choice might affect the market value of its securities, and we describe four theories that attempt to explain the optimal debt-equity mix. The chapter concludes with a look at how companies approach the debt-equity mix decision in practice and how the mix differs by industry. Appendixes 15A–D present more of the theory and mechanics of debt-equity relationships.

Chapter 16 is devoted to risk management, the debt maturity mix, and the use of temporary working capital. After introducing hedging and showing how it can be used to reduce financial risks, we describe the four-step sequence of making working capital decisions and apply hedging to two of the four steps. Appendix 16A presents models of optimal transfers between cash and marketable securities.

Chapter 17 examines dividend theory and practice. We review how shareholders get their returns, describe five classes of dividend theories, and discuss patterns of dividends and how they are declared and paid. The chapter concludes by looking at three alternatives to cash dividends.

CHAPTER 15

LEVERAGE AND THE DEBT-EQUITY MIX

Debbie Curtis looked again at the figures on the screen of her computer and shook her head slowly. She now had five sets of figures, and each was quite different from the others. "How to proceed?" she thought.

Debbie was assistant chief financial officer of her company, a business that was growing and in need of new capital funds. She was in the process of contacting several investment banks and other advisors for recommendations on what form the new financing should take.

Debbie's problem was that each person she called gave her another point of view. One investment banker told her that her firm could benefit from greater financial leverage and should issue long-term debt. Another pointed out the company's strong stock price and recommended a sizeable equity issue. An analyst at a large investment fund reminded her that her company's debt ratio was not in line with the industry—perhaps her company should attend to that. But a distinguished professor at the nearby university told her that her firm's choice of financing wasn't very important, so the firm could raise its money any way it found most convenient. There seemed to be no agreement on what was right for her company.

In an effort to sort through the conflicting recommendations, Debbie had constructed pro-forma financial statements for each recommendation using the spreadsheet program on her personal computer. The differences among the pro-forma statements were significant. As she looked at the computer screen again, she found herself wondering just what was the best financing mix for her firm.

debt-equity mix—the combination of debt and equity financing employed by a firm

capital structure—the combination of long-term debt and equity financing employed by a firm, often used as a synonym for *the debt-equity mix*

The **debt-equity mix** refers to the composition of the right side of a company's balance sheet—in particular, how much of the firm's financing comes from borrowing (debt) and how much is contributed by stock investors (equity). It is also called the firm's **capital structure,** where *capital* refers to long-term financing, even though most firms include some short-term debt in their financing mix.

Financial theorists disagree on the importance of the debt-equity mix to the value of the firm. On the one extreme are the "traditionalists," who say that it is important to get the mix of funds just right to generate high value for investors. On the other extreme are Professors Modigliani and Miller, both Nobel laureates in economics, who argue that if it were not for imperfections in the financial markets, the debt-equity mix would play no role at all in establishing the value of the firm. In between are a full spectrum of financial theorists and practitioners for whom the debt-equity mix decision carries some degree of importance. In this chapter we will meet them all. Debbie will have to understand the competing views on the debt-equity mix decision if she is to help her firm make a reasoned choice.

Key Points You Should Learn from This Chapter

After reading this chapter you should be able to:

- Define operating and financial leverage and describe their relationship to fixed costs.
- Discuss why a company's financing choice might affect the market value of its securities.
- Describe four theories that attempt to explain the optimal mix of debt and equity financing.
- Describe how companies approach the debt-equity mix decision in practice.
- Explain why the debt-equity mix differs by industry.

Introductory Concepts—Leverage

Leverage is magnification. We are all familiar with common examples of leverage in the physical world: a screwdriver that magnifies the force of a hand to turn a screw, a crowbar that magnifies the force of an arm to lift a heavy weight, a power braking system that magnifies the force of a foot to stop a car. An automobile or bicycle transmission, with its multiple gears to magnify the engine's or rider's power, is a particularly sophisticated form of leverage, adjusting the amount of magnification as needed to meet road conditions.[1]

In business, leverage is also magnification. But instead of the magnification taking a physical form, business leverage deals with the magnification of profits. Rather than a crowbar or screwdriver or gear, the lever in a business is its fixed costs. And, instead of there being some physical force pressing against the lever, in business it is changing sales that pushes the firm toward higher or lower profitability.

We introduced the nature of variable and fixed costs in Chapter 4.[2] The same concepts hold here. A variable cost is one that changes with changes in sales, while a fixed cost is one that remains constant as the level of sales varies. Although it is likely that most costs are neither totally variable nor totally fixed, we will continue to make the convenient assumption that all costs can be classified as either fixed or variable.

1. Two Types of Fixed Costs: Operating and Financial

Fixed costs come in two varieties: operating and financial. Figure 15.1 is an income statement with its top half in managerial form.[3] The top half of the statement (lightly shaded) is the operating half. It begins with sales and ends with EBIT, and records operating revenues and expenses. In this half of the statement, fixed operating costs—those incurred in the production and delivery of the firm's products and services—are identified directly. The bottom half of the statement (more darkly shaded) is the financial half. It begins with EBIT and includes the division of earnings after taxes (EAT) by the number of outstanding common shares to produce earnings per share (EPS). This half of the statement details how operating earnings (EBIT) are distributed: to creditors (interest), to the government (taxes), and to shareholders (earnings per share).[4] The fixed financing cost

---

[1] **Observation:** In British business English, leverage is referred to as *gearing*, a usage based on this form of physical magnification.

[2] **Cross-reference:** Chapter 4, pp. 81–82.

[3] **Explanation:** Rather than the GAAP cost categories of "cost of goods sold" and "operating expenses" required for public reporting, this form of the income statement groups operating costs by their behavior: variable or fixed, making it easier for financial analysts to project costs should revenues change.

[4] **Observation and cross-reference:** We have omitted dividends paid to preferred shareholders from Figure 15.1 since their inclusion adds complexity to the illustration. The income statement of a company that pays a preferred dividend is presented in Appendix 15C in both statement and algebraic form.

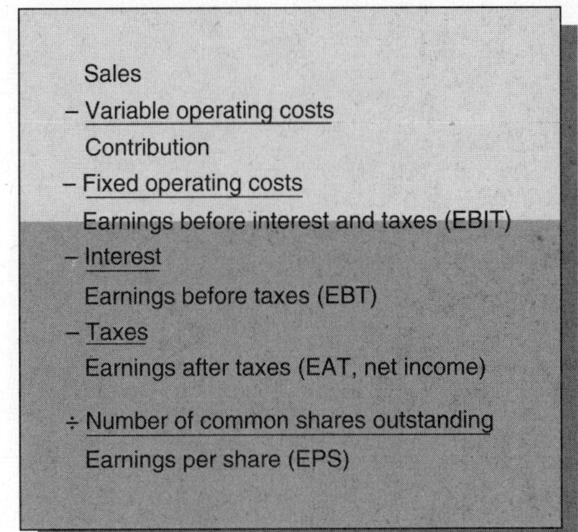

Sales
– Variable operating costs
Contribution
– Fixed operating costs
Earnings before interest and taxes (EBIT)
– Interest
Earnings before taxes (EBT)
– Taxes
Earnings after taxes (EAT, net income)
÷ Number of common shares outstanding
Earnings per share (EPS)

FIGURE 15.1
A simplified income statement in managerial form. The statement can be divided into an operating half and financial half, each with fixed costs.

is interest, which must be paid regardless of the level of earnings,[5] and it arises when a company elects to finance with debt.

Choosing between fixed and variable operating costs Often a company has limited choice over its fixed operating costs. Some firms' resources are heavily weighted toward capital equipment because of the technology of their industries and they have no viable variable cost alternatives. For example, it is hard to imagine how a steel mill could replace a foundry with a more variable cost resource such as temporary labor. Other companies are characterized by costs that are primarily variable and have no practical fixed cost alternatives. An example is the hairdressing industry, where the personal skill of the practitioner and the relationship between hairdresser and customer cannot easily be replaced by machinery. On the other hand, some companies face a choice of operating resources that permits them to choose between variable and fixed costs. For example, a computer may be built in an automated factory with fixed assembly costs or it may be constructed by piecework laborers, making assembly costs quite variable.

As suggested in the preceding paragraph, the operating resource-mix decision has traditionally been framed in terms of labor versus machinery. Labor has been considered the variable cost, easy to add and subtract as business volume changes, while machinery has been seen as the fixed cost, one that does not increase if the firm's sales rise but equally cannot easily be reduced if sales fall. Today we are discovering that the division of operating costs between variable and fixed is not as simple as labor versus machinery. Leasing and other rental agreements have

[5] **Observation:** Corporate debt often carries a "variable interest rate," making interest costs a function of the level of interest rates. With respect to a company's profitability, however, interest costs are fixed since they are not tied to sales or EBIT.

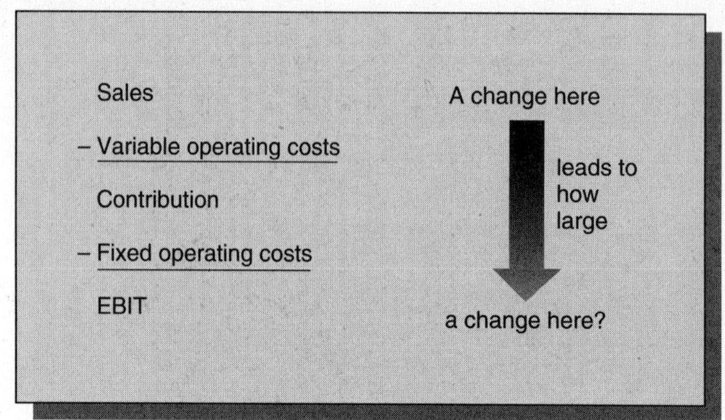

FIGURE 15.2
The operating half of the income statement. Operating leverage is the responsiveness of EBIT to change in sales.

made it possible for some costs once thought to be fixed to be made variable instead. And some firms, highly committed to their employees, have ceased treating labor as a variable cost.[6]

Choosing between fixed and variable financing costs Unlike the choice between fixed and variable operating costs, there are typically no technological barriers that prevent a firm from financing with different mixes of debt and equity. However, there often are practical limitations. Small firms rarely have good access to the capital markets. They cannot sell stock easily and often cannot place long-term debt. Their sole sources of external financing are through banks, insurance companies, etc., and their financing choices are limited to short- and intermediate-term debt. Larger firms do have good capital market access and can select more freely between debt and equity financing. To the extent a company can finance with either debt or equity funds, it can determine its level of fixed financing costs—by its debt-equity mix.

2. Two Types of Leverage: Operating and Financial

operating leverage—magnification of changes in operating earnings (EBIT) in response to changes in sales that is caused by the existence of fixed operating costs in the firm's cost structure

financial leverage—magnification of changes in earnings per share (EPS) in response to changes in EBIT that is caused by the existence of fixed financing costs (interest obligations) in the firm's cost structure

Since there are two types of fixed costs, there are also two types of leverage. **Operating leverage** is caused by the fixed costs of operations and is the magnification in the operating (top) half of the income statement—how EBIT responds to a change in sales as diagrammed in Figure 15.2. When a company's sales change, its EBIT changes as well, but the amount of the change depends on the firm's operating leverage. In a firm with no operating leverage (no fixed costs), profits change at the same rate as sales. For example, if a firm with no fixed operating costs experiences a 10% sales increase, its EBIT will be up by 10% as well. A firm with operating leverage (with fixed costs) will find its EBIT changing by more than the change to sales. For this type of firm, a 10% sales increase will lead to a greater-than-10% increase in EBIT.

Financial leverage is caused by fixed financing costs and is the magnification in the financial (bottom) half of the income statement—how earnings per share responds to a change in EBIT as sketched in Figure 15.3. In a firm with no financial

[6] **Cross-reference:** These points are discussed further in Appendix 15A.

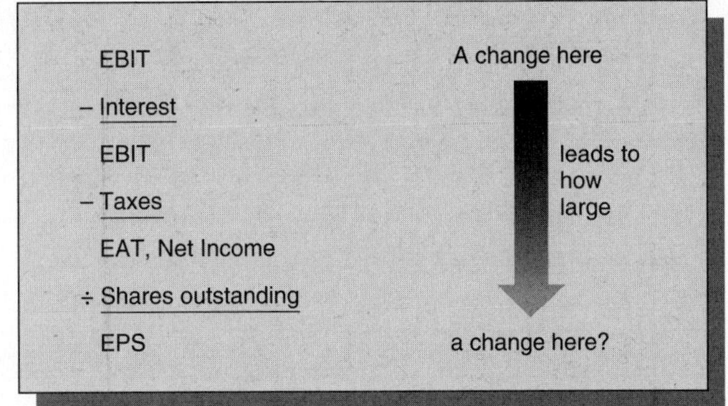

FIGURE 15.3
The financial half of the income statement. Financial leverage is the responsiveness of EPS to changes in EBIT.

leverage (no interest costs), EPS changes at the same rate as EBIT. For example, if a firm financed solely with equity experiences a 10% increase in its EBIT, its per-share earnings will be up by 10% as well. By contrast, a firm financed partly with debt (and, therefore, responsible for interest costs) will find its earnings per share changing by more than the change to EBIT. For this kind of firm, a 10% increase to EBIT would lead to a greater-than-10% increase in its EPS.[7]

Financing Choice Might Change a Company's Value

A company's financial leverage affects both the returns and risk it provides to its stakeholders. Returns change due to the magnification of profits. Risk changes because magnified profits are more volatile. As a firm adds to its debt, increasing its financial leverage, it becomes increasingly sensitive to changes in its level of operating profits (EBIT). Small increases in EBIT produce large increases in earnings per share (EPS). And, small decreases in EBIT produce large decreases in earnings per share.

For high amounts of debt, all stakeholders are exposed to the increased risk—a firm that is having trouble making interest payments will also have trouble making other payments and providing a stable environment for its stakeholders. For low amounts of debt, the increased risk from leverage is felt primarily by the company's stockholders since they bear the residual variability of the firm's income stream. For this reason, and because corporate finance theory has been derived with the goal of shareholder wealth maximization, the issue of leverage is usually evaluated from the point of view of the firm's stockholders.

The best debt-equity mix will depend on the way in which investors react to the risk and return issues contained in financial leverage. As customers of the firm, investors deserve the highest value for their participation in the business. Management should select the financing mix that produces the risk-return combination most satisfying to the financial markets, hence that produces the highest value for the firm's securities.

[7] **Cross-reference:** Appendix 15B discusses the impact of leverage on the income statement in more detail and presents three useful financial ratios that measure the amount of magnification.

1. How Financial Leverage Changes Returns and Risk

To understand these ideas better, Debbie Curtis constructs the bottom half of her company's income statement for two levels of debt. First, she assumes that interest costs are $20,000 and that there are 8,000 shares outstanding. For the second case, she assumes the company has financed with more debt and, correspondingly, less equity, so that interest costs are $30,000 and there are 7,000 shares outstanding.

Examples

The Impact of Financial Leverage on Returns and Risk

Debbie's company has EBIT of $100,000 and is in the 35% tax bracket.

Question: Construct the bottom half of the company's income statement for Debbie's two cases.

Solution steps:

	Case 1	Case 2
EBIT	$ 100,000	$ 100,000
− Interest	20,000	30,000
EBT	80,000	70,000
− Taxes	28,000	24,500
EAT	$ 52,000	$ 45,500
÷ Number of shares	8,000	7,000
EPS	$ 6.50	$ 6.50

Question: Repeat the analysis for EBIT of $80,000.

Solution steps:

	Case 1	Case 2
EBIT	$ 80,000	$ 80,000
−Interest	20,000	30,000
EBT	60,000	50,000
−Taxes	21,000	17,500
EAT	$ 39,000	$ 32,500
÷ Number of shares	8,000	7,000
EPS	$ 4.88	$ 4.64

Question: Repeat the analysis for EBIT of $120,000.

Solution steps:

	Case 1	Case 2
EBIT	$ 120,000	$ 120,000
−Interest	20,000	30,000
EBT	100,000	90,000
−Taxes	35,000	31,500
EAT	$ 65,000	$ 58,500
÷ Number of shares	8,000	7,000
EPS	$ 8.13	$ 8.36

Answer: For EBIT of $100,000, both financing plans produce the same EPS of $6.50. However, when EBIT changes, EPS changes by a greater amount when there is $30,000 of interest (down to $4.64, up to $8.36), than when there is only $20,000 of interest (down to $4.88, up to 8.13).

EBIT-EPS analysis—a graph showing how EPS responds to EBIT for various financing alternatives

Figure 15.4, produced from the data of this example and referred to as an **EBIT-EPS analysis,** summarizes Debbie's findings.

2. Finding the Indifference Point

indifference point—the level of EBIT which produces the same EPS regardless of the debt-equity mix

On the right-hand side of the graph of Figure 15.4, EPS is higher if Debbie's company uses a debt level with $30,000 of interest costs. On the left-hand side, EPS is higher if interest costs are $20,000. It will be important for Debbie to locate the **indifference point** at which the two lines intersect. At this level of EBIT, the two financing alternatives produce the same value of EPS, in this case, $6.50. To find this point, we use the algebraic representation of the bottom half of the income statement as given below,[8] fill in the numbers for each alternative, and then equate the two since we are looking for the point where EPS is equal.

$$EPS = \frac{(EBIT - interest) \times (1 - tax\ rate)}{number\ of\ shares}$$

FIGURE 15.4
An EBIT-EPS analysis showing the effect of financial leverage on earnings per share. As a company's interest costs increase, its EPS becomes more volatile, rising and falling by greater amounts.

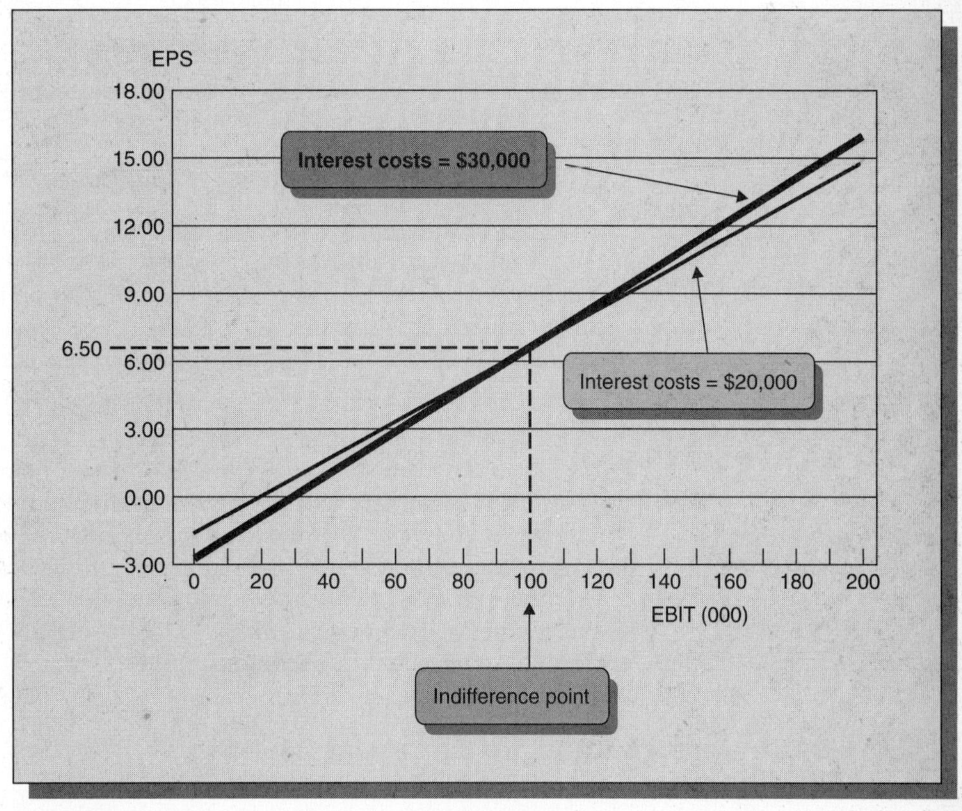

[8] **Cross-reference:** This equation is derived in Appendix 15C.

Example

Finding the Indifference Point

Debbie Curtis wishes to locate the point at which the two lines in Figure 15.4 intersect.

Question: What is the indifference point between these two alternatives?

Solution steps:

1. Write the algebraic representation of the bottom half of each income statement for each alternative:

$$\text{Alternative 1: EPS} = \frac{(\text{EBIT} - 20{,}000)(1 - .35)}{8{,}000}$$

$$\text{Alternative 2: EPS} = \frac{(\text{EBIT} - 30{,}000)(1 - .35)}{7{,}000}$$

2. Equate and solve for EBIT:

$$\frac{(\text{EBIT} - 20{,}000)(1 - .35)}{8{,}000} = \frac{(\text{EBIT} - 30{,}000)(1 - .35)}{7{,}000}$$

$$7{,}000(\text{EBIT} - 20{,}000) = 8{,}000(\text{EBIT} - 30{,}000)$$

$$7{,}000(\text{EBIT}) - 140{,}000{,}000 = 8{,}000(\text{EBIT}) - 240{,}000{,}000$$

$$1{,}000(\text{EBIT}) = 100{,}000{,}000$$

$$\text{EBIT} = 100{,}000$$

Answer: Earnings per share will be the same at EBIT of $100,000.

3. Summarizing the Effects of Leverage

To the right of the indifference point (EBIT > $100,000) higher levels of debt increase earnings per share. To the left of the indifference point (EBIT < $100,000) higher debt levels depress earnings per share. And on both sides, risk rises along with debt since debt increases the volatility of EPS. As we have seen throughout this book, high return with low risk is the return-risk combination that provides the highest financial value. Debbie Curtis summarizes what she has learned about financial leverage in this framework:

If EBIT is forecast to be *less than* the indifference point of $100,000, it is best to *avoid debt* since low debt leads to higher profits with less risk. However, if EBIT is forecast to be *greater than* the indifference point of $100,000, there is a *tradeoff between risk and return*. Higher debt increases profits but also increases risk; lower debt reduces risk but also reduces profits. In this case there is no clear financing strategy—the best debt-equity mix will be the one that gives investors the combination of returns and risk they most prefer.

How Investors React to Financial Leverage

The study of the way investors react to alternative debt-equity combinations is typically done by looking for the mix that minimizes the company's cost of capital. This is because the minimum cost of capital corresponds precisely to the maximum value of the firm. The reason is straightforward. In Chapter 9 we saw that the price of any security is inversely related to investors' required rate of return: as required rates of return fall, security prices rise, and vice versa. The weighted-average cost of capital is a measure of the combined required rates of return of all investors in the firm. Accordingly, as the cost of capital falls, the combined value of all the firm's securities rises, and vice versa.

There are several ways a firm's cost of capital can be lowered, thereby raising the company's value. One, not under the control of the financial manager, is if the general level of interest rates falls due to a declining pure rate of interest or, more likely, due to falling inflation expectations. The others *are* manageable. The financial manager can be diligent in raising money from those investors who perceive the least amount of risk, hence have lower required rates of return than other investors. The cost of any financing source can be kept down by minimizing flotation costs and by maximizing opportunities for tax deductions. Finally, the cost of capital can be reduced by selecting the mix of debt and equity that produces the lowest weighted-average cost, the subject of this chapter.

In the discussion that follows, we present competing theories of how investors react to various debt-equity combinations. Each is illustrated with a graph showing how the cost of debt (k_d), the cost of equity (k_e), and the resulting weighted-average cost of capital (k_w) change as the financing mix is varied from 100% equity and no debt to 100% debt and no equity. To keep the graphs easy to read, we have assumed that the firm uses only one type of debt and one type of equity. In every case, the minimum value on the weighted-average cost of capital line indicates the optimal debt-equity mix: the mix that maximizes the value of the firm.

1. The Traditional Approach

In the 1950s Professor David Durand summarized prevailing thought about the debt-equity mix and identified three approaches to the issue. The first two, the "net income approach" and the "net operating income approach" seemed illogi-

SERVING FINANCE'S CUSTOMERS

Keeping Shareholders Well Informed at Corning, Incorporated

Reducing perceived risks to raise security prices often goes well beyond selecting investors who think highly of the company. In December 1992, the controversy over the potential dangers from failures of breast implants manufactured by Dow Corning hit the news. Investors, seeing increased risk from the possibility of costly, class-action lawsuits, quickly bid down Dow Corning's stock price, as well as that of Corning, Incorporated. But Corning, Incorporated's Investor Relations group had been working for several years to understand their stockholders' and financial analysts' information requirements and had put an effective communication network in place. The open lines of communication helped investors understand that Dow Corning was a distinctly different company than Corning, Incorporated, and the fall in Corning, Incorporated's stock price, although initially severe, was only temporary.

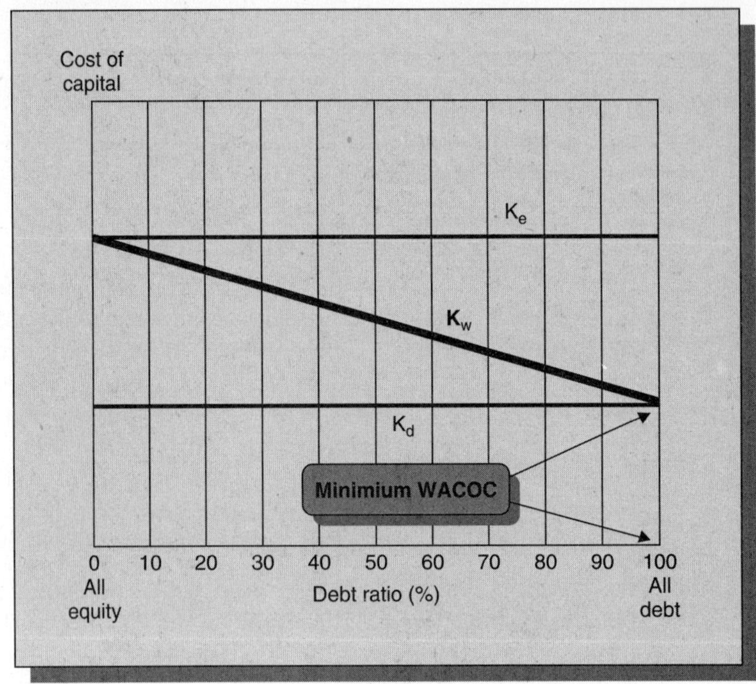

FIGURE 15.5
Capital costs under the net income approach. The optimal debt-equity mix is 100% debt.

cal in both their assumptions and conclusions and were dismissed by most financial managers. The third philosophy, which Durand called the "traditional approach," made assumptions and reached conclusions deemed much more reasonable and was widely accepted. The three approaches differ primarily in their assumptions about how investors react to increased levels of debt.[9]

The net income approach This approach assumes that neither creditors nor stockholders perceive that increased borrowing adds to their risks, so the firm's cost of debt and cost of equity remain constant regardless of its level of debt. Figure 15.5 summarizes this point of view. The lines for the costs of debt (k_d) and equity (k_e) are drawn horizontally to indicate that they are not changing as the financing mix goes from all equity to all debt. However, since the cost of debt is typically less than the cost of equity, the weighted-average cost of capital (k_w) declines as cheaper debt is substituted for the more expensive equity. The minimum cost of capital, corresponding to maximum value, is reached at the far right-hand side of the graph. As a result, the net income approach concludes that the best financing mix is 100% debt and no equity.

[9] **Elaboration:** The net income and net operating income approaches get their names from the way the value of the firm's stock is calculated. Under the net income approach, the value that belongs to shareholders is priced directly by taking the present value of the firm's projected *net income*, using the cost of equity as the discount rate. Under the net operating income approach, we first evaluate the company's total income stream by taking the present value of the firm's projected *net operating income* (EBIT) using the weighted-average cost ofcapital as the discount rate. Then, since EBIT is claimed by all investors, we subtract the value of the company's debt—the remainder must be the value of the firm's stock.

The net operating income approach Like the net income approach, this approach also assumes that creditors do not react to increased debt levels. Stockholders do find a higher debt ratio more risky, but their required rate of return increases to precisely cancel out the advantage of cheaper debt, making the firm's cost of capital constant regardless of its debt-equity mix. Figure 15.6 summarizes this point of view. The line for the cost of debt (k_d) is drawn horizontally to indicate it is not changing as the debt-equity mix goes from all equity to all debt. The line for the cost of equity (k_e) slopes upward, capturing stockholders' increasing required rate of return. The weighted-average cost of capital (k_w) remains constant (horizontal)—as the financing mix is changed to include more debt, the cheaper debt is exactly offset by the increasing cost of the remaining equity. Since there is no low point on the cost of capital line, there is no financing mix that maximizes the firm's value. The net operating income approach concludes that the debt-equity mix is irrelevant. Value comes only from the firm's operating income (EBIT), and any financing mix is as good as any other.

The traditional approach This approach assumes that both creditors and stockholders perceive that increased borrowing adds to their risks. As a firm increases its debt ratio, both its cost of debt and cost of equity increase. Figure 15.7 summarizes this point of view. The lines for the cost of debt (k_d) and the cost of equity (k_e) are now both drawn with an upward slope. The weighted-average cost of capital (k_w) first declines as cheaper debt is substituted for more expensive equity and then increases, swept up by the rising k_d and k_e. The cost of capital reaches a low point, and the firm's value reaches its maximum, in the middle of the graph. Accordingly, the traditional approach concludes that the best debt-

FIGURE 15.6

Capital costs under the net operating income approach. The debt-equity mix is irrelevant since no one mix produces a lower cost of capital, hence higher value, than any other.

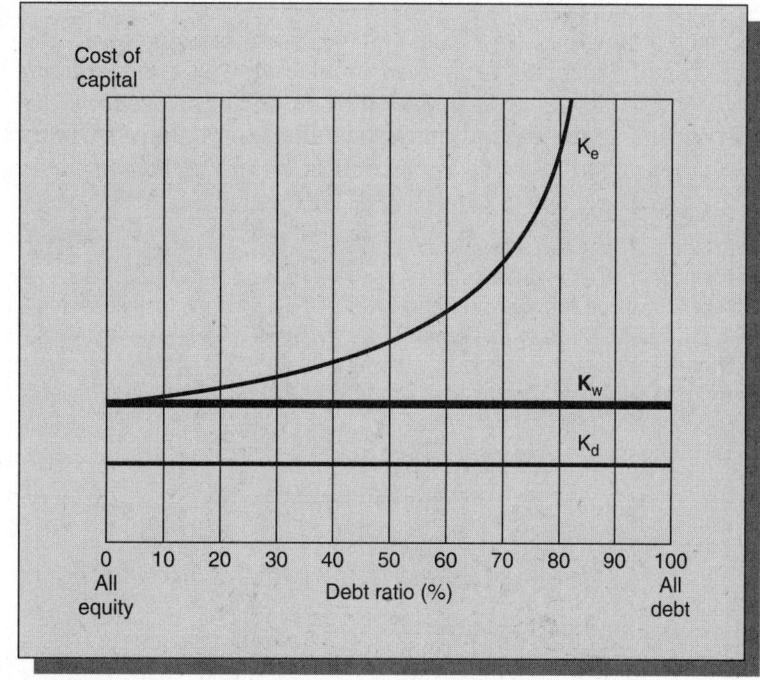

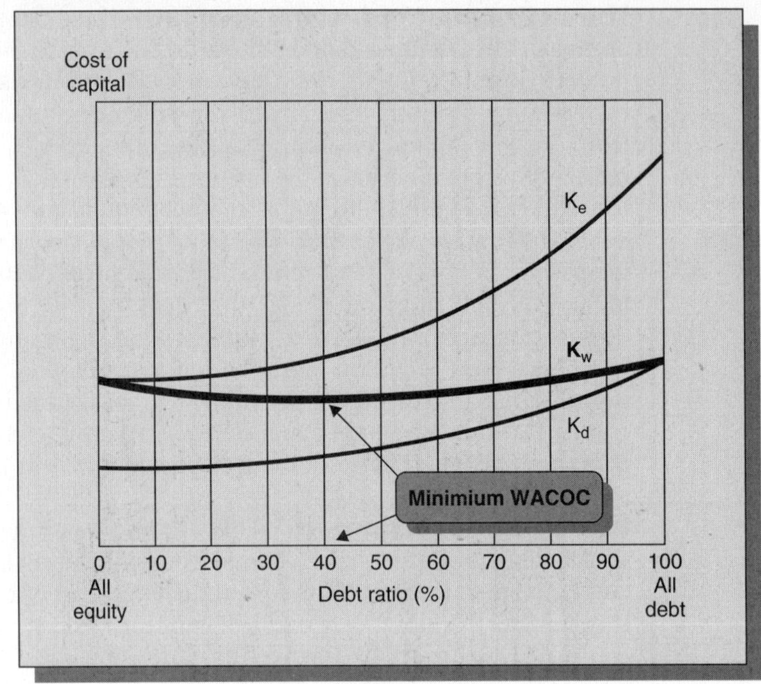

FIGURE 15.7
Capital costs under the traditional approach. The optimal debt-equity mix includes some debt and some equity.

equity mix is somewhere in the middle, a function of the rate at which the risks perceived by investors increase.

Example

The Traditional Approach to the Optimal Debt-Equity Mix

Debbie Curtis is experimenting with the traditional approach as a guide to the best way to finance her company. She has made the following forecasts of how the financial markets would react to alternative mixes of financing:

Debt Ratio	Cost of Debt	Cost of Equity
0%	5.0%	11.0%
10	5.0	11.0
20	5.0	11.2
30	5.3	11.6
40	5.7	12.2
50	6.2	13.2
60	6.8	14.8
70	7.8	16.8
80	9.0	19.2
90	10.4	22.0

Question: What is the optimum debt-equity mix?

Solution steps:

1. Calculate the weighted-average cost of capital for each mix:

Debt Ratio	Debt Proportion × Cost	+	Equity Proportion × Cost	=	WACOC
0%	0% × 5.0%	+	100% × 11.0%	=	11.00%
10	10% × 5.0	+	90% × 11.0	=	10.40
20	20% × 5.0	+	80% × 11.2	=	9.96
30	30% × 5.3	+	70% × 11.6	=	9.71
40	40% × 5.7	+	60% × 12.2	=	**9.60**
50	50% × 6.2	+	50% × 13.2	=	9.70
60	60% × 6.8	+	40% × 14.8	=	10.00
70	70% × 7.8	+	30% × 16.8	=	10.50
80	80% × 9.0	+	20% × 19.2	=	11.04
90	90% × 10.4	+	10% × 22.0	=	11.56

2. Locate the lowest weighted-average cost of capital: The cost of capital reaches a minimum value of 9.60% at a debt ratio of 40%.

Answer: The optimal debt-equity mix is 40% debt and 60% equity. At that mix, the weighted-average cost of capital is minimized, hence the value of the firm is at a maximum.

2. Modigliani-Miller Theory

In the late 1950s, Professors Franco Modigliani and Merton Miller (we'll refer to them as "MM") stunned the finance community by publishing a "proof" that, under certain circumstances, the conclusion of the net operating income approach was in fact correct: there is no optimal financing mix. Although MM's conclusions were the same as those of the net operating income approach, the way they reached their conclusions was very different.

Perfect market assumptions MM began their analysis by making some simplifying assumptions, in particular, that the financial markets were uncomplicated and without any imperfections. Specifically, MM assumed:

1. Unlimited borrowing and lending is available to both companies and investors at one common interest rate. Individual borrowing to purchase stock is secured by the shares purchased, and the borrowers' liability is limited to the value of the shares. Should a company default on its debt, its creditors would seize the remaining assets and the company would suffer no further loss of value (there are no bankruptcy costs).
2. Firms can be grouped into "equivalent risk classes," groups of companies with the same business risk.
3. Securities trade in perfect capital markets in which every participant is a "price taker," too small to influence prices directly; no transactions costs (brokerage, flotation, transfer taxes, etc.) exist; complete and free information is available to all traders; and securities are infinitely divisible.
4. No taxes are paid on corporate income.
5. Shareholders are indifferent to receiving their returns in the form of dividends or capital gains, and ordinary income and capital gains are taxed at the same rate.

The MM argument The net effect of assumption 1 is that personal borrowing and lending has the same cost and risk as corporate borrowing and lending. MM argued that if individuals could borrow and lend in the same way as corporations, they would not pay a higher stock price for corporations to do the borrowing or lending for them. What matter to investors are the total return and risk from their investment position, including the impact of corporate borrowing plus the impact of any borrowing or lending they do themselves. Should a company's level of debt be different than desired, each investor could personally borrow or lend to add to or undo any undesired corporate borrowing themselves. For example, if a company borrowed more than an investor thought prudent, that investor could lend (to the government, for example, by investing in Treasury bills) to offset the corporate debt. On the other hand, if a company borrowed less than an investor thought wise, the investor could **buy the stock on margin,** using borrowed funds to help pay for the stock thereby adding more debt to the investment position. Through the use of this **homemade leverage** investors could exactly duplicate corporate leverage, producing the same changes to returns and risk. Accordingly, investors would not care about the debt-equity mix chosen by any corporation.

buying stock on margin—purchasing stock using borrowed money for part of the purchase price

homemade leverage—borrowing by stock investors to leverage their investment portfolio

Assumptions 2 and 3 insure that two companies with the same operating earnings (EBIT) cannot have different stock prices. By assumption 2, investors can identify companies that have the same business risk. Should two companies with the same earnings stream and the same business risk have different stock prices, investors would arbitrage between them, simultaneously selling the higher-priced stock and purchasing the lower-priced security, leaving their risk-return exposure unchanged while pocketing the difference in price. Assumption 3 guarantees that this would be an easy and costless procedure.

Assumptions 4 and 5 complete the MM argument. If there are no corporate income taxes, the tax system cannot create a value difference between debt and equity financing by allowing companies to deduct some payments to investors (interest) while not others (dividends). If investors are indifferent to the form of their returns, management cannot make the company more valuable to investors by directing the firm's returns into interest versus dividends and capital gains.

Corporate income taxes Of all MM's assumptions, finance theorists consider the assuming away of corporate income taxes the one most at odds with the real world. Several years after their pathbreaking analysis, MM rederived their conclusions incorporating corporate income taxes. Not surprisingly, they found that in the United States, where interest payments are deductible but dividends are not, a firm can reduce its tax bill by tilting its financing mix toward debt. MM concluded that as long as a firm was profitable and would otherwise pay taxes, the best financing mix was to use as much debt as possible to reduce taxes by as much as possible. MM had revised their prescription for the debt-equity mix from the improbable conclusion of the net operating income approach to the even more improbable conclusion of the net income approach!

3. The Miller (Personal Tax) Model

In 1976, Merton Miller presented another version of the MM model which incorporated personal income taxes. In doing so, he relaxed the assumption that investors are indifferent to the form of their returns. Miller pointed out that: (1) creditors receive the majority of their returns as interest payments while stockholders' returns are far more likely to be in the form of capital gains, and (2) in the United States, interest is taxed at a higher rate than capital gains for two reasons. First, interest is lumped in with other income and taxed at the investor's marginal tax rate while capital gains receive a preferential lower rate. Second, interest is taxed when received while capital gains are not taxed until the security is sold, often many years later. Therefore, to minimize their personal taxes, investors would prefer to see a firm issue equity rather than debt. Miller concluded that the personal tax system's favoring of equity offset some or all of the corporate tax system's favoring of debt financing, and he returned to the original MM conclusion: the debt-equity mix was (essentially) irrelevant to the firm's value.

When Professor Miller studied personal taxes in 1976, capital gains were taxed at only 40% of the taxpayer's marginal tax rate, so the difference he identified was quite significant. Today, however, capital gains are taxed at the same (or nearly the same) rate as interest.[10] Only the difference in the timing of payments separates the tax treatment of interest and capital gains for many taxpayers. The result: personal taxes play a much smaller role in the financing mix decision in today's tax environment.

4. Compromise Theory

In the years since MM's contributions, finance theorists have been exploring the importance of each of MM's perfect market assumptions—how necessary each assumption is for the MM conclusions to hold. In effect, they have been searching for a compromise between the extreme results of MM and the more intuitively appealing conclusions of the traditional approach. Today, the majority opinion seems to be that there are three significant "imperfections" in the financial environment which tip the financing mix decision toward either equity or debt. These are: (1) the corporate income tax as considered by MM, (2) the costs of corporate bankruptcy, and (3) agency costs.

Corporate income taxes As MM pointed out, the corporate income tax favors debt financing. Interest payments are tax-deductible while dividends are not. A firm that borrows is rewarded with lower income tax payments while a firm that uses equity financing sees no comparable tax reduction.

bankruptcy—the condition of being unable to make payments on debt

Bankruptcy costs The costs associated with **bankruptcy** favor equity financing. MM simplified their analysis by assuming that there are no costs if a firm defaults on its debt. In practice, this is rarely true. When a firm defaults, it generally experiences one or more of the following costs: (1) fees paid to attorneys to control the legal damage; (2) court costs if a legal declaration of bankruptcy is sought

[10] **Elaboration and cross-reference:** There is a ceiling rate of 28% applied to capital gains. For investors at or below the 28% marginal tax bracket, interest income and capital gains are taxed at the same rate. Taxpayers in higher brackets save on capital gains taxes. Refer to Appendix 4B for more information on the U.S. personal income tax system.

to keep creditors at bay; (3) lost sales due to skeptical customers; (4) poor performance by pessimistic employees who might spend part or all of their work time looking for other work; (5) impaired long-run viability from management decisions that sacrifice the long run to raise short-run cash; (6) interruptions of business process flow if creditors seize assets; (7) deterioration, obsolescence, and/or vandalism of plant and inventories due to suspension of business activities; and (8) sale of assets at less than full market value to satisfy creditors. Both creditors and stockholders perceive this risk which rises with increased debt levels.

Agency costs Agency costs also favor equity financing. As a company assumes greater levels of debt, management faces a more difficult task in balancing and aligning the needs of the firm's investment stakeholders. Creditors, concerned that management might act contrary to their best interests, typically impose loan covenants on the firm which restrict management's financial freedom and which must be monitored, usually at the firm's expense. All investors, observing these added costs and management issues, forecast lower EBIT and greater risk as more debt is taken on.

The compromise Summarizing these effects, the impact of leverage on the value of a firm is often written as follows:

$$V_{levered} = V_{unlevered} + CT - BC - AC$$

where:

$V_{levered}$ = the value of a firm with leverage

$V_{unlevered}$ = the value of the same firm if it had no debt financing

CT = the added value from the corporate tax effect

BC = the reduction in value from the bankruptcy cost effect

AC = the reduction in value from the agency cost effect

acceptable range—the set of debt-equity mixes that produce a weighted-average cost of capital at or near its minimum value

Figure 15.8 depicts the conclusions of the compromise theory. As the firm begins to take on debt, the first impact comes from the corporate tax subsidy which lowers the cost of debt (k_d) and pushes down the cost of capital (k_w). As the firm continues to borrow, both the cost of debt (k_d) and cost of equity (k_e) lines rise due to the increased risk perceptions from estimates of bankruptcy and agency costs pushing the cost of capital (k_w) line back up. The weighted-average cost of capital (k_w) first declines and then rises. While there is a minimum cost of capital, and hence a corresponding maximum value of the firm, the k_w line is shallow at the bottom, and the precise minimum point is difficult to find. Instead, it is more useful to identify an **acceptable range** within which the cost of capital is at or near its minimum. Any debt-equity mix within the acceptable range is close enough to the optimum so that the cost of being more precise exceeds the possible added value.

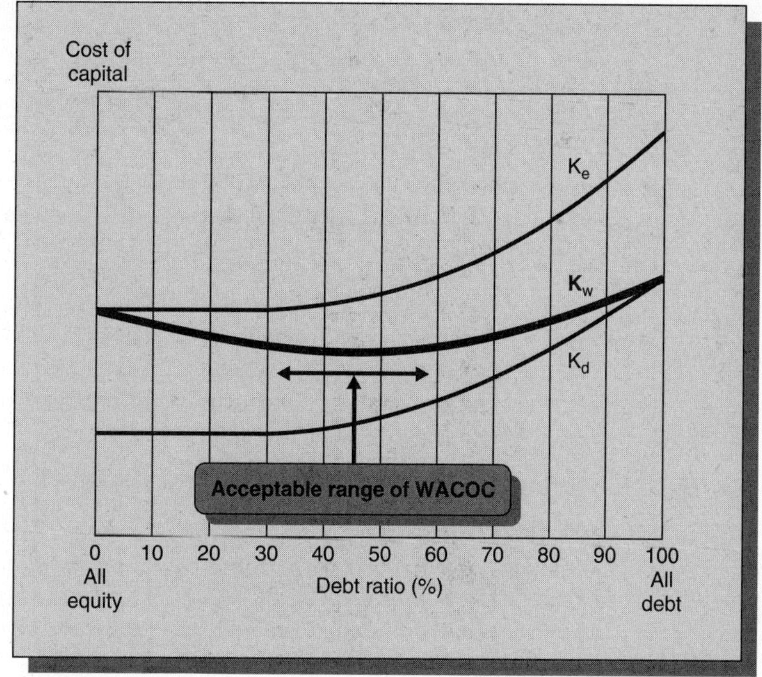

FIGURE 15.8
Capital costs under the compromise approach. The cost of capital first falls, due to the corporate income tax effect, and then rises as bankruptcy and agency costs become significant.

Example

Compromise Theory

Debbie Curtis has estimated the unlevered value of her firm ($V_{unlevered}$) to be $50,000,000, and has also estimated the corporate income tax effect (CT), bankruptcy cost effect (BC), and agency cost effect (AC) for alternative mixes of financing:

Debt Ratio	CT	BC	AC
0%	$ 0	$ 0	$ 0
10	1,700,000	0	200,000
20	3,400,000	0	500,000
30	5,100,000	1,000,000	900,000
40	6,800,000	3,000,000	1,400,000
50	8,500,000	6,000,000	2,000,000
60	10,200,000	10,000,000	2,800,000
70	11,900,000	15,000,000	3,800,000
80	13,600,000	21,000,000	5,000,000
90	15,300,000	28,000,000	6,400,000

Question: What is the acceptable range of the debt-equity mix?

Solution steps:

1. Use the compromise theory relationship to calculate the value of the firm at each possible debt ratio:

$$V_{unlevered} + CT - BC - AC = V_{levered}$$

Debt Ratio	Value of the Firm								
0%:	$50,000,000	+	0	−	0	−	0	=	$50,000,000
10:	$50,000,000	+	1,700,000	−	0	−	200,000	=	$51,500,000
20:	$50,000,000	+	3,400,000	−	0	−	500,000	=	**$52,900,000**
30:	$50,000,000	+	5,100,000	−	1,000,000	−	900,000	=	**$53,200,000**
40:	$50,000,000	+	6,800,000	−	3,000,000	−	1,400,000	=	**$52,400,000**
50:	$50,000,000	+	8,500,000	−	6,000,000	−	2,000,000	=	$50,500,000
60:	$50,000,000	+	10,200,000	−	10,000,000	−	2,800,000	=	$47,400,000
70:	$50,000,000	+	11,900,000	−	15,000,000	−	3,800,000	=	$43,100,000
80:	$50,000,000	+	13,600,000	−	21,000,000	−	5,000,000	=	$37,600,000
90:	$50,000,000	+	15,300,000	−	28,000,000	−	6,400,000	=	$30,900,000

2. Locate the greatest value. The value of Debbie's firm reaches a maximum of $53,200,000 at a debt ratio of 30%.

Answer: From her calculations, Debbie determines the optimal debt-equity mix to be 30% debt and 70% equity. However, recognizing the uncertainty in her estimates, she identifies the acceptable range from 20% debt to 40% debt.

Notice that Figure 15.8 looks very much like Figure 15.7, the one for the traditional approach. The only difference, in fact, is how we arrived at our conclusions. In a sense, finance theory has come full circle in its view of the debt-equity mix. We began with the traditional approach, which identified an optimal combination of debt and equity; moved to MM theory, which concluded that any debt-equity combination was okay; then moved on to "MM with corporate taxes," with its call for 100% debt; next flirted with Miller's personal tax theory, which returned us to the original MM position of financing irrelevance; and now have the compromise theory, which once again claims that an optimal combination of debt and equity exists for each company. We anticipate that in the coming years financial managers will see further developments as academics and practitioners make new contributions to the theory, as the government continues to tinker with the income tax code, and as quality-management approaches to the alignment of the firm, its managers, and its stakeholders suggest new factors to consider and/or provide new insights into agency and bankruptcy costs.

Setting the Capital Structure in Practice

Because the theories of the debt-equity mix offer conflicting advice and because it is difficult to forecast the numbers required to implement the compromise theory, most financial managers seem to supplement the theories with other, more practical methods of making the financing mix decision. In this section we look at two of the more widely used: (1) a collection of techniques summarized by the acronym FRICTO and (2) a pattern of financing choice called the "pecking-order approach."

1. The FRICTO Approach

FRICTO—an acronym (flexibility, risk, income, control, timing, other) summarizing practical considerations in setting the debt-equity mix

FRICTO is an acronym for the words: flexibility, risk, income, control, timing, and other. The FRICTO approach assumes the financial manager is concerned about the form the next financing issue should take. Although theory suggests the firm should stick closely to its target capital structure by issuing a mix of debt and equity every year, to do so would be very expensive in practice. It is far more common for a company to fund itself only with debt in some years and only with equity in others. FRICTO serves as a reminder to financial managers as they sort through the practical issues surrounding this choice. Each concept addresses one of the important effects of the financing mix decision on the firm's value and financial health.

Flexibility Flexibility refers to the freedom to raise funds in the form of debt or equity whenever desired. A firm in need of funds but with limited financing choices is often at the mercy of the financial markets. For example, restrictive

"Would you care to assist, sir, in reducing my debt to equity ratio?"

covenants on existing debt or a high debt load relative to the firm's cash flow often close off further debt financing, leaving equity as the only alternative. Each time a firm obtains funding, it must be careful not to limit its opportunities the next time around. In fact, a well-planned sequence of funding creates more, not less, opportunities for future financing.

Flexibility comes from proficient financial planning, identifying the amounts and timing of future security issues. It is increased by good communication with existing and potential investor stakeholders, so that bankers and capital market participants understand the company's financial strategy. Flexibility is further maintained by avoiding a debt-equity mix near the high end of (or above) the acceptable range—when a company's debt-equity mix is considered to be high, it can be difficult or quite costly to issue additional debt.

Risk As we have seen in this chapter, the risk associated with the debt-equity mix has three components. One is the added volatility of the earnings stream that comes from financial leverage. Another is the danger of bankruptcy that comes from committing to fixed interest payments. The third is the risk from the overhead built into the firm's management because of agency considerations—for example, the potential loss of control that comes from loan documents that give lenders power over the firm's assets and actions if it defaults on its debt.

Risk can be quantified by a variety of measures, including financial leverage ratios such as the debt ratio, the funded debt ratio, the debt/equity ratio, times interest earned, and fixed charge coverage; the ratios that capture the magnification of leverage: degree of operating leverage, degree of financial leverage, and degree of total leverage; and the firm's levered beta.[11]

Financial managers must monitor the stability of the firm's earnings stream and the likelihood of default or bankruptcy, communicating with financial market participants to ensure that the firm is not perceived as excessively risky. This is done by keeping leverage ratios within accepted norms and by conducting an ongoing dialog with lenders, analysts, bankers, debt rating agencies, etc., to inform them of the firm's financial plans.

Income Income refers to the ability of financial leverage to magnify the firm's earnings per share and reminds the financial manager to do the EBIT-EPS analysis of Figure 15.4.

dilute—to reduce the percentage of a firm owned by each common share by increasing the number of shares outstanding

Control If the firm finances by selling additional common shares, ownership of the firm is **diluted.** While the new financing may enable the company to earn sufficient additional income to restore earnings per share, investors have no way to restore their lost voting control other than by buying a proportionate share of the new issue.

[11] **Cross-reference:** Financial leverage ratios are discussed in Appendix 4D, pp. 130–135; degree of leverage measures are presented in Appendix 15B; and the levered beta appears in Appendix 15D.

In a widely held company in which no single shareholder owns a significant number of shares, control is normally not a relevant issue. However, for the major shareholders of a **closely held firm,** dilution might represent a severe cost. Fortunately in this case, the financial manager can speak directly with those shareholders to learn their preferences and incorporate them into the financing mix decision.

closely held firm—a company in which a small number of shareholders own a significant percentage of the outstanding common stock

Timing Market conditions often favor the issue of one type of security or the other. When interest rates are at a historical low, debt issues become attractive. When stock prices are at a historical high, equity issues are favored. Financial managers must remain on top of financial market conditions to sequence debt and equity issues at the most favorable rates.

Other This category refers to a potpourri of miscellaneous considerations. Examples are: limits on debt or outstanding shares in the firm's charter, government regulations, the ability to use assets as collateral to reduce interest costs, the speed with which funds are needed, the amount of funds required, and the impact of the features of a new security issue on those currently outstanding.

2. The Pecking-Order Approach

Studies of how companies raise funds in practice have shown that a large number ignore the recommendations of all the debt-equity mix theories. Instead, many seem to follow a consistent pattern year after year, financing first with retained earnings, next with the easier-to-obtain forms of borrowing such as payables and bank debt, then with more complex debt forms such as bond issues, and last with issues of common stock. Professor Stewart Meyers has labelled this pattern the **pecking-order approach.**

pecking-order approach—a pattern of financing in which a company raises funds in the same sequence each year

Since observing this phenomenon, Myers and others finance theorists have proposed several possible explanations. One suggestion is that the pecking order is the path of least resistance, the easiest way for financial managers to obtain funds. Retained earnings and payables are available with little or no effort, but it requires much more work to raise money in the public markets. However, it is difficult to believe that so many financial managers would choose financing that consistently ignores opportunities to add value to their companies just because it is easy.

Two other explanations do have a theoretical basis. First, the sequence of financing in the pecking-order approach is consistent with increasing flotation costs—from zero for retained earnings and payables, through moderate flotation costs for debt issues, through higher flotation costs for stock issues. Using the pecking-order approach keeps flotation costs to a minimum—important if flotation costs are a significant part of the cost of capital.

asymmetric information hypothesis—a theory that explores the ramifications of management having better information about a company's prospects than investors

A second, theoretically-based explanation attempts to show why selling stock is last in the pecking order. Financial managers may want to avoid stock sales because the announcement of a stock issue tends to depress the stock's price by sending a negative signal to investors. This has been explained by the **asymmetric information hypothesis,** which studies financial behavior by observing that management typically knows more about the company than investors. In this application of the hypothesis, the argument is that management only wants to sell stock when it is at a relatively high price. This minimizes dilution since fewer shares will have to be sold to raise a given amount of money. However, investors realize that management is better informed than they are and treat a stock issue as "signalling" important new information: if management is willing to sell shares at this price, the stock could well be overvalued. In response, investors bid down the company's stock price.

In companies where the financial manager follows the pecking-order approach, the debt-equity mix is an accident of how much financing is needed each year. In years where the firm requires little funding, the money will come from retained earnings and the mix will tilt toward equity. If more funding is needed, the firm will borrow and the mix will tilt back toward debt. And if large amounts of new financing are required, the firm will have to issue common stock and the mix will tilt back toward more equity.

Typical Capital Structures

Capital structures differ significantly by industry. Figure 15.9 reports the industry-average debt ratios for representative industries in the United States.

FIGURE 15.9
Debt ratios of selected U.S. industries. Industries with good collateral, stable EBIT, or seasonal needs finance with high amounts of debt.

Source: Leo Troy, *Almanac of Business and Industrial Financial Ratios,* 1994 Edition. (Englewood Cliffs, NJ: Prentice Hall, 1994.)

Industry	Average debt ratio	Comment
Airlines	92.8%	Make extensive use of debt to finance aircraft
Commercial banks	91.4	Highly stable EBIT due to regulation
Real estate developers	88.0	Property used for collateral
Furniture stores	65.4	Representative retailers
Grocery stores	83.7	
Drug stores	59.9	
Furniture wholesalers	69.2	Representative wholesalers
Grocery wholesalers	70.7	
Pharmaceutical wholesalers	68.9	
Furniture manufacturers	64.2	Representative manufacturers
Grain milling	59.2	
Pharmaceutical manufacturing	52.6	
Regulated investment companies (mutual funds)	3.6	Funding is overwhelmingly from investors' deposits; charter typically prohibits borrowing to leverage investments

Debbie Curtis walked back into her office and turned on the computer. She loaded her spreadsheet program and looked again at her stock price model. Over the past week she had improved her figures several times to incorporate her new insights into the effects of financing on stakeholder value.

Debbie now understood why she had received such conflicting advice—the debt-equity mix decision was one of the least well understood in all of finance. If all the perfect market assumptions of Modigliani and Miller were correct, it wouldn't matter how her firm raised its money, since the financing mix would not change the firm's value. But it was more likely that the financial markets were not perfect. The tax treatment of interest, and stakeholders' concerns about the costs associated with bankruptcy and agency were very real and could change the company's worth. What was clear to Debbie was the need to understand the reactions of all the firm's stakeholders to the returns and risks from each financing alternative. And it would require a lot of judgment to quantify those reactions.

Debbie reviewed her calculations once more and ranked the financing alternatives in order of their estimated impact on the company's value. Then she began to write her report for the CFO. She outlined the theoretical issues and then organized her analyses and observations using the FRICTO framework. As she printed out her results, a colleague stuck his head into her office and asked how she was doing. "I think it came out well," she replied. "There's no clear answer, but I sure have plenty to tell the CFO tomorrow."

Summary of Key Points

- **Define operating and financial leverage and describe their relationship to fixed costs.** Operating leverage is the magnification of operating profits (EBIT) in response to changes in a firm's sales. Financial leverage is the magnification of earnings per share (EPS) in response to changes in a firm's operating profits (EBIT). Both are caused by the existence of fixed costs in the firm's cost structure. Operating fixed costs come from commitments to productive resources—human or technological. Financial fixed costs come primarily from interest on debt financing. Control over operating fixed costs is often limited due to technological constraints. While small companies typically have little choice about their financial leverage due to their inability to access the financial markets, larger firms can choose between debt and equity financing.
- **Discuss why a company's financing choice might affect the market value of its securities.** Through its choice of financing, a company can modify the pattern of risk and return it provides to its stakeholders. As a firm's financial leverage rises, the behavior of its EPS changes: at high levels of EBIT, EPS is increased while at low EBIT levels, EPS is decreased. It is important to locate the crossover, or indifference, point. High financial leverage also adds volatility to a firm's EPS stream. A firm with EBIT below the indifference point should avoid debt financing—at this level of EBIT low leverage produces higher returns and lower risk. A firm with EBIT above the indifference point must weigh the tradeoff from adding leverage: greater returns but also greater risk. The best financing mix will be the one that produces the most value for the firm's stakeholders.
- **Describe four theories that attempt to explain the optimal mix of debt and equity financing.** The traditional approach studies how investors perceive the risks of increased debt, concluding there is an optimal financing mix. MM show that if financial markets are "perfect," the financing mix decision is irrelevant to firm value; adding corporate income taxes, MM conclude that the optimal financing mix is 100% debt. Miller shows that personal income taxes partially offset the effects of the corporate income tax. Compromise theory focuses on "imperfections" in the financial markets, concluding that there is an op-

timal financing mix due to the corporate income tax, bankruptcy costs, and agency costs.

- **Describe how companies approach the debt-equity mix decision in practice.** Some firms use the acronym FRICTO (flexibility, risk, income, control, timing, other) to organize their analysis of the debt-equity mix. Others appear to use the pecking-order approach, in which they consistently finance first with retained earnings, then debt, then stock sales.
- **Explain why the debt-equity mix differs by industry.** Values of the debt-equity mix vary widely among companies in different industries, due primarily to the level of operating leverage and the stability of the industry's sales and EBIT. Often stability is due to government regulation.

Questions

1. In what way is business leverage similar to physical leverage?
2. Distinguish between operating leverage and financial leverage.
3. How much choice does a firm have over its operating leverage? over its financial leverage?
4. Describe the way in which earnings per share responds to changing EBIT in a firm with:
   a. No fixed financing costs
   b. Some fixed financing costs
5. How does a firm's financial leverage affect:
   a. Its profitability?
   b. Its level of risk?
6. A firm is considering two alternative capital structures and has calculated its profitability at various EBIT levels under each structure. What should the firm do if its projected EBIT is:
   a. Below the indifference point?
   b. Above the indifference point?
7. Compare and contrast the net income approach, net operating income approach, and traditional approach to the optimal debt-equity mix. Which assumptions do you find reasonable? Unreasonable?
8. What role does each of MM's assumptions play in their theory of the debt-equity mix?
9. Describe "homemade leverage."
10. Is Professor Miller's personal tax model relevant in today's tax environment?
11. What are the variables that enter compromise theory? What is the effect of each on the optimal debt-equity mix?
12. Define the meaning of each letter of *FRICTO*, and give an illustration of each.
13. What is meant by the *pecking-order approach*? Give three explanations why it is an observed phenomenon.

Problems

1. **(Magnification)** A firm has sales of $5 million of which 45% are variable costs. Fixed operating costs are $1 million but the firm has no debt and therefore no interest expenses. The firm is in the 35% tax bracket and has 1 million shares outstanding.
   a. Calculate the company's EBIT and EPS.
   b. Calculate EBIT and EPS if sales goes up by 5% and if sales goes down by 5%.
   c. For each case of part b, by what percent did EBIT and EPS change?
   d. Compare the results of part c for EBIT and EPS.
2. **(Magnification)** A firm has sales of $5,000,000 of which 65% are variable costs. There are no fixed operating costs, but interest expense totals $750,000. The company is in the 35% tax bracket and has 1,000,000 shares outstanding.
   a. Calculate the company's EBIT and EPS.
   b. Calculate EBIT and EPS if sales goes up by 5% and if sales goes down by 5%.
   c. For each case of part b, by what percent did EBIT and EPS change?
   d. Compare the results of part c for EBIT and EPS.
3. **(Leverage, returns, and risk)** A company with EBIT of $1,000,000 is considering two financing alternatives. The first would have interest expense of $250,000 and 200,000 outstanding shares, whereas the second would have interest expense of $350,000 but only 150,000 shares outstanding. The company is in the 35% federal income tax bracket.
   a. Construct the bottom half of the income statement for each financing alternative.
   b. Repeat part a if EBIT rises to $1,100,000.
   c. Repeat part a if EBIT falls to $900,000.
   d. What do you observe about the behavior of EPS?
4. **(Leverage, returns, and risk)** A company with EBIT of $8,000,000 is considering two financing alternatives. The first would have interest expense of $2,250,000 and 1,000,000 outstanding shares, whereas the second would have interest expense of $4,000,000 but only 800,000 shares outstanding. The company is in the 35% federal income tax bracket.
   a. Construct the bottom half of the income statement for each financing alternative.

b. Repeat part a if EBIT rises to $9,200,000.
c. Repeat part a if EBIT falls to $6,800,000.
d. What do you observe about the behavior of EPS?

5. **(Indifference point)** A company is considering two debt-equity mixes. Under Plan A its annual interest costs will be $500,000 and it will have 400,000 shares of common stock outstanding. Under Plan B its annual interest costs will be $800,000, but it will only issue 250,000 common shares. The company pays taxes at a 35% rate.
   a. Sketch a graph of EPS versus EBIT for EBIT in the range of zero to $3,000,000. Your graph should have two lines on it, one for Plan A and one for Plan B.
   b. Locate the indifference point between Plans A and B.
   c. What is the firm's EPS at the indifference point?
   d. On which side of the indifference point is EPS higher under Plan A? Plan B?

6. **(Indifference point)** A company is considering two debt-equity mixes. Under Plan X its annual interest costs will be $2,000,000 and it will have 250,000 shares of common stock outstanding. Under Plan Y its annual interest costs will be only $1,200,000, although it would issue 450,000 common shares. The company pays taxes at a 35% rate.
   a. Sketch a graph of EPS versus EBIT for EBIT in the range of zero to $6,000,000. Your graph should have two lines on it, one for Plan X and one for Plan Y.
   b. Locate the indifference point between Plans X and Y.
   c. What is the firm's EPS at the indfference point?
   d. On which side of the indifference point is EPS higher under Plan X? Plan Y?

7. **(The traditional approach)** A company has gathered the following data about its cost of capital:

Debt ratio	Cost of debt	Cost of equity
0%	4.0%	10.5%
10	4.0	11.0
20	4.0	11.6
30	4.2	12.4
40	4.5	13.6
50	4.9	15.3
60	5.4	17.8
70	6.2	21.5
80	7.5	26.0

   a. What is the relationship between the cost of capital and the optimal debt-equity mix?
   b. Calculate the cost of capital at each debt ratio.
   c. Which debt-equity mix is optimal?
   d. According to the traditionalists, why do the cost of debt and cost of equity exhibit the above patterns?

8. **(The traditional approach)** A company has gathered the following data about its cost of capital:

Debt ratio	Cost of debt	Cost of equity
0%	3.5%	9.0%
10	3.5	9.0
20	3.5	9.2
30	3.5	9.6
40	3.7	10.2
50	4.0	11.4
60	4.5	13.0
70	5.2	15.2
80	6.2	18.2

   a. Calculate the cost of capital at each debt ratio.
   b. Which debt-equity mix is optimal?
   c. Calculate the increase in the cost of debt and the cost of equity for each 10% increase in the debt ratio. Explain the pattern you discover.
   d. Calculate the difference between the cost of debt and the cost of equity at each debt ratio. Explain the pattern you discover.

9. **(Compromise theory)** The stock of a company with no debt has a market value of $35,000,000. Its investment bankers have helped it gather the following information, where:

   CT = present value of federal income taxes saved from deducting interest expenses
   BC = present value of bankruptcy costs
   AC = present value of agency costs

Debt ratio	CT	BC	AC
0%	$ 0	$ 0	$ 0
10	1,000,000	0	200,000
20	2,000,000	1,000,000	400,000
30	3,000,000	2,000,000	700,000
40	4,000,000	4,000,000	1,100,000
50	5,000,000	7,000,000	1,600,000
60	6,000,000	11,000,000	2,200,000
70	7,000,000	16,000,000	2,900,000
80	8,000,000	22,000,000	3,700,000

   a. Calculate the value of the firm at each debt ratio.
   b. Which debt-equity mix is optimal?
   c. Locate the acceptable range.

d. Why do the CT numbers increase at a constant rate while the BC and AC numbers increase at an increasing rate?

10. **(Compromise theory)** The stock of a company with no debt has a market value of $80,000,000. Its investment bankers have helped it gather the following information, where:

CT = present value of federal income taxes saved from deducting interest expenses

BC = present value of bankruptcy costs

AC = present value of agency costs

Debt ratio	CT	BC	AC
0%	$ 0	$ 0	$ 0
10	3,000,000	0	1,000,000
20	6,000,000	0	1,500,000
30	9,000,000	4,000,000	2,200,000
40	12,000,000	8,000,000	3,100,000
50	15,000,000	14,000,000	4,200,000
60	18,000,000	22,000,000	5,500,000
70	21,000,000	32,000,000	7,000,000
80	24,000,000	44,000,000	8,700,000

a. Calculate the value of the firm at each debt ratio.
b. Which debt-equity mix is optimal?
c. Locate the acceptable range.
d. Why are there agency costs at a 10% and 20% debt ratio while bankruptcy costs remain at zero?

11. **(Changing the capital structure)** A company with $10 million in assets currently has $3 million of debt financing. The cost of this debt is 5%, and the company's cost of equity is now 12%. The company's treasurer has suggested borrowing another $2 million and using the proceeds to retire an equivalent amount of common stock. The new debt would have a cost of 6.5%, and the treasurer estimates the company's stockholders would respond to the change in financing mix by raising the cost of equity to 14%.

a. Calculate the company's debt ratio now and after the proposed change.
b. Calculate the cost of debt after the change (assume it is the weighted average of the two debt issues).
c. Calculate the company's weighted-average cost of capital now and after the proposed change.
d. Should the company alter its debt-equity mix as suggested by the treasurer?

12. **(Changing the capital structure)** A company with $50 million in assets currently has $40 million of debt financing as a result of a recent leveraged buyout. The cost of this debt is 10%, and the company's cost of equity is now 19%. Now the company's management wishes to take the company public again by selling $15 million of equity and using the proceeds to retire an equivalent amount of debt. The treasurer estimates the company's stockholders would respond to the change in financing mix by reducing the cost of equity to 12%.

a. Calculate the company's debt ratio now and after the proposed change.
b. Calculate the company's weighted-average cost of capital now and after the proposed change.
c. Now assume the company used this opportunity to call its debt and replace it with new debt with a cost of 6%. Calculate the company's weighted-average cost of capital after the proposed change.
d. Should the company alter its debt-equity mix, and if so, should it refund its debt?

APPENDIX 15A

THE BLURRING OF FIXED AND VARIABLE OPERATING COSTS

Traditionally it has been easy to identify which operating costs were variable and which were fixed. Labor resources were the variable costs, because labor could be hired or laid off as needed. This was because much labor was not too highly skilled. One worker was very much like another, and there was little cost to the business if there were turnover in the workforce. Capital resources were the fixed costs since it was often difficult to add or reduce plant and machine capacity at will. Plant took a while to build and place on-line. It was not easy to sell off unused plant and equipment since there was not a good market for those resources.

Today it is far more difficult to identify a type of operating cost with a type of resource. In many cases, evolving business characteristics and practices have made labor a relatively fixed cost of operations while developments in the markets for capital resources have made plant and equipment a variable cost. Several trends are behind this shift:

1. As business has moved toward the use of higher technology, the typical worker brings a much greater degree of skill to the workplace than in the past. In fact, for many companies, the knowledge, skill, and capability of their employees is now their most critical resource. It is more difficult than in the past to lay off workers and then rehire comparable employees.
2. Management often has invested a significant amount of money in training, and the cost of training new workers exceeds the cost savings from reducing staff in a downturn.

"Seems like only yesterday it was serving drinks and doing little chores around the house."

3. Insights gained from companies pursuing quality management have convinced many companies that the improvement in productivity and quality of output from a work force that knows its jobs are safe more than compensates for the inability to reduce staff in periods of slow business activity.
4. Improvements in leasing have made many kinds of capital resources available to businesses on a temporary basis.
5. Modular plant and multipurpose equipment have been designed so that resources that are unneeded in one area of the business can be redeployed elsewhere.
6. Advances in transportation and communications have lessened the importance of having all capital resources in one location, thus broadening the market for unused plant and equipment.
7. The concept of the "virtual corporation," a fluid series of joint ventures with other companies, means highly complex resources can be obtained and released quickly as required.

In today's environment, financial managers can no longer rely on broad classifications such as "labor" and "capital" to assess which operating costs are variable and which are fixed. Rather, each element of cost must be studied to understand its overall role in the firm's production resource mix.

APPENDIX 15B

MEASURING THE DEGREE OF LEVERAGE

In this appendix we explore the relationship of fixed costs to leverage in more detail. We identify the factors that contribute to higher or lower magnification of earnings and show how to measure leverage with a set of useful ratios.

1. The Impact of Fixed Operating Costs on EBIT

Debbie Curtis, who we met at the beginning of this chapter, has gathered information about the following companies:

Varicost, Inc.—a firm with only variable (and no fixed) operating costs

Mixco, Inc.—a firm with both variable and fixed operating costs

Debbie first studies Varicost, constructing pro-forma income statements for several levels of sales. She discovers that if all operating costs are variable they go up and down at the same rate as sales, hence so do profits. Varicost is an example of a company with *no operating leverage* since it has no fixed operating costs. This means that when sales changes by a given percentage amount, the firm's EBIT will change by *the same* percentage.[1]

Example

A Firm with No Operating Leverage

Varicost's sales is now $100,000 per year. Operating costs (all variable) total $80,000; as a result, the firm's variable cost percentage is 80% ($80,000 / $100,000).

Question: What would happen to Varicost's EBIT if sales rose by 20%?

Solution steps: Construct two managerial/analytical income statements for Varicost and compare:

	Before	After	
Sales	$ 100,000	$ 120,000	up by 20%
– Variable costs	80,000	96,000	80% of sales
Contribution	20,000	24,000	
– Fixed costs	0	0	
EBIT	$ 20,000	$ 24,000	also up 20%

Answer: Varicost's EBIT is up by 20%, mirroring the 20% rise in sales. There is no operating leverage here since EBIT rises by exactly the same percentage rate as sales, not at a greater (magnified) rate.

Next, Debbie turns her attention to Mixco, the company with both variable and fixed operating costs, and constructs similar pro-forma statements. She discovers that if a firm has fixed operating costs, not all costs go up and down with sales. Mixco is an example of a company *with operating leverage* since it has fixed operating costs. This means that when sales changes by a given percentage amount, the firm's EBIT will change by *a greater* percentage.

Example

A Firm with Operating Leverage

Mixco's sales is also $100,000 per year. Operating costs total $80,000, of which $50,000 is variable and the remaining $30,000 is fixed; as a result, the firm's variable cost percentage is 50% ($50,000 / $100,000).

Question: What would happen to Mixco's EBIT if sales rose by 20%?

Solution steps: Construct two managerial/analytical income statements for Mixco and compare:

[1] **Elaboration:** This is an "elasticity" concept, similar to those you might have seen in your studies of economics. Elasticity measures are based on percentage changes rather than absolute amounts. They are commonly used since they can be applied to any business regardless of its size.

	Before	After	
Sales	$ 100,000	$ 120,000	up by 20%
− Variable costs	50,000	60,000	50% of sales
Contribution	50,000	60,000	
− Fixed costs	30,000	30,000	
EBIT	$ 20,000	$ 30,000	up by 50%

Answer: Mixco's EBIT is up by 50%, greater than the 20% rise in sales. There is operating leverage here since EBIT rises at a greater percentage rate than sales.

The amount of operating leverage a firm has depends on two factors: (1) the level of its fixed operating costs, and (2) the level of its EBIT.

Fixed Operating Costs As fixed operating costs rise, so does operating leverage.

Example

A Firm's Operating Leverage Depends on the Level of Its Fixed Operating Costs

Debbie Curtis is wondering what would happen to Mixco's leverage if its operating cost structure changed so that fixed operating costs increased to $40,000 while variable operating costs declined to $40,000 (variable cost percentage goes to 40%).

Question: With this new operating cost structure, what would happen to Mixco's EBIT if sales rose by 20%?

Solution steps:

	Before	After	
Sales	$ 100,000	$ 120,000	up by 20%
− Variable costs	40,000	48,000	40% of sales
Contribution	60,000	72,000	
− Fixed costs	40,000	40,000	
EBIT	$ 20,000	$ 32,000	up by 60%

Answer: With $40,000 of fixed costs, Mixco's EBIT is up by 60%, compared to a 50% increase when fixed costs were $30,000.

EBIT The other factor that determines a firm's operating leverage is its level of EBIT. Firms with a low EBIT have greater leverage than firms whose EBIT is high.

Example

A Firm's Operating Leverage Depends on Its Level of EBIT

Debbie is wondering what would happen to Mixco's (fixed costs = $30,000, variable cost percentage = 50%) leverage if its EBIT increased due to greater sales.

Question: If Mixco's sales were $150,000 instead of $100,000, what would happen to EBIT if sales rose by 20%?

Solution steps:

	Before	After	
Sales	$ 150,000	$ 180,000	up by 20%
– Variable costs	75,000	90,000	50% of sales
Contribution	75,000	90,000	
– Fixed costs	30,000	30,000	
EBIT	$ 45,000	$ 60,000	up by 33.33%

Answer: With $45,000 of EBIT, Mixco has less leverage than when EBIT was $20,000. With $20,000 of EBIT, a 20% change in sales increased EBIT by 50%. Here EBIT only rose 33.33% in response to the same 20% sales increase.

2. The Degree of Operating Leverage

degree of operating leverage (DOL)—a ratio measuring the amount of magnification built into a firm's operating cost structure.

The **degree of operating leverage (DOL)** is a financial ratio that measures a firm's operating leverage. It is defined as the percentage change in EBIT that results from a given percentage change in sales. Thus, if a 20% change in sales produces a 33.33% change in EBIT (as in the above example), the firm's degree of operating leverage is 33.33% / 20% = 1.67. In general:

$$DOL = \frac{contribution}{EBIT}$$

By multiplying a projected sales increase by a firm's DOL ratio, we can project its new level of EBIT.

Example

Calculating and Using the DOL Ratio

Looking back at the four examples of operating leverage, Debbie uses the DOL formula to calculate the DOL ratio in each case and confirm her results.

Question: What is the DOL ratio in each example?

Solution steps:

1. Varicost: DOL = $20,000 / $20,000 = 1
2. Mixco—Example 1: DOL = $50,000 / $20,000 = 2.5
3. Mixco—Example 2: DOL = $60,000 / $20,000 = 3
4. Mixco—Example 3: DOL = $75,000 / $45,000 = 1.67

Answer: With no operating leverage, Varicost has a DOL of 1. Mixco's DOL is greater than 1 (2.5, 3, 1.67), reflecting its operating leverage.

Check:

1. For Varicost, a 20% sales increase produces a 20% × 1 = 20% rise in EBIT. ✓✓

2. For Mixco (example 1), a 20% sales increase produces a 20% × 2.5 = 50% rise in EBIT. ✓✓
3. For Mixco (example 2), a 20% sales increase produces a 20% × 3 = 60% rise in EBIT. ✓✓
4. For Mixco (example 3), a 20% sales increase produces a 20% × 1.67 = 33.33% rise in EBIT. ✓✓

The DOL ratio may be easily derived with a few basic algebraic variables. To start with, let:

P = **P**rice at which each unit is sold

Q = **Q**uantity of units produced and sold

V = **V**ariable production cost per unit

F = **F**ixed cost level

Then, EBIT may be represented as unit sales multiplied by the firm's contribution margin minus fixed costs:

$$\begin{aligned} \text{EBIT} &= \text{Sales} - \text{Variable cost} - \text{Fixed cost} \\ &= \text{PQ} - \text{VQ} - \text{F} \\ &= \text{Q(P} - \text{V)} - \text{F} \end{aligned}$$

The DOL ratio asks about EBIT if sales changes. Let:

ΔQ = **change in Q**uantity of units produced and sold

so that the total quantity of units sold becomes:

$$\text{Q} + \Delta\text{Q}$$

This would change EBIT to be:

$$\begin{aligned} \text{EBIT}_{\text{new}} &= \text{Sales} - \text{Variable cost} - \text{Fixed cost} \\ &= \text{P(Q} + \Delta\text{Q)} - \text{V(Q} + \Delta\text{Q)} - \text{F} \\ &= \text{(Q} + \Delta\text{Q)(P} - \text{V)} - \text{F} \end{aligned}$$

And the change to EBIT becomes the change to sales multiplied by the firm's contribution margin:

$$\begin{aligned} \Delta\text{EBIT} &= \text{EBIT}_{\text{new}} - \text{EBIT} \\ &= [\text{(Q} + \Delta\text{Q)(P} - \text{V)} - \text{F}] - [\text{Q(P} - \text{V)} - \text{F}] \\ &= \text{Q(P} - \text{V)} + \Delta\text{Q(P} - \text{V)} - \text{F} - \text{Q(P} - \text{V)} + \text{F} \\ &= \Delta\text{Q(P} - \text{V)} \end{aligned}$$

Since DOL is an elasticity concept, we need the percentage change to sales and the percentage change to EBIT:

$$\begin{aligned} \text{percentage change to sales} &= \Delta\text{Q} \,/\, \text{Q} \\ \text{percentage change to EBIT} &= \Delta\text{EBIT} \,/\, \text{EBIT} \\ &= \Delta\text{Q(P} - \text{V)} \,/\, \text{EBIT} \end{aligned}$$

finally:

$$\text{DOL} = \frac{\text{percentage change to EBIT}}{\text{percentage change to sales}}$$

$$= \frac{\dfrac{\Delta Q(P - V)}{\text{EBIT}}}{\dfrac{\Delta Q}{Q}} = \frac{\Delta Q(P - V)}{\text{EBIT}} \times \frac{Q}{\Delta Q} = \frac{Q(P - V)}{\text{EBIT}}$$

$$DOL = \frac{Q(P - V)}{Q(P - V) - F} \quad or \quad \frac{contribution}{EBIT}$$

By examining the algebraic form of the DOL ratio, we can confirm some conclusions of this appendix:

1. When a firm has no fixed operating costs ($F = 0$), DOL equals 1 no matter what the firm's level of sales. A given percentage change in sales will lead to a "one-times" (identical) percentage change to EBIT. This is the case of no operating leverage.
2. When a firm does have fixed operating costs ($F > 0$), the denominator of DOL becomes lower than the numerator and DOL takes on a value greater than 1. A given percentage change in sales will lead to a greater percentage change in EBIT. This is the case of operating leverage.
3. The denominator of DOL is EBIT. As this number approaches zero, the DOL ratio rises, indicating that magnification is increased near the point where EBIT = 0.

3. The Impact of Fixed Financing Costs on EPS

Debbie Curtis has also gathered information about the following companies:

Equico, Inc.—a firm financed only with equity.

Levered, Inc.—a firm financed with both debt and equity funds.

Debbie first studies Equico, constructing pro-forma income statements for several levels of EBIT. She discovers that if all financial costs are variable they go up and down at the same rate as EBIT, hence so does EPS. Equico is an example of an "all-equity firm," a company with *no financial leverage,* since it has no fixed financial costs. This means that when EBIT changes by a given percentage amount, the firm's earnings per share will change by *the same* percentage.

Example

A Firm with No Financial Leverage

Equico, Inc. has no debt, hence no fixed financing costs. EBIT is now $100,000 per year, the firm's tax rate is 35%, and there are 10,000 shares of common stock outstanding.

Question: What would happen to Equico's EPS if EBIT rose by 20%?

Solution steps: Construct the bottom halves of two income statements for Equico and compare:

	Before	After	
EBIT	$ 100,000	$ 120,000	up by 20%
− Interest	0	0	
EBT	100,000	120,000	
− Taxes	35,000	42,000	
EAT	$ 65,000	$ 78,000	
÷ Number of shares	10,000	10,000	
EPS	$ 6.50	$ 7.80	also up 20%

Answer: Equico's EPS is up by 20%, mirroring the 20% rise in EBIT. There is no financial leverage here since EPS rises by exactly the same percentage rate as EBIT, not at a greater (magnified) rate.

Next, Debbie turns her attention to Levered, Inc., the company with both debt and equity financing, and constructs similar pro-forma statements. She discovers that if a firm has fixed financing costs, not all costs go up and down with sales. Levered, Inc. is an example of a company *with financial leverage* since it has fixed financing costs (interest expenses). This means that when EBIT changes by a given percentage amount, the firm's EPS will change by *a greater* percentage.

Example

A Firm with Financial Leverage

Levered, Inc.'s interest costs total $20,000. EBIT is now $100,000 per year, the firm's tax rate is 35%, and there are 8,000 shares of common stock outstanding.

Question: What would happen to Levered's EPS if EBIT rose by 20%?

Solution steps: Construct the bottom halves of two income statements for Levered, Inc. and compare:

	Before	After	
EBIT	$ 100,000	$ 120,000	up by 20%
− Interest	20,000	20,000	
EBT	80,000	100,000	
− Taxes	28,000	35,000	
EAT	$ 52,000	$ 65,000	
÷ Number of shares	8,000	8,000	
EPS	$ 6.50	$ 8.125	up by 25%

Answer: Levered, Inc.'s EPS is up by 25%, greater than the 20% rise in sales. There is financial leverage here since EPS rises at a greater percentage rate than EBIT.

As with operating leverage, the amount of financial leverage a firm has depends on two factors. For financial leverage these are: (1) the level of the firm's interest or fixed financial costs, and (2) the level of its earnings before taxes.

Fixed financial costs As fixed financial costs rise, so does financial leverage.

Example

A Firm's Financial Leverage Depends on the Level of Its Interest Costs

Debbie Curtis is wondering what would happen to Levered, Inc.'s financial leverage if it borrowed more money, increasing interest costs to $30,000 and used the loan proceeds to buy back some of its common stock, reducing the number of outstanding shares to 7,000.

Question: With this new debt-equity mix, what would happen to Levered, Inc.'s EPS if EBIT rose by 20%?

Solution steps: Construct the bottom halves of two income statements for Levered, Inc., and compare:

	Before	After	
EBIT	$ 100,000	$ 120,000	up by 20%
− Interest	30,000	30,000	
EBT	70,000	90,000	
− Taxes	24,500	31,500	
EAT	$ 45,500	$ 58,500	
÷ Number of shares	7,000	7,000	
EPS	$ 6.50	$ 8.36	up by 28.6%

Answer: With $30,000 of interest costs, Levered Inc.'s EPS is up by 28.6%, compared to a 25% increase when interest costs were $20,000.

EBT The other factor that determines a firm's financial leverage is its level of earnings before taxes. Firms with a low EBT have greater leverage than firms whose EBT is high.

Example

A Firm's Financial Leverage Depends on Its Level of EBT

Debbie Curtis is wondering what would happen to Levered, Inc.'s financial leverage if its EBT increased due to greater EBIT.

Question: If Levered's EBIT were $150,000 instead of $100,000, what would happen to EPS if EBIT rose by 20%?

Solution steps: Construct the bottom halves of two income statements for Levered, Inc. and compare:

	Before	After	
EBIT	$ 150,000	$ 180,000	up by 20%
− Interest	20,000	20,000	
EBT	130,000	160,000	
− Taxes	45,500	56,000	
EAT	$ 84,500	$ 104,000	
÷ Number of shares	8,000	8,000	
EPS	$ 10.56	$ 13.00	up by 23.1%

Answer: With $130,000 of EBT, Levered, Inc. has less leverage than when EBT is $80,000. If $80,000 of EBT is the starting point, EPS rises 25% in response to a 20% change in sales. Here EPS only rose 23.1% in response to the same 20% sales increase.

4. The Degree of Financial Leverage

degree of financial leverage (DFL)—a ratio measuring the amount of magnification built into a firm's financial cost structure

The **degree of financial leverage (DFL)** is a financial ratio that measures a firm's financial leverage. It is defined as the percentage change in earnings per share that results from a given percentage change in EBIT. Thus, if a 20% change in EBIT produces a 23% change in EPS (as in the example at the bottom of the previous page), the firm's degree of financial leverage is 23.1% / 20% = 1.15. In general:

$$DFL = \frac{EBIT}{earnings\ before\ taxes}$$

By multiplying a projected change to EBIT by a firm's DFL ratio, we can project its new level of EPS.

Example

Calculating and Using the DFL Ratio

Looking back at the four examples of operating leverage, Debbie Curtis uses the DFL formula to calculate the DFL ratio in each case and confirm her results.

Question: What is the DFL ratio in each example?

Solution steps:

1. Equico: DFL = $100,000 / $100,000 = 1
2. Levered—Example 1: DFL = $100,000 / $80,000 = 1.25
3. Levered—Example 2: DFL = $100,000 / $70,000 = 1.43
4. Levered—Example 3: DFL = $150,000 / $130,000 = 1.15

Answer: With no financial leverage, Equico has a DFL of 1. Levered's DFL is greater than 1 (1.25, 1.43, 1.15) reflecting its financial leverage.

Check:

1. For Equico, a 20% increase in EBIT produces a 20% × 1 = 20% rise in EPS. ✓✓
2. For Levered, Inc. (example 1), a 20% increase in EBIT produces a 20% × 1.25 = 25% rise in EPS. ✓✓
3. For Levered, Inc. (example 2), a 20% increase in EBIT produces a 20% × 1.43 = 28.6% rise in EPS. ✓✓
4. For Levered, Inc. (example 3), a 20% increase in EBIT produces a 20% × 1.15 = 23% rise in EBIT. ✓✓

The DFL ratio is also easy to derive. Let:

EBIT = **E**arnings **B**efore **I**nterest and **T**axes

I = **I**nterest expense

t = **t**ax rate

S = **S**hares of common stock outstanding

Then, EPS may be represented as EBIT minus interest and taxes, and divided by the number of common shares outstanding:

$$\begin{aligned} EPS &= (EBIT - interest - taxes) \,/\, shares \\ &= [EBIT - I - (EBIT - I)t] \,/\, S \\ &= (EBIT - I)(1 - t) \,/\, S \end{aligned}$$

The DFL ratio asks about EPS if EBIT changes. Let:

ΔEBIT = **change in** Earnings **B**efore **I**nterest and **T**axes

so that the new value of EBIT, $EBIT_{new}$, becomes:

$$EBIT + \Delta EBIT$$

This would change EPS to be equal to be:

$$\begin{aligned} EPS_{new} &= (EBIT_{new} - interest - taxes) \,/\, shares \\ &= [(EBIT + \Delta EBIT) - I - (EBIT + \Delta EBIT - I)t] \,/\, S \\ &= (EBIT + \Delta EBIT - I)(1 - t) \,/\, S \end{aligned}$$

And the change to EPS becomes the change to EBIT multiplied by (1 minus the firm's tax rate) and then divided by the number of shares outstanding:

$$\begin{aligned} \Delta EPS &= EPS_{new} - EPS \\ &= [(EBIT + \Delta EBIT - I)(1 - t) \,/\, S] - [(EBIT - I)(1 - t) \,/\, S] \\ &= EBIT(1 - t)/S + \Delta EBIT(1 - t)/S - I(1 - t)/S - \\ &\qquad EBIT(1 - t)/S + I(1 - t)/S \\ &= \Delta EBIT(1 - t) \,/\, S \end{aligned}$$

Since DFL is an elasticity concept, we need the percentage change to EBIT and the percentage change to EPS:

$$\begin{aligned} \text{percentage change to EBIT} &= \Delta EBIT \,/\, EBIT \\ \text{percentage change to EPS} &= \Delta EPS \,/\, EPS \\ &= [\Delta EBIT(1 - t)/S] \,/\, [(EBIT - I)(1 - t)/S] \\ &= \Delta EBIT \,/\, (EBIT - I) \end{aligned}$$

and:

$$DFL = \frac{\text{percentage change to EPS}}{\text{percentage change to EBIT}}$$

$$= \frac{\dfrac{\Delta EBIT}{EBIT - I}}{\dfrac{\Delta EBIT}{EBIT}} = \frac{\Delta EBIT}{EBIT - I} \times \frac{EBIT}{\Delta EBIT}$$

$$\boldsymbol{DFL = \frac{EBIT}{EBIT - I} \quad or \quad \frac{EBIT}{earnings\ before\ taxes}}$$

"... and these are our children, Leverage and Equity."

By examining the algebraic form of the DFL ratio, we can confirm some further conclusions of this appendix:

1. When a firm has no interest costs (I = 0), DFL equals 1 no matter what the firm's level of EBIT. A given percentage change in EBIT will lead to a "one-times" (identical) percentage change to EPS. This is the case of no financial leverage.
2. When a firm does have interest costs (I > 0), the denominator of DFL becomes lower than the numerator and DFL takes on a value greater than 1. A given percentage change in EBIT will lead to a greater percentage change in EPS. This is the case of financial leverage.
3. The denominator of DFL is earnings before taxes. As this number approaches zero, the DFL ratio rises, indicating that magnification is increased near the point where EBT = 0.

5. The Degree of Total Leverage

degree of total leverage (DTL)—a ratio measuring the amount of magnification built into a firm's overall cost structure

Operating leverage describes how EBIT will change in response to changing sales. But this change to EBIT will be further magnified into a change to EPS if the firm has financial leverage. To understand leverage from top to bottom on the income statement, we must combine the two leverage effects. The **degree of total leverage (DTL)** is a financial ratio that measures a firm's combined operating and financial leverage. It is defined as the percentage change in earnings per share that results from a given percentage change in sales. Thus, if a 20% change in sales produces an 80% change in EPS, the firm's degree of total leverage is 80% / 20% = 4. In general:

$$DTL = \frac{contribution}{earnings\ before\ taxes}$$

The DTL ratio may easily be decomposed into the product of the DOL and DFL ratios:

$$\text{DTL} = \frac{\text{contribution}}{\text{earnings before taxes}}$$

$$= \frac{\text{contribution}}{\text{EBIT}} \times \frac{\text{EBIT}}{\text{earnings before taxes}}$$

$$DTL = DOL \times DFL$$

By multiplying a forecasted change to sales by a firm's DTL ratio, we can project its new level of EPS.

Example

Calculating and Using the DTL Ratio

To understand total leverage, Debbie Curtis projects a full income statement for her company and then increases sales by 20%.

Question: What are the DOL, DFL, and DTL ratios?

Solution steps:

	Before	After	
Sales	$ 500,000	$ 600,000	up by 20%
− Variable costs	250,000	300,000	50% of sales
Contribution	250,000	300,000	
− Fixed costs	150,000	150,000	
EBIT	$ 100,000	$150,000	up by 50%
− Interest	30,000	30,000	
EBT	70,000	120,000	
− Taxes	24,500	42,000	
EAT	$ 45,500	$ 78,000	
÷ Number of shares	7,000	7,000	
EPS	$ 6.50	$ 11.14	up by 71.4%

DOL = $250,000 / $100,000 = 2.5

DFL = $100,000 / $70,000 = 1.429

DTL = $250,000 / $70,000 = 3.57, also = 2.5 × 1.429

Answer: Debbie's company has a DOL of 2.5, a DFL of 1.429, and a DTL of 3.57 which is the product of the DOL and DFL.

Check:

1. DOL: A 20% increase in sales produces a 20% × 2.5 = 50% rise in EBIT. ✓✓
2. DFL: A 50% increase in EBIT produces a 50% × 1.429 = 71.4% rise in EPS. ✓✓
3. DTL: A 20% increase in sales produces a 20% × 3.57 = 71.4% rise in EPS. ✓✓

Problems

1. **(The impact of fixed costs on EBIT)** A company with a variable cost percentage of 40% has sales of $300,000. What is the company's EBIT if its fixed operating costs equal:
   a. $0?
   b. $40,000?
   c. $80,000?
   d. $120,000?

2. **(The impact of fixed costs on EBIT)** A company with a variable cost percentage of 65% has sales of $1,750,000. What is the company's EBIT if its fixed operating costs equal:
   a. $0?
   b. $150,000?
   c. $300,000?
   d. $450,000?

3. **(Operating leverage and fixed costs)** For the company of Problem 1, calculate the dollar and percentage change to EBIT for each level of fixed operating costs if sales increase to $400,000.

4. **(Operating leverage and fixed costs)** For the company of Problem 2, calculate the dollar and percentage change to EBIT for each level of fixed operating costs if sales increase to $2 million.

5. **(Operating leverage and EBIT)** A company with a variable cost percentage of 50% has fixed operating costs of $300,000. For each level of sales below, calculate the company's: (1) EBIT, (2) new level of EBIT if sales increases by 10%, and (3) percentage change to EBIT when sales increases by 10%.
   a. Sales of $700,000
   b. Sales of $800,000
   c. Sales of $900,000
   d. Sales of $1,000,000

6. **(Operating leverage and EBIT)** A company with a variable cost percentage of 40% has fixed operating costs of $120,000. For each level of sales below, calculate the company's: (1) EBIT, (2) new level of EBIT if sales increases by 25%, and (3) percentage change to EBIT when sales increases by 25%.
   a. Sales of $250,000
   b. Sales of $300,000
   c. Sales of $350,000
   d. Sales of $400,000

7. **(Degree of operating leverage)** For the company of Problem 1, calculate the degree of operating leverage for each level of fixed costs and use the resulting DOL numbers to check the percentage increases in EBIT from Problem 3.

8. **(Degree of operating leverage)** For the company of Problem 2, calculate the degree of operating leverage for each level of fixed costs and use the resulting DOL numbers to check the percentage increases in EBIT from Problem 4.

9. **(Degree of operating leverage)** For the company of Problem 5, calculate the degree of operating leverage, both prior to and after the sales increase, for each level of fixed costs.

10. **(Degree of operating leverage)** For the company of Problem 6, calculate the degree of operating leverage, both prior to and after the sales increase, for each level of fixed costs.

11. **(The impact of fixed financing costs on EPS)** A company with 20,000 shares of common stock outstanding has EBIT of $500,000 and is in the 35% marginal income tax bracket. What is the company's EPS if its interest costs equal:
    a. $0?
    b. $100,000?
    c. $200,000?
    d. $300,000?

12. **(The impact of fixed financing costs on EPS)** A company with 150,000 shares of common stock outstanding has EBIT of $2,500,000 and is in the 35% marginal income tax bracket. What is the company's EPS if its interest costs equal:
    a. $0?
    b. $500,000?
    c. $1,000,000?
    d. $1,500,000?

13. **(Financial leverage and fixed financing costs)** For the company of Problem 11, calculate the dollar and percentage change to EPS for each level of interest costs if EBIT increases to $550,000.

14. **(Financial leverage and fixed financing costs)** For the company of Problem 12, calculate the dollar and percentage change to EPS for each level of interest costs if EBIT increases to $3 million.

15. **(Financial leverage and EPS)** A company with 35,000 outstanding common shares has interest costs of $200,000 and is in the 35% tax bracket. For each level of EBIT below, calculate the company's: (1) EPS, (2) new level of EPS if EBIT increases by 10%, and (3) percentage change to EPS when EBIT increases by 10%.
    a. EBIT of $400,000
    b. EBIT of $600,000
    c. EBIT of $800,000
    d. EBIT of $1,000,000

16. **(Financial leverage and EPS)** A company with 12,000 outstanding common shares has interest costs of \$80,000 and is in the 35% tax bracket. For each level of EBIT below, calculate the company's: (1) EPS, (2) new level of EPS if EBIT increases by 25%, and (3) percentage change to EPS when EBIT increases by 25%.

    a. EBIT of \$250,000
    b. EBIT of \$300,000
    c. EBIT of \$350,000
    d. EBIT of \$400,000

17. **(Degree of financial leverage)** For the company of Problem 11, calculate the degree of financial leverage for each level of interest costs and use the resulting DFL numbers to check the percentage increases in EPS from Problem 13.

18. **(Degree of financial leverage)** For the company of Problem 12, calculate the degree of financial leverage for each level of interest costs and use the resulting DFL numbers to check the percentage increases in EPS from Problem 14.

19. **(Degree of financial leverage)** For the company of Problem 15, calculate the degree of financial leverage, both prior to and after the increase in EBIT, for each level of EBIT.

20. **(Degree of financial leverage)** For the company of Problem 16, calculate the degree of financial leverage, both prior to and after the increase in EBIT, for each level of EBIT.

21. **(Degree of total leverage)** A firm has sales of \$2,000,000, a variable cost ratio of 55%, and fixed operating costs of \$600,000. Interest costs are \$100,000. The firm is in the 35% tax bracket and has 150,000 common shares outstanding.

    a. Prepare an income statement for the firm.
    b. Calculate the firm's DOL, DFL, and DTL.
    c. Show that DTL is the product of DOL and DFL.
    d. Prepare a second income statement for a sales increase of 15%. Show that the three leverage ratios accurately predict the EBIT and EPS on this statement.

22. **(Degree of total leverage)** A firm has sales of \$500,000, a variable cost ratio of 35%, and fixed operating costs of \$125,000. Interest costs are \$50,000. The firm is in the 35% tax bracket and has 75,000 common shares outstanding.

    a. Prepare an income statement for the firm.
    b. Calculate the firm's DOL, DFL, and DTL.
    c. Show that DTL is the product of DOL and DFL.
    d. Prepare a second income statement for a sales increase of 25%. Show that the three leverage ratios accurately predict the EBIT and EPS on this statement.

APPENDIX 15C

THE BOTTOM HALF OF THE INCOME STATEMENT

The bottom half of the income statement has the form:

EBIT	
− Interest	______
Earnings before taxes (EBT)	
− Taxes	______
Earnings after taxes (EAT)	
÷ Number of shares	______
Earnings per share (EPS)	======

Working down the statement step-by-step:

$$\text{EBT} = \text{EBIT} - \text{interest}$$

$$\begin{aligned}\text{Taxes} &= \text{EBT} \times (\text{tax rate}) \\ &= (\text{EBIT} - \text{interest}) \times (\text{tax rate})\end{aligned}$$

$$\begin{aligned}\text{EAT} &= \text{EBT} - \text{taxes} \\ &= (\text{EBIT} - \text{interest}) - (\text{EBIT} - \text{interest}) \times (\text{tax rate}) \\ &= (\text{EBIT} - \text{interest}) \times (1 - \text{tax rate})\end{aligned}$$

and:

$$\text{EPS} = \text{EAT} \;/\; (\text{number of shares})$$

$$EPS = \frac{(EBIT - interest) \times (1 - tax\ rate)}{number\ of\ shares}$$

If a firm has issued preferred stock, the bottom half of the income statement becomes:

EBIT	
− Interest	______
Earnings before taxes (EBT)	
− Taxes	______
Earnings after taxes (EAT)	
− Preferred dividend (D_p)	______
Earnings available to common	
÷ Number of shares	______
Earnings per share (EPS)	======

and:

$$EPS = \frac{(EBIT - interest) \times (1 - tax\ rate) - D_p}{number\ of\ shares}$$

APPENDIX 15D

DEBT-EQUITY MIX RELATIONSHIPS

In this appendix we present the algebraic forms of the Modigliani-Miller conclusions—both without and with corporate income taxes, the Miller personal tax model, and the beta of a levered firm. The following variables are used throughout (as always, lower case letters represent rates while upper case letters are dollar amounts):

EBIT = net operating income (Earnings Before Interest and Taxes)

t = the firm's tax rate

t_d = investors' tax rate on interest income from owning corporate debt

t_e = investors' tax rate (averaged) on dividend and capital gains income from equity investments

k_d = the cost of debt

k_{eU} = the cost of equity capital for an Unlevered firm (a firm with no leverage)

k_{eL} = the cost of equity for a Levered firm (a firm with financial leverage)

D = the (market) value of the firm's Debt

E = the (market) value of the firm's Equity

and:

D/E = the firm's (market value) debt/equity ratio

1. The Basic Modigliani-Miller Propositions

Modigliani and Miller (MM) summarized their results in three propositions.

Proposition I *The total value of a company is the present value of its operating income (EBIT) capitalized (discounted) at the cost of capital appropriate for the firm's level of business risk.* MM simplified their algebra by assuming that investors forecast EBIT to be constant forever, and used the perpetuity model to calculate present value:

$$V = \frac{EBIT}{k_{eU}}$$

Note that neither EBIT nor k_{eU} change as the firm's debt-equity mix is varied. Therefore, the value of a firm is independent of the way it is financed.

Proposition II *The cost of equity of a levered firm equals the cost of equity of an unlevered firm plus a risk premium which depends on the firm's financial leverage.* The risk premium is the product of the firm's debt/equity ratio and the difference between the firm's unlevered cost of equity and cost of debt.

$$k_{eL} = k_{eU} + (k_{eU} - k_d)\left(\frac{D}{E}\right)$$

As a firm changes its financing mix toward more debt, its debt/equity ratio increases, increasing the risk premium demanded by equity investors and therefore the cost of equity capital. However, the increase in the cost of equity follows a precise formula whose effect is to keep the weighted-average cost of capital constant, no matter what the debt-equity mix.

Proposition III *The weighted-average cost of capital is the appropriate "hurdle" rate for investment decisions, and the value of any investment alternative is independent of how the investment is financed.* This follows directly from Propositions I and II, since the cost of capital is unchanged by the debt-equity mix. Proposition III is the basis for separating the analysis of investment decisions and financing decisions as we have done in this book.[1]

2. The MM Propositions Including Corporate Taxes

Proposition I *The total value of a company is the present value of its* after-tax *operating income (EBIT) capitalized (discounted) at the cost of capital appropriate for the firm's level of business risk plus the present value of the tax savings from interest deductions.*

$$V = \frac{EBIT\,(1 - t)}{k_{eU}} + tD$$

Corporate income taxes have two effects on a company's value. First, they lower the worth of all companies since the government takes a fraction of net operating income. Notice that the numerator of the first term is now *EBIT(1 − t)*, the firm's operating earnings after taxes have been taken away. This effect is independent of the firm's financing mix. Second, if a firm borrows, its value is increased by the annual tax reduction due to interest expense. The second term is the present value of a perpetuity of such benefits. The more the company borrows, the higher the value of this term, hence the higher the value of the firm.

Proposition II *The cost of equity of a levered firm equals the cost of equity of an unlevered firm plus a risk premium that depends on the firm's financial leverage and tax rate.*

$$k_{eL} = k_{eU} + (k_{eU} - k_d)\,(1 - t)\left(\frac{D}{E}\right)$$

[1] **Elaboration:** We saw in Chapter 15 that market imperfections do exist, so that MM's conclusions are not perfectly true. In practice there are some interactions between the investment and financing decisions, but these are more properly the subject of a more advanced text.

This equation differs from MM's proposition II without taxes in that the term $(1 - t)$ enters the risk premium. Since $(1 - t)$ will always have a value less than one, its effect is to reduce the risk premium. The cost of equity capital rises at a slower rate than if there were no taxes. As the firm increases the debt in its financing mix, the cost of equity does not fully offset the lower cost of debt, and the weighted-average cost of capital rises.

Proposition III *The weighted average cost of capital is the appropriate "hurdle" rate for investment decisions, but it should be calculated using the firm's target capital structure as weights for the value of any investment alternative to be independent of how the investment is financed.* Unlike Proposition III without taxes, the weighted-average cost of capital now depends on the financing mix. The firm must establish its optimal financing mix prior to separating the investment and financing decisions. For MM, the optimal mix would be as close to 100% debt as the financial markets would allow.

3. The Miller (Personal Tax) Model

The value of an unlevered firm *The total value of a company is the present value of its after-both-corporate-and-personal-tax operating income (EBIT) capitalized (discounted) at the cost of capital appropriate for the firm's level of business risk.*

$$V = \frac{EBIT\ (1 - t)\ (1 - t_e)}{k_{eu}}$$

Now investors' personal tax rate on income from stock investments enters the equation, further reducing the value of the firm to them.

The value of a levered firm *The total value of a company is the present value of its after-both-corporate-and-personal-tax operating income (EBIT) capitalized (dicounted) at the cost of capital appropriate for the firm's level of business risk plus the present value of the tax savings from interest deductions.*

$$V = \frac{EBIT\ (1 - t)\ (1 - t_e)}{k_{eu}} + \left[1 - \frac{(1 - t)\ (1 - t_e)}{(1 - t_d)}\right] D$$

This equation is much like MM's Proposition II with taxes, except that investors' personal tax rates enter. Notice that the basic MM conclusion from their Proposition II with taxes still holds: the value of a firm with leverage exceeds the value of an unlevered firm by the present value of the tax benefits due to tax-deductible interest.

4. Beta with Leverage

MM's Proposition II shows that equity investors see corporate borrowing as risky and increase their required rate of return in response. This means that the beta of a levered firm must exceed the beta of an unlevered firm. The following expression captures this relationship:

$$\beta_L = \beta_u \left[1 + (1 - t)\left(\frac{D}{E}\right)\right]$$

where:

$$\beta_L = \text{beta of a } \textbf{L}\text{evered firm}$$

$$\beta_U = \text{beta of an } \textbf{U}\text{nlevered firm}$$

Notice that this relationship is quite parallel to MM's Proposition II with taxes, in that the increase in risk is captured by multiplying by the "after-tax" term $(1 - t)$ by the debt/equity ratio.

CHAPTER 16
RISK MANAGEMENT AND TEMPORARY WORKING CAPITAL

Clif Carlton finished writing on the flip-chart and turned back to the conference table. "My concern is that our cash and accounts receivable balances are becoming more variable. They have always been seasonal, but recently they have been fluctuating over a wider range on a weekly basis. And since we expanded our overseas business last year, the problem has become worse. Not only do we have more rapidly changing current asset balances, but the currencies we hold are changing almost as quickly. Yet we've been slow to respond to these changes."

Clif was treasurer of a medium-sized transportation company. Among his responsibilities were selecting and obtaining the firm's liabilities. Recently he had become concerned about changing patterns of the company's cash flows and balance sheet accounts, and he had called today's meeting to address his concerns. Around the table were members of each finance group that reported to him—domestic cash management, international cash management, investment management, and financial planning and research—but he had also invited several colleagues from other areas of the company who could contribute to the discussion or might be affected by the alternatives his group would consider.

Clif continued his remarks. "I'm convinced it's time to rethink our liability strategy. With rapidly changing asset balances, our risk exposure is constantly changing as well. I'm not convinced that our existing policies are up to the job of dealing with that. We also need to look again at the mix of debt financing we use and how that affects the company's risk posture. Let's put together a team to study the way our business has changed and recommend whether new approaches are required."

Clif is concerned about financial risk management, using financial managing methods and products to reduce the financial risks faced by his company. As Clif's team re-examines the company's liability strategy, it will find itself studying how well the company uses these risk management techniques in both its overall financing strategy and its day-to-day operations. Modern finance has developed powerful tools for limiting risks. Used wisely, they can enable a company to be involved in business activities that might otherwise be far too risky to take on.

However, financial risk management has an important role to play even in companies that normally shun risky ventures. Like Clif's firm, every company is exposed to potential losses from many of its business activities. Some risks, such as product liability, involve the firm's customers. Other risks are employee-related, for example the risk of on-the-job injury. The possibility of fire, theft, or damage to property poses yet another risk. In this chapter we look at the way financial risk management is used to address two types of risk that arise from the firm's financial transactions: (1) the risk of being unable to repay and refinance debt, and (2) the risk of losses due to fluctuations in interest and foreign exchange rates. The first is addressed by matching the maturities of assets and liabilities across the balance sheet, the second through the use of financial insurance contracts and derivative securities. These two activities are worth investigating for another reason as well. As we will see, they are the third and fourth steps in a four-step process of managing a company's working capital that begins with the incremental decisions about permanent working capital we discussed in Chapter 12.

Key Points You Should Learn from This Chapter

After reading this chapter you should be able to:

- Discuss how hedging can reduce financial risks.
- Describe the four-step sequence of working capital decisions.
- Discuss how companies set their debt maturity mix.
- Relate how temporary working capital arises in the current accounts.
- Discuss the basics of hedging against foreign currency and interest rate movements including the use of derivative securities.

Introductory Concepts—Hedging

Suppose a professional basketball player's contract specifies that he will get a $200,000 bonus if his team wins the championship. In effect the player faces some financial risk: depending on the outcome of the season, he could receive a bonus payment of either $0 or $200,000. One way the player could deal with this risk would be to make a $100,000 bet against his team winning the championship. If the team wins, he would receive the $200,000 bonus but would have to pay the $100,000, for a net take of $100,000. If the team loses, he would get no bonus but would receive the $100,000 from the bet. Effectively, the bet would change his risky position into a riskless one: either way he would get $100,000.

Of course, it would be wrong (and illegal!) for a basketball pro to bet against his own team. Fortunately, however, betting of this kind is not illegal in business. Consider, for example, the problem of a farmer who grows corn. The farmer's financial position is quite risky since the amount of money the crop will bring in will depend on corn prices at harvest time. The risk is that corn prices will fall. One way for the farmer to obtain protection is to "bet against himself" by selling futures contracts that require the farmer to deliver a set amount of corn at a specified price, contracts whose value is tied to the price of corn. If corn prices fall, the futures position will increase in value, offsetting the loss, since the contracts would be cheaper to fulfill. Cereal manufacturers are in a position precisely opposite to that of the farmer, running the risk that corn prices will rise. They can reduce their risk by purchasing the futures contracts so that if corn prices rise, their loss will be offset by the increased value of owning contracts which fix (limit) the price they have to pay.[1]

hedging—balancing a risky financial position with an opposite position to cancel out the risk

Each of these examples is an illustration of **hedging,** offsetting a financial risk with an equal and opposite position so that changes in the value of the two positions cancel each other out. While many financial risk positions can be addressed with hedging, in this chapter we concentrate on two: balancing assets and liabilities, and balancing cash inflows and outflows.

In this book, we first encountered the concept of hedging in Chapter 6, when we looked at the "segmentation or hedging hypothesis" for explaining the yield curve.[2] That theory supposes that bond investors choose the maturities of the bonds they buy based upon when they will need the cash back. They do so to lock in a known dollar value at a specified time and ensure that cash will be available as needed. The hedging we examine in this chapter is done for the same reasons: to guarantee values and to improve a company's liquidity.

By hedging across the balance sheet, financial managers ensure that the correct amount of cash will be available to pay each of the firm's liabilities when they fall due and that there will be financing for every asset.

---

[1] **Acknowledgment:** These examples were suggested by Professor Robert G. Schweback of the University of Wyoming.

[2] **Cross-reference:** The segmentation or hedging hypothesis appears on pp. 217–218.

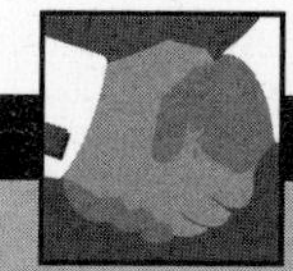

SERVING FINANCE'S CUSTOMERS

Risk Management at Corning, Incorporated

Corning, Incorporated's treasury has redefined the scope of its financial risk management activities. In addition to the hedging conducted by domestic and international cash management professionals, another group, known formally as "Risk Management and Prevention," looks at the potential for financial loss from product liability claims. The group defines Corning's operating units as its customers. Once seen simply as a buyer of insurance, today the group includes both finance specialists and Ph.D. scientists who work together to identify, assess, and reduce the customer units' risk exposure. The goal is to drive down avoidable litigation costs, those that would not have happened if Corning made no errors, to a tiny fraction of total litigation costs. As a result of its innovative use of quality-management approaches, the Risk Management and Prevention group within Corning, Incorporated's treasury is recognized within the profession as world class.

Example

Hedging Across the Balance Sheet

Belleco Resources recently issued $10 million of 20-year bonds to finance its investment in an off-shore oil platform. Cash from the oil platform project will be used to pay the bonds' interest and principal. Belleco's treasurer chose 20 years as the bonds' maturity to match the forecasted 20-year life of the platform.

By hedging individual cash flows, financial managers ensure that every receipt can be efficiently used and that there is a known cost to every obligation.

Example

Hedging a Cash Flow

Belleco Resources has an obligation to pay ¥1.5 million to a Japanese supplier in 30 days. To guarantee the exchange rate, which might fluctuate during the next month, Belleco's treasurer has entered into a forward exchange contract with its bank.[3]

Notice that while hedging reduces risk, it also takes away the opportunity to benefit from favorable results. The basketball player gave up the possibility to receive $200,000 by hedging his bonus. The farmer gave up the opportunity to sell his crop at a higher price had corn prices risen. The cereal producer lost the chance to purchase the corn at a lower price had prices fallen. Hedging eliminates variability, upward changes as well as downward changes.

To further understand the benefits of hedging, it is useful to consider what happens when financial managers do not hedge. Whereas hedged receipts are

[3] **Cross-reference:** Forward exchange rates, the quotes for forward exchange contracts, were introduced in Chapter 7, pp. 238–239.

promptly used, unhedged receipts become excess cash, over and above the firm's needs. Although this money can be invested, it often earns interest at a lower rate than better-planned investments. Unhedged obligations force a company to obtain funds for their payment in today's markets. The money might carry a high interest rate, or, if in another currency, might only be available at a foreign exchange rate less favorable than could have been obtained with prior planning.

Throughout this chapter we study how risk management activities can *reduce* financial risks. However, it is quite possible to use the insights, tools, and instruments of financial risk management to speculate in risky situations, effectively *increasing* a company's risk exposure in the hope of greater returns. Although some treasurers engage in this kind of speculation, most do not, treating it as not supportive of the company's activities and as a business they do not want to be in. Accordingly, we have not looked at the speculative side of financial risk management in this chapter.

The Four-Step Sequence of Working Capital Decisions

Working capital is put in place in a sequence with four steps, much like a set of building blocks. As we consider this process, it is useful to recall the concepts of permanent and temporary working capital, a distinction we made in Chapter 12.[4]

1. Permanent and Temporary Working Capital Revisited

Recall from Chapter 12 that permanent working capital is the base level of current accounts, the amount that remains in place regardless of variations in business activity. Temporary working capital is the remainder, the additions to working capital that come from cyclical, seasonal, and daily fluctuations. Figure 16.1, a repeat of Figure 12.1, illustrates the division of both current assets and current liabilities into permanent and temporary portions.

2. The Four Steps in Establishing Working Capital Balances

In the order in which they are typically conceptualized, the four steps in the process of setting a company's working capital levels are:

1. Put the permanent current assets into place.
2. Use attractive short-term financing opportunities as permanent current liabilities.
3. Add additional permanent debt, if needed, to hedge the maturities of the balance sheet.

[4] **Cross-reference:** The distinction between permanent and temporary working capital appears throughout Chapter 12, but it is explicitly discussed on pp. 426–427.

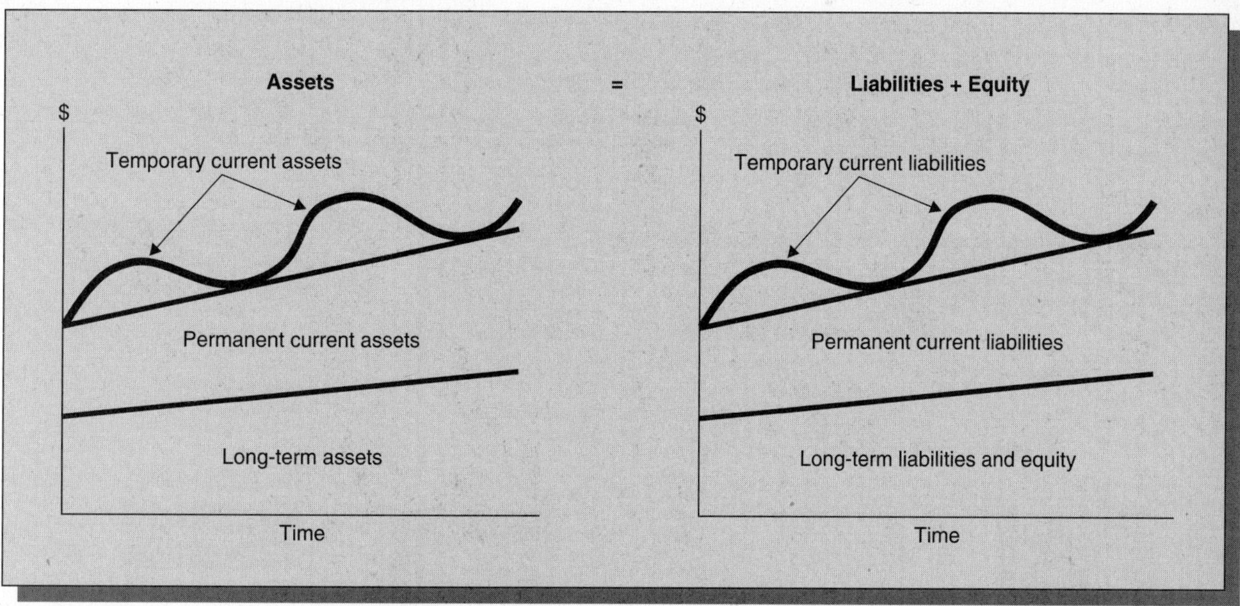

FIGURE 16.1
Levels of assets and claims across time for a growing firm. Current assets and liabilities can be divided into a permanent level plus temporary fluctuations.

4. Respond to temporary working capital needs and opportunities.

However, since business and financial market conditions regularly change, the process is not quite as neat and linear as our description makes it sound. It is common for each step to be revisited regularly and for the four steps to be rethought on an ongoing basis.

Figure 16.2 illustrates the four steps. In addition, the figure illustrates another important point. At the same time that working capital opportunities are being analyzed, two other financial managing balance-sheet-related activities are taking place. In Chapter 11 we studied capital budgeting, the evaluation and selection of noncurrent asset investments. Chapter 15 was devoted to setting the debt-equity mix. Both analyses are done in parallel to working capital decisions, and there is some amount of interaction between all of them. However, to simplify our presentation, we will assume that these other two decisions have already been made as we enter the four working capital steps. The top of Figure 16.2, which shows a balance sheet containing some amount of noncurrent assets and with a target split between debt and equity financing, will therefore be our starting point for considering working capital.

The four steps are described further below:

First: Set the permanent current asset balances In Chapter 12 we discovered that investments in permanent current asset balances are analyzed in

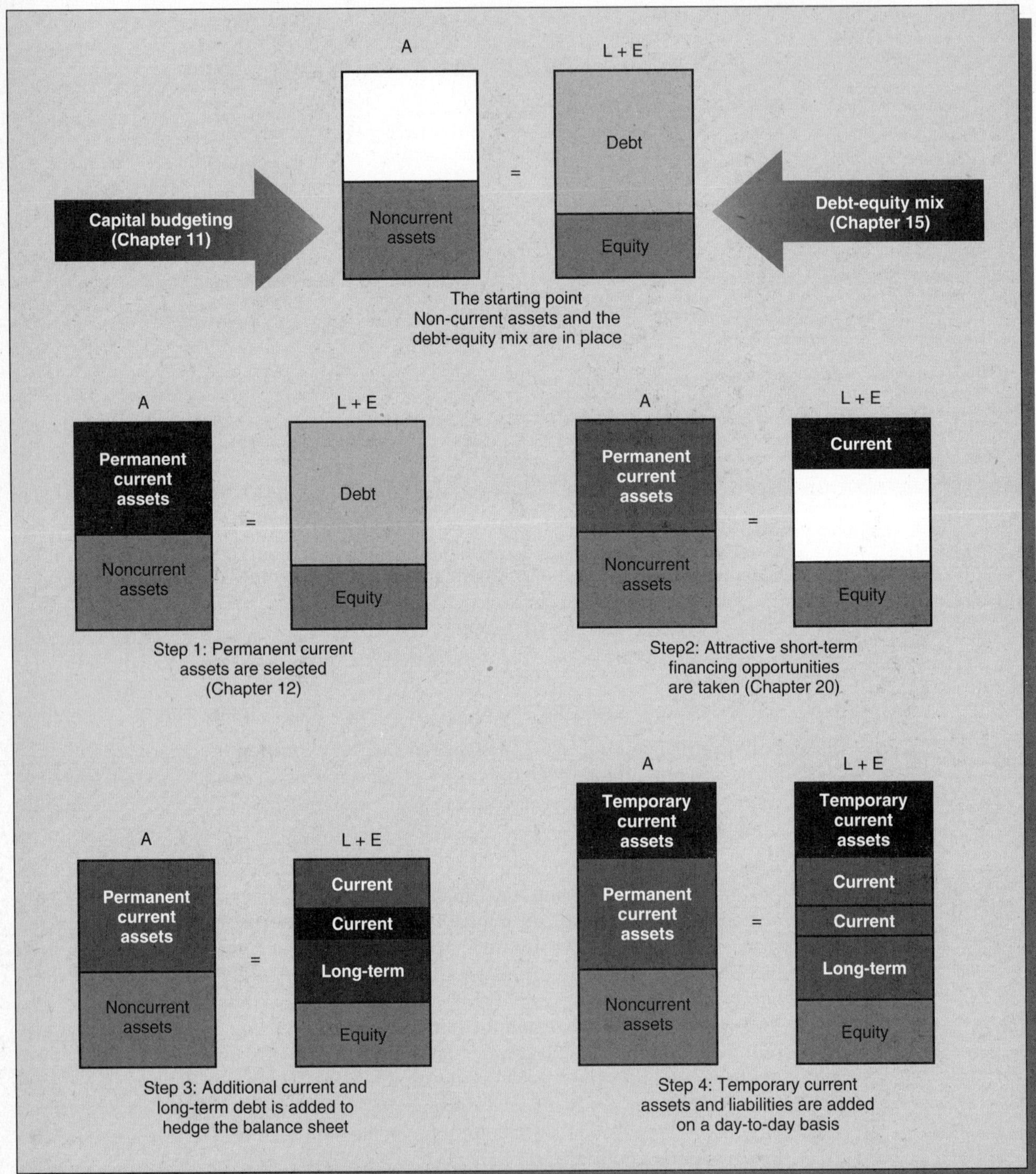

FIGURE 16.2

The four steps in working capital decisions. In order, the steps involve: (1) permanent current assets, (2) low-or-no-cost permanent current liabilities, (3) other permanent debt, and (4) temporary working capital.

much the same way as long-term assets.[5] For each opportunity to adjust permanent current assets we estimate incremental cash flows, establish a cost of capital appropriate for the level of risk, and apply time value of money calculations. A company should invest in all permanent working capital assets that produce a positive net present value. Accordingly, the appropriate level for the permanent component of each current asset is the amount that produces a positive NPV, and a company's total permanent working capital asset balance becomes the sum of these figures. Step 1 of Figure 16.2 builds on the starting point by adding in a balance of permanent current assets.

Second: Use attractive short-term financing opportunities as the first permanent current liabilities A company should use short-term payables for financing whenever the interest rate is favorable and the supplier is happy with the relationship. The rate of interest on most institutional payables (wages payable, taxes payable) is typically zero, hence it benefits a company to use as much of this financing as is available. For trade credit (accounts payable), an interest rate must be calculated as we will demonstrate in Chapter 20[6]; in cases where the effective interest rate is consistently below market levels, the company should take this credit as well. The total of these low-or-no-cost current liabilities becomes the first part of the firm's permanent current liability balance. Step 2 of Figure 16.2 builds on Step 1 by adding in a balance of low (or no) cost permanent current liabilities.

Third: Add additional current liabilities and long-term debt to hedge the balance sheet Steps 1 and 2 establish current asset and current liability balances without reference to one another. But from the point of view of hedging, it makes sense for the two current portions of the balance sheet to be related. Current assets, those expected to produce cash in the near term, are normally the primary means of paying current liabilities. The current ratio—current assets divided by current liabilities—used by many financial analysts to measure the overall relationship of the current accounts, captures this concept.[7] At the same time, it is prudent for the firm's noncurrent assets—expected to be around for many years—to be financed primarily with long-term funds. In this step, the financial manager adds appropriate amounts of permanent current liabilities and long-term debt to move the balance sheet toward the desired relationship between the current assets and current liabilities, and between noncurrent assets and long-term financing. The "debt-maturity mix," the split between short- and longer-term debt financing employed by the firm, results from these choices. This is shown in Step 3 of Figure 16.2.

Fourth: Respond to temporary working capital needs and opportunities Cyclicality, seasonality, and day-to-day events require a company to take on additional, temporary working capital assets and provide opportunities for

---

[5] **Cross-reference:** This insight is presented on pp. 427–430, and is illustrated throughout the remainder of Chapter 12.

[6] **Cross-reference and observation:** See pp. 725–729 for the calculation of interest rates in trade credit terms. As we discuss in Chapter 20, it is important not to miss the "relationship" issues that surround the company's payables as they can have a significant impact on the total cost of doing business.

[7] **Cross-reference:** The current ratio is discussed in Appendix 4D, pp. 122–123.

temporary working capital financing. These issues are handled on a day-to-day basis as they arise. Step 4 of Figure 16.2 adds temporary current assets and liabilities to the balance sheet to illustrate these changes.

Example

The Four-Step Working Capital Sequence

The treasurer of Belleco Resources has determined the following:

- Investment opportunities in current assets totalling $36 million are available with positive net present values when evaluated at the appropriate risk-adjusted cost of capital.
- The company's payroll and tax systems create wages payable and taxes payable totalling $8 million. No interest or other payments are required to support these payables.
- A sensitivity analysis of Belleco's liquidity indicates the need for a minimum current ratio of 1.8 times.
- Daily fluctuations in working capital balances are anticipated throughout the coming year.

Question: How should the working capital balances be set?

Solution steps: Belleco's treasurer follows the four-step process:

1. "Set the permanent current asset balances." Invest the $36 million in working capital assets.
2. "Use attractive short-term financing opportunities as the first permanent current liabilities." Make the $8 million of institutional payables the first portion of permanent current liabilities since they have zero cost.
3. "Set the split between current liabilities and long-term financing."

   a. With $36 million of permanent current assets and a minimum current ratio of 1.8 times, the target number for Belleco's total permanent current liabilities can easily be determined:

   $$\text{Current assets/current liabilities} = 1.8$$

   so:

   $$\text{Current liabilities} = \$36\text{ million}/1.8 = \$20\text{ million}$$

   b. Since $8 million of permanent current liabilities is already in place from Step 2, add another $12 million of short-term debt.

4. "Respond to temporary working capital needs and opportunities." Use the methods discussed later in this chapter, including investment in marketable securities and the hedging of cash flows, to reduce day-to-day risks as working capital levels deviate from the permanent balances throughout the year.

In the remainder of this chapter we look in more detail at the third and fourth steps in this process: achieving a desired level of working capital by setting the split between current and long-term financing, and making use of temporary working capital.

The Debt Maturity Mix

debt maturity mix—the blend of debt maturities used by a firm

The term **debt maturity mix** refers to the relative amounts of each maturity of debt in a company's capital structure. It is important to include all maturities in the analysis, as each can play a role in hedging the company's assets. However, since the balance sheet divides liabilities into "current" and "long-term," it is common and convenient to think of the debt maturity mix as referring to these two categories. When a company hedges its balance sheet as the third step in setting its working capital balances, it sets its debt maturity mix.

1. The Risk-Return Tradeoff

By setting its debt maturity mix, a company establishes an important part of its risk-return posture. A firm can normally lower its financing costs by weighting its debt maturities toward the short term since yield curves have historically been upward-sloping, with current liabilities costing less than long-term debt. However, a company's liquidity goes down, hence its risk goes up, as its current liabilities increase relative to its current assets. The initial step in setting the debt maturity mix is evaluating this classic risk-return tradeoff.

Example

The Risk-Return Tradeoff in the Debt Maturity Mix

Rumat Industries is considering three alternative approaches to setting its debt maturity mix. Strategy A is aggressive, emphasizing short-term debt. Strategy C is conservative, emphasizing long-term debt. Strategy B lies between the other two. Rumat's treasurer has organized the following data (in millions of dollars) to use in the analysis:

- The company has $1,000 of assets of which $400 are current.
- $400 of liabilities will be obtained. If Strategy A is adopted, $300 of this will be current; $200 will be current under strategy B; and $100 under Strategy C.
- EBIT is forecasted to be $200, and Rumat is in the 35% income tax bracket.
- The yield curve is currently upward-sloping: the interest rate on bank notes is 6%, and long-term debt yields 10%.

Question: What will Rumat's balance sheet and the financial half of its income statement look like under each strategy?

Solution steps:

1. Organize the asset, liability, and equity data into a balance sheet format. Note that with $1,000 of assets and $400 of liabilities, owners equity will equal $600 under each alternative.

	Strategy A	Strategy B	Strategy C
Assets:			
Current	$ 400	$ 400	$ 400
Noncurrent	600	600	600
Total	$ 1,000	$ 1,000	$ 1,000

	Strategy A	Strategy B	Strategy C
Liabilities:			
Current	$ 300	$ 200	$ 100
Long-term	100	200	300
Equity:	600	600	600
Total	$ 1,000	$ 1,000	$ 1,000

2. Construct the financial half of Rumat's income statement under each alternative:

   a. Calculate interest expense under each alternative (from the yield curve data equal to 6% of current liabilities plus 10% of long-term liabilities):

$$\text{Strategy A: } (6\% \times \$300) + (10\% \times \$100) = \$28$$

$$\text{Strategy B: } (6\% \times \$200) + (10\% \times \$200) = \$32$$

$$\text{Strategy C: } (6\% \times \$100) + (10\% \times \$300) = \$36$$

   b. Organize the information of the income statements:

	Strategy A	Strategy B	Strategy C
EBIT	$200	$200	$200
− Interest	28	32	36
EBT	172	168	164
− Taxes(35%)	60	59	57
EAT	$112	$109	$107

Question: What will Rumat's return and liquidity risk look like under each alternative as measured by its return on equity and current ratios?

Solution steps:

Return on equity = EAT/owners equity
Current ratio = Current assets/current liabilities

	Strategy A	Strategy B	Strategy C
Return on equity	$\frac{112}{600} = 18.7\%$	$\frac{109}{600} = 18.2\%$	$\frac{107}{600} = 17.8\%$
Current ratio	$\frac{400}{300} = 1.33$	$\frac{400}{200} = 2.00$	$\frac{400}{100} = 4.00$

Answer: Rumat's rate of return and liquidity move in opposite directions. While Strategy A increases Rumat's rate of return, it reduces the firm's liquidity. Strategy C provides a high degree of liquidity at the cost of a lowered rate of return. Strategy B lies in the middle.

2. Using Hedging to Reduce Risk

Currently, finance theory offers no clear formula for finding the best debt maturity mix. However, the technique of hedging can be used to reduce a company's repayment and liquidity risks. If this can be done at low cost, it is possible to improve the firm's risk-return posture. In this section we look at three strategies for using hedging to set the debt maturity mix: (1) individual asset/liability hedging, (2) maturity-range hedging, and (3) maturity-range hedging with deviations.

Individual asset/liability hedging This approach is the ultimate application of hedging: the financial manager attempts to offset each liability with an asset of identical size and maturity. This would ensure that every cash flow could be used fully and every liability would have a cash flow to pay it when due. A financial company with many discrete liabilities, such as a bank or insurance company, can often come close to this ideal. For a nonfinancial firm such as a manufacturing company, with a small number of individual items on the right-hand side of the balance sheet, this approach is both impractical and very costly. Nevertheless, the concept of hedging individual assets and liabilities serves as a useful starting point for further analysis.

Maturity-range hedging With this approach, the overall *level* of assets with a given range of maturities is matched with a similar level of liabilities and/or equity with the same maturity range. Figure 16.3 illustrates this approach. Maturity-range hedging would have the firm set the following relationships among its balances:

Current liabilities = current assets

Long-term liabilities and equity = noncurrent assets

FIGURE 16.3
Maturity-range hedging. The level of current assets is matched by a similar level of current liabilities.

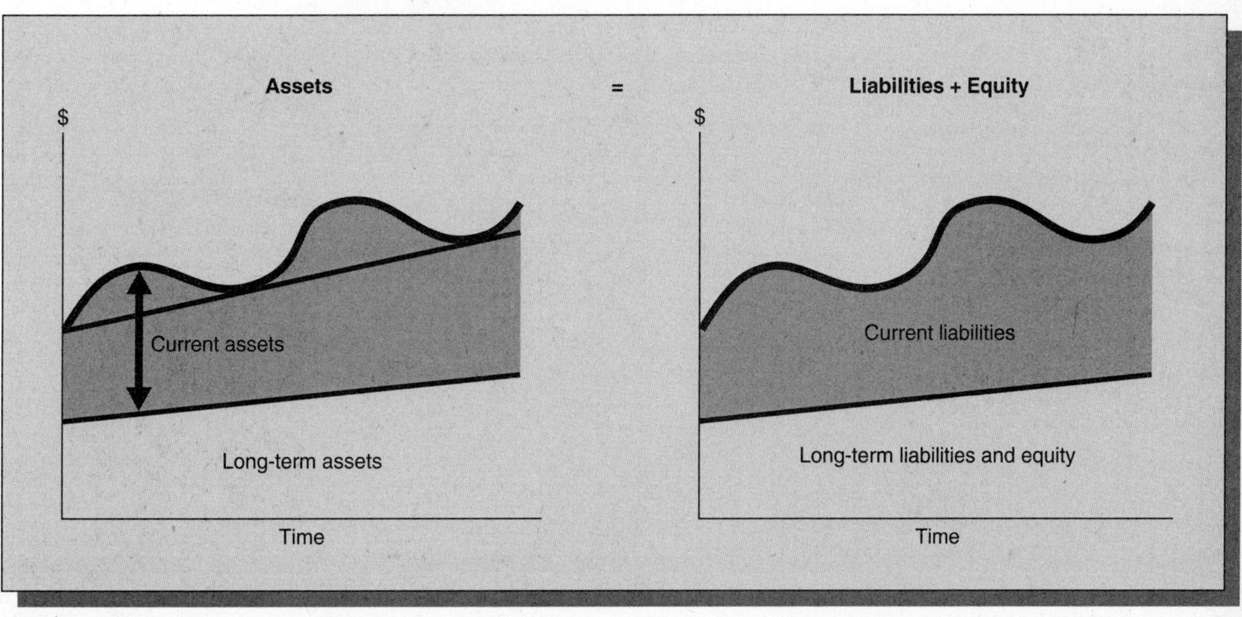

We can improve upon maturity-range hedging by allowing for permanent current assets. Since, as we saw in Chapter 12, permanent current assets are treated as having an infinite (long-term) lifetime, a more consistent use of maturity-range hedging is to set:

Current liabilities = temporary current assets

Long-term liabilities and equity = permanent current assets plus noncurrent assets

This approach is illustrated in Figure 16.4.

Deviations from maturity-range hedging Some companies elect to move away from precise maturity-range hedging, especially if they are small or if their asset needs are unpredictable. Firm size plays a role in how well maturity-range hedging can be achieved. Small firms find it difficult and costly to issue long-term securities; they tend to deviate from the hedging goal by weighting their financing toward short and intermediate sources. And the more unpredictable a company's asset levels, hence its financing needs, the more difficult it is to hedge.

However, many larger companies deviate from maturity-range hedging by choice. Some firms choose to have a higher level of current liabilities than maturity-range hedging would prescribe. They finance some portion of their permanent current assets and possibly even some of their noncurrent assets with short-term sources, as Figure 16.5 illustrates. This strategy has three effects: (1) Since yield curves nor-

FIGURE 16.4
Improved maturity-range hedging. Long-term financing is used for permanent current assets as well as noncurrent assets; current liabilities finance temporary current assets.

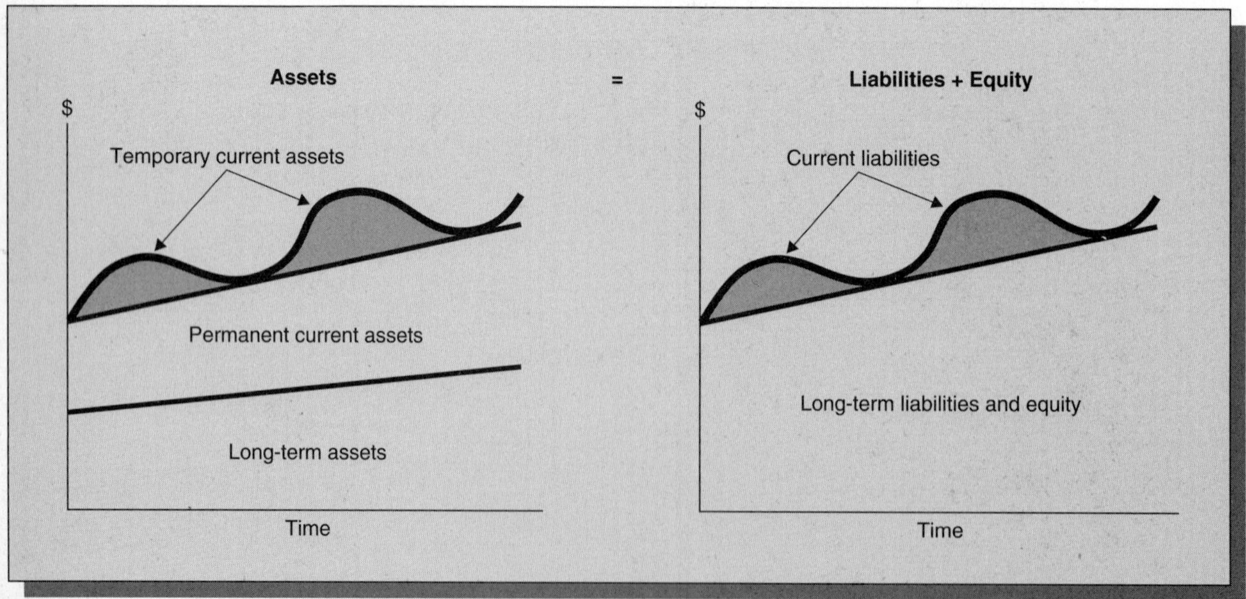

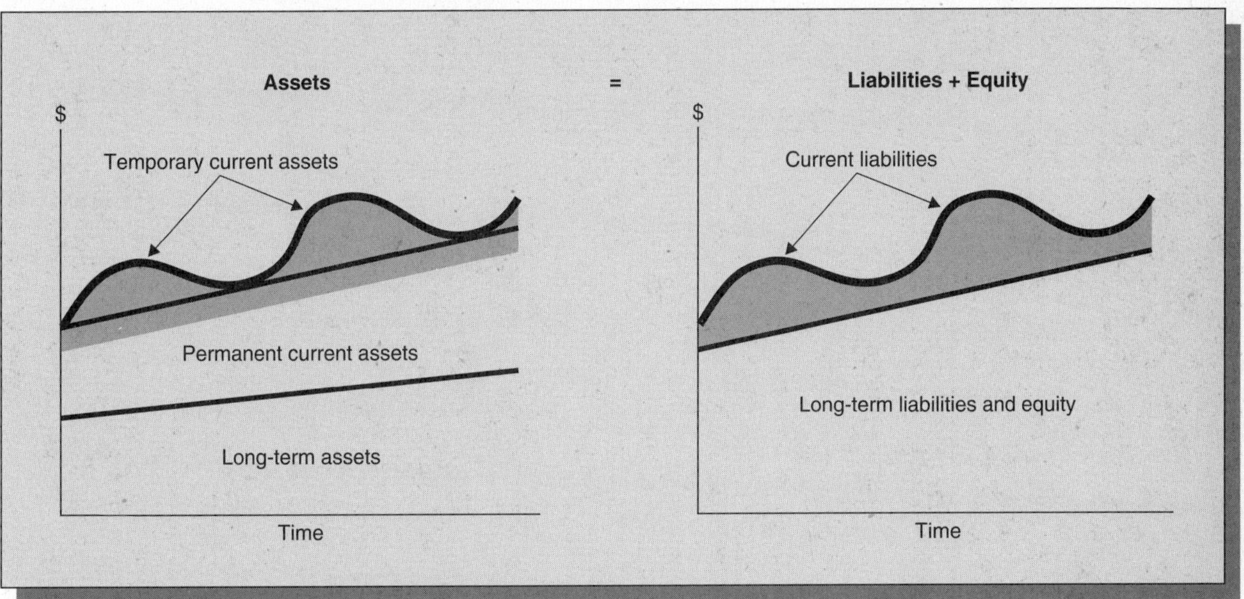

FIGURE 16.5
Increased current liabilities. Current liabilities finance temporary current assets plus some permanent current assets.

mally slope upwards, additional short-term debt usually reduces financing costs. (2) Offsetting this saving is a possible increase to the administrative costs and fees associated with obtaining debt since high levels of short-term financing imply more frequent debt contract renewals. (3) It is relatively easy to adjust the level of short-term financing (as compared to long-term debt or equity), especially bank borrowing. With a high level of current debt, the firm can more exactly match its financing to its needs.

Other companies elect to use a lower level of current liabilities than maturity-range hedging would dictate. Thus they finance some portion of temporary current assets with long-term sources. This strategy has four effects. (1) The company's risk of near-term bankruptcy is reduced. Lower current liabilities means less debt coming due in the near future. This removes pressure from the firm to have the liquidity necessary to repay this debt. (2) The company faces less exposure to changing interest rates. Whereas short-term debt maturities mean regular renewal at changing interest rates, long-term debt maturities typically lock in the cost of debt financing so the firm can more easily plan its long-term capital budget. (3) The company will generally have a better credit rating, since having a small amount of current debt—which implies more working capital and better liquidity ratios—is seen as a conservative financing strategy. (4) When temporary current assets drop below the level of long-term financing, the firm has extra funds which, practically, cannot go toward reducing debt. The most common use for these funds is marketable securities that earn at a rate lower than the cost of debt. Thus, the firm loses money on these excess funds. Figure 16.6 illustrates this approach.

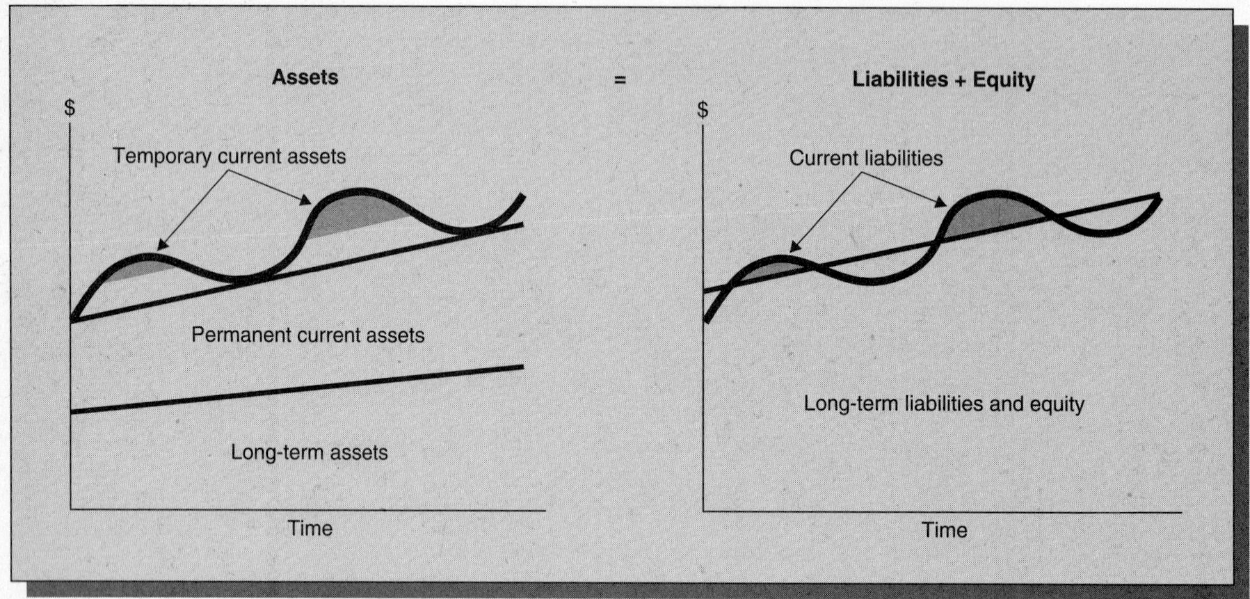

FIGURE 16.6
Decreased short-term debt. In this strategy, current liabilities finance only a portion of temporary current assets.

Temporary Working Capital

In this section we look first at patterns in a typical firm's temporary working capital. Then we examine more closely the nature of the temporary balances in each of the working capital accounts: cash, marketable securities, accounts receivable, inventory, and payables. Finally we point out some dangers of poor temporary working capital management.

1. Patterns of Working Capital

working capital cycle—the flow of value through current asset accounts

There is a pattern to the ebb and flow of temporary current assets within the working capital accounts. Figure 16.7 illustrates this **working capital cycle,** and Figure 16.8 shows schematically how each working capital asset bulges in turn as the pattern progresses.

The flow of value through the working capital asset accounts begins on the left-hand side of Figure 16.7, when the financial manager provides the necessary funds to the cash balance. The cash is used to purchase inventory, either directly in the form of raw materials and merchandise, or indirectly through the payment of wages to employees who convert raw materials into work-in-process and finished goods. When the inventory is sold, the value it contains moves to accounts receivable and eventually returns to cash when the receivables are collected. Some returning cash remains in working capital to finance the next round. Other cash may be removed from the working capital cycle if the need for temporary working capital is forecasted to decline.

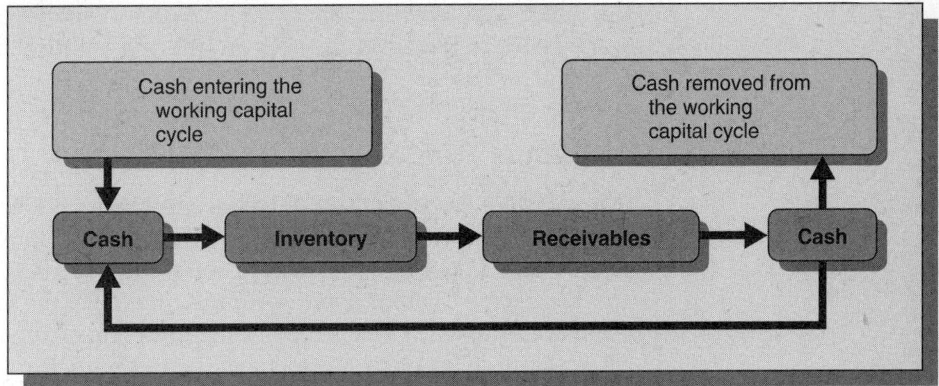

FIGURE 16.7
The working capital cycle. Cash enters the cycle to purchase and/or manufacture inventory and returns when accounts receivable are collected.

As the working capital cycle progresses, a company first builds up its temporary inventory and then its temporary accounts receivable before the cash invested in the cycle returns to the firm—as shown in Figure 16.8. At the same time, on the right-hand side of the balance sheet, temporary accounts payable and wages payable grow when inventory grows, and they return to their base levels when these liabilities are paid. In practice, however, the pattern is rarely this clear. In many firms the cycle repeats itself so fast that the bulges are not clearly visible; each bulge follows the prior one so closely that the flow appears to be continuous. Also, since temporary working capital includes the impacts of cyclicality,

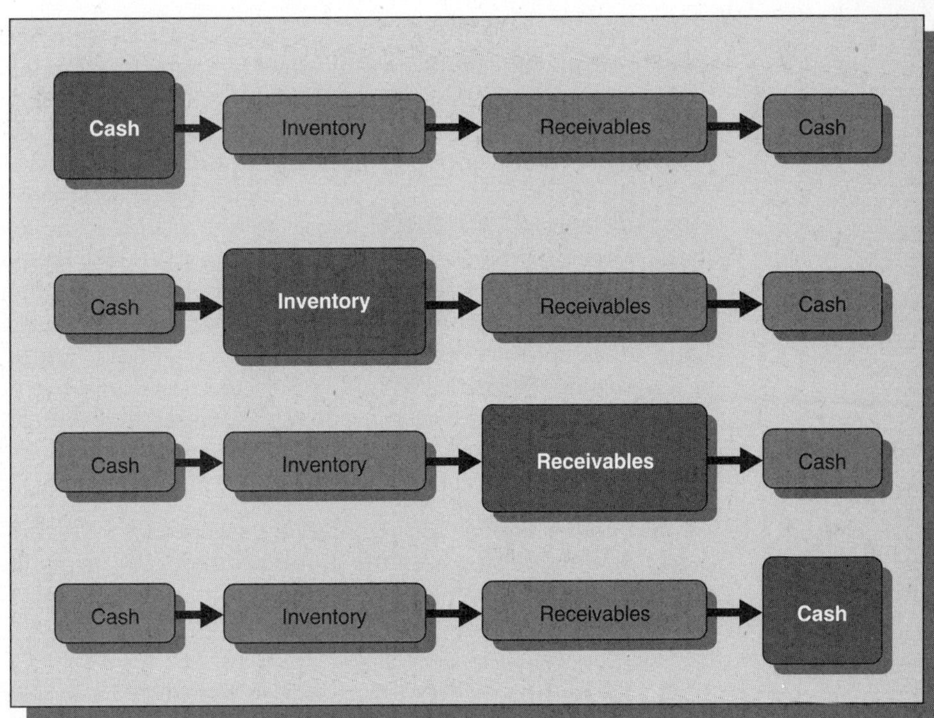

FIGURE 16.8
Buildups in working capital assets. The bulge moves from cash to inventory to receivables and back to cash.

seasonality, and circumstance, the working capital cycle is typically not a single simple pattern but several cycles of differing lengths superimposed one upon the other.

2. Temporary Cash

It is common for a firm's cash balance to rise above its target minimum amount. Inflows and outflows of cash are rarely equal on a day-to-day basis. When a company sells a major asset or raises capital funds by selling bonds or stock, it usually has excess cash for some period of time until the money is spent. Companies often accumulate cash when planning for a large expenditure, such as a major asset acquisition, debt principal repayment, or stock repurchase. A treasurer who expects interest rates to rise or stock prices to fall might find it attractive to raise cash in today's market environment, even if the money could not be used fully for some time.

3. Marketable Securities

marketable security—investments with a ready market which may be sold easily to obtain their value in cash

When the cash balance rises above target, the excess is normally invested to earn interest. Treasurers look for **marketable securities,** low-risk, highly liquid investments that may be resold easily without loss of principal. Among the alternative investment choices for excess U.S. dollar funds are U.S. Treasury securities (bonds, notes, and bills),[8] federal agency issues, state and local bonds, banker's acceptances, negotiable certificates of deposit, repurchase agreements, commercial paper, Euronotes, money market mutual funds, and variable-rate preferred stock. Figure 16.9 summarizes some of the key characteristics of each of these investment instruments.

A firm with significant inflows of temporary cash might find itself holding a portfolio of marketable securities. In Chapter 8 we looked at the dynamics of a portfolio and discovered that systematic risk can be reduced by diversifying the portfolio to lower its beta.[9] For a portfolio of marketable securities, however, diversification of this kind is not possible. In practice, the primary systematic factor affecting the risk of marketable securities is the level of interest rates—when rates rise, marketable securities fall in value together, and vice versa. As a result, the risk of one security does not offset that of another, and a portfolio of many marketable securities has much the same risk as a large holding of only one. This does not mean that financial managers should ignore the mix of marketable securities. Securities should be selected based on their maturity dates to hedge the timing of future cash needs. This ensures that the company will receive known face values from redeeming the securities rather than having to sell them in the market and receive uncertain future market values.

Because there is a cost to buying and selling marketable securities—the banker's or broker's fee plus the administrative cost of managing the transaction—it is

---

[8] **Cross-reference:** U.S. Treasury obligations first appeared in Chapter 6, pp. 211–213, in our discussion of the yield curve.

[9] **Cross-reference:** Diversification and its implications are discussed in the second half of Chapter 8, beginning on p. 276.

Treasury bills	Maturities of 91 days (13 weeks), 182 days (26 weeks), 270 days (52 weeks). Sold on discount basis. New issue weekly: auction every Monday with bills sold to highest bidders (lowest yield). Small buyers can buy at average bid price.
Treasury notes	Maturities of one to seven years. Sold on coupon basis. Shorter maturities are bearer bonds; longer maturities are registered.
Treasury bonds	Maturities over five years. Sold on coupon basis; registered.
Federal agency issues	Maturities of one month to 15 years with 2/3 less than one year. Guaranteed by specific agency, not a general obligation of the Treasury. Issued by "government agencies" (the public has no ownership interest) and "government-sponsored enterprises" (some public ownership).
State and local bonds	Maturities of more than one year. Income exempt from federal taxes and local taxes in state and/or city of issue. Rated by rating agencies; AAA-rated bonds very safe.
Banker's acceptances	Drafts accepted by banks for later payment. Obligations of the bank. Maturities of one to six months.
Negotiable certificates of deposit (CDs)	Large denomination term borrowing by banks. Maturities between a few days and 18 months. Banks encourage secondary market to help primary issuance.
Repurchase agreements (Repos)	Borrowing by selling securities and simultaneously agreeing to repurchase them at a specified date. Maturities very short; most frequent maturity: overnight.
Commercial paper and Euronotes	Short-term unsecured borrowings of large corporations. Maturities of less than nine months—tailored to parties' needs.
Money market mutual funds	Pooled money owning a portfolio of money market securities. Company can write checks directly on the fund to convert the investment back to cash. Particularly suitable for small firms that cannot afford to manage a portfolio of marketable securities themselves.
Variable-rate preferred stock	Seventy percent of dividends are tax-free to corporations. Variable interest rate means the stock always sells close to par value, thus avoiding the interest rate risk that would accompany such a perpetual-life issue.

FIGURE 16.9
Marketable securities. Characteristics of the more common investments used by companies to earn interest on temporary excess cash.

not always efficient to invest every dollar of excess cash in marketable securities. Appendix 16A presents several models that attempt to find an optimal cash-marketable securities policy.

4. Temporary Accounts Receivable

Beyond the effects of seasonality or the business cycle, a company's balance of accounts receivable will vary about its base level when special terms of payment are negotiated with individual customers. This happens when the volume or riskiness of the customer's business differs from the company's norms or when one party can raise funds more cheaply than the other due to financial strength or superior financial market access. A financially strong seller often lengthens the payment period to aid a weaker buyer. A financially strong buyer can often pay rapidly to aid a weaker seller by substituting other forms of credit for trade payables.

Individual customers are evaluated for credit against a set of criteria often summarized as the "five Cs": character, capacity, capital, collateral, and conditions.

Character Does the credit applicant honor obligations? This is assessed by learning about the applicant's past behavior. Individuals and organizations with whom the applicant has done business in the past, including suppliers and commercial banks, can provide some information. Other data come from credit reporting and rating services, such as Dun & Bradstreet.

Capacity Does the applicant have the ability to pay? This question is typically answered through a formal credit analysis, a study of the applicant's financial statements to predict its future liquidity and cash flows.

Capital Does the applicant have sufficient financial strength to withstand reverses and still make payments? The same credit analysis that studies capacity to pay is used to answer this question by projecting the applicant's liquidity and cash flows under a variety of downside scenarios.

Collateral Does the applicant have assets that can be seized and sold to provide cash in case of lack of payment? For most banks and other companies that extend credit, collateral is not considered the primary basis for repayment. Rather it provides a "second way out" in case the applicant cannot or will not pay. Potential collateral is appraised to ensure its value exceeds the amount of the loan.

Conditions What outside factors, such as a downturn in economic activity, might alter the situation and make repayment difficult? What is the probability of each downside scenario, and what is the effect of each on the applicant?

If an exchange of currency is taking place, other considerations enter the credit decision: the choice of currency in which to denominate the transaction and the impact of changing foreign exchange values on the payment terms. As recipient of the payment, the seller will prefer the sale to be denominated in the stronger currency, whereas the buyer will prefer to pay with the weaker currency. If the buying firm's currency is the stronger of the two, there is a tendency for the seller to be generous with payment terms to keep the amount denominated in the strong currency as long as possible. Conversely, if the selling firm's currency is the stronger, the tendency is to shorten terms in order to move the money to the stronger currency as quickly as possible. The relative bargaining power of the parties and the extent to which they have created alignment in their relationship, coupled with their exchange-rate forecasts, usually determines the outcome of this negotiation. Also, one or both parties might favor the other's currency for cash flow reasons. The seller might need the buyer's currency to meet local payment obligations or to retire debt. The buyer might have a supply of the seller's currency obtained from foreign revenues or borrowing.

5. Temporary Inventory

Companies adjust their finished goods and merchandise inventories about the permanent base level in response to seasonal manufacturing or selling peaks. They tend to accumulate raw materials when price increases are anticipated, either domestically or because of a change in foreign exchange rates. They also stock up when price or exchange controls are forecasted that would limit the company's future ability to acquire materials.

When a commodity is a critical raw material, companies often buy large amounts in advance of their needs to lock in a price. This can be through direct purchase or by buying forward contracts, futures, or options to guarantee a price for later delivery. Examples are grain for cereal producers or fuel for airlines.

6. Temporary Payables

When productive resources are purchased on credit, accounts payable will rise and fall with inventories. Wages payable will vary during seasonal peaks. Accounts payable will vary around its base level due to the same factors that affect accounts receivable.

Special terms of payment might be negotiated with individual suppliers when the volume or riskiness of the customer's business differs from the company's norms or when one party can raise funds more cheaply than the other due to financial strength or superior financial market access. As part of a customer-supplier alignment, a financially strong buyer often shortens the payment period to aid a weaker supplier while a financially strong supplier can extend credit for a longer period of time. Also, the same foreign currency considerations discussed above under accounts receivable apply to the buyer as the other party to the transaction.

7. Poor Temporary Working Capital Management

Although temporary working capital may appear to be a small part of a company's resources, poor temporary current working capital management can lead to financial distress and perhaps even insolvency. This is because a firm's liquidity is intimately connected to its working capital balances. When working capital is out of control, it is easy for a company to become illiquid and be unable to pay its bills.

It is important for a company's risk management systems to protect against losses due to leakages from the working capital cycle. A traditional view of losses has

FINANCE IN PRACTICE

Freeing Up Working Capital Resources at American Standard

In 1988, American Standard Companies, the diversified international manufacturer of air conditioning, braking, and bathroom/kitchen products, adopted a "demand flow" (just-in-time) manufacturing system. Today, rather than produce to a forecast of demand, American Standard manufactures mainly in response to specific customer orders. In addition to improving quality, reducing costs, and decreasing cycle time, this manufacturing change has created other savings. Demand flow has freed up large amounts of both permanent and temporary working capital as raw materials, work-in-process, and finished goods inventories have all been cut to a fraction of their earlier levels. Long-term assets needed for production have been reduced as well—machinery is used more effectively and far less manufacturing and warehouse space are required for each level of output. Even internal audit has been affected, because the new manufacturing processes have changed the auditors' work considerably. For example, the auditors used to compare production schedules against forecasts—investigating variances between forecast and actual. With traditional manufacturing forecasts no longer appropriate, this job has disappeared. They also used to devote considerable time to monitoring the use and control of inventories, but with far fewer inventories on hand there is a much lower probability of theft, damage, or obsolescence to guard against. Now that significant parts of their traditional job are no longer necessary, American Standard's internal audit group has been freed up to add further value by playing much more of a change-agent role in the company. For example, auditors now take demand flow technology beyond manufacturing operations, applying it in audits of the administrative areas.

Source: James A.F. Stoner and Frank M. Werner, *Internal Audit and Innovation in Financial Management* (Morristown, N.J.: FInancial Executives Research Foundation, forthcoming).

been in terms of fraud and theft: cash that is embezzled or diverted for inappropriate uses, credit that is extended to cronies and becomes bad debts, and inventory that is stolen. Beyond illegalities, however, financial managers must look at the nature of the working capital to prevent poorly performing assets: idle cash; receivables with an unexpectedly long collection period; or inventory that has lost value due to obsolescence, damage, or being out of fashion.

The financial management function with the responsibility to protect against these losses is internal audit. Recent research into the internal audit function at some quality-leading companies is disclosing that several of the new management approaches characteristic of quality management—empowerment, team-based analysis, just-in-time inventory, etc.—are permitting control to change in ways that lead to better working capital management, with more control, yet at significantly lower cost than under traditional systems.

Hedging Temporary Working Capital Flows

The day-to-day cash flows of a company are rarely in balance, either with respect to their timing or their currency. As a result, the firm is exposed to the daily interest and exchange-rate fluctuations of the financial markets. Hedging plays an important role in limiting or eliminating these risks. In this section we look briefly at the tools for hedging temporary working capital and how they are used.

1. Not All Cash Positions Are Square

square cash position—the condition in which receivables and payables are perfectly hedged

A company is in a **square cash position** when its receivables and payables (trade account or otherwise) are perfectly matched with equal and opposite cash flows of the same currency. Every receipt is used immediately to pay an obligation; every obligation is paid with a cash flow that was just received. A square cash position is a no-risk position. Since no time elapses between each receipt and its use, the firm has no need to invest or borrow temporarily and is not exposed to fluctuating interest rates. Since no currency exchanges take place, the firm is not exposed to fluctuating foreign exchange rates. Of course, while a square cash position represents an ideal scenario for temporary working capital, it is a rarity in practice. Far more realistic is a receipt that cannot be used immediately, an outflow that exceeds the firm's available cash balance, or a cash flow that must be converted to another currency before it can be used.

The time lags between the receipt and payment of cash and the need to convert currencies expose the firm to financial market risks. What interest rate will be available next month between the payments for production and sales and the collection of the resulting accounts receivable? What will the exchange rate be in 90 days when a large inflow denominated in a foreign currency is expected to arrive? Because of its ability to reduce or eliminate these exposures, hedging is used extensively to stabilize the value of many cash obligations and receipts.

Since the purpose of hedging an obligation is to ensure that the correct amount and type of money is available when it is needed, a common technique is to invest in an asset that pays back the required amount of cash on the due date of the obligation.

Example

Hedging a Liability

Suppose you have a $5,000 tuition bill to pay next September. You could guarantee you will have the money when you need it by investing in a $5,000 face value certificate of deposit that matures on September 1.

In the previous example, the obligation was a dollar amount. In the next example, we hedge an amount in another currency.

Example

Hedging a Liability in a Foreign Currency

Your company has placed an order with a British supplier which requires a payment of £20,000 in 30 days when the goods are expected to arrive. You could hedge that obligation by entering into a forward exchange contract and depositing the present value of the contractual amount at your bank. In return for your deposit, the bank will provide the £20,000 in 30 days.

Hedging an anticipated receipt that will be spent at a later date can prevent the money from earning an unacceptably low interest rate until it is needed. A common technique for doing this is to estimate the time until the funds will be needed and obtain a security that guarantees a fixed rate over that time period.

Example

Hedging a Receipt

Your company expects to receive $30,000 from customers during the first week of next month; however, the money will not be required to cover accounts payable for another 20 days. Rather than wait and invest the money at the floating rate available next month, you could guarantee the rate the money will earn by purchasing a forward rate note today for that 20-day period.

2. Forward Contracts

forward contract—a contract binding the parties to a future transaction on a specified date and at a specified price or rate

One way to eliminate risk is to pay another party to assume it. A **forward contract** is an agreement committing the parties to enter into an exchange at a specified future date at a specified price. Because the price at which the exchange will take place is specified, forward contracts insulate the company from changes in prices or rates between the date the contract is signed and the date of the exchange.

forward rate agreement (FRA)—a contract binding the parties to a future loan on a specified date, for a specified period, and at a specified interest rate

We introduced the concept of forward foreign exchange contracts in Chapter 7.[10] These contracts are available for periods of a few days to about one year and are widely used to hedge cash flows from day-to-day transactions with foreign customers and suppliers. Forward contracts known as **forward rate agreements (FRAs)** are also available on interest rates and are used to lock in a borrowing or lending rate for a future time period.

The primary suppliers of forward contracts are commercial banks. This might make it appear that banks are assuming huge risks—all the risks offloaded by the companies that enter into the forward contracts. However, this is not the case. Each bank is also engaged in hedging, in this case to offset its exposures. For example, if a bank commits to provide Swiss francs to one customer in 90 days, it looks to enter another 90-day contract in which it commits to purchase the same number of Swiss francs at the same price. It can then simply deliver the francs from one customer to the other, without having to exchange currencies. While it is difficult, if not impossible, to offset each exposure with a precisely opposite contract, it is possible to net out the bank's exposure across all forward contracts to a substantial degree. (Notice that this is much like the maturity-range hedging we looked at earlier in this chapter: it is difficult to hedge individual assets and liabilities, but it is very possible to hedge ranges of maturities.) By balancing its foreign exchange "book," the bank nets out its own risks while it reduces the risks faced by its customers.

Although forward contracts can eliminate the risk of future price and rate changes, they do not eliminate all risks. Forward contracts are a commitment; the firm must go through with the exchange. If a company enters into a forward contract to hedge an anticipated receipt that never comes, the company must honor the contract, even if there is now a high cost to obtaining the money.

[10] **Cross-reference:** See Chapter 7, pp. 238–239.

3. Derivative Securities

derivative security—a contract whose value is defined by a financial market rate or the price of a financial instrument

Derivative securities are contracts whose value changes with the price of a specified ("underlying") security, money rate, or economic index. Because their value is driven by the underlying economic variable, they are particularly useful for hedging the risk of being exposed to that variable. Some derivatives, such as futures and options, come in relatively standard forms and are traded on the organized securities exchanges. Others are custom-designed to meet the specific needs of investors and financial managers.

Puts and calls on common stock,[11] the oldest form of derivatives, have been around for a long time. However, the increased volatility of interest and exchange rates stemming from the oil price shocks of the early 1970s and the subsequent liberalization and globalization of world trade made financial managers eager to find new risk management opportunities. Formalized trading of options began in the mid-1970s, and the number of types and uses for derivatives exploded dramatically during the 1980s. Today, for example, some $10–15 billion of stock index futures changes hands on the Chicago Mercantile Exchange on a typical trading day, and trading of U.S. Treasury futures on the Chicago Board of Trade exceeds $12 billion daily.

When used for hedging, derivatives are purchased or sold to create an exposure that is equal and opposite to the risk to be hedged. In this way, the movement of one cancels out the other.

Example

Using Derivatives to Hedge Temporary Working Capital

Belleco Resources expects to accumulate an inventory of petroleum over the next three months and sell it at the end of that period. Belleco's treasurer is concerned, however, that spot oil prices will decline over the three-month period, reducing the value of the inventory. To hedge this risk, the treasurer has sold futures contracts whose value is tied to the price of oil and which commit Belleco to deliver the oil in three months. Should the price of oil decline, the contracts would increase in value (since they would be cheaper to fulfill) and would offset Belleco's loss of inventory value.

Four basic types of derivatives are (1) options, (2) futures, (3) swaps, and (4) synthetic securities.

Options Options represent a right to purchase or sell some asset at a prespecified price and within a certain time. Exchange-traded options are available on common stocks, stock indexes such as the Standard & Poor's 500 index, interest rates, major international currencies, futures contracts, and commodities.

future—an exchange-traded standardized forward contract

Futures Like a forward contract, a **future** is also a contract committing the parties to enter into an exchange at a specified future date at a specified price. However, unlike forward contracts, which are tailored to the needs of the parties,

[11] **Cross-reference:** Puts and calls, the basic types of options, are introduced in Chapter 9, pp. 318–321. See Appendix 9A for a discussion of the Black-Scholes model used to price options.

futures contracts are standardized so they can be traded on the securities exchanges. As with options, futures are available for common stocks, stock indexes, interest rates, currencies, and commodities.

swap—an exchange of financial obligations

Swap A **swap** is an exchange of obligations between two parties, for example a dollar loan for a pound sterling loan. It permits a company to trade away a risky exposure for one considered less risky. Swaps are individually arranged by commercial or investment banks which maintain an active resale market for swap contracts, allowing a company to get out of a swap it previously entered or assume the obligations of an existing swap arrangement. Since swaps are often used to obtain long-term financing at a preferred interest rate or in a desired currency, we examine them more fully in Chapter 21 as part of our look at intermediate and long-term debt.[12]

synthetic security—an artificial security constructed from real securities and derivatives

Synthetic securities **Synthetic securities** are securities constructed from a combination of real securities and derivatives. Sometimes the new security's cash flow pattern is the same as an already existing security; other times the pattern is something brand new. When they recreate the pattern of cash flows of an already existing security, their purpose is to get around regulatory, tax, or accounting limitations, or to make that cash flow pattern available to a market participant who otherwise would find it unavailable. New cash flow patterns create new hedging opportunities, as well as new investment and financing opportunities for financial managers.

---

[12] **Cross-reference:** See Chapter 21, pp. 754–755.

exchange position—an anticipated cash flow not fully hedged against exchange-rate movements

4. Hedging Exchange Rates

An **exchange position** is a cash flow position that is not fully hedged with respect to foreign exchange-rate movements.

Example

Exchange Position

Belleco Resources expects to receive ¥4 million from a Japanese customer in 120 days. The dollar amount to which this will translate will depend upon the yen-dollar exchange rate prevailing on that date. Since Belleco does not have an offsetting ¥4 million cash outflow, this anticipated cash flow represents an exchange position

Belleco can respond to its exchange position in one of two ways. It can "let the position stand" by doing nothing, either out of ignorance of the hedging possibilities or because its analysis shows the cost of hedging the position to exceed the expected loss from the exposure. Alternatively Belleco can hedge this receipt through a forward exchange contract, by using a derivative security such as a currency future or option, or with a money market hedge—a foreign loan combined with a domestic investment to lock in the receipt's dollar value.[13] If Belleco elects to hedge, it should choose the technique that will provide the greatest receipt. As the benefits of various hedging techniques tend to be quite similar, given the efficiency of these markets, the best hedging method is often a function of the firm's marginal income tax rate. A secondary consideration is the appearance of the hedge on the company's financial statements. Whereas a money market hedge appears in the body of the financial statements as a loan and offsetting investment, forward, future, and option transactions appear only in footnotes (off-balance sheet).

interest rate position—an anticipated cash flow not fully hedged against interest rate movements

5. Hedging Interest Rates

An **interest rate position** is a cash flow position that is not fully hedged with respect to interest rate movements.

Example

Interest Rate Position

Belleco Resources expects to receive $10,000 from a good customer in 30 days. It forecasts it will have to spend the money 90 days after that. The amount Belleco can earn on this cash will depend upon the 90-day interest rate available 30 days from now. Since Belleco does not have offsetting flows for the receipt and expenditure, the cash flows represent an interest rate position.

[13] **Elaboration:** A money market hedge operates in much the same way as covered interest arbitrage, using a loan and a parallel investment to lock in a profit (see Chapter 7, pp. 247–249, if you wish to review this topic). In this case Belleco would borrow a yen amount to be repaid, along with interest, by the future receipt. Belleco would then convert the borrowed yen to dollars at today's spot rate and invest the dollar amount for the 120-day period. The result: the yen receipt does not have to be exchanged to dollars, and Belleco knows precisely how much it will get in dollars at the end of 120 days.

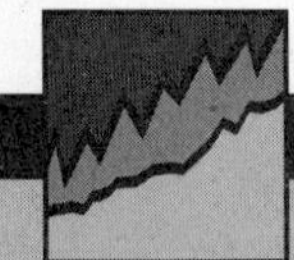

IMPROVING FINANCE'S PROCESSES

Managing the Cost of Capital at Molson

Brian Crombie, VP of planning and corporate development at the large Canadian brewer Molson, uses hedging to reduce the company's cost of capital, a proactive financial managing strategy to add value to the company. Says Crombie,

> I believe that the cost of capital is one of the most important competitive advantages around, . . . My point is that people look at the cost of capital as a given, rather than managing it down.
>
> A number of strategies are needed to reduce the cost of capital, some operational and some financial. On the financial side, companies can try to broaden the investor base for their securities, issue in new markets and institute a sophisticated treasury operation.
>
> While the majority of a company's value is essentially derived from operations, a finely tuned financial policy will often significantly add to . . . overall value creation by lowering the cost of capital to maximize share price and shareholder value.
>
> This is achieved not only through effective asset and liability management and by optimizing capital structure, but through interest rate, forex, and commodity price risk management. The objective of risk management in this process should be to stabilize earnings and lower equity risk.
>
> Through managing risk, a company may reduce expected taxes by ensuring that losses are not incurred, losing a tax shield. It may decrease its potential cost of financial distress, increase its sustainable debt capacity and also reduce its borrowing costs. . . . Stability gives you a lower beta, the factor that determines the riskiness of a firm relative to the market, which means you can invest in more projects because you have a lower cost of capital.

Reference: Lawerence Quinn, "Hedging in Perspective," in *Corporate Finance*, Jun. 1994, pp. 36–38.

In much the same manner as dealing with an exchange position, Belleco can respond to its interest rate position in one of two ways. It can "let the position stand" by doing nothing, or it can hedge this cash flow using one of several techniques: by contracting for a forward rate note (a committed interest rate for the future time period), by using a derivative security such as an interest rate future or option, or with a money market hedge (in this case a 30-day loan combined with a 120-day investment).[14]

[14] **Elaboration:** For this money-market hedge, Belleco would borrow an amount for 30 days to be repaid, along with interest, by the future receipt. Belleco would then invest the borrowed amount for 120-days and use a portion of the proceeds to cover its anticipated cash outflow. The result: the receipt does not have to be invested at an uncertain interest rate and Belleco knows precisely how much it will have at the end of 120 days.

Clif Carlton walked into the conference room with a big smile on his face and tossed the stack of computer reports on the table. "Nice job, gang," he said, provoking the usual mock protest from one team member who kept insisting that he had no desire to be part of a gang. "We're making great progress in getting our risk exposure under better control."

Three months had elapsed since Clif first called the team together. In that time, the team had studied the company's increasing risk exposure, met with the company's bankers, and laid out a strategy for improving the firm's risk management activities.

The team began its work with a look at the maturities of the company's assets and liabilities. A comparison with past balance sheets identified that the company's asset maturities had changed over the past five years but no comparable changes had been made to the firm's liability structure. The team identified the mismatched maturities and then invited the company's investment bankers to join them in a discussion of how to adjust the company's financing. Together, they recommended a moderate increase in intermediate-term borrowing plus the refinancing of one bond issue, a transaction that had just been completed this past week.

Next the team turned its attention to improving how the company hedged its daily cash flows. After passing around two books and countless magazine articles taken from the company library, they attended a seminar on financial derivatives, sponsored by their commercial bank. On returning to the office, they made a modest proposal to begin testing some of the newer derivative products. Clif had approved the experiment enthusiastically, and the early results were quite encouraging.

Clif looked around the room, and it was clear he was genuinely pleased. "Last month when I was over at our bank, their risk management specialists walked me through the exposure book they maintain to be sure their interest rate and currency risks are as fully hedged as possible. It seems to me we're well on the way to running our own little 'bank' a whole lot better than we used to."

Summary of Key Points

- **Discuss how hedging can reduce financial risks.** Hedging is balancing a risky financial position with an opposite position to cancel risk. It includes offsetting assets and liabilities with equal amounts and maturities. Hedging balance sheet aggregate numbers ensures that cash will be available to pay liabilities as they fall due. Hedging individual cash flows guarantees that receipts can be used efficiently and that obligations have a known cost.
- **Describe the four-step sequence of working capital decisions.** Current account balances are the result of a four-step decision process: (1) permanent current asset alternatives with positive NPV are accepted, creating the permanent current asset balance, (2) current liabilities with a low or zero interest rate are taken, creating the first portion of the permanent current liability balance, (3) additional debt is divided among maturities to hedge the balance sheet; the short-term portion completes the current liability balance, and (4) temporary current assets and liabilities are taken as they arise naturally in day-to-day operations.
- **Discuss how companies set their debt maturity mix.** The debt maturity mix is a product of the third step of the working capital sequence. Debt maturities are selected to hedge the balance sheet, establishing a risk-return position between debt costs and liquidity risk. While financial institutions can hedge individual assets and liabilities, nonfinancial companies

hedge maturity ranges. Because of their long-term presence in the firm, permanent current assets are included with noncurrent assets for this analysis. Some companies elect to deviate from maturity-range hedging to reach a preferred combination of risk and return.

- **Relate how temporary working capital arises in the current accounts.** Temporary working capital comes from the working capital cycle, imbalances in cash inflows and outflows, and special opportunities to use working capital to reduce costs or improve dealings with suppliers or customers. Temporary cash also comes from large dollar transactions. Marketable securities permit the firm to earn interest on otherwise idle excess cash. Temporary accounts receivable often represent the tailoring of the firm's receivables policy to its customers. Temporary inventory often reflects business seasonalities or large-scale commodities purchases. Temporary payables follow the production cycle and also arise for the same reasons as temporary accounts receivable. At some quality-leading companies, risk management activities directed at the current accounts are shifting from external control through inspection to internal control through improved management systems.
- **Discuss the basics of hedging against foreign currency and interest rate movements including the use of derivative securities.** Companies use forward contracts and derivative securities to deal with exchange and interest rate positions. Forward contracts guarantee that the other party, often a commercial bank, will provide an agreed-upon price, or interest rate, or exchange rate at some future date. Derivative securities—options, futures, swaps, and synthetic securities—move in value opposite to the firm's exposure, creating a gain (or loss) that balances out any loss (or gain) suffered by the firm due to price or rate movements.

Questions

1. Why does hedging reduce risk?
2. What is the difference between hedging across the balance sheet and hedging individual cash flows?
3. What are the four steps in putting working capital on the balance sheet?
4. Why are the "attractive short-term financing opportunities," described in the second step of the four-step process, considered before other debt financing?
5. How is the current ratio used in setting the debt maturity mix? Can you think of any other financial measures that also could be used in this analysis?
6. Why is the debt maturity mix normally simplified to short- versus long-term debt? What, if anything, is lost in making this simplification?
7. What role does the debt maturity mix play in the firm's overall risk-return posture?
8. Distinguish between individual asset/liability hedging and maturity-range hedging? What type of company can do each?
9. What role do permanent current assets play in maturity-range hedging?
10. Why do companies deviate from maturity-range hedging?
11. What factor(s) enter the decisions about the composition of a portfolio of marketable securities?
12. Which financial instruments are most commonly used as marketable securities?
13. What is meant by the "five Cs"?
14. In what way(s) are quality-leading companies changing their approach to the control of working capital?
15. Some financial professionals consider forward contracts to be another kind of derivative security. Why do you think this is so?
16. How does a forward contract work as a hedging device?
17. How does a derivative security work as a hedging device?
18. A new finance student was overheard making the following statement: "In efficient financial markets, all hedging devices should be perfect substitutes!" Discuss.
19. Draw a flow chart of the four-step working capital process.

Problems

1. **(Four-step sequence)** A company with \$2 million of low-cost current financing opportunities wishes to target a current ratio of 2.5. How much additional short-term financing should it raise if its permanent current asset balance is:

   a. \$10 million?
   b. \$8 million?
   c. \$5 million?
   d. \$2 million?

2. **(Four-step sequence)** A company with \$25 million of permanent current assets has \$4 million of low-cost current financing opportunities. How much additional short-term financing should it raise if its target current ratio is:

a. 1.8?
b. 2.0?
c. 2.4?
d. 2.8?

3. **(Debt-maturity mix)** A company has $25 million of current assets and another $25 million of noncurrent assets. It forecasts an EBIT of $5 million and is in the 35% income tax bracket. Currently the yield curve is normal; bank notes carry a 7% interest rate, and the company can issue long-term bonds at 12%. The company has set a target debt ratio of 40%. For each of the following debt maturity mixes: (1) construct the company's balance sheet, (2) construct the financial half of its income statement, and (3) evaluate its risk and return using the return on equity and current ratios.
   a. 20% of the debt is current, 80% long-term
   b. 40% of the debt is current, 60% long-term
   c. 60% of the debt is current, 40% long-term
   d. 80% of the debt is current, 20% long-term
4. **(Debt-maturity mix)** A company has $400 million of assets of which $250 are current assets. It forecasts a basic earning power ratio of 15% and is in the 35% income tax bracket. Currently the yield curve is normal; bank notes carry a 5% interest rate, and the company can issue long-term bonds at 10%. The company has set a target debt ratio of 50%. For each of the following debt maturity mixes: (1) construct the company's balance sheet, (2) construct the financial half of its income statement, and (3) evaluate its risk and return using the return on equity and current ratios.
   a. 20% of the debt is current, 80% long-term
   b. 40% of the debt is current, 60% long-term
   c. 60% of the debt is current, 40% long-term
   d. 80% of the debt is current, 20% long-term

APPENDIX 16A

TRANSFERRING MONEY BETWEEN CASH AND MARKETABLE SECURITIES

A firm that accumulates excess temporary cash desires to move that cash to "marketable securities," an investment in which it can earn interest. In this appendix, we look at three models of the cash-to-securities transfer. All three are premised on balancing the opportunity to earn interest with the transaction costs of moving the money. They differ in the assumptions they make about how accurately financial managers can predict a firm's daily cash flows.

1. The Baumol Model

Professor William Baumol adapted the economic order quantity (EOQ) model[1] to the cash-to-securities transfer problem by considering the cash balance as an in-

[1] **Cross-reference:** The economic order quantity model is presented in Appendix 12B.

ventory. The model assumes that the financial manager can predict the firm's cash flows with certainty and that cash arrives and is spent at an unchanging rate throughout the year. Ordering cost is the cost to transfer funds between cash and securities. Carrying cost is the interest forgone by holding money in the cash balance rather than in securities. The model minimizes the total cost of holding cash: transactions cost plus forgone interest.

The solution to the model is the same as the EOQ solution, with different letters used for the variables:

$$Z = \sqrt{\frac{2NF}{i}}$$

where the variables are (equivalent EOQ variables in parentheses):

Z = **Z**ero point: the cash balance return point (the EOQ)

N = annual cash **N**eed (the usage rate, S)

F = (**F**ixed) cost of each cash-securities transaction (the order cost, O)

i = **i**nterest rate per year on marketable securities (the carrying cost, C)

The other results of the EOQ model hold as well. The average cash balance becomes Z/2. There will be N/Z transfers from securities to cash during the year with a frequency (assuming a 360-day year) of 360/(transfers per year). For high transaction costs the firm tends to increase its cash balances to minimize the number of securities-to-cash movements. On the other hand, when interest rates are high, cash balances tend to fall as there is a high opportunity cost of holding idle cash.

Example

Baumol Model

Clif Carlton is curious to apply the Baumol model to his company's cash-to-securities transfer activities. He estimates that cash disbursements total $50 million per year and it costs $75 on average each time securities are sold for cash. Short-term Treasury bill rates are now at 5%.

Question: If Clif uses the Baumol model, what will be the zero point, the average cash level, the number of transfers per year, and the frequency of securities-to-cash transfers?

Solution steps:

1. Zero point

$$Z = \sqrt{\frac{2NF}{i}} = \sqrt{\frac{2 \times 50{,}000{,}000 \times 75}{.05}} = \sqrt{150{,}000{,}000{,}000} = 387{,}298$$

2. Average cash balance

$$Z/2 = 387{,}298/2 = 193{,}649$$

3. Number of transfers per year

$$N/Z = 50{,}000{,}000/387{,}298 = 129$$

4. Transfer frequency

$$360/\text{transfers per year} = 360/129 = \text{every 2.8 days}$$

Answer: The Baumol model calls for a zero point of $387,298, obtained by moving cash from securities every 2.8 days. The company will make 129 transactions per year and maintain an average cash balance of $193,649.

Although it is a good first approach to the cash-to-securities transfer problem, the Baumol model suffers from its unrealistic assumptions. For any seasonal or cyclical business, cash does not flow in and out at a predictable, unchanging rate throughout the year. The possibility of accumulating excess cash cannot be ignored. Also, transaction costs often do not have a fixed component regardless of the size of the cash transfer. For example, many banks offer their business clients money market sweep accounts in which excess cash balances are automatically moved ("swept") into an interest-bearing account with no per-transaction fee.

2. The Miller-Orr Model

Professors Merton Miller and Daniel Orr extended the Baumol model in two key respects. First, they allowed cash to arrive and be spent in an irregular and unpredictable pattern. Second, they made the model bidirectional. Whereas the Baumol model looks only at cash outflows to determine when to replenish the cash balance, the Miller-Orr model tracks both cash inflows and outflows. It identifies two thresholds, a minimum cash balance at which securities are sold to replenish cash and also a maximum cash balance at which the cash balance is reduced by investing the excess cash in securities.

Figure 16A.1 illustrates the cash pattern of a company using the Miller-Orr model. The company begins with its cash at level Z, the zero or return point. Every day,

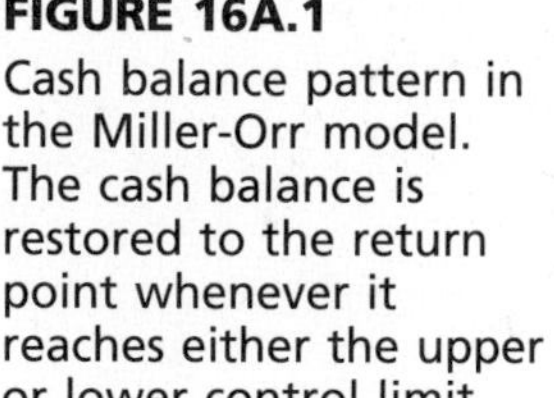

FIGURE 16A.1
Cash balance pattern in the Miller-Orr model. The cash balance is restored to the return point whenever it reaches either the upper or lower control limit.

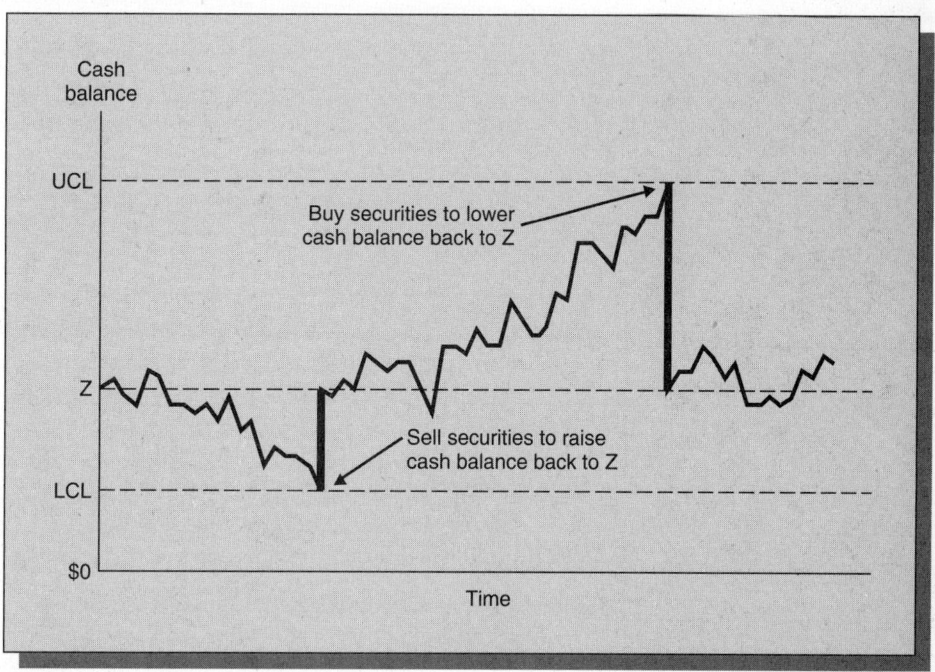

the cash balance varies upward or downward by a random amount. Should the balance decline far enough to reach the lower control limit (LCL), securities are sold to bring the cash back to level Z. Should the balance increase sufficiently to reach the upper control limit (UCL), securities are purchased reducing the cash balance down to level Z. As long as the balance remains between the LCL and UCL, no cash-to-securities transactions are undertaken.

The solution to the Miller-Orr model is similar to that of the Baumol model:

$$Z = \sqrt[3]{\frac{3F\sigma^2}{4i}} + LCL$$

Two of the variables are identical to those in the Baumol model:

Z = **Zero** point: the cash balance return point

F = (**Fixed**) cost of each cash-securities transaction

A third is nearly identical:

i = **interest** rate per day on marketable securities
(in the Baumol model the rate was for the full year)

The new variable deals with the unpredictability of cash inflows and outflows. While the model assumes each day's flows are not known, it does assume financial managers can estimate the statistical variability of the daily cash change.

σ^2 = **variance** of the net daily cash flow

The lower control limit is up to management's discretion. If the firm can obtain cash immediately when the cash balance drops to the lower limit, the LCL can be set to zero. However, the LCL will be set above zero if the company's bank requires that the firm maintain a minimum balance or if immediate securities-to-cash transfers are not possible. The upper control limit solves to:

$$UCL = 3Z - 2(LCL)$$

and the average cash balance is:

$$Average\ cash\ balance = \frac{4Z - LCL}{3}$$

Example

Miller-Orr Model

Clif Carlton is also interested in the Miller-Orr model. He continues to estimate that it costs $75 on average for each securities transaction. Short-term Treasury bill rates are now at 5%. By studying his company's cash flow pattern, he determines the variance of the change to the daily cash balance to be $20,000,000,000 (standard deviation of $141,421). Loan agreements currently in place require a $50,000 balance at all times, and Clif sees no reason to maintain a higher minimum balance.

Question: If Clif uses the Miller-Orr model, what will be the lower control limit, the zero point, the upper control limit, and the average cash balance?

Solution steps:

1. Obtain the daily interest rate. Assuming that 5% is an effective market quote for 365 days:

$$i = (1.05)^{(1/365)} - 1 = .0001337$$

2. Lower control limit = $50,000 balance requirement.
3. Zero point:

$$Z = \sqrt[3]{\frac{3F\sigma^2}{4i}} + LCL = \sqrt[3]{\frac{3 \times 75 \times 20{,}000{,}000{,}000}{4 \times .0001337}} + 50{,}000$$

$$= 203{,}395 + 50{,}000 = 253{,}395$$

4. Upper control limit:

$$UCL = 3 \times 253{,}395 - 2 \times 50{,}000 = 660{,}185$$

5. Average cash balance:

$$\text{Average} = \frac{4 \times 253{,}395 - 50{,}000}{3} = 321{,}193$$

Answer: The Miller-Orr model calls for keeping the cash balance between $50,000 and $660,185. Should the balance fall to $50,000, the company treasurer would sell $203,395 of securities to raise the cash balance to the zero point of $253,395. If the balance should rise to $660,185, $406,790 of securities would be purchased to reduce the cash balance to $253,395. The average cash balance will be $321,193.

3. The Stone Variation on the Miller-Orr Model

Professor Bernell Stone extended the Miller-Orr model to incorporate knowledge of future cash flows. Although the Miller-Orr model assumes that daily changes to the cash balance are random, corporate treasurers can often predict cash flow activity for some days ahead. Companies routinely pay a large number of bills or collect a disproportionate fraction of their receivables on a certain day—for example, the first of the month. Large inflows and outflows often receive special financial management attention. To the extent that the next several days' cash flows are predictable, it might pay to override the instructions of the Miller-Orr model.

In the Stone model, the treasurer makes one additional test when the cash balance reaches the upper or lower control limits, rather than reacting automatically. If, in the next several days, the cash balance is forecasted to remain outside the control limits, the Miller-Orr model's prescription is followed and the cash balance is reset to the zero point. However, if the balance is forecasted to return to within the limits on its own, no action is taken saving the cost of a cash-to-securities transaction.

Problems

1. **(Baumol model)** A company has annual cash disbursements of $20 million and pays $50 each time it makes a securities-to-cash transaction. Short-term Treasury bill rates are currently 6%. Using the Baumol model, calculate:

   a. The zero point (Z)
   b. The average cash balance
   c. The number of securities-to-cash transfers each year
   d. The frequency of transfers

2. **(Baumol model)** A company has annual cash disbursements of $5 million and pays $75 each time it makes a securities-to-cash transaction. Short-term Treasury bill rates are currently 4%. Using the Baumol model, calculate:

   a. The zero point (Z)
   b. The average cash balance
   c. The number of securities-to-cash transfers each year
   d. The frequency of transfers

3. **(Miller-Orr model)** A company's treasurer has calculated the variance of its daily cash balance to be $1,000,000,000. Short-term Treasury bill rates are currently (an effective annual) 5%, and the company pays $60 for each transfer of funds between cash and securities. The company has no minimum cash balance requirements. Using the Miller-Orr model, calculate:

   a. The lower control limit (LCL)
   b. The zero point (Z)
   c. The upper control limit (UCL)
   d. The average cash balance

4. **(Miller-Orr model)** A company's treasurer has calculated the variance of its daily cash balance to be $100,000,000,000. Short-term Treasury bill rates are currently (an effective annual) 4.5%, and the company pays $40 for each transfer of funds between cash and securities. The company's bank requires a $25,000 minimum cash balance. Using the Miller-Orr model, calculate:

   a. The lower control limit (LCL)
   b. The zero point (Z)
   c. The upper control limit (UCL)
   d. The average cash balance

5. **(Miller-Orr model—sensitivity)** Using the data of Problem 3, recalculate the lower control limit, zero point, upper control limit, and average cash balance if the Treasury bill rate changes to:

   a. 3%
   b. 4%
   c. 6%
   d. 7%

6. **(Miller-Orr model—sensitivity)** Using the data of Problem 4, recalculate the lower control limit, zero point, upper control limit, and average cash balance if the cost of a funds transfer changes to:

   a. $20
   b $30
   c. $50
   d. $60

CHAPTER 17
DIVIDEND POLICY

Bob Forrest looked up from his pad of paper but continued to scribble furiously, making notes of everything the CFO said. Bob was a new member of the finance organization of his company. As part of his training, he had been invited to join a team to recommend a new dividend policy to the board of directors at their next meeting. The CFO had just finished outlining the company's past dividend practice and was turning to the current policy issue.

"It seems as if everybody has their own idea about what our dividend should be. You all know that the son of our founder sits on the board and lives on the dividends we pay him. He would love to see the dividend raised. Some other board members have strong feelings about keeping continuity in our payout policy. So, if they have their way, not only can't we pay less than last quarter, we can't pay so much that the dividend becomes unsustainable and we might have to reduce it later. Now the president talks about reducing the dividend because of the taxes it forces our shareholders to pay. On the other hand, the chairman believes we must be more aggressive in distributing our profits to shareholders, not only through traditional cash dividends but also through share repurchases. As for me, sometimes I wonder why we pay a dividend at all. If we retained the money we could avoid raising other funds with all the costs and problems that entails."

After the CFO's presentation, the team got into an animated discussion over how to approach the problem. Bob found the talk fascinating—there certainly were conflicting opinions about what to do. But he was bothered by the sense that he hadn't heard any solid basis for making the decision, only a collection of observations and "gut feelings." As he left the meeting, Bob headed to the company library to read all he could about dividend policy.

The problem Bob and his colleagues are grappling with is a difficult one for most financial managers because there is no single comprehensive theory to guide a company's dividend payments. The situation is quite similar to the debt-equity mix and debt maturity mix decisions, described in Chapters 15 and 16: there are conflicting points of view over what dividend payment stream maximizes the value of a firm to its stockholders, as well to any other stakeholders who might be affected by the decision. Bob's team will have to balance a variety of ideas to arrive at a policy appropriate for his company.

dividend policy—a company's plan for the level and pattern of its dividend payments

In this chapter we look at the theoretical and practical considerations financial managers face in establishing a corporation's **dividend policy.** We use the word *policy* intentionally because it is not enough to decide solely on the next dividend. Both theory and practice tell us that the pattern of dividend payments is as important a consideration as the amount of each payment.

Key Points You Should Learn from This Chapter

After reading this chapter you should be able to:

- Explain how shareholders get their returns.
- Describe five classes of theory that attempt to identify a company's optimal dividend policy.
- Discuss seven practical considerations in setting a firm's dividend.
- Describe the mechanics of how dividends are declared and paid.
- Analyze three alternatives to cash dividends.

Introductory Concepts—Does It Matter How Shareholders Get Their Returns?

dividend—a payment made by a corporation directly to its stockholders

A **dividend** is any direct payment from a firm to its stockholders. Dividends may be paid in cash, but they may also be in the form of stock or other noncash distributions. This includes stock splits and stock dividends, as well as spinoffs of units of the business. An alternative to cash dividends is the repurchase of common shares. In this chapter we will look at each.

Dividends are one of the two methods by which stockholders receive value from their investment (the other is via capital gains—*if* the price of their shares goes up). Dividends put cash or other valuable paper into the hands of investors, money that can be spent or reinvested. Other things equal, then, investors should prefer to receive high and regular dividends. But are other things equal?

In Chapter 9, we applied the growing cash stream model—renamed the *dividend-growth model* for this application—to common stock. We assumed a constant rate of dividend growth to simplify the mathematics and calculated the value of a share as the present value of the firm's dividend stream. We concluded that a stock's market value depends on the upcoming dividend (D_1), investors' required rate of return from the common stock (r_c), and the firm's rate of growth[1] (g):

$$\textit{Stock value} = \textit{PV of dividend stream} = \frac{D_1}{r_c - g}$$

This relationship is consistent with our earlier observation: other things equal, a higher dividend produces a higher stock value. In fact, if investors do not change their growth forecast or required rate of return, the value of a share will rise by the same proportion as the increase in the dividend.

Examples

A Dividend Increase, Other Things Equal

Yesterday, investors forecast that the Dolan Company would pay a $1.00 per share dividend three months from now, and would increase the dividend at the rate of 2% per quarter. Investors require a 4% quarterly rate of return.

Question: What was the value of one share of Dolan's stock yesterday?

Solution steps: Use the dividend-growth model:

$$\text{Stock value} = \frac{D_1}{r_c - g} = \frac{\$1.00}{.04 - .02}$$

$$= \frac{\$1.00}{.02} = \$50.00$$

Answer: Dolan's stock was worth $50.00 per share.

In today's newspaper, Dolan's CFO was quoted as saying that the company expects to pay a dividend of $1.10 per share in the next quarter.

[1] **Observation:** Strictly speaking, g is the growth rate of the firm's dividend stream, the cash flow that is being evaluated in this present value model. However, in estimating a value for g, many analysts also look at the growth rate of the variables that underlie the firm's ability to pay a dividend, such as sales and earnings, especially if the company's dividend stream has been low (or zero) or erratic, making future dividends difficult to forecast.

Question: What will Dolan's share value be after the announcement if investors do not revise their growth forecast or change their required rate of return?

Solution steps:

$$\text{Stock value} = \frac{D_1}{r_c - g} = \frac{\$1.10}{.04 - .02}$$
$$= \frac{\$1.10}{.02} = \$55.00$$

Answer: The value of one share of Dolan's stock will rise by 10%, from \$50.00 to \$55.00 in response to the 10% rise in the next estimated dividend.

Even if investors change their growth forecast or required rate of return, increased dividends could lead to an increase in a stock's value. This would occur if stockholders' required rate of return (r_c) declines or the growth rate (g) anticipated by investors increases. However, if raising the dividend reduces investors' forecasts of the firm's growth rate or increases their required rate of return, increasing the dividend could depress the value of the company's stock.

Example

A Dividend Increase, Other Things *Not* Equal

In response to Dolan Company's announcement of a dividend increase, investors do not modify their 4% required quarterly rate of return. However, they conclude that the company will have less money to reinvest in the business and reduce their growth forecast to 1.5% per quarter.

Question: What will happen to Dolan's share value?

Solution steps: Use the dividend-growth model:

$$\text{Stock value} = \frac{D_1}{r_c - g} = \frac{\$1.10}{.04 - .015}$$
$$= \frac{\$1.10}{.025} = \$44.00$$

Answer: The value of Dolan's stock will fall from \$50.00 to \$44.00. Rather than add to shareholders' wealth, the dividend increase reduced value.

The critical question about dividends then is whether—and if so, how—a dividend paid today changes investors' forecasts of future dividends or their required rate of return. The combination of dividends and investors' reactions that produces the highest value for shareholders will define a company's optimal dividend policy.

Dividend Theories

Finance thinkers have identified many factors that might affect investors' reaction to dividends. Unfortunately, there is little theory to join them into a coherent picture. In fact, the various arguments are downright contradictory in many respects. In the discussion below we present these factors grouped under five headings: (1) theories that argue for the payment of dividends, (2) theories that argue against the payment of dividends, (3) a theory that concludes that dividends are irrelevant since they have nothing to do with the value of the firm, (4) theories that argue that any dividend is acceptable as long as the company is consistent, and (5) a theory that argues against setting a dividend policy in the first place.

1. Theories That Argue for the Payment of Dividends

These theories claim that the benefits from dividends exceed any offsetting changes in investors' forecasts of growth or required rates of return.

Risk-reduction theories These three theories argue that the payment of a dividend reduces investors' perceived risk, reducing their required rate of return. The cash from the dividend and the reduced risk combine to increase the value of a share of stock.

- Resolution of uncertainty: Payment of a dividend resolves some of investors' uncertainty about their returns. This is because dividends are more difficult to forecast, hence riskier, the further they are into the future.[2] In the context of the present value model, investors apply a lower required rate of return to evaluate current dividends than to evaluate future dividends. As a result, paying current dividends reduces investors' net (averaged over time) required rate of return, yielding a higher stock value.
- Information transmittal: Dividends, especially changes in dividends, convey useful data to investors permitting better predictions of the company's future performance. For example, an increase in the dividend often signals management's confidence that the firm can support a higher payout while an unchanging dividend when earnings rise suggests a cautious management attitude. Note that only firms with truly good prospects can credibly raise their dividends, or else the dividend signal would quickly backfire as investors discovered that management was bluffing. For the announcement of a dividend increase to send a meaningful signal, the higher dividend must be sustainable. Improved information lowers investors' uncertainty, reducing their risk and lowering their required rate of return. A company that does not pay a dividend forgoes this opportunity to communicate with the financial markets.
- Liquidity: Dividends increase investors' liquidity by converting a portion of their investment value into cash. By contrast, investors who need cash but receive their returns in the form of stock price appreciation, risk having to sell some of their shares in what could turn out to be poor market conditions. Payment of dividends permits investors to manage their liquidity better, reducing the risk of their investment position and, correspondingly, reducing their required rate of return.

Market imperfection theories Financial markets are imperfect if the law does not treat all investors equally. These two theories argue that investors find

[2] **Elaboration:** This argument is sometimes called the "bird in the hand" theory after the old, familiar proverb. In this context: "$1 in the hand is worth $2 still inside the corporate bush."

the shares of companies that pay dividends particularly attractive due to regulatory or tax law and are willing to accept a lower rate of return. Investors increase the demand for dividend-paying shares raising their value.

- Legal restrictions: Some institutional investors can only acquire shares of stock if they pay dividends. For example, life insurance companies are restricted by the laws of most states to invest only in securities that pay interest or dividends. Other investors, such as endowment funds, are often prohibited by their charters from touching the fund's principal and depend on dividends for income.
- Tax preferences: Two provisions of the tax code make dividend-paying stocks particularly attractive to investors. First, corporate investors benefit from the rule that 70% of the dividends paid by one corporation to another are tax-free. For an investor corporation in the 35% bracket, intercompany dividends are taxed at an effective rate of only (35% × 30% =) 10.5% raising the after-tax rate of return. Second, a company that does not pay dividends risks a tax penalty if the Internal Revenue Service determines it has "improperly accumulated" retained earnings. Paying a regular dividend lessens the chance of running afoul of the IRS.[3]

Efficiency theory Financial market efficiency is enhanced when investors have the freedom to direct new investment dollars to the best available opportunities. This theory argues that investors prefer firms that pay dividends since this permits them to reinvest their earnings where they desire. By contrast, a company that retains earnings limits its shareholders' opportunities, forcing them to reinvest only in that company. Investors are willing to pay a premium (accept a lower rate of return) for reinvestment flexibility, a premium that directly increases the value of dividend-paying stocks.

2. Theories That Argue Against the Payment of Dividends

These theories argue that adverse changes to investors' forecasts of growth or required rates of return outweigh any benefits from paying dividends.

Supply-demand theory When the supply of a company's stock goes up, its price faces downward pressure. A company in need of additional equity can avoid selling shares of its stock by not paying dividends and retaining its earnings instead. Figure 17.1, a traditional supply-demand graph, illustrates how selling new shares can lower a company's stock price. S_{old} (old supply) and S_{new} (new supply) represent the number of shares outstanding before and after a new stock issue. The intersection of the supply and demand curves determines the market equilibrium price, which declines from P_{old} to P_{new}. Effectively, to attract new stockholders—people who previously chose not to invest in the company—the stock must provide a higher rate of return; and the market price of the new shares, and therefore the market price of *all* shares, must fall.

---

[3] **Cross-reference:** See Appendix 4C, pp. 107 and 110, for more detail about these provisions of the corporate tax code.

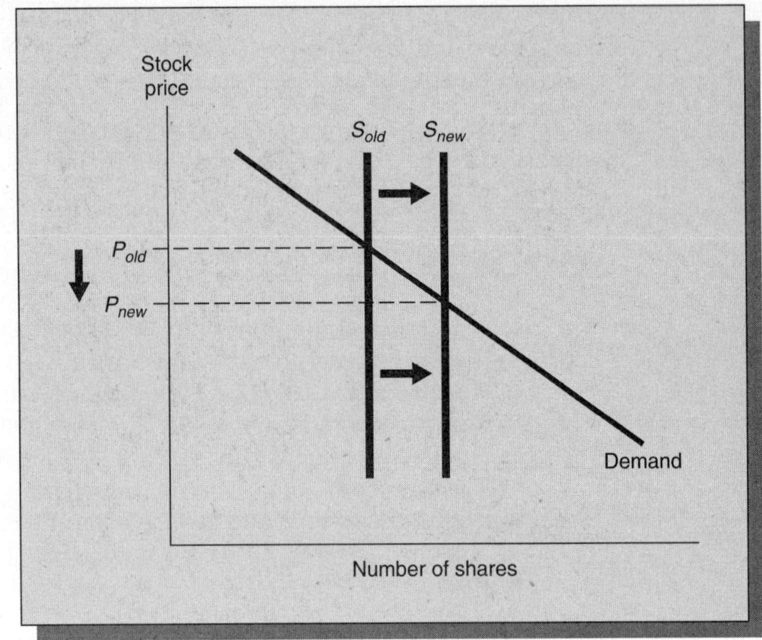

FIGURE 17.1
Supply-demand theory. Dividends should be avoided because they force companies to sell new shares, increasing their supply and lowering their price.

Market imperfection theories These financial market imperfections are "frictions," costs arising from the payment of dividends that remove value from the firm and its shareholders. Each one either reduces after-tax dividends today or lowers investors' forecast of future growth. A company can avoid these costs by not paying dividends.

- Processing costs: Paying dividends incurs the costs of writing and mailing checks.
- Flotation costs: In Chapter 10 we saw that flotation costs make the cost of external equity greater than the cost of retained earnings. Since companies that pay dividends eventually substitute external equity for the earnings they are not retaining, they raise their cost of capital. But high company value is consistent with minimizing the cost of capital, as we saw in Chapter 15.[4] This problem is especially acute for firms needing limited amounts of new equity financing as small stock issues are particularly costly to sell.
- Tax differences: Dividends are effectively taxed twice, once as corporate income and once as personal income to the investor.[5] Firms that do not pay dividends do not expose their shareholders to this double taxation. By contrast, capital gains are taxed only once to the investor; are not taxed until the security is sold; and, for high tax-bracket investors, are taxed at a lower rate (28% versus 31%, 36%, or 39.6%).

[4] **Cross-reference:** Chapter 10, pp. 350–352; Chapter 15, pp. 534–535.

[5] **Cross-reference:** See Appendix 4C, pp. 108–109.

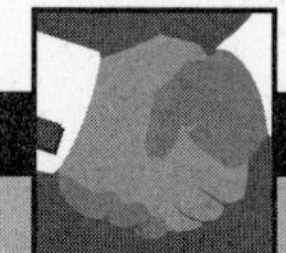

SERVING FINANCE'S CUSTOMERS

Reducing the Dividend at IBM

In 1992 the IBM Corporation lost nearly $5 billion, the second consecutive year the company suffered a multibillion-dollar loss. As part of its plan to restructure and reinvigorate its business, IBM management realized it needed to restore the equity lost through unprofitable operations. However, the company's stock price was at an all-time low, and selling new shares would lead to an unacceptable degree of dilution. Instead IBM's management elected to retain more of its operating income. In December 1992 and again in June 1993, IBM reduced its dividend from $4.84 per share to $2.16 and then to $1.00 per share. By resetting its dividend policy, IBM provided the equity funds for its future growth in a way management felt would best serve its shareholders.

Control theory Reliance on external sources of equity financing results in the continued dilution of each shareholder's percentage ownership. For some investors, dilution translates to lower future dividends. For others, dilution means added risk—and a higher required rate of return—as it reduces their influence on the firm. A company can minimize dilution by not selling new shares, hence by retaining its earnings and not paying dividends.

Sustainable growth theory Sustainable growth refers to the ability of a firm to grow without selling additional common shares.[6] As a company grows, it typically needs additional financing, and the new money must come from both debt and equity sources if the firm is to maintain a target debt-equity mix. However, retained earnings is the sole source of equity financing for small or financially weak companies that cannot (and for larger companies that choose not to) access the equity markets. A company that cannot sell new shares yet pays a dividend limits its growth potential. In response, investors lower their forecast of future growth, reducing the value of the firm's stock.

3. A Theory That Concludes Dividends Are Irrelevant

In Chapter 15 we met Professors Modigliani and Miller (MM), who proved that if the capital markets were "perfect" a firm's value would be independent of its debt-equity mix.[7] MM have made a similar argument for dividends, concluding that the dividend decision also does not affect the value of the firm's stock.

Once again, MM begin by assuming the same perfect market conditions used in their proof of the irrelevance of financing choice. They show that payment of a dividend decreases shareholders' value by exactly the amount of the dividend. The sum of the remaining market value and the dividend is constant regardless of the amount of the dividend, thus the dividend does not change shareholders' wealth.

[6] **Cross-reference:** Sustainable growth is the subject of Appendix 18C.

[7] **Cross-reference:** See pp. 539–540.

Examples

Modigliani-Miller Dividend Theory

The Dolan Company is financed only with equity. Stockholders require a 15% rate of return and forecast a perpetuity of earnings after taxes (EAT) of $600. Dolan's policy is to pay out 100% of its EAT as dividends at year end.

Question: What is the market value of Dolan's stock on January 1?

Solution steps: Use the dividend-growth model with growth equal to zero (which is the same as the perpetuity model):

$$\text{Stock value} = \frac{D_1}{r_c - g} = \frac{\$600}{.15 - .00} = \$4{,}000$$

Dolan is considering a change to its 100% payout ratio. At the end of the year, the company will divide its EAT of $600 between a cash dividend and retained earnings.

Question: What will Dolan's stock be worth on December 31 if the dividend is $0, $200, $400, or $600?

Solution steps: To the January 1 value of $4,000, add this year's income and subtract the dividend:

Possible dividend	$0	$200	$400	$600
Value, January 1	$4,000	$4,000	$4,000	$4,000
+ EAT this year	600	600	600	600
– Dividend	0	200	400	600
Value, December 31	$4,600	$4,400	$4,200	$4,000

Question: How much total value will Dolan's stockholders have on December 31 if the dividend is $0, $200, $400, or $600?

Solution steps: Add the stock value and the dividend:

Possible dividend	$0	$200	$400	$600
Stock value, December 31	$4,600	$4,400	$4,200	$4,000
+ Dividend	0	200	400	600
Total shareholder value	$4,600	$4,600	$4,600	$4,600

Answer: Dolan's shareholders will have $4,600 of total value regardless of the company's dividend. The effect of the dividend is only to split shareholders' value between cash (from the dividend) and stock.

homemade dividends—selling shares of stock to augment a company's dividends

MM rely on their proof of financing irrelevance to claim that their conclusion holds for any firm, regardless of its debt-equity mix, and not just for the all-equity firm in the above example. They also show that the company's choice of dividend cannot reduce the worth of investors who would have preferred a different payout since these investors can easily reallocate their value between cash and stock. Investors who want a larger dividend can create it personally by simply selling some shares—a process called **homemade dividends,** while investors who prefer a lower dividend can reinvest some or all of the dividends they received. With perfect financial markets, these reallocations would take place with no loss in value due to brokerage costs, taxes, etc.

4. Theories That Argue for Consistency

These theories conclude that a firm's dividend policy does not matter as long as the firm is consistent in its payout.

clientele—a group of investors with a similar preference for dividends

Clientele theory A **clientele** is an investor group with a distinct dividend preference. For example, a clientele of retired senior citizens might desire high and regular dividends for income while a clientele of high-income professionals might prefer not to receive dividends since they would be taxed at high marginal rates. This theory argues that investors will naturally gravitate toward those firms whose dividend policies meet their needs. Over time, a company's shareholders will reflect its dividend policy; there is no need to craft a dividend policy in advance to meet the needs of any particular shareholder group. Any dividend payout policy is acceptable as long as it is consistently maintained.

Market imperfection theories These financial market imperfections prevent MM's homemade dividend process from being costless. Investors who receive a dividend different from what they prefer cannot easily reallocate their investment between cash and stock. To prevent placing shareholders in the position of having to reallocate their investment, a company should establish and maintain an announced, consistent dividend policy.

- Indivisibility of securities: Investors who hold a stock that does not pay dividends but who prefer income must sell an integral number of shares. However, this may not yield the amount of income desired. Investors who hold a stock that pays dividends but who prefer share value must buy an integral number of shares. But this may not match the amount of the dividend received. For companies with a low share price this is not a significant problem, but where share price is high, buying or selling the right amount of stock can be problematic. Consider, for example the stock of Berkshire Hathaway, Inc., which in mid-1994, sold for over $15,000 per share.
- Brokerage costs: The cost to buy or sell a small number of shares is high relative to the amount of the transaction. Investors selling a few shares for income will pay excessive brokerage fees which could be avoided entirely if a dividend were paid. Investors buying a few shares with an unwanted dividend will also pay excessive brokerage fees which could be avoided entirely if no dividend were paid.

5. A Theory That Argues Against Setting a Dividend Policy

Each theory we have discussed so far in this chapter began with the assumption that it is useful to look at a company's dividend policy as a variable for the financial manager to optimize. This theory turns the subject upside down. Dividends are one-half of the decision of how to dispose of a firm's earnings after taxes (EAT). The other half is retained earnings. This theory argues that the dividend is not the important decision, rather it is the retained earnings decision that should be optimized. The dividend should merely be the residual result of the decision to retain or not to retain earnings.

According to the residual approach, a company should arrive at its dividend as follows:

1. Determine the total need for new financing from the operating and capital budgets.
2. Determine how much new financing should be equity, using the target debt-equity mix.
3. Use retained earnings to the greatest extent possible since it is the cheapest and most convenient source of new equity.
4. Make the dividend payout
   a. 100% of earnings after taxes (EAT), if no new equity funds are needed,
   b. the earnings not required for new investments, if EAT is more than sufficient to finance new equity needs, or
   c. zero, if equity needs exceed EAT.

Examples

Residual Theory of Dividends

The Dolan Company has determined it will require $850 million of new financing in the coming year. Its target debt ratio is 40%.

Question: How much of the new financing should come from equity to maintain the target debt-equity mix?

Solution steps: 40% of the new financing should come from debt, so 60% should come from equity.

$$60\% \times \$850 \text{ million} = \$510 \text{ million}$$

Question: What should Dolan's dividend be if it uses the residual theory of dividends and its EAT is $400 million? $600 million?

Solution steps: Compare EAT to the equity needed:

1. If EAT = $400 million. Retain all $400 million since the $510 million of equity needed exceeds EAT. Nothing is left for a dividend.
2. If EAT = $600 million. Retain $510 million and pay out the remaining $90 million.

Answer: If EAT is less than the $510 million of equity needed, retain it all and pay a dividend of $0. If EAT exceeds $510 million, retain $510 million and pay out the difference.

The residual theory of dividends is very much at odds with the prescription of those theories that argue for consistency of dividend payments. A firm adhering to residual theory will appear to be following an irregular dividend pattern since EAT and capital needs will vary from year to year. As a result, residual theory is not used by many financial managers.

Dividends in Practice

Given the conflicting advice of the various dividend theories, most companies use a combination of theory and practical guidelines to establish their dividend policy. Perhaps the most commonly followed rule is to maintain stability of dividend payments. A company's stage in its life cycle also plays an important role in its dividend policy. Other considerations are the availability of cash to pay the dividend, alternative uses for the cash, access to banks and financial markets to replace the cash used for dividends, shareholder preferences if ascertainable, and legal or charter restrictions on dividend payments.

1. Stability of Payments

Several of the theories identify that stability is a value-adding strategy. Stability lowers the volatility of investors' cash flows, reducing the risk of that component of their rate of return. Maintaining a stable dividend during a temporary downturn in earnings conveys management's optimism to investors and could limit a drop in stock price. Some investors look to dividends for current income and will pay more for a predictable dividend. Regular dividends attract institutional investors increasing the demand for a stock, and hence its price.

There are three common approaches to achieving stability of dividend payments: (1) maintaining a stable payout ratio, (2) maintaining a stable dollar dividend, and (3) maintaining a stable dollar dividend plus a year-end dividend bonus.

Stable payout ratio Recall that the payout ratio equals dividends divided by earnings. Under this approach, per-share dividends are kept equal to a fixed

WANTED: CLASS CLOWNS, ARTISTS, AND WACKY STUDENTS!

Send us your cartoon ideas for this chapter, or any other chapter. If we use your cartoon suggestion, you'll receive your choice of any three HarperCollins College textbooks or HarperCollins Business titles, and we'll also acknowledge your editorial contribution in the preface of the next edition of *Modern Financial Managing.* Mail your suggestions to: Frank Werner and Jim Stoner, c/o Finance Editor, HarperCollins College Publishers, 10 East 53rd Street, New York, NY, 10022-5299. (Accounting majors need not apply . . . just kidding.)

"A cartoon campaign! You read my mind!
WEBER

percentage of earnings per share (EPS). Of course, if followed exactly, this approach will produce a stable dividend only if EPS is stable. Figure 17.2 shows the more common scenario in which fluctuating EPS leads to a fluctuating dividend stream. As a result, financial managers who target a stable payout ratio rarely use the current quarter's or year's earnings as the basis for the dividend. Rather, they apply this method with a time lag; for example, dividends might be set equal to a percentage of average earnings over the last several years.

Example

Stable Payout Ratio

The Dolan Company reported the following earnings per share (EPS) over the past 12 quarters (three years).

Quarter	EPS	Quarter	EPS
1	$1.00	7	$1.30
2	1.20	8	1.40
3	1.30	9	1.70
4	1.25	10	1.80
5	1.45	11	2.00
6	1.50	12	2.10

Question: What quarterly dividend per share (DPS) should Dolan have paid to maintain a stable payout ratio of 40%?

Solution steps: Multiply each EPS figure by 40%:

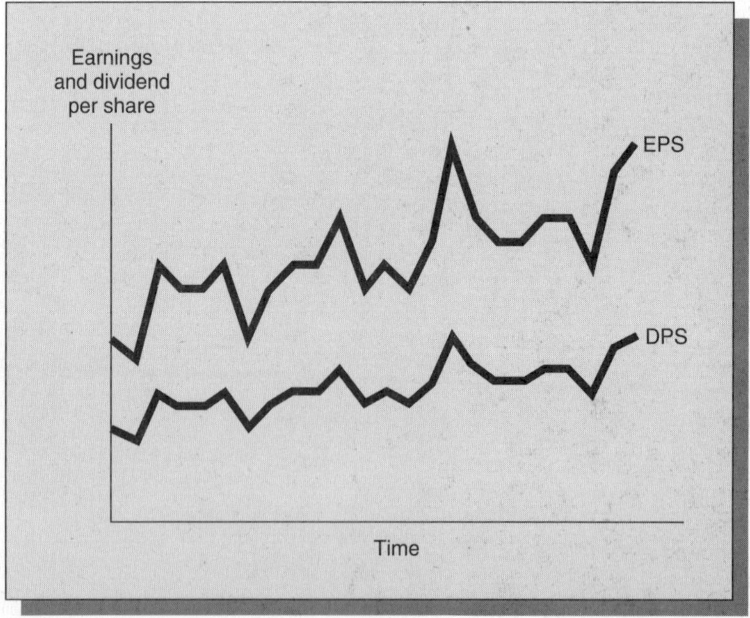

FIGURE 17.2
Stable payout ratio. Dividends are a fixed percentage of earnings.

Quarter	DPS	Quarter	DPS
1	$0.40	7	$0.52
2	0.48	8	0.56
3	0.52	9	0.68
4	0.50	10	0.72
5	0.58	11	0.80
6	0.60	12	0.84

Stable dollar dividend Under this approach, dividends are set equal to a fixed dollar amount, independent of the precise value of EPS. As Figure 17.3 illustrates, when EPS trends upward, the dividend is increased in a series of steps. Should EPS drop, the dividend would be maintained as long as possible. The result is a much smoother pattern of dividends than with the stable payout ratio approach. Investors are insulated from some of the variability of EPS and receive the benefits of a less volatile cash stream.

Example

Stable Dollar Dividend

The Dolan Company reported the following earnings per share (EPS) over the past 12 quarters (three years):

Quarter	EPS	Quarter	EPS
1	$1.00	7	$1.30
2	1.20	8	1.40
3	1.30	9	1.70
4	1.25	10	1.80
5	1.45	11	2.00
6	1.50	12	2.10

FIGURE 17.3
Stable dollar dividend. Dividends are kept constant for a while and are changed when the overall level of earnings changes.

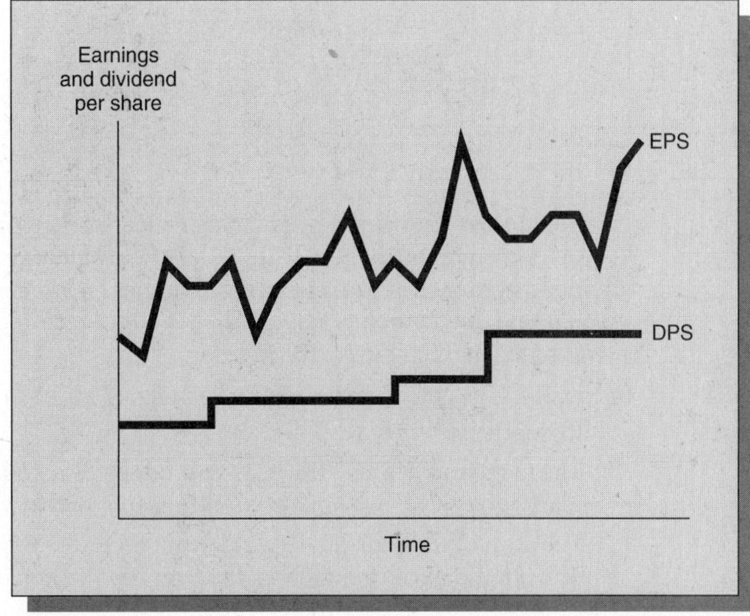

Question: What quarterly dividend per share (DPS) should Dolan have paid to maintain a stable dollar dividend, beginning at $0.40 in quarter 1 and increasing to 40% of EPS whenever EPS reached a level 20% above its value at the last dividend change?

Solution steps: Proceed quarter by quarter as in the following table. Calculate the change to EPS in each quarter relative to its value the last time dividends were raised and reset the dividend if EPS is up by at least 20%. For example, in quarter 5:

1. EPS was $1.45.
2. The last time the dividend was changed was in quarter 2 when EPS was $1.20.
3. $1.45 represents a 20.8% increase over $1.20 (a change of $0.25, which equals $0.25/$1.20 = 20.8%).
4. Since 20.8% is above the 20% threshold, the dividend should be reset.
5. The new dividend will be 40% × $1.45 = $0.58.

Quarter	(1) EPS	(2) EPS When Dividend Last Changed	(3) Percentage Change to EPS	(4) Reset the Dividend?	(5) Dividend
1	$1.00	—	—	—	$0.40
2	1.20	$1.00	20.0%	Yes	0.48
3	1.30	1.20	8.3	No	0.48
4	1.25	1.20	4.2	No	0.48
5	**1.45**	**1.20**	**20.8**	**Yes**	**0.58**
6	1.50	1.45	3.4	No	0.58
7	1.30	1.45	−10.3	No	0.58
8	1.40	1.45	−3.4	No	0.58
9	1.70	1.45	17.2	No	0.58
10	1.80	1.45	24.1	Yes	0.72
11	2.00	1.80	11.1	No	0.72
12	2.10	1.80	16.7	No	0.72

Stable dollar dividend plus a year-end bonus payment This method attempts to combine the best features of the stable payout ratio and stable dollar dividend approaches. The quarterly dividend is held constant throughout the year. At year end, the company pays a "bonus dividend" if appropriate. There are four advantages to this approach.

1. Dividends appear stable to investors since they do not fluctuate from quarter to quarter.
2. The company can use the year-end bonus to reward stockholders in a particularly good year without committing to a higher regular dividend.
3. The sum of the four quarterly dividends is less than the planned annual payout. Should earnings decline, the firm has the flexibility to decrease its annual

dividend without losing quarterly stability, by simply reducing or eliminating the bonus dividend.

4. The year-end bonus can be adjusted to keep the annual payout proportional to earnings if the company wishes to maintain a constant payout ratio.

Example

Stable Dollar Dividend with Year-End Bonus

The Dolan Company reported the following earnings per share (EPS) over the past 12 quarters (three years):

Quarter	EPS	Quarter	EPS
1	$1.00	7	$1.30
2	1.20	8	1.40
3	1.30	9	1.70
4	1.25	10	1.80
5	1.45	11	2.00
6	1.50	12	2.10

Question: What regular and bonus dividend per share (DPS) should Dolan have paid to maintain a stable dollar dividend plus year-end bonus if the regular quarterly dividend is set to 40% of first quarter EPS and the year-end bonus is calculated to bring the annual payout ratio up to 40%?

Solution steps:

Year 1 (quarters 1–4):

1. Quarterly dividend = 40% × $1.00 = $0.40
2. Bonus:

40% of annual EPS = 40% ($1.00 + 1.20 + 1.30 + 1.25)
= 40% × $4.75 = $1.90
Less: regular dividend paid = 4 × $0.40 = 1.60
$0.30

Year 2 (quarters 5–8):

1. Quarterly dividend = 40% × $1.45 = $0.58
2. Bonus:

40% of annual EPS = 40% ($1.45 + 1.50 + 1.30 + 1.40)
= 40% × $5.65 = $2.26
Less: regular dividend paid = 4 × $0.58 = 2.32
− $0.06

Dolan would not pay a bonus dividend in this year since its regular quarterly dividend payments have distributed more than 40% of EPS.

Year 3 (quarters 9–12):

1. Quarterly dividend = 40% × $1.70 = $0.68

2. Bonus:

40% of annual EPS	= 40% ($1.70 + 1.80 + 2.00 + 2.10)		
	= 40% × $7.60	=	$3.04
Less: regular dividend paid	= 4 × $0.68	=	2.72
			$0.32

2. Company Maturity

A second practical consideration in setting a dividend policy is the position of a company in its life cycle. Companies pass through a series of stages as they grow and mature. Each stage is characterized by different needs and access to cash, hence different pressures on retaining earnings. Each stage is also characterized by different growth rates, hence different abilities to produce returns for investors in the form of capital gains. Both factors affect dividend policy. We look briefly at three of these stages below: (1) birth, (2) rapid growth, and (3) maturity.

Birth At birth, few companies are able to pay dividends. Almost all companies begin their lives in a cash-poor position, requiring every dollar they can get their hands on to survive and grow. At this stage, firms generally have poor access to external resources since they are unknown and have not yet established successful financial histories. Their equity financing is normally from their founder(s) or venture capitalists—investors who intimately understand the company's need to conserve every bit of its cash and who are willing to postpone receiving dividends in the hope of much larger returns later.

Rapid growth During rapid growth, most companies choose not to pay a dividend. As described in Chapter 18, when companies grow quickly they need significant infusions of cash to acquire assets. At the same time, rapid growth may now be providing their stockholders with a high rate of return in the form in capital gains, mitigating the need for dividends. If a firm in this stage pays a dividend at all, it tends to be quite modest.

Maturity At maturity, companies tend to pay moderate to high dividends. As companies mature, their rate of growth settles down. They can no longer generate high returns for investors through stock price appreciation and must use dividends to provide stockholders with a reasonable rate of return. They no longer need large amounts of new cash to expand their asset base and often do not have good internal uses for all the money they earn. At the extreme, a profitable company that ceases to grow may pay out all its earnings as dividends.

3. Other Practical Considerations

In addition to a desire for stability and stage in life cycle, several other practical concerns shape a company's dividend policy.

Availability of cash To pay regular dividends, a company must have sufficient cash on hand each quarter. A firm with a predictable and stable cash flow finds it easier to commit to regular dividend payments than one whose cash flow is uncertain or erratic.

Alternative uses for cash Closely connected to the availability of cash is the lack of competing uses for the money. Companies that regularly have a large selection of attractive investment opportunities or consistently need funds to repay debt principal may have difficulty finding the cash for dividends.

Access to banks and financial markets Companies that can obtain funds easily can pay dividends without worrying too much about securing replacement financing if needed. Such companies also typically pay low flotation costs when they issue stock, which keeps down the cost differential between external equity and retained earnings. If investors in these companies accept a wide range of debt-equity mixes, the firm can borrow as required to maintain its dividend and a higher dividend can be sustained.

Shareholder preferences To the extent the financial manager can determine them, the firm's dividend policy can be directly responsive to shareholders' tax positions and control preferences. This is possible in closely held companies where there are few key shareholders and is difficult if the company's stock is widely held.

Legal or charter restrictions Provisions of a company's charter, contracts it has entered, or the law can place boundaries around a company's dividend policy. Most state corporation laws have a "capital impairment rule" that limits dividends to the sum of a firm's retained earnings and/or an "insolvency rule" that prohibits insolvent firms (those with negative equity) from paying dividends. Loan agreements are often written to limit or prohibit dividend payments to prevent money that should be used for debt service from leaving the firm. In the other direction, recall the provision of the federal tax code that subjects excess retained earnings to a special "improper accumulation" penalty.

How a Dividend Is Paid

date of declaration—the date a company's board of directors votes to pay a dividend

date of record—the date a company determines who will receive a dividend

payment date—the date a dividend is paid

The decision to pay a dividend is made by a company's board of directors. Most boards meet quarterly, and a regular item on their agenda is consideration of the next dividend. If the board votes to pay or "declares" a dividend, that date is identified as the **date of declaration.** With the advice of the financial manager, the board also establishes two other dates that define the remaining mechanics of paying the dividend. The first is the **date of record,** the date on which the company will look at its list of shareholders to determine who will receive the dividend. The second is the **payment date,** on which dividend checks will be mailed.

Figure 17.4 is the card that accompanied the Quaker Oats Company's dividend payment of April 15, 1994. At the top of the card, Quaker communicated the stability of its dividend policy by informing its stockholders that this was the 365th dividend paid by the company. In the first paragraph, Quaker related the other relevant information: the dividend was in the amount of $0.53 per share, had been declared on March 9, 1994, and was paid on April 15 to shareholders whose name appeared on the company's records at the end of the business day on March 18.

The Quaker Oats Company
Common Stock Dividend No. 365

April 15, 1994

Current Dividend Payment

On March 9, 1994, the Board of Directors declared a dividend of 53 cents per share on the outstanding common stock. The dividend is payable April 15, 1994 to shareholders of record at the close of business on March 18, 1994.

Safekeeping of Stock Certificates

As a participant in the Dividend Reinvestment and Stock Purchase Plan, you may deposit for safekeeping any stock certificates now registered in your name for credit to your account under the Plan. There is no charge for this service, and by making a deposit, you will be relieved of the responsibility for loss, theft, or destruction of the certificates. If you decide to deposit the shares with Harris Trust and Savings Bank for safekeeping, you may use the top portion of your dividend reinvestment statement.

If you have other information needs concerning your shareholder account, please feel free to write or call the ***Shareholder Hotline*** toll-free at ***1-800-344-1198*** and your request will be answered as quickly as possible.

Harris Trust and Savings Bank
Shareholder Services
P.O. Box 755
311 West Monroe Street
Chicago, IL 60690-0755

FIGURE 17.4
Announcement of a dividend. The announcement specifies the amount of the dividend as well as the date of declaration, record date, and payment date.

ex-dividend date—the date by which stock must be purchased to receive the next dividend

There is a fourth date relevant to dividend payments. It takes several days for information about stock transactions to make its way to a company. Suppose some investors bought Quaker stock on March 16. Would their names reach the company by March 18 so they would be eligible for the April 15 dividend? To protect investors and assure them that they will (or will not) get the next dividend, each stock exchange establishes an **ex-dividend date,** usually four business days prior to the date of record. For the Quaker dividend, the ex-dividend date was Monday, March 14. Investors who purchased the stock on or before March 14 were assured by the New York Stock Exchange that their name would reach the company by March 18, in time to be included in the company's records and receive the next dividend. At the end of trading on March 14, Quaker stock went "ex-dividend"; an investor who purchased the stock after that date did not receive the next dividend—rather it was paid to the former stockholder.

The four dates for the Quaker Oats dividend are diagrammed in a time line in Figure 17.5.

Alternatives to Cash Dividends

To this point in the chapter we have looked at traditional cash dividends. However, there are other forms of distributions companies make to their common stockholders. In this section we look at dividend reinvestment plans, stock dividends and stock splits, and stock repurchases.

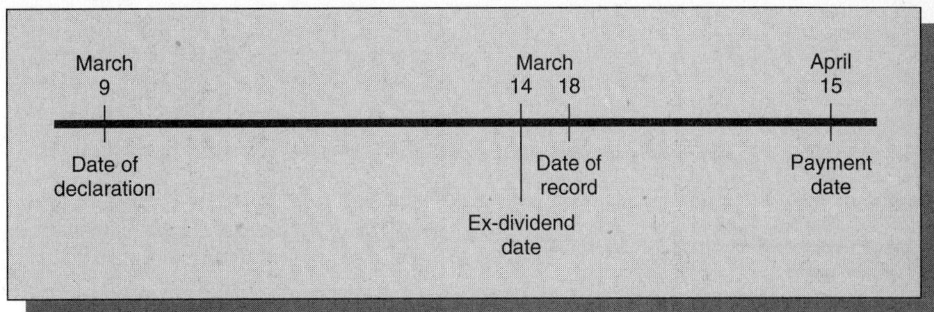

FIGURE 17.5
Quaker Oats dividend timetable. Four dates define the payment of a dividend.

1. Dividend Reinvestment Plans

Many large companies offer their stockholders the option of participating in a dividend reinvestment plan. By joining the plan, stockholders elect to receive additional shares of stock instead of cash dividends, permitting them to "reinvest" their dividends in the company. Although investors forgo a cash payment, the additional shares increase the total value of their investment.[8]

Dividend reinvestment plans can be classified into "old stock plans" and "new stock plans." In an old stock plan, the company engages a commercial bank to purchase blocks of shares in the market with the money that would have been paid as the dividend. The bank then apportions the newly acquired shares to the plan members and holds the shares for investors in accounts at the bank. Per-share transaction costs are low since a large number of shares is purchased and the company often picks up the brokerage fee. Under a new stock plan, the company keeps the cash that would have gone to the dividend payment and issues new shares of stock with market value equal to the dividend. Some companies

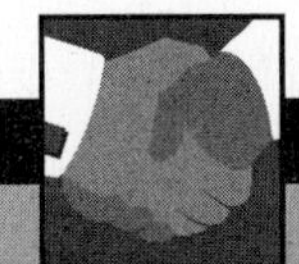

SERVING FINANCE'S CUSTOMERS

Enhancing a Dividend Reinvestment Plan at Quaker Oats

The Quaker Oats Company's dividend reinvestment plan provides that shareholders may keep all their shares at Harris Trust and Savings Bank, the bank that administers the plan. As the dividend announcement of Figure 17.4 reminds shareholders, by depositing their stock certificates with Harris Trust they "will be relieved of the responsibility for loss, theft, or destruction of the certificates." Records of the investment position are centralized at the bank. And if shareholders elect to sell some or all of their shares, the bank can handle the transaction directly, often at the same low transaction costs applied to the dividend reinvestment.

[8] **Observation:** The Internal Revenue Service treats dividend reinvestment as if a cash dividend had been paid and the investor then used the money to purchase the additional shares. Accordingly, investors must pay tax on the amount of their dividends, even though they receive no cash. The new shares are treated as having a cost equal to the amount of the dividend.

offer a discount (5% is common) off the market price since they are saving on flotation costs, thus distributing more shares than the dividend could purchase.

2. Stock Dividends and Stock Splits

stock dividend—the distribution of additional shares to common shareholders

stock split—the replacement of all outstanding shares of common stock with a different number of new shares

A **stock dividend** is the distribution of new common shares to existing shareholders. For example, in a 10% stock dividend, each shareholder receives one new share for every ten held, a 10% increase. In a **stock split,** a company replaces all existing common shares with a different number of new shares. For example, if a company splits its stock "2 for 1," each shareholder receives two new shares for each old share. Although they are defined in different terms, stock dividends and stock splits are identical in outcome. In fact, most companies implement a 2 for 1 split by simply sending shareholders one additional share for each share owned, the same mechanics as a 100% stock dividend.

Accounting for stock dividends and splits Financial accounting rules distinguish between a stock split and a stock dividend by the number of additional shares issued, regardless of which description the company uses. According to Generally Accepted Accounting Principles, which treat splits and dividends slightly differently, a distribution which increases the number of outstanding shares by less than 20–25% is a stock dividend while one which increases outstanding shares by more than that amount is a stock split. The New York Stock Exchange places the dividing line at 25%.

The value of stock dividends and splits In both stock dividends and stock splits, the number of outstanding common shares changes, which makes earnings per share, dividends per share, and the company's stock price adjust proportionally. However, the *total* market value of the firm's stock will not change if the cash flows received by investors or their expectations of the firm's future performance remain the same. It is somewhat like cutting a cake into more slices—while the number of slices increases, the total amount of cake does not and each slice is proportionately smaller.

Examples

A Stock Split That Does Not Change Value

The Dolan Company has decided to split its common stock 2 for 1. Currently there are 10 million shares outstanding with a market price per share of \$80.00. In the most recent year the company earned \$8.00 per share and paid a dividend of \$3.20 per share.

Question: What will earnings per share (EPS) and dividends per share (DPS) be after the split?

Solution steps:

1. Shares outstanding after the split:

$$10 \text{ million} \times 2 = 20 \text{ million}$$

2. Net income now = 10 million shares × \$8.00 = \$80 million

EPS after the split = $80 million/20 million shares = $4.00

3. Total dividend now = 10 million shares × $3.20 = $32 million

DPS after the split = $32 million/20 million shares = $1.60

Answer: Since the number of shares will double, both EPS and DPS will fall to half their presplit values.

Question: Assuming investors do not revise their forecast of the company's future performance, what will Dolan's total stock value and share price be after the split? How will each shareholder fare?

Solution steps:

1. Total value now = 10 million shares × $80 = $800 million
2. Value after the split = $800 million (unchanged since investors do not change their forecasts)
3. Share price after the split = $800 million/20 million shares = $40

Answer: Dolan's total stock value will not change, although its share price will fall by half. Since each shareholder will have twice as many shares, every shareholder's value will remain the same.

Stock dividends and splits do have value if they make a stock more attractive to investors by increasing cash flow (actual or forecasted) or reducing risk.

- Small dividend increase: A stock dividend can be a device for increasing the cash dividend by a small amount. If investors do not offset the higher dividend flow by raising their required rate of return or lowering their growth forecast, the value of the company's stock will rise.

Examples

Increasing the Cash Dividend Through a Stock Dividend

The Dolan Company, which currently pays a dividend of $3.20 per share, is considering a 10% stock dividend. Bob Forrest owns 100 shares of Dolan common stock.

Question: How much does Bob currently receive in cash dividends?

Solution steps: 100 shares × $3.20 = $320.00

Question: If Dolan pays the 10% stock dividend without reducing the per-share cash dividend, how much will Bob receive?

Solution steps: Bob will receive an additional 10 shares (10% of 100) bringing his ownership up to 110 shares.

110 shares × $3.20 = $352.00

Answer: Bob's cash dividend will increase by 10%, from $320.00 to $352.00 as a result of the stock dividend.

- Information content: Management's decision to split the company's stock might communicate to investors its belief that the firm has positive prospects for the future. Recently, financial researchers have identified a small but positive stock price reaction to stock split announcements, supporting this hypothesis.
- Favored trading range: Many financial managers prefer to see their stock sell in the $20–$50 per share price range. They fear that a price below $20 would make the company appear too cheap, while shares priced much above $50 would become too expensive for small investors and reduce demand for the stock. They use stock splits to move their stock price down to the favored range, an act that signals management's confidence that the stock is strong enough not to fall below $50 on its own.

A bad reason for a stock dividend Some companies use a stock dividend as a substitute for a cash dividend, claiming shareholders receive the "best of both worlds": both a dividend in hand and reinvestment in the company. Savvy investors will see through this argument and realize that cash cannot be in two places at one time. In fact, a company making this claim could see its stock price fall if investors interpret the stock dividend as an admission of inability to pay a cash dividend.

reverse split—a stock split that reduces the number of outstanding shares

A difference between stock dividends and splits Stock splits and stock dividends differ in one respect. Unlike stock dividends, which always increase the number of shares outstanding, it is possible to have a **reverse split** in which the number of outstanding shares declines. For example, in a "1 to 4 reverse split," each shareholder would receive one new share for every four old shares. If the purpose of a split that increases the number of shares is to communicate management's optimism and bring down a stock price that otherwise would not fall to the favored trading range, imagine the message of a reverse split!

3. Stock Repurchase

In recent years, some companies have elected to use cash that might otherwise go toward a dividend to repurchase their shares on the open market. To some extent, repurchase is a substitute for cash dividends since both techniques put cash in the

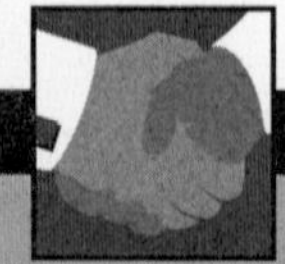

SERVING FINANCE'S CUSTOMERS

Adjusting a Stock's Price Through Stock Splits At Coca-Cola

In May 1993, the Coca-Cola Company split its stock 2 for 1. Prior to the split, the stock was trading in the $80 range; the split brought the company's share price down to just above $40, a number management felt would be more attractive to its shareholders. This was the second time in two years Coca-Cola stock had split 2 for 1. Had the splits not occurred, Coke's stock would have been selling for over $160 per share!

hands of shareholders. But there are several important differences that can make repurchase a superior alternative to cash dividends under certain circumstances.

Shareholders might prefer a stock repurchase offer to cash dividends since it changes the nature of their returns. An investor who sells shares back to the company effectively creates a dividend. However, since this "dividend" comes from selling stock, only the appreciation in value (the capital gain and not the entire amount) is taxed.

For the company, there are several benefits from repurchasing stock rather than paying a cash dividend.

- Repurchase increases demand for the company's shares, supporting their price in a weak market. A recent example came after the "crash" of October 19, 1987, a day on which the Dow Jones Industrial Average lost 508 points—more than 1/5 of its total value. Many companies entered the market on October 20 to repurchase their stock, which helped stabilize stock prices and prevent a further drastic fall.
- Repurchase permits a company to benefit when its stock price is low. If management feels its shares are undervalued, repurchase becomes a use of funds with a high rate of return. However, departing shareholders will lose out if management has inside information that the stock price will subsequently rise and eventually reissues the stock at a higher price.
- Repurchase removes stock from the hands of those shareholders most willing to sell, reducing the possibility that an outside party could acquire sufficient shares to mount a takeover or greenmail attempt.
- Repurchase adds to the number of shares available within the company for stock option and bonus plans.

If the repurchase is made at the prevailing stock price, there is no transfer of value between those shareholders who sell their shares back to the company and those who do not. However, a repurchase at a different price does transfer value between the two groups.

Example

Stock Repurchase

The Dolan Company, which currently has 10 million shares outstanding at a price of $80, is thinking of repurchasing 5% of the outstanding shares. Bob Forrest owns 100 shares of Dolan stock.

Question: What happens to Dolan's stock price if Dolan repurchases the stock at $80 per share? At $85 per share? At $75 per share?

Solution steps:

1. Calculate the company's current market value:

$$10{,}000{,}000 \text{ shares} \times \$80 = \$800{,}000{,}000$$

2. Calculate the number of shares involved:

$$\text{Shares repurchased} = 5\% \times 10{,}000{,}000 = 500{,}000$$
$$\text{Shares remaining} = 10{,}000{,}000 - 500{,}000 = 9{,}500{,}000$$

3. Repurchase at \$80:

   Amount spent on repurchase: \$80 × 500,000 = \$40,000,000
   Company value goes to: \$800,000,000 – 40,000,000 = \$760,000,000
   Price of remaining shares = \$760,000,000/9,500,000 = \$80

   Repurchase at \$85:

   Amount spent on repurchase: \$85 × 500,000 = \$42,500,000
   Company value goes to: \$800,000,000 – 42,500,000 = \$757,500,000
   Price of remaining shares = \$757,500,000/9,500,000 = \$79.74

   Repurchase at \$75:

   Amount spent on repurchase: \$75 × 50,000 = \$37,500,000
   Company value goes to: \$800,000,000 – 37,500,000 = \$762,500,000
   Price of remaining shares = \$762,500,000/9,500,000 = \$80.26

Question: What happens to Bob's worth if he sells his stock back to the company under each of the three scenarios?

Solution steps:

1. Calculate Bob's current worth: 100 shares × \$80 = \$800
2. Repurchase at \$80:

   Bob receives: 100 shares × \$80 = \$800
   Change to worth: \$800 – 800 = \$0

   Repurchase at \$85:

   Bob receives: 100 shares × \$85 = \$850
   Change to worth: \$850 – 800 = \$50

   Repurchase at \$75:

   Bob receives: 100 shares × \$75 = \$750
   Change to worth: \$750 – 800 = –\$50

Question: What happens to Bob's worth if he does not sell his stock back to the company under each of the three scenarios?

Solution steps:

1. Calculate Bob's current worth: 100 shares × \$80 = \$800
2. Repurchase at \$80:

   Bob now has: 100 shares × \$80 = \$800
   Change to worth: \$800 – 800 = \$0

Repurchase at $85:

Bob now has: 100 shares × $79.74 = $797.40
Change to worth: $797.40 − 800 = −$2.60

Repurchase at $75:

Bob now has: 100 shares × $80.26 = $802.60
Change to worth: $802.60 − 800 = $2.60

Answer: If the repurchase takes place at current stock price of $80, Bob's wealth remains unchanged, regardless of whether he sells or keeps his shares. At a repurchase price above $80, value is transferred from the remaining shareholders to those who sell; Bob should sell his shares. At a repurchase price below $80, value is transferred from shareholders who sell to those who remain; Bob should keep his shares.

FINANCE IN PRACTICE

Repurchasing Stock

Back in the 1980s it was a defensive move. Many companies bought back big chunks of their stock—often with borrowed money—as a way to keep the shares away from unfriendly takeover types. But the demise of the dealmeisters in the early 1990s made buybacks less urgent. The recession forced Corporate America to focus on shrinking debt, not equity.

By mid-1993, however, many companies were repurchasing stock as an offensive move, to boost earnings per share and share price. As *Business Week* reported in its August 23rd issue:

> So far this year, there have been 359 announcements of stock buybacks worth about $23.5 billion, according to Securities Data Co. That compares with 599 announcements of $35.6 billion in 1992 and only 437 worth $20.2 billion for all of 1991. Among the companies whose boards have authorized repurchases recently are H.J. Heinz, Nike, PepsiCo, Quaker Oats, Reebok International, and Wachovia.

Fueling the buyback boom is improved cash flow from the dramatic reduction in corporate expenses over the last few years. Interest rates have fallen to 20-year lows saving billions of dollars in interest expenses. Corporate restructuring, driven in part by the global quality revolution, has reduced overhead and other costs of doing business by further billions.

> "We spend on new products, we make acquisitions, and we raise the dividend, and we still can't soak up all the cash," says Janet K. Cooper, Quaker's treasurer. The company has repurchased 20 million shares in the last five years and recently authorized acquisition of an additional 5 million.

Reference: "The Great Buyback Boom of '93," *Business Week,* Aug. 23, 1993, pp. 76–77.

On occasion a company repurchases stock from one or a small group of shareholders, especially if that group owns a substantial number of shares. This can be to accommodate a particular shareholder's needs, such as a member of the family of the company's founder. It can also be the payoff for **greenmail**. In greenmail, an outside investor acquires a large number of a company's shares and then threatens a hostile takeover unless the company repurchases the shares at an above-market price, transferring wealth from other shareholders to the greenmailer.

greenmail—demanding that a company repurchase its shares at an inflated price by threatening a hostile takeover

One problem with aggressive share repurchase is that it might signal to the financial markets that the company sees a lack of good investment opportunities. All companies must maintain a program of investing in employees, processes, research and development, and facilities to grow or simply keep up with their competitors. It is important that financial managers keep investors and security analysts well informed of the place of a repurchase program in the company's overall strategic plan.

Bob Forrest looked at his watch and was surprised at how much time had passed. He had spent the last several hours in a comfortable chair in the back corner of the company library reading all he could about dividend policy. Bob stood up and stretched, then placed some books back on the shelf and gathered up his notes. As he returned to his office, Bob mulled over what he had learned.

Dividend policy was an area in which finance theory gave very mixed signals. Some theories argued that the payment of dividends added value to shareholders while others claimed that dividends lowered stock values. Professors Modigliani and Miller were convinced that dividends had nothing to do with value. The other theories were in conflict as well: one argued for stable payments while another made dividends the unstable residual of the retained earnings decision.

Dividend practice seemed a bit more settled than the theory since there was broad agreement that stability of payments was of value. Yet there were different ways to achieve stability, and they all seemed so contradictory.

Back in his office, Bob rewrote his notes, organizing his findings into a series of pros and cons and matching them with the opinions expressed in that morning's meeting. He had the sense that a pattern of ideas was emerging. After reading through his notes one more time, Bob went down the hall to seek out other members of the team and test out his new insights.

Summary of Key Points

- **Explain how shareholders get their returns.** Shareholders' returns come in the form of dividends (direct distributions from the corporation) and capital gains (increased stock value). The dividend growth model shows the relationship between current dividends, investors' required rate of return, and investors' growth forecast and identifies the tradeoffs financial managers face in planning a dividend policy.
- **Describe five classes of theory that attempt to identify a company's optimal dividend policy.** Dividend theories may be classified into five categories: (1) theories that conclude that dividends add value, (2) theories that conclude that dividends reduce value, (3) MM theory which concludes that dividends have nothing to do with value, (4) theories that conclude that consistency adds value, and (5) residual theory which turns our attention away from dividends and toward retained earnings. The theories all improve our knowledge of dividend policy, yet are wildly contradictory in their advice.
- **Discuss seven practical considerations in setting a firm's dividend.** One important consideration is stability of payments. Three approaches to stability are a stable payout ratio, a stable dollar dividend, and a stable dollar dividend plus a year-end bonus payment. A second factor is where the company is in its life cycle. Other practical considerations are the availability of cash, alternative uses for the cash, access to banks and financial markets, shareholder preferences regarding taxes and control, and legal or charter restrictions on dividend payments.
- **Describe the mechanics of how dividends are declared and paid.** When a board of directors declares a dividend, it determines the amount to be paid and sets a date of record and a payment date. In response, the relevant stock exchange establishes an ex-dividend date, the last day to buy the stock and receive the coming dividend.
- **Analyze three alternatives to cash dividends.** Many companies maintain a dividend reinvestment plan through which some shareholders elect to receive their dividends in the form of additional shares of stock. Companies not wishing to distribute cash often substitute stock dividends. Stock splits can be used to change the number of outstanding shares and move the stock price to a more favorable level. Recently, share repurchase has become popular to substitute for or augment a regular cash dividend.

Questions

1. Why do we talk of a dividend *policy* and not just a dividend in this chapter?
2. Under what circumstances does a dividend increase raise the value of a corporation's stock?
3. How can the payment of a dividend reduce investors' risk?
4. What market imperfections enter into the planning of a corporation's dividend policy?
5. "If all companies paid dividends the financial markets would be more efficient!" Comment on this assertion.
6. What conditions must be true for MM's dividend irrelevance theory to be correct?
7. What is a homemade dividend?
8. What is a clientele? Describe three groups of investors who might form a clientele.
9. The consistency theories and the residual theory of dividends reach opposite conclusions. What are those conclusions, and why are they so different?
10. Can a stable payout policy ever produce a stable dollar dividend? Under what condition(s)?
11. What is the relationship of a company's dividend policy to its stage in its life cycle?
12. In today's environment, which of the practical considerations that guide corporations' dividend policies are most important?
13. Distinguish between the following events:
    a. Declaration date
    b. Ex-dividend date
    c. Date of record
    d. Payment date
14. Compare and contrast a 100% stock dividend and a 2-for-1 stock split.
15. Why is stock repurchase particularly attractive to many companies today?

Problems

1. **(Dividend-growth model)** Investors who require a 3.5% quarterly rate of return forecast that a company will pay a dividend of $0.50 three months from now. What will the value of a share of stock be if investors forecast a quarterly growth rate of:
    a. 0%?
    b. 1%?

c. 2%?
d. 3%?

2. **(Dividend-growth model)** Investors forecast that a company will pay a dividend of $1.00 three months from now, which will grow thereafter at a quarterly rate of 1%. What will the value of a share of stock be if investors require a quarterly rate of return of:

   a. 2.00%?
   b. 2.75%?
   c. 3.50%?
   d. 4.25%?

3. **(Dividend-growth model)** A company is thinking of announcing an increase in its next quarterly dividend from $1.50 to $1.65. Currently investors forecast a quarterly growth rate of 2.5% and have a 3.75% quarterly required rate of return. Calculate:

   a. The value of one share of the company's stock today
   b. The value of a share after the announcement if investors do not change their growth forecast or their required rate of return
   c. The value of a share after the announcement if investors lower their quarterly growth forecast to 2% but do not change their required rate of return
   d. The value of a share after the announcement if investors do not change their growth forecast but increase their quarterly required rate of return to 4%

4. **(Dividend-growth model)** A company is thinking of announcing an increase in its next quarterly dividend from $1.00 to $1.10. Currently investors forecast a quarterly growth rate of 2% and have a 4% quarterly required rate of return. Calculate:

   a. The value of one share of the company's stock today
   b. The value of a share after the announcement if investors do not change their growth forecast nor their required rate of return
   c. The value of a share after the announcement if investors lower their quarterly growth forecast to 1.5% but do not change their required rate of return
   d. The value of a share after the announcement if investors lower their quarterly growth forecast to 1.5% but decrease their quarterly required rate of return to 3.25%

5. **(Risk reduction)** A company is considering the following two dividend policies for the next four quarters (one year):

Policy A	Policy B
$1.00	$0.00
1.00	0.00
1.00	2.10
1.00	2.10

   a. How much in dividends per share will a stockholder receive over the year under each policy?
   b. If investors see no difference in risk between the two policies and apply a quarterly discount rate of 3% to both, what is the present value of each dividend stream?
   c. Now suppose investors see the Policy B as the riskier of the two. They apply a 3% quarterly discount rate to policy A but a 4% quarterly rate to Policy B. What is the present value of each dividend stream?
   d. Why might investors see Policy B as riskier?

6. **(Risk reduction)** A company is considering the following two dividend policies for the next four quarters (one year):

Policy X	Policy Y
$3.00	$2.00
3.00	4.00
3.00	2.50
3.00	4.00

   a. How much in dividends per share will a stockholder receive over the year under each policy?
   b. If investors see no difference in risk between the two policies and apply a quarterly discount rate of 2.75% to both, what is the present value of each dividend stream?
   c. Suppose investors see the Policy Y as the riskier of the two. They apply a 2.75% quarterly discount rate to Policy X but a 3.5% quarterly rate to Policy Y. What is the present value of each dividend stream?
   d. Now suppose investors apply a 2.75% quarterly discount rate to Policy X but a 4.25% quarterly rate to Policy Y. What is the present value of each dividend stream?

7. **(Taxation)** Among the stockholders of the Dolan company are Dorothy, a widow in the 15% marginal federal income tax bracket; Josh, a successful young businessman in the 36% bracket; and Kateco, a corporation in the 35% bracket. Dolan's financial managers are considering the effect of either paying a dividend of $2.00 per share on March 1 or retaining the income, in which case they forecast that their

share price will rise by the same $2.00 on or about March 1.

a. Calculate the after-tax benefit of the dividend and the capital gain to Dorothy.
b. Calculate the after-tax benefit of the dividend and the capital gain to Josh.
c. Calculate the after-tax benefit of the dividend and the capital gain to Kateco.
d. What is the message from this exercise for Dolan's financial managers?

8. **(Taxation)** Among the stockholders of the Dolan company are Edwin, a retired businessman in the 15% marginal federal income tax bracket; Sylvia, a rich widow in the 39.6% bracket; and Ernco, a corporation in the 35% bracket. Dolan's financial managers are considering whether to increase the dividend by $1.00 per share.

a. Calculate the after-tax benefit of the proposed dividend increase to Edwin.
b. Calculate the after-tax benefit of the proposed dividend increase to Sylvia.
c. Calculate the after-tax benefit of the proposed dividend increase to Ernco.
d. How should Dolan's financial managers react to the tax consequences of increasing the dividend if they believe the company's shareholders are primarily corporations?

9. **(Residual theory)** A corporation forecasts it will require $3 million of new financing in the coming year. Its target debt ratio is 30%, and it plans to use the residual theory to determine its dividend.

a. How much new financing should come from debt and how much from equity to meet the target debt ratio?
b. What should the corporation's dividend be if its earnings after taxes (EAT) is $1 million?
c. What should the corporation's dividend be if its EAT is $2 million?
d. What should the corporation's dividend be if its EAT is $3 million?

10. **(Residual theory)** A corporation forecasts it will require $800,000 of new financing in the coming year. Its target debt ratio is 50%, and it plans to use the residual theory to determine its dividend.

a. How much new financing should come from debt and how much from equity to meet the target debt ratio?
b. What should the corporation's dividend be if its earnings after taxes (EAT) is $600,000?
c. What should the corporation's dividend be if its EAT is $400,001?
d. What should the corporation's dividend be if its EAT is $200,000?

11. **(Dividends in practice)** On the basis of the following (admittedly very limited) information, recommend a dividend policy—high, moderate, or low payout ratio—for the following companies:

a. Growth rate: 2%, target cash balance: 2% of total assets
b. Growth rate: 2%, target cash balance: 15% of total assets
c. Growth rate: 15%, target cash balance: 2% of total assets
d. Growth rate: 15%, target cash balance: 15% of total assets

12. **(Dividends in practice)** On the basis of the following (admittedly very limited) information, recommend a dividend policy—high, moderate, or low payout ratio—for the following companies:

a. Growth rate: 3%, good access to financial markets
b. Growth rate: 3%, poor access to financial markets
c. Growth rate: 12%, good access to financial markets
d. Growth rate: 12%, poor access to financial markets

13. **(Stability)** A company predicts the following quarterly earnings per share for the next three years:

Quarter	EPS	Quarter	EPS
1	$1.00	7	$1.30
2	1.20	8	1.40
3	1.30	9	1.70
4	1.25	10	1.80
5	1.45	11	2.00
6	1.50	12	2.10

What quarterly dividend per share (DPS) should the company pay if it follows:

a. A stable payout ratio of 50%?
b. A stable dollar dividend beginning at $0.50 in Quarter 1 and increasing to 50% of EPS whenever EPS reaches a level 15% above its value at the last dividend change?
c. A stable dollar dividend plus a year-end bonus if the regular quarterly dividend is set to 50% of first quarter EPS and the year-end bonus is calculated to bring the annual payout ratio up to 50%?
d. How well do each of these three methods achieve the goal of a stable dividend?

14. **(Stability)** A company predicts the following quarterly earnings per share for the next three years:

Quarter	EPS	Quarter	EPS
1	$2.00	7	$3.00
2	2.50	8	3.50
3	2.00	9	3.50
4	2.75	10	3.80
5	3.00	11	4.00
6	3.10	12	4.50

What dividends should the company pay if it follows:

a. A stable payout ratio of 40%?
b. A stable dollar dividend beginning at $0.80 in Quarter 1 and increasing to 40% of EPS whenever EPS reaches a level 25% above its value at the last dividend change?
c. A stable dollar dividend plus a year-end bonus if the regular quarterly dividend is set to 40% of first quarter EPS, and the year-end bonus is calculated to bring the annual payout ratio up to 40%?
d. Why might a financial manager prefer the plan of part c to those of parts a and b?

15. **(Stock dividend)** A company that pays a $2 per share cash dividend has decided to pay a 15% stock dividend. Currently there are 20 million shares outstanding, with a price of $40 each.

a. How many new shares will the company issue?
b. What will happen to the company's share price if investors do not change the total market value of the company's stock?
c. What will happen to the cash dividend of an investor who owns 100 shares (prior to the stock dividend) if the per share cash dividend is reduced proportionally to the stock dividend?
d. What will happen to the cash dividend of an investor who owns 100 shares (prior to the stock dividend) if the per share cash dividend is unchanged?

16. **(Stock dividend)** A company that pays a $1 per share cash dividend has decided to pay a 20% stock dividend. Currently there are 8 million shares outstanding, with a price of $60 each.

a. How many new shares will the company issue?
b. What will happen to the company's share price if investors do not change the total market value of the company's stock?
c. What will happen to the cash dividend of an investor who owns 500 shares (prior to the stock dividend) if the per share cash dividend is reduced proportionally to the stock dividend?
d. What will happen to the cash dividend of an investor who owns 500 shares (prior to the stock dividend) if the per share cash dividend is unchanged?

17. **(Stock split)** A company has decided to split its stock since its share price has reached $140. Currently there are 5 million common shares outstanding. In the most recent year, the company earned $5 per share and paid a dividend of $1. Calculate EPS, DPS, share price, and the number of shares outstanding after the split assuming the split is:

a. 2 for 1
b. 3 for 1
c. 4 for 1
d. 5 for 1

18. **(Stock split)** A company has decided to engineer a reverse split of its stock since its share price has fallen to $5.00. Currently there are 10 million common shares outstanding. In the most recent year, the company earned $0.25 per share and paid a dividend of $0.10. Calculate EPS, DPS, share price, and the number of shares outstanding after the split assuming the split is:

a. 1 for 2
b. 1 for 3
c. 1 for 5
d. 1 for 10

19. **(Stock repurchase)** A company has announced it will repurchase 10% of its outstanding shares. Currently there are 8 million shares outstanding with market price of $30.

a. Calculate the company's current market value, the number of shares the company will repurchase, and the number of shares that will remain outstanding.
b. If the company repurchases the shares at $30, what will happen to the worth of an investor who owns 500 shares and elects to sell? elects not to sell?
c. If the company repurchases the shares at $28, what will happen to the worth of an investor who owns 500 shares and elects to sell? elects not to sell?
d. If the company repurchases the shares at $32, what will happen to the worth of an investor who owns 500 shares and elects to sell? elects not to sell?

20. **(Stock repurchase)** A company has announced that it will repurchase 20% of its outstanding shares. Currently there are 6 million shares outstanding, with a market price of $45.

a. Calculate the company's current market value, the number of shares the company will repurchase, and the number of shares that will remain outstanding.

b. If the company repurchases the shares at $45, what will happen to the worth of an investor who owns 200 shares and elects to sell? elects not to sell?

c. If the company repurchases the shares at $43, what will happen to the worth of an investor who owns 200 shares and elects to sell? elects not to sell?

d. If the company repurchases the shares at $47, what will happen to the worth of an investor who owns 200 shares and elects to sell? elects not to sell?

PART VII SOURCES OF FINANCING

In Part VII we survey the various financial instruments used by businesses to raise funds. Our goal is to mix description and analysis and to demonstrate that the same time-value techniques we have been using throughout the book remain fully applicable to financial instruments.

Chapter 18 looks at the process of financial planning and budgeting. After introducing specific-item forecasting, we explore the percentage-of-sales method through an extended example. Appendixes 18A–D cover additional forecasting relationships and formulas and extend the chapter examples.

Chapter 19 introduces the financial markets and the institutions that operate within them. We discuss the roles of these markets including how new securities are brought to market and traded. We also discuss the regulatory environment and identify relevant legislation and regulatory bodies.

Chapter 20 explores short-term debt. We study the costs and characteristics of trade credit, accruals, and loans and describe how commercial paper and Euronotes have become important competitors to bank lending.

Chapter 21 studies intermediate- and long-term debt. We discuss fixed and floating interest rates and how caps, collars, and swaps can be used to reduce rate exposure. Then we examine term debt, leases, bonds, and floating rate notes, which are further explored in Appendixes 21A–C.

Chapter 22 examines equity financing. After identifying alternative ways to view a company's equity, we look at the characteristics of preferred and common stock. We also describe warrants and convertible securities.

CHAPTER 18
PREDICTING FINANCIAL NEEDS

Carol May left the vice president's office with a puzzled look on her face. She had been asked to prepare an analysis of how much financing her firm, the Jefferson Company, would need to raise in the financial markets in the coming year. She was to present her conclusions at a meeting of the executive committee in two weeks' time.

At first Carol thought the answer was obvious—the company would need enough money to pay for the construction of new plant and the purchase of equipment that had been ordered for delivery in the coming year. But the more she thought about it, the more uncertain she became. There were other things the company had to pay for: labor, materials, operating costs, and so on. The Jefferson Company would surely need additional money to pay for those items. On the other hand, the company was expected to earn profits next year; some of this money ought to be available to help cover the firm's costs. Conceivably, not all of the firm's funding needs would have to come from outside sources. But Carol was sure this was only a part of the story. Perhaps there were other money flows she was overlooking.

As she returned to her desk, one thing was clear in Carol's mind. She would need a systematic way to organize the firm's resources and needs if she were to determine accurately the amount of financing her company required.

Few business firms are precisely self-sufficient, generating exactly as much cash as they need to spend. Many companies, especially those that are young and growing, need to acquire assets faster than they can generate the cash to pay for them. These businesses go to the financial markets to raise the additional funds they require. Other companies—especially older, more mature firms—find they have become "**cash cows,**" with little or no need for outside financing.

cash cow—a firm that regularly generates more cash than it needs for operations and growth

To know which type of company the Jefferson Company is, Carol will have to study the firm's growth rate as well as its economic and financial structure. In this chapter we will look at techniques Carol can use to help her company plan for its future financial needs.[1]

Key Points You Should Learn from This Chapter

After reading this chapter you should be able to:

- Describe the functions and limitations of planning and budgeting, including financial planning.
- Recognize when specific-item forecasting is an appropriate financial planning technique.
- Identify financial statement accounts that relate to sales and establish those relationships.
- Use the percentage-of-sales technique to project a firm's financial statements.
- Determine a company's external financing needs and calculate the limit to its ability to grow using internal financing.
- Interpret pro-forma financial statements.

[1] **Observation:** The same concepts also apply to individuals. When you are young, you typically need to buy more assets than you can self-finance, and so you borrow. As you get older, your income rises but your need for assets declines until, eventually, you can repay your debts and accumulate money for your later years. As you read this chapter, you might find it interesting to apply the planning techniques that we discuss to your personal financial situation and begin a financial plan for yourself.

Introductory Concepts—The Role of Planning

All successful businesses plan for the future. Without effective planning, a firm drifts from day to day with no direction and a very low probability of survival. Planning significantly increases a firm's chances of success.

1. Planning

Planning begins with a corporate mission statement, a broad statement of purpose intended to underlie all the firm's activities. Mission statements frequently include beliefs about ethics, quality, the worth of people, and other fundamental convictions to guide all personal interactions and decision making. Without a clear and well-defined statement of mission and beliefs, a firm's employees are left to decide for themselves what actions are consistent with the interests and intentions of the firm. They are forced to base decisions on their own or others' subjective impressions of managements' philosophy or to give up trying to understand the firm's intentions and resign themselves to doing whatever seems to work. They very often end up working at cross purposes relative to others who make differing interpretations of the firm's mission.

The second step in planning is to focus on the firm's customers and other stakeholders: to identify them and to understand their expectations for the products and services they receive. Remember that a critical day-to-day goal of any firm is to exceed customer expectations. The firm cannot do this if it does not know who its customers are and what they want.

Once an organization has identified its goals and has learned from its customers what it takes to exceed their expectations, it devises a strategy for achieving them. To be effective, the strategy must place the firm in alignment—that is, consistent—with its internal culture and strengths and also with its environment. Next, the company develops operating plans consistent with its strategy and designed to move the firm toward its objectives. As with all aspects of the firm, strategies and plans must be continuously revised and improved as new information becomes available and as the firm and its environment change.

Traditionally, planning has been seen as the first, and most important, job of the manager.[2] Planning helps the organization to establish its goals and identifies the role that each unit of the organization is to play in achieving them. It sets activities in motion at the right time and in the right scale. It identifies the individuals within the organization who will do each task. It establishes benchmarks against which to test results. It enforces an objective rationality on the activities of the firm.

2. Budgeting

budget—a time-oriented statement of the financial resources allocated to carry out an organization's activities

A key tool of the planning process is the **budget,** the translation of the organization's plan into its dollar impacts. The common denominator of money forces the

[2] **Elaboration:** The other traditional roles of the manager have been organizing (establishing the structure of the organization, delegating and coordinating work, dealing with internal conflict), leading (providing motivation and reward, developing employees), and controlling (testing actual results against budgets, auditing performance, making changes).

plan to be consistent with the accounting system and encourages managers to focus efforts on maximizing financial value. Budgets divide the firm's plan into time units, permitting their use as performance standards. Managers use budgets to guide their planning process, to allocate resources, and to test performance against the plan. Deviation from budget is often taken as a signal that something is wrong and that corrective action needs to be taken.

As companies adopt modern management practices, emphasizing customer-focused quality, planning continues to be a necessary activity but the planning process tends to change. It becomes less of a top-down activity—a set of instructions from the boss—and more of a team-oriented one. Organization members at all levels participate earlier and more fully than they did in the past, as managers attempt to take advantage of the knowledge of those near the "bottom of the traditional organization chart."

Although necessary for managing an organization, budgets have long been recognized as having some unintended, and often damaging, side-effects. Individuals may be penalized for not making their budgets, even though the shortfall is due to events or conditions over which they have no control. Above-average performers often achieve their budget goals with ease and then produce no more. They fear they will be criticized as "rate-busters" by their peers or will be forced to achieve a higher budget next year. Below-average performers may produce poor-quality output as they rush or cheat to achieve the targets in their budgets. When compensation is tied to performance against budget, organizational members are encouraged to become competitive instead of cooperative, failing to assist each other in reaching the firm's goals or even interfering with each others' efforts.

Recently, increased understanding of quality-management concepts has called attention to another type of problem with budgets, which only a few managers were fully aware of in the past. Budgets can lead managers to overreact to apparent changes in the environment. Some deviation from budget is inevitable: there is variation in the world, and it is impossible to predict the future with certainty. As a result, the firm will rarely, if ever, perform exactly on budget. However, it is wrong for management to intervene in response to every variation.

As we noted in Chapter 13, an important part of managing is to separate special causes of variation from common causes of variation. Common causes produce problems that recur many times, for example, untrained workers who perform poorly day after day. Management should work on common causes of variation, studying them and removing them (in this case, by developing and using appropriate training programs).

Special causes, on the other hand, are one-time events which will not recur on a regular basis—for example, normally high-performing workers who do a poor job on a specific day when they are ill. Special causes deserve unique responses (in this case, perhaps, encouraging sick workers to go home for the day). There is no benefit to changing the firm in response to something that will not happen regularly or perhaps ever again. A management that is overly concerned with budgets as performance targets is susceptible to **tampering,** making changes in processes and systems in response to special causes. Such changes will tend to make the firm's performance worse, not better.

tampering—modifying a system in response to special causes of variation, further destabilizing the system's performance

3. Financial Planning

Financial planning is an important component of the firm's overall planning effort. To be effective in carrying out its operating plans, the firm must obtain and deploy financial resources as needed. Good financial planning permits the finance function to provide the appropriate money resources to the rest of the firm.

Tasks of financial planning Financial planning is designed to accomplish six tasks, as tabulated in Figure 18.1: (1) make assumptions explicit and shared, (2) identify actions consistent with health, (3) identify needed financial resources, (4) provide guidelines for external financing, (5) be a benchmark for results, and (6) assist in communicating with stakeholders.

1. *Make assumptions explicit and shared.* Financial planning forces assumptions about the firm's financial future to be made explicit and shared throughout the company. Arranging for wide participation in developing the plan improves its quality by separating realistic assumptions from the unrealistic ones. It also contributes to a shared assessment of the firm's prospects and the steps necessary to achieve success; from a shared assessment, organization members can derive a shared commitment toward achieving the firm's goals.
2. *Identify healthy actions.* Financial planning identifies company actions that are consistent with financial health, and vice-versa. By locating courses of action that have a high probability of leading to financial success, financial planning provides important input to management's choices. By identifying impending financial problems, and often nonfinancial problems as well, it permits management to address issues early, before they have a serious effect on the firm. In addition, management can develop contingency plans to handle alternative economic scenarios.
3. *Identify financial resources.* Financial planning identifies the financial resources required for the firm to carry out its plans. In particular it identifies: (a) how much money the firm will need, (b) whether the money can be generated internally or will have to come from sources external to the firm, and (c) the timing of the firm's needs.
4. *Guide financing choices.* Financial planning provides guidelines in the choice of external funding sources. If the firm requires outside money, it might have

FIGURE 18.1
Six tasks of financial planning. Done well, financial planning helps the financial manager support the organization's business activities.

1. Make assumptions explicit and shared throughout the organization.
2. Identify actions consistent (and inconsistent) with company health.
3. Identify financial resources needed to carry out plans.
4. Provide guidelines for external financing choices.
5. Serve as a benchmark against which to compare results.
6. Help communicate with stakeholders.

Cartoon by Henry Martin

the luxury of choosing from a variety of available sources. Financial planning generates some of the data necessary to make those choices.

5. *Benchmark results.* Financial planning serves as a benchmark against which to compare the firm's actual results. Of course, it is unrealistic to expect that actual performance will agree perfectly with the financial plan—too many unpredictable things happen. However, deviations from the forecast provide new information to help management understand the forces acting on the firm and to improve the planning process.
6. *Communicate with stakeholders.* Financial planning helps the firm communicate with its stakeholders, who must be partners in achieving the firm's goals.

Parts of the financial plan The financial plan consists of several parts, including (1) the long-run financial plan, (2) the capital budget, and (3) the operating or cash budget.

1. *The long-run financial plan:* This is a look at the firm's financial needs over the next several years. Five years is a commonly used planning horizon. The long-run financial plan is designed to identify major financial trends the firm will face and permit an early start at large-scale, long-term financing.
2. *The capital budget:* This is an analysis of available long-term investment opportunities, testing each to see if it adds financial value to the firm.
3. *The operating or cash budget:* This is a short-run, more detailed look at the firm's money needs, usually over the next year. It is normally done on a monthly basis, although a shorter period (weekly or daily) might be appropriate if the insights from greater detail outweigh the costs of producing the more extensive plan.

pro-forma financial statement—a financial statement that projects a firm's condition or operating results into the future

Pro-forma financial statements A primary device used in financial planning is the preparation of **pro-forma financial statements.** These projected statements give management insight into many of the "what-if" questions they need to explore. They show what the firm would look like under each of the economic and competitive scenarios forecasted. They permit management to see the results of different decisions it might make. With the arrival of personal computers and spreadsheet programs, it is easier than ever to generate pro-forma statements.

Specific-Item Forecasting

specific-item forecasting—a forecasting technique in which each account on a firm's financial statements is projected without reference to the other accounts

A first strategy for forecasting financial variables is to project each financial statement account independent of the other accounts. This approach is called **specific-item forecasting.** Each account is studied individually to determine the factors that produce its value. A relationship is then derived relating the account to its causal factors.

Example

Establishing a Forecasting Relationship

Luz Iluminata has been asked to forecast the cost of lighting a building. Looking at past records, she discovers that lighting costs consist of: (1) the cost of electricity, (2) the cost of light bulbs, and (3) the cost of replacing blown-out bulbs. In turn, these costs depend upon the number of bulbs in use; the life of each bulb; the power consumption of each bulb; and the prices of electricity, light bulbs; and maintenance services. Luz combines her findings into a formula relating lighting cost to the causal variables.

Specific-item forecasting is particularly appropriate for a firm whose financial statement accounts are not closely related to one another.

Example

Deciding to Use Specific-Item Forecasting

Helen Leonia runs a real-estate company that owns and rents space in a number of office buildings. As she examines the accounts on her income statement, she discovers:

Line Item	Depends on:
Rental revenue	Occupancy rate
Depreciation	Historical cost, GAAP rules
Maintenance	Level of service, age of buildings
Repairs	Type of tenant, weather
Salaries	Needs of management
Interest	Debt level, interest rates
Taxes	Net income, tax law

Helen concludes that specific-item forecasting is appropriate for her income statement since the accounts do not appear to be related to one another.

The advantage of specific-item forecasting is its flexibility. We can search for the relationship that best explains each variable we wish to forecast. The disadvantage is that we ignore relationships among the variables that, if taken into account, might improve our forecasting accuracy.

Forecasts That Relate to Sales

In Appendix 4D we saw that many financial ratios contain sales in their calculation. This is because the value of so many accounts depends on sales (and vice-versa). We can take advantage of this observation to improve our financial statement forecasting. If we believe that an account relates to sales, then it makes sense to study that relationship and incorporate it into our projections. By doing so we increase the internal consistency of our forecasts and hence the likelihood that they will be good predictors of the future.

Example

Accounts That Relate to Sales

Whenever the Washington Company makes a sale, it makes two related accounting entries. The first debits "cash" or "accounts receivable" and credits "sales" to record revenue. The second debits "cost of goods sold" and credits "inventory" to record expense. As a result, the balances of the cash, accounts receivable, inventory, and cost of goods sold accounts change whenever sales changes. They are related to sales.

While we might consider relating accounts to some other variable, none works as well as sales. Companies are in business to deliver products and services to their customers; sales demand is the outside force to which the firm must respond. A firm that faces high demand is justified in spending to acquire resources to produce additional products and services. A firm with declining demand is best advised to limit its spending on existing activities, or costs will exceed revenue and the firm will lose money. Rather, it must refocus its attention to identifying and meeting changing customer needs. To survive and prosper, the company must match its resources and commitments to the demand from its customers.

Of course, not everything relates to sales. Some accounts relate to other causal factors. For example, interest expense depends on the amount of money a firm has borrowed and the interest rate it must pay, neither of which will change automatically as sales changes. Other accounts, such as accumulated depreciation, depend primarily on history and accounting rules. Still others vary only if management chooses to change them—for example, bonds payable or common stock. We must be careful not to find connections to sales that do not exist.

For a forecast based on sales to be useful, we must: (1) start with a good sales forecast, (2) correctly identify the accounts that relate to sales, and (3) accurately establish the relationship of those accounts to sales.

1. Start with a Good Sales Forecast

Since so many accounts relate to sales, a good independent sales forecast is critical if the firm's financial projections are to be useful. A small error in the sales forecast can easily be magnified into a large error in the firm's pro-forma statements.

2. Identify Accounts That Relate to Sales

To produce a forecast containing relationships to sales, we must separate the firm's accounts into two broad categories: those that relate to sales and those that do not.

It is useful to ask three questions to help make this separation. First, *why is the firm spending this particular amount of money?* If the money is going to purchase a resource that is intimately associated with the production or sales process, and that needs to be acquired only if production or sales takes place, this amount relates to sales.

Example

Identifying an Amount as Related to Sales

Adams Company uses a just-in-time inventory system, buying production materials only when it is ready to produce and sell. It concludes that the cost of materials is closely related to sales.

On the other hand, if the money is going for a resource not associated with the production or sales process, which would be acquired regardless of the firm's level of sales, this amount does not relate to sales.

Example

Identifying an Amount as Not Related to Sales

Adams Company identifies the cost of power for heat and light in their office building as not related to sales since the amount they spend varies with utility rates and not with their volume of business.

Second, *what is the time horizon of the account?* Some assets, a plant for example, take time to acquire or to sell. In the short-run,[3] some costs are fixed simply because the firm cannot change them fast enough, even though it might wish to do so. In the long-run, by definition, no costs are fixed.

Example

Identifying an Amount as Not Related to Sales Due to Time Horizon

One of Adams Company's product lines has become obsolete. Sales go to zero immediately, but it will take the firm two years to dispose of related machinery. The book value of this machinery will not fully respond to sales until two years have passed.

Third, *how will management respond to changes in sales?* If management views a change in sales as a temporary phenomenon, it will likely respond with temporary or variable resources. However, if it perceives a change in sales as permanent, management might commit to additional fixed resources.

[3] **Elaboration:** You may recall that the economic definition of *short-run* is that period of time during which the firm faces constraints on its ability to change and cannot adjust its resources as desired. By contrast, the *long-run* is defined as that period of time long enough so that the firm faces no limitations on its choice or use of resources.

Example

How a Management Decision Can Determine if a Cost Is Related to Sales

Adams Company is experiencing a 20% increase in orders this month, requiring additional usage of production machinery. Management could lease time on another firm's machinery, making the cost vary with sales. Alternatively, management could purchase new machinery, fixing the new cost independent of sales. Whether the additional cost is variable or fixed will depend on the choice management makes.

In Chapter 4 we saw that income statement accounts that change with sales are identified as *variable costs;* examples are: direct production labor, materials used in production, and commissions and bonuses based on sales. Income statement accounts that do *not* change with sales—such as production overhead, the base level of administrative salaries, and interest costs—are identified as *fixed costs.*[4]

spontaneous account—a balance sheet account whose value changes with sales without the need for specific management action

There is a comparable classification for the balance sheet. Accounts on the balance sheet that change with sales are termed **spontaneous accounts.** This is because their value responds to a change in sales automatically, or "spontaneously," without the need for specific management action. In general, the following accounts are spontaneous:

- Assets that support the firm's operations—operating cash, accounts receivable, inventories, prepaids, plant and equipment.
- Trade and institutional liabilities—accounts payable, accrued payables (wages payable, taxes payable).
- Earned equity—the income component of retained earnings.

discretionary account—a balance sheet account whose value does not change with sales but rather is set by a management decision

Balance sheet accounts that do *not* change with sales are called **discretionary accounts** since their value is solely up to the judgment or "discretion" of management. In general, the following accounts are discretionary:

- Assets unrelated to the firm's operations—marketable securities apart from the operating cash balance, investments in other companies.
- Contractual liabilities—bank notes payable, commercial paper, leases, term loans, bonds payable.
- Managed equity—common and preferred stock, treasury stock, the dividend component of retained earnings.

3. Establish the Relationship to Sales

Once an account is identified as varying with sales, we must specify the form of variation. While many relationships are possible, it is useful to develop the concepts of this chapter assuming that the most simple relationship holds: all ac-

---

[4] **Cross-reference:** Variable and fixed costs are introduced on pp. 81–82.

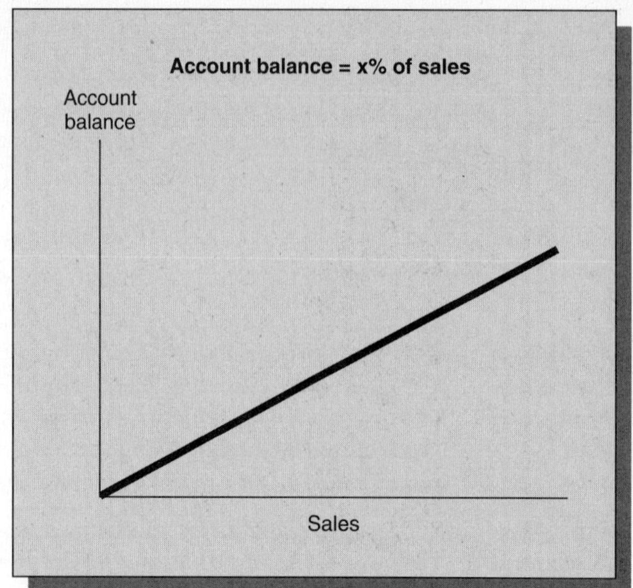

FIGURE 18.2
The percentage-of-sales relationship. The balance of an account is projected to remain a given fraction of sales.

counts that change with sales do so in a strictly linear fashion. This is the *percentage-of-sales relationship*. It is illustrated graphically in Figure 18.2.

Although percentage of sales is clearly a simplification in many cases,[5] it provides a basic forecast that is typically quite useful. In particular, if sales is difficult to project, the use of more complex relationships may not materially improve the quality of the forecast. In addition, percentage of sales gives us a forecasting relationship that is easy to understand and build upon. For these reasons, percentage of sales is widely used, both within companies and by banks and other stakeholders who analyze the firm.

The Percentage-of-Sales Method Illustrated

The percentage-of-sales method consists of seven steps:

1. *Forecast sales.* Obtain a good sales forecast.
2. *Classify accounts.* Identify the variable and spontaneous accounts, the ones that vary with sales. Also identify the fixed and discretionary accounts as well as accounts that are connected to some other variable.
3. *Determine relationships.* Calculate the percentage-of-sales relationship for all variable and spontaneous accounts. For accounts that vary with some other variable, obtain that relationship as well.

[5] **Cross-reference:** See Appendix 18A for a discussion of other possible relationships.

4. *Project new values.* Calculate the anticipated value of each variable and spontaneous account by applying its percentage of sales to the new sales number. Also determine the value of those accounts that vary with other variables by applying the appropriate relationship determined in Step 2.
5. *Fill in the pro-forma income statement and balance sheet.* Insert the new values for all accounts calculated in Step 3. Transfer the values of all fixed and discretionary items unchanged, making the forecast independent of discretionary management actions. Use projected net income and dividends to calculate end-of-year retained earnings.
6. *Force the pro-forma balance sheet to balance.* Since each account is forecasted individually, we do not adhere to double-entry bookkeeping, and it is almost certain that the pro-forma balance sheet will not yet balance. If liabilities plus equity exceed assets, we learn that the firm will bring in more resources than it has plans to use, and we balance the statement by adding a new asset called "excess cash." If assets exceed liabilities plus equity, we learn that the firm needs more assets than it has money for; in this case, we balance the statement by adding a new item on the right-hand side called "external financing needed."
7. *Produce the pro-forma cash flow statement.* Rearrange the numbers on the pro-forma income statement and on the beginning-of-year and end-of-year pro-forma balance sheets.

We illustrate the percentage-of-sales method by following Carol May as she forecasts the 1995 pro-forma financial statements for the Jefferson Company. The numbers have purposely been kept simple to focus on the process. Since we last left Carol, in the introduction to this chapter, she has read up on financial planning and forecasting and has chosen to use the percentage-of-sales method for her task. Carol begins with the financial statements in Jefferson's 1994 annual report:

THE JEFFERSON COMPANY
Income Statement
For the year ended December 31, 1994

Sales		$2,500
– Cost of goods sold		1,738
Gross profit		762
– Operating expenses	$550	
– Depreciation	40	
		590
EBIT		172
– Interest expense		18
EBT		154
– Tax expense		54
EAT		$ 100
– Dividends		33
Addition to retained earnings		$ 67

THE JEFFERSON COMPANY Balance Sheet December 31, 1994			
Cash	$ 100	Accounts payable	$ 150
Marketable securities	50	Accrued payables	200
Accounts receivable	150	Bonds payable	200
Inventories	200	Common stock	150
Plant, net	500	Retained earnings	300
Total assets	$1,000	Total liability and equity	$1,000

Carol follows the seven steps we discussed above:

Step 1—Obtain a Good Sales Forecast

Carol talks to her peers in marketing. Together they review the state of the economy and the competitive picture for the company's products. They conclude that the most likely number for 1995 sales is $3,000.

Step 2—Classify Accounts

Carol studies her company's accounts carefully. She examines past relationships and asks questions about the role of each account. She concludes:

a. Fixed costs—$175 of operating expense and all $40 of depreciation expense will not vary with sales.

b. Variable costs—all of cost of goods sold and the remainder of operating expense ($375 in 1994) will vary with sales.

c. Spontaneous accounts—cash, accounts receivable, inventories, net plant, accounts payable, and accrued payables will change with sales.

d. Discretionary accounts—marketable securities, bonds payable, and common stock will not change with sales.

Carol also discovers the following:

e. Bonds payable—$50 of the $200 of bonds payable falls due on December 31, 1995. The bonds carry a 9% interest coupon. (Carol notes that this explains the interest expense of $18 in 1994 since 9% of $200 = $18.)

f. Income taxes—the firm pays taxes on income at a flat 35% rate. (Carol notes that this explains the tax expense of $54 in 1994 since 35% of $154 = $54.)

g. Dividends—management's announced policy is to target a payout ratio of 1/3 of earnings after tax. (Carol notes that this explains the dividend of $33 in 1994 since 1/3 of $100 = $33).

Step 3—Determine Relationships

Carol studies the relationship of each variable cost and spontaneous account to sales. She concludes that 1994 was a representative year and, therefore, the relationships in the 1994 financial statements are appropriate to use. Using 1994 data, she calculates:

a. Variable costs:

Cost of goods sold/sales	= $1,738/$2,500	= 69.52%
Operating expense/sales	= $ 375/$2,500	= 15.00%

b. Spontaneous accounts:

Cash/sales	= $ 100/$2,500	= 4.00%
Accounts receivable/sales	= $ 150/$2,500	= 6.00%
Inventories/sales	= $ 200/$2,500	= 8.00%
Net plant/sales	= $ 500/$2,500	= 20.00%
Accounts payable/sales	= $ 150/$2,500	= 6.00%
Accrued payables/sales	= $ 200/$2,500	= 8.00%

Step 4—Project New Values

Carol next uses the sales forecast from Step 1 and the relationships from Step 3 to project 1995 values:

a. Variable costs:

Cost of goods sold = 69.52% of sales = 69.52% × $3,000 = $ 2,086

Variable operating expense = 15.00% of sales = 15.00% × $3,000 = $ 450

(Therefore, total operating expense = the variable component of $450 plus the fixed component of $175 = $625.)

b. Spontaneous accounts:

Cash	= 4.00% of sales	= 4.00% × $3,000	= $120
Accounts receivable	= 6.00% of sales	= 6.00% × $3,000	= $180
Inventories	= 8.00% of sales	= 8.00% × $3,000	= $240
Net plant	= 20.00% of sales	= 20.00% × $3,000	= $600
Accounts payable	= 6.00% of sales	= 6.00% × $3,000	= $180
Accrued payables	= 8.00% of sales	= 8.00% × $3,000	= $240

Carol also uses the other information she has discovered to project the following:

c. Bonds payable—since $50 will be repaid in 1995, the end-of-year balance should be $200 − $50 = $150. However, since the repayment will not take place until December, the balance of debt throughout the year will remain $200 and interest expense should again be $18—just as in 1994.

Step 5—Fill in the Pro-Forma Statements

Carol now compiles her projections into a pro-forma income statement and balance sheet. She uses the same format as was used in 1994.

THE JEFFERSON COMPANY Pro-Forma Income Statement For the year ending December 31, 1995			Data obtained from:
Sales		$3,000	Step 1—forecast
− Cost of goods sold		2,086	Step 4a—projection
Gross profit		914	
− Operating expenses	$625		Step 4a—projection
− Depreciation	40		Step 2a—fixed cost
		665	
EBIT		249	
− Interest expense		18	Step 4c—projection
EBT		231	
− Tax expense (35%)		81	Step 2f—calculation
EAT		$ 150	
− Dividends		50	Step 2g—calculation
Addition to retained earnings		$ 100	

From the statement of retained earnings at the bottom of the pro-forma income statement, Carol discovers that $100 will be added to retained earnings in 1995. This will increase the retained earnings balance to $300 + $100 = $400.

THE JEFFERSON COMPANY Pro-Forma Balance Sheet December 31, 1995		Data obtained from:
Cash	$ 120	Step 4b—projection
Marketable securities	50	Step 2d—discretionary
Accounts receivable	180	Step 4b—projection
Inventories	240	Step 4b—projection
Plant, net	600	Step 4b—projection
Total assets	$1,190	
Accounts payable	$ 180	Step 4b—projection
Accrued payables	240	Step 4b—projection
Bonds payable	150	Step 4c—projection
Common stock	150	Step 2d—discretionary
Retained earnings	400	Step 5—pro-forma income statement
	$1,120	
External Financing Needed	70	Step 6—force a balance
Total liability and equity	$1,190	

Step 6—Force the Pro-Forma Balance Sheet to Balance

Carol's balance sheet does not balance! Her projection shows that by December 1995, Jefferson Company will require $1,190 of assets to support sales of $3,000, an increase of $190 from December 1994. But spontaneous sources will provide only $120 of new money. (Accounts payable will increase by $30, accrued payables will increase by $40, and retained earnings will increase by $100, for a total of $170 of new financing. However, the firm will have to use $50 of this to refund its bonds payable. This will leave it with a net spontaneous increase in financing of $120, raising the liability-equity side of its balance sheet to $1,120.)

external financing needed—the amount of financing a firm must raise from outside sources to acquire the assets necessary to support its forecasted level of sales

Carol forces the balance sheet to balance by adding a "plug figure" to the side with the smaller amount, in this case the liability-equity side. This is the **external financing needed (EFN),** the financing the firm must raise from outside sources. For sales to grow to $3,000, the firm must acquire $190 of new assets. To do so it will need $190 of new financing, yet internal operations will only produce $120 of that amount. The extra $70 must come from outside, or external, sources.[6]

Carol is careful to write the EFN of $70 into her pro-forma balance sheet as a separate line and not to include it in any other account. Management must still decide how to raise the $70, and Carol does not want to assume any decision before it is made.

Although Carol found that her firm will need external funds in 1995, this is not always the case. As we will see in the next section, EFN typically comes with rapidly growing sales. Had Carol's sales forecast been much lower, she would have projected a smaller growth in assets, and spontaneous liabilities and equity would be more than sufficient to pay for this. The plug figure to make the balance sheet balance would now be placed on the asset side and would be labeled **excess cash.** Now, management's decision would be how best to use this cash which is not needed to support sales.

excess cash—the amount of spontaneous financing produced by a firm over and above what it needs to acquire the assets necessary to support its sales forecast

Step 7—Produce the Pro-Forma Cash Flow Statement

Carol can now produce a cash flow statement by rearranging the data of her pro-forma income statement and balance sheet:[7]

THE JEFFERSON COMPANY
Pro-forma Statement of Cash Flows
For the year ending December 31, 1995

		Data obtained from:
CASH FLOW FROM OPERATIONS		
Received from customers	$2,970	Pro-forma statements[8]
Paid to suppliers and employees	(2,681)	Pro-forma statements[9]
Interest paid	(18)	New income statement
Income taxes paid	(81)	New income statement

[6] **Observation:** The firm could also use some or all of its $50 of marketable securities to meet this need.

[7] **Tip:** If you feel the need for a review of the relationship among these three statements, see your introductory accounting textbook.

[8] **Calculation:** This is the projected sales of $3,000 less the $30 projected increase in accounts receivable—sales that will not be collected in 1995.

[9] **Calculation:** This is the projected cost of goods sold plus operating expenses ($2,086 + 625 = $2,711) plus the $40 projected increase in inventories—an additional payment—less the $70 projected increase in accounts and accrued payables—expenses that will not be paid in 1995.

New cash provided by operating activities	190	
CASH FLOWS FROM INVESTMENTS		
Payments for purchase of property, plant, and equipment	(140)	Both balance sheets[10]
CASH FLOWS FROM FINANCING		
External financing	70	New balance sheet
Repayment of long-term debt	(50)	Both balance sheets[11]
Dividends paid	(50)	New income statement
Net cash used by financing activities	(30)	
NET INCREASE (DECREASE) IN CASH	20	
Cash and equivalents, beginning of year	150	
Cash and equivalents, end of year	$ 170	
RECONCILIATION OF NET INCOME TO CASH PROVIDED BY OPERATIONS		
Net income	$ 150	New income statement
Add back: Depreciation	40	New income statement
Subtract increase in:		
Accounts receivable	(30)	Both balance sheets
Inventories	(40)	Both balance sheets
Add increase in		
Accounts payable	30	Both balance sheets
Accrued payables	40	Both balance sheets
Net cash provided by operations	$ 190	

Relating EFN to a Company's Growth Rate

sensitivity analysis—a test to examine how the result of an analysis will vary with changes in inputs

Carol used the best sales forecast she could get as the basis for her projection. Yet it is quite likely that Jefferson Company's sales in 1995 will not be $3,000. For her forecast to be useful, Carol should perform a **sensitivity analysis,** testing how the results of her forecast will vary for other values of sales. This will produce a range of possible outcomes so that management can plan for reasonable contingencies.

EFN relationship—a formula which relates external financing needed to growth in sales

1. The EFN Relationship

Since Carol is particularly interested in the possible range of EFN, she can take advantage of the **EFN relationship.** This formula captures the structural charac-

[10] **Calculation:** Plant is now $500. During 1995, depreciation will be $40, reducing plant to $460. If the account is to go up to $600, $140 of new plant must be purchased during 1995. The following T-account summarizes this:

Plant, net

Beginning Balance	$500		
Buy new plant	140	Depreciation	$40
Ending balance	$600		

[11] **Calculation:** Subtract the beginning-of-year balance sheet number from the forecasted end-of-year number.

teristics of the firm and calculates the external financing needed for any level of sales.[12]

$$EFN = [P - R] + [a - \ell - m(1 - d)]\ \Delta S$$

The variables[13] have the following meaning (the Jefferson Company's numbers are in parentheses):

S = sales last year ($2500)

ΔS = **change** to sales forecasted ($3,000 − $2,500 = $500)—we will leave this as a variable to make the relationship apply to any value of additional sales

P = **principal** of financing that must be repaid this year ($50)

R = **retained** earnings increase if sales does not change this year ($66.67, just as in 1994—note that this number is rounded to $67.00 on the income statement on p. 655.)

a = "spontaneous **asset** percentage," the firm's total spontaneous assets as a percentage of sales (4% for cash + 6% for accounts receivable + 8% for inventories + 20% for net plant = 38%)

ℓ = "spontaneous **liability** percentage," the firm's total spontaneous liabilities as a percentage of sales (6% for accounts payable + 8% for accrued payables = 14%)

m = net **margin**, the profit from each incremental dollar of sales (10.06% [14])

d = **dividend** payout ratio (1/3)

The EFN relationship has two terms. The first term, [P − R], gives the need for external funds if sales do not change. It consists of two parts:

---

[12] **Cross-reference:** The EFN relationship is derived in Appendix 18B.

[13] **Notation:** We continue to use the convention that a capital letter stands for a money (dollar) value while a lower-case letter represents a rate or percentage.

[14] **Calculation:** We obtain a value for the variable m by completing a pro-forma income statement for $1.00 of incremental sales:x

Sales	$1.0000
−Incremental variable costs:	
Cost of goods sold	.6952*
Operating expenses	.1500*
−Incremental fixed costs	0.0000
Incremental EBIT	0.1548
−Incremental interest expense	0.0000
Incremental EBT	0.1548
−Incremental tax expense (35%)	0.0542
Incremental EAT	$0.1006

m = Incremental EAT/incremental sales = $0.1006/$1.0000 = 10.06%

* These are the percentages-of-sales numbers Carol calculated in Step 3a of her forecast.

P—money to repay debt that is falling due, less

R—the contribution to retained earnings which comes from maintaining the same level of sales.

The second term, $[a - \ell - m(1 - d)]\Delta S$, gives the additional need for external funds if the firm's sales grow. It equals zero when ΔS, the forecasted growth in sales, equals zero. ΔS multiplies the term in the square brackets which consists of three parts:

a—money to buy new assets to support each dollar of additional sales, less

ℓ—the increase in liabilities coming from each dollar of additional sales, less

m(1 − d)—the increase in retained earnings coming from each dollar of additional sales, consisting of the incremental profit less incremental dividends paid.

For the Jefferson Company:

$$\begin{aligned} EFN &= [50 - 66.67] + [.3800 - .1400 - .1006(2/3)]\ \Delta S \\ &= [50 - 66.67] + [.3800 - .1400 - .0671]\ \Delta S \\ &= \underline{\underline{-16.67 + .1729\ \Delta S}} \end{aligned}$$

If the Jefferson Company's sales remain at \$2,500 in 1995, ($\Delta S = 0$), EFN is −\$16.67. This means Jefferson will not need external funds. Rather, the company will generate \$16.67 of excess cash, consisting of \$66.67 of new retained earnings less \$50 paid to retire debt. Should Jefferson's sales grow, each dollar of sales growth requires Jefferson to buy \$0.38 of new assets. But internal sources do not provide sufficient money to pay for this: spontaneous liabilities provide \$0.14 while incremental retained earnings adds another \$0.0671, for a total of \$0.2071. Jefferson will need to find \$0.1729 of external incremental financing. Note that Carol's forecast was based on a sales growth of \$500, for which:

$$\begin{aligned} EFN &= -16.67 + .1729 \times 500 \\ &= -16.67 + 86.45 \\ &= \$69.78 \text{ or, within round-off error, } \underline{\underline{\$70}} \end{aligned}$$

the number she obtained.

It is useful to draw the EFN relationship on a graph, as we have done in Figure 18.3. The formula calculates EFN as a function of the change in sales, so EFN becomes the vertical axis and ΔS the horizontal axis. The relationship graphs as a straight line with intercept of [P − R], and a slope of $[a - \ell - m(1 - d)]$.

We have drawn the graph with a negative intercept and a positive slope because this was the case for the Jefferson Company. In fact, we chose to make the example this way because many companies are like this.

2. The Limit to Internally Financed Growth

Looking at the graph of the EFN relationship, Carol realizes that if the Jefferson Company's sales grow at a low rate, EFN calculates negative, which means the firm would generate excess cash. But as the rate of sales growth increases, EFN rises and

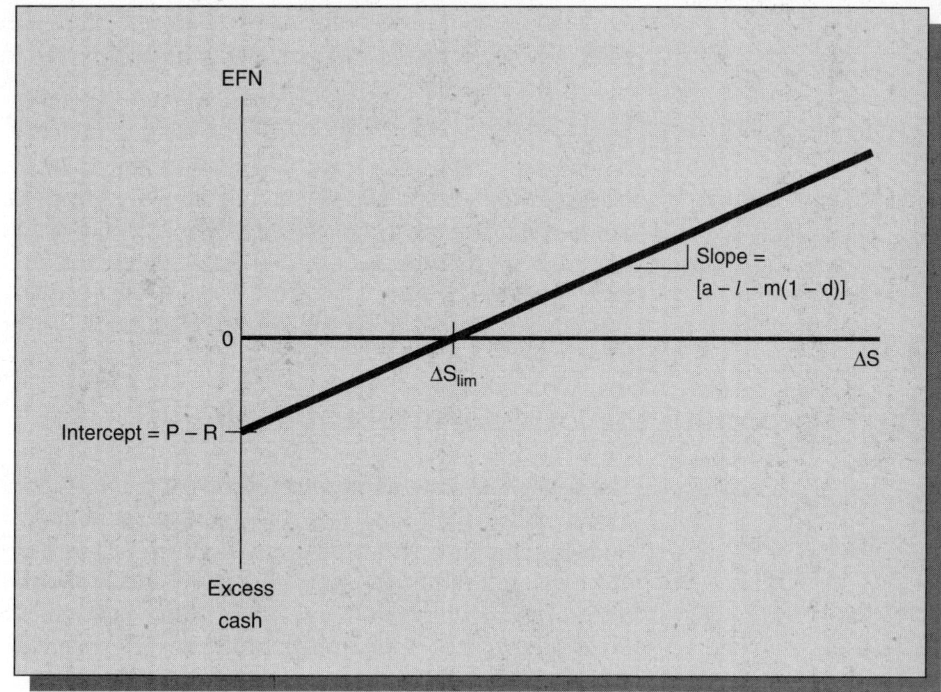

FIGURE 18.3
The EFN relationship. For low sales growth the firm generates excess cash, while for sales growth greater than ΔS_{lim} the firm requires external financing

eventually becomes positive, indicating that the firm would then require external funds. At some growth rate in sales, EFN equals zero—the firm is in perfect balance, without excess cash and with no need for external funds. At this growth rate, money generated spontaneously is exactly sufficient to buy new assets.

limit to internally-financed growth—the maximum amount by which a company's sales can grow in a year before the firm must turn to external financing

We identify this one particular value of ΔS as ΔS_{lim}, the **limit to internally-financed growth.** On the graph of Figure 18.3, this is the point on the horizontal axis at which the EFN line crosses over from negative to positive. Mathematically, when EFN equals zero:

$$\text{EFN} = 0$$

$$[P - R] + [a - \ell - m(1 - d)]\,\Delta S_{lim} = 0$$

Solving for ΔS_{lim}, the change in sales at which EFN equals zero, gives:

$$[a - \ell - m(1 - d)]\,\Delta Slim = -[P - R] = [R - P]$$

$$\Delta S_{lim} = \frac{R - P}{a - \ell - m(1 - d)}$$

Applying this idea to the Jefferson Company's data, Carol obtains:

$$\Delta S_{lim} = [66.67 - 50]/[.3800 - .1400 - .1006(2/3)]$$

$$= 16.67/.1729 = \underline{\underline{96.41}}$$

If sales grow by less than \$96.41 in 1995 (that is, 1995 sales is less than \$2,500 + \$96.41 = \$2,596.41), the Jefferson Company will have excess cash and will not need external financing. If sales grow by more than \$96.41 in 1995 (to above \$2,596.41), the Jefferson Company will require funding from external sources. However, if sales grow by exactly $96.41 (to just equal $2,596.41), the Jefferson Company will neither have excess cash nor need external financing. Therefore, a sales increase of $96.41 is the limit of Jefferson's ability to grow through internal financing.

While Carol knows that it would be quite a coincidence if the Jefferson Company's sales grew by exactly $96.41, she immediately grasps the importance of this number. If 1995 sales are forecasted with some confidence to be below $2,596.41, Carol can conclude that finding external funds will not be an issue for her in the coming year. However, if sales will grow by more than $96.41, external funding will be needed, and Carol can get a headstart on defining and obtaining that financing.

Interpreting the Pro-Forma Statements

The pro-forma statements give important clues as to the future behavior and condition of the firm. From them, the financial manager can begin to learn how much financing the firm will need and why, and can get a first sense of which source(s) of financing might be a good choice. In addition, the financial manager can use the pro-forma statements to anticipate financial trends within the firm. In all cases, the objective is to be in a position to provide resources and financial guidance at an early stage so financial problems do not arise.

1. There Are Two Reasons Why Firms Need External Funds

As Carol prepared the pro-forma balance sheet, she discovered an external financing need (EFN) of $70: on December 31, the Jefferson Company would need $70 of additional financing. The EFN was required because of the firm's *growth.* Projected growth in sales meant the firm would have to purchase additional assets, yet the company would be unable to generate sufficient funds internally. It would have to raise external money.

When she prepares her cash budget, Carol will see that the financing needs of her company go beyond the EFN of $70 due to the firm's *seasonality.* This need is independent of its growth.[15]

The insight that her firm needs financing for two distinct reasons prompts Carol to think about where the financing might come from. The cash budget points out that the seasonal cash requirements will be short-term in nature. Perhaps, muses Carol, a short-term financing source, such as a bank loan or commercial paper, will be appropriate for this. On the other hand, the EFN of $70 is due to the growth of the firm, a long-term trend. Carol wonders whether some long-term source of money, such as bonds or stock, might be appropriate to cover this part of Jefferson's needs.

[15] **Cross-reference and elaboration:** Carol prepares a cash budget consistent with her income statement and balance sheet forecasts in Appendix 18D. The line "Cumulative financing needed" on her cash budget (p. 682) shows that the firm's cash position is projected to be seasonal during the year—beginning with excess cash, then changing to a need which peaks at $152 in March, returning to excess cash during the summer, and reverting to a need for external financing in the last four months of the year.

2. The Cash-Flow Statement Gives Additional Clues to Funding

According to the pro-forma cash flow statement, the Jefferson Company will use cash for three major purposes other than operations in 1995: to pay dividends ($50), to purchase plant ($140), and to retire bonds ($50). These uses total $240 and are all long-term in nature. None will result in cash coming back to the firm in the near future.

Jefferson's sources of cash are projected to be from operations ($190) and external funds ($70). The funds from operations are long-term in the sense that management may choose to retain them forever. The external financing, however, may be either short- or long-term at management's discretion.

One reasonable financing strategy would be to hedge the balance sheet, matching the long-term uses of cash with long-term sources. Since there are $240 of long-term uses, roughly $240 of the sources, including most or all of the external funds, would then be long-term in character.

3. Financial (Ratio) Analysis Can Be Used to Examine the Results

Financial ratios can be used to test the pro-forma statements in the same way as they are used to evaluate past and present performance. In particular, ratios calculated from the pro-forma data can be compared to prior values of the same ratios to search for improvement or deterioration of the firm's condition.

Not all ratios are useful for this test. For example, the gross margin ratio and the various asset turnover ratios define the percentage-of-sales relationships used to forecast gross profit and asset balances in the first place. These ratios calculated from the pro-forma statements should be exactly the same as ratios taken from the data used to obtain the percentage-of-sales figures. A change in these ratios indicates an error of calculation and not a company trend.

Certain ratios can be used to anticipate general trends within the business. These are the ratios that are not directly related to sales and therefore do not define the percentage-of-sales relationships used in constructing the pro-forma statements. Examples are times interest earned, net profit margin, and return on assets.

Example

Using Ratios to Test the Pro-Forma Statements for Trends

Carol calculates the following ratios:

	1994 Actual	1995 Pro-Forma
Times interest earned	9.6 times	13.8 times
Net profit margin	4.00%	5.00%
Return on assets	10.0%	12.6%

If these changes are meaningful and not merely natural variation, and if the forecast comes to pass, the Jefferson Company will strengthen on all three of these dimensions in 1995.

Another group of ratios is particularly sensitive to how the firm chooses to finance its EFN.[16] They can be used both to look for trends in the company and to study the impact of the financing choice on the firm's structure.

Example

Using Ratios to Test the Choice of EFN Source

Carol calculates the following ratios assuming an EFN of 70:

	1994 Actual	1995 Pro-Forma: EFN Financed by: Current Liabilities	Long-term Liabilities	Common Equity
Current ratio	1.25	1.20	1.40	1.40
Quick ratio	0.75	0.71	0.83	0.83
Debt ratio	50.0%	49.6%	49.6%	43.7%
Return on equity	22.2%	27.3%	27.3%	24.2%

From the 1995 pro-forma balance sheet (p. 658), current assets are forecast to be 590 (120 of cash + 50 of marketable securities + 180 of accounts receivable + 240 of inventories) and current liabilities are forecasted to be 420 (180 of accounts payable + 240 of accrued payables) prior to determining the form of the EFN. If Jefferson finances its EFN using short-term liabilities, current liabilities will rise to 490 (420 + 70) and its current ratio will be:

$$590/490 = \underline{\underline{1.20}}$$

If, on the other hand, Jefferson uses long-term liabilities or equity to finance its EFN, its current liabilities will remain 420 and its current ratio will be:

$$590/420 = \underline{\underline{1.40}}$$

Carol uses the same logic to get each of the other ratios above.

The Jefferson Company has a strong profitability (return on equity) which will improve no matter how the EFN is financed. Liquidity (current and quick ratios) is weak. It would weaken further with current liability financing but would improve if long-term money were used. Leverage (debt ratio) can be improved if equity financing is used; otherwise it would not be significantly changed.

4. Relationships Are Changing

In our example of the Jefferson Company, Carol used the percentage relationships from the 1994 financial statements to project 1995. In doing so she assumed that the structure of the company would not change in any significant way during the coming year. In today's environment, this assumption may well be incorrect.

As companies respond to the pressures of global competition, many are reexamining the way they conduct each part of their business. As they change their

[16] **Observation:** To the extent that the choice of financing impacts interest expense, the prior group of ratios will change as well.

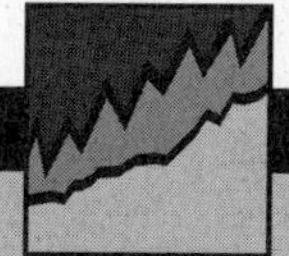

IMPROVING FINANCE'S PROCESSES

Budgeting for Improvement at Southern Pacific

Southern Pacific Transportation Company has created a new planning process in the context of its long-term objective of becoming the lowest-cost, highest-quality provider of transportation services in its industry. The process integrates the company's strategic, operational, financial, and quality objectives and is driven and managed by the company's assistant vice president—finance. Each year is seen not as a separate, stand-alone phenomenon but rather a step on the way to a series of goals with a seven- to eight-year time horizon. These goals include satisfactory and regular profitability which will permit the restructuring of the company's long-term debt to remove existing restrictive covenants. The plan contains explicit objectives for quality improvement and cost reduction based upon each organizational unit's key performance indicators (KPIs), which identify prime opportunities for operating expense reductions and service-quality improvements. A senior management committee selects, prioritizes, and designates responsibilities for KPIs, thus setting a series of intermediate-term targets for the entire company to follow. The cost reductions projected to flow from quality improvements are built into the company's financial plans and budgets for each year.

production methodologies and use of resources, the percentage relationship of virtually every account to sales may change. For example, the move toward just-in-time manufacturing systems dramatically reduces inventory balances, and inventory as a percentage of sales declines sharply. It also reduces the need for much factory space, reducing many overhead costs. The elimination of rework and inspection costs lowers cost of goods sold. As customers perceive higher quality, they are willing to pay more and revenue rises. These changes reduce the percentage relationship of costs to sales. As companies become progressively more skilled at continuously improving their work processes, relationship between sales and other financial accounts are likely to continue to change year after year.

Astute financial managers build these changes into their financial forecasts and budgets. They work with others throughout the organization to understand and be part of the improvements taking place. Correspondingly, they encourage others to help shape the financial forecasts. Doing so makes the forecasts more accurate and permits them to capture the dynamic nature of the business. Further, to the extent that the financial forecast truly reflects the aspirations of the company, predicting improvement may actually help make it happen!

Carol May put the finishing touches on her last transparency and sat back with a satisfied feeling. Her presentation to the executive committee was the next day, and she was confident it would go well. She put the transparencies in order and began to practice what she would say.

Carol would start her presentation with the assumptions she had pieced together from her interviews with others in the organization. Next, she would present her pro-forma financial statements for the coming year. She would highlight the external financing needs number and then show how that amount would vary over a range of alternative sales forecasts. Finally, she would show how the financial condition of the company would change if the sales forecast proved accurate.

As she thought back to the past two weeks, Carol was amazed at how much she had learned. She had been surprised at the extent to which her forecasts took advantage of accounting relationships and was certainly glad she had done well in her accounting courses. But she also had a new appreciation of the value of accounting information and how it could be used in financial planning.

Summary of Key Points

- **Describe the functions and limitations of planning and budgeting, including financial planning.** Planning begins with a mission statement: a statement of goals and beliefs to guide all activities of the firm. It focuses on customers and on exceeding their expectations. It leads to strategies that are aligned with the firm's culture, strengths, and environment. Although planning traditionally has been a job for managers, in modern management practice planning is becoming the responsibility of all members of the organization. The use of budgets, a key component of planning, is also changing. Whereas budgets traditionally have been targets for performance, today they are seen more as guides for planning and acquiring resources.

  Financial planning accomplishes six tasks. It (1) forces assumptions to be made explicit, (2) identifies actions that are consistent or inconsistent with financial health, (3) identifies the financial resources required to support the firm's plans, (4) provides guidance in the choice of financing sources, (5) becomes a benchmark against which to compare results so as to improve the planning process, and (6) helps the firm communicate with its stakeholders. A financial plan consists of a long-run financial plan, a capital budget, and an operating budget. An important technique used in financial planning is the construction of pro-forma financial statements, projections of the firm's future financial activity and position.

- **Recognize when specific-item forecasting is an appropriate financial planning technique.** Specific-item forecasting is a technique for estimating values independently of one another. It is particularly appropriate when the variables are not related through a central causal variable. A more commonly used forecasting technique is the percentage-of-sales method, in which many accounts are related to sales to ensure an internal consistency to the forecast.

- **Identify financial statement accounts that relate to sales and establish those relationships.** A percentage-of-sales forecast requires a good understanding of how the firm's financial accounts relate to each other. To identify which accounts relate to sales we ask: (1) why is this money being spent? (2) what is the account's time horizon? and (3) how will management respond to a change in sales? For those accounts determined to be spontaneous, we construct a relationship connecting the account balance to the level of sales.

- **Use the percentage-of-sales technique to project a firm's financial statements.** The percentage-of-sales technique consists of seven steps: (1) forecast sales, (2) classify accounts as variable and spontaneous, and fixed and discretionary, (3) determine relationships between the variable and discretionary accounts and sales, (4) project new values for all accounts, (5) fill in the pro-forma statements with the projected amounts, (6) force the pro-forma-balance sheet to balance with "external financing needed (EFN)" or "excess cash," and (7) produce the pro-forma cash flow statement.

- **Determine a company's external financing needs and calculate the limit to its ability to grow using internal financing.** An important output of pro-forma statements is the EFN figure, the amount of financing a company will have to raise from outside sources to acquire the resources necessary to meet its sales projection. One advantage of relating variables to sales is the ability to construct an EFN relationship so that external financing needs can be studied for a range of possible sales figures. The EFN relationship can also be used to determine the range of sales for which the firm will be financially self-sufficient and the range for which it will need external financing.

- **Interpret pro-forma financial statements.** Pro-forma statements help the financial manager to separate needs caused by growth from needs caused by seasonality. The cash flow statement may be examined to see if sources and uses of cash match. Ratios may be calculated from the pro-forma income statement and balance sheet to gauge the future condition of the firm. As companies adopt quality-management methods, the relationships among the numbers on their financial statements are changing. Accurate forecasting requires that the financial manager work closely with others in the company to understand and be part of quality improvements and to incorporate them into financial forecasts.

Questions

1. What is the role of planning in management?
2. How can budgets hurt rather than help a firm?
3. Identify the six tasks that financial planning can help a firm to accomplish.
4. What is the distinction between specific-item forecasting and forecasts that relate to sales?
5. In the percentage-of-sales forecasting method, what is the significance of:
   a. Having a good sales forecast?
   b. Relating accounts to sales?
6. Identify the following concepts. What is their relationship to financial forecasting?
   a. Variable cost
   b. Fixed cost
   c. Spontaneous account
   d. Discretionary account
7. What is the relationship between external financing needed and excess cash?
8. A firm with a high growth rate typically requires external financing. In what other situations would a firm require external financing?
9. How is the use of total quality management changing the relationships appropriate for financial forecasting?

Problems

1. **(Percentage of sales—income statement)** Using the percentage-of-sales method, forecast the income statement of a company with the following data and forecasts:

Sales last year	$8,000,000
Variable expenses:	
Cost of goods sold	$4,800,000
Operating expense	$1,760,000
Fixed operating expense	$ 750,000
Interest bearing debt:	
Average balance next year	$2,500,000
Average interest rate next year	10%
Tax rate	35%

   if the company's sales forecast for the coming year is:
   a. $8,000,000
   b. $8,800,000
   c. $9,500,000
   d. $10,000,000

2. **(Percentage of sales—income statement)** Using the percentage-of-sales method, forecast the income statement of a company with the following data and forecasts:

Sales last year	$3,000,000
Variable expenses:	
Cost of goods sold	$1,200,000
Operating expense	$ 960,000
Fixed operating expense	$ 200,000
Interest bearing debt:	
Average balance next year	$1,000,000
Average interest rate next year	12%
Tax rate	35%

   if the company's sales forecast for the coming year is:
   a. $3,400,000
   b. $3,900,000
   c. $4,200,000
   d. $4,500,000

3. **(Percentage of sales—spontaneous accounts)** A company had sales of $4,500,000 last year and ended the year with $450,000 of accounts receivable, $200,000 of inventory, and $300,000 of accounts payable—all of which are considered spontaneous accounts. Forecast the end-of-coming-year balances for these three accounts using the percentage-of-sales method if the sales forecast for the coming year is:
   a. $4,000,000
   b. $4,500,000
   c. $5,000,000
   d. $6,000,000

4. **(Percentage of sales—spontaneous accounts)** A company had sales of $1,500,000 last year and ended the year with $75,000 of accrued payables, which is considered a spontaneous account. Using the percentage-of-sales method, determine the level of sales that can be supported by the following end-of-coming-year accrued payables balances:

   a. $65,000
   b. $75,000
   c. $90,000
   d. $120,000

5. **(Percentage of sales—spontaneous accounts)** In the past, a company's collection period has been 45 days. Using the percentage-of-sales method, determine the end-of-coming-year level of accounts receivable that would accompany the following sales levels if accounts receivable were a spontaneous asset:

   a. $200,000
   b. $400,000
   c. $800,000
   d. $1,600,000

6. **(Percentage of sales—spontaneous accounts)** In the past, a company's accounts receivable turnover ratio has been 12 times, and the company does not expect this relationship to change in the coming year. Using the percentage-of-sales method, determine the level of sales that can be supported by the following end-of-coming-year accounts receivable balances if accounts receivable were a spontaneous asset:

   a. $100,000
   b. $250,000
   c. $500,000
   d. $1,000,000

7. **(Percentage of sales—spontaneous and discretionary accounts)** A company had sales of $3,500,000 last year and forecasts sales of $4,000,000 in the coming year. It ended last year with $140,000 in its cash balance and with another $100,000 of marketable securities. Cash is considered a spontaneous asset. Forecast the end-of-coming-year balances of cash and marketable securities under each of the following alternatives:

   a. 100% of the marketable securities balance is considered part of the company's operating cash and therefore spontaneous.
   b. 70% of the marketable securities balance is considered part of the company's operating cash and therefore spontaneous. The remainder is considered discretionary.
   c. 30% of the marketable securities balance is considered part of the company's operating cash and therefore spontaneous. The remainder is considered discretionary.
   d. None of the marketable securities balance is considered part of the company's operating cash, but rather it is all considered discretionary.

8. **(Percentage of sales—spontaneous and discretionary accounts)** A company had sales of $10,000,000 last year and forecasts sales of $12,000,000 in the coming year. It ended last year with $250,000 in its cash balance and with another $175,000 of marketable securities. Cash is considered a spontaneous asset. Forecast the end-of-coming-year balances of cash and marketable securities under each of the following alternatives:

   a. 100% of the marketable securities balance is considered part of the company's operating cash and therefore spontaneous.
   b. 60% of the marketable securities balance is considered part of the company's operating cash and therefore spontaneous. The remainder is considered discretionary.
   c. 25% of the marketable securities balance is considered part of the company's operating cash and therefore spontaneous. The remainder is considered discretionary.
   d. None of the marketable securities balance is considered part of the company's operating cash, but rather it is all considered discretionary.

9. **(Percentage of sales—plant and equipment)** A company had sales last year of $16,000,000 and forecasts sales of $20,000,000 in the coming year. It ended the year with $5,000,000 of plant and equipment. Forecast the end-of-coming-year balance for plant and equipment under each of the following alternatives.

   a. Plant and equipment is now at capacity and will be increased proportionally to sales.
   b. Plant and equipment is now at capacity. New plant and equipment must be purchased in $750,000 increments.
   c. Plant and equipment is now being used at 90% of capacity. New plant and equipment will be purchased in the exact amount needed.
   d. Plant and equipment is now being used at 90% of capacity. New plant and equipment must be purchased in $750,000 increments.

10. **(Percentage of sales—plant and equipment)** A company had sales last year of $30,000,000 and forecasts sales of $40,000,000 in the coming year. It ended the year with $12,000,000 of plant and equipment. Forecast the end-of-coming-year balance for plant and equipment under each of the following alternatives.

a. Plant and equipment is now at capacity and will be increased proportionally to sales.

b. Plant and equipment is now at capacity. New plant and equipment must be purchased in $2,500,000 increments.

c. Plant and equipment is now being used at 90% of capacity. New plant and equipment will be purchased in the exact amount needed.

d. Plant and equipment is now being used at 70% of capacity. New plant and equipment must be purchased in $2,500,000 increments.

11. **(Percentage of sales—bonds payable)** A company listed bonds payable in its year-end balance sheet, of which $500,000 was reported as a current liability. Next year another $500,000 will become current. Forecast its end-of-coming-year balance of "bonds payable—current" and "bonds payable—long term" if this year's year-end balance of bonds payable—long-term is:

a. $500,000

b. $2,500,000

c. $5,000,000

d. $10,000,000

12. **(Percentage of sales—bonds payable)** A company listed bonds payable in its year-end balance sheet, of which $125,000 was reported as a current liability. Next year $75,000 will become current. Forecast its end-of-coming-year balance of "bonds payable—current" and "bonds payable—long term" if this year's year-end total balance of bonds payable is:

a. $250,000

b. $500,000

c. $1,000,000

d. $1,500,000

13. **(Percentage of sales—retained earnings)** A company reported $250,000 of retained earnings on its balance sheet last year. In the coming year it expects sales of $800,000. Forecast the end-of-coming-year balance of retained earnings if the company has a:

a. Net margin ratio of 12% and a dividend payout ratio of 40%

b. Net margin ratio of 8% and a dividend payout ratio of 15%

c. Net margin ratio of 5% and a dividend payout ratio of 75%

d. Net margin ratio of 8% and a dividend payout ratio of 100%

14. **(Percentage of sales—retained earnings)** A company reported $6,000,000 of retained earnings on its balance sheet last year. In the coming year it expects sales of $4,500,000. Forecast the end-of-coming-year balance of retained earnings if the company has a:

a. Net margin ratio of 3% and a dividend payout ratio of 80%

b. Net margin ratio of 7% and a dividend payout ratio of 25%

c. Net margin ratio of 9% and a dividend payout ratio of 100%

d. Net margin ratio of 14% and a dividend payout ratio of 40%

15. **(Percentage of sales—full projection)** A company published the following financial statements in its 1994 annual report:

Income Statement
For the year ended December 31, 1994

Sales		$70,000
−Cost of goods sold		45,000
Gross profit		25,000
−Operating expenses	$8,000	
−Depreciation	5,000	
		13,000
EBIT		12,000
−Interest expense		1,300
EBT		10,700
−Tax expense		3,745
EAT		$ 6,955
−Dividends		3,000
Addition to retained earnings		$ 3,955

Balance Sheet
December 31, 1994

Cash	$ 8,000
Marketable securities	2,000
Accounts receivable	10,000
Inventories	6,000
Plant, net	20,000
Total assets	$46,000
Accounts payable	$ 7,000
Accrued payables	3,000
Bonds payable	10,000
Common stock	15,000
Retained earnings	11,000
Total liabilities and equity	$46,000

1995 sales is estimated to be $80,000. Forecast the 1995 income statement, balance sheet, and statement of cash flow assuming: (1) cost of goods sold and $5,000 of the operating expenses are variable; (2) depreciation and the remainder of operating expenses are fixed; (3) cash, accounts receivable, inventories, net plant, accounts payable, and accrued payables are spontaneous; (4) marketable securities, bonds payable, and common stock are discretionary; (5) $500 of bonds payable are current and will be repaid at the beginning of the year; and (6) the firm will maintain its 1994 dividend payout ratio in 1995.

16. **(Percentage of sales—full projection)** A company published the following financial statements in its 1994 annual report:

Income Statement
For the year ended December 31, 1994

Sales		$500,000
−Cost of goods sold		350,000
Gross profit		150,000
−Operating expenses	$75,000	
−Depreciation	20,000	
		95,000
EBIT		55,000
−Interest expense		20,000
EBT		35,000
−Tax expense		12,250
EAT		$ 22,750
−Dividends		10,000
Addition to retained earnings		$ 12,750

Balance Sheet
December 31, 1994

Cash	$ 25,000
Marketable securities	10,000
Accounts receivable	50,000
Inventories	85,000
Plant, net	200,000
Total assets	$370,000
Accounts payable	$ 60,000
Accrued payables	35,000
Bonds payable	140,000
Common stock	105,000
Retained earnings	30,000
Total liabilities and equity	$370,000

1995 sales is estimated to be $650,000. Forecast the 1995 income statement, balance sheet and statement of cash flow assuming: (1) cost of goods sold, $30,000 of the operating expenses, and depreciation expense are variable; (2) the remainder of operating expenses is fixed; (3) cash, accounts receivable, inventories, net plant, accounts payable, and accrued payables are spontaneous; (4) marketable securities, bonds payable, and common stock are discretionary; (5) $10,000 of bonds payable are current and will be repaid at the beginning of the year; and (6) the firm will maintain its 1994 dividend payout ratio in 1995.

17. **(EFN relationship)** We have the following information about a firm:

Sales last year	$5,500,000
Sales forecast, this year	$6,000,000
Current portion of debt principal	$ 150,000
Increase to retained earnings last year	$ 250,000
Spontaneous assets as a percentage of sales	56%
Spontaneous liabilities as a percentage of sales	23%
Net profit margin ratio	6%
Dividend payout ratio	45%
Year-end debt/equity ratio	60%

a. Construct the firm's EFN relationship.
b. Explain the meaning of the two "square-bracket" terms.
c. Use the EFN relationship to forecast EFN.
d. Use the EFN relationship to forecast EFN if the sales forecast changes to:
(1) $5,600,000
(2) $6,600,000

18. **(EFN relationship)** We have the following information about a firm:

Sales last year	$1,800,000
Sales forecast, this year	$2,000,000
Current portion of debt principal	$ 50,000
Increase to retained earnings last year	$ 150,000
Spontaneous assets as a percentage of sales	75%
Spontaneous liabilities as a percentage of sales	18%
Net profit margin ratio	14%
Dividend payout ratio	25%
Year-end debt/equity ratio	42%

a. Construct the firm's EFN relationship.
b. Explain the meaning of the two "square-bracket" terms.
c. Use the EFN relationship to forecast EFN.
d. Use the EFN relationship to forecast EFN if the sales forecast changes to:
(1) $1,850,000
(2) $2,250,000

19. **(Limit to internally financed growth)** Use your answers to Problem 17 to calculate the limit to internally financed growth for that firm. What does this mean?

20. **(Limit to internally financed growth)** Use your answers to Problem 18 to calculate the limit to internally financed growth for that firm. What does this mean?

21. **(Evaluating the pro-forma statements)** Analyze the pro-forma statements you prepared for the firm of Problem 15, using those financial ratios that are not used in the percentage-of-sales projection by:
a. Calculating ratios from the 1994 statements
b. Calculating ratios from the 1995 pro-forma statements assuming:
(1) EFN is financed with current liabilities
(2) EFN is financed with long-term liabilities
(3) EFN is financed with common equity
c. Commenting on the direction of change of the ratios. Which financing alternative (if any) does the best job of improving the firm's financial ratios (or at least not degrading them too much)?

22. **(Evaluating the pro-forma statements)** Analyze the pro-forma statements you prepared for the firm of Problem 16, using those financial ratios that are not used in the percentage-of-sales projection by:
a. Calculating ratios from the 1994 statements
b. Calculating ratios from the 1995 pro-forma statements assuming:
(1) EFN is financed with current liabilities
(2) EFN is financed with long-term liabilities
(3) EFN is financed with common equity
c. Commenting on the direction of change of the ratios. Which financing alternative (if any) does the best job of improving the firm's financial ratios (or at least not degrading them too much)?

APPENDIX 18A

MORE-COMPLEX FORECASTING RELATIONSHIPS

We developed the concepts of financial forecasting in this chapter using the simple percentage-of-sales relationship. That model assumes that any variable which changes with sales does so in a strictly linear fashion. Yet, other relationships between a company's account balances and sales level are quite possible, and their use might improve the accuracy of our forecasts. Although it complicates the form of the EFN relationship, it is not very difficult to re-derive the EFN relationship using these formulations.

Among the more common alternate relationships are:

- *Variable with fixed base:* The balance of the account is treated as consisting of a fixed component plus a variable component that is strictly proportional to sales, as illustrated in Figure 18A.1.

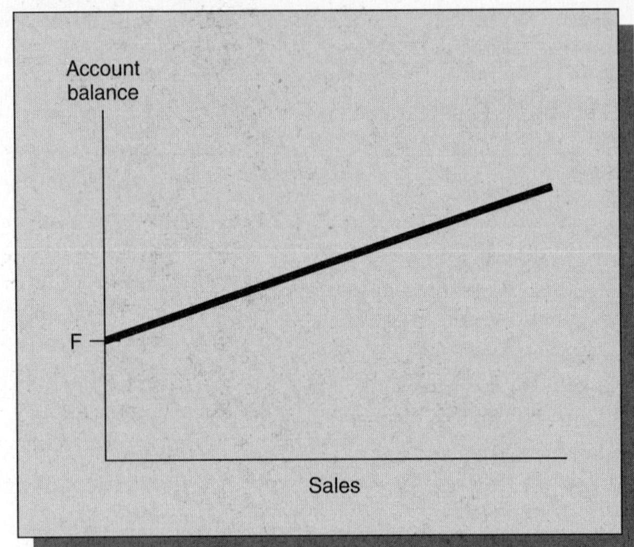

FIGURE 18A.1
Variable costs with a fixed base. Total cost equals a fixed level (F) plus a variable component that rises linearly with sales.

- *Economies of scale:* Cost increases taper off as the firm grows. The account balance grows with sales—quickly at first and then more slowly as sales increases still further. Figure 18A.2 shows this pattern.
- *Diseconomies of scale:* The opposite of economies of scale (as drawn in Figure 18A.3). Cost increases accelerate as the firm grows. The balance of the account grows with sales—slowly at first and then more quickly as sales increases still further.

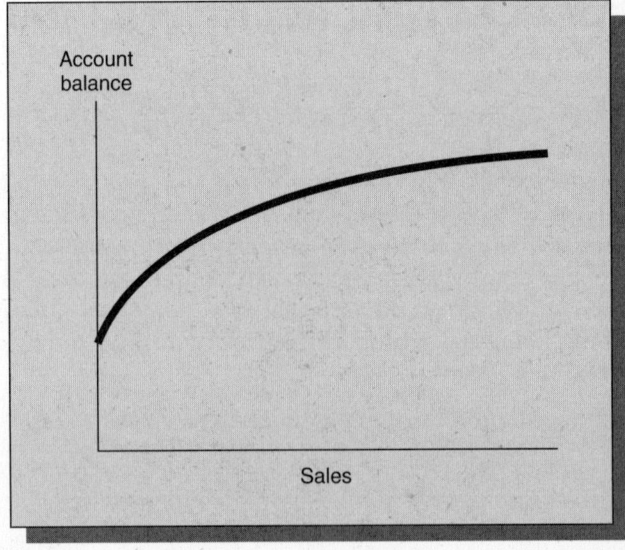

FIGURE 18A.2
Economies of scale. Costs increase with sales at a decreasing rate.

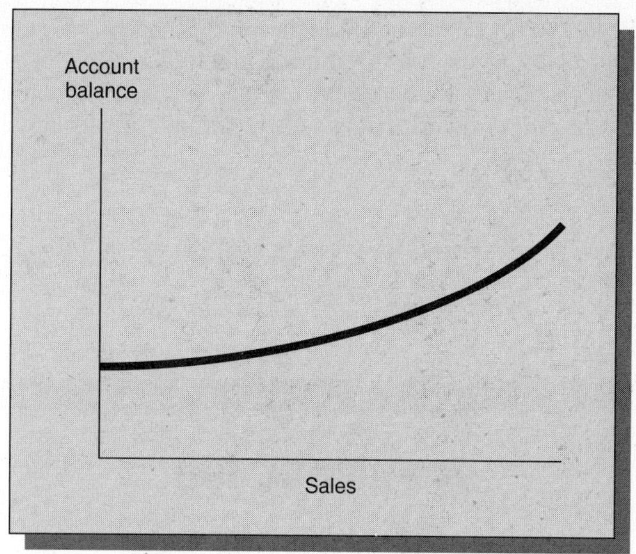

FIGURE 18A.3
Diseconomies of scale. Costs increase with sales at an increasing rate.

- *Lumpy resource:* The resource can only be acquired in large discrete quantities. The account balance jumps sharply as the resource is purchased and then stays constant until more must be acquired. The resulting "step function" is shown in Figure 18A.4. Plant is the typical example since it is bought in large amounts but then no more plant need be purchased until the existing plant's capacity has been reached.

To determine if one of these relationships better describes any of the firm's accounts, statistical modeling techniques such as regression analysis may be used.

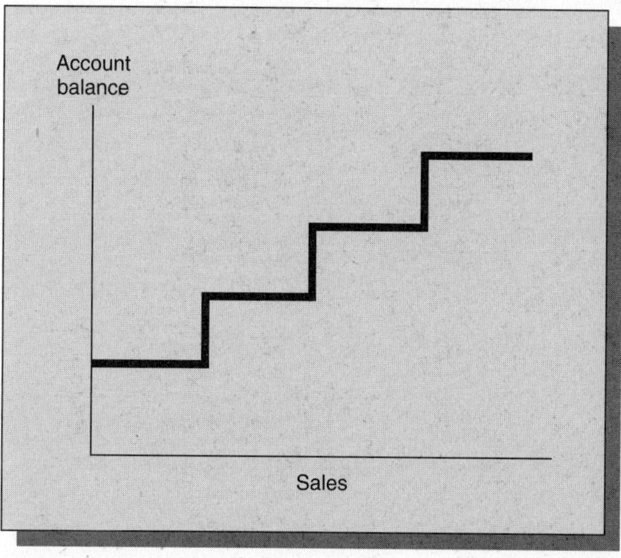

FIGURE 18A.4
Costs from a lumpy resource. Costs increase in steps each time more of the resource is acquired.

Past data for the account balance and for sales are graphed and a statistical computer package is used to find the line that gives the best fit. Alternatively, the statistical analysis done as part of the company's continuous improvement plan might point toward one of these relationships for a particular account.

APPENDIX 18B

DERIVATION OF THE EFN RELATIONSHIP

The EFN relationship comes from the fundamental accounting identity:

$$\text{Assets} = \text{Liabilities} + \text{Owners' equity}$$

This equation must be true at all times. In particular, it is true at the beginning and at the end of the year, so that for the period of the year (where Δ stands for "change in"):

$$\Delta\text{Assets} = \Delta\text{Liabilities} + \Delta\text{Owners' equity}$$

In the percentage-of-sales forecasting technique, the changes to each category come from the following:

1. New assets required by the firm are the spontaneous assets which change with sales. The "spontaneous asset percentage" captures this relationship:

$$\Delta\text{Assets} = \text{new spontaneous assets} = a\Delta S$$

2. Liabilities change for two reasons. Spontaneous liabilities change with sales. The "spontaneous liability percentage" captures this relationship:

$$\text{New spontaneous liabilities} = \ell\Delta S$$

Liabilities also change when debt is repaid. This is represented by the variable P:

$$\text{Debt repayment} = P$$

And the total change to liabilities is:

$$\Delta\text{Liabilities} = \ell\Delta S - P$$

3. Owners' equity changes due to the retention of earnings and the payment of dividends. For convenience, we divide earnings into two sources, the earnings the firm would have if sales do not change (we represent this by E here) and the earnings from growth of sales, which is obtained by multiplying the forecasted sales growth, ΔS, by the net profit margin ratio,[1] m:

$$\text{Earnings after taxes} = E + \Delta Sm$$

Dividends are calculated by multiplying earnings after taxes by the dividend payout ratio, d:

$$\text{Dividends} = d\,(E + \Delta Sm)$$

And the total change to equity is income less dividends:

$$\begin{aligned}\Delta\text{Owners' equity} &= (E + \Delta Sm) - d\,(E + \Delta Sm)\\ &= (E + \Delta Sm)\,(1 - d)\\ &= E(1 - d) + \Delta Sm(1 - d)\end{aligned}$$

But $E(1 - d)$ is our variable R, the addition to retained earnings should the firm's sales not grow this year, so:

$$\Delta\text{Owners' equity} = R + \Delta Sm(1 - d)$$

Substituting these expressions into the accounting identity gives:

$$\begin{aligned}\Delta\text{Assets} &= \Delta\text{Liabilities} + \Delta\text{Owners' equity}\\ a\Delta S &= [\ell\Delta S - P] + [R + \Delta Sm(1 - d)] + EFN\end{aligned}$$

We must add the EFN term to the right-hand side of the equation since there is no reason to believe that the equation will balance when each item is estimated independently of the others and calculated without using double-entry bookkeeping. Solving for EFN and rearranging gives the EFN relationship:

$$\begin{aligned}EFN &= a\Delta S - [\ell\Delta S - P] - [R + \Delta Sm(1 - d)]\\ &= a\Delta S - \ell\Delta S + P - R - \Delta Sm(1 - d)\\ &= P - R + a\Delta S - \ell\Delta S - m(1 - d)\Delta S\end{aligned}$$

$$\boldsymbol{EFN = [P - R] + [a - \ell - m(1 - d)]\,\Delta S}$$

[1] **Cross-reference:** Recall from Appendix 4D, p. 119, that:

Net profit margin = earnings after taxes/sales

APPENDIX 18C

SUSTAINABLE GROWTH

Financial managers and analysts study the connection between a firm's rate of growth and its financial leverage ratios.

Since financial managers are often hesitant to sell additional common stock for fear of diluting owners' equity, the need for external financing frequently leads a firm to borrow. However, there is a concern that rapid growth with its need for external financing could lead to excessive borrowing and a debt/equity ratio that is too high.

sustainable growth rate—the rate of growth that does not change a firm's debt/equity ratio, assuming any external financing needed comes from debt

A firm's **sustainable growth rate** (ΔS_{sgr}) is the amount its sales can grow in a year without changing (and particularly without increasing) its debt/equity ratio. The analysis assumes that any external financing needed comes from borrowing. Mathematically, this point is calculated as:

$$\Delta S_{sgr} = \frac{m(1 - d)(der + 1)}{a - m(1 - d)(der + 1)} \times S$$

where all the variables are as previously defined and:

der = the firm's beginning-of-year debt/equity ratio (on its 1994 balance sheet, the Jefferson Company had \$500 of debt and \$500 of equity, so at the beginning of 1995, der = \$500/\$500 = 1)

For the Jefferson Company, Carol calculates:

$$\Delta S_{sgr} = \frac{.1011(2/3)(2)}{.3800 - .1011(2/3)(2)} \times 2{,}500 = \frac{.1348}{.2452} \times 2500 = \underline{\underline{\$1{,}374}}$$

If sales grow by less than \$1,374 in 1995 (that is, 1995 sales is less than \$2,500 + \$1,374 = \$3,874), the Jefferson Company's debt/equity ratio will decline. If sales grow by more than \$1,374 in 1995 (to above \$3,874), the Jefferson Company's debt equity ratio will rise. \$1,374 defines Jefferson's sustainable growth rate.

In each year, a firm's debt/equity ratio is affected by the following three forces:

1. If a company does not grow at all, the only change to its balance sheet is from the new year's retained earnings and the repayment of any debt falling due. Typically, this increases equity and reduces debt and the firm's debt/equity ratio falls.
2. For internally financed growth, right-hand-side balance sheet changes come from new spontaneous liabilities and incremental retained earnings. Typi-

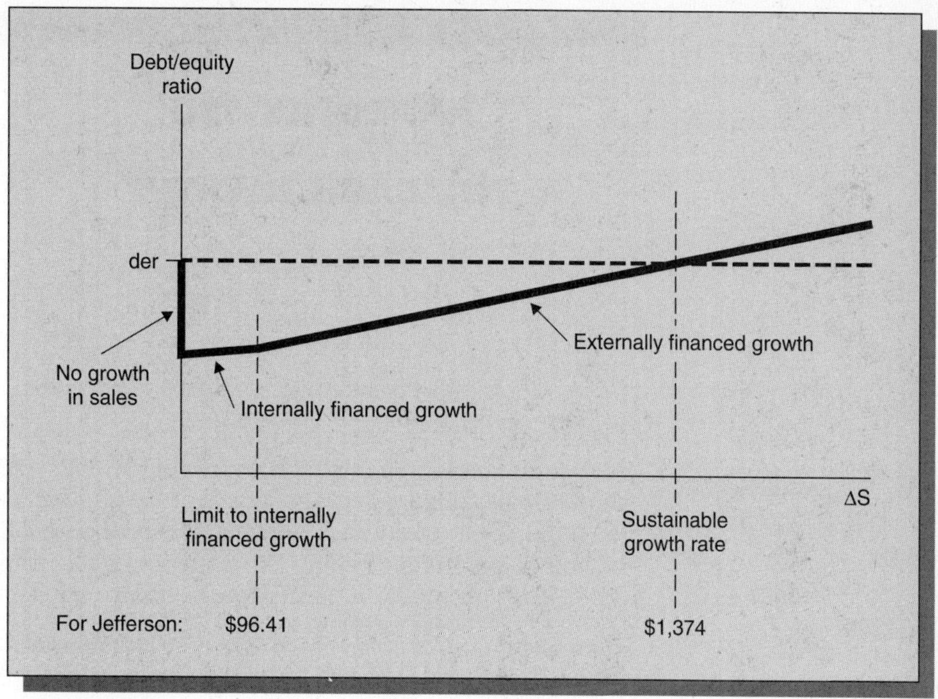

FIGURE 18C.1
How a company's debt/equity ratio changes with sales. If sales growth exceeds the sustainable growth rate, the firm's debt/equity ratio will rise.

cally the spontaneous liabilities arrive faster than retained earnings. Debt rises faster than equity, and the debt/equity ratio creeps upward.

3. Should the firm grow beyond its limit to internally financed growth, external financing becomes another addition to the right-hand side of the balance sheet. If the external financing comes from debt, the debt/equity ratio begins to rise at a still faster rate.

Figure 18C.1 summarizes these forces and identifies the relevant numbers for the Jefferson Company. At the increase in sales where the debt/equity ratio crosses through its starting level, the firm has reached its sustainable growth rate.

Problems

1. **(Sustainable growth)** Use your answers to Problem 17 of Chapter 18 to calculate the sustainable growth rate for that firm. What does this mean?

2. **(Sustainable growth)** Use your answers to Problem 18 of Chapter 18 to calculate the sustainable growth rate for that firm. What does this mean?

APPENDIX 18D

THE CASH BUDGET

cash budget—a time-oriented statement of projected cash flows

A **cash budget** is an itemized schedule of predicted cash inflows and outflows. It shows financial managers the details of the company's cash flows and identifies the timing of its likely cash excesses and cash shortfalls. It is typically done on a monthly basis unless a shorter time period gives insights that are worth the additional cost of preparing such detailed information.

We return to Carol May who needs to prepare a cash budget for 1995 for the Jefferson Company. First she breaks down her 1995 sales forecast of $3,000 into monthly sales figures:

January	$250	May	$350	September	$150
February	200	June	250	October	200
March	250	July	250	November	300
April	300	August	200	December	300

She notes that sales was $250 in both November and December 1994.

Carol also projects the following:

Regarding Inflows

1. 50% of sales will be for cash, with the other 50% for credit.
2. Of the credit sales, 80% will be collected in the following month; the remaining 20% will be collected two months after the sale.

Regarding Outflows

3. Payments for all production and operating costs will be made equally throughout the year.
4. The $140 investment in plant is scheduled for March.
5. The bond payable has an annual coupon so that annual interest is paid in one sum; interest is due along with the $50 of principal in December.
6. The tax expense of $81 is to be paid in equal quarterly installments in March, June, September, and December.
7. The $50 dividend will be paid in semi-annual payments of $25 each in February and August.

Target cash balance

8. The firm will set a target cash balance of $100 through June and $120 from July to December.

Carol begins with her sales projections, just as she began with sales when forecasting the pro-forma income statement and balance sheet. First she prepares the worksheet portion of the cash budget to organize her information about sales. (Carol's worksheet and cash budget are on page 682). She lists the monthly sales forecasts and breaks the data into cash sales and credit sales (50% cash, 50% credit from her Projection No. 1) to make it easier to identify when cash from sales is collected.

1. Cash Inflows

Next, Carol prepares the "Cash inflows" section of the cash budget. Since cash sales result in an immediate inflow of cash, she transcribes each monthly cash sales figure on the worksheet directly below to the line "Cash sales."

Example

Preparing the Line "Cash Sales" on the Cash Budget

On the worksheet, cash sales are projected to be $125 in January. This amount will be collected in January, therefore $125 becomes the January figure for the line "Cash sales" in the "Cash inflows" section of the cash budget. Carol continues the pattern for the remainder of the year.

Credit sales, on the other hand, are not collected immediately but pass through accounts receivable and are collected at a later date. From her projections (Projection No. 2), she expects 80% of credit sales to be collected one month after sale with the other 20% collected two months after the sale date. Accordingly, Carol applies these percentages to each figure for credit sales from the worksheet.

Example

Preparing the Lines "Collections—One Month" and "Collections—Two Months" on the Cash Budget

On the worksheet, credit sales are projected to be $125 in January. According to Carol's forecast, 80% or $100 will be collected one month later in February—this amount becomes the February figure for the line "Collections—1 month" in the "Cash inflows" section of the cash budget. The other 20% or $25 will be collected two months later in March—this amount becomes the March figure for the line "Collections—2 months" in the "Cash inflows" section of the cash budget. Carol continues the pattern for the remainder of the year.

Carol adds up the monthly cash inflows to produce the line "Total inflows."

2. Cash Outflows

Next Carol starts to work on cash outflows. From her pro-forma income statement (p. 658), she knows she must account for cost of goods sold, operating expenses, depreciation, interest expense, tax expense, and dividends.

Worksheet:

	1994		1995												
	Nov.	Dec.	Jan.	Feb.	Mar.	Apr.	May	June	July	Aug.	Sept.	Oct.	Nov.	Dec.	Total
Sales	250	250	250	200	250	300	350	250	250	200	150	200	300	300	3,000
Cash (50%)	125	125	125	100	125	150	175	125	125	100	75	100	150	150	1,500
Credit (50%)	125	125	125	100	125	150	175	125	125	100	75	100	150	150	1,500

THE JEFFERSON COMPANY
Pro-Forma Cash Budget for the Year 1995

	Jan.	Feb.	Mar.	Apr.	May	June	July	Aug.	Sept.	Oct.	Nov.	Dec.	Total
Cash inflows:													
Cash sales	125	100	125	150	175	125	125	100	75	100	150	150	1,500
Collections—1 month	100	100	80	100	120	140	100	100	80	60	80	120	1,180
—2 months	25	25	25	20	25	30	35	25	25	20	15	20	290
Total inflows	250	225	230	270	320	295	260	225	180	180	245	290	2,970
Cash outflows:													
Production costs	175	175	174	175	175	174	175	175	174	175	175	174	2,096
Operating costs	49	49	49	48	49	49	49	48	49	49	49	48	585
Purchase plant			140										140
Bonds—pay interest												18	18
—pay principal												50	50
Pay taxes			21			20			20			20	81
Pay dividends		25						25					50
Total outflows	224	249	384	223	224	243	224	248	243	224	224	310	3,020
Net In(out)flow	26	(24)	(154)	47	96	52	36	(23)	(63)	(44)	21	(20)	(50)
+ Beginning cash balance	100	100	100	100	100	100	100	120	120	120	120	120	
= Cash prior to financing	126	76	(54)	147	196	152	136	97	57	76	141	100	Total
+ Financing needed/Sell securities		**24**	**154**					**23**	**63**	**44**		**20**	**328**
− Financing repaid/Buy securities	**26**			**47**	**96**	**52**	**16**				**21**		**258**
= Ending (target) cash balance	100	100	100	100	100	100	120	120	120	120	120	120	**70**
Cumulative financing needed	–	–	*152*	*105*	*9*	–	–	–	*27*	*71*	*50*	***70***	
*Marketable securities balance**	*26*	*2*	–	–	–	*43*	*59*	*36*	–	–	–	–	

* Does not include the beginning-of-year balance of $50

Cost of goods sold Tracing through the accounting system, Carol recalls that when cost of goods sold is debited, the credit is to the inventory account, not to cash. When inventory is purchased, the credit is to accounts payable, not to cash. It is only when accounts payable is debited that cash is finally credited, that is, cash flows out from the firm. Carol uses this logic to calculate the cash to be spent in 1995 on production.

Example

Preparing the Line "Production Costs" on the Cash Budget

Since inventory and accounts payable come between cost of goods sold and cash, Carol examines those accounts. She compares the company's 1994 balance sheet (p. 656) and her pro-forma balance sheet for 1995 (p. 658), and discovers that inventory is projected to increase by $40—from $200 to $240—and accounts payable is projected to increase by $30—from $150 to $180. The $40 increase in inventory means that purchases will exceed the cost of goods sold as the firm increases its inventory balance and the firm will *spend more cash* than its cost of goods suggest. The $30 increase in accounts payable means that the firm will increase its obligations and *spend less cash* than its purchases suggest. Carol summarizes these numbers:

Cost of goods sold	$2,086
+ ΔInventory	40
− ΔAccounts payable	(30)
= Cash for production	$2,096

As she expects this amount to be paid equally throughout the year (her Projection No. 3), Carol divides $2,096 by 12 to get $174.67 per month. To avoid working with decimal figures, she rounds this to $175 for two months, followed by $174 for the third month; and she enters these figures on the cash budget.

Operating expenses Carol applies the same logic to operating expenses. From the accounting system she learns that operating expenses pass through accrued payables before they are paid.

Example

Preparing the Line "Operating Costs" on the Cash Budget

Since accrued payables comes between operating expenses and cash, Carol examines this account. She compares the company's 1994 balance sheet (p. 656) and her pro-forma balance sheet for 1995 (p. 658), and discovers that accrued payables is projected to increase by $40—from $200 to $240. This means that the firm will increase its obligations and *spend less cash* than its operating expenses suggest. Carol summarizes these numbers:

Operating expenses	$625
− ΔAccrued payables	(40)
= Cash for operations	$585

As she expects this amount to be paid equally throughout the year (her Projection No. 3), Carol divides $585 by 12 to get $48.75 per month. Again, to avoid working with decimal figures, she rounds this to $49 for three months, followed by $48 for the fourth month, and she enters these figures on the cash budget.

Depreciation Carol knows that *depreciation is not a cash flow* and has no place on a cash budget. However, looking at the line on her pro-forma income statement for depreciation expense reminds her that her company will be purchasing $140 of plant and equipment in 1995 (refer back to footnote 10 on page 660). Using her Projection No. 4, she records the $140 outflow on the cash budget in the column for March.

Interest expense, tax expense, dividends, and bond principal Next, Carol discovers that there are no accrual issues with interest expense, tax expense and dividends—the amount on the pro-forma income statement is the amount that will have to be paid in 1995. Using her projections (Nos. 5, 6, and 7), she places these figures in the cash budget. She also records the anticipated outflow of $50 in December to repay the bond principal falling due in 1995.

3. Net In(Out) Flow

Carol adds up the monthly cash outflows to produce the line "Total outflows." She then subtracts this from "Total inflows" to get the "Net in(out)flow" each month.

4. Monthly Cash Position

Finally Carol summarizes each month's cash flows to produce her forecast of the monthly cash balance and the monthly cash excess or shortfall.

1. She adds the beginning cash balance (the ending balance of $100 on the December 31, 1994, balance sheet becomes the beginning balance on January 1, 1995) to the month's net in(out)flow to get "Cash prior to financing." If the firm did nothing with respect to financing, this would be the month-end cash balance.
2. She imposes the firm's target cash balance (from her Projection No. 8).[1]
3. If cash prior to financing is below the target cash balance (as in February, March, August, September, October, and December), the firm will need to acquire additional funds. It can do this by selling off marketable securities, if any, or through external financing. If cash prior to financing is above the target cash balance (as in January, April, May, June, July, and November), the firm will have excess funds. It can use this money to repay external financing or to purchase marketable securities. Carol enters the difference between cash prior to financing and the target cash balance on the lines "Financing needed/sell securities" and "Financing repaid/buy securities."
4. Carol summarizes the firm's financing needs on the bottom of the cash budget using the lines "Cumulative financing needed" and "Marketable securities balance."

---

[1]**Elaboration:** Since business cash balances often do not earn interest, most firms try to minimize this amount, setting it equal to the sum of their transactions plus precautionary needs. Smaller firms sometimes find they must keep a higher cash balance when their bank requires a minimum balance in the firm's account. By contrast, large firms can use sophisticated "cash management systems" to push the noninterest-bearing cash balance as close to zero as possible.

5. As a last step, Carol checks the cash budget against the pro-forma income statement, balance sheet, and cash flow statement to ensure consistency. One indication of consistency is immediately apparent. The year-end cumulative financing needed on the cash budget is $70, exactly the EFN from the pro-forma balance sheet.

Problems

1. **(Cash budget—inflows)** A firm has the following data for sales:

	Cash sales	Credit sales
Actual:		
January	$25,000	$55,000
February	30,000	60,000
Forecast:		
March	40,000	80,000
April	35,000	75,000
May	30,000	70,000

Past experience is that 35% of credit sales are collected in the month of sale, 50% one month after sale, 13% two months after sale, and the remaining 2% of credit sales becomes bad debts. Prepare a schedule of cash inflows for the months of March, April, and May.

2. **(Cash budget—inflows)** A firm has the following data for sales:

	Cash sales	Credit sales
Actual:		
July	$95,000	$150,000
August	110,000	175,000
Forecast:		
September	150,000	250,000
October	185,000	300,000
November	200,000	350,000

Past experience is that 20% of credit sales is collected in the month of sale, 60% one month after sale, 17% two months after sale, and the remaining 3% of credit sales becomes bad debts. Prepare a schedule of cash inflows for the months of September, October, and November.

3. **(Cash budget—outflows)** The firm of Problem 1 projects the following cash outflows for the months of March, April, and May:

Production costs	$45,000 per month
Operating costs	30,000 per month
Tax payment	8,000 in April
Purchase of plant	12,000 in May
Payment of interest on debt	2,000 in March
Payment of debt principal	5,000 in March
Payment of dividends	6,000 in April

Prepare a schedule of cash outflows for the months of March, April, and May.

4. **(Cash budget—outflows)** The firm of Problem 2 projects the following cash outflows for the months of September, October, and November:

Production costs	$250,000 per month
Operating costs	125,000 per month
Tax payment	40,000 in October
Purchase of plant	50,000 in September
Payment of interest on debt	20,000 in September
Payment of debt principal	45,000 in September
Payment of dividends	20,000 in November

Prepare a schedule of cash outflows for the months of September, October, and November.

5. **(Cash budget—full Projection)** The firm of Problems 1 and 3 has a cash balance of $20,000 on March 1, which is its target cash balance. Prepare the bottom section of its cash budget showing net in(out)flow and monthly cash reconciliation for the months of March, April, and May.

6. **(Cash budget—full projection)** The firm of Problems 2 and 4 has a cash balance of $35,000 on September 1, which is its target cash balance. Prepare the bottom section of its cash budget showing net in(out)flow and monthly cash reconciliation for the months of September, October, and November.

APPENDIX 18E

FINANCIAL FEEDBACK

financial feedback—the iterative process of incorporating the cost of new financing into pro-forma statements

Jefferson Company requires external financing, yet the pro-forma statements do not yet contain the impact of the EFN on interest and dividend payments. This is the effect known as **financial feedback.** If Jefferson borrows, interest expense will go up. If Jefferson sells shares of stock, dividend payments will likely rise. Carol needs to do a couple of iterations through the pro-forma statements to incorporate the costs associated with the new financing.

Carol notices from the cash budget (p. 682) that the maximum need for external funds is $152.00 (in March). To get a sense of what financial feedback means, Carol does the following analysis, assuming that the company will borrow the additional $152.00 (and any other amount the analysis reveals that the Jefferson Company will need) at a 10% interest rate on January 1 and will keep this amount outstanding throughout the year.[1]

Example

Financial Feedback

The $152.00 of new debt will result in additional interest of 10% of $152.00 = $15.20. Carol adds this to the original $18.00 of interest, raising interest expense to $33.20 and does a "second iteration":

	Original Projection[2]	Second Iteration	Third Iteration	Fourth Iteration
EBIT	$249	$249.00	$249.00	$249.00
−Interest	18	33.20	33.85	33.88
EBT	231	215.80	215.15	215.12
−Tax exp. (35%)	81	75.53	75.30	75.29
EAT	$150	$140.27	$139.85	$139.83
−Dividend (1/3)	50	46.76	46.62	46.61
Add to RE	$100	$ 93.51	$ 93.23	$ 93.22
EFN	$ 70	$ 76.49	$ 76.77	$ 76.78

[1]**Observation:** As we have seen from the cash budget, Jefferson needs no funds until February, and needs $152 only for a short time. We have purposely kept this example simple to make it easier to understand. In reality, with a different amount and possible source of financing each month, we would have to consider each month's added financing costs separately. We would also have to include the interest earnings from excess cash invested in marketable securities.

[2]**Cross-reference:** Taken from the pro-forma income and balance sheet statement on p. 658.

After the second iteration, the addition to retained earnings is down to $93.51, $6.49 less than the figure of $100.00 from the original projection. Carol adds this shortfall (the $6.49) to the EFN and performs a "third iteration," in which the firm borrows $308.49 (the original $150.00 of bonds payable plus another $158.49: $152.00 from the original projection plus the new $6.49). Interest expense now becomes $33.85 (the original $18.00 plus 10% of $158.49).

After the third iteration, the addition to retained earnings is down to $93.23, $6.77 less than the figure of $100.00 from the original projection. Carol adjusts the EFN and performs a "fourth iteration" in which the firm borrows $308.77 (the original $150.00 of bonds payable, plus another $158.77: $152.00 from the original projection, plus the new $6.77). Interest expense now becomes $33.88 (the original $18.00 plus 10% of $158.77).

Carol observes that there is very little difference between the third and fourth iterations—the process has converged. There is no need to go further. If the firm borrows $158.77 at 10% for the full year, it will raise its end-of-year EFN to $76.78.

CHAPTER 19
FINANCIAL MARKETS AND INSTITUTIONS

Glenn Morton reached for one of the dozen books on the chair beside his desk, located the passage he was looking for, and wrote several notes on one of the 20 or so pieces of paper covering his desk. Replacing the book, he grabbed a second sheet of paper and wrote down another thought. After about 40 minutes of this, he sat back and surveyed his desk with a shake of his head. How would he make sense of all this information?

Glenn was a vice president and lending officer of a large bank. He had recently completed his M.B.A. degree with honors at a local university and had been asked by the chair of the finance faculty to speak on financial markets and institutions at a session of the introductory finance class. Glenn's problem was to organize the material in a way that would be interesting and useful to the students—all within one 90-minute class period.

Glenn looked over his notes. One page was labeled "primary markets." Another was titled "secondary markets." There were several pages on investment and commercial banks, insurance companies, mutual funds, and other members of the "financial industry." Directly in front of him were notes about the way security prices behaved. To the right was a page on the regulation of the financial markets. Glenn moved several of the pages around, cocked his head, and looked over the papers again. Slowly, the pattern was making sense. Glenn took out a clean sheet of paper and sketched out a summary outline of the topics. He could see the class session beginning to take shape. One by one he reorganized the pages, turning them into the materials that would guide him during the class.

The financial markets provide the setting in which much financial activity occurs. Within these markets, individuals and companies obtain money for the present and save and invest for the future. Securities are issued and traded, loans are made and repaid, and risks are shared and shifted. Companies' prospects are analyzed and priced. Financial institutions—including investment and commercial banks, insurance companies, mutual funds, and pension and endowment funds—are key players in these markets, bringing savers and investors together and handling the transfer of billions of dollars daily.

As students of finance, we all struggle with the same problem facing Glenn. The world of financial markets and institutions is a marvelously rich and complex one, with many participants and organizations providing a wide variety of financial products and services. The study of financial markets and institutions is legitimately a full course in itself. Like Glenn's 90-minute class, this chapter can only hope to scratch the surface and provide a description of the most important players and concepts.

Key Points You Should Learn from This Chapter

After reading this chapter you should be able to:

- Describe seven roles of financial markets and institutions, three methods of channeling funds from net savers to net investors, and the difference between the money and capital markets.
- Discuss how newly created securities are issued, including the role of the investment banker, flotation costs, and private placement.
- Describe the nature of the secondary financial markets, including the securities exchanges and other trading mechanisms.
- Identify indexes that measure financial market activity; and compare technical analysis, fundamental analysis, the efficient market hypothesis, and the random walk as descriptions of security price behavior.
- Describe three types of financial intermediaries and five types of financial intermediation.
- Relate the basics of the regulatory environment in which the financial markets and financial institutions function.

Introductory Concepts—The Functions and Functioning of Financial Markets and Institutions

Of all the roles played by the financial system, the movement of funds from individuals and companies with surplus resources to those in need of money is one of the most important. In this section, we look briefly at the wide range of roles played by financial markets and institutions, identify three ways in which funds move within the system, and draw the distinction between the money and capital markets.

1. Functions of Financial Markets and Institutions

Financial markets and institutions perform at least seven functions in the economic system. They are: (1) a payments mechanism, (2) a vehicle for savings, (3) a supplier of credit, (4) a storehouse of wealth, (5) a means of obtaining liquidity, (6) a mechanism for risk shifting, and (7) a vehicle for public policy.

Payments mechanism Most payments for goods and services are made by checks or electronic transfers processed by the banking system, a key financial institution.

Savings vehicle Individuals use financial markets and institutions such as banks and stock brokers to move their savings into bank deposits, notes, bonds, and stocks.

Credit supplier Financial institutions such as banks, as well as companies and individual investors operating in the financial markets, provide loans that permit companies and individuals to supplement their income and purchase assets.

Wealth storehouse Most individuals and companies that have accumulated liquid capital use financial instruments traded in the financial markets to store their wealth.

Liquidity source The many participants in the financial markets provide savers with the ability to convert most financial assets to cash if and when required.

Risk reducer Financial intermediaries such as banks and insurance companies sell a wide variety of products to reduce the risk of exposure to financial and physical damages.

Policy vehicle The federal government uses its ability to affect the financial markets to influence the stability and rate of growth of the economy.

2. Imbalances in Income and Expenses

Consider what a typical year in your life looks like from a financial point of view. Most likely, you earn some money from a job, which may be supplemented by earnings from a bank account or other investments. From your income you must pay your living expenses: food, clothing, shelter, education, entertainment, etc. As we saw in Chapter 18, if you earn more than you spend, you face the decision of how best to deploy your excess cash. On the other hand, if you spend more than you earn, your problem is to obtain external financing to make up the deficit. The same is true for every other individual and business in the economy.

deficit-budget unit—an individual or business that spends more than it earns

balanced-budget unit—an individual or business that spends exactly what it earns

surplus-budget unit—an individual or business that spends less than it earns

Accordingly, over any period of time, every individual, business, and government falls into one of three categories: (1) a **deficit-budget unit,** (2) a **balanced-budget unit,** or (3) a **surplus-budget unit.** A deficit-budget unit is one whose expenditures exceed its revenues; to make up the deficit it must acquire additional funds. A balanced-budget unit (a rarity) is one whose expenditures exactly equal its revenues; it is able to take Polonius's advice in *Hamlet* and: "neither a borrower nor a lender be." A surplus-budget unit is one whose revenues exceed its expenditures; it looks for ways to invest its excess funds.

It is normal for any individual or business to move back and forth between these three states. Individuals tend to be deficit-budget units in the early stages of their working lives when their income is relatively low and when they are starting families and acquiring assets. Later in life, individuals often switch over to be surplus-budget units as their income increases and their children grow up and leave home. As the external financing needs (EFN) model of Chapter 18 illustrated, companies tend to be deficit-budget units during periods of rapid growth and surplus-budget units when they reach a more mature stage.

3. Moving Funds from Surplus Units to Deficit Units

In a world with both surplus-budget units looking to invest funds and deficit-budget units looking to obtain them, it is natural that the financial markets have created mechanisms to channel funds from the former to the latter. It is common to classify these routes into three categories: (1) direct transfer, (2) semidirect transfer, and (3) indirect transfer or intermediation. Figure 19.1 illustrates these three paths. For simplicity, surplus-budget units are identified as "lenders" and deficit-budget units as "borrowers" in Figure 19.1, even though the transaction they engage in might not have the legal form of a loan.

Direct transfer The simplest method for moving funds is direct transfer from lender to borrower. If you have ever borrowed money from a relative or friend, you have used this method. Some corporations and investment funds also use direct transfer. However, since this method requires both parties to know of and have access to each other, it is the least used of the three routes.

broker—an individual or company that locates buyers and sellers and brings them together

Semidirect transfer Semidirect transfer involves the use of a professional **broker** to locate buyers and sellers and bring them together. Imagine trying to sell a house using direct transfer. The odds of your knowing a buyer with the desire and the money to buy your house when you want to sell it are minuscule. You could advertise in the local paper or put a sign on the lawn to attract passers-by, but this might not bring in sufficient potential buyers. As a result, most people use a real-estate broker when they sell their houses. As Figure 19.1 indicates, in the financial markets this role is primarily played by investment bankers. Like direct transfer, the money and securities are exchanged directly

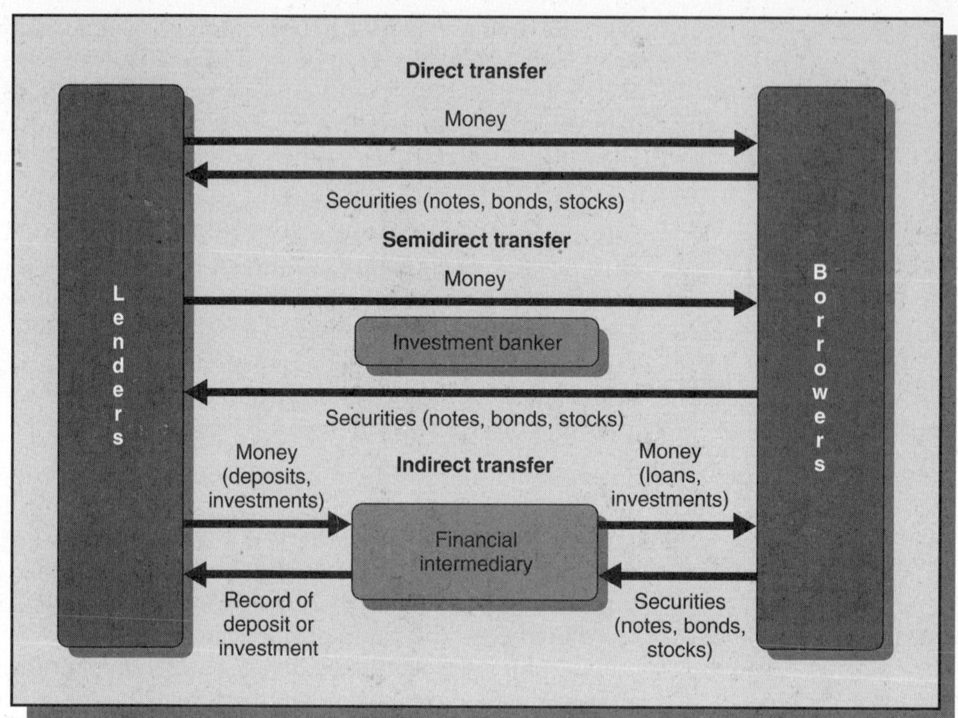

FIGURE 19.1
Methods of funds transfer. Money moves from lenders to borrowers in one of three ways: direct, semidirect, or indirect.

by the lender and borrower. The broker does not handle the funds but simply earns a finder's fee.

financial intermediary—an organization that takes funds from surplus-budget units and provides them to deficit-budget units

intermediation —moving funds through financial intermediaries

Indirect transfer The third method of moving funds is through a **financial intermediary,** an organization that places itself between savers and investors. Because of the participation of intermediaries, this route is called **intermediation.** It is quite common for the needs of lenders and borrowers not to match. For example, suppose you had $1,000 you wished to invest for the next 60 days. What are the odds that you, or a broker hired by you, will find a deficit-budget unit with exactly that requirement for funds? Financial intermediaries solve this and other problems of mismatched needs by combining the loans of many lenders, repackaging the money in other forms, and then relending the funds to a variety of borrowers.

A commercial bank would be a typical financial intermediary represented in Figure 19.1. You could deposit your $1,000 in a savings account at a bank and be able to withdraw your funds in 60 days. The bank would combine your money with the deposits of other lenders and make loans of many different types to its customers—the deficit-budget units—in the amounts and for the periods of time they desire. Note that you never deal with the ultimate borrowers of your money—in fact you never even learn who those persons or organizations are. Both your needs and those of the borrower are met by the intermediary.

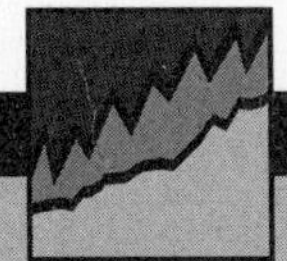

IMPROVING FINANCE'S PROCESSES

Improving the Funds Transfer Process at Corning, Incorporated

The cash management group of Corning Incorporated's treasury now defines its requirements to banks in the same terms used for other suppliers. The company invites bankers to attend its in-house quality-management seminars, where they learn what Corning expects from product and service providers. Corning's assistant treasurer for cash management relates that "It is resulting in 'bells going off.' Now they are using quality terminology and beginning to get some customer focus." The banks are invited to become partners in Corning's treasury processes to improve their service. In one example, Citibank and Wachovia have tailored their cash management systems to tie into Corning's general ledger system. Corning gets the data in a form immediately useful, saving considerable rework. As a by-product, the banks are developing a heightened level of customer awareness and an expanded product line they can sell to others.

Source: James A.F. Stoner and Frank M. Werner, *Finance in the Quality Revolution* (Morristown, N.J.: Financial Executives Research Foundation, 1993), pp. 19–20.

As you study and use the services of the financial markets and financial institutions, it is useful to view funds transfer as a process, similar in many ways to the other financial processes we discussed in Chapters 13 and 14. Surplus-budget units are the suppliers, investment bankers and financial intermediaries are the process operators, and the deficit-budget units are the customers. Like any process, there are typically numerous ways to make improvements to better meet customer requirements and reduce costs.

4. Money Vs. Capital Markets

money markets—the markets for (debt) securities with maturity of one year or less

capital markets—the markets for securities with maturity greater than one year

The term **money markets** is used for the financial markets where debt securities with a maturity of one year or less trade. The **capital markets** are the markets for securities with maturity longer than one year, including intermediate and long-term notes, bonds, and stocks.

With its short-term focus, the primary function of the money markets is to help individuals and organizations manage their liquidity, i.e., their day-to-day cash position. Individuals use the money markets for short-term personal loans, cash advances against their credit cards, and to cover overdrafts against their checking accounts. As we saw in Chapter 16, companies use the money markets to finance temporary working capital needs. Governments borrow heavily in the money markets as well; for example, the federal government sells the Treasury bills we discussed in Chapter 6 to balance its tax receipts and expenditures. And investors, both individuals and institutions, use funds from the money markets to finance the purchase of securities on margin, a topic we covered in Chapter 15. In Chapter 20, we will study the common money market instruments used by businesses.

The capital markets provide intermediate and long-term financing for assets of comparable maturity. Individuals use the capital markets to finance the purchase of homes, automobiles, and other durable goods. Companies raise funds in the capital markets to build plant and equipment, to finance permanent working capital, and for mergers and acquisitions. Governments use capital market funds to build schools and highways and to finance their long-term deficits. In Chapters 21 and 22 we will look at common capital market instruments that businesses use.

Although the maturities of the instruments traded and the functions of the money and capital markets are clearly distinct, in practice the distinction blurs quite a bit both in terms of the participants and the places where market activity takes place. Most individuals and organizations participate in both markets. For example, a commercial bank may make short-term and intermediate-term loans in the same day, the federal government may sell 90-day Treasury bills and 15-year Treasury bonds in the same week, or a family may take a one-month cash advance on its credit card and refinance its 30-year home mortgage in the same month. Also, both money market and capital market securities are often traded in the same location. For example, a commercial bank retail office may be the site of loan transactions of many maturities, and one-month Treasury bills trade along with the common stock of many companies on the "over-the-counter market."

Primary Financial Markets

primary financial markets—the markets for the initial issue of securities

initial public offering (IPO)—the first public sale of a company's stock

The **primary financial markets** are the markets where securities are issued for the first time. For example, when Great Lakes Aviation, Ltd., sold 2,500,000 new shares of its common stock in January 1994, it did so in the primary markets. In 1992, new stock and bond issues in the United States totaled $851.2 billion and nearly 600 companies came to market for the first time with **initial public offerings** worth $39.4 billion.[1]

1. The Investment Banker

A key player in the primary markets is the investment banker, a specialist in the distribution of new securities. Most firms go to the capital markets infrequently and find it costly to develop the skills and resources needed to issue securities. Investment bankers have the expertise, contacts, and scale of operations to perform this function efficiently and at comparatively low cost.

Companies hire investment bankers through one of two processes. Most common is negotiation, in which the investment bankers work closely with the firm providing a full range of services from planning to distribution of the issue. Terms are negotiated directly between the firm and its investment bankers. The alternative is competitive bidding, where each interested investment banker submits a sealed bid to purchase the new issue and the highest bidder gets the job. Because of the need of governments for a public display of fairness, competitive bid-

[1] **Reference:** *Fact Book for the Year 1992* (New York: New York Stock Exchange, 1993), p. 8.

ding is typical for government issues. Companies pursuing modern quality management appear to be moving further toward negotiation as part of their desire to structure a customer-supplier alignment with this important supplier of financial services.

Investment bankers provide a variety of services to companies issuing securities, including: (1) analysis and advice,(2) underwriting, (3) selling, and (4) market stabilization.

Analysis and advice As experts in the issuance of securities, investment bankers advise companies on the amount and timing of a new issue, the combination of features to include in the issue, how to price the issue, and the legal aspects of bringing the issue to market (although most of the detailed legal work generally is done by outside counsel who are specialists in the complex area of Securities and Exchange Commission (SEC) registration requirements).

For a publicly traded stock, it is typical for an issue of additional shares to be priced at slightly below market in order to attract new investors. For an initial public offering, however, there is no market price on which to base the offering price of the new issue, and the investment banker will conduct an analysis of the company, conditions in the stock market, and comparable firms to recommend a fair price. Either way, since market conditions change daily, the actual offering price normally is not finalized until the last moment. Note the potential conflict of interest: the issuing firm wants a high price to raise the maximum amount possible while the investment banker would benefit from a low price to make the issue easy to sell.

Underwriting Companies need to plan their cash flow and usually wish to avoid the risk of not knowing the proceeds of a security issue until after the fact. In response, investment bankers offer a service known as **underwriting** that ensures that the firm will receive a given amount from the sale. The investment banker purchases the issue at the agreed-upon price and then assumes the responsibility for reselling the issue to the public. Notice that when investment bankers assume this role, they go beyond the simple broker relationship between buyer and seller and act as intermediaries.

underwriting—guaranteeing the proceeds of a security issue by purchasing the issue at an agreed-upon price

Two levels of underwriting commitment are available. In a firm commitment, the investment banker purchases the entire issue, thus assuming all the risk of sale. In a standby commitment, the investment banker purchases only the portion of the issue that cannot be sold by the firm directly, for example, the shares leftover from an offering to existing shareholders.

The investment banker normally creates an underwriting group, or syndicate, to spread the risk of underwriting an issue. Within the syndicate, the firm's investment banker is known as the *originating house* and usually takes on the responsibility of lead underwriter or manager of the syndicate.

Selling The investment banker puts together a selling group, consisting of the syndicate members plus up to several hundred additional securities dealers who actually place the securities with their customers. To further reduce the risk of underwriting, the selling group typically lines up buyers even before the offering is made. Since the Securities and Exchange Commission prohibits offering a security without a disclosure statement known as a **prospectus**, a preliminary prospectus, popularly known as a *red herring*, is used at this stage.

prospectus—a booklet of data about a company which must be given to potential investors prior to soliciting any money

If the issue is underwritten, two alternative selling responsibilities are possible. In an undivided account—the usual arrangement—each syndicate member remains liable for a portion of all shares that cannot be sold by the members of the selling group. In a divided account, each syndicate member is liable only for its portion of the issue. If the issue is not underwritten, the selling group engages in a best-efforts offering, committing only to do its best to place the securities.

Market stabilization The manager typically agrees to "make a market in" (buy and sell) the newly issued securities for a specified period after the issue date—normally 30 days—guaranteeing that the original investors can resell the securities if they desire.

Figure 19.2,[2] is an announcement of Great Lakes Aviation, Ltd.'s public offering of 2.5 million shares of common stock, popularly known as a *tombstone*. In addition to identifying the company and the number and type of securities, tombstones list the investment bankers who participated in the issue. The investment banker(s) who arranged the issue are listed first (in this case Alex. Brown & Sons and Piper Jaffray Inc.). Following are the names of the other investment banks in the syndicate, listed in the order of the number of shares each purchased.

2. Flotation Cost

Flotation cost, the cost of issuing new securities, generally consists of two components: the spread, or investment bankers' fees; and administrative costs including registration of the issue with the SEC, legal fees, printing costs, trustee's fees, outside auditors' fees, and taxes.

Example

Underwriting Spread

In advising a company on its planned security issue, Glenn Morton has proposed a spread equal to 4% of the issue's face value, subdivided as follows:

Managing underwriter's fee	0.60% of issue
Underwriting (risk) fee	1.40% of issue
Concession (selling) fees	2.00% of issue
	4.00%

Flotation costs vary with the risk of placing the issue—how difficult it will be for the investment banker to sell the securities. One factor is the riskiness of the security itself. In general it is more difficult to sell stock than bonds, so the flotation cost for stock is normally greater than that for bonds. For the same reason,

[2] **Reference:** *The Wall Street Journal*, Jan. 21, 1994, p. C16.

This advertisement is neither an offer to sell nor a solicitation of an offer to buy any of these securities. The offering is made only by the Prospectus.

January 21, 1994

2,500,000 Shares

GREAT LAKES AVIATION, LTD.

Common Stock

Price $11 Per Share

Copies of the Prospectus may be obtained from such of the Underwriters as may legally offer these securities in compliance with the securities laws of the respective states.

ALEX. BROWN & SONS
INCORPORATED

PIPER JAFFRAY INC.

CS FIRST BOSTON
DEAN WITTER REYNOLDS INC.
DONALDSON, LUFKIN & JENRETTE
SECURITIES CORPORATION
A.G. EDWARDS & SONS, INC.
KIDDER, PEABODY & CO.
INCORPORATED
MERRILL LYNCH & CO.
MORGAN STANLEY & CO.
INCORPORATED
OPPENHEIMER & CO., INC.
PAINEWEBBER INCORPORATED
PRUDENTIAL SECURITIES INCORPORATED
SMITH BARNEY SHEARSON INC.
ROBERT W. BAIRD & CO.
INCORPORATED
GEORGE K. BAUM & COMPANY
WILLIAM BLAIR & COMPANY
THE CHICAGO CORPORATION
DAIN BOSWORTH
INCORPORATED
D. A. DAVIDSON & CO.
INCORPORATED
FIRST OF MICHIGAN CORPORATION
HANIFEN, IMHOFF INC.
KEMPER SECURITIES, INC.
JOHN G. KINNARD AND COMPANY
INCORPORATED
MCDONALD & COMPANY
SECURITIES, INC.
THE ROBINSON-HUMPHREY COMPANY, INC.
RONEY & CO.

FIGURE 19.2
A tombstone. These announcements of new security issues identify the number of shares (or amount of debt), company, type of security, offering price, and the investment bankers.

large, stable firms pay lower flotation costs than small, speculative firms. Flotation costs also vary with the size of the issue. In general, large issues cost less to float on a percentage basis due to the ability to spread the fixed costs of the issue across many securities, the ease of selling better-known issues, and competition among investment bankers for major clients.

3. Private Placement

private placement—the sale of a new issue of securities directly to an investor

A **private placement** is the sale of a security issue directly to one or a small group of investors without going through the public markets. For example, a company might sell $10 million of its debt to a life insurance company rather than offering

This announcement appears as a matter of record only.

$30,000,000

Subordinated Notes due 2001

New Vision Television L.P.

The undersigned acted as financial advisor to the Company and arranged the private placement of the securities with institutional investors.

Bank of Montreal

December 1993

FIGURE 19.3
Announcement of a private placement. The company borrowed $30 million from an unidentified lender.

it to the general public. Both bonds and stock are privately placed, although the volume of debt transactions far exceeds that of privately placed equity.

Private placements are done both with and without the services of an investment banker. Large, experienced companies that are known to the private investment community often use private placements to avoid engaging a broker and paying flotation costs. However, smaller companies and those with less exposure to financial markets typically still require the services of an investment banker to locate investors and to provide advice about market conditions, timing, and how to structure the issue. Banks that assist companies in privately placing their debt like to advertise in the financial press to celebrate their success and to attract new customers. Figure 19.3, taken from *The Wall Street Journal*,[3] is the announcement of the private placement of $30 million of notes by New Vision Television, L.P.

[3] **Reference:** *The Wall Street Journal*, Jan. 13, 1994, p. C13.

Four advantages of private placements relate to: (1) speed, (2) privacy, (3) terms of the issue, and (4) size of the issue.

Speed Compared to public offerings, private placements can be made far more quickly. There is no requirement for registration with the SEC, avoiding the time it takes to prepare and file extensive paperwork, and no mandated waiting period between filing and offering dates as there is with a public issue. In 1982, however, in response to concerns over long lead time, the time to issue securities to the public was lessened considerably when the SEC approved a system known as **shelf registration.** Under shelf registration, a company files the required paperwork for a public issue in advance of its intention to issue the securities. The company then can issue the securities in small batches via auction without further SEC authorization.

shelf registration—advance SEC approval to make small public security issues

Privacy Because there is no public filing or announcement in a private issue, the company is not required to disclose any information to the public about its operations, finances, or management. This can be appealing to companies concerned about competitors' potential use of the data or to wealthy stockholders and managers who might prefer not to make their financial status public.

Terms In a private placement, the terms of the issue are tailored to the needs of the borrower and lender through direct negotiation. There is far less pressure to make the issue conform to the standard terms and forms preferred in the public markets.

Size Private placement permits small issues to be sold without excessive flotation costs. For example, while a small public issue might be anything below $10,000,000 a small private issue could easily be as small as $100,000.

There are also some disadvantages to private placements. Privately placed securities tend to be difficult to resell since a public market for the issue has not been established. The lender, desiring to benefit from the issue for its full term, often insists on a covenant prohibiting refinancing at the borrowers' option. And even though flotation costs are typically lower than for a public issue, overall costs are usually higher since private lenders demand a higher interest rate and also often negotiate some form of "sweetener," such as warrants or a convertible feature.[4]

Secondary Financial Markets

secondary financial markets—the markets for trading existing securities

The **secondary financial markets** are the markets for the reselling or trading of previously issued securities. In this section we look at the functions of secondary

[4] **Cross-reference:** Warrants and convertibles are covered in Chapter 22, pp. 808–813.

markets and explore the exchanges and other mechanisms by which securities are traded.

1. Functions of the Secondary Markets

Five functions of the secondary markets are: (1) to permit trading, (2) to provide information, (3) to create continuity, (4) to protect participants, and (5) to improve the distribution of capital funds.

Permit trading The secondary markets are places where a large number of buyers and sellers can come together. By centralizing the activities of many participants, the probability becomes very high that every buyer will find a seller and every seller will find a buyer quickly and for the same amount of securities. Participants can invest for the long term or, if so inclined, can speculate on future price movements of securities.

Provide information Trading activities in the organized secondary markets are public and highly visible. The ticker tape reporting security trades—no longer a physical tape but now a computerized record—is made available to the public in real time. It is displayed in brokerage houses and on television channels, and is accessible to anyone by computer. In addition, fair and competitive price quotations are available for the asking.

Create continuity With so many trades taking place, the secondary markets guarantee that securities are highly liquid and marketable. This not only makes it easy for investors to cash out of their positions, it also ensures that securities are good loan collateral, permitting trading on margin and enhancing individuals' and companies' ability to borrow.

Protect participants The regulation of the secondary markets by the Securities and Exchange Commission and the rules of activity established by each exchange (which must be approved by the SEC) create a set of publicly known and accepted ground rules for trading activities. Security brokers and dealers must be licensed—a designation requiring the passing of examinations covering market procedures and securities law—and must act within a strict set of guidelines defining legal and ethical behavior. Market activities are supervised by regulatory authorities on a continuous basis in a further attempt to identify and eliminate any fraudulent activities.

Improve capital distribution An active secondary market makes investors more willing to purchase securities in the primary market, since it becomes possible to resell the securities should an investor's needs or opinion of the investment change. In addition, to the extent that there are many participants in the secondary market, security prices reflect investors' consensus estimate of each firm's opportunities. An investor looking to invest new funds is more likely to direct the money to a company with good business opportunities when investment prices are realistic than if a company's opportunity set and security prices are disconnected.

2. The Security Exchanges

At the core of the secondary markets are the security exchanges, the places where buyers and sellers come together. Originally, security exchanges were central locations where brokers met in person to trade securities for themselves and their customers. Today, they are equally likely to be computer networks linking brokers and traders around the world. In what follows, we look first at the physical security exchanges and then at the "over the counter" or NASDAQ market, the primary electronic exchange in the United States.

The physical exchanges When most people think of the securities markets, they think of the organized exchanges of national scope: the New York Stock Exchange and the American Stock Exchange. These two markets are indeed central to stock trading in the United States, handling more than 60% of all trades by dollar volume. But there are other domestic stock exchanges as well. Some are regional in orientation, such as the Philadelphia Stock Exchange serving the east coast, the Midwest Stock Exchange in Chicago, and the Pacific Stock Exchange in San Francisco. Others, such as the Boston Stock Exchange, are primarily local in orientation. Each of the regional and local markets trades shares of companies in its geographical area, including some that are also listed on the New York and American exchanges.

There are, of course, security exchanges in each major financial center: London, Tokyo, Frankfurt, Paris, Rome, Toronto, Zurich, Hong Kong, etc., on which the

securities of companies headquartered in that country trade. Until recently, it was unusual for securities of a company to trade on an exchange outside its home country. However, there is currently a trend for multinational companies to list their shares on stock exchanges in more than one country, for example, Diamler-Benz, whose stock is now traded both in Frankfurt and on the New York Stock Exchange. This reflects the increasing desire of these companies to see themselves as global in all aspects: strategy, products, facilities, employees, and—in part through the international trading of their securities—ownership.

A membership in a stock exchange is called a "seat," although most members spend the majority of their time at the exchange on their feet. There are 1,366 seats on the New York Stock Exchange, a number that has remained constant since 1953. Seats may be bought and sold, just like securities; in 1992, 28 New York Stock Exchange seats changed hands at prices ranging from $375,000 to $600,000. As you might imagine, the price of a seat, just like the price of a security, is the present value of the benefits forecasted—in this case potential commission income and the opportunity to resell the seat at a later date. As of the end of 1992, the 1,366 members belonged to 503 companies, of which 318 were qualified to do business with the public.[5]

There are four types of members on the New York Stock Exchange: commission brokers, independent brokers, floor traders, and specialists. Commission brokers are the individuals most associated with the exchange in the public's mind, the people who execute trades for customers. Independent brokers, also called "floor brokers" or "$2 brokers" after an early commission rate, offer their services to other brokers rather than to the public, handling overflow business during periods of high activity. Floor traders offer their services to no one; they are wealthy individuals who own a seat to be part of the action on the exchange floor and to trade for their own account.

The fourth type of member is the "specialist," whose role is significantly different from the other three. Each specialist is located at a specific trading location on the floor and is responsible for the trading activity of one or more securities on the exchange. Specialists record all trades in their assigned securities and send the information to the ticker tape. They quote prices on request: the last trade and the current bid and asked prices. They are the "broker's brokers," accepting trading instructions from other brokers and executing them when an opposite party arrives. They are also responsible for maintaining a continuous, orderly market by trading for their own accounts, becoming the opposite side to any unmatched trade.

listing—arranging for a company's securities to trade on a stock exchange

A company that wishes its securities to trade on an organized exchange must meet the exchange's **listing** requirements. Each exchange has its own standards, both for initial listing and for a company to remain listed. Although there are some complexities and flexibilities in its rules, the primary listing requirements of the New York Stock Exchange are given in Figure 19.4.[6] In addition each exchange

[5] **Reference:** *Fact Book for the Year 1992.* (New York: New York Stock Exchange, 1993), p. 73.

[6] **Reference:** *Fact Book for the Year 1992.* (New York: New York Stock Exchange, 1993), pp. 29–32.

Requirement	Initial listing	Continued listing
Earning power	Earnings before taxes of at least $2.5 million in the most recent year and $2 million in the two years prior, or $6.5 million in total for the last three years plus $4.5 million in the most recent year	
Asset value	Net tangible assets of at least $18 million	
Market value of publicly held shares	At least $18 million	At least $5 million
Shares outstanding	At least 1.1 million	At least 600,000
Shareholders	At least 2,000 holders of 100 shares or more, or 2,200 holders plus average monthly trading volume of at least 100,000 shares over the most recent six months	At least 1,200 holders of 100 shares or more

FIGURE 19.4
New York Stock Exchange listing requirements. The requirements for initial listing are more stringent than those to remain listed.

requires listed companies to adhere to its rules of operation and all SEC requirements for listed companies.

Listing on an exchange provides a company with free advertising and publicity since its financial activities and the prices of its securities are reported daily in the financial press. Since only large companies can meet the listing requirements, listing conveys some prestige and an enhanced reputation as a financially sound firm, a reputation that might lower the company's cost of capital. However, some companies, including Apple Computer and Intel, recently have chosen not to list on the organized exchanges due to the emergence of the NASDAQ system as a viable alternative to physical exchange trading.

NASDAQ NASDAQ (pronounced "NAZ-DAK") is the acronym of the National Association of Securities Dealers Automated Quotation system, a computerized trading system for securities not listed on the physical exchanges. Prior to the 1930s, this market was popularly called the "over the counter market," as trading took place over teller counters in commercial bank branches. In 1933, the Glass-Steagall Act removed securities trading from commercial banks, and trading in these securities moved to brokerage houses. Although the popular name is still used by many people, today NASDAQ is a computerized network of some 10,000 securities dealers who offer to buy and sell ("make a market in") securities. Trading is done by direct negotiation with the dealer over the telephone, and quotations and settlement are provided by the computer network. Among the securities traded in the NASDAQ system are roughly half of all industrial stocks, all government bonds, and about 90% of corporate bonds. In 1993, $1.35 trillion of securities were traded via the NASDAQ system.[7]

3. Other Trading Mechanisms

Although the vast majority of securities are traded on the exchanges, there are two other vehicles for trading: (1) institutional block trading and (2) trading through private computerized services.

Institutional block trading Large blocks of securities are often traded directly through stockbrokers, usually by large institutional investors. Often it is difficult to buy or sell a large number of shares without moving the market price in an adverse direction. For example, a portfolio manager wishing to sell 50,000 shares of General Motors might be concerned that such an increase in the number of shares available for sale would drive down the price. Institutional block trades are handled much like a primary market issue. The broker locates buyers through its network of customers instead of finding them via the exchanges. It is only as a final step, when all the buyers have been located and confirmed, that the actual trade(s) are passed through the exchange floor to meet the broker's obligation to funnel trades to the exchanges of which it is a member.

Computerized trading services Several computer services, Instinet for example, have set up private systems to trade securities through a computer network. These trades are cheap, fast, and anonymous, although they represent a very small portion of all securities trading.

The Behavior of Financial Markets

Measuring and predicting the future of security prices, especially stock prices, has fascinated financial observers ever since the first securities were traded in Venice in the thirteenth century. Today, there are many ways to measure security price movements and four major schools of thought about how stock prices change and can be forecasted.

1. Measuring the Markets

Investment professionals, securities exchanges, and the financial press have created a wide variety of devices to measure the performance of securities in the financial markets. Among these are: (1) market indexes, (2) supply-demand indicators, (3) opinion indicators, (4) relative strength indicators, and (5) graphs.

[7] **Reference:** *Securities Industry Association Yearbook.* (New York, Securities Industry Association, 1994), p. 961.

Market indexes Market indexes attempt to capture the overall performance of a group of securities or of a financial market as a whole. Among the most popularly followed are:

- The Dow Jones indexes—based on the sum of the prices of a select number of New York Stock Exchange stocks representing sectors of the economy. There is the Dow Jones Industrial Average, an index of 30 large industrial stocks; the Dow Jones Transportation Average, an index of 20 transportation stocks; and the Dow Jones Utility Average, an index of 15 utility stocks. Dow Jones also publishes an index consisting of the 65 stocks that make up the three other averages.[8]
- The Standard & Poor's (S&P) indexes—based on the market value of a large number of New York Stock Exchange stocks representing sectors of the economy. Best known is the S&P 500, an index of 500 stocks drawn from across many industries. The 500 stocks are also subdivided to produce indexes of 400 industrial stocks, 20 transportation stocks, 40 financial stocks, and 40 utility stocks.
- Exchange indexes—a measure of the market value of all stocks traded on an exchange, such as the New York Stock Exchange Index and the American Stock Exchange Index.
- NASDAQ indexes—comparable to the S&P indexes but reflecting samples of stocks traded in the NASDAQ system.
- Multimarket indexes—indexes that span several exchanges and markets such as the Value Line Stock Index which draws from both the New York and American exchanges, and the Wilshire 5000 index, a very broad index of the value of 5,000 exchange and NASDAQ stocks.
- Foreign indexes—indexes measuring the activity on major stock exchanges such as the Financial Times Stock Exchange 100 (abbreviated FT-SE 100 and pronounced "Footsie 100") in London, the Nikkei-Dow 225 in Tokyo, the FAZ in Frankfurt, the Hang Sen in Hong Kong, and others in each major financial market.

Figure 19.5 is the top of the "Markets Diary" column, which appears daily on the first page of the "Money & Investing" section of *The Wall Street Journal*.[9] The column contains graphs of the Dow Jones Industrial Average and the Lehman Brothers Treasury-Bond Index for the last 18 months, with an exploded graph for the last week. Data from several other popular stock and bond indexes are also presented. Not shown in Figure 19.5 is the remainder of the column which contains similar presentations for interest rates, exchange rates, and commodities prices.

Supply-demand indicators These measures attempt to gauge the supply versus demand for stocks, to predict the overall direction in which stock prices will move. Popular supply-demand measures are:

- Market breadth—a comparison of the number of stocks advancing in price vs. the number declining in price each day.

---

[8] **Cross-reference:** The 65 Dow Jones stocks appear in Figure 8.8 on p. 285, where they were presented to illustrate the betas of companies in various industries.

[9] **Reference:** *The Wall Street Journal*, May 26, 1994, p. C1.

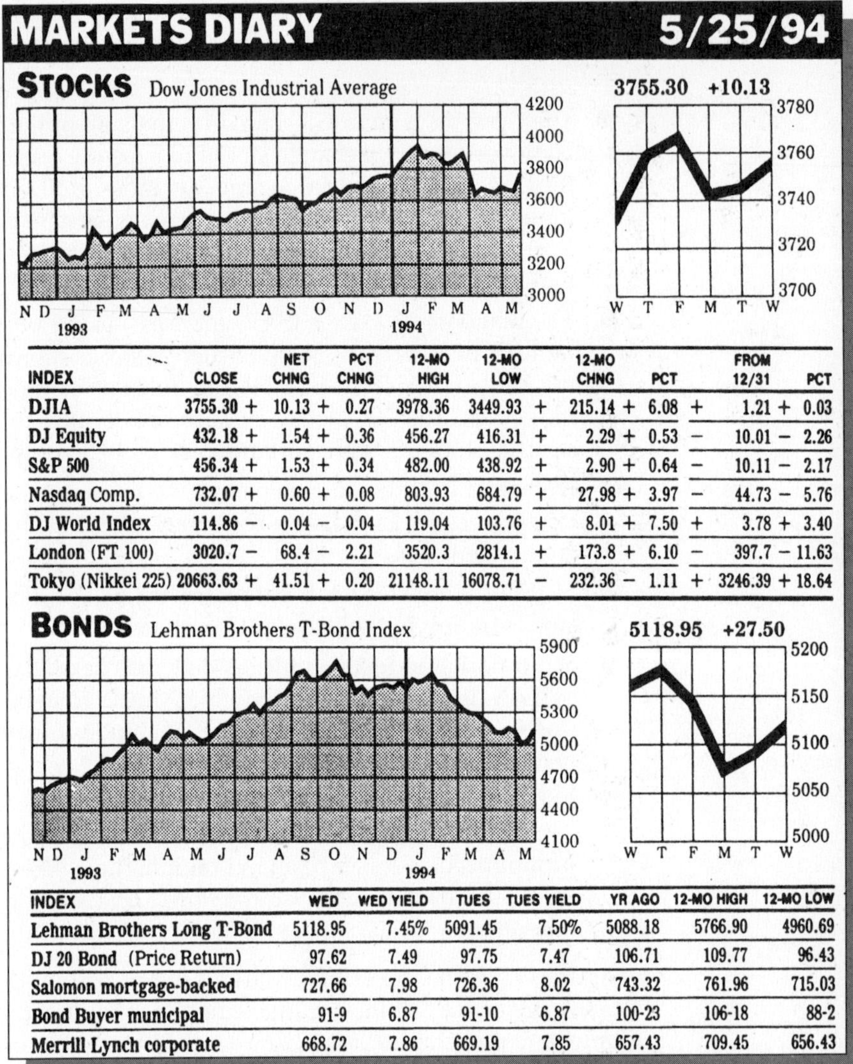

MARKETS DIARY 5/25/94

STOCKS Dow Jones Industrial Average 3755.30 +10.13

INDEX	CLOSE	NET CHNG	PCT CHNG	12-MO HIGH	12-MO LOW	12-MO CHNG	PCT	FROM 12/31	PCT
DJIA	3755.30	+ 10.13	+ 0.27	3978.36	3449.93	+ 215.14	+ 6.08	+ 1.21	+ 0.03
DJ Equity	432.18	+ 1.54	+ 0.36	456.27	416.31	+ 2.29	+ 0.53	− 10.01	− 2.26
S&P 500	456.34	+ 1.53	+ 0.34	482.00	438.92	+ 2.90	+ 0.64	− 10.11	− 2.17
Nasdaq Comp.	732.07	+ 0.60	+ 0.08	803.93	684.79	+ 27.98	+ 3.97	− 44.73	− 5.76
DJ World Index	114.86	− 0.04	− 0.04	119.04	103.76	+ 8.01	+ 7.50	+ 3.78	+ 3.40
London (FT 100)	3020.7	− 68.4	− 2.21	3520.3	2814.1	+ 173.8	+ 6.10	− 397.7	− 11.63
Tokyo (Nikkei 225)	20663.63	+ 41.51	+ 0.20	21148.11	16078.71	− 232.36	− 1.11	+ 3246.39	+ 18.64

BONDS Lehman Brothers T-Bond Index 5118.95 +27.50

INDEX	WED	WED YIELD	TUES	TUES YIELD	YR AGO	12-MO HIGH	12-MO LOW
Lehman Brothers Long T-Bond	5118.95	7.45%	5091.45	7.50%	5088.18	5766.90	4960.69
DJ 20 Bond (Price Return)	97.62	7.49	97.75	7.47	106.71	109.77	96.43
Salomon mortgage-backed	727.66	7.98	726.36	8.02	743.32	761.96	715.03
Bond Buyer municipal	91-9	6.87	91-10	6.87	100-23	106-18	88-2
Merrill Lynch corporate	668.72	7.86	669.19	7.85	657.43	709.45	656.43

FIGURE 19.5
The Wall Street Journal Markets Diary. Widely followed stock and bond indexes are reported daily.

- Confidence index—the ratio of the average yield of high-grade bonds to that of low-grade bonds. The difference is the risk premium demanded for accepting lower bond ratings and is read as a measure of investors' concerns about the level of risk in investing.
- Volume—the number of shares traded in each trading session compared to average trading volume.

Opinion indicators These indicators attempt to measure the optimism or pessimism of particular investor groups.

- Odd-lot (less than 100 shares) volume—a measure of what the small investor is doing. Many market observers believe that small investors are always the "last to know" and their activity reflects the end of a trend.

- Short interest—the volume of uncovered short sales, sales of securities made by people who do not own the stock but plan to purchase it and deliver it to the buyer at a later date. Short sellers profit when stock prices fall, so this measure is used as a gauge of market pessimism.

Relative strength There are several indicators that attempt to assess investors' interest in any particular security by calculating its price movement or volume of trading relative to market averages.

Charts Many different graphs of stock and market activity are used to visualize security price movements. Figure 19.6 is an example of one of these, a "high-low" chart for the last five years. Each vertical bar represents the range of the company's stock price for that unit of time (about three weeks). Below is a bar chart showing trading volume in hundreds of thousands of shares.

FIGURE 19.6
A high-low chart. Some market analysts use charts such as this one to look for patterns in stock price movements.

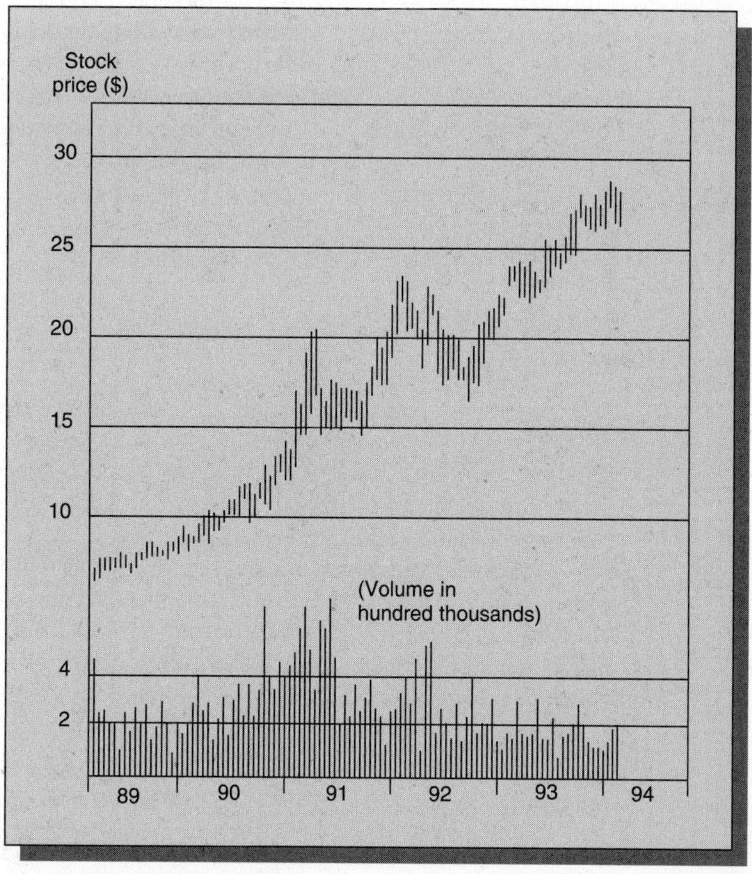

2. Models of Stock Price Behavior

Four models of the way stock prices are determined are widely discussed, debated, and followed in the financial markets: (1) technical theory and analysis, (2) fundamental theory and analysis, (3) the efficient market hypothesis, and (4) the random walk.

Technical theory and analysis Technical theory argues that the price and not the value of a security is the foundation of investment decisions. Prices are the result of supply and demand interaction; and with the supply of a firm's stock fixed in the short run, it is investors' demand that sets prices. Demand is both rational and irrational, with rational forces in control of long-run movements in price and irrational forces in control in the short-run. Irrationality depends on human psychological behavior: most people follow the lead of others, hence prices move in trends. And, because human nature is consistent through the ages, trends (patterns of price movement) repeat themselves.

Technical theorists point to various episodes in economic history as evidence of irrationality. Two of the more widely recounted are the "tulipomania" in Holland during the 1630s when the price of selected tulip bulbs quickly rose to levels rivaling a year's wages . . . and fell just as fast, and the "South Seas Bubble" in England in the 1710s when public excitement over newly opened exotic foreign trade routes led investors to pay enormous sums for the stock of companies of dubious prospects—including one that described itself in its prospectus as "A company for carrying on an undertaking of great advantage, but nobody to know what it is."[10] A more recent illustration cited by technical theorists is stock prices on Wall Street in the late 1920s. For example, consider whether the price history of RCA stock, perhaps the hottest high-technology stock of the decade, might reflect any irrationality on the part of investors:

- March 3, 1928: 94 1/2
- September 3, 1929: 505
- November 3, 1929: 28
- 1932 low: 2 1/2

Perhaps the best known exponent of technical theory was the British economist John Maynard Keynes, who used technical methods to increase tenfold the worth of the endowment fund of his employer, Kings College of Cambridge University, during the depths of the Great Depression of the 1930s. Keynes likened investing to beauty contests of the times in which newspaper readers were asked to select, from pictures in the paper, the contestant that the judges would eventually pick as the winner. As Keynes pointed out, the decision depends on what the judges will do, not on which contestant the reader finds most beautiful. Similarly, Keynes argued, choosing stocks depends on what other investors will do, not on which securities an investor finds most attractive.

---

[10] **Reference:** This quotation is from a delightful book first published in 1841 which recounts many episodes of mass hysteria: Charles Mackay, *Extraordinary Popular Delusions and the Madness of Crowds* (New York: Harmony Books), 1980.

intrinsic value—the true economic worth of an asset

Fundamental theory and analysis Fundamental theory takes a very different approach, arguing that every financial asset has a "true" or **intrinsic value** equal to the economic benefit of owning that asset. Skilled analysis of economic data will lead to the discovery of a security's intrinsic value. For a bond this would involve analysis of the issuer to determine risk of default and of interest rates to quantify interest rate and reinvestment risk. For a stock, fundamental analysis would include an examination of the company's products and growth potential, costs and earnings quality, business risks, etc.

Fundamental analysts attempt to purchase a security when it is selling for a price that is some "margin of safety" below its intrinsic value, to allow for a margin of error in the analysis. Then, they argue, the odds are in favor of the security's price rising to (or above) intrinsic value over the medium-to-long term.

The efficient market hypothesis A capital market is efficient if it channels money accurately and quickly to those real investments that result in the greatest benefits to society. For this to be true, companies' security prices must accurately reflect their earnings opportunities. The importance of this market function has motivated economists and students of finance to study the capital markets extensively. However, researchers have found it difficult to measure directly the distributive power of the markets.

One fruitful line of study is an information arrival model, a model of stock price formulation that bears directly on efficiency and can be formulated in a way that lends itself to testing. In its simple form, the model is written out in Figure 19.7. At any point in time there exists a set of stock prices. There is no reason for these prices to change unless new, relevant information becomes available to market participants. However, new information arrives regularly, and once the new information is processed and its meaning understood, prices will change and a new equilibrium will be established.

The key issue for market efficiency is the time lag between the arrival of information in the marketplace and the establishment of revised stock prices. If the time lag is extended, the market is inefficient, with old prices existing long after the new information shows them to be no longer correct. However, if the time lag is short, the market is efficient; stock prices are adjusting quickly to the import of the new information, and there is little if any time during which they give wrong signals to investors.

FIGURE 19.7

The information arrival model. Stock prices change when new information reaches the capital markets.

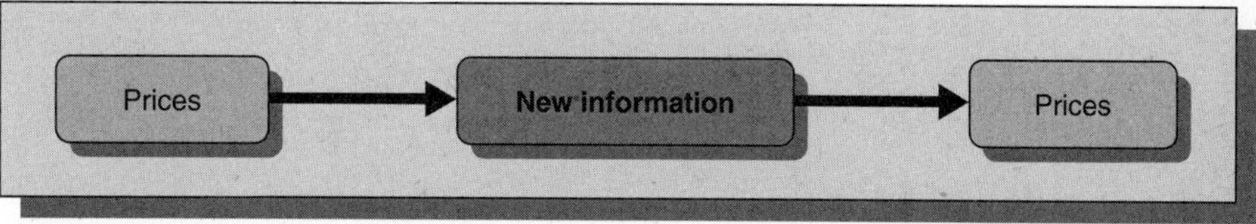

For formal testing purposes, the premise that the capital markets are efficient with respect to their reaction to the arrival of new information has been formulated as the efficient market hypothesis:

Prices contain all relevant information.

If the hypothesis is true and stock prices react quickly to the arrival of new information, the markets are efficient—at least with respect to the incorporation of information into investment values. The hypothesis is further subdivided into three versions depending upon the amount of information under study.[11]

- *The weak form:* In this version of the hypothesis, all relevant information is defined to be past stock prices. Thus the hypothesis becomes "Prices contain all that can be known from the study of past prices." If the weak form is true, technical analysis, with its emphasis on the patterns and trends of stock price movements, is worthless for locating investment opportunities. Academic studies of commodities prices, comparisons of stock prices to computer-generated random numbers and the Brownian motion of gaseous atoms, tests for serial correlation between stock price movements, tests for patterns of stock price changes, and tests of investment rules based on price patterns have consistently supported the weak form.
- *The semistrong form:* This strangely named version of the hypothesis equates all relevant information to all public information. Thus the hypothesis becomes "Prices contain all that can be known from the study of all public information." If the semistrong form is true, fundamental analysis with its emphasis on economic analysis of public data is worthless. Early academic studies of stock market responses to leading economic indicators, income statement data release, stock splits, Fed discount rate changes, etc. have supported the semistrong form. More recently there have been some studies of inflation, takeover offers, etc. that point out some lack of efficiency with respect to public information. While substantially supporting the semistrong form of the hypothesis, the research results here are somewhat mixed.
- *The strong form:* In the strong form, all relevant information means *all* information, public or private. Thus the hypothesis becomes "Prices contain all that can be known—period!" If this form of the efficient market hypothesis is true, no amount of analysis can predict the movement of stock prices better than purely random selection. Academic studies of trading by stock exchange specialists and corporate insiders, individuals who might have inside information, have not supported this form of the hypothesis. It appears that private information is quite useful in stock price prediction.

In summary, many financial market practitioners argue that they are successful using technical and fundamental analysis to earn returns above the market averages. Academics are split. The true believers of most of the research argue that it is impossible to use technical or fundamental analysis consistently to beat the market. Other academics accept at least some of the more recent research as showing

[11] **References:** An excellent summary of the efficient market hypothesis and early tests of all three forms is Chapter 4 of James H. Lorie and Mary T. Hamilton, *The Stock Market—Theories and Evidence* (Homewood, Il: Richard D. Irwin, 1973).

that there are areas of inefficiency in the financial markets. All agree that: (1) originality of analysis and better-than-average insight on a regular basis, kept secret from other analysts, should lead to a superior investment record, and (2) tests of efficiency have been done primarily on New York Stock Exchange stocks due to the availability of data. Other markets, served by fewer stock analysts and with less widely circulated data, may well be less efficient.

The efficient market hypothesis gives rise to a fascinating paradox. In its semistrong form, the hypothesis argues that fundamental analysis is worthless, yet it is the existence of many fundamental analysts, disseminating new information quickly and analyzing voluminous data, that most likely accounts for the measured efficiency of the market.

random walk—a process in which successive changes are independent of each other

The random walk The movement of stock prices has been characterized by some academics as a **random walk.** This is an attempt to quantify the concept of the efficient market hypothesis in statistical terms. The random walk is a stronger statement than the efficient market hypothesis due to the quantification.

The concept of the random walk is that successive percentage price changes of a given security appear to be independently drawn from a single probability distribution (representing the set of possible percentage price changes)—much like rolling a pair of dice produces a set of random numbers drawn from the distribution of possible results of dice rolls. Although the form of the distribution has been studied, research conclusions are a bit problematic. It would be convenient if the distribution were a normal distribution, the one consistent with the capital asset pricing model and the other statistical risk modeling we examined in Chapter 8. Unfortunately, the distribution that best fits the data has an infinite standard deviation, presenting a problem for current statistical models that use the standard deviation as their measure of risk.

Financial Intermediaries

Financial intermediaries separate surplus budget units and deficit budget units, permitting each to enter into their desired financial transaction without the need to find a counterparty on their own. In this section we identify three classes of intermediaries and five types of intermediation.

1. Classes of Intermediaries

Financial intermediaries can be grouped into three classes: (1) deposit intermediaries, (2) contractual intermediaries, and (3) investment intermediaries.

Deposit intermediaries Deposit intermediaries include commercial banks, savings and loan associations, mutual savings banks, and credit unions. They take deposits from lenders and make loans to borrowers. In return they collect interest and principal repayments from the borrowers and return the lenders' deposits with interest earned.

Contractual intermediaries Contractual intermediaries include insurance companies—both life, and property and casualty—pension funds, and endowment funds. They take premiums and contributions from their customers and contributors and invest the proceeds, lending the money to governments and corporations. In return, the earnings and principal of their investment portfolio are used to pay insurance claims, pay retirement benefits, or support the endowed institution.

Investment intermediaries Investment intermediaries are primarily mutual funds. They aggregate money from investors and purchase many kinds of investment portfolios, providing each investor the ability to own a piece of a broadly diversified portfolio. They manage the portfolios for their investors and return the money when requested.

2. Types of Intermediation

Financial intermediaries provide five kinds of separation between lending and borrowing: (1) amount intermediation, (2) risk intermediation, (3) maturity intermediation, (4) portfolio mix intermediation, and (5) information intermediation.

Amount intermediation Intermediaries serve lenders and borrowers who have and need different amounts of money. For example, a commercial bank aggregates deposits of all sizes from its many depositor-lenders and then makes loans of different amounts to its many customer-borrowers.

Risk intermediation Intermediaries serve lenders and borrowers with different attitudes toward and perceptions of risk. For example, a property and casualty insurance company collects premium money from its customers and assumes risks associated with loss to the insured assets. It lends the money to governments and corporations by buying bonds with quite different levels of risk and uses some of the proceeds to compensate its customers for the losses that occur.

Maturity intermediation Intermediaries serve lenders and borrowers with different maturity needs. For example, a savings and loan association takes in short-term deposits and provides money to homebuyers in the form of mortgage loans of up to 30 years.

Portfolio mix intermediation Intermediaries serve lenders and borrowers who desire to change the combination of investments they are holding. For example, a mutual fund takes deposits from its investors and provides each with a share of ownership in a broadly diversified investment portfolio.

Information intermediation Intermediaries serve borrowers and lenders with different access to information. For example pension funds construct retirement packages based on sophisticated actuarial analyses not easily available to many workers. Mutual funds base their investment decisions on extensive data collection and analyses most investors would not have the time or the skills to accomplish.

The Regulatory Environment

Financial markets and institutions have a long and colorful history dating from the "money-changers" of ancient times. Throughout, an ongoing concern of governments has been maintaining the balance between an aggressive, vital financial industry and the prevention of fraud and abuse. Since the mid-nineteenth century for banks, and the 1930s for the securities industry, financial institutions and markets in the United States have been governed by a succession of laws and regulatory agencies.

1. Regulation of Primary Markets

The primary financial markets have been regulated since the passage of the Securities Act of 1933, the law that established the rules for new security issues. A key role of the law is to make better information available to the public when they are invited to invest in a new issue. Prior to issuing securities, a firm must register the issue with the Securities and Exchange Commission (SEC)[12], filing audited financial statements, information about key personnel, the intended use of the proceeds, information on the underwriting agreement, and other supporting data. The SEC makes this information available to the public at its offices and also requires companies to provide a prospectus, a document containing substantially all the above information, to all potential buyers before any money may be solicited. The law gives both the SEC and investors the right to sue a company and its management for any misrepresentation.

The act applies to securities issues offered for sale in more than one state, with value over $500,000 and with maturity over 270 days. Exempt are industries regulated by another federal agency—for example the railroads, which fall under the jurisdiction of the Interstate Commerce Commission.

2. Regulation of Secondary Markets

In 1934, Congress passed the Securities Exchange Act extending regulation to the securities markets and establishing the SEC as the central regulatory agency. Among the key provisions of this law were:

- All exchanges were required to register with the SEC, which was given the power to regulate them.
- The requirements of the 1933 act were extended to apply to all listed companies on an annual basis, leading to today's annual reports.
- Insider trading was curtailed. Officers, directors, and stockholders with over a 5% ownership of a firm's common stock were required to file monthly reports of their trading activity. Also, all profits from trading on inside information were to go to the company.

---

[12] **Historical note:** The SEC did not exist in 1933 when the Securities Act was passed but was created in 1934 with the Securities Exchange Act to administer both laws. The 1933 act was administered by the Federal Trade Commission until the SEC was up and running.

- Certain manipulative trading techniques were outlawed, including pools (groups coordinating their trades to move the price of a stock), wash sales (sales among friends to increase reported trading volume), and price pegging except in support of a new issue.
- Proxies were regulated in an attempt to limit management's control over stockholders.
- The Federal Reserve was given the authority to set margin requirements limiting the amount that could be borrowed when purchasing stock. Today FED Regulation T specifies the maximum margin borrowed from broker-dealers and Regulation U the maximum margin borrowed from domestic commercial banks.

3. Regulation of Intermediaries

Each type of financial intermediary is regulated through a different mix of laws and regulatory agencies.

Bank regulation The U.S. banking system has been regulated since 1863, when the National Banking Act established a uniform national currency and created the office of the Comptroller of the Currency to charter and supervise bank activities. Since then, several important pieces of legislation have shaped the industry into the form we have today.

- The Federal Reserve Act of 1913 created the Fed as the nation's central bank and ultimate guarantor of liquidity in the financial system. The act gave the Fed significant control over banking activities, especially through its ability to set reserve requirements—the fraction of deposits banks must hand over to the Fed and, therefore, which are not available for lending to customers.
- The McFadden Act of 1927 was an attempt to limit the growing power of large, big city, "money center" banks. The act gave states the right to limit retail bank offices (branches) within their states and prohibited interstate bank branches unless specifically approved by the states in question. The states responded by either: (1) permitting branches throughout the state, such as California; (2) permitting branches only in a local area, such as New York, which required banks to limit their branches to one of three regions, thus protecting small upstate banks from competition from the big New York City companies; or (3) prohibiting branching at all, such as Illinois, which limited its banks to only one branch. As a result of McFadden, the United States still has some 12,000 commercial banks (there were 30,000 in 1930) while most other Western countries have fewer than 20—for example, Canada has only 13 commercial banks of which five are significantly larger than the rest).
- The Glass-Steagall Act (officially the Banking Act of 1933) separated the industry into commercial banks, those permitted to take deposits and make loans, and investment banks, those permitted to underwrite and deal in securities. The law was a reaction to a widespread belief that the stock market crash of 1929 and the subsequent loss of economic activity were exacerbated by a too-powerful banking industry. The act also prohibited commercial banks

from paying interest on demand deposits and created the Federal Deposit Insurance Corporation (FDIC) to restore some of the confidence in the banking system lost by the rash of bank failures in the early years of the Great Depression.

- The International Banking Act of 1978 subjected foreign banks operating in the United States to U.S. banking regulation, leveling the playing field between domestic and foreign competitors within the country.
- The Depository Institutions Deregulation and Monetary Control Act of 1980 eliminated many of the differences between commercial banks and thrift institutions. The act phased out the limits on the interest rates banks and thrifts could pay, abolished most restrictions on the types of accounts they could offer depositors and the loans they could make, and unified reserve requirements.
- The Garn-St. Germain Depository Institutions Act of 1982 extended the deregulation of the 1980 act by permitting banks and thrifts to offer deposit products previously available only through the securities industry, such as money market accounts. The act also dealt with bank failures and the belief of many bankers and economists that consolidation would produce a healthier industry by giving stronger institutions the authority to merge with those in financial trouble.
- The Riegle-Neal Interstate Banking and Branching Efficiency Act of 1994 effectively repealed the McFadden Act, allowing banks to operate branches in more than one state. Under the new law, a bank can purchase another bank operating in a different state and fully integrate the two. Banks which had previously purchased others under the terms of the Garn-St. Germain Act no longer must operate each bank independently but may now combine them, eliminating duplicate management and operating systems.

Insurance company regulation Insurance companies are regulated by state authorities. To minimize fraud, the states insist that anyone selling policies be licensed. To protect those who have purchased policies, the kinds of investments insurance companies can make are limited. Each state has created some form of state insurance commission to administer and enforce the relevant legislation.

Pension regulation Pension plans are regulated by the federal government through the Internal Revenue Service. The relevant legislation is the Employee Retirement Income Security Act of 1974 (ERISA) which specifies who can join a pension plan, when they can join, and how soon they own the benefits set aside for them. ERISA created the Pension Benefit Guaranty Corporation as an insurance fund for pension benefits, although the act also required employers to provide full funding for all pension plans over the following 40 years to remove the need for governmental guarantees and eliminate the possibility that if a company fails, employees would be left without the pensions they earned.

Mutual fund regulation Mutual funds are regulated at the federal level through the Investment Company Act of 1940 and the Investment Advisers Act, also passed in 1940. Funds must register with the SEC and must conform to all laws affecting public securities. Shareholders (investors) in the fund vote for a board of directors, just as in a public corporation, and also vote to set the fund's investment policies and objectives. The fund must engage a separate management or investment advisory company to manage its portfolio, and investors must approve the contract between the fund and portfolio manager at least every two years.

Glenn Morton spoke animatedly and pointed to a diagram he had drawn on the blackboard. His class at the local university had just ended, and he found himself surrounded by a half-dozen eager students with lots of questions. The class had gone by quickly—too quickly—both because he had brought much more material to class than the time allowed and because he had genuinely enjoyed the experience.

Glenn had opened the class by relating several of his recent experiences in designing loan packages tailored to the needs of his customers. He talked about the different ways his customers could raise financing and discussed the benefits of each. Then he presented some of the important characteristics of the primary and secondary financial markets. For the remainder of the class, he led the group in a discussion of financial intermediation and the role of his bank in bridging the needs of its various depositors and borrowers, always coming back to his perspective of the importance of understanding and meeting his customers' financing needs.

As the last student left the classroom, the chair of the finance faculty walked up to Glenn from the back of the room where she had observed the class. "That was a fabulous presentation," she said. "Judging from the students' level of attention and questioning you were a big hit!"

"It was a really great experience," Glenn replied with a smile "Your students are excellent." He looked at the blackboard thoughtfully. "They taught me something as well. I live in the financial markets every day, and think I know a lot about them. But so much is going on out there that it really is important to step back every once in a while to review the roles they play and the ways they operate."

Summary of Key Points

- **Describe seven roles of financial markets and institutions, three methods of channeling funds from net savers to net investors, and the difference between the money and capital markets.** Financial markets and institutions serve as a conduit for the movement of money from surplus-budget economic units to deficit-budget economic units. They do so by providing mechanisms for making payments, vehicles for savings, supplies of credit, investments in which to store wealth, sources of liquidity, mechanisms for shifting and reducing risk, and vehicles for government economic policy. Funds move from net savers to net investors through direct transfer when the parties know each other, semidirect transfer using the services of a broker, or indirect transfer with the funds passing through a financial intermediary.

We separate the financial markets into the money markets and capital markets based on maturities of the instruments traded.

- **Discuss how newly created securities are issued, including the role of the investment banker, flotation costs, and private placement.** New securities are sold in the primary markets. Public issues are normally brought to market by an investment banker who can provide advice, underwriting, selling, and market stabilization services. Private placements, with or without the services of an investment banker, have the advantages of faster speed to market, greater privacy, more-tailored terms, and fewer limitations on the amount of the issue. Flotation costs, the costs of bringing a new security issue to market, include the investment banker's spread and all administrative costs.

- **Describe the nature of the secondary financial markets, including the securities exchanges and other trading mechanisms.** Previously issued securities trade in the secondary markets. These markets bring buyers and sellers together, provide information to investors, create continuity of trading which enhances investors' liquidity, protect market participants through regulation, and improve capital distribution in the economy. The exchanges include the physical exchanges, such as the New York Stock Exchange and American Stock Exchange, where brokers and traders come together in person, and the electronic exchanges, such as the NASDAQ computer network. Other trading mechanisms are block trading among financial institutions, and computerized trading services.

- **Identify indexes that measure financial market activity; and compare technical analysis, fundamental analysis, the efficient market hypothesis, and the random walk as descriptions of security price behavior.** Among the many indexes that capture financial market activity are market indexes, supply-demand indicators, opinion indicators, and measures of relative strength. Charts are widely used to make security price and other data visual and to look for trends. Technical analysis looks at these trends to predict future security prices. Fundamental analysis looks at economic and business information to calculate a security's true or intrinsic value. By contrast, the efficient market hypothesis—in its weak and semistrong forms—concludes that security prices react so quickly to new information that technical and fundamental analysis are useless in making investment decisions. If the strong form of the efficient market hypothesis is true, even inside information does not give investors an edge over other market participants. The random walk attempts to quantify security price movements in statistical terms.

- **Describe three types of financial intermediaries and five types of financial intermediation.** Financial intermediaries are commonly grouped into: (1) deposit intermediaries—banks and thrift institutions, (2) contractual intermediaries—insurance companies and pension and endowment funds, and (3) investment intermediaries—primarily mutual funds. They separate lenders and borrowers, enabling funds to flow when the individual parties differ in: (1) the amount of money they wish to move, (2) the risks they wish to take, (3) the time over which they wish to invest, (4) the mix of their investment portfolios, and (5) their access to investment information.

- **Relate the basics of the regulatory environment in which the financial markets and financial institutions function.** A large number of laws limit and shape the activities of financial market participants and financial institutions. The securities markets and the public financing activities of corporations that use them are regulated by the federal government through the Securities and Exchange Commission. Banks and thrifts are primarily regulated by the Federal Reserve Board and Comptroller of the Currency. Insurance companies are regulated at the state level, while oversight of pension and mutual funds is by federal agencies.

Questions

1. Identify seven functions of financial markets and institutions.
2. What is the difference among a deficit-budget unit, a balanced-budget unit, and a surplus-budget unit? Is it possible for an individual or company to be one of the three in one year and another in the next?
3. Distinguish among direct transfer, semidirect transfer, and indirect transfer. Which financial organizations play an important role in each?
4. In what ways are the money markets and capital markets different? In what ways are they similar?
5. Distinguish between the primary financial markets and secondary financial markets.
6. Identify four services provided by investment bankers in helping companies issue securities.
7. How does underwriting work?
8. Describe what the components of a $1 million flotation cost might be.

9. What are the differences between a public security issue and a private placement?
10. What is shelf registration? Why was it created? What do you think is its impact on the way companies issue securities?
11. Identify five functions of secondary financial markets.
12. Why did Diamler-Benz list its stock on the New York Stock Exchange when it was already trading in Frankfurt?
13. Why do you think Apple Computer chose not to list its securities on a physical exchange?
14. What are the differences between the Dow Jones indexes and the Standard & Poor's indexes?
15. Contrast technical analysis and fundamental analysis as methods for finding good stock investments.
16. Describe the three forms of the efficient market hypothesis.
17. Why does:
    a. The weak form of the efficient market hypothesis invalidate technical analysis?
    b. The semistrong form of the efficient market hypothesis invalidate fundamental analysis?
18. Why is it possible to earn above-normal rates of return in the stock market if you have inside information? What does this suggest about laws regulating the investment activities of corporate officers?
19. What is the random walk? What is its relationship to the efficient market hypothesis?
20. Identify three classes of financial intermediaries. In what way(s) are they different?
21. Identify five types of intermediation. Describe a situation in which you might wish to use each one.
22. What are the primary laws and government bodies that regulate:
    a. The primary markets?
    b. The secondary markets?
    c. Banks and thrifts?
    d. Insurance companies?
    e. Pension funds?
    f. Mutual funds?

CASE

JEAN MEREDITH

Jean Meredith twirled a strand of her long brown hair as she listened attentively to the speaker's presentation. He was the last speaker of the first day of the seminar. It had been a full day, but surprisingly Jean did not feel tired. She was enjoying the program and felt she was learning a lot, although an answer to the central question of the seminar—how will changes in the financial environment over the next decade affect the financial markets—remained very foggy in her mind.

Jean was a financial analyst for a large international consumer products company. She was attending a seminar entitled "The Future of the Financial Markets" at which several well known economists and financial authors were the featured speakers. As she looked around the room, she saw roughly 100 people, many who appeared to be her own age. "Probably in similar positions at other companies," she thought. She spotted the three people she had spoken to at the last coffee break and made a mental note to ask them to join her for dinner.

Jean turned her attention back to the speaker, a popular author and technology expert, who was concluding his talk. "And so, over the next decade, I expect to see computing power continue to double every 18 months at the same price, as it has for the past 10 years. This will continue to have an immense effect on the way financial market transactions are carried out and on the financial products that market professionals will be able to create and support. In fact, this may well be the most important factor that will influence the markets for the next decade—certainly it's an important one to watch. In any event, I look forward to attending this conference again in ten years to see just how correct, or wrong, all our projections are!"

As the seminar host finished his wrap-up of the day to scattered applause, Jean quickly worked her way through the crowd to the spot where her newly-made friends were chatting. They agreed to have dinner together and made plans to meet in the hotel lobby in one hour. Jean went back to her room to change and freshen up.

The dinner conversation was lively. Jean and her companions found themselves vigorously discussing the content of the day's session, especially which environmental factors would be the ones to change the financial markets in the next decade. One agreed with the last speaker and argued for the continuing changes in telecommunications and computing. Another felt the most important influences would be legal and regulatory as economic barriers continued to fall. The third believed the markets would spend most of their time adapting to continued financial volatility as more countries deregulated their industries and exposed them to market forces. As for Jean, she was convinced that unless a new international monetary order were designed, increasing currency and interest-rate risks would dominate the financial markets. They all agreed that the next decade was going to be a period of continued and accelerating change.

Back at her room after dinner, Jean sat down at the desk and jotted down some notes. All her dinner companions seemed to have good points, echoing many of those made by the speakers earlier that day. Most likely, all the environmental factors would continue to change the markets. But which would have the most important impacts? What would they be? And was there a factor no one had yet mentioned that would also be important?

CHAPTER 20

SHORT-TERM DEBT

Alicia Vasquez chewed on the end of her pen as she glanced around the conference room. She recognized everyone there, a cross-section of her company's finance organization called together by the company's treasurer. In front of her on the table, full of her notes, was a pad with the emblem of the local university where she was finishing her business degree at night.

Alicia had recently joined the treasury group of a large multinational company. Among the group's responsibilities was managing the company's short-term financing. Because of the company's size, it was regularly approached by commercial and investment banks with recommendations for raising short-term funds. But the proposals were often presented in dissimilar terms and were difficult to compare, and there was some concern in the group that the best offers were not always the ones accepted.

Alicia refocused her attention toward the flip-charts at the corner of the room where the treasurer was finishing his presentation. "The discrepancies in proposals have become too significant to ignore. Sometimes the interest rate we are offered is very different from the effective rate we would pay if we took that financing. And, I suspect, sometimes the most important costs of the financing are not even part of the offer but reflect savings we can realize in our internal operations or through a better relationship with our bankers and suppliers. What we need is a consistent way to look at our short-term financing alternatives."

As the meeting broke up, Alicia found herself thinking of how the company's problem was similar to the topics she was covering in her finance class at the university. She decided to bring her notes from the meeting to class later that week to see if that would help her learn more about the company's problem.

Short-term debt—trade credit, accruals, bank loans and other negotiated credit, and money raised through the capital markets—constitutes an important source of financing for many companies. Yet the sources of short-term financing are often not directly comparable to one another, as Alicia's company has discovered. Sometimes the form in which they arise disguises their costs. In other cases, their true costs are hidden by banking practices and financial market conventions. And, as the treasurer of Alicia's company suspects, there can often be large, nonfinancing-related costs associated with short-term debt.

To make intelligent choices among short-term financing alternatives, Alicia's company must understand their features and determine the cost of each in a consistent manner. In Chapter 16 where we studied hedging, we saw that short-term financing sources can reduce risk, in particular, interest-rate risk and foreign-exchange risk. In this chapter we look at each short-term financing source in turn to understand its characteristics and its costs.

Key Points You Should Learn from This Chapter

After reading this chapter you should be able to:

- Identify three reasons why short-term debt is an attractive financing source.
- Describe trade credit by its legal arrangement and terms of sale, and evaluate the cost of trade credit and forgoing trade discounts.
- Describe the worth of accruals.
- Calculate the effective interest rate and understand the characteristics of unsecured and secured bank loans.
- Describe two alternatives to bank debt developed in the domestic and international capital markets.

Introductory Concepts—The Appeal of Short-Term Debt

Short-term debt is particularly attractive to financial managers for three reasons: it is generally (1) easily available to most companies, (2) the cheapest form of financing available, and (3) a form of financing that provides the company a high degree of financial flexibility.

Of all types of financing, short-term debt is typically the easiest to obtain. Accruals (wages payable, taxes payable, interest payable) are built into the firm's normal business arrangements and require no further effort to acquire. Many suppliers routinely extend trade credit without any special negotiation. Banks and finance companies compete to make short-term loans to companies of all sizes. In fact, for small firms, short-term debt may be the *only* source of financing available from sources outside the company.

Short-term debt is normally a low-cost source of financing relative to debt of longer maturities. As we will see in this chapter, some short-term financing is actually free. For debt carrying an interest rate set in the public markets, short-term debt is usually cheaper than long-term debt since the yield curve is normally upward-sloping, with short-term rates lower than long-term rates.[1] And, as we saw when we looked at the cost of capital in Chapter 10, lower risk and favorable tax treatment of interest payments make debt cheaper than equity financing.

Short-term financing also provides a high degree of flexibility in that a company can change its level of funding quickly and easily as its needs change. In fact, most commercial bank lines of credit and related short-term debt sources are specifically designed with this feature in mind. By contrast, long-term debt financing is more difficult to obtain and often more difficult to repay.

Trade Credit

Trade credit is a company's accounts payable—the opportunity to purchase supplies and other resources without paying for them immediately. For some companies, especially small firms without good access to the capital markets, trade credit can represent a large percentage of their financing.

1. Types of Trade Credit

We can distinguish trade credit by two characteristics: the legal arrangement between the parties and the terms of payment requested by the seller.

Legal arrangement The legal arrangement encompasses whether there is a formal note or not and, if so, whether the note is backed by the buyer alone or by the buyer plus some financially stronger third party.

[1] **Cross-reference:** The yield curve is discussed in Chapter 6, pp. 211–218.

The most common form of trade credit is the open account or "account payable." An open account is characterized by no formal legal agreement between the parties. The seller delivers goods or provides a service at the request of the buyer and follows up with an invoice asking for payment. This arrangement is normally preceded by a credit check to ensure that the buyer will pay the invoice.

If the buyer's creditworthiness is questionable, if the buyer has not paid as requested in the past, or if an open account is past due, the seller might require the buyer to sign a formal promissory note upon shipment of the goods or provision of the service. This amount appears on the company's books as a "note payable." Compared to an open account, the note gives the seller a stronger legal position should the buyer not pay.

For financially weak or unknown buyers—for example, newly formed firms or foreign companies—a seller might require the buyer to sign a draft payable to the seller before any goods are shipped or services are performed. The buyer designates a commercial bank to process payment of the draft when due. If the buyer's credit is good, the draft may be marketable and the seller can sell it immediately at a discount and receive payment. If the buyer's credit is questionable, the seller might request the buyer to have a third party—such as a parent company or a bank—guarantee payment. When the guarantee comes from a bank it is termed a **banker's acceptance,** a service banks regularly sell for a fee. Now the draft is very marketable since the bank's credit stands behind the payment.

banker's acceptance—a promissory note which carries a bank's promise of payment

Figure 20.1 summarizes these three legal forms.

Terms of sale Figure 20.2 lists common terms of sale from the most liberal to the most restrictive. Although called *terms of sale,* they really define the terms of payment—when payment is due. They differ primarily in how much time a buyer has before payment must be received. Liberal terms of sale are appropriate when the buyer is reputable but financially weak; stricter terms are used in dealings with unknown customers or those with questionable reputations.

At the liberal end of the scale is **consignment,** a practice often used when the buyer is financially quite weak. The seller ships goods to the buyer but retains title to them. In effect, the seller initially treats the buyer as a warehouse rather than as a customer. Payment for the goods becomes due only when the buyer resells the goods to its customer.

consignment—shipping goods to a buyer but not requiring payment until the goods are resold

FIGURE 20.1
Types of legal payable arrangements. Weaker or less-known buyers are often asked to sign a note or provide a third-party guarantee.

Legal Form	Characteristic
Account payable	Informal agreement based on relationship and creditworthiness
Note payable	Formal note, usually giving the seller a senior claim to other payables
Acceptance	Formal note guaranteed by a third party

Terms	Payment is due
Consignment	Whenever the buyer resells the goods
Seasonal dating	After an agreed-upon date corresponding to a high point in the buyer's cash flow cycle
Monthly billing	Upon receipt of a monthly statement
Discount, net	By a specified date; however, a discount is offered for early payment
Net	By a specified date
Cash on delivery (COD)	When the goods are delivered
Cash before delivery	Prior to shipment of the goods

FIGURE 20.2
Terms of sale. The terms, which specify when payment is due, range from liberal (consignment) to highly restrictive (cash before delivery).

seasonal dating—invoicing several months' worth of shipments at a strong point in the buyer's seasonal pattern

In **seasonal dating,** all purchases made before a specified date are treated as if made on that date for billing purposes. For example, a seller might ship goods throughout the year but not send an invoice to the buyer until October 1. Seasonal dating is used when the customer's business is highly seasonal and the customer is only able to pay at certain points in its cash flow cycle (for example retail toy stores) or when selling high-cost items to financially weak but reliable customers (such as jewelry to small retail stores). It is also often used strategically, for example to support a customer's plans for expansion or when introducing a new product line.

Many companies use "monthly billing," a practice by which all sales made before a certain date (often the 25th of the month) are invoiced at month's end. Payment is due during the following month. This method is particularly appropriate when many transactions are made during the month. For example, professionals such as attorneys and consultants often bill monthly rather than send an invoice for every hour of work. Monthly billing is also the method used to bill customers using retail credit cards such as Discover, MasterCard, and Visa.

Traditionally, the most common terms of sale extended to other businesses have been "discount, net" and "net." Examples are "2/10, net 30" and "net 45." With terms of 2/10, net 30, full payment is due 30 days after the invoice date but a 2% discount is granted if payment is made by day 10. Net 45 asks for full payment 45 days after the invoice date with no discount offered for early payment.

The strictest terms of sale, used for high-risk customers or when no credit information about the buyer is available, are "cash on delivery (COD)" and "cash before delivery." With cash on delivery, goods are shipped but are released from the shipper to the buyer only upon payment by cash or certified check. Cash before delivery requires the buyer to pay in full before the seller will ship the goods or perform the service.

2. When to Say Yes (or No) to Trade Credit

Companies with limited access to financing often find trade credit one of the few available sources of funding and take the credit without further analysis for lack of a better alternative. However, companies that can choose from among alternative financing sources should first determine the cost of each set of trade credit terms and only finance with trade credit when it is cheaper than the alternatives.

Free trade credit Sometimes trade credit is truly free financing—there is no explicit interest rate or other incremental cost to taking it. In this case, it is wise to take the credit.

Examples

Free Trade Credit

Dasgupta Transport Corp. is examining two strategies: paying cash for all purchases versus buying on credit terms that average 60 days. Purchases total $100,000 per month regardless of how Dasgupta pays for them.

Question: What is the difference in Dasgupta's financial position between the alternatives?

Solution steps:

1. Examine Dasgupta's cash flows over the next several months under each alternative. If it pays cash, Dasgupta's cash outflows begin immediately along with its purchases. On the other hand, if it takes the credit, it can delay its payments by 60 days so that the payment for Month 1's purchases is made in Month 3, etc.

	Month					
	1	2	3	4	5	. . .
Pay cash						
Purchases	100	100	100	100	100	. . .
Cash outflow	100	100	100	100	100	. . .
Take 60 days credit						
Purchases	100	100	100	100	100	. . .
Cash outflow			100	100	100	. . .

2. Compute the difference in cash outflows between the two alternatives to obtain the cash saved by taking the credit:

	Month					
	1	2	3	4	5	. . .
Cash saved	100	100				

Answer: By taking the credit, Dasgupta will have retained an additional $200,000 in cash by the end of the second month. This will be offset on the balance sheet by accounts payable of $200,000, a source of financing with no interest charge.

Question: Should Dasgupta take the trade credit?

Answer: Yes. In effect, Dasgupta's creditors are acting exactly like a commercial bank, making monthly loans to the firm of $100,000 each: all loans of two months duration, immediately renewable, and at a zero interest rate.

Trade credit with a cost In other cases, trade credit does carry an interest rate and we must calculate the rate to make a decision about taking the credit. Sometimes the rate is explicit—stated directly by the seller, but in most cases the rate is implicit in the difference between a cash price and a credit price.

Examples

Trade Credit with a Cost

Dasgupta Transport Corp. can purchase gasoline for its fleet of trucks for cash or on credit. If it takes the credit, the price will be 3% higher and payment will be due in 45 days on average. Dasgupta's management considers trade credit an alternative to short-term bank loans which currently have an effective annual rate (EAR) of 7.5%.

Question: What is the interest rate embedded in this trade credit?

Solution steps:

1. Organize the cash flows Dasgupta experiences if it takes the credit. For every $100 (cash price) of gasoline it purchases, Dasgupta retains the $100 but pays $103, 45 days later.

Day 0	Day 45
$100	($103)

2. Solve for the interest rate embedded in these cash flows:[2]

CLEAR the time value part of your calculator

Key in 100 and press PV

Key in −103 and press FV

Key in 45/365 and press n (45/365th of a year)

Compute i = 27.09%

Answer: Taking this trade credit is identical to taking a 45-day loan at an effective annual interest rate of 27.09%.

[2] **Calculator tip:** For HP-12C users only—be sure your calculator is in the "compound mode" rather than the "nominal mode" (press the **STO** then **EEX** keys so the letter "C" shows in the display) or it will compute a nominal, not effective interest rate. Setting this mode becomes important when the value of **n** is not an integer.

Question: Should Dasgupta take the trade credit?

Answer: No. It would be cheaper for Dasgupta to borrow from its bank at an EAR of 7.5% and use the proceeds to pay cash for the fuel.

3. When Not to Take a Discount

When the terms of sale are "discount, net," the buyer faces a second trade credit decision: whether to pay quickly and take the discount or wait until the net date to make payment. Forgoing a discount creates additional trade credit. The buyer avoids paying the discounted price on the discount date, the equivalent of taking a loan for that amount, but pays the full price (the loan principal plus "interest") on the net date. Notice that if the buyer pays on the discount date, there is no further trade credit; it is by *forgoing* the discount that the buyer extends the seller's "loan"! Again, the decision depends on the interest rate embedded in the terms.

Example

Analysis of a Trade Discount

Dasgupta Transport Corp. has been offered terms of 2/10, net 45 by a supplier. Dasgupta's management considers trade credit an alternative to short-term bank loans which currently have an effective annual rate (EAR) of 7.5%.

Question: Should Dasgupta take this discount?

Solution steps:

1. Organize the cash flows Dasgupta experiences if it forgoes the discount. For every $100 (gross) of purchases, Dasgupta would pay $98 on Day 10 if it took the discount. By forgoing the discount, Dasgupta keeps the $98 but pays the full $100 on Day 45, 35 days later.

Day 10	Day 45
$98	($100)

2. Solve for the interest rate embedded in these cash flows:

CLEAR the time value part of your calculator

Key in 98 and press PV

Key in −100 and press FV

Key in 35/365 and press n (35/365th of a year)

Compute i = 23.45%

Answer: Yes. Forgoing the discount creates a loan at an EAR of 23.45%, which is too much to pay for financing given that a 7.5% bank loan is an available alternative.

It is standard practice for company treasurers to do the above calculation for each set of discount terms offered by their suppliers, and to forgo only those discounts that create low-cost financing.

Example

Analysis of Several Trade Discounts

Dasgupta Transport Corp. is offered the following terms from its several suppliers:

1/10, net 30	2/10, net 30
1/10, net 60	2/10, net 60
1/10, net 90	2/10, net 90

Dasgupta's management considers trade credit an alternative to short-term bank loans which currently have an effective annual rate (EAR) of 7.5%.

Question: Which of these discounts should Dasgupta take?

Solution steps:

1. Organize the cash flows Dasgupta experiences if it forgoes each discount. For every $100 (gross) of purchases:

Terms	Day 10	Day 30	Day 60	Day 90
1/10, net 30	$99	($100)		
1/10, net 60	99		($100)	
1/10, net 90	99			($100)
2/10, net 30	98	(100)		
2/10, net 60	98		(100)	
2/10, net 90	98			(100)

2. Solve for the interest rates embedded in these cash flows. Note that the loan period is the time *between* discount date and net date:

CLEAR the time value part of your calculator

Key in 99 and press PV

Key in −100 and press FV

Terms	n		
1/10, net 30	20/365	Compute i	= 20.13%
1/10, net 60	50/365	Compute i	= 7.61%
1/10, net 90	80/365	Compute i	= 4.69%

Key in 98 and press PV

Key in −100 and press FV

Terms	n		
2/10, net 30	20/365	Compute i	= 44.59%
2/10, net 60	50/365	Compute i	= 15.89%
2/10, net 90	80/365	Compute i	= 9.66%

Answer: Dasgupta should take the discount on all these terms except 1/10, net 90 to avoid taking expensive loans. For 1/10, net 90, Dasgupta should forgo the discount and pay on day 90 since this creates an 80-day loan at a rate of 4.69%, well below its bank rate. (Should the bank rate increase to above 7.61%, Dasgupta should now forgo the discount on 1/10, net 60, etc.)

4. Stretching Payables

Look back to the interest rates we calculated in the previous example. If a company is offered terms of 2/10, net 30 and pays on the net date, it has taken a "loan" at a high 44.59% interest rate. However, if it waits until Day 60 to pay (in violation of its supplier's instructions), it has reduced the rate to 15.89%, clearly a more reasonable rate. And if it can wait until Day 90, it has brought the rate down to 9.66%.

Figure 20.3 illustrates this pattern. The interest rate on the loan from forgoing a discount is extremely high if payment is made immediately after the discount date, but drops quickly the more the payable can be stretched. Eventually, if the payable is stretched long enough, the interest rate will drop below the rate on alternative financing. This provides a motivation for some firms to delay their payments.

FIGURE 20.3
Stretching payables. The interest rate in the "loan" decreases rapidly as the payable is stretched further.

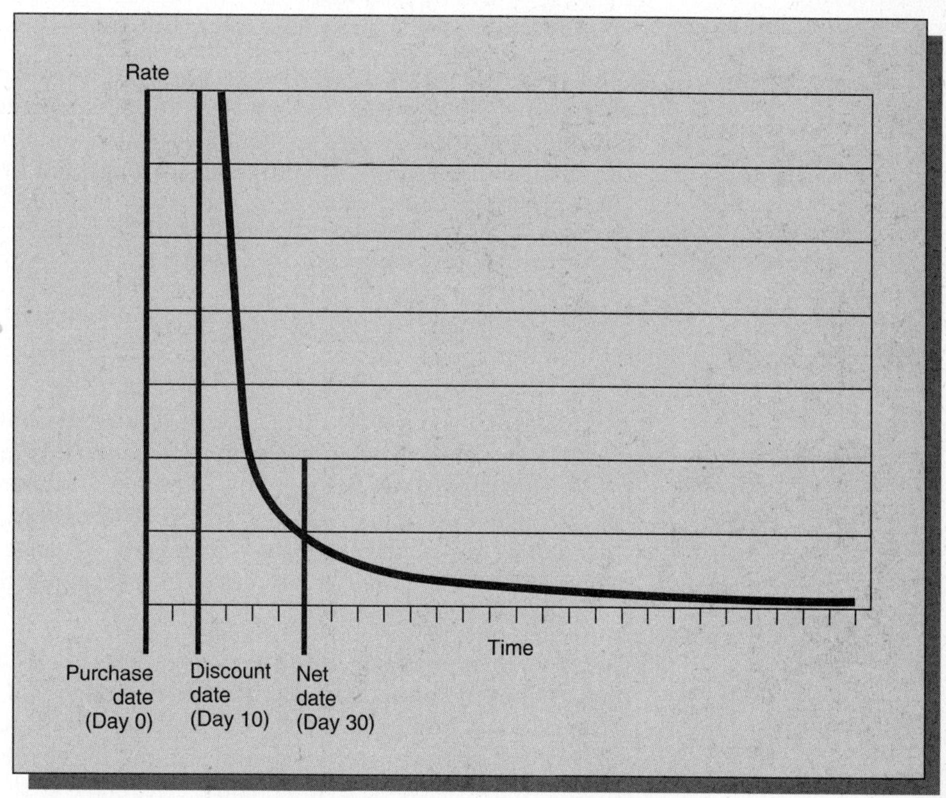

If a company stretches its payables, it is borrowing from its supplier, substituting increased trade credit for bank or other financing. A strong firm that stretches its payables is often taking advantage of its supplier; a weak company may have no alternative funding sources. In either case, the relationship between the firm and its supplier is placed in jeopardy and the long-term cost of doing business with that supplier may well increase, as it typically does when customer requirements are not met. If stretching payables seems desirable, there is almost always a superior approach than simply paying late. It is far better to work closely with the supplier, informing it of the financial difficulties that make stretching payables an alternative under consideration and making the supplier a participant in the decision to stretch. Many suppliers seek to build strong long-term relationships with their customers and will work closely with them in times of financial difficulty.

5. Net Credit

We can combine trade credit extended (accounts receivable) and trade credit used (accounts payable) into a measure of a company's overall trade credit position:

Net credit = accounts receivable − accounts payable

If a company's accounts receivable balance is greater than its accounts payable balance, its net credit measure is positive and it is a net supplier of trade credit. Positive net credit is appropriate for large firms with good access to financial markets which can raise funds more cheaply than their customers and can support their customers by passing on the low financing cost through trade credit. It is inappropriate for small and financially weak firms.

If a company's accounts receivable balance is less than its accounts payable balance, its net credit measure is negative and it is a net user of trade credit. A negative net credit position is appropriate for small and financially weak firms which can finance through low-cost trade credit provided by strong suppliers. It is inappropriate for large firms with good access to financial markets.

Accruals

Accruals are a company's other payables: wages payable, interest payable, taxes payable, etc. They arise spontaneously because it is normal business practice to pay certain obligations at intervals even though they are incurred on a day-by-day basis (for example, wages—which are paid weekly, biweekly, or monthly even though they are earned every day). In general, accruals do not lead to higher payments and are therefore free sources of financing, just like the free trade credit we discussed on pp. 725 and 726.

However, there may be hidden costs to some accruals. Perhaps employees would prefer to be paid at more frequent intervals and would reward the company with greater loyalty and productivity. Or perhaps a bank would reduce the firm's interest rate if payments were scheduled more frequently. There might be costs associated with a payable that offset the advantage of float. For example, suppliers may treat customers who pay quickly as "preferred customers," providing special treatment without charge. A thorough analysis of accruals incorporates these effects to determine if the accruals are truly free or contain any of these or other hidden costs.

Bank Loans

Loans from commercial banks are an important way companies acquire short-term funds beyond those provided by trade credit and accruals. And for small firms, bank loans may be the only other financing alternative. A bank loan is discretionary financing since the amount and timing of the loan request is up to a firm's management.

1. Arranging a Bank Loan

Companies obtain short-term bank loans in two ways. The most common is through prenegotiation, in which the company and bank agree on a relationship at the beginning of the year. Other short-term bank loans are made on an offering, or as-needed basis.

Prenegotiated loans In Appendix 18D we prepared a cash budget and discovered that it is normal for a firm's cash balance to vary significantly throughout the year. Most companies use their cash budget to project a maximum need for external short-term funds and then negotiate with their bank the ability to borrow up to that amount. Both parties subsequently monitor the relationship by comparing the company's actual cash flows to the cash budget.

There are two methods of borrowing under a prenegotiated loan, called *taking down $X against the facility.* In one, the company signs a note payable to the bank

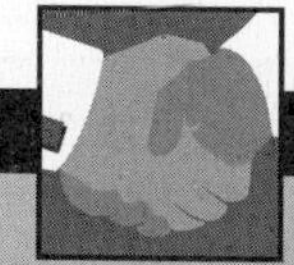

SERVING FINANCE'S CUSTOMERS

Settling Expense Reports Promptly at Federal Express

At one time, it took several weeks for employees of Federal Express to be reimbursed for travel and other out-of-pocket expenses. Incorrectly filled-in expense reports were regularly returned to employees to be redone. When a correct form was submitted, it often took days to be processed and even longer for a check to be cut and mailed. Today, expense reports are filed on-line and the computer program catches most input errors. The vendor services/finance group regularly meets its target of turning around properly filled out reports within one business day. Federal Express employees are delighted with the improvement. Now they can charge their expenses on their personal credit cards and be reimbursed well before the bill arrives. Federal Express has significantly reduced the cost of processing reports. And as a bonus, the company has been able to reduce its petty cash balance and the costs associated with making, tracking, and collecting advances, since there is far less demand for cash advances now that employees know they will be reimbursed so quickly.

for each portion of the facility taken down. Each note has a specific maturity date, usually 30 to 90 days, and is either repaid or rolled over when it matures. In the second method, the company signs a general overdraft agreement, permitting it to write checks in excess of its deposit balance. The bank covers each overdraft up to the prenegotiated limit, effectively making a loan to the company. Deposits to the account are first applied toward reducing the loan balance. With an overdraft agreement, loans typically have no specific maturity.

Since banks want their customers to view short-term borrowing as temporary financing, they normally insist that the outstanding loan balance be reduced to zero for some portion of the year (one or two months is common). Called the *cleanup period, out-of-debt period,* or *out-of-bank period,* this practice ensures that the company does not use the loan facility as part of its long-term financing.

line of credit—a relationship in which a bank offers to lend up to a specified amount for a given time period with no guarantee that funds will be available

Prenegotiated loans come in two forms: the line of credit and the revolving credit line (revolver). In a **line of credit,** the bank makes no commitment to its customer that money will be available and the bank does not have to honor any request for funds under the line. Most banks, however, treat a line of credit as a commitment unless the borrower is delinquent or has fallen significantly in creditworthiness. A familiar form of a line of credit is contained in a bank credit card (MasterCard, Visa). The cardholder can borrow up to the amount of the credit line as desired, but the bank reserves the right to cancel the card at its discretion.

revolving credit line—a line of credit containing a guarantee that funds will be available for the period of the line

Unlike a line of credit, a **revolving credit line** is legally binding. It contains a commitment that the bank will honor any request by the customer up to the limit of the line. In return for taking this additional risk, the bank normally charges a "commitment fee" on the unused portion of the facility.

Example

Commitment Fee

Dasgupta Transport Corp. has taken down $400,000 against a $1,000,000 revolving credit line. It maintains this position for three months. Terms of the revolver call for 8% interest on the amount borrowed, plus a commitment fee of 1/2% on the unused portion of the line. Both rates are nominal and applied quarterly.

Question: What payment of interest and fees will Dasgupta make at the end of the three months?

Solution steps:

1. Calculate the quarterly rates. Since they are nominal rates to be applied quarterly:

$$8\%/4 = 2\%$$

$$1/2\%/4 = 1/8\%$$

2. Obtain the unused portion of the line:

$$\$1{,}000{,}000 - 400{,}000 = \$600{,}000$$

3. Calculate the sum of the interest and the fee:

Interest	2% × \$400,000 =	\$8,000
Commitment fee	1/8% × \$600,000 =	750
		\$8,750

Answer: The payment will be \$8,750. Note that if Dasgupta increases its borrowing against the line, the interest component of the payment will rise but the fee component will decline, and vice-versa.

offering basis loan—a short-term loan with no prenegotiation

Offering basis loans The alternative to a prenegotiated loan is an **offering basis loan.** A familiar example is an automobile loan. There is no prior negotiation between the bank and borrower, and the loan proceeds are intended for a specific purpose.

2. Loan Pricing

prime rate—a reference rate used in the United States, traditionally the rate available to the most creditworthy customers

reference rate—a base rate for loan pricing

London inter-bank offering rate (LIBOR)—a reference rate used for dollar-denominated loans made outside the United States

Banks quote interest rates on most loans relative to a base rate of interest. For many years, the base rate in the United States was the **prime rate,** which served as the "minimum commercial loan rate," the rate charged to the most creditworthy customers on the shortest-term loans. However, increased competition in the 1980s from foreign banks not subject to U.S. banking regulations led many domestic banks to make loans at rates below prime. Today, banks use several base rates which are generically called **reference rates.** Within the United States, the prime rate is still widely used. Banks making U.S.-dollar denominated loans outside the United States most often use as the reference rate the **London inter-bank offering rate (LIBOR),** the rate at which the large British clearing banks lend to each other.

Since the banking industry is an oligopoly, the prime rate is set by a price leader, usually one of the large New York banks. To determine whether the prime rate should be changed, the price leader looks at comparable financing instruments whose rates are set in the marketplace (such as commercial paper) or at the cost of funds to the bank (e.g., CD rates, Fed funds, etc.). In most cases other banks quickly follow the leader and adopt the new prime rate, although sometimes the other banks disagree with the leader and force the leader to rescind the change. Differences among banks do not last long since their product (cash) has limited differentiation and since bank customers, many of whom maintain multiple banking relationships, can easily shift their borrowing to the bank with the lowest rates.

"Mr. Jones, we'd like to talk again about that loan application of yours."

credit analysis—a study to determine the ability of a customer to repay a loan

When a company applies for a bank loan, officers of the bank perform a **credit analysis** to assess the company's creditworthiness—its ability to repay the loan. The credit analysis reviews the firm's financial condition using financial ratio analysis and the other techniques for examining financial accounting data we studied in Appendix 4D. It also looks at the intended use of the loan proceeds and the integrity of the company's management. Credit analysis quantifies the risks of making the loan—if the bank elects to proceed, the analysis specifies the premium over the reference rate to charge and indicates the need for any special terms and conditions in the loan contract.[3]

The final loan quote is usually in the form of "reference plus," for example, "prime plus 1" which identifies that the interest rate will be 1% above the reference rate—in this case the prime rate of interest. Should the prime rate change, the loan rate is reset accordingly.

3. Effective Annual Rate

Toward the end of Chapter 5, we learned how compounding within a year changes cash flows and produces an effective annual interest rate (EAR) greater than the nominal or quoted rate. A similar effect often occurs in bank loan pricing. Sometimes bank loan cash flows are changed by within-year compounding, but they can also be changed by the required timing of interest and/or principal payments or by other loan costs such as fees and compensating balances.

[3] **Cross-reference:** The "5 Cs," a convenient summary of the primary steps in credit analysis, appear on p. 592 as part of the discussion of temporary accounts receivable.

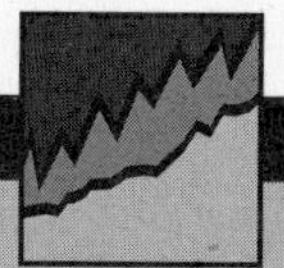

IMPROVING FINANCE'S PROCESSES

Using Quality Initiatives to Support a Loan Request at Southern Pacific

In February 1992, senior executives of the Southern Pacific Transportation Company made a presentation to the company's lead bank, Bank of America, and a syndicate group of 20 other banks to convince the bankers to move forward with a $125 million revolving credit facility. At the time, Southern Pacific had no bank credit lines and was without backup liquidity, the result of a decade of poor financial results due to its slow response to the deregulation of the railroad industry and the failure of a planned merger with the Atchison Topeka and Santa Fe. But a year and a half prior, Southern Pacific had adopted a program of systematic quality management throughout the company, and its presentation to the bankers identified dozens of cost-reduction opportunities made possible through the application of quality-improvement methods. Even though Bank of America had originally advised Southern Pacific to delay the loan syndication, the inclusion of quality goals in the company's plans convinced the bankers to proceed with the financing.

In the following section we illustrate how these cash flow changes modify loan rates. We start with a simple ordinary payment or "collect" loan, in which principal and interest are due at the end of the loan period and there are no other cash flows. We then add in the other cash flows one at a time, observing how the effective annual rate changes.

Example

Ordinary Payment (Collect) Loan

The First National Bank has quoted a rate to Dasgupta Transport Corp. of "prime plus 2" on a $100,000, one-year collect loan. Prime is now 6%.

Question: What is the effective annual rate (EAR) on the loan?

Solution steps:

1. Organize the loan's cash flows:

	Year 0	Year 1	
Principal	$100,000	($100,000)	
Interest		(8,000)	8% of $100,000
	$100,000	($108,000)	

2. Solve for the interest rate embedded in these cash flows:

CLEAR the time value part of your calculator

Key in 100,000 and press PV

Key in −108,000 and press FV

Key in 1 and press n (1 year)

Compute i = 8.00%

Answer: The EAR is 8.00%, the same as the quoted rate.

Fees Banks often charge fees—one-time charges—in addition to interest to compensate them for the cost of processing a loan. A common example is in the market for home mortgage loans, where fees are called "points"—each point representing a fee of 1% of the loan principal to be paid at the time the loan originates.

Example

Ordinary Payment Loan with an Origination Fee

The Second National Bank has quoted a rate of "prime plus 2" plus a 2% origination fee on a $100,000, one-year collect loan to Dasgupta Transport Corp. Prime is now 6%.

Question: What is the effective annual rate (EAR) on the loan?

Solution steps:

1. Organize the loan's cash flows:

	Year 0	Year 1	
Principal	$100,000	($100,000)	
Interest		(8,000)	8% of $100,000
Fee	(2,000)		2% of $100,000
	$ 98,000	($108,000)	

2. Solve for the interest rate embedded in these cash flows:

CLEAR the time value part of your calculator

Key in 98,000 and press PV

Key in −108,000 and press FV

Key in 1 and press n (1 year)

Compute i = 10.20%

Answer: The EAR is 10.20%. The fee adds 2.20% to the EAR: 2% from the fee itself plus 20 basis points since the fee is at the beginning of the loan period rather than the end.

compensating balance—a deposit that must remain at the bank as long as a loan is outstanding

Compensating balances A **compensating balance** is cash that must remain on deposit at the bank as long as a loan is outstanding. The bank pays no interest on this amount and can invest it for the period of the loan. Whereas banks tend to use fees to cover one-time costs, such as the cost of preparing loan documents, compensating balances have been traditionally used to "compensate" the bank for ongoing services provided to the customer but not directly billed, such as check clearing, maintaining records, advice, credit information, etc.

Compensating balances are quoted in several ways—a common form is simply a percentage of the loan principal. The balance required by a bank is a function of its earning opportunities, costs, allocation of fixed costs, profitability of specific accounts, aggressiveness, etc. It differs from bank to bank; thus, it pays for financial managers to shop around. Recently, some banks have moved toward charging separately for each bank service—a trend called *unbundling*—as they have made improvements in the ways they measure and control their costs.

If a compensating balance requirement results in a firm keeping a higher balance than it otherwise would, the balance requirement raises the EAR on a loan.

Example

Collect Loan with a Compensating Balance

The Third National Bank has quoted a rate of "prime plus 2" plus a 15% compensating balance on a $100,000, one-year ordinary payment loan to Dasgupta Transport Corp. Prime is now 6%, and Dasgupta currently has no deposits at that bank.

Question: What is the effective annual rate (EAR) on the loan?

Solution steps:

1. Organize the loan's cash flows. Since Dasgupta has no balances at the bank, the full 15% requirement would have to be deposited at the bank for the duration of the loan (note that Dasgupta retrieves the balance amount when the loan is repaid):

	Year 0	Year 1	
Principal	$100,000	($100,000)	
Interest		(8,000)	8% of $100,000
Balance	(15,000)	15,000	15% of $100,000
	$ 85,000	($ 93,000)	

2. Solve for the interest rate embedded in these cash flows:

CLEAR the time value part of your calculator

Key in 85,000 and press PV

Key in −93,000 and press FV

Key in 1 and press n (1 year)

Compute i = 9.41%

Answer: The EAR is 9.41%. The balance requirement adds 1.41% to the interest rate. Effectively, Dasgupta still pays $8,000 interest on a loan of only $85,000.

Timing of principal and interest payments In the previous examples, each loan was an ordinary payment loan with interest and principal due at the end of the loan period. It is also possible that interest and/or some of the principal might be due at an earlier date.

discount loan—a loan in which interest is paid at the beginning of the loan period

A **discount loan** is one in which the interest is paid at the time the loan is taken, not at repayment. If the interest is calculated on the full loan amount, however, the result is an increase to the effective annual rate.

Example

Discount Loan

The Fourth National Bank has quoted a rate of "prime plus 2" to Dasgupta Transport Corp. on a $100,000, one-year discount loan. The prime rate is now 6%.

Question: What is the effective annual rate (EAR) on the loan?

Solution steps:

1. Organize the loan's cash flows. Note that interest is paid at "Year 0" and not at "Year 1":

	Year 0	Year 1	
Principal	$100,000	($100,000)	
Interest	(8,000)		8% of $100,000
	$ 92,000	($100,000)	

2. Solve for the interest rate embedded in these cash flows:

CLEAR the time value part of your calculator

Key in 92,000 and press PV

Key in −100,000 and press FV

Key in 1 and press n (1 year)

Compute i = 8.70%

Answer: The EAR is 8.70%. Requiring the interest payment in advance adds 70 basis points to the interest rate. Effectively, Dasgupta still pays $8,000 interest on a loan of only $92,000.

4. Asset-Based Loans

Banks want their loans to be repaid from the cash flows generated by their customers' operations. However, in cases where the borrower is not of the highest creditworthiness, banks often ask for a claim on some or all of the borrower's assets to give them a "second way out" of the loan. When this happens, we have an **asset-based loan.**

asset-based loan—a loan backed with a pledge of assets

The property pledged to back the repayment of a loan is called **collateral.** If the loan is repaid, the bank's claim on the collateral expires. But if the borrower defaults, the bank can institute legal proceedings to claim the collateral, sell it, and use the proceeds to satisfy the loan obligation.

collateral—property pledged in support of a loan

The use of collateral is governed by the Uniform Commercial Code (UCC), the commercial law adopted by all 50 states.The borrower signs a security agreement, a standard document by which property is pledged as collateral. The agreement is then filed with the state government ("perfected"), after which it has legal force and the lender obtains a security interest in the pledged property. The state makes all security agreements public so other lenders can know the extent of pledged assets and so anyone who disputes the agreement can know of its existence.

The most common collateral for short-term lending is working capital assets: the accounts receivable and inventories financed by the loan.

Assignment of receivables Assignment is the normal way that accounts receivable are pledged as loan collateral. The procedure is as follows: The borrower extends credit to its customers and then sends the invoices and supporting information to the bank. Upon receipt of the documentation, the bank does a credit evaluation of the borrower's customers and accepts some or all of the receivables as collateral. In general, the bank will accept receivables only from firms with an established credit rating. Also, banks prefer large accounts (i.e., receivables from the sale of "big-ticket" items) to minimize administrative costs as a percent of the loan. The bank then advances some fraction of the accepted receivables as a loan to the borrower.

Usually the borrower's customer is unaware of the agreement and is instructed to mail its payment to a lock box picked up by the bank. When a payment arrives, the bank takes the fraction advanced to the borrower plus interest and remits (or credits the borrower's demand account for) the rest. Should a receivable become uncollectible, the bank has recourse to the borrower.

factoring—selling accounts receivable

factor—a company that purchases accounts receivable

Factoring **Factoring** is similar to assignment except that the accounts receivable are *sold* to the bank. The bank has no further recourse to the borrower if a receivable becomes uncollectible. When acting in this capacity, the bank is known as a **factor.**[4]

The procedure for factoring is a bit different and a bit more complex than for assignment. The borrower first notifies the factor that a potential customer wishes to buy on credit. In response the factor does a credit evaluation of the borrower's customer before credit has been extended. If the borrower's customer is acceptable, the factor notifies the borrower to proceed with the credit sale. However, if the borrower's customer is not acceptable, the factor advises the borrower to proceed with the sale only if the borrower wishes to bear the risk of collection. As these are the riskiest customers, the borrower ordinarily agrees with the factor's analysis and does not extend the credit.

The factor then pays some fraction of the amount of the receivable to purchase it from the borrower. In making this calculation, the factor deducts three amounts from the face amount of the receivable: (1) a "reserve" to cover sales returns and allowances, and disputes between the borrower and its customer; (2) a fee for administrative services, and (3) interest. Upon receipt of payment from the borrower's customer, the factor pays the reserve to the borrower and keeps the remainder.

Although the explicit costs of factoring are high, there are significant savings for the borrower. In factoring, the bank: (1) does credit analysis for the borrower and

[4] **Elaboration:** Throughout this section we have been referring to banks as if they were the only source of short-term loans. In fact, quite a few other organizations—some independent such as Credit Centers, Inc., some affiliated with banks such as CIT, and some affiliated with industrial corporations such as GE Credit—make short-term loans, especially asset-based loans.

(2) protects it from incurring bad debts. These savings often outweigh the costs of factoring, making it a value-adding activity.

Examples

Factoring

Dasgupta Transport Corp. has an average receivables balance of $2 million which turns over eight times/year (roughly every 45 days). A factor will buy the receivables, advancing Dasgupta face value less a 10% reserve, a 1% fee, and interest at a nominal annual rate of "prime plus 10." Prime is now 6%, and fees and interest are based on face value less the reserve.

Question: What is the effective annual rate (EAR) from the factoring arrangement?

Solution steps:

1. Calculate the 45-day (1/8th year) interest rate:

$$16\%/8 = 2\%$$

2. Calculate the reserve, and the fees and interest charged every 45 days:

$$\text{Reserve} = 10\% \times \$2{,}000{,}000 = \$200{,}000$$

$$\text{Fee} = 1\% \times \$1{,}800{,}000 = \$\ 18{,}000$$

$$\text{Interest} = 2\% \times \$1{,}800{,}000 = \$\ 36{,}000$$

3. Organize the cash flows:

	Day 0	Day 45
Receivables balance	$2,000,000	($2,000,000)
Less: reserve	(200,000)	200,000
Gross advance	1,800,000	(1,800,000)
Less: fee	(18,000)	
interest	(36,000)	
Net cash flows	$1,746,000	($1,800,000)

4. Solve for the interest rate embedded in these cash flows:

CLEAR the time value part of your calculator

Key in 1,746,000 and press PV

Key in −1,800,000 and press FV

Key in .125 and press n (1/8 year)

Compute i = 27.59%

Answer: The EAR is 27.59%.

Question: If Dasgupta can save $40,000 as of the end of each 45-day period in credit analysis and bad debt costs, how does the EAR change?

Solution steps:

1. Recalculate the cash flows:

	Day 0	Day 45
Cash flows before savings	$1,746,000	($1,800,000)
Additional savings		40,000
Cash flows after savings	$1,746,000	($1,760,000)

2. Solve for the interest rate embedded in these cash flows:

CLEAR the time value part of your calculator

Key in 1,746,000 and press PV

Key in −1,760,000 and press FV

Key in .125 and press n (1/8 year)

Compute i = 6.60%

Answer: The EAR is reduced to 6.60%. All things considered, this is very low-cost financing.

Pledging inventories The collateral value of inventory depends on its perishability, marketability, market prices, and cost of disposing the inventory if necessary. In general, raw material is acceptable collateral if it is a commodity, but work-in-process is rarely acceptable because it is difficult to sell. The worth of finished goods and merchandise as collateral depends on the product: for example, appliances, canned foods, building materials, and fuels are generally acceptable while clothing, fresh foods, and specialized products are not.

There are four common methods by which a lender secures its interest in inventory collateral: (1) a floating lien, (2) a chattel mortgage, (3) a trust receipt, or (4) a warehouse receipt. They differ by the degree of control over the inventory demanded by the lender.

1. A *floating lien* is a general claim to all inventory owned by the borrower, either now or in the future as long as any part of the loan remains outstanding. Because of its broad coverage, it is also known as a "blanket lien." A floating lien is the least restrictive claim on inventory. The borrower retains full control of the goods, and the lender must first locate and identify the inventory and then take legal possession should it be needed to satisfy a loan.
2. A *chattel mortgage* is a claim on specific items of inventory, usually identified by serial number. Inventory remains with the borrower, however the borrower cannot sell it without the lender's consent. This form of security is particularly suitable for low-turnover, easily identifiable items.
3. With a *trust receipt*, the inventory collateral and any proceeds from selling it must be held by the borrower in a legal trust for the benefit of the lender. For example, trust receipts are often used to finance an inventory of automobiles at a retail showroom (where the process is known as "floor planning"). The

FINANCE IN PRACTICE

Sometimes Even a Terminal Warehouse Isn't Enough

In the early 1960s, officers of the Allied Crude Vegetable Oil Company approached the Bank of America for an asset-based loan to finance an inventory of salad oil. Because the president of Allied, Angelo (Tino) DeAngelis, had a criminal record and was known to associate with organized-crime figures, the bank hired American Express Field Warehousing Company, a unit of American Express, to establish and manage a terminal warehouse facility. American Express Field Warehousing posted a 24-hour-per-day armed guard. However, even these precautions proved insufficient. Tino DeAngelis arranged for his associates to be hired as guards who then looked the other way while he removed the oil. He also bribed American Express inspectors not to take a physical inventory and modified the oil tanks so spot checks would make it appear as if the oil were still there.

The theft was ultimately discovered, and DeAngelis spent years in federal prison for the "Great Salad Oil Swindle." But the salad oil was never recovered. Bank of America and the lending syndicate lost over $200 million, and the resulting lawsuits and bad publicity nearly put American Express out of business.

cars on the lot are effectively owned by the lender and can be sold only if the dealer "buys" them by placing the sale proceeds in the lender's name. As a result of this degree of control, the lender's permission is not required prior to each sale.

4. A *warehouse receipt* is the most restrictive form of an inventory claim. Under this system, goods serving as collateral must be separated from the borrower's other inventory and kept in a warehouse under the control of a third party. The lender advances funds against each inventory item upon obtaining a receipt from the warehouse manager certifying that the item is indeed in the warehouse. Goods can be released from the warehouse only with the lender's permission. A warehouse located on the borrower's property is termed a "field warehouse." This arrangement is appropriate when the inventory is difficult or costly to move or when the borrower needs access to the inventory for technical or marketing reasons. A lender concerned that goods might be removed from the warehouse without permission will often require that the pledged inventory be taken from the borrower and stored in a "terminal warehouse" located away from the borrower's facilities.

5. Choosing a Bank

Even though the basic product of commercial banks (the use of money) is a commodity and cannot be differentiated, banks are very different in many respects. Among the differences financial managers evaluate are:

- The range of their products and services (e.g., cash management, capital markets advice and access, private placement, foreign-currency expertise, etc.)

- Practices that increase quoted rates, such as fees and compensating balances.
- Their loyalty in adverse conditions.
- Their understanding of the firm's business.
- Their creativity in packaging financing.
- Their professional contacts.
- The size of loans they can make available.
- Their attitude toward risk, which is a function of the bank's size, the stability of its loan portfolio, the stability of its demand deposits, and the stability of its cost of funds.

Capital Market Alternatives to Bank Loans

In Chapter 19 we noted that commercial banks and investment banks in the United States, separated by the Glass-Steagall Act of 1933, have recently been looking for ways to recapture some of the business each lost to the other in the split-up. Two creations of investment banks to reenter the world of short-term lending are commercial paper (a substitute for an offering basis loan) and Euronotes (a substitute for a revolving line of credit).

1. Commercial Paper

commercial paper—short-term, unsecured notes issued by large corporations

Commercial paper—short-term, unsecured, negotiable promissory notes—represents direct borrowing and lending between large corporations without the use of a commercial bank. It is typically issued at a discount to its face value, much like Treasury bills, and carries no interest coupon.

The sale of commercial paper is arranged by investment bankers who bring together the issuer and buyer (lender) for a broker's fee. Because the issuer and buyer deal directly, the amount and maturity of each issue is tailored to the parties' needs rather than to any standard amount or time period. Maturities range from a few days to nine months, but are rarely longer since paper with maturity of 270 days or less does not have to be registered with the Securities and Exchange Commission.

To encourage lenders to buy commercial paper, the major investment banks maintain an active secondary market for high-quality paper. This guarantees that a lender can resell the paper if it needs to retrieve its funds prior to maturity. In addition, most issuers maintain a commercial-bank revolving-credit line to back the issue.[5] Should the issuer be unable to refund the paper at maturity due to low cash flow or the inability to issue new paper ("roll over the issue"), it can obtain the needed funds by borrowing against the revolver.

---

[5] **Elaboration:** In fact, many investment banks will not handle a commercial paper issue unless the issuer obtains a backup revolving line of credit.

Example

Commercial Paper

Oliver, Thomas & Co., the investment bank, has proposed to Dasgupta Transport Corp. that it sell $10 million of 30-day commercial paper at a discount to face value of 5.5%. The bank will take a fee of 1/8% of face value to place the issue.

Question: What is the effective annual rate (EAR) on the paper?

Solution steps:

1. Calculate the discounted issue price:

   CLEAR the time value part of your calculator

   Key in −10,000,000 and press FV

   Key in 5.5 and press i

   Key in .0822 and press n (30/365 year)

   Compute PV = 9,956,086

2. Organize the issue's cash flows:

	Day 0	Day 30	
Principal	$9,956,086	($10,000,000)	
Fee	(12,500)		1/8% of $10,000,000
	$9,943,586	($10,000,000)	

3. Solve for the interest rate embedded in these cash flows:

   CLEAR the time value part of your calculator

   Key in 9,943,586 and press PV

   Key in −10,000,000 and press FV

   Key in .0822 and press n (30/365 year)

   Compute i = 7.12%

Answer: The EAR is 7.12%.

Commercial paper has become very popular among large corporations for at least five reasons:

- It is low-cost financing. The interest rate on paper is normally below the reference rate by 1/4% to 2%, since investment banks bear none of the costs or risks of intermediation.
- There are no compensating balance or fee requirements (other than the commitment fee for a backup revolving credit line) to add to the effective cost of the issue.
- There are no institutional restrictions on the size of the financing. By contrast, the amount a bank can lend to any one customer is limited both by law and prudence to prevent excessive exposure to that customer's risks.

- The investment bank serves as a resource. It provides market-oriented advice which may be of help in other capital-market-related decisions.
- There is prestige in the ability to issue commercial paper. Only the largest, most creditworthy firms can enter this market.

There are some disadvantages to commercial paper as compared to commercial bank loans. Firms that issue paper reduce their business with their banks, potentially weakening that relationship. The interest rate on commercial paper, determined in the open market, is more volatile than the reference rate, exposing issuers of paper to greater uncertainty in their cost of funds. Also, the market for paper is impersonal and cannot handle variations in the issuer's plans, such as a change in cash needs or the desire to extend the maturity of a loan in a bad market.

Nevertheless, most large corporations have found the advantages of commercial paper to be so significant that they now use it for much of their negotiated short-term debt. Today, the dollar amount of commercial paper outstanding rivals total bank lending. Banks that once specialized in lending to the largest corporations have seen much of that business evaporate and now lend primarily to middle-sized ("middle market") and small companies.

2. Euronotes

Euronotes—short-term, unsecured, standardized notes issued by large corporations and governments in the Eurodollar market

Euronotes are short-term, unsecured, promissory notes issued by corporations and governments in the Eurodollar market outside the United States. They are most commonly denominated in dollars, although there is a growing demand for other currencies including European Currency Units (ECUs), the common currency created by the European Community. Like commercial paper, they are issued at a discount to face value. However, unlike commercial paper, they tend to have standardized face values—typically multiples of $250,000—and standardized maturities of one, three, or six months.

Euronote facility—a contract for the issuance of Euronotes

Euronotes are commonly issued through a **Euronote facility,** a contract between a bank (or syndicate of banks)[6] and the borrowing organization. The contract provides that the borrower may issue a series of Euronotes with a predetermined interest rate (normally referenced to LIBOR), typically over a period of five to seven years. The bank commits to purchase all the notes as issued up to a specified maximum amount for resale to investors. In return, the borrower pays a commitment fee to the financial institution.

A Euronote facility provides the equivalent of a revolving line of credit guaranteed for the life of the contract. In addition, Euronote financing is usually cheaper than domestic borrowing for two reasons: (1) the facility is priced in relation to LIBOR and not the higher U.S. prime rate, and (2) since Euronotes are resold to the general investing public, they have broadened the market for corporate debt by offering investors the ability to buy the paper of top-quality credits previously held only by banks.

---

[6] **Observation:** Since Euronotes are created and sold outside the United States, the Glass-Steagall Act does not apply. Both U.S. investment and commercial banks are active participants in this market.

Alicia Vasquez walked out of her finance class talking animatedly to her classmates. There was a palpable excitement in her voice. Speaking faster than some of her friends could follow, she related her assignment at work and how she had taken advantage of that evening's class to learn more about short-term debt.

The effective rates on short-term debt were not always apparent from their quotes. However, there was a consistent method to calculate them based on the same time value analysis of cash flows Alicia had learned in her first finance course. And the treasurer had been correct to conclude that some costs of short-term financing were hidden in the way the company operated internally and with its customers. These impacts were much more difficult to quantify and include in cash flows, but it was important to improve continuously the company's ability to do so. The after-class discussion was so lively that an hour passed before anyone looked at a watch and the group finally said good-bye.

Alicia got into her car and tossed her books on the seat beside her. A well-chewed pen fell out of her notebook and onto the floor. Alicia laughed out loud as the pen caught her eye. "Well, that pen earned its keep today," she thought as she turned the key and backed out of the parking space. As she drove home, she began to look forward to going to work the next day and sharing her new insights with her colleagues.

Summary of Key Points

- **Identify three reasons why short-term debt is an attractive financing source.** Short-term debt is attractive because of its availability, low cost, and flexibility. For small companies, short-term debt is often the only financing source accessible outside the company.
- **Describe trade credit by its legal arrangement and terms of sale, and evaluate the cost of trade credit and forgoing trade discounts.** Trade credit can be in the form of an account payable, a note payable, or a third-party acceptance. A wide range of terms of sale—really terms of payment—are common, from the most liberal consignment to the most restrictive cash before delivery. Some trade credit is free and should be taken automatically. Nonfree trade credit must be evaluated by calculating the effective annual interest rate embedded in the terms of sale. The same is true of trade discounts where forgoing a discount creates a further loan for the period between the discount and payment dates. Some companies stretch payables to reduce their cost, but it is becoming more common for companies to work closely with their suppliers to create terms of sale that are mutually beneficial.
- **Describe the worth of accruals.** Accruals—wages payable, taxes payable, interest payable, etc.—provide free financing since the delayed payment requires no increase in obligation. However, accruals can hide performance-related costs which must be thoroughly understood to evaluate the total cost of this financing.
- **Calculate the effective interest rate and understand the characteristics of unsecured and secured bank loans.** Lines of credit and revolving credit lines are prenegotiated, while offering basis loans are not. Bank loans are normally priced relative to a reference rate of interest: the prime rate in the United States and the London inter-bank offering rate (LIBOR) in the Euromarkets. The effective annual interest rate (EAR) on the loan is a function of the borrower's risk as determined by a credit analysis and can be obtained by applying time value of money calculations to the loan's cash flows. For all but the most creditworthy customers, it is common for the bank to ask for collateral— accounts receivable or inventories—as security in case the loan cannot be repaid from the borrowers' operating cash flows. An alternative to a loan collateralized by accounts receivable is factoring, in which the borrower sells its receivables to the bank. It is worthwhile for borrowers to choose their

banks with care, even though money is a commodity product, since banks differ considerably in their policies and capabilities.

■ **Describe two alternatives to bank debt developed in the domestic and international capital markets.** Commercial paper is direct borrowing and lending between large corporations, tailored to their specific needs. Euronotes are notes of standard size and maturity, issued by large corporations and governments and purchased by a bank for resale to investors. A Euronote facility guarantees that a company can issue Euronotes up to a maximum amount for the length of the contract.

Questions

1. Why is short-term debt an attractive source of financing to financial managers?
2. Why might a seller not be happy with an open account payable? What are the alternatives?
3. Under what conditions would a seller be willing to sell on consignment? on terms of cash before delivery? Under what conditions would a buyer be comfortable with each of these two extreme terms of sale?
4. What distinguishes free trade credit from nonfree trade credit?
5. Why is the time period from the date of sale until the discount date not included in the analysis of a trade discount?
6. Why is it the forgoing of a trade discount that creates the loan and not the taking of the discount?
7. Why is stretching payables not a good thing to do in practice, even though it lowers the interest rate on trade credit?
8. What is net credit? What kind of company should have positive net credit? negative net credit?
9. Identify some of the hidden costs associated with accruals.
10. What are the differences among a line of credit, revolving credit line, and an offering basis loan?
11. What is a reference rate? What are the rates most commonly used for dollar-denominated loans?
12. Why do banks charge fees and compensating balances?
13. What is collateral? Why do banks usually insist that it be part of a loan agreement?
14. What is the difference between assignment of receivables and factoring?
15. Why did investment banks create commercial paper and Euronotes? Distinguish between them.

Problems

1. **(Trade credit)** Determine the effective interest rate for trade credit if a company can pay 2% over the cash price to obtain credit terms of:
   a. 20 days
   b. 35 days
   c. 50 days
   d. 65 days
2. **(Trade credit)** Determine the effective interest rate for trade credit if a company can obtain credit terms of "net 60" by paying an increment over the cash price of:
   a. 0%
   b. 1%
   c. 2%
   d. 3%
3. **(Trade discount)** Calculate the interest rate on the loan obtained by forgoing the following trade discounts:
   a. 1/10, net 75
   b. 2/10, net 35
   c. 3/10, net 60
   d. 4/10, net 30
4. **(Trade discount)** Calculate the interest rate on the loan obtained by forgoing the following trade discounts:
   a. 4/15, net 40
   b. 3/10, net 40
   c. 2/20, net 40
   d. 1/5, net 40
5. **(Trade discount)** A company can obtain short-term bank debt at an effective annual rate of 8.5%. For which of the four terms of sale given in Problem 3 should the company take the discount?
6. **(Trade discount)** A company can obtain short-term bank debt at an effective annual rate of 12%. For which of the four terms of sale given in Problem 4 should the company forgo the discount?
7. **(Net credit)** A company has accounts receivable of $1 million. Calculate the company's net credit and whether it is a net supplier or net user of trade credit if its accounts payable equals:
   a. $600,000
   b. $800,000
   c. $1,000,000
   d. $1,200,000

8. **(Net credit)** A company has accounts payable of $4 million. Calculate the company's net credit and whether it is a net supplier or net user of trade credit, if its accounts receivable equals:
   a. $6 million
   b. $5 million
   c. $4 million
   d. $3 million
9. **(Commitment fee)** A company has borrowed $300,000 against a $750,000 revolving credit line with an interest rate of prime plus 2 on the amount borrowed and a 1/2% commitment fee on the unused portion of the line. Both rates are nominal and applied quarterly. Determine the quarterly interest-plus-fee payment that will be due if the company maintains this position for three months and the prime rate is:
   a. 4%
   b. 6%
   c. 8%
   d. 10%
10. **(Commitment fee)** A company has arranged a $5 million revolving credit line with an interest rate of prime plus 1 on the amount borrowed and a 1/2% commitment fee on the unused portion of the line. Both rates are nominal and applied quarterly. Determine the quarterly interest-plus-fee payment that will be due at the end of three months if the prime rate is 6% and company borrows:
    a. $0
    b. $2 million
    c. $4 million
    d. $5 million
11. **(Bank loan)** A bank is willing to make a collect loan of $500,000 to a company for one year at prime plus 1. Prime is now 6%. Calculate the effective annual rate on the loan if:
    a. There are no fees or compensating balances.
    b. There is a 2% origination fee.
    c. There is a 15% compensating balance requirement.
    d. There are both a 2% origination fee and a 15% compensating balance requirement.
12. **(Bank loan)** A bank is willing to make a collect loan of $2,500,000 to a company for one year at prime plus 1/2. Prime is now 6%. Calculate the effective annual rate on the loan if:
    a. There are no fees or compensating balances.
    b. There is a 1% origination fee.
    c. There is a 12% compensating balance requirement.
    d. There are both a 1% origination fee and a 12% compensating balance requirement.
13. **(Bank loan)** Redo Problem 11 assuming the loan is a discount loan instead of a collect loan.
14. **(Bank loan)** Redo Problem 12 assuming the loan is a discount loan instead of a collect loan.
15. **(Factoring)** A company has sales of $10 million and an average collection period of 36 days (use a 360-day year). A factor will buy its receivables and advance the company face value less an 8% reserve, a 3/4% fee, and interest at a nominal annual rate of prime plus 7. Fees and interest are based on face value less the reserve. The prime rate is now 7%.
    a. Determine the net cash flows of this financing.
    b. Calculate the effective annual rate (EAR) of the arrangement with the factor.
    c. Now assume the firm can reduce its costs every receivables cycle by $15,000 (at day 36) by engaging the factor. Recalculate the EAR including this savings.
    d. Redo part c assuming the cost reduction is $30,000.
16. **(Factoring)** A company has sales of $60 million and an average collection period of 30 days (use a 360-day year). A factor will buy its receivables and advance the company face value less an 5% reserve, a 1/2% fee, and interest at a nominal annual rate of prime plus 6. Fees and interest are based on face value less the reserve. The prime rate is now 6%.
    a. Determine the net cash flows of this financing.
    b. Calculate the effective annual rate (EAR) of the arrangement with the factor.
    c. Now assume the firm can reduce its costs every receivables cycle by $60,000 (at day 30) by engaging the factor. Recalculate the EAR including this savings.
    d. Redo part c assuming the cost reduction is $150,000.
17. **(Commercial paper)** What is the effective annual rate on a 30-day, $25 million commercial paper issue with a 1/10% placement fee if it is sold at a discount to face value of:
    a. 4.5%?
    b. 5.0%?
    c. 5.5%?
    d. 6.0%?
18. **(Commercial paper)** What is the effective annual rate on a 60-day, $15 million commercial paper issue sold at a discount to face value of 5% if it has a placement fee of:
    a. 0.20%?
    b. 0.25%?
    c. 0.30%?
    d. 0.35%?

19. **(Choice of short-term financing)** A company that needs to raise $7 million in financing for a period of 30 days to finance a seasonal buildup of retail inventories is considering three choices:

- Forgo discounts of 1/10, net 40 on its trade credit.
- Borrow on a collect loan from its commercial bank at a nominal rate of prime plus 1 applied monthly with a 1/4% origination fee and a 20% compensating balance requirement. The prime rate is now 6%.
- Issue commercial paper at a discount to face value of 7% with a 0.4% placement fee.

a. Calculate the effective annual rate of each choice.
b. Which alternative has the lowest EAR?
c. What other considerations might enter your analysis?

20. **(Choice of short-term financing)** A company that needs to raise $10 million in financing for a period of 60 days to finance its customers' purchases is considering three choices:

- Forgo discounts of 1/5, net 50 on its trade credit.
- Borrow on a collect loan from its commercial bank at a nominal rate of prime plus 3/4 applied bimonthly with a 1/8% origination fee and a 14% compensating balance requirement. The prime rate is now 6%.
- Factor its $10 million of accounts receivable which turns over six times per year. The factor will advance face value less a 10% reserve, a 1% fee, and interest at a nominal annual rate of prime plus 6. Fees and interest are based on face value less the reserve.

a. Calculate the effective annual rate of each choice.
b. Which alternative has the lowest EAR?
c. What other considerations might enter your analysis?

CHAPTER 21
INTERMEDIATE- AND LONG-TERM DEBT

Dean Hite stared at the telephone on his desk. It had been so long since he had spoken to his old classmate, Fred. His mind flashed back to school and the rock band they had formed—it brought back warm memories. Whose fault was it that they had not spoken in years, or did it really matter? Letting out a sigh, he picked up the receiver and dialed.

Dean had recently been appointed treasurer of a rapidly growing manufacturing company. Fred was now a senior partner at the investment bank of North, Stream, and Valley. Dean had decided to make the call because his company was about to enter a major expansion and would be requiring additional debt financing. He wanted to learn more about the forms of intermediate and long-term debt available to his company. Dean's relationship with the company's previous investment bank had not gone well, and he was looking for advice from his old friend.

After the first few hesitant words, it was as if their paths had never separated. Dean and Fred spoke quickly about their families, jobs, and other interests—especially their love of music. Then Dean explained his company's situation and his thoughts about alternate forms the debt might take: how the company would be building a new plant and equipping the facility with state-of-the-art machinery, how its success over the past decade had left it with excellent borrowing capacity, and how the company's most recent cash flow forecast indicated a strong ability to service the new debt financing. Dean agreed to send Fred the company's most recent financial statements and some other supporting information.

As the conversation wound down, Fred offered to call back in a couple of days with his reaction to the company's financial position and debt requirements, and both friends promised to meet for lunch a week later. As Dean hung up the phone, he told himself this was a promise he certainly would keep.

Most financial managers share the problem Dean is facing: selecting the type of debt most appropriate for their company. We have already considered various sides of this question. In Chapter 15 we studied the debt-equity mix to determine how much debt was appropriate. Then in Chapter 16 we asked about the mix of debt and looked at issues of maturity and risk. In this chapter we examine the most common forms of intermediate- and long-term debt—term loans, leases, floating-rate notes, and bonds—to learn more about their characteristics and use.

Financial accountants classify debt with a maturity longer than one year as long-term, but the division between current and long-term is somewhat arbitrary and awkward. A note that matures in 13 months would be classified as long-term on the balance sheet, but is not very different from a 12-month note and is clearly not long-term in any meaningful sense. To deal with this distinction, financial professionals have coined the term "intermediate-term debt" for the middle maturities. While the dividing line between the intermediate term and long term is a matter of some debate and opinion, most financial observers place it somewhere in the range of seven to ten years.

Key Points You Should Learn from This Chapter

After reading this chapter you should be able to:

- Discuss the distinction between fixed-rate and floating-rate debt.
- Describe term debt and construct a repayment schedule for three different kinds of term loans.
- Discuss the nature and benefits of a lease.
- Describe the characteristics and life cycle of a bond.
- Describe floating-rate notes.

Introductory Concepts—Fixed and Floating Rates

Fixed-rate debt is debt on which the interest rate remains constant over the life of the loan. A quote of "prime plus 1" means "prime at the time the loan is taken plus 1%." By contrast, the interest rate on floating rate debt changes with the general level of interest rates; "prime plus 1" translates to "today's prime rate plus 1%." Floating rates are reset whenever the reference rate changes or at predetermined intervals such as monthly, quarterly, annually, etc.

1. Interest Rate Risk

In our discussion of short-term debt in Chapter 20, we said nothing about whether the interest rate on a bank loan was fixed or floating since it was of little importance. Short-term loans mature quickly, and it is easy to adjust the rate when they are renewed. As debt maturities lengthen past one year, however, the distinction between fixed and floating rates becomes far more important.

For intermediate- and long-term debt, the decision to make the interest rate fixed or floating determines the exposure of each party to interest rate changes. Figure 21.1 summarizes the possibilities. A fixed rate offers the lender protection if rates fall but prevents the lender from benefiting if rates should rise. It shields a borrower from a rise in rates but also from the benefit of lowered interest payments should rates decline. The opposite is true for floating-rate debt. If rates rise, the lender benefits from higher interest earnings, but the lender is hurt by falling rates. The borrower enjoys falling rates but must pay more if rates should rise.

Prior to the interest rate volatility of the 1970s, banks were willing to make fixed-rate loans. Since that time, almost all bank lending has become floating-rate debt, passing on the risk of rising rates to the banks' customers. A borrower who desires a fixed rate must pay a higher interest rate than on floating-rate debt or purchase interest rate insurance from the same or another bank.

2. Rate Insurance

Interest rate insurance is available from commercial banks in the form of caps, floors, and collars.

cap—a limit to how high the interest rate on a loan can rise

A **cap** is a rate ceiling. Should the interest rate remain at or below the ceiling, no payment is made by the insurer—much like an automobile insurance policy where

FIGURE 21.1
Risk vs. rates. The choice between a fixed and floating rate changes the interest rate exposure of the borrower and lender.

	Borrower runs the risk that:	Lender runs the risk that:
Fixed rate	Rates will fall	Rates will rise
Floating rate	Rates will rise	Rates will fall

there are no accidents. However, if the interest rate rises above the cap, the insurer pays the remaining interest.

Examples

Interest Rate Cap

Dean Hite's company borrows $1 million from the First National Bank at a floating rate which is now 7%. Concerned that rates might rise, Dean purchases a 9% cap from the Second National Bank.

Question: What rate does the company pay if the interest rate rises to 8%?

Answer: Since 8% is below the 9% cap, Dean's company pays the full 8% to the First National Bank. The Second National Bank pays nothing.

Question: What rate does the company pay if the interest rate rises to 10%?

Answer: Since 10% is above the 9% cap, Dean's company only pays 9% to the First National Bank. The Second National Bank pays the First National Bank the remaining 1%.

floor—a limit to how low the interest rate on a loan can fall

collar—a combination of a cap and a floor

A **floor** is a minimum rate. It functions as the opposite of a cap: the borrower never pays less than the floor rate, even if the loan rate falls below that level. In return, the insurer pays a fee to the borrower. Floors are rarely sold on a standalone basis; instead they accompany caps. In effect, the role of a floor is to lower the cost of a cap by giving something back to the insurer. When a borrower purchases a cap and a floor together, the combination is called a **collar.**

Example

Interest Rate Collar

Dean Hite's company borrows $1 million from the First National Bank at a floating rate which is now 7%. Concerned that rates might change, Dean purchases a collar from the Second National Bank, limiting his exposure to the band of 5% to 9%.

Question: What rate does the company pay if the interest rate falls to 4%?

Answer: Four percent is below the 5% floor. Dean's company still pays 5%: 4% to the First National Bank against the loan and 1% to the Second National Bank against the collar.

Caps, floors, and collars can be set to provide any level of interest rate protection desired by the borrower. Figure 21.2 shows two possibilities for a collar in a volatile interest rate environment. The fluctuating line represents the rate the borrower would pay without insurance. In the first graph, the collar is wide and has little effect—only the most extreme rate spikes are eliminated. In the second graph, the band is much narrower and the borrower's rate is much closer to being fixed. Effectively, by combining a floating-rate loan and a collar with the desired bandwidth, a borrower can adjust its rate exposure to any point along a range from floating to fixed.

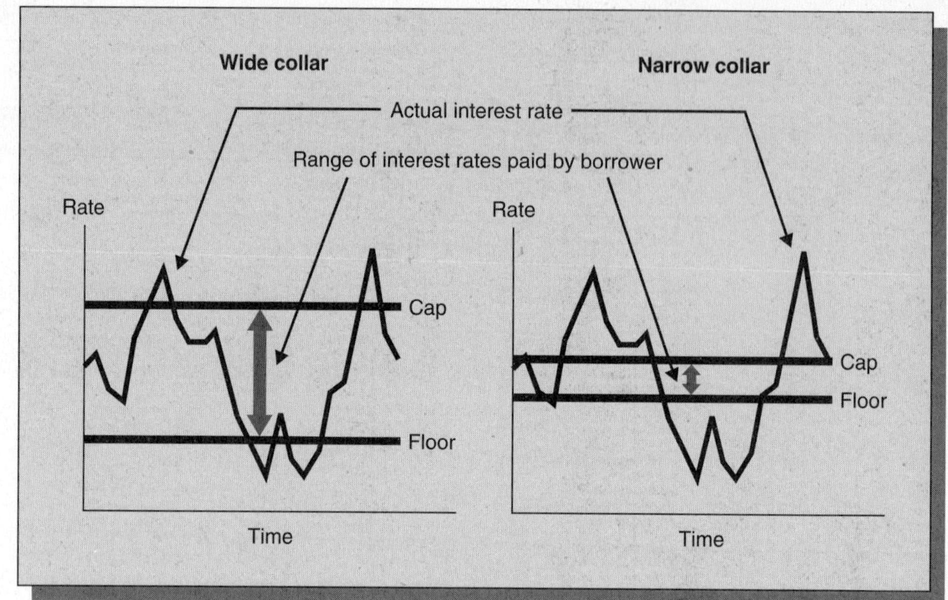

FIGURE 21.2
Interest rate collar. A floating rate may be changed any distance toward a fixed rate by selecting the width of the band.

3. Swaps

swap—an exchange of loan obligations

counterparties—the participants in a swap

A **swap** is an exchange of loan obligations. Two companies, known as **counterparties,** each borrow money and then exchange either their loan principals, repayment obligations, or both. Swaps make sense when each borrower can reduce the cost of (or only obtain) the financing it wants by letting the counterparty obtain it.

Swaps come in three basic forms: the "basis swap," the "fixed for floating swap," and the "currency swap." In a basis swap, the parties borrow at two different reference rates—for example, one loan might be based on the U.S. prime rate while the other is based on LIBOR. In a fixed for floating swap, one loan carries a fixed interest rate and the other a floating rate of interest. In a currency swap, the two loans are denominated in different currencies.

Because swaps allow companies to switch their obligations between fixed and floating rates, among reference rates, and among currencies, they provide additional risk-reduction possibilities and an extra degree of flexibility in intermediate- and long-term debt financing.

Examples

Swap

Dean Hite's company can borrow $1 million at a fixed rate of 8% or at a floating rate of prime. To hedge its assets, Dean prefers the fixed-rate financing. However, Dean's banker at the First National Bank has suggested that Dean raise the funds at the floating rate and swap with a counterparty that wants floating-rate debt. The counterparty's bank has quoted a floating rate of prime plus 2 and a fixed rate of 9% for a $1 million loan.

Question: What is the interest rate savings from the swap?

Solution steps:

1. Calculate the sum of the rates if the two companies raise what they want directly:

Dean's company:	fixed rate of	8%
Counterparty:	floating rate of	prime + 2
Sum		prime + 10

2. Calculate the sum of the rates if the two companies raise the opposite of what they want in anticipation of a swap:

Dean's company:	floating rate of	prime
Counterparty:	fixed rate of	9%
Sum		prime + 9

3. Compare the two sums:

$$(\text{prime} + 10) - (\text{prime} + 9) = 1\%$$

Answer: The two parties can save 1% through the swap.

Question: If the 1% savings is allocated between Dean's company, the counterparty, and the bank so that Dean's company saves 1/2%, what rate will it pay for its financing?

Answer: Dean's company will pay 7.5% for its financing, 1/2% less than the 8% it would pay without the swap.

Question: What will be the impact of a 1% increase in the prime rate on the rate Dean's company is paying?

Answer: Nothing. Since Dean has swapped the floating-rate loan for a fixed rate, the change to prime will affect the counterparty's rate. Dean's company will still pay 7.5%.

Term Loans

term loan—a loan with a maturity of more than one year

Term loans are loans with a maturity greater than one year. The use of the word *term*, a synonym for *maturity*, emphasizes the extended time frame. Term loans are made primarily by commercial banks and life insurance companies. However, while banks are specialists in credit analysis, life insurance companies generally are not. As a result, banks lend to companies of all sizes and financial conditions, while the insurance companies lend primarily to large, financially sound companies.

1. The Use of Term Loans

Term loans are particularly appropriate financing in three circumstances: (1) when used to purchase an asset with an intermediate-term life, (2) as a substitute for a line of credit for a company whose operating cycle is longer than one year, and (3) as a "bridge loan."

Hedging intermediate-life assets Often a company wishes to acquire an asset with an intermediate-term life which will generate cash benefits and provide good collateral value over that lifetime and not beyond. Such an asset matches the payment and collateral requirements of a term loan.

Financing a long operating cycle A company with an operating cycle longer than one year—for example, a construction company whose natural cycle is the business cycle—may find short-term financing *too* short-term. A term loan guarantees the availability of financing for more than a year and avoids the out-of-bank clean-up period common to short-term loans.

bridge loan—a loan to provide temporary financing until future, more permanent financing is arranged

Bridge loan When market conditions are unfavorable for long-term financing, a term loan is often used to finance the firm until a bond issue becomes less costly. In this use the term loan is a **bridge loan,** spanning the gulf between today's position and the future financing. Term loans are also used as a bridge when long-term needs are uncertain and the company is unwilling to commit long-term to an amount or maturity of debt.

2. Term-Loan Maturities

The maturity of a term loan depends on the needs of both borrower and lender.

From the borrower's point of view, the maturity should match the reason for the loan, either the productive life of the asset the loan is financing, the longer-than-one-year operating cycle, or the forecasted period of uncertainty the loan is intended to bridge.

The lender has two considerations in establishing the maturity of a term loan. First the lender is concerned about being repaid and wants to match the term to the borrower's projected cash flows. Second the lender wants to hedge its own balance sheet, hence wants to tie loan maturities (its assets) to the maturities of its liabilities. Banks, with a high level of short-term deposit liabilities, tend to restrict the term over which they will lend to about 5–7 years. Life insurance companies, with much more predictable and stable liability demands (death and disability benefits that can be forecasted to a fairly high degree of accuracy by its actuaries), prefer to lend for longer terms, generally 5 to 15 years with preference for over 10 years, and generally insist on penalties for early repayment.

For term loans with longer lives, it is common for a syndicate (group) of lenders, consisting of both banks and insurance companies, to make the loan jointly. The borrower makes interest and principal payments to the banks for the first 5 to 7 years until they are fully repaid and makes the remaining payments to the insurance companies.

3. Term-Loan Structures

amortize—to repay a loan

The structure of a term loan refers to the way in which the loan will be **amortized,** or repaid. Three structures are particularly common: (1) equal payments, (2) equal amortization, and (3) balloon and bullet loans.

Equal payment An equal-payment term loan calls for principal and interest to be repaid together in equal installments over the lifetime of the loan. The payment stream forms an annuity with a present value equal to the loan amount. Since an annuity payment can only be determined if the interest rate is known, the equal-payment structure is generally used for loans with a fixed interest rate.[1] Examples familiar to most of us are an automobile loan with equal monthly payments for a 3- to 5-year period and a home mortgage loan which calls for equal monthly payments for anywhere from 10 to 30 years.

Examples

Equal-Payment Loan

Dean Hite's company arranges a two-year term loan of $500,000 with its bank repayable in eight equal end-of-quarter payments at a nominal annual rate of 8%.

Question: How much is each quarterly payment?

Solution steps:

1. Calculate the quarterly interest rate:

$$8\%/4 = 2\%$$

2. Solve for the payment with present value equal to the loan amount:

CLEAR the time value part of your calculator, set END

Key in 500,000 and press PV

Key in 2 and press i

Key in 8 and press n (8 quarters)

Compute PMT = −68,255

Answer: There will be eight payments of $68,255, each containing interest and repayment of principal.

Question: Construct a repayment schedule detailing the composition of each payment.

Solution steps: Fill out each line of the table as follows (calculations for the first line are in parentheses):

---

[1] **Elaboration:** When an equal-payment structure is used for a floating-rate loan, the entire amortization schedule must be recalculated whenever the interest rate changes. Either the payment is held constant and the loan term is lengthened or shortened, or the term of the loan remains constant and the payment is changed (in which case the loan has "equal payments" only if the interest rate remains constant).

1. Start with the $500,000 beginning balance in Quarter 1.
2. The interest payment equals 2% of the beginning balance (2% × $500,000 = $10,000).
3. The principal repayment equals the remainder of the payment: $68,255 minus the interest payment ($68,255 – 10,000 = $58,255).
4. The ending balance for the quarter is the beginning balance less the principal repaid that quarter ($500,000 – 58,255 = $441,745). Make this the beginning balance for the next quarter, and continue with Step 2.

Answer:

Qtr.	Beginning Balance	Interest Payment	Principal Repayment	Ending Balance
1	$500,000	$10,000	$58,255	$441,745
2	441,745	8,835	59,420	382,325
3	382,325	7,647	60,608	321,717
4	321,717	6,434	61,821	259,896
5	259,896	5,198	63,057	196,839
6	196,839	3,937	64,318	132,521
7	132,521	2,651	65,604	66,917
8	66,917	1,338	66,917	0

Sums to $68,255 in each quarter

Notice from the above example that in an equal-payment loan, the first payments contain a larger amount of interest and a correspondingly smaller amount of principal repayment than the final payments. This is because the outstanding balance is greater at the beginning of the loan than at the end, and interest is proportional to the outstanding balance.

Equal amortization An equal-amortization loan calls for the principal to be repaid in equal installments. Interest is calculated separately and is added to the principal repayment to obtain the total payment in each period. Since interest is treated separately from principal and is calculated at each payment point, the equal-amortization structure is particularly appropriate for floating-rate loans and is widely used in commercial lending.

Example

Equal-Amortization Loan

Dean Hite's company arranges a two-year term loan of $500,000 with its bank. The principal is due in eight equal end-of-quarter payments with interest at "prime plus 1." For the first three quarters prime is 7%; it falls to 6.5% for the next two quarters and then falls again to 6%, where it remains for the lifetime of the obligation.

Question: Construct a repayment schedule detailing the composition of each payment.

Solution steps:

1. Calculate the amount of principal repaid with each payment:

$$\$500{,}000/8 = \$62{,}500$$

2. Calculate the quarterly interest rate for each value of the prime rate:

$$7\% + 1\% = 8\%, \quad \text{and} \quad 8\%/4 = 2\%$$

$$6.5\% + 1\% = 7.5\% \quad \text{and} \quad 7.5\%/4 = 1.875\%$$

$$6\% + 1\% = 7\% \quad \text{and} \quad 7\%/4 = 1.75\%$$

3. Fill out each column of the table:
   a. The beginning balance starts at $500,000 and declines by $62,500 each quarter.
   b. The interest rate is from step 2 above.
   c. The interest payment is the interest rate multiplied by the beginning balance.
   d. The principal repayment is a constant $62,500 per quarter.
   e. The total payment is the sum of the interest and principal repayment.

Answer:

Qtr.	Beginning Balance	Interest Rate	Interest Payment	Principal Repayment	Total Payment
1	$500,000	2.00%	$10,000	$62,500	$72,500
2	437,500	2.00	8,750	62,500	71,250
3	375,000	2.00	7,500	62,500	70,000
4	312,500	1.875	5,859	62,500	68,359
5	250,000	1.875	4,688	62,500	67,188
6	187,500	1.75	3,281	62,500	65,781
7	125,000	1.75	2,188	62,500	64,688
8	62,500	1.75	1,094	62,500	63,594
				constant	

balloon—a large final loan payment

Balloon and bullet Often a loan is structured with a disproportionally large final payment, known as a **balloon.** A balloon structure is commonly used when the borrower's cash flows are not expected to be sufficient to service the loan over its lifetime. Making the final payment a balloon reduces the size of the earlier payments, making them more manageable. At maturity, the borrower will sell assets to repay the loan or will simply roll the loan over, extending its maturity.

Example

Equal-Amortization Loan with a Balloon

Dean Hite's company arranges a two-year, 7% fixed-rate term loan of $500,000 with its bank. The principal is due in seven equal end-of-quarter payments plus a balloon payment of $325,000.

Question: Construct a repayment schedule detailing the composition of each payment.

Solution steps:

1. Calculate the amount of principal repaid with each of the first seven payments:

$$(\$500{,}000 - 325{,}000)/7 = \$175{,}000/7 = 25{,}000$$

2. Calculate the quarterly interest rate:

$$7\%/4 = 1.75\%$$

3. Fill out each column of the table:
   a. The beginning balance starts at $500,000, declines by $25,000 in each of the first seven quarters and by $325,000 in the eighth quarter.
   b. The interest payment is 1.75% of the beginning balance.
   c. The principal repayment is a constant $25,000 per quarter until the last quarter, when it is the balloon of $325,000.
   d. The total payment is the sum of the interest and principal repayment.

Answer:

Qtr.	Beginning Balance	Interest Payment	Principal Repayment	Total Payment
1	$500,000	$8,750	$ 25,000	$ 33,750
2	475,000	8,313	25,000	33,313
3	450,000	7,875	25,000	32,875
4	425,000	7,438	25,000	32,438
5	400,000	7,000	25,000	32,000
6	375,000	6,563	25,000	31,563
7	350,000	6,125	25,000	31,125
8	325,000	5,688	325,000	330,688

bullet—a single payment equal to the total principal amount of a loan

The extreme case of a balloon is a **bullet** loan, a loan that requires no principal repayment until its maturity date (the large principal repayment is the "bullet"). It is used when the financing is a bridge loan and will be rolled over into longer-term financing. The interest rate on bullet loans is generally higher than on other term loans as they have a greater risk of nonpayment compared to loans where the principal is repaid in installments.

Example

Bullet Loan

Dean Hite's company arranges a two-year, 7% fixed-rate term loan of $500,000 with its bank. The principal is due as a bullet at maturity.

Question: Construct a repayment schedule detailing the composition of each payment.

Solution steps:

1. Calculate the quarterly interest rate:

$$7\%/4 = 1.75\%$$

2. Fill out each column of the table:
   a. The beginning balance remains $500,000 throughout the lifetime of the loan.
   b. The interest payment is 1.75% of the beginning balance.
   c. The principal repayment is zero until the last quarter, when it is the bullet of $500,000.
   d. The total payment is the sum of the interest and principal repayment.

Answer:

Qtr.	Beginning Balance	Interest Payment	Principal Repayment	Total Payment
1	$500,000	$8,750	$ 0	$ 8,750
2	500,000	8,750	0	8,750
3	500,000	8,750	0	8,750
4	500,000	8,750	0	8,750
5	500,000	8,750	0	8,750
6	500,000	8,750	0	8,750
7	500,000	8,750	0	8,750
8	500,000	8,750	500,000	508,750

4. Term-Loan Contracts

chattel mortgage—a collateral claim on property other than real estate

protective covenants—loan terms designed to assure repayment

A term-loan contract serves three purposes. First, it specifies the loan's characteristics—amount, maturity, interest rate, repayment schedule, penalties for early repayment if any, etc. Second, it identifies the loan collateral which is normally required from all but the largest borrowers. Collateral requested by banks includes compensating balances, financial assets such as stocks and bonds, and a **chattel mortgage** on the assets financed by the loan. Insurance companies typically ask for a mortgage on equipment or real estate.

Third, the contract contains **protective covenants,** restrictions on the financial behavior of the borrower intended to decrease the probability that the loan will not be repaid. Covenants can be grouped into three categories: (1) the "boilerplate"—those terms that rarely change, (2) terms that appear in most agreements but whose details change to fit the specific circumstances, and (3) terms that appear only if the lender deems them necessary.

Boilerplate Common standard loan terms require the borrower to: (1) pay all its debts on time to avoid claims on its assets by other lenders, (2) regularly give its financial statements to the lender, (3) insure collateral assets to at least the value of the loan, (4) not sell collateral assets without approval of the lender, (5) not pledge its other assets to a third party (the "negative pledge clause"), and (6) not assume certain other liabilities or guarantee a third party's debt.

Changing details Typical of the terms whose details change with each loan are those that require the borrower to: (1) maintain a specified level of working capital or a minimum current ratio, (2) not remove cash from the business through excessive cash dividends, stock repurchase, or capital expenditures; and (3) not take on additional obligations via other term loans or leases.

Special terms Terms that may be included in the loan agreement when appropriate include: (1) a limitation on the use of the loan proceeds, (2) limits on executive salaries, and (3) a requirement that employment contracts and life insurance be arranged for key people.

Leasing

A lease is a rental agreement in which the owner of an asset (the lessor) gives another party (the lessee) the right to use the asset in return for a series of payments. An early use of leasing was to make the monthly cost of real estate affordable. Many companies did not have the desire or the cash to purchase the land and buildings they required, and banks were unwilling to make loans for the temporary use of someone else's property. As other benefits of leasing were discovered, leasing was extended to virtually all types of business assets. Recently, there has been an explosion in nonbusiness leases, in particular individuals leasing automobiles. Today the value of assets leased by businesses and individuals is approaching $1 trillion.

Several types of organizations are active as lessors. Manufacturers often lease their own products, as IBM did for many years with its mainframe computers. Some manufacturers have set up leasing subsidiaries to purchase their products and provide them to customers via lease. The three domestic automobile manufacturers are examples: Chrysler through Chrysler Credit Corporation, Ford through Ford Motor Credit, and GM through General Motors Acceptance Corporation (GMAC). Most major banks have a sister leasing company; examples are Citicorp Leasing, Chase Manhattan Leasing, etc. Leasing is also provided by some financing companies unaffiliated with a manufacturer or bank—"independents" such as Comdisco and ITEL Leasing.

1. Types of Leases

There are various ways to classify leases. In this section we look briefly at five classification schemes: (1) by the number of lessors, (2) by the previous ownership of the asset, (3) by the extent of the services purchased by the lessee, (4) by the nature of the lease terms, and (5) by financial accounting rules.

direct lease—a lease with only one investor, the lessor, who owns the leased asset

leveraged lease—a lease with both equity (the lessor) and debt investors

Number of lessors In some leases, called **direct leases,** the lessor manufactures or purchases the asset to be leased. Other leases are **leveraged leases,** in which the lessor invests only a portion of the cost of the asset and borrows the remainder, leveraging its investment position and increasing its rate of return. Figure 21.3 illustrates this difference. Leveraged leases are particularly popular for expensive assets with good collateral value such as airplanes, which can cost over $100 million apiece. A more detailed example of a leveraged lease is presented in Appendix 21A.

sale and leaseback—a transaction in which a company sells an asset to a lessor and then leases it back

Previous ownership Some leases are for equipment that is purchased directly by the lessor from its manufacturer or some other vendor. An alternative is the **sale and leaseback,** in which the lessor purchases the asset from the lessee and then leases it back to that company. Figure 21.4 diagrams the relationships in a

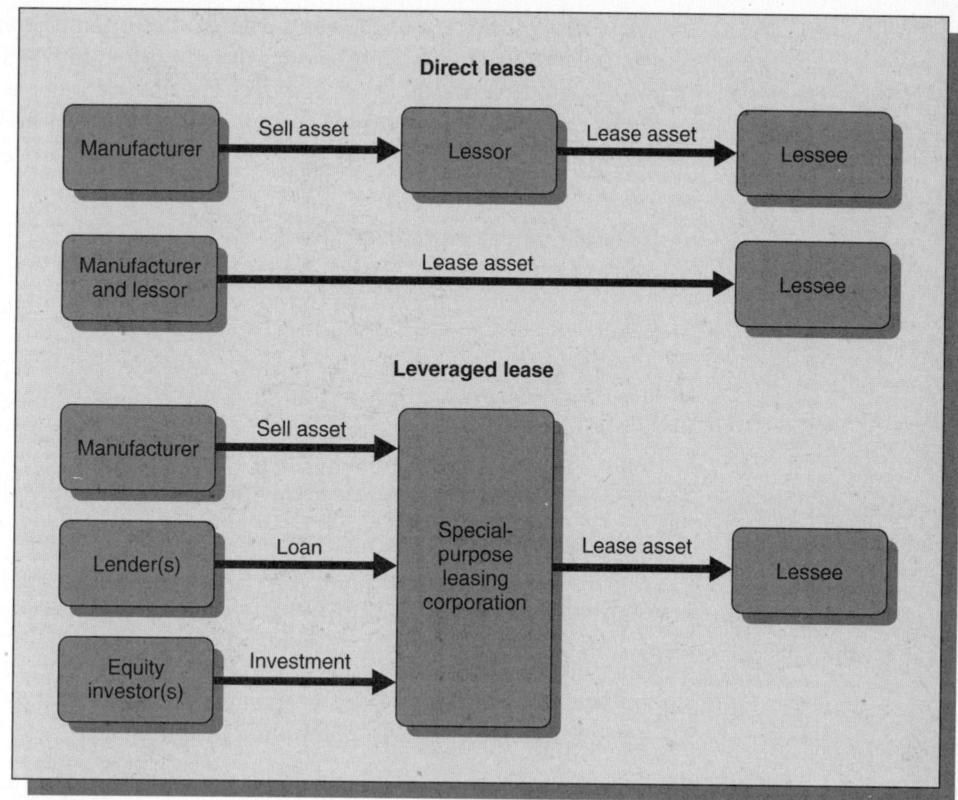

FIGURE 21.3
Direct and leveraged leases. In a leveraged lease, the lessor/investor leverages its position by borrowing to purchase the asset.

sale and leaseback. A sale and leaseback is a way for a company to turn its investment in an asset into cash without losing the use of that asset. In recent years, several major New York banks have entered into sale and leaseback arrangements in which they have sold their headquarters office building to a lessor and then leased them back. The banks freed up millions of dollars to use for lending while retaining the use of the buildings.

full-service lease—a lease for an asset and also its operation and maintenance

Services purchased Lessors use the term **full-service lease** to describe a lease in which they provide both the use of an asset and its operation; the lessee's pay-

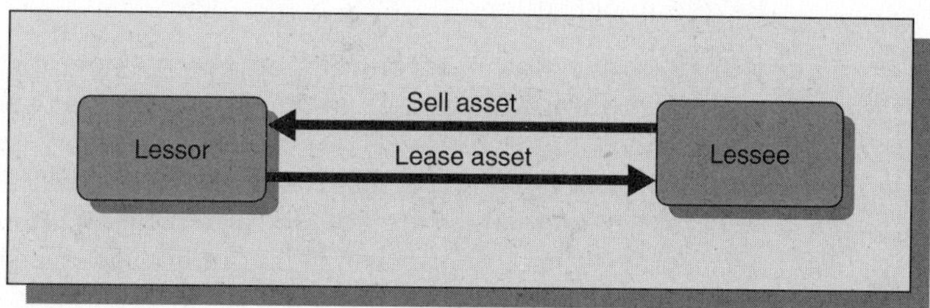

FIGURE 21.4
Sale and leaseback. A company sells an asset to a lessor, who promptly leases it back to the company.

ment covers the cost of the asset itself and of operating and maintaining it. Mainframe computers and large-scale xerography equipment are examples of assets often obtained on full-service leases. The alternative is a **net lease,** a lease for the asset under which operating and maintaining the asset is the responsibility of the lessee. Automobile and aircraft leases are typically net leases.

net lease—a lease for an asset without any supporting services

Nature of lease terms Based on its terms, a lease may be classified into one of two categories: an "operating lease" or "financial lease." An **operating lease** is similar to renting an apartment for a year—the lessee gains temporary use of the asset. The lease term is small relative to the life of the asset, and the lessee often can cancel the lease prior to its end. Lease payments represent only a fraction of the asset's worth. At the end of the lease, the asset generally returns to the lessor who may lease it to another party. Operating leases are used for assets required on a temporary basis such as office space, for assets subject to rapid obsolescence such as computers, and for assets that have short lives such as automobiles.

operating lease—a lease providing temporary use of an asset

A **financial lease** is similar to purchasing a house with a mortgage loan—the lessee gains use of the asset for or near its full life. The lease term is long relative to the life of the asset and rarely has a cancellation clause. Total lease payments are greater than the cost of the asset. At the end of the lease, the asset often becomes the property of the lessee, either automatically or for a nominal payment such as $1. Financial leases are generally used for assets required for long periods of time such as core plant and equipment.

financial lease—a lease providing long-term use of an asset

Financial leases are of particular interest to financial managers because they are very similar to purchasing the asset using a term loan as financing. In both cases the company gets the use of the equipment over its full life. In both cases there is no way to cancel the acquisition of the asset. And in both cases the payments are greater than the asset's cost and may be seen as comprising the purchase price of the asset plus interest on the debt taken to procure it. Appendix 21B illustrates a method for making the decision between borrowing and buying an asset vs. acquiring it via a financial lease.

Financial accounting rules Regardless of whether a lease is an operating or financial lease, the only transactions between lessee and lessor are the regular lease payments. As a result, there is a natural tendency to account for leases by simply recording each payment as an expense when it is made. Since the lessee does not own the asset, it does not appear on the lessee's books; neither is any obligation included in the lessee's liabilities. This accounting treatment makes sense for an operating lease in which there is no suggestion of ownership or any long-term obligation.

However, this simple accounting approach is inappropriate for financial leases since they duplicate the combination of a term loan and the purchase of an asset. Using this simple accounting approach, a company could use financial leases to hide both the existence of its leased assets and the associated payment obligations. When companies are able to raise funds without putting the liabilities on their balance sheet they are engaging in **off-balance-sheet financing.**

off-balance-sheet financing—financing that is not included in balance sheet liabilities

Examples

Off-Balance-Sheet Financing

Dean Hite's company currently has $50 million of assets financed by $30 million of liabilities and $20 million of equity. Net income last year was $5 million. Dean is wondering about the change to two financial ratios—return on assets and debt/equity—if $10 million of the assets financed by debt had been leased instead of purchased.

Question: Calculate the company's return on assets and debt/equity ratios at present.

Solution steps:

1. Return on assets (ROA) = net income/assets
   = $5 million/$50 million = 10%
2. Debt/equity ratio = liabilities/equity
   = $30 million/$20 million = 1.5

Question: Recalculate these ratios assuming that $10 million of assets owned by the company and financed with $10 million of debt had been leased instead and could have been kept off the balance sheet.

Solution steps:

1. Calculate what assets and liabilities would have been:

   Assets = $50 million − $10 million = $40 million

   Liabilities = $30 million − $10 million = $20 million

2. Recalculate the ratios:

   Return on assets = $5 million/$40 million = 12.5%

   Debt/equity ratio = $20 million/$20 million = 1.0

Answer: If the debt and assets could be kept off the balance sheet, the company's return on assets would increase from 10% to 12.5% and its debt/equity ratio would decline from 1.5 to 1.0.

Since the use of off-balance-sheet financing can provide an inaccurate picture of a firm's financial condition, financial accounting rules have been designed to identify financial leases (also called *capital leases* by the accountants) and require companies to treat them as if the firm had indeed taken a term loan and used the proceeds to purchase the asset. The asset appears on the lessee's books under a category called *leased assets* and is offset by a liability titled *obligations under capital leases*, representing the loan.

Statement of Financial Accounting Standards No. 13 subjects every lease to four tests to determine if it is a financial lease. A lease that passes any one of the tests must be treated as a financial lease on the company's accounting records. The tests are:

1. Is the term of the lease at least 75% of the economic life of the asset?

2. Is the present value of the minimum amount that must be paid to the lessor equal to or greater than 90% of the value of the asset?
3. Does the asset become the property of the lessee by the end of the lease term?
4. Can the lessee purchase the asset at a "bargain" price?

2. Benefits of a Lease to the Lessee

A company that obtains the use of an asset through a lease can obtain one or more of four benefits: (1) tax savings, (2) cost savings, (3) risk avoidance, and (4) financing flexibility.

Tax savings A primary benefit of leasing is tax benefits that might otherwise be unavailable. A company that purchases an asset can reduce its taxes through depreciation and any other deductions and credits it is permitted to put on its tax return. However, the amount of the tax benefit depends on the firm's level of income. A company with low income might be in a low tax bracket and get only a small tax reduction. A company with negative income would get no tax benefit immediately and would have to carry the loss forward until a profitable year. By contrast, if a lessor in a high income tax bracket owns the asset, it can take full advantage of tax deductions in the current year and pass a portion of the savings along to the lessee in the form of lower lease payments.

Leasing real estate provides another tax benefit. Owned land cannot be depreciated. However, payments made to lease property are fully tax deductible.

Cost savings A lessor that regularly deals in a particular asset can often purchase it or maintain it for less than the lessee. The lessor can offer advice about the selection of the asset and can dispose of it more efficiently than the lessee at the end of its useful life.

Risk avoidance By leasing an asset on an operating lease instead of purchasing it, a lessee shifts the risk of obsolescence to the lessor. Obsolescence can be of two types: obsolescence of the asset itself due to a change in technology, or obsolescence of use in which the company's needs have changed and the asset is no longer useful. Either way, the lessee can return the asset to the lessor and not have to concern itself with disposal of the asset.

Financing flexibility Leasing is readily available for many assets without the need for a formal loan application or an extensive credit review. Unlike term loans, in which a bank might only lend 80% of the value of an asset, 100% financing is standard. There are rarely any protective covenants restricting the firm or its financial activities. In addition, many financial leases are structured with an annuity of lease payments, making the term loan embedded within them a fixed-rate loan. This provides companies the opportunity to acquire fixed-rate financing at rates that are often better than fixed-rate term loans.

3. Benefits of a Lease to the Lessor

For the lessor, a lease is the equivalent of a profitable loan. In an operating lease, the loan is a loan of property, and the lessor recoups some of the asset's cost. In

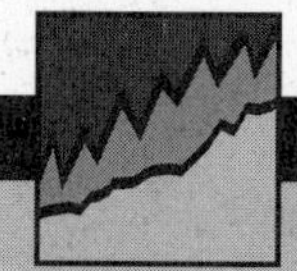

IMPROVING FINANCE'S PROCESSES

Reducing Cycle Time for Credit Approval at IBM Credit Corporation

At one time it took six days on average and sometimes as long as two weeks for IBM Credit Corporation, the financing subsidiary of IBM Corporation, to approve a request for leasing or other financing. Salespersons and customers were frustrated with the slow process which often resulted in losing a customer to a competing financing company. After several traditional approaches to the problem, which only succeeded in increasing the turnaround time, two senior managers walked a loan request through each step in the credit approval process to understand what was going on. Much to their surprise they found that the work required to process the request took only 90 minutes; the remainder of the time was devoted to moving the paper and waiting for the next step to be taken. IBM Credit redesigned the process, eliminating much of the paper handling, so it now takes only four hours from start to finish. The new system is so efficient that over the past several years IBM Credit has been able to handle over 100 times the number of credit applications each year without any increase in personnel. And while the cost savings of the improved process were dramatic and fairly easy to measure, the revenue increases arising from better service were far greater—and much more difficult to estimate.

Source: Michael Hammer and James Champy, *Reengineering the Corporation* (New York: HarperCollins, 1993), pp. 36–39.

a financial lease, the loan is one of money. The lessor makes or purchases the asset and is promised a series of payments that fully pay for the asset plus provide an acceptable rate of return. Also, the lessor has a superior position in bankruptcy compared with a bank that has made a collateralized loan, as it owns the asset and does not have to wait for legal authority to repossess it should the lessee stop making payments.

Bonds

A bond issue is a loan divided into uniform pieces or "bonds," designed to enable a company to raise funds from many lenders. Corporate bonds normally are in units of $1,000 each, municipals $5,000, and U.S. Treasurys $10,000 to $1,000,000. By dividing the bond issue in this way, it becomes possible for investors of virtually any size to loan money to the issuing company. Thus a $10,000,000 corporate bond issue might be subdivided into 10,000 bonds, each with a $1,000 face value; and any one investor needs to lend only $1,000 to participate in the loan.

When issued, a bond may be described by three numbers: (1) its maturity—the length of the loan, (2) its coupon—the cash interest to be paid at intervals over its life, and (3) its maturity value (also, called *par value* or *face value*)—the amount to be paid to the lender at maturity. In Chapter 9, where we looked at bond valuation, we saw that investors attach two other numbers to each bond: (1) its market price and (2) its yield-to-maturity.[2] In this chapter we explore the nature of bonds in more detail.

As described in Chapter 19, bonds may be privately placed with a professional investor, or may be offered for sale to the public.[3]

1. The Bond Indenture

bond indenture—the formal agreement between a bond's issuer and buyer

A **bond indenture** is the formal agreement spelling out the relationship between the lenders who purchase the bond and the borrower, the organization that issues the bond. In many ways, the indenture is much like a term loan contract, specifying the bond's characteristics, collateral, and any restrictions placed on the company during the life of the financing.

trustee—a third party to a bond indenture, responsible for representing the bondholders to the issuing company

When bonds are held by the general public, it is normal for the issuer to appoint and pay a **trustee** to represent the interests of what can be a diverse and geographically separated group of investors. Most large commercial banks maintain a corporate trust department that offers this service. The trustee acts as an auditor, monitoring the issuer's activities against the requirements of the indenture and mailing to each bondholder an annual certification that the issuer is in compliance with the terms of the indenture. Should the issuer violate the indenture, the trustee can take action, legal if necessary, to protect the investor group.

mortgage bond—a bond with collateral

Bonds with collateral are called **mortgage bonds,** since the lenders receive a claim or mortgage on asset(s) of the borrower. A "first mortgage bond" has the most senior claim. Should the company be unable to repay its debts and have to sell the collateral, first mortgage bondholders would receive their money before any other claim. Next in line are any "second mortgage bonds," "third mortgage bonds," etc. Some mortgages are "open-ended," meaning that any amount of additional debt of the same seniority may be issued using the same assets as collateral. Other mortgages are "limited open-ended" where a specified amount of additional debt of the same seniority may be issued using the assets as collateral, or "closed-ended," in which no additional debt of the same seniority may be issued against the named assets. Still other indentures have an "after-acquired clause" requiring that any new assets purchased by the company become additional collateral.

debenture—a bond with no collateral

A bond without collateral is a **debenture.** With a debenture, the lender's ability to be repaid depends on the firm's general financial strength, hence debentures are issued only by large, financially sound firms. Debentures often contain a "negative pledge clause" preventing both present and future assets from being pledged as collateral to any other lender, an action that would weaken the debenture holders' position should the issuer enter bankruptcy. Debentures may be "subordinated" to other financing, ranking below nonsubordinated debt in order of their claim to income and assets.

---

[2] **Cross-reference:** See Chapter 9, pp. 300–310.

[3] **Cross-reference:** See Chapter 19, pp. 694–699.

2. Bond Ratings

default—to breach a loan agreement

A borrower that violates one or more provisions of a bond indenture is said to be in **default.** There are two types of default. Financial default is the failure to make interest or principal payments on time. Technical default is the failure to comply with some other indenture provision—for example, maintaining ratios, insuring collateral, or providing information. Both types of default, however, can reduce a bond's value, either directly through changed cash flows, or indirectly through changed risk perceptions. When a company issues a bond, the interest rate it must pay depends in part on the risk of default perceived by investors. In an effort to sell their bonds at the lowest possible interest rate, many issuers hire a credit rating agency to evaluate the issue's default risk.[4]

The two major credit rating agencies for bonds are Standard & Poor's (S&P) and Moody's Investor Services. To establish their ratings they study a variety of factors which might provide clues to the issuer's future ability and willingness to meet its obligations. These include the issuer's business risk and stability of earnings, financial leverage, cash flow and interest coverage, and quality of management. Techniques used include financial ratio analysis, interviews with employees of the issuer and its key stakeholders, and a study of published information about the issuer and its industry. In general the agencies do not place much weight on collateral unless it is real property, due to the difficulty of predicting liquidation values.

The rating systems employed by S&P and Moody's are very similar and are listed in Figure 21.5. (Several of the classifications are further subdivided where finer distinctions are possible and worthwhile, such as category AA, which is divided into AA1, AA2, and AA3.) For both companies, a bond rated in any one of the top four categories is considered to be "investment grade," a bond with a sufficiently low probability of default to be legitimately considered a sound investment. Bonds rated below the first four categories are "speculative grade," too risky to be included in an investment portfolio.

In general there is a good correlation between bond ratings and yields, just as finance theory would predict. New bond issues rated highly by the agencies are accepted in the financial markets as having a low risk of default and carry lower interest rates than bonds with lower ratings. However, the rating agencies generally lag the financial markets in analyzing changes to a bond's risk. Therefore, the ratings of seasoned issues tend to confirm what investors have already discovered about the bonds, rather than provide much new information. Figure 21.6 illustrates the relationship between bond ratings and yields for 30-year maturity, investment grade bonds.

In the 1980s, some investment professionals, most notably Michael Milken of the investment bank of Drexel, Burnham, Lambert, argued that the additional return from speculative grade bonds was high relative to the added risk, making them

---

[4] **Elaboration:** Although sometimes the rating agencies will evaluate the default risk of a widely held bond on their own to make their rating books more complete, for the most part they only rate bonds when an issuer hires them to do so.

Moody's	S&P	Comment
Aaa	AAA	Highest grade obligation
Aa	AA	High grade; little difference from "triple-As"
A	A	Upper-medium grade; may be affected by changes in economic conditions
Baa	BBB	Medium grade; borderline between sound and speculative; good coverage under normal conditions but susceptible to downturns; lowest-quality commercial bank investment
Ba	BB	Lower medium grade; poor performance likely in downturns
B	B	Speculative; not desirable investments; small assurance of performance over long-term
Caa	CCC	Speculative (Moody's: may be in default)
Ca	CC	Speculative to a high degree; marked shortcomings (Moody's: usually in default)
C	C	Moody's: in default; S&P: an income bond with no payment
	D	S&P: in default

FIGURE 21.5
Bond ratings. Bonds in the first four categories are considered suitable for investment while those with lower ratings are described as speculative.

junk bond—a speculative grade bond

an excellent investment opportunity. Known throughout the 1980s as **junk bonds,** speculative grade bonds were in great demand. In prior decades, all bonds were investment grade when issued and only became speculative grade if the issuer fell on hard times. However, in the 1980s, the demand for junk bonds grew to be so high—fueled in large part by Milken's success in publicizing his claims—that many companies came to market with bonds that were speculative to begin with.

FIGURE 21.6
Bond yields as a function of their ratings. As concerns about default risk increase, required yields increase as well.

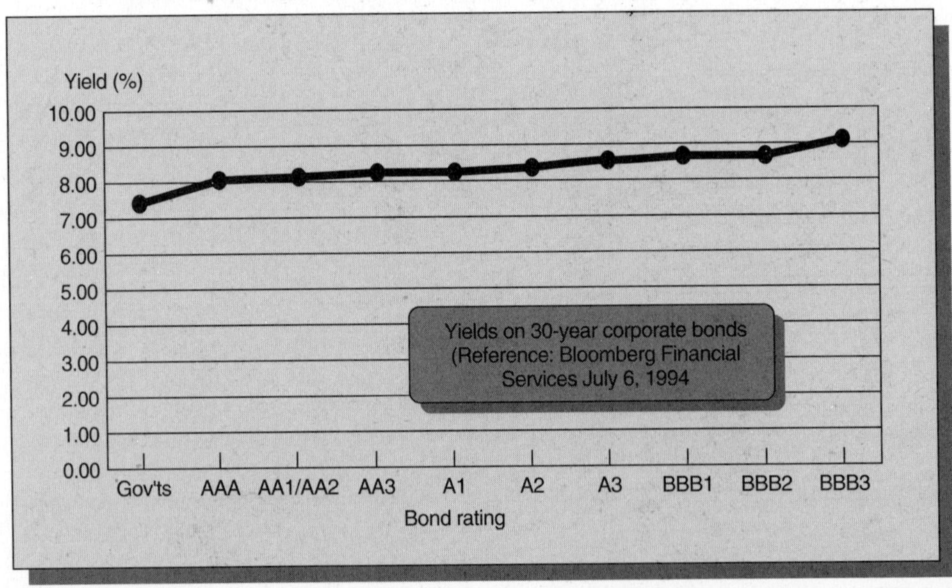

"Tell me again–is it junk food or junk bonds that you're very big in?"

As long as business was booming, Milken's assertion held: the returns were high and incidents of default were low. But by the end of the decade, the economy had entered a recession, defaults on junk bonds had increased significantly, and the financial markets returned to the conventional wisdom that junk bonds were truly speculative.

3. International Bonds

With the globalization of the financial markets, it is now possible for an issuer to raise funds in many currencies and in many countries. In general, a bond issued outside the borrower's home country is considered an **international bond.** It is useful to separate international bonds into three categories: (1) foreign bonds, (2) Eurobonds, and (3) multicurrency bonds.

international bond—a bond issued outside the borrower's home country

foreign bond—a bond issued by a foreign borrower in the currency of the country of issue

Foreign bonds A **foreign bond** is a bond issued by a foreign borrower and denominated in the currency of the country in which it is issued. For example, an Italian lira bond issued in the Italian capital markets by PepsiCo to fund its operations in that country would be a foreign bond. Other than the fact that the issuer is not an Italian company, this bond would be similar to other bonds issued in the Italian capital markets. The issue would be denominated in Italian lira, handled by Italian investment bankers, offered to Italian investors, and would trade in the Italian bond markets.

Eurobond—a bond denominated in a currency other than that of the country in which it is sold

Eurobonds A **Eurobond** is a bond denominated in a currency other than that of the country in which it is initially sold. Eurobonds are brought to market by one or a syndicate of investment bankers with global operations. The Eurobond market is an "off-shore" market, conducted outside the national boundaries of any one country. This gives Eurobonds several advantages over comparable domestic bonds:

- Eurobond issues escape regulation by the various domestic security laws. They do not have to be registered with governmental regulatory agencies. This reduces transactions cost and cycle time making them cheaper and less time consuming to issue.
- Because no prospectus is required, disclosure requirements are minimal—an attraction for some issuers.
- Since Eurobonds are bearer bonds, the identity of the bonds' owners is not recorded. Investors may remain anonymous, either to protect their privacy or to avoid the scrutiny of tax authorities. Some investors are willing to pay more for these bonds than comparable registered bonds, and borrowers obtain a lower interest rate.
- In most markets, Eurobonds escape tax withholding regulations. Because investors receive the full interest paid by the bond, the coupon can be less than on a comparable bond where taxes are withheld.

multicurrency bond—a bond denominated in more than one currency

Multicurrency bonds A **multicurrency bond** is a bond in which the principal, interest payments, or both are denominated in more than one currency. Three types of multicurrency bonds are:

- Multiple currency bonds—giving the lender the right to request that interest and/or principal be paid in any one of several specified currencies. Since the exchange rates to be used for this calculation are determined when the bond is issued, investors request the currency that has appreciated the most against the others. In return for assuming the risk that its bond obligation will increase, the borrower receives a lower interest rate on the issue.
- Currency cocktail bonds—denominated in a currency unit based on a mix of currencies, such as the European Currency Unit (ECU: a mixture of European Community currencies) or the Special Drawing Right (SDR: the mixture of five strong currencies—United States, Germany, United Kingdom, France, and Japan—used by the International Monetary Fund as an international reserve currency). Financing with these bonds provides some degree of exchange-rate stability for both lender and borrower since the risk from exposure to a portfolio of currencies is less than the risk from being exposed to any one of them alone.
- Dual currency bonds—in which interest payments are made in one currency and principal payments in another. These bonds appeal to lenders and borrowers whose year-by-year currency needs differ from their long-term capital requirements.

In addition to the cost reductions discussed in the preceding paragraphs—lowered transaction costs and lowered interest rates from lack of registration and tax withholding—there is another reason why international borrowing can often be done at a lower rate of interest than domestic borrowing. Unlike the short-term foreign exchange markets, where covered-interest arbitrage ensures that forward exchange rates are closely related to interest rates,[5] there is no comparable mechanism for long-term debt. Forward contracts are rarely available for longer than one year. Without an active market for long-term exchange rates, long-term interest rates among countries do not necessarily reach an equilibrium with forecasts of future exchange rates. It is often possible to issue a bond in another country at an interest rate that, when combined with the financial manager's forecast of future exchange rates, produces a cheaper total financing package than a domestic bond.

Corporate treasurers use international bonds for one more reason: they can hedge anticipated future cash flows in another currency. PepsiCo may choose to issue lira bonds because the company expects to generate profits in Italy over the next decades. Rather than take the risk of what future lira-dollar exchange rates will be available when the company desires to repatriate its profits to the United States, it can use the lira to repay its Italian debt and avoid exchanging the currency altogether.

4. Retiring Bonds

Bonds terminate their natural lives in one of several ways: (1) by full payment at maturity, (2) by being called or converted to equity, or (3) by periodic repayment over their lifetime.[6]

Full payment at maturity Many bond issues remain in place for their full lifetime. On the maturity date the face value of each bond in the issue is paid to the bondholders and the bond issue ceases to exist.

sinking fund—an account set up to accumulate the cash to retire debt

Companies use three strategies to obtain the cash to retire a bond issue. First, if they are highly profitable, they might have sufficient cash on hand as a result of their ongoing operations. Second, they might set up a **sinking fund** to accumulate the money and make deposits to the fund at intervals over the issue's life. Third, and very common for growing firms, they might simply "roll the issue over," issuing new debt and using the proceeds of the new issue to refund the old.

Options Many bond issues contain built-in options permitting the issuer or bondholder to retire some or all of the bonds prior to their maturity date. A call option gives the issuer the right to retire the bonds for cash. A conversion option gives the bondholder the right to trade in the bond for shares of stock.[7] In Appendix 21C, we look at one common case of calling a bond issue: replacing a high coupon issue with a less costly issue when interest rates have fallen.

serial bond issue—a bond issue composed of bonds of many maturities

Periodic repayment Some bond issues are structured so that a portion of the issue is retired prior to the final maturity date. One technique is to issue **serial bonds,** an issue consisting of bonds with different maturities. For example, in a

[5] **Cross-reference:** Covered interest arbitrage, and interest rate parity—the relationship between the spot and forward exchange rates between two countries and the short-term interest rates in each—are discussed in Chapter 7, pp. 246–249.

[6] **Observation and cross-reference:** Bonds also can end their lives after a default, with the bondholders receiving less than full value.

[7] **Cross-reference:** We explore these and other equity options more fully in Chapter 22.

20-year issue of 10,000 bonds, 500 of the bonds might mature after one year, another 500 after two years, and so on, with the last 500 maturing at the end of the twentieth year. To identify the different maturities, each bond carries a serial number and the indenture specifies which bonds mature on which date. A second method, used when the bonds in the issue do not carry serial numbers, is through a sinking fund. The fund is given to the issue's trustee who either calls the required number of bonds (chosen by lottery) or purchases the bonds in the open market, whichever is less expensive.

Floating-Rate Notes

Floating-rate notes (FRNs) are bonds issued for intermediate and long-term maturities with a variable rate of interest. They are primarily issued in U.S. dollars, but also in U.K. pounds sterling, German marks, Canadian dollars, Hong Kong dollars, SDRs, and ECUs. Although FRNs originated in the Eurocurrency markets, the FRN concept has spread to many domestic capital markets, including the United States, Switzerland, France, Italy, Belgium, and others.

1. Characteristics of FRNs

FRNs take the form of a bearer, promissory note, typically issued at a $1,000 face value with a variable interest coupon paid semi-annually. The interest rate is the reference rate (normally LIBOR) plus an increment typically in the range of 1/16% to 1/8% for the most creditworthy issuers. The rate is normally reset once each coupon period, and there is often a rate floor. Maturities are generally from 5 to 20 years, although some FRNs issued by governments are perpetual. FRNs are often redeemable after 10 or 15 years. Issues are sized from $5 million to $500 million, with $100 million typical.

Floating-rate notes have been issued with call provisions, convertible provisions (usually to some fixed-rate debt instrument), and with warrants attached. Most FRNs are traded either as listed securities on major foreign stock exchanges or are traded actively by broker-dealers.

2. Other Floating Rate Instruments

The FRN has led to the creation of a family of similar securities among which are: (1) floating-rate certificates of deposit (FRCDs)—negotiable receipts for dollar-denominated bank deposits held in the United States; (2) Eurodollar floating rate certificates of deposit—FRCDs for dollar deposits outside the United States; (3) floating/fixed-rate notes—convertible FRNs which may be exchanged for a traditional fixed-rate bond, either at the lender's option or automatically as provided at issue; and (4) mismatched floating-rate notes—FRNs in which the rate is reset with each change in the reference rate, rather than once each coupon period.

Dean Hite hung up the telephone and smiled. He had just received a very satisfying call from his old buddy Fred. Since the last time they had spoken, Fred had researched Dean's company and looked at the financial statements Dean had sent him, and he had some useful insights into the position in which Dean's company found itself.

As a financially strong company, Dean's firm had a full range of intermediate-term and long-term debt financing alternatives available to it. To finance intermediate-life assets, it could enter into a lease or use term-loan financing from its commercial banks, whichever was cheaper. Term loans would also be appropriate when the company's money needs were uncertain or to finance a division with an operating cycle longer than a year. Assets with long-term lives would be better financed by long-term bonds. Fred talked about the possibility of issuing floating-rate notes to take advantage of opportunities in the international financial markets. He also suggested that Dean consider using swaps and insurance products—such as caps and collars—to match the company's interest rate exposure to its cash flow patterns.

Dean took out his date book and looked at his entries for the coming week. Penciled in for Wednesday was the lunch date with Fred. Dean added the name of his favorite restaurant and made a mental note to make a reservation. "The food might as well be as good as the company," he thought as he put his date book aside and turned back to his desk.

Summary of Key Points

- **Discuss the distinction between fixed-rate and floating-rate debt.** The interest rate on debt may either be fixed (unchanging over the loan term) or floating (following the movement of interest rates). The choice of a fixed or floating rate determines which type of interest rate risk is borne by lender or borrower. A borrower exposed to interest rate risk can purchase insurance in the form of a cap or collar or can enter into a swap arrangement, exchanging the undesired rate exposure for a preferred risk position.
- **Describe term debt and construct a repayment schedule for three different kinds of term loans.** Term loans are loans with maturities of greater than one year. They are used to hedge intermediate-life assets, finance a long operating cycle, or serve as a bridge loan in an uncertain environment. Term loans can be structured with equal payments, equal amortization of principal, a balloon payment, or as a bullet loan. The term-loan contract contains protective covenants designed to insure repayment.
- **Discuss the nature and benefits of a lease.** A lease is a type of rental agreement. Leases can be direct or leveraged, or can involve the sale and leaseback of assets. An important distinction is between operating leases (short-term rentals), and financial leases (those that are very similar to the combination of a term loan and asset purchase). Because the financial accounting profession is concerned about off-balance-sheet financing, financial leases must be accounted for as if a loan had been taken and the proceeds used to purchase the asset. Benefits to lessees include tax savings, cost savings, risk avoidance, and financing flexibility. Lessors use leases to construct a profitable loan arrangement with superior bankruptcy protection.
- **Describe the characteristics and life cycle of a bond.** Bonds are characterized by a maturity date, interest coupon, and face value. When sold to the general public, a trustee is engaged to represent the multiple bondholders. Mortgage bonds are those with collateral; bonds with no collateral are termed debentures. To obtain lower interest rates, bond issuers often employ the services of credit rating agencies to evaluate and publicize the issue's risk of default. Those with low default risk are termed investment grade; bonds with greater risk of default are speculative grade or junk bonds. As companies have become global and access to international capital markets has grown,

many bonds are now issued in foreign countries and/or foreign currencies. Bonds end their lives by full payment at maturity, through the exercise of an option prior to maturity, through periodic repayment of principal over the issue's lifetime, or by default.

Describe floating-rate notes. Floating-rate notes are intermediate- and long-term, variable-rate bonds. Originated in the Euromarkets, their popularity has spread to many domestic capital markets.

Questions

1. Which party bears which type of interest rate risk exposure in a fixed-rate loan? in a floating-rate loan?
2. Why are caps and collars considered insurance products?
3. Why would any company sell a floor, since it keeps its interest payments up when interest rates fall?
4. How does a collar make a floating-rate loan become more like a fixed-rate loan?
5. Why would a company enter into:
   a. A basis swap?
   b. A fixed-floating swap?
   c. A currency swap?
6. Identify three conditions in which term-loan financing is particularly appropriate.
7. What are the similarities and differences between:
   a. An equal payment term loan?
   b. An equal amortization term loan?
8. Distinguish between a "balloon" and a "bullet."
9. What are the three purposes of a term-loan contract?
10. Identify the following lease concepts:
    a. Direct lease
    b. Leveraged lease
    c. Sale and leaseback
    d. Full service lease
    e. Net lease
    f. Operating lease
    g. Financial lease
11. Why do many companies find off-balance-sheet financing attractive? How might a company's other investors—bondholders and stockholders—react?
12. Identify four benefits of a lease to the lessee and two benefits to the lessor.
13. Identify the following bond concepts:
    a. Indenture
    b. Trustee
    c. Mortgage
    d. Debenture
    e. Sinking fund
    f. Serial bond
14. What is the difference between technical default and financial default? Which is more critical to bondholders?
15. What is a junk bond? Why were junk bonds so popular in the 1980s? Why are they less popular today?
16. Distinguish between a foreign bond, Eurobond, and multicurrency bond. What are the advantages and disadvantages of each to both lender and borrower.
17. What is a floating-rate note?

Problems

1. **(Interest rate cap, floor, collar)** A company borrows \$6 million for one year at a floating rate. For the first three months the rate is 7%. The rate then goes to 10% for the next three months, back to 7% for the three months after that, and then to 5% for the last three months of the year. All rates are nominal applied quarterly. How much total interest will be paid during the year if the company:
   a. Does not purchase rate insurance?
   b. Purchases an 8% cap?
   c. Purchases a collar set at 5% and 9%?
   d. Purchases a collar set at 6% and 8%?
2. **(Interest rate cap, floor, collar)** A company borrows \$20 million for one year at a floating rate. For the first three months the rate is 6.5%. The rate then goes to 5.5% for the next three months, to 7% for the three months after that, and then to 8% for the last three months of the year. All rates are nominal applied quarterly. How much total interest will be paid during the year if the company:
   a. Does not purchase rate insurance?
   b. Purchases an 8% cap?
   c. Purchases a collar set at 4.5% and 9.5%?
   d. Purchases a collar set at 6% and 7%?
3. **(Fixed-floating swap)** A company can borrow \$25 million at a fixed rate of 7% or at a floating rate of prime plus 1. To hedge its assets it prefers the fixed-rate financing. Its banker, however, has suggested that it raise the funds at the floating rate and swap with a counterparty that wants floating-rate debt. The counterparty's bank has quoted a floating rate of prime plus 2 and a fixed rate of 7.5% for a \$25 million loan.
   a. What is the interest rate savings from this swap?
   b. If the company saves 1/4%, what will it pay for its financing?

c. If the counterparty saves 1/8%, what will it pay for its financing?
d. If the company could borrow at prime rather than prime plus 1, and all other data remained the same, should the company still enter into the swap agreement?

4. **(Fixed-floating swap)** A company can borrow $10 million at a fixed rate of 8.5% or at a floating rate of prime plus 3. To hedge its assets it prefers the floating-rate financing. Its banker, however, has suggested that it raise the funds at the fixed rate and swap with a counterparty that wants fixed-rate debt. The counterparty's bank has quoted a fixed rate of 7.5% and a floating rate of prime plus 1 for a $10 million loan.
   a. What is the interest rate savings from this swap?
   b. If the company saves 3/8%, what will it pay for its financing?
   c. If the counterparty saves 3/8%, what will it pay for its financing?
   d. If the company could borrow at prime plus 2 rather than prime plus 3, and all other data remained the same, should the company still enter into the swap agreement?

5. **(Term-loan structure)** A company has taken a two-year term loan of $1 million, calling for quarterly payments at a nominal annual rate of 8%. Prepare a repayment schedule detailing the amount and composition (interest versus principal repayment) of each payment if the loan is:
   a. An equal payment loan
   b. An equal amortization loan
   c. An equal amortization loan with a $300,000 balloon
   d. A bullet loan

6. **(Term-loan structure)** A company has taken a two-year term loan of $4 million calling for quarterly payments at a nominal annual rate of 6%. Prepare a repayment schedule detailing the amount and composition (interest versus principal repayment) of each payment if the loan is:
   a. An equal payment loan
   b. An equal amortization loan
   c. An equal amortization loan with a $1,200,000 balloon
   d. A bullet loan

7. **(Floating-rate term loan)** A company has arranged a two-year term loan of $2 million with its commercial bank. The principal is due in eight equal end-of-quarter payments with interest at prime plus 2. The prime rate is 6% for the first two quarters, drops to 5.5% for the next year, and then returns to 6% for the remainder of the loan period.
   a. Calculate the amount of principal repaid with each payment.
   b. Determine the interest rate charged each quarter.
   c. Calculate the amount of interest paid each quarter.
   d. Prepare a repayment schedule detailing the amount and composition (interest versus principal repayment) of each payment.

8. **(Floating-rate term loan)** A company has arranged a three-year term loan of $15 million with its commercial bank. The principal is due in 12 equal end-of-quarter payments with interest at prime plus 1. The prime rate is 6.5% for the first three quarters, increases to 7% for the next two quarters, drops to 6.75% for the next year, and then drops further to 6% for the remainder of the loan period.
   a. Calculate the amount of principal repaid with each payment.
   b. Determine the interest rate charged each quarter.
   c. Calculate the amount of interest paid each quarter.
   d. Prepare a repayment schedule detailing the amount and composition (interest versus principal repayment) of each payment.

9. **(Off-balance-sheet financing)** A company currently has $100 million of assets financed with $50 million of debt and $50 million of equity. Net income last year was $10 million. Calculate the company's return on assets ratio and debt/equity ratio:
   a. Now
   b. Assuming the company had leased $5 million of its assets off the balance sheet
   c. Assuming the company had leased $15 million of its assets off the balance sheet
   d. Assuming the company had leased $25 million of its assets off the balance sheet

10. **(Off-balance-sheet financing)** A company currently has $400 million of assets financed with $250 million of debt and $150 million of equity. Net income last year was $20 million. Calculate the company's return on assets ratio and debt/equity ratio:
   a. Now
   b. Assuming the company had leased $25 million of its assets off the balance sheet
   c. Assuming the company had leased $50 million of its assets off the balance sheet
   d. Assuming the company had leased $75 million of its assets off the balance sheet

APPENDIX 21A

THE LEVERAGED LEASE

In a leveraged lease, funds for the purchase of the asset are provided by a combination of investment and borrowing. The lessor is the investor, contributing some of its own funds and borrowing the remainder of the asset's purchase price from one or more lenders using the asset as collateral.

The lessor creates a special-purpose leasing corporation to purchase and lease the asset. As in bond financing, a trustee—known as the *indenture trustee*—is appointed by the lessor to represent the lenders' interests in the deal. The lessee's payments for the use of the asset go to the indenture trustee, which first pays the creditors and then forwards the remaining amount to the lessor.

Figure 21A.1 expands on Figure 21.3 to show all the parties and the cash flows in a leveraged lease. On the left side of the diagram are the initial cash flows to finance and purchase the asset. The lessor sets up the leasing corporation and funds it through a combination of investment and borrowing. The corporation then purchases the asset from a manufacturer/vendor and instructs the vendor to deliver it to the lessee. On the right side of the diagram are the ongoing cash flows—the lease payments flowing through the indenture trustee which repay the lenders and provide returns to the lessor's equity position.

As the following example demonstrates, the purpose of leveraging the lease is to increase significantly the lessor's rate of return.

Examples

Leveraged Lease

JONCO Financial Co. has entered into an agreement to lease EastWest Airlines a new Boeing 747 airplane for a period of five years. The 747 costs $100 million; JONCO will invest $20 million of its own funds as equity and will borrow the other $80 million from a syndicate of insurance companies using the airplane as collateral. The loan will be repaid in five equal end-of-year payments of $21 million. The lease calls for EastWest Airlines to make five annual beginning-of-year payments of $25 million each. The airplane will be depreciated for tax purposes over the five year lease period to a zero salvage value using the straight-line method; however, at the end of the lease term JONCO expects to sell the airplane for $50 million. JONCO is in the 35% tax bracket.

Question: What interest rate will the lenders receive?

Solution steps: The loan has an $80 million principal with five annual end-of-year payments of $21 million.

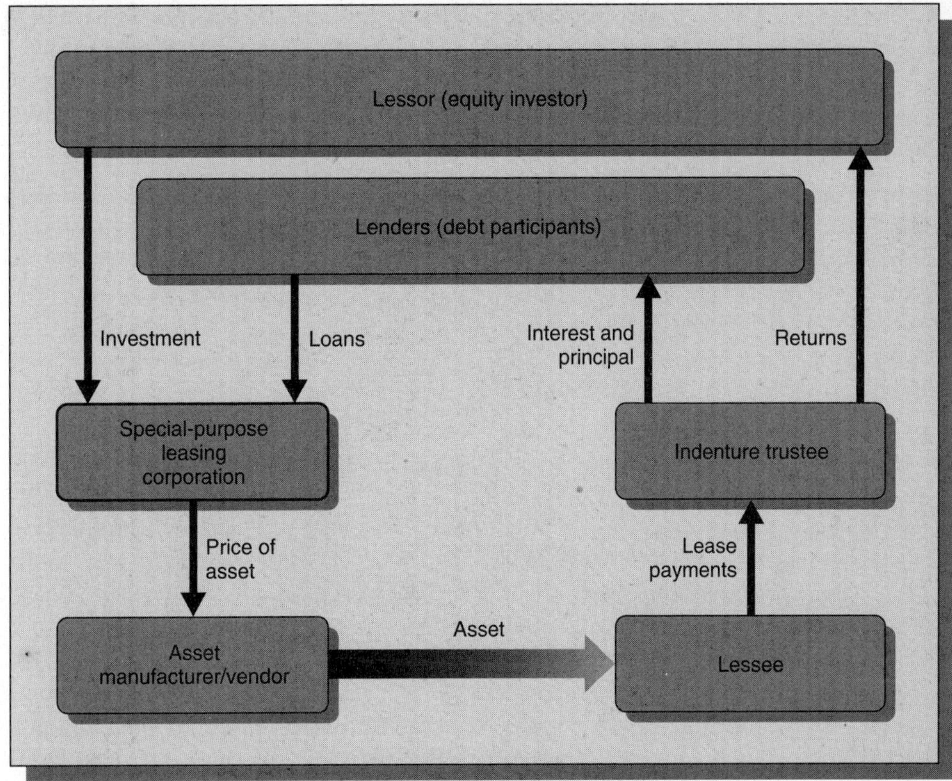

FIGURE 21A.1
A leveraged lease. The leased asset is financed with a combination of equity and debt investment.

CLEAR the time value part of your calculator

Key in −80,000,000 and press PV

Key in 21,000,000 and press PMT, set END

Key in 5 and press n

Compute i = 9.81%

Question: What interest rate is implicit in the lease payment?

Solution steps: The lessee acquires an asset worth \$100 million by making five annual beginning-of-year payments of \$25 million each.

CLEAR the time value part of your calculator

Key in 100,000,000 and press PV

Key in −25,000,000 and press PMT, set BEG

Key in 5 and press n

Compute i = 12.59%

Question: What is the rate of return on the lease to JONCO?

Solution steps:

1. Construct a loan amortization table to determine the tax benefit from deducting interest payments. The last column, the tax benefit, is the interest payment multiplied by the 35% tax rate (000 omitted).

Yr.	Beginning Balance	Interest Payment	Principal Repayment	Ending Balance	Tax Benefit
1	$80,000	$7,846	$13,154	$66,846	$2,746
2	66,846	6,556	14,444	52,402	2,295
3	52,402	5,139	15,861	36,541	1,799
4	36,541	3,584	17,416	19,125	1,254
5	19,125	1,875	19,125	0	656

2. Determine the annual depreciation tax deductions from depreciating the airplane. JONCO will be able to take this benefit since it owns the leasing corporation that owns the airplane:

$$\text{Depreciation/year} = \$100{,}000{,}000/5 = \$20{,}000{,}000$$

$$\text{Tax savings/year} = 35\% \times \$20{,}000{,}000 = \$7{,}000{,}000$$

3. Construct a cash flow table for JONCO incorporating the results of steps 1 and 2. In return for its $20 million investment, JONCO will receive the lease payments (less taxes at 35% on this revenue) plus the tax benefits from interest and depreciation, less the loan repayment. JONCO will also get the salvage value of $50 million but will have to pay a capital gains tax equal to 35% of this amount: all $50 million will be a capital gain since the airplane will be depreciated to a zero salvage value (000 omitted).

	Year 0	Year 1	Year 2	Year 3	Year 4	Year 5
Invest	(20,000)					
Lease payment	25,000	25,000	25,000	25,000	25,000	
Tax	(8,750)	(8,750)	(8,750)	(8,750)	(8,750)	
Repay loan		(21,000)	(21,000)	(21,000)	(21,000)	(21,000)
Tax-interest		2,746	2,295	1,799	1,254	656
Tax-depreciation		7,000	7,000	7,000	7,000	7,000
Sell plane						50,000
Tax-gain						(17,500)
Net cash flows	(3,750)	4,996	4,545	4,049	3,504	19,156

4. Calculate the rate of return embedded in JONCO's cash flows using the cash flow part of your calculator:[1]

[1] **Calculator observation:** This problem requires the cash flow list feature of your calculator because the cash flows do not form an annuity. This is due to the tax benefits from interest: since the interest component of an equal payment loan is not uniform from year to year, neither are the associated tax benefits.

CLEAR the cash flow list part of your calculator

Key in −3,750 as FLOW 0

Key in 4,996 as FLOW 1

Key in 4,545 as FLOW 2

Key in 4,049 as FLOW 3

Key in 3,504 as FLOW 4

Key in 19,156 as FLOW 5

Compute IRR = 131.25%

Answer: By borrowing at 9.81%, JONCO has created a lease that costs the lessee 12.59% but returns 131.25% to JONCO.

Structured properly, a leveraged lease benefits all parties by reducing costs and shifting risks.

1. Cost Reduction

Leveraged leases provide multiple opportunities for cost reduction; five are listed below. While the first four opportunities are available in any lease, the fifth is particular to a leveraged lease.

- If it regularly deals in the asset to be leased, the lessor may be able to purchase it at a low price.
- If the tax benefits associated with the leased asset can be increased by shifting tax deductions from an unprofitable company where they do no good to a profitable one, the overall cost of acquiring the asset is further reduced.
- Maintenance of the asset is normally done by the party able to do it at the lowest cost.
- If the lessor is financially stronger or more creditworthy than the lessee, it can normally raise funds for purchasing the asset at a cost lower than the lessee could obtain by itself.
- By adding lenders to the deal, the lessor can further lower the cost of funds. In part this comes from the lenders' high creditworthiness and ability to raise additional money at low cost. It is also due to the lessor's more limited risk exposure—the lessor now puts up only a fraction of the asset's cost—which can reduce its required rate of return.

2. Risk Shifting

The various risks of the deal—the possibility of default on the loan, risks from operating the asset, the asset's salvage value, etc.—are assumed by the party most able to bear them, reducing the overall cost of risk-bearing. Default risk is shared by the lessor and lenders, most often commercial banks or finance companies with many loans across which to spread the risk. Operating risks fall to the lessee, an expert in using the leased asset. Salvage value risk is assumed by the lessor, a company that is often active in the resale market for the leased asset.

In summary, the lessee obtains the use of the asset at an attractive price. Lenders get the opportunity to participate in a secured loan carrying an attractive interest rate. Most notably, the lessor earns a high rate of return on its capital in return for the risks it bears and for setting up and administering the deal.

Problems

1. **(Leveraged lease)** A lessor in the 35% tax bracket is creating a leveraged lease structure for a large-scale mainframe computer. The computer costs $35 million; the lessor plans to invest $10 million and borrow the other $25 million on a three-year equal-payment loan with end-of-year payments of $10 million. The lessee would make three beginning-of-year payments of $13 million. The computer would be depreciated over the three-year lease period to a zero salvage value using the straight-line method. At the end of the lease term the lessor expects to sell the computer for $10 million.
   a. What interest rate will the lenders receive?
   b. What interest rate is implicit in the lease payment?
   c. Construct a cash flow table for the lessor.
   d. What is the lessor's rate of return?
2. **(Leveraged lease)** A lessor in the 35% tax bracket is creating a leveraged lease structure for ten railroad boxcars. The boxcars cost $20 million; the lessor plans to invest $5 million and borrow the other $15 million on a four-year equal (end-of-year) payment loan at an interest rate of 8.75%. The lessee would make four beginning-of-year payments of $5.8 million. The boxcars would be depreciated over the four-year lease period to a zero salvage value using the straight-line method. At the end of the lease term the lessor expects to sell the boxcars for $12 million.
   a. What is the amount of the loan payment?
   b. What interest rate is implicit in the lease payment?
   c. Construct a cash flow table for the lessor.
   d. What is the lessor's rate of return?

APPENDIX 21B

THE LEASE VS. BORROW-AND-BUY DECISION

In Chapter 21 we identified that a financial lease is remarkably similar to purchasing the asset using the proceeds of a term loan. As a result, any company needing the use of an asset faces the choice of leasing it or borrowing and buying it. The decision depends on which alternative provides the greater value.

net advantage to leasing—the net present value of leasing an asset rather than borrowing and buying it

We define the **net advantage to leasing (NAL)** as the difference between the present value of the borrow-and-buy cash outflows and the present value of the cash outflows from leasing. If the net advantage to leasing is positive, leasing is cheaper than borrowing and buying, and vice-versa.

Throughout this book we have discussed the importance of using interest rates that accurately reflect the risk of each cash flow when calculating present values. In this analysis, the cash flows fall into two distinct risk categories. Financing cash flows are of relatively low risk, and the appropriate discount rate—reflecting the cost of that capital—is the after-tax interest rate on the term loan. Tax savings from depreciation are included with the financing flows as they too have relatively low risk. Operating cash flows, including maintenance costs and salvage values, share the asset's generally higher risk level and are discounted at the cost of capital for the asset.

Example

Lease Vs. Borrow-and-Buy Decision

Dean Hite's Company has decided to acquire a medium-sized computer. The computer can be purchased for $350,000. If the decision is to buy, the firm will obtain the funds from a five-year, 10% term loan repayable in equal payments at the end of each year. The computer would be depreciated using the straight line method to zero salvage value over a five year life; however the computer's economic salvage value is forecasted to be $25,000. Alternatively, the company could lease the computer by making five annual beginning-of-year payments of $100,000 each. Maintenance of the computer, expected to be $15,000 per year, would be paid by the lessor under the lease. The firm is in the 35% tax bracket, and the cost of capital for the computer is 12%.

Question: Should the company lease the asset or buy it using the term loan?

Solution steps:

1. Lease alternative:

   a. Construct a cash flow table. (Note that the lease payments are at the beginning of each year, hence at "Years 0–4"):

	Years 0–4
Lease payment	(100,000)
Tax	35,000
Net cash flows	(65,000)

   b. Calculate the after-tax debt rate:

$$10\% \ (1 - .35) = 10\% \times .65 = 6.50\%$$

   c. Calculate the present value of the lease outflows:

CLEAR the time value part of your calculator

Key in −65,000 and press PMT, set BEG

Key in 6.50 and press i

Key in 5 and press n

Compute PV = 287,677

2. Borrow-and-buy alternative:

a. Calculate the loan payment:

CLEAR the time value part of your calculator

Key in 350,000 and press PV

Key in 10 and press i

Key in 5 and press n

Set END, compute PMT = −92,329

b. Construct a loan amortization table to determine the tax benefit from deducting interest payments. The last column, the tax benefit, is the interest payment multiplied by the 35% tax rate.

Yr.	Beginning Balance	Interest Payment	Principal Repayment	Ending Balance	Tax Benefit
1	$350,000	$35,000	$57,329	$292,671	$12,250
2	292,671	29,267	63,062	229,609	10,243
3	229,609	22,961	69,368	160,241	8,036
4	160,241	16,024	76,305	83,936	5,608
5	83,936	8,393	83,936	0	2,938

c. Determine the annual depreciation tax deductions from depreciating the computer.

Depreciation/year = $350,000/5 = $70,000

Tax savings/year = 35% × $70,000 = $24,500

d. Construct a cash flow table incorporating the results of steps a, b, and c which separates financing and operating cash flows:

	Year 0	Year 1	Year 2	Year 3	Year 4	Year 5
Borrow	350,000					
Repay loan		(92,329)	(92,329)	(92,329)	(92,329)	(92,329)
Tax-interest		12,250	10,243	8,036	5,608	2,938
Buy	(350,000)					
Tax-depreciation		24,500	24,500	24,500	24,500	24,500
Net **financing** flows		(55,579)	(57,586)	(59,793)	(62,221)	(64,891)
Maintenance		(15,000)	(15,000)	(15,000)	(15,000)	(15,000)
Tax		5,250	5,250	5,250	5,250	5,250
Salvage						25,000
Tax-gain						(8,750)
Net **operating** flows		(9,750)	(9,750)	(9,750)	(9,750)	6,500

e. Calculate the present value of the borrow-and-buy flows. The financing flows are evaluated at the after-tax cost of debt:

CLEAR the time value part of your calculator

Key in 6.50 and press i

Key in −55,579 and press FV

Key in 1 and press n

Compute PV = 52,187

Repeat for FV = −57,586, n = 2, compute PV = 50,771

Repeat for FV = −59,793, n = 3, compute PV = 49,500

Repeat for FV = −62,221, n = 4, compute PV = 48,366

Repeat for FV = −64,891, n = 5, compute PV = 47,363

The operating flows are evaluated at the cost of capital for the computer:

CLEAR the time value part of your calculator

Key in 12 and press i

Key in −9,750 and press PMT, set END

Key in 4 and press n

Compute PV = 29,614

CLEAR the time value part of your calculator

Key in 12 and press i

Key in 6,500 and press FV

Key in 5 and press n

Compute PV = −3,688

Sum the present values to obtain the total present value of the borrow-and-buy cash outflows:

52,187 + 50,771 + 49,500 + 48,366 + 47,363 + 29,614 − 3,688 = 274,113

3. Calculate the net advantage to leasing:

NAL = PV of borrow-and-buy − PV of leasing
= 274,113 − 287,677 = −13,564

Answer: The net advantage to leasing is −$13,564. Since the net advantage to leasing is negative, the company should borrow and buy the computer. This will lower the present value of their costs by $13,564.

Problems

1. **(Lease vs. borrow-and-buy)** A company is considering whether to purchase or lease a copying machine that costs $40,000. If the machine is purchased it will be financed by a four-year, 8% term loan repayable in equal payments at the end of each year. The machine would be depreciated using the straight-line method to zero salvage value over a four year life; however, the machine's economic salvage value is forecasted to be $5,000. Alternatively, the company could lease the copier by making four annual beginning-of-year payments of $12,000 each. Maintenance of the copier, expected to be $3,000 per year, would be paid by the lessor under the lease. The firm is in the 35% tax bracket, and the cost of capital for the copying machine is 14%.

a. Calculate the present value of the lease cash outflows.
b. Calculate the present value of the borrow-and-buy cash outflows.
c. Calculate the net advantage to leasing.
d. Should the company purchase or lease the machine?

2. **(Lease vs. borrow-and-buy)** A company is considering whether to purchase or lease a fleet of ten automobiles. The cost of the autos is $250,000. If the automobiles are purchased they will be financed by a three-year, 9% term loan repayable in equal payments at the end of each year. The autos would be depreciated using the straight-line method to zero salvage value over a three-year life; however their economic salvage value is forecasted to be $100,000. Alternatively, the company could lease the automobiles by making three annual beginning-of-year payments of $95,000. Maintenance of the autos, expected to be $10,000 per year, would be paid by the lessor under the lease. The firm is in the 35% tax bracket, and the cost of capital for the automobiles is 11%.
a. Calculate the present value of the lease cash outflows.
b. Calculate the present value of the borrow-and-buy cash outflows.
c. Calculate the net advantage to leasing.
d. Should the company purchase or lease the automobiles?

APPENDIX 21C

THE BOND REFUNDING DECISION

Many bond issues have a "call feature" built into their indenture, an option permitting the company that issued the bond to retire it prior to maturity. From the issuer's side, a call feature provides the flexibility to terminate or refinance debt without waiting until the bond's maturity date. For the bondholder, a call feature creates uncertainty and increases the possibility of loss.

1. Increased Risk

A call feature increases the risk of owning a bond in two ways. First, the existence of a call feature makes a bond's lifetime uncertain. Instead of maturing on a known date, the bond's life can now end on any day within a time period that may stretch over many years. Second, issuers only call a bond when it is in their interest to do so, which often does not coincide with the interests of the lenders.

Lenders insist on a combination of additional compensation and/or protection when asked to assume call risk. This comes in one or more of three forms: a higher interest yield, a premium upon call, or freedom from being called for some period of time.

Higher compensation Callable bonds generally yield more than comparable noncallable bonds.

Call penalty The indenture of a callable bond generally requires the issuer to make a penalty payment—a premium over face value—in the event of a call. The premium is typically in the range of one year's interest and often declines over the life of the bond since the later the bond is called, the less has been taken away from the lenders.

Deferred call Many callable bonds may not be called for several years after their issue date, guaranteeing lenders a period of time during which they bear no risk of a call.

Example

Deferred and Declining Call Penalty

Dean Hite's Company has an issue of $1,000 face value bonds outstanding with a 12% coupon and a 30-year maturity. The bond may not be called during the first six years of its life. After that date, the call penalty depends upon the year in which the company calls the bonds, as follows:

Year	Penalty	Year	Penalty
7–9	$120	19–21	$60
10–12	105	22–24	45
13–15	90	25–27	30
16–18	75	28–30	15

2. Why Are Bonds Called?

Issuers terminate their debt prior to maturity for one of two reasons: to retire it or to replace it with a more favorable issue.[1] Companies retire bonds when their financial needs have changed. For example, a newly profitable company might elect to pay down its debt from earnings to reduce its debt ratio. Companies refinance their debt when they think they can do better in today's market. For example, a company that has become financially stronger since issuing its bonds might replace them to eliminate indenture terms it finds onerous or inhibiting to its current business activities. The most common reason to refinance a bond issue is to reduce interest costs when interest rates have fallen.

3. When Are Bonds Called?

A company desiring to terminate debt with a call feature has the choice of calling it or simply repurchasing it in the market. Companies call their bonds when it is cheaper to call the debt than to repurchase it.

---

[1] **Observation:** There is a good analogy between calling corporate bonds and paying off a home mortgage loan early. Homeowners pay off a loan because their needs have changed—perhaps they are moving or have come into some money—or to refinance the debt when interest rates have fallen.

Example

Calling Rather Than Repurchasing a Bond

It has been 20 years since Dean Hite's company issued the bonds of the prior example, and management has decided to retire the debt. Since interest rates have fallen in the interim, the bonds are now selling at a premium. The company can repurchase the bonds at their current market price of $1,100 or call them for their face value of $1,000 plus a $60 penalty, for a total payment of $1,060. It is cheaper to use the call feature to retire the bonds than to repurchase them in the bond market.

4. The Refunding Decision

net advantage of refunding—the net present value of the bond refunding analysis

We define the **net advantage of refunding (NAR)** as the difference between the present value of the cash savings from refunding a bond issue and the present value of the costs of the refunding transaction. If the net advantage of refunding is positive, it is worthwhile to replace the existing debt issue.

The cash flows in this decision are the principal amounts of the old and new issues, the penalty payment for calling the outstanding bonds, flotation costs of the new issue, interest payments, and associated tax flows. There is also usually an "overlap period," several days between issuing the new bonds and using the proceeds to retire the old issue, during which both issues are outstanding. Interest is still owed on the old bonds during the overlap period, but the proceeds of the new issue can be invested to offset some of the double interest obligation.

Recall from our discussion of the cost of capital in Chapter 10 that under U.S. tax law, flotation costs must be capitalized and written off on a straight-line basis over the life of the security. When a bond is retired its life ends; accordingly any remaining unamortized flotation cost on the old issue may be expensed immediately for tax purposes.[2]

As in the case of the lease vs. borrow-and-buy decision of Appendix 21B, it is important to use an interest rate in calculating present values that accurately reflects the risk of the cash flows. In a refunding analysis, all future cash flows are financial: interest and principal payments and the associated taxes. Accordingly the appropriate interest rate is the after-tax cost of the new debt reflecting today's cost of that capital.

Example

Bond Refunding Analysis

Dean Hite's company has outstanding a $10 million, 12% semi-annual coupon, 25-year bond issue with 15 years remaining to maturity and callable at a price of $108. Market rates have fallen to 8% for debt of this risk and Dean is considering refunding the outstanding issue with a new $10 million, 15 year, 10% semi-annual offering. The flotation cost of the existing issue was $100,000; it is being amortized, straight-line, over the bond's life. The new bond issue would have a flotation cost of $150,000 which would be capitalized and amortized in the same manner. There would be a four day "overlap" period during which

[2] **Cross-reference:** The tax treatment of bond flotation cost appears on p. 346.

interest would still be paid on the old issue, and the new funds would be invested to earn 4%. The company's marginal tax rate is 35%.

Question: Should the bond issue be refunded?

Solution steps:

1. Calculate the amount (face value plus penalty) the company will pay to call the bonds:

   "$108" means 108% of face value = $10,000,000 + $800,000 = $10,800,000

2. Calculate the semi-annual interest on the old and new issues:

   Old issue: (12%/2) × $10,000,000 = $600,000
   New issue: (8%/2) × $10,000,000 = $400,000

3. Analyze the flotation costs of the outstanding bond issue. Fifteen of the original 25 years of life remain:
   a. The original amount is a sunk cost and is ignored in this analysis.
   b. Unamortized amount

      (15/25) × $100,000 = $60,000

   c. Tax benefit from writing it all off today

      35% × $60,000 = $21,000

   d. Tax benefit forgone in each of the next 30 half-years

      35% × ($60,000/30) = $700/half-year

4. Analyze the flotation costs of the proposed new bond issue.
   a. Semi-annual amortization

      $150,000/30 = $5,000/half-year

   b. Tax benefit each half-year

      35% × $5,000 = $1,750

5. Analyze the overlap period:
   a. Interest paid on the old issue:

      Four-day rate = $(1.12)^{4/365} - 1$ = .001243
      Four days' interest = $10,000,000 (.001243) = $12,430
      Tax benefit = 35% × $12,430 = $4,351

   b. Interest earned by temporarily investing the proceeds of the new issue:

      Four-day rate = $(1.04)^{4/365} - 1$ = .0004299
      Four day's interest = $10,000,000 (.0004299) = $4,299
      Tax obligation = 35% × $4,299 = $1,505

6. Construct a cash flow table incorporating the results of steps 1 through 5:

	Year 0	Half-years 1–30	Half-year 30 (Year 15)
Redeem old bond:			
Principal	($10,000,000)		$10,000,000
Call penalty	(800,000)		
Tax	280,000		
Interest		$600,000	
Tax		(210,000)	
Tax-flotation	21,000	(700)	
Issue new bond:			
Principal	10,000,000		(10,000,000)
Interest		(400,000)	
Tax		140,000	
Flotation	(150,000)		
Tax		1,750	
Overlap period:			
Interest paid	(12,430)		
Tax	4,351		
Interest earned	4,299		
Tax	(1,505)		
Net cash flows	($ 654,285)	$131,050	$ 0

7. Calculate the half-year after-tax rate on the new debt:

$$(8\%/2) \times (1 - .35) = 4\% \times .65 = 2.60\%$$

8. Calculate the net advantage of refunding (NAR):
   a. Present value of cash savings:

      CLEAR the time value part of your calculator
      Key in 131,050 and press PMT, set END
      Key in 30 and press n
      Key in 2.60 and press i
      Compute PV = −2,706,696

      (Note that this number represents a benefit, even though the financial calculator produces a negative number.)

   b. Calculate the NAR

      NAR = PV of cash savings − PV of refunding costs
      = $2,706,696 − 654,285 = $2,052,411

Answer: The net advantage of refunding is $2,052,411. Since the net advantage of refunding is positive, the company should refund the outstanding bond issue.

Problems

1. **(Bond refunding)** A company in the 35% tax bracket is considering whether to refund a $25,000,000 bond issue. The outstanding issue has a 10% semi-annual coupon, a 25-year life, was issued 15 years ago, and could be called today for a price of $105. The proposed new issue would have a 7.5% semi-annual coupon and a 10-year life. Flotation costs on the old issue were $250,000; the company's investment banker quotes a cost of $400,000 to float the new bond issue. During a five-day overlap period, the proceeds of the new issue would be invested to earn 3.5%.

   a. Construct a cash flow table for this refunding decision.
   b. Calculate the appropriate discount rate for the refunding analysis.
   c. Calculate the net advantage of refunding.
   d. Should the company refund the outstanding bond issue?

2. **(Bond refunding)** A company in the 35% tax bracket is considering whether to refund a $70,000,000 bond issue. The outstanding issue has a 11.5% semi-annual coupon, a 30-year life, was issued 10 years ago, and could be called today for a price of $109. The proposed new issue would have a 9% semi-annual coupon and a 20-year life. Flotation costs on the old issue were $750,000; the company's investment banker quotes a cost of $900,000 to float the new bond issue. During a five-day overlap period, the proceeds of the new issue would be invested to earn 4.5%.

   a. Construct a cash flow table for this refunding decision.
   b. Calculate the appropriate discount rate for the refunding analysis.
   c. Calculate the net advantage of refunding.
   d. Should the company refund the outstanding bond issue?

CHAPTER 22
EQUITY

Ivan Wolff fired up the spreadsheet program on his laptop computer. He typed in several numbers and recalculated the analysis. Frowning, he changed several more numbers and recalculated again.

Ivan was a venture capitalist with Malcolm Vernon Partners. He was reaching the final stage of a negotiation to invest in a small startup company whose R&D activities, innovative products, and potential markets looked particularly promising. Ivan had done all the traditional tests of strength and value such as ratio analysis, financial statement projections, and discounted cash flow analyses. But he was most excited about the way the company was collecting and using customer satisfaction data and how rapidly it was improving its production and business processes. He was convinced the company had jumped ahead of its competition and was rapidly establishing itself with its customers as the highest-quality, lowest-cost competitor in its young industry.

The question on the table was the form of the equity to be issued to the venture capitalists and eventually to public shareholders when the company was taken public, a move that was expected within the next two to three years. Ivan was evaluating the type of stock: common versus preferred, the division of ownership privileges through creating different classes of stock, and whether any "sweeteners," such as warrants or conversion options, should be added to the issue.

As Ivan worked over his numbers one more time, he thought about all the inputs to his decision and how important it was to have a thorough understanding of corporate equity and equity options to do a complete analysis.

To accountants, owners' equity represents the portion of a company's assets not offset by liabilities and hence belonging to the company's owner(s). Finance professionals see a company's equity holders in a variety of additional ways: as the legal owners of the firm, as the firm's investors, as residual claimants of income and value, and as risk bearers. And equity now comes in numerous forms and flavors, each with its own set of privileges and characteristics. Ivan will have to sift through these views to determine the best form of equity for the company in which his venture capital firm is investing.

In this chapter we look first at these various concepts of owners' equity. Then we discuss the characteristics of the two primary types of equity securities: common stock and preferred stock. Common stock is the stock held by a corporation's owner-investors, the people we generally refer to as its "stockholders" or "shareholders." Preferred stock is a financial instrument with features that make it "preferable" to common stock in some respects and, by necessity, other features that make it less attractive. We also examine two types of call options issued by corporations on their equity: warrants and those embedded within convertible securities.

Key Points You Should Learn from This Chapter

After reading this chapter you should be able to:

- Identify five concepts of owners' equity.
- Describe the characteristics of common stock, including share and value concepts, benefits of share ownership, and classified common stock.
- Describe how preferred stock combines the features of bonds and common stock, and understand the cumulative feature.
- Discuss how warrants and convertibles function and how they are used as financing techniques.

Introductory Concepts—Concepts of Equity

The owners' equity of a company represents several concepts rolled into one: (1) an accounting measure, (2) a legal status, (3) an investment position, (4) a claim on value, and (5) a risk.

1. Equity as an accounting measure. In financial accounting, owners' equity is defined by the fundamental accounting equation:

   $$\text{Assets} = \text{liabilities} + \text{owners' equity}$$

   or, rearranging the equation:

   $$\text{Owners' equity} = \text{assets} - \text{liabilities}$$

   Owners' equity equals the total value of the company's assets less the amount of its debts. Accordingly, from the accounting point of view, equity represents the measure of the company's value that belongs to stockholders.
2. Equity as the legal ownership of the firm. From a legal point of view, the important word in the term owners' equity is owners. Regardless of the legal form of the organization—proprietorship, partnership, or corporation—equity holders are considered to own the company. Acting directly if proprietors or partners, or acting through the board of directors if shareholders in a corporation, equity holders have full power to hire and fire, to purchase and sell, and to make or buy any resources required by the firm. They have the authority to choose the company's products and markets. They can expand or contract the company's operations, and can sell the company in its entirety or even terminate its existence if they desire. Most importantly, as owners, the equity holders set the company's strategy and policies including its goals and the systems and measures to achieve those goals.
3. Equity as the investor in the firm. Equity holders invest their money in the firm. In this respect they are no different from most of the company's other stakeholders, each of which has invested time or money in the hope of a reasonable return.
4. Equity as the residual claimant to the firm's value. Equity holders are last in the line of creditors and investors who have a financial claim on the firm. In a going concern, their claim is to any income remaining after all other stakeholders are paid. Should the company terminate its operations, equity holders receive whatever value is left over after every other claimant is fully satisfied.
5. Equity as the ultimate risk bearer. Because equity holders are last in the line of financial claimants, they bear the greatest amount of risk. Their income stream is the most volatile of any stakeholder, and their investment value depends in part on the collective judgment of the firm by the financial markets. They receive no income and no value in bankruptcy unless all other claimants are paid. By their willingness to accept these risks, equity holders permit companies to pursue risky but potentially rewarding business opportunities.

Figure 22.1 is the owners' equity section of the Gillette Company balance sheet published in the company's 1993 annual report. It shows that Gillette has two types of stock outstanding: an issue of cumulative preferred stock paying an 8% dividend and held by the company's employees through an employee stock ownership plan (ESOP), and its common stock. The statement provides additional details about both financial instruments:

- Unearned ESOP compensation—some of the value of the preferred stock has not yet been "earned" by the ESOP, much like unearned revenue represents payments to a company for goods and services to be delivered in the future.
- Common stock/additional paid-in capital—the claim for money paid to the company for its shares has been recorded in these two accounts according to accounting's par value convention.
- Earnings reinvested in the business—Gillette's retained earnings.
- Cumulative foreign currency translation adjustments—the change to retained earnings due to losses from the declining value of foreign-currency-denominated investments and activities.
- Treasury stock—shares repurchased by the company from investors.

You might find it interesting to refer back to this statement as you read further in the chapter about the characteristics of equity.

Common Stock

common stock—ownership shares in a corporation

In a corporation, owners' equity takes the form of shares of **common stock.** Each share represents a fraction of the ownership of the corporation; for example, if a company has 1 million shares in the hands of its shareholders, each share owns one-millionth of the company.

FIGURE 22.1
Gillette's owners' equity. The company has both preferred and common stock outstanding.

	1993	1992
Stockholders' equity		
8.0% Cumulative Series C ESOP Convertible Preferred, without par value,		
Issued: 1993—164,243 shares; 1992—164,608 shares	$ 99.0	$ 99.2
Unearned ESOP compensation	(53.8)	(64.8)
Common stock, par value $1 per share		
Authorized 580,000,000 shares		
Issued: 1993—278,587,610 shares; 1992—277,874,114 shares	278.6	277.9
Additional paid-in capital	259.4	236.9
Earnings reinvested in the business	2,357.9	2,259.6
Cumulative foreign currency translation adjustments	(415.0)	(265.2)
Treasury stock, at cost:		
1993—57,697,990 shares; 1992—57,705,301 shares	(1,047.1)	(1,047.2)
Total stockholders' equity	$ 1,479.0	$ 1,496.4

The earliest companies depended on retained earnings or a few wealthy investors for their equity capital. The development of shares of stock permitted companies to raise equity funds from many investors, each contributing a relatively small amount of money, which significantly broadened companies' ability to raise funds.

1. Share Concepts

The common stock of a corporation may be subdivided into several groups. These are: (1) authorized shares, (2) issued shares, (3) outstanding shares, and (4) treasury shares. Figure 22.2 illustrates the relationship among these groups.

Authorized shares Authorized shares are the maximum number of shares the firm has the legal authority to issue. When a company incorporates, it must specify in its charter (the legal document of its corporate powers) the number of shares it plans to issue, now or in the future. By accepting the firm's charter, the state effectively authorizes the firm to issue up to this number of shares. Most companies do not immediately issue the full number of authorized shares but issue a lesser amount and reserve the remaining shares for subsequent issues. As long as the company stays within the limit of its authorization, it does not need to obtain state approval to issue additional shares. However, should the company desire to issue more shares than authorized, it must ask the state to amend its charter. All states require a stockholder vote before agreeing to such an amendment (since additional shares will **dilute** the shares already issued) but routinely approve the amended charter if stockholders agree.

dilute—to weaken the rights, power, or value of a security

Issued shares Issued shares are the number of shares the firm has distributed to investors. Management may elect to issue any amount from one to the full number of authorized shares. The number of unissued shares become those "authorized but not issued."

Outstanding shares Outstanding shares are the portion of the issued shares currently in the hands of investors. At any time, the company may repurchase some of the issued shares. Those remaining with shareholders are the outstanding shares.

Treasury shares Treasury shares are the portion of the issued shares no longer held by investors due to their having been repurchased by the firm. They remain

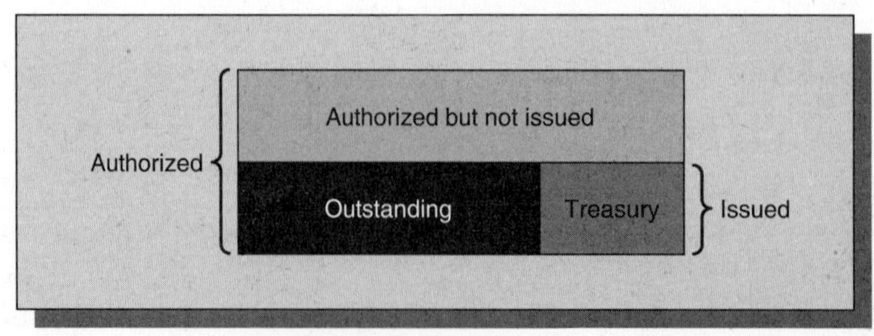

FIGURE 22.2
Common stock share relationships. Some portion of the authorized shares are issued; issued shares not repurchased for the corporate treasury remain outstanding.

authorized and may be reissued again whenever management finds it appropriate to do so.

Example

Share Concepts

The end-of-year balance sheet in the Gillette Company's 1993 annual report discloses the following numbers about common stock:

Shares authorized:	580,000,000
Shares issued:	278,587,610
Treasury shares:	57,697,990

Question: How many shares were outstanding at the end of 1993?

Solution steps:

Shares outstanding = shares issued − treasury shares
= 278,587,610 − 57,697,990 = 220,889,620

Answer: There were 220,889,620 shares outstanding.

2. Value Measures

The value of a share of common stock is measured in several ways: (1) par value, (2) book value, (3) market value, and (4) liquidation value.

par value—the minimum amount of money per share a shareholder is required to invest

Par value When it refers to common stock, **par value** is a legal term representing the minimum capital contribution per share for which shareholders are liable. The concept was developed during the nineteenth century when a company's creditors looked to contributed capital as the firm's major source of funds for repaying its debts. Lenders felt more comfortable making a loan knowing the corporation could call on its shareholders for additional capital. Today, however, par value is not very relevant. Creditors have learned to look to operating cash flow as the source of funds for debt repayment. Further, par value is often set to a nominal (or zero) value so stockholders have fully met their capital requirement upon initial purchase of the stock. In fact, some states permit common stock to be issued without a par value.

Example

Par Value

The common stock of the Gillette Company has a par value of $1.00 per share. An investor who bought the stock from the company many years ago for $0.40 per share would be required to invest up to another $0.60 per share at the request of management. An investor who purchased a more recent issue at a price of $50.00 per share, however, would have no further obligation to invest.

Book value Book value is the accounting measure of a share's worth: the value of owners' equity on the accounting records divided by the number of shares outstanding. By the fundamental accounting identity, owners' equity is equal to total assets less total liabilities. Thus, book value depends on the valuation rules (monetary versus nonmonetary, cash equivalent versus historical cost) and recognition (accrual) rules of Generally Accepted Accounting Principles for assets and liabilities. Since accounting asset values tend toward the conservative—using historical cost rather than market value for many numbers—while liabilities are usually carried at full value, book value is sometimes used by financial analysts as a lower limit when estimating the firm's worth.

Example

Book Value

The Gillette Company reported total stockholders' equity of $1,479,000,000 as of December 31, 1993. There were 220,889,620 shares outstanding at that time.

Question: What was the company's book value per share on that date?

Solution steps:

$$\text{Book value per share} = \text{total book value/shares outstanding}$$
$$= \$1{,}479{,}000{,}000/220{,}889{,}620 = \$6.70$$

Answer: Gillette's book value per share was $6.70.

Market value Market value is the price of the firm's stock as it trades in the securities markets. In theory, it represents investors' aggregate judgment of the present value of all benefits to be received from the firm discounted at investors' required rate of return. As we have seen throughout this book, market value is the measure of shareholder wealth and is used to represent the value of the equity stakeholder in financial analysis and decision making.

Example

Market Value

Gillette Company common stock closed at a price of $59 5/8 per share on December 31, 1993. There were 220,889,620 shares outstanding at that time.

Question: What was the total market value of Gillette stock on that date?

Solution steps:

$$\text{Total market value} = \text{share price} \times \text{shares outstanding}$$
$$= \$59.625 \times 220{,}889{,}620 = \$13{,}170{,}543{,}593$$

Answer: The total market value of Gillette's stock was $13,170,543,593.

Liquidation value Liquidation value is the amount left over for distribution to common shareholders in the event the firm terminates the business, sells its assets, and settles all prior claims. It is used primarily when a company is in or approaching bankruptcy and liquidation is expected.

3. Benefits of Ownership

The owner of a share of common stock has purchased a set of rights and benefits. These include: (1) income, (2) control, (3) information, (4) freedom to sell, (5) limited liability, and (6) a residual claim to assets should the company terminate its business.

Income Each share of common stock has the right to a fraction of the company's earnings, its earnings per share (EPS). Primary earnings per share is the net income of the firm divided by average number of shares outstanding during the year. Fully diluted earnings per share is a recalculation of EPS assuming that every investor holding an option to acquire additional shares exercised that option at the beginning of the year; it is net income divided by the maximum possible number of average outstanding shares. Shareholders receive their income in one of two ways: as cash if management elects to pay a dividend; and/or as an increase in the value of their stock if management retains the company's earnings and stock market analysts and investors feel this will lead to even greater future benefits.

Example

Earnings per Share

The Gillette Company reported earnings available to common shareholders (EAC) of $283,600,000 in 1993. While there were 220,889,620 shares outstanding at December 31, 1993, the average number of outstanding shares during 1993 was 220,400,000. Had all holders of options to buy the stock done so at the beginning of 1993, EAC would have been $285,600,000 and there would have been 225,500,000 shares outstanding on average.

Question: What was the company's primary and fully diluted earnings per share for 1993?

Solution steps: Earnings per share numbers are based on earnings available to common shareholders

1. Primary EPS = EAC/average shares outstanding
   = $283,600,000/220,400,000 = $1.29
2. Fully diluted EPS = adjusted EAC/maximum average shares
   = $285,600,000/225,500,000 = $1.27

Answer: In 1993, Gillette earned $1.29 per share, and $1.27 per share fully diluted.

Control Each share of common stock carries with it the right to vote on company affairs. Normally each share has one vote, although, as we will see below, there are examples of shares with greater or lesser voting power. Shareholders vote annually for members of the board of directors, to ratify management's selection of an external auditor and to amend the company's charter and/or by-laws. They also vote on any other issue that must be submitted to the shareholders according to the company's charter or the corporation law of the state under which the company is incorporated. Examples are the authorization of a new stock issue and the authorization of major investment plans (e.g., mergers and acquisitions).

Voting typically takes place at the company's annual meeting, a get-together of management and stockholders at which management reports on their stewardship of the corporation and asks for approval of corporate initiatives.[1] A closely held company often has most of its shareholders attend. A widely held company, however, may attract only a small number of shareholders to its annual meeting.

---

[1] **Observation:** Although the stated purpose of an annual meeting is for stockholders to review the stewardship of the company's management, stockholders rarely have any real input to the proceedings. In part this is due to the cumbersome nature of transacting business in such a large meeting. But it is also due to the proxy system, discussed in this section, which gives management the ability to determine the outcome of almost all votes. For many managements, the annual meeting is seen as a "necessary evil" and a disruption of their work.

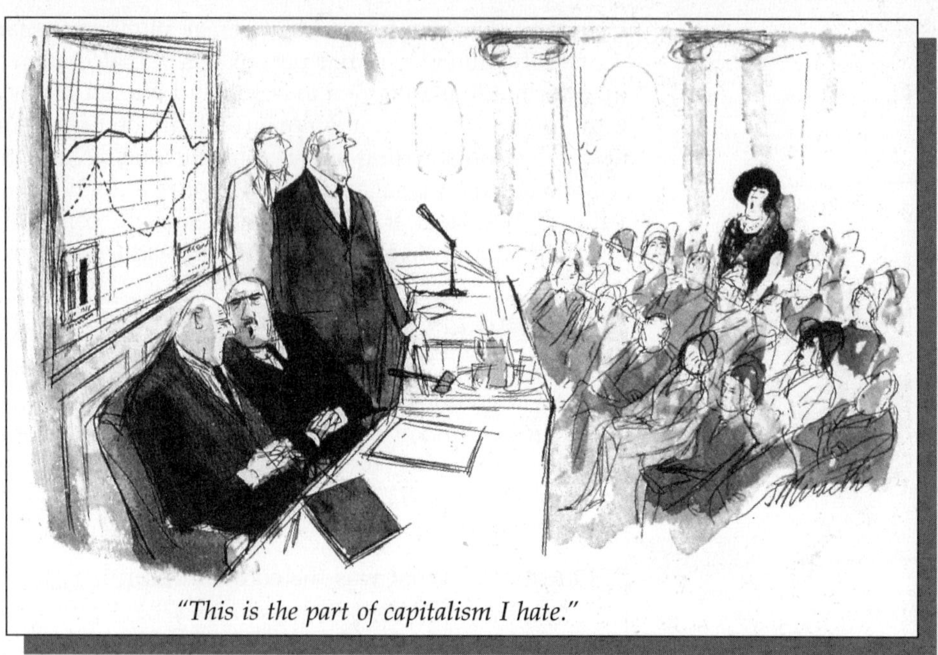

"This is the part of capitalism I hate."

proxy—a combined absentee ballot and assignment of the right to vote, used to obtain a majority of shareholder votes

In order to have a quorum of voting shares at the meeting, usually a simple majority, corporations use the device of a **proxy,** a combination absentee ballot and assignment of the right to vote on issues not on the ballot. Proxies are prepared and collected by the firm's officers, who typically name themselves as recipients of the assignment of voting power. They are therefore used by management to maintain control. Proxies are sometimes (although rarely) solicited by an outsider hoping to gain some control of the firm.

There are two common systems for voting for directors, the majority system and the cumulative system. In both, each share has a number of votes equal to the number of directors' seats on the ballot. For example, if five directors are to be elected, each share has five votes.[2] They differ by whether shareholders can bunch their votes behind a preferred candidate. Under a majority system, shareholders must spread the votes of each share among the candidates. However, under a cumulative system, shareholders may group the votes of each share behind a favored candidate. The effect of cumulative voting is to permit a minority of shares to be represented on the board of directors.

Example

Voting Systems

The charter of one of the companies Ivan Wolff has invested in specifies majority voting for its board of directors. Four directors are to be elected this year. Each share owned by Malcolm Vernon Partners must cast its four votes for four different people.

[2] **Observation:** This is consistent with the way we vote for public office in the United States. Even though it is popular to describe the U.S. system with the phrase "one person, one vote," each of us may cast several votes when we enter the voting booth, one for each contest.

The charter of another of Ivan Wolff's companies specifies cumulative voting for its board of directors. Four directors are also to be elected this year. Each share owned by Malcolm Vernon Partners will cast all four votes for Ivan, increasing his chances to win a seat on the board but forgoing the opportunity to vote for other candidates.

The cumulative system is an option under the corporation law of many states. Nevertheless, many senior managers dislike it because it increases the chance that a dissident shareholder group can win a seat on the board of directors. A management operating under a cumulative system can reduce the probability of a minority presence on the board in either of two ways. One is to decrease the number of directors up for election at any one time by reducing the size of the board or by staggering the terms of directors. This increases the number of shares a minority group must hold to be guaranteed of winning a seat. Another tactic is to issue additional shares, forcing the minority group to increase its investment or see its voting power diluted.

preemptive right—the right to purchase a proportionate amount of any newly issued stock

To protect each shareholder's income and voting power, most state corporation laws insist that when a company issues additional common shares, it must give existing shareholders the right of first refusal in proportion to their ownership position. This privilege is known as the **preemptive right.** Often the company offers the new shares to existing shareholders at a discount since it is saving the costs of hiring an investment banker to sell the shares to the public. Shareholders who elect to purchase the additional shares maintain their proportional ownership of the company.

Examples

Preemptive Right

The Gillette Company had 220,889,620 shares outstanding, with market price of $59 5/8 per share as of the end of 1993. Gillette's charter contains a requirement for preemptive rights. Susan Joseph owns 500 shares of Gillette common.

Question: If Gillette had elected to issue 2,208,896 additional shares on December 31, 1993, how many shares would Susan be entitled to purchase using her preemptive rights?

Solution steps:

1. Calculate the percentage of new shares:

$$2{,}208{,}896/220{,}889{,}620 = .01 = 1\%$$

2. Apply this percentage to Susan's holding:

$$1\% \times 500 \text{ shares} = 5 \text{ shares}$$

Question: If Gillette gives its shareholders the opportunity to purchase the new shares at a 5% discount to the market price on December 31, how much would Susan have to pay for her new shares?

Solution steps:

1. Calculate the price available to shareholders:

$$\$59.625 - (5\% \times \$59.625) = \$59.625 - 2.981 = \$56.644$$

2. Use this price to determine Susan's cost:

$$5 \text{ shares} \times \$56.644 = \$283.22$$

Answer: Susan will be able to purchase five shares from the new issue at a total cost of $283.22.

Information As owners and investors in a corporation, stockholders are entitled under the law to information about the company's financial condition. Traditionally this right has been written into corporations' charters as the right to "inspect the firm's books." However, it is rarely interpreted literally for fear of damaging the firm's competitive position—otherwise a competitor could buy one share of a company's stock and then demand to see internal firm documents. Instead, access to information is normally satisfied through the annual report and other public reporting documents, such as the 10K form—the annual report from corporations to the Securities and Exchange Commission. Any shareholder also has the right to gain access to the list of all shareholders for purposes of soliciting their proxies to challenge the company's management.

Freedom to sell Shareholders have the right to sell their shares whenever and to whomever they desire. All rights and privileges of ownership transfer with the sale, and no approval is required from the company, from a governmental agency, or from other shareholders.

Limited liability The corporate form of organization limits the liability of investors to the amount of their investment—they can lose that amount but no more. Accordingly, limited liability translates to freedom from responsibility for the firm's errors.

Residual claim The contracts between a company and its creditors supplemented by state corporation laws create a sequence of claims on the company's income stream and assets. In an ongoing operation, shareholders have ownership of all earnings not claimed by other creditors and investors. Should the company be dissolved, shareholders receive the value of any assets remaining after all other claimants have been satisfied.

4. Classified Common Stock

A firm wishing to separate the rights and claims of its various owners may issue several types of common stock. Each type is described as a "class" of stock.

Separation of voting rights One classification is for the purpose of allocating voting rights on a basis other than one vote per share.

Example

Separation of Voting Rights

The 1969 balance sheet of the Ford Motor Company reported the following number of common shares of three classes of common stock:

Class A	27,971,187	26%
Class B	12,174,972	11%
Common (Class C)	69,168,884	63%
	109,315,043	100%

All three classes of stock shared equally in dividends and liquidation benefits. However, they differed in voting rights. Class A shares were owned by the Ford Foundation and had no voting rights to preserve the foundation's tax-free status. In this way the Ford Foundation could receive dividends on its shares without being considered the majority controlling shareholder of the Ford Motor Company, an arrangement worked out with the Internal Revenue Service. Class B shares were owned by the Ford family and were guaranteed 40% of the voting power, regardless of the number outstanding. Common shares were owned by the general public and had one vote each.

By 1969, the Ford Foundation had decided to diversify its investment portfolio to be less dependent on the dividend stream from Ford Motor Company. But without the right to vote, Class A shares were saleable only at a discount. To remedy this problem, the foundation arranged with the IRS and Ford Motor Company to exchange its Class A stock for common shares which it could sell. By the end of 1974, Class A shares had been fully retired. Today there are only two classes of Ford stock outstanding: Class B and common.

To give the Class B shares 40% control, each share has more than one vote. The number of votes per share is recalculated regularly based on the total number of shares of each class outstanding. For example, at the end of 1969, each Class B share had 3.79 votes:

	Shares		Votes/Share		Total Votes		
Class B	12,174,972	×	3.79	=	46,143,144	40%	✓✓
Common	69,168,884				69,168,884	60%	
					115,312,028	100%	

Separation of income rights A second stock classification involves allocating a company's income on a basis other than equally per share.

Example

Separation of Income Rights

In 1984, when General Motors acquired Ross Perot's EDS, Inc., through an exchange of stock, it faced a problem. EDS employees held a substantial amount of EDS stock and were accustomed to receiving some of their bonus compensation through EDS dividends which reflected the earnings of their company. GM stock, by contrast, paid a much smaller dividend and reflected the performance of the much stodgier automobile company. In response, GM created a new class (Class E) of common stock especially for the exchange. In addition to receiving GM stock, EDS stockholders also received Class E shares. Dividends on the new stock were tied to the performance of EDS, effectively restoring the bonus program. In 1985, GM created Class H stock for the same purpose upon acquiring Hughes Aircraft Co. Since then, GM has sold additional shares of Class E and Class H stock to the general public, and both trade alongside the parent company stock on the New York Stock Exchange.

Founder's shares A frequent use of classified common is in new ventures when it is desired to give control to the managers who founded the company but give income to the investors. Often no dividend is paid on the managers' shares until the firm reaches a specified milestone (e.g., sales, profits, asset size, time in

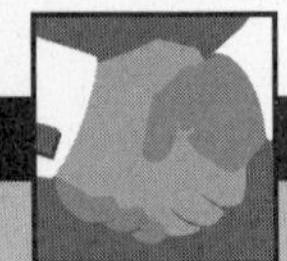

SERVING FINANCE'S CUSTOMERS

Investor Relations at Corning, Incorporated

The investor relations group of Corning, Incorporated, conveys both strategic and financial information to financial analysts so they can accurately assess the company's market value. The group works to move the investment community away from a short-term valuation approach by putting events in strategic context and by acting as a teacher, helping analysts perform better analyses. The group considers a good investor relations program as one marked by availability, listening, preparation, and credibility. While they constantly deal with how much they can tell their analyst customers—given the availability of information and legal and ethical boundaries—they want to "leave them all feeling they got the best information available."

business). Ivan Wolff will probably consider founder's shares a good alternative for the new company he is financing.

5. Investor Relations

Most corporations operate a shareholder relations function to deal with the information requirements and other needs of financial analysts and the company's equity holders.

Preferred Stock

preferred stock—stock with one or more features better than common stock and without any ownership claim

Preferred stock, also called *preference stock,* is stock that has no claim of ownership on the firm. In return, it has one or more features that are better than the comparable features of the company's common stock. Examples are a stated, unchanging dividend versus common stock's variable and uncertain dividend, and seniority to common stock in the event of bankruptcy or liquidation.

1. A Stock-Bond Hybrid

In concept and on the balance sheet, preferred stock resides between long-term debt and common equity (although as stock, it is often grouped with the owners' equity for reporting purposes). This location is appropriate for, in many ways, preferred stock is a hybrid between a bond and a share of stock.

Like a bond Among the characteristics of preferred stock that make it resemble bonds are the following:

- Preferred stock has a face value, also called *maturity value* and *par value,* representing the amount to be paid to the investor when the relationship is terminated. (Unlike bonds, which have face values of $1,000 or higher, the most common face value for preferred stock is $100 per share.)
- Preferred stock pays its holder a fixed amount each year which may be stated as a dollar amount or a percentage of face value.

Example

Preferred Stock Payment

Malcolm Vernon Partners, Ivan Wolff's venture capital firm, owns 40,000 shares of "$10 preferred stock" and also 100,000 shares of "11%, $100 face value preferred stock" issued to it by two of the companies in which it invested.

Question: How much does Malcolm Vernon Partners receive in dividends each year from these two investments?

Solution steps:

1. The "$10 preferred stock" pays $10 per share per year.

   40,000 shares × $10 = $400,000

2. The "11%, $100 face value preferred stock" pays 11% × $100 = $11 per share per year.

   100,000 shares × $11 = $1,100,000

Answer: Malcolm Vernon Partners receives $400,000 plus $1,100,000 or $1,500,000 in total.

- Preferred stock normally has no voting privileges so preferred stockholders cannot participate in choosing directors and making major corporate decisions.
- Preferred stock has priority above common stock in liquidation.
- Preferred stock may contain a call feature.
- Preferred stock may be convertible to common stock.
- A preferred stock issue may require a sinking fund for retirement. The sinking fund is often combined with a call feature so the firm has the ability to retire the issue at the lower of market price or call price.
- A preferred issue may contain indenture provisions—for example, a restriction on the firm's ability to issue senior claims or a requirement for a minimum level of liquidity.

Like common stock Among the characteristics of preferred stock that make it resemble common stock are the following:

- Preferred stock rarely has a fixed maturity.
- The payment to investors in preferred stock is a dividend. It is paid at the discretion of the firm and is not tax-deductible.
- Some preferred issues permit preferred stockholders to vote in company affairs if an issue before the board of directors has a major effect on them or if the preferred dividend is not paid. Some issues give the preferred shareholders control over a fixed minority of seats on the board of directors.
- Preferred stock has priority after all debt in liquidation.
- The dividend on some preferred issues, known as *participating preferred stock,* can be increased if the firm has a particularly good year. Participating preferred stock may be "partially participating," in which case any extra preferred dividend is some fraction of the common dividend, or "fully

participating" where any extra preferred dividend is equal to the dividend on the common stock.

Examples

Participating Preferred Stock

Malcolm Vernon Partners owns shares of $12 *partially* participating preferred, requiring that if the common dividend exceeds $8.00 per share, the preferred dividend will rise by $0.50 for each additional $1.00 of common dividend.

Question: If a $10.00 per share common dividend is paid, what will happen to the preferred dividend?

Solution steps:

1. Determine the amount by which the common dividend exceeds the threshold of $8.00 per share:

$$\$10.00 - 8.00 = \$2.00$$

2. Add $0.50 per dollar of extra common dividend to the $12.00 preferred dividend:

$$\$12.00 + (2 \times \$0.50) = \$13.00$$

Answer: The preferred dividend will rise to $13.00 per share.

Malcolm Vernon Partners also owns shares of $9 *fully* participating preferred which pays a $9 per share dividend if the common dividend is $9 per share or less and pays a dividend equal to the common dividend if the latter is above $9 per share.

Question: If a $12 per share common dividend is paid, what will happen to the preferred dividend?

Answer: The preferred dividend will rise to $12 per share to match the common stock dividend.

2. Cumulative Feature

Because preferred stockholders are concerned that the company's management may elect not to pay the preferred dividend, most preferred stock has a protection built in known as the "cumulative feature." The cumulative feature prohibits payment of dividends on common stock if any preferred dividends have not been paid. A company that has not fully paid all preferred dividends is said to be *in arrears,* and the cumulative amount of preferred dividends owed is known as *arrearages.*[3]

[3] **Observation and cross-reference:** Recall that the word *arrears* first made an appearance in this book in Chapter 5, p. 172, to describe an annuity in which cash flows come at the end of each period of time. In general, the word *arrears* implies *later in time,* which explains its use here.

Example

Arrearages on Preferred Stock

A company is three years in arrears on its 8%, $100 face value issue of cumulative preferred stock. At the end of the fourth year management desires to pay a common stock dividend.

Question: How much must the company pay to preferred stockholders before they can pay the common dividend?

Answer: The company must first pay a $32 per share preferred dividend ($24 arrearages plus $8 for the current year).

Arrearages on preferred stock create (or confirm) problems for the company and its common stockholders as well as for the preferred stockholders. The company may suffer a decline in its credit rating and a lessened ability to sell additional securities. Resumption of common dividends requires a large cash payment to the preferred shareholders, something that may be quite difficult for a cash-strapped firm. Common stockholders are prevented from receiving dividends as long as the arrearages remain outstanding, leading to a downward pressure on the market value of their stock. Preferred stockholders see their stock fall in price. Also, arrearages earn no interest; even if they are subsequently paid, the preferred shareholder has lost the time value of this money.

A company falls in arrears on its preferred stock when it is seriously short of cash. If the cash shortage persists, the arrearages will increase, and the company will find it even more difficult to find the cash to clear them up. Accordingly, a company several years in arrears might make an "exchange offering" to its preferred stockholders, offering to satisfy the arrearages with shares of common stock rather than cash.

Example

Exchange Offering

A company has come to Ivan Wolff for advice on how to clear up the arrearages on its 8%, $100 face value issue of cumulative preferred stock. The company has not paid a preferred dividend for five years. As a result the preferred stock is selling at $40 per share and the company's common stock is down (from a much higher value) to $15 per share.

Ivan suggests the following possible exchange offerings:

1. Three common shares for all arrearages, leaving the preferred shares outstanding, or
2. Five common shares for each preferred share including arrearages.

When an exchange offering is for the preferred stock itself, it is often made contingent on a majority vote of the preferred shareholders so the entire issue may be retired, thus eliminating the arrearage problem in its entirety.

3. Advantages and Disadvantages of Issuing Preferred Stock

Preferred stock can be an attractive source of funds for many companies for several reasons:

- Preferred financing preserves a company's debt capacity while raising funds in a manner similar to long-term debt. The preferred issue is fixed-rate financing, collateral is not required, and voting control is not diluted.
- Preferred stock is accepted as equity by some regulatory authorities, permitting utilities and banks to maintain legally required equity levels without diluting their common stock.
- Compared to common stock, preferred stock usually has a lower capital cost.
- Preferred stock provides tax benefits to its holders, making it an attractive alternative to long-term debt for investors looking for steady income. As we saw in Appendix 4B, 70% of dividends paid by one corporation to another are tax free. In addition, if preferred stock is acquired in a stock swap, any capital gain may be deferred until the preferred stock is sold, possibly years later.

There are also some important limitations to preferred stock.

- Like dividends on common stock, preferred dividends are not tax-deductible to the issuing company, making the explicit cost of preferred stock capital high relative to debt.
- Investors often see preferred stock as a particularly risky investment. The market price of preferred is volatile, swinging over a large range in response to interest rate fluctuations since preferred stock has an infinite life. Also, investors have no legal claim to preferred dividends, and historically many arrearages have not been paid in full.
- A missed dividend could result in a strong negative reaction from creditors and stockholders, closing access to other financing.

Equity Options

Companies commonly issue call options on their own common stock. Two common examples are (1) warrants and (2) the call option embedded in convertible securities.

1. Warrants

warrant—a call option issued by the company whose stock may be called

A **warrant** is a call option issued by the company against whose stock the option is written. For example, the Gillette company might issue an option giving the holder the right to buy stock directly from the company. Two common examples of warrants are the "stock subscription warrant," the mechanism used to convey preemptive rights to shareholders, and "employee stock options" used as incentive compensation for employees.

Warrants are often used as extra compensation for lenders and preferred stockholders to reduce interest and dividend rates. When used this way they are often called "kickers" or "sweeteners." However, in return for the savings in financing costs, the firm risks giving away common shares at a bargain price.

Some warrants must always remain "attached" to the securities with which they are issued; they trade together in the market. Other warrants are not issued with another security or may be "detached" from their sister securities and traded as separate financial instruments.

The value of a warrant At minimum, a warrant's value is the potential savings from using it. When the stock the warrant can purchase is selling below the warrant's exercise or strike price, the warrant's minimum value is zero. When the stock price is above the exercise price, the warrant's minimum value is the savings from using it to purchase the stock.

Example

The Minimum Value of a Warrant

A company has outstanding warrants with an exercise price of $20, each warrant good for the purchase of five shares of common stock.

Question: What is the minimum value of each warrant for stock prices in the range of $5 to $50?

Solution steps: Construct a table showing the savings at various stock prices:

Stock Price	Savings per Share	Savings for Five Shares
$ 5	$ 0	$ 0
10	0	0
15	0	0
20	0	0
25	5	25
30	10	50
35	15	75
40	20	100
45	25	125
50	30	150

Answer: The warrant's minimum value is zero until the stock reaches $20. For stock prices above $20, the minimum warrant value equals the savings on the five shares that can be purchased using the warrant.

Figure 22.3 graphs the minimum value of the warrant in the example above. Note that it graphs as a kinked line, the characteristic graph of an option's minimum value.[4]

[4] **Observation and cross-reference:** If this graph and the comparable graph for a convertible bond on p. 812 look familiar, you may find it interesting to refer back to the graph of the value of a call option at expiration on p. 327. Since a warrant is a call option and since a convertible bond is the combination of a bond and a call option, it is no wonder that the three graphs are very similar.

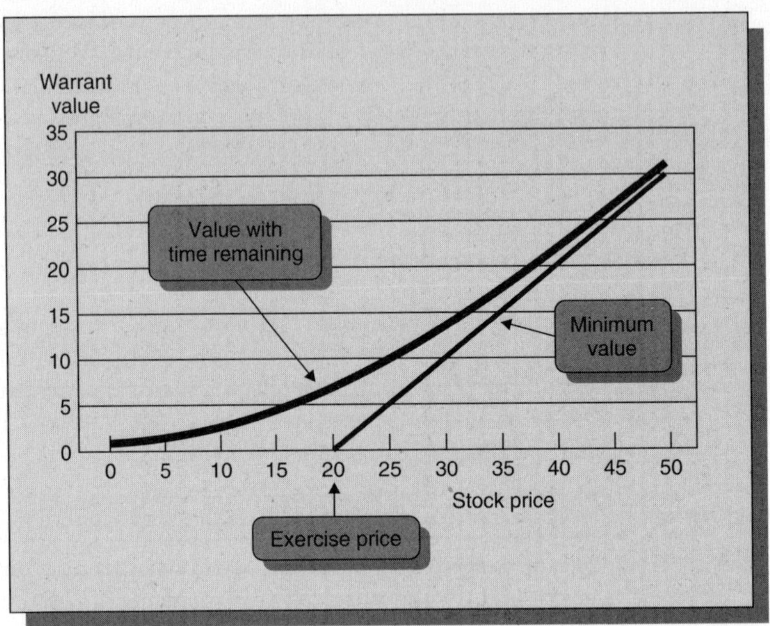

FIGURE 22.3
The value of a warrant. If time remains until expiration, the warrant's value will exceed its minimum value.

The minimum value of a warrant will be its market value on the date the warrant expires since on that date the warrant must be used or left to perish. If there is time remaining until the warrant expires, however, the stock might go up in price, increasing the savings from using the warrant. As a result, when there is time remaining to expiration, a warrant's value exceeds its minimum value.[5] The curved line on the graph of Figure 22.3 approximates the warrant's value assuming there is time left until the warrant expires.

Exercise of warrants Investors will exercise warrants if two conditions are true: (1) they are in the money and (2) they are about to expire or otherwise lose their value. Note that management has only partial control over the timing of the exercise of warrants, and then primarily through prior decisions: exercise price and expiration date. It can, however, hope to influence investors' decisions by increasing the common dividend, thus making the acquisition of common stock more attractive.

Examples

Exercise of Warrants

Several years ago, a company issued bonds with detachable warrants. Each warrant gives its holder the right to purchase ten shares of the company's com-

[5] **Elaboration:** The same factors are at work as in any option: the longer the time to expiration and the more volatile the underlying security, the greater the spread between the option's market value and minimum (expiration) value.

mon stock (now trading at $35 per share) for $30 per share. The warrants expire tomorrow.

Question: How much is one warrant worth?

Answer: An investor may submit one warrant plus $300 and receive ten shares of common worth $350 in the market today, a $50 benefit. Alternatively, the investor could sell the warrant to another investor and receive the $50 directly.

Question: How will the exercise of the warrant affect the company?

Answer: The company will receive $300 in cash and issue ten shares of new stock. It will add the $300 to its "common stock" and "additional paid-in-capital" accounts.

2. Convertible Securities

convertible security—a security that may be exchanged for another

A **convertible security** is a bond or preferred stock that may be exchanged for another security, usually common stock, at the option of the holder. The exchange is made by the issuing firm. The number of shares obtained from the conversion is given by one of two measures: the *conversion price*—the dollars of face value of the convertible security that must be exchanged for one share of common stock, or the *conversion ratio*—the number of shares of common stock received by converting one convertible security.

Example

Conversion Price and Ratio

A company has an issue of $1,000 face value convertible bonds outstanding, each bond convertible to 25 common shares.

Question: Calculate the convertible's conversion price and conversion ratio.

Solution steps:

1. Conversion price = $1,000/25 = $40 per share
2. Conversion ratio = 25 shares per bond

The value of a convertible bond To understand the value of a convertible bond, it is useful to view it first as a bond and then as common stock. The graph of Figure 22.4 summarizes this. The convertible's bond value is shown as a horizontal line, independent of the price of the company's stock. If the convertible were exchanged for stock, its value would simply be the value of the stock, shown as the line sloping upward to the right at a 45% angle. These two lines taken together form the minimum value for the convertible as shown by the solid sections of each line. However, if there is time remaining before conversion, the convertible's value will be above the minimum as investors pay a premium for the possibility that interest rates might fall or the stock price will rise. Note the similarity of Figures 22.3 and 22.4; effectively, a convertible bond is a composite of a bond and a warrant.

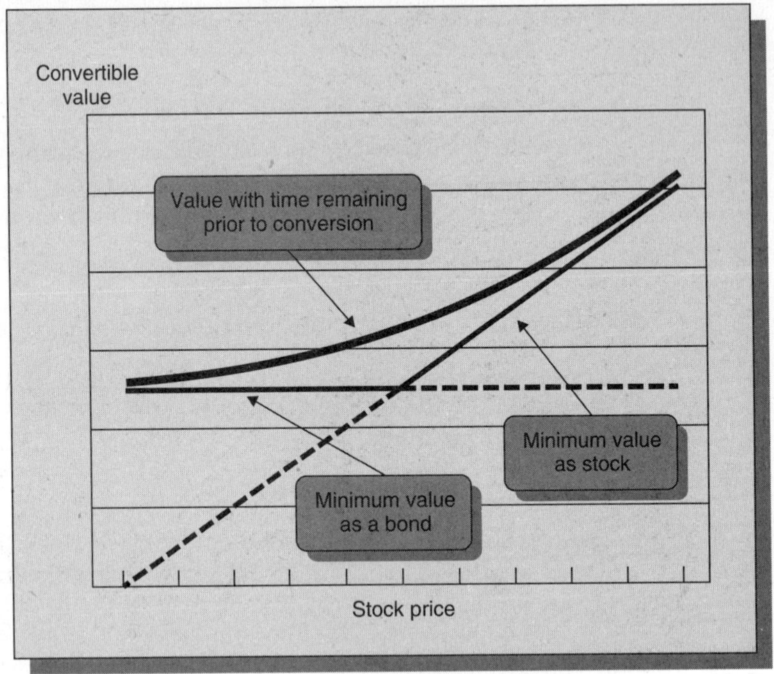

FIGURE 22.4
The value of a convertible bond. The convertible is the combination of a bond plus a warrant.

Conversion of convertible bonds Investors, in general, do not want to convert a convertible bond to common stock since, as Figure 22.4 shows, the convertible is more valuable than the stock to which it can be converted. Accordingly, companies use the call feature to force conversion when desired.

Examples

Conversion of a Convertible Bond Issue

A company's $1,000 face value bonds are each convertible to 50 common shares. They may be called at a price of $104 (104% of face value). The bonds were issued when the company's stock price was $18; today the stock price is $25 per share. In an effort to force conversion, the company has just called the bonds.

Question: How will the bondholders react to the call?

Solution steps:

1. Calculate the value of a bond if submitted in response to the call:

$$104\% \times \$1{,}000 = \$1{,}040$$

2. Calculate the value of a bond if converted:

$$50 \text{ shares} \times \$25 = \$1{,}250$$

Answer: Bondholders will immediately convert rather than submit to the call.

Question: How will the conversion affect the company?

Answer: The firm will pay out nothing and will have achieved the desired conversion. It will remove the debt from its books, replacing it with an identical amount of equity which will increase the number of shares outstanding.

To make conversion attractive and likely, the "rule of thumb" is to set the exercise or conversion price 15–20% above the stock price at the time of issue.

Conversion depends on the stock price being high enough to make converting worthwhile. If the stock price remains low, investors will neither convert voluntarily nor convert in response to a call. Rather, investors will turn their bonds in upon a call requiring the firm to pay out substantial cash to redeem the issue.

Examples

A Failed Attempt to Convert a Convertible Bond Issue

A company's $1,000 face value bonds are each convertible to 50 common shares. They may be called at a price of $104. The bonds were issued when the company's stock price was $18; today the stock price is still $18 per share. In an effort to force conversion, the company is thinking of calling the bonds.

Question: How would the bondholders react to the call?

Solution steps:

1. Calculate the value of a bond if submitted in response to the call:

$$104\% \times \$1{,}000 = \$1{,}040$$

2. Calculate the value of a bond if converted:

$$50 \text{ shares} \times \$18 = \$900$$

Answer: Bondholders would submit to the call rather than convert.

Question: How would calling the bonds affect the company?

Answer: The firm would pay out $1,040 per bond, removing the debt from its books and reducing its cash. It would have failed to increase its equity balance.

Financial managers find convertible securities attractive for several reasons:

- The interest rate on convertible debt is less than on a comparable nonconvertible security as investors get the benefit of the conversion privilege.
- If stock market conditions are currently poor, a company can still raise funds that will very likely become equity at a price to the company appreciably above the currently depressed stock price.
- The company adds leverage at first which disappears naturally with conversion.
- Debt capacity is used and then freed up automatically.

Ivan Wolff connected the video output of his laptop computer to the overhead projector, adjusted the focus, and began his talk. He was presenting his analysis about financing the exciting startup company to his firm's partners. He remained convinced that this was an excellent opportunity with a good probability of a high rate of return on investment.

Ivan began with a review of the company's background, products, and management—paying particular attention to the company's successes in satisfying its early customers and improving its processes. Next he summarized his numerical analyses and projections and identified the company's strengths and weaknesses. Finally he turned to the best way for Malcolm Vernon Partners to provide the financing, a complex combination of preferred and common stock and warrants that would give the company the funds it needed while providing the partnership with income, growth potential, and a fair share of control. After an extended discussion, the partners approved Ivan's plan.

Ivan picked up the phone and placed a long-distance call to the president of the young company. He informed the president of the good news and made arrangements to visit the company within the next week to work with them on the next stage of their growth. As he hung up the phone, Ivan accepted hearty handshakes from the partners. He had a good feeling that this was going to be a winning deal for all the participants.

Summary of Key Points

- **Identify five concepts of owners' equity.** Owners' equity can be seen as an accounting measure based on the fundamental accounting identity, a legal concept defining the ownership of a company, a financial position deriving from investment in the firm, a residual position in relation to others who have a claim on the company's income and resources, and a risk-taking posture since equity holders are the ultimate bearers of the company's risks.
- **Describe the characteristics of common stock, including share and value concepts, benefits of share ownership, and classified common stock.** Common stock is the form of ownership in a corporation providing its owners with income, control, information, the freedom to sell, limited liability, and a residual claim. A company arranges for the state to authorize shares, some of which are issued to the public. Those not repurchased for the company's treasury are identified as outstanding. Equity can be measured by its par value, book value, market value, and liquidation value. Of these, market value is the theoretically correct way to measure the company's worth to its shareholders. By using classified common stock and founder's shares, a company can separate the rights of ownership among its stockholders.
- **Describe how preferred stock combines the features of bonds and common stock, and understand the cumulative feature.** Features such as its face value, fixed payment, lack of voting privileges, and priority above common stock, cause preferred stock to resemble a bond. However, other features such as lack of a fixed maturity, discretionary payment, and priority below debt, make preferred look like common stock. To prevent management from skipping the preferred dividend, most preferred stock issues have a cumulative feature preventing payment of a common stock dividend if the preferred dividend is in arrears.
- **Discuss how warrants and convertibles function and how they are used as financing techniques.** Companies issue call options directly in the form of warrants and convertible bonds. Warrants are used as extra compensation in financing, to convey preemptive rights to shareholders, and as incentive compensation. Convertibles are used to lower the interest rate on debt, place equity in poor financial markets, and control the firm's leverage.

Questions

1. In what way can owners' equity been seen as:
   a. An accounting measure?
   b. A legal concept?
   c. An investment concept?
   d. A value claim concept?
   e. A risk concept?
2. Distinguish among the following common stock concepts:
   a. Authorized shares
   b. Issued shares
   c. Outstanding shares
   d. Treasury shares
3. Distinguish among the following common stock concepts:
   a. Par value
   b. Book value
   c. Market value
   d. Liquidation value

4. What are six benefits to owning common stock? Rank them in order of importance to you.
5. What is the difference between primary and fully diluted earnings per share?
6. In what way does a proxy give significant power to a corporation's management?
7. Is there any advantage to having preemptive rights as a stockholder? Is there any disadvantage?
8. Why can't a stockholder "inspect the company's books"?
9. When would a stockholder be willing to purchase a class of common stock that did not have full shareholders' rights?
10. Why is preferred stock often called a hybrid between bonds and common stock?
11. Is there any difference in value between cumulative and noncumulative preferred stock? Why, or why not?
12. Why do companies issue warrants?
13. Why do companies issue convertible bonds?
14. What is the relationship of a warrant and a convertible bond to a call option?
15. Under what circumstances can a company successfully force conversion of a convertible bond? Under what circumstances will the company fail?

Problems

1. **(Number of shares)** A company whose charter authorizes 10 million shares, has sold 6 million to the public. Of these, 5 million are in the hands of investors today.
   a. How many shares are issued?
   b. How many shares are authorized but not issued?
   c. How many shares are outstanding?
   d. How many shares are in the treasury?
2. **(Number of shares)** A company whose charter authorizes 40 million shares, has sold 25 million to the public. Of these, 7 million have been repurchased by the company.
   a. How many shares are authorized but not issued?
   b. How many shares are outstanding?
   c. How many shares are in the treasury?
   d. Could the company split its stock 2 for 1 without getting authorization for additional shares?
3. **(Share value)** At the end of last year a company had 12 million shares ($2.50 par value) outstanding and total owners' equity of $96 million. Net income in the past year was $25 million, and 11.5 million shares were outstanding on average during the year.
   a. What is the remaining obligation, if any, of a shareholder who purchased shares from the company at $1.00 per share?
   b. What is the remaining obligation, if any, of a shareholder who purchased shares from the company at $10.00 per share?
   c. Calculate the company's book value per share at year-end.
   d. Calculate the company's earnings per share for the year.
4. **(Share value)** At the end of last year a company had 25 million shares ($1.00 par value) outstanding, and total owners' equity of $100 million. Net income in the past year was $75 million, and 24 million shares were outstanding on average during the year.
   a. What is the remaining obligation, if any, of a shareholder who purchased shares from the company at $0.40 per share?
   b. What is the remaining obligation, if any, of a shareholder who purchased shares from the company at $40.00 per share?
   c. Calculate the company's book value per share at year-end.
   d. Calculate the company's earnings per share for the year.
5. **(Voting systems)** A company has 1,000,000 shares outstanding. One investor who owns 50,000 shares is interested in running for a seat on the board of directors. What is the maximum number of votes the investor can cast for herself if:
   a. There is a majority voting system and two directors' seats are up for vote?
   b. There is a cumulative voting system and two directors' seats are up for vote?
   c. There is a majority voting system and five directors' seats are up for vote?
   d. There is a cumulative voting system and five directors' seats are up for vote?
6. **(Voting systems)** A company has 6,000,000 shares outstanding. One investor who owns 150,000 shares is interested in running for a seat on the board of directors. What is the maximum number of votes the investor can cast for himself if:
   a. There is a majority voting system and three directors' seats are up for vote?
   b. There is a cumulative voting system and three directors' seats are up for vote?
   c. There is a majority voting system and seven directors' seats are up for vote?
   d. There is a cumulative voting system and seven directors' seats are up for vote?

7. **(Preemptive rights)** A company with 25 million shares outstanding is planning a new equity issue of 5 million shares. Existing stockholders have preemptive rights, and the company will first offer them the new shares at a 5% discount from the stock's current market value of $30. You own 1,000 shares of the company's stock.
   a. What fraction of the company's shares do you own?
   b. How many of the new shares are you entitled to?
   c. At what price can you purchase the new shares?
   d. What will you pay in total for the new shares?

8. **(Preemptive rights)** A company with 50 million shares outstanding is planning a new equity issue of 15 million shares. Existing stockholders have preemptive rights, and the company will first offer them the new shares at a 4% discount from the stock's current market value of $75. You own 500 shares of the company's stock.
   a. To how many of the new shares are you entitled?
   b. At what price can you purchase the new shares?
   c. What will you pay in total for the new shares?
   d. How is your percentage ownership of the company affected if you do not purchase the new shares?

9. **(Classified common)** A company has two classes of common stock. There are 25 million shares of Class B stock outstanding held by the general public, each with one vote. There are also 5 million shares of Class A stock held by the company's founding family. How many votes does each Class A share have if Class A stock has:
   a. 30% of the voting power?
   b. 40% of the voting power?
   c. 50% of the voting power?
   d. 60% of the voting power?

10. **(Classified common)** A company has two classes of common stock. There are 2,000,000 shares of Class B stock outstanding held by the company's venture capitalists. There are also 500,000 shares of Class A stock held by the engineers who founded the company. The company just declared a $1 per share dividend on the Class B stock. How much should the per-share dividend on the Class A stock be if the Class A stock is entitled to:
    a. 5% of the total Class B dividend?
    b. 10% of the total Class B dividend?
    c. 20% of the total Class B dividend?
    d. 35% of the total Class B dividend?

11. **(Preferred dividend)** A company has an outstanding issue of $100.00 par value preferred stock. It recently declared a $7.00 per share dividend on its common stock. How much will the company pay in annual per-share preferred dividends if the preferred is:
    a. "$12.00 preferred stock"?
    b. "14% preferred stock"?
    c. $10.00 partially participating preferred, requiring that the preferred dividend increase by $0.25 for every dollar the common dividend exceeds $5.00?
    d. $6.00 fully participating preferred, requiring that the preferred dividend increase to equal the common dividend if the latter exceeds $6.00?

12. **(Preferred dividend)** A company has an outstanding issue of $100.00 par value preferred stock. It recently declared a $12.00 per share dividend on its common stock. How much will the company pay in annual per-share preferred dividends if the preferred is:
    a. "$13.00 preferred stock"?
    b. "11% preferred stock"?
    c. $8.00 partially participating preferred, requiring that the preferred dividend increase by $0.60 for every dollar the common dividend exceeds $8.00?
    d. $8.00 fully participating preferred requiring that the preferred dividend increase to equal the common dividend if the latter exceeds $8.00?

13. **(Preferred arrearages)** A company is in arrears on its $12 cumulative preferred stock. However, the company's fortunes have improved and it now wishes to resume its common stock dividend. How much must it first pay to each preferred shareholder if it is:
    a. One year in arrears?
    b. Three years in arrears?
    c. Five years in arrears?
    d. Eight years in arrears but the preferred stock is not cumulative?

14. **(Preferred arrearages)** A company is ten years in arrears on its $14.00 cumulative preferred stock and sees no hope of paying them off. However, management desires to resume paying a $0.50 per share dividend on its common stock. The company has 100,000 shares of preferred and 3,000,000 shares of common stock outstanding.
    a. How much must the company pay to preferred shareholders to eliminate the arrearages?
    b. What is the total cash outlay required to pay $0.50 per share to the common stockholders?
    c. How much would each preferred shareholder receive if the company made them an exchange offering consisting of ten common shares for each preferred share including arrearages and then paid the $0.50 common dividend?
    d. How would your answers to parts a, b, and c change if the preferred stock were not cumulative?

15. **(Warrant)** A company has issued warrants with an exercise price of $25, each warrant redeemable for one share of the company's common stock.
    a. What is the minimum value of the warrant if the stock is trading at a per share price of $10? $15? $20? $25? $30? $35? $40? $45? $50?
    b. Graph your results from part a. Your graph should have stock price on the horizontal axis and minimum warrant value on the vertical axis.
    c. If the warrants have six months until they expire, what will the warrants' value be in comparison to their minimum value? Why?
    d. What will happen to the holder of one warrant and to the company if the stock is selling for $35 and the warrants are due to expire today?
16. **(Warrant)** A company has issued warrants with an exercise price of $50, each warrant redeemable for five shares of the company's common stock.
    a. What is the minimum value of the warrant if the stock is trading at a per share price of $20? $30? $40? $50? $60? $70? $80? $90? $100?
    b. Graph your results from part a. Your graph should have stock price on the horizontal axis and minimum warrant value on the vertical axis.
    c. What will happen to the holder of one warrant and to the company if the stock is selling for $55 and the warrants are due to expire today?
    d. What will happen to the holder of one warrant and to the company if the stock is selling for $45 and the warrants are due to expire today?
17. **(Convertible bond)** A company's $1,000 face value bonds, each convertible to 40 common shares, were called today at a price of $108.
    a. If the company's stock is currently selling for $30 per share, how will the bondholders react to the call?
    b. If the company's stock is currently selling for $30 per share, how will the bondholders' response affect the company?
    c. If the company's stock is currently selling for $20 per share, how will the bondholders react to the call?
    d. If the company's stock is currently selling for $20 per share, how will the bondholders' response affect the company?
18. **(Convertible bond)** A company's $1,000 face value bonds, each convertible to 50 common shares, were called today at a price of $107.
    a. If the company's stock is currently selling for $23 per share, how will the bondholders react to the call?
    b. If the company's stock is currently selling for $23 per share, how will the bondholders' response affect the company?
    c. If the company's stock is currently selling for $17 per share, how will the bondholders react to the call?
    d. If the company's stock is currently selling for $17 per share, how will the bondholders' response affect the company?

PART VIII LOOKING AHEAD

Chapter 23

The Continuing Evolution of Financial Managing

Part VIII consists of only one chapter, one that is somewhat different from the others in this book. We have stepped back from our study of financial managing to summarize where we are: what we know and what we don't know about finance. We know quite a bit, yet in many respects what we don't know is as striking as what we do know. An ongoing part of every finance professional's work is to continue to learn the new as it develops and integrate it with the old, to maintain continuity while embracing change.

Chapter 23 looks ahead, but first we look back by summarizing seven central concepts of financial managing that have appeared repeatedly throughout the book. Then, we focus our attention toward the future. We identify forces for change in finance theory and discuss innovations in important financial concepts and practices that may be occurring as a result of changes in the global competitive environment and the evolution of financial thought. We distinguish between analytical and operational finance theory and summarize five central concepts in operational finance theory. We identify the benefits and dangers of using a financial perspective in thinking about business decisions and highlight ways to avoid the dangers. Finally we discuss reasons for being humble about what we know about financial managing.

CHAPTER 23
THE CONTINUING EVOLUTION OF FINANCIAL MANAGING

"FINANCIAL MANAGEMENT THEORY AND PRACTICE: WHAT'S STABLE AND WHAT'S CHANGING?" Carrie Finch wrote in big block letters on the flip-chart. "Okay," she said to the other five members of her group, "here's how I tried to organize my thoughts."

For four days the seminar speakers and participants from Carrie's company had discussed key concepts in financial managing and how they are used. During the week, Carrie found herself particularly interested when seminar members speculated about the future of finance or emphasized what is not known about financial managing. Perhaps those parts especially interested her because a dozen years in various finance jobs and an MBA with a finance minor made her reasonably comfortable with the finance concepts that were widely accepted. Or perhaps it was because she knew this question would be discussed at the end of the seminar. Now was the time for each of the groups to bring their thoughts together and to prepare to share their ideas with the seminar leaders and the other teams.

"Four themes keep coming up for me," she said and wrote four words on the flip-chart: *THEORY, PRACTICE, CAUSALITY,* and *SO?* "First, theory. What do we think we know about finance, what don't we know, and how is what we don't know likely to change what we think we do know? Second, practice. What's being done the same in finance as it was 5, 10, or 20 years ago, and what's likely to be done differently? I am not convinced that theory and practice are always the same. Third, causality. What is likely to cause these changes we are predicting? I guess I need a theory of change—some sense of causality—so I can have some grounding for talking about what might be stable and what might be changing. And finally, so? as in 'so what?' Why do we care what's changing, and what does it imply for how we do our jobs?

"I'd like to hear what you people think about all of these, but we have only a little time. So which ones do we get to talk about?"

We find ourselves in a situation much like Carrie's. This is the book's last chapter, and we have many remaining thoughts—and questions—about modern financial managing we'd like to share. And we have only a moderate amount of space for doing so. We also feel we have a "last chapter" opportunity we should not miss—a chance to review and bring together some of the things we discussed in earlier chapters.

As a result, this chapter is a combination of review and speculation. We return once again to the subtitle of the book, *Continuity and Change,* and in doing so we try to touch on each of the four items on Carrie's list.

Key Points You Should Learn from This Chapter

After reading this chapter, you should be able to:

- Understand why we wrote this chapter the way we did.
- Summarize seven central concepts of financial managing.
- Identify three possible forces for change in finance theory and discuss five changes in important financial concepts that may be occurring as a result of changes in the global competitive environment and the evolution of financial thought.
- Distinguish between analytical and operational finance theory and summarize five central concepts in operational finance theory.
- Describe the area of financial practice that seems to be changing the most as a result of changes in the global competitive environment and the evolution of financial thought.
- Describe the benefits and dangers of using a financial perspective in thinking about business decisions and ways to avoid the dangers.
- Discuss three reasons for being humble about what we know about financial managing.

Introductory Concepts—The Last-Chapter Game Plan

The subject of finance is a bit like the subject of medicine. We have made significant strides in the past 50 years in understanding the financial aspects of the organism we call the business organization, in helping it function better, and in curing some of its worst financial diseases. But there is still much we do not know and many ailments that remain uncured. We are in the same position as the doctor who can do so very much yet still does not have the answers to many medical questions.

In this last chapter we have taken a step back from our study of financial managing to summarize where we are: what we know and what we don't know about finance. We know quite a bit, yet in many respects what we don't know is as striking as what we do know. Like doctors, an ongoing part of every finance professional's work is to continue to learn the new as it develops and integrate it with the old, to maintain continuity while embracing change.

We begin the chapter by reviewing seven key concepts in the book. They have been recognized as important for a number of years and are recognized as important right now. We think most professors are likely to agree that Carrie, you, and we will continue finding them useful 10 or 20 years from now. They are so important and enduring that we have devoted about 80% of the book to presenting them. These things fit well with the subtitle word *continuity.*

Then we shift to *change,* and we simultaneously become much more speculative in our writing. We do so in part because it is easy to make mistakes in recognizing which changes are important and which are not. We continue to consider the seven key concepts and speculate about forces that may lead to changes in them and what some of those changes might be. Also, we have introduced a number of topics in this book that are not normally found in finance texts but we believe are important—for example, managing financial processes in Chapters 13 and 14; and we have reported some things that are new to finance practice and that only a few companies are currently doing. As textbook authors we see these topics as suggesting possible changes in how finance defines itself as a field and in the ways finance is practiced. Accordingly, in this part of the chapter, we intentionally go well beyond simply reviewing what we have written earlier—we speculate about what may be emerging in the future.

Next we try to make clear a distinction we see between two aspects of financial managing: one that normally receives a great deal of attention in textbooks and research and one that does not. In making the distinction we even have had to invent some phrases because we cannot find this distinction written about in terminology we can use. We then look at changes that are occurring in the second of the two areas.

Finally, we close with a review of the value of the finance perspective, some dangers in using it, ideas on how to avoid the dangers, and thoughts about maintaining some humility about what the field of finance knows about financial managing and the world in which financial managing takes place.

Important Concepts in Financial Managing

Much of the content of this book is a report on the established insights of finance theory. In the section that follows, we summarize seven of the most important conclusions of finance theory and connect them to their appearance(s) in this text. We anticipate that each of these concepts will continue to be useful to Carrie and her co-workers for many years to come. They have been widely discussed in the finance literature, are widely taught in finance courses, and influence the day-to-day decisions of all financial managers. The seven concepts are: (1) the importance of cash flows, (2) time value as an evaluation tool, (3) the risk-return relationship, (4) perfect market learnings and the importance of market imperfections, (5) insights from financial economics, (6) the importance of stakeholder alignments, and (7) the value of options.

1. Importance of Cash Flows

A core concept in finance is that financial value depends upon cash flows. An investor who purchases a single asset, a share of a company, or an entire business exchanges cash today for anticipated cash in the future. This has two major implications.

Cash flows vs. accrual accounting One implication of the recognition that cash flows are the underpinnings of value is that accrual accounting numbers—income, asset values, book value, and so on—are the wrong numbers to use in financial valuation analysis. While financial accounting numbers can provide one useful picture of a company, their dependence on accrual accounting conventions means that they are not always consistent with cash flows. In 1987, this understanding led the Financial Accounting Standards Board, the rule-making body for financial accounting, to include a "statement of cash flows" as one of the required outputs of public financial reporting. In Chapter 4 we introduced the concept of cash flows as the basis for financial decision making and illustrated the dangers of using accrual accounting data.

Expectations vs. historical flows A second implication is that historical cash flows, such as those reported in financial statements and other accounting data do not contribute to financial value. It is future cash flows that matter. Historical information is useful only to the extent that it enables individuals to predict or improve future flows. Expectations of cash flows influence financial decisions. The importance of expectations and the corresponding lesser importance of historical data were discussed throughout the book, but particularly in Chapters 1 (Overview), 4 (Data), 6 (Interest Rates), 7 (Exchange Rates), 9 (Valuation), 11 (Capital Budgeting), 12 (Permanent Working Capital), 16 (Risk Management), and 18 (Planning).

Book value vs. market value Concerns about accrual accounting and historical flows have led finance theorists and practitioners to make the important distinction between book values and market values. Book values, the numbers on a company's accounting books that are made public on its financial statements, are historical in nature and contain the effects of accrual accounting. Market values, on the other hand, represent investors' evaluation of future cash flows and are the relevant measures for financial decision making.

2. Time Value as an Evaluation Tool

A corollary to the framework of cash flow analysis is the importance of time to the worth of those cash flows. In Chapter 5 we introduced the concept of time value: that the value of money depends not only on its amount but also on when it is paid or received. Since virtually all business exchanges involve paying (or receiving) cash now in return for receiving (or paying) cash later, it is impossible to evaluate financial opportunities without applying time value.

Chapter 5 presented the calculations for basic and some more-complex time value analyses and introduced the power of the financial calculator as an analytical aid. We then applied these time value concepts to some common financial analyses and decisions. In Chapter 9 we showed that the price of long-term securities can be modeled as the present value of the cash flows anticipated by investors. In Chapter 11 we used time value concepts to perform a cost-benefit analysis of the long-term investments available to a company; we extended the analysis to permanent working capital decisions in Chapter 12. Later, in Chapters 20 and 21, we used time value to understand debt instruments in more detail.

3. The Risk-Return Relationship

A third core concept of finance is that value depends on a tradeoff between returns and risk. It is not enough to estimate the amount and timing of future cash flows because not all anticipated cash flows are equally likely, hence equally desirable to investors. In Chapter 8 we introduced the concept of risk as the uncertainty of future cash flows. We identified investors as risk averters—requiring higher returns to assume greater risk.

Chapter 8 also contained an introduction to the statistical risk modeling commonly done in finance. For an asset held by itself—for example, a small business owned by an investor-manager without substantial other assets—the total risk model applied and risk could be measured by the standard deviation of returns. However, for an asset held in a portfolio, the relevant risk is the systematic risk, the incremental risk from adding that asset to the portfolio deriving from sources that impact all investments in the economy. Systematic risk is measured by an asset's beta, the relationship of its returns to those from the overall market. These powerful concepts of portfolio risk are summarized in the capital asset pricing model.

The importance of risk to value appears elsewhere in the book as well. In Chapter 6, we saw from the Fisher model that risk enters the determination of every interest rate. In Chapter 10, we showed how a company's cost of capital—the composite rate it must earn on an investment to justify raising the funds—depends on the risks its investors are asked to take: the risk of the assets the company is investing in compounded by the risk of the financial instruments they hold. In later chapters we saw that the financial industry has developed a full set of tools for reducing risks by shifting them to individuals and organizations better able to assume them. Chapter 16 introduced hedging tools—forward contracts, futures, and options on interest rates, currencies, and the timing of cash flows. In Chapter 21, we looked at caps, floors, collars, and swaps—devices for reducing the risk of intermediate- and long-term floating-rate debt. Equity options were examined in Chapter 22.

4. Perfect Market Learnings and the Importance of Market Imperfections

A particularly fruitful line of finance research has come from the analysis of perfect markets, markets with complete and fully shared information, universal and equal access to borrowing and lending, and no taxes or transactions costs. In such perfect markets, several decisions of financial managers, which seem on the surface to be of critical importance, become irrelevant to the value of the firm. In particular, in Chapter 15 and Chapter 17 we highlighted the work of Professors Modigliani and Miller who showed that if markets were perfect, a company's debt/equity mix and dividend decisions would not change its value.

It is the imperfections in financial markets that create opportunities for adding value. In these realistic markets, some companies have the opportunity to act on better information than their competitors. Others have superior access to resources. Still other companies can structure their activities to reduce tax obligations and other operating costs. Investors in imperfect markets cannot always substitute their own financing activities for those of corporations and, in contrast to MM's perfect-market conclusions, are no longer indifferent to corporate financing activity.

Since it is the imperfections in financial markets that make many investment and financing choices meaningful, financial managers have learned to focus their attention on imperfections rather than those market conditions that approach economic perfection.

5. Insights from Financial Economics

Several financial economic concepts play a vitally important role in finance thought and action. In Chapter 6 we discussed the model of interest rates developed by Professor Irving Fisher. That model demonstrated that interest rates are critically dependent on anticipated inflation and risk; it also provided a valuable framework for many subsequent analyses. In Chapter 7, we looked at foreign exchange relationships—purchasing power parity, the international Fisher effect, interest rate parity—and discovered important relationships among currencies and between spot and forward exchange rates.

In both Chapters 6 and 7, we saw how financial markets tend toward an equilibrium that unifies interest rates and exchange rates. The opportunity to profit from arbitrage when rates are not in equilibrium is a powerful force which prevents out-of-equilibrium rates from existing for very long. It is foolhardy to do financial analysis without assuming that interest rates, spot exchange rates, and near-term forward exchange rates are in equilibrium.

6. Importance of Stakeholder Alignments

Agency theory, as noted in Chapter 2, has provided a powerful way to examine a major issue in finance theory—the need to establish alignments between the organization and its various stakeholders. In corporations where ownership and management are separated, the interests of managers and shareholders are not always the same. Managers have many ways to enrich themselves and other stakeholders at the expense of shareholders, thus violating their implicit responsibility as agents to their shareholder-principals.

Agency theory was framed initially in terms of conflicts of interests between professional managers and shareholders. However, it can be looked at as raising a more encompassing and more important issue—the requirement to create ways of aligning and balancing the needs and interests of all stakeholders of the organization. The legal system origin of agency theory has not encouraged either this larger view nor has it emphasized the positive potential of seeking such alignments. So far, discussions of the "agency problem" have emphasized the abuses arising from manager-shareholder conflicts. Suggested solutions have tended to emphasize either legalistic, contractual ways to restrain self-interested managers from exploiting shareholders, or economic incentives in an attempt to ensure that shareholders benefit from managers' self-interest. Finance theory is likely to continue to address the importance of seeking stakeholder alignments and is likely to broaden the scope and creativity of its analysis and possible solutions.

7. The Value of Options

It is difficult to look very long at finance opportunities without finding options embedded in them, either explicitly or in some implicit form. Once a sleepy backwater of financial activity, options jumped to front and center with the development of the option pricing model by Professors Black and Scholes. Today the discovery and explicit valuation of options is a major part of financial analysis.

In Chapter 9 we introduced options and we presented the Black-Scholes model in detail in Appendix 9A; however, options appear in many places throughout this book. Call options on bonds were introduced in Chapter 6 and were considered in more detail in Chapter 21 and Appendix 21C as part of a bond refunding analysis. In Chapter 11 we discussed real options in capital budgeting, such as the ability to abandon a previously accepted project or the ability to move forward on another opportunity because of the learnings from the project under consideration. In Chapter 16 we considered the use of interest rate and foreign currency options as devices to hedge the risks of day-to-day financial activities. In Chapter 22 we looked at warrants and convertible bonds, call options on corporate equity.

Changes in Finance Theory

In this section, we look at three sets of forces that lead to the continual evolution of finance theory, identify three sources of change we have emphasized in this book, and then speculate on possible changes in finance theory that might come from these forces.

1. Three Sets of Forces for Change

Finance theory is like all other theory—subject to change and evolution—and it is changing in many ways for many reasons. Some new theory is coming from academic researchers who are using logical and mathematical tools to find relationships that have not been seen before or to disprove relationships previously thought to hold. Other new theory is coming from researchers who study financial practice and synthesize and explain what they observe.

Three sets of forces that have led to changes in finance theory in the past are likely to lead to additional changes in the future. These are: (1) changes in the environment in which finance is practiced, (2) new discoveries within the framework of existing finance theory, and (3) the adoption of insights from other fields into finance theory.

Environmental changes Changes in the environment in which finance is practiced bring new issues onto the agenda of financial managers and onto the plate of finance theory. As Figure 1.3 summarized, finance theory has regularly added new topics and insights and raised new issues for managers and scholars as the economy and technology have evolved. For example, in Chapter 16 we discussed how the increasing volatility of interest rates and exchange rates led to the need for and a proliferation of risk management techniques and products.

Discoveries in finance Discoveries within the framework of existing finance theory lead to adjusting, refining, and even overthrowing existing theoretical formulations. For example, the theory of the debt-equity mix, presented in Chapter 15, has changed dramatically over the past 40 years from the traditional theory of Durand, to the perfect market theory of Modigliani and Miller, to the market imperfection theories of today—and yet we still have much to learn. The continual testing of theory against data that is the heart of the scientific process supports some theories and not others, leading to further changes in finance theory.

Borrowing insights Borrowing from other fields also contributes greatly to finance—just as it does to all fields. Much of finance theory comes from economics, particularly those parts dealing with markets and incremental and optimization decision making. Portfolio theory has its roots in statistics. In deriving the option pricing model, Black and Scholes used an equation well known in physics. Many of the concepts of agency theory, including the name itself, derive from the field of law.

2. Three Important Sources of Change

In this book we have emphasized the impacts on financial theory and practice arising from three sources: changes brought about by the increasing globalization of business, changes brought about by revolutionary rates of quality improvement, and changes brought about by the borrowing (adopting) of quality-management practices by financial managers. All of these are hinted at in the phrase *the global quality revolution.*

In paying particular attention to the worldwide changes in management practice that we call *the global quality revolution,* we do not rest on uncontested ground. The concept of a quality revolution is not universally accepted. As the cartoon indicates, for many individuals the jury is still out on the value of quality management. Many believe it is just one more management fad, likely to pass away after a short period of attention.

In Chapters 3 and 13 we provided brief descriptions of the management technology we believe is fueling the global quality revolution. There are a great many other ways in which these changes can be described, such as a "new theory of management," the "end of the Taylor system of management," a new management "paradigm," "fourth-generation management," and "the quality imperative."[1] We believe all these interpretations are describing the same basic phenomenon and that they all are more striking in their similarities than in their differences.

---

[1] **References:** W. Edwards Deming, *Out of the Crisis* (Cambridge, Mass.: MIT Center for Advanced Management Studies, 1986); Joseph M. Juran, "The Upcoming Century of Quality" (Keynote speech at the 1984 ASQC Annual Quality Congress, May 24, 1994); Joel Barker, *Paradigms: The Business of Discovering the Future* (New York: Harper Business, 1993); Brian Joiner, *Fourth Generation Management: The Business Consciousness* (New York: McGraw-Hill, 1993); Myron Tribus and Yoshikazu Tsuda, *The Quality Imperative in the New Economic Era* (Cambridge, Mass.: MIT Center for Advanced Management Studies, August 1985).

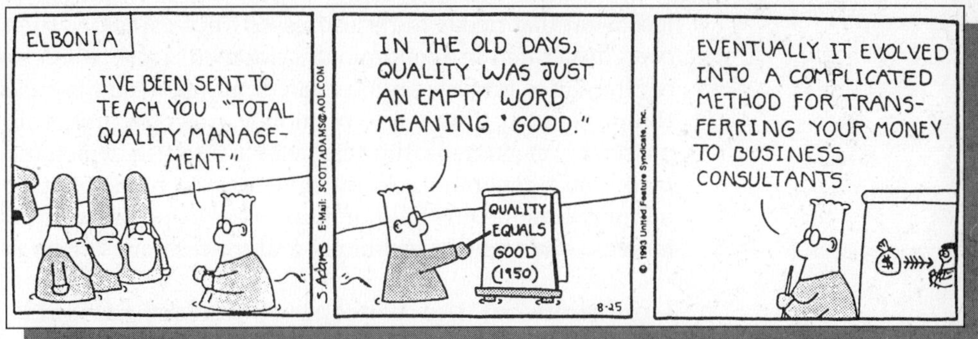

3. Possible Changes in Well-Established Finance Concepts

As we have indicated throughout this book, these global competitive developments seem to be changing the practice of corporate finance in a number of ways. And, as practice changes, finance theory is also likely to change, although what those changes will be is not clear. Five areas of possible change relate to: (1) the purpose(s) of the firm, (2) agency theory, (3) time value of money, (4) the theory of perfect and imperfect markets, and (5) option theory.

The purpose(s) of the firm As we discussed in Chapter 2, defining the purpose of the firm as the maximizing of share price has been a very attractive simplification for analytical finance theory for many years. However, like every theoretical concept in the social sciences, it is not in any sense an ultimate truth—nor is it an indispensable piece of finance theory. It is a simplification of a complex set of relationships, a value judgment, and a view of the world that carries significant risks with its advantages. The continuing global competitive successes of companies apparently pursuing alternative purposes seem to be reducing the advantages of this simplification and calling for new attempts to integrate the valuable insights of this perspective with alternate and often broader views of the purposes of all organizations.

Rethinking agency theory As we also noted in Chapter 2, agency theory is in a very similar situation. It is a powerful and useful framing, containing a major and important kernel of truth that is ripe for greater intellectual development and increased conceptual sophistication. One possible way of achieving a fuller contribution of the insights of agency theory is to shift from a relatively negative and competitive framing to a more positive and collaborative framing. In the coming years, finance theory may offer powerful insights and guidance to managers working to align the interests of all stakeholders.

Intergenerational implications of the timing of benefits and costs Money today is clearly worth more than the same amount of money tomorrow. However, it is not at all clear that social, environmental, political, or any other benefits are worth more today than tomorrow. Thus, any attempt to put monetary values on noncash items and then discount them to the present is a value judgment that needs to be addressed very explicitly. (Just such an approach has been used often in economic development work where social costs and benefits of alternative projects are translated into monetary terms and then discounted to the present.) If time value of money concepts are applied uncritically to non-monetary phenomena, they can lead to a selfish exploitation of future generations by our own generation. As the inventor and home of this powerful financial evaluation technique, the field of finance has a special responsibility for learning how to avoid abusing this technique and for teaching others to use it properly.

Limitations of the concept of perfect markets Financial markets are amazingly efficient in many respects. Like many other markets, they have proven to be very powerful disciplinarians of those who think they are smarter than the markets, those who feel they can fool them forever, or those who think that somehow the realities that drive the forces of supply and demand in those markets do not apply to them. However, the wisdom of financial markets can be exaggerated and may not capture every social value we assume they capture. In particular, we are asking an enormous amount from financial markets if we assume they respond quickly and accurately enough to be a useful guide to managerial decisions in the short run. In the coming years, finance theory may make rich discoveries about when and how financial markets are useful guides to financial and other managerial decisions and when they are not.

Using option theory and/or agency theory as vehicles for enriching finance theory The insights of both option theory and agency theory have the potential of breaking down some of the intellectual and conceptual barriers that separate finance theory from other theoretical approaches. Both option theory and agency theory contain behavioral aspects. They both look beyond the core valuation framework of finance theory to ask questions about when and how decisions should be made or are made in practice. These two areas are promising places to start integrating sophisticated behavioral perspectives into finance theory.

A Second Focus for Finance Theory

As we consider ways in which increased global competitiveness may be influencing the evolution of finance theory and practice, one observation stands out for us. The things finance theory historically has paid the most attention to seem more objective and analytical than subjective and behavioral. Finance theory seems to deal largely with *what* should be done in managing corporate finance—which decisions to make and the mathematical techniques for doing the analysis. Much less attention seems to be paid to *how* things should be done—how decisions should be made and how they should be carried into action. Let's try to illustrate this distinction.

1. What Vs. How

The first area encompasses many topics, including the value today of receiving $100 next year, the forward discount on pounds sterling in today's market, and the cost of capital for a particular firm. Some of these topics—like the present value of $100—are *relatively* simple, in the sense that they are factual, definitional, or involve only a few related assumptions or data. Others are more complex, involve more assumptions, and frequently require considerable amounts of data in their construction, like the cost of capital of a large, diversified firm. Whether fairly simple or fairly complex, these topics have a long and respected history in the field of finance and have usually carried a label such as *finance theory and decision making*. Research and conceptualization on topics such as these give managers a better sense of the workings of the financial environment and a better understanding of financial analytical techniques. It tells them what they *should* do in making decisions about a company's financial resources and what to expect in the financial markets important to those decisions. It has made many contributions to the successful management of organizations.

The second area focuses on how finance actually gets done in organizations. This area includes such topics as the factors that determine which approach to capital budgeting a particular firm chooses to use, how a firm chooses to manage its accounts payable function, how financial managers perceive and execute their role in a particular firm, and which data are collected to make financial decisions. Relative to finance theory and decision making, this aspect of finance has received scant attention from teachers and researchers in the field of finance, and it does not even have a widely accepted name to distinguish it from finance theory and decision making.

Although finance theory and research have focused almost exclusively on the first area, there is no reason why theory and research are not appropriate for the second area as well. In fact, the very modest attention paid so far to the second area makes it a particularly promising one for research contributions. For many organizations, major improvements in the practice of financial operations (translating theory and decisions into action) will make great contributions to organizational performance, contributions that may well match or exceed the benefits from increased conceptual understanding of financial frameworks, tools, and techniques.

analytical finance theory—theory about the factual nature of finance and what decisions should be made

operational finance theory—theory about how financial actions are taken in an organization

To call attention to the importance of finance theory for both of these areas of finance, we have chosen to call the first area **analytical finance theory** and the second **operational finance theory.** We are neither enchanted with nor wedded to those labels and expect better ones to emerge in the future. We use them for the present simply because we have not found in the literature widely accepted alternative labels that we could adopt in their place. In understanding and meeting the financial needs of organizations, both areas are important and both are necessary and appropriate fields of research, theory, and conceptualization by finance practitioners, researchers, and teachers.

2. Possible Important Concepts Related to Financial Operations

Although the operational theory of finance is not yet as developed as the analytical theory, at least five central concepts seem to be emerging. Each has influenced the writing of much of this book on financial managing. The concepts relate to: (1) internal and external customers, (2) quality, (3) business processes, (4) continuous improvement, and (5) stakeholders.

Internal and external customers The concept of finance's customers has appeared throughout this book. The logical application, that finance members can look at their work as "serving finance's customers," has been illustrated in virtually every chapter. This customer focus has been changing the ways in which finance members look at their jobs and how they do their work. It fits well with the changes described by Patrick J. Keating and Stephen F. Jablonsky in a series of studies of the changing roles of financial managers.[2]

Quality In many places, this book suggests that a broad definition of *financial quality* is emerging in the field of financial management. Although some people still think of financial quality largely in terms of the analytical sophistication of financial decisions or the lack of default risk in financial instruments, broader, more pervasive, and more dynamic definitions are coming into use. They include explicit recognition that finance's customers define quality financial work and that internal as well as external customers need to be served. They include the ideas of anticipating customer needs, exceeding expectations, and even delighting customers—not just meeting needs. They include providing finance's services more quickly—reducing cycle time. And they include "joy in work"—making finance people more fun to work with and finance work more fun for finance people to do.

Business processes In Chapters 13 and 14 we looked at the financial processes that exist in an organization. Because finance is so intimately involved in all parts of the company, much of finance's work is intertwined with the work of other organizational units. Said another way, many finance processes are really cross-functional business processes.

Chapter 13's key point about financial processes—that they *exist*—comes as a new insight to many finance professionals. Recognizing the existence of financial processes has not always been a part of the perspective of many financial managers. Chapter 14's key point about financial processes—that it is important that those processes be well managed—is becoming increasingly apparent to financial managers.

Continuous improvement In Chapter 14 we examined how financial and other business processes can be improved. The importance of "improving finance's processes" is the natural corollary of recognizing their existence and their importance to the organization's competitive success.

On the basis of the accumulating experience and successes of finance professionals, we can predict with some confidence that there soon will be considerable agreement about the usefulness of quality-management tools in financial operations. The tools of process planning, control, and improvement that have emerged from the global quality revolution apply to financial processes—just as to every other part of the organization. When finance people use process-improvement tools, either alone or in collaboration with other organizational members, they can

[2] **References:** Patrick J. Keating and Stephen F. Jablonsky, *Changing Roles of Financial Management: Getting Close to the Business* (Morristown, N.J.: Financial Executives Research Foundation, 1990) and Stephen F. Jablonsky, Patrick J. Keating, and James B. Heian, *Business Advocate or Corporate Policeman? Assessing Your Role as a Financial Executive* (Morristown, N.J.: Financial Executives Research Foundation, 1993).

add significant value to their companies. In the growing number of places where these tools are being used skillfully and appropriately, revolutionary rates of defect reduction, cycle time reduction, customer satisfaction improvement, and cost reduction are being achieved.[3]

Stakeholders In many places, this book also suggests that finance is coming to recognize that it has an important role to play in identifying and seeking to exceed the expectations of the organization's many stakeholders. Chapters 2 and 3 paid particular attention to this possibility. Many financial managers who once held the view that finance has a special obligation to serve only one stakeholder—the owners of equity shares—are coming to see that serving all stakeholders is often a superior way to serve the company's shareholders.

Changes in Financial Practice

To explore ways in which global competitive developments may be changing financial practice, we continue to focus our attention on possible changes arising from using customer-focused quality-management approaches. Returning to the final words of Chapter 1, we will expand the start, continue, stop questions into four pieces: "What's new in financial practice as finance functions adopt quality-management approaches?" "What continues to be done but in new ways?" "What continues to be done in well-established ways?" and "What is no longer done?"

Figures 23.1 to 23.4 suggest some possible answers to those questions. However, one early warning about Figures 23.1 to 23.4: the suggestions in these figures and the accompanying text must be considered to be very tentative. These questions are just starting to be asked, and the field of finance knows very little about the

FIGURE 23.1
What's new. Examples of activities that are new to financial practice as finance functions adopt quality-management approaches.

Some Examples – What's New

- Using quality-management tools in finance
- Conducting team-based improvements of finance processes
- Competitive benchmarking in financial processes and by finance
- Developing, collecting, and reporting new financial measures
- "Distributing" financial activities and functions to nonfinancial people

[3] **Reference:** James A.F. Stoner and Frank M. Werner, *Managing Finance for Quality: Bottom-Line Results from Top-Level Commitment* (Milwaukee: Quality Press, and Morristown, NJ: Financial Executives Research Foundation, 1994).

answers. And, as we will argue at the very end of this chapter, there are a variety of reasons why even the few things we might *think* we know may be inaccurate.

1. What's New in Financial Practice?

Adoption of systematic quality-management practices brings with it the use of all of the tools of quality management introduced in Chapters 3 and 14. The quantitative and analytical tools, such as run charts, control charts, Pareto charts, and cause and effect diagrams, are as useful in finance as anywhere else in the organization. And because of the "numerical literacy" of most finance people, these tools are often grasped quickly and enthusiastically.

The behavioral tools, such as task force management approaches, quality-improvement teams, nominal group technique, and active listening, are also useful in financial managing as are the techniques of competitive benchmarking. The behavioral tools may be more difficult for many finance members to master than the quantitative /analytical ones because of the preference of many finance members for the "hard" side of management versus the "soft" side. However, this greater difficulty of mastering the "soft tools" of quality management is not unique to finance. David Kearns, ex-CEO and chairman of the board of Xerox, has echoed many other quality champions in noting that, for many people, "the hard stuff is easy and the soft stuff is hard."

Competitive benchmarking for financial and other organizational processes also comes naturally to many finance members because of its large analytical component. It is attractive to finance members because of its superiority to a somewhat similar process, the comparing of elements of organizational performance against the average of comparable companies. Competitive benchmarking stimulates strong organizations to new initiatives by revealing how far they lag behind the very best practices; comparisons against averages run the risk of encouraging complacency in organizations that are near or above average.

Developing, collecting, and reporting new measures to capture key success factors that are not captured in existing financial measures are a challenge both to companies and to the field of finance as a whole. The greatest progress in this field, as in many others, is occurring in companies that are working to align their reward systems with their emerging quality-management systems.

The empowerment and increased training that are part of systematic quality management support and encourage aggressive efforts of finance members to train nonfinancial members in the tools and skills of financial analysis. These efforts include the development of new computer programs for doing financial analysis. Together, these efforts to "distribute" financial tools, skills, and capabilities resemble the "distributed data processing" phenomenon occurring with personal computers and other technological changes in information systems and practices.

2. What's Done Differently?

The first three activities shown in Figure 23.2—planning and budgeting, capital project analysis, and measuring the performance of the total organization—are long-established financial processes which, in some leading companies, are being

Some Examples – What's Done Differently

- Planning and budgeting
- Capital project analysis
- Measuring contributions and performance of the total organization
- Measuring and publicly reporting finance's performance in quality-management terms (e.g. SQIs, KRIs, KPIs)
- Working with finance's external and internal suppliers and customers

FIGURE 23.2
What's done differently. Examples of financial activities that are done differently as finance functions adopt quality-management approaches.

performed at least somewhat differently from the ways they were in the past. Examples of such changes are given in Chapters 4, 11, and 18, and each was the result of using the tools of quality management to perform well-established financial practices more effectively and more efficiently.

Corning Incorporated's Treasury KRIs (key results indicators) in Chapter 4 is an example of the new steps taken to measure and report finance's performance within the corporation and even to outsiders.

Finance organizations are also beginning to frame and treat the people and organizations with which they work as "customers." In Chapter 3, we noted the framing of all relationships, both inside and outside the organization, as customer/supplier alignments. Doing so improves communication and reduces unnecessary work and rework. It also leads to reductions in operating costs and increases in profitability that are sometimes quite dramatic.

3. What's Done the Same?

As Figure 23.3 indicates, not everything in financial practice is changing as a result of developments in global competitiveness. To the contrary, many financial activities do not seem to be changing appreciably. A large number of financial analyses are performed today much as they were 20 or more years ago. Cost of capital calculations, financing mix analyses, and dividend policy seem to be relatively unchanged. It is difficult to predict the future of these activities as finance functions gain in mastery of modern quality-management approaches and as those approaches themselves evolve and change. The quality revolution is still very new in American business and even newer in corporate finance, so the future may yield much greater impact on finance than can be seen today. But, at present, changes in these areas, if there are any at all, are much more difficult to detect than in the others.

Some Examples – What's Done the Same

- Analytical techniques:
  - Marginal analysis
  - Break-even
  - Cash flows
  - Time value of money
- Interest rate, foreign-exchange analysis
- Most aspects of risk analysis
- Stock and bond evaluation
- Cost of capital calculation
- Financing mix analysis
- Hedging liability exposure–domestically and internationally
- Dividend policy
- Most aspects of financing and the use of financial instruments:
  - Acquiring and granting short-term credit
  - Acquiring, servicing, and retiring long-term debt and equity
  - Issuing and investing in contingent claims and derivatives

FIGURE 23.3
What's done the same. Examples of financial activities that do not appear to be changing appreciably—at least at present—as finance functions adopt quality-management approaches.

4. What's No Longer Done?

A major contribution of quality-management approaches involves uncovering nonvalue-added activities that can be eliminated. Figure 23.4 suggests two areas where some finance functions have eliminated activities or changed attitudes and behaviors. When finance takes a customer-serving approach to its relationships with internal and external customers and suppliers, an early question is "What do you need from me and why?" The answers frequently reveal that finance toils to produce reports and analyses not really needed in the form provided—or not needed in any form. In a similar way, cycle time and defect-reducing projects of-

FIGURE 23.4
What's no longer done. Examples of financial activities that are done much less frequently as finance functions adopt quality-management approaches.

Some Examples – What's No Longer Done

- Nonvalue-added activities:
  - Some standardized widely distributed reports
  - Many inspections–reviewing and summarizing the work of others for the next level up
- Finance as the "only adults in the company" (police, judge, inspector)

ten remove multiple steps from financial and cross-functional processes: removing inspections, analyses, reports, rework, and other nonvalue-added work.

The shift in roles of finance members to more collaborative, team-based partnerships with other organizational members has also eliminated many aspects of the police, judge, and inspector roles of finance.

So What? Benefits and Dangers of the Financial Perspective

And now we come to Carrie's last question: "So what?" We take her question considerably further than merely the implications of these changes for financial practice, and we take it in three pieces. First, we look at the benefits of the financial perspective as presented in this book (and essentially in all other finance texts). What special contributions will you bring to an organization when you put your financial manager's hat on? Second, we look at the dangers that accompany finance thinking, what unintended consequences might flow from the approaches and analyses used in the name of finance. And third, we suggest ways to capture the benefits of the financial perspective without being ensnared by the dangers. Naturally, we are pretty positive about what finance has to contribute—it is inconceivable to us that a modern company could be run without drawing heavily on the contributions of finance theory. However, we do not feel that the financial perspective, or the perspective on any single discipline or philosophy for that matter, can be embraced without careful regard for possible blind spots it may encourage.

1. Benefits—Finance Thinking as a Useful Mindset

The finance perspective—looking at the money flows through an organization with an eye toward shareholder value—has proven to be a particularly valuable perspective for managers, investors, and analysts of organizational performance. The value of this perspective comes from at least five sources: (1) focus, (2) tools and concepts, (3) a big, integrated picture, (4) wide acceptance, and (5) separation of signal from noise.

Focus The finance perspective is grounded in a fundamental truth which gives focus to managerial actions: all organizations need to achieve a balance among their money flows in both the longer and the shorter terms. For businesses this need for balance is immediate and obvious, but it also applies to not-for-profit organizations and even to governments. Ongoing surpluses in funds flows are associated with short-term organizational health and long-term survival; ongoing deficits are associated with crisis and termination. An obvious and major contribution of the financial perspective is its call to managers to take explicit account of the impact of business decisions on the financial health of the organization.

Tools and concepts This first benefit is made real by the second, a set of tools and concepts to analyze the financial implications of organizational actions.

Big, integrated picture The financial perspective provides a big, integrated picture of the organization that enables us to capture the enormous complexity of its many activities in a small group of numbers. Perhaps the most widely reported is net income, but other accounting numbers such as return on assets and earnings per share, and cash-flow-based numbers such as net cash from operations and net present value are also recognized as valuable "integrators" of the organization's performance. Analytical finance theory argues that summary numbers such as these are effective in capturing the most important activities of an organization, providing a powerful merging and netting out of a wide range of managerial behavior. Nobel laureate in economics Milton Friedman has made perhaps the most famous argument about the value of one of these measures, net economic profit. He has concluded that corporate profit captures so many of the benefits of an organization's impact on society that it provides a safe and uniquely correct measure of those benefits. In this view, the only social responsibility of managers is to maximize profit.[4]

Widely accepted The finance perspective is widely accepted. Many people have learned to think very comfortably in terms of budgets, revenues, expenses, and time value of money. The financial perspective provides a language for communicating within and about organizations.

Signal from noise Like any useful framework or theory, the finance perspective enables us to separate what is important from what is not—to separate the "signal" from the "noise," to use Professor Stewart Myers's terms.[5] In one of its boldest manifestations, analytical finance theory has concluded that data and actions that impact share price are important—the true signals—and those that do not are simply noise.

2. Dangers of Using the Finance Perspective Carelessly

As valuable as the finance perspective is, its use is not without danger. At least three sources of danger exist: (1) expecting too much from analytical finance theory, (2) acting as though the financial perspective is the only important one, (3) acting as though it is always a complete and accurate one.

Expecting too much It is possible to ask too much from analytical finance theory. The benefits of the focus and tools described above can be carried to extremes, such as suggesting that managers make moment-by-moment managerial decisions to maximize moment-by-moment share price. Thus, omniscient financial markets enable managers to choose among alternative courses of action by selecting the one that will increase share price the most today. This *reductio ad absurdum* of analytical finance theory is based upon a misconception of the research findings that financial markets are remarkably efficient in the short term. The research has shown that for widely followed stocks public information is im-

[4] **Reference:** Milton Friedman, *Capitalism and Freedom* (Chicago: Univ. of Chicago Press, 1963), p. 133.

[5] **Reference:** Stewart Myers, "The Evaluation of an Acquisition Target," in Joel M. Stern and Donald H. Chew Jr., ed., *The Revolution in Corporate Finance* (New York: Basil Blackwell, 1986), p. 394.

"Our new young MBAs really lend a tone. But dammit, what do they mean by 'reductio ad absurdum'?"

pounded into stock prices very quickly. But not all stocks are widely followed, nor is all information bearing on a company's worth necessarily public—making it incorrect to conclude that a company's stock price accurately captures its value in real time.

This distortion of valuable financial insights is directly contrary to the experience of most managers we have spoken to, who believe they are regularly faced with the choice between decisions with differing shorter- versus longer-run impacts on organizational performance (and share price.) These managers believe they know ways they can make their own and the organization's performance look better for a day or a week or month or even a year or two before the piper has to be paid. Contrary to the predictions of agency theory, they believe that one of their major challenges is to avoid unwise, self-serving decisions that benefit them in the short run and harm the organization and its stakeholders in the longer run. To the extent that analytical finance theory appears to urge managers to focus on today's share price, it both misses an opportunity to contribute and does a significant disservice to the practice of management.

Only important perspective Because financial losses can eventually lead to the end of any organization, the big financial picture of the company may be mistaken for the only one that matters. James B. Stewart's description of the very public fall of the investment banking firm Drexel, Burnham, Lambert at the end of the 1980s repeatedly calls attention to top management's unwillingness to uncover and correct the questionable practices of Michael Milken's incredibly profitable Beverly Hills junk bond operation. Top management was so mesmerized by the financial success of Milken and his group that it allowed them to pile one questionable practice upon another until illegal acts became so blatant and so extensive that they eventually destroyed the entire company.[6]

Complete and accurate perspective The financial perspective is never a complete picture of the organization, and it is not even always an accurate one. As David Halberstam reports in *The Reckoning,* his study of the American and Japanese automobile industries, the deep competitive hole the American auto industry made for itself in the 1950s through the 1970s was dug with shovels that seemed to be unearthing endless lodes of gold. Record operating profits and high share prices masked deteriorating product quality, declining customer satisfaction, inefficient management practices, poor industrial relations, and steady market share incursions by Japanese and other competitors. During this period, Ford's financial and analytical "whiz kid," Robert McNamara, first played the role of hero and then the role of villain. His heroic role involved bringing badly needed financial discipline to a company whose finances were in disarray, building sophistication and talent into Ford's finance function, and increasing its influence in business decision making. The role of villain arose from too much of a good thing: the finance function's growing dominance over company decisions, even product and manufacturing decisions. As David Halberstam noted, "The coming of McNamara to the Ford Motor Company, his protege Lee Iacocca once said, was one of the best things that ever happened to the company, and his leaving it, Iacocca added, was also one of the best things that ever happened."[7]

3. Capturing the Benefits Without Being Captured by the Dangers

Financial managers are widely recognized as key players in bringing the benefits of the financial perspective to their organizations. However, they are also well placed to protect their organizations from being captured by the dangers of the financial perspective. Unfortunately, their training may make them slow to see this second opportunity and may cause them to increase the dangers by pushing too aggressively for the use of financial perspectives at the expense of others. Four things they can do to avoid those dangers relate to: (1) multiple perspectives, (2) nonfinancial factors, (3) serving multiple stakeholders, and (4) work styles.

Multiple perspectives Finance is in a strong position to support other organizational functions and other managers in insisting that a variety of framings or perspectives be used on an on-going basis: that customer satisfaction be emphasized, that investments in the organization's human resources be sustained and increased, that continuous quality improvements be given high priority, and that progressively higher ethical standards be sought and achieved. Insisting that increased profits, increased shareholder value, or other financial measures be pur-

---

[6] **Reference:** James B. Stewart, *Den of Thieves* (New York: Simon and Schuster, 1991). See also: Jesse Kornbluth, *Highly Confident: The Crime and Punishment of Michael Milken* (New York: William Morrow, 1992).

[7] **Reference:** David Halberstam, *The Reckoning* (New York: William Morrow, 1986), (p.207 in Avon paperback edition).

sued in concert with these other goals rather than in conflict with them reduces the danger that the financial perspective will become an excuse for what later turn out to be very bad business decisions.

Measuring nonfinancial dimensions Finance has a well-established role in collecting the numbers and defining and calculating the scorecard by which organizational and unit performance are measured. This traditional role puts it in the ideal position to add new, nontraditional measures to that scorecard and to play a leading role in collecting and reporting those numbers. Finance members are well placed to be key players in doing the conceptual and intellectual work required to figure out how to measure the frequently soft and qualitative dimensions that are not caught in traditional financial measures.

Serving all stakeholders Finance traditionally has played the role of and been seen as the guardian of shareholder interests—the police officers in the company, making certain that corporate members do not neglect their obligations to the company's owners. From this historical position finance is particularly well placed to insist that the interests of all stakeholders be kept in mind and that all members of the organization are just as responsible as finance for safeguarding organizational assets and the interests of all stakeholders.

Modeling the new organizational style Finance's traditional roles have not always supported collaborative, team-based working methods. To the extent that finance has perceived the shareholder as its prime or only customer, finance has been tempted to downplay the arguments of other organizational units advocating the needs of other stakeholder groups. When finance members use collaborative, team-based, customer-focused work styles, they set an example that is noticed throughout the organization.

The Appropriateness of Humility—Some Closing Thoughts

Finance provides a very powerful way of looking at organizations, and the tools of financial analysis are key tools for managing those organizations. Financial officers play important roles in making things happen, as well as figuring out afterwards what actually did happen. So, it is very tempting to be confident and proud of the power of the finance perspective. While that confidence and feeling of power are appropriate, there are also at least three reasons for tempering those feelings with some modesty and intellectual caution—or even a healthy dose of humility.

First, although many current theories of finance have held up well, it is in the very nature of theories to be replaced. It is normal for newer theories to replace older ones. What we know to be true today will very likely no longer be true in the future—either because the situation will have changed or because new insights will have taught us that what we thought we knew to be true never was true. Ewald Nyquist, former chancellor of the board of education of the state of New York, expressed this concern eloquently in a commencement address when he told the graduating class, "I'm convinced that half of everything I say to students is false. The problem is that I don't know which half!"

Second, even our best theories are partial in scope and limited in applicability. All theories, and thus all knowledge, are based upon enormous simplifications of reality, so what we "know" is always limited and partial.

However, the third reason is in may ways the most important. During a period of major change of the kind we appear to be undergoing now, it is particularly difficult to know what is really happening and why. A time of major change is a time of replacement of a whole network of theories, an entire reframing of the way we look at the relevant part of the world. During such times, major errors of interpretation and prediction are particularly likely. For example, throughout the 1960s and 1970s most American business leaders and academics completely misinterpreted the early stages of the global quality revolution. Initially they believed the Japanese were not producing high-quality goods but rather that they were producing low-quality goods with cheap labor and selling them below cost overseas to buy market share. Later they accepted that Japan actually was producing high-quality goods but by a unique national and culture-based management system unavailable to the West—"Japanese management." Only in the 1980s did many American observers discover that Japanese companies were adopting a new way of managing more rapidly than companies elsewhere and were reaping the competitive benefits. Those early mistakes may seem almost ridiculous today, but they were not so illogical at the time—and a few still make them.

Ultimately, the major changes in management methods and global competitive patterns that are occurring provide the possibility for great contributions by those who see the newly emerging world more accurately and ahead of others. Leadership involves discovering what we do not yet know and applying it before it becomes conventional wisdom. Great opportunities come from worlds in flux; great contributions come from those who can combine the timeless basics and newly emerging framings, approaches, and tools.

Carrie Finch looked around the table and smiled. "These last four days have been an outstanding experience," she said. "It was great to work with the five of you."

Carrie and the other members of her seminar group were at a restaurant two blocks from the hotel where the seminar had been held. They had become close during the past four days, and had eagerly agreed to go to dinner together to celebrate the end of their experience.

Carrie continued exuberantly, "This was a special week for me. Of course, you five are a good part of what made it so special. But there was so much more. During this week, I got the chance to review finance theory and practice. It was a good feeling to realize how much I remembered, and it was fascinating to see how much the field has evolved in just the past ten years. Of course, the big eye-opener for me was how finance practice is changing. I never thought of it in terms of analytical and operational finance, but that seems to capture a distinction I was sure existed but never could explain. And while I guess we've made some progress in improving our financial operations around the office, the things the speakers told us about what other companies are doing was just wonderful. Also, now I think I understand a little more about what is causing all these changes, especially how much is coming from the globalization of business and the new management systems of quality and continuous improvement. My goodness! Until this week, I never even connected the words *continuous improvement* to finance work."

Carrie paused, and the others picked up the conversation, sharing their feelings about what they had learned. There was a general consensus that the seminar had been very worthwhile. When it was Carrie's turn to speak again, she was quieter and more thoughtful. "This afternoon, my last question was 'So what? Why do we care about the changes in financial managing?' It wasn't all that clear to me then, but it's a lot clearer now. I think we're really lucky. We're at the right place at the right time. The changes in financial managing we talked about are giving us the knowledge and tools to make a big difference in our careers and for our company."

Carrie picked up her glass and raised it in the air. "I want to make a toast," she said. "To us. There are few things better than being with friends like you and knowing we can make a difference."

Summary of Key Points

- **Understand why we wrote this chapter the way we did.** Finance, like all disciplines, continues to experience continuity and change. We see this last chapter as an opportunity to share our thoughts about what is known in financial managing and what is less well known. It gives us the chance to review key financial managing concepts that we believe will endure (continuity) and speculate on where financial managing research and practice might be heading (change).
- **Summarize seven central concepts of financial managing.** Seven central concepts in the analytical theory of corporate finance are: (1) the importance of cash flows, (2) the time value of money as an evaluation tool, (3) the significance of risk in determining value, (4) the necessity to study perfect markets to understand the meaning of market imperfections, (5) the market equilibrium insights from financial economics, (6) the importance of stakeholder alignment which traditionally has been characterized as the problem of principal-agent conflicts, and (7) the value of financial and other options.
- **Identify three possible forces for change in finance theory and discuss five changes in important financial concepts that may be occurring as a result of changes in the global competitive environment and the evolution of financial thought.** Three forces that have led to changes in finance theory in the past and are likely to lead to additional changes in the future are changes in the environment in which finance is practiced, new discoveries within the framework of existing finance theory, and the adoption of insights from other fields into finance theory. The need to pursue multiple goals, the limitations of agency theory, the intergenerational implications of careless use of time value of money as an evaluation tool, the dangers of reading too much into the concept of perfect markets, and the possibility of using option theory and agency theory to enrich finance theory all may offer insights and guidance in the future considerably different from those of the past.
- **Distinguish between analytical and operational finance theory and summarize five central concepts in operational finance theory.** Analytical finance theory deals with the content of financial decision making, the ways in which markets operate, and the tools of financial analysis. It emphasizes how financial decisions *should* be made. Operational finance theory deals with the ways in which the financial operations of an organization are performed—particularly how finance's own productive processes are designed, executed, and improved—and *how* financial decisions are actually made (the behavioral processes of decision making). Five central concepts in the operational theory of financial practice are internal and external customers, business processes, quality, continuous improvement, and stakeholders.

- **Describe the area of financial practice that seems to be changing the most as a result of changes in the global competitive environment and the evolution of financial thought.** Although each of the five areas of financial practice discussed in this book appears to be changing, the greatest change may be occurring in the planning, using, and improving of financial processes. In connection with this increased focus on financial processes, the roles, attitudes, and actions of many financial practitioners are changing significantly. Finance members are becoming more like partners and less like judges and police officers in their day-to-day work. They are spending more time improving their own financial processes and working as team members to improve cross-functional processes.
- **Describe the benefits and dangers of using a financial perspective in thinking about business decisions and ways to avoid the dangers.** A financial perspective provides a simple integrated framework for the many complex costs and outcomes of business activities. It uses a language that is widely used and understood inside and outside the organization, and it emphasizes the fundamental importance of financial health for organizational survival. However, the financial picture of the company may be mistaken for the only framework important for managers to use, as a complete framework that captures all aspects of organizational performance, and as one based on full and accurate data. Four things financial managers can do to avoid the dangers are: (1) learning and supporting the use of multiple perspectives to guide organizational decisions, (2) measuring and reporting the organization's key nonfinancial dimensions, (3) looking for opportunities to serve multiple stakeholders, and (4) modeling modern, collaborative, team-based managerial styles.
- **Discuss three reasons for being humble about what we know about financial managing.** Our current theories very likely will be replaced. It is normal for newer theories to replace older ones. All theories, and thus all knowledge, are based upon enormous simplifications of reality, so even what we "know" is limited and partial. During a period of major change—a "shift of paradigms"—it is particularly difficult to know what is truly happening, making errors of interpretation and prediction particularly likely. Yet, even with this humility, it is important to remember that without theory there is no knowledge and that often we must take action—no matter how limited our knowledge.

Questions

1. What is the difference between analytical finance theory and operational finance theory?
2. Select any task done by financial people in an organization. Which portions of the task are best approached through analytical finance and which through operational finance?
3. Give five reasons why the finance mindset is valuable. What might happen to someone who attempted to address business issues without this mindset? Why?
4. Why might careless use of financial thinking lead to conclusions and actions that could be detrimental to an organization?
5. How can finance professionals reap the benefits of the finance perspective without falling into the potential traps?
6. Identify seven concepts that are central to analytical finance. Why is each so important to understand?
7. Identify five concepts that are central to operational finance. Why is each so important to understand?
8. Why are global competitive developments changing the practice of financial management? Identify five areas where this might be happening.
9. What's new in financial practice? Why?
10. What's done differently in financial practice? Why?
11. What's done the same in financial practice? Why?
12. What's no longer done in financial practice? Why?
13. Why do we feel the need to caution you about humility in thinking about and applying financial theory?

CASE

EDWARD LOWE

Edward Lowe ran out of the classroom building, threw his hands up in the air, and let out a big yell. "Well, that one's over with!" he said with a big smile. Turning to his buddies who had also taken the same final examination, he asked, "Howd'ya do? I've got a feeling I just aced that puppy!" Ed and his friends had just finished the introductory finance course at their university. "You know," Ed continued more thoughtfully, "When we started the course, I couldn't wait for it to end. But then the subject turned out to be really interesting. Now I'm sort of sorry its over. I really think finance is a subject I could spend a lot of time with—maybe even make a career out of. I just wish I had a sense of what I should be looking for as I continue to learn finance."

The friends decided to head for the cafeteria for a bite of lunch. After selecting their food and finding a table, Ed pulled out the university's course catalog. He searched for the finance offerings. "Hey guys, listen to this," he said. "There are plenty of additional finance courses we can take." A lively discussion of what to take next and the reputations of the different teachers ensued. As the course catalog was passed around the table, Ed and his friends discovered that at their school, advanced finance courses were grouped into five categories:

- corporate financial management
- investment analysis and portfolio management
- derivatives, including options and futures, and financial engineering
- financial markets and management of financial institutions
- real estate finance

The friends debated the different areas, the courses offered in each, and the career opportunities that might be waiting for them.

After lunch, Ed decided to see his finance professor for further advice. The professor grinned when he saw Ed at the office door. "So soon? Generally, students don't come in to discuss the final exam until at least a day has passed."

Ed smiled. "That's not why I'm here," he said earnestly. "Actually, I think I did very well on the exam. I really liked the course. In fact, that's what got me thinking. I'd like your advice on what finance courses to take next—on what to look for if I go on in finance."

"Have a seat," the professor offered. Together, they went over the catalog. The professor described the various courses and course sequences and the careers that each might lead to. "Most important, think of learning finance as a life-long affair. The field is constantly changing as the environment shifts, as new theoretical discoveries are made, and as practitioners discover better ways to do their jobs. That's one of the reasons finance is such an exciting field. I suspect you'll discover your problem is not having too little to choose from but rather not enough time to pursue all the good alternatives."

After some further discussion, Ed left the professor's office, feeling glad he had stopped in. He liked what he had heard and felt sure he wanted to study more finance. He tentatively made up his mind about which finance courses to register for in the next term. And he knew he would keep returning to his initial question, "What should I be looking for as I continue to learn finance?"

SUMMARY OF MATHEMATICAL RELATIONSHIPS

Numbers in parentheses refer to the chapter and page on which the definition appears, e.g., (5:6) means Chapter 5, page 6.

Chapter 4—Data for Financial Decision Making

1. Break-even point in units (4A:96)

$$Q_{be} = \frac{F}{P - V}$$

where: Q_{be} = break-even sales in units sold
F = fixed cost level
P = sales price per unit
V = variable production cost per unit

2. Break-even point in dollars (4A:96)

$$S_{be} = \frac{F}{1 - v}$$

where: S_{be} = break-even sales in dollars
F = fixed cost level
v = variable cost percentage

3. Basic du Pont relationship (4E:143)

Return on assets = net profit margin × total asset turnover

4. Extended du Pont relationship (4E:144)

$$\textit{Return on equity} = \textit{return on assets} \times \frac{\textit{assets}}{\textit{equity}}$$

Chapter 5—The Time Value of Money

1. Compound interest (5:154–155)

$$FV = PV(1 + r)^n$$

where: FV = future value
PV = present value
r = interest rate per period
n = number of time periods

2. Present value (5:160)

$$PV = \frac{FV}{(1 + r)^n}$$

where: PV = present value
FV = future value
r = interest rate per period
n = number of time periods

3. Future value of an annuity (5:167)

$$FV = PMT\left(\frac{(1 + r)^n - 1}{r}\right)$$

where: FV = future value
PMT = annuity amount
r = interest rate per period
n = number of time periods

4. Present value of an annuity (5:167)

$$PV = PMT\left(\frac{1 - \frac{1}{(1 + r)^n}}{r}\right)$$

where: PV = present value
PMT = annuity amount
r = interest rate per period
n = number of time periods

5. Growing cash stream (5:176)

$$PV = \frac{CF_1}{r - g}$$

where: PV = present value
CF_1 = first cash flow, one period past PV
r = interest rate per period
g = growth rate of cash flows

6. Perpetuity (5:177)

$$PV = \frac{PMT}{r}$$

where: PV = present value
PMT = annuity amount
r = interest rate per period

7. Effective interest rate (from nominal rate) (5:180)

$$Effective\ rate = \frac{nominal\ rate}{p}$$

where: p = number of times compounding takes place

8. Nominal interest rate (from effective rate) (5:182)

$$Nominal\ rate = effective\ rate \times p$$

where: p = number of times compounding takes place

9. Longer period effective rate (from shorter period effective rate) (5:182)

$$EPR_{longer\ period} = (1 + EPR_{shorter\ period})^{p} - 1$$

where: EPR = effective periodic rate
p = number of times compounding takes place

10. Shorter period effective rate (from longer period effective rate) (5:183)

$$EPR_{shorter\ period} = (1 + EPR_{longer\ period})^{1/p} - 1$$

where: EPR = effective periodic rate
p = number of times compounding takes place

11. Future value—continuous compounding (5A:190)

$$FV = PV \times e^{rt}$$

where: FV = future value
e = 2.718281828, a constant
r = interest rate per year prior to compounding
t = time measured in years

12. Effective periodic rate—continuous compounding (5A:190)

$$EPR = e^{rt} - 1$$

where: EPR = effective periodic rate
e = 2.718281828, a constant
r = interest rate per year prior to compounding
t = time measured in years

Chapter 6—Interest Rates

1. Fisher model of interest rates (6:206)

$$\textit{Nominal rate} = (1 + r_p)(1 + r_i)(1 + r_r) - 1$$

where:
r_p = pure rate of interest
r_i = inflation premium
r_r = risk premium

2. Real rate of interest (6:208)

$$\textit{Real rate} = (1 + r_p)(1 + r_r) - 1$$

where:
r_p = pure rate of interest
r_r = risk premium

3. Risk-free rate of interest (6:208)

$$\textit{Risk-free rate} = (1 + r_p)(1 + r_i) - 1$$

where:
r_p = pure rate of interest
r_i = inflation premium

4. Expectations hypothesis equilibrium (6:214)

$$(1 + r_N)^N = (1 + r_1)(1 + r_2)(1 + r_3) \ldots (1 + r_n)$$

where:
r_N = interest rate available today on an N-year security
r_1 = interest rate available today on a 1-year security
r_2 = interest rate forecasted for second year on a 1-year security
r_3 = interest rate forecasted for third year on a 1-year security
r_n = interest rate forecasted for n^{th} year on a 1-year security

Chapter 7—Exchange Rates

1. Forward discount or premium (7:240)

$$\textit{Forward discount or premium} = \frac{\textit{forward} - \textit{spot}}{\textit{spot}} \times \frac{12}{\textit{months forward}}$$

2. Daily percentage change in exchange rate (7:241)

$$\textbf{Daily percentage change} = \frac{\textbf{today's rate} - \textbf{yesterday's rate}}{\textbf{yesterday's rate}}$$

3. Interest rate parity (7:246)

$$\textit{Forward rate}_{\left(\frac{\textit{currency A}}{\textit{currency B}}\right)} = \textit{spot rate}_{\left(\frac{\textit{currency A}}{\textit{currency B}}\right)} \times \frac{1 + r_A}{1 + r_B}$$

where: r_A = interest rate in country (currency) A for the period of the forward rate
r_B = interest rate in country (currency) B for the period of the forward rate

Chapter 8—Risk

1. Expected value (8:270–271)

$$E(r) = \sum_i p_i \times r_i$$

where: E(r) = expected rate of return
Σ = summation operator
p_i = probability of ith forecasted rate of return
r_i = i^{th} forecasted rate of return

2. Variance and standard deviation (8:271–274)

$$\sigma^2(r) = \sum_i p_i[r_i - E(r)]^2$$

$$\sigma(r) = \sqrt{\sigma^2(r)}$$

where: σ^2(r) = variance of returns
Σ = summation operator
p_i = probability of ith forecasted rate of return
r_i = i^{th} forecasted rate of return
E(r) = expected rate of return
σ(r) = standard deviation of returns

3. Coefficient of variation (8:274–275)

$$\textit{Coefficient of variation} = \frac{\sigma(r)}{E(r)}$$

where: σ(r) = standard deviation of returns
E(r) = expected rate of return

4. Capital market line (CML) (8:276)

$$\textit{Required rate of return} = r_f + (\textit{price of total risk}) \times \sigma$$

where: r_f = risk-free rate of interest
σ = standard deviation of returns

5. Security market line (SML) (8:286)

$$\textit{Required rate of return} = r_f + (\textit{market price of risk}) \times \beta$$

$$= r_f + (r_m - r_f) \times \beta$$

where: r_f = risk-free rate of interest
β = relationship between investment's returns and market returns
r_m = required rate of return on the "market portfolio"

Chapter 9—Valuation

1. Traditional bond value (9:300)

$$\textit{Price of bond} = \textit{PV of interest annuity} + \textit{PV of face value}$$

$$= PMT\left(\frac{1 - \dfrac{1}{(1+r)^n}}{r}\right) + FV\left(\frac{1}{(1+r)^n}\right)$$

where: PMT = bond coupon
FV = face value
n = number of interest periods until the bond's maturity date
r = bond investors' required rate of return per interest period

2. Perpetual bond value (9:305)

$$\textit{Value} = PV = \frac{C}{r_b}$$

where: C = bond coupon
r_b = bond investors' required rate of return

3. Current yield from a bond (9:307)

$$\textit{Current yield} = \frac{\textit{periodic interest coupon}}{\textit{beginning-of-period market price}}$$

4. Capital gains yield from a bond (9:307)

$$\textit{Capital gains yield} = \frac{\textit{change in market price}}{\textit{beginning-of-period market price}}$$

5. Preferred stock value (9:311)

$$\textit{Value} = PV = \frac{D_p}{r_p}$$

where: D_p = preferred stock dividend
r_p = preferred stock investors' required rate of return

6. Preferred stock yield (9:312)

$$Yield = r_p = \frac{D_p}{market\ price}$$

where: D_p = preferred stock dividend

7. Common stock value (9:314)

$$Value = PV = \frac{D_1}{r_c - g}$$

where:

D_1 = investors' next anticipated dividend
r_c = common stock investors' required rate of return
g = investors' anticipated growth rate of dividends

8. Rate of return on common stock (9:317)

$$Rate\ of\ return = r_c = \frac{D_1}{stock\ price} + g$$

where:

D_1 = investors' next anticipated dividend
g = investors' anticipated growth rate of dividends

9. Black-Scholes option pricing model (9A:329–330)

$$C = SN(d_1) - \frac{E}{e^{rt}}N(d_2)$$

and:

$$d_1 = \frac{\ln\left(\frac{S}{E}\right) + \left(r + \frac{\sigma^2}{2}\right)t}{\sigma\sqrt{t}}$$

$$d_2 = \frac{\ln\left(\frac{S}{E}\right) + \left(r - \frac{\sigma^2}{2}\right)t}{\sigma\sqrt{t}} = d_1 - \sigma\sqrt{t}$$

where:

C = Call option price
S = Stock price
E = Exercise price of the option
e = 2.718281828, a constant
r = the annual risk-free interest rate
t = the time until expiration in years
σ^2 = the variance of the rate of return of the stock
N(d) = the cumulative standard normal probability function: the probability that a normally distributed random variable with mean of zero and standard deviation of 1 will be less than d

Chapter 10—The Cost of Capital

1. Break point (10:354)

$$\textit{Total new financing} = \frac{\textit{amount of money from each source}}{\textit{its proportion}}$$

Chapter 12—Permanent Working Capital

1. Definition of working capital (12:426)

$$\textit{Working capital} = \textit{current assets} - \textit{current liabilities}$$

2. Economic order quantity (EOQ) (12B:456)

$$EOQ = \sqrt{\frac{2SO}{C}}$$

where: EOQ = economic order quantity
S = annual usage or sales
O = ordering cost per order
C = carrying cost per unit per year

3. Orders per year using EOQ (12B:457)

$$\textit{Orders per year} = \frac{S}{EOQ}$$

where: EOQ = economic order quantity
S = annual usage or sales

4. Order frequency using EOQ (12B:457)

$$\textit{Order frequency} = \frac{360}{\textit{orders per year}}$$

Chapter 15—Leverage and the Debt-Equity Mix

1. Bottom half of the income statement (15:533, 15C:568)

$$EPS = \frac{(EBIT - \textit{interest}) \times (1 - \textit{tax rate})}{\textit{number of shares}}$$

where: EPS = earnings per share
EBIT = earnings before interest and taxes

2. Compromise (market imperfections) approach to the value of a firm with leverage (15:542)

$$V_{levered} = V_{unlevered} + CT - BC - AC$$

where:

$V_{levered}$ = the value of a firm with leverage
$V_{unlevered}$ = the value of the same firm if it had no debt financing
CT = the added value from the corporate tax effect
BC = the reduction in value from the bankrupty cost effect
AC = the reduction in value from the agency cost effect

3. Degree of operating leverage (DOL) (15B:557–559)

$$DOL = \frac{\text{percentage change to EBIT}}{\text{percentage change to sales}}$$

$$= \frac{Q(P - V)}{Q(P - V) - F} \quad or \quad \frac{\text{contribution}}{EBIT}$$

where:

Q = quantity of units produced and sold
P = price at which each unit is sold
V = variable production cost per unit
F = fixed cost level
EBIT = earnings before interest and taxes

4. Degree of financial leverage (DFL) (15:562–563)

$$DFL = \frac{\text{percentage change to EPS}}{\text{percentage change to EBIT}}$$

$$= \frac{EBIT}{EBIT - I} \quad or \quad \frac{EBIT}{\text{earnings before taxes}}$$

where:

EBIT = earnings before interest and taxes
I = interest expense

5. Degree of total leverage (DTL) (15B:564)

$$DTL = \frac{\text{contribution}}{\text{earnings before taxes}}$$

$$= DOL \times DFL$$

where:

DOL = degree of operating leverage
DFL = degree of financial leverage

6. Bottom half of the income statement with a preferred stock dividend (15C:568)

$$EPS = \frac{(EBIT - interest) \times (1 - tax\ rate) - D_p}{\text{number of shares}}$$

where: EPS = earnings per share
EBIT = earnings before interest and taxes
D_P = preferred dividend

7. Modigliani-Miller Proposition I without corporate income taxes—the value of a firm (15D:569)

$$V = \frac{EBIT}{k_{eU}}$$

where:
EBIT = earnings before interest and taxes
K_{eU} = cost of equity capital for an unlevered firm

8. Modigliani-Miller Proposition II without corporate income taxes—the cost of equity of a levered firm (15D:570)

$$k_{eL} = k_{eU} + (k_{eU} - k_d)\left(\frac{D}{E}\right)$$

where:
k_{eL} = cost of equity for a levered firm
k_{eU} = cost of equity capital for an unlevered firm
k_d = cost of debt
D = market value of the firm's debt
E = market value of the firm's equity

9. Modigliani-Miller Proposition I with corporate income taxes—the value of a firm (15D:570)

$$V = \frac{EBIT(1 - t)}{k_{eU}} + tD$$

where: EBIT = earnings before interest and taxes
t = the firm's tax rate
K_{eU} = cost of equity capital for an unlevered firm
D = market value of the firm's debt

10. Modigliani-Miller Proposition II with corporate income taxes—the cost of equity of a levered firm (15D:570)

$$k_{eL} = k_{eU} + (k_{eU} - k_d)(1 - t)\left(\frac{D}{E}\right)$$

where:
k_{eL} = cost of equity for a levered firm
k_{eU} = cost of equity capital for an unlevered firm
k_d = cost of debt
t = the firm's tax rate
D = market value of the firm's debt
E = market value of the firm's equity

11. The Miller personal tax model—value of an unlevered firm (15D:571)

$$V = \frac{EBIT(1 - t)(1 - t_e)}{k_{eU}}$$

where: EBIT = earnings before interest and taxes
t = the firm's tax rate
t_e = investors' average tax rate on dividends and capital gains from equity investments
K_{eU} = cost of equity capital for an unlevered firm

12. The Miller personal tax model—value of a levered firm (15D:571)

$$V = \frac{EBIT(1 - t)(1 - t_e)}{k_{eU}} + \left[1 - \frac{(1 - t)(1 - t_e)}{(1 - t_d)}\right]D$$

where: EBIT = earnings before interest and taxes
t = the firm's tax rate
t_e = investors' average tax rate on dividends and capital gains from equity investments
t_d = investors' tax rate on interest income from owning corporate debt
K_{eU} = cost of equity capital for an unlevered firm
D = market value of the firm's debt

13. Beta with leverage (15D:571–572)

$$\beta_L = \beta_U\left[1 + (1 - t)\left(\frac{D}{E}\right)\right]$$

where:
β_L = beta of a levered firm
β_U = beta of an unlevered firm
t = the firm's tax rate
D = market value of the firm's debt
E = market value of the firm's equity

Chapter 16—Risk Management and Temporary Working Capital

1. Baumol cash-securities transfer model (16A:604)

$$Z = \sqrt{\frac{2NF}{i}}$$

where:
Z = the cash balance return (zero) point
N = annual cash need
F = fixed cost of each cash-securities transaction
i = interest rate per year on marketable securities

2. Miller-Orr cash-securities transfer model (16A:606)

$$Z = \sqrt[3]{\frac{3F\sigma^2}{4i}} + LCL$$

and:

$$UCL = 3Z - 2(LCL)$$

where:

Z = the cash balance return (zero) point
F = fixed cost of each cash-securities transaction
σ^2 = variance of the net daily cash flow
i = interest rate per day on marketable securities
LCL = lower control limit
UCL = upper control limit

3. Average cash balance using Miller-Orr (16A:606)

$$Average\ cash\ balance = \frac{4Z - LCL}{3}$$

where:
Z = the cash balance return (zero) point
LCL = lower control limit

Chapter 17—Dividend Policy

1. Dividend-growth model (17:612)

$$Stock\ Value = PV\ of\ dividend\ stream = \frac{D_1}{r_c - g}$$

where:

D_1 = investors' next anticipated dividend
r_c = common stock investors' required rate of return
g = investors' anticipated growth rate of dividends

Chapter 18—Predicting Financial Needs

1. The EFN relationship (18:661 and 18B:677)

$$EFN = [P - R] + [a - \ell - m(1 - d)]\Delta S$$

where:

EFN = external financing needed
P = financing principal to be repaid this year
R = retained earnings increase if sales do not change
a = spontaneous asset percentage
ℓ = spontaneous liability percentage
m = net margin ratio
d = dividend payout ratio
ΔS = forecasted change in sales

2. Limit to internally-financed growth (18:663)

$$\Delta S_{lim} = \frac{R - P}{a - \ell - m(1 - d)}$$

where:
ΔS_{lim} = maximum change in sales that can be financed internally
R = retained earnings increase if sales do not change
P = financing principal to be repaid this year
a = spontaneous asset percentage
ℓ = spontaneous liability percentage
m = net margin ratio
d = dividend payout ratio

3. Sustainable growth rate (18C:678)

$$\Delta S_{sgr} = \frac{m(1 - d)(der + 1)}{a - m(1 - d)(der + 1)} \times S$$

where:
ΔS_{sgr} = rate of growth that leaves the debt/equity ratio unchanged
m = net margin ratio
d = dividend payout ratio
der = beginning-of-year debt/equity ratio
a = spontaneous asset percentage
S = sales last year

Chapter 20—Short-Term Debt

1. Net credit (20:730)

$$\textit{Net credit} = \textit{accounts receivable} - \textit{accounts payable}$$

SUMMARY OF FINANCIAL RATIOS

Ratios that Measure Profitability

1. Profitability compared to sales

$$\textit{Gross profit margin} = \frac{\textit{gross profit}}{\textit{sales}}$$

- Measures pricing policy relative to production costs.

$$\textit{Operating profit margin} = \frac{\textit{EBIT}}{\textit{sales}}$$

- Measures economic earnings from delivering products and services to customers.

$$\textit{Pretax profit margin} = \frac{\textit{earnings before taxes}}{\textit{sales}}$$

- Measures profit after satisfying creditors but before taxes and shareholders.

$$\textit{Net profit margin} = \frac{\textit{earnings after taxes}}{\textit{sales}}$$

- Measures profitability as seen by shareholders.

$$\textit{Contribution margin} = \frac{\textit{contribution}}{\textit{sales}}$$

- Measures the change to profit from a $1 change in sales.

2. Profitability compared to assets

$$\textit{Basic earning power} = \frac{\textit{EBIT}}{\textit{average total assets}}$$

- Shows economic earnings in relation to investment in assets.

$$\textit{Return on assets (ROA)} = \frac{\textit{earnings after taxes}}{\textit{average total assets}}$$

- Shows total earnings in relation to investment in assets.

3. Profitability compared to equity

$$\textit{Return on equity (ROE)} = \frac{\textit{earnings after taxes}}{\textit{average total equity}}$$

- Shows total earnings in relation to equity funding.

Ratios that Measure Effective Use of Working Capital

1. Measures of overall liquidity

$$\textit{Current ratio} = \frac{\textit{current assets}}{\textit{current liabilities}}$$

- Measures ability to generate cash to meet upcoming obligations.

$$\textit{Quick ratio} = \frac{\textit{quick assets}}{\textit{current liabilities}}$$

- Measures ability to generate immediate cash to meet existing or emergency obligations.

2. Measures of the effective use of accounts receivable

$$\textit{Accounts receivable turnover} = \frac{\textit{credit sales}}{\textit{average accounts receivable}}$$

- The number of times per year that credit is extended and accounts receivable collected.

$$\textit{Collection period} = \frac{\textit{average accounts receivable}}{\textit{credit sales}} \times 360$$

- The number of days it takes to collect the typical account receivable.

3. Measures of the effective use of inventories

$$\textit{Inventory turnover} = \frac{\textit{cost of goods sold}}{\textit{average inventory}}$$

- The number of times per year that inventories are sold and replenished.

$$\textit{Inventory days} = \frac{\textit{average inventory}}{\textit{cost of goods sold}} \times 360$$

- The number of days the average item remains in inventory.

4. Measures of the effective use of accounts payable

$$\textit{Accounts payable turnover} = \frac{\textit{purchases}}{\textit{average accounts payable}}$$

- The number of times per year that purchases are made and accounts payable paid.

$$\text{Payables period} = \frac{\text{average accounts payable}}{\text{purchases}} \times 360$$

- The number of days it takes to pay the typical account payable.

5. The cash conversion cycle

$$\text{Cash conversion cycle} = \text{inventory days} + \text{collection period} - \text{payables period}$$

- The number of days it takes to recover the funds invested in inventories and accounts receivable.

Ratios that Measure the Use of Fixed and Total Assets

1. A measure of the productivity of fixed assets

$$\text{Fixed asset turnover} = \frac{\text{sales}}{\text{average fixed assets}}$$

- Measures the effectiveness of fixed assets in generating sales.

2. A measure of the productivity of total assets

$$\text{Total asset turnover} = \frac{\text{sales}}{\text{average total assets}}$$

- Summarizes the relationship of all assets to sales.

Ratios that Measure the Choice and Management of Funding

1. Measures of the financing mix

$$\text{The debt ratio} = \frac{\text{total liabilities}}{\text{total assets}}$$

- Measures the fraction of assets financed with debt.

$$\text{The funded debt ratio} = \frac{\text{funded debt}}{\text{total assets}}$$

- Measures the fraction of assets financed with interest-bearing debt.

$$\text{The debt/equity ratio} = \frac{\text{total debt}}{\text{total equity}}$$

- Measures the amount of debt relative to equity financing.

$$\textit{The assets/equity ratio} = \frac{\textit{total assets}}{\textit{total equity}}$$

- Measures the amount of assets supported by each dollar of equity financing.

2. Measures of the ability to service debt

$$\textit{Times interest earned} = \frac{\textit{EBIT}}{\textit{interest}}$$

- Tests the ability of operating earnings to cover interest obligations.

$$\textit{Cash-flow-based times interest earned} = \frac{\textit{cash from operations}}{\textit{interest}}$$

- Tests the ability of cash flow from operations to cover interest obligations.

$$\textit{Fixed charge coverage} = \frac{\textit{EBIT}}{\textit{interest} + \textit{principal}\left(\frac{1}{1-t}\right)}$$

- Tests the ability of operating earnings to cover interest and principal repayment obligations.

3. Measures of payments against equity

$$\textit{Dividend payout ratio} = \frac{\textit{dividends}}{\textit{earnings after taxes}}$$

- Measures the fraction of earnings paid to shareholders in the form of dividends.

$$\textit{Retention ratio} = \frac{\textit{earnings retained}}{\textit{earnings after taxes}}$$

- Measures the fraction of earnings retained within the firm.

Ratios that Measure the Market's Reaction to the Firm

$$\textit{Price/earnings ratio} = \frac{\textit{stock price}}{\textit{earnings per share}}$$

- Compares stock price to earnings.

$$\textit{Market/book ratio} = \frac{\textit{stock price}}{\textit{book value per share}}$$

- Compares the market value of equity to its accounting value.

$$\textit{Tobin's q ratio} = \frac{\textit{market value of debt + equity}}{\textit{replacement cost of assets}}$$

- Compares the market value of a firm to the cost of replacing its assets.

Measures of Leverage

$$\textit{Degree of operating leverage (DOL)} = \frac{\textit{contribution}}{\textit{EBIT}}$$

- Measures the sensitivity of operating profit to changes in sales.

$$\textit{Degree of financial leverage (DFL)} = \frac{\textit{EBIT}}{\textit{earnings before taxes}}$$

- Measures the sensitivity of earnings per share to changes in operating profit.

$$\textit{Degree of total leverage (DTL)} = \frac{\textit{contribution}}{\textit{earnings before taxes}}$$

- Measures the sensitivity of earnings per share to changes in sales.

USING YOUR FINANCIAL CALCULATOR

In this section we show where to locate the time-value keys on 6 popular financial calculators which can handle the full range of time value calculations in this book. One page is devoted to each calculator. Notes at the bottom of each page give additional helpful pointers.

The featured calculators are:

- Hewlett-Packard 10B, 12C, 17BII, 19BII
- Sharp EL-733
- Texas Instruments BAII PLUS

The following examples translate the notation employed throughout the book to the keystrokes for each of the six calculators.

Example

Using your financial calculator to solve a basic time value problem

A problem requires you to find the future value of an annuity of $1,000 paid at the beginning of each of the next 15 years, at an interest rate of 9%.

Question: Solve this problem using your financial calculator.

Solution steps:

Step	As described in the text	Using a HP–10B	Using a HP–12C	Using a HP–17BII or HP–19BII	Using an EL–733	Using a BAII PLUS
Select the correct menu				**MAIN** (Gold **EXIT**) **FIN** then **TVM**		
Set payments per year to 1		1 **P/YR** (Gold **PMT**)		**OTHER** 1 **P/YR** **EXIT**		**P/Y** 1 **ENTER** **QUIT**
Clear	CLEAR the time value part of your calculator	**CLEAR ALL** (Gold **INPUT**)	**CLEAR FIN** (**f x≷y**)	**CLEAR DATA** (Gold **INPUT**)	**CA** (**2ndF C•CE**)	**CLR TVM** (**2nd FV**)
Enter data	Key in −1,000 and press PMT	1000 **+/− PMT**	1000 **CHS PMT**	1000 **+/− PMT**	1000 **+/− PMT**	1000 **+/− PMT**
	Key in 15 and press n	15 **N**	15 **n**	15 **N**	15 **n**	15 **N**
	Key in 9 and press i	9 **I/YR**	9 **i**	9 **I%YR**	9 **i**	9 **I/Y**
	Set for BEG	**Gold** then **0** until begin appears	**g 7**	**OTHER BEG EXIT**	**BGN** until BGN appears	**BGN** then **SET** until BGN appears, then **QUIT**
Calculate the result	FV	**FV**	**FV**	**FV**	**COMP FV**	**CPT FV**

Answer: The annuity has a future value of $32,003.40.

Example

Using your financial calculator to solve a cash flow list problem

A problem requires you to find the present value of an investment which costs $10,000 and returns the following cash flows. The interest rate is 7.5%.

Year	Cash flow	Year	Cash flow	Year	Cash flow
1	$1,000	5	4,000	8	$ 0
2	2,000	6	4,000	9	3,000
3	2,000	7	1,000	10	3,000
4	2,000				

Question: Solve this problem using your financial calculator.

Solution steps:

Step	As described in the text	Using a HP–10B	Using a HP–12C	Using a HP–17BII or HP–19BII	Using an EL–733	Using a BAII PLUS
Select the correct menu				MAIN (Gold EXIT) FIN then CFLO		CF
Clear	CLEAR the cash-flow-list part of your calculator	CLEAR ALL (Gold INPUT)	CLEAR REG (f CLx)	CLEAR DATA (Gold INPUT) then YES	CA (2ndF C • CE)	CLR Work (2nd CE/C)
Enter data	Key in −10,000 as FLOW 0	10,000 +/− CF_j	10000 CHS CF_0 (g PV)	10000 +/− INPUT	10000 +/− CF_i	10000 +/− ENTER ↓
	Key in 1000 as FLOW 1	1000 CF_j	1000 CF_j (g PMT)	1000 INPUT INPUT	1000 CF_i	1000 ENTER ↓ ↓
	Key in 2000 as FLOW 2, 3 TIMES	2000 CF_j 3 N_j (Gold CF_j)	2000 CF_j (g PMT) 3 N_j (g FV)	2000 INPUT 3 INPUT	3 N_i (2nd CF_i) 2000 CF_i	2000 ENTER ↓ 3 ENTER ↓
	Key in 4000 as FLOW 3, 2 TIMES	4000 CF_j 2 N_j (Gold CF_j)	4000 CF_j (g PMT) 2 N_j (g FV)	4000 INPUT 2 INPUT	2 N_i (2nd CF_i) 4000 CF_i	4000 ENTER ↓ 2 ENTER ↓
	Key in 1000 as FLOW 4	1000 CF_j	1000 CF_j	1000 INPUT INPUT	1000 CF_i	1000 ENTER ↓ ↓
	Key in 0 as FLOW 5	0 CF_j	0 CF_j (g PMT)	0 INPUT INPUT	0 CF_i	0 ENTER ↓ ↓
	Key in 3000 as FLOW 6, 2 TIMES	3000 CF_j 2 N_j (Gold CF_j)	3000 CF_j (g PMT) 2 N_j (g FV)	3000 INPUT 2 INPUT	2 N_i (2nd CF_i) 3000 CF_i	3000 ENTER ↓ 2 ENTER ↓
Switch to the calculation menu				17BII: EXIT CALC 19BII: CALC		NPV
Enter the interest rate	Enter 7.5 and press i	7.5 I/YR	7.5 i	7.5 I%	7.5 i	7.5 ENTER ↓
Calculate the result	Compute NPV	NPV (Gold PRC)	NPV (f PV)	NPV	NPV	CPT

Answer: The investment has a present value of $4,769.59.

Hewlett-Packard HP–10B

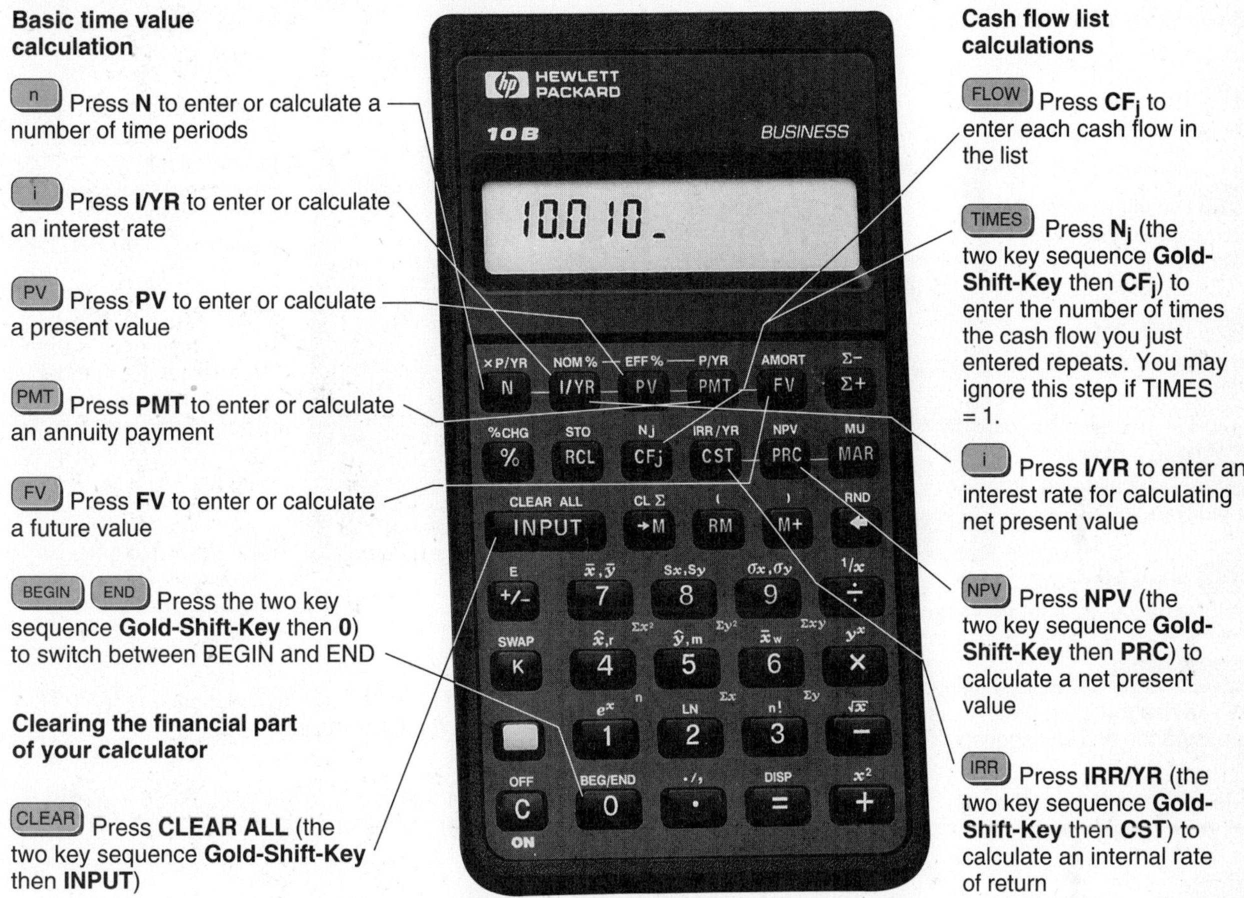

Basic time value calculation
n Press **N** to enter or calculate a number of time periods
i Press **I/YR** to enter or calculate an interest rate
PV Press **PV** to enter or calculate a present value
PMT Press **PMT** to enter or calculate an annuity payment
FV Press **FV** to enter or calculate a future value
BEGIN END Press the two key sequence **Gold-Shift-Key** then **0**) to switch between BEGIN and END
Clearing the financial part of your calculator
CLEAR Press **CLEAR ALL** (the two key sequence **Gold-Shift-Key** then **INPUT**)
HEWLETT PACKARD
10B
BUSINESS
10.0 10_
Cash flow list calculations
FLOW Press $\mathbf{CF_j}$ to enter each cash flow in the list
TIMES Press $\mathbf{N_j}$ (the two key sequence **Gold-Shift-Key** then $\mathbf{CF_j}$) to enter the number of times the cash flow you just entered repeats. You may ignore this step if TIMES = 1.
i Press **I/YR** to enter an interest rate for calculating net present value
NPV Press **NPV** (the two key sequence **Gold-Shift-Key** then **PRC**) to calculate a net present value
IRR Press **IRR/YR** (the two key sequence **Gold-Shift-Key** then **CST**) to calculate an internal rate of return

Other Helpful Hints about the HP–10B Calculator

1. To enter data, key in the number and then press the key describing that item. To calculate a result, press the appropriate key without first keying in a number.
2. Be sure to set payments-per-year equal to 1 prior to doing any annuity calculations to avoid unwanted compounding within each period. The keystroke sequence is:

   Key in the number 1 then press **P/YR** (the two key sequence **Gold-Shift-Key** then **PMT**)
3. In the **BEG** mode, the word "BEGIN" appears in the display. If "BEGIN" does not appear, you are in the **END** mode.
4. If you hold down the **CLEAR ALL** key when you clear, the setting for payments-per-year will be displayed. Also, if you hold down the $\mathbf{CF_j}$ and $\mathbf{N_j}$ keys as you enter cash-flow-list data items, the value of j will be displayed.
5. To set the number of decimal places displayed, press **DISP** (the two key sequence **GOLD-Shift-Key** then **=**) followed by the number of decimal places desired (for example, **DISP** then **2** sets the display to show 2 decimal places).

Hewlett-Packard HP–12C

Basic time value calculations

Cash flow list calculations

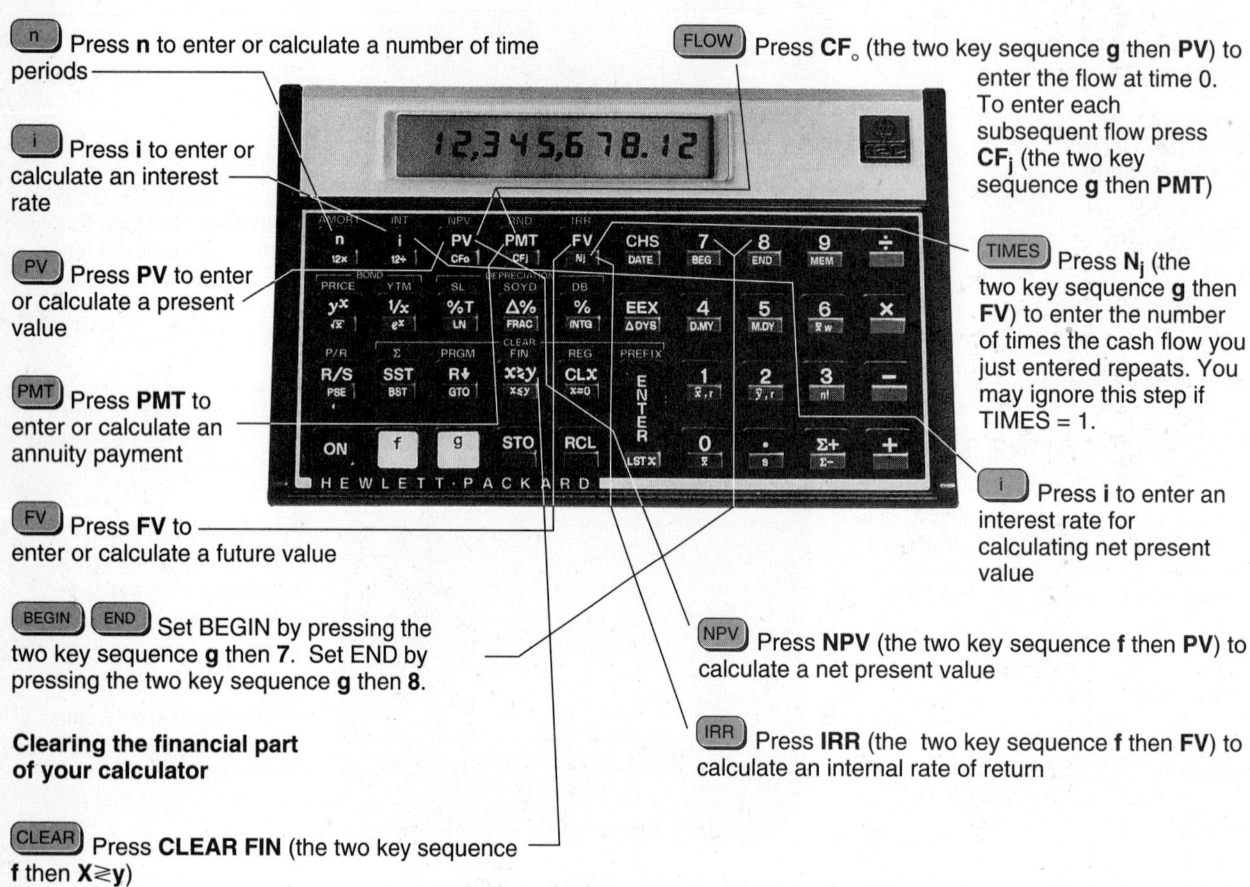
n Press **n** to enter or calculate a number of time periods
i Press **i** to enter or calculate an interest rate
PV Press **PV** to enter or calculate a present value
PMT Press **PMT** to enter or calculate an annuity payment
FV Press **FV** to enter or calculate a future value
BEGIN END Set BEGIN by pressing the two key sequence **g** then **7**. Set END by pressing the two key sequence **g** then **8**.
Clearing the financial part of your calculator
CLEAR Press **CLEAR FIN** (the two key sequence **f** then **X≷y**)
FLOW Press **CF**$_0$ (the two key sequence **g** then **PV**) to enter the flow at time 0. To enter each subsequent flow press **CF**$_j$ (the two key sequence **g** then **PMT**)
TIMES Press **N**$_j$ (the two key sequence **g** then **FV**) to enter the number of times the cash flow you just entered repeats. You may ignore this step if TIMES = 1.
i Press **i** to enter an interest rate for calculating net present value
NPV Press **NPV** (the two key sequence **f** then **PV**) to calculate a net present value
IRR Press **IRR** (the two key sequence **f** then **FV**) to calculate an internal rate of return
12,345,678.12
HEWLETT·PACKARD

Other Helpful Hints about the HP–12C Calculator

1. To enter data, key in the number and then press the key describing that item. To calculate a result, press the appropriate key without first entering a number.
2. In the **BEG** mode, the word "BEGIN" appears in the display. If "BEGIN" does not appear, you are in the **END** mode.
3. When calculating n, the HP–12C rounds the answer up to the nearest integer. If you enter a non-integer value for **n**—for example, n = 1/2 to represent 1/2 year—be sure the calculator is set properly for nominal or compound calculations. Toggle between "nominal mode" and "compound mode" using the two key sequence **STO** then **EEX**. In the compound mode, the letter "C" appears in the display. If "C" does not appear, you are in the nominal mode.
4. To set the number of decimal places displayed, press the two key sequence **f** then the number of decimal places desired (for example, **f** then **2** sets the display to show 2 decimal places).

Hewlett-Packard HP–17BII

You must first display the correct menu for the kind of problem you are doing. For basic time value problems, display the TVM menu (from the main menu press **FIN** then **TVM**). For cash flow list problems, display the cash flow menu (from the main menu press **FIN** then **CFLO**).

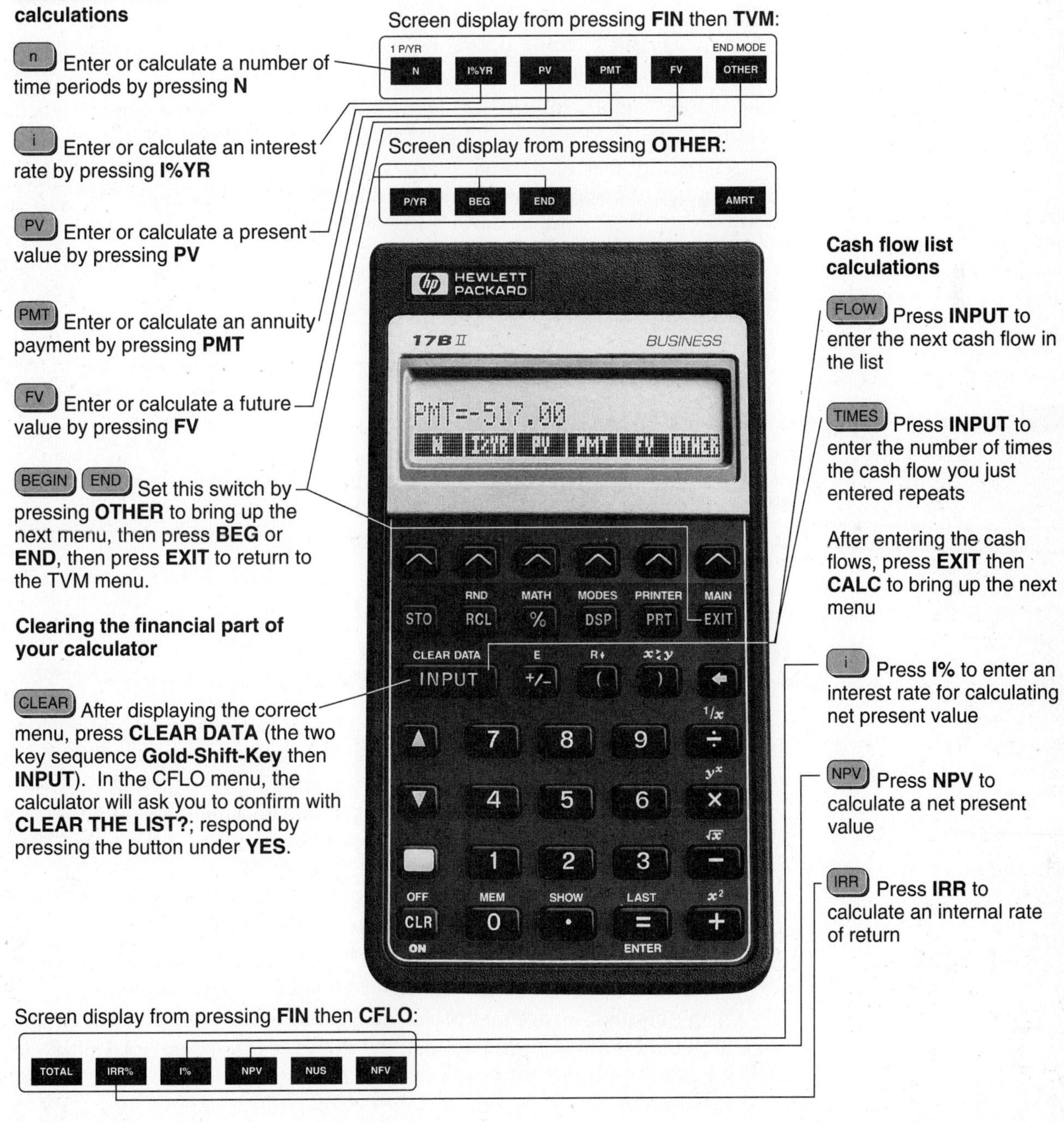

Basic time value calculations
n Enter or calculate a number of time periods by pressing **N**
i Enter or calculate an interest rate by pressing **I%YR**
PV Enter or calculate a present value by pressing **PV**
PMT Enter or calculate an annuity payment by pressing **PMT**
FV Enter or calculate a future value by pressing **FV**
BEGIN END Set this switch by pressing **OTHER** to bring up the next menu, then press **BEG** or **END**, then press **EXIT** to return to the TVM menu.
Clearing the financial part of your calculator
CLEAR After displaying the correct menu, press **CLEAR DATA** (the two key sequence **Gold-Shift-Key** then **INPUT**). In the CFLO menu, the calculator will ask you to confirm with **CLEAR THE LIST?**; respond by pressing the button under **YES**.
Screen display from pressing **FIN** then **TVM**:
1 P/YR
END MODE
N
I%YR
PV
PMT
FV
OTHER
Screen display from pressing **OTHER**:
P/YR
BEG
END
AMRT
HEWLETT PACKARD
17BII
BUSINESS
PMT=-517.00
RND
MATH
MODES
PRINTER
MAIN
STO
RCL
%
DSP
PRT
EXIT
CLEAR DATA
INPUT
OFF
MEM
SHOW
LAST
CLR
ON
ENTER
Cash flow list calculations
FLOW Press **INPUT** to enter the next cash flow in the list
TIMES Press **INPUT** to enter the number of times the cash flow you just entered repeats
After entering the cash flows, press **EXIT** then **CALC** to bring up the next menu
i Press **I%** to enter an interest rate for calculating net present value
NPV Press **NPV** to calculate a net present value
IRR Press **IRR** to calculate an internal rate of return
Screen display from pressing **FIN** then **CFLO**:
TOTAL
IRR%
I%
NPV
NUS
NFV

Other Helpful Hints about the HP–17BII Calculator

1. To enter basic time value data, key in the number and press the key describing that item. To calculate a result, press the appropriate key without first keying in a number.
2. Be sure to set payments-per-year equal to 1 prior to doing any annuity calculations to avoid unwanted compounding within each period. From the TVM menu, the keystroke sequence is:

   Press **OTHER** to bring up the next menu, then key in the number 1 and press **P/YR**, then press **EXIT** to return to the TVM menu
3. The words "BEGIN MODE" or "END MODE" appear in the display when you enter the TVM menu to let you know which mode you are in.
4. To set the number of decimal places displayed, press **DSP** then **FIX** then the number of decimal places desired, then **INPUT** (for example **DSP FIX** 2 **INPUT** sets the display to show 2 decimal places).

Hewlett-Packard HP–19BII

You must first display the correct menu for the kind of problem you are doing. For basic time value problems, display the TVM menu (from the main menu press **FIN** then **TVM**). For cash flow list problems, display the cash flow menu (from the main menu press **FIN** then **CFLO**).

Other Helpful Hints about the HP–19BII Calculator

1. To enter basic time value data, key in the number and press the key describing that item. To calculate a result, press the appropriate key without first keying in a number.
2. Be sure to set payments-per-year equal to 1 prior to doing any annuity calculations to avoid unwanted compounding within each period. From the TVM menu, the keystroke sequence is:

   Press **OTHER** to bring up the next menu, then key in the number 1 and press **P/YR**, then press **EXIT** to return to the TVM menu
3. The words "BEGIN MODE" or "END MODE" appear in the display when you enter the TVM menu to let you know which mode you are in.
4. To set the number of decimal places displayed, press **DISP** then **FIX** then the number of decimal places desired, then **INPUT** (for example **DISP FIX** 2 **INPUT** sets the display to show 2 decimal places).

Screen display from pressing **OTHER**:

P/YR | BEG | END | AMRT

Screen display from pressing **FIN** then **CFLO**:

TOTAL | IRR% | I% | NPV | NUS | NFV

Basic time value calculations

(n) Enter or calculate a number of time periods by pressing **N**

(i) Enter or calculate an interest rate by pressing **I%YR**

(PV) Enter or calculate a present value by pressing **PV**

(PMT) Enter or calculate an annuity payment by pressing **PMT**

(FV) Enter or calculate a future value by pressing **FV**

(BEGIN) (END) Set this switch by pressing **OTHER** to bring up the next menu, then press **BEG** or **END**, then press **EXIT** to return to the TVM menu.

Clearing the financial part of your calculator

(CLEAR) After displaying the correct menu, press **CLEAR DATA** (the two key sequence **Gold-Shift-Key** then **INPUT**). In the CFLO menu, the calculator will ask you to confirm with **CLEAR THE LIST?**; respond by pressing the button under **YES**.

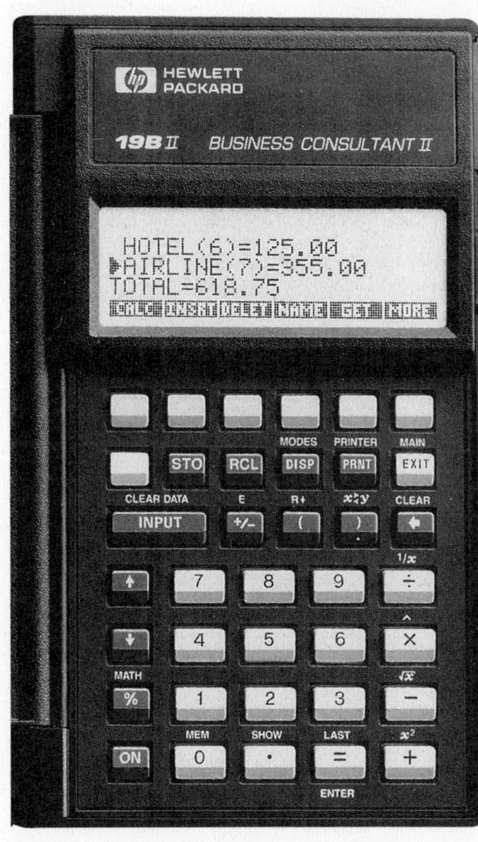

Cash flow list calculations

(FLOW) Press **INPUT** to enter the next cash flow in the list

(TIMES) Press **INPUT** to enter the number of times the cash flow you just entered repeats

After entering the cash flows, press **CALC** to bring up the next menu

(i) Press **I%** to enter an interest rate for calculating net present value

(NPV) Press **NPV** to calculate a net present value

(IRR) Press **IRR** to calculate an internal rate of return

Screen display from pressing **FIN** then **TVM**:

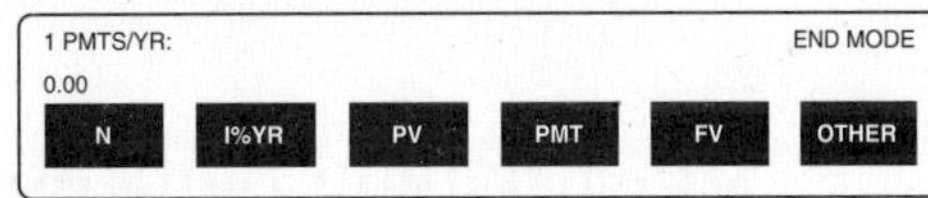

Sharp EL–733

Be sure your calculator is in the "FINANCIAL" mode prior to doing any time value calculations. If it is, "FIN" will appear in the display. If not, press the two key sequence **2ndF** then **MODE** repeatedly until "FIN" appears.

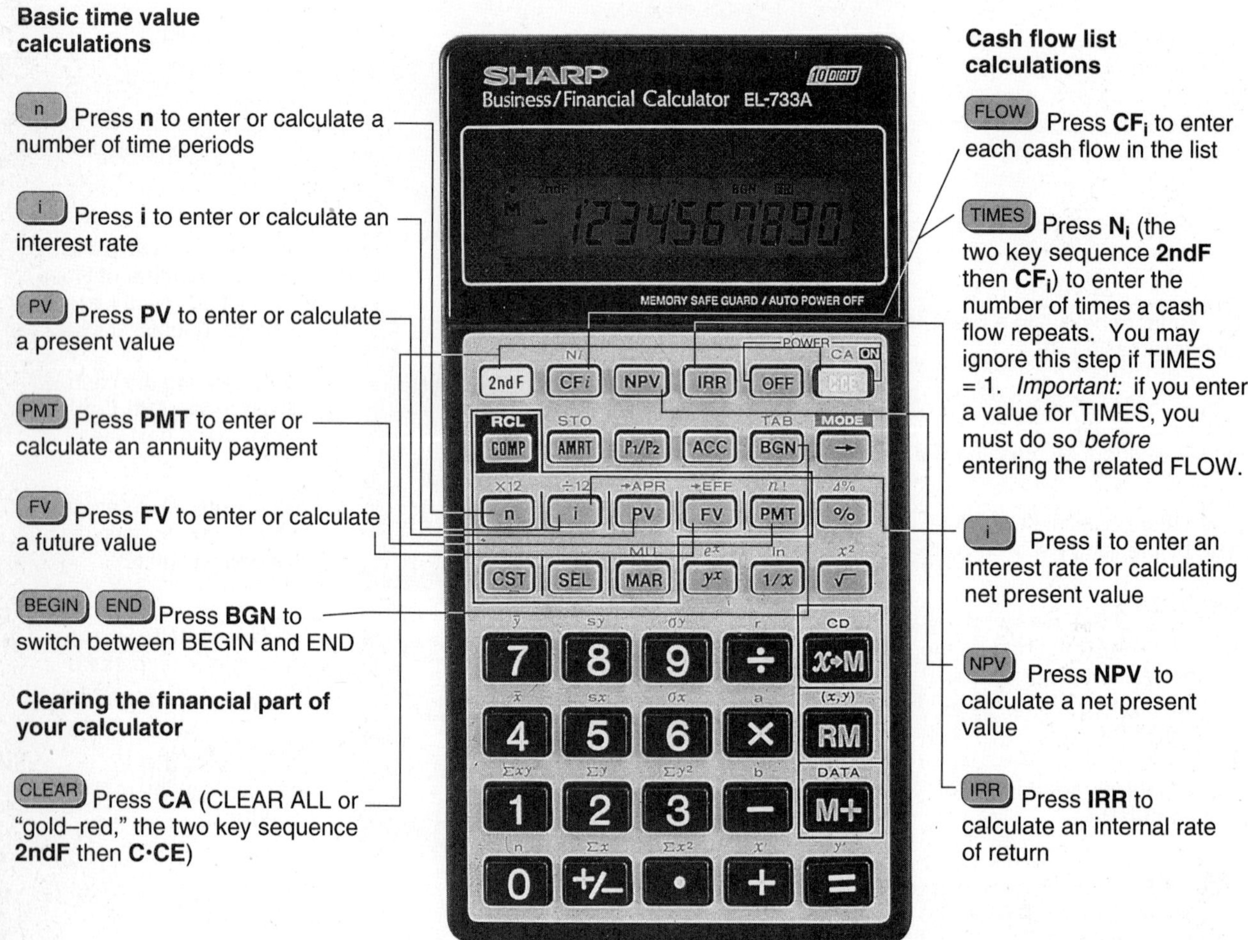

Basic time value calculations
n Press n to enter or calculate a number of time periods
i Press i to enter or calculate an interest rate
PV Press PV to enter or calculate a present value
PMT Press PMT to enter or calculate an annuity payment
FV Press FV to enter or calculate a future value
BEGIN END Press BGN to switch between BEGIN and END
Clearing the financial part of your calculator
CLEAR Press CA (CLEAR ALL or "gold–red," the two key sequence 2ndF then C•CE)
SHARP
Business/Financial Calculator EL-733A
MEMORY SAFE GUARD / AUTO POWER OFF
Cash flow list calculations
FLOW Press CFi to enter each cash flow in the list
TIMES Press Ni (the two key sequence 2ndF then CFi) to enter the number of times a cash flow repeats. You may ignore this step if TIMES = 1. Important: if you enter a value for TIMES, you must do so before entering the related FLOW.
i Press i to enter an interest rate for calculating net present value
NPV Press NPV to calculate a net present value
IRR Press IRR to calculate an internal rate of return

Other Helpful Hints About the Sharp EL–733 Calculator

1. To enter data, key in the number and then press the key describing that item. To calculate a result, first press the **COMP** key (the key surrounded in brown) then press the appropriate key.
2. In the **BEG** mode, the indication "BEG" appears in the display. If "BEG" does not appear, you are in the **END** mode.
3. To set the number of decimal places displayed, press the key sequence **TAB** (**2ndF** then **BGN**) then the number of decimal places desired (for example, **TAB** then **2** sets the display to show 2 decimal places).

Texas Instruments BAII PLUS

Cash-flow-list calculations, switching between BEGIN and END, setting the display, and many other calculations and settings are done in "prompted worksheets." Once in a worksheet, use the keys on the top row:

- Use ↑ and ↓ to move around within a worksheet.
- Key in a number and press **ENTER** to enter data into a worksheet.
- Press **SET** (the two key sequence **2nd** then **ENTER**) to switch a setting among alternatives within a worksheet.
- Press **QUIT** (the two key sequence **2nd** then **CPT**) to exit a worksheet.

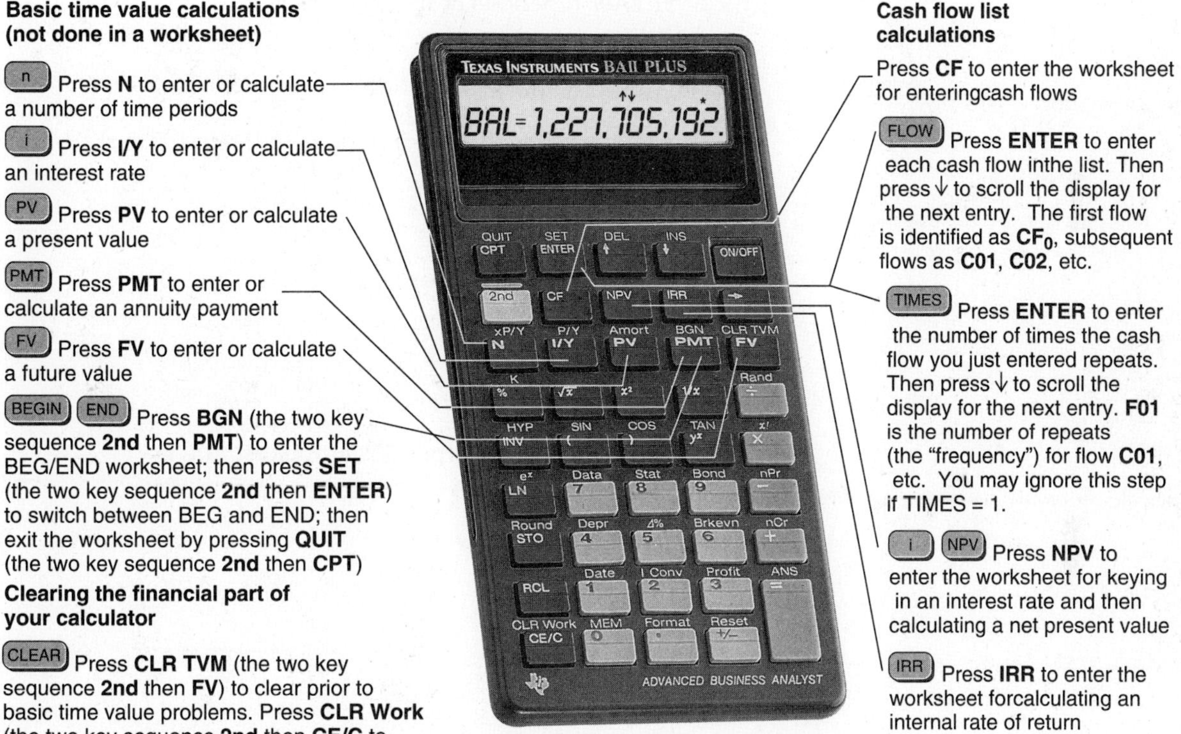

Basic time value calculations (not done in a worksheet)
n Press N to enter or calculate a number of time periods
i Press I/Y to enter or calculate an interest rate
PV Press PV to enter or calculate a present value
PMT Press PMT to enter or calculate an annuity payment
FV Press FV to enter or calculate a future value
BEGIN END Press BGN (the two key sequence 2nd then PMT) to enter the BEG/END worksheet; then press SET (the two key sequence 2nd then ENTER) to switch between BEG and END; then exit the worksheet by pressing QUIT (the two key sequence 2nd then CPT)
Clearing the financial part of your calculator
CLEAR Press CLR TVM (the two key sequence 2nd then FV) to clear prior to basic time value problems. Press CLR Work (the two key sequence 2nd then CE/C to clear prior to cash flow list problems.
TEXAS INSTRUMENTS BAII PLUS
BAL= 1,227,705,192.
ADVANCED BUSINESS ANALYST
Cash flow list calculations
Press CF to enter the worksheet for enteringcash flows
FLOW Press ENTER to enter each cash flow inthe list. Then press ↓ to scroll the display for the next entry. The first flow is identified as CF0, subsequent flows as C01, C02, etc.
TIMES Press ENTER to enter the number of times the cash flow you just entered repeats. Then press ↓ to scroll the display for the next entry. F01 is the number of repeats (the "frequency") for flow C01, etc. You may ignore this step if TIMES = 1.
i NPV Press NPV to enter the worksheet for keying in an interest rate and then calculating a net present value
IRR Press IRR to enter the worksheet forcalculating an internal rate of return

Other Helpful Hints About the Texas Instruments BAII PLUS Calculator

1. To enter data, key in the number and then press the key describing that item. To calculate a result, press the **CPT** key then press the appropriate key.
2. In the **BEG** mode, the indication "BGN" appears in the display. If "BGN" does not appear, you are in the **END** mode.
3. To set the number of decimal places displayed, press the key sequence **FORMAT** (**2ndF** then **.**), then the number of decimal places desired followed by **ENTER**, then **QUIT** (the two key sequence **2nd** then **CPT**). For example, **FORMAT** then **2** then **ENTER** then **QUIT** sets the display to show 2 decimal places.

TIME VALUE TABLES

- Table 1 Future Value Factors $= (1 + r)^n$
  (**FV** of $1 after **n** periods at interest rate **r**)

- Table 2 Present Value Factors $= \frac{1}{(1 + r)^n}$
  (**PV** of $1 to be received after **n** periods at interest rate **r**)

- Table 3 Future Value Annuity Factors $= \frac{(1 + r)^n - 1}{r}$
  (**FV** of $1 per period for **n** periods at interest rate **r**)

- Table 4 Present Value Annuity Factors $= \frac{1 - \frac{1}{(1 + r)^n}}{r}$
  (**PV** of $1 per period for **n** periods at interest rate **r**)

TABLE 1 Future Value Factors = $(1 + r)^n$ (FV of $1 after n periods at interest rate r)

n	1%	2%	3%	4%	5%	6%	7%	8%	9%	10%	11%	12%	13%	14%	15%	20%	25%	30%	35%	40%
1	1.0100	1.0200	1.0300	1.0400	1.0500	1.0600	1.0700	1.0800	1.0900	1.1000	1.1100	1.1200	1.1300	1.1400	1.1500	1.2000	1.2500	1.3000	1.3500	1.4000
2	1.0201	1.0404	1.0609	1.0816	1.1025	1.1236	1.1449	1.1664	1.1881	1.2100	1.2321	1.2544	1.2769	1.2996	1.3225	1.4400	1.5625	1.6900	1.8225	1.9600
3	1.0303	1.0612	1.0927	1.1249	1.1576	1.1910	1.2250	1.2597	1.2950	1.3310	1.3676	1.4049	1.4429	1.4815	1.5209	1.7280	1.9531	2.1970	2.4604	2.7440
4	1.0406	1.0824	1.1255	1.1699	1.2155	1.2625	1.3108	1.3605	1.4116	1.4641	1.5181	1.5735	1.6305	1.6890	1.7490	2.0736	2.4414	2.8561	3.3215	3.8416
5	1.0510	1.1041	1.1593	1.2167	1.2763	1.3382	1.4026	1.4693	1.5386	1.6105	1.6851	1.7623	1.8424	1.9254	2.0114	2.4883	3.0518	3.7129	4.4840	5.3782
6	1.0615	1.1262	1.1941	1.2653	1.3401	1.4185	1.5007	1.5869	1.6771	1.7716	1.8704	1.9738	2.0820	2.1950	2.3131	2.9860	3.8147	4.8268	6.0534	7.5295
7	1.0721	1.1487	1.2299	1.3159	1.4071	1.5036	1.6058	1.7138	1.8280	1.9487	2.0762	2.2107	2.3526	2.5023	2.6600	3.5832	4.7684	6.2749	8.1722	10.541
8	1.0829	1.1717	1.2668	1.3686	1.4775	1.5938	1.7182	1.8509	1.9926	2.1436	2.3045	2.4760	2.6584	2.8526	3.0590	4.2998	5.9605	8.1573	11.032	14.758
9	1.0937	1.1951	1.3048	1.4233	1.5513	1.6895	1.8385	1.9990	2.1719	2.3579	2.5580	2.7731	3.0040	3.2519	3.5179	5.1598	7.4506	10.604	14.894	20.661
10	1.1046	1.2190	1.3439	1.4802	1.6289	1.7908	1.9672	2.1589	2.3674	2.5937	2.8394	3.1058	3.3946	3.7072	4.0456	6.1917	9.3132	13.786	20.107	28.925
11	1.1157	1.2434	1.3842	1.5395	1.7103	1.8983	2.1049	2.3316	2.5804	2.8531	3.1518	3.4785	3.8359	4.2262	4.6524	7.4301	11.642	17.922	21.144	40.496
12	1.1268	1.2682	1.4258	1.6010	1.7959	2.0122	2.2522	2.5182	2.8127	3.1384	3.4985	3.8960	4.3345	4.8179	5.3503	8.9161	14.552	23.298	36.644	56.694
13	1.1381	1.2936	1.4685	1.6651	1.8856	2.1329	2.4098	2.7196	3.0658	3.4523	3.8833	4.3635	4.8980	5.4924	6.1528	10.699	18.190	30.288	49.470	79.371
14	1.1495	1.3195	1.5126	1.7317	1.9799	2.2609	2.5785	2.9372	3.3417	3.7975	4.3104	4.8871	5.5348	6.2613	7.0757	12.839	22.737	39.374	66.784	111.12
15	1.1610	1.3459	1.5580	1.8009	2.0789	2.3966	2.7590	3.1722	3.6425	4.1772	4.7846	5.4736	6.2543	7.1379	8.1371	15.407	28.422	51.186	90.158	155.57
16	1.1726	1.3728	1.6047	1.8730	2.1829	2.5404	2.9522	3.4259	3.9703	4.5950	5.3109	6.1304	7.0673	8.1372	9.3576	18.488	35.527	66.542	121.71	217.80
17	1.1843	1.4002	1.6528	1.9479	2.2920	2.6928	3.1588	3.7000	4.3276	5.0545	5.8951	6.8660	7.9861	9.2765	10.761	22.186	44.409	86.504	164.31	304.91
18	1.1961	1.4282	1.7024	2.0258	2.4066	2.8543	3.3799	3.9960	4.7171	5.5599	6.5436	7.6900	9.0243	10.575	12.375	26.623	55.511	112.46	221.82	426.88
19	1.2081	1.4568	1.7535	2.1068	2.5270	3.0256	3.6165	4.3157	5.1417	6.1159	7.2633	8.6128	10.197	12.056	14.232	31.948	69.389	146.19	299.46	597.63
20	1.2202	1.4859	1.8061	2.1911	2.6533	3.2071	3.8697	4.6610	5.6044	6.7275	8.0623	9.6463	11.523	13.743	16.367	38.338	86.736	190.05	404.27	836.68
21	1.2324	1.5157	1.8603	2.2788	2.7860	3.3996	4.1406	5.0338	6.1088	7.4002	8.9492	10.804	13.021	15.668	18.822	46.005	108.42	247.06	545.77	1171.4
22	1.2447	1.5460	1.9161	2.3699	2.9253	3.6035	4.4304	5.4365	6.6586	8.1403	9.9336	12.100	14.714	17.861	21.645	55.206	135.53	321.18	736.79	1639.9
23	1.2572	1.5769	1.9736	2.4647	3.0715	3.8197	4.7405	5.8715	7.2579	8.9543	11.026	13.552	16.627	20.362	24.891	66.247	169.41	417.54	994.66	2295.9
24	1.2697	1.6084	2.0328	2.5633	3.2251	4.0489	5.0724	6.3412	7.9111	9.8497	12.239	15.179	18.788	23.212	28.625	79.497	211.76	542.80	1342.8	3214.2
25	1.2824	1.6406	2.0938	2.6658	3.3864	4.2919	5.4274	6.8485	8.6231	10.835	13.585	17.000	21.231	26.462	32.919	95.396	264.70	705.64	1812.8	4499.9
26	1.2953	1.6734	2.1566	2.7725	3.5557	4.5494	5.8074	7.3964	9.3992	11.918	15.080	19.040	23.991	30.167	37.857	114.48	330.87	917.33	2447.2	6299.8
27	1.3082	1.7069	2.2213	2.8834	3.7335	4.8223	6.2139	7.9881	10.245	13.110	16.739	21.325	27.109	34.390	43.535	137.37	413.59	1192.5	3303.8	8819.8
28	1.3213	1.7410	2.2879	2.9987	3.9201	5.1117	6.6488	8.6271	11.167	14.421	18.580	23.884	30.633	39.204	50.066	164.84	516.99	1550.3	4460.1	12348
29	1.3345	1.7758	2.3566	3.1187	4.1161	5.4184	7.1143	9.3173	12.172	15.863	20.624	26.750	34.616	44.693	57.575	197.81	646.23	2015.4	6021.1	17287
30	1.3478	1.8114	2.4273	3.2434	4.3219	5.7435	7.6123	10.063	13.268	17.449	22.892	29.960	39.116	50.950	66.212	237.38	807.79	2620.0	8128.5	24201
31	1.3613	1.8476	2.5001	3.3731	4.5380	6.0881	8.1451	10.868	14.462	19.194	25.410	33.555	44.201	58.083	76.144	284.85	1009.7	3406.0	10974	33882
32	1.3749	1.8845	2.5751	3.5081	4.7649	6.4534	8.7153	11.737	15.763	21.114	28.206	37.582	49.947	66.215	87.565	341.82	1262.2	4427.8	14814	47435
33	1.3887	1.9222	2.6523	3.6484	5.0032	6.8406	9.3253	12.676	17.182	23.225	31.308	42.092	56.440	75.485	100.70	410.19	1577.7	5756.1	19999	66409
34	1.4026	1.9607	2.7319	3.7943	5.2533	7.2510	9.9781	13.690	18.728	25.548	34.752	47.143	63.777	86.053	115.80	492.22	1972.2	7483.0	26999	92972
35	1.4166	1.9999	2.8139	3.9461	5.5160	7.6861	10.677	14.785	20.414	28.102	38.575	52.800	72.069	98.100	133.18	590.67	2465.2	9727.9	36449	130161
40	1.4889	2.2080	3.2620	4.8010	7.0400	10.286	14.974	21.725	31.409	45.259	65.001	93.051	132.78	188.88	267.86	1469.8	7523.2	36119	*******	*******
50	1.6446	2.6916	4.3839	7.1067	11.467	18.420	29.457	46.902	74.358	117.39	184.56	289.00	450.74	700.23	1083.7	9100.4	70065	*******	*******	*******
60	1.8167	3.2810	5.8916	10.520	18.679	32.988	57.946	101.26	176.03	304.48	524.06	897.60	1530.1	2595.9	4384.0	56348	*******	*******	*******	*******
70	2.0068	3.9996	7.9178	15.572	30.426	59.076	113.99	218.61	416.73	789.75	1488.0	2787.8	5193.9	9623.6	17736	*******	*******	*******	*******	*******
80	2.2167	4.8754	10.641	23.050	49.561	105.80	224.23	471.95	986.55	2048.4	4225.1	8658.5	17631	35677	71751	*******	*******	*******	*******	*******
360	35.950	1247.6	41822	*******	*******	*******	*******	*******	*******	*******	*******	*******	*******	*******	*******	*******	*******	*******	*******	*******

******* Factor > 99999

TABLE 2 Present Value Factors = $\frac{1}{(1+r)^n}$ (PV of $1 to be received after n periods at interest rate r)

	1%	2%	3%	4%	5%	6%	7%	8%	9%	10%	11%	12%	13%	14%	15%	20%	25%	30%	35%	40%
1	0.9901	0.9804	0.9709	0.9615	0.9524	0.9434	0.9346	0.9259	0.9174	0.9091	0.9009	0.8929	0.8850	0.8772	0.8696	0.8333	0.8000	0.7692	0.7407	0.7143
2	0.9803	0.9612	0.9426	0.9246	0.9070	0.8900	0.8734	0.8573	0.8417	0.8264	0.8116	0.7972	0.7831	0.7695	0.7561	0.6944	0.6400	0.5917	0.5487	0.5102
3	0.9706	0.9423	0.9151	0.8890	0.8638	0.8396	0.8163	0.7938	0.7722	0.7513	0.7312	0.7118	0.6931	0.6750	0.6575	0.5787	0.5120	0.4552	0.4064	0.3644
4	0.9610	0.9238	0.8885	0.8548	0.8227	0.7921	0.7629	0.7350	0.7084	0.6830	0.6587	0.6355	0.6133	0.5921	0.5718	0.4823	0.4096	0.3501	0.3011	0.2603
5	0.9515	0.9057	0.8626	0.8219	0.7835	0.7473	0.7130	0.6806	0.6499	0.6209	0.5935	0.5674	0.5428	0.5194	0.4972	0.4019	0.3277	0.2693	0.2230	0.1859
6	0.9420	0.8880	0.8375	0.7903	0.7462	0.7050	0.6663	0.6302	0.5963	0.5645	0.5346	0.5066	0.4803	0.4556	0.4323	0.3349	0.2621	0.2072	0.1652	0.1328
7	0.9327	0.8706	0.8131	0.7599	0.7107	0.6651	0.6627	0.5835	0.5470	0.5132	0.4817	0.4523	0.4251	0.3996	0.3759	0.2791	0.2097	0.1594	0.1224	0.0949
8	0.9235	0.8535	0.7894	0.7307	0.6768	0.6274	0.5820	0.5403	0.5019	0.4665	0.4339	0.4039	0.3762	0.3506	0.3269	0.2326	0.1678	0.1226	0.0906	0.0678
9	0.9143	0.8368	0.7664	0.7026	0.6446	0.5919	0.5439	0.5002	0.4604	0.4241	0.3909	0.3606	0.3329	0.3075	0.2843	0.1938	0.1342	0.0943	0.0671	0.0484
10	0.9053	0.8203	0.7441	0.6756	0.6139	0.5584	0.5083	0.4632	0.4224	0.3855	0.3522	0.3220	0.2946	0.2697	0.2472	0.1615	0.1074	0.0725	0.0497	0.0346
11	0.8963	0.8043	0.7224	0.6496	0.5847	0.5268	0.4751	0.4289	0.3875	0.3505	0.3173	0.2875	0.2607	0.2366	0.2149	0.1346	0.0859	0.0558	0.0368	0.0247
12	0.8874	0.7885	0.7014	0.6246	0.5568	0.4970	0.4440	0.3971	0.3555	0.3186	0.2858	0.2567	0.2307	0.2076	0.1869	0.1122	0.0687	0.0429	0.0273	0.0176
13	0.8787	0.7730	0.6810	0.6006	0.5303	0.4688	0.4150	0.3677	0.3262	0.2897	0.2575	0.2292	0.2042	0.1821	0.1625	0.0935	0.0550	0.0330	0.0202	0.0126
14	0.8700	0.7579	0.6611	0.5775	0.5051	0.4423	0.3878	0.3405	0.2992	0.2633	0.2320	0.2046	0.1807	0.1597	0.1413	0.0779	0.0440	0.0254	0.0150	0.0090
15	0.8613	0.7430	0.6419	0.5553	0.4810	0.4173	0.3624	0.3152	0.2745	0.2394	0.2090	0.1827	0.1599	0.1401	0.1229	0.0649	0.0352	0.0195	0.0111	0.0064
16	0.8528	0.7284	0.6232	0.5339	0.4581	0.3936	0.3387	0.2919	0.2519	0.2176	0.1883	0.1631	0.1415	0.1229	0.1069	0.0541	0.0281	0.0150	0.0082	0.0046
17	0.8444	0.7142	0.6050	0.5134	0.4363	0.3714	0.3166	0.2703	0.2311	0.1978	0.1696	0.1456	0.1252	0.1078	0.0929	0.0451	0.0225	0.0116	0.0061	0.0033
18	0.8360	0.7002	05874	0.4936	0.4155	0.3503	0.2959	0.2502	0.2120	0.1799	0.1528	0.1300	0.1108	0.0946	0.0808	0.0376	0.0180	0.0089	0.0045	0.0023
19	0.8277	0.6864	0.5703	0.4746	0.3957	0.3305	0.2765	0.2317	0.1945	0.1635	0.1377	0.1161	0.0981	0.0829	0.0703	0.0313	0.0144	0.0068	0.0033	0.0017
20	0.8195	0.6730	0.5537	0.4564	0.3769	0.3118	0.2584	0.2145	0.1784	0.1486	0.1240	0.1037	0.0868	0.0728	0.0611	0.0261	0.0115	0.0053	0.0025	0.0012
21	0.8114	0.6598	0.5375	0.4386	0.3589	0.2942	0.2415	0.1987	0.1637	0.1351	0.1117	0.0926	0.0768	0.0638	0.0531	0.0217	0.0092	0.0040	0.0018	0.0009
22	0.8034	0.6468	0.5219	0.4220	0.3418	0.2775	0.2257	0.1839	0.1502	0.1228	0.1007	0.0826	0.0680	0.0560	0.0462	0.0181	0.0074	0.0031	0.0014	0.0006
23	0.7954	0.6342	0.5067	0.4057	0.3256	0.2618	0.2109	0.1703	0.1378	0.1117	0.0907	0.0738	0.0601	0.0491	0.0402	0.0151	0.0059	0.0024	0.0010	0.0004
24	0.7876	0.6217	0.4919	0.3901	0.3101	0.2470	0.1971	0.1577	0.1264	0.1015	0.0817	0.0659	0.0532	0.0431	0.0349	0.0126	0.0047	0.0018	0.0007	0.0003
25	0.7798	0.6095	0.4776	0.3751	0.2953	0.2330	0.1842	0.1460	0.1160	0.0923	0.0736	0.0588	0.0471	0.0378	0.0304	0.0105	0.0038	0.0014	0.0006	0.0002
26	0.7720	0.5976	0.4637	0.3607	0.2812	0.2198	0.1722	0.1352	0.1064	0.0839	0.0663	0.0525	0.0417	0.0331	0.0264	0.0087	0.0030	0.0011	0.0004	0.0002
27	0.7644	0.5859	0.4502	0.3468	0.2678	0.2074	0.1609	0.1252	0.0976	0.0763	0.0597	0.0469	0.0369	0.0291	0.0230	0.0073	0.0024	0.0008	0.0003	0.0001
28	0.7568	0.5744	0.4371	0.3335	0.2551	0.1956	0.1504	0.1159	0.0895	0.0693	0.0538	0.0419	0.0326	0.0255	0.0200	0.0061	0.0019	0.0006	0.0002	0.0001
29	0.7493	0.5631	0.4243	0.3207	0.2429	0.1846	0.1406	0.1073	0.0822	0.0630	0.0485	0.0374	0.0289	0.0224	0.0174	0.0051	0.0015	0.0005	0.0002	0.0001
30	0.7419	0.5521	0.4120	0.3083	0.2314	0.1741	0.1314	0.0994	0.0754	0.0573	0.0437	0.0334	0.0256	0.0196	0.0151	0.0042	0.0012	0.0004	0.0001	*******
31	0.7346	0.5412	0.4000	0.2965	0.2204	0.1643	0.1228	0.0920	0.0691	0.0521	0.0394	0.0298	0.0226	0.0172	0.0131	0.0035	0.0010	0.0003	0.0001	*******
32	0.7273	0.5306	0.3883	0.2851	0.2099	0.1550	0.1147	0.0852	0.0634	0.0474	0.0355	0.0266	0.0200	0.0151	0.0114	0.0029	0.0008	0.0002	0.0001	*******
33	0.7201	0.5202	0.3770	0.2741	0.1999	0.1462	0.1072	0.0789	0.0582	0.0431	0.0319	0.0238	0.0177	0.0132	0.0099	0.0024	0.0006	0.0002	0.0001	*******
34	0.7130	0.5100	0.3660	0.2636	0.1904	0.1379	0.1002	0.0730	0.0534	0.0391	0.0288	0.0212	0.0157	0.0116	0.0086	0.0020	0.0005	0.0001	*******	*******
35	0.7059	0.5000	0.3554	0.2534	0.1813	0.1301	0.0937	0.0676	0.0490	0.0356	0.0259	0.0189	0.0139	0.0102	0.0075	0.0017	0.0004	0.0001	*******	*******
40	0.6717	0.4529	0.3066	0.2083	0.1420	0.0972	0.0668	0.0460	0.0318	0.0221	0.0154	0.0107	0.0075	0.0053	0.0037	0.0007	0.0001	*******	*******	*******
50	0.6080	0.3715	0.2281	0.1407	0.0872	0.0543	0.0339	0.0213	0.0134	0.0085	0.0054	0.0035	0.0022	0.0014	0.0009	0.0001	*******	*******	*******	*******
60	0.5504	0.3048	0.1697	0.0951	0.0535	0.0303	0.0173	0.0099	0.0057	0.0033	0.0019	0.0011	0.0007	0.0004	0.0002	*******	*******	*******	*******	*******
70	0.4983	0.2500	0.1263	0.0642	0.0329	0.0169	0.0088	0.0046	0.0024	0.0013	0.0007	0.0004	0.0002	0.0001	0.0001	*******	*******	*******	*******	*******
80	0.4511	0.2051	0.0940	0.0434	0.0202	0.0095	0.0045	0.0021	0.0010	0.0005	0.0002	0.0001	0.0001	*******	*******	*******	*******	*******	*******	*******
360	0.0278	0.0008	*******	*******	*******	*******	*******	*******	*******	*******	*******	*******	*******	*******	*******	*******	*******	*******	*******	*******

******* Factor < 0.0001

TABLE 3 Future Value Annuity Factors = $\dfrac{(1 + r)^n - 1}{r}$ (**FV** of $1 per period for **n** periods at interest rate **r**)

	1%	2%	3%	4%	5%	6%	7%	8%	9%	10%	11%	12%	13%	14%	15%	20%	25%	30%	35%	40%
1	1.0000	1.0000	1.0000	1.0000	1.0000	1.0000	1.0000	1.0000	1.0000	1.0000	1.0000	1.0000	1.0000	1.0000	1.0000	1.0000	1.0000	1.0000	1.0000	1.0000
2	2.0100	2.0200	2.0300	2.0400	2.0500	2.0600	2.0700	2.0800	2.0900	2.1000	2.1100	2.1200	2.1300	2.1400	2.1500	2.2000	2.2500	2.3000	2.3500	2.4000
3	3.0301	3.0604	3.0909	3.1216	3.1525	3.1836	3.2149	3.2464	3.2781	3.3100	3.3421	3.3744	3.4069	3.4396	3.4725	3.6400	3.8125	3.9900	4.1725	4.3600
4	4.0604	4.1216	4.1836	4.2465	4.3101	4.3746	4.4399	4.5061	4.5731	4.6410	4.7097	4.7793	4.8498	4.9211	4.9934	5.3680	5.7656	6.1870	6.6329	7.1040
5	5.1010	5.2040	5.3091	5.4163	5.5256	5.6371	5.7507	5.8686	5.9847	6.1051	6.2278	6.3528	6.4803	6.6101	6.7424	7.4416	8.2070	9.0431	9.9544	10.946
6	6.1520	6.3081	6.4684	6.6330	6.8019	6.9753	7.1533	7.3359	7.5233	7.7156	7.9129	8.1152	8.3227	8.5355	8.7537	9.9299	11.259	12.756	14.438	16.324
7	7.2135	7.4343	7.6625	7.8983	8.1420	8.3938	8.6540	8.9228	9.2004	9.4872	9.7833	10.089	10.405	10.730	11.067	12.916	15.073	17.583	20.492	23.853
8	8.2857	8.5830	8.8923	9.2142	9.5491	9.8975	10.260	10.637	11.028	11.436	11.859	12.300	12.757	13.233	13.727	16.499	19.842	23.858	28.664	34.395
9	9.3685	9.7546	10.159	10.583	11.027	11.491	11.978	12.488	13.021	13.579	14.164	14.776	15.416	16.085	16.786	20.799	25.802	32.015	39.696	49.153
10	10.462	10.950	11.464	12.006	12.578	13.181	13.816	14.487	15.193	15.937	16.722	17.549	18.420	19.337	20.304	25.959	33.253	42.619	54.590	69.814
11	11.567	12.169	12.808	13.486	14.207	14.972	15.784	16.645	17.560	18.531	19.561	20.655	21.814	23.045	24.349	32.150	42.566	56.405	74.697	98.739
12	12.683	13.412	14.192	15.026	15.917	16.870	17.888	18.977	20.141	21.384	22.713	24.133	25.650	27.271	29.002	39.581	54.208	74.327	101.84	139.23
13	13.809	14.680	15.618	16.627	17.713	18.882	20.141	21.495	22.953	24.523	26.212	28.029	29.985	32.089	34.352	48.497	68.760	97.625	138.48	195.93
14	14.947	15.974	17.086	18.292	19.599	21.015	22.550	24.215	26.019	27.975	30.095	32.393	34.883	37.581	40.505	59.196	86.949	127.91	187.95	275.30
15	16.097	17.293	18.599	20.024	21.579	23.276	25.129	27.152	29.361	31.772	34.405	37.280	40.417	43.842	47.580	72.035	109.69	167.29	254.74	386.42
16	17.258	18.639	20.157	21.825	23.657	25.673	27.888	30.324	33.003	35.950	39.190	42.753	46.672	50.980	55.717	87.442	138.11	218.47	344.90	541.99
17	18.430	20.012	21.762	23.698	25.840	28.213	30.840	33.750	36.974	40.545	44.501	48.884	53.739	59.118	65.075	105.93	173.64	285.01	466.61	759.78
18	19.615	21.412	23.414	25.645	28.132	30.906	33.999	37.450	41.301	45.599	50.396	55.750	61.725	68.394	75.836	128.12	218.04	371.52	630.92	1064.7
19	20.811	22.841	25.117	27.671	30.539	33.760	37.379	41.446	46.018	51.159	56.939	63.440	70.749	78.969	88.212	154.74	273.56	483.97	852.75	1491.6
20	22.019	24.297	26.870	29.778	33.066	36.786	40.995	45.762	51.160	57.275	64.203	72.052	80.947	91.025	102.44	186.69	342.94	630.17	1152.2	2089.2
21	23.239	25.783	28.676	31.969	35.719	39.993	44.865	50.423	56.765	64.002	72.265	81.699	92.470	104.77	118.81	225.03	429.68	820.22	1556.5	2925.9
22	24.472	27.299	30.537	34.248	38.505	43.392	49.006	55.457	62.873	71.403	81.214	92.503	105.49	120.44	137.63	271.03	538.10	1067.3	2102.3	4097.2
23	25.716	28.845	32.453	36.618	41.430	46.996	53.436	60.893	69.532	79.543	91.148	104.60	120.20	138.30	159.28	326.24	673.63	1388.5	2839.0	5737.1
24	26.973	30.422	34.426	39.083	44.502	50.816	58.177	66.765	76.790	88.497	102.17	118.16	136.83	158.66	184.17	392.48	843.03	1806.0	3833.7	8033.0
25	28.243	32.030	36.459	41.646	47.727	54.865	63.249	73.106	84.701	98.347	114.41	133.33	155.62	181.87	212.79	471.98	1054.8	2348.8	5176.5	11247
26	29.526	33.671	38.553	44.312	51.113	59.156	68.676	79.954	93.324	109.18	128.00	150.33	176.85	208.33	245.71	567.38	1319.5	3054.4	6989.3	15747
27	30.821	35.344	40.710	47.084	54.669	63.706	74.484	87.351	102.72	121.10	143.08	169.37	200.84	238.50	283.57	681.85	1650.4	3971.8	9436.5	22047
28	32.129	37.051	42.931	49.968	58.403	68.528	80.698	95.339	112.97	134.21	159.82	190.70	227.95	272.89	327.10	819.22	2064.0	5164.3	12740	30867
29	33.450	38.792	45.219	52.966	62.323	73.640	87.347	103.97	124.14	148.63	178.40	214.58	258.58	312.09	377.17	984.07	2580.9	6714.6	17200	43214
30	34.785	40.568	47.575	56.085	66.439	79.058	94.461	113.28	136.31	164.49	199.02	241.33	293.20	356.79	434.75	1181.9	3227.2	8730.0	23222	60501
31	36.133	42.379	50.003	59.328	70.761	84.802	102.07	123.35	149.58	181.94	221.94	271.29	332.32	407.74	500.96	1419.3	4035.0	11350	31350	84703
32	37.494	44.227	52.503	62.701	75.299	90.890	110.22	134.21	164.04	201.14	247.32	304.85	376.52	465.82	577.10	1704.1	5044.7	14756	42324	*******
33	38.869	46.112	55.078	66.210	80.064	97.343	118.93	145.95	179.80	222.25	275.53	342.43	426.46	532.04	664.67	2045.9	6306.9	19184	57138	*******
34	40.258	48.034	57.730	69.858	85.067	104.18	128.26	158.63	196.98	245.48	306.84	384.52	482.90	607.52	765.37	2456.1	7884.6	24940	77137	*******
35	41.660	49.994	60.462	73.652	90.320	111.43	138.24	172.32	215.71	271.02	341.59	431.66	546.68	693.57	881.17	2948.3	9856.8	32423	*******	*******
40	48.886	60.402	75.401	95.026	120.80	154.76	199.64	259.06	337.88	442.59	581.83	767.09	1013.7	1342.0	1779.1	7343.9	30089	********	********	*******
50	64.463	84.579	112.80	152.67	209.35	290.34	406.53	573.77	815.08	1163.9	1668.8	2400.0	3459.5	4994.5	7217.7	45497	*******	********	*******	*******
60	81.670	114.05	163.05	237.99	353.58	533.13	813.52	1253.2	1944.8	3034.8	4755.1	7471.6	11762	18535	29220	*******	*******	*******	*******	*******
70	100.68	149.98	230.59	364.29	588.53	967.93	1614.1	2720.1	4619.2	7887.5	13518	23223	39945	68733	*******	*******	*******	*******	*******	*******
80	121.67	193.77	321.36	551.24	971.23	1746.6	3189.1	5886.9	10951	20474	38401	72146	*******	*********	*******	*******	*******	*******	*******	*******

Factor > 99999

TABLE 4 **Present Value Annuity Factors** $= \dfrac{1 - \dfrac{1}{(1+r)^n}}{r}$ **(PV of $1 per period for n periods at interest rate r)**

n	1%	2%	3%	4%	5%	6%	7%	8%	9%	10%	11%	12%	13%	14%	15%	20%	25%	30%	35%	40%
1	0.9901	0.9804	0.9709	0.9615	0.9524	0.9434	0.9346	0.9529	0.9174	0.9091	0.9009	0.8929	0.8850	0.8772	0.8896	0.8333	0.8000	0.7692	0.7407	0.7143
2	1.9704	1.9416	1.9135	1.8861	1.8594	1.8334	1.8080	1.7833	1.7591	1.7355	1.7125	1.6901	1.6681	1.6467	1.6257	1.5278	1.4400	1.3609	1.2894	1.2245
3	2.9410	2.8839	2.8286	2.7751	2.7232	2.6730	2.6243	2.5771	2.5313	2.4869	2.4437	2.4018	2.3612	2.3216	2.2832	2.1065	1.9520	1.8161	1.6959	1.5889
4	3.9020	3.8077	3.7171	3.6299	3.5460	3.4651	3.3872	3.3121	3.2397	3.1699	3.1024	3.0373	2.9745	2.9137	2.8550	2.5887	2.3616	2.1662	1.9969	1.8492
5	4.8534	4.7135	4.5797	4.4518	4.3295	4.2124	4.1002	3.9927	3.8897	3.7908	3.6959	3.6048	3.5172	3.4331	3.3522	2.9906	2.6893	2.4356	2.2200	2.0352
6	5.7955	5.6014	5.4172	5.2421	5.0757	4.9173	4.7665	4.6229	4.4859	4.3553	4.2305	4.1114	3.9975	3.8887	3.7845	3.3255	2.9514	2.6427	2.3852	2.1680
7	6.7282	6.4720	6.2303	6.0021	5.7864	5.5824	5.3893	5.2064	5.0330	4.8684	4.7122	4.5638	4.4226	4.2883	4.1604	3.6046	3.1611	2.8021	2.5075	2.2628
8	7.6517	7.3255	7.0197	6.7327	6.4632	6.2098	5.9713	5.7466	5.5348	5.3349	5.1461	4.9676	4.7988	4.6389	4.4873	3.8372	3.3289	2.9247	2.5982	2.3306
9	8.5660	8.1622	7.7861	7.4353	7.1078	6.8017	6.5152	6.2469	5.9952	5.7590	5.5370	5.3282	5.1317	4.9464	4.7716	4.0310	3.4631	3.0190	2.6653	2.3790
10	9.4713	8.9826	8.5302	8.1109	7.7217	7.3601	7.0236	6.7101	6.4177	6.1446	5.8892	5.6502	5.4262	5.2161	5.0188	4.1925	3.5705	3.0915	2.7150	2.4136
11	10.368	9.7868	9.2526	8.7605	8.3064	7.8869	7.4987	7.1390	6.8052	6.4951	6.2065	5.9377	5.6869	5.4527	5.2337	4.3271	3.6564	3.1473	2.7519	2.4383
12	11.255	10.575	9.9540	9.3851	8.8633	8.3838	7.9427	7.5361	7.1607	6.8137	6.4924	6.1944	5.9176	5.6603	5.4206	4.4392	3.7251	3.1903	2.7792	2.4559
13	12.134	11.348	10.635	9.9856	9.3936	8.8527	8.3577	7.9038	7.4869	7.1034	6.7499	6.4235	6.1218	5.8424	5.5831	4.5327	3.7801	3.2233	2.7994	2.4685
14	13.004	12.106	11.296	10.563	9.8986	9.2950	8.7455	8.2442	7.7862	7.3667	6.9819	6.6282	6.3025	6.0021	5.7245	4.6106	3.8241	3.2487	2.8144	2.4775
15	13.865	12.849	11.938	11.118	10.380	9.7122	9.1079	8.5595	8.0607	7.6061	7.1909	6.8109	6.4624	6.1422	5.8474	4.6755	3.8593	3.2682	2.8255	2.4839
16	14.718	13.578	12.561	11.652	10.838	10.106	9.4466	8.8514	8.3126	7.8237	7.3792	6.9740	6.6039	6.2651	5.9542	4.7296	3.8874	3.2832	2.8337	2.4885
17	15.562	14.292	13.166	12.166	11.274	10.477	9.7632	9.1216	8.5436	8.0216	7.5488	7.1196	6.7291	6.3729	6.0472	4.7746	3.9099	3.2948	2.8398	2.4918
18	16.398	14.992	13.754	12.659	11.690	10.828	10.059	9.3719	8.7556	8.2014	7.7016	7.2497	6.8399	6.4674	6.1280	4.8122	3.9279	3.3037	2.8443	2.4941
19	17.226	15.678	14.324	13.134	12.085	11.158	10.336	9.6036	8.9501	8.3649	7.8393	7.3658	6.9380	6.5504	6.1982	4.8435	3.9424	3.3105	2.8476	2.4958
20	18.046	16.351	14.877	13.590	12.462	11.470	10.594	9.8181	9.1285	8.5136	7.9633	7.4694	7.0248	6.6231	6.2593	4.8696	3.9539	3.3158	2.8501	2.4970
21	18.857	17.011	15.415	14.029	12.821	11.764	10.836	10.017	9.2922	8.6487	8.0751	7.5620	7.1016	6.6870	6.3125	4.8913	3.9631	3.3198	2.8519	2.4979
22	19.660	17.658	15.937	14.451	13.163	12.042	11.061	10.201	9.4424	8.7715	8.1757	7.6446	7.1695	6.7429	6.3587	4.9094	3.9705	3.3230	2.8533	2.4985
23	20.456	18.292	16.444	14.857	13.489	12.303	11.272	10.371	9.5802	8.8832	8.2664	7.7184	7.2297	6.7921	6.3988	4.9245	3.9764	3.3254	2.8543	2.4989
24	21.243	18.914	16.936	15.247	13.799	12.550	11.469	10.529	9.7066	8.9847	8.3481	7.7843	7.2829	6.8351	6.4338	4.9371	3.9811	3.3272	2.8550	2.4992
25	22.023	19.523	17.413	15.622	14.094	12.783	11.654	10.675	9.8226	9.0770	8.4217	7.8431	7.3300	6.8729	6.4641	4.9476	3.9849	3.3286	2.8556	2.4994
26	22.795	20.121	17.877	15.983	14.375	13.003	11.826	10.810	9.9290	9.1609	8.4881	7.8957	7.3717	6.9061	6.4906	4.9563	3.9879	3.3297	2.8560	2.4996
27	23.560	20.707	18.327	16.330	14.643	13.211	11.987	10.935	10.027	9.2372	8.5478	7.9426	7.4086	6.9352	6.5135	4.9636	3.9903	3.3305	2.8563	2.4997
28	24.316	21.281	18.764	16.663	14.898	13.406	12.137	11.051	10.116	9.3066	8.6016	7.9844	7.4412	6.9607	6.5335	4.9697	3.9923	3.3312	2.8565	2.4998
29	25.066	21.844	19.188	16.984	15.141	13.591	12.278	11.158	10.198	9.3696	8.6501	8.0218	7.4701	6.9830	6.5509	4.9747	3.9938	3.3317	2.8567	2.4999
30	25.808	22.396	19.600	17.292	15.372	13.765	12.409	11.258	10.274	9.4269	8.6938	8.0552	7.4957	7.0027	6.5660	4.9789	3.9950	3.3321	2.8568	2.4999
31	26.542	22.938	20.000	17.588	15.593	13.929	12.532	11.350	10.343	9.4790	8.7331	8.0850	7.5183	7.0199	6.5791	4.9824	3.9960	3.3324	2.8569	2.4999
32	27.270	23.468	20.389	17.874	15.803	14.084	12.647	11.435	10.406	9.5264	8.7686	8.1116	7.5383	7.0350	6.5905	4.9854	3.9968	3.3326	2.8569	2.4999
33	27.990	23.989	20.766	18.148	16.003	14.230	12.754	11.514	10.464	9.5694	8.8005	8.1354	7.5560	7.0482	6.6005	4.9878	3.9975	3.3328	2.8570	2.5000
34	28.703	24.499	21.132	18.411	16.193	14.368	12.854	11.587	10.518	9.6086	8.8293	8.1566	7.5717	7.0599	6.6091	4.9898	3.9980	3.3329	2.8570	2.5000
35	29.409	24.999	21.487	18.665	16.374	14.498	12.948	11.655	10.567	9.6442	8.8552	8.1755	7.5856	7.0700	6.6166	4.9915	3.9984	3.3330	2.8571	2.5000
40	32.835	27.355	23.115	19.793	17.159	15.046	13.332	11.925	10.757	9.7791	8.9511	8.2438	7.6344	7.1050	6.6418	4.9966	3.9995	3.3332	2.8571	2.5000
50	39.196	31.424	25.730	21.482	18.256	15.762	13.801	12.233	10.962	9.9148	9.0417	8.3045	7.6752	7.1327	6.6605	4.9995	3.9999	3.3333	2.8571	2.5000
60	44.955	34.761	27.676	22.623	18.929	16.161	14.039	12.377	11.048	9.9672	9.0736	8.3240	7.6873	7.1401	6.6651	4.9999	4.0000	3.3333	2.8571	2.5000
70	50.169	37.499	29.123	23.395	19.343	16.385	14.160	12.443	11.084	9.9873	9.0848	8.3303	7.6908	7.1421	6.6663	5.0000	4.0000	3.3333	2.8571	2.5000
80	54.888	39.745	30.201	23.915	19.596	16.509	14.222	12.474	11.100	9.9951	9.0888	8.3324	7.6919	7.1427	6.6666	5.0000	4.0000	3.3333	2.8571	2.5000
360	97.218	49.960	33.333	25.000	20.000	16.667	14.286	12.500	11.111	10.000	9.0909	8.3333	7.6923	7.1429	6.6667	5.0000	4.0000	3.3333	2.8571	2.5000
999	99.995	50.000	33.333	25.000	20.000	16.667	14.286	12.500	11.111	10.000	9.0909	8.3333	7.6923	7.1429	6.6667	5.0000	4.0000	3.3333	2.8571	2.5000

GLOSSARY

Numbers in parentheses refer to the chapter and page on which the definition appears, e.g., (7:243) means Chapter 7, page 243.

absolute purchasing power parity—a relationship that holds that, at equilibrium, the spot exchange rate between two currencies is equal to the ratio of the price levels between the countries (7:243)

accelerated cost recovery system—the depreciation method required for tax calculations in the United States (4C:106)

acceptable range—the set of debt-equity mixes that produces a weighted-average cost of capital at or near its minimum value (15:542)

accounting profits—the bottom number on an income statement using rules of measurement determined by accounting authorities (2:28)

accrual accounting—a system of recording accounting numbers when economic events have been achieved (4:79)

activity-based costing—a cost allocation method based on cost driver activities (4:83)

adding value—making the output of a process worth more for its customers (13:473)

adjusted gross income—a tax term referring to gross income less permitted subtractions (4B:102)

agency cost—the reduction in a principal's wealth when an agent does not act in the principal's best interests (2:35)

agency problem—the possibility that an agent will not act in the best interests of his/her principal (2:33)

agent—a person who acts on behalf of and by the authority of another (2:33)

aggressive security—an investment with a beta greater than 1 (8:284)

amortize—to repay a loan (21:756)

analytical finance theory—theory about the factual nature of finance and what decisions should be made (23:831)

annual percentage rate—a standardized interest rate which must be disclosed to borrowers and lenders under U.S. law (5:184)

annuity—a series of cash flows that is equal in amount, direction of flow, and time distance apart (5:166)

annuity due (annuity in advance, BEGIN annuity)—an annuity in which the cash flows occur at the beginning of each time period (5:172)

annuity in advance (annuity due, BEGIN annuity)—an annuity in which the cash flows occur at the beginning of each time period (5:172)

annuity in arrears (ordinary annuity, END annuity)—an annuity in which the cash flows occur at the end of each time period (5:172)

asset-based loan—a loan backed with a pledge of assets (20:738)

asymmetric information hypothesis—a theory that explores the ramifications of management having better information about a company's prospects than investors (15:547)

average cost—total cost divided by the number of units made (4:80)

average tax rate—the single number which, if multiplied by taxable income, produces the total amount of tax (4:88)

balanced-budget unit—an individual or business that spends exactly what it earns (19:691)

balance of payments—the net difference between money inflows and outflows for a country during a period of time (7:231)

balloon—a large final loan payment (21:759)

banker's acceptance—a promissory note which carries a bank's promise of payment (20:723)

bankruptcy—the condition of being unable to make payments on debt (15:541)

base level of interest rates—the level of interest rates common to all financial instruments in the economy (6:201)

BEGIN annuity (annuity due, annuity in advance)—an annuity in which the cash flows occur at the beginning of each time period (5:172)

benchmark comparison—comparison to a norm which is valid across many companies and/or industries (4:90)

beta—the numerical relationship between the returns from an investment and the returns from the overall market (8:284)

bond—a type of financial instrument that is a long-term loan, giving the holder the right to receive interest payments and repayment of the loan principal (1:8)

bond indenture—the formal agreement between a bond's issuer and buyer (21:768)

break-even point—the level of sales at which revenues equal operating costs so that operating profit (EBIT) equals zero (4A:95)

break point—a point on the cost of capital schedule where the firm's cost of capital increases (10:354)

bridge loan—a loan to provide temporary financing until future, more permanent financing is arranged (21:756)

broker—an individual or company that locates buyers and sellers and brings them together (19:691)

budget—a time-oriented statement of the financial resources allocated to carry out an organization's activities (18:646)

bullet—a single payment equal to the total principal amount of a loan (21:760)

business risk—the total variability of a firm's operating results (8:268)

business system—the set of integrated and overlapping work processes that constitutes an entire business organization (13:466)

buying stock on margin—purchasing stock using borrowed money for part of the purchase price (15:540)

call—an option to buy (9:318)

call risk—the risk that a lender will retire a security prior to maturity, taking a good earning opportunity away from an investor (6:220)

cap—a limit to how high the interest rate on a loan can rise (21:753)

capital asset pricing model (CAPM)—the finance model relating asset prices and rates of return to the asset's beta, its impact on the risk of a well-diversified portfolio (8:288)

capital budget—a financial plan showing a firm's intended outlays for long-term assets (11:372)

capital budgeting—the process of discovering, evaluating, and deciding whether to pursue investments in long-term assets (11:372)

capital gains income—a tax term referring to income from asset sales (4B:101)

capital gains yield—the portion of a security's yield coming from growth in value (9:307)

capitalist economic system—an economy marked by private ownership of businesses and the resources necessary for producing goods and services (2:27)

capital market line (CML)—a graph of investors' required rate of return as a function of an asset's total risk (8:275)

capital markets—the markets for securities with maturity greater than one year (19:693)

capital structure—the combination of long-term debt and equity financing employed by a firm, often used as a synonym for *the debt-equity mix* (15:527)

carrying costs—the annual costs of storing inventory (12B:455)

cash budget—a time-oriented statement of projected cash flows (18D:680)

cash conversion cycle—the length of time from the outflow of cash to purchase inventory until the inflow of cash from the collection of accounts receivable (4D:127)

cash cow—a firm that regularly generates more cash than it needs for operations and growth (18:645)

cash flow—money received or paid by an organization (4:78)

certificate of deposit—a receipt for a bank deposit in which the depositor commits not to withdraw funds from the bank for a specified period of time in return for a better rate of interest (5:170)

characteristic line—the relationship of an investment's rate of return to the overall rate of return available in the market (8:282)

chattel mortgage—a collateral claim on property other than real estate (21:761)

chief financial officer (CFO)—the senior finance professional responsible for all of a company's financial activities (1:9)

classical theory of interest rates—a theory of interest rate determination focusing on household savings and business investment (6:201)

clientele—a group of investors with a similar preference for dividends (17:619)

closely held firm—a company in which a small number of shareholders own a significant percentage of the outstanding common stock (15:547)

coefficient of variation—standard deviation divided by expected value (8:274)

collar—a combination of a cap and a floor (21:753)

collateral—property pledged in support of a loan (20:738)

commercial banker—an individual or organization that specializes in taking deposits from investors and in making loans to individuals and organizations (1:9)

commercial paper—short-term, unsecured notes issued by large corporations (20:743)

common causes of variation—factors that cause natural variation in a stable process (13:482)

common size financial statement—a financial statement in which the numbers are presented as percentages of the statement's total number, rather than in absolute money terms (4D:115)

common stock—ownership shares in a corporation (22:795)

compensating balance—a deposit that must remain at the bank as long as a loan is outstanding (20:736)

competitive benchmarking—using the best example available, regardless of source, as the firm's target (4:91)

competitive market—a market in which no participant has enough economic power to influence prices (2:28)

compounding—adding compound interest to a present value to produce a future value (5:156)

compound interest—interest paid on both the initial principal and previously paid interest (5:154)

concentration banking—the practice of instructing customers to mail payments to a local bank which then forwards the payment electronically (12:433)

consignment—shipping goods to a buyer but not requiring payment until the goods are resold (20:723)

consolidated tax return—a tax return combining the income of a parent company and one or more of its subsidiaries (4C:109)

contract—an agreement between parties specifying each party's role in the relationship (2:35)

contribution margin—the net amount brought into the firm by the production and sale of one unit of its product (4A:95)

contribution percentage—the net amount brought into the fim by the production and sale of one dollar of its product (4A:95)

controller—the finance/accounting professional responsible for a company's financial record-keeping and reporting (1:17)

convertible security—a security that may be exchanged for another (22:811)

correlation coefficient—a measure of the relationship between the returns from two investments (8:278)

cost driver—an activity that results in costs being incurred in operations (4:82)

cost of a source of funds—the rate a firm must earn from the use of funds to provide the rate of return required by that investor (10:338)

cost of capital—the minimum rate of return a firm must earn on new investments to satisfy its creditors and stockholders (10:336)

cost of capital schedule—a graph showing how a firm's cost of capital will increase with the amount of capital it attempts to raise (10:354)

cost of poor quality—the sum of all unnecessary costs due to process and product quality being less than perfect (13:480)

counterparties—the participants in a swap (21:754)

coupon—the amount of cash interest paid annually by a bond (9:300)

covered interest arbitrage—simultaneous borrowing and lending in two currencies, coupled with spot and forward exchange contracts to take advantage of a discrepancy in the interest rate parity relationship (7:247)

credit analysis—a study to determine the ability of a customer to repay a loan (20:734)

cross rate—the price of one foreign currency in terms of another, calculated via their relationships to a third currency (7:235)

cross-section comparison—comparison of some number to equivalent data from other companies or from the industry over a common period of time (4:91)

current yield—the portion of a bond's yield coming from interest payments (9:307)

customer-processor-supplier—the three simultaneous roles played by everyone involved in a process (13:473)

customer-supplier alignment—a close working relationship between two parties, one of whom supplies the other, to ensure that the needs of each are being met (2:42)

cycle time—the time from the beginning to the end of any process or process step (4:78)

date of declaration—the date a company's board of directors votes to pay a dividend (17:627)

date of record—the date a company determines who will receive a dividend (17:627)

debenture—a bond with no collateral (21:768)

debt equity mix—the combination of debt and equity financing employed by a firm (15:527)

debt maturity mix—the blend of debt maturities used by a firm (16:583)

deep discount bond—a bond with a price significantly less than its face value (9:305)

default—to breach a loan agreement (21:769)

default risk—the risk that a borrower will delay or not make scheduled payments, or otherwise violate a loan agreement (6:217)

defensive security—an investment with a beta less than 1 (8:284)

deficit-budget unit—an individual or business that spends more than it earns (19:691)

degree of financial leverage (DFL)—a ratio measuring the amount of magnification built into a firm's financial cost structure (15B:562)

degree of operating leverage (DOL)—a ratio measuring the amount of magnification built into a firm's operating cost structure (15B:557)

degree of total leverage (DTL)—a ratio measuring the amount of magnification built into a firm's overall cost structure (15B:564)

derivative security—a contract whose value is defined by a financial market rate or the price of a financial instrument (16:597)

dilute—to reduce the percentage of a firm owned by each common share by increasing the number of shares outstanding (15:546); to weaken the rights, power, or value of a security (22:796)

direct cost—a cost directly traceable to the manufacture of a product or delivery of a service (4:82)

direct exchange rate—the number of units of domestic currency required to purchase one unit of a foreign currency (7:232)

direct lease—a lease with only one investor, the lessor, who owns the leased asset (21:762)

director of financial analysis—the finance professional responsible for a company's financial analysis and planning (1:17)

discount bond—a bond with a price less than its face value (9:302)

discounting—removing compound interest from a future value to produce a present value (5:160)

discount loan—a loan in which interest is paid at the beginning of the loan period (20:737)

discretionary account—a balance sheet account whose value does not change with sales but rather is set by a management decision (18:653)

diversify—to spread your money across several investments, i.e., to purchase a portfolio (8:276)

dividend—a payment made by a corporation directly to its stockholders (17:612)

dividend policy—a company's plan for the level and pattern of its dividend payments (17:611)

dividend unit—the right to receive the dividends paid on a specific number of shares of stock as if the stock itself were owned (2B:51)

dividend yield—the portion of a stock's rate of return coming from dividend payments (9:317)

double taxation—the taxing of income twice: first as business income and then as income of the owner of the business (4C:108)

earned income—a tax term referring to income from personal services (4B:101)

EBIT-EPS analysis—a graph showing how EPS responds to EBIT for various financing alternatives (15:533)

econometric model—a computer-based model of all or some part of the macroeconomy, in which the relationships between variables are represented by a set of simultaneous equations (6:205)

economic exposure—exposure to a reduction in monetary asset values, an increase in monetary liabilities, or a reduction in cash flow due to adverse exchange rate movements (7:250)

economic order quantity—the quantity of inventory to purchase with each order to minimize inventory costs (12B:455)

economic profits—the money returns to the investors in a firm (2:28)

effective interest rate—a true rate of interest which summarizes the total change in value over some period of time (5:179)

efficient allocation of resources—directing the resources of an economy (money, labor, machinery, land, etc.) to those businesses where they can produce goods and services of the greatest value (2:28)

efficient capital market—a financial market in which security prices fully contain the meaning of all known information (2:30)

EFN relationship—a formula which relates external financing needed to growth in sales (18:660)

END annuity (ordinary annuity, annuity in arrears)—an annuity in which the cash flows occur at the end of each time period (5:172)

environmental risk—unexpected changes outside the firm that impact its operations (8:268)

Eurobond—a bond denominated in a currency other than that of the country in which it is sold (21:771)

Euronote facility—a contract for the issuance of Euronotes (20:745)

Euronotes—short-term, unsecured, standardized notes issued by large corporations and governments in the Eurodollar market (20:745)

excess cash—the amount of spontaneous financing produced by a firm over and above what it needs to acquire the assets necessary to support its sales forecast (18:659)

exchange position—an anticipated cash flow not fully hedged against exchange-rate movements (16:599)

(foreign) exchange rate—the value of one currency in terms of another (7:230)

ex-dividend date—the date by which stock must be purchased to receive the next dividend (17:628)

exemptions—a tax term referring to family size which determines a subtraction from income (4B:103)

expectations hypothesis—a theory of the term structure focusing on investors' forecasts of future interest rates (6:211)

expected value—the weighted average of the forecasted rates of return from an investment (8:270)

external financing needed—the amount of financing a firm must raise from outside sources to acquire the assets necessary to support its forecasted level of sales (18:659)

factor—a company that purchases accounts receivable (20:739)

factoring—selling accounts receivable (20:739)

finance—the study and practice of how money is raised and used by organizations (1:6)

financial analysis—the use of financial and other data to understand the financial health of an organization (4:74)

financial environment—the business and social forces which impact the financial operations of an organization (1:8)

financial feedback—the iterative process of incorporating the cost of new financing into pro-forma statements (18E:686)

financial instrument—a document giving the holder a claim to present or future cash flows (1:8)

financial intermediary—an organization that takes funds from surplus-budget units and provides them to deficit-budget units (19:692)

financial lease—a lease providing long-term use of an asset (21:764)

financial leverage—the use of debt to magnify the returns to equity investors (4D:130); more specifically magnification of changes in earnings per share (EPS) in response to changes in EBIT that is caused by the existence of fixed financing costs (interest obligations) in the firm's cost structure (15:530)

financial manager—a person responsible for analyzing and improving the money flows of an organization (1:9)

financial managing—the art of integrating financial theory and practice with the rest of an organization's management systems to support the delivery of low-cost, high-quality goods and services to customers and to maximize the value of the organization to its stockholders and other stakeholders (1:5)

financial risk—the increased variability in a firm's financial results caused by its financing mix (8:268)

Fisher effect—a relationship that holds that, at equilibrium, real rates are the same in all currencies (7:242)

fixed cost—a cost that remains constant when sales changes (4:81)

fixed exchange rate system—a system in which exchange rates are kept constant by government policy (7:230)

flat rate tax system—a tax system with a single rate independent of income level (4:88)

floating exchange rate system—a system in which exchange rates are allowed to change freely with market conditions (7:231)

floor—a limit to how low the interest rate on a loan can fall (21:753)

flotation costs—the total amount paid to third parties in order to raise funds (10:338)

foreign bond—a bond issued by a foreign borrower in the currency of the country of issue (21:771)

(foreign) exchange rate—the value of one currency in terms of another (7:230)

foreign exchange risk—the possibility of variation in exchange rates which makes uncertain the value of assets, liabilities, cash flows, and income denominated in a foreign currency (7:230)

forward contract—a contract binding the parties to a future transaction on a specified date and at a specified price or rate (16:596)

forward discount—the condition when forward rates are less than the spot rate, also the amount of the difference (7:239)

forward exchange contract—a contract binding the parties to a future trade of currencies on a specified date and at a specified exchange rate, the forward rate (7:238)

forward (exchange) rate—an exchange rate for a contract to be entered into today (forward exchange contract) but with the trade of currencies to take place on a specified future date (7:239)

forward premium—the condition when forward rates are greater than the spot rate, also the amount of the difference (7:239)

forward rate agreement (FRA)—a contract binding the parties to a future loan on a specified date, for a specified period, and at a specified interest rate (16:596)

FRICTO—an acronym (flexibility, risk, income, control, timing, other) summarizing practical considerations in setting the debt-equity mix (15:545)

full-service lease—a lease for an asset and also its operation and maintenance (21:763)

fully invested IRR (IRR*)—the rate of return from the combination of a project and any subsequent reinvestment (11C:413)

fully invested NPV (NPV*)—the total net present value of a project and any subsequent reinvestment (11C:413)

future—an exchange-traded standardized forward contract (16:597)

future value—a single cash flow or value at the end of a time frame (5:156)

general partnership—a partnership in which all partners share equally in decision-making authority and liability (2A:48)

geographic arbitrage—the simultaneous buying and selling of two currencies to take advantage of a discrepancy in their reciprocal relationship (7:234)

goal—the objective of (a business's) actions (2:26)

greenmail—demanding that a company repurchase its shares at an inflated price by threatening a hostile takeover (17:635)

gross income—a tax term referring to total income (4B:101)

growing cash stream—an infinitely long series of equally spaced cash flows in which each flow is greater than the previous one by a constant rate of growth (5:176)

hedge (hedging)—to balance liabilities with assets of equal amount and maturity (6:217); also balancing a risky financial position with an opposite position to cancel out the risk (16:576)

holding-period yield—the rate of return an investor actually earns from an investment (9:309)

homemade dividends—selling shares of stock to augment a company's dividends (17:618)

homemade leverage—borrowing by stock investors to leverage their investment port-folio (15:540)

improper accumulation—a tax term referring to the "excessive" retention of earnings, hence not paying dividends, to avoid double taxation (4C:109)

incremental cost—the additional cost from taking a particular action (4:81)

independent investment projects—investment projects where acceptance of one does not have anything to do with the decision to accept or reject the other (11C:407)

indifference point—the level of EBIT which produces the same EPS regardless of the debt-equity mix (15:533)

indirect (overhead) cost—a cost not directly traceable to a product or service (4:82)

industry-average ratio—a ratio calculated by averaging the ratios of firms within an industry (4:92)

inflation premium—the component of interest rates demanded by investors as compensation for anticipated inflation (6:207)

information asymmetry—the condition in which a firm's manager-agents know more about the firm than its shareholder-principals (2:35)

initial public offering (IPO)—the first public sale of a company's stock (19:694)

interest rate parity—a relationship that holds that, at equilibrium, interest rate differentials between two countries are offset by the differences between spot and forward rates. (7:246)

interest rate position—an anticipated cash flow not fully hedged against interest rate movements (16:599)

interest-rate risk—the risk that interest rates will rise, reducing the value of securities (6:217)

intermediation—moving funds through financial intermediaries (19:692)

internal rate of return—the rate of return from an investment (5B:193); also the discount rate that equates the present value of all benefits from a proposed investment to the present value of all costs (11:388)

international bond—a bond issued outside the borrower's home country (21:771)

international Fisher effect—a relationship that holds that, at equilibrium, the difference in interest rates between two countries is an unbiased predictor of the future spot rate (7:245)

intrinsic value—the true economic worth of an asset (19:709)

inverted yield curve—a downward-sloping yield curve in which short-term rates exceed long-term rates (6:211)

investment banker—an individual or organization that specializes in helping firms issue new securities and in trading existing securities (1:8)

investment income—a tax term referring to income from investment in financial assets (4B:101)

itemized deductions—a tax term referring to a detailed listing of expenses permitted as subtractions from income (4B:103)

joint float—a system in which several currencies are fixed against each other but float as a unit against other currencies (7:232)

junk bond—a speculative grade bond (21:770)

just-in-time inventory system—a system in which inventory is received and produced only as needed keeping the balance of inventory-on-hand as close as possible to zero (4D:125)

just-in-time manufacturing—a system of integrating purchasing, production, and sales so each task is done only when required (12:447)

Kaizen—small- and moderate-scale continuous improvement in all phases of an organization (14:496)

leveraged lease—a lease with both equity (the lessor) and debt investors (21:762)

life-cycle numbers—numbers which cover the full life-span of some activity and which are not limited to any time period (11:375)

limited partnership—a partnership in which some partners receive limited liability in return for limited authority (2A:48)

limit to internally-financed growth—the maximum amount by which a company's sales can grow in a year before the firm must turn to external financing (18:663)

line of credit—a relationship in which a bank offers to lend up to a specified amount for a given time period with no guarantee that funds will be available (20:732)

liquidity—the ability to have access to cash quickly and in full amount (4D:121, also 6:203)

liquidity preference hypothesis—a theory of the term structure focusing on investors' loss of liquidity as maturities lengthen (6:217)

liquidity preference theory—a theory of interest rate determination focusing on individuals' reasons for holding cash and on the money supply as determined by the central bank (6:203)

listing—arranging for a company's securities to trade on a stock exchange (19:702)

loanable funds—money, in whatever form, available for borrowing and lending (6:205)

loanable funds theory—a theory of interest rate determination focusing on money available for borrowing and lending (6:205)

lock box—a post office box to which customers mail their payments (12:433)

London inter-bank offering rate (LIBOR)—a reference rate used for dollar-denominated loans made outside the United States (20:733)

loss carryback—a tax term referring to the offsetting of income in prior years with a current loss to obtain a refund of taxes paid (4C:110)

loss carryforward—a tax term referring to the offsetting of current income with a loss in a prior year to reduce the firm's tax obligation (4C:110)

macroeconomics—the study of the functioning of economies taken as a whole (1:6)

managed (dirty) float—a system in which government influences a floating exchange rate system through central bank intervention in the currency markets (7:231)

marginal cost—the cost of making one additional unit (4:80)

marginal cost of capital (MCC)—a synonym for "cost of capital" emphasizing its use as a measure of the marginal cost of capital funds (10:352)

marginal tax rate—the tax rate applicable to an incremental dollar of income (4:88)

marketability risk—the risk that a security will be difficult, hence costly, to sell (6:220)

marketable security—investments with a ready market which may be sold easily to obtain their value in cash (16:590)

market price of risk—the additional return demanded by investors to take on one unit of portfolio risk (8:286)

market return—the rate of return from the economy, commonly measured by a major stock market index (8:284)

maturity—the time remaining until the expiration of a security (6:211)

microeconomics—the study of individual units within an economy, specifically consumers and producing firms (1:6)

modified internal rate of return (MIRR)—the fully invested IRR of a project plus reinvestment at the cost of capital (11D:422)

money markets—the markets for (debt) securities with maturity of one year or less (19:693)

mortgage bond—a bond with collateral (21:768)

multicurrency bond—a bond denominated in more than one currency (21:772)

municipal bond—a bond issued by any government or government agency other than the federal government (4B:101)

mutual fund—a pool of money from many investors which is invested in a portfolio of securities (8:281)

mutually exclusive investment projects—investment projects where acceptance of one precludes acceptance of the other, and vice-versa (11C:407)

naive diversification—the construction of a portfolio at random (8:281)

natural variation—the random variation inherent in any process (13:481)

net annual benefit (NAB)—the amount by which the annual benefit from an investment exceeds the amount required to cover the firm's cost of capital (12:429)

net lease—a lease for an asset without any supporting services (21:764)

net present value—the present value of all benefits from a proposed investment less the present value of all costs, using the weighted-average cost of capital as the discount rate (5B:192, also 11:384)

net present value profile—a graph of an investment project's net present value as a function of the discount rate (11B:402)

nexus of contracts—an interconnection of many contracts (2:36)

nominal interest rate (nominal rate of interest)—a quoted rate of interest (5:178); in the context of the Fisher model, the rate of interest including the premiums for inflation and risk (6:206)

normal yield curve—an upward-sloping yield curve in which long-term rates exceed short-term rates (6:211)

off-balance-sheet financing—financing that is not included in balance sheet liabilities (21:764)

offering basis loan—a short-term loan with no prenegotiation (20:733)

operating lease—a lease providing temporary use of an asset (21:764)

operating leverage—magnification of changes in operating earnings (EBIT) in response to changes in sales that is caused by the existence of fixed operating costs in the firm's cost structure (15:530)

operational finance theory—theory about how financial actions are taken in an organization (23:831)

opportunity cost—a benefit forgone by the making of a financial decision (4:81)

opposite project—an investment project in which all cash inflows precede all cash outflows (11B:402)

option—the right to buy or sell an asset at an agreed-upon price during a specified time period (9:318)

ordering costs—the annual costs of acquiring inventory (12B:455)

ordinary annuity (annuity in arrears, END annuity)—an annuity in which the cash flows occur at the end of each time period (5:172)

ordinary income—a tax term referring to income from providing goods and services (4B:101)

paper loss—a loss according to tax calculations not accompanied by a similar loss of cash or market value (4B:101)

par bond—a bond with a price equal to its face value (9:302)

par value—the minimum amount of money per share a shareholder is required to invest (22:797)

passive income—a tax term referring to income from business activities in which the individual plays little part (4B:101)

payables float—the dollar amount of outgoing checks that have been written but have not yet been covered by bank deposits (12:432)

payback period—the length of time until an investment project has returned its initial investment (11D:417)

payment—one of the cash flows in an annuity (5:167)

payment date—the date a dividend is paid (17:627)

pecking-order approach—a pattern of financing in which a company raises funds in the same sequence each year (15:547)

pegged float—a system in which a currency is fixed against another which itself is free to float against other currencies (7:231)

performance units and shares—deferred compensation which may be converted to cash only if a company achieves its performance goals (2B:50)

permanent working capital—the level of working capital required at all times (12:426)

perpetual bond—a bond with no maturity date (9:305)

perpetuity—an annuity that continues forever; also, a growing cash stream with a zero rate of growth (5:177)

perquisite ("perq")—compensation in a form other than money (2:35)

portfolio—a group of investments held at the same time (8:276)

precautionary motive—the desire to hold cash for unanticipated spending needs (6:203)

preemptive right—the right to purchase a proportionate amount of any newly issued stock (22:801)

preferred habitat hypothesis—a theory of the term structure that incorporates elements of the other three theories (6:218)

preferred stock—stock with one or more features better than common stock and without any ownership claim (22:804)

premium bond—a bond with a price greater than its face value (9:302)

present value—a single cash flow or value at the beginning of a time frame (5:160)

price of total risk—the additional return demanded by investors to take on one unit of total risk (8:276)

primary financial markets—the markets for the initial issue of securities (19:694)

prime rate—a reference rate used in the United States, traditionally the rate available to the most credit worthy customers (20:733)

principal—a person who employs another to act in his/her behalf (2:33)

private placement—the sale of a new issue of securities directly to an investor (19:697)

probability distribution—a listing of all possible results of some activity showing the chance of each result taking place (8:269)

process adaptability—the ease and speed with which a process can be modified (13:483)

process boundary—the line separating a process from other business activities (13:473)

process capability—how well a process functions under normal operating conditions (13:483)

process risk—unnecessary variability caused by systems within the firm that are out of control (8:268)

process robustness—the ability of a process to meet performance objectives when inputs and operating conditions vary (13:484)

professional managers—individuals employed by a firm to direct its activities because of their expertise. They are distinguished from owner-managers, individuals who find themselves managing a firm because they own it (2:28)

profitablity index—the net present value of benefits per dollar invested (11D:419)

profit maximization—the act of managing a firm so as to increase its economic profits to the maximum possible level (2:28)

pro-forma financial statement—a financial statement that projects a firm's condition or operating results into the future (18:650)

progressive tax system—a tax system in which the tax rate rises with income level (4:88)

prospectus—a booklet of data about a company which must be given to potential investors prior to soliciting any money (19:696)

protective covenants—loan terms designed to assure repayment (21:761)

proxy—a combined absentee ballot and assignment of the right to vote, used to obtain a majority of shareholder votes (22:800)

purchasing power—the value of money measured by the goods and services it can purchase (6:207)

pure rate of interest—the interest rate prior to inclusion of the premiums for inflation and risk (6:207)

put—an option to sell (9:318)

random walk—a process in which successive changes are independent of each other (19:711)

rational expectations theory—a theory of interest rate determination focusing on the way in which individuals predict and process information (6:205)

real rate of interest—the rate of interest excluding the premium for inflation (6:208)

receivables float—the dollar amount of incoming checks that have been mailed but have not yet been collected (12:432)

reciprocal exchange rate—the number of units of a foreign currency required to purchase one unit of domestic currency (7:232)

reference rate—a base rate for loan pricing (20:733)

reinvestment risk—the risk that interest rates will fall, limiting reinvestment opportunities (6:220)

relative purchasing power parity—a relationship that holds that, at equilibrium, the change in the spot exchange rate between two currencies is equal to the ratio of the changes in relative price levels between the countries (7:244)

required rate of return—the minimum acceptable rate of return on an investment which will appropriately compensate the investor for time and risk (9:296)

restricted stock—stock that cannot be sold prior to some trigger event taking place (2B:50)

reverse split—a stock split that reduces the number of outstanding shares (17:632)

revolving credit line—a line of credit containing a guarantee that funds will be available for the period of the line (20:732)

rework—an activity performed to correct an error or omission in an earlier stage of a work process (13:475)

risk—the possibility that the result of some activity will not be exactly as (and particularly, will be worse than) forecast (2:28)

risk averter—an individual willing to pay to avoid risk (8:264)

risk-free rate of interest—the rate of interest excluding the premium for risk; it is the rate available on a risk-free investment (6:208)

riskless hedge—a combination of investments which have a certain outcome (9A:326)

risk neutral—indifferent to risk (8:264)

risk premium—the component of interest rates demanded by investors as compensation for risk (6:207)

risk seeker—an individual willing to pay to assume additional risk (8:264)

root cause—the single cause most important in creating a problem (14:503)

safety stock—extra inventory kept on hand to minimize the chance the firm will stock out (12B:459)

sale and leaseback—a transaction in which a company sells an asset to a lessor and then leases it back (21:762)

seasonal—a firm or market whose activity varies in a pattern throughout the year (4D:122)

seasonal dating—invoicing several months' worth of shipments at a strong point in the buyer's seasonal pattern (20:724)

secondary financial markets—the markets for trading existing securities (19:699)

security—a financial instrument such as a bond or share of stock (1:8)

security market line (SML)—a graph of investors' required rate of return as a function of an asset's portfolio (systematic) risk (8:286)

segmentation or hedging hypothesis—a theory of the term structure focusing on investors' desire for specific maturity instruments to hedge their liabilities (6:217)

sensitivity analysis—a test to examine how the result of an analysis will vary with changes in inputs (18:660)

serial bond issue—a bond issue composed of bonds of many maturities (21:773)

shareholder wealth—the total value of an investment in the common stock of a company, measured by the price at which the stock could be sold (2:30)

shelf registration—advance SEC approval to make small public security issues (19:699)

shrinkage—the loss of inventory for any reason (12:445)

signaling—the process of conveying economic information (2:31)

simple interest—interest paid only on the initial principal and not on previously paid interest (5:154)

sinking fund—an account set up to accumulate the cash to retire debt (21:773)

six sigma—a statistical measure of process accuracy, only 3.4 errors per million opportunities (4:77)

special causes of variation—factors that cause excessive variation and make a process unstable (13:482)

specific-item forecasting—a forecasting technique in which each account on a firm's financial statements is projected without reference to the other accounts (18:650)

speculative motive—the desire to hold cash for investment purposes in anticipation of rising interest rates (6:204)

spontaneous account—a balance sheet account whose value changes with sales without the need for specific management action (18:653)

spot (exchange) rate—an exchange rate available for the immediate trade of currencies (7:238)

square cash position—the condition in which receivables and payables are perfectly hedged (16:595)

stakeholders—persons and organizations affected by the actions of a business firm (1:6)

standard deduction—a tax term referring to a statutory number that may be used instead of itemizing deductions (4B:103)

standard deviation—the square root of the variance (8:273)

standard project—an investment project in which all cash outflows precede all cash inflows (11B:401)

stock—a type of financial instrument that gives the holder ownership of a portion of a corporation (1:8)

stock appreciation rights—the right to be paid the difference between a company's stock price and some specified price (2B:50)

stock dividend—the distribution of additional shares to common shareholders (17:630)

stock option—the right to buy shares of a company's common stock at a specified price within a specified time frame (2B:50)

stock out—to run out of inventory (12B:459)

stock split—the replacement of all outstanding shares of common stock with a different number of new shares (17:630)

sunk cost—money previously spent (4:81)

surplus-budget unit—an individual or business that spends less than it earns (19:691)

sustainable growth rate—the rate of growth that does not change a firm's debt/equity ratio, assuming any external financing needed comes from debt (18C:678)

swap—an exchange of financial obligations (16:598); one possibility is an exchange of loan obligations (21:754)

synthetic security—an artificial security constructed from real securities and derivatives (16:598)

systematic risk—the variability in an investment's rate of return caused by factors that impact all investments (8:281)

tampering—modifying a system in response to special causes of variation, further destabilizing the system's performance (18:647)

target capital structure—the percentage mix of financing sources management plans to use in the future (10:352)

taxable income—a tax term referring to the amount of income subject to tax (4B:103)

tax avoidance—reducing a tax obligation within the framework of the law (4:87)

tax evasion—not paying taxes which are owed to a government (4:87)

tax shelter—an investment whose purpose is to generate losses to reduce taxable income, hence taxes (4B:101)

temporary working capital—increases to working capital due to fluctuations in business activity (12:427)

terminal value—the projected future value of a sum of money consisting of the value added by investing it in a project currently under consideration plus the additional value added by reinvesting the proceeds up to the end of a common time horizon (11C:412)

term loan—a loan with a maturity of more than one year (21:755)

term structure of interest rates—the relationship between a security's yield and maturity (6:211)

time-series comparison—a tracking of some number across time to see if it is changing, and if so, the direction and amount of change (4:91)

time value of money—the concept that the value of money depends on the date of its receipt or payment (5:151)

total cost—the sum of the costs of making each unit (4:80)

traditional bond—a bond that returns a fixed periodic interest payment plus a fixed principal value at maturity (9:300)

transaction exposure—exposure to foreign exchange losses on day-to-day transactions due to adverse exchange rate movements (7:249)

transactions motive—the desire to hold cash for day-to-day spending needs (6:203)

translation exposure—exposure to reduction of accounting income and values due to adverse exchange rate movements (7:249)

treasurer—the finance professional responsible for funding a company and for its day-to-day money flows (1:16)

triangular arbitrage—the simultaneous buying and selling of three currencies to take advantage of a discrepancy in a cross rate (7:236)

trustee—a third party to a bond indenture, responsible for representing the bondholders to the issuing company (21:768)

underwriting—guaranteeing the proceeds of a security issue by purchasing the issue at an agreed-upon price (19:695)

unsystematic risk—the variability in an investment's rate of return caused by factors that only impact that investment (8:281)

variable cost—a cost that changes with changes in sales (4:81)

variance—a measure of the variability of rates of return (8:273)

warrant—a call option issued by the company whose stock may be called (22:808)

weighted-average cost of capital (WACOC)—a synonym for "cost of capital" emphasizing the method by which it is constructed (10:352)

working capital—a firm's current assets minus its current liabilities (4D:121); also liquid resources available for the day-to-day operations of the firm (12:426)

working capital cycle—the flow of value through current asset accounts (16:588)

work process—a series of work activities intended to produce a specific result (13:466)

yield—the rate of return available from a security (6:211)

yield curve—a graph of the term structure, most commonly of U.S. Treasury securities (6:211)

yield-to-first-call—the rate of return an investor would earn from a bond if it were purchased at today's price, made all promised payments, and were then called at the first possible opportunity (9:308)

yield-to-maturity—the rate of return an investor would earn from a bond if it were purchased at today's price and held until its maturity date—provided it made all promised payments (9:306)

zero-coupon bond—a bond which makes no cash interest payments (9:303)

CREDITS

Art: p. xviii, Drawing by Booth: © 1982 *The New Yorker Magazine, Inc.;* p. xxiv, Reprinted by permission of Eric Werner; p. xxx, From the *Wall Street Journal*-Permission, Cartoon Features Syndicate; p. 19, © 1994 by Sidney Harris-*Harvard Business Review;* p. 26, *The Far Side* © 1986 FarWorks, Inc. Dist. by Universal Press Syndicate. Reprinted with permission. All rights reserved; p. 48, © 1986 by Sidney Harris-*Harvard Business Review;* p. 76, Reprinted by permission: Tribune Media Services; p. 103, From the *Wall Street Journal*-Permission, Cartoon Features Syndicate; p. 122, Drawing by H. Martin; © 1976 *The New Yorker Magazine, Inc.;* p. 186, *The Far Side* © 1985 FarWorks, Inc. Dist. by Universal Press Syndicate. Reprinted with permission. All rights reserved; p. 208, By permission of Johnny Hart & Creator's Syndicate, Inc.; p. 244, From the *Wall Street Journal*-Permission, Cartoon Features Syndicate; p. 264, *Calvin and Hobbes* © 1986 Watterson. Reprinted with permission of Universal Press Syndicate. All rights reserved; p. 300, From the *Wall Street Journal*-Permission, Cartoon Features Syndicate; p. 331, From the *Wall Street Journal*-Permission, Cartoon Features Syndicate; p. 336, From the *Wall Street Journal*-Permission, Cartoon Features Syndicate; p. 375, From the *Wall Street Journal*-Permission, Cartoon Features Syndicate; p. 449, © 1991 Lee Lorenz; p. 484, © 1993 by S. Harris-*Harvard Business Review;* p. 497, © Permission by Leo Cullum; p. 506, EXCERPT DRAWN FROM "IBM CREDIT" from REENGINEERING THE CORPORATION by MICHAEL HAMMER and JAMES CHAMPY. Copyright © 1993 by Michael Hammer & James Champy. Reprinted by permission of HarperCollins Publishers, Inc.; p. 545, Reprinted by permission of James L. Stevenson-*Harvard Business Review,* March/April 1988, p. 112; p. 553, Reprinted by permission of Dana Fradon-*Harvard Business Review,* July/August 1989, p. 107; p. 564, Drawing by D. Reilly. Reprinted from *Harvard Business Review* by permission of artist; p. 598, Reprinted by permission of Roger Beale-*Financial Times of London;* p. 621, Reprinted by permission of Valen Associates, Inc.; p. 649, Cartoon by Henry R. Martin; p. 701, Drawing by Michael Thompson, reprinted from the *State Journal Register;* p. 734, Reprinted by permission of David Brion; p. 771, Drawing by D. Reilly, reprinted from the *Harvard Business Review* by permission of artist; p. 800, Drawing by Joe Mirachi; © 1965 *The New Yorker Magazine, Inc.;* p. 829, DILBERT reprinted by permission of UFS, Inc.; p. 839, Reprinted by permission of Ed Fisher-*Harvard Business Review;* Literary: Chapter 1: "Lifting American Competitiveness," *Fortune,* April 23, 1990, pp. 56–58. Peter Petre, FORTUNE © 1990 Time Inc. All rights reserved; "Rewriting the Export Rules," *Fortune,* April 23, 1990, p. 92. Monci Joe Williams, FORTUNE © 1990 Time Inc. All rights reserved; "Lessons From U.S. Business Blunders," *Fortune,* April 23, 1990, p. 129. Thomas A. Stewart, FORTUNE © 1990 Time Inc. All rights reserved; "Quality: Small and Midsize Companies

Seize the Challenge—Not a Moment Too Soon," *Business Week,* November 30, 1992, p. 72. Reprinted from November 30, 1992 issue of Business Week by special permission copyright © 1992 by McGraw Hill, Inc.; Peters, Tom, *Thriving on Chaos.* New York: Alfred A. Knopf, 1987, p. 370. From THRIVING ON CHAOS by Tom Peters copyright © 1987 by Excel, a California Limited Partnership Reprinted by permission of Alfred A. Knopf, Inc.; Chapter 4: Gabel, Natalie, "Is 99.9% Good Enough?," A Supplement to Training, March 1991, Lakewood Publications. Reprinted with permission from the March supplement 1991 issue of TRAINING Magazine. Copyright 1991. Lakewood Publications, MN. All rights reserved. Not for resale; Chapter 5: "Get Receipts Sooner and Pay Bills Later is New Federal Rule," *Wall Street Journal,* August 18, 1980. p. 3. Reprinted by permission of The Wall Street Journal, © 1980 Dow Jones & Company, Inc. All rights reserved worldwide; Chapter 6: "A Stampede for Cheaper Money," *Business Week,* January 20, 1992, p 26–27. Reprinted from January 20, 1992 issue of Business Week by special permission copyright © 1992 by McGraw Hill, Inc.; "Can GM Remodel Itself?," *Fortune,* January 13, 1992, p. 26–34. By Alex Taylor III, FORTUNE © 1992 Time Inc. All rights reserved; Chapter 11: *Fortune,* May 21, 1990, p. 75–76 by Terence p. Pare credit line; by Terence Pare, FORTUNE © 1990 Time Inc. All rights reserved; WSJ, 1991, by Amal Kumar Naj. Reprinted by permission of The Wall Street Journal © 1991 Dow Jones & Company, Inc. All right reserved worldwide; Chapter 13: Juran Institute, Inc. Three part classification. Reprinted by permission of Juran Institute, Inc.; Chapter 14: Masaaki Imai, Kaizen: The Key to Japan's Competitive Success. NY: McGraw Hill 1986. Masaaki Imai, Kaizen: The Key to Japan's Competitive Success, copyright 1986. Reprinted by special permission of McGraw Hill, Inc.; Juran Institute, Inc. Example. Reprinted by permission of Juran Institute, Inc.; Michael Hammer and James Champy, Reengineering the Corporation, NY, HarperCollins, 1992. p. 39–44 also Michael Hammer, "Reengineering work: Don't Automate, obliterate." Harvard Business Review, July-Aug 1990; 104–112. © 1990 by the President and Fellows of Harvard College. All rights reserved. Reprinted by permission of Harvard Business Review. Reengineering work: Don't Automate, obliterate, by Michael Hammer and James Champy, July-August 1990; Chapter 17: "The Great Buyback boom of '93" Business Week, Aug. 23, 1992, p. 76–77. Reprinted from August 23, 1993 issue of Business Week by special permission copyright © 1993 by McGraw Hill, Inc.; Chapter 19: Barrons, February 28, 1994. p. 43. Reprinted by permission of Barrons, © 1994 Dow Jones & Company, Inc. All rights reserved worldwide; Chapter 23: Keating & Jablonsky, Changing Roles of Financial Mgmt: Getting Close to the Business (FInancial Exec Research Foundation, 1990) Copyright © 1990 Keating and Jablonsky, Changing Roles of Financial Management: Getting Close to the Business, Financial Executive Research Foundation, Morristown, NJ; Milton Friedman, Capitalism and Freedom (Chicago: Univ. of Chicago Press, 1963) p. 133. Milton Friedman, Capitalism and Freedom, copyright © 1963 University of Chicago Press; Figure 6.4, 7.1, 9.2, 9.3, 9.4—The Wall Street Journal. Reprinted by permission of The Wall Street Journal, © 1994 Dow Jones & Company, Inc. All rights reserved worldwide; Figure 8.8—Value Line Investment Survey. Copyright 1994 by Value Line Publishing Inc. Reprinted by permission. All rights reserved; Figure 14.7—Reprinted by permission of the Juran Institute, Inc.; Figure 17.4—Reprinted by permission of Harris Trust & Savings Bank-Quaker Oats Co.

INDEX